Algorithm Design:

Foundations, Analysis, and Internet Examples

Michael T. Goodrich
Department of Information and Computer Science
University of California, Irvine

Roberto Tamassia
Department of Computer Science
Brown University

John Wiley & Sons, Inc.

ACQUISITIONS EDITOR	Paul Crockett
MARKETING MANAGER	Katherine Hepburn
SENIOR PRODUCTION EDITOR	Sharon Prendergast
SENIOR DESIGNER	Harry Nolan
COVER DESIGN	Howard Grossman

Cover painting: Joan Miro, *Carnival of Harlequin*, 1925. Oil on canvas, 36-3/4 × 47 × 3-1/4 inches.
© 2001 ART, New York/ADAGP, Paris. Photo provided courtesy of Albright-Knox Gallery.

This book was set in LaTeX by the authors and printed and bound by R.R. Donnelley, Crawfordsville. The cover was printed by Phoenix Color Corporation.

This book is printed on acid free paper. ∞

ISBN 0-471-38365-1

Printed in the United States of America

10 9 8 7 6 5 4 3 2 1

To my children, Paul, Anna, and Jack

– *Michael T. Goodrich*

To Isabel

– *Roberto Tamassia*

Preface

This book is designed to provide a comprehensive introduction to the design and analysis of computer algorithms and data structures. In terms of the computer science and computer engineering curricula, we have written this book to be primarily focused on the Junior-Senior level Algorithms (CS7) course, which is taught as a first-year graduate course in some schools.

Topics

The topics covered in this book are taken from a broad spectrum of discrete algorithm design and analysis, including the following:

- ***Design and analysis of algorithms***, including asymptotic notation, worst-case analysis, amortization, randomization and experimental analysis
- ***Algorithmic design patterns***, including greedy method, divide-and-conquer, dynamic programming, backtracking and branch-and-bound
- ***Algorithmic frameworks***, including NP-completeness, approximation algorithms, on-line algorithms, external-memory algorithms, distributed algorithms, and parallel algorithms
- ***Data structures***, including lists, vectors, trees, priority queues, AVL trees, 2-4 trees, red-black trees, splay trees, B-trees, hash tables, skip-lists, union-find trees
- ***Combinatorial algorithms***, including heap-sort, quick-sort, merge-sort, selection, parallel list ranking, parallel sorting
- ***Graph algorithms***, including traversals (DFS and BFS), topological sorting, shortest paths (all-pairs and single-source), minimum spanning tree, maximum flow, minimum-cost flow, and matching
- ***Geometric algorithms***, including range searching, convex hulls, segment intersection, and closest pairs
- ***Numerical algorithms***, including integer, matrix, and polynomial multiplication, the Fast Fourier Transform (FFT), extended Euclid's algorithm, modular exponentiation, and primality testing
- ***Internet algorithms***, including packet routing, multicasting, leader election, encryption, digital signatures, text pattern matching, information retrieval, data compression, Web caching, and Web auctions

About the Authors

Professors Goodrich and Tamassia are well-recognized researchers in data structures and algorithms, having published many papers in this field, with applications to Internet computing, information visualization, geographic information systems, and computer security. They have an extensive record of research collaboration and have served as principal investigators in several joint projects sponsored by the National Science Foundation, the Army Research Office, and the Defense Advanced Research Projects Agency. They are also active in educational technology research, with special emphasis on algorithm visualization systems and infrastructure support for distance learning.

Michael Goodrich received his Ph.D. in Computer Science from Purdue University in 1987. He is currently a professor in the Department of Information and Computer Science at University of California, Irvine. Prior to this service we was Professor of Computer Science at Johns Hopkins University, and director of the Hopkins Center for Algorithm Engineering. He is an editor for the *International Journal of Computational Geometry & Applications*, *Journal of Computational and System Sciences*, and *Journal of Graph Algorithms and Applications*.

Roberto Tamassia received his Ph.D. in Electrical and Computer Engineering from the University of Illinois at Urbana-Champaign in 1988. He is currently a professor in the Department of Computer Science and the director of the Center for Geometric Computing at Brown University. He is an editor for *Computational Geometry: Theory and Applications* and the *Journal of Graph Algorithms and Applications*, and he has previously served on the editorial board of IEEE *Transactions on Computers*.

In addition to their research accomplishments, the authors also have extensive experience in the classroom. For example, Dr. Goodrich has taught data structures and algorithms courses since 1987, including Data Structures as a freshman-sophomore level course and Introduction to Algorithms as a upper level course. He has earned several teaching awards in this capacity. His teaching style is to involve the students in lively interactive classroom sessions that bring out the intuition and insights behind data structuring and algorithmic techniques, as well as in formulating solutions whose analysis is mathematically rigorous. Dr. Tamassia has taught Data Structures and Algorithms as an introductory freshman-level course since 1988. He has also attracted many students (including several undergraduates) to his advanced course on Computational Geometry, which is a popular graduate-level CS course at Brown. One thing that has set his teaching style apart is his effective use of interactive hypermedia presentations, continuing the tradition of Brown's "electronic classroom." The carefully designed Web pages of the courses taught by Dr. Tamassia have been used as reference material by students and professionals worldwide.

For the Instructor

This book is intended primarily as a textbook for a Junior-Senior Algorithms (CS7) course, which is also taught as a first-year graduate course in some schools. This book contains many exercises, which are divided between reinforcement exercises, creativity exercises, and implementation projects. Certain aspects of this book were specifically designed with the instructor in mind, including:

- ***Visual justifications (that is, picture proofs)***, which make mathematical arguments more understandable for students, appealing to visual learners. An example of visual justifications is our analysis of bottom-up heap construction. This topic has traditionally been difficult for students to understand; hence, time consuming for instructors to explain. The included visual proof is intuitive, rigorous, and quick.
- ***Algorithmic design patterns***, which provide general techniques for designing and implementing algorithms. Examples include divide-and-conquer, dynamic programming, the decorator pattern, and the template method pattern.
- ***Use of randomization***, which takes advantage of random choices in an algorithm to simplify its design and analysis. Such usage replaces complex average-case analysis of sophisticated data structures with intuitive analysis of simple data structures and algorithms. Examples include skip lists, randomized quick-sort, randomized quick-select, and randomized primality testing.
- ***Internet algorithmics topics***, which either motivate traditional algorithmic topics from a new Internet viewpoint or highlight new algorithms that are derived from Internet applications. Examples include information retrieval, Web crawling, packet routing, Web auction algorithms, and Web caching algorithms. We have found that motivating algorithms topics by their Internet applications significantly improves student interest in the study of algorithms.
- ***Java implementation examples***, which cover software design methods, object-oriented implementation issues, and experimental analysis of algorithms. These implementation examples, provided in separate sections of various chapters, are optional, so that instructors can either cover them in their lectures, assign them as additional reading, or skip them altogether.

This book is also structured to allow the instructor a great deal of freedom in how to organize and present the material. Likewise, the dependence between chapters is rather flexible, allowing the instructor to customize an algorithms course to highlight the topics that he or she feels are most important. We have extensively discussed Internet Algorithmics topics, which should prove quite interesting to students. In addition, we have included examples of Internet application of traditional algorithms topics in several places as well.

We show in Table 0.1 how this book could be used for a traditional Introduction to Algorithms (CS7) course, albeit with some new topics motivated from the Internet.

Ch.	Topics	Option
1	Algorithm analysis	Experimental analysis
2	Data structures	Heap Java example
3	Searching	Include one of § 3.2–3.5
4	Sorting	In-place quick-sort
5	Algorithmic techniques	The FFT
6	Graph algorithms	DFS Java example
7	Weighted graphs	Dijkstra Java example
8	Matching and flow	Include at end of course
9	Text processing (at least one section)	Tries
12	Computational geometry	Include at end of course
13	NP-completeness	Backtracking
14	Frameworks (at least one)	Include at end of course

Table 0.1: Example syllabus schedule for a traditional Introduction to Algorithms (CS7) course, including optional choices for each chapter.

This book can also be used for a specialized Internet Algorithmics course, which reviews some traditional algorithms topics, but in a new Internet-motivated light, while also covering new algorithmic topics that are derived from Internet applications. We show in Table 0.2 how this book could be used for a such a course.

Ch.	Topics	Option
1	Algorithm analysis	Experimental analysis
2	Data structures (inc. hashing)	Quickly review
3	Searching (inc. § 3.5, skip lists)	Search tree Java example
4	Sorting	In-place quick-sort
5	Algorithmic techniques	The FFT
6	Graph algorithms	DFS Java example
7	Weighted graphs	Skip one MST alg.
8	Matching and flow	Matching algorithms
9	Text processing	Pattern matching
10	Security & Cryptography	Java examples
11	Network algorithms	Multi-casting
13	NP-completeness	Include at end of course
14	Frameworks (at least two)	Include at end of course

Table 0.2: Example syllabus schedule for an Internet Algorithmics course, including optional choices for each chapter.

Of course, other options are also possible, including a course that is a mixture of a traditional Introduction to Algorithms (CS7) course and an Internet Algorithmics course. We do not belabor this point, however, leaving such creative arrangements to the interested instructor.

Web Added-Value Education

This book comes accompanied by an extensive Web site:

http://www.wiley.com/college/goodrich/

This Web site includes an extensive collection of educational aids that augment the topics of this book. Specifically for students we include:

- Presentation handouts (four-per-page format) for most topics in this book
- A database of hints on selected assignments, indexed by problem number
- Interactive applets that animate fundamental data structures and algorithms
- Source code for the Java examples in this book

We feel that the hint server should be of particular interest, particularly for creativity problems that can be quite challenging for some students.

For instructors using this book, there is a dedicated portion of the Web site just for them, which includes the following additional teaching aids:

- Solutions to selected exercises in this book
- A database of additional exercises and their solutions
- Presentations (one-per-page format) for most topics covered in this book

Readers interested in the implementation of algorithms and data structures can download ***JDSL*** the ***Data Structures Library in Java***, from

http://www.jdsl.org/

Prerequisites

We have written this book assuming that the reader comes to it with certain knowledge. In particular, we assume that the reader has a basic understanding of elementary data structures, such as arrays and linked lists, and is at least vaguely familiar with a high-level programming language, such as C, C++, or Java. Even so, all algorithms are described in a high-level "pseudo-code," and specific programming language constructs are only used in the optional Java implementation example sections.

In terms of mathematical background, we assume the reader is familiar with topics from first-year college mathematics, including exponents, logarithms, summations, limits, and elementary probability. Even so, we review most of these facts in Chapter 1, including exponents, logarithms, and summations, and we give a summary of other useful mathematical facts, including elementary probability, in Appendix A.

Contents

I Fundamental Tools 1

1 Algorithm Analysis 3
1.1 Methodologies for Analyzing Algorithms 5
1.2 Asymptotic Notation 13
1.3 A Quick Mathematical Review 21
1.4 Case Studies in Algorithm Analysis 31
1.5 Amortization 34
1.6 Experimentation 42
1.7 Exercises 47

2 Basic Data Structures 55
2.1 Stacks and Queues 57
2.2 Vectors, Lists, and Sequences 65
2.3 Trees 75
2.4 Priority Queues and Heaps 94
2.5 Dictionaries and Hash Tables 114
2.6 Java Example: Heap 128
2.7 Exercises 131

3 Search Trees and Skip Lists 139
3.1 Ordered Dictionaries and Binary Search Trees 141
3.2 AVL Trees 152
3.3 Bounded-Depth Search Trees 159
3.4 Splay Trees 185
3.5 Skip Lists 195
3.6 Java Example: AVL and Red-Black Trees 202
3.7 Exercises 212

4 Sorting, Sets, and Selection 217
4.1 Merge-Sort 219
4.2 The Set Abstract Data Type 225
4.3 Quick-Sort 235
4.4 A Lower Bound on Comparison-Based Sorting 239
4.5 Bucket-Sort and Radix-Sort 241
4.6 Comparison of Sorting Algorithms 244
4.7 Selection 245
4.8 Java Example: In-Place Quick-Sort 248
4.9 Exercises 251

5 Fundamental Techniques **257**
5.1 The Greedy Method 259
5.2 Divide-and-Conquer 263
5.3 Dynamic Programming 274
5.4 Exercises 282

II Graph Algorithms **285**

6 Graphs **287**
6.1 The Graph Abstract Data Type 289
6.2 Data Structures for Graphs 296
6.3 Graph Traversal 303
6.4 Directed Graphs 316
6.5 Java Example: Depth-First Search 329
6.6 Exercises 335

7 Weighted Graphs **339**
7.1 Single-Source Shortest Paths 341
7.2 All-Pairs Shortest Paths 354
7.3 Minimum Spanning Trees 360
7.4 Java Example: Dijkstra's Algorithm 373
7.5 Exercises 376

8 Network Flow and Matching **381**
8.1 Flows and Cuts 383
8.2 Maximum Flow 387
8.3 Maximum Bipartite Matching 396
8.4 Minimum-Cost Flow 398
8.5 Java Example: Minimum-Cost Flow 405
8.6 Exercises 412

III Internet Algorithmics **415**

9 Text Processing **417**
9.1 Strings and Pattern Matching Algorithms 419
9.2 Tries 429
9.3 Text Compression 440
9.4 Text Similarity Testing 443
9.5 Exercises 447

10 Number Theory and Cryptography **451**
10.1 Fundamental Algorithms Involving Numbers 453
10.2 Cryptographic Computations 471
10.3 Information Security Algorithms and Protocols 481
10.4 The Fast Fourier Transform 488
10.5 Java Example: FFT 500
10.6 Exercises 508

11 Network Algorithms **511**
11.1 Complexity Measures and Models 513
11.2 Fundamental Distributed Algorithms 517
11.3 Broadcast and Unicast Routing 530
11.4 Multicast Routing 535
11.5 Exercises 541

IV Additional Topics **545**

12 Computational Geometry **547**
12.1 Range Trees 549
12.2 Priority Search Trees 556
12.3 Quadtrees and k-D Trees 561
12.4 The Plane Sweep Technique 565
12.5 Convex Hulls 572
12.6 Java Example: Convex Hull 583
12.7 Exercises 587

13 NP-Completeness **591**
13.1 **P** and **NP** 593
13.2 **NP**-Completeness 599
13.3 Important **NP**-Complete Problems 603
13.4 Approximation Algorithms 618
13.5 Backtracking and Branch-and-Bound 627
13.6 Exercises 638

14 Algorithmic Frameworks **643**
14.1 External-Memory Algorithms 645
14.2 Parallel Algorithms 657
14.3 Online Algorithms 667
14.4 Exercises 680

A Useful Mathematical Facts **685**
Bibliography **689**
Index **698**

Acknowledgments

There are a number of individuals who have helped us with the contents of this book. Specifically, we thank Jeff Achter, Ryan Baker, Devin Borland, Ulrik Brandes, Stina Bridgeman, Robert Cohen, David Emory, David Ginat, Natasha Gelfand, Mark Handy, Benoît Hudson, Jeremy Mullendore, Daniel Polivy, John Schultz, Andrew Schwerin, Michael Shin, Galina Shubina, and Luca Vismara.

We are grateful to all our former teaching assistants who helped us in developing exercises, programming assignments, and algorithm animation systems. There have been a number of friends and colleagues whose comments have lead to improvements in the text. We are particularly thankful to Karen Goodrich, Art Moorshead, and Scott Smith for their insightful comments. We are also truly indebted to the anonymous outside reviewers for their detailed comments and constructive criticism, which were extremely useful.

We are grateful to our editors, Paul Crockett and Bill Zobrist, for their enthusiastic support of this project. The production team at Wiley has been great. Many thanks go to people who helped us with the book development, including Susannah Barr, Katherine Hepburn, Bonnie Kubat, Sharon Prendergast, Marc Ranger, Jeri Warner, and Jennifer Welter.

This manuscript was prepared primarily with LaTeX for the text and Adobe FrameMaker® and Visio® for the figures. The LGrind system was used to format Java code fragments into LaTeX. The CVS version control system enabled smooth coordination of our (sometimes concurrent) file editing.

Finally, we would like to warmly thank Isabel Cruz, Karen Goodrich, Giuseppe Di Battista, Franco Preparata, Ioannis Tollis, and our parents for providing advice, encouragement, and support at various stages of the preparation of this book. We also thank them for reminding us that there are things in life beyond writing books.

Michael T. Goodrich
Roberto Tamassia

Part

I Fundamental Tools

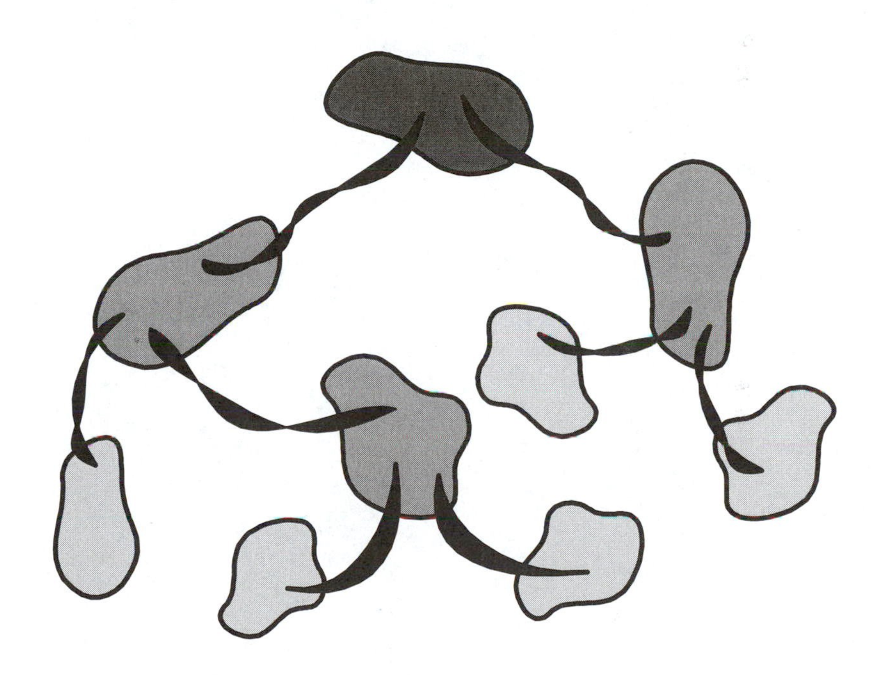

Chapter

1 Algorithm Analysis

Contents

1.1 Methodologies for Analyzing Algorithms 5
1.1.1 Pseudo-Code 7
1.1.2 The Random Access Machine (RAM) Model 9
1.1.3 Counting Primitive Operations 10
1.1.4 Analyzing Recursive Algorithms 12
1.2 Asymptotic Notation 13
1.2.1 The "Big-Oh" Notation 13
1.2.2 "Relatives" of the Big-Oh 16
1.2.3 The Importance of Asymptotics 19
1.3 A Quick Mathematical Review 21
1.3.1 Summations 21
1.3.2 Logarithms and Exponents 23
1.3.3 Simple Justification Techniques 24
1.3.4 Basic Probability 28
1.4 Case Studies in Algorithm Analysis 31
1.4.1 A Quadratic-Time Prefix Averages Algorithm 32
1.4.2 A Linear-Time Prefix Averages Algorithm 33
1.5 Amortization 34
1.5.1 Amortization Techniques 36
1.5.2 Analyzing an Extendable Array Implementation . . . 39
1.6 Experimentation 42
1.6.1 Experimental Setup 42
1.6.2 Data Analysis and Visualization 45
1.7 Exercises 47

In a classic story, the famous mathematician Archimedes was asked to determine if a golden crown commissioned by the king was indeed pure gold, and not part silver, as an informant had claimed. Archimedes discovered a way to determine this while stepping into a (Greek) bath. He noted that water spilled out of the bath in proportion to the amount of him that went in. Realizing the implications of this fact, he immediately got out of the bath and ran naked through the city shouting, "Eureka, eureka!," for he had discovered an analysis tool (displacement), which, when combined with a simple scale, could determine if the king's new crown was good or not. This discovery was unfortunate for the goldsmith, however, for when Archimedes did his analysis, the crown displaced more water than an equal-weight lump of pure gold, indicating that the crown was not, in fact, pure gold.

In this book, we are interested in the design of "good" algorithms and data structures. Simply put, an ***algorithm*** is a step-by-step procedure for performing some task in a finite amount of time, and a ***data structure*** is a systematic way of organizing and accessing data. These concepts are central to computing, but to be able to classify some algorithms and data structures as "good," we must have precise ways of analyzing them.

The primary analysis tool we will use in this book involves characterizing the running times of algorithms and data structure operations, with space usage also being of interest. Running time is a natural measure of "goodness," since time is a precious resource. But focusing on running time as a primary measure of goodness implies that we will need to use at least a little mathematics to describe running times and compare algorithms.

We begin this chapter by describing the basic framework needed for analyzing algorithms, which includes the language for describing algorithms, the computational model that language is intended for, and the main factors we count when considering running time. We also include a brief discussion of how recursive algorithms are analyzed. In Section 1.2, we present the main notation we use to characterize running times—the so-called "big-Oh" notation. These tools comprise the main theoretical tools for designing and analyzing algorithms.

In Section 1.3, we take a short break from our development of the framework for algorithm analysis to review some important mathematical facts, including discussions of summations, logarithms, proof techniques, and basic probability. Given this background and our notation for algorithm analysis, we present some case studies on theoretical algorithm analysis in Section 1.4. We follow these examples in Section 1.5 by presenting an interesting analysis technique, known as amortization, which allows us to account for the group behavior of many individual operations. Finally, in Section 1.6, we conclude the chapter by discussing an important and practical analysis technique—experimentation. We discuss both the main principles of a good experimental framework as well as techniques for summarizing and characterizing data from an experimental analysis.

1.1 Methodologies for Analyzing Algorithms

The running time of an algorithm or data structure operation typically depends on a number of factors, so what should be the proper way of measuring it? If an algorithm has been implemented, we can study its running time by executing it on various test inputs and recording the actual time spent in each execution. Such measurements can be taken in an accurate manner by using system calls that are built into the language or operating system for which the algorithm is written. In general, we are interested in determining the dependency of the running time on the size of the input. In order to determine this, we can perform several experiments on many different test inputs of various sizes. We can then visualize the results of such experiments by plotting the performance of each run of the algorithm as a point with x-coordinate equal to the input size, n, and y-coordinate equal to the running time, t. (See Figure 1.1.) To be meaningful, this analysis requires that we choose good sample inputs and test enough of them to be able to make sound statistical claims about the algorithm, which is an approach we discuss in more detail in Section 1.6.

In general, the running time of an algorithm or data structure method increases with the input size, although it may also vary for distinct inputs of the same size. Also, the running time is affected by the hardware environment (processor, clock rate, memory, disk, etc.) and software environment (operating system, programming language, compiler, interpreter, etc.) in which the algorithm is implemented, compiled, and executed. All other factors being equal, the running time of the same algorithm on the same input data will be smaller if the computer has, say, a much faster processor or if the implementation is done in a program compiled into native machine code instead of an interpreted implementation run on a virtual machine.

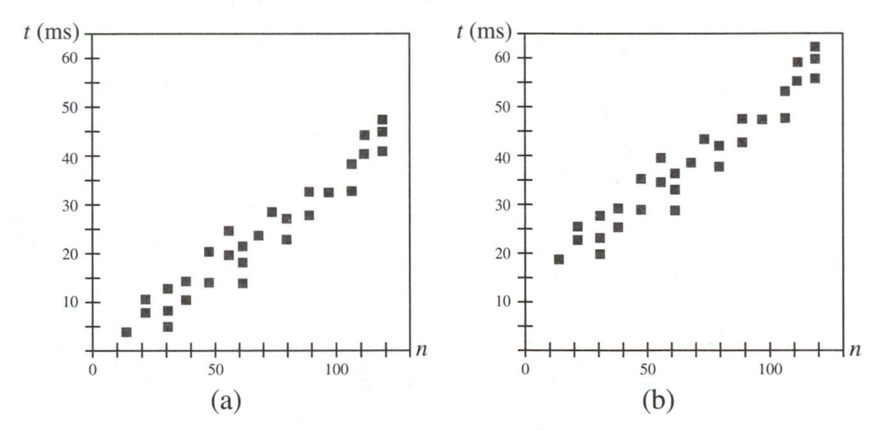

Figure 1.1: Results of an experimental study on the running time of an algorithm. A dot with coordinates (n,t) indicates that on an input of size n, the running time of the algorithm is t milliseconds (ms). (a) The algorithm executed on a fast computer; (b) the algorithm executed on a slow computer.

Requirements for a General Analysis Methodology

Experimental studies on running times are useful, as we explore in Section 1.6, but they have some limitations:

- Experiments can be done only on a limited set of test inputs, and care must be taken to make sure these are representative.
- It is difficult to compare the efficiency of two algorithms unless experiments on their running times have been performed in the same hardware and software environments.
- It is necessary to implement and execute an algorithm in order to study its running time experimentally.

Thus, while experimentation has an important role to play in algorithm analysis, it alone is not sufficient. Therefore, in addition to experimentation, we desire an analytic framework that:

- Takes into account all possible inputs
- Allows us to evaluate the relative efficiency of any two algorithms in a way that is independent from the hardware and software environment
- Can be performed by studying a high-level description of the algorithm without actually implementing it or running experiments on it.

This methodology aims at associating with each algorithm a function $f(n)$ that characterizes the running time of the algorithm in terms of the input size n. Typical functions that will be encountered include n and n^2. For example, we will write statements of the type "Algorithm A runs in time proportional to n," meaning that if we were to perform experiments, we would find that the actual running time of algorithm A on ***any*** input of size n never exceeds cn, where c is a constant that depends on the hardware and software environment used in the experiment. Given two algorithms A and B, where A runs in time proportional to n and B runs in time proportional to n^2, we will prefer A to B, since the function n grows at a smaller rate than the function n^2.

We are now ready to "roll up our sleeves" and start developing our methodology for algorithm analysis. There are several components to this methodology, including the following:

- A language for describing algorithms
- A computational model that algorithms execute within
- A metric for measuring algorithm running time
- An approach for characterizing running times, including those for recursive algorithms.

We describe these components in more detail in the remainder of this section.

1.1.1 Pseudo-Code

Programmers are often asked to describe algorithms in a way that is intended for human eyes only. Such descriptions are not computer programs, but are more structured than usual prose. They also facilitate the high level analysis of a data structure or algorithm. We call these descriptions ***pseudo-code***.

An Example of Pseudo-Code

The array-maximum problem is the simple problem of finding the maximum element in an array A storing n integers. To solve this problem, we can use an algorithm called arrayMax, which scans through the elements of A using a **for** loop.

The pseudo-code description of algorithm arrayMax is shown in Algorithm 1.2.

Algorithm arrayMax(A, n):
  Input: An array A storing $n \geq 1$ integers.
  Output: The maximum element in A.

  $currentMax \leftarrow A[0]$
  for $i \leftarrow 1$ **to** $n-1$ **do**
    if $currentMax < A[i]$ **then**
      $currentMax \leftarrow A[i]$
  return $currentMax$

Algorithm 1.2: Algorithm arrayMax.

Note that the pseudo-code is more compact than an equivalent actual software code fragment would be. In addition, the pseudo-code is easier to read and understand.

Using Pseudo-Code to Prove Algorithm Correctness

By inspecting the pseudo-code, we can argue about the correctness of algorithm arrayMax with a simple argument. Variable $currentMax$ starts out being equal to the first element of A. We claim that at the beginning of the ith iteration of the loop, $currentMax$ is equal to the maximum of the first i elements in A. Since we compare $currentMax$ to $A[i]$ in iteration i, if this claim is true before this iteration, it will be true after it for $i+1$ (which is the next value of counter i). Thus, after $n-1$ iterations, $currentMax$ will equal the maximum element in A. As with this example, we want our pseudo-code descriptions to always be detailed enough to fully justify the correctness of the algorithm they describe, while being simple enough for human readers to understand.

What Is Pseudo-Code?

Pseudo-code is a mixture of natural language and high-level programming constructs that describe the main ideas behind a generic implementation of a data structure or algorithm. There really is no precise definition of the ***pseudo-code*** language, however, because of its reliance on natural language. At the same time, to help achieve clarity, pseudo-code mixes natural language with standard programming language constructs. The programming language constructs we choose are those consistent with modern high-level languages such as C, C++, and Java. These constructs include the following:

- ***Expressions:*** We use standard mathematical symbols to express numeric and Boolean expressions. We use the left arrow sign ($\leftarrow$) as the assignment operator in assignment statements (equivalent to the $=$ operator in C, C++, and Java) and we use the equal sign ($=$) as the equality relation in Boolean expressions (equivalent to the "$==$" relation in C, C++, and Java).
- ***Method declarations:*** **Algorithm** name($param1, param2, \ldots$) declares a new method "name" and its parameters.
- ***Decision structures:*** **if** condition **then** true-actions [**else** false-actions]. We use indentation to indicate what actions should be included in the true-actions and false-actions.
- ***While-loops:*** **while** condition **do** actions. We use indentation to indicate what actions should be included in the loop actions.
- ***Repeat-loops:*** **repeat** actions **until** condition. We use indentation to indicate what actions should be included in the loop actions.
- ***For-loops:*** **for** variable-increment-definition **do** actions. We use indentation to indicate what actions should be included among the loop actions.
- ***Array indexing:*** $A[i]$ represents the ith cell in the array A. The cells of an n-celled array A are indexed from $A[0]$ to $A[n-1]$ (consistent with C, C++, and Java).
- ***Method calls:*** object.method(args) (object is optional if it is understood).
- ***Method returns:*** **return** value. This operation returns the value specified to the method that called this one.

When we write pseudo-code, we must keep in mind that we are writing for a human reader, not a computer. Thus, we should strive to communicate high-level ideas, not low-level implementation details. At the same time, we should not gloss over important steps. Like many forms of human communication, finding the right balance is an important skill that is refined through practice.

Now that we have developed a high-level way of describing algorithms, let us next discuss how we can analytically characterize algorithms written in pseudo-code.

1.1.2 The Random Access Machine (RAM) Model

As we noted above, experimental analysis is valuable, but it has its limitations. If we wish to analyze a particular algorithm without performing experiments on its running time, we can take the following more analytic approach directly on the high-level code or pseudo-code. We define a set of high-level ***primitive operations*** that are largely independent from the programming language used and can be identified also in the pseudo-code. Primitive operations include the following:

- Assigning a value to a variable
- Calling a method
- Performing an arithmetic operation (for example, adding two numbers)
- Comparing two numbers
- Indexing into an array
- Following an object reference
- Returning from a method.

Specifically, a primitive operation corresponds to a low-level instruction with an execution time that depends on the hardware and software environment but is nevertheless constant. Instead of trying to determine the specific execution time of each primitive operation, we will simply ***count*** how many primitive operations are executed, and use this number t as a high-level estimate of the running time of the algorithm. This operation count will correlate to an actual running time in a specific hardware and software environment, for each primitive operation corresponds to a constant-time instruction, and there are only a fixed number of primitive operations. The implicit assumption in this approach is that the running times of different primitive operations will be fairly similar. Thus, the number, t, of primitive operations an algorithm performs will be proportional to the actual running time of that algorithm.

RAM Machine Model Definition

This approach of simply counting primitive operations gives rise to a computational model called the ***Random Access Machine*** (RAM). This model, which should not be confused with "random access memory," views a computer simply as a CPU connected to a bank of memory cells. Each memory cell stores a word, which can be a number, a character string, or an address, that is, the value of a base type. The term "random access" refers to the ability of the CPU to access an arbitrary memory cell with one primitive operation. To keep the model simple, we do not place any specific limits on the size of numbers that can be stored in words of memory. We assume the CPU in the RAM model can perform any primitive operation in a constant number of steps, which do not depend on the size of the input. Thus, an accurate bound on the number of primitive operations an algorithm performs corresponds directly to the running time of that algorithm in the RAM model.

1.1.3 Counting Primitive Operations

We now show how to count the number of primitive operations executed by an algorithm, using as an example algorithm arrayMax, whose pseudo-code was given back in Algorithm 1.2. We do this analysis by focusing on each step of the algorithm and counting the primitive operations that it takes, taking into consideration that some operations are repeated, because they are enclosed in the body of a loop.

- Initializing the variable *currentMax* to $A[0]$ corresponds to two primitive operations (indexing into an array and assigning a value to a variable) and is executed only once at the beginning of the algorithm. Thus, it contributes two units to the count.
- At the beginning of the for loop, counter i is initialized to 1. This action corresponds to executing one primitive operation (assigning a value to a variable).
- Before entering the body of the for loop, condition $i < n$ is verified. This action corresponds to executing one primitive instruction (comparing two numbers). Since counter i starts at 0 and is incremented by 1 at the end of each iteration of the loop, the comparison $i < n$ is performed n times. Thus, it contributes n units to the count.
- The body of the for loop is executed $n-1$ times (for values $1,2,\ldots,n-1$ of the counter). At each iteration, $A[i]$ is compared with *currentMax* (two primitive operations, indexing and comparing), $A[currentMax]$ is possibly assigned to *currentMax* (two primitive operations, indexing and assigning), and the counter i is incremented (two primitive operations, summing and assigning). Hence, at each iteration of the loop, either four or six primitive operations are performed, depending on whether $A[i] \leq currentMax$ or $A[i] > currentMax$. Therefore, the body of the loop contributes between $4(n-1)$ and $6(n-1)$ units to the count.
- Returning the value of variable *currentMax* corresponds to one primitive operation, and is executed only once.

To summarize, the number of primitive operations $t(n)$ executed by algorithm arrayMax is at least

$$2+1+n+4(n-1)+1 = 5n$$

and at most

$$2+1+n+6(n-1)+1 = 7n-2.$$

The best case ($t(n) = 5n$) occurs when $A[0]$ is the maximum element, so that variable *currentMax* is never reassigned. The worst case ($t(n) = 7n-2$) occurs when the elements are sorted in increasing order, so that variable *currentMax* is reassigned at each iteration of the for loop.

Average-Case and Worst-Case Analysis

Like the arrayMax method, an algorithm may run faster on some inputs than it does on others. In such cases we may wish to express the running time of such an algorithm as an average taken over all possible inputs. Although such an ***average case*** analysis would often be valuable, it is typically quite challenging. It requires us to define a probability distribution on the set of inputs, which is typically a difficult task. Figure 1.3 schematically shows how, depending on the input distribution, the running time of an algorithm can be anywhere between the worst-case time and the best-case time. For example, what if inputs are really only of types "A" or "D"?

An average-case analysis also typically requires that we calculate expected running times based on a given input distribution. Such an analysis often requires heavy mathematics and probability theory.

Therefore, except for experimental studies or the analysis of algorithms that are themselves randomized, we will, for the remainder of this book, typically characterize running times in terms of the ***worst case***. We say, for example, that algorithm arrayMax executes $t(n) = 7n - 2$ primitive operations ***in the worst case***, meaning that the maximum number of primitive operations executed by the algorithm, taken over all inputs of size n, is $7n - 2$.

This type of analysis is much easier than an average-case analysis, as it does not require probability theory; it just requires the ability to identify the worst-case input, which is often straightforward. In addition, taking a worst-case approach can actually lead to better algorithms. Making the standard of success that of having an algorithm perform well in the worst case necessarily requires that it perform well on ***every*** input. That is, designing for the worst case can lead to stronger algorithmic "muscles," much like a track star who always practices by running up hill.

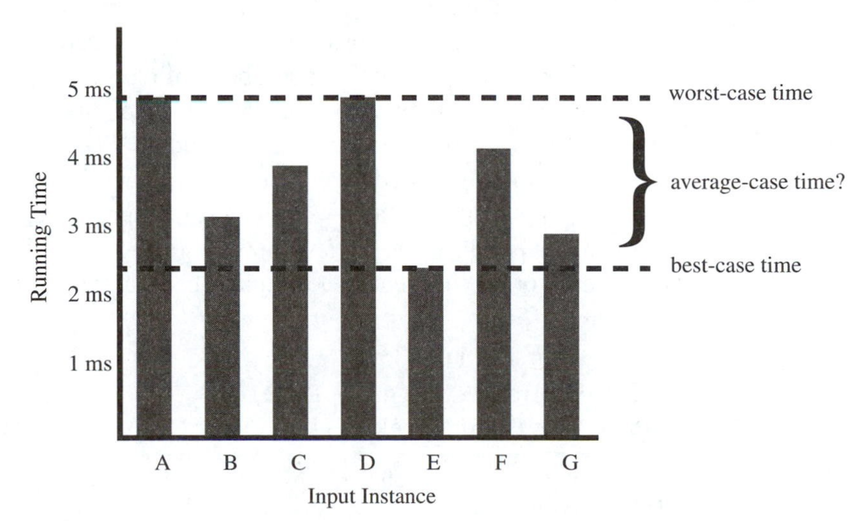

Figure 1.3: The difference between best-case and worst-case time. Each bar represents the running time of some algorithm on a different possible input.

1.1.4 Analyzing Recursive Algorithms

Iteration is not the only interesting way of solving a problem. Another useful technique, which is employed by many algorithms, is to use ***recursion***. In this technique, we define a procedure P that is allowed to make calls to itself as a subroutine, provided those calls to P are for solving subproblems of smaller size. The subroutine calls to P on smaller instances are called "recursive calls." A recursive procedure should always define a ***base case***, which is small enough that the algorithm can solve it directly without using recursion.

We give a recursive solution to the array maximum problem in Algorithm 1.4. This algorithm first checks if the array contains just a single item, which in this case must be the maximum; hence, in this simple base case we can immediately solve the problem. Otherwise, the algorithm recursively computes the maximum of the first $n-1$ elements in the array and then returns the maximum of this value and the last element in the array.

As with this example, recursive algorithms are often quite elegant. Analyzing the running time of a recursive algorithm takes a bit of additional work, however. In particular, to analyze such a running time, we use a ***recurrence equation***, which defines mathematical statements that the running time of a recursive algorithm must satisfy. We introduce a function $T(n)$ that denotes the running time of the algorithm on an input of size n, and we write equations that $T(n)$ must satisfy. For example, we can characterize the running time, $T(n)$, of the recursiveMax algorithm as

$$T(n) = \begin{cases} 3 & \text{if } n = 1 \\ T(n-1) + 7 & \text{otherwise,} \end{cases}$$

assuming that we count each comparison, array reference, recursive call, max calculation, or **return** as a single primitive operation. Ideally, we would like to characterize a recurrence equation like that above in ***closed form***, where no references to the function T appear on the righthand side. For the recursiveMax algorithm, it isn't too hard to see that a closed form would be $T(n) = 7(n-1) + 3 = 7n - 2$. In general, determining closed form solutions to recurrence equations can be much more challenging than this, and we study some specific examples of recurrence equations in Chapter 4, when we study some sorting and selection algorithms. We study methods for solving recurrence equations of a general form in Section 5.2.

Algorithm recursiveMax(A, n):
  Input: An array A storing $n \geq 1$ integers.
  Output: The maximum element in A.

 if $n = 1$ **then**
  return $A[0]$
 return $\max\{\text{recursiveMax}(A, n-1), A[n-1]\}$

Algorithm 1.4: Algorithm recursiveMax.

1.2 Asymptotic Notation

We have clearly gone into laborious detail for evaluating the running time of such a simple algorithm as arrayMax and its recursive cousin, recursiveMax. Such an approach would clearly prove cumbersome if we had to perform it for more complicated algorithms. In general, each step in a pseudo-code description and each statement in a high-level language implementation corresponds to a small number of primitive operations that does not depend on the input size. Thus, we can perform a simplified analysis that estimates the number of primitive operations executed up to a constant factor, by counting the steps of the pseudo-code or the statements of the high-level language executed. Fortunately, there is a notation that allows us to characterize the main factors affecting an algorithm's running time without going into all the details of exactly how many primitive operations are performed for each constant-time set of instructions.

1.2.1 The "Big-Oh" Notation

Let $f(n)$ and $g(n)$ be functions mapping nonnegative integers to real numbers. We say that $f(n)$ is $O(g(n))$ if there is a real constant $c > 0$ and an integer constant $n_0 \geq 1$ such that $f(n) \leq cg(n)$ for every integer $n \geq n_0$. This definition is often referred to as the "big-Oh" notation, for it is sometimes pronounced as "$f(n)$ is ***big-Oh*** of $g(n)$." Alternatively, we can also say "$f(n)$ is ***order*** $g(n)$." (This definition is illustrated in Figure 1.5.)

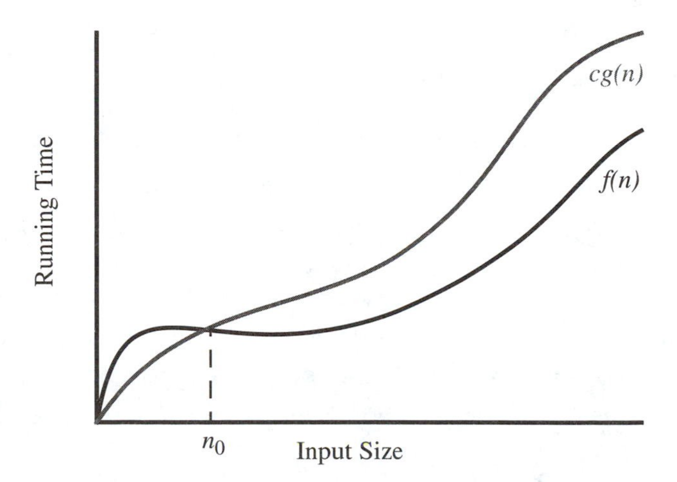

Figure 1.5: Illustrating the "big-Oh" notation. The function $f(n)$ is $O(g(n))$, for $f(n) \leq c \cdot g(n)$ when $n \geq n_0$.

Example 1.1: *$7n-2$ is $O(n)$.*

Proof: *By the big-Oh definition, we need to find a real constant $c>0$ and an integer constant $n_0 \geq 1$ such that $7n-2 \leq cn$ for every integer $n \geq n_0$. It is easy to see that a possible choice is $c=7$ and $n_0=1$. Indeed, this is one of infinitely many choices available because any real number greater than or equal to 7 will work for c, and any integer greater than or equal to 1 will work for n_0.* ■

The big-Oh notation allows us to say that a function of n is "less than or equal to" another function (by the inequality "$\leq$" in the definition), up to a constant factor (by the constant c in the definition) and in the ***asymptotic*** sense as n grows toward infinity (by the statement "$n \geq n_0$" in the definition).

The big-Oh notation is used widely to characterize running times and space bounds in terms of some parameter n, which varies from problem to problem, but is usually defined as an intuitive notion of the "size" of the problem. For example, if we are interested in finding the largest element in an array of integers (see arrayMax given in Algorithm 1.2), it would be most natural to let n denote the number of elements of the array. For example, we can write the following precise statement on the running time of algorithm arrayMax from Algorithm 1.2.

Theorem 1.2: *The running time of algorithm* arrayMax *for computing the maximum element in an array of n integers is $O(n)$.*

Proof: As shown in Section 1.1.3, the number of primitive operations executed by algorithm arrayMax is at most $7n-2$. We may therefore apply the big-Oh definition with $c=7$ and $n_0=1$ and conclude that the running time of algorithm arrayMax is $O(n)$. ■

Let us consider a few additional examples that illustrate the big-Oh notation.

Example 1.3: *$20n^3 + 10n\log n + 5$ is $O(n^3)$.*

Proof: $20n^3 + 10n\log n + 5 \leq 35n^3$, *for $n \geq 1$.* ■

In fact, any polynomial $a_k n^k + a_{k-1} n^{k-1} + \cdots + a_0$ will always be $O(n^k)$.

Example 1.4: *$3\log n + \log\log n$ is $O(\log n)$.*

Proof: $3\log n + \log\log n \leq 4\log n$, *for $n \geq 2$. Note that $\log\log n$ is not even defined for $n=1$. That is why we use $n \geq 2$.* ■

Example 1.5: *2^{100} is $O(1)$.*

Proof: $2^{100} \leq 2^{100} \cdot 1$, *for $n \geq 1$. Note that variable n does not appear in the inequality, since we are dealing with constant-valued functions.* ■

Example 1.6: *$5/n$ is $O(1/n)$.*

Proof: $5/n \leq 5(1/n)$, *for $n \geq 1$ (even though this is actually a* **decreasing** *function).* ■

In general, we should use the big-Oh notation to characterize a function as closely as possible. While it is true that $f(n) = 4n^3 + 3n^{4/3}$ is $O(n^5)$, it is more accurate to say that $f(n)$ is $O(n^3)$. Consider, by way of analogy, a scenario where a hungry traveler driving along a long country road happens upon a local farmer walking home from a market. If the traveler asks the farmer how much longer he must drive before he can find some food, it may be truthful for the farmer to say, "certainly no longer than 12 hours," but it is much more accurate (and helpful) for him to say, "you can find a market just a few minutes' drive up this road."

Instead of always applying the big-Oh definition directly to obtain a big-Oh characterization, we can use the following rules to simplify notation.

Theorem 1.7: *Let $d(n)$, $e(n)$, $f(n)$, and $g(n)$ be functions mapping nonnegative integers to nonnegative reals. Then*

1. *If $d(n)$ is $O(f(n))$, then $ad(n)$ is $O(f(n))$, for any constant $a > 0$.*
2. *If $d(n)$ is $O(f(n))$ and $e(n)$ is $O(g(n))$, then $d(n)+e(n)$ is $O(f(n)+g(n))$.*
3. *If $d(n)$ is $O(f(n))$ and $e(n)$ is $O(g(n))$, then $d(n)e(n)$ is $O(f(n)g(n))$.*
4. *If $d(n)$ is $O(f(n))$ and $f(n)$ is $O(g(n))$, then $d(n)$ is $O(g(n))$.*
5. *If $f(n)$ is a polynomial of degree d (that is, $f(n) = a_0 + a_1 n + \cdots + a_d n^d$), then $f(n)$ is $O(n^d)$.*
6. *n^x is $O(a^n)$ for any fixed $x > 0$ and $a > 1$.*
7. *$\log n^x$ is $O(\log n)$ for any fixed $x > 0$.*
8. *$\log^x n$ is $O(n^y)$ for any fixed constants $x > 0$ and $y > 0$.*

It is considered poor taste to include constant factors and lower order terms in the big-Oh notation. For example, it is not fashionable to say that the function $2n^2$ is $O(4n^2 + 6n\log n)$, although this is completely correct. We should strive instead to describe the function in the big-Oh in ***simplest terms***.

Example 1.8: $2n^3 + 4n^2 \log n$ *is* $O(n^3)$.

Proof: *We can apply the rules of Theorem 1.7 as follows:*

- *$\log n$ is $O(n)$ (Rule 8).*
- *$4n^2 \log n$ is $O(4n^3)$ (Rule 3).*
- *$2n^3 + 4n^2 \log n$ is $O(2n^3 + 4n^3)$ (Rule 2).*
- *$2n^3 + 4n^3$ is $O(n^3)$ (Rule 5 or Rule 1).*
- *$2n^3 + 4n^2 \log n$ is $O(n^3)$ (Rule 4).* ■

Some functions appear often in the analysis of algorithms and data structures, and we often use special terms to refer to them. Table 1.6 shows some terms commonly used in algorithm analysis.

logarithmic	linear	quadratic	polynomial	exponential
$O(\log n)$	$O(n)$	$O(n^2)$	$O(n^k)$ $(k \geq 1)$	$O(a^n)$ $(a > 1)$

Table 1.6: Terminology for classes of functions.

Using the Big-Oh Notation

It is considered poor taste, in general, to say "$f(n) \leq O(g(n))$," since the big-Oh already denotes the "less-than-or-equal-to" concept. Likewise, although common, it is not completely correct to say "$f(n) = O(g(n))$" (with the usual understanding of the "$=$" relation), and it is actually incorrect to say "$f(n) \geq O(g(n))$" or "$f(n) > O(g(n))$." It is best to say "$f(n)$ ***is*** $O(g(n))$." For the more mathematically inclined, it is also correct to say,

$$\text{“}f(n) \in O(g(n)),\text{”}$$

for the big-Oh notation is, technically speaking, denoting a whole collection of functions.

Even with this interpretation, there is considerable freedom in how we can use arithmetic operations with the big-Oh notation, provided the connection to the definition of the big-Oh is clear. For instance, we can say,

$$\text{“}f(n) \text{ is } g(n) + O(h(n)),\text{”}$$

which would mean that there are constants $c > 0$ and $n_0 \geq 1$ such that $f(n) \leq g(n) + ch(n)$ for $n \geq n_0$. As in this example, we may sometimes wish to give the exact leading term in an asymptotic characterization. In that case, we would say that "$f(n)$ is $g(n) + O(h(n))$," where $h(n)$ grows slower than $g(n)$. For example, we could say that $2n\log n + 4n + 10\sqrt{n}$ is $2n\log n + O(n)$.

1.2.2 "Relatives" of the Big-Oh

Just as the big-Oh notation provides an asymptotic way of saying that a function is "less than or equal to" another function, there are other notations that provide asymptotic ways of making other types of comparisons.

Big-Omega and Big-Theta

Let $f(n)$ and $g(n)$ be functions mapping integers to real numbers. We say that $f(n)$ is $\Omega(g(n))$ (pronounced "$f(n)$ is big-Omega of $g(n)$") if $g(n)$ is $O(f(n))$; that is, there is a real constant $c > 0$ and an integer constant $n_0 \geq 1$ such that $f(n) \geq cg(n)$, for $n \geq n_0$. This definition allows us to say asymptotically that one function is greater than or equal to another, up to a constant factor. Likewise, we say that $f(n)$ is $\Theta(g(n))$ (pronounced "$f(n)$ is big-Theta of $g(n)$") if $f(n)$ is $O(g(n))$ and $f(n)$ is $\Omega(g(n))$; that is, there are real constants $c' > 0$ and $c'' > 0$, and an integer constant $n_0 \geq 1$ such that $c'g(n) \leq f(n) \leq c''g(n)$, for $n \geq n_0$.

The big-Theta allows us to say that two functions are asymptotically equal, up to a constant factor. We consider some examples of these notations below.

Example 1.9: $3\log n + \log\log n$ *is* $\Omega(\log n)$.

Proof: $3\log n + \log\log n \geq 3\log n$, *for* $n \geq 2$. ■

This example shows that lower order terms are not dominant in establishing lower bounds with the big-Omega notation. Thus, as the next example sums up, lower order terms are not dominant in the big-Theta notation either.

Example 1.10: $3\log n + \log\log n$ *is* $\Theta(\log n)$.

Proof: *This follows from Examples 1.4 and 1.9.* ■

Some Words of Caution

A few words of caution about asymptotic notation are in order at this point. First, note that the use of the big-Oh and related notations can be somewhat misleading should the constant factors they "hide" be very large. For example, while it is true that the function $10^{100}n$ is $\Theta(n)$, if this is the running time of an algorithm being compared to one whose running time is $10n\log n$, we should prefer the $\Theta(n\log n)$ time algorithm, even though the linear-time algorithm is asymptotically faster. This preference is because the constant factor, 10^{100}, which is called "one googol," is believed by many astronomers to be an upper bound on the number of atoms in the observable universe. So we are unlikely to ever have a real-world problem that has this number as its input size. Thus, even when using the big-Oh notation, we should at least be somewhat mindful of the constant factors and lower order terms we are "hiding."

The above observation raises the issue of what constitutes a "fast" algorithm. Generally speaking, any algorithm running in $O(n\log n)$ time (with a reasonable constant factor) should be considered efficient. Even an $O(n^2)$ time method may be fast enough in some contexts, that is, when n is small. But an algorithm running in $\Theta(2^n)$ time should never be considered efficient. This fact is illustrated by a famous story about the inventor of the game of chess. He asked only that his king pay him 1 grain of rice for the first square on the board, 2 grains for the second, 4 grains for the third, 8 for the fourth, and so on. But try to imagine the sight of 2^{64} grains stacked on the last square! In fact, this number cannot even be represented as a standard long integer in most programming languages.

Therefore, if we must draw a line between efficient and inefficient algorithms, it is natural to make this distinction be that between those algorithms running in polynomial time and those requiring exponential time. That is, make the distinction between algorithms with a running time that is $O(n^k)$, for some constant $k \geq 1$, and those with a running time that is $\Theta(c^n)$, for some constant $c > 1$. Like so many notions we have discussed in this section, this too should be taken with a "grain of salt," for an algorithm running in $\Theta(n^{100})$ time should probably not be considered "efficient." Even so, the distinction between polynomial-time and exponential-time algorithms is considered a robust measure of tractability.

"Distant Cousins" of the Big-Oh: Little-Oh and Little-Omega

There are also some ways of saying that one function is strictly less than or strictly greater than another asymptotically, but these are not used as often as the big-Oh, big-Omega, and big-Theta. Nevertheless, for the sake of completeness, we give their definitions as well.

Let $f(n)$ and $g(n)$ be functions mapping integers to real numbers. We say that $f(n)$ is $o(g(n))$ (pronounced "$f(n)$ is little-oh of $g(n)$") if, for any constant $c > 0$, there is a constant $n_0 > 0$ such that $f(n) \leq cg(n)$ for $n \geq n_0$. Likewise, we say that $f(n)$ is $\omega(g(n))$ (pronounced "$f(n)$ is little-omega of $g(n)$") if $g(n)$ is $o(f(n))$, that is, if, for any constant $c > 0$, there is a constant $n_0 > 0$ such that $g(n) \leq cf(n)$ for $n \geq n_0$. Intuitively, $o(\cdot)$ is analogous to "less than" in an asymptotic sense, and $\omega(\cdot)$ is analogous to "greater than" in an asymptotic sense.

Example 1.11: *The function $f(n) = 12n^2 + 6n$ is $o(n^3)$ and $\omega(n)$.*

Proof: *Let us first show that $f(n)$ is $o(n^3)$. Let $c > 0$ be any constant. If we take $n_0 = (12+6)/c$, then, for $n \geq n_0$, we have*

$$cn^3 \geq 12n^2 + 6n^2 \geq 12n^2 + 6n.$$

Thus, $f(n)$ is $o(n^3)$.

To show that $f(n)$ is $\omega(n)$, let $c > 0$ again be any constant. If we take $n_0 = c/12$, then, for $n \geq n_0$, we have

$$12n^2 + 6n \geq 12n^2 \geq cn.$$

Thus, $f(n)$ is $\omega(n)$. ■

For the reader familiar with limits, we note that $f(n)$ is $o(g(n))$ if and only if

$$\lim_{n \to \infty} \frac{f(n)}{g(n)} = 0,$$

provided this limit exists. The main difference between the little-oh and big-Oh notions is that $f(n)$ is $O(g(n))$ if ***there exist*** constants $c > 0$ and $n_0 \geq 1$ such that $f(n) \leq cg(n)$, for $n \geq n_0$; whereas $f(n)$ is $o(g(n))$ if ***for all*** constants $c > 0$ there is a constant n_0 such that $f(n) \leq cg(n)$, for $n \geq n_0$. Intuitively, $f(n)$ is $o(g(n))$ if $f(n)$ becomes insignificant compared to $g(n)$ as n grows toward infinity. As previously mentioned, asymptotic notation is useful because it allows us to concentrate on the main factor determining a function's growth.

To summarize, the asymptotic notations of big-Oh, big-Omega, and big-Theta, as well as little-oh and little-omega, provide a convenient language for us to analyze data structures and algorithms. As mentioned earlier, these notations provide convenience because they let us concentrate on the "big picture" rather than low-level details.

1.2.3 The Importance of Asymptotics

Asymptotic notation has many important benefits, which might not be immediately obvious. Specifically, we illustrate one important aspect of the asymptotic viewpoint in Table 1.7. This table explores the maximum size allowed for an input instance for various running times to be solved in 1 second, 1 minute, and 1 hour, assuming each operation can be processed in 1 microsecond (1 μs). It also shows the importance of algorithm design, because an algorithm with an asymptotically slow running time (for example, one that is $O(n^2)$) is beaten in the long run by an algorithm with an asymptotically faster running time (for example, one that is $O(n \log n)$), even if the constant factor for the faster algorithm is worse.

Running Time	Maximum Problem Size (n) 1 second	1 minute	1 hour
$400n$	2,500	150,000	9,000,000
$20n\lceil\log n\rceil$	4,096	166,666	7,826,087
$2n^2$	707	5,477	42,426
n^4	31	88	244
2^n	19	25	31

Table 1.7: Maximum size of a problem that can be solved in one second, one minute, and one hour, for various running times measured in microseconds.

The importance of good algorithm design goes beyond just what can be solved effectively on a given computer, however. As shown in Table 1.8, even if we achieve a dramatic speedup in hardware, we still cannot overcome the handicap of an asymptotically slow algorithm. This table shows the new maximum problem size achievable for any fixed amount of time, assuming algorithms with the given running times are now run on a computer 256 times faster than the previous one.

Running Time	New Maximum Problem Size
$400n$	$256m$
$20n\lceil\log n\rceil$	approx. $256((\log m)/(7+\log m))m$
$2n^2$	$16m$
n^4	$4m$
2^n	$m+8$

Table 1.8: Increase in the maximum size of a problem that can be solved in a certain fixed amount of time, by using a computer that is 256 times faster than the previous one, for various running times of the algorithm. Each entry is given as a function of m, the previous maximum problem size.

Ordering Functions by Their Growth Rates

Suppose two algorithms solving the same problem are available: an algorithm A, which has a running time of $\Theta(n)$, and an algorithm B, which has a running time of $\Theta(n^2)$. Which one is better? The little-oh notation says that n is $o(n^2)$, which implies that algorithm A is ***asymptotically better*** than algorithm B, although for a given (small) value of n, it is possible for algorithm B to have lower running time than algorithm A. Still, in the long run, as shown in the above tables, the benefits of algorithm A over algorithm B will become clear.

In general, we can use the little-oh notation to order classes of functions by asymptotic growth rate. In Table 1.9, we show a list of functions ordered by increasing growth rate, that is, if a function $f(n)$ precedes a function $g(n)$ in the list, then $f(n)$ is $o(g(n))$.

Functions Ordered by Growth Rate
$\log n$
$\log^2 n$
$\sqrt{n}$
n
$n \log n$
n^2
n^3
2^n

Table 1.9: An ordered list of simple functions. Note that, using common terminology, one of the above functions is logarithmic, two are polylogarithmic, three are sublinear, one is linear, one is quadratic, one is cubic, and one is exponential.

In Table 1.10, we illustrate the difference in the growth rate of all but one of the functions shown in Table 1.9.

n	$\log n$	$\sqrt{n}$	n	$n \log n$	n^2	n^3	2^n
2	1	1.4	2	2	4	8	4
4	2	2	4	8	16	64	16
8	3	2.8	8	24	64	512	256
16	4	4	16	64	256	4,096	65,536
32	5	5.7	32	160	1,024	32,768	4,294,967,296
64	6	8	64	384	4,096	262,144	1.84×10^{19}
128	7	11	128	896	16,384	2,097,152	3.40×10^{38}
256	8	16	256	2,048	65,536	16,777,216	1.15×10^{77}
512	9	23	512	4,608	262,144	134,217,728	1.34×10^{154}
1,024	10	32	1,024	10,240	1,048,576	1,073,741,824	1.79×10^{308}

Table 1.10: Growth of several functions.

1.3 A Quick Mathematical Review

In this section, we briefly review some of the fundamental concepts from discrete mathematics that will arise in several of our discussions. In addition to these fundamental concepts, Appendix A includes a list of other useful mathematical facts that apply in the context of data structure and algorithm analysis.

1.3.1 Summations

A notation that appears again and again in the analysis of data structures and algorithms is the ***summation***, which is defined as

$$\sum_{i=a}^{b} f(i) = f(a) + f(a+1) + f(a+2) + \cdots + f(b).$$

Summations arise in data structure and algorithm analysis because the running times of loops naturally give rise to summations. For example, a summation that often arises in data structure and algorithm analysis is the geometric summation.

Theorem 1.12: *For any integer $n \geq 0$ and any real number $0 < a \neq 1$, consider*

$$\sum_{i=0}^{n} a^i = 1 + a + a^2 + \cdots + a^n$$

(remembering that $a^0 = 1$ if $a > 0$). This summation is equal to

$$\frac{1 - a^{n+1}}{1 - a}.$$

Summations as shown in Theorem 1.12 are called ***geometric*** summations, because each term is geometrically larger than the previous one if $a > 1$. That is, the terms in such a geometric summation exhibit exponential growth. For example, everyone working in computing should know that

$$1 + 2 + 4 + 8 + \cdots + 2^{n-1} = 2^n - 1,$$

for this is the largest integer that can be represented in binary notation using n bits.

Another summation that arises in several contexts is

$$\sum_{i=1}^{n} i = 1 + 2 + 3 + \cdots + (n-2) + (n-1) + n.$$

This summation often arises in the analysis of loops in cases where the number of operations performed inside the loop increases by a fixed, constant amount with each iteration. This summation also has an interesting history. In 1787, a German elementary schoolteacher decided to keep his 9- and 10-year-old pupils occupied with the task of adding up all the numbers from 1 to 100. But almost immediately after giving this assignment, one of the children claimed to have the answer—5,050.

That elementary school student was none other than Karl Gauss, who would grow up to be one of the greatest mathematicians of the 19th century. It is widely suspected that young Gauss derived the answer to his teacher's assignment using the following identity.

Theorem 1.13: *For any integer $n \geq 1$, we have*

$$\sum_{i=1}^{n} i = \frac{n(n+1)}{2}.$$

Proof: We give two "visual" justifications of Theorem 1.13 in Figure 1.11, both of which are based on computing the area of a collection of rectangles representing the numbers 1 through n. In Figure 1.11a we draw a big triangle over an ordering of the rectangles, noting that the area of the rectangles is the same as that of the big triangle ($n^2/2$) plus that of n small triangles, each of area $1/2$. In Figure 1.11b, which applies when n is even, we note that 1 plus n is $n+1$, as is 2 plus $n-1$, 3 plus $n-2$, and so on. There are $n/2$ such pairings. ■

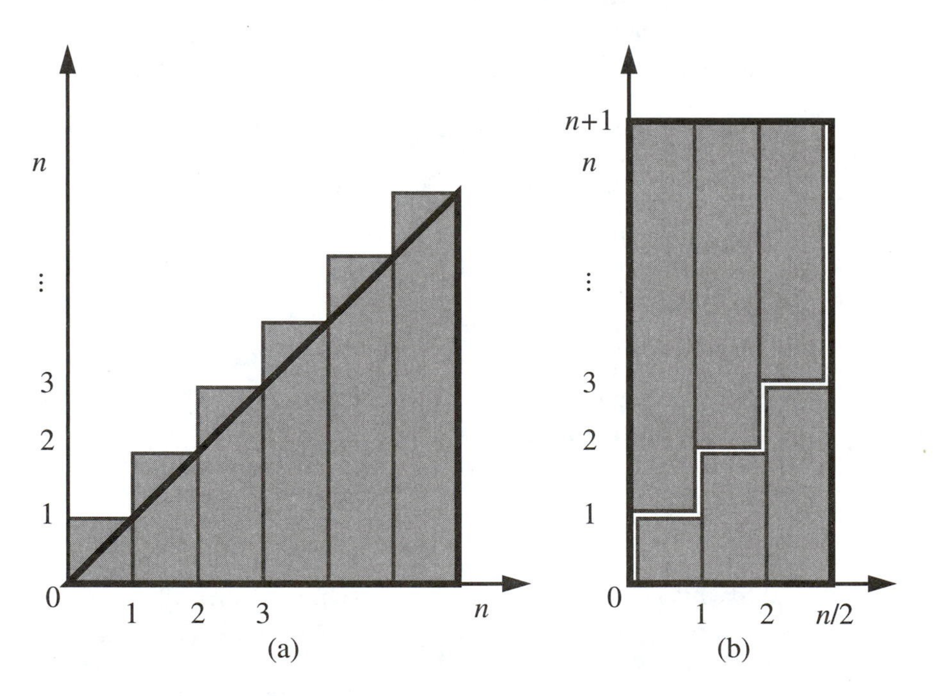

Figure 1.11: Visual justifications of Theorem 1.13. Both illustrations visualize the identity in terms of the total area covered by n unit-width rectangles with heights $1, 2, \ldots, n$. In (a) the rectangles are shown to cover a big triangle of area $n^2/2$ (base n and height n) plus n small triangles of area $1/2$ each (base 1 and height 1). In (b), which applies only when n is even, the rectangles are shown to cover a big rectangle of base $n/2$ and height $n+1$.

1.3.2 Logarithms and Exponents

One of the interesting and sometimes even surprising aspects of the analysis of data structures and algorithms is the ubiquitous presence of logarithms and exponents, where we say

$$\log_b a = c \qquad \text{if} \qquad a = b^c.$$

As is the custom in the computing literature, we omit writing the base b of the logarithm when $b = 2$. For example, $\log 1024 = 10$.

There are a number of important rules for logarithms and exponents, including the following:

Theorem 1.14: *Let a, b, and c be positive real numbers. We have:*

1. $\log_b ac = \log_b a + \log_b c$
2. $\log_b a/c = \log_b a - \log_b c$
3. $\log_b a^c = c \log_b a$
4. $\log_b a = (\log_c a)/\log_c b$
5. $b^{\log_c a} = a^{\log_c b}$
6. $(b^a)^c = b^{ac}$
7. $b^a b^c = b^{a+c}$
8. $b^a/b^c = b^{a-c}$.

Also, as a notational shorthand, we use $\log^c n$ to denote the function $(\log n)^c$ and we use $\log \log n$ to denote $\log(\log n)$. Rather than show how we could derive each of the above identities, which all follow from the definition of logarithms and exponents, let us instead illustrate these identities with a few examples of their usefulness.

Example 1.15: *We illustrate some interesting cases when the base of a logarithm or exponent is 2. The rules cited refer to Theorem 1.14.*

- $\log(2n \log n) = 1 + \log n + \log \log n$, *by rule 1 (twice)*
- $\log(n/2) = \log n - \log 2 = \log n - 1$, *by rule 2*
- $\log \sqrt{n} = \log(n)^{1/2} = (\log n)/2$, *by rule 3*
- $\log \log \sqrt{n} = \log(\log n)/2 = \log \log n - 1$, *by rules 2 and 3*
- $\log_4 n = (\log n)/\log 4 = (\log n)/2$, *by rule 4*
- $\log 2^n = n$, *by rule 3*
- $2^{\log n} = n$, *by rule 5*
- $2^{2 \log n} = (2^{\log n})^2 = n^2$, *by rules 5 and 6*
- $4^n = (2^2)^n = 2^{2n}$, *by rule 6*
- $n^2 2^{3 \log n} = n^2 \cdot n^3 = n^5$, *by rules 5, 6, and 7*
- $4^n/2^n = 2^{2n}/2^n = 2^{2n-n} = 2^n$, *by rules 6 and 8*

The Floor and Ceiling Functions

One additional comment concerning logarithms is in order. The value of a logarithm is typically not an integer, yet the running time of an algorithm is typically expressed by means of an integer quantity, such as the number of operations performed. Thus, an algorithm analysis may sometimes involve the use of the so-called "floor" and "ceiling" functions, which are defined respectively as follows:

- $\lfloor x \rfloor =$ the largest integer less than or equal to x.
- $\lceil x \rceil =$ the smallest integer greater than or equal to x.

These functions give us a way to convert real-valued functions into integer-valued functions. Even so, functions used to analyze data structures and algorithms are often expressed simply as real-valued functions (for example, $n \log n$ or $n^{3/2}$). We should read such a running time as having a "big" ceiling function surrounding it.[1]

1.3.3 Simple Justification Techniques

We will sometimes wish to make strong claims about a certain data structure or algorithm. We may, for example, wish to show that our algorithm is correct or that it runs fast. In order to rigorously make such claims, we must use mathematical language, and in order to back up such claims, we must justify or ***prove*** our statements. Fortunately, there are several simple ways to do this.

By Example

Some claims are of the generic form, "There is an element x in a set S that has property P." To justify such a claim, we need only produce a particular $x \in S$ that has property P. Likewise, some hard-to-believe claims are of the generic form, "Every element x in a set S has property P." To justify that such a claim is false, we need to only produce a particular x from S that does not have property P. Such an instance is called a ***counterexample***.

Example 1.16: *A certain Professor Amongus claims that every number of the form* $2^i - 1$ *is a prime, when* i *is an integer greater than* 1. *Professor Amongus is wrong.*

Proof: *To prove Professor Amongus is wrong, we need to find a counter-example. Fortunately, we need not look too far, for* $2^4 - 1 = 15 = 3 \cdot 5$. ■

[1]Real-valued running-time functions are almost always used in conjunction with the asymptotic notation described in Section 1.2, for which the use of the ceiling function would usually be redundant anyway. (See Exercise R-1.24.)

The "Contra" Attack

Another set of justification techniques involves the use of the negative. The two primary such methods are the use of the ***contrapositive*** and the ***contradiction***. The use of the contrapositive method is like looking through a negative mirror. To justify the statement "if p is true, then q is true" we instead establish that "if q is not true, then p is not true." Logically, these two statements are the same, but the latter, which is called the ***contrapositive*** of the first, may be easier to think about.

Example 1.17: *If ab is odd, then a is odd or b is even.*

Proof: *To justify this claim, consider the contrapositive, "If a is even and b is odd, then ab is even." So, suppose $a = 2i$, for some integer i. Then $ab = (2i)b = 2(ib)$; hence, ab is even.* ■

Besides showing a use of the contrapositive justification technique, the previous example also contains an application of ***DeMorgan's Law***. This law helps us deal with negations, for it states that the negation of a statement of the form "p or q" is "not p and not q." Likewise, it states that the negation of a statement of the form "p and q" is "not p or not q."

Another negative justification technique is proof by ***contradiction***, which also often involves using DeMorgan's Law. In applying the proof by contradiction technique, we establish that a statement q is true by first supposing that q is false and then showing that this assumption leads to a contradiction (such as $2 \neq 2$ or $1 > 3$). By reaching such a contradiction, we show that no consistent situation exists with q being false, so q must be true. Of course, in order to reach this conclusion, we must be sure our situation is consistent before we assume q is false.

Example 1.18: *If ab is odd, then a is odd or b is even.*

Proof: *Let ab be odd. We wish to show that a is odd or b is even. So, with the hope of leading to a contradiction, let us assume the opposite, namely, suppose a is even and b is odd. Then $a = 2i$ for some integer i. Hence, $ab = (2i)b = 2(ib)$, that is, ab is even. But this is a contradiction: ab cannot simultaneously be odd and even. Therefore a is odd or b is even.* ■

Induction

Most of the claims we make about a running time or a space bound involve an integer parameter n (usually denoting an intuitive notion of the "size" of the problem). Moreover, most of these claims are equivalent to saying some statement $q(n)$ is true "for all $n \geq 1$." Since this is making a claim about an infinite set of numbers, we cannot justify this exhaustively in a direct fashion.

We can often justify claims such as those above as true, however, by using the technique of ***induction***. This technique amounts to showing that, for any particular $n \geq 1$, there is a finite sequence of implications that starts with something known to be true and ultimately leads to showing that $q(n)$ is true. Specifically, we begin a proof by induction by showing that $q(n)$ is true for $n=1$ (and possibly some other values $n=2,3,\ldots,k$, for some constant k). Then we justify that the inductive "step" is true for $n>k$, namely, we show "if $q(i)$ is true for $i<n$, then $q(n)$ is true." The combination of these two pieces completes the proof by induction.

Example 1.19: *Consider the Fibonacci sequence:* $F(1)=1$, $F(2)=2$, *and* $F(n)=F(n-1)+F(n-2)$ *for* $n>2$. *We claim that* $F(n)<2^n$.

Proof: *We will show our claim is right by induction.*
Base cases: *(*$n\leq 2$*).* $F(1)=1<2=2^1$ and $F(2)=2<4=2^2$.
Induction step: *(*$n>2$*). Suppose our claim is true for* $n'<n$. *Consider* $F(n)$. *Since* $n>2$, $F(n)=F(n-1)+F(n-2)$. *Moreover, since* $n-1<n$ *and* $n-2<n$, *we can apply the inductive assumption (sometimes called the "inductive hypothesis") to imply that* $F(n)<2^{n-1}+2^{n-2}$. *In addition,*

$$2^{n-1}+2^{n-2}<2^{n-1}+2^{n-1}=2\cdot 2^{n-1}=2^n.$$

This completes the proof. ■

Let us do another inductive argument, this time for a fact we have seen before.

Theorem 1.20: *(which is the same as Theorem 1.13)*

$$\sum_{i=1}^{n} i=\frac{n(n+1)}{2}.$$

Proof: We will justify this equality by induction.
Base case: $n=1$. Trivial, for $1=n(n+1)/2$, if $n=1$.
Induction step: $n\geq 2$. Assume the claim is true for $n'<n$. Consider n.

$$\sum_{i=1}^{n} i=n+\sum_{i=1}^{n-1} i.$$

By the induction hypothesis, then

$$\sum_{i=1}^{n} i=n+\frac{(n-1)n}{2},$$

which we can simplify as

$$n+\frac{(n-1)n}{2}=\frac{2n+n^2-n}{2}=\frac{n^2+n}{2}=\frac{n(n+1)}{2}.$$

This completes the proof. ■

We may sometimes feel overwhelmed by the task of justifying something true for *all* $n\geq 1$. We should remember, however, the concreteness of the inductive technique. It shows that, for any particular n, there is a finite step-by-step sequence of implications that starts with something true and leads to the truth about n. In short, the inductive argument is a formula for building a sequence of direct justifications.

Loop Invariants

The final justification technique we discuss in this section is the ***loop invariant***.

> To prove some statement $\mathcal{S}$ about a loop is correct, define $\mathcal{S}$ in terms of a series of smaller statements $\mathcal{S}_0, \mathcal{S}_1, \ldots, \mathcal{S}_k$, where:
>
> 1. The ***initial*** claim, $\mathcal{S}_0$, is true before the loop begins.
> 2. If $\mathcal{S}_{i-1}$ is true before iteration i begins, then one can show that $\mathcal{S}_i$ will be true after iteration i is over.
> 3. The final statement, $\mathcal{S}_k$, implies the statement $\mathcal{S}$ that we wish to justify as being true.

We have, in fact, already seen the loop-invariant justification technique at work in Section 1.1.1 (for the correctness of arrayMax), but let us nevertheless give one more example here. In particular, let us consider applying the loop invariant method to justify the correctness of Algorithm arrayFind, shown in Algorithm 1.12, which searches for an element x in an array A.

To show arrayFind to be correct, we use a loop invariant argument. That is, we inductively define statements, $\mathcal{S}_i$, for $i = 0, 1, \ldots, n$, that lead to the correctness of arrayFind. Specifically, we claim the following to be true at the beginning of iteration i:

$\mathcal{S}_i$: x is not equal to any of the first i elements of A.

This claim is true at the beginning of the first iteration of the loop, since there are no elements among the first 0 in A (this kind of a trivially-true claim is said to hold ***vacuously***). In iteration i, we compare element x to element $A[i]$ and return the index i if these two elements are equal, which is clearly correct. If the two elements x and $A[i]$ are not equal, then we have found one more element not equal to x and we increment the index i. Thus, the claim $\mathcal{S}_i$ will be true for this new value of i, for the beginning of the next iteration. If the while-loop terminates without ever returning an index in A, then $\mathcal{S}_n$ is true—there are no elements of A equal to x. Therefore, the algorithm is correct to return the nonindex value -1, as required.

Algorithm arrayFind(x,A):
    Input: An element x and an n-element array, A.
    Output: The index i such that $x = A[i]$ or -1 if no element of A is equal to x.

```
i ← 0
while i < n do
   if x = A[i] then
      return i
   else
      i ← i + 1
return −1
```

Algorithm 1.12: Algorithm arrayFind.

1.3.4 Basic Probability

When we analyze algorithms that use randomization or if we wish to analyze the average-case performance of an algorithm, then we need to use some basic facts from probability theory. The most basic is that any statement about a probability is defined upon a ***sample space*** S, which is defined as the set of all possible outcomes from some experiment. We leave the terms "outcomes" and "experiment" undefined in any formal sense, however.

Example 1.21: *Consider an experiment that consists of the outcome from flipping a coin five times. This sample space has 2^5 different outcomes, one for each different ordering of possible flips that can occur.*

Sample spaces can also be infinite, as the following example illustrates.

Example 1.22: *Consider an experiment that consists of flipping a coin until it comes up heads. This sample space is infinite, with each outcome being a sequence of i tails followed by a single flip that comes up heads, for $i \in \{0,1,2,3,\ldots\}$.*

A ***probability space*** is a sample space S together with a probability function, Pr, that maps subsets of S to real numbers in the interval $[0,1]$. It captures mathematically the notion of the probability of certain "events" occurring. Formally, each subset A of S is called an ***event***, and the probability function Pr is assumed to possess the following basic properties with respect to events defined from S:

1. $\Pr(\emptyset) = 0$.
2. $\Pr(S) = 1$.
3. $0 \le \Pr(A) \le 1$, for any $A \subseteq S$.
4. If $A, B \subseteq S$ and $A \cap B = \emptyset$, then $\Pr(A \cup B) = \Pr(A) + \Pr(B)$.

Independence

Two events A and B are ***independent*** if

$$\Pr(A \cap B) = \Pr(A) \cdot \Pr(B).$$

A collection of events $\{A_1, A_2, \ldots, A_n\}$ is ***mutually independent*** if

$$\Pr(A_{i_1} \cap A_{i_2} \cap \cdots \cap A_{i_k}) = \Pr(A_{i_1}) \Pr(A_{i_2}) \cdots \Pr(A_{i_k}).$$

for any subset $\{A_{i_1}, A_{i_2}, \ldots, A_{i_k}\}$.

Example 1.23: *Let A be the event that the roll of a die is a 6, let B be the event that the roll of a second die is a 3, and let C be the event that the sum of these two dice is a 10. Then A and B are independent events, but C is not independent with either A or B.*

Conditional Probability

The ***conditional probability*** that an event A occurs, given an event B, is denoted as $\Pr(A|B)$, and is defined as

$$\Pr(A|B) = \frac{\Pr(A \cap B)}{\Pr(B)},$$

assuming that $\Pr(B) > 0$.

Example 1.24: *Let A be the event that a roll of two dice sums to 10, and let B be the event that the roll of the first die is a 6. Note that $\Pr(B) = 1/6$ and that $\Pr(A \cap B) = 1/36$, for there is only one way two dice can sum to 10 if the first one is a 6 (namely, if the second is a 4). Thus, $\Pr(A|B) = (1/36)/(1/6) = 1/6$.*

Random Variables and Expectation

An elegant way for dealing with events is in terms of ***random variables***. Intuitively, random variables are variables whose values depend upon the outcome of some experiment. Formally, a ***random variable*** is a function X that maps outcomes from some sample space S to real numbers. An ***indicator random variable*** is a random variable that maps outcomes to the set $\{0, 1\}$. Often in algorithm analysis we use a random variable X that has a discrete set of possible outcomes to characterize the running time of a randomized algorithm. In this case, the sample space S is defined by all possible outcomes of the random sources used in the algorithm. We are usually most interested in the typical, average, or "expected" value of such a random variable. The ***expected value*** of a discrete random variable X is defined as

$$E(X) = \sum_x x \Pr(X = x),$$

where the summation is defined over the range of X.

Theorem 1.25 (The Linearity of Expectation): *Let X and Y be two arbitrary random variables. Then $E(X+Y) = E(X) + E(Y)$.*

Proof:

$$\begin{aligned} E(X+Y) &= \sum_x \sum_y (x+y) \Pr(X = x \cap Y = y) \\ &= \sum_x \sum_y x \Pr(X = x \cap Y = y) + \sum_x \sum_y y \Pr(X = x \cap Y = y) \\ &= \sum_x \sum_y x \Pr(X = x \cap Y = y) + \sum_y \sum_x y \Pr(Y = y \cap X = x) \\ &= \sum_x x \Pr(X = x) + \sum_y y \Pr(Y = y) \\ &= E(X) + E(Y). \end{aligned}$$

Note that this proof does not depend on any independence assumptions about the events when X and Y take on their respective values. ■

Example 1.26: *Let X be a random variable that assigns the outcome of the roll of two fair dice to the sum of the number of dots showing. Then $E(X) = 7$.*

Proof: *To justify this claim, let X_1 and X_2 be random variables corresponding to the number of dots on each die, respectively. Thus, $X_1 = X_2$ (that is, they are two instances of the same function) and $E(X) = E(X_1 + X_2) = E(X_1) + E(X_2)$. Each outcome of the roll of a fair die occurs with probability $1/6$. Thus*

$$E(X_i) = \frac{1}{6} + \frac{2}{6} + \frac{3}{6} + \frac{4}{6} + \frac{5}{6} + \frac{6}{6} = \frac{7}{2},$$

for $i = 1,2$. Therefore, $E(X) = 7$. ■

Two random variables X and Y are ***independent*** if

$$\Pr(X = x | Y = y) = \Pr(X = x),$$

for all real numbers x and y.

Theorem 1.27: *If two random variables X and Y are independent, then*

$$E(XY) = E(X)E(Y).$$

Example 1.28: *Let X be a random variable that assigns the outcome of a roll of two fair dice to the product of the number of dots showing. Then $E(X) = 49/4$.*

Proof: *Let X_1 and X_2 be random variables denoting the number of dots on each die. The variables X_1 and X_2 are clearly independent; hence*

$$E(X) = E(X_1 X_2) = E(X_1)E(X_2) = (7/2)^2 = 49/4.$$

■

Chernoff Bounds

It is often necessary in the analysis of randomized algorithms to bound the sum of a set of random variables. One set of inequalities that makes this tractable is the set of Chernoff Bounds. Let $X_1, X_2, \ldots, X_n$ be a set of mutually independent indicator random variables, such that each X_i is 1 with some probability $p_i > 0$ and 0 otherwise. Let $X = \sum_{i=1}^{n} X_i$ be the sum of these random variables, and let μ denote the mean of X, that is, $\mu = E(X) = \sum_{i=1}^{n} p_i$. We give the following without proof.

Theorem 1.29: *Let X be as above. Then, for $\delta > 0$,*

$$\Pr(X > (1+\delta)\mu) < \left[\frac{e^{\delta}}{(1+\delta)^{(1+\delta)}} \right]^{\mu},$$

and, for $0 < \delta \leq 1$,

$$\Pr(X < (1-\delta)\mu) < e^{-\mu\delta^2/2}.$$

1.4 Case Studies in Algorithm Analysis

Having presented the general framework for describing and analyzing algorithms, we now consider some case studies in algorithm analysis. Specifically, we show how to use the big-Oh notation to analyze two algorithms that solve the same problem but have different running times.

The problem we focus on in this section is the one of computing the so-called ***prefix averages*** of a sequence of numbers. Namely, given an array X storing n numbers, we want to compute an array A such that $A[i]$ is the average of elements $X[0], \ldots, X[i]$, for $i = 0, \ldots, n-1$, that is,

$$A[i] = \frac{\sum_{j=0}^{i} X[j]}{i+1}.$$

Computing prefix averages has many applications in economics and statistics. For example, given the year-by-year returns of a mutual fund, an investor will typically want to see the fund's average annual returns for the last year, the last three years, the last five years, and the last ten years. The prefix average is also useful as a "smoothing" function for a parameter that is quickly changing, as illustrated in Figure 1.13.

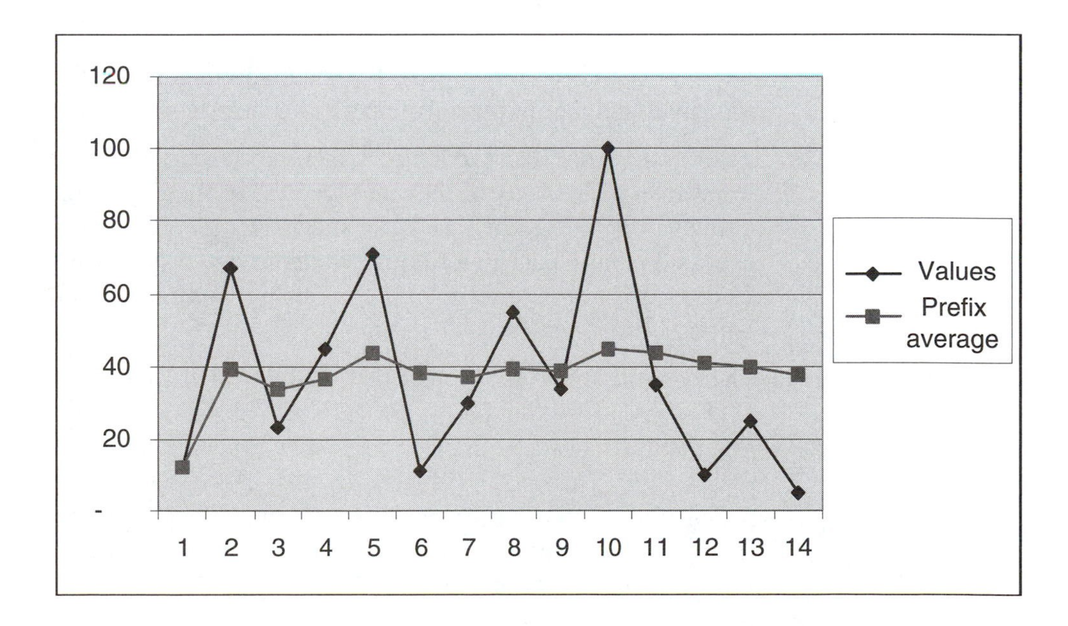

Figure 1.13: An illustration of the prefix average function and how it is useful for smoothing a quickly changing sequence of values.

1.4.1 A Quadratic-Time Prefix Averages Algorithm

Our first algorithm for the prefix averages problem, called prefixAverages1, is shown in Algorithm 1.14. It computes every element of A separately, following the definition.

Algorithm prefixAverages1(X):
  Input: An n-element array X of numbers.
  Output: An n-element array A of numbers such that $A[i]$ is the average of elements $X[0],\ldots,X[i]$.
 Let A be an array of n numbers.
 for $i \leftarrow 0$ **to** $n-1$ **do**
  $a \leftarrow 0$
  for $j \leftarrow 0$ **to** i **do**
   $a \leftarrow a + X[j]$
  $A[i] \leftarrow a/(i+1)$
 return array A

Algorithm 1.14: Algorithm prefixAverages1.

Let us analyze the prefixAverages1 algorithm.

- Initializing and returning array A at the beginning and end can be done with a constant number of primitive operations per element, and takes $O(n)$ time.
- There are two nested **for** loops, which are controlled by counters i and j, respectively. The body of the outer loop, controlled by counter i, is executed n times, for $i = 0,\ldots,n-1$. Thus, statements $a = 0$ and $A[i] = a/(i+1)$ are executed n times each. This implies that these two statements, plus the incrementing and testing of counter i, contribute a number of primitive operations proportional to n, that is, $O(n)$ time.
- The body of the inner loop, which is controlled by counter j, is executed $i+1$ times, depending on the current value of the outer loop counter i. Thus, statement $a = a + X[j]$ in the inner loop is executed $1+2+3+\cdots+n$ times. By recalling Theorem 1.13, we know that $1+2+3+\cdots+n = n(n+1)/2$, which implies that the statement in the inner loop contributes $O(n^2)$ time. A similar argument can be done for the primitive operations associated with incrementing and testing counter j, which also take $O(n^2)$ time.

The running time of algorithm prefixAverages1 is given by the sum of three terms. The first and the second term are $O(n)$, and the third term is $O(n^2)$. By a simple application of Theorem 1.7, the running time of prefixAverages1 is $O(n^2)$.

1.4.2 A Linear-Time Prefix Averages Algorithm

In order to compute prefix averages more efficiently, we can observe that two consecutive averages $A[i-1]$ and $A[i]$ are similar:

$$\begin{aligned} A[i-1] &= (X[0]+X[1]+\cdots+X[i-1])/i \\ A[i] &= (X[0]+X[1]+\cdots+X[i-1]+X[i])/(i+1). \end{aligned}$$

If we denote with S_i the ***prefix sum*** $X[0]+X[1]+\cdots+X[i]$, we can compute the prefix averages as $A[i]=S_i/(i+1)$. It is easy to keep track of the current prefix sum while scanning array X with a loop. We present the details in Algorithm 1.15 (prefixAverages2).

Algorithm prefixAverages2(X):
  Input: An n-element array X of numbers.
  Output: An n-element array A of numbers such that $A[i]$ is the average of elements $X[0],\ldots,X[i]$.

  Let A be an array of n numbers.
  $s \leftarrow 0$
  for $i \leftarrow 0$ **to** $n-1$ **do**
    $s \leftarrow s+X[i]$
    $A[i] \leftarrow s/(i+1)$
  return array A

Algorithm 1.15: Algorithm prefixAverages2.

The analysis of the running time of algorithm prefixAverages2 follows:

- Initializing and returning array A at the beginning and end can be done with a constant number of primitive operations per element, and takes $O(n)$ time.
- Initializing variable s at the beginning takes $O(1)$ time.
- There is a single **for** loop, which is controlled by counter i. The body of the loop is executed n times, for $i=0,\ldots,n-1$. Thus, statements $s=s+X[i]$ and $A[i]=s/(i+1)$ are executed n times each. This implies that these two statements plus the incrementing and testing of counter i contribute a number of primitive operations proportional to n, that is, $O(n)$ time.

The running time of algorithm prefixAverages2 is given by the sum of three terms. The first and the third term are $O(n)$, and the second term is $O(1)$. By a simple application of Theorem 1.7, the running time of prefixAverages2 is $O(n)$, which is much better than the quadratic-time algorithm prefixAverages1.

1.5 Amortization

An important analysis tool useful for understanding the running times of algorithms that have steps with widely varying performance is ***amortization***. The term "amortization" itself comes from the field of accounting, which provides an intuitive monetary metaphor for algorithm analysis, as we shall see in this section.

The typical data structure usually supports a wide variety of different methods for accessing and updating the elements it stores. Likewise, some algorithms operate iteratively, with each iteration performing a varying amount of work. In some cases, we can effectively analyze the performance of these data structures and algorithms on the basis of the worst-case running time of each individual operation. Amortization takes a different viewpoint. Rather than focusing on each operation separately, it considers the interactions between all the operations by studying the running time of a series of these operations.

The Clearable Table Data Structure

As an example, let us introduce a simple abstract data type (ADT), the ***clearable table***. This ADT stores a table of elements, which can be accessed by their index in the table. In addition, the clearable table also supports the following two methods:

add(e): Add the the element e to the next available cell in the table.

clear(): Empty the table by removing all its elements.

Let S be a clearable table with n elements implemented by means of an array, with a fixed upper bound, N, on its size. Operation clear takes $\Theta(n)$ time, since we should dereference all the elements in the table in order to really empty it.

Now consider a series of n operations on an initially empty clearable table S. If we take a worst-case viewpoint, we may say that the running time of this series of operations is $O(n^2)$, since the worst case of a single clear operation in the series is $O(n)$, and there may be as many as $O(n)$ clear operations in this series. While this analysis is correct, it is also an overstatement, since an analysis that takes into account the interactions between the operations shows that the running time of the entire series is actually $O(n)$.

Theorem 1.30: *A series of n operations on an initially empty clearable table implemented with an array takes $O(n)$ time.*

Proof: Let $M_0, \ldots, M_{n-1}$ be the series of operations performed on S, and let $M_{i_0}, \ldots, M_{i_{k-1}}$ be the k clear operations within the series. We have

$$0 \le i_0 < \ldots < i_{k-1} \le n-1.$$

Let us also define $i_{-1} = -1$. The running time of operation M_{i_j} (a clear operation) is $O(i_j - i_{j-1})$, because at most $i_j - i_{j-1} - 1$ elements could have been added into the table (using the add operation) since the previous clear operation $M_{i_{j-1}}$ or since the beginning of the series. Thus, the running time of all the clear operations is

$$O\left(\sum_{j=0}^{k-1}(i_j - i_{j-1})\right).$$

A summation such as this is known as a ***telescoping sum***, for all terms other than the first and last cancel each other out. That is, this summation is $O(i_{k-1} - i_{-1})$, which is $O(n)$. All the remaining operations of the series take $O(1)$ time each. Thus, we conclude that a series of n operations performed on an initially empty clearable table takes $O(n)$ time. ■

Theorem 1.30 indicates that the average running time of any operation on a clearable table is $O(1)$, where the average is taken over an arbitrary series of operations, starting with an initially empty clearable table.

Amortizing an Algorithm's Running Time

The above example provides a motivation for the amortization technique, which gives us a worst-case way of performing an average-case analysis. Formally, we define the ***amortized running time*** of an operation within a series of operations as the worst-case running time of the series of operations divided by the number of operations. When the series of operations is not specified, it is usually assumed to be a series of operations from the repertoire of a certain data structure, starting from an empty structure. Thus, by Theorem 1.30, we can say that the amortized running time of each operation in the clearable table ADT is $O(1)$ when we implement that clearable table with an array. Note that the actual running time of an operation may be much higher than its amortized running time (for example, a particular clear operation may take $O(n)$ time).

The advantage of using amortization is that it gives us a way to do a robust average-case analysis without using any probability. It simply requires that we have some way of characterizing the worst-case running time for performing a series of operations. We can even extend the notion of amortized running time so as to assign each individual operation in a series of operations its own amortized running time, provided the total actual time taken to process the entire series of operations is no more than the sum of amortized bounds given to the individual operations.

There are several ways of doing an amortized analysis. The most obvious way is to use a direct argument to derive bounds on the total time needed to perform a series of operations, which is what we did in the proof of Theorem 1.30. While direct arguments can often be found for a simple series of operations, performing an amortized analysis of a nontrivial series of operations is often easier using special techniques for amortized analysis.

1.5.1 Amortization Techniques

There are two fundamental techniques for performing an amortized analysis, one based on a financial model—the accounting method—and the other based on an energy model—the potential function method.

The Accounting Method

The ***accounting method*** for performing an amortized analysis is to use a scheme of credits and debits for keeping track of the running time of the different operations in the series. The basis of the accounting method is simple. We view the computer as a coin-operated appliance that requires the payment of one ***cyber-dollar*** for a constant amount of computing time. We also view an operation as a sequence of constant time ***primitive operations***, which each cost one ***cyber-dollar*** to be executed. When an operation is executed, we should have enough cyber-dollars available to pay for its running time. Of course, the most obvious approach is to charge an operation a number of cyber-dollars equal to the number of primitive operations performed. However, the interesting aspect of using the accounting method is that we do not have to be fair in the way we charge the operations. Namely, we can overcharge some operations that execute few primitive operations and use the profit made on them to help out other operations that execute many primitive operations. This mechanism may allow us to charge the same amount a of cyber-dollars to each operation in the series, without ever running out of cyber-dollars to pay for the computer time. Hence, if we can set up such a scheme, called an ***amortization scheme***, we can say that each operation in the series has an amortized running time that is $O(a)$. When designing an amortization scheme, it is often convenient to think of the unspent cyber-dollars as being "stored" in certain places of the data structure, for example, at the elements of a table.

An alternative amortization scheme charges different amounts to the various operations. In this case, the amortized running time of an operation is proportional to the total charges made divided by the number of operations.

We now go back to the clearable table example and present an amortization scheme for it that yields an alternative proof of Theorem 1.30. Let us assume that one cyber-dollar is enough to pay for the execution of operation of an index access or an add operation, and for the time spent by operation clear to dereference one element. We shall charge each operation two cyber-dollars. This means undercharging operation clear and overcharging all the other operations by one cyber-dollar. The cyber-dollar profited in an add operation will be stored at the element inserted by the operation. (See Figure 1.16.) When a clear operation is executed, the cyber-dollar stored at each element in the table is used to pay for the time spent dereferencing it. Hence, we have a valid amortization scheme, where each operation is charged two cyber-dollars, and all the computing time is paid for. This simple amortization scheme implies the result of Theorem 1.30.

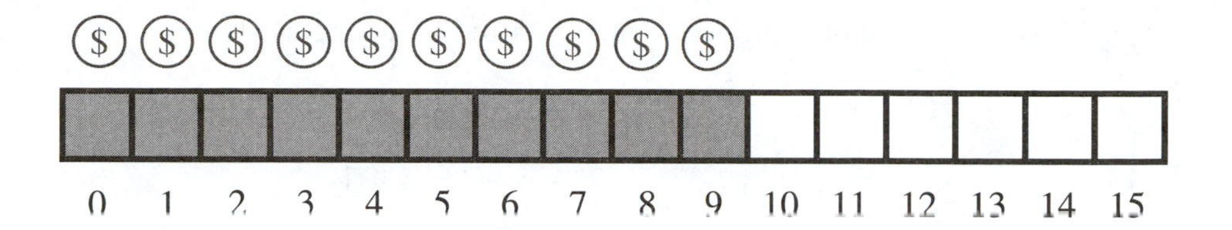

Figure 1.16: Cyber-dollars stored at the elements of a clearable table S in the amortized analysis of a series of operations on S.

Notice that the worst case for the running time occurs for a series of add operations followed by a single clear operation. In other cases, at the end of the series of operations, we may end up with some unspent cyber-dollars, which are those profited from index access operations and those stored at the elements still in the sequence. Indeed, the computing time for executing a series of n operations can be paid for with the amount of cyber-dollars between n and $2n$. Our amortization scheme accounts for the worst case by always charging two cyber-dollars per operation.

At this point, we should stress that the accounting method is simply an analysis tool. It does not require that we modify a data structure or the execution of an algorithm in any way. In particular, it does not require that we add objects for keeping track of the cyber-dollars spent.

Potential Functions

Another useful technique for performing an amortized analysis is based on an energy model. In this approach, we associate with our structure a value, Φ, which represents the current energy state of our system. Each operation that we perform will contribute some additional amount, known as the amortized time, to Φ, but then also extracts value from Φ in proportion to the amount of time actually spent. Formally, we let $\Phi_0 \geq 0$ denote the initial value of Φ, before we perform any operations, and we use Φ_i to denote the value of the potential function, Φ, after we perform the ith operation. The main idea of using the potential function argument is to use the change in potential for the ith operation, $\Phi_i - \Phi_{i-1}$, to characterize the amortized time needed for that operation.

Let us focus more closely on the action of the ith operation, letting t_i denote its actual running time. We define the amortized running time of the ith operation as

$$t'_i = t_i + \Phi_i - \Phi_{i-1}.$$

That is, the amortized cost of the ith operation is the actual running time plus the net change in potential that operation causes (which may be positive or negative). Or, put another way,

$$t_i = t'_i + \Phi_{i-1} - \Phi_i,$$

that is, the actual time spent is the amortized cost plus the net drop in potential.

Denote by T' the total amortized time for performing n operations on our structure. That is,

$$T' = \sum_{i=1}^{n} t'_i.$$

Then the total actual time, T, taken by our n operations can be bounded as

$$\begin{aligned} T &= \sum_{i=1}^{n} t_i \\ &= \sum_{i=1}^{n} \left(t'_i + \Phi_{i-1} - \Phi_i\right) \\ &= \sum_{i=1}^{n} t'_i + \sum_{i=1}^{n} (\Phi_{i-1} - \Phi_i) \\ &= T' + \sum_{i=1}^{n} (\Phi_{i-1} - \Phi_i) \\ &= T' + \Phi_0 - \Phi_n, \end{aligned}$$

since the second term above forms a telescoping sum. In other words, the total actual time spent is equal to the total amortized time plus the net drop in potential over the entire sequence of operations. Thus, so long as $\Phi_n \geq \Phi_0$, then $T \leq T'$, the actual time spent is no more than the amortized time.

To make this concept more concrete, let us repeat our analysis of the clearable table using a potential argument. In this case, we choose the potential Φ of our system to be the actual number of elements in our clearable table. We claim that the amortized time for any operation is 2, that is, $t'_i = 2$, for $i = 1, \ldots, n$. To justify this, let us consider the two possible methods for the ith operation.

- add(e): inserting the element e into the table increases Φ by 1 and the actual time needed is 1 unit of time. So, in this case,

  $$1 = t_i = t'_i + \Phi_{i-1} - \Phi_i = 2 - 1,$$

  which is clearly true.
- clear(): removing all m elements from the table requires no more than $m+2$ units of time—m units to do the removal plus at most two units for the method call and its overhead. But this operation also drops the potential Φ of our system from m to 0 (we even allow for $m = 0$). So, in this case

  $$m + 2 = t_i = t'_i + \Phi_{i-1} - \Phi_i = 2 + m,$$

  which clearly holds.

Therefore, the amortized time to perform any operation on a clearable table is $O(1)$. Moreover, since $\Phi_i \geq \Phi_0$, for any $i \geq 1$, the actual time, T, to perform n operations on an initially empty clearable table is $O(n)$.

1.5.2 Analyzing an Extendable Array Implementation

A major weakness of the simple array implementation for the clearable table ADT given above is that it requires advance specification of a fixed capacity, N, for the total number of elements that may be stored in the table. If the actual number of elements, n, of the table is much smaller than N, then this implementation will waste space. Worse, if n increases past N, then this implementation will crash.

Let us provide a means to grow the array A that stores the elements of a table S. Of course, in any conventional programming language, such as C, C++, and Java, we cannot actually grow the array A; its capacity is fixed at some number N. Instead, when an ***overflow*** occurs, that is, when $n = N$ and method add is called, we perform the following steps:

1. Allocate a new array B of capacity $2N$
2. Copy $A[i]$ to $B[i]$, for $i = 0, \ldots, N-1$
3. Let $A = B$, that is, we use B as the array supporting S.

This array replacement strategy is known as an ***extendable array***. (See Figure 1.17.) Intuitively, this strategy is much like that of the hermit crab, which moves into a larger shell when it outgrows its previous one.

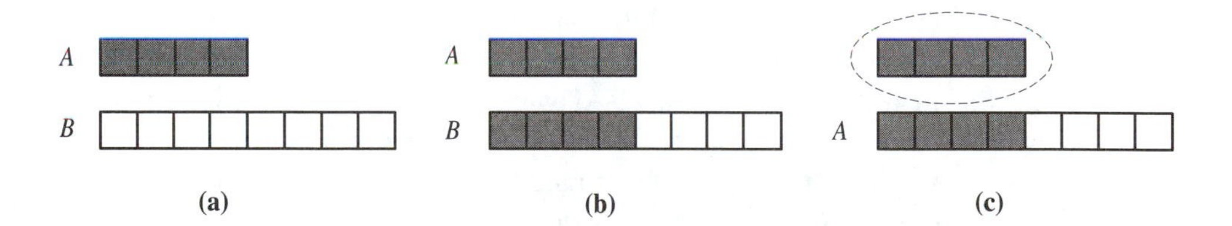

Figure 1.17: An illustration of the three steps for "growing" an extendable array: (a) create new array B; (b) copy elements from A to B; (c) reassign reference A to the new array. Not shown is the future garbage collection of the old array.

In terms of efficiency, this array replacement strategy might at first seem slow, for performing a single array replacement of size n required by some element insertion takes $\Theta(n)$ time. Still, notice that after we perform an array replacement, our new array allows us to add n new elements to the table before the array must be replaced again. This simple fact allows us to show that the running time of a series of operations performed on an initially empty extendable table is actually quite efficient. As a shorthand notation, let us refer to the insertion of an element to be the last element in a vector as an "add" operation. Using ***amortization***, we can show that performing a sequence of such add operations on a table implemented with an extendable array is actually quite efficient.

Theorem 1.31: *Let S be a table implemented by means of an extendable array A, as described above. The total time to perform a series of n* add *operations in S, starting from S being empty and A having size $N = 1$, is $O(n)$.*

Proof: We justify this theorem using the accounting method for ***amortization***. To perform this analysis, we again view the computer as a coin-operated appliance that requires the payment of one ***cyber-dollar*** for a constant amount of computing time. When an operation is executed, we should have enough cyber-dollars available in our current "bank account" to pay for that operation's running time. Thus, the total amount of cyber-dollars spent for any computation will be proportional to the total time spent on that computation. The beauty of this analysis is that we can over charge some operations to save up cyber-dollars to pay for others.

Let us assume that one cyber-dollar is enough to pay for the execution of each add operation in S, excluding the time for growing the array. Also, let us assume that growing the array from size k to size $2k$ requires k cyber-dollars for the time spent copying the elements. We shall charge each add operation three cyber-dollars. Thus, we over charge each add operation not causing an overflow by two cyber-dollars. Think of the two cyber-dollars profited in an insertion that does not grow the array as being "stored" at the element inserted. An overflow occurs when the table S has 2^i elements, for some integer $i \geq 0$, and the size of the array used by S is 2^i. Thus, doubling the size of the array will require 2^i cyber-dollars. Fortunately, these cyber-dollars can be found at the elements stored in cells 2^{i-1} through $2^i - 1$. (See Figure 1.18.) Note that the previous overflow occurred when the number of elements became larger than 2^{i-1} for the first time, and thus the cyber-dollars stored in cells 2^{i-1} through $2^i - 1$ were not previously spent. Therefore, we have a valid amortization scheme in which each operation is charged three cyber-dollars and all the computing time is paid for. That is, we can pay for the execution of n add operations using $3n$ cyber-dollars. ■

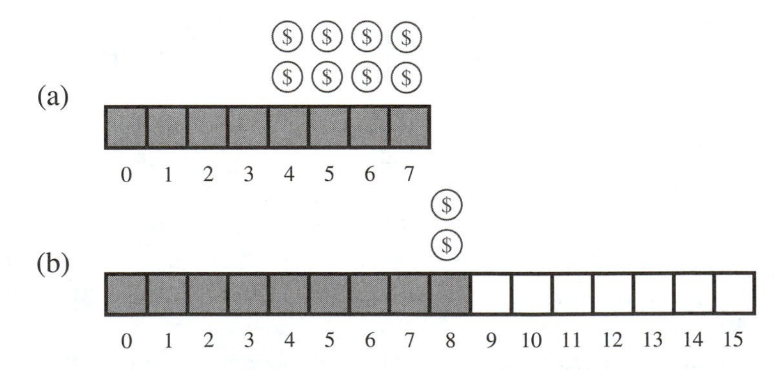

Figure 1.18: A costly add operation: (a) a full 8-cell with two cyber-dollars for cells 4 through 7; (b) an add doubles the capacity. Copying elements spends the cyber-dollars in the table, inserting the new element spends one cyber-dollar charged to the add, and two cyber-dollars profited are stored at cell 8.

A table can be doubled in size with each extension, as we have described it, or we can specify an explicit capacityIncrement parameter that determines the fixed amount an array should grow with each expansion. That is, this parameter is set to a value, k, then the array adds k new cells when it grows. We must utilize such a parameter with caution, however. For most applications, doubling in size is the right choice, as the following theorem shows.

Theorem 1.32: *If we create an initially empty table with a fixed positive* capacityIncrement *value, then performing a series of n* add *operations on this vector takes* $\Omega(n^2)$ *time.*

Proof: Let $c > 0$ be the capacityIncrement value, and let $c_0 > 0$ denote the initial size of the array. An overflow will be caused by an add operation when the current number of elements in the table is $c_0 + ic$, for $i = 0, \ldots, m-1$, where $m = \lfloor (n - c_0)/c \rfloor$. Hence, by Theorem 1.13, the total time for handling the overflows is proportional to

$$\sum_{i=0}^{m-1} (c_0 + ci) = c_0 m + c \sum_{i=0}^{m-1} i = c_0 m + c\frac{m(m-1)}{2},$$

which is $\Omega(n^2)$. Thus, performing the n add operations takes $\Omega(n^2)$ time. ■

Figure 1.19 compares the running times of a series of add operations on an initially empty table, for two initial values of capacityIncrement.

We discuss applications of amortization further when we discuss splay trees (Section 3.4) and a tree structure for performing unions and finds in set partitions (Section 4.2.2).

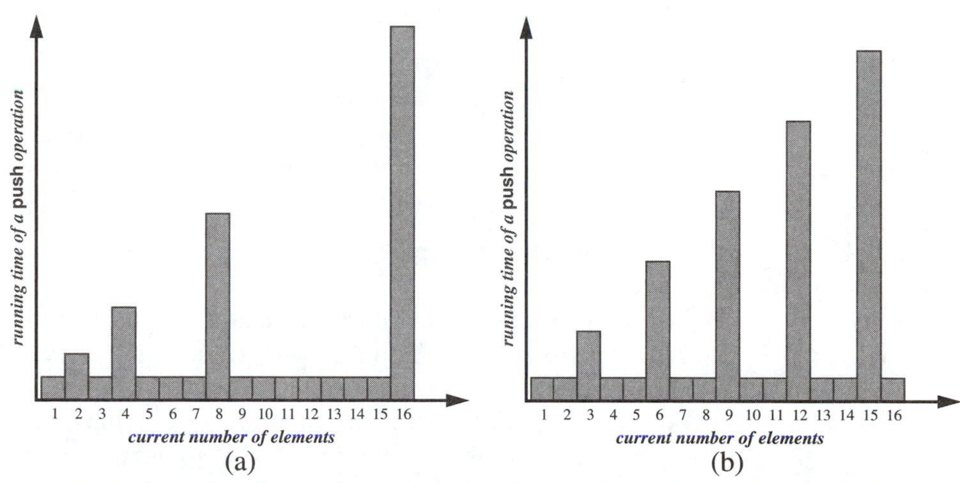

Figure 1.19: Running times of a series of add operations on an extendable table. In (a) the size is doubled with each expansion, and in (b) it is simply incremented by capacityIncrement $= 3$.

1.6 Experimentation

Using asymptotic analysis to bound the running time of an algorithm is a deductive process. We study a pseudo-code description of the algorithm. We reason about what would be worst-case choices for this algorithm, and we use mathematical tools, such as amortization, summations, and recurrence equations, to characterize the running time of the algorithm.

This approach is very powerful, but it has its limitations. The deductive approach to asymptotic analysis doesn't always provide insight into the constant factors that are "hiding" behind the big-Oh in an algorithm analysis. Likewise, the deductive approach gives us little guidance into the breakpoint between when we should use an asymptotically slow algorithm with a small constant factor and an asymptotically fast algorithm with a larger constant. In addition, the deductive approach focuses primarily on worst-case inputs, which may not be representative of the typical input for a certain problem. Finally, the deductive approach breaks down when an algorithm is too complicated to allow us to effectively bound its performance. In such cases, experimentation can often help us perform our algorithm analysis.

In this section, we discuss some techniques and principles for performing experimental algorithm analysis.

1.6.1 Experimental Setup

In performing an experiment, there are several steps that must be performed in order to set it up. These steps require thought and deliberation, and should be performed with care.

Choosing the Question

The first thing to determine in setting up an experiment is to decide what to test. In the realm of algorithm analysis, there are several possibilities:

- Estimate the asymptotic running time of an algorithm in the average case.
- Test which of two competing algorithms is faster for a given range of input values $[n_0, n_1]$.
- For an algorithm that has numeric parameters, such as constants α or ε, that determine its behavior, find the values of these parameters that yield the best performance.
- For an algorithm that tries to minimize or maximize some function of an input, test how close the algorithm comes to the optimal value.

Once we have determined which of these questions, or even an alternative question, we would like to answer empirically, we can then move to the next step in our experimental setup.

Deciding What to Measure

Once we know what question to ask, we should next focus on quantitative measurements that can be used to answer that question. In the case of an optimization problem, we should measure the function that we wish to maximize or minimize. In the case of running time, the factor to measure is not as obvious as we might at first think.

We can, of course, measure that actual running time of an algorithm. Using a procedure call that returns the time of day, we can measure the time of day before and after running our algorithm and then subtract to determine how much time passed as the algorithm was running. This measurement of time is most useful, however, if the computer we are running on is representative of "typical" computers that we will wish to use for this algorithm.

Moreover, we should recognize that the so-called "wall clock" time for running an implementation of an algorithm can be affected by other factors, including programs that are running concurrently on our computer, whether or not our algorithm makes effective use of a memory cache, and whether or not our algorithm uses so much memory that its data is swapping in and out from secondary memory. All of these additional factors can slow down an otherwise fast algorithm, so if we are using wall clock time to measure algorithm speed, we should make sure these effects are minimized.

An alternative approach is to measure speed in a platform-independent manner, counting the number of times some primitive operation is used repeatedly in our algorithm. Examples of such primitive operations that have been used effectively in algorithm analysis include the following:

- ***Memory references***. By counting memory references in a data intensive algorithm we get a measure that will correlate highly with the running time for this algorithm on any machine.

- ***Comparisons***. In an algorithm, such as sorting, that processes data primarily by performing comparisons between pairs of elements, a count of the comparisons made by the algorithm will be highly correlated to the running time of that algorithm.

- ***Arithmetic operations***. In numerical algorithms, which are dominated by many arithmetic computations, counting the number of additions and/or multiplications can be an effective measure of running time. Such a measure can be translated into running times on a given computer, by factoring in the performance achieved by whether this computer has a math co-processor or not.

Once we have decided what it is we wish to measure, we then must generate test data upon which to run our algorithm and collect statistics.

Generating Test Data

Our goals in generating test data include the following:

- We wish to generate enough samples so that taking averages yields statistically significant results.
- We wish to generate sample inputs of varying sizes, to be able to make educated guesses about the performance of our algorithm over wide ranging input sizes.
- We wish to generate test data that is representative of the kind of data that we expect our algorithm to be given in practice.

Generating data that satisfies the first two points is simply a matter of coverage; satisfying the third criteria takes thought. We need to think about the input distribution, and generate test data according to that distribution. Simply generating data uniformly at random is often not the appropriate choice here. For example, if our algorithm performs searches based on words found in a natural language document, then the distribution of requests should not be uniform. Ideally, we would like to find some way of gathering actual data in a sufficient enough quantity that it gives rise to statistically valid conclusions. When such data is only partially available, we can compromise by generating random data that matches key statistical properties of the available actual data. In any case, we should strive to create test data that will enable us to derive general conclusions that support or refute specific hypotheses about our algorithm.

Coding the Solution and Performing the Experiment

The necessary step of coding up our algorithm correctly and efficiently involves a certain amount of programming skill. Moreover, if we are comparing our algorithm to another, then we must be sure to code up the competing algorithm using the same level of skill as we are using for our own. The degree of code optimization between two algorithm implementations that we wish to compare should be as close as possible. Achieving a level playing field for comparing algorithms empirically is admittedly subjective, but we should still work as hard as we can to achieve a fair comparison in such cases. Ultimately, we should strive for results that are ***reproducible***, that is, a different programmer with similar skill should be able to reproduce the same results by performing similar experiments.

Once we have our program completed and we have generated our test data, then we are ready to actually perform our experiments and collect our data. Of course, we should perform our experiments in as "sterile" an environment as possible, eliminating as best we can any sources of noise in our data collection. We should take specific note of the details of the computational environment we are using, including the number of CPUs, the speed of the CPUs, the main memory size, and the speed of the memory bus.

1.6.2 Data Analysis and Visualization

Viewing data in tables is common, but it is often not nearly as useful as a graphical plot. A complete discussion of such data analysis and visualization techniques is beyond the scope of this book, but we nevertheless discuss two analysis and visualization techniques useful for algorithm analysis in this section.

The Ratio Test

In the ***ratio test***, we use knowledge of our algorithm to derive a function $f(n) = n^c$ for the main term in our algorithm's running time, for some constant $c > 0$. Our analysis is then designed to test if the average running time of our algorithm is $\Theta(n^c)$ or not. Let $t(n)$ denote the actual running time of our algorithm on a specific problem instance of size n. The ratio test is to plot the ratio $r(n) = t(n)/f(n)$, using several experimentally gathered values for $t(n)$. (See Figure 1.20.)

If $r(n)$ grows as n increases, then our $f(n)$ under estimates the running time $t(n)$. If, on the other hand, $r(n)$ converges to 0, then our $f(n)$ is an over estimate. But if the ratio function $r(n)$ converges to some constant b greater than 0, then we have found a good estimate for the growth rate of $t(n)$. In addition, the constant b gives us a good estimate for the constant factor in the running time $t(n)$.

Still, we should recognize that any empirical study can only test a finite number of inputs and input sizes; hence, the ratio test approach cannot be used to find an exact value of the exponent $c > 0$. Also, its accuracy is limited to polynomial functions for $f(n)$, and even then studies have shown that the best it can achieve for determining the exponent c is to within the range $[c - 0.5, c + 0.5]$.

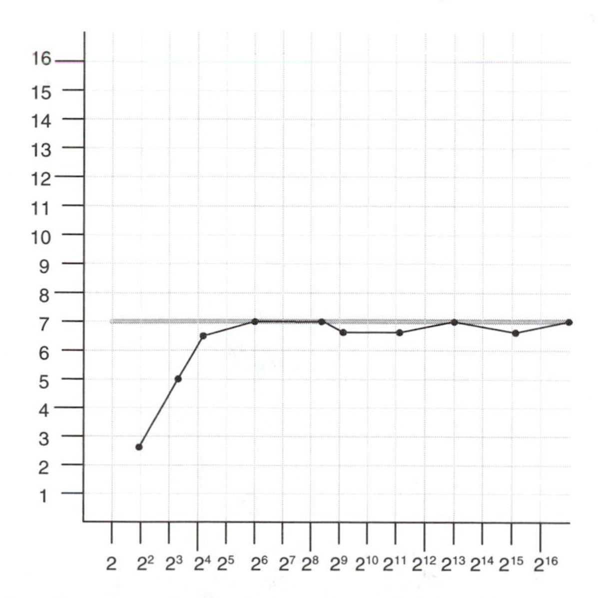

Figure 1.20: An example plot of a ratio test estimating that $r(n) = 7$.

The Power Test

In the ***power test*** we can produce a good estimate for the running time, $t(n)$, of an algorithm without producing a good guess for that running time in advance. The idea is to take experimentally gathered data pairs (x,y) such that $y = t(x)$, where x is the size of a sample input, and apply the transformation $(x,y) \rightarrow (x',y')$ where $x' = \log x$ and $y' = \log y$. Then we plot all the (x',y') pairs and examine the results.

Note that if $t(n) = bn^c$ for some constants $b > 0$ and $c > 0$, then the log-log transformation implies that $y' = cx' + b$. Thus, if the (x',y') pairs are close to forming a line, then by a simple line fit we can determine the values of the constants b and c. The exponent c corresponds to the slope of the line in this log-log scale, and the coefficient b corresponds to this line's y-axis intercept. (See Figure 1.21.) Alternatively, if (x',y') pairs grow in a significant way, then we can safely deduce that $t(n)$ is super-polynomial, and if the (x',y') pair converge to a constant, then it is likely that $t(n)$ is sublinear. In any case, because of the finiteness of testable input sizes, as with the ratio test, it is difficult to estimate c better than the range $[c-0.5, c+0.5]$ with the power test.

Even so, the ratio test and the power test are generally considered good approaches to estimating the empirical running time of an algorithm. They are considerably better, for example, than trying to directly fit a polynomial to the test data through regression techniques. Such curve-fitting techniques tend to be overly sensitive to noise; hence, they may not give good estimates to the exponents in polynomial running times.

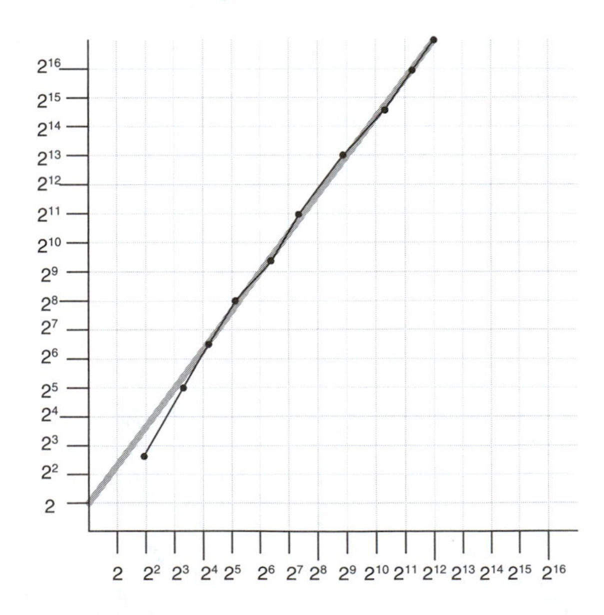

Figure 1.21: An example plot of a power test. In this case we would estimate that $y' = (4/3)x' + 2$; hence, we would estimate $t(n) = 2n^{4/3}$.

1.7 Exercises

Reinforcement

R-1.1 Graph the functions $12n$, $6n\log n$, n^2, n^3, and 2^n using a logarithmic scale for the x- and y-axes; that is, if the function value $f(n)$ is y, plot this as a point with x-coordinate at $\log n$ and y-coordinate at $\log y$.

R-1.2 Algorithm A uses $10n\log n$ operations, while algorithm B uses n^2 operations. Determine the value n_0 such that A is better than B for $n \geq n_0$.

R-1.3 Repeat the previous problem assuming B uses $n\sqrt{n}$ operations.

R-1.4 Show that $\log^3 n$ is $o(n^{1/3})$.

R-1.5 Show that the following two statements are equivalent:

(a) The running time of algorithm A is $O(f(n))$.

(b) In the worst case, the running time of algorithm A is $O(f(n))$.

R-1.6 Order the following list of functions by the big-Oh notation. Group together (for example, by underlining) those functions that are big-Theta of one another.

$$\begin{array}{ccccc} 6n\log n & 2^{100} & \log\log n & \log^2 n & 2^{\log n} \\ 2^{2^n} & \lceil\sqrt{n}\rceil & n^{0.01} & 1/n & 4n^{3/2} \\ 3n^{0.5} & 5n & \lfloor 2n\log^2 n\rfloor & 2^n & n\log_4 n \\ 4^n & n^3 & n^2\log n & 4^{\log n} & \sqrt{\log n} \end{array}$$

Hint: When in doubt about two functions $f(n)$ and $g(n)$, consider $\log f(n)$ and $\log g(n)$ or $2^{f(n)}$ and $2^{g(n)}$.

R-1.7 For each function $f(n)$ and time t in the following table, determine the largest size n of a problem that can be solved in time t assuming that the algorithm to solve the problem takes $f(n)$ microseconds. Recall that $\log n$ denotes the logarithm in base 2 of n. Some entries have already been completed to get you started.

	1 Second	1 Hour	1 Month	1 Century
$\log n$	$\approx 10^{300000}$			
$\sqrt{n}$				
n				
$n\log n$				
n^2				
n^3				
2^n				
$n!$		12		

R-1.8 Bill has an algorithm, find2D, to find an element x in an $n \times n$ array A. The algorithm find2D iterates over the rows of A and calls the algorithm arrayFind, of Algorithm 1.12, on each one, until x is found or it has searched all rows of A. What is the worst-case running time of find2D in terms of n? Is this a linear-time algorithm? Why or why not?

R-1.9 Consider the following recurrence equation, defining $T(n)$, as

$$T(n) = \begin{cases} 4 & \text{if } n = 1 \\ T(n-1) + 4 & \text{otherwise.} \end{cases}$$

Show, by induction, that $T(n) = 4n$.

R-1.10 Give a big-Oh characterization, in terms of n, of the running time of the Loop1 method shown in Algorithm 1.22.

R-1.11 Perform a similar analysis for method Loop2 shown in Algorithm 1.22.

R-1.12 Perform a similar analysis for method Loop3 shown in Algorithm 1.22.

R-1.13 Perform a similar analysis for method Loop4 shown in Algorithm 1.22.

R-1.14 Perform a similar analysis for method Loop5 shown in Algorithm 1.22.

Algorithm Loop1(n):
  $s \leftarrow 0$
  for $i \leftarrow 1$ **to** n **do**
    $s \leftarrow s + i$

Algorithm Loop2(n):
  $p \leftarrow 1$
  for $i \leftarrow 1$ **to** $2n$ **do**
    $p \leftarrow p \cdot i$

Algorithm Loop3(n):
  $p \leftarrow 1$
  for $i \leftarrow 1$ **to** n^2 **do**
    $p \leftarrow p \cdot i$

Algorithm Loop4(n):
  $s \leftarrow 0$
  for $i \leftarrow 1$ **to** $2n$ **do**
    for $j \leftarrow 1$ **to** i **do**
      $s \leftarrow s + i$

Algorithm Loop5(n):
  $s \leftarrow 0$
  for $i \leftarrow 1$ **to** n^2 **do**
    for $j \leftarrow 1$ **to** i **do**
      $s \leftarrow s + i$

Algorithm 1.22: A collection of loop methods.

R-1.15 Show that if $f(n)$ is $O(g(n))$ and $d(n)$ is $O(h(n))$, then the summation $f(n)+d(n)$ is $O(g(n)+h(n))$.

R-1.16 Show that $O(\max\{f(n),g(n)\}) = O(f(n)+g(n))$.

R-1.17 Show that $f(n)$ is $O(g(n))$ if and only if $g(n)$ is $\Omega(f(n))$.

R-1.18 Show that if $p(n)$ is a polynomial in n, then $\log p(n)$ is $O(\log n)$.

R-1.19 Show that $(n+1)^5$ is $O(n^5)$.

R-1.20 Show that 2^{n+1} is $O(2^n)$.

R-1.21 Show that n is $o(n \log n)$.

R-1.22 Show that n^2 is $\omega(n)$.

R-1.23 Show that $n^3 \log n$ is $\Omega(n^3)$.

R-1.24 Show that $\lceil f(n) \rceil$ is $O(f(n))$ if $f(n)$ is a positive nondecreasing function that is always greater than 1.

R-1.25 Justify the fact that if $d(n)$ is $O(f(n))$ and $e(n)$ is $O(g(n))$, then the product $d(n)e(n)$ is $O(f(n)g(n))$.

R-1.26 What is the amortized running time of an operation in a series of n add operations on an initially empty extendable table implemented with an array such that the capacityIncrement parameter is always maintained to be $\lceil \log(m+1) \rceil$, where m is the number of elements of the stack? That is, each time the table is expanded by $\lceil \log(m+1) \rceil$ cells, its capacityIncrement is reset to $\lceil \log(m'+1) \rceil$ cells, where m is the old size of the table and m' is the new size (in terms of actual elements present).

R-1.27 Describe a recursive algorithm for finding both the minimum and the maximum elements in an array A of n elements. Your method should return a pair (a,b), where a is the minimum element and b is the maximum. What is the running time of your method?

R-1.28 Rewrite the proof of Theorem 1.31 under the assumption that the the cost of growing the array from size k to size $2k$ is $3k$ cyber-dollars. How much should each add operation be charged to make the amortization work?

R-1.29 Plot on a semi-log scale, using the ratio test, the comparison of the set of points

$$S = \{(1,1),(2,7),(4,30),(8,125),(16,510),(32,2045),(64,8190)\}$$

against each of the following functions:

a. $f(n) = n$
b. $f(n) = n^2$
c. $f(n) = n^3$.

R-1.30 Plot on a log-log scale the set of points

$$S = \{(1,1),(2,7),(4,30),(8,125),(16,510),(32,2045),(64,8190)\}.$$

Using the power rule, estimate a polynomial function $f(n) = bn^c$ that best fits this data.

Creativity

C-1.1 What is the amortized running time of the operations in a sequence of n operations $P = p_1 p_2 \ldots p_n$ if the running time of p_i is $\Theta(i)$ if i is a multiple of 3, and is constant otherwise?

C-1.2 Let $P = p_1 p_2 \ldots p_n$ be a sequence of n operations, each either a red or blue operation, with p_1 being a red operation and p_2 being a blue operation. The running time of the blue operations is always constant. The running time of the first red operation is constant, but each red operation p_i after that runs in time that is twice as long as the previous red operation, p_j (with $j < i$). What is the amortized time of the red and blue operations under the following conditions?

a. There are always $\Theta(1)$ blue operations between consecutive red operations.
b. There are always $\Theta(\sqrt{n})$ blue operations between consecutive red operations.
c. The number of blue operations between a red operation p_i and the previous red operation p_j is always twice the number between p_j and its previous red operation.

C-1.3 What is the total running time of counting from 1 to n in binary if the time needed to add 1 to the current number i is proportional to the number of bits in the binary expansion of i that must change in going from i to $i+1$?

C-1.4 Consider the following recurrence equation, defining a function $T(n)$:

$$T(n) = \begin{cases} 1 & \text{if } n = 1 \\ T(n-1) + n & \text{otherwise,} \end{cases}$$

Show, by induction, that $T(n) = n(n+1)/2$.

C-1.5 Consider the following recurrence equation, defining a function $T(n)$:

$$T(n) = \begin{cases} 1 & \text{if } n = 1 \\ T(n-1) + 2^n & \text{otherwise,} \end{cases}$$

Show, by induction, that $T(n) = 2^{n+1} - 1$.

C-1.6 Consider the following recurrence equation, defining a function $T(n)$:

$$T(n) = \begin{cases} 1 & \text{if } n = 1 \\ 2T(n-1) & \text{otherwise,} \end{cases}$$

Show, by induction, that $T(n) = 2^n$.

C-1.7 Al and Bill are arguing about the performance of their sorting algorithms. Al claims that his $O(n \log n)$-time algorithm is *always* faster than Bill's $O(n^2)$-time algorithm. To settle the issue, they implement and run the two algorithms on many randomly generated data sets. To Al's dismay, they find that if $n < 100$, the $O(n^2)$-time algorithm actually runs faster, and only when $n \geq 100$ is the $O(n \log n)$-time algorithm better. Explain why this scenario is possible. You may give numerical examples.

C-1.8 Communication security is extremely important in computer networks, and one way many network protocols achieve security is to encrypt messages. Typical *cryptographic* schemes for the secure transmission of messages over such networks are based on the fact that no efficient algorithms are known for factoring large integers. Hence, if we can represent a secret message by a large prime number p, we can transmit over the network the number $r = p \cdot q$, where $q > p$ is another large prime number that acts as the *encryption key*. An eavesdropper who obtains the transmitted number r on the network would have to factor r in order to figure out the secret message p.

Using factoring to figure out a message is very difficult without knowing the encryption key q. To understand why, consider the following naive factoring algorithm:

> For every integer p such that $1 < p < r$, check if p divides r. If so, print "The secret message is p!" and stop; if not, continue.

a. Suppose that the eavesdropper uses the above algorithm and has a computer that can carry out in 1 microsecond (1 millionth of a second) a division between two integers of up to 100 bits each. Give an estimate of the time that it will take in the worst case to decipher the secret message if r has 100 bits.

b. What is the worst-case time complexity of the above algorithm? Since the input to the algorithm is just one large number r, assume that the input size n is the number of bytes needed to store r, that is, $n = (\log_2 r)/8$, and that each division takes time $O(n)$.

C-1.9 Give an example of a positive function $f(n)$ such that $f(n)$ is neither $O(n)$ nor $\Omega(n)$.

C-1.10 Show that $\sum_{i=1}^{n} i^2$ is $O(n^3)$.

C-1.11 Show that $\sum_{i=1}^{n} i/2^i < 2$.

Hint: Try to bound this sum term by term with a geometric progression.

C-1.12 Show that $\log_b f(n)$ is $\Theta(\log f(n))$ if $b > 1$ is a constant.

C-1.13 Describe a method for finding both the minimum and maximum of n numbers using fewer than $3n/2$ comparisons.

Hint: First construct a group of candidate minimums and a group of candidate maximums.

C-1.14 Suppose you are given a set of small boxes, numbered 1 to n, identical in every respect except that each of the first i contain a pearl whereas the remaining $n-i$ are empty. You also have two magic wands that can each test if a box is empty or not in a single touch, except that a wand disappears if you test it on an empty box. Show that, without knowing the value of i, you can use the two wands to determine all the boxes containing pearls using at most $o(n)$ wand touches. Express, as a function of n, the asymptotic number of wand touches needed.

C-1.15 Repeat the previous problem assuming that you now have k magic wands, with $k > 2$ and $k < \log n$. Express, as a function of n and k, the asymptotic number of wand touches needed to identify all the magic boxes containing pearls.

C-1.16 An n-degree ***polynomial*** $p(x)$ is an equation of the form

$$p(x) = \sum_{i=0}^{n} a_i x^i,$$

where x is a real number and each a_i is a constant.

a. Describe a simple $O(n^2)$ time method for computing $p(x)$ for a particular value of x.

b. Consider now a rewriting of $p(x)$ as

$$p(x) = a_0 + x(a_1 + x(a_2 + x(a_3 + \cdots + x(a_{n-1} + xa_n)\cdots))),$$

which is known as ***Horner's method***. Using the big-Oh notation, characterize the number of multiplications and additions this method of evaluation uses.

C-1.17 Consider the following induction "proof" that all sheep in a flock are the same color:

Base case: One sheep. It is clearly the same color as itself.

Induction step: A flock of n sheep. Take a sheep, a, out of the flock. The remaining $n-1$ are all the same color by induction. Now put sheep a back in the flock, and take out a different sheep, b. By induction, the $n-1$ sheep (now with a in their group) are all the same color. Therefore, a is the same color as all the other sheep; hence, all the sheep in the flock are the same color.

What is wrong with this "proof"?

C-1.18 Consider the following "proof" that the Fibonacci function, $F(n)$, defined as $F(1) = 1$, $F(2) = 2$, $F(n) = F(n-1) + F(n-2)$, is $O(n)$:
Base case ($n \leq 2$): $F(1) = 1$, which is $O(1)$, and $F(2) = 2$, which is $O(2)$.
Induction step ($n > 2$): Assume the claim is true for $n' < n$. Consider n. $F(n) = F(n-1) + F(n-2)$. By induction, $F(n-1)$ is $O(n-1)$ and $F(n-2)$ is $O(n-2)$. Then, $F(n)$ is $O((n-1)+(n-2))$, by the identity presented in Exercise R-1.15. Therefore, $F(n)$ is $O(n)$, since $O((n-1)+(n-2))$ is $O(n)$.
What is wrong with this "proof"?

C-1.19 Consider the Fibonacci function, $F(n)$, from the previous exercise. Show by induction that $F(n)$ is $\Omega((3/2)^n)$.

C-1.20 Draw a visual justification of Theorem 1.13 analogous to that of Figure 1.11b for the case when n is odd.

C-1.21 An array A contains $n-1$ unique integers in the range $[0, n-1]$, that is, there is one number from this range that is not in A. Design an $O(n)$-time algorithm for finding that number. You are allowed to use only $O(1)$ additional space besides the array A itself.

C-1.22 Show that the summation $\sum_{i=1}^{n} \lceil \log_2 i \rceil$ is $O(n \log n)$.

C-1.23 Show that the summation $\sum_{i=1}^{n} \lceil \log_2 i \rceil$ is $\Omega(n \log n)$.

C-1.24 Show that the summation $\sum_{i=1}^{n} \lceil \log_2 (n/i) \rceil$ is $O(n)$. You may assume that n is a power of 2.

Hint: Use induction to reduce the problem to that for $n/2$.

C-1.25 An evil king has a cellar containing n bottles of expensive wine, and his guards have just caught a spy trying to poison the king's wine. Fortunately, the guards caught the spy after he succeeded in poisoning only one bottle. Unfortunately, they don't know which one. To make matters worse, the poison the spy used was very deadly; just one drop diluted even a billion to one will still kill someone. Even so, the poison works slowly; it takes a full month for the person to die. Design a scheme that allows the evil king to determine exactly which one of his wine bottles was poisoned in just one month's time while expending at most $O(\log n)$ of his taste testers.

C-1.26 Let S be a set of n lines such that no two are parallel and no three meet in the same point. Show by induction that the lines in S determine $\Theta(n^2)$ intersection points.

C-1.27 Suppose that each row of an $n \times n$ array A consists of 1's and 0's such that, in any row of A, all the 1's come before any 0's in that row. Assuming A is already in memory, describe a method running in $O(n)$ time (not $O(n^2)$ time) for finding the row of A that contains the most 1's.

C-1.28 Suppose that each row of an $n \times n$ array A consists of 1's and 0's such that, in any row i of A, all the 1's come before any 0's in that row. Suppose further that the number of 1's in row i is at least the number in row $i+1$, for $i = 0, 1, \ldots, n-2$. Assuming A is already in memory, describe a method running in $O(n)$ time (not $O(n^2)$ time) for counting the number of 1's in the array A.

C-1.29 Describe, using pseudo-code, a method for multiplying an $n \times m$ matrix A and an $m \times p$ matrix B. Recall that the product $C = AB$ is defined so that $C[i][j] = \sum_{k=1}^{m} A[i][k] \cdot B[k][j]$. What is the running time of your method?

C-1.30 Give a recursive algorithm to compute the product of two positive integers m and n using only addition.

C-1.31 Give complete pseudo-code for a new class, ShrinkingTable, that performs the add method of the extendable table, as well as methods, remove(), which removes the last (actual) element of the table, and shrinkToFit(), which replaces the underlying array with an array whose capacity is exactly equal to the number of elements currently in the table.

C-1.32 Consider an extendable table that supports both add and remove methods, as defined in the previous exercise. Moreover, suppose we grow the underlying array implementing the table by doubling its capacity any time we need to increase the size of this array, and we shrink the underlying array by half any time the number of (actual) elements in the table dips below $N/4$, where N is the current capacity of the array. Show that a sequence of n add and remove methods, starting from an array with capacity $N = 1$, takes $O(n)$ time.

C-1.33 Consider an implementation of the extendable table, but instead of copying the elements of the table into an array of double the size (that is, from N to $2N$) when its capacity is reached, we copy the elements into an array with $\lceil \sqrt{N} \rceil$ additional cells, going from capacity N to $N + \lceil \sqrt{N} \rceil$. Show that performing a sequence of n add operations (that is, insertions at the end) runs in $\Theta(n^{3/2})$ time in this case.

Projects

P-1.1 Program the two algorithms, prefixAverages1 and prefixAverages2 from Section 1.4, and perform a careful experimental analysis of their running times. Plot their running times as a function of their input sizes as scatter plots on both a linear-linear scale and a log-log scale. Choose representative values of the size n, and run at least five tests for each size value n in your tests.

P-1.2 Perform a careful experimental analysis that compares the relative running times of the methods shown in Algorithm 1.22. Use both the ratio test and the power test to estimate the running times of the various methods.

P-1.3 Implement an extendable table using arrays that can increase in size as elements are added. Perform an experimental analysis of each of the running times for performing a sequence of n add methods, assuming the array size is increased from N to the following possible values:

a. $2N$
b. $N + \lceil \sqrt{N} \rceil$
c. $N + \lceil \log N \rceil$
d. $N + 100$.

Chapter Notes

The topics discussed in this chapter come from diverse sources. Amortization has been used to analyze a number of different data structures and algorithms, but it was not a topic of study in its own right until the mid 1980's. For more information about amortization, please see the paper by Tarjan [201] or the book by Tarjan [200].

Our use of the big-Oh notation is consistent with most authors' usage, but we have taken a slightly more conservative approach than some. The big-Oh notation has prompted several discussions in the algorithms and computation theory community over its proper use [37, 92, 120]. Knuth [118, 120], for example, defines it using the notation $f(n) = O(g(n))$, but he refers to this "equality" as being only "one way," even though he mentions that the big-Oh is actually defining a set of functions. We have chosen to take a more standard view of equality and view the big-Oh notation truly as a set, following the suggestions of Brassard [37]. The reader interested in studying average-case analysis is referred to the book chapter by Vitter and Flajolet [207].

We include a number of useful mathematical facts in Appendix A. The reader interested in further study into the analysis of algorithms is referred to the books by Graham, Knuth, and Patashnik [90], and Sedgewick and Flajolet [184]. The reader interested in learning more about the history of mathematics is referred to the book by Boyer and Merzbach [35]. Our version of the famous story about Archimedes is taken from [155]. Finally, for more information about using experimentation to estimate the running time of algorithms, we refer the interested reader to several papers by McGeoch and coauthors [142, 143, 144].

Chapter 2 Basic Data Structures

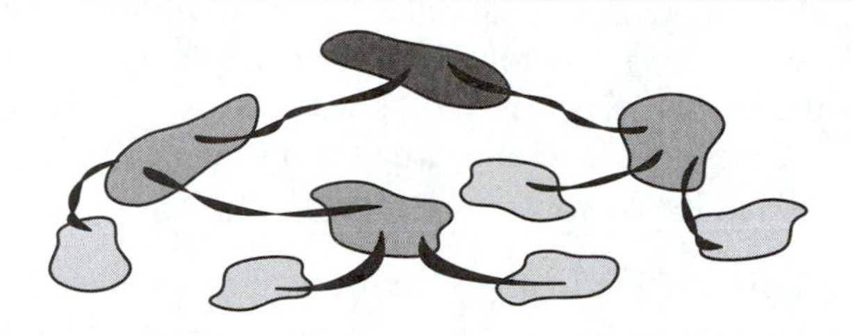

Contents

2.1 Stacks and Queues **57**
- 2.1.1 Stacks 57
- 2.1.2 Queues 61

2.2 Vectors, Lists, and Sequences **65**
- 2.2.1 Vectors 65
- 2.2.2 Lists 68
- 2.2.3 Sequences 73

2.3 Trees **75**
- 2.3.1 The Tree Abstract Data Type 77
- 2.3.2 Tree Traversal 78
- 2.3.3 Binary Trees 84
- 2.3.4 Data Structures for Representing Trees 90

2.4 Priority Queues and Heaps **94**
- 2.4.1 The Priority Queue Abstract Data Type 94
- 2.4.2 PQ-Sort, Selection-Sort, and Insertion-Sort 96
- 2.4.3 The Heap Data Structure 99
- 2.4.4 Heap-Sort 107

2.5 Dictionaries and Hash Tables **114**
- 2.5.1 The Unordered Dictionary ADT 114
- 2.5.2 Hash Tables 116
- 2.5.3 Hash Functions 117
- 2.5.4 Compression Maps 119
- 2.5.5 Collision-Handling Schemes 120
- 2.5.6 Universal Hashing 125

2.6 Java Example: Heap **128**

2.7 Exercises **131**

Basic data structures, such as stacks and queues, are used in a host of different applications. Using good data structures often makes the difference between an efficient algorithm and an inefficient one. Thus, we feel it important to review and discuss several basic data structures.

We begin our discussion in this chapter by studying stacks and queues, including how they can be used to implement recursion and multiprogramming. We follow this discussion by presenting the ***vector***, ***list***, and ***sequence*** ADTs, each of which represents a collection of linearly arranged elements and provides methods for accessing, inserting, and removing arbitrary elements. An important property of a sequence is that, just as with stacks and queues, the order of the elements in a sequence is determined by the operations in the abstract data type specification, and not by the values of the elements.

In addition to these linear data structures we also discuss nonlinear structures, which use organizational relationships richer than the simple "before" and "after" relationships. Specifically, we discuss the ***tree*** abstract data type, which defines relationships that are ***hierarchical***, with some objects being "above" and some "below" others. The main terminology for tree data structures comes from family trees, by the way, with the terms "parent," "child," "ancestor," and "descendent" being the most common words used to describe hierarchical relationships.

In this chapter, we also study data structures that store "prioritized elements," that is, elements that have priorities assigned to them. Such a priority is typically a numerical value, but we can view priorities as arbitrary objects, so long as there is a consistent way of comparing pairs of such objects. A priority queue allows us to select and remove the element of first priority, which we define, without loss of generality, to be an element with the smallest key. This general viewpoint allows us to define a generic abstract data type, called the ***priority queue***, for storing and retrieving prioritized elements. This ADT is fundamentally different from the position-based data structures we discuss in this chapter, such as stacks, queues, sequences, and even trees. These other data structures store elements at specific positions, which are often positions in a linear arrangement of the elements determined by the insertion and deletion operations performed. The priority queue ADT stores elements according to their priorities, and has no notion of "position."

The final structure we discuss is the dictionary, which stores elements so that they can be located quickly using keys. The motivation for such searches is that each element in a dictionary typically stores additional useful information besides its search key, but the only way to get at that information is to use the search key. Like a priority queue, a dictionary is a container of key-element pairs. Nevertheless, a total order relation on the keys is always required for a priority queue; it is optional for a dictionary. Indeed, the simplest form of a dictionary, which uses a hash table, assumes only that we can assign an integer to each key and determine whether two keys are equal.

2.1 Stacks and Queues

2.1.1 Stacks

A ***stack*** is a container of objects that are inserted and removed according to the ***last-in first-out*** (***LIFO***) principle. Objects can be inserted into a stack at any time, but only the most-recently inserted (that is, "last") object can be removed at any time. The name "stack" is derived from the metaphor of a stack of plates in a spring-loaded cafeteria plate dispenser. In this case, the fundamental operations involve the "pushing" and "popping" of plates on the stack.

Example 2.1: *Internet Web browsers store the addresses of recently visited sites on a stack. Each time a user visits a new site, that site's address is "pushed" onto the stack of addresses. The browser then allows the user to "pop" back to previously visited sites using the "back" button.*

The Stack Abstract Data Type

A stack S is an abstract data type (ADT) supporting the following two methods:

push(o): Insert object o at the top of the stack.

pop(): Remove from the stack and return the top object on the stack, that is, the most recently inserted element still in the stack; an error occurs if the stack is empty.

Additionally, let us also define the following supporting methods:

size(): Return the number of objects in the stack.

isEmpty(): Return a Boolean indicating if the stack is empty.

top(): Return the top object on the stack, without removing it; an error occurs if the stack is empty.

A Simple Array-Based Implementation

A stack is easily implemented with an N-element array S, with elements stored from $S[0]$ to $S[t]$, where t is an integer that gives the index of the top element in S. Note that one of the important details of such an implementation is that we must specify some maximum size N for our stack, say, $N = 1,000$. (See Figure 2.1.)

Figure 2.1: Implementing a stack with an array S. The top element is in cell $S[t]$.

Recalling that the convention in this book is that arrays start at index 0, we initialize t to -1, and we use this value for t to identify when the stack is empty. Likewise, we can use this variable to determine the number of elements in a stack $(t+1)$. We also must signal an error condition that arises if we try to insert a new element and the array S is full. Given this new exception, we can then implement the main methods of the stack ADT as described in Algorithm 2.2.

Algorithm push(o):
  if size() $= N$ **then**
    indicate that a stack-full error has occurred
  $t \leftarrow t+1$
  $S[t] \leftarrow o$

Algorithm pop():
  if isEmpty() **then**
    indicate that a stack-empty error has occurred
  $e \leftarrow S[t]$.
  $S[t] \leftarrow$ **null**
  $t \leftarrow t-1$
  return e

Algorithm 2.2: Implementation of a stack by means of an array.

Pseudo-code descriptions for performing the supporting methods of the Stack ADT in constant time are fairly straightforward. Thus, each of the stack methods in the array realization executes a constant number of statements involving arithmetic operations, comparisons, and assignments. That is, in this implementation of the stack ADT, each method runs in $O(1)$ time.

The array implementation of a stack is both simple and efficient, and is widely used in a variety of computing applications. Nevertheless, this implementation has one negative aspect; it must assume a fixed upper bound N on the ultimate size of the stack. An application may actually need much less space than this, in which case we would be wasting memory. Alternatively, an application may need more space than this, in which case our stack implementation may "crash" the application with an error as soon as it tries to push its $(N+1)$st object on the stack. Thus, even with its simplicity and efficiency, the array-based stack implementation is not necessarily ideal. Fortunately, there are other implementations, discussed later in this chapter, that do not have a size limitation and use space proportional to the actual number of elements stored in the stack. Alternatively, we could also use an extendable table, as discussed in Section 1.5.2. In cases where we have a good estimate on the number of items needing to go in the stack, however, the array-based implementation is hard to beat. Stacks serve a vital role in a number of computing applications, so it is helpful to have a fast stack ADT implementation, such as the simple array-based implementation.

Using Stacks for Procedure Calls and Recursion

Stacks are an important application to the run-time environments of modern procedural languages, such as C, C++, and Java. Each thread in a running program written in one of these languages has a private stack, called the ***method stack***, which is used to keep track of local variables and other important information on methods, as they are invoked during execution. (See Figure 2.3.)

More specifically, during the execution of a program thread, the runtime environment maintains a stack whose elements are descriptors of the currently active (that is, nonterminated) invocations of methods. These descriptors are called ***frames***. A frame for some invocation of method "cool" stores the current values of the local variables and parameters of method cool, as well as information on the method that called cool and on what needs to be returned to this method.

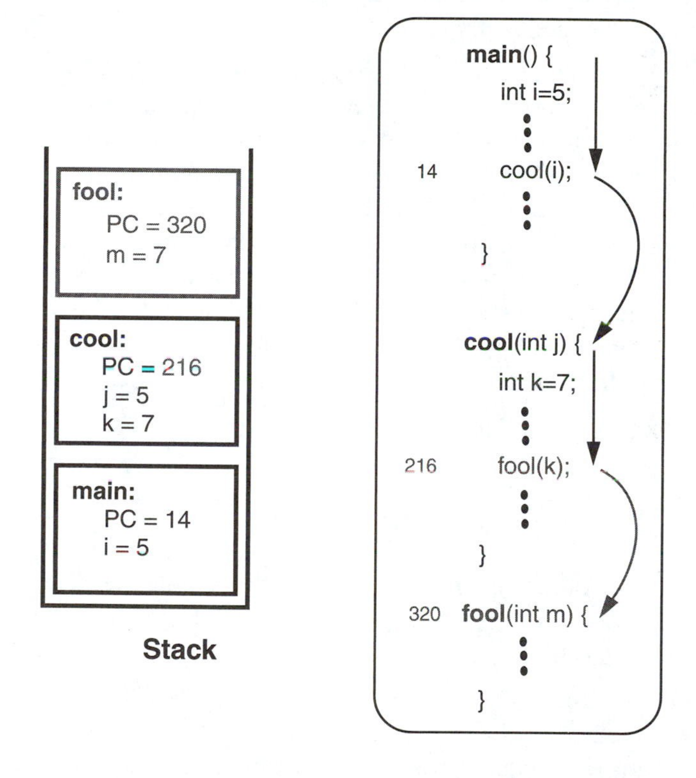

Figure 2.3: An example of a method stack: Method fool has just been called by method cool, which itself was previously called by method main. Note the values of the program counter, parameters, and local variables stored in the stack frames. When the invocation of method fool terminates, the invocation of method cool will resume its execution at instruction 217, which is obtained by incrementing the value of the program counter stored in the stack frame.

The runtime environment keeps the address of the statement the thread is currently executing in the program in a special register, called the ***program counter***. When a method "cool" invokes another method "fool", the current value of the program counter is recorded in the frame of the current invocation of cool (so the computer will "know" where to return to when method fool is done).

At the top of the method stack is the frame of the ***running method***, that is, the method that currently has control of the execution. The remaining elements of the stack are frames of the ***suspended methods***, that is, methods that have invoked another method and are currently waiting for it to return control to them upon its termination. The order of the elements in the stack corresponds to the chain of invocations of the currently active methods. When a new method is invoked, a frame for this method is pushed onto the stack. When it terminates, its frame is popped from the stack and the computer resumes the processing of the previously suspended method.

The method stack also performs parameter passing to methods. Specifically, many languages, such as C and Java, use the ***call-by-value*** parameter passing protocol using the method stack. This means that the current ***value*** of a variable (or expression) is what is passed as an argument to a called method. In the case of a variable x of a primitive type, such as an int or float, the current value of x is simply the number that is associated with x. When such a value is passed to the called method, it is assigned to a local variable in the called method's frame. (This simple assignment is also illustrated in Figure 2.3.) Note that if the called method changes the value of this local variable, it will ***not*** change the value of the variable in the calling method.

Recursion

One of the benefits of using a stack to implement method invocation is that it allows programs to use ***recursion*** (Section 1.1.4). That is, it allows a method to call itself as a subroutine.

Recall that in using this technique correctly, we must always design a recursive method so that it is guaranteed to terminate at some point (for example, by always making recursive calls for "smaller" instances of the problem and handling the "smallest" instances nonrecursively as special cases). We note that if we design an "infinitely recursive" method, it will not actually run forever. It will instead, at some point, use up all the memory available for the method stack and generate an out-of-memory error. If we use recursion with care, however, the method stack will implement recursive methods without any trouble. Each call of the same method will be associated with a different frame, complete with its own values for local variables. Recursion can be very powerful, as it often allows us to design simple and efficient programs for fairly difficult problems.

2.1.2 Queues

Another basic data structure is the ***queue***. It is a close "cousin" of the stack, as a queue is a container of objects that are inserted and removed according to the ***first-in first-out*** (***FIFO***) principle. That is, elements can be inserted at any time, but only the element that has been in the queue the longest can be removed at any time. We usually say that elements enter the queue at the ***rear*** and are removed from the ***front***.

The Queue Abstract Data Type

The queue ADT keeps objects in a sequence, where element access and deletion are restricted to the first element in the sequence, which is called the ***front*** of the queue, and element insertion is restricted to the end of the sequence, which is called the ***rear*** of the queue. Thus, we enforce the rule that items are inserted and removed according to the FIFO principle. The ***queue*** ADT supports the following two fundamental methods:

enqueue(o): Insert object o at the rear of the queue.

dequeue(): Remove and return from the queue the object at the front; an error occurs if the queue is empty.

Additionally, the queue ADT includes the following supporting methods:

size(): Return the number of objects in the queue.

isEmpty(): Return a Boolean value indicating whether queue is empty.

front(): Return, but do not remove, the front object in the queue; an error occurs if the queue is empty.

A Simple Array-Based Implementation

We present a simple realization of a queue by means of an array, Q, with capacity N, for storing its elements. Since the main rule with the queue ADT is that we insert and delete objects according to the FIFO principle, we must decide how we are going to keep track of the front and rear of the queue.

To avoid moving objects once they are placed in Q, we define two variables f and r, which have the following meanings:

- f is an index to the cell of Q storing the first element of the queue (which is the next candidate to be removed by a dequeue operation), unless the queue is empty (in which case $f = r$)
- r is an index to the next available array cell in Q.

Initially, we assign $f = r = 0$, and we indicate that the queue is empty by the condition $f = r$. Now, when we remove an element from the front of the queue, we can simply increment f to index the next cell. Likewise, when we add an element, we can simply increment r to index the next available cell in Q. We have to be a little careful not to overflow the end of the array, however. Consider, for example, what happens if we repeatedly enqueue and dequeue a single element N different times. We would have $f = r = N$. If we were then to try to insert the element just one more time, we would get an array-out-of-bounds error (since the N valid locations in Q are from $Q[0]$ to $Q[N-1]$), even though there is plenty of room in the queue in this case. To avoid this problem and be able to utilize all of the array Q, we let the f and r indices "wrap around" the end of Q. That is, we now view Q as a "circular array" that goes from $Q[0]$ to $Q[N-1]$ and then immediately back to $Q[0]$ again. (See Figure 2.4.)

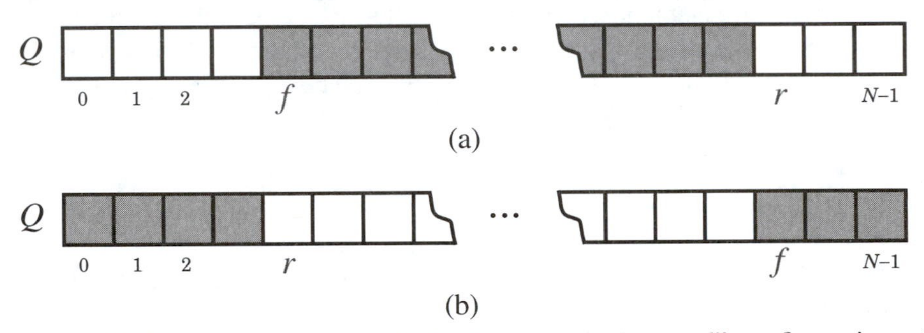

Figure 2.4: Using array Q in a circular fashion: (a) the "normal" configuration with $f \leq r$; (b) the "wrapped around" configuration with $r < f$. The cells storing queue elements are highlighted.

Implementing this circular view of Q is pretty easy. Each time we increment f or r, we simply compute this increment as "$(f+1) \bmod N$" or "$(r+1) \bmod N$," respectively, where the operator " mod " is the ***modulo*** operator, which is computed by taking the remainder after an integral division, so that, if y is nonzero, then

$$x \bmod y = x - \lfloor x/y \rfloor y.$$

Consider now the situation that occurs if we enqueue N objects without dequeuing them. We would have $f = r$, which is the same condition as when the queue is empty. Hence, we would not be able to tell the difference between a full queue and an empty one in this case. Fortunately, this is not a big problem, and a number of ways for dealing with it exist. For example, we can simply insist that Q can never hold more than $N-1$ objects. The above simple rule for handling a full queue takes care of the final problem with our implementation, and leads to the pseudo-coded descriptions of the main queue methods given in Algorithm 2.5. Note that we may compute the size of the queue by means of the expression $(N - f + r) \bmod N$, which gives the correct result both in the "normal" configuration (when $f \leq r$) and in the "wrapped around" configuration (when $r < f$).

Algorithm dequeue():
  if isEmpty() **then**
    throw a QueueEmptyException
  $temp \leftarrow Q[f]$
  $Q[f] \leftarrow$ **null**
  $f \leftarrow (f+1) \bmod N$
  return $temp$

Algorithm enqueue(o):
  if size() $= N-1$ **then**
    throw a QueueFullException
  $Q[r] \leftarrow o$
  $r \leftarrow (r+1) \bmod N$

Algorithm 2.5: Implementation of a queue by means of an array, which is viewed circularly.

As with our array-based stack implementation, each of the queue methods in the array realization executes a constant number of statements involving arithmetic operations, comparisons, and assignments. Thus, each method in this implementation runs in $O(1)$ time.

Also, as with the array-based stack implementation, the only real disadvantage of the array-based queue implementation is that we artificially set the capacity of the queue to be some number N. In a real application, we may actually need more or less queue capacity than this, but if we have a good estimate of the number of elements that will be in the queue at the same time, then the array-based implementation is quite efficient.

Using Queues for Multiprogramming

Multiprogramming is a way of achieving a limited form of parallelism, even on a computer that has only one CPU. This mechanism allows us to have multiple tasks or computational ***threads*** running at the same time, with each thread being responsible for some specific computation. Multiprogramming is useful in graphical applications. For example, one thread can be responsible for catching mouse clicks while several others are responsible for moving parts of an animation around in a screen canvas. Even if the computer has only one CPU, these different computational threads can all seem to be running at the same time because:

1. The CPU is so fast relative to our perception of time.
2. The operating system is providing each thread with a different "slice" of the CPU's time.

The time slices given to each different thread occur with such rapid succession that the different threads appear to be running simultaneously, in parallel.

For example, Java has a built-in mechanism for achieving multiprogramming—Java threads. Java threads are computational objects that can cooperate and communicate with one another to share other objects in memory, the computer's screen, or other kinds of resources and devices. Switching between different threads in a Java program occurs rapidly because each thread has its own Java stack stored in the memory of the Java Virtual Machine. The method stack for each thread contains the local variables and the frames for the methods that that thread is currently running. Thus, to switch from a thread T to another thread U, all the CPU needs to do is to "remember" where it left off in the thread T before it switches to the thread U. We have already discussed a way for this to be done, namely, by storing the current value of T's program counter, which is a reference to the next instruction T is to perform, at the top of T's Java stack. By saving the program counter for each active thread in the top of its Java stack, the CPU can pick up where it left off in some other thread U, by restoring the value of the program counter to the value that was stored at the top of U's Java stack (and using U's stack as the "current" Java stack).

When designing a program that uses multiple threads, we must be careful not to allow an individual thread to monopolize the CPU. Such CPU monopolization can lead to an application or applet ***hanging***, where it is technically running, but not actually doing anything. In some operating systems, CPU monopolizing by threads is not an issue, however. These operating systems utilize a queue to allocate CPU time to the runnable threads in the ***round-robin*** protocol.

The main idea of the round-robin protocol is to store all runnable threads in a queue Q. When the CPU is ready to provide a time slice to a thread, it performs a dequeue operation on the queue Q to get the next available runnable thread; let's call it T. Before the CPU actually begins executing instructions for T, however, it starts a timer running in hardware set to expire a fixed amount of time later. The CPU now waits until either (a) thread T blocks itself (by one of the blocking methods mentioned above), or (b) the timer expires. In the latter case, the CPU stops the execution of T and and performs an enqueue operation to place T at the end of the line of currently runnable threads. In either case, the CPU saves the current value of T's program counter at the top of T's method stack and processes the next available runnable thread by extracting it from Q with a dequeue operation. In this way, the CPU ensures that each runnable thread is given its fair share of time. Thus, by using a simple queue data structure and a hardware stopwatch, the operating system can avoid CPU monopolization.

While this queue-based solution solves the multiprogramming problem, we should mention that this solution is actually an oversimplification of the protocol used by most operating systems that do round-robin time slicing, as most systems give threads priorities. Thus, they use a ***priority queue*** to implement time slicing. We discuss priority queues in Section 2.4.

2.2 Vectors, Lists, and Sequences

Stacks and queues store elements according to a linear sequence determined by update operations that act on the "ends" of the sequence. The data structures we discuss in this section maintain linear orders while allowing for accesses and updates in the "middle."

2.2.1 Vectors

Suppose we are given a linear sequence S that contains n elements. We can uniquely refer to each element e of S using an integer in the range $[0, n-1]$ that is equal to the number of elements of S that precede e in S. We define the ***rank*** of an element e in S to be the number of elements that are before e in S. Hence, the first element in a sequence has rank 0 and the last element has rank $n-1$.

Note that rank is similar to an array index, but we do ***not*** insist that an array should be used to implement a sequence in such a way that the element at rank 0 is stored at index 0 in the array. The rank definition offers us a way to refer to the "index" of an element in a sequence without having to worry about the exact implementation of that list. Note that the rank of an element may change whenever the sequence is updated. For example, if we insert a new element at the beginning of the sequence, the rank of each of the other elements increases by one.

A linear sequence that supports access to its elements by their ranks is called a ***vector***. Rank is a simple yet powerful notion, since it can be used to specify where to insert a new element into a vector or where to remove an old element. For example, we can give the rank that a new element will have after it is inserted (for example, insert at rank 2). We could also use rank to specify an element to be removed (for example, remove the element at rank 2).

The Vector Abstract Data Type

A ***vector*** S storing n elements supports the following fundamental methods:

elemAtRank(r): Return the element of S with rank r; an error condition occurs if $r < 0$ or $r > n-1$.

replaceAtRank(r, e): Replace with e the element at rank r and return it; an error condition occurs if $r < 0$ or $r > n-1$.

insertAtRank(r, e): Insert a new element e into S to have rank r; an error condition occurs if $r < 0$ or $r > n$.

removeAtRank(r): Remove from S the element at rank r; an error condition occurs if $r < 0$ or $r > n-1$.

In addition, a vector supports the usual methods size() and isEmpty().

A Simple Array-Based Implementation

An obvious choice for implementing the vector ADT is to use an array A, where $A[i]$ stores (a reference to) the element with rank i. We choose the size N of array A sufficiently large, and we maintain in an instance variable the number $n < N$ of elements in the vector. The details of the implementation of the methods of the vector ADT are reasonably simple. To implement the elemAtRank(r) operation, for example, we just return $A[r]$. Implementations of methods insertAtRank(r,e) and removeAtRank(r) are given in Algorithm 2.6. An important (and time-consuming) part of this implementation involves the shifting of elements up or down to keep the occupied cells in the array contiguous. These shifting operations are required to maintain our rule of always storing an element of rank i at index i in A. (See Figure 2.7 and also Exercise C-2.5.)

Algorithm insertAtRank(r,e):
  for $i = n-1, n-2, \ldots, r$ **do**
    $A[i+1] \leftarrow A[i]$ {make room for the new element}
  $A[r] \leftarrow e$
  $n \leftarrow n+1$

Algorithm removeAtRank(r):
  $e \leftarrow A[r]$ {e is a temporary variable}
  for $i = r, r+1, \ldots, n-2$ **do**
    $A[i] \leftarrow A[i+1]$ {fill in for the removed element}
  $n \leftarrow n-1$
  return e

Algorithm 2.6: Methods in an array implementation of the vector ADT.

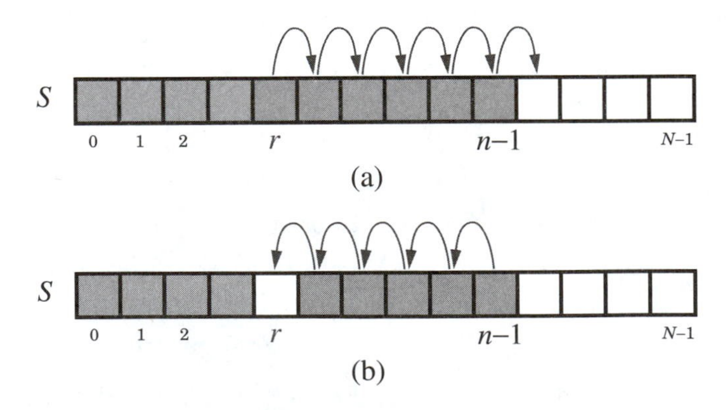

Figure 2.7: Array-based implementation of a vector S storing n elements: (a) shifting up for an insertion at rank r; (b) shifting down for a removal at rank r.

Table 2.8 shows the running times of the methods of a vector realized by means of an array. The methods isEmpty, size, and elemAtRank clearly run in $O(1)$ time, but the insertion and removal methods can take much longer than this. In particular, insertAtRank(r,e) runs in time $\Theta(n)$ in the worst case. Indeed, the worst case for this operation occurs when $r = 0$, since all the existing n elements have to be shifted forward. A similar argument applies to the method removeAtRank(r), which runs in $O(n)$ time, because we have to shift backward $n-1$ elements in the worst case ($r = 0$). In fact, assuming that each possible rank is equally likely to be passed as an argument to these operations, their average running time is $\Theta(n)$, for we will have to shift $n/2$ elements on average.

Method	Time
size()	$O(1)$
isEmpty()	$O(1)$
elemAtRank(r)	$O(1)$
replaceAtRank(r,e)	$O(1)$
insertAtRank(r,e)	$O(n)$
removeAtRank(r)	$O(n)$

Table 2.8: Worst-case performance of a vector with n elements realized by an array. The space usage is $O(N)$, where N is the size of the array.

Looking more closely at insertAtRank(r,e) and removeAtRank(r), we note that they each run in time $O(n-r+1)$, for only those elements at rank r and higher have to be shifted up or down. Thus, inserting or removing an item at the end of a vector, using the methods insertAtRank(n,e) and removeAtRank$(n-1)$, respectively take $O(1)$ time each. That is, inserting or removing an element at the end of a vector takes constant time, as would inserting or removing an element within a constant number of cells from the end. Still, with the above implementation, inserting or removing an element at the beginning of a vector requires shifting every other element by one; hence, it takes $\Theta(n)$ time. Thus, there is an asymmetry to this vector implementation—updates at the end are fast, whereas updates at the beginning are slow.

Actually, with a little effort, we can produce an array-based implementation of the vector ADT that achieves $O(1)$ time for insertions and removals at rank 0, as well as insertions and removals at the end of the vector. Achieving this requires that we give up on our rule that an element at rank i is stored in the array at index i, however, as we would have to use a circular array approach like we used in Section 2.1.2 to implement a queue. We leave the details of this implementation for an exercise (C-2.5). In addition, we note that a vector can also be implemented efficiently using an extendable table (Section 1.5.2), which in fact is the default implementation of the vector ADT in Java.

2.2.2 Lists

Using a rank is not the only means of referring to the place where an element appears in a list. We could alternatively implement the list S so that each element is stored in a special ***node*** object with references to the nodes before and after it in the list. In this case, it could be more natural and efficient to use a node instead of a rank to identify where to access and update a list. In this section, we explore a way of abstracting the node concept of "place" in a list.

Positions and Node-Based Operations

We would like to define methods for a list S that take nodes of the list as parameters and provide them as return types. For instance, we could define a hypothetical method removeAtNode(v) that removes the element of S stored at node v of the list. Using a node as a parameter allows us to remove an element in $O(1)$ time by simply going directly to the place where that node is stored and then "linking out" this node through an update of the referring links of its neighbors.

Defining methods of a list ADT by adding such node-based operations raises the issue of how much information we should be exposing about the implementation of our list. Certainly, it is desirable for us to be able to use such an implementation without revealing this detail to a user. Likewise, we do not wish to allow a user to modify the internal structure of a list without our knowledge. To abstract and unify the different ways of storing elements in the various implementations of a list, we introduce the concept of ***position*** in a list, which formalizes the intuitive notion of "place" of an element relative to others in the list.

In order to safely expand the set of operations for lists, we abstract a notion of "position" that allows us to enjoy the efficiency of node-based list implementations without violating object-oriented design principles. In this framework, we view a list as a container of elements that stores each element at a position and that keeps these positions arranged in a linear order. A position is itself an abstract data type that supports the following simple method:

element(): Return the element stored at this position.

A position is always defined ***relatively***, that is, in terms of its neighbors. In a list, a position p will always be "after" some position q and "before" some position s (unless p is the first or last position). A position p, which is associated with some element e in a list S, does not change, even if the rank of e changes in S, unless we explicitly remove e (and, hence, destroy position p). Moreover, the position p does not change even if we replace or swap the element e stored at p with another element. These facts about positions allow us to define a rich set of position-based list methods that take position objects as parameters and also provide position objects as return values.

The List Abstract Data Type

Using the concept of position to encapsulate the idea of "node" in a list, we can define another type of sequence ADT, called simply the ***list*** ADT. This ADT supports the following methods for a list S:

first(): Return the position of the first element of S; an error occurs if S is empty.

last(): Return the position of the last element of S; an error occurs if S is empty.

isFirst(p): Return a Boolean value indicating whether the given position is the first one in the list.

isLast(p): Return a Boolean value indicating whether the given position is the last one in the list.

before(p): Return the position of the element of S preceding the one at position p; an error occurs if p is the first position.

after(p): Return the position of the element of S following the one at position p; an error occurs if p is the last position.

The above methods allow us to refer to relative positions in a list, starting at the beginning or end, and to be able to move incrementally up or down the list. These positions can intuitively be thought of as nodes in the list, but note that there are no specific references to node objects nor links to previous or next nodes in these methods. In addition to the above methods and the generic methods size and isEmpty, we also include the following update methods for the list ADT.

replaceElement(p,e): Replace the element at position p with e, returning the element formerly at position p.

swapElements(p,q): Swap the elements stored at positions p and q, so that the element that is at position p moves to position q and the element that is at position q moves to position p.

insertFirst(e): Insert a new element e into S as the first element.

insertLast(e): Insert a new element e into S as the last element.

insertBefore(p,e): Insert a new element e into S before position p in S; an error occurs if p is the first position.

insertAfter(p,e): Insert a new element e into S after position p in S; an error occurs if p is the last position.

remove(p): Remove from S the element at position p.

The list ADT allows us to view an ordered collection of objects in terms of their places, without worrying about the exact way those places are represented. Also, note that there is some redundancy in the above repertoire of operations for the list ADT. Namely, we can perform operation isFirst(p) by checking whether p is equal to the position returned by first(). We can also perform operation insertFirst(e) by performing the operation insertBefore(first(), e). The redundant methods should be viewed as shortcuts.

An error condition occurs if a position passed as argument to one of the list operations is invalid. Reasons for a position p to be invalid include its being null, a position of a different list, or previously deleted from the list.

The list ADT, with its built-in notion of position, is useful in a number of settings. For example, a simple text editor embeds the notion of positional insertion and removal, since such editors typically perform all updates relative to a ***cursor***, which represents the current position in the list of characters of text being edited.

Linked List Implementation

The ***linked list*** data structure allows for a great variety of operations, including insertion and removal at various places, to run in $O(1)$ time. A node in a ***singly linked*** list stores in a ***next*** link a reference to the next node in the list. Thus, a singly linked list can only be traversed in one direction—from the head to the tail. A node in a ***doubly linked*** list, on the other hand, stores two references—a ***next*** link, which points to the next node in the list, and a ***prev*** link, which points to the previous node in the list. Therefore, a doubly linked list can be traversed in either direction. Being able to determine the previous and next node from any given node in a list greatly simplifies list implementation; so let us assume we are using a doubly linked list to implement the list ADT.

To simplify updates and searching, it is convenient to add special nodes at both ends of the list: a ***header*** node just before the head of the list, and a ***trailer*** node just after the tail of the list. These "dummy" or ***sentinel*** nodes do not store any element. The header has a valid *next* reference but a null *prev* reference, while the trailer has a valid *prev* reference but a null *next* reference. A doubly linked list with these sentinels is shown in Figure 2.9. Note that a linked list object would simply need to store these two sentinels and a size counter that keeps track of the number of elements (not counting sentinels) in the list.

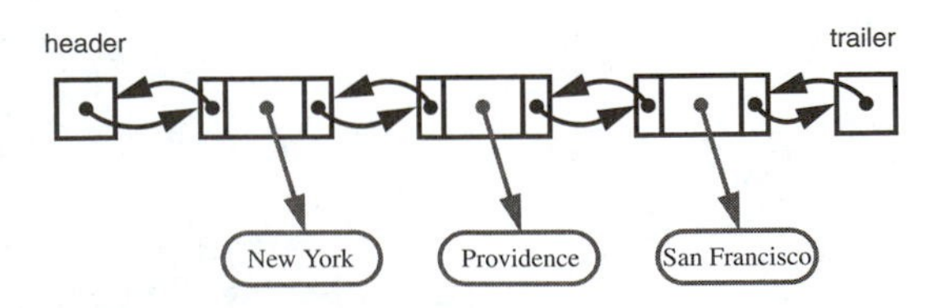

Figure 2.9: A doubly linked list with sentinels, header and trailer, marking the ends of the list. An empty list would have these sentinels pointing to each other.

We can simply make the nodes of the linked list implement the position ADT, defining a method element(), which returns the element stored at the node. Thus, the nodes themselves act as positions.

Consider how we might implement the insertAfter(p, e) method, for inserting an element e after position p. We create a new node v to hold the element e, link v into its place in the list, and then update the next and prev references of v's two new neighbors. This method is given in pseudo-code in Algorithm 2.10, and is illustrated in Figure 2.11.

Algorithm insertAfter(p, e):
  Create a new node v
  v.element $\leftarrow e$
  v.prev $\leftarrow p$ {link v to its predecessor}
  v.next $\leftarrow p$.next {link v to its successor}
  (p.next).prev $\leftarrow v$ {link p's old successor to v}
  p.next $\leftarrow v$ {link p to its new successor, v}
  return v {the position for the element e}

Algorithm 2.10: Inserting an element e after a position p in a linked list.

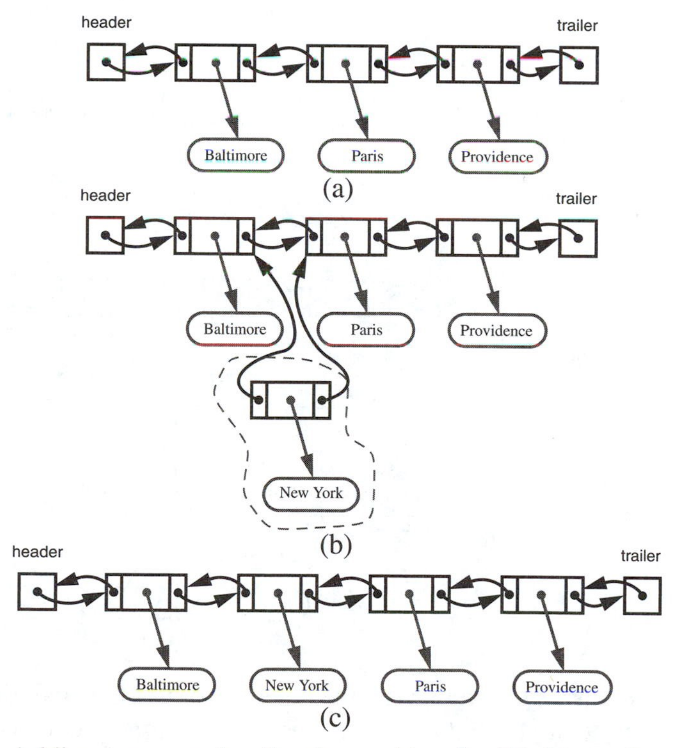

Figure 2.11: Adding a new node after the position for "Baltimore": (a) before the insertion; (b) creating node v and linking it in; (c) after the insertion.

The algorithms for methods insertBefore, insertFirst, and insertLast are similar to that for method insertAfter; we leave their details as an exercise (R-2.1). Next, consider the remove(p) method, which removes the element e stored at position p. To perform this operation we link the two neighbors of p to refer to one another as new neighbors—linking out p. Note that after p is linked out, no nodes will be pointing to p; hence, a garbage collector can reclaim the space for p. This algorithm is given in Algorithm 2.12 and is illustrated in Figure 2.13. Recalling our use of sentinels, note that this algorithm works even if p is the first, last, or only real position in the list.

Algorithm remove(p):
  $t \leftarrow p$.element {a temporary variable to hold the return value}
  (p.prev).next $\leftarrow p$.next {linking out p}
  (p.next).prev $\leftarrow p$.prev
  p.prev $\leftarrow$ **null** {invalidating the position p}
  p.next $\leftarrow$ **null**
  return t

Algorithm 2.12: Removing an element e stored at a position p in a linked list.

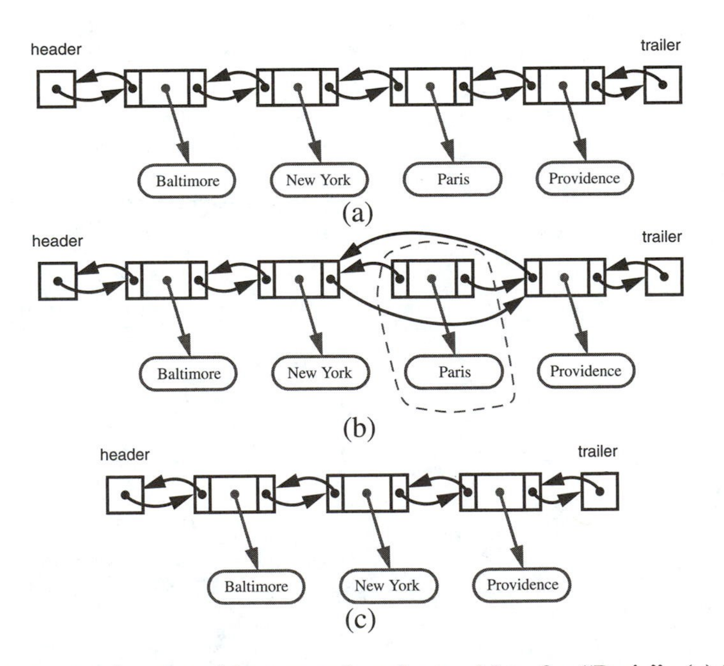

Figure 2.13: Removing the object stored at the position for "Paris": (a) before the removal; (b) linking out the old node; (c) after the removal (and garbage collection).

2.2.3 Sequences

In this section, we define a generalized sequence ADT that includes all the methods of the vector and list ADTs. This ADT therefore provides access to its elements using both ranks and positions, and is a versatile data structure for a wide variety of applications.

The Sequence Abstract Data Type

A ***sequence*** is an ADT that supports all the methods of both the vector ADT (discussed in Section 2.2.1) and the list ADT (discussed in Section 2.2.2), plus the following two "bridging" methods that provide connections between ranks and positions:

atRank(r): Return the position of the element with rank r.

rankOf(p): Return the rank of the element at position p.

A general sequence can be implemented with either a doubly linked list or an array, with natural tradeoffs between these two implementations. Table 2.14 compares the running times of the implementations of the general sequence ADT, by means of an array (used in a circular fashion) and by means of a doubly linked list.

Operations	Array	List
size, isEmpty	$O(1)$	$O(1)$
atRank, rankOf, elemAtRank	$O(1)$	$O(n)$
first, last, before, after	$O(1)$	$O(1)$
replaceElement, swapElements	$O(1)$	$O(1)$
replaceAtRank	$O(1)$	$O(n)$
insertAtRank, removeAtRank	$O(n)$	$O(n)$
insertFirst, insertLast	$O(1)$	$O(1)$
insertAfter, insertBefore,	$O(n)$	$O(1)$
remove	$O(n)$	$O(1)$

Table 2.14: Comparison of the running times of the methods of a sequence implemented with either an array (used in a circular fashion) or a doubly linked list. We denote with n the number of elements in the sequence at the time the operation is performed. The space usage is $O(n)$ for the doubly linked list implementation, and $O(N)$ for the array implementation, where N is the size of the array.

Summarizing this table, we see that the array-based implementation is superior to the linked-list implementation on the rank-based access operations (atRank, rankOf, and elemAtRank), and it is equal in performance to the linked-list implementation on all the other access operations. Regarding update operations, the linked-list implementation beats the array-based implementation in the position-based update operations (insertAfter, insertBefore, and remove). Even so, the array-based and linked-list implementations have the same worst-case performance on the rank-based update methods (insertAtRank and removeAtRank), but for different reasons. In update operations insertFirst and insertLast, the two implementations have comparable performance.

Considering space usage, note that an array requires $O(N)$ space, where N is the size of the array (unless we utilize an extendable array), while a doubly linked list uses $O(n)$ space, where n is the number of elements in the sequence. Since n is less than or equal to N, this implies that the asymptotic space usage of a linked-list implementation is superior to that of a fixed-size array, although there is a small constant factor overhead that is larger for linked lists, since arrays do not need links to maintain the ordering of their cells.

The array and linked-list implementations each have their advantages and disadvantages. The correct one for a particular application depends on the kinds of operations that are to be performed and the memory space available. Designing the sequence ADT in a way that does not depend on the way it is implemented allows us to easily switch between implementations, enabling the use of the implementation that best suits our applications, with few changes to our program.

Iterators

A typical computation on a vector, list, or sequence is to march through its elements in order, one at a time, for example, to look for a specific element.

An ***iterator*** is a software design pattern that abstracts the process of scanning through a collection of elements one element at a time. An iterator consists of a sequence S, a current position in S, and a way of stepping to the next position in S and making it the current position. Thus, an iterator extends the concept of the position ADT we introduced in Section 2.2.2. In fact, a position can be thought of as an iterator that doesn't go anywhere. An iterator encapsulates the concepts of "place" and "next" in a collection of objects.

We define the iterator ADT as supporting the following two methods:

hasNext: Test whether there are elements left in the iterator.

nextObject: Return and remove the next element in the iterator.

Note that this ADT has the notion of the "current" element in a traversal through a sequence. The first element in an iterator is returned by the first call to the method nextObject, assuming of course that the iterator contains at least one element.

An iterator provides a unified scheme to access all the elements of a container (a collection of objects) in a way that is independent from the specific organization of the collection. An iterator for a sequence should return the elements according to their linear ordering.

2.3 Trees

A ***tree*** is an abstract data type that stores elements hierarchically. With the exception of the top element, each element in a tree has a ***parent*** element and zero or more ***children*** elements. A tree is usually visualized by placing elements inside ovals or rectangles, and by drawing the connections between parents and children with straight lines. (See Figure 2.15.) We typically call the top element the ***root*** of the tree, but it is drawn as the highest element, with the other elements being connected below (just the opposite of a botanical tree).

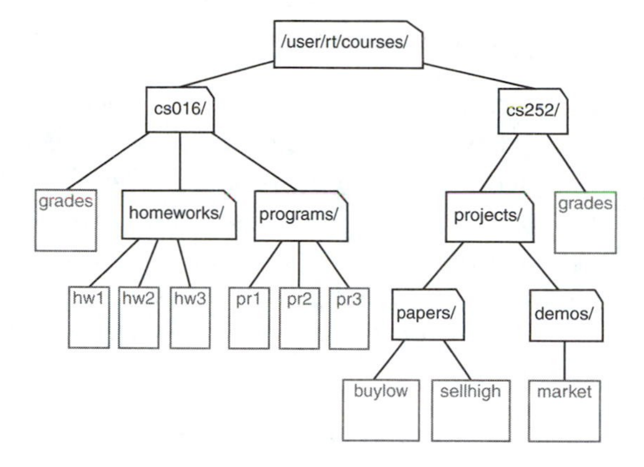

Figure 2.15: A tree representing a portion of a file system.

A ***tree*** T is a set of ***nodes*** storing elements in a ***parent-child*** relationship with the following properties:

- T has a special node r, called the ***root*** of T.
- Each node v of T different from r has a ***parent*** node u.

Note that according to the above definition, a tree cannot be empty, since it must have at least one node, the root. One could also allow the definition to include empty trees, but we adopt the convention that a tree always has a root so as to keep our presentation simple and to avoid having to always deal with the special case of an empty tree in our algorithms.

If node u is the parent of node v, then we say that v is a ***child*** of u. Two nodes that are children of the same parent are ***siblings***. A node is ***external*** if it has no children, and it is ***internal*** if it has one or more children. External nodes are also known as ***leaves***. The ***subtree*** of T ***rooted*** at a node v is the tree consisting of all the descendents of v in T (including v itself). An ***ancestor*** of a node is either the node itself or an ancestor of the parent of the node. Conversely, we say that a node v is a ***descendent*** of a node u if u is an ancestor of v.

Example 2.2: *In most operating systems, files are organized hierarchically into nested directories (also called folders), which are presented to the user in the form of a tree. (See Figure 2.15.) More specifically, the internal nodes of the tree are associated with directories and the external nodes are associated with regular files. In the UNIX/Linux operating system, the root of the tree is appropriately called the "root directory," and is represented by the symbol "/." It is the ancestor of all directories and files in a UNIX/Linux file system.*

A tree is ***ordered*** if there is a linear ordering defined for the children of each node; that is, we can identify children of a node as being the first, second, third, and so on. Ordered trees typically indicate the linear order relationship existing between siblings by listing them in a sequence or iterator in the correct order.

Example 2.3: *A structured document, such as a book, is hierarchically organized as a tree whose internal nodes are chapters, sections, and subsections, and whose external nodes are paragraphs, tables, figures, the bibliography, and so on. (See Figure 2.16.) We could in fact consider expanding the tree further to show paragraphs consisting of sentences, sentences consisting of words, and words consisting of characters. In any case, such a tree is an example of an ordered tree, because there is a well-defined ordering among the children of each node.*

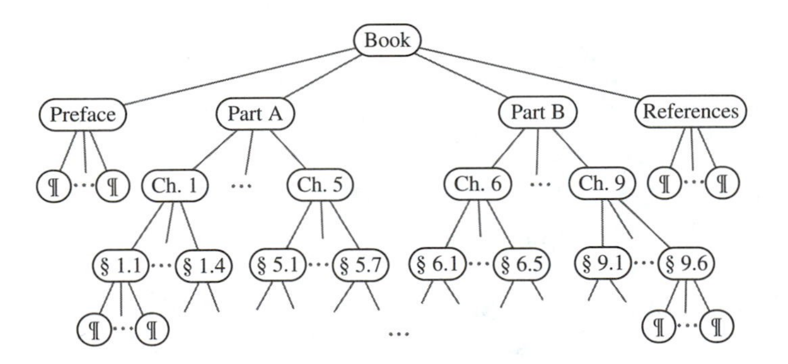

Figure 2.16: A tree associated with a book.

A ***binary tree*** is an ordered tree in which every node has at most two children. A binary tree is ***proper*** if each internal node has two children. For each internal node in a binary tree, we label each child as either being a ***left child*** or a ***right child***. These children are ordered so that a left child comes before a right child. The subtree rooted at a left or right child of an internal node v is called a ***left subtree*** or ***right subtree***, respectively, of v. We make the convention in this book that, unless otherwise stated, every binary tree is a proper binary tree. Of course, even an improper binary tree is still a general tree, with the property that each internal node has at most two children. Binary trees have a number of useful applications, including the following.

Example 2.4: *An arithmetic expression can be represented by a tree whose external nodes are associated with variables or constants, and whose internal nodes are associated with one of the operators* $+$, $-$, $\times$, *and* $/$. *(See Figure 2.17.) Each node in such a tree has a value associated with it.*

- *If a node is external, then its value is that of its variable or constant.*
- *If a node is internal, then its value is defined by applying its operation to the values of its children.*

Such an arithmetic expression tree is a proper binary tree, since each of the operators $+$, $-$, $\times$, *and* $/$ *take exactly two operands. Of course, if we were to allow for unary operators, like negation* ($-$), *as in "*$-x$*," then we could have an improper binary tree.*

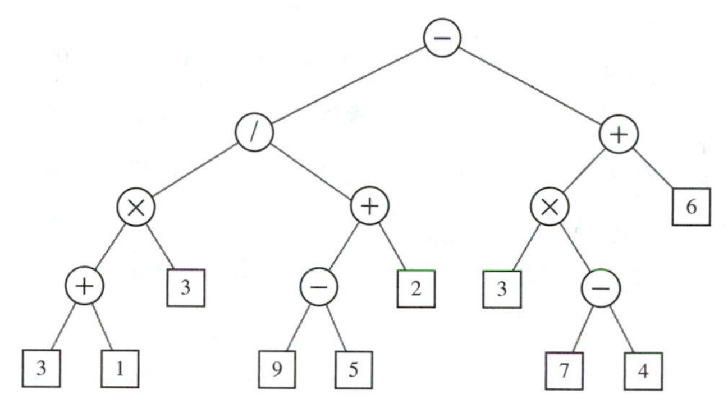

Figure 2.17: A binary tree representing an arithmetic expression. This tree represents the expression $((((3+1)\times 3)/((9-5)+2))-((3\times(7-4))+6))$. The value associated with the internal node labeled "/" is 2.

2.3.1 The Tree Abstract Data Type

The tree ADT stores elements at positions, which, as with positions in a list, are defined relative to neighboring positions. The ***positions*** in a tree are its ***nodes***, and neighboring positions satisfy the parent-child relationships that define a valid tree. Therefore we use the terms "position" and "node" interchangeably for trees. As with a list position, a position object for a tree supports the element() method, which returns the object at this position. The real power of node positions in a tree, however, comes from the following ***accessor methods*** of the tree ADT:

root(): Return the root of the tree.

parent(v): Return the parent of node v; an error occurs if v is root.

children(v): Return an iterator of the children of node v.

If a tree T is ordered, then the iterator children(v) provides access to the children of v in order. If v is an external node, then children(v) is an empty iterator.

In addition, we also include the following ***query methods***:

isInternal(v): Test whether node v is internal.

isExternal(v): Test whether node v is external.

isRoot(v): Test whether node v is the root.

There are also a number of methods a tree should support that are not necessarily related to its tree structure. Such ***generic methods*** include the following:

size(): Return the number of nodes in the tree.

elements(): Return an iterator of all the elements stored at nodes of the tree.

positions(): Return an iterator of all the nodes of the tree.

swapElements(v, w): Swap the elements stored at the nodes v and w.

replaceElement(v, e): Replace with e and return the element stored at node v.

We do not define any specialized update methods for a tree here. Instead, let us reserve the potential to define different tree update methods in conjunction with specific tree applications.

2.3.2 Tree Traversal

In this section, we present algorithms for performing computations on a tree by accessing it through the tree ADT methods.

Assumptions

In order to analyze the running time of tree-based algorithms, we make the following assumptions on the running times of the methods of the tree ADT.

- The accessor methods root() and parent(v) take $O(1)$ time.
- The query methods isInternal(v), isExternal(v), and isRoot(v) take $O(1)$ time, as well.
- The accessor method children(v) takes $O(c_v)$ time, where c_v is the number of children of v.
- The generic methods swapElements(v, w) and replaceElement(v, e) take $O(1)$ time.
- The generic methods elements() and positions(), which return iterators, take $O(n)$ time, where n is the number of nodes in the tree.
- For the iterators returned by methods elements(), positions(), and children(v), the methods hasNext(), nextObject() or nextPosition() take $O(1)$ time each.

In Section 2.3.4, we will present data structures for trees that satisfy the above assumptions. Before we describe how to implement the tree ADT using a concrete data structure, however, let us describe how we can use the methods of the tree ADT to solve some interesting problems for trees.

Depth and Height

Let v be a node of a tree T. The ***depth*** of v is the number of ancestors of v, excluding v itself. Note that this definition implies that the depth of the root of T is 0. The depth of a node v can also be recursively defined as follows:

- If v is the root, then the depth of v is 0.
- Otherwise, the depth of v is one plus the depth of the parent of v.

Based on the above definition, the recursive algorithm depth, shown in Algorithm 2.18, computes the depth of a node v of T by calling itself recursively on the parent of v, and adding 1 to the value returned.

```
Algorithm depth(T, v):
  if T.isRoot(v) then
    return 0
  else
    return 1 + depth(T, T.parent(v))
```

Algorithm 2.18: Algorithm depth for computing the depth of a node v in a tree T.

The running time of algorithm depth(T, v) is $O(1+d_v)$, where d_v denotes the depth of the node v in the tree T, because the algorithm performs a constant-time recursive step for each ancestor of v. Thus, in the worst case, the depth algorithm runs in $O(n)$ time, where n is the total number of nodes in the tree T, since some nodes may have nearly this depth in T. Although such a running time is a function of the input size, it is more accurate to characterize the running time in terms of the parameter d_v, since this will often be much smaller than n.

The ***height*** of a tree T is equal to the maximum depth of an external node of T. While this definition is correct, it does not lead to an efficient algorithm. Indeed, if we were to apply the above depth-finding algorithm to each node in the tree T, we would derive an $O(n^2)$-time algorithm to compute the height of T. We can do much better, however, using the following recursive definition of the ***height*** of a node v in a tree T:

- If v is an external node, then the height of v is 0.
- Otherwise, the height of v is one plus the maximum height of a child of v.

The ***height*** of a tree T is the height of the root of T.

Algorithm height, shown in Algorithm 2.19 computes the height of tree T in an efficient manner by using the above recursive definition of height. The algorithm is expressed by a recursive method height(T, v) that computes the height of the subtree of T rooted at a node v. The height of tree T is obtained by calling height$(T, T.\mathrm{root}())$.

Algorithm height(T, v):
  if T.isExternal(v) **then**
    return 0
  else
    $h = 0$
    for each $w \in T$.children(v) **do**
      $h = \max(h, \mathrm{height}(T, w))$
    return $1 + h$

Algorithm 2.19: Algorithm height for computing the height of the subtree of tree T rooted at a node v.

The height algorithm is recursive, and if it is initially called on the root of T, it will eventually be called once on each node of T. Thus, we can determine the running time of this method by an amortization argument where we first determine the amount of time spent at each node (on the nonrecursive part), and then sum this time bound over all the nodes. The computation of an iterator children(v) takes $O(c_v)$ time, where c_v denotes the number of children of node v. Also, the **while** loop has c_v iterations, and each iteration of the loop takes $O(1)$ time plus the time for the recursive call on a child of v. Thus, algorithm height spends $O(1 + c_v)$ time at each node v, and its running time is $O(\sum_{v \in T}(1 + c_v))$. In order to complete the analysis, we make use of the following property.

Theorem 2.5: *Let T be a tree with n nodes, and let c_v denote the number of children of a node v of T. Then*

$$\sum_{v \in T} c_v = n - 1.$$

Proof: Each node of T, with the exception of the root, is a child of another node, and thus contributes one unit to the summation $\sum_{v \in T} c_v$. ■

By Theorem 2.5, the running time of Algorithm height when called on the root of T is $O(n)$, where n is the number of nodes of T.

A ***traversal*** of a tree T is a systematic way of accessing, or "visiting," all the nodes of T. We next present basic traversal schemes for trees, called preorder and postorder traversals.

Preorder Traversal

In a ***preorder*** traversal of a tree T, the root of T is visited first and then the subtrees rooted at its children are traversed recursively. If the tree is ordered, then the subtrees are traversed according to the order of the children. The specific action associated with the "visit" of a node v depends on the application of this traversal, and could involve anything from incrementing a counter to performing some complex computation for v. The pseudo-code for the preorder traversal of the subtree rooted at a node v is shown in Algorithm 2.20. We initially call this routine as preorder$(T, T.\text{root}())$.

Algorithm preorder(T, v):
  perform the "visit" action for node v
  for each child w of v **do**
    recursively traverse the subtree rooted at w by calling preorder(T, w)

Algorithm 2.20: Algorithm preorder.

The preorder traversal algorithm is useful for producing a linear ordering of the nodes of a tree where parents must always come before their children in the ordering. Such orderings have several different applications; we explore a simple instance of such an application in the next example.

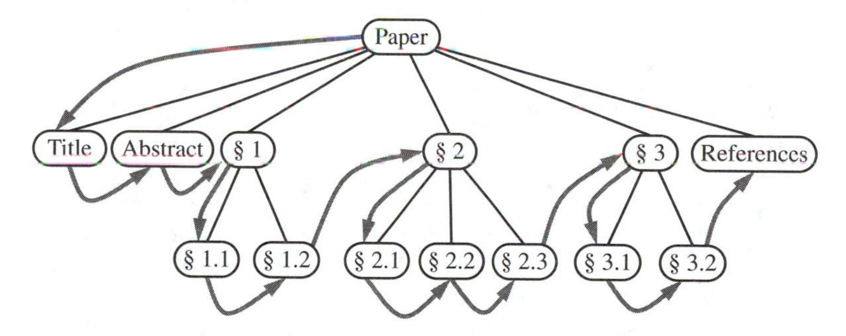

Figure 2.21: Preorder traversal of an ordered tree.

Example 2.6: *The preorder traversal of the tree associated with a document, as in Example 2.3, examines an entire document sequentially, from beginning to end. If the external nodes are removed before the traversal, then the traversal examines the table of contents of the document. (See Figure 2.21.)*

The analysis of preorder traversal is actually similar to that of algorithm height given above. At each node v, the nonrecursive part of the preorder traversal algorithm requires time $O(1 + c_v)$, where c_v is the number of children of v. Thus, by Theorem 2.5, the overall running time of the preorder traversal of T is $O(n)$.

Postorder Traversal

Another important tree traversal algorithm is the ***postorder*** traversal. This algorithm can be viewed as the opposite of the preorder traversal, because it recursively traverses the subtrees rooted at the children of the root first, and then visits the root. It is similar to the preorder traversal, however, in that we use it to solve a particular problem by specializing an action associated with the "visit" of a node v. Still, as with the preorder traversal, if the tree is ordered, we make recursive calls for the children of a node v according to their specified order. Pseudo-code for the postorder traversal is given in Algorithm 2.22.

Algorithm postorder(T, v):
  for each child w of v **do**
    recursively traverse the subtree rooted at w by calling postorder(T, w)
  perform the "visit" action for node v

Algorithm 2.22: Method postorder.

The name of the postorder traversal comes from the fact that this traversal method will visit a node v after it has visited all the other nodes in the subtree rooted at v. (See Figure 2.23.)

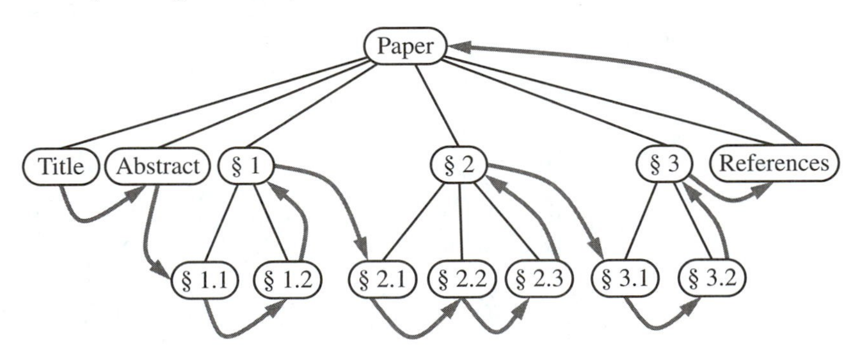

Figure 2.23: Postorder traversal of the ordered tree of Figure 2.21.

The analysis of the running time of a postorder traversal is analogous to that of a preorder traversal. The total time spent in the nonrecursive portions of the algorithm is proportional to the time spent visiting the children of each node in the tree. Thus, a postorder traversal of a tree T with n nodes takes $O(n)$ time, assuming that visiting each node takes $O(1)$ time. That is, the postorder traversal runs in linear time.

The postorder traversal method is useful for solving problems where we wish to compute some property for each node v in a tree, but computing that property for v requires that we have already computed that same property for v's children. Such an application is illustrated in the following example.

Example 2.7: *Consider a file system tree T, where external nodes represent files and internal nodes represent directories (Example 2.2). Suppose we want to compute the disk space used by a directory, which is recursively given by the sum of:*

- *The size of the directory itself*
- *The sizes of the files in the directory*
- *The space used by the children directories.*

(See Figure 2.24.) This computation can be done with a postorder traversal of tree T. After the subtrees of an internal node v have been traversed, we compute the space used by v by adding the sizes of the directory v itself and of the files contained in v, to the space used by each internal child of v, which was computed by the recursive postorder traversals of the children of v.

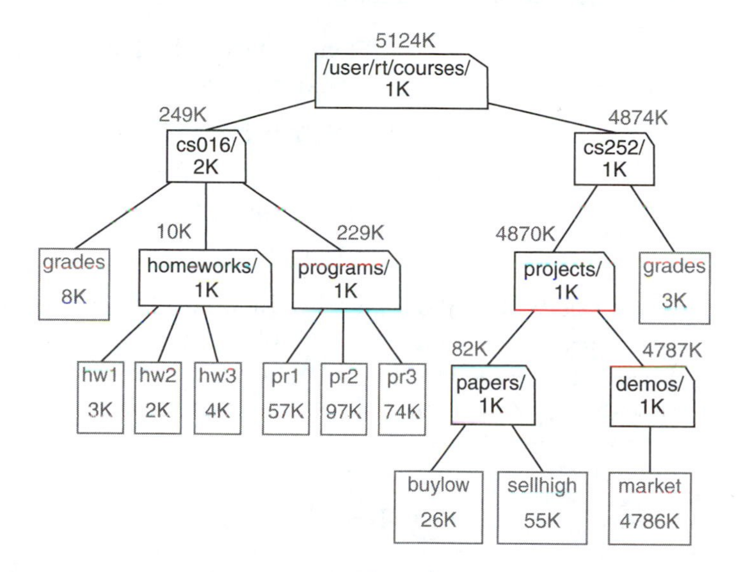

Figure 2.24: The tree of Figure 2.15 representing a file system, showing the name and size of the associated file/directory inside each node, and the disk space used by the associated directory above each internal node.

Although the preorder and postorder traversals are common ways of visiting the nodes of a tree, we can also imagine other traversals. For example, we could traverse a tree so that we visit all the nodes at depth d before we visit the nodes at depth $d+1$. Such a traversal could be implemented, for example, using a queue, whereas the preorder and postorder traversals use a stack (this stack is implicit in our use of recursion to describe these methods, but we could make this use explicit, as well, to avoid recursion). In addition, binary trees, which we discuss next, support an additional traversal method, known as the inorder traversal.

2.3.3 Binary Trees

One kind of tree that is of particular interest is the binary tree. As we mentioned in Section 2.3.1, a proper ***binary tree*** is an ordered tree in which each internal node has exactly two children. We make the convention that, unless otherwise stated, binary trees are assumed to be proper. Note that our convention for binary trees is made without loss of generality, for we can easily convert any improper binary tree into a proper one, as we explore in Exercise C-2.14. Even without such a conversion, we can consider an improper binary tree as proper, simply by viewing missing external nodes as "null nodes" or place holders that still count as nodes.

The Binary Tree Abstract Data Type

As an abstract data type, a binary tree is a specialization of a tree that supports three additional accessor methods:

leftChild(v): Return the left child of v; an error condition occurs if v is an external node.

rightChild(v): Return the right child of v; an error condition occurs if v is an external node.

sibling(v): Return the sibling of node v; an error condition occurs if v is the root.

Note that these methods must have additional error conditions if we are dealing with improper binary trees. For example, in an improper binary tree, an internal node may not have the left child or right child. We do not include here any methods for updating a binary tree, for such methods can be created as required in the context of specific needs.

Properties of Binary Trees

We denote the set of all nodes of a tree T at the same depth d as the ***level*** d of T. In a binary tree, level 0 has one node (the root), level 1 has at most two nodes (the children of the root), level 2 has at most four nodes, and so on. (See Figure 2.25.) In general, level d has at most 2^d nodes, which implies the following theorem (whose proof is left to Exercise R-2.4).

Theorem 2.8: *Let T be a (proper) binary tree with n nodes, and let h denote the height of T. Then T has the following properties:*

1. *The number of external nodes in T is at least $h+1$ and at most 2^h.*
2. *The number of internal nodes in T is at least h and at most $2^h - 1$.*
3. *The total number of nodes in T is at least $2h+1$ and at most $2^{h+1} - 1$.*
4. *The height of T is at least $\log(n+1) - 1$ and at most $(n-1)/2$, that is, $\log(n+1) - 1 \leq h \leq (n-1)/2$.*

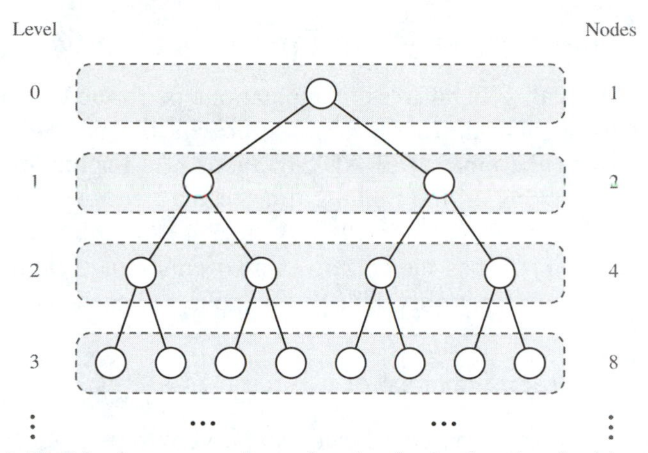

Figure 2.25: Maximum number of nodes in the levels of a binary tree.

In addition, we also have the following.

Theorem 2.9: *In a (proper) binary tree T, the number of external nodes is* 1 *more than the number of internal nodes.*

Proof: The proof is by induction. If T itself has only one node v, then v is external, and the proposition clearly holds. Otherwise, we remove from T an (arbitrary) external node w and its parent v, which is an internal node. If v has a parent u, then we reconnect u with the former sibling z of w, as shown in Figure 2.26. This operation, which we call removeAboveExternal(w), removes one internal node and one external node, and it leaves the tree being a proper binary tree. Thus, by the inductive hypothesis, the number of external nodes in this tree is one more than the number of internal nodes. Since we removed one internal and one external node to reduce T to this smaller tree, this same property must hold for T. ■

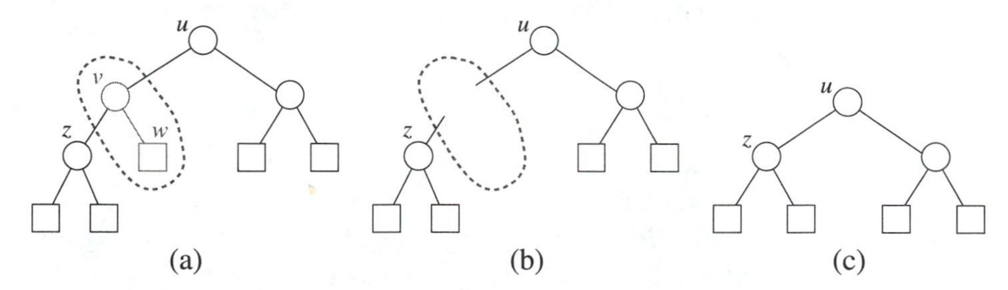

Figure 2.26: Operation removeAboveExternal(w), which removes an external node and its parent node, used in the justification of Theorem 2.9.

Note that the above relationship does not hold, in general, for nonbinary trees.

In subsequent chapters, we explore some important applications of the above facts. Before we can discuss such applications, however, we should first understand more about how binary trees are traversed and represented.

Traversals of a Binary Tree

As with general trees, computations performed on binary trees often involve tree traversals. In this section, we present binary tree traversal algorithms expressed using the binary tree ADT methods. As for running times, in addition to the assumptions on the running time of the tree ADT methods made in Section 2.3.2, we assume that, for a binary tree, method children(v) takes $O(1)$ time, because each node has either zero or two children. Likewise, we assume that methods leftChild(v), rightChild(v), and sibling(v) each take $O(1)$ time.

Preorder Traversal of a Binary Tree

Since any binary tree can also be viewed as a general tree, the preorder traversal for general trees (Code Fragment 2.20) can be applied to any binary tree. We can simplify the pseudo-code in the case of a binary tree traversal, however, as we show in Algorithm 2.27.

```
Algorithm binaryPreorder(T, v):
  perform the "visit" action for node v
  if v is an internal node then
    binaryPreorder(T, T.leftChild(v))       {recursively traverse left subtree}
    binaryPreorder(T, T.rightChild(v))      {recursively traverse right subtree}
```

Algorithm 2.27: Algorithm binaryPreorder that performs the preorder traversal of the subtree of a binary tree T rooted at node v.

Postorder Traversal of a Binary Tree

Analogously, the postorder traversal for general trees (Algorithm 2.22) can be specialized for binary trees, as shown in Algorithm 2.28.

```
Algorithm binaryPostorder(T, v):
  if v is an internal node then
    binaryPostorder(T, T.leftChild(v))      {recursively traverse left subtree}
    binaryPostorder(T, T.rightChild(v))     {recursively traverse right subtree}
  perform the "visit" action for the node v
```

Algorithm 2.28: Algorithm binaryPostorder for performing the postorder traversal of the subtree of a binary tree T rooted at node v.

Interestingly, the specialization of the general preorder and postorder traversal methods to binary trees suggests a third traversal in a binary tree that is different from both the preorder and postorder traversals.

Inorder Traversal of a Binary Tree

An additional traversal method for a binary tree is the ***inorder*** traversal. In this traversal, we visit a node between the recursive traversals of its left and right subtrees, as shown in in Algorithm 2.29.

Algorithm inorder(T, v):
  if v is an internal node **then**
    inorder$(T, T.$leftChild$(v))$ {recursively traverse left subtree}
  perform the "visit" action for node v
  if v is an internal node **then**
    inorder$(T, T.$rightChild$(v))$ {recursively traverse right subtree}

Algorithm 2.29: Algorithm inorder for performing the inorder traversal of the subtree of a binary tree T rooted at a node v.

The inorder traversal of a binary tree T can be informally viewed as visiting the nodes of T "from left to right." Indeed, for every node v, the inorder traversal visits v after all the nodes in the left subtree of v and before all the nodes in the right subtree of v. (See Figure 2.30.)

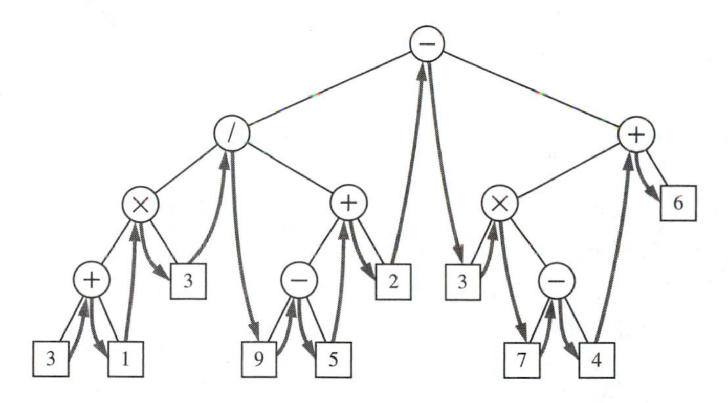

Figure 2.30: Inorder traversal of a binary tree.

A Unified Tree Traversal Framework

The tree-traversal algorithms we have discussed so far are all forms of iterators. Each traversal visits the nodes of a tree in a certain order, and is guaranteed to visit each node exactly once. We can unify the tree-traversal algorithms given above into a single design pattern, however, by relaxing the requirement that each node be visited exactly once. The resulting traversal method is called the ***Euler tour traversal***, which we study next. The advantage of this traversal is that it allows for more general kinds of algorithms to be expressed easily.

The Euler Tour Traversal of a Binary Tree

The Euler tour traversal of a binary tree T can be informally defined as a "walk" around T, where we start by going from the root toward its left child, viewing the edges of T as being "walls" that we always keep to our left. (See Figure 2.31.) Each node v of T is encountered three times by the Euler tour:

- "On the left" (before the Euler tour of v's left subtree)
- "From below" (between the Euler tours of v's two subtrees)
- "On the right" (after the Euler tour of v's right subtree).

If v is external, then these three "visits" actually all happen at the same time.

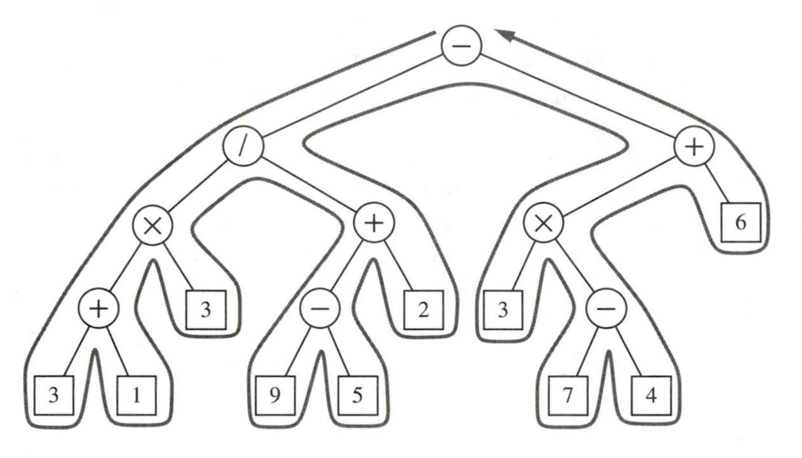

Figure 2.31: Euler tour traversal of a binary tree.

We give pseudo-code for the Euler tour of the subtree rooted at a node v in Algorithm 2.32.

Algorithm eulerTour(T, v):
  perform the action for visiting node v on the left
  if v is an internal node **then**
    recursively tour the left subtree of v by calling eulerTour$(T, T$.leftChild$(v))$
  perform the action for visiting node v from below
  if v is an internal node **then**
    recursively tour the right subtree of v by calling eulerTour$(T, T$.rightChild$(v))$
  perform the action for visiting node v on the right

Algorithm 2.32: Algorithm eulerTour for computing the Euler tour traversal of the subtree of a binary tree T rooted at a node v.

The preorder traversal of a binary tree is equivalent to an Euler tour traversal such that each node has an associated "visit" action occur only when it is encountered on the left. Likewise, the inorder and postorder traversals of a binary tree are equivalent to an Euler tour such that each node has an associated "visit" action occur only when it is encountered from below or on the right, respectively.

The Euler tour traversal extends the preorder, inorder, and postorder traversals, but it can also perform other kinds of traversals. For example, suppose we wish to compute the number of descendents of each node v in an n node binary tree T. We start an Euler tour by initializing a counter to 0, and then increment the counter each time we visit a node on the left. To determine the number of descendents of a node v, we compute the difference between the values of the counter when v is visited on the left and when it is visited on the right, and add 1. This simple rule gives us the number of descendents of v, because each node in the subtree rooted at v is counted between v's visit on the left and v's visit on the right. Therefore, we have an $O(n)$-time method for computing the number of descendents of each node in T.

The running time of the Euler tour traversal is easy to analyze, assuming visiting a node takes $O(1)$ time. Namely, in each traversal, we spend a constant amount of time at each node of the tree during the traversal, so the overall running time is $O(n)$ for an n node tree.

Another application of the Euler tour traversal is to print a fully parenthesized arithmetic expression from its expression tree (Example 2.4). The method printExpression, shown in Algorithm 2.33, accomplishes this task by performing the following actions in an Euler tour:

- "On the left" action: if the node is internal, print "("
- "From below" action: print the value or operator stored at the node
- "On the right" action: if the node is internal, print ")."

```
Algorithm printExpression(T, v):
  if T.isExternal(v) then
    print the value stored at v
  else
    print "("
    printExpression(T, T.leftChild(v))
    print the operator stored at v
    printExpression(T, T.rightChild(v))
    print ")"
```

Algorithm 2.33: An algorithm for printing the arithmetic expression associated with the subtree of an arithmetic expression tree T rooted at v.

Having presented these pseudo-code examples, we now describe a number of efficient ways of realizing the tree abstract data type by concrete data structures, such as sequences and linked structures.

2.3.4 Data Structures for Representing Trees

In this section, we describe concrete data structures for representing trees.

A Vector-Based Structure for Binary Trees

A simple structure for representing a binary tree T is based on a way of numbering the nodes of T. For every node v of T, let $p(v)$ be the integer defined as follows.

- If v is the root of T, then $p(v) = 1$.
- If v is the left child of node u, then $p(v) = 2p(u)$.
- If v is the right child of node u, then $p(v) = 2p(u) + 1$.

The numbering function p is known as a ***level numbering*** of the nodes in a binary tree T, because it numbers the nodes on each level of T in increasing order from left to right, although it may skip some numbers. (See Figure 2.34.)

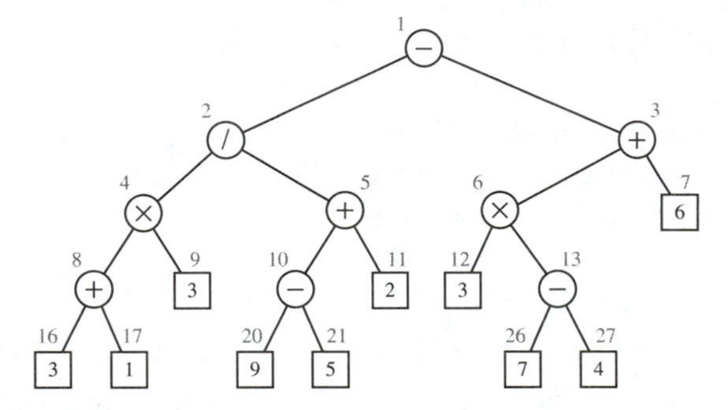

Figure 2.34: An example binary tree level numbering.

The level numbering function p suggests a representation of a binary tree T by means of a vector S such that node v of T is associated with the element of S at rank $p(v)$. (See Figure 2.35.) Typically, we realize the vector S by means of an extendable array. (See Section 1.5.2.) Such an implementation is simple and fast, for we can use it to easily perform the methods root, parent, leftChild, rightChild, sibling, isInternal, isExternal, and isRoot by using simple arithmetic operations on the numbers $p(v)$ associated with each node v involved in the operation. That is, each position object v is simply a "wrapper" for the index $p(v)$ into the vector S. We leave the details of such implementations as a simple exercise (R-2.7).

Let n be the number of nodes of T, and let p_M be the maximum value of $p(v)$ over all the nodes of T. Vector S has size $N = p_M + 1$ since the element of S at rank 0 is not associated with any node of T. Also, vector S will have, in general, a number of empty elements that do not refer to existing nodes of T. These empty slots could, for example, correspond to empty external nodes or even slots where descendents of such nodes would go. In fact, in the worst case, $N = 2^{(n+1)/2}$,

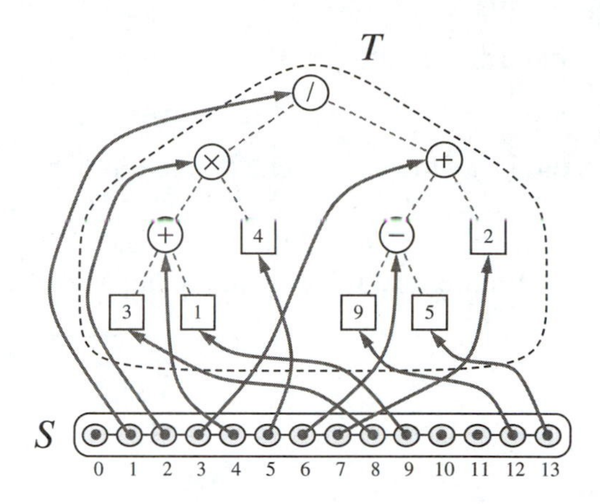

Figure 2.35: Representation of a binary tree T by means of a vector S.

the justification of which is left as an exercise (R-2.6). In Section 2.4.3, we will see a class of binary trees, called "heaps" for which $N = n + 1$. Moreover, if all external nodes are empty, as will be the case in our heap implementation, then we can save additional space by not even extending the size of the vector S to include external nodes whose index is past that of the last internal node in the tree. Thus, in spite of the worst-case space usage, there are applications for which the vector representation of a binary tree is space efficient. Still, for general binary trees, the exponential worst-case space requirement of this representation is prohibitive.

Table 2.36 summarizes the running times of the methods of a binary tree implemented with a vector. In this table, we do not include any methods for updating a binary tree.

Operation	Time
positions, elements	$O(n)$
swapElements, replaceElement	$O(1)$
root, parent, children	$O(1)$
leftChild, rightChild, sibling	$O(1)$
isInternal, isExternal, isRoot	$O(1)$

Table 2.36: Running times of the methods of a binary tree T implemented with a vector S, where S is realized by means of an array. We denote with n the number of nodes of T, and N denotes the size of S. Methods hasNext(), nextObject(), and nextPosition() of the iterators elements(), positions(), and children(v) take $O(1)$ time. The space usage is $O(N)$, which is $O(2^{(n+1)/2})$ in the worst case.

The vector implementation of a binary tree is fast and simple, but it can be very space inefficient if the height of the tree is large. The next data structure we discuss for representing binary trees does not have this drawback.

A Linked Structure for Binary Trees

A natural way to realize a binary tree T is to use a ***linked structure***. In this approach we represent each node v of T by an object with references to the element stored at v and the positions associated with the children and parent of v. We show a linked structure representation of a binary tree in Figure 2.37.

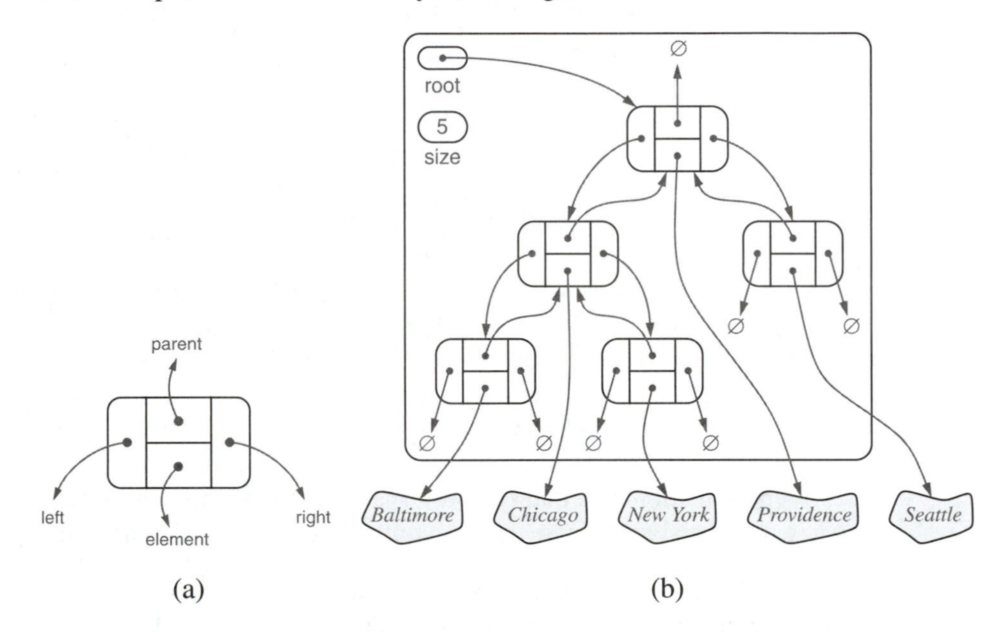

Figure 2.37: An example linked data structure for representing a binary tree: (a) object associated with a node; (b) complete data structure for a binary tree with five nodes.

If v is the root of T, then the reference to the parent node is null, and if v is an external node, then the references to the children of v are null.

If we wish to save space for cases when external nodes are empty, then we can have references to empty external nodes be null. That is, we can allow a reference from an internal node to an external node child to be null.

In addition, it is fairly straightforward to implement each of the methods size(), isEmpty(), swapElements(v,w), and replaceElement(v,e) in $O(1)$ time. Moreover, the method positions() can be implemented by performing an inorder traversal, and implementing the method elements() is similar. Thus, methods positions() and elements() take $O(n)$ time each.

Considering the space required by this data structure, note that there is a constant-sizer object for every node of tree T. Thus, the overall space requirement is $O(n)$.

A Linked Structure for General Trees

We can extend the linked structure for binary trees to represent general trees. Since there is no limit on the number of children that a node v in a general tree can have, we use a container (for example, a list or vector) to store the children of v, instead of using instance variables. This structure is schematically illustrated in Figure 2.38, assuming we implement the container for a node as a sequence.

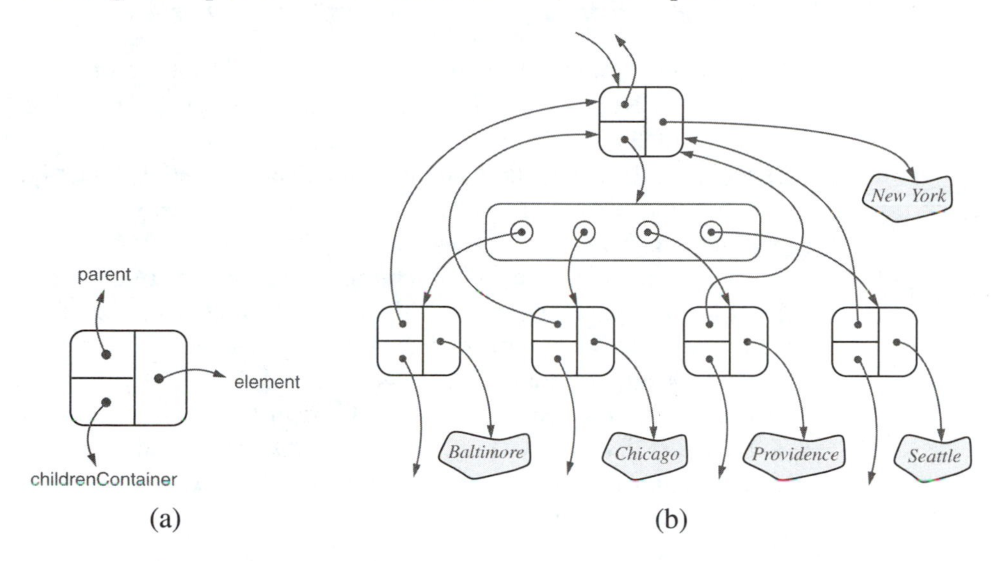

Figure 2.38: The linked structure for a tree: (a) the object associated with a node; (b) the portion of the data structure associated with a node and its children.

We note that the performance of a linked implementation of the tree ADT, shown in Table 2.39, is similar to that of the linked implementation of a binary tree. The main difference is that in the implementation of the tree ADT we use an efficient container, such as a list or vector, to store the children of each node v, instead of direct links to exactly two children.

Operation	Time
size, isEmpty	$O(1)$
positions, elements	$O(n)$
swapElements, replaceElement	$O(1)$
root, parent	$O(1)$
children(v)	$O(c_v)$
isInternal, isExternal, isRoot	$O(1)$

Table 2.39: Running times of the methods of an n-node tree implemented with a linked structure. We let c_v denote the number of children of a node v.

2.4 Priority Queues and Heaps

In this section, we provide a framework for studying priority queues, based on the concepts of key and comparator.

2.4.1 The Priority Queue Abstract Data Type

Applications commonly require comparing and ranking objects according to parameters or properties, called "keys," that are assigned for each object in a collection. Formally, we define a ***key*** to be an object that is assigned to an element as a specific attribute for that element, which can be used to identify, rank, or weight that element. Note that the key is assigned to an element, typically by a user or application.

The concept of a key as an arbitrary object type is therefore quite general. But, in order to deal consistently with such a general definition for keys and still be able to discuss when one key has priority over another, we need a way of robustly defining a rule for comparing keys. That is, a priority queue needs a comparison rule that will never contradict itself. In order for a comparison rule, denoted by $\leq$, to be robust in this way, it must define a ***total order*** relation, which is to say that the comparison rule is defined for every pair of keys and it must satisfy the following properties:

- **Reflexive property**: $k \leq k$.
- **Antisymmetric property**: if $k_1 \leq k_2$ and $k_2 \leq k_1$, then $k_1 = k_2$.
- **Transitive property**: if $k_1 \leq k_2$ and $k_2 \leq k_3$, then $k_1 \leq k_3$.

Any comparison rule, $\leq$, that satisfies these three properties will never lead to a comparison contradiction. In fact, such a rule defines a linear ordering relationship among a set of keys. Thus, if a (finite) collection of elements has a total order defined for it, then the notion of a ***smallest*** key, $k_{\min}$, is well defined. Namely, it is a key in which $k_{\min} \leq k$, for any other key k in our collection.

A ***priority queue*** is a container of elements, each having an associated key that is provided at the time the element is inserted. The name "priority queue" comes from the fact that keys determine the "priority" used to pick elements to be removed. The two fundamental methods of a priority queue P are as follows:

insertItem(k,e): Insert an element e with key k into P.

removeMin(): Return and remove from P an element with the smallest key, that is, an element whose key is less than or equal to that of every other element in P.

By the way, some people refer to the removeMin method as the "extractMin" method, so as to stress that this method simultaneously removes and returns a smallest element in P. We can additionally augment these two fundamental methods, with supporting methods, such as size(), and isEmpty(). Also, we can add accessor methods, such as the following:

minElement(): Return (but do not remove) an element of P with the smallest key.

minKey(): Return (but do not remove) the smallest key in P.

Both of these methods return error conditions if the priority queue is empty.

One of the interesting aspects of the priority queue ADT, which should now be obvious, is that the priority queue ADT is much simpler than the sequence ADT. This simplicity is due to the fact that elements in a priority queue are inserted and removed based entirely on their keys, whereas elements are inserted and removed in a sequence based on their positions and ranks.

Comparators

The priority queue ADT implicitly makes use of a software engineering design pattern, the comparator. This pattern specifies the way in which we compare keys, and is designed to support the most general and reusable form of a priority queue. For such a design, we should not rely on the keys to provide their comparison rules, for such rules might not be what a user desires (particularly for multi-dimensional data). Instead, we use special ***comparator*** objects that are external to the keys to supply the comparison rules. A comparator is an object that compares two keys. We assume that a priority queue P is given a comparator when P is constructed, and we might also imagine the ability of a priority queue to be given a new comparator if its old one ever becomes "out of date." When P needs to compare two keys, it uses the comparator it was given to perform the comparison. Thus, a programmer can write a general priority queue implementation that can work correctly in a wide variety of contexts. Formally, a comparator object provides the following methods, each of which takes two keys and compares them (or reports an error if the keys are incomparable). The methods of the comparator ADT include:

isLess(a,b): True if and only if a is less than b.

isLessOrEqualTo(a,b): True if and only if a is less than or equal to b.

isEqualTo(a,b): True if and only if a and b are equal.

isGreater(a,b): True if and only if a is greater than b.

isGreaterOrEqualTo(a,b): True if and only if a is greater than or equal to b.

isComparable(a): True if and only if a can be compared.

2.4.2 PQ-Sort, Selection-Sort, and Insertion-Sort

In this section, we discuss how to use a priority queue to sort a set of elements.

PQ-Sort: Using a Priority Queue to Sort

In the ***sorting*** problem, we are given a collection C of n elements that can be compared according to a total order relation, and we want to rearrange them in increasing order (or at least in nondecreasing order if there are ties). The algorithm for sorting C with a priority queue Q is quite simple and consists of the following two phases:

1. In the first phase, we put the elements of C into an initially empty priority queue P by means of a series of n insertItem operations, one for each element.
2. In the second phase, we extract the elements from P in nondecreasing order by means of a series of n removeMin operations, putting them back into C in order.

We give pseudo-code for this algorithm in Algorithm 2.40, assuming that C is a sequence (such as a list or vector). The algorithm works correctly for any priority queue P, no matter how P is implemented. However, the running time of the algorithm is determined by the running times of operations insertItem and removeMin, which do depend on how P is implemented. Indeed, PriorityQueueSort should be considered more a sorting "scheme" than a sorting "algorithm," because it does not specify how the priority queue P is implemented. The PriorityQueueSort scheme is the paradigm of several popular sorting algorithms, including selection-sort, insertion-sort, and heap-sort, which we discuss in the remainder of this section.

Algorithm PQ-Sort(C,P):
  Input: An n-element sequence C and a priority queue P that compares keys, which are elements of C, using a total order relation
  Output: The sequence C sorted by the total order relation
  while C is not empty **do**
    $e \leftarrow C$.removeFirst() {remove an element e from C}
    P.insertItem(e,e) {the key is the element itself}
  while P is not empty **do**
    $e \leftarrow P$.removeMin() {remove a smallest element from P}
    C.insertLast(e) {add the element at the end of C}

Algorithm 2.40: Algorithm PQ-Sort. Note that the elements of the input sequence C serve both as keys and elements of the priority queue P.

Using a Priority Queue Implemented with an Unordered Sequence

As our first implementation of a priority queue P, let us consider storing the elements of P and their keys in a sequence S. Let us say that S is a general sequence implemented with either an array or a doubly linked list (the choice of specific implementation will not affect performance, as we will see). Thus, the elements of S are pairs (k,e), where e is an element of P and k is its key. A simple way of implementing method insertItem(k,e) of P is to add the new pair object $p = (k,e)$ at the end of sequence S, by executing method insertLast(p) on S. This implementation of method insertItem takes $O(1)$ time, independent of whether the sequence is implemented using an array or a linked list (see Section 2.2.3). This choice means that S will be unsorted, for always inserting items at the end of S does not take into account the ordering of the keys. As a consequence, to perform operation minElement, minKey, or removeMin on P, we must inspect all the elements of sequence S to find an element $p = (k,e)$ of S with minimum k. Thus, no matter how the sequence S is implemented, these search methods on P all take $O(n)$ time, where n is the number of elements in P at the time the method is executed. Moreover, these methods run in $\Omega(n)$ time even in the best case, since they each require searching the entire sequence to find a minimum element. That is, these methods run in $\Theta(n)$ time. Thus, by using an unsorted sequence to implement a priority queue, we achieve constant-time insertion, but the removeMin operation takes linear time.

Selection-Sort

If we implement the priority queue P with an unsorted sequence, then the first phase of PQ-Sort takes $O(n)$ time, for we can insert each element in constant time. In the second phase, assuming we can compare two keys in constant time, the running time of each removeMin operation is proportional to the number of elements currently in P. Thus, the bottleneck computation in this implementation is the repeated "selection" of the minimum element from an unsorted sequence in phase 2. For this reason, this algorithm is better known as ***selection-sort***.

Let us analyze the selection-sort algorithm. As noted above, the bottleneck is the second phase, where we repeatedly remove an element with smallest key from the priority queue P. The size of P starts at n and incrementally decreases with each removeMin until it becomes 0. Thus, the first removeMin operation takes time $O(n)$, the second one takes time $O(n-1)$, and so on, until the last (nth) operation takes time $O(1)$. Therefore, the total time needed for this second phase is

$$O(n+(n-1)+\cdots+2+1) = O\left(\sum_{i=1}^{n} i\right).$$

By Theorem 1.13, we have $\sum_{i=1}^{n} i = \frac{n(n+1)}{2}$. Thus, the second phase takes time $O(n^2)$, as does the entire selection-sort algorithm.

Using a Priority Queue Implemented with a Sorted Sequence

An alternative implementation of a priority queue P also uses a sequence S, except that this time let us store items ordered by key values. We can implement methods minElement and minKey in this case simply by accessing the first element of the sequence with the first method of S. Likewise, we can implement the removeMin method of P as S.remove(S.first()). Assuming that S is implemented with a linked list or an array that supports constant-time, front-element removal (see Section 2.2.3), finding and removing the minimum in P takes $O(1)$ time. Thus, using a sorted sequence allows for simple and fast implementations of priority queue access and removal methods.

This benefit comes at a cost, however, for now the method insertItem of P requires that we scan through the sequence S to find the appropriate position to insert the new element and key. Thus, implementing the insertItem method of P now requires $O(n)$ time, where n is the number of elements in P at the time the method is executed. In summary, when using a sorted sequence to implement a priority queue, insertion runs in linear time whereas finding and removing the minimum can be done in constant time.

Insertion-Sort

If we implement the priority queue P using a sorted sequence, then we improve the running time of the second phase of the PQ-Sort method to $O(n)$, for each operation removeMin on P now takes $O(1)$ time. Unfortunately, the first phase now becomes the bottleneck for the running time. Indeed, in the worst case, the running time of each insertItem operation is proportional to the number of elements that are currently in the priority queue, which starts out having size zero and increases in size until it has size n. The first insertItem operation takes time $O(1)$, the second one takes time $O(2)$, and so on, until the last (nth) operation takes time $O(n)$, in the worst case. Thus, if we use a sorted sequence to implement P, then the first phase becomes the bottleneck phase. This sorting algorithm is therefore better known as ***insertion-sort***, for the bottleneck in this sorting algorithm involves the repeated "insertion" of a new element at the appropriate position in a sorted sequence.

Analyzing the running time of insertion-sort, we note that the first phase takes $O(\sum_{i=1}^{n} i)$ time in the worst case. Again, by recalling Theorem 1.13, the first phase runs in $O(n^2)$ time, and hence so does the entire algorithm. Therefore, both selection-sort and insertion-sort both have a running time that is $O(n^2)$.

Still, although selection-sort and insertion-sort are similar, they actually have some interesting differences. For instance, note that selection-sort always takes $\Omega(n^2)$ time, for selecting the minimum in each step of the second phase requires scanning the entire priority-queue sequence. The running time of insertion-sort, on the other hand, varies depending on the input sequence. For example, if the input sequence S is in reverse order, then insertion-sort runs in $O(n)$ time.

2.4.3 The Heap Data Structure

A realization of a priority queue that is efficient for both insertions and removals uses a data structure called a ***heap***. This data structure allows us to perform both insertions and removals in logarithmic time. The fundamental way the heap achieves this improvement is to abandon the idea of storing elements and keys in a sequence and store elements and keys in a binary tree instead.

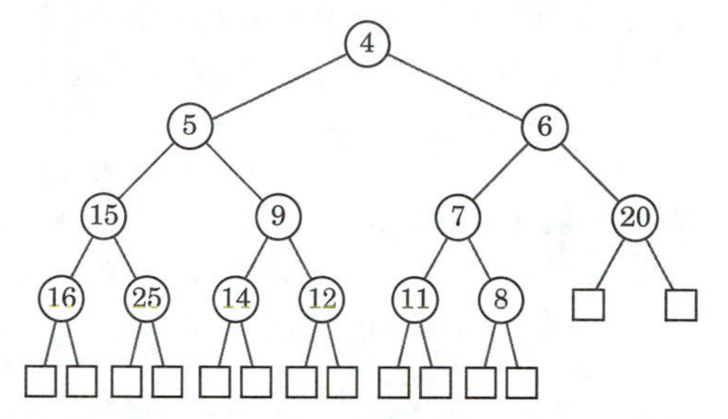

Figure 2.41: Example of a heap storing 13 integer keys. The last node is the one storing key 8, and external nodes are empty.

A heap (see Figure 2.41) is a binary tree T that stores a collection of keys at its internal nodes and that satisfies two additional properties: a relational property defined in terms of the way keys are stored in T and a structural property defined in terms of T itself. We assume that a total order relation on the keys is given, for example, by a comparator. Also, in our definition of a heap the external nodes of T do not store keys or elements and serve only as "place-holders." The relational property for T is the following:

Heap-Order Property: In a heap T, for every node v other than the root, the key stored at v is greater than or equal to the key stored at v's parent.

As a consequence of this property, the keys encountered on a path from the root to an external node of T are in nondecreasing order. Also, a minimum key is always stored at the root of T. For the sake of efficiency, we want the heap T to have as small a height as possible. We enforce this desire by insisting that the heap T satisfy an additional structural property:

Complete Binary Tree: A binary tree T with height h is ***complete*** if the levels $0, 1, 2, \ldots, h-1$ have the maximum number of nodes possible (that is, level i has 2^i nodes, for $0 \leq i \leq h-1$) and in level $h-1$ all the internal nodes are to the left of the external nodes.

By saying that all the internal nodes on level $h-1$ are "to the left" of the external nodes, we mean that all the internal nodes on this level will be visited before any external nodes on this level in an inorder traversal. (See Figure 2.41.)

By insisting that a heap T be complete, we identify another important node in a heap T, other than the root, namely, the ***last node*** of T, which we define to be the right-most, deepest internal node of T. (See Figure 2.41.)

Implementing a Priority Queue with a Heap

Our heap-based priority queue consists of the following (see Figure 2.42):

- ***heap***: A complete binary tree T whose elements are stored at internal nodes and have keys satisfying the heap-order property. We assume the binary tree T is implemented using a vector, as described in Section 2.3.4. For each internal node v of T, we denote the key of the element stored at v as $k(v)$.
- ***last***: A reference to the last node of T. Given the vector implementation of T, we assume that the instance variable, last, is an integer index to the cell in the vector storing the last node of T.
- ***comp***: A a comparator that defines the total order relation among the keys. Without loss of generality, we assume that ***comp*** maintains the minimum element at the root. If instead we wish the maximum element to be at the root, then we can redefine our comparison rule accordingly.

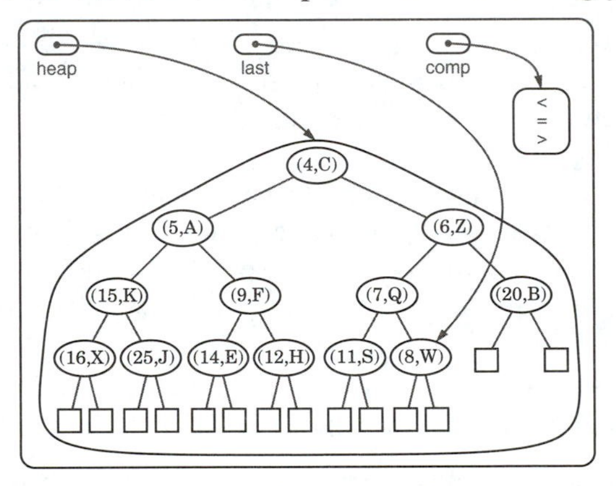

Figure 2.42: A heap-based priority queue storing integer keys and text elements.

The efficiency of this implementation is based on the following fact.

Theorem 2.10: *A heap T storing n keys has height $h = \lceil \log(n+1) \rceil$.*

Proof: Since T is complete, the number of internal nodes of T is at least

$$1+2+4+\cdots+2^{h-2}+1 = 2^{h-1}-1+1 = 2^{h-1}.$$

This lower bound is achieved when there is only one internal node on level $h-1$. Alternately, we observe that the number of internal nodes of T is at most

$$1+2+4+\cdots+2^{h-1} = 2^h-1.$$

This upper bound is achieved when all the 2^{h-1} nodes on level $h-1$ are internal. Since the number of internal nodes is equal to the number n of keys, $2^{h-1} \le n$ and $n \le 2^h-1$. Thus, by taking logarithms of both sides of these two inequalities, we see that $h \le \log n + 1$ and $\log(n+1) \le h$, which implies that $h = \lceil \log(n+1) \rceil$. ■

Thus, if we can perform update operations on a heap in time proportional to its height, then those operations will run in logarithmic time.

The Vector Representation of a Heap

Note that when the heap T is implemented with a vector, the index of the last node w is always equal to n, and the first empty external node z has index equal to $n+1$. (See Figure 2.43.) Note that this index for z is valid even for the following cases:

- If the current last node w is the right-most node on its level, then z is the left-most node of the bottom-most level (see Figure 2.43b).
- If T has no internal nodes (that is, the priority queue is empty and the last node in T is not defined), then z is the root of T.

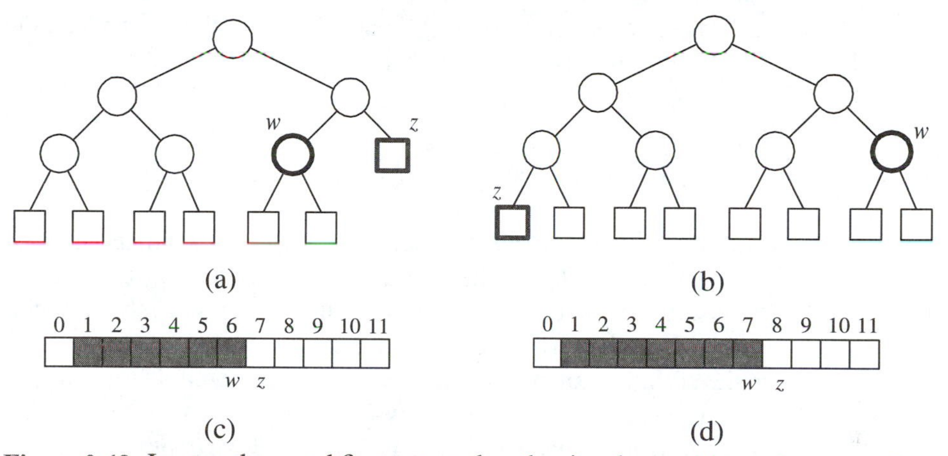

Figure 2.43: Last node w and first external node z in a heap: (a) regular case where z is right of w; (b) case where z is left-most on bottom level. The vector representation of (a) is shown in (c); similarly, the representation of (b) is shown in (d).

The simplifications that come from representing the heap T with a vector aid in our methods for implementing the priority queue ADT. For example, the update methods expandExternal(z) and removeAboveExternal(z) can also be performed in $O(1)$ time (assuming no vector expansion is necessary), for they simply involve allocating or deallocating a single cell in the vector. With this data structure, methods size and isEmpty take $O(1)$ time, as usual. In addition, methods minElement and minKey can also be easily performed in $O(1)$ time by accessing the element or key stored at the root of the heap (which is at rank 1 in the vector). Moreover, because T is a complete binary tree, the vector associated with heap T in a vector-based implementation of a binary tree has $2n+1$ elements, $n+1$ of which are place-holder external nodes by our convention. Indeed, since all the external nodes have indices higher than any internal node, we don't even have to explicitly store all the external nodes. (See Figure 2.43.)

Insertion

Let us consider how to perform method insertItem of the priority queue ADT using the heap T. In order to store a new key-element pair (k,e) into T, we need to add a new internal node to T. In order to keep T as a complete binary tree, we must add this new node so that it becomes the new last node of T. That is, we must identify the correct external node z where we can perform an expandExternal(z) operation, which replaces z with an internal node (with empty external-node children), and then insert the new element at z. (See Figure 2.44a-b.) Node z is called the ***insertion position***.

Usually, node z is the external node immediately to the right of the last node w. (See Figure 2.43a.) In any case, by our vector implementation of T, the insertion position z is stored at index $n+1$, where n is the current size of the heap. Thus, we can identify the node z in constant time in the vector implementing T. After then performing expandExternal(z), node z becomes the last node, and we store the new key-element pair (k,e) in it, so that $k(z)=k$.

Up-Heap Bubbling after an Insertion

After this action, the tree T is complete, but it may violate the heap-order property. Hence, unless node z is the root of T (that is, the priority queue was empty before the insertion), we compare key $k(z)$ with the key $k(u)$ stored at the parent u of z. If $k(u) > k(z)$, then we need to restore the heap-order property, which can be locally achieved by swapping the key-element pairs stored at z and u. (See Figure 2.44c–d.) This swap causes the new key-element pair (k,e) to move up one level. Again, the heap-order property may be violated, and we continue swapping going up in T until no violation of heap-order property occurs. (See Figure 2.44e–h.)

The upward movement by means of swaps is conventionally called ***up-heap bubbling***. A swap either resolves the violation of the heap-order property or propagates it one level up in the heap. In the worst case, up-heap bubbling causes the new key-element pair to move all the way up to the root of heap T. (See Figure 2.44.) Thus, in the worst case, the running time of method insertItem is proportional to the height of T, that is, it is $O(\log n)$ because T is complete.

If T is implemented with a vector, then we can find the new last node z immediately in $O(1)$ time. For example, we could extend a vector-based implementation of a binary tree, so as to add a method that returns the node with index $n+1$, that is, with level number $n+1$, as defined in Section 2.3.4. Alternately, we could even define an add method, which adds a new element at the first external node z, at rank $n+1$ in the vector. In Algorithm 2.60, shown later in this chapter, we show how to use this method to efficiently implement the method insertItem. If, on the other hand, the heap T is implemented with a linked structure, then finding the insertion position z is a little more involved. (See Exercise C-2.27.)

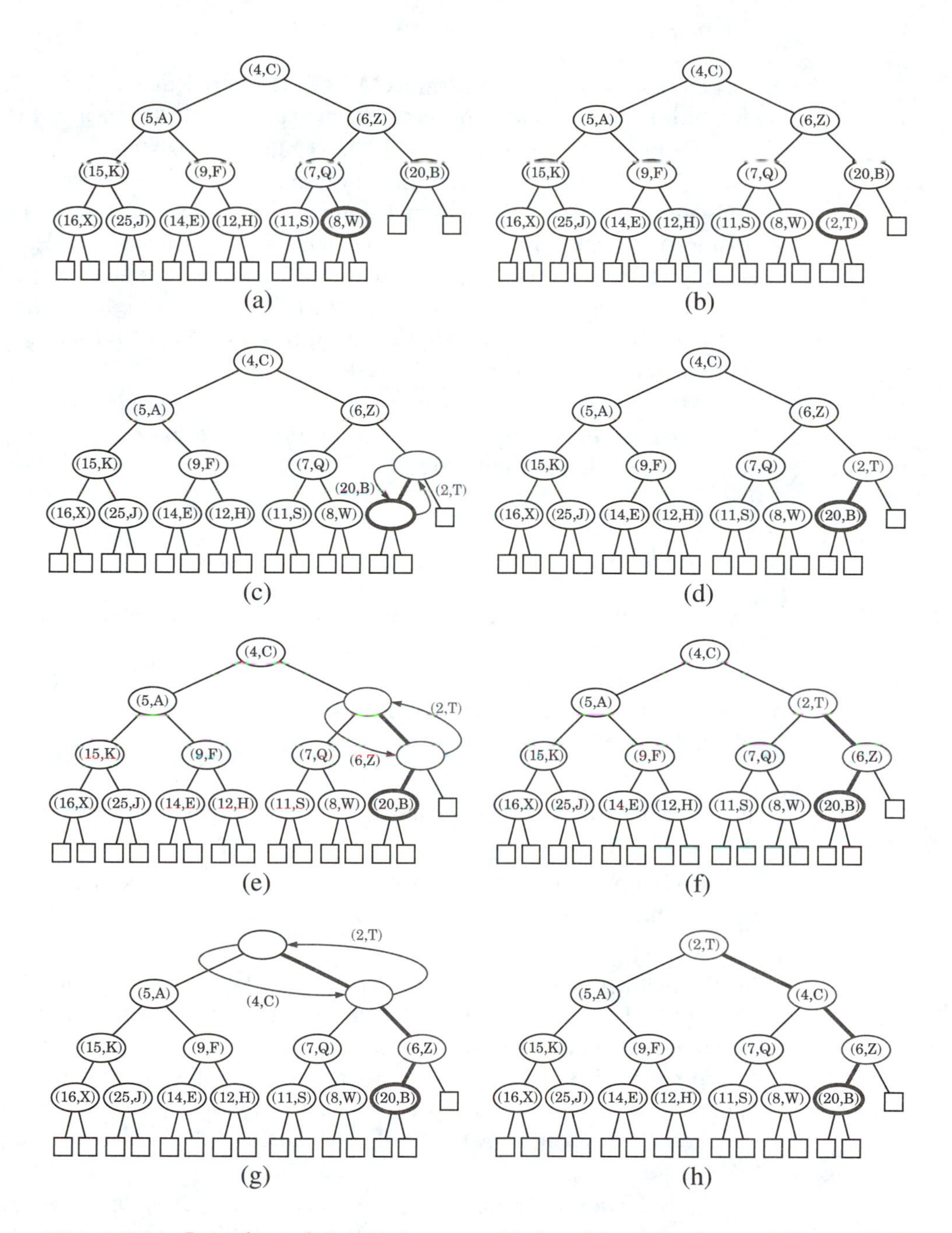

Figure 2.44: Insertion of a new element with key 2 into the heap of Figure 2.42: (a) initial heap; (b) adding a new last node to the right of the old last node; (c)–(d) swap to locally restore the partial order property; (e)–(f) another swap; (g)–(h) final swap.

Removal

Let us now turn to method removeMin of the priority queue ADT. The algorithm for performing method removeMin using heap T is illustrated in Figure 2.45.

We know that an element with the smallest key is stored at the root r of the heap T (even if there is more than one smallest key). However, unless r is the only internal node of T, we cannot simply delete node r, because this action would disrupt the binary tree structure. Instead, we access the last node w of T, copy its key-element pair to the root r, and then delete the last node by performing the update operation removeAboveExternal(u), where $u = T$.rightChild(w)). This operation removes the parent, w, of u, together with the node u itself, and replaces w with its left child. (See Figure 2.45a–b.)

After this constant-time action, we need to update our reference to the last node, which can be done simply by referencing the node at rank n (after the removal) in the vector implementing the tree T.

Down-Heap Bubbling after a Removal

We are not done, however, for, even though T is now complete, T may now violate the heap-order property. To determine whether we need to restore the heap-order property, we examine the root r of T. If both children of r are external nodes, then the heap-order property is trivially satisfied and we are done. Otherwise, we distinguish two cases:

- If the left child of r is internal and the right child is external, let s be the left child of r.
- Otherwise (both children of r are internal), let s be a child of r with the smallest key.

If the key $k(r)$ stored at r is greater than the key $k(s)$ stored at s, then we need to restore the heap-order property, which can be locally achieved by swapping the key-element pairs stored at r and s. (See Figure 2.45c–d.) Note that we shouldn't swap r with s's sibling. The swap we perform restores the heap-order property for node r and its children, but it may violate this property at s; hence, we may have to continue swapping down T until no violation of the heap-order property occurs. (See Figure 2.45e–h.)

This downward swapping process is called ***down-heap bubbling***. A swap either resolves the violation of the heap-order property or propagates it one level down in the heap. In the worst case, a key-element pair moves all the way down to the level immediately above the bottom level. (See Figure 2.45.) Thus, the running time of method removeMin is, in the worst case, proportional to the height of heap T, that is, it is $O(\log n)$.

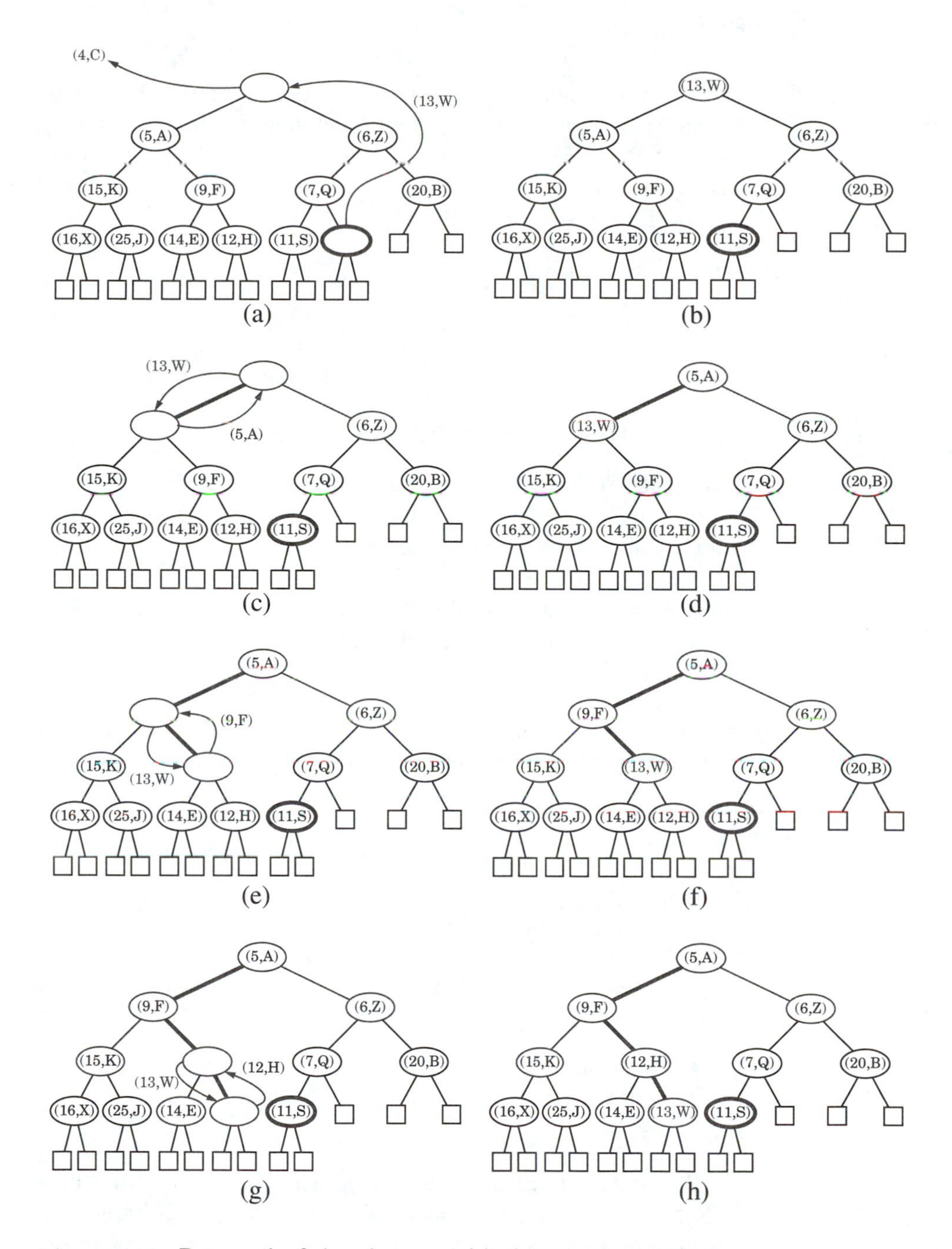

Figure 2.45: Removal of the element with the smallest key from a heap: (a)–(b) deletion of the last node, whose key-element pair gets stored into the root; (c)–(d) swap to locally restore the heap-order property; (e)–(f) another swap; (g)–(h) final swap.

Performance

Table 2.46 shows the running time of the priority queue ADT methods for the heap implementation of a priority queue, assuming that the heap T is realized by a data structure for binary trees that supports the binary tree ADT methods (except for elements()) in $O(1)$ time. The linked structure and vector-based structure from Section 2.3.4 easily satisfy this requirement.

Operation	Time
size, isEmpty	$O(1)$
minElement, minKey	$O(1)$
insertItem	$O(\log n)$
removeMin	$O(\log n)$

Table 2.46: Performance of a priority queue realized by means of a heap, which is in turn implemented with a vector-based structure for binary trees. We denote with n the number of elements in the priority queue at the time a method is executed. The space requirement is $O(n)$ if the heap is realized with a linked structure, and is $O(N)$ if the heap is realized with a vector-based structure, where $N \geq n$ is the size of the array used to implement the vector.

In short, each of the priority queue ADT methods can be performed in $O(1)$ or in $O(\log n)$ time, where n is the number of elements at the time the method is executed. The analysis of the running time of the methods is based on the following:

- The height of heap T is $O(\log n)$, since T is complete.
- In the worst case, up-heap and down-heap bubbling take time proportional to the height of T.
- Finding the insertion position in the execution of insertItem and updating the last node position in the execution of removeMin takes constant time.
- The heap T has n internal nodes, each storing a reference to a key and a reference to an element, and $n+1$ external nodes.

We conclude that the heap data structure is a very efficient realization of the priority queue ADT, independent of whether the heap is implemented with a linked structure or a sequence. The heap implementation achieves fast running times for both insertion and removal, unlike the sequence-based priority queue implementations. Indeed, an important consequence of the efficiency of the heap-based implementation is that it can speed up priority-queue sorting to be much faster than the sequence-based insertion-sort and selection-sort algorithms.

2.4.4 Heap-Sort

Let us consider again the PQ-Sort sorting scheme from Section 2.4.2, which uses a priority queue P to sort a sequence S. If we implement the priority queue P with a heap, then, during the first phase, each of the n insertItem operations takes time $O(\log k)$, where k is the number of elements in the heap at the time. Likewise, during the second phase, each of the n removeMin operations also runs in time $O(\log k)$, where k is the number of elements in the heap at the time. Since we always have $k \leq n$, each such operation runs in $O(\log n)$ time in the worst case. Thus, each phase takes $O(n \log n)$ time, so the entire priority-queue sorting algorithm runs in $O(n \log n)$ time when we use a heap to implement the priority queue. This sorting algorithm is better known as ***heap-sort***, and its performance is summarized in the following theorem.

Theorem 2.11: *The heap-sort algorithm sorts a sequence S of n comparable elements in $O(n \log n)$ time.*

Recalling Table 1.7, we stress that the $O(n \log n)$ running time of heap-sort is much better than the $O(n^2)$ running time for selection-sort and insertion-sort. In addition, there are several modifications we can make to the heap-sort algorithm to improve its performance in practice.

Implementing Heap-Sort In-Place

If the sequence S to be sorted is implemented by means of an array, we can speed up heap-sort and reduce its space requirement by a constant factor using a portion of the sequence S itself to store the heap, thus avoiding the use of an external heap data structure. This is accomplished by modifying the algorithm as follows:

1. We use a reverse comparator, which corresponds to a heap where the largest element is at the top. At any time during the execution of the algorithm, we use the left portion of S, up to a certain rank $i-1$, to store the elements in the heap, and the right portion of S, from rank i to $n-1$ to store the elements in the sequence. Thus, the first i elements of S (at ranks $0, \ldots, i-1$) provide the vector representation of the heap (with modified level numbers starting at 0 instead of 1), that is, the element at rank k is greater than or equal to its "children" at ranks $2k+1$ and $2k+2$.
2. In the first phase of the algorithm, we start with an empty heap and move the boundary between the heap and the sequence from left to right, one step at a time. In step i ($i = 1, \ldots, n$), we expand the heap by adding the element at rank $i-1$.
3. In the second phase of the algorithm, we start with an empty sequence and move the boundary between the heap and the sequence from right to left, one step at a time. At step i ($i = 1, \ldots, n$), we remove a maximum element from the heap and store it at rank $n-i$.

The above variation of heap-sort is said to be ***in-place***, since we use only a constant amount of space in addition to the sequence itself. Instead of transferring elements out of the sequence and then back in, we simply rearrange them. We illustrate in-place heap-sort in Figure 2.47. In general, we say that a sorting algorithm is in-place if it uses only a constant amount of memory in addition to the memory needed for the objects being sorted themselves. The advantage of an in-place sorting algorithm in practice is that such an algorithm can make the most efficient use of the main memory of the computer it is running on.

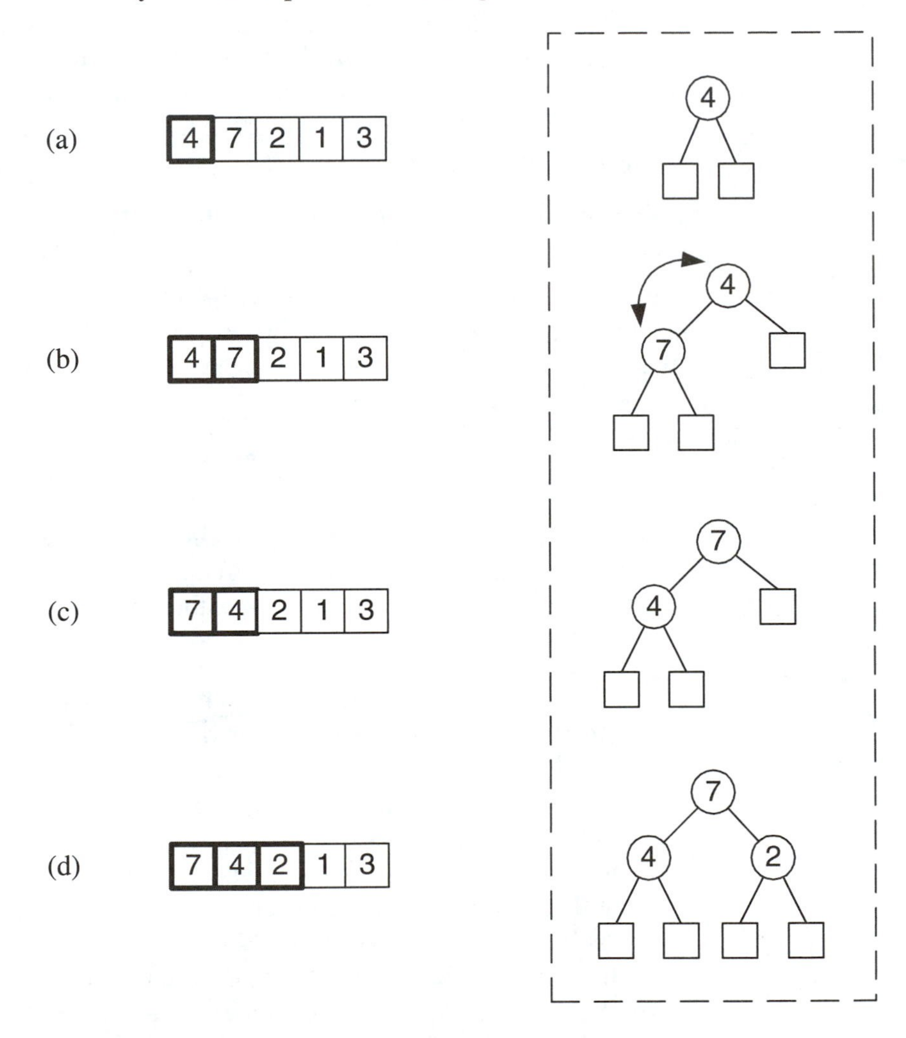

Figure 2.47: First three steps of Phase 1 of in-place heap-sort. The heap portion of the vector is highlighted with thick lines. Next to the vector, we draw a binary tree view of the heap, even though this tree is not actually constructed by the in-place algorithm.

Bottom-Up Heap Construction

The analysis of the heap-sort algorithm shows that we can construct a heap storing n key-element pairs in $O(n \log n)$ time, by means of n successive insertItem operations, and then use that heap to extract the elements in order. However, if all the keys to be stored in the heap are given in advance, there is an alternative ***bottom-up*** construction method that runs in $O(n)$ time.

We describe this method in this section, observing that it could be included as one of the constructors in a Heap class, instead of filling a heap using a series of n insertItem operations. For simplicity of exposition, we describe this bottom-up heap construction assuming the number n of keys is an integer of the type

$$n = 2^h - 1.$$

That is, the heap is a complete binary tree with every level being full, so the heap has height

$$h = \log(n+1).$$

We describe bottom-up heap construction as a recursive algorithm, as shown in Algorithm 2.48, which we call by passing a sequence storing the keys for which we wish to build a heap. We describe the construction algorithm as acting on keys, with the understanding that their elements accompany them. That is, the items stored in the tree T are key-element pairs.

Algorithm BottomUpHeap(S):
    Input: A sequence S storing $n = 2^h - 1$ keys
    Output: A heap T storing the keys in S.
    if S is empty **then**
        return an empty heap (consisting of a single external node).
    Remove the first key, k, from S.
    Split S into two sequences, S_1 and S_2, each of size $(n-1)/2$.
    $T_1 \leftarrow$ BottomUpHeap(S_1)
    $T_2 \leftarrow$ BottomUpHeap(S_2)
    Create binary tree T with root r storing k, left subtree T_1, and right subtree T_2.
    Perform a down-heap bubbling from the root r of T, if necessary.
    return T

Algorithm 2.48: Recursive bottom-up heap construction.

This construction algorithm is called "bottom-up" heap construction because of the way each recursive call returns a subtree that is a heap for the elements it stores. That is, the "heapification" of T begins at its external nodes and proceeds up the tree as each recursive call returns. For this reason, some authors refer to the bottom-up heap construction as the "heapify" operation.

We illustrate bottom-up heap construction in Figure 2.49 for $h = 4$.

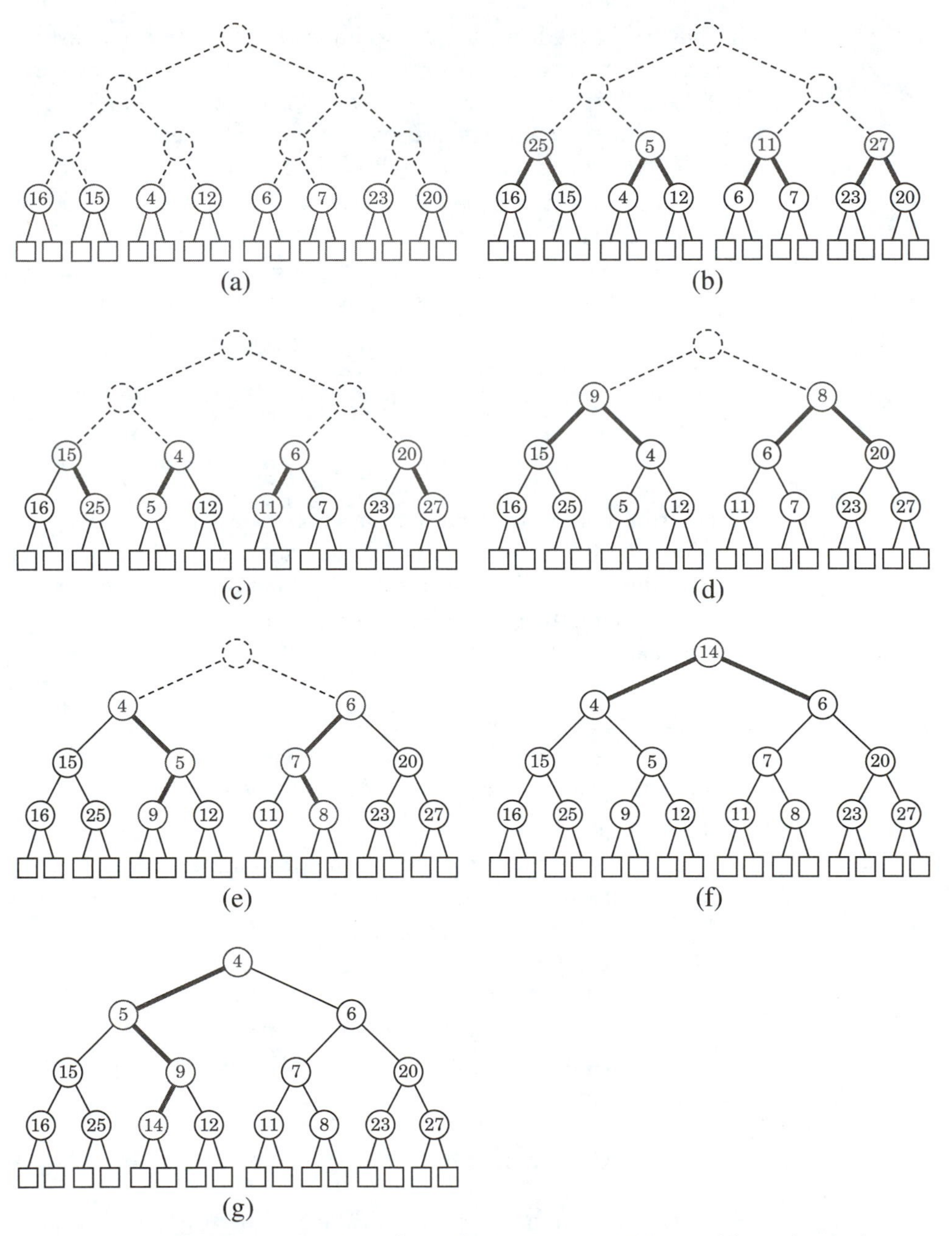

Figure 2.49: Bottom-up construction of a heap with 15 keys: (a) we begin by constructing 1-key heaps on the bottom level; (b)–(c) we combine these heaps into 3-key heaps and then (d)–(e) 7-key heaps, until (f)–(g) we create the final heap. The paths of the down-heap bubblings are highlighted with thick lines.

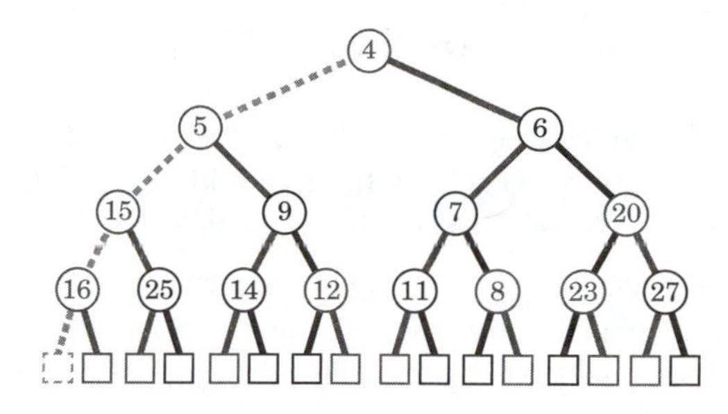

Figure 2.50: Visual justification of the linear running time of bottom-up heap construction, where the paths associated with the internal nodes have been highlighted alternating grey and black. For example, the path associated with the root consists of the internal nodes storing keys 4, 6, 7, and 11, plus an external node.

Bottom-up heap construction is asymptotically faster than incrementally inserting n keys into an initially empty heap, as the following theorem shows.

Theorem 2.12: *The bottom-up construction of a heap with n items takes $O(n)$ time.*

Proof: We analyze bottom-up heap construction using a "visual" approach, which is illustrated in Figure 2.50.

Let T be the final heap, let v be an internal node of T, and let $T(v)$ denote the subtree of T rooted at v. In the worst case, the time for forming $T(v)$ from the two recursively formed subtrees rooted at v's children is proportional to the height of $T(v)$. The worst case occurs when down-heap bubbling from v traverses a path from v all the way to a bottom-most external node of $T(v)$. Consider now the path $p(v)$ of T from node v to its inorder successor external node, that is, the path that starts at v, goes to the right child of v, and then goes down leftward until it reaches an external node. We say that path $p(v)$ is ***associated with*** node v. Note that $p(v)$ is not necessarily the path followed by down-heap bubbling when forming $T(v)$. Clearly, the length (number of edges) of $p(v)$ is equal to the height of $T(v)$. Hence, forming $T(v)$ takes time proportional to the length of $p(v)$, in the worst case. Thus, the total running time of bottom-up heap construction is proportional to the sum of the lengths of the paths associated with the internal nodes of T.

Note that for any two internal nodes u and v of T, paths $p(u)$ and $p(v)$ do not share edges, although they may share nodes. (See Figure 2.50.) Therefore, the sum of the lengths of the paths associated with the internal nodes of T is no more than the number of edges of heap T, that is, no more than $2n$. We conclude that the bottom-up construction of heap T takes $O(n)$ time. ■

To summarize, Theorem 2.12 says that the first phase of heap-sort can be implemented to run in $O(n)$ time. Unfortunately, the running time of the second phase of heap-sort is $\Omega(n \log n)$ in the worst case. We will not justify this lower bound until Chapter 4, however.

The Locator Design Pattern

We conclude this section by discussing a design pattern that allows us to extend the priority queue ADT to have additional functionality, which will be useful, for example, in some of the graph algorithms discussed later in this book.

As we saw with lists and binary trees, abstracting positional information in a container is a very powerful tool. The position ADT, described in Section 2.2.2, allows us to identify a specific "place" in a container that can store an element. A position can have its element changed, for example, as a consequence of a swapElements operation, but the position stays the same.

There are also applications where we need to keep track of elements as they are being moved around inside a container, however. A design pattern that fulfills this need is the ***locator***. A locator is a mechanism for maintaining the association between an element and its current position in a container. A locator "sticks" with a specific element, even if the element changes its position in the container.

A locator is like a coat check; we can give our coat to a coat-room attendant, and we receive back a coat check, which is a "locator" for our coat. The position of our coat relative to the other coats can change, as other coats are added and removed, but our coat check can always be used to retrieve our coat. The important thing to remember about a locator is that it follows its item, even if it changes position.

Like a coat check, we can now imagine getting something back when we insert an element in a container—we can get back a locator for that element. This locator in turn can be used later to refer to the element within the container, for example, to specify that this element should be removed from the container. As an abstract data type, a locator ℓ supports the following methods:

element(): Return the element of the item associated with ℓ.

key(): Return the key of the item associated with ℓ.

For the sake of concreteness, we next discuss how we can use locators to extend the repertoire of operations of the priority queue ADT to include methods that return locators and take locators as arguments.

Locator-Based Priority Queue Methods

We can use locators in a very natural way in the context of a priority queue. A locator in such a scenario stays attached to an item inserted in the priority queue, and allows us to access the item in a generic manner, independent of the specific implementation of the priority queue. This ability is important for a priority queue implementation, for there are no positions, *per se*, in a priority queue, since we do not refer to items by any notions of "rank," "index," or "node."

Extending the Priority Queue ADT

By using locators, we can extend the priority queue ADT with the following methods that access and modify a priority queue P:

- min(): Return the locator to an item of P with smallest key.
- insert(k,e): Insert a new item with element e and key k into P and return a locator to the item.
- remove(ℓ): Remove from P the item with locator ℓ.
- replaceElement(ℓ,e): Replace with e and return the element of the item of P with locator ℓ.
- replaceKey(ℓ,k): Replace with k and return the key of the item of P with locator ℓ.

Locator-based access runs in $O(1)$ time, while a key-based access, which must look for the element via a search in an entire sequence or heap, runs in $O(n)$ time in the worst case. In addition, some applications call for us to restrict the operation replaceKey so that it only increases or decreases the key. This restriction can be done by defining new methods increaseKey or decreaseKey, for example, which would take a locator as an argument. Further applications of such priority queue methods are given in Chapter 7.

Comparison of Different Priority Queue Implementations

In Table 2.51, we compare running times of the priority queue ADT methods defined in this section for the unsorted-sequence, sorted-sequence, and heap implementations.

Method	Unsorted Sequence	Sorted Sequence	Heap
size, isEmpty, key, replaceElement	$O(1)$	$O(1)$	$O(1)$
minElement, min, minKey	$O(n)$	$O(1)$	$O(1)$
insertItem, insert	$O(1)$	$O(n)$	$O(\log n)$
removeMin	$O(n)$	$O(1)$	$O(\log n)$
remove	$O(1)$	$O(1)$	$O(\log n)$
replaceKey	$O(1)$	$O(n)$	$O(\log n)$

Table 2.51: Comparison of the running times of the priority queue ADT methods for the unsorted-sequence, sorted-sequence, and heap implementations. We denote with n the number of elements in the priority queue at the time a method is executed.

2.5 Dictionaries and Hash Tables

A computer dictionary is similar to a paper dictionary of words in the sense that both are used to look things up. The main idea is that users can assign keys to elements and then use those keys later to look up or remove elements. (See Figure 2.52.) Thus, the dictionary abstract data type has methods for the insertion, removal, and searching of elements with keys.

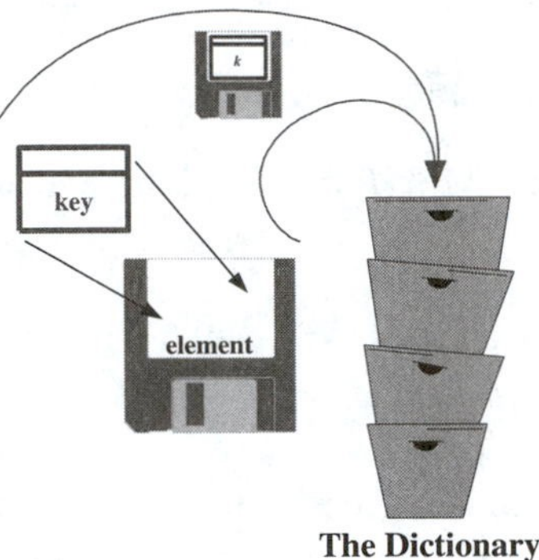

Figure 2.52: A conceptual illustration of the dictionary ADT. Keys (labels) are assigned to elements (diskettes) by a user. The resulting items (labeled diskettes) are inserted into the dictionary (file cabinet). The keys can be used later to retrieve or remove the items.

2.5.1 The Unordered Dictionary ADT

A dictionary stores key-element pairs (k, e), which we call ***items***, where k is the key and e is the element. For example, in a dictionary storing student records (such as the student's name, address, and course grades), the key might be the student's ID number. In some applications, the key may be the element itself.

We distinguish two types of dictionaries, the ***unordered dictionary*** and the ***ordered dictionary***. We study ordered dictionaries in Chapter 3; we discuss unordered dictionaries here. In either case, we use a ***key*** as an identifier that is assigned by an application or user to an associated element.

For the sake of generality, our definition allows a dictionary to store multiple items with the same key. Nevertheless, there are applications in which we want to disallow items with the same key (for example, in a dictionary storing student records, we would probably want to disallow two students having the same ID). In such cases when keys are unique, then the key associated with an object can be viewed as an "address" for that object in memory. Indeed, such dictionaries are sometimes referred to as "associative stores," because the key associated with an object determines its "location" in the dictionary.

As an ADT, a ***dictionary*** D supports the following fundamental methods:

findElement(k): If D contains an item with key equal to k, then return the element of such an item, else return a special element NO_SUCH_KEY.

insertItem(k,e): Insert an item with element e and key k into D.

removeElement(k): Remove from D an item with key equal to k, and return its element. If D has no such item, then return the special element NO_SUCH_KEY.

Note that if we wish to store an item e in a dictionary so that the item is itself its own key, then we would insert e with the method call insertItem(e,e). When operations findElement(k) and removeElement(k) are unsuccessful (that is, the dictionary D has no item with key equal to k), we use the convention of returning a special element NO_SUCH_KEY. Such a special element is known as a ***sentinel***.

In addition, a dictionary can implement other supporting methods, such as the usual size() and isEmpty() methods for containers. Moreover, we can include a method, elements(), which returns the elements stored in D, and keys(), which returns the keys stored in D. Also, allowing for nonunique keys could motivate our including methods such as findAllElements(k), which returns an iterator of all elements with keys equal to k, and removeAllElements(k), which removes from D all the items with key equal to k, returning an iterator of their elements.

Log Files

A simple way of realizing a dictionary D uses an unsorted sequence S, which in turn is implemented using a vector or list to store the key-element pairs. Such an implementation is often called a ***log file*** or ***audit trail***. The primary applications of a log file are situations where we wish to store small amounts of data or data that is unlikely to change much over time. We also refer to the log file implementation of D as an ***unordered sequence implementation***.

The space required for a log file is $\Theta(n)$, since both the vector and linked list data structures can maintain their memory usage to be proportional to their size. In addition, with a log file implementation of the dictionary ADT, we can realize operation insertItem(k,e) easily and efficiently, just by a single call to the insertLast method on S, which runs in $O(1)$ time.

Unfortunately, a findElement(k) operation must be performed by scanning the entire sequence S, examining each of its items. The worst case for the running time of this method clearly occurs when the search is unsuccessful, and we reach the end of the sequence having examined all of its n items. Thus, the findElement method runs in $O(n)$ time. Similarly, a linear amount of time is needed in the worst case to perform a removeElement(k) operation on D, for in order to remove an item with a given key, we must first find it by scanning through the entire sequence S.

2.5.2 Hash Tables

The keys associated with elements in a dictionary are often meant as "addresses" for those elements. Examples of such applications include a compiler's symbol table and a registry of environment variables. Both of these structures consist of a collection of symbolic names where each name serves as the "address" for properties about a variable's type and value. One of the most efficient ways to implement a dictionary in such circumstances is to use a ***hash table***. Although, as we will see, the worst-case running time of the dictionary ADT operations is $O(n)$ when using a hash table, where n is the number of items in the dictionary. A hash table can perform these operations in $O(1)$ expected time. It consists of two major components, the first of which is a bucket array.

Bucket Arrays

A ***bucket array*** for a hash table is an array A of size N, where each cell of A is thought of as a "bucket" (that is, a container of key-element pairs) and the integer N defines the ***capacity*** of the array. If the keys are integers well distributed in the range $[0,N-1]$, this bucket array is all that is needed. An element e with key k is simply inserted into the bucket $A[k]$. Any bucket cells associated with keys not present in the dictionary are assumed to hold the special NO_SUCH_KEY object. (See Figure 2.53.)

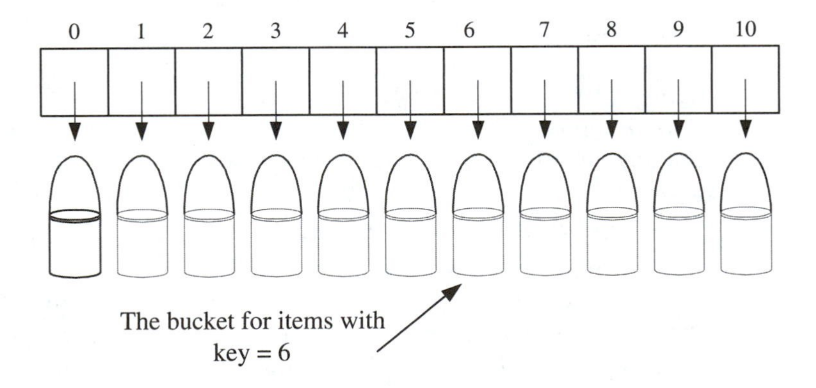

Figure 2.53: An illustration of a bucket array.

Of course, if keys are not unique, then two different elements may be mapped to the same bucket in A. In this case, we say that a ***collision*** has occurred. Clearly, if each bucket of A can store only a single element, then we cannot associate more than one element with a single bucket, which is a problem in the case of collisions. To be sure, there are ways of dealing with collisions, which we will discuss later, but the best strategy is to try to avoid them in the first place.

Analysis of the Bucket Array Structure

If keys are unique, then collisions are not a concern, and searches, insertions, and removals in the hash table take worst-case time $O(1)$. This sounds like a great achievement, but it has two major drawbacks. The first is that it uses space $O(N)$, which is not necessarily related to the number of items, n, actually present in the dictionary. Indeed, if N is large relative to n, then this implementation is wasteful of space. The second drawback is that the bucket array requires keys be unique integers in the range $[0,N-1]$, which is often not the case. Since these two drawbacks are so common, we define the hash table data structure to consist of a bucket array together with a "good" mapping from our keys to integers in the range $[0,N-1]$.

2.5.3 Hash Functions

The second part of a hash table structure is a function, h, called a ***hash function***, that maps each key k in our dictionary to an integer in the range $[0,N-1]$, where N is the capacity of the bucket array for this table. Equipped with such a hash function, h, we can apply the bucket array method to arbitrary keys. The main idea of this approach is to use the hash function value, $h(k)$, as an index into our bucket array, A, instead of the key k (which is most likely inappropriate for use as a bucket array index). That is, we store the item (k,e) in the bucket $A[h(k)]$.

We say that a hash function is "good" if it maps the keys in our dictionary so as to minimize collisions as much as possible. For practical reasons, we also would like the evaluation of a given hash function to be fast and easy to compute. Following a common convention, we view the evaluation of a hash function, $h(k)$, as consisting of two actions—mapping the key k to an integer, called the ***hash code***, and mapping the hash code to an integer within the range of indices of a bucket array, called the ***compression map***. (See Figure 2.54.)

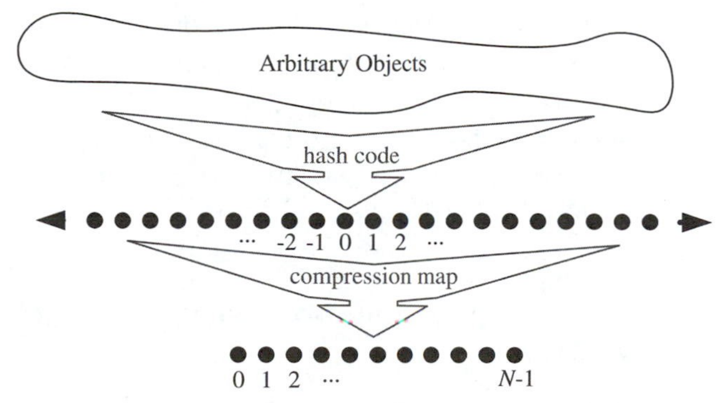

Figure 2.54: The two parts of a hash function: a hash code and a compression map.

Hash Codes

The first action that a hash function performs is to take an arbitrary key k and assign it an integer value. The integer assigned to a key k is called the ***hash code*** or ***hash value*** for k. This integer value need not be in the range $[0, N-1]$, and may even be negative, but we desire that the set of hash codes assigned to our keys should avoid collisions as much as possible. In addition, to be consistent with all of our keys, the hash code we use for a key k should be the same as the hash code for any key that is equal to k.

Summing Components

For base types whose bit representation is double that of a hash code, the above scheme is not immediately applicable. Still, one possible hash code, and indeed one that is used by many Java implementations, is to simply cast a (long) integer representation of the type down to an integer the size of a hash code. This hash code, of course, ignores half of the information present in the original value, and if many of the keys in our dictionary only differ in these bits, then they will collide using this simple hash code. An alternative hash code, then, which takes all the original bits into consideration, is to sum an integer representation of the high-order bits with an integer representation of the low-order bits. Indeed, the approach of summing components can be extended to any object x whose binary representation can be viewed as a k-tuple $(x_0, x_1, \ldots, x_{k-1})$ of integers, for we can then form a hash code for x as $\sum_{i=0}^{k-1} x_i$.

Polynomial Hash Codes

The summation hash code, described above, is not a good choice for character strings or other multiple-length objects that can be viewed as tuples of the form $(x_0, x_1, \ldots, x_{k-1})$, where the order of the x_i's is significant. For example, consider a hash code for a character string s that sums the ASCII (or Unicode) values of the characters in s. This hash code unfortunately produces lots of unwanted collisions for common groups of strings. In particular, `"temp01"` and `"temp10"` collide using this function, as do `"stop"`, `"tops"`, `"pots"`, and `"spot"`. A better hash code should somehow take into consideration the positions of the x_i's. An alternative hash code, which does exactly this, is to choose a nonzero constant, $a \neq 1$, and use as a hash code the value

$$x_0 a^{k-1} + x_1 a^{k-2} + \cdots + x_{k-2} a + x_{k-1},$$

which, by Horner's rule (see Exercise C-1.16), can be rewritten as

$$x_{k-1} + a(x_{k-2} + a(x_{k-3} + \cdots + a(x_2 + a(x_1 + a x_0)) \cdots)),$$

which, mathematically speaking, is simply a polynomial in a that takes the components $(x_0, x_1, \ldots, x_{k-1})$ of an object x as its coefficients. This hash code is therefore called a ***polynomial hash code***.

An Experimental Hash Code Analysis

Intuitively, a polynomial hash code uses multiplication by the constant a as a way of "making room" for each component in a tuple of values while also preserving a characterization of the previous components. Of course, on a typical computer, evaluating a polynomial will be done using the finite bit representation for a hash code; hence, the value will periodically overflow the bits used for an integer. Since we are more interested in a good spread of the object x with respect to other keys, we simply ignore such overflows. Still, we should be mindful that such overflows are occurring and choose the constant a so that it has some nonzero, low-order bits, which will serve to preserve some of the information content even as we are in an overflow situation.

We have done some experimental studies that suggest that 33, 37, 39, and 41 are particularly good choices for a when working with character strings that are English words. In fact, in a list of over 50,000 English words formed as the union of the word lists provided in two variants of Unix, we found that taking a to be 33, 37, 39, or 41 produced less than 7 collisions in each case! It should come as no surprise, then, to learn that many actual character string implementations choose the polynomial hash function, using one of these constants for a, as a default hash code for strings. For the sake of speed, however, some implementations only apply the polynomial hash function to a fraction of the characters in long strings, say, every eight characters.

2.5.4 Compression Maps

The hash code for a key k will typically not be suitable for immediate use with a bucket array, because the range of possible hash codes for our keys will typically exceed the range of legal indices of our bucket array A. That is, incorrectly using a hash code as an index into our bucket array may result in an array out-of-bounds exception being thrown, either because the index is negative or it exceeds the capacity of A. Thus, once we have determined an integer hash code for a key object k, there is still the issue of mapping that integer into the range $[0, N-1]$. This compression step is the second action that a hash function performs.

The Division Method

One simple ***compression map*** to use is

$$h(k) = |k| \bmod N,$$

which is called the ***division method***.

If we take N to be a prime number, then the division compression map helps "spread out" the distribution of hashed values. Indeed, if N is not prime, there is a higher likelihood that patterns in the distribution of keys will be repeated in the distribution of hash codes, thereby causing collisions. For example, if we hash the keys $\{200, 205, 210, 215, 220, \ldots, 600\}$ to a bucket array of size 100, then each hash code will collide with three others. But if this same set of keys is hashed to a bucket array of size 101, then there will be no collisions. If a hash function is chosen well, it should guarantee that the probability of two different keys getting hashed to the same bucket is at most $1/N$. Choosing N to be a prime number is not always enough, however, for if there is a repeated pattern of key values of the form $iN + j$ for several different i's, then there will still be collisions.

The MAD Method

A more sophisticated compression function, which helps eliminate repeated patterns in a set of integer keys is the ***multiply add and divide*** (or "MAD") method. In using this method we define the compression function as

$$h(k) = |ak + b| \bmod N,$$

where N is a prime number, and a and b are nonnegative integers randomly chosen at the time the compression function is determined so that $a \bmod N \neq 0$. This compression function is chosen in order to eliminate repeated patterns in the set of hash codes and get us closer to having a "good" hash function, that is, one such that the probability any two different keys will collide is at most $1/N$. This good behavior would be the same as we would have if these keys were "thrown" uniformly into A at random.

With a compression function such as this, that spreads n integers fairly evenly in the range $[0, N-1]$, and a mapping of the keys in our dictionary to integers, we have an effective hash function. Together, such a hash function and a bucket array define the key ingredients of a hash table implementation of the dictionary ADT.

But before we can give the details of how to perform such operations as findElement, insertItem, and removeElement, we must first resolve the issue of how we will be handling collisions.

2.5.5 Collision-Handling Schemes

Recall that the main idea of a hash table is to take a bucket array, A, and a hash function, h, and use them to implement a dictionary by storing each item (k, e) in the "bucket" $A[h(k)]$. This simple idea is challenged, however, when we have two distinct keys, k_1 and k_2, such that $h(k_1) = h(k_2)$. The existence of such ***collisions*** prevents us from simply inserting a new item (k, e) directly in the bucket $A[h(k)]$. They also complicate our procedure for performing the findElement(k) operation. Thus, we need consistent strategies for resolving collisions.

Separate Chaining

A simple and efficient way for dealing with collisions is to have each bucket $A[i]$ store a reference to a list, vector, or sequence, S_i, that stores all the items that our hash function has mapped to the bucket $A[i]$. The sequence S_i can be viewed as a miniature dictionary, implemented using the unordered sequence or ***log file*** method, but restricted to only hold items (k,e) such that $h(k) = i$. This ***collision resolution*** rule is known as ***separate chaining***. Assuming that we implement each nonempty bucket in a miniature dictionary as a log file in this way, we can perform the fundamental dictionary operations as follows:

- findElement(k):

  $B \leftarrow A[h(k)]$
  if B is empty **then**
    return NO_SUCH_KEY
  else
    {search for the key k in the sequence for this bucket}
    return B.findElement(k)

- insertItem(k,e):

  if $A[h(k)]$ is empty **then**
    Create a new initially empty, sequence-based dictionary B
    $A[h(k)] \leftarrow B$
  else
    $B \leftarrow A[h(k)]$
  B.insertItem(k,e)

- removeElement(k):

  $B \leftarrow A[h(k)]$
  if B is empty **then**
    return NO_SUCH_KEY
  else
    return B.removeElement(k)

Thus, for each of the fundamental dictionary operations involving a key k, we delegate the handling of this operation to the miniature sequence-based dictionary stored at $A[h(k)]$. So, an insertion will put the new item at the end of this sequence, a find will search through this sequence until it reaches the end or finds an item with the desired key, and a remove will additionally remove an item after it is found. We can "get away" with using the simple log-file dictionary implementation in these cases, because the spreading properties of the hash function help keep each miniature dictionary small. Indeed, a good hash function will try to minimize collisions as much as possible, which will imply that most of our buckets are either empty or store just a single item.

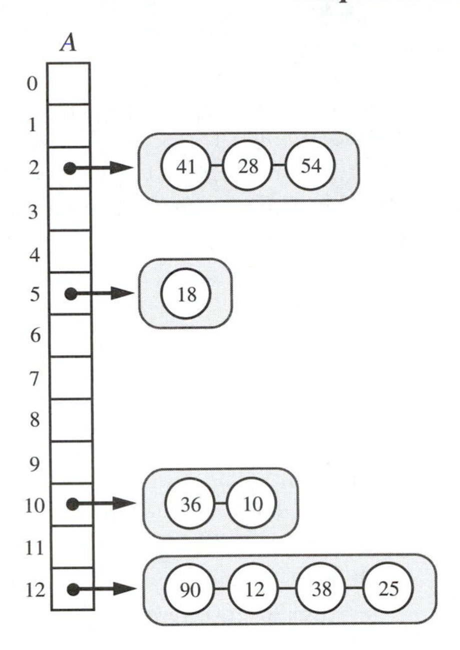

Figure 2.55: Example of a hash table of size 13, storing 10 integer keys, with collisions resolved by the chaining method. The compression map in this case is $h(k) = k \bmod 13$.

In Figure 2.55, we give an illustration of a simple hash table that uses the division compression function and separate chaining to resolve collisions.

Load Factors and Rehashing

Assuming that we are using a good hash function for holding the n items of our dictionary in a bucket array of capacity N, we expect each bucket to be of size n/N. This parameter, which is called the ***load factor*** of the hash table, should therefore be kept below a small constant, preferably below 1. For, given a good hash function, the expected running time of operations findElement, insertItem, and removeElement in a dictionary implemented with a hash table that uses this function is $O(\lceil n/N \rceil)$. Thus, we can implement the standard dictionary operations to run in $O(1)$ expected time, provided we know that n is $O(N)$.

Keeping a hash table's load factor a constant (0.75 is common) requires additional work whenever we add elements so as to exceed this bound. In such cases, in order to keep the load factor below the specified constant, we need to increase the size of our bucket array and change our compression map to match this new size. Moreover, we must then insert all the existing hash-table elements into the new bucket array using the new compression map. Such a size increase and hash table rebuild is called ***rehashing***. Following the approach of the extendable array (Section 1.5.2), a good choice is to rehash into an array roughly double the size of the original array, choosing the size of the new array to be a prime number.

Open Addressing

The separate chaining rule has many nice properties, such as allowing for simple implementations of dictionary operations, but it nevertheless has one slight disadvantage: it requires the use of an auxiliary data structure—a list, vector, or sequence—to hold items with colliding keys as a log file. We can handle collisions in other ways besides using the separate chaining rule, however. In particular, if space is of a premium, then we can use the alternative approach of always storing each item directly in a bucket, at most one item per bucket. This approach saves space because no auxiliary structures are employed, but it requires a bit more complexity to deal with collisions. There are several methods for implementing this approach, which is referred to as ***open addressing***.

Linear Probing

A simple open addressing collision-handling strategy is ***linear probing***. In this strategy, if we try to insert an item (k,e) into a bucket $A[i]$ that is already occupied, where $i = h(k)$, then we try next at $A[(i+1) \bmod N]$. If $A[(i+1) \bmod N]$ is occupied, then we try $A[(i+2) \bmod N]$, and so on, until we find an empty bucket in A that can accept the new item. Once this bucket is located, we simply insert the item (k,e) here. Of course, using this collision resolution strategy requires that we change the implementation of the findElement(k) operation. In particular, to perform such a search we must examine consecutive buckets, starting from $A[h(k)]$, until we either find an item with key equal to k or we find an empty bucket (in which case the search is unsuccessful). (See Figure 2.56.)

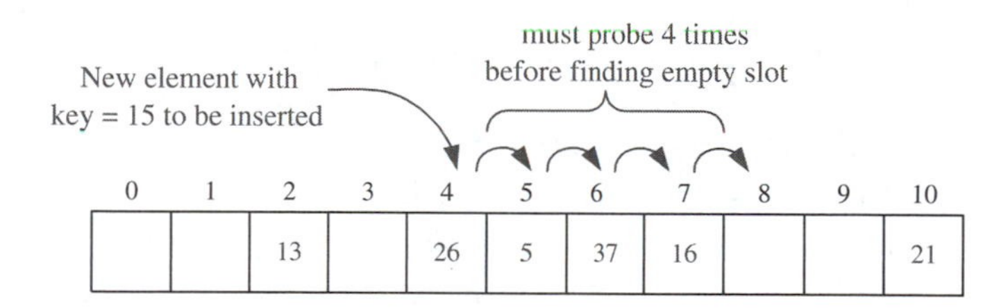

Figure 2.56: An insertion into a hash table using linear probing to resolve collisions. Here we use the compression map $h(k) = k \bmod 11$.

The operation removeElement(k) is more complicated than this, however. Indeed, to fully implement this method, we should restore the contents of the bucket array to look as though the item with key k was never inserted in its bucket $A[i]$ in the first place. Although performing such a restoration is certainly possible, it requires that we shift items down in buckets above $A[i]$, while not shifting others in this group (namely, the items that are already in their correct location). A typical way we can get around this difficulty is to replace the deleted item with a special "deactivated item" object. This object must be marked in some way so that we can immediately detect when it is occupying a given bucket. With this special marker possibly occupying buckets in our hash table, we modify our search algorithm for removeElement(k) or findElement(k), so that the search for a key k should skip over deactivated items and continue probing until reaching the desired item or an empty bucket. But our algorithm for the insertItem(k,e) should instead stop at a deactivated item and replace it with the new item to be inserted.

Linear probing saves space, but it complicates removals. Even with the use of the deactivated item object, the linear-probing collision-handling strategy suffers from an additional disadvantage. It tends to cluster the items of the dictionary into contiguous runs, which causes searches to slow down considerably.

Quadratic Probing

Another open addressing strategy, known as ***quadratic probing***, involves iteratively trying the buckets $A[(i+f(j)) \bmod N]$, for $j=0,1,2,\ldots$, where $f(j)=j^2$, until finding an empty bucket. As with linear probing, the quadratic probing strategy complicates the removal operation, but it does avoid the kinds of clustering patterns that occur with linear probing. Nevertheless, it creates its own kind of clustering, called ***secondary clustering***, where the set of filled array cells "bounces" around the array in a fixed pattern. If N is not chosen as a prime, then the quadratic probing strategy may not find an empty bucket in A even if one exists. In fact, even if N is prime, this strategy may not find an empty slot, if the bucket array is at least half full.

Double Hashing

Another open addressing strategy that does not cause clustering of the kind produced by linear probing or the kind produced by quadratic probing is the ***double hashing*** strategy. In this approach, we choose a secondary hash function, h', and if h maps some key k to a bucket $A[i]$, with $i=h(k)$, that is already occupied, then we iteratively try the buckets $A[(i+f(j)) \bmod N]$ next, for $j=1,2,3,\ldots$, where $f(j)=j\cdot h'(k)$. In this scheme, the secondary hash function is not allowed to evaluate to zero; a common choice is $h'(k)=q-(k \bmod q)$, for some prime number $q<N$. Also, N should be a prime. Moreover, we should choose a secondary hash function that will attempt to minimize clustering as much as possible.

These ***open addressing*** schemes save some space over the separate chaining method, but they are not necessarily faster. In experimental and theoretical analyses, the chaining method is either competitive or faster than the other methods, depending on the load factor of the bucket array. So, if memory space is not a major issue, the collision-handling method of choice seems to be separate chaining. Still, if memory space is in short supply, then one of these open addressing methods might be worth implementing, provided our probing strategy minimizes the clustering that can occur from open addressing.

2.5.6 Universal Hashing

In this section, we show how a hash function can be guaranteed to be good. In order to do this carefully, we need to make our discussion a bit more mathematical.

As we mentioned earlier, we can assume without loss of generality that our set of keys are integers in some range. Let $[0, M-1]$ be this range. Thus, we can view a hash function h as a mapping from integers in the range $[0, M-1]$ to integers in the range $[0, N-1]$, and we can view the set of candidate hash functions we are considering as a ***family*** H of hash functions. Such a family is ***universal*** if for any two integers j and k in the range $[0, M-1]$ and for a hash function chosen uniformly at random from H,

$$\Pr(h(j) = h(k)) \leq \frac{1}{N}.$$

Such a family is also known as a ***2-universal*** family of hash functions. The goal of choosing a good hash function can therefore be viewed as the problem of selecting a small universal family H of hash functions that are easy to compute. The reason universal families of hash functions are useful is that they result in a low expected number of collisions.

Theorem 2.13: *Let j be an integer in the range $[0, M-1]$, let S be a set of n integers in this same range, and let h be a hash function chosen uniformly, at random, from a universal family of hash functions from integers in the range $[0, M-1]$ to integers in the range $[0, N-1]$. Then the expected number of collisions between j and the integers in S is at most n/N.*

Proof: Let $c_h(j, S)$ denote the number of collisions between j and integers in S (that is, $c_h(j, S) = |\{k \in S : h(j) = h(k)\}|$). The quantity we are interested in is the expected value $E(c_h(j, S))$. We can write $c_h(j, S)$ as

$$c_h(j, S) = \sum_{k \in S} X_{j,k},$$

where $X_{j,k}$ is a random variable that is 1 if $h(j) = h(k)$ and is 0 otherwise (that is, $X_{j,k}$ is an ***indicator*** random variable for a collision between j and k). By the linearity of expectation,

$$E(c_h(j, S)) = \sum_{s \in S} E(X_{j,k}).$$

Also, by the definition of a universal family, $E(X_{j,k}) \leq 1/N$. Thus,

$$E(c_h(j, S)) \leq \sum_{s \in S} \frac{1}{N} = \frac{n}{N}.$$

■

Put another way, this theorem states that the expected number of collisions between a hash code j and the keys already in a hash table (using a hash function chosen at random from a universal family H) is at most the current load factor of the hash table. Since the time to perform a search, insertion, or deletion for a key j in a hash table that uses the chaining collision-resolution rule is proportional to the number of collisions between j and the other keys in the table, this implies that the expected running time of any such operation is proportional to the hash table's load factor. This is exactly what we want.

Let us turn our attention, then, to the problem of constructing a small universal family of hash functions that are easy to compute. The set of hash functions we construct is actually similar to the final family we considered at the end of the previous section. Let p be a prime number greater than or equal to the number of hash codes M but less than $2M$ (and there must always be such a prime number, according to a mathematical fact known as ***Bertrand's Postulate***).

Define H as the set of hash functions of the form

$$h_{a,b}(k) = (ak + b \bmod p) \bmod N.$$

The following theorem establishes that this family of hash functions is universal.

Theorem 2.14: *The family $H = \{h_{a,b} : 0 < a < p \text{ and } 0 \le b < p\}$ is universal.*

Proof: Let Z denote the set of integers in the range $[0, p-1]$. Let us separate each hash function $h_{a,b}$ into the functions

$$f_{a,b}(k) = ak + b \bmod p$$

and

$$g(k) = k \bmod N,$$

so that $h_{a,b}(k) = g(f_{a,b}(k))$. The set of functions $f_{a,b}$ defines a family of hash functions F that map integers in Z to integers in Z. We claim that each function in F causes no collisions at all. To justify this claim, consider $f_{a,b}(j)$ and $f_{a,b}(k)$ for some pair of different integers j and k in Z. If $f_{a,b}(j) = f_{a,b}(k)$, then we would have a collision. But, recalling the definition of the modulo operation, this would imply that

$$aj + b - \left\lfloor \frac{aj+b}{p} \right\rfloor p = ak + b - \left\lfloor \frac{ak+b}{p} \right\rfloor p.$$

Without loss of generality, we can assume that $k < j$, which implies that

$$a(j-k) = \left(\left\lfloor \frac{aj+b}{p} \right\rfloor - \left\lfloor \frac{ak+b}{p} \right\rfloor \right) p.$$

Since $a \neq 0$ and $k < j$, this in turn implies that $a(j-k)$ is a multiple of p. But $a < p$ and $j - k < p$, so there is no way that $a(j-k)$ can be a positive multiple of p, because p is prime (remember that every positive integer can be factored into a product of primes). So it is impossible for $f_{a,b}(j) = f_{a,b}(k)$ if $j \neq k$. To put this another way, each $f_{a,b}$ maps the integers in Z to the integers in Z in a way that defines a one-to-one correspondence. Since the functions in F cause no collisions, the only way that a function $h_{a,b}$ can cause a collision is for the function g to cause a collision.

Let j and k be two different integers in Z. Also, let $c(j,k)$ denote the number of functions in H that map j and k to the same integer (that is, that cause j and k to collide). We can derive an upper bound for $c(j,k)$ by using a simple counting argument. If we consider any integer x in Z, there are p different functions $f_{a,b}$ such that $f_{a,b}(j) = x$ (since we can choose a b for each choice of a to make this so). Let us now fix x and note that each such function $f_{a,b}$ maps k to a unique integer

$$y = f_{a,b}(k)$$

in Z with $x \neq y$. Moreover, of the p different integers of the form $y = f_{a,b}(k)$, there are at most

$$\lceil p/N \rceil - 1$$

such that $g(y) = g(x)$ and $x \neq y$ (by the definition of g). Thus, for any x in Z, there are at most $\lceil p/N \rceil - 1$ functions $h_{a,b}$ in H such that

$$x = f_{a,b}(j) \quad \text{and} \quad h_{a,b}(j) = h_{a,b}(k).$$

Since there are p choices for the integer x in Z, the above counting arguments imply that

$$\begin{aligned} c(j,k) &\leq p\left(\left\lceil \frac{p}{N} \right\rceil - 1\right) \\ &\leq \frac{p(p-1)}{N}. \end{aligned}$$

There are $p(p-1)$ functions in H, since each function $h_{a,b}$ is determined by a pair (a,b) such that $0 < a < p$ and $0 \leq b < p$. Thus, picking a function uniformly at random from H involves picking one of $p(p-1)$ functions. Therefore, for any two different integers j and k in Z,

$$\begin{aligned} \Pr(h_{a,b}(j) = h_{a,b}(k)) &\leq \frac{p(p-1)/N}{p(p-1)} \\ &= \frac{1}{N}. \end{aligned}$$

That is, the family H is universal. ■

In addition to being universal, the functions in H have a number of other nice properties. Each function in H is easy to select, since doing so simply requires that we select a pair of random integers a and b such that $0 < a < p$ and $0 \leq b < p$. In addition, each function in H is easy to compute in $O(1)$ time, requiring just one multiplication, one addition, and two applications of the modulus function. Thus, any hash function chosen uniformly at random in H will result in an implementation of the dictionary ADT so that the fundamental operations all have expected running times that are $O(\lceil n/N \rceil)$, since we are using the chaining rule for collision resolution.

2.6 Java Example: Heap

In order to better illustrate how the methods of the tree ADT and the priority queue ADT could interact in a concrete implementation of the heap data structure, we discuss a case study implementation of the heap data structure in Java in this section. Specifically, a Java implementation of a heap-based priority queue is shown in Algorithms 2.57–2.60. To aid in modularity, we delegate the maintenance of the structure of the heap itself to a data structure, called ***heap-tree***, that extends a binary tree and provides the following additional specialized update methods:

add(o): Performs the following sequence of operations:
expandExternal(z);
replaceElement(z,o);
return z;
such that z becomes the last node of the tree at the end of the operation.

remove(): Performs the following sequence of operations:
$t \leftarrow z$.element();
removeAboveExternal(rightChild(z));
return t;
where z is the last node at the beginning of the operation.

That is, the add operation adds a new element at the first external node, and the remove operation removes the element at the last node. Using a vector-based implementation of a tree (see Section 2.3.4), operations add and remove take $O(1)$ time. The heap-tree ADT is represented by the Java interface HeapTree shown in Algorithm 2.57. We assume that a Java class VectorHeapTree (not shown) implements the HeapTree interface with a vector and supports methods add and remove in $O(1)$ time.

```
public interface HeapTree extends InspectableBinaryTree, PositionalContainer {
  public Position add(Object elem);
  public Object remove();
}
```

Code Fragment 2.57: Interface HeapTree for a heap-tree. It extends the interface InspectableBinaryTree with methods replaceElement and swapElements, inherited from the PositionalContainer interface, and adds the specialized update methods add and remove.

Class HeapPriorityQueue implements the PriorityQueue interface using a heap. It is shown in Algorithms 2.58 and 2.60. Note that we store key-element items of class Item, which is simply a class for key-element pairs, into the heap-tree.

```
public class HeapPriorityQueue implements PriorityQueue {
  HeapTree T;
  Comparator comp;

  public HeapPriorityQueue(Comparator c) {
    if ((comp = c) == null)
      throw new IllegalArgumentException("Null comparator passed");
    T = new VectorHeapTree();
  }

  public int size() {
    return (T.size() - 1) / 2;
  }

  public boolean isEmpty() {
    return T.size() == 1; }

  public Object minElement() throws PriorityQueueEmptyException {
    if (isEmpty())
      throw new PriorityQueueEmptyException("Empty Priority Queue");
    return element(T.root());
  }

  public Object minKey() throws PriorityQueueEmptyException {
    if (isEmpty())
      throw new PriorityQueueEmptyException("Empty Priority Queue");
    return key(T.root());
  }

⋮
```

Code Fragment 2.58: Instance variables, constructor, and methods size, isEmpty, minElement, and minKey of class HeapPriorityQueue, which implements a priority queue by means of a heap. Other methods of this class are shown in Algorithm 2.60. The auxiliary methods key and element extract the key and element of an item of the priority queue stored at at given position of the heap-tree.

```
public void insertItem(Object k, Object e) throws InvalidKeyException {
  if (!comp.isComparable(k))
    throw new InvalidKeyException("Invalid Key");
  Position z = T.add(new Item(k, e));
  Position u;
  while (!T.isRoot(z)) { // up-heap bubbling
    u = T.parent(z);
    if (comp.isLessThanOrEqualTo(key(u), key(z)))
      break;
    T.swapElements(u, z);
    z = u;
  }
}

public Object removeMin() throws PriorityQueueEmptyException {
  if (isEmpty())
    throw new PriorityQueueEmptyException("Empty priority queue!");
  Object min = element(T.root());
  if (size() == 1)
    T.remove();
  else {
    T.replaceElement(T.root(), T.remove());
    Position r = T.root();
    while (T.isInternal(T.leftChild(r))) { // down-heap bubbling
      Position s;
      if (T.isExternal(T.rightChild(r)) ||
          comp.isLessThanOrEqualTo(key(T.leftChild(r)), key(T.rightChild(r))))
        s = T.leftChild(r);
      else
        s = T.rightChild(r);
      if (comp.isLessThan(key(s), key(r))) {
        T.swapElements(r, s);
        r = s;
      }
      else
        break;
    }
  }
  return min;
}
```

Code Fragment 2.60: Methods insertItem and removeMin of class HeapPriorityQueue. Other methods of this class are shown in Algorithm 2.58.

2.7 Exercises

Reinforcement

R-2.1 Describe, using pseudo-code, implementations of the methods insertBefore(p,e), insertFirst(e), and insertLast(e) of the list ADT, assuming the list is implemented using a doubly linked list.

R-2.2 Draw an expression tree that has four external nodes, storing the numbers 1, 5, 6, and 7 (with each number stored one per external node but not necessarily in this order), and has three internal nodes, each storing an operation from the set $\{+,-,\times,/\}$ of binary arithmetic operators, so that the value of the root is 21. The operators are assumed to return rational numbers (not integers), and an operator may be used more than once (but we only store one operator per internal node).

R-2.3 Let T be an ordered tree with more than one node. Is it possible that the preorder traversal of T visits the nodes in the same order as the postorder traversal of T? If so, give an example; otherwise, argue why this cannot occur. Likewise, is it possible that the preorder traversal of T visits the nodes in the reverse order of the postorder traversal of T? If so, give an example; otherwise, argue why this cannot occur.

R-2.4 Answer the following questions so as to justify Theorem 2.8.

a. Draw a binary tree with height 7 and maximum number of external nodes.
b. What is the minimum number of external nodes for a binary tree with height h? Justify your answer.
c. What is the maximum number of external nodes for a binary tree with height h? Justify your answer.
d. Let T be a binary tree with height h and n nodes. Show that

$$\log(n+1)-1 \le h \le (n-1)/2.$$

e. For which values of n and h can the above lower and upper bounds on h be attained with equality?

R-2.5 Let T be a binary tree such that all the external nodes have the same depth. Let D_e be the sum of the depths of all the external nodes of T, and let D_i be the sum of the depths of all the internal nodes of T. Find constants a and b such that

$$D_e + 1 = aD_i + bn,$$

where n is the number of nodes of T.

R-2.6 Let T be a binary tree with n nodes, and let p be the level numbering of the nodes of T, as given in Section 2.3.4.

a. Show that, for every node v of T, $p(v) \le 2^{(n+1)/2}-1$.
b. Show an example of a binary tree with at least five nodes that attains the above upper bound on the maximum value of $p(v)$ for some node v.

R-2.7 Let T be a binary tree with n nodes that is realized with a vector, S, and let p be the level numbering of the nodes in T, as given in Section 2.3.4. Give pseudo-code descriptions of each of the methods root, parent, leftChild, rightChild, isInternal, isExternal, and isRoot.

R-2.8 Illustrate the performance of the selection-sort algorithm on the following input sequence: $(22, 15, 36, 44, 10, 3, 9, 13, 29, 25)$.

R-2.9 Illustrate the performance of the insertion-sort algorithm on the input sequence of the previous problem.

R-2.10 Give an example of a worst-case sequence with n elements for insertion-sort, and show that insertion-sort runs in $\Omega(n^2)$ time on such a sequence.

R-2.11 Where may an item with largest key be stored in a heap?

R-2.12 Illustrate the performance of the heap-sort algorithm on the following input sequence: $(2, 5, 16, 4, 10, 23, 39, 18, 26, 15)$.

R-2.13 Suppose a binary tree T is implemented using a vector S, as described in Section 2.3.4. If n items are stored in S in sorted order, starting with index 1, is the tree T a heap?

R-2.14 Is there a heap T storing seven distinct elements such that a preorder traversal of T yields the elements of T in sorted order? How about an inorder traversal? How about a postorder traversal?

R-2.15 Show that the sum $\sum_{i=1}^{n} \log i$, which appears in the analysis of heap-sort, is $\Omega(n \log n)$.

R-2.16 Show the steps for removing key 16 from the heap of Figure 2.41.

R-2.17 Show the steps for replacing 5 with 18 in the heap of Figure 2.41.

R-2.18 Draw an example of a heap whose keys are all the odd numbers from 1 to 59 (with no repeats), such that the insertion of an item with key 32 would cause up-heap bubbling to proceed all the way up to a child of the root (replacing that child's key with 32).

R-2.19 Draw the 11-item hash table resulting from hashing the keys 12, 44, 13, 88, 23, 94, 11, 39, 20, 16, and 5, using the hash function $h(i) = (2i + 5) \bmod 11$ and assuming collisions are handled by chaining.

R-2.20 What is the result of the previous exercise, assuming collisions are handled by linear probing?

R-2.21 Show the result of Exercise R-2.19, assuming collisions are handled by quadratic probing, up to the point where the method fails because no empty slot is found.

R-2.22 What is the result of Exercise R-2.19 assuming collisions are handled by double hashing using a secondary hash function $h'(k) = 7 - (k \bmod 7)$?

R-2.23 Give a pseudo-code description of an insertion into a hash table that uses quadratic probing to resolve collisions, assuming we also use the trick of replacing deleted items with a special "deactivated item" object.

R-2.24 Show the result of rehashing the hash table shown in Figure 2.55 into a table of size 19 using the new hash function $h(k) = 2k \bmod 19$.

Creativity

C-2.1 Describe, in pseudo-code, a link-hopping method for finding the middle node of a doubly linked list with header and trailer sentinels, and an odd number of real nodes between them. (Note: This method must only use link hopping; it cannot use a counter.) What is the running time of this method?

C-2.2 Describe how to implement the queue ADT using two stacks, so that the amortized running time for dequeue and enqueue is $O(1)$, assuming that the stacks support constant time push, pop, and size methods. What is the running time of the enqueue() and dequeue() methods in this case?

C-2.3 Describe how to implement the stack ADT using two queues. What is the running time of the push() and pop() methods in this case?

C-2.4 Describe a recursive algorithm for enumerating all permutations of the numbers $\{1,2,\ldots,n\}$. What is the running time of your method?

C-2.5 Describe the structure and pseudo-code for an array-based implementation of the vector ADT that achieves $O(1)$ time for insertions and removals at rank 0, as well as insertions and removals at the end of the vector. Your implementation should also provide for a constant-time elemAtRank method.

C-2.6 In the children's game "hot potato," a group of n children sit in a circle passing an object, called the "potato," around the circle (say in a clockwise direction). The children continue passing the potato until a leader rings a bell, at which point the child holding the potato must leave the game, and the other children close up the circle. This process is then continued until there is only one child remaining, who is declared the winner. Using the sequence ADT, describe an efficient method for implementing this game. Suppose the leader always rings the bell immediately after the potato has been passed k times. (Determining the last child remaining in this variation of hot potato is known as the ***Josephus problem***.) What is the running time of your method in terms of n and k, assuming the sequence is implemented with a doubly linked list? What if the sequence is implemented with an array?

C-2.7 Using the Sequence ADT, describe an efficient way of putting a sequence representing a deck of n cards into random order. Use the function randomInt(n), which returns a random number between 0 and $n-1$, inclusive. Your method should guarantee that every possible ordering is equally likely. What is the running time of your method, if the sequence is implemented with an array? What if it is implemented with a linked list?

C-2.8 Design an algorithm for drawing a binary tree, using quantities computed in a tree traversal.

C-2.9 Design algorithms for the following operations for a node v in a binary tree T:

- preorderNext(v): return the node visited after v in a preorder traversal of T
- inorderNext(v): return the node visited after v in an inorder traversal of T
- postorderNext(v): return the node visited after v in a postorder traversal of T.

What are the worst-case running times of your algorithms?

C-2.10 Give an $O(n)$-time algorithm for computing the depth of all the nodes of a tree T, where n is the number of nodes of T.

C-2.11 The ***balance factor*** of an internal node v of a binary tree is the difference between the heights of the right and left subtrees of v. Show how to specialize the Euler tour traversal to print the balance factors of all the nodes of a binary tree.

C-2.12 Two ordered trees T' and T'' are said to be ***isomorphic*** if one of the following holds:

- Both T' and T'' consist of a single node
- Both T' and T'' have the same number k of subtrees, and the ith subtree of T' is isomorphic to the ith subtree of T'', for $i = 1, \ldots, k$.

Design an algorithm that tests whether two given ordered trees are isomorphic. What is the running time of your algorithm?

C-2.13 Let a visit action in the Euler tour traversal be denoted by a pair (v,a), where v is the visited node and a is one of ***left***, ***below***, or ***right***. Design an algorithm for performing operation tourNext(v,a), which returns the visit action (w,b) following (v,a). What is the worst-case running time of your algorithm?

C-2.14 Show how to represent an improper binary tree by means of a proper one.

C-2.15 Let T be a binary tree with n nodes. Define a ***Roman node*** to be a node v in T, such that the number of descendents in v's left subtree differ from the number of descendents in v's right subtree by at most 5. Describe a linear-time method for finding each node v of T, such that v is not a Roman node, but all of v's descendents are Roman nodes.

C-2.16 In pseudo-code, describe a nonrecursive method for performing an Euler tour traversal of a binary tree that runs in linear time and does not use a stack.

Hint: You can tell which visit action to perform at a node by taking note of where you are coming from.

C-2.17 In pseudo-code, describe a nonrecursive method for performing an inorder traversal of a binary tree in linear time.

C-2.18 Let T be a binary tree with n nodes (T may or may not be realized with a vector). Give a linear-time method that uses the methods of the BinaryTree interface to traverse the nodes of T by increasing values of the level numbering function p given in Section 2.3.4. This traversal is known as the ***level order traversal***.

C-2.19 The ***path length*** of a tree T is the sum of the depths of all the nodes in T. Describe a linear-time method for computing the path length of a tree T (which is not necessarily binary).

C-2.20 Define the ***internal path length***, $I(T)$, of a tree T to be the sum of the depths of all the internal nodes in T. Likewise, define the ***external path length***, $E(T)$, of a tree T to be the sum of the depths of all the external nodes in T. Show that if T is a binary tree with n internal nodes, then $E(T) = I(T) + 2n$.

C-2.21 Let T be a tree with n nodes. Define the ***lowest common ancestor*** (LCA) between two nodes v and w as the lowest node in T that has both v and w as descendents (where we allow a node to be a descendent of itself). Given two nodes v and w, describe an efficient algorithm for finding the LCA of v and w. What is the running time of your method?

C-2.22 Let T be a tree with n nodes, and, for any node v in T, let d_v denote the depth of v in T. The ***distance*** between two nodes v and w in T is $d_v + d_w - 2d_u$, where u is the LCA u of v and w (as defined in the previous exercise). The ***diameter*** of T is the maximum distance between two nodes in T. Describe an efficient algorithm for finding the diameter of T. What is the running time of your method?

C-2.23 Suppose we are given a collection S of n intervals of the form $[a_i, b_i]$. Design an efficient algorithm for computing the union of all the intervals in S. What is the running time of your method?

C-2.24 Assuming the input to the sorting problem is given in an array A, describe how to implement the selection-sort algorithm using only the array A and at most six additional (base-type) variables.

C-2.25 Assuming the input to the sorting problem is given in an array A, describe how to implement the insertion-sort algorithm using only the array A and at most six additional (base-type) variables.

C-2.26 Assuming the input to the sorting problem is given in an array A, describe how to implement the heap-sort algorithm using only the array A and at most six additional (base-type) variables.

C-2.27 Suppose the binary tree T used to implement a heap can be accessed using only the methods of the binary tree ADT. That is, we cannot assume T is implemented as a vector. Given a reference to the current last node, v, describe an efficient algorithm for finding the insertion point (that is, the new last node) using just the methods of the binary tree interface. Be sure and handle all possible cases. What is the running time of this method?

C-2.28 Show that, for any n, there is a sequence of insertions in a heap that requires $\Omega(n \log n)$ time to process.

C-2.29 We can represent a path from the root to a node of a binary tree by means of a binary string, where 0 means "go to the left child" and 1 means "go to the right child." Design a logarithmic-time algorithm for finding the last node of a heap holding n elements based on the this representation.

C-2.30 Show that the problem of finding the kth smallest element in a heap takes at least $\Omega(k)$ time in the worst case.

C-2.31 Develop an algorithm that computes the kth smallest element of a set of n distinct integers in $O(n + k \log n)$ time.

C-2.32 Let T be a heap storing n keys. Give an efficient algorithm for reporting all the keys in T that are smaller than or equal to a given query key x (which is not necessarily in T). For example, given the heap of Figure 2.41 and query key $x = 7$, the algorithm should report 4, 5, 6, 7. Note that the keys do not need to be reported in sorted order. Ideally, your algorithm should run in $O(k)$ time, where k is the number of keys reported.

C-2.33 The hash table dictionary implementation requires that we find a prime number between a number M and a number $2M$. Implement a method for finding such a prime by using the ***sieve algorithm***. In this algorithm, we allocate a $2M$ cell Boolean array A, such that cell i is associated with the integer i. We then initialize the array cells to all be "true" and we "mark off" all the cells that are multiples of 2, 3, 5, 7, and so on. This process can stop after it reaches a number larger than $\sqrt{2M}$.

C-2.34 Give the pseudo-code description for performing a removal from a hash table that uses linear probing to resolve collisions where we do not use a special marker to represent deleted elements. That is, we must rearrange the contents of the hash table so that it appears that the removed item was never inserted in the first place.

C-2.35 The quadratic probing strategy has a clustering problem that relates to the way it looks for open slots when a collision occurs. Namely, when a collision occurs at bucket $h(k)$, we check $A[(h(k)+f(j)) \bmod N]$, for $f(j) = j^2$, using $j = 1,2,\ldots,N-1$.

a. Show that $f(j) \bmod N$ will assume at most $(N+1)/2$ distinct values, for N prime, as j ranges from 1 to $N-1$. As a part of this justification, note that $f(R) = f(N-R)$ for all R.

b. A better strategy is to choose a prime N such that N is congruent to 3 modulo 4 and then to check the buckets $A[(h(k) \pm j^2) \bmod N]$ as j ranges from 1 to $(N-1)/2$, alternating between addition and subtraction. Show that this alternate type of quadratic probing is guaranteed to check every bucket in A.

Projects

P-2.1 Write a program that takes as input a fully parenthesized arithmetic expression and converts it to a binary expression tree. Your program should display the tree in some way and also print the value associated with the root. For an additional challenge, allow for the leaves to store variables of the form x_1, x_2, x_3, and so on, which are initially 0 and which can be updated interactively by your program, with the corresponding update in the printed value of the root of the expression tree.

P-2.2 Write an applet or stand-alone graphical program that animates a heap. Your program should support all the priority queue operations and it should visualize the operations of the up-heap and down-heap bubbling procedures. (Extra: Visualize bottom-up heap construction as well.)

P-2.3 Perform a comparative analysis that studies the collision rates for various hash codes for character strings, such as various polynomial hash codes for different values of the parameter a. Use a hash table to determine collisions, but only count collisions where different strings map to the same hash code (not if they map to the same location in this hash table). Test these hash codes on text files found on the Internet.

P-2.4 Perform a comparative analysis as in the previous exercise but for 10-digit telephone numbers instead of character strings.

Chapter Notes

The basic data structures of stacks, queues, and linked lists discussed in this chapter belong to the folklore of computer science. They were first chronicled by Knuth in his seminal book on *Fundamental Algorithms* [117]. In this chapter, we have taken the approach of defining the basic data structures of stacks, queues, and deques, first in terms of their ADTs and then in terms of concrete implementations. This approach to data structure specification and implementation is an outgrowth of software engineering advances brought on by the object-oriented design approach, and is now considered a standard approach for teaching data structures. We were introduced to this approach to data structure design by the classic books by Aho, Hopcroft, and Ullman on data structures and algorithms [7, 8]. For further study of abstract data types, please see the book by Liskov and Guttag [135], the survey paper by Cardelli and Wegner [44], or the book chapter by Demurjian [57]. The naming conventions we use for the methods of the stack, queue, and deque ADTs are taken from JDSL [86]. JDSL is a data structures library in Java that builds on approaches taken for C++ in the libraries STL [158] and LEDA [151]. We shall use this convention throughout this text. In this chapter, we motivated the study of stacks and queues from implementation issues in Java. The reader interested in learning more about the Java run-time environment known as the Java Virtual Machine (JVM) is referred to the book by Lindholm and Yellin [134] that defines the JVM.

Sequences and iterators are pervasive concepts in the C++ Standard Template Library (STL) [158], and they play fundamental roles in JDSL, the data structures library in Java. The sequence ADT is a generalization and extension of the Java java.util.Vector API (for example, see the book by Arnold and Gosling [13]) and the list ADTs proposed by several authors, including Aho, Hopcroft, and Ullman [8], who introduce the "position" abstraction, and Wood [211], who defines a list ADT similar to ours. Implementations of sequences via arrays and linked lists are discussed in Knuth's seminal book, *Fundamental Algorithms* [118]. Knuth's companion volume, *Sorting and Searching* [119], describes the bubble-sort method and the history of this and other sorting algorithms.

The concept of viewing data structures as containers (and other principles of object-oriented design) can be found in object-oriented design books by Booch [32] and Budd [42]. The concept also exists under the name "collection class" in books by Golberg and Robson [79] and Liskov and Guttag [135]. Our use of the "position" abstraction derives from the "position" and "node" abstractions introduced by Aho, Hopcroft, and Ullman [8]. Discussions of the classic preorder, inorder, and postorder tree traversal methods can be found in Knuth's *Fundamental Algorithms* book [118]. The Euler tour traversal technique comes from the parallel algorithms community, as it is introduced by Tarjan and Vishkin [197] and is discussed by JáJá [107] and by Karp and Ramachandran [114]. The algorithm for drawing a tree is generally considered to be a part of the "folklore" of graph drawing algorithms. The reader interested in graph drawing is referred to works by Tamassia [194] and Di Battista *et al.* [58, 59]. The puzzler in Exercise R-2.2 was communicated by Micha Sharir.

Knuth's book on sorting and searching [119] describes the motivation and history for the selection-sort, insertion-sort, and heap-sort algorithms. The heap-sort algorithm is due to Williams [210], and the linear-time heap construction algorithm is due to Floyd [70]. Additional algorithms and analyses for heaps and heap-sort variations can be found in papers by Bentley [29], Carlsson [45], Gonnet and Munro [82], McDiarmid and Reed [141], and Schaffer and Sedgewick [178]. The locator pattern (also described in [86]), appears to be new.

Chapter

3 Search Trees and Skip Lists

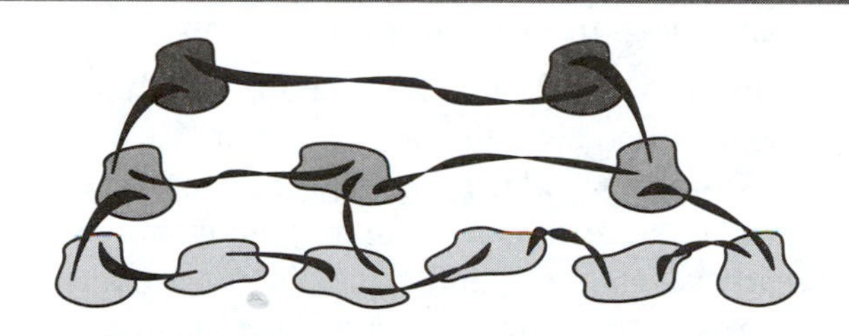

Contents

3.1 Ordered Dictionaries and Binary Search Trees 141

3.1.1 Sorted Tables 142

3.1.2 Binary Search Trees 145

3.1.3 Searching in a Binary Search Tree 146

3.1.4 Insertion in a Binary Search Tree 148

3.1.5 Removal in a Binary Search Tree 149

3.1.6 Performance of Binary Search Trees 151

3.2 AVL Trees 152

3.2.1 Update Operations 154

3.2.2 Performance 158

3.3 Bounded-Depth Search Trees 159

3.3.1 Multi-Way Search Trees 159

3.3.2 (2,4) Trees 163

3.3.3 Red-Black Trees 170

3.4 Splay Trees 185

3.4.1 Splaying 185

3.4.2 Amortized Analysis of Splaying 191

3.5 Skip Lists 195

3.5.1 Searching 197

3.5.2 Update Operations 198

3.5.3 A Probabilistic Analysis of Skip Lists 200

3.6 Java Example: AVL and Red-Black Trees 202

3.6.1 Java Implementation of AVL Trees 206

3.6.2 Java Implementation of Red-Black Trees 209

3.7 Exercises 212

People like choices. We like to have different ways of solving the same problem, so that we can explore different trade-offs and efficiencies. This chapter is devoted to the exploration of different ways of implementing an ordered dictionary. We begin this chapter by discussing binary search trees, and how they support a simple tree-based implementation of an ordered dictionary, but do not guarantee efficient worst-case performance. Nevertheless, they form the basis of many tree-based dictionary implementations, and we discuss several in this chapter. One of the classic implementations is the AVL tree, presented in Section 3.2, which is a binary search tree that achieves logarithmic-time search and update operations.

In Section 3.3, we introduce the concept of bounded-depth trees, which keep all external nodes at the same depth or "pseudo-depth." One such tree is the multi-way search tree, which is an ordered tree where each internal node can store several items and have several children. A multi-way search tree is a generalization of the binary search tree, and like the binary search tree, it can be specialized into an efficient data structure for ordered dictionaries. A specific kind of multi-way search tree discussed in Section 3.3 is the $(2,4)$ tree, which is a bounded-depth search tree in which each internal node stores 1, 2, or 3 keys and has 2, 3, or 4 children, respectively. The advantage of these trees is that they have algorithms for inserting and removing keys that are simple and intuitive. Update operations rearrange a $(2,4)$ tree by means of natural operations that split and merge "nearby" nodes or transfer keys between them. A $(2,4)$ tree storing n items uses $O(n)$ space and supports searches, insertions, and removals in $O(\log n)$ worst-case time. Another kind of bounded-depth search tree studied in this section is the red-black tree. These are binary search trees whose nodes are colored "red" and "black" in such a way that the coloring scheme guarantees each external node is at the same (logarithmic) "black depth." The pseudo-depth notion of black depth results from an illuminating correspondence between red-black and $(2,4)$ trees. Using this correspondence, we motivate and provide intuition for the somewhat more complex algorithms for insertion and removal in red-black trees, which are based on rotations and recolorings. An advantage that a red-black tree achieves over other binary search trees (such as AVL trees) is that it can be restructured after an insertion or removal with only $O(1)$ rotations.

In Section 3.4, we discuss splay trees, which are attractive due to the simplicity of their search and update methods. Splay trees are binary search trees that, after each search, insertion, or deletion, move the node accessed up to the root by means of a carefully choreographed sequence of rotations. This simple "move-to-the-top" heuristic helps this data structure ***adapt*** itself to the kinds of operations being performed. One of the results of this heuristic is that splay trees guarantee that the amortized running time of each dictionary operation is logarithmic.

Finally, in Section 3.5, we discuss skip lists, which are not a tree data structure, but nevertheless have a notion of depth that keeps all elements at logarithmic depth. These structures are randomized, however, so their depth bounds are probabilistic. In particular, we show that with very high probability the height of a skip list storing

n elements is $O(\log n)$. This is admittedly not as strong as a true worst-case bound, but the update operations for skip lists are quite simple and they compare favorably to search trees in practice.

We focus on the practice of implementing binary search trees in Section 3.6, giving Java implementations for both AVL and red-black trees. We highlight how both of these data structures can build upon the tree ADT discussed in Section 2.3.

There are admittedly quite a few kinds of search structures discussed in this chapter, and we recognize that a reader or instructor with limited time might be interested in studying only selected topics. For this reason, we have designed this chapter so that each section can be studied independent of any other section except for the first section, which we present next.

3.1 Ordered Dictionaries and Binary Search Trees

In an ordered dictionary, we wish to perform the usual dictionary operations, discussed in Section 2.5.1, such as the operations findElement(k), insertItem(k,e), and removeElement(k), but also maintain an order relation for the keys in our dictionary. We can use a comparator to provide the order relation among keys, and, as we will see, such an ordering helps us to efficiently implement the dictionary ADT. In addition, an ordered dictionary also supports the following methods:

closestKeyBefore(k): Return the key of the item with largest key less than or equal to k.

closestElemBefore(k): Return the element for the item with largest key less than or equal to k.

closestKeyAfter(k): Return the key of the item with smallest key greater than or equal to k.

closestElemAfter(k): Return the element for the item with smallest key greater than or equal to k.

Each of these methods returns the special NO_SUCH_KEY object if no item in the dictionary satisfies the query.

The ordered nature of the above operations makes the use of a log file or a hash table inappropriate for implementing the dictionary, for neither of these data structures maintains any ordering information for the keys in the dictionary. Indeed, hash tables achieve their best search speeds when their keys are distributed almost at random. Thus, we should consider new dictionary implementations when dealing with ordered dictionaries.

Having defined the dictionary abstract data type, let us now look at some simple ways of implementing this ADT.

3.1.1 Sorted Tables

If a dictionary D is ordered, we can store its items in a vector S by nondecreasing order of the keys. We specify that S is a vector, rather than a general sequence, for the ordering of the keys in the vector S allows for faster searching than would be possible had S been, say, a linked list. We refer to this ordered vector implementation of a dictionary D as a ***lookup table***. We contrast this implementation with the log file, which uses an unordered sequence to implement the dictionary.

The space requirement of the lookup table is $\Theta(n)$, which is similar to the log file, assuming we grow and shrink the array supporting the vector S to keep the size of this array proportional to the number of items in S. Unlike a log file, however, performing updates in a lookup table takes a considerable amount of time. In particular, performing the insertItem(k,e) operation in a lookup table requires $O(n)$ time in the worst case, since we need to shift up all the items in the vector with key greater than k to make room for the new item (k,e). The lookup table implementation is therefore inferior to the log file in terms of the worst-case running times of the dictionary update operations. Nevertheless, we can perform the operation findElement much faster in a sorted lookup table.

Binary Search

A significant advantage of using an array-based vector S to implement an ordered dictionary D with n items is that accessing an element of S by its ***rank*** takes $O(1)$ time. We recall from Section 2.2.1 that the rank of an element in a vector is the number of elements preceding it. Thus, the first element in S has rank 0, and the last element has rank $n-1$.

The elements in S are the items of dictionary D, and since S is ordered, the item at rank i has a key no smaller than keys of the items at ranks $0,\ldots,i-1$, and no larger than keys of the items at ranks $i+1,\ldots,n-1$. This observation allows us to quickly "home in" on a search key k using a variant of the children's game "high-low." We call an item I of D a ***candidate*** if, at the current stage of the search, we cannot rule out that I has key equal to k. The algorithm maintains two parameters, low and high, such that all the candidate items have rank at least low and at most high in S. Initially, $\mathsf{low}=0$ and $\mathsf{high}=n-1$, and we let $\mathsf{key}(i)$ denote the key at rank i, which has $\mathsf{elem}(i)$ as its element. We then compare k to the key of the median candidate, that is, the item with rank

$$\mathsf{mid} = \lfloor(\mathsf{low}+\mathsf{high})/2\rfloor.$$

We consider three cases:

- If $k=\mathsf{key}(\mathsf{mid})$, then we have found the item we were looking for, and the search terminates successfully returning $\mathsf{elem}(\mathsf{mid})$.
- If $k<\mathsf{key}(\mathsf{mid})$, then we recur on the first half of the vector, that is, on the range of ranks from low to $\mathsf{mid}-1$.
- If $k>\mathsf{key}(\mathsf{mid})$, we recur on the range of ranks from $\mathsf{mid}+1$ to high.

This search method is called ***binary search***, and is given in pseudo-code in Algorithm 3.1. Operation findElement(k) on an n-item dictionary implemented with a vector S consists of calling BinarySearch($S,k,0,n-1$).

Algorithm BinarySearch(S,k, low, high):
  Input: An ordered vector S storing n items, whose keys are accessed with method key(i) and whose elements are accessed with method elem(i); a search key k; and integers low and high
  Output: An element of S with key k and rank between low and high, if such an element exists, and otherwise the special element NO_SUCH_KEY

  if low > high **then**
    return NO_SUCH_KEY
  else
    mid ← ⌊(low + high)/2⌋
    if k = key(mid) **then**
      return elem(mid)
    else if k < key(mid) **then**
      return BinarySearch(S,k, low, mid − 1)
    else
      return BinarySearch(S,k, mid + 1, high)

Algorithm 3.1: Binary search in an ordered vector.

We illustrate the binary search algorithm in Figure 3.2.

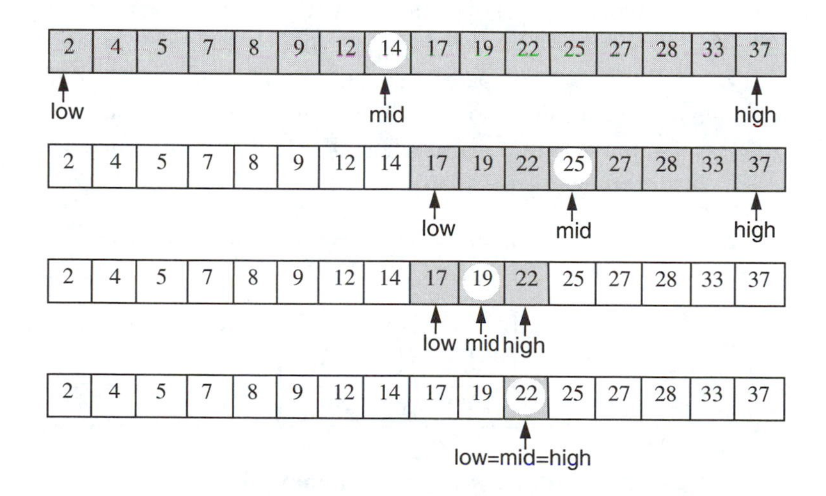

Figure 3.2: Example of a binary search to perform operation findElement(22), in a dictionary with integer keys, implemented with an array-based ordered vector. For simplicity, we show the keys stored in the dictionary but not the elements.

Considering the running time of binary search, we observe that a constant number of operations are executed at each recursive call. Hence, the running time is proportional to the number of recursive calls performed. A crucial fact is that with each recursive call the number of candidate items still to be searched in the sequence S is given by the value $\mathsf{high} - \mathsf{low} + 1$. Moreover, the number of remaining candidates is reduced by at least one half with each recursive call. Specifically, from the definition of mid the number of remaining candidates is either

$$(\mathsf{mid} - 1) - \mathsf{low} + 1 = \left\lfloor \frac{\mathsf{low} + \mathsf{high}}{2} \right\rfloor - \mathsf{low} \leq \frac{\mathsf{high} - \mathsf{low} + 1}{2}$$

or

$$\mathsf{high} - (\mathsf{mid} + 1) + 1 = \mathsf{high} - \left\lfloor \frac{\mathsf{low} + \mathsf{high}}{2} \right\rfloor \leq \frac{\mathsf{high} - \mathsf{low} + 1}{2}.$$

Initially, the number of candidate is n; after the first call to BinarySearch, it is at most $n/2$; after the second call, it is at most $n/4$; and so on. That is, if we let a function, $T(n)$, represent the running time of this method, then we can characterize the running time of the recursive binary search algorithm as follows:

$$T(n) \leq \begin{cases} b & \text{if } n < 2 \\ T(n/2) + b & \text{else,} \end{cases}$$

where b is a constant. In general, this recurrence equation shows that the number of candidate items remaining after each recursive call is at most $n/2^i$. (We discuss recurrence equations like this one in more detail in Section 5.2.1.) In the worst case (unsuccessful search), the recursive calls stop when there are no more candidate items. Hence, the maximum number of recursive calls performed is the smallest integer m such that $n/2^m < 1$. In other words (recalling that we omit a logarithm's base when it is 2), $m > \log n$. Thus, we have $m = \lfloor \log n \rfloor + 1$, which implies that $\mathsf{BinarySearch}(S, k, 0, n-1)$ runs in $O(\log n)$ time.

Table 3.3 compares the running times of the methods of a dictionary realized by either a log file or a lookup table. A log file allows for fast insertions but slow searches and removals, whereas a lookup table allows for fast searches but slow insertions and removals.

Method	**Log File**	**Lookup Table**
findElement	$O(n)$	$O(\log n)$
insertItem	$O(1)$	$O(n)$
removeElement	$O(n)$	$O(n)$
closestKeyBefore	$O(n)$	$O(\log n)$

Table 3.3: Comparison of the running times of the primary methods of an ordered dictionary realized by means of a log file or a lookup table. We denote the number of items in the dictionary at the time a method is executed with n. The performance of the methods closestElemBefore, closestKeyAfter, closestElemAfter is similar to that of closestKeyBefore.

3.1.2 Binary Search Trees

The data structure we discuss in this section, the binary search tree, applies the motivation of the binary search procedure to a tree-based data structure. We define a binary search tree to be a binary tree in which each internal node v stores an element e such that the elements stored in the left subtree of v are less than or equal to e, and the elements stored in the right subtree of v are greater than or equal to e. Furthermore, let us assume that external nodes store no elements; hence, they could in fact be null or references to a NULL_NODE object.

An inorder traversal of a binary search tree visits the elements stored in such a tree in nondecreasing order. A binary search tree supports searching, where the question asked at each internal node is whether the element at that node is less than, equal to, or larger than the element being searched for.

We can use a binary search tree T to locate an element with a certain value x by traversing down the tree T. At each internal node we compare the value of the current node to our search element x. If the answer to the question is "smaller," then the search continues in the left subtree. If the answer is "equal," then the search terminates successfully. If the answer is "greater," then the search continues in the right subtree. Finally, if we reach an external node (which is empty), then the search terminates unsuccessfully. (See Figure 3.4.)

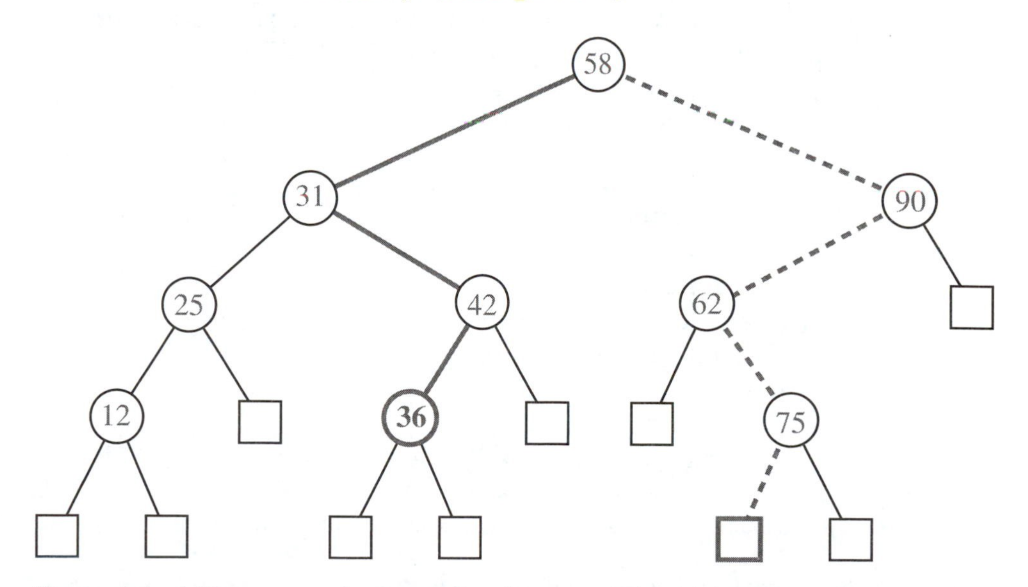

Figure 3.4: A binary search tree storing integers. The thick solid path drawn with thick lines is traversed when searching (successfully) for 36. The thick dashed path is traversed when searching (unsuccessfully) for 70.

3.1.3 Searching in a Binary Search Tree

Formally, a ***binary search tree*** is a binary tree T in which each internal node v of T stores an item (k,e) of a dictionary D, and keys stored at nodes in the left subtree of v are less than or equal to k, while keys stored at nodes in the right subtree of v are greater than or equal to k.

In Algorithm 3.5, we give a recursive method TreeSearch, based on the above strategy for searching in a binary search tree T. Given a search key k and a node v of T, method TreeSearch returns a node (position) w of the subtree $T(v)$ of T rooted at v, such that one of the following two cases occurs:

- w is an internal node of $T(v)$ that stores key k.
- w is an external node of $T(v)$. All the internal nodes of $T(v)$ that precede w in the inorder traversal have keys smaller than k, and all the internal nodes of $T(v)$ that follow w in the inorder traversal have keys greater than k.

Thus, method findElement(k) can be performed on dictionary D by calling the method TreeSearch(k, T.root()) on T. Let w be the node of T returned by this call of the TreeSearch method. If node w is internal, we return the element stored at w; otherwise, if w is external, then we return NO_SUCH_KEY.

Algorithm TreeSearch(k,v):
Input: A search key k, and a node v of a binary search tree T
Output: A node w of the subtree $T(v)$ of T rooted at v, such that either w is an internal node storing key k or w is the external node where an item with key k would belong if it existed

```
if v is an external node then
    return v
if k = key(v) then
    return v
else if k < key(v) then
    return TreeSearch(k, T.leftChild(v))
else
    {we know k > key(v)}
    return TreeSearch(k, T.rightChild(v))
```

Algorithm 3.5: Recursive search in a binary search tree.

Note that the running time of searching in a binary search tree T is proportional to the height of T. Since the height of a tree with n nodes can be as small as $O(\log n)$ or as large as $\Omega(n)$, binary search trees are most efficient when they have small height.

Analysis of Binary Tree Searching

The formal analysis of the worst-case running time of searching in a binary search tree T is simple. The binary tree search algorithm executes a constant number of primitive operations for each node it traverses in the tree. Each new step in the traversal is made on a child of the previous node. That is, the binary tree search algorithm is performed on the nodes of a path of T that starts from the root and goes down one level at a time. Thus, the number of such nodes is bounded by $h+1$, where h is the height of T. In other words, since we spend $O(1)$ time per node encountered in the search, method findElement (or any other standard search operation) runs in $O(h)$ time, where h is the height of the binary search tree T used to implement the dictionary D. (See Figure 3.6.)

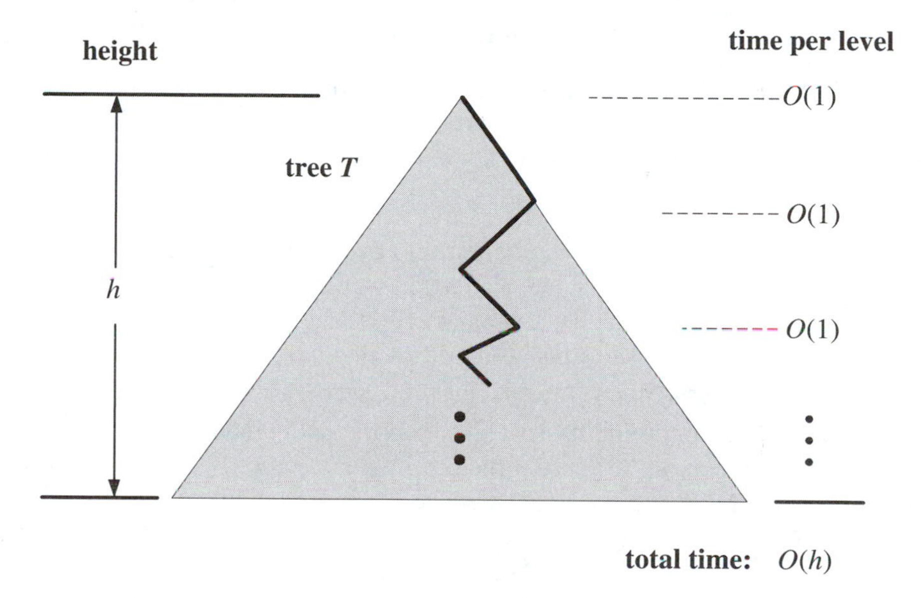

Figure 3.6: Illustrating the running time of searching in a binary search tree. The figure uses standard visualization shortcuts of viewing a binary search tree as a big triangle and a path from the root as a zig-zag line.

We can also show that a variation of the above algorithm performs operation findAllElements(k), which finds all the items in the dictionary with key k, in time $O(h+s)$, where s is the number of elements returned. However, this method is slightly more complicated, and the details are left as an exercise (C-3.3).

Admittedly, the height h of T can be as large as n, but we expect that it is usually much smaller. Indeed, we will show in subsequent sections in this chapter how to maintain an upper bound of $O(\log n)$ on the height of a search tree T. Before we describe such a scheme, however, let us describe implementations for dictionary update methods in a possibly unbalanced binary search tree.

3.1.4 Insertion in a Binary Search Tree

Binary search trees allow implementations of the insertItem and removeElement operations using algorithms that are fairly straightforward, but not trivial.

To perform the operation insertItem(k,e) on a dictionary D implemented with a binary search tree T, we start by calling the method TreeSearch$(k, T.$root$())$ on T. Let w be the node returned by TreeSearch.

- If w is an external node (no item with key k is stored in T), we replace w with a new internal node storing the item (k,e) and two external children, by means of operation expandExternal(w) on T (see Section 2.3.3). Note that w is the appropriate place to insert an item with key k.
- If w is an internal node (another item with key k is stored at w), we call TreeSearch$(k,$ rightChild$(w))$ (or, equivalently, TreeSearch$(k,$ leftChild$(w))$) and recursively apply the algorithm to the node returned by TreeSearch.

The above insertion algorithm eventually traces a path from the root of T down to an external node, which gets replaced with a new internal node accommodating the new item. Hence, an insertion adds the new item at the "bottom" of the search tree T. An example of insertion into a binary search tree is shown in Figure 3.7.

The analysis of the insertion algorithm is analogous to that for searching. The number of nodes visited is proportional to the height h of T in the worst case. Also, assuming a linked structure implementation for T (see Section 2.3.4), we spend $O(1)$ time at each node visited. Thus, method insertItem runs in $O(h)$ time.

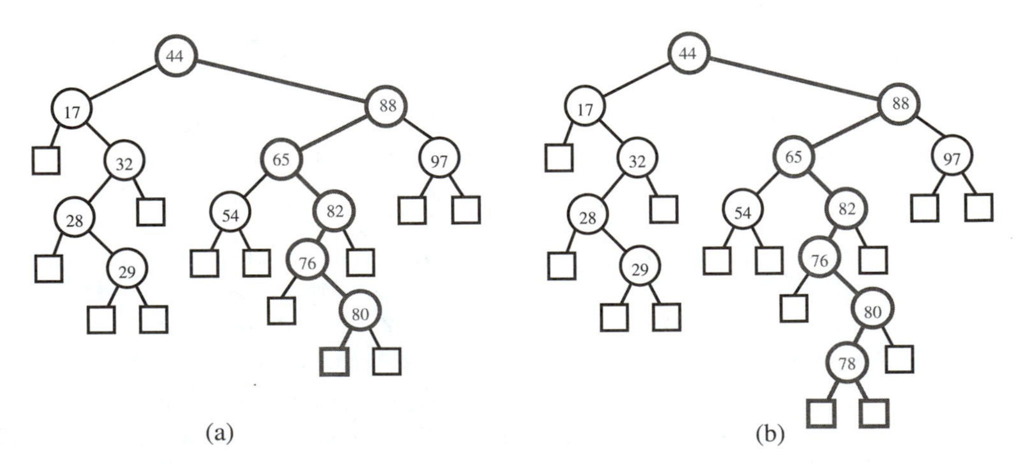

Figure 3.7: Insertion of an item with key 78 into a binary search tree. Finding the position to insert is shown in (a), and the resulting tree is shown in (b).

3.1.5 Removal in a Binary Search Tree

Performing the removeElement(k) operation on a dictionary D implemented with a binary search tree T is a bit more complex, since we do not wish to create any "holes" in the tree T. Such a hole, where an internal node would not store an element, would make it difficult if not impossible for us to correctly perform searches in the binary search tree. Indeed, if we have many removals that do not restructure the tree T, then there could be a large section of internal nodes that store no elements, which would confuse any future searches.

The removal operation starts out simple enough, since we begin by executing algorithm TreeSearch$(k, T.\text{root}())$ on T to find a node storing key k. If TreeSearch returns an external node, then there is no element with key k in dictionary D, and we return the special element NO_SUCH_KEY and we are done. If TreeSearch returns an internal node w instead, then w stores an item we wish to remove.

We distinguish two cases (of increasing difficulty) of how to proceed based on whether w is a node that is easily removed or not:

- If one of the children of node w is an external node, say node z, we simply remove w and z from T by means of operation removeAboveExternal(z) on T. This operation (also see Figure 2.26 and Section 2.3.4) restructures T by replacing w with the sibling of z, removing both w and z from T.

This case is illustrated in Figure 3.8.

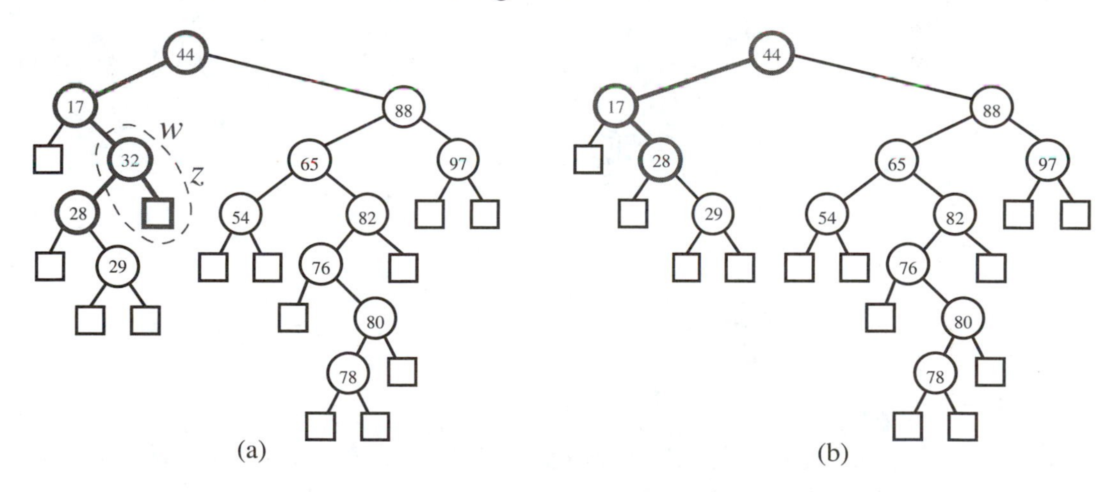

Figure 3.8: Removal from the binary search tree of Figure 3.7b, where the key to remove (32) is stored at a node (w) with an external child: (a) shows the tree before the removal, together with the nodes affected by the removeAboveExternal(z) operation on T; (b) shows the tree T after the removal.

- If both children of node w are internal nodes, we cannot simply remove the node w from T, since this would create a "hole" in T. Instead, we proceed as follows (see Figure 3.9):

  1. We find the first internal node y that follows w in an inorder traversal of T. Node y is the left-most internal node in the right subtree of w, and is found by going first to the right child of w and then down T from there, following left children. Also, the left child x of y is the external node that immediately follows node w in the inorder traversal of T.
  2. We save the element stored at w in a temporary variable t, and move the item of y into w. This action has the effect of removing the former item stored at w.
  3. We remove x and y from T using operation removeAboveExternal(x) on T. This action replaces y with x's sibling, and removes both x and y from T.
  4. We return the element previously stored at w, which we had saved in the temporary variable t.

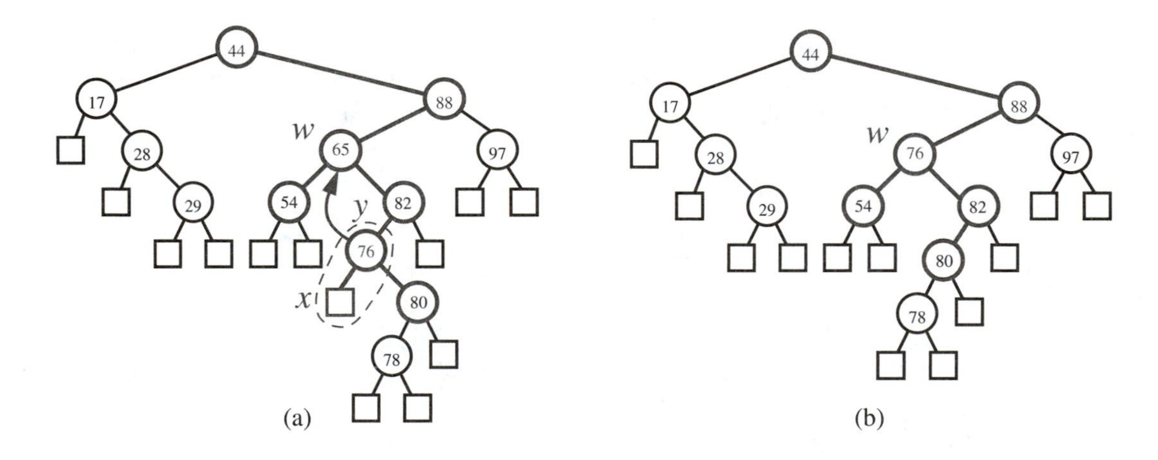

Figure 3.9: Removal from the binary search tree of Figure 3.7b, where the key to remove (65) is stored at a node whose children are both internal: (a) before the removal; (b) after the removal.

The analysis of the removal algorithm is analogous to that of the insertion and search algorithms. We spend $O(1)$ time at each node visited, and, in the worst case, the number of nodes visited is proportional to the height h of T. Thus, in a dictionary D implemented with a binary search tree T, the removeElement method runs in $O(h)$ time, where h is the height of T.

We can also show that a variation of the above algorithm performs operation removeAllElements(k) in time $O(h+s)$, where s is the number of elements in the iterator returned. The details are left as an exercise (C-3.4).

3.1.6 Performance of Binary Search Trees

The performance of a dictionary implemented with a binary search is summarized in the following theorem and in Table 3.10.

Theorem 3.1: *A binary search tree T with height h for n key-element items uses $O(n)$ space and executes the dictionary ADT operations with the following running times. Operations* size *and* isEmpty *each take $O(1)$ time. Operations* findElement, insertItem, *and* removeElement *each take time $O(h)$ time. Operations* findAllElements *and* removeAllElements *each take $O(h+s)$ time, where s is the size of the iterators returned.*

Method	Time
size, isEmpty	$O(1)$
findElement, insertItem, removeElement	$O(h)$
findAllElements, removeAllElements	$O(h+s)$

Table 3.10: Running times of the main methods of a dictionary realized by a binary search tree. We denote with h the current height of the tree and with s the size of the iterators returned by findAllElements and removeAllElements. The space usage is $O(n)$, where n is the number of items stored in the dictionary.

Note that the running time of search and update operations in a binary search tree varies dramatically depending on the tree's height. We can nevertheless take comfort that, on average, a binary search tree with n keys generated from a random series of insertions and removals of keys has expected height $O(\log n)$. Such a statement requires careful mathematical language to precisely define what we mean by a random series of insertions and removals, and sophisticated probability theory to justify; hence, its justification is beyond the scope of this book. Thus, we can be content knowing that random update sequences give rise to binary search trees that have logarithmic height on average, but, keeping in mind their poor worst-case performance, we should also take care in using standard binary search trees in applications where updates are not random.

The relative simplicity of the binary search tree and its good average-case performance make binary search trees a rather attractive dictionary data structure in applications where the keys inserted and removed follow a random pattern and occasionally slow response time is acceptable. There are, however, applications where it is essential to have a dictionary with fast worst-case search and update time. The data structures presented in the next sections address this need.

3.2 AVL Trees

In the previous section, we discussed what should be an efficient dictionary data structure, but the worst-case performance it achieves for the various operations is linear time, which is no better than the performance of sequence-based dictionary implementations (such as log files and lookup tables). In this section, we describe a simple way of correcting this problem so as to achieve logarithmic time for all the fundamental dictionary operations.

Definition

The simple correction is to add a rule to the binary search tree definition that will maintain a logarithmic height for the tree. The rule we consider in this section is the following ***height-balance property***, which characterizes the structure of a binary search tree T in terms of the heights of its internal nodes (recall from Section 2.3.2 that the height of a node v in a tree is the length of a longest path from v to an external node):

Height-Balance Property: For every internal node v of T, the heights of the children of v can differ by at most 1.

Any binary search tree T that satisfies this property is said to be an ***AVL tree***, which is a concept named after the initials of its inventors: Adel'son-Vel'skii and Landis. An example of an AVL tree is shown in Figure 3.11.

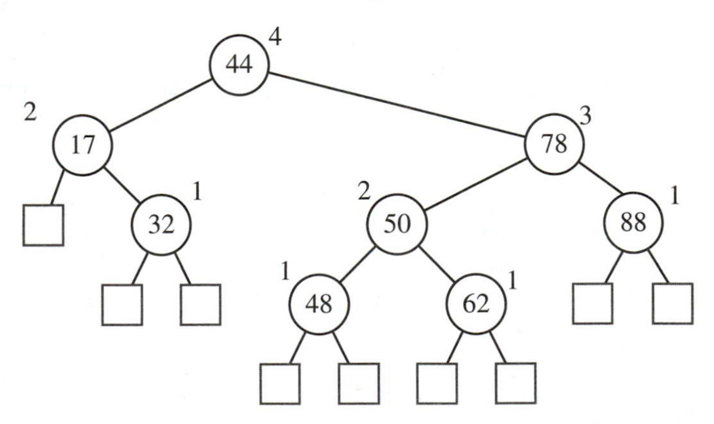

Figure 3.11: An example of an AVL tree. The keys are shown inside the nodes, and the heights are shown next to the nodes.

An immediate consequence of the height-balance property is that a subtree of an AVL tree is itself an AVL tree. The height-balance property has also the important consequence of keeping the height small, as shown in the following proposition.

Theorem 3.2: *The height of an AVL tree T storing n items is $O(\log n)$.*

Proof: Instead of trying to find an upper bound on the height of an AVL tree directly, it is easier to work on the "inverse problem" of finding a lower bound on the minimum number of internal nodes $n(h)$ of an AVL tree with height h. We will show that $n(h)$ grows at least exponentially, that is, $n(h)$ is $\Omega(c^h)$ for some constant $c > 1$. From this, it will be an easy step to derive that the height of an AVL tree storing n keys is $O(\log n)$.

Notice that $n(1) = 1$ and $n(2) = 2$, because an AVL tree of height 1 must have at least one internal node and an AVL tree of height 2 must have at least two internal nodes. Now, for $h \geq 3$, an AVL tree with height h and the minimum number of nodes is such that both its subtrees are AVL trees with the minimum number of nodes: one with height $h-1$ and the other with height $h-2$. Taking the root into account, we obtain the following formula that relates $n(h)$ to $n(h-1)$ and $n(h-2)$, for $h \geq 3$:

$$n(h) = 1 + n(h-1) + n(h-2). \tag{3.1}$$

Formula 3.1 implies that $n(h)$ is a strictly increasing function of h (corresponding to the Fibonacci progression). Thus, we know that $n(h-1) > n(h-2)$. Replacing $n(h-1)$ with $n(h-2)$ in Formula 3.1 and dropping the 1, we get, for $h \geq 3$,

$$n(h) \; > \; 2 \cdot n(h-2). \tag{3.2}$$

Formula 3.2 indicates that $n(h)$ at least doubles each time h increases by 2, which intuitively means that $n(h)$ grows exponentially. To show this fact in a formal way, we apply Formula 3.2 repeatedly, by a simple inductive argument, to show that

$$n(h) > 2^i \cdot n(h-2i), \tag{3.3}$$

for any integer i, such that $h - 2i \geq 1$. Since we already know the values of $n(1)$ and $n(2)$, we pick i so that $h - 2i$ is equal to either 1 or 2. That is, we pick $i = \lceil h/2 \rceil - 1$. By substituting the above value of i in Formula 3.3, we obtain, for $h \geq 3$,

$$\begin{aligned} n(h) \; &> \; 2^{\lceil \frac{h}{2} \rceil - 1} \cdot n\left(h - 2\left\lceil \frac{h}{2} \right\rceil + 2\right) \\ &\geq \; 2^{\lceil \frac{h}{2} \rceil - 1} n(1) \\ &\geq \; 2^{\frac{h}{2} - 1}. \end{aligned} \tag{3.4}$$

By taking logarithms of both sides of Formula 3.4, we obtain $\log n(h) \; > \; \frac{h}{2} - 1$, from which we get

$$h \; < \; 2\log n(h) + 2, \tag{3.5}$$

which implies that an AVL tree storing n keys has height at most $2\log n + 2$. ■

By Theorem 3.2 and the analysis of binary search trees given in Section 3.1.2, the operation findElement in a dictionary implemented with an AVL tree, runs in $O(\log n)$ time, where n is the number of items in the dictionary.

3.2.1 Update Operations

The important issue remaining is to show how to maintain the height-balance property of an AVL tree after an insertion or removal. The insertion and removal operations for AVL trees are similar to those for binary search trees, but with AVL trees we must perform additional computations.

Insertion

An insertion in an AVL tree T begins as in an insertItem operation described in Section 3.1.4 for a (simple) binary search tree. Recall that this operation always inserts the new item at a node w in T that was previously an external node, and it makes w become an internal node with operation expandExternal. That is, it adds two external node children to w. This action may violate the height-balance property, however, for some nodes increase their heights by one. In particular, node w, and possibly some of its ancestors, increase their heights by one. Therefore, let us describe how to restructure T to restore its height balance.

Given the binary search tree T, we say that a node v of T is ***balanced*** if the absolute value of the difference between the heights of the children of v is at most 1, and we say that it is ***unbalanced*** otherwise. Thus, the height-balance property characterizing AVL trees is equivalent to saying that every internal node is balanced.

Suppose that T satisfies the height-balance property, and hence is an AVL tree, prior to our inserting the new item. As we have mentioned, after performing the operation expandExternal(w) on T, the heights of some nodes of T, including w, increase. All such nodes are on the path of T from w to the root of T, and these are the only nodes of T that may have just become unbalanced. (See Figure 3.12a.) Of course, if this happens, then T is no longer an AVL tree; hence, we need a mechanism to fix the "unbalance" that we have just caused.

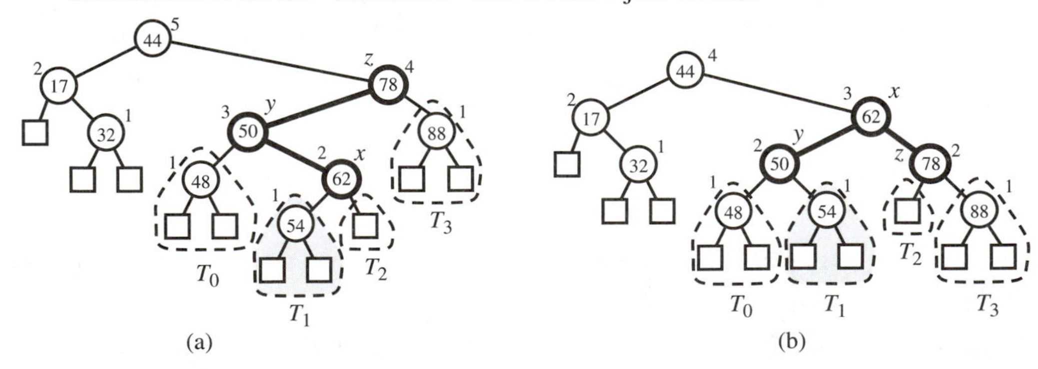

Figure 3.12: An example insertion of an element with key 54 in the AVL tree of Figure 3.11: (a) after adding a new node for key 54, the nodes storing keys 78 and 44 become unbalanced; (b) a trinode restructuring restores the height-balance property. We show the heights of nodes next to them, and we identify the nodes x, y, and z.

Algorithm restructure(x):

Input: A node x of a binary search tree T that has both a parent y and a grandparent z

Output: Tree T after a trinode restructuring (which corresponds to a single or double rotation) involving nodes x, y, and z

1: Let (a,b,c) be a left-to-right (inorder) listing of the nodes x, y, and z, and let (T_0,T_1,T_2,T_3) be a left-to-right (inorder) listing of the four subtrees of x, y, and z not rooted at x, y, or z.

2: Replace the subtree rooted at z with a new subtree rooted at b.

3: Let a be the left child of b and let T_0 and T_1 be the left and right subtrees of a, respectively.

4: Let c be the right child of b and let T_2 and T_3 be the left and right subtrees of c, respectively.

Algorithm 3.13: The trinode restructure operation in a binary search tree.

We restore the balance of the nodes in the binary search tree T by a simple "search-and-repair" strategy. In particular, let z be the first node we encounter in going up from w toward the root of T such that z is unbalanced. (See Figure 3.12a.) Also, let y denote the child of z with higher height (and note that y must be an ancestor of w). Finally, let x be the child of y with higher height (and if there is a tie, choose x to be an ancestor of w). Note that node x could be equal to w and x is a grandchild of z. Since z became unbalanced because of an insertion in the subtree rooted at its child y, the height of y is 2 greater than its sibling. We now rebalance the subtree rooted at z by calling the ***trinode restructuring*** method, restructure(x), described in Algorithm 3.13 and illustrated in Figures 3.12 and 3.14. A trinode restructure temporarily renames the nodes x, y, and z as a, b, and c, so that a precedes b and b precedes c in an inorder traversal of T. There are four possible ways of mapping x, y, and z to a, b, and c, as shown in Figure 3.14, which are unified into one case by our relabeling. The trinode restructure then replaces z with the node called b, makes the children of this node be a and c, and makes the children of a and c be the four previous children of x, y, and z (other than x and y) while maintaining the inorder relationships of all the nodes in T.

The modification of a tree T caused by a trinode restructure operation is often called a ***rotation***, because of the geometric way we can visualize the way it changes T. If $b = y$ (see Algorithm 3.13), the trinode restructure method is called a ***single rotation***, for it can be visualized as "rotating" y over z. (See Figure 3.14a and b.) Otherwise, if $b = x$, the trinode restructure operation is called a ***double rotation***, for it can be visualized as first "rotating" x over y and then over z. (See Figure 3.14c and d, and Figure 3.12.) Some researchers treat these two kinds as separate methods, each with two symmetric types; we have chosen, however, to unify these four types of rotations. No matter how we view it, note that the trinode restructure method modifies parent-child relationships of $O(1)$ nodes in T, while preserving the inorder traversal ordering of all the nodes in T.

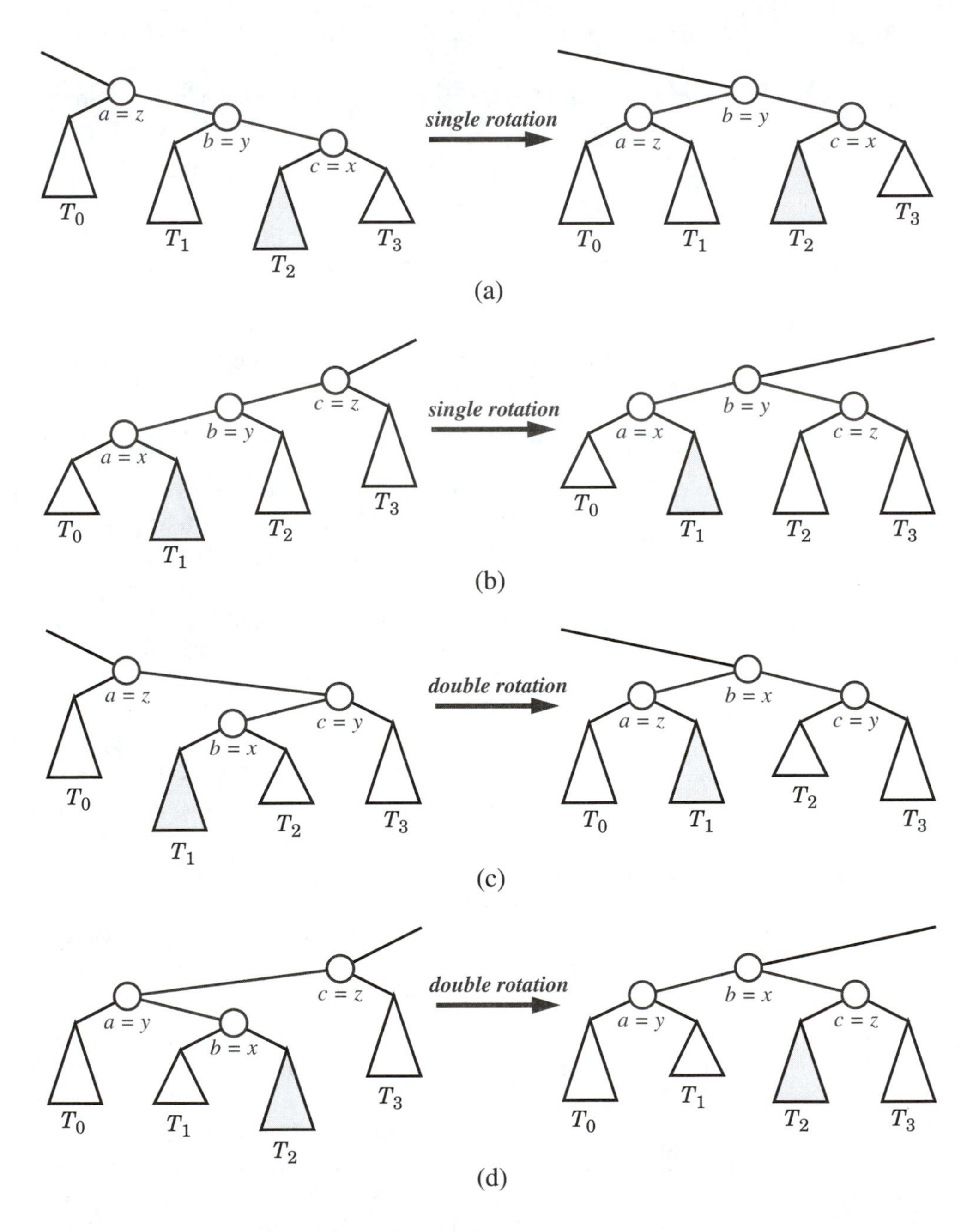

Figure 3.14: Schematic illustration of a trinode restructure operation (Algorithm 3.13). Parts (a) and (b) show a single rotation, and parts (c) and (d) show a double rotation.

In addition to its order-preserving property, a trinode restructuring operation changes the heights of nodes in T, so as to restore balance. Recall that we execute the method restructure(x) because z, the grandparent of x, is unbalanced. Moreover, this unbalance is due to one of the children of x now having too large a height relative to the height of z's other child. As a result of a rotation, we move up the "tall" child of x while pushing down the "short" child of z. Thus, after performing restructure(x), all the nodes in the subtree now rooted at the node we called b are balanced. (See Figure 3.14.) Thus, we restore the height-balance property ***locally*** at the nodes x, y, and z.

In addition, since after performing the new item insertion the subtree rooted at b replaces the one formerly rooted at z, which was taller by one unit, all the ancestors of z that were formerly unbalanced become balanced. (See Figure 3.12.) (The justification of this fact is left as Exercise C-3.13.) Therefore, this one restructuring also restores the height-balance property ***globally***. That is, one rotation (single or double) is sufficient to restore the height-balance in an AVL tree after an insertion.

Removal

As was the case for the insertItem dictionary operation, we begin the implementation of the removeElement dictionary operation on an AVL tree T by using the algorithm for performing this operation on a regular binary search tree. The added difficulty in using this approach with an AVL tree is that it may violate the height-balance property.

In particular, after removing an internal node with operation removeAboveExternal and elevating one of its children into its place, there may be an unbalanced node in T on the path from the parent w of the previously removed node to the root of T. (See Figure 3.15a.) In fact, there can be one such unbalanced node at most. (The justification of this fact is left as Exercise C-3.12.)

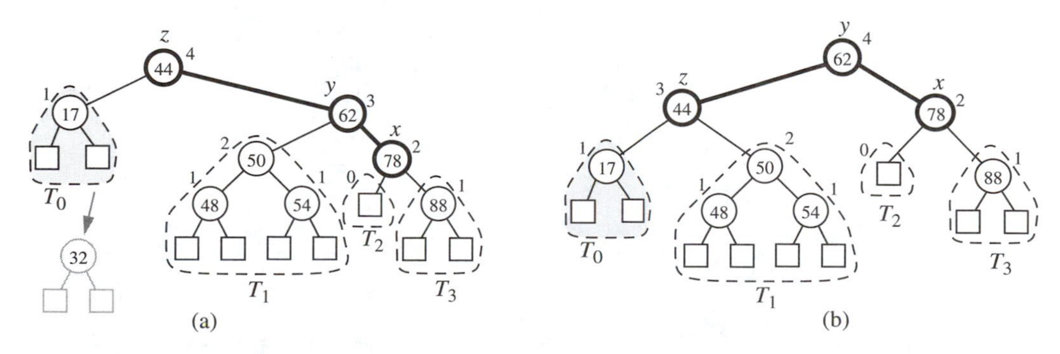

Figure 3.15: Removal of the element with key 32 from the AVL tree of Figure 3.11: (a) after removing the node storing key 32, the root becomes unbalanced; (b) a (single) rotation restores the height-balance property.

As with insertion, we use trinode restructuring to restore balance in the tree T. In particular, let z be the first unbalanced node encountered going up from w toward the root of T. Also, let y be the child of z with larger height (note that node y is the child of z that is not an ancestor of w), and let x be a child of y with larger height. The choice of x may not be unique, since the subtrees of y may have the same height. In any case, we then perform a restructure(x) operation, which restores the height-balance property ***locally***, at the subtree that was formerly rooted at z and is now rooted at the node we temporarily called b. (See Figure 3.15b.)

Unfortunately, this trinode restructuring may reduce the height of the subtree rooted at b by 1, which may cause an ancestor of b to become unbalanced. Thus, a single trinode restructuring may not restore the height-balance property globally after a removal. So, after rebalancing z, we continue walking up T looking for unbalanced nodes. If we find another, we perform a restructure operation to restore its balance, and continue marching up T looking for more, all the way to the root. Still, since the height of T is $O(\log n)$, where n is the number of items, by Theorem 3.2, $O(\log n)$ trinode restructurings are sufficient to restore the height-balance property.

3.2.2 Performance

We summarize the analysis of the AVL tree as follows. Operations findElement, insertItem, and removeElement visit the nodes along a root-to-leaf path of T, plus, possibly their siblings, and spend $O(1)$ time per node. Thus, since the height of T is $O(\log n)$ by Theorem 3.2, each of the above operations takes $O(\log n)$ time. We illustrate this performance in Figure 3.16.

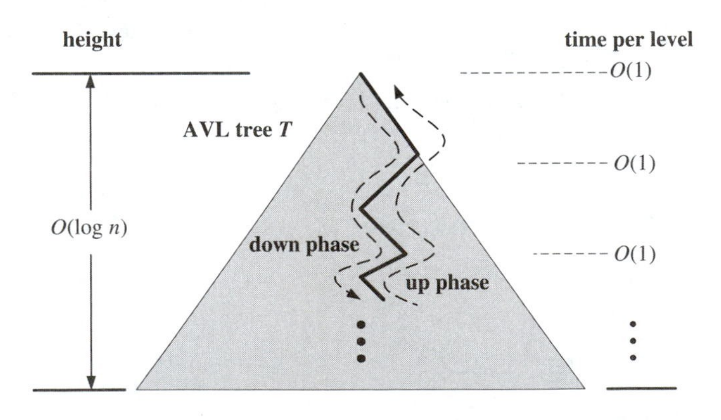

Figure 3.16: Illustrating the running time of searches and updates in an AVL tree. The time performance is $O(1)$ per level, broken into a down phase, which typically involves searching, and an up phase, which typically involves updating height values and performing local trinode restructurings (rotations).

3.3 Bounded-Depth Search Trees

Some search trees base their efficiency on rules that explicitly bound their depth. In fact, such trees typically define a depth function, or a "pseudo-depth" function closely related to depth, so that every external node is at the same depth or pseudo-depth. In so doing, they maintain every external node to be at depth $O(\log n)$ in a tree storing n elements. Since tree searches and updates usually run in times that are proportional to depth, such a ***depth-bounded tree*** can be used to implement an ordered dictionary with $O(\log n)$ search and update times.

3.3.1 Multi-Way Search Trees

Some bounded-depth search trees are multi-way trees, that is, trees with internal nodes that have two or more children. In this section, we describe how multi-way trees can be used as search trees, including how multi-way trees store items and how we can perform search operations in multi-way search trees. Recall that the ***items*** that we store in a search tree are pairs of the form (k,x), where k is the ***key*** and x is the element associated with the key.

Let v be a node of an ordered tree. We say that v is a ***d-node*** if v has d children. We define a ***multi-way search tree*** to be an ordered tree T that has the following properties (which are illustrated in Figure 3.17a):

- Each internal node of T has at least two children. That is, each internal node is a d-node, where $d \geq 2$.
- Each internal node of T stores a collection of items of the form (k,x), where k is a key and x is an element.
- Each d-node v of T, with children $v_1,\ldots,v_d$, stores $d-1$ items $(k_1,x_1),\ldots,$ (k_{d-1},x_{d-1}), where $k_1 \leq \cdots \leq k_{d-1}$.
- Let us define $k_0 = -\infty$ and $k_d = +\infty$. For each item (k,x) stored at a node in the subtree of v rooted at v_i, $i = 1,\ldots,d$, we have $k_{i-1} \leq k \leq k_i$.

That is, if we think of the set of keys stored at v as including the special fictitious keys $k_0 = -\infty$ and $k_d = +\infty$, then a key k stored in the subtree of T rooted at a child node v_i must be "in between" two keys stored at v. This simple viewpoint gives rise to the rule that a node with d children stores $d-1$ regular keys, and it also forms the basis of the algorithm for searching in a multi-way search tree.

By the above definition, the external nodes of a multi-way search do not store any items and serve only as "placeholders." Thus, we view a binary search tree (Section 3.1.2) as a special case of a multi-way search tree. At the other extreme, a multi-way search tree may have only a single internal node storing all the items. In addition, while the external nodes could be **null**, we make the simplifying assumption here that they are actual nodes that don't store anything.

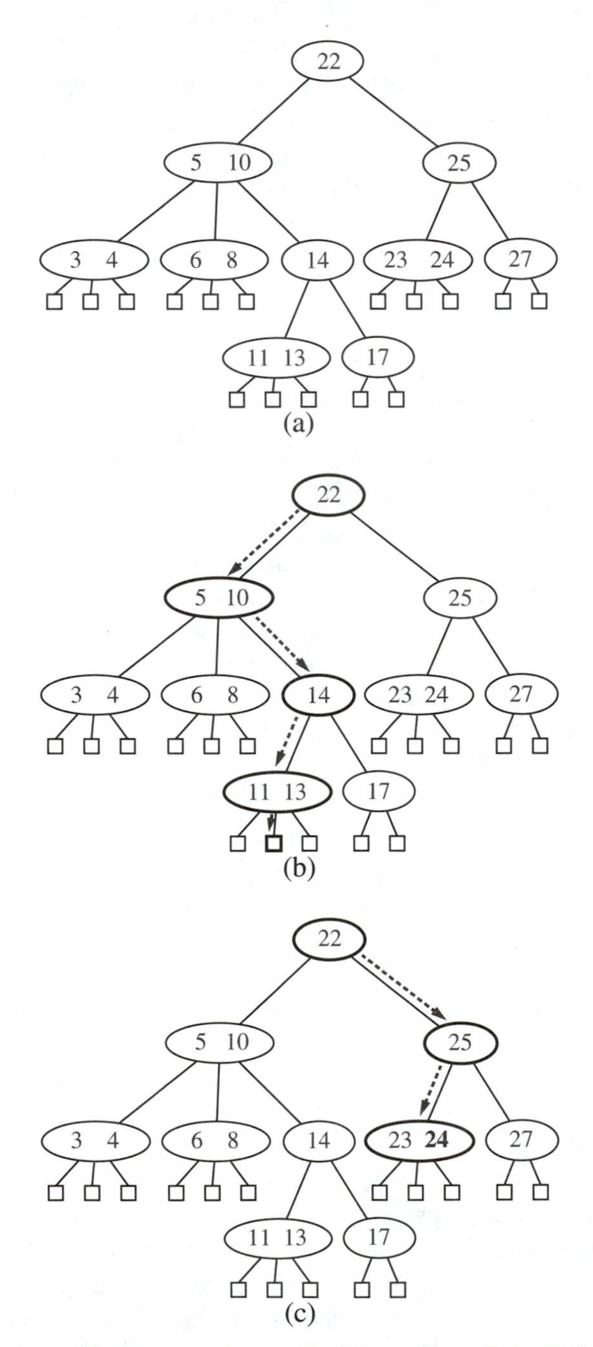

Figure 3.17: (a) A multi-way search tree T; (b) search path in T for key 12 (unsuccessful search); (c) search path in T for key 24 (successful search).

Whether internal nodes of a multi-way tree have two children or many, however, there is an interesting relationship between the number of items and the number of external nodes.

Theorem 3.3: *A multi-way search tree storing n items has $n+1$ external nodes.*

We leave the justification of this theorem as an exercise (C-3.16).

Searching in a Multi-Way Tree

Given a multi-way search tree T, searching for an element with key k is simple. We perform such a search by tracing a path in T starting at the root. (See Figure 3.17b and c.) When we are at a d-node v during this search, we compare the key k with the keys $k_1,\ldots,k_{d-1}$ stored at v. If $k = k_i$ for some i, the search is successfully completed. Otherwise, we continue the search in the child v_i of v such that $k_{i-1} < k < k_i$. (Recall that we consider $k_0 = -\infty$ and $k_d = +\infty$.) If we reach an external node, then we know that there is no item with key k in T, and the search terminates unsuccessfully.

Data Structures for Multi-Way Search Trees

In Section 2.3.4, we discussed different ways of representing general trees. Each of these representations can also be used for multi-way search trees. In fact, in using a general multi-way tree to implement a multi-way search tree, the only additional information that we need to store at each node is the set of items (including keys) associated with that node. That is, we need to store with v a reference to some container or collection object that stores the items for v.

Recall that when we use a binary tree to represent an ordered dictionary D, we simply store a reference to a single item at each internal node. In using a multi-way search tree T to represent D, we must store a reference to the ordered set of items associated with v at each internal node v of T. This reasoning may at first seem like a circular argument, since we need a representation of an ordered dictionary to represent an ordered dictionary. We can avoid any circular arguments, however, by using the ***bootstrapping*** technique, where we use a previous (less advanced) solution to a problem to create a new (more advanced) solution. In this case, bootstrapping consists of representing the ordered set associated with each internal node using a dictionary data structure that we have previously constructed (for example, a lookup table based on an ordered vector, as shown in Section 3.1.1). In particular, assuming we already have a way of implementing ordered dictionaries, we can realize a multi-way search tree by taking a tree T and storing such a dictionary at each d-node v of T.

The dictionary we store at each node v is known as a ***secondary*** data structure, for we are using it to support the bigger, ***primary*** data structure. We denote the dictionary stored at a node v of T as $D(v)$. The items we store in $D(v)$ will allow us to find which child node to move to next during a search operation. Specifically, for each node v of T, with children $v_1, \ldots, v_d$ and items $(k_1,x_1), \ldots, (k_{d-1},x_{d-1})$, we store in the dictionary $D(v)$ the items $(k_1,x_1,v_1), (k_2,x_2,v_2), \ldots, (k_{d-1},x_{d-1},v_{d-1})$, $(+\infty, null, v_d)$. That is, an item (k_i,x_i,v_i) of dictionary $D(v)$ has key k_i and element (x_i,v_i). Note that the last item stores the special key $+\infty$.

With the above realization of a multi-way search tree T, processing a d-node v while searching for an element of T with key k can be done by performing a search operation to find the item (k_i,x_i,v_i) in $D(v)$ with smallest key greater than or equal to k, such as in the closestElemAfter(k) operation (see Section 3.1). We distinguish two cases:

- If $k < k_i$, then we continue the search by processing child v_i. (Note that if the special key $k_d = +\infty$ is returned, then k is greater than all the keys stored at node v, and we continue the search processing child v_d.)
- Otherwise ($k = k_i$), then the search terminates successfully.

Performance Issues for Multi-Way Search Trees

Consider the space requirement for the above realization of a multi-way search tree T storing n items. By Theorem 3.3, using any of the common realizations of ordered dictionaries (Section 2.5) for the secondary structures of the nodes of T, the overall space requirement for T is $O(n)$.

Consider next the time spent answering a search in T. The time spent at a d-node v of T during a search depends on how we realize the secondary data structure $D(v)$. If $D(v)$ is realized with a vector-based sorted sequence (that is, a lookup table), then we can process v in $O(\log d)$ time. If instead $D(v)$ is realized using an unsorted sequence (that is, a log file), then processing v takes $O(d)$ time. Let $d_{\max}$ denote the maximum number of children of any node of T, and let h denote the height of T. The search time in a multi-way search tree is either $O(hd_{\max})$ or $O(h \log d_{\max})$, depending on the specific implementation of the secondary structures at the nodes of T (the dictionaries $D(v)$). If $d_{\max}$ is a constant, the running time for performing a search is $O(h)$, irrespective of the implementation of the secondary structures.

Thus, the prime efficiency goal for a multi-way search tree is to keep the height as small as possible, that is, we want h to be a logarithmic function of n, the number of total items stored in the dictionary. A search tree with logarithmic height, such as this, is called a ***balanced search tree***. Bounded-depth search trees satisfy this goal by keeping each external node at exactly the same depth level in the tree.

Next, we discuss a bounded-depth search tree that is a multi-way search tree that caps $d_{\max}$ at 4. In Section 14.1.2, we discuss a more general kind of multi-way search tree that has applications where our search tree is too large to completely fit into the internal memory of our computer.

3.3.2 (2,4) Trees

In using a multi-way search tree in practice, we desire that it be balanced, that is, have logarithmic height. The multi-way search tree we study next is fairly easy to keep balanced. It is the $(2,4)$ tree, which is sometimes also called the 2-4 tree or 2-3-4 tree. In fact, we can maintain balance in a $(2,4)$ tree by maintaining two simple properties (see Figure 3.18):

***Size Property*:** Every node has at most four children.

***Depth Property*:** All the external nodes have the same depth.

Enforcing the size property for $(2,4)$ trees keeps the size of the nodes in the multi-way search tree constant, for it allows us to represent the dictionary $D(v)$ stored at each internal node v using a constant-sized array. The depth property, on the other hand, maintains the balance in a $(2,4)$ tree, by forcing it to be a bounded-depth structure.

Theorem 3.4: *The height of a $(2,4)$ tree storing n items is $\Theta(\log n)$.*

Proof: Let h be the height of a $(2,4)$ tree T storing n items. Note that, by the size property, we can have at most 4 nodes at depth 1, at most 4^2 nodes at depth 2, and so on. Thus, the number of external nodes in T is at most 4^h. Likewise, by the depth property and the definition of a $(2,4)$ tree, we must have at least 2 nodes at depth 1, at least 2^2 nodes at depth 2, and so on. Thus, the number of external nodes in T is at least 2^h. In addition, by Theorem 3.3, the number of external nodes in T is $n+1$. Therefore, we obtain

$$2^h \leq n+1 \quad \text{and} \quad n+1 \leq 4^h.$$

Taking the logarithm in base 2 of each of the above terms, we get that

$$h \leq \log(n+1) \quad \text{and} \quad \log(n+1) \leq 2h,$$

which justifies our theorem. ■

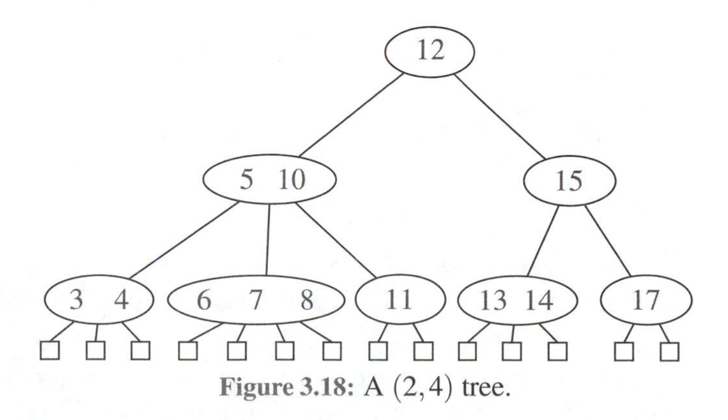

Figure 3.18: A $(2,4)$ tree.

Insertion in a (2,4) Tree

Theorem 3.4 states that the size and depth properties are sufficient for keeping a multi-way tree balanced. Maintaining these properties requires some effort after performing insertions and removals in a $(2,4)$ tree, however. In particular, to insert a new item (k,x), with key k, into a $(2,4)$ tree T, we first perform a search for k. Assuming that T has no element with key k, this search terminates unsuccessfully at an external node z. Let v be the parent of z. We insert the new item into node v and add a new child w (an external node) to v on the left of z. That is, we add item (k,x,w) to the dictionary $D(v)$.

Our insertion method preserves the depth property, since we add a new external node at the same level as existing external nodes. Nevertheless, it may violate the size property. Indeed, if a node v was previously a 4-node, then it may become a 5-node after the insertion, which causes the tree T to no longer be a $(2,4)$ tree. This type of violation of the size property is called an ***overflow*** at node v, and it must be resolved in order to restore the properties of a $(2,4)$ tree. Let $v_1,\ldots,v_5$ be the children of v, and let $k_1,\ldots,k_4$ be the keys stored at v. To remedy the overflow at node v, we perform a ***split*** operation on v as follows (see Figure 3.19):

- Replace v with two nodes v' and v'', where
  - v' is a 3-node with children v_1,v_2,v_3 storing keys k_1 and k_2
  - v'' is a 2-node with children v_4,v_5 storing key k_4.
- If v was the root of T, create a new root node u; else, let u be the parent of v.
- Insert key k_3 into u and make v' and v'' children of u, so that if v was child i of u, then v' and v'' become children i and $i+1$ of u, respectively.

We show a sequence of insertions in a $(2,4)$ tree in Figure 3.20.

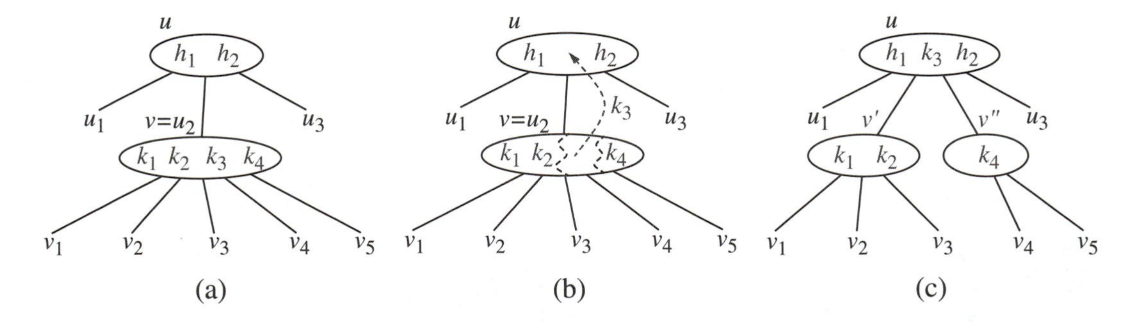

Figure 3.19: A node split: (a) overflow at a 5-node v; (b) the third key of v inserted into the parent u of v; (c) node v replaced with a 3-node v' and a 2-node v''.

A split operation affects a constant number of nodes of the tree and $O(1)$ items stored at such nodes. Thus, it can be implemented to run in $O(1)$ time.

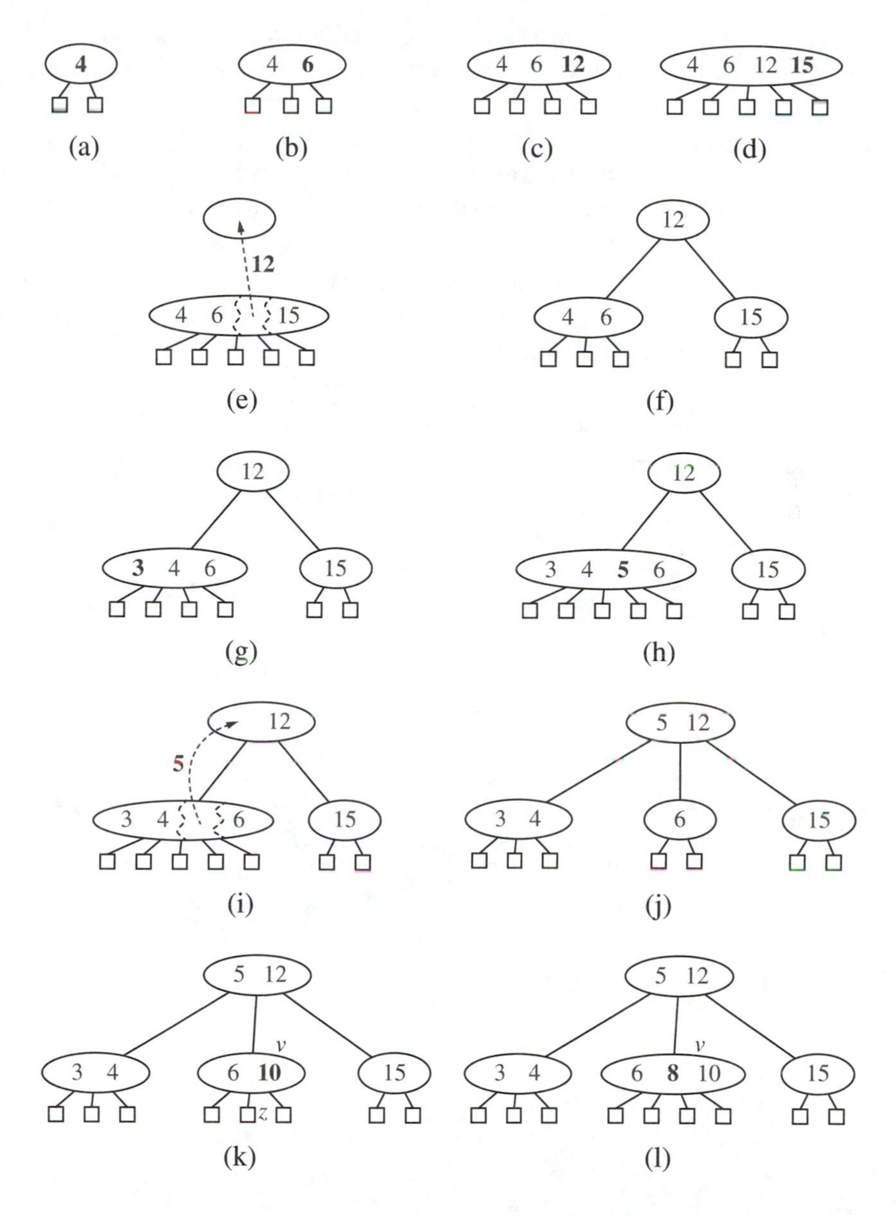

Figure 3.20: A sequence of insertions into a $(2,4)$ tree: (a) initial tree with one item; (b) insertion of 6; (c) insertion of 12; (d) insertion of 15, which causes an overflow; (e) split, which causes the creation of a new root node; (f) after the split; (g) insertion of 3; (h) insertion of 5, which causes an overflow; (i) split; (j) after the split; (k) insertion of 10; (l) insertion of 8.

Performance of (2,4) Tree Insertion

As a consequence of a split operation on node v, a new overflow may occur at the parent u of v. If such an overflow occurs, it triggers, in turn, a split at node u. (See Figure 3.21.) A split operation either eliminates the overflow or propagates it into the parent of the current node. Indeed, this propagation can continue all the way up to the root of the search tree. But if it does propagate all the way to the root, it will finally be resolved at that point. We show such a sequence of splitting propagations in Figure 3.21.

Thus, the number of split operations is bounded by the height of the tree, which is $O(\log n)$ by Theorem 3.4. Therefore, the total time to perform an insertion in a $(2,4)$ tree is $O(\log n)$.

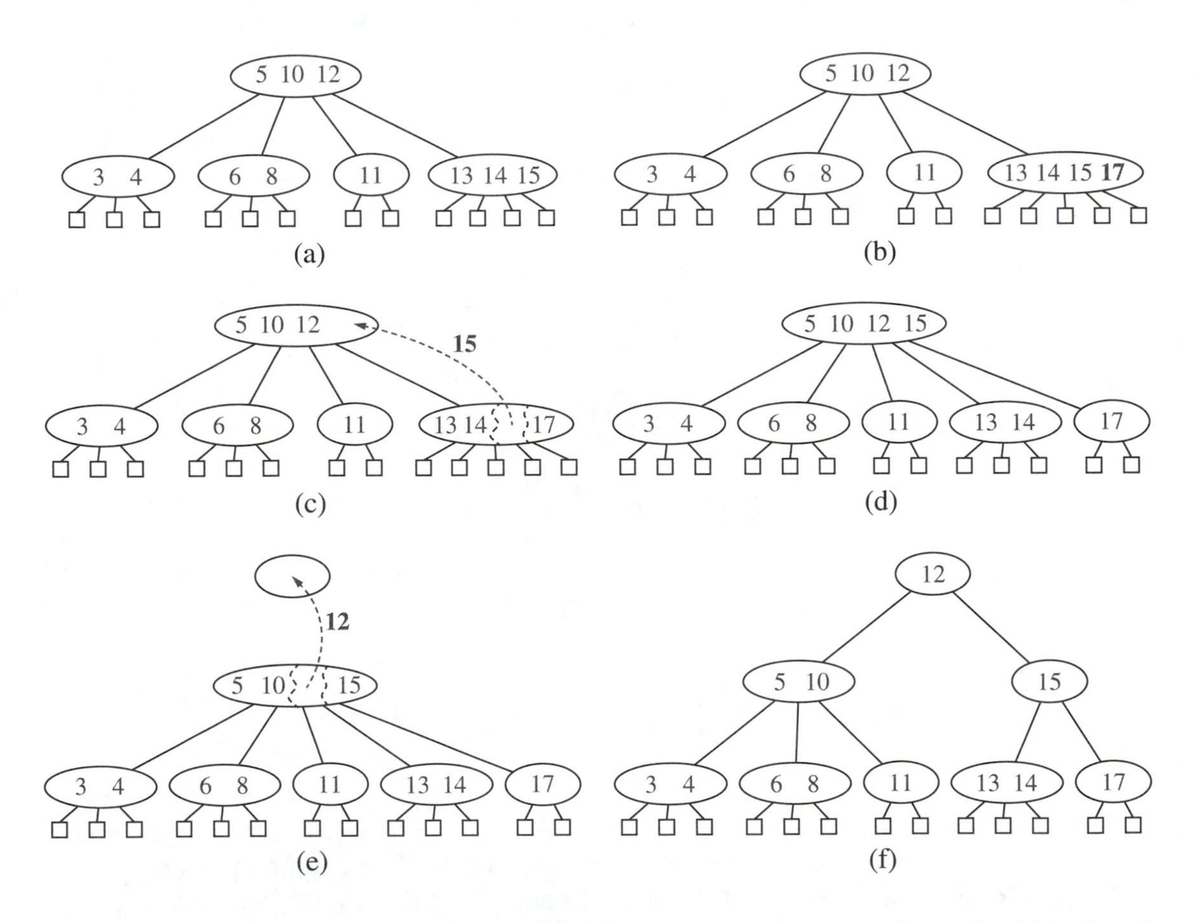

Figure 3.21: An insertion in a $(2,4)$ tree that causes a cascading split: (a) before the insertion; (b) insertion of 17, causing an overflow; (c) a split; (d) after the split a new overflow occurs; (e) another split, creating a new root node; (f) final tree.

Removal in a (2,4) Tree

Let us now consider the removal of an item with key k from a $(2,4)$ tree T. We begin such an operation by performing a search in T for an item with key k. Removing such an item from a $(2,4)$ tree can always be reduced to the case where the item to be removed is stored at a node v whose children are external nodes. Suppose, for instance, that the item with key k that we wish to remove is stored in the ith item (k_i,x_i) at a node z that has only internal-node children. In this case, we swap the item (k_i,x_i) with an appropriate item that is stored at a node v with external-node children as follows (Figure 3.22d):

1. We find the right-most internal node v in the subtree rooted at the ith child of z, noting that the children of node v are all external nodes.
2. We swap the item (k_i,x_i) at z with the last item of v.

Once we ensure that the item to remove is stored at a node v with only external-node children (because either it was already at v or we swapped it into v), we simply remove the item from v (that is, from the dictionary $D(v)$) and remove the ith external node of v.

Removing an item (and a child) from a node v as described above preserves the depth property, for we always remove an external node child from a node v with only external-node children. However, in removing such an external node we may violate the size property at v. Indeed, if v was previously a 2-node, then it becomes a 1-node with no items after the removal (Figure 3.22d and e), which is not allowed in a $(2,4)$ tree. This type of violation of the size property is called an ***underflow*** at node v. To remedy an underflow, we check whether an immediate sibling of v is a 3-node or a 4-node. If we find such a sibling w, then we perform a ***transfer*** operation, in which we move a child of w to v, a key of w to the parent u of v and w, and a key of u to v. (See Figure 3.22b and c.) If v has only one sibling, or if both immediate siblings of v are 2-nodes, then we perform a ***fusion*** operation, in which we merge v with a sibling, creating a new node v', and move a key from the parent u of v to v'. (See Figure 3.23e and f.)

A fusion operation at node v may cause a new underflow to occur at the parent u of v, which in turn triggers a transfer or fusion at u. (See Figure 3.23.) Hence, the number of fusion operations is bounded by the height of the tree, which is $O(\log n)$ by Theorem 3.4. If an underflow propagates all the way up to the root, then the root is simply deleted. (See Figure 3.23c and d.) We show a sequence of removals from a $(2,4)$ tree in Figures 3.22 and 3.23.

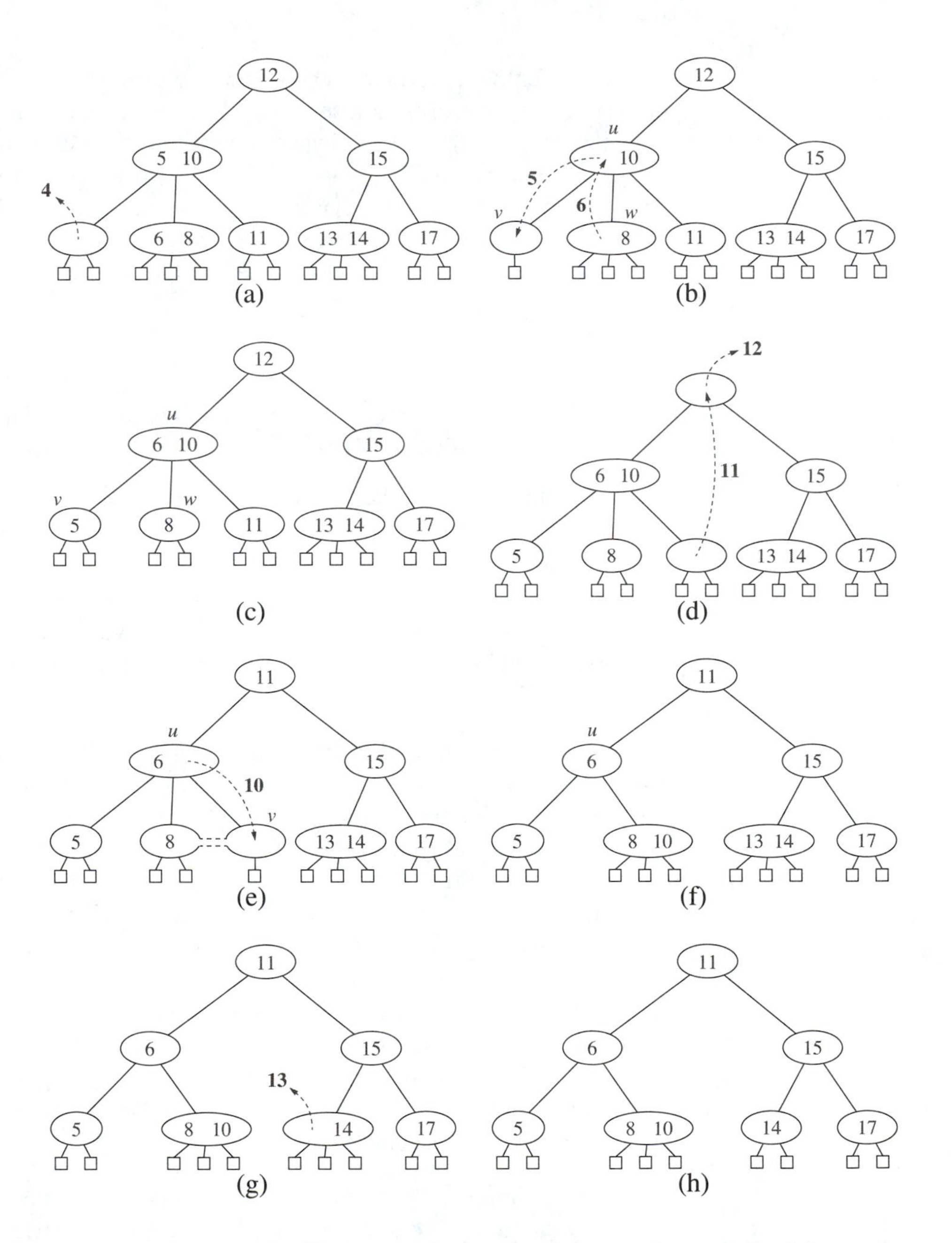

Figure 3.22: A sequence of removals from a $(2,4)$ tree: (a) removal of 4, causing an underflow; (b) a transfer operation; (c) after the transfer operation; (d) removal of 12, causing an underflow; (e) a fusion operation; (f) after the fusion operation; (g) removal of 13; (h) after removing 13.

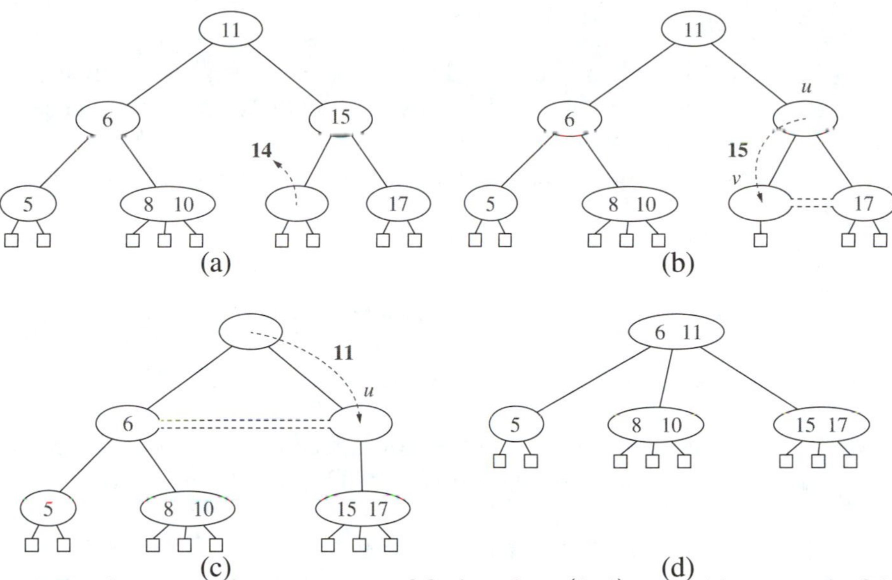

Figure 3.23: A propagating sequence of fusions in a $(2,4)$ tree: (a) removal of 14, which causes an underflow; (b) fusion, which causes another underflow; (c) second fusion operation, which causes the root to be removed; (d) final tree.

Performance of a $(2,4)$ Tree

Table 3.24 summarizes the running times of the main operations of a dictionary realized with a $(2,4)$ tree. The time complexity analysis is based on the following:

- The height of a $(2,4)$ tree storing n items is $O(\log n)$, by Theorem 3.4.
- A split, transfer, or fusion operation takes $O(1)$ time.
- A search, insertion, or removal of an item visits $O(\log n)$ nodes.

Operation	Time
size, isEmpty	$O(1)$
findElement, insertItem, removeElement	$O(\log n)$
findAllElements, removeAllElements	$O(\log n + s)$

Table 3.24: Performance of an n-element dictionary realized by a $(2,4)$ tree, where s denotes the size of the iterators returned by findAllElements and removeAllElements. The space usage is $O(n)$.

Thus, $(2,4)$ trees provide for fast dictionary search and update operations. $(2,4)$ trees also have an interesting relationship to the data structure we discuss next.

3.3.3 Red-Black Trees

The data structure we discuss in this section, the red-black tree, is a binary search tree that uses a kind of "pseudo-depth" to achieve balance using the approach of a depth-bounded search tree. In particular, a ***red-black tree*** is a binary search tree with nodes colored red and black in a way that satisfies the following properties:

***Root Property*:** The root is black.

***External Property*:** Every external node is black.

***Internal Property*:** The children of a red node are black.

Depth Property*:** All the external nodes have the same ***black depth, which is defined as the number of black ancestors minus one.

An example of a red-black tree is shown in Figure 3.25. Throughout this section, we use the convention of drawing ***black nodes*** and their parent edges with ***thick lines***.

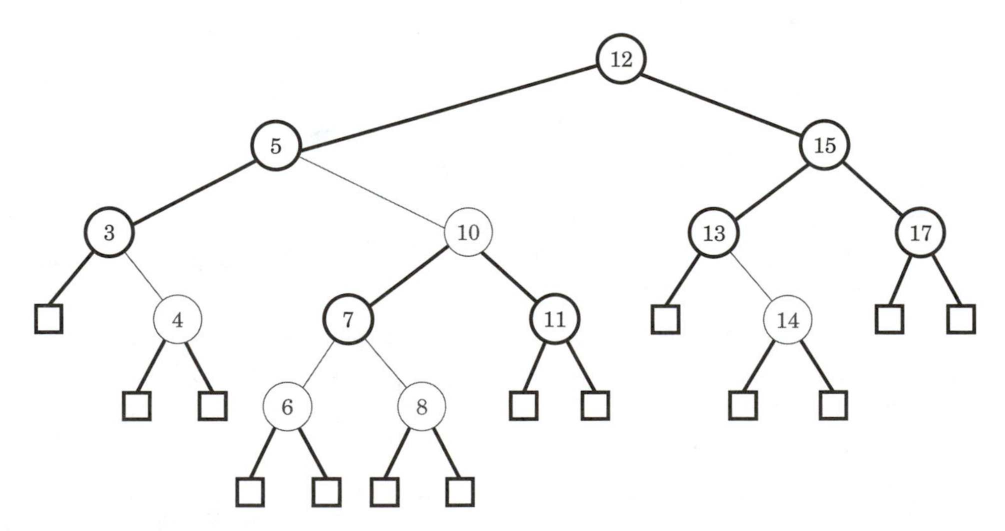

Figure 3.25: Red-black tree associated with the $(2,4)$ tree of Figure 3.18. Each external node of this red-black tree has three black ancestors; hence, it has black depth 3. Recall that we use thick lines to denote black nodes.

As has been the convention in this chapter, we assume that items are stored in the internal nodes of a red-black tree, with the external nodes being empty placeholders. Also, we describe our algorithms assuming external nodes are real, but we note in passing that at the expense of slightly more complicated search and update methods, external nodes could be **null** or references to a NULL_NODE object.

The red-black tree definition becomes more intuitive by noting an interesting correspondence between red-black and $(2,4)$ trees, as illustrated in Figure 3.26. Namely, given a red-black tree, we can construct a corresponding $(2,4)$ tree by merging every red node v into its parent and storing the item from v at its parent. Conversely, we can transform any $(2,4)$ tree into a corresponding red-black tree by coloring each node black and performing a simple transformation for each internal node v.

- If v is a 2-node, then keep the (black) children of v as is.
- If v is a 3-node, then create a new red node w, give v's first two (black) children to w, and make w and v's third child be the two children of v.
- If v is a 4-node, then create two new red nodes w and z, give v's first two (black) children to w, give v's last two (black) children to z, and make w and z be the two children of v.

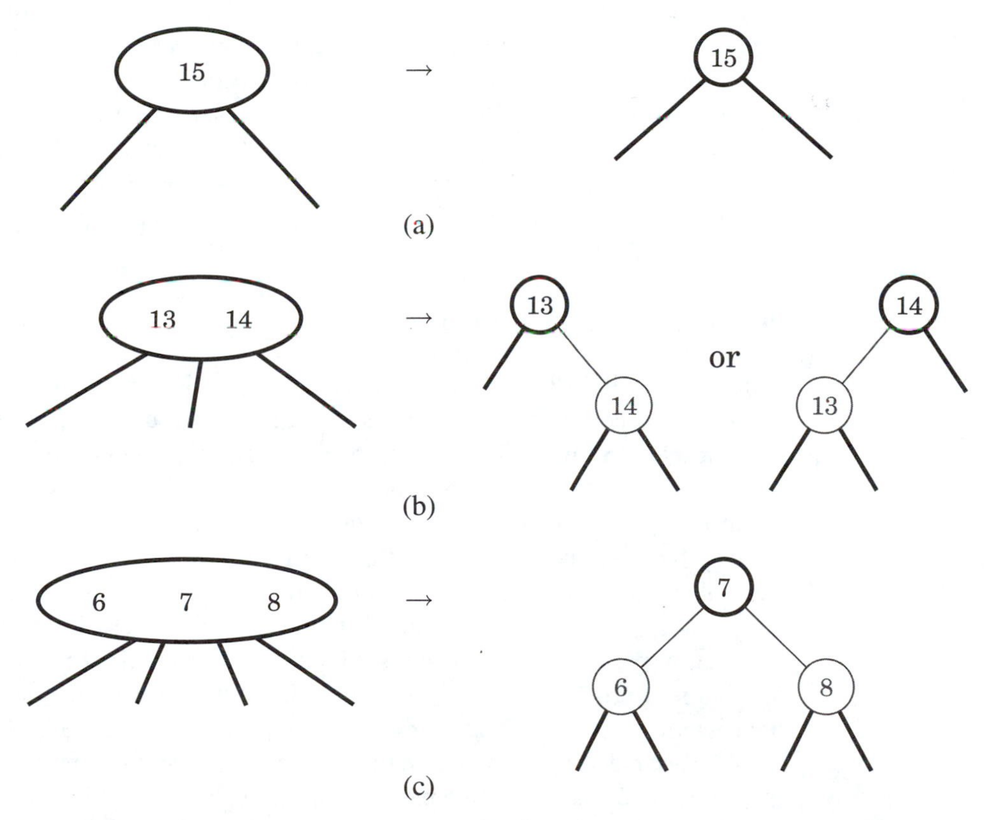

Figure 3.26: Correspondence between a $(2,4)$ tree and a red-black tree: (a) 2-node; (b) 3-node; (c) 4-node.

This correspondence between (2,4) trees and red-black trees provides important intuition that we will use in our discussions. In fact, the update algorithms for red-black trees are mysteriously complex without this intuition. We also have the following property for red-black trees.

Theorem 3.5: *The height of a red-black tree storing n items is $O(\log n)$.*

Proof: Let T be a red-black tree storing n items, and let h be the height of T. We justify this theorem by establishing the following fact:

$$\log(n+1) \leq h \leq 2\log(n+1).$$

Let d be the common black depth of all the external nodes of T. Let T' be the (2,4) tree associated with T, and let h' be the height of T'. We know that $h' = d$. Hence, by Theorem 3.4, $d = h' \leq \log(n+1)$. By the internal node property, $h \leq 2d$. Thus, we obtain $h \leq 2\log(n+1)$. The other inequality, $\log(n+1) \leq h$, follows from Theorem 2.8 and the fact that T has n internal nodes. ■

We assume that a red-black tree is realized with a linked structure for binary trees (Section 2.3.4), in which we store a dictionary item and a color indicator at each node. Thus the space requirement for storing n keys is $O(n)$. The algorithm for searching in a red-black tree T is the same as that for a standard binary search tree (Section 3.1.2). Thus, searching in a red-black tree takes $O(\log n)$ time.

Performing the update operations in a red-black tree is similar to that of a binary search tree, except that we must additionally restore the color properties.

Insertion in a Red-Black Tree

Consider the insertion of an element x with key k into a red-black tree T, keeping in mind the correspondence between T and its associated (2,4) tree T' and the insertion algorithm for T'. The insertion algorithm initially proceeds as in a binary search tree (Section 3.1.4). Namely, we search for k in T until we reach an external node of T, and we replace this node with an internal node z, storing (k,x) and having two external-node children. If z is the root of T, we color z black, else we color z red. We also color the children of z black. This action corresponds to inserting (k,x) into a node of the (2,4) tree T' with external children. In addition, this action preserves the root, external and depth properties of T, but it may violate the internal property. Indeed, if z is not the root of T and the parent v of z is red, then we have a parent and a child (namely, v and z) that are both red. Note that by the root property, v cannot be the root of T, and by the internal property (which was previously satisfied), the parent u of v must be black. Since z and its parent are red, but z's grandparent u is black, we call this violation of the internal property a ***double red*** at node z.

To remedy a double red, we consider two cases.

Case 1: ***The Sibling* w *of* v *is Black.*** (See Figure 3.27.) In this case, the double red denotes the fact that we have created a malformed replacement for a corresponding 4-node of the $(2,4)$ tree T' in our red-black tree, which has as its children the four black children of u, v, and z. Our malformed replacement has one red node (v) that is the parent of another red node (z), while we want it to have the two red nodes as siblings instead. To fix this problem, we perform a ***trinode restructuring*** of T. The trinode restructuring is done by the operation restructure(z), which consists of the following steps (see again Figure 3.27; this operation is also discussed in Section 3.2):

- Take node z, its parent v, and grandparent u, and temporarily relabel them as a, b, and c, in left-to-right order, so that a, b, and c will be visited in this order by an inorder tree traversal.
- Replace the grandparent u with the node labeled b, and make nodes a and c the children of b, keeping inorder relationships unchanged.

After performing the restructure(z) operation, we color b black and we color a and c red. Thus, the restructuring eliminates the double-red problem.

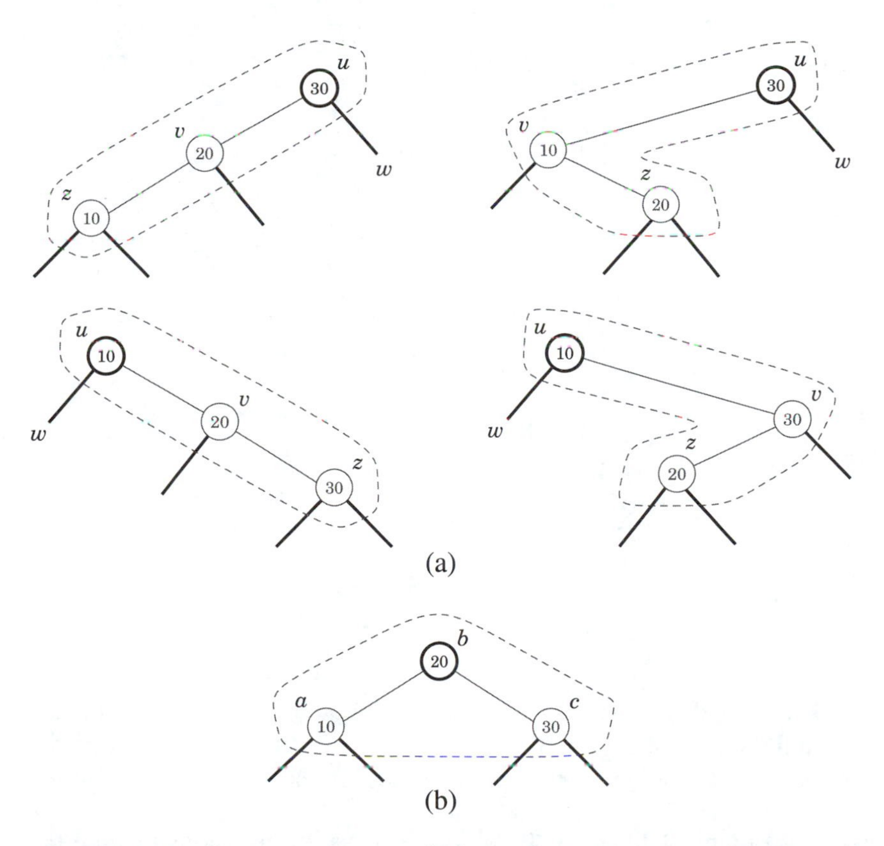

Figure 3.27: Restructuring a red-black tree to remedy a double red: (a) the four configurations for u, v, and z before restructuring; (b) after restructuring.

Case 2: ***The Sibling* w *of* v *is Red.*** (See Figure 3.28.) In this case, the double red denotes an overflow in the corresponding $(2,4)$ tree T. To fix the problem, we perform the equivalent of a split operation. Namely, we do a ***recoloring***: we color v and w black and their parent u red (unless u is the root, in which case, it is colored black). It is possible that, after such a recoloring, the double-red problem reappears, albeit higher up in the tree T, since u may have a red parent. If the double-red problem reappears at u, then we repeat the consideration of the two cases at u. Thus, a recoloring either eliminates the double-red problem at node z, or propagates it to the grandparent u of z. We continue going up T performing recolorings until we finally resolve the double-red problem (with either a final recoloring or a trinode restructuring). Thus, the number of recolorings caused by an insertion is no more than half the height of tree T, that is, no more than $\log(n+1)$ by Theorem 3.5.

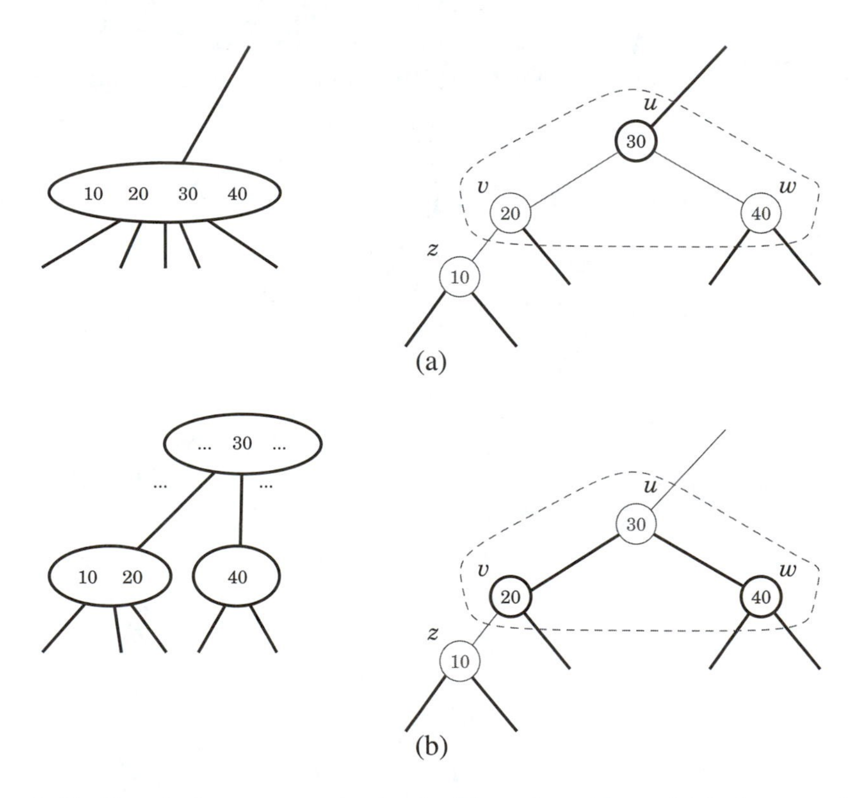

Figure 3.28: Recoloring to remedy the double-red problem: (a) before recoloring and the corresponding 5-node in the associated $(2,4)$ tree before the split; (b) after the recoloring (and corresponding nodes in the associated $(2,4)$ tree after the split).

Figures 3.29 and 3.30 show a sequence of insertions in a red-black tree.

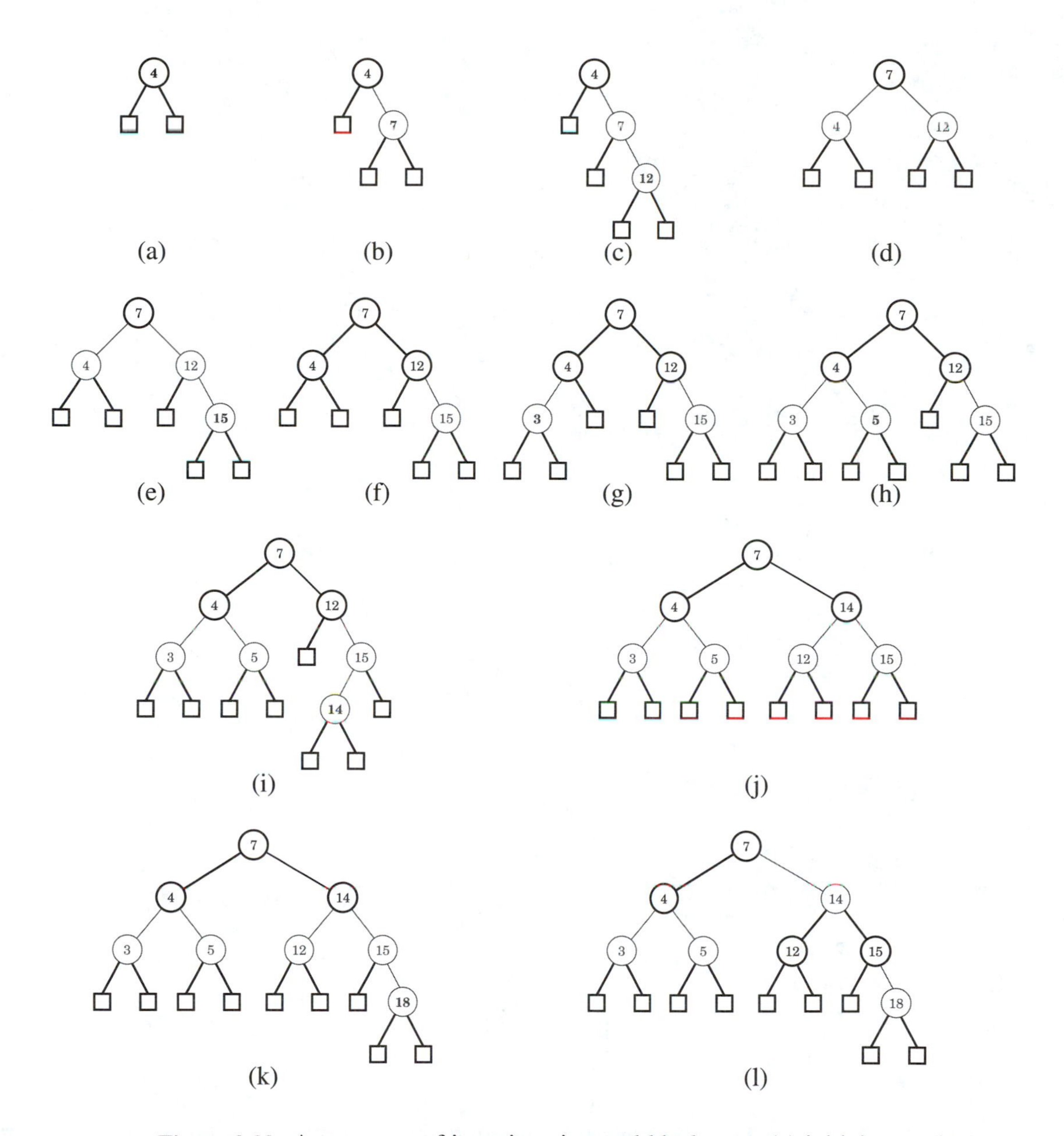

Figure 3.29: A sequence of insertions in a red-black tree: (a) initial tree; (b) insertion of 7; (c) insertion of 12, which causes a double red; (d) after restructuring; (e) insertion of 15, which causes a double red; (f) after recoloring (the root remains black); (g) insertion of 3; (h) insertion of 5; (i) insertion of 14, which causes a double red; (j) after restructuring; (k) insertion of 18, which causes a double red; (l) after recoloring. (Continued in Figure 3.30.)

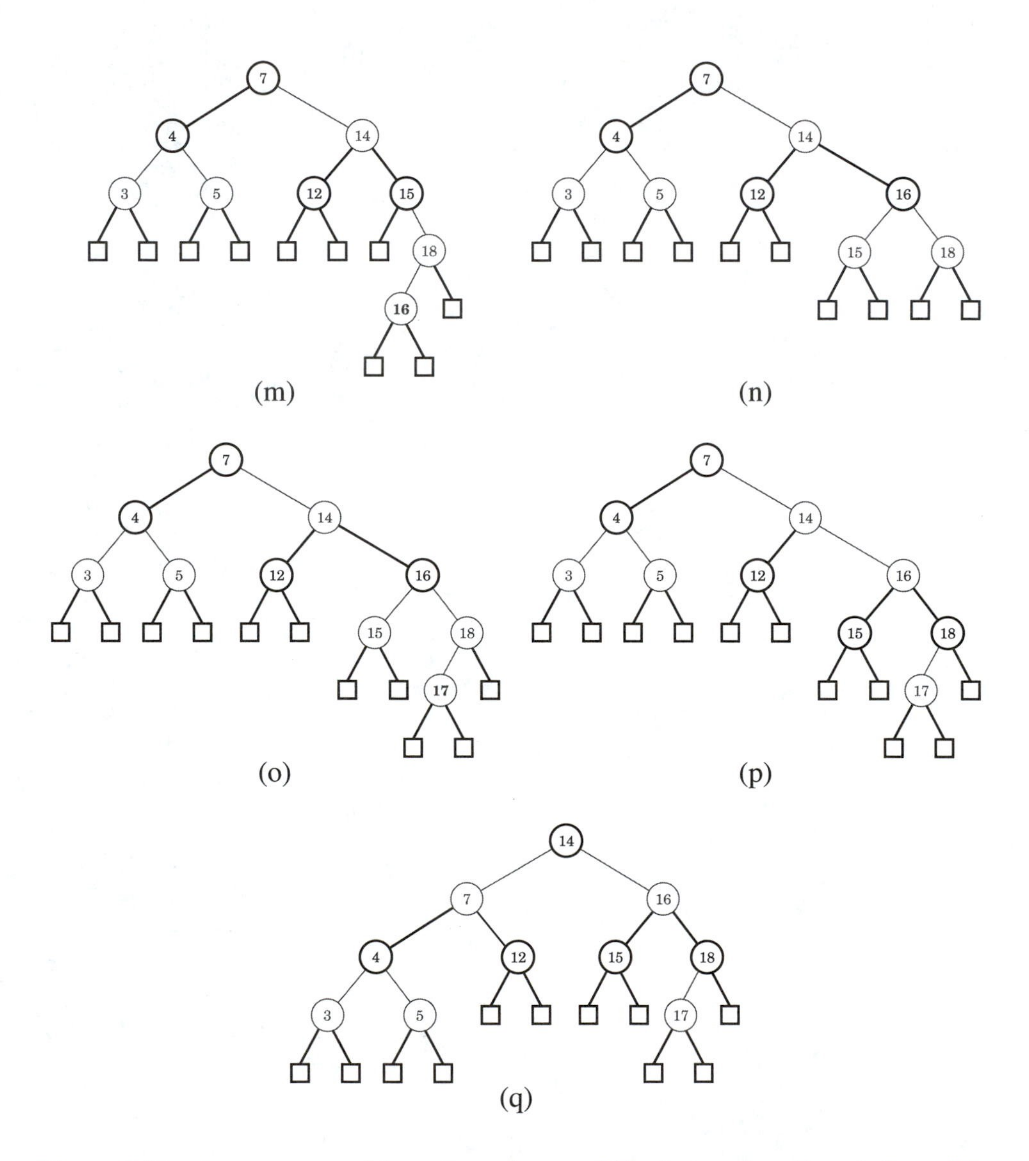

Figure 3.30: A sequence of insertions in a red-black tree (continued from Figure 3.29): (m) insertion of 16, which causes a double red; (n) after restructuring; (o) insertion of 17, which causes a double red; (p) after recoloring there is again a double red, to be handled by a restructuring; (q) after restructuring.

The cases for insertion imply an interesting property for red-black trees. Namely, since the Case 1 action eliminates the double-red problem with a single trinode restructuring and the Case 2 action performs no restructuring operations, at most one restructuring is needed in a red-black tree insertion. By the above analysis and the fact that a restructuring or recoloring takes $O(1)$ time, we have the following:

Theorem 3.6: *The insertion of a key-element item in a red-black tree storing n items can be done in $O(\log n)$ time and requires at most $O(\log n)$ recolorings and one trinode restructuring (a* restructure *operation).*

Removal in a Red-Black Tree

Suppose now that we are asked to remove an item with key k from a red-black tree T. Removing such an item initially proceeds as for a binary search tree (Section 3.1.5). First, we search for a node u storing such an item. If node u does not have an external child, we find the internal node v following u in the inorder traversal of T, move the item at v to u, and perform the removal at v. Thus, we may consider only the removal of an item with key k stored at a node v with an external child w. Also, as we did for insertions, we keep in mind the correspondence between red-black tree T and its associated $(2,4)$ tree T' (and the removal algorithm for T').

To remove the item with key k from a node v of T with an external child w we proceed as follows. Let r be the sibling of w and x be the parent of v. We remove nodes v and w, and make r a child of x. If v was red (hence r is black) or r is red (hence v was black), we color r black and we are done. If, instead, r is black and v was black, then, to preserve the depth property, we give r a fictitious ***double-black*** color. We now have a color violation, called the double-black problem. A double black in T denotes an underflow in the corresponding $(2,4)$ tree T'. Recall that x is the parent of the double-black node r. To remedy the double-black problem at r, we consider three cases.

Case 1: ***The Sibling* y *of* r *is Black and has a Red Child* z.** (See Figure 3.31.) Resolving this case corresponds to a transfer operation in the $(2,4)$ tree T'. We perform a ***trinode restructuring*** by means of operation restructure(z). Recall that the operation restructure(z) takes the node z, its parent y, and grandparent x, labels them temporarily left to right as a, b, and c, and replaces x with the node labeled b, making it the parent of the other two. (See also the description of restructure in Section 3.2.) We color a and c black, give b the former color of x, and color r black. This trinode restructuring eliminates the double-black problem. Hence, at most one restructuring is performed in a removal operation in this case.

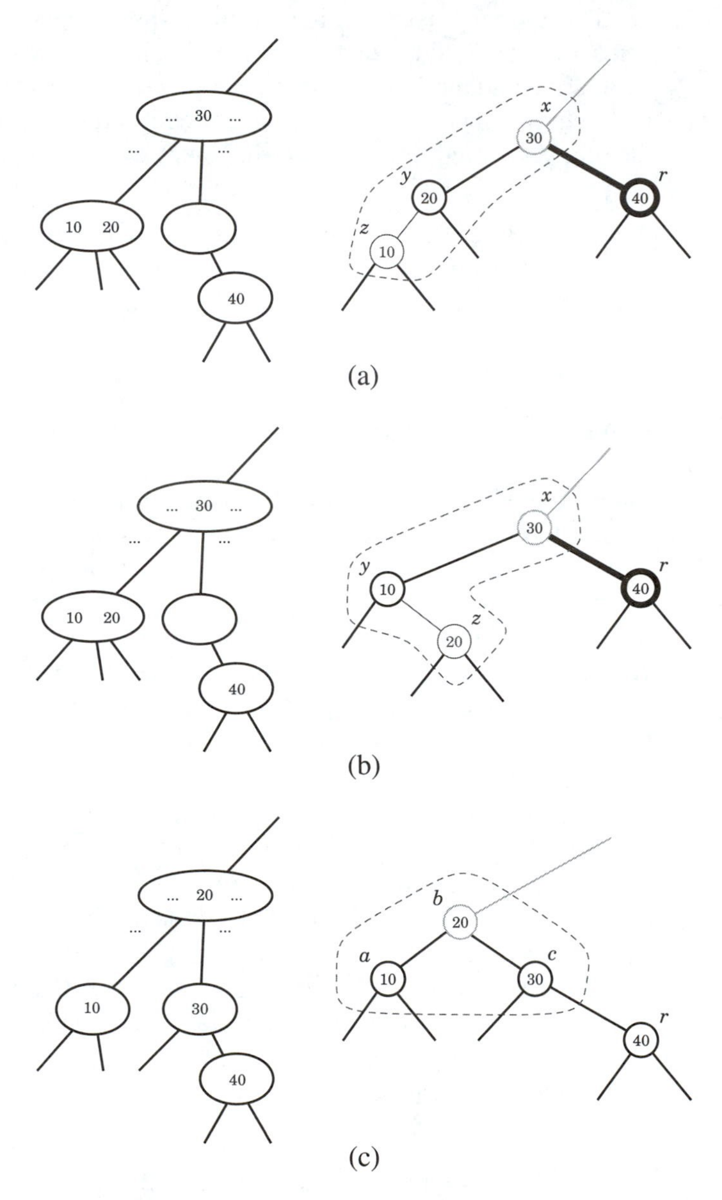

Figure 3.31: Restructuring of a red-black tree to remedy the double-black problem: (a) and (b) configurations before the restructuring, where r is a right child and the associated nodes in the corresponding $(2,4)$ tree before the transfer (two other symmetric configurations where r is a left child are possible); (c) configuration after the restructuring and the associated nodes in the corresponding $(2,4)$ tree after the transfer. Node x in parts (a) and (b) and node b in part (c) may be either red or black.

Case 2: ***The Sibling* y *of* r *is Black and Both Children of* y *are Black*.** (See Figures 3.32 and 3.33.) Resolving this case corresponds to a fusion operation in the corresponding $(2,4)$ tree T'. We do a ***recoloring***; we color r black, we color y red, and, if x is red, we color it black (Figure 3.32); otherwise, we color x ***double black*** (Figure 3.33). Hence, after this recoloring, the double-black problem may reappear at the parent x of r. (See Figure 3.33.) That is, this recoloring either eliminates the double-black problem or propagates it into the parent of the current node. We then repeat a consideration of these three cases at the parent. Thus, since Case 1 performs a trinode restructuring operation and stops (and, as we will soon see, Case 3 is similar), the number of recolorings caused by a removal is no more than $\log(n+1)$.

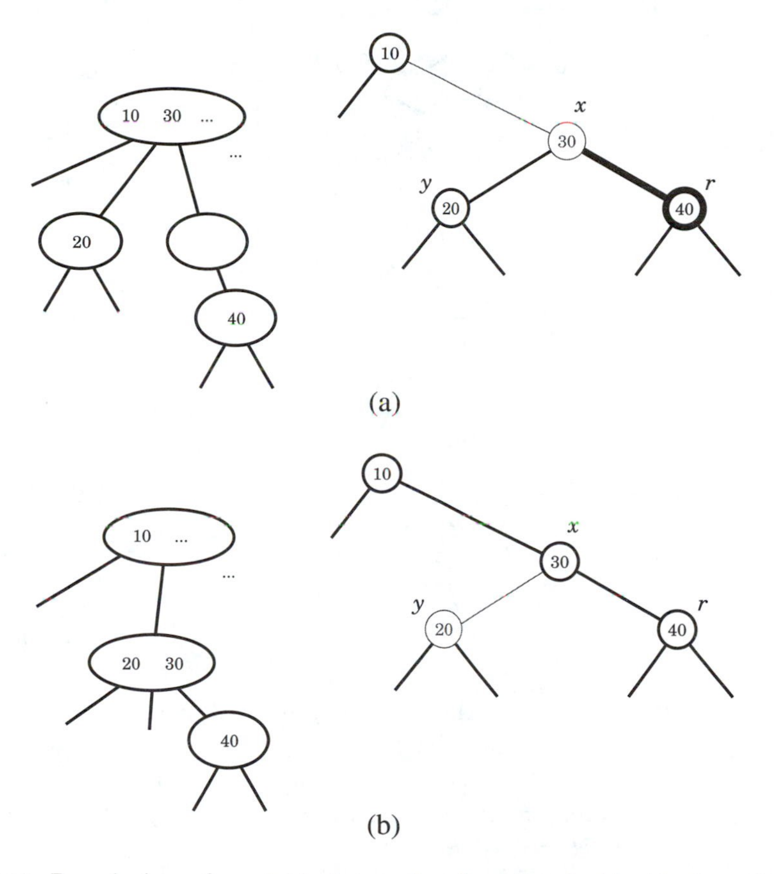

Figure 3.32: Recoloring of a red-black tree that fixes the double-black problem: (a) before the recoloring and corresponding nodes in the associated $(2,4)$ tree before the fusion (other similar configurations are possible); (b) after the recoloring and corresponding nodes in the associated $(2,4)$ tree after the fusion.

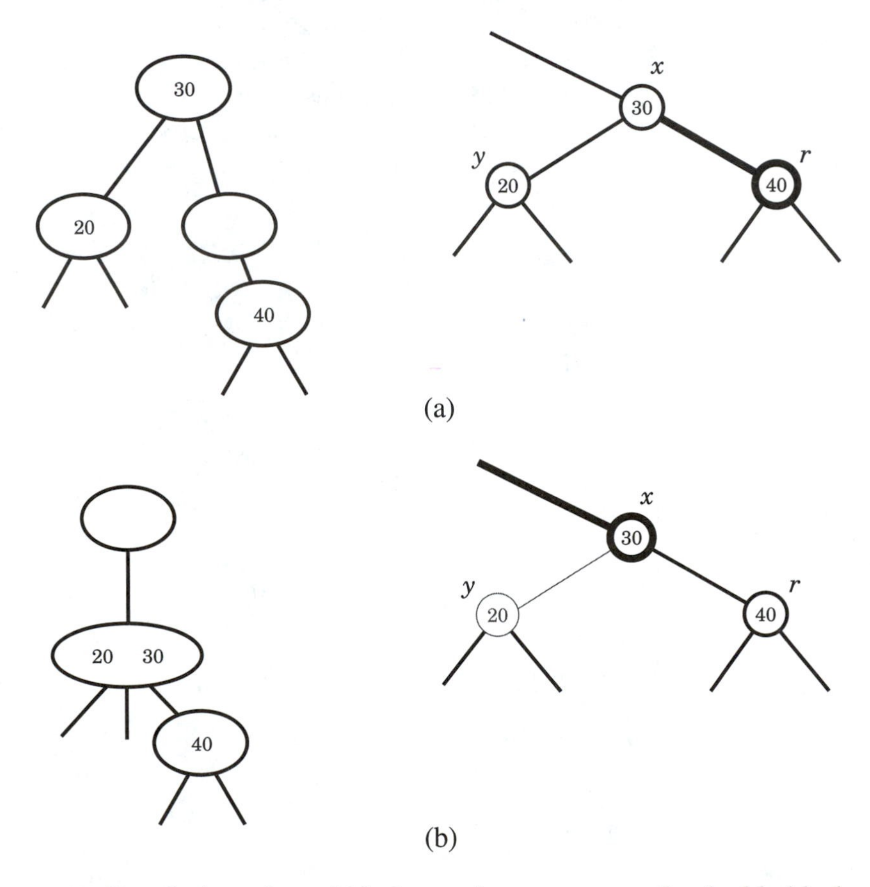

Figure 3.33: Recoloring of a red-black tree that propagates the double black problem: (a) configuration before the recoloring and corresponding nodes in the associated $(2,4)$ tree before the fusion (other similar configurations are possible); (b) configuration after the recoloring and corresponding nodes in the associated $(2,4)$ tree after the fusion.

Case 3: ***The Sibling* y *of* r *is Red.*** (See Figure 3.34.) In this case, we perform an ***adjustment*** operation, as follows. If y is the right child of x, let z be the right child of y; otherwise, let z be the left child of y. Execute the trinode restructure operation restructure(z), which makes y the parent of x. Color y black and x red. An adjustment corresponds to choosing a different representation of a 3-node in the $(2,4)$ tree T'. After the adjustment operation, the sibling of r is black, and either Case 1 or Case 2 applies, with a different meaning of x and y. Note that if Case 2 applies, the double-black problem cannot reappear. Thus, to complete Case 3 we make one more application of either Case 1 or Case 2 above and we are done. Therefore, at most one adjustment is performed in a removal operation.

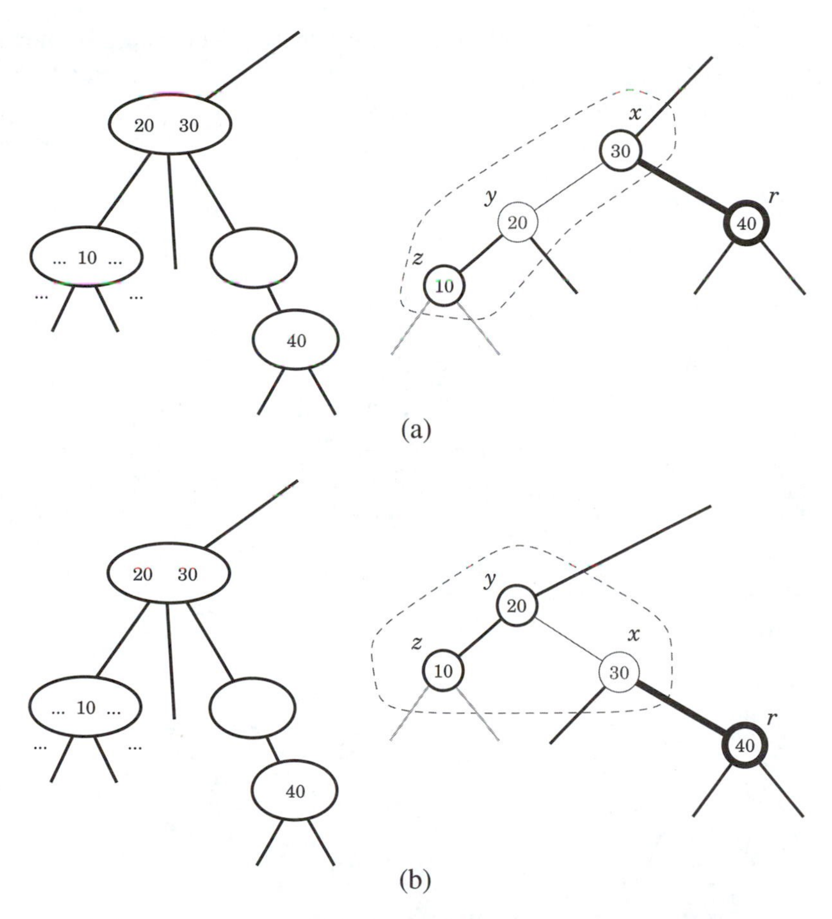

Figure 3.34: Adjustment of a red-black tree in the presence of a double black problem: (a) configuration before the adjustment and corresponding nodes in the associated $(2,4)$ tree (a symmetric configuration is possible); (b) configuration after the adjustment with the same corresponding nodes in the associated $(2,4)$ tree.

From the above algorithm description, we see that the tree updating needed after a removal involves an upward march in the tree T, while performing at most a constant amount of work (in a restructuring, recoloring, or adjustment) per node. The changes we make at any node in T during this upward march takes $O(1)$ time, because it affects a constant number of nodes. Moreover, since the restructuring cases terminate upward propagation in the tree, we have the following.

Theorem 3.7: *The algorithm for removing an item from a red-black tree with n items takes $O(\log n)$ time and performs $O(\log n)$ recolorings and at most one adjustment plus one additional trinode restructuring. Thus, it performs at most two* restructure *operations.*

In Figures 3.35 and 3.36, we show a sequence of removal operations on a red-black tree. We illustrate Case 1 restructurings in Figure 3.35c and d. We illustrate Case 2 recolorings at several places in Figures 3.35 and 3.36. Finally, in Figure 3.36i and j, we show an example of a Case 3 adjustment.

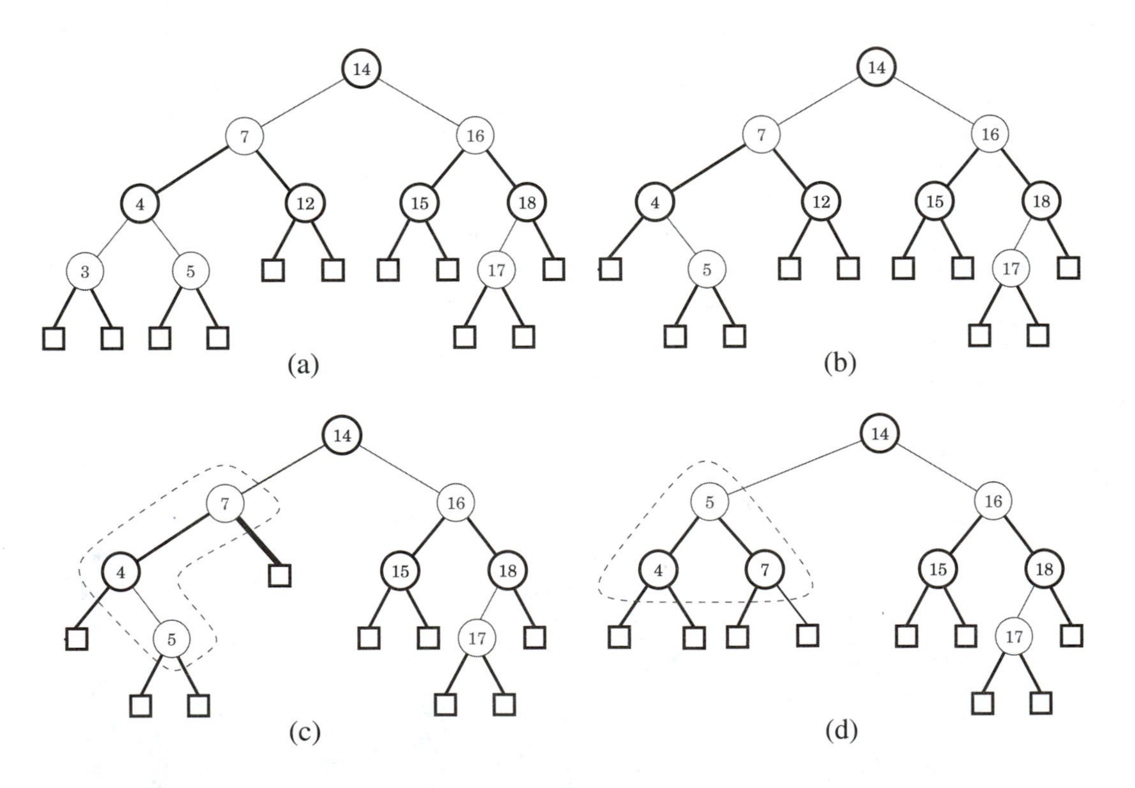

Figure 3.35: Sequence of removals from a red-black tree: (a) initial tree; (b) removal of 3; (c) removal of 12, causing a double black (handled by restructuring); (d) after restructuring.

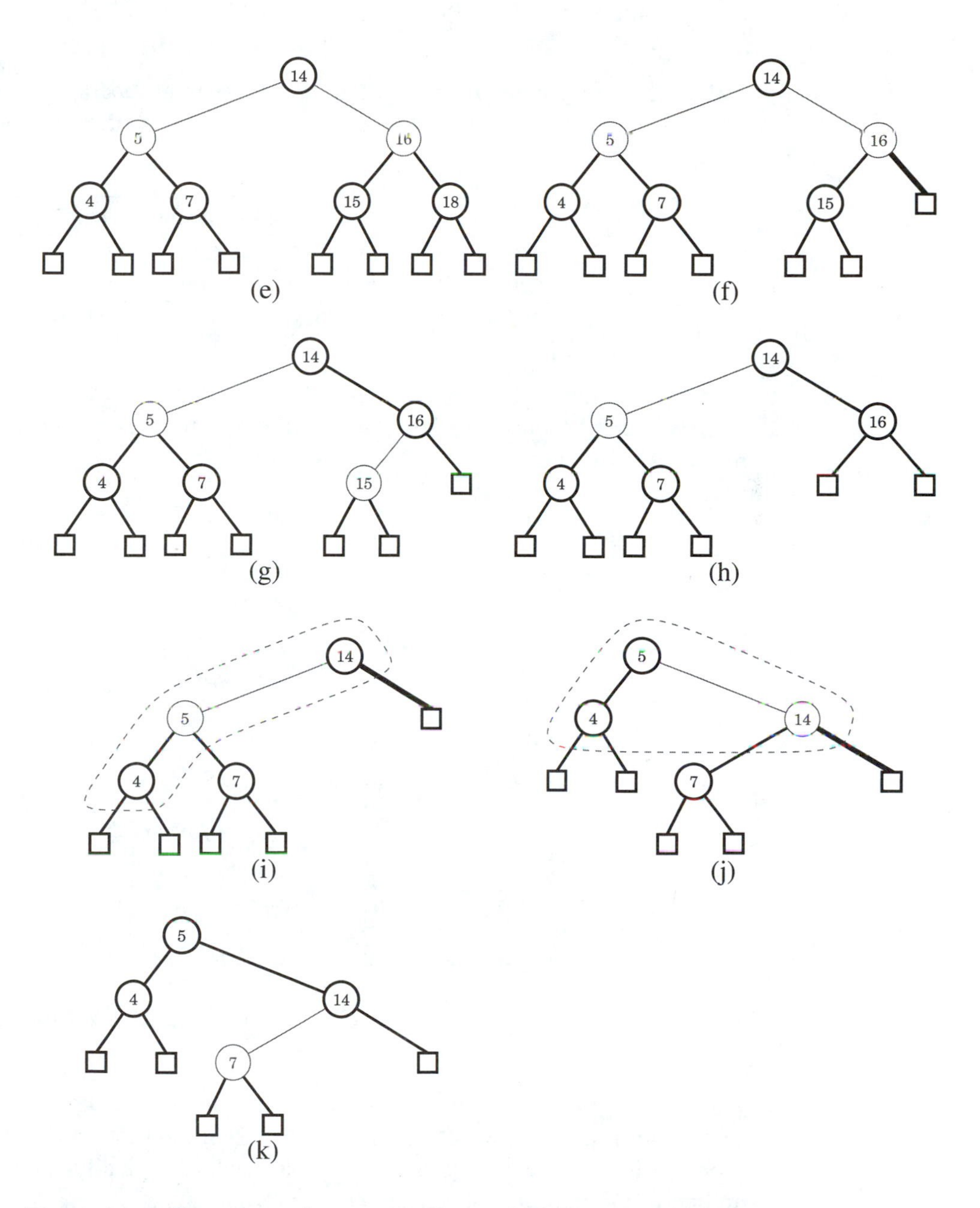

Figure 3.36: Sequence of removals in a red-black tree (continued): (e) removal of 17; (f) removal of 18, causing a double black (handled by recoloring); (g) after recoloring; (h) removal of 15; (i) removal of 16, causing a double black (handled by an adjustment); (j) after the adjustment, the double black needs to be handled by a recoloring; (k) after the recoloring.

Performance of a Red-Black Tree

Table 3.37 summarizes the running times of the main operations of a dictionary realized by means of a red-black tree. We illustrate the justification for these bounds in Figure 3.38.

Operation	Time
size, isEmpty	$O(1)$
findElement, insertItem, removeElement	$O(\log n)$
findAllElements, removeAllElements	$O(\log n + s)$

Table 3.37: Performance of an n-element dictionary realized by a red-black tree, where s denotes the size of the iterators returned by findAllElements and removeAllElements. The space usage is $O(n)$.

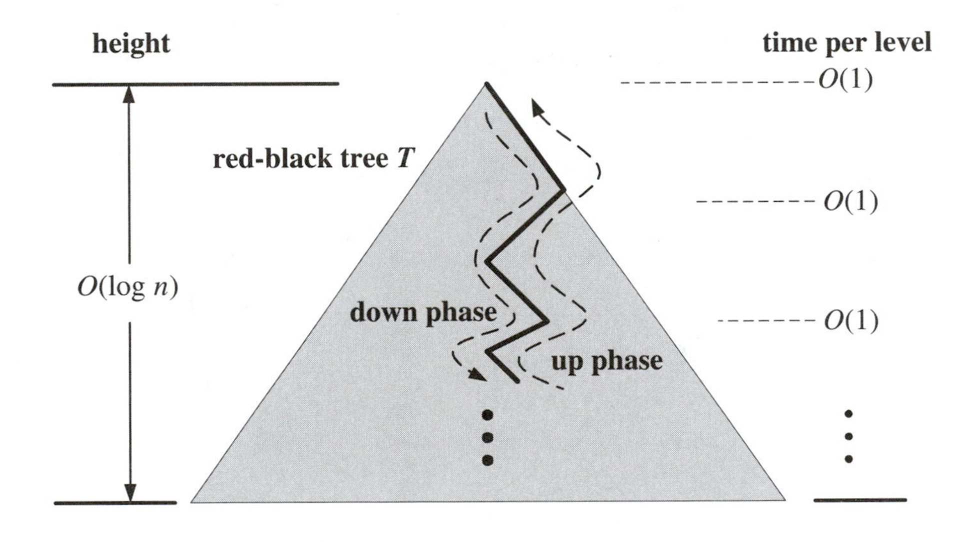

Figure 3.38: Illustrating the running time of searches and updates in a red-black tree. The time performance is $O(1)$ per level, broken into a down phase, which typically involves searching, and an up phase, which typically involves recolorings and performing local trinode restructurings (rotations).

Thus, a red-black tree achieves logarithmic worst-case running times for both searching and updating in a dictionary. The red-black tree data structure is slightly more complicated than its corresponding $(2,4)$ tree. Even so, a red-black tree has a conceptual advantage that only a constant number of trinode restructurings are ever needed to restore the balance in a red-black tree after an update.

3.4 Splay Trees

The final balanced search tree data structure we discuss in this chapter is the ***splay tree***. This structure is conceptually quite different from the previously discussed balanced search trees (AVL, red-black, and (2,4) trees), for a splay tree does not use any explicit rules to enforce its balance. Instead, it applies a certain move-to-root operation, called ***splaying*** after every access, in order to keep the search tree balanced in an amortized sense. The splaying operation is performed at the bottom-most node x reached during an insertion, deletion, or even a search. The surprising thing about splaying is that it allows us to guarantee amortized running times for insertions, deletions, and searches that are logarithmic. The structure of a ***splay tree*** is simply a binary search tree T. In fact, there are no additional height, balance, or color labels that we associate with the nodes of this tree.

3.4.1 Splaying

Given an internal node x of a binary search tree T, we ***splay*** x by moving x to the root of T through a sequence of restructurings. The particular restructurings we perform are important, for it is not sufficient to move x to the root of T by just any sequence of restructurings. The specific operation we perform to move x up depends upon the relative positions of x, its parent y, and (if it exists) x's grandparent z. There are three cases that we consider.

zig-zig: The node x and its parent y are both left or right children. (See Figure 3.39.) We replace z by x, making y a child of x and z a child of y, while maintaining the inorder relationships of the nodes in T.

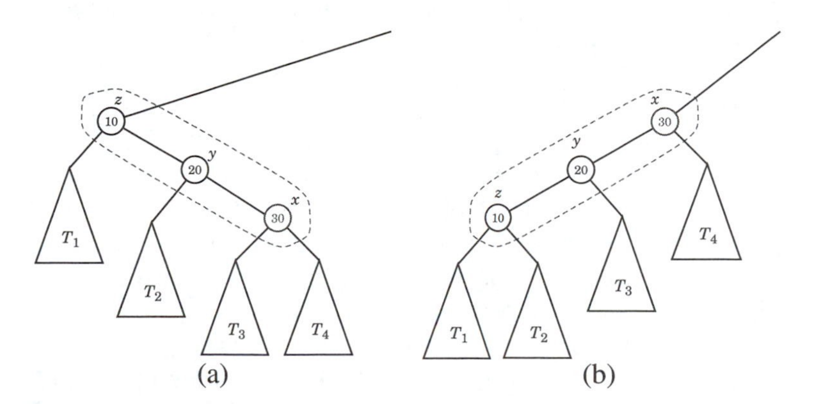

Figure 3.39: Zig-zig: (a) before; (b) after. There is another symmetric configuration where x and y are left children.

***zig-zag*:** One of x and y is a left child and the other is a right child. (See Figure 3.40.) In this case, we replace z by x and make x have as its children the nodes y and z, while maintaining the inorder relationships of the nodes in T.

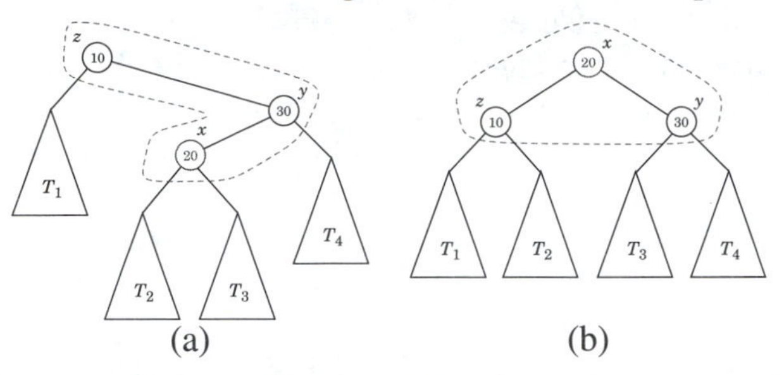

Figure 3.40: Zig-zag: (a) before; (b) after. There is another symmetric configuration where x is a right child and y is a left child.

***zig*:** x does not have a grandparent (or we are not considering x's grandparent for some reason). (See Figure 3.41.) In this case, we rotate x over y, making x's children be the node y and one of x's former children w, so as to maintain the relative inorder relationships of the nodes in T.

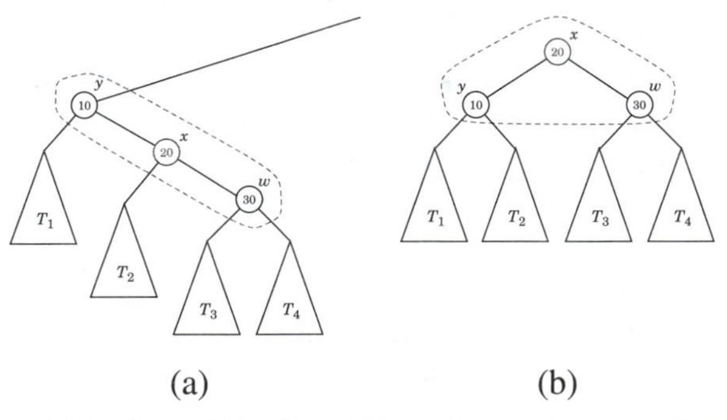

Figure 3.41: Zig: (a) before; (b) after. There is another symmetric configuration where x and w are left children.

We perform a zig-zig or a zig-zag when x has a grandparent, and we perform a zig when x has a parent but not a grandparent. A ***splaying*** step consists of repeating these restructurings at x until x becomes the root of T. Note that this is not the same as a sequence of simple rotations that brings x to the root. An example of the splaying of a node is shown in Figures 3.42 and 3.43.

After a zig-zig or zig-zag, the depth of x decreases by two, and after a zig the depth of x decreases by one. Thus, if x has depth d, splaying x consists of a sequence of $\lfloor d/2 \rfloor$ zig-zigs and/or zig-zags, plus one final zig if d is odd. Since a single zig-zig, zig-zag, or zig affects a constant number of nodes, it can be done in $O(1)$ time. Thus, splaying a node x in a binary search tree T takes time $O(d)$, where d is the depth of x in T. In other words, the time for performing a splaying step for a node x is asymptotically the same as the time needed just to reach that node in a top-down search from the root of T.

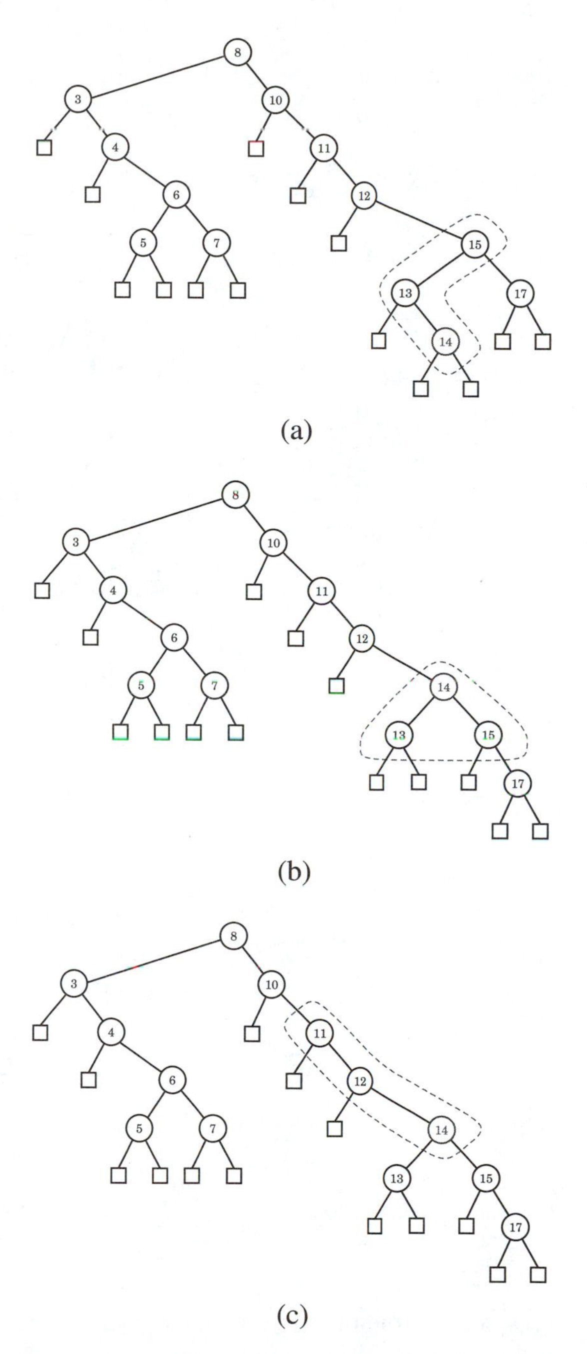

Figure 3.42: Example of splaying a node: (a) splaying the node storing 14 starts with a zig-zag; (b) after the zig-zag; (c) the next step is a zig-zig.

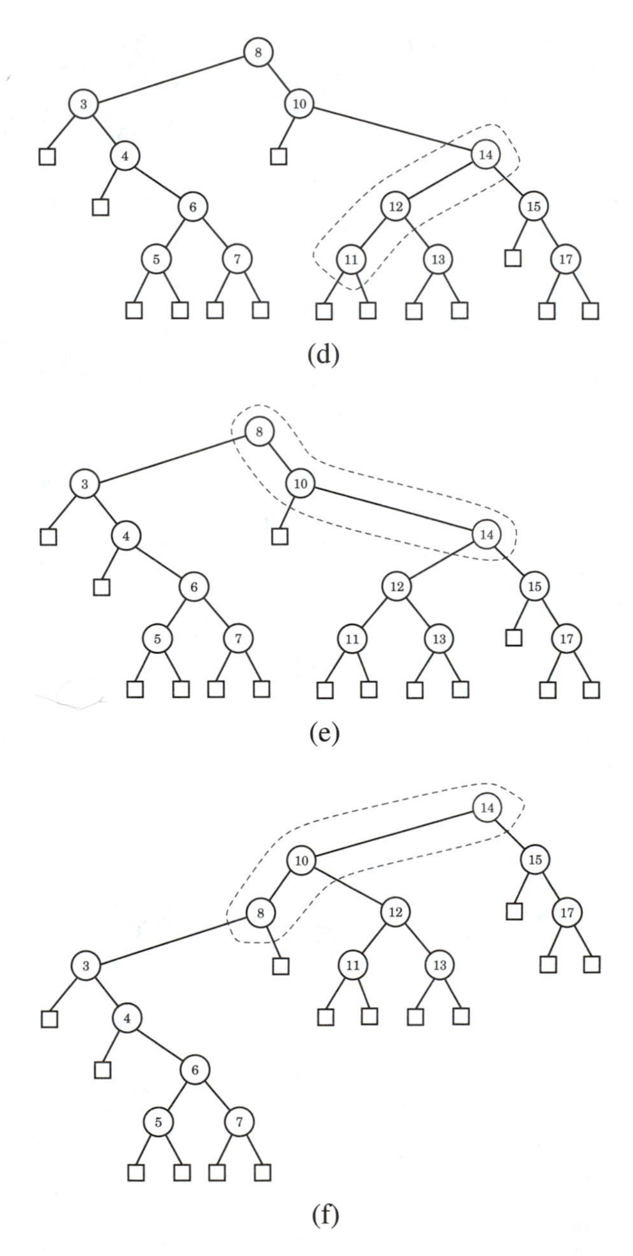

Figure 3.43: Example of splaying a node (continued from Figure 3.42): (d) after the zig-zig; (e) the next step is again a zig-zig; (f) after the zig-zig.

When to Splay

The rules that dictate when splaying is performed are as follows:

- When searching for key k, if k is found at a node x, we splay x, else we splay the parent of the external node at which the search terminates unsuccessfully. For example, the splaying in Figures 3.42 and 3.43 would be performed after searching successfully for key 14 or unsuccessfully for key 14.5.
- When inserting key k, we splay the newly created internal node where k gets inserted. For example, the splaying in Figures 3.42 and 3.43 would be performed if 14 were the newly inserted key. We show a sequence of insertions in a splay tree in Figure 3.44.

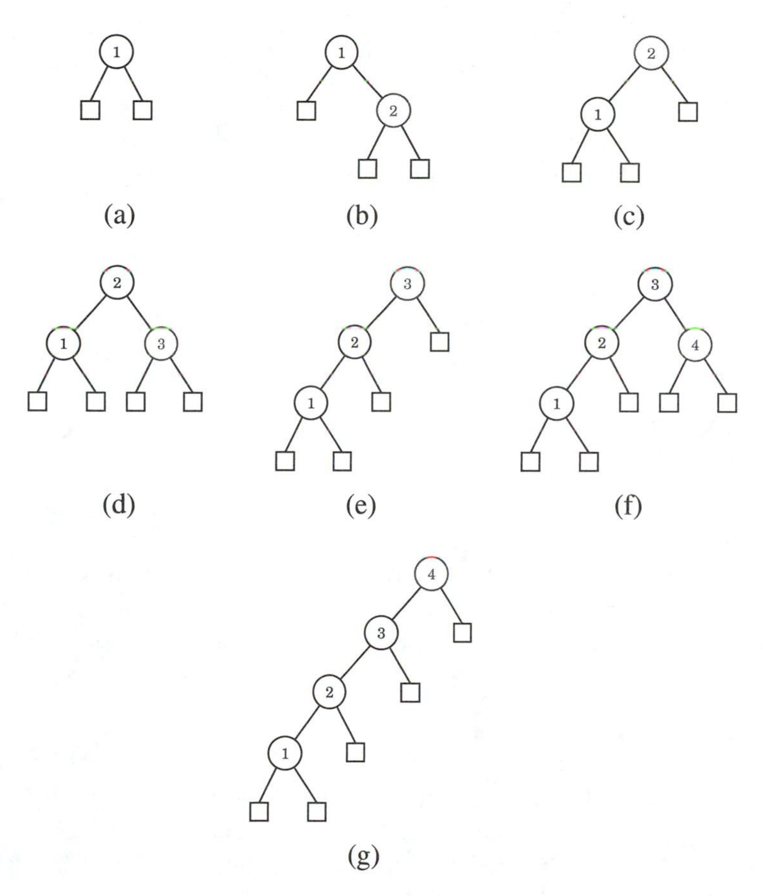

Figure 3.44: A sequence of insertions in a splay tree: (a) initial tree; (b) after inserting 2; (c) after splaying; (d) after inserting 3; (e) after splaying; (f) after inserting 4; (g) after splaying.

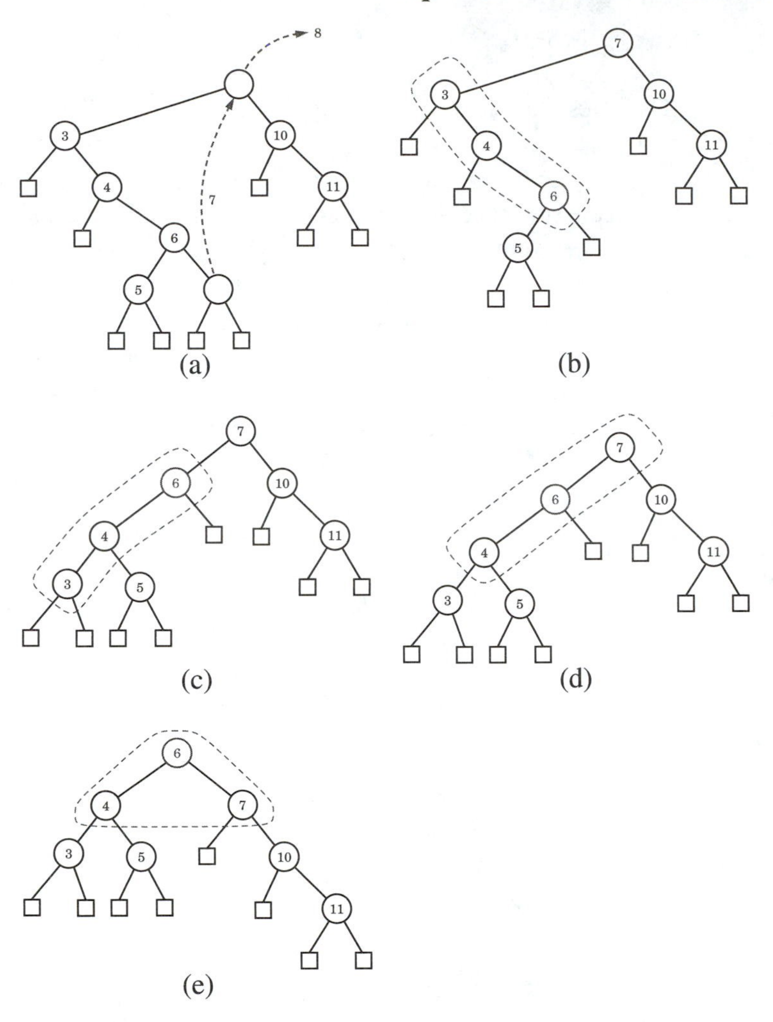

Figure 3.45: Deletion from a splay tree: (a) the deletion of 8 from node r is performed by moving to r the key of the right-most internal node v, in the left subtree of r, deleting v, and splaying the parent u of v; (b) splaying u starts with a zig-zig; (c) after the zig-zig; (d) the next step is a zig; (e) after the zig.

- When deleting a key k, we splay the parent of the node w that gets removed, that is, w is either the node storing k or one of its descendents. (Recall the deletion algorithm for binary search trees given in Section 3.1.2.) An example of splaying following a deletion is shown in Figure 3.45.

In the worst case, the overall running time of a search, insertion, or deletion in a splay tree of height h is $O(h)$, since the node we splay might be the deepest node in the tree. Moreover, it is possible for h to be $\Omega(n)$, as shown in Figure 3.44. Thus, from a worst-case point of view, a splay tree is not an attractive data structure.

3.4.2 Amortized Analysis of Splaying

In spite of its poor worst-case performance, a splay tree performs well in an amortized sense. That is, in a sequence of intermixed searches, insertions, and deletions, each operation takes on average logarithmic time. We note that the time for performing a search, insertion, or deletion is proportional to the time for the associated splaying; hence, in our analysis, we consider only the splaying time.

Let T be a splay tree with n keys, and let v be a node of T. We define the ***size*** $n(v)$ of v as the number of nodes in the subtree rooted at v. Note that the size of an internal node is one more than the sum of the sizes of its two children. We define the ***rank*** $r(v)$ of a node v as the logarithm in base 2 of the size of v, that is, $r(v) = \log n(v)$. Clearly, the root of T has the maximum size $2n+1$ and the maximum rank, $\log(2n+1)$, while each external node has size 1 and rank 0.

We use cyber-dollars to pay for the work we perform in splaying a node x in T, and we assume that one cyber-dollar pays for a zig, while two cyber-dollars pay for a zig-zig or a zig-zag. Hence, the cost of splaying a node at depth d is d cyber-dollars. We keep a virtual account, storing cyber dollars, at each internal node of T. Note that this account exists only for the purpose of our amortized analysis, and does not need to be included in a data structure implementing the splay tree T. When we perform a splaying, we pay a certain number of cyber-dollars (the exact value will be determined later). We distinguish three cases:

- If the payment is equal to the splaying work, then we use it all to pay for the splaying.
- If the payment is greater than the splaying work, we deposit the excess in the accounts of several nodes.
- If the payment is less than the splaying work, we make withdrawals from the accounts of several nodes to cover the deficiency.

We show that a payment of $O(\log n)$ cyber-dollars per operation is sufficient to keep the system working, that is, to ensure that each node keeps a nonnegative account balance. We use a scheme in which transfers are made between the accounts of the nodes to ensure that there will always be enough cyber-dollars to withdraw for paying for splaying work when needed. We also maintain the following invariant:

Before and after a splaying, each node v ***of*** T ***has*** $r(v)$ ***cyber-dollars.***

Note that the invariant does not require us to endow an empty tree with any cyber-dollars. Let $r(T)$ be the sum of the ranks of all the nodes of T. To preserve the invariant after a splaying, we must make a payment equal to the splaying work plus the total change in $r(T)$. We refer to a single zig, zig-zig, or zig-zag operation in a splaying as a splaying ***substep***. Also, we denote the rank of a node v of T before and after a splaying substep with $r(v)$ and $r'(v)$, respectively. The following lemma gives an upper bound on the change of $r(T)$ caused by a single splaying substep.

Lemma 3.8: *Let δ be the variation of $r(T)$ caused by a single splaying substep (a zig, zig-zig, or zig-zag) for a node x in a splay tree T. We have the following:*

- $\delta \le 3(r'(x) - r(x)) - 2$ *if the substep is a zig-zig or zig-zag.*
- $\delta \le 3(r'(x) - r(x))$ *if the substep is a zig.*

Proof: We shall make use of the following mathematical fact (see Appendix A): If $a > 0$, $b > 0$, and $c > a + b$, then

$$\log a + \log b \le 2\log c - 2. \tag{3.6}$$

Let us consider the change in $r(T)$ caused by each type of splaying substep.

***zig-zig*:** (Recall Figure 3.39.) Since the size of each node is one more than the size of its two children, note that only the ranks of x, y, and z change in a zig-zig operation, where y is the parent of x and z is the parent of y. Also, $r'(x) = r(z)$, $r'(y) \le r'(x)$, and $r(y) \ge r(x)$. Thus

$$\begin{aligned}\delta &= r'(x) + r'(y) + r'(z) - r(x) - r(y) - r(z) \\ &\le r'(y) + r'(z) - r(x) - r(y) \\ &\le r'(x) + r'(z) - 2r(x).\end{aligned} \tag{3.7}$$

Observe that $n(x) + n'(z) \le n'(x)$. Thus, by 3.6, $r(x) + r'(z) \le 2r'(x) - 2$. That is,

$$r'(z) \le 2r'(x) - r(x) - 2.$$

This inequality and 3.7 imply

$$\begin{aligned}\delta &\le r'(x) + (2r'(x) - r(x) - 2) - 2r(x) \\ &\le 3(r'(x) - r(x)) - 2.\end{aligned}$$

***zig-zag*:** (Recall Figure 3.40.) Again, by the definition of size and rank, only the ranks of x, y, and z change, where y denotes the parent of x and z denotes the parent of y. Also, $r'(x) = r(z)$ and $r(x) \le r(y)$. Thus

$$\begin{aligned}\delta &= r'(x) + r'(y) + r'(z) - r(x) - r(y) - r(z) \\ &\le r'(y) + r'(z) - r(x) - r(y) \\ &\le r'(y) + r'(z) - 2r(x).\end{aligned} \tag{3.8}$$

Observe that $n'(y) + n'(z) \le n'(x)$. Thus, by 3.6, $r'(y) + r'(z) \le 2r'(x) - 2$. This inequality and 3.8 imply

$$\begin{aligned}\delta &\le 2r'(x) - 2 - 2r(x) \\ &\le 3(r'(x) - r(x)) - 2.\end{aligned}$$

***zig*:** (Recall Figure 3.41.) In this case, only the ranks of x and y change, where y denotes the parent of x. Also, $r'(y) \le r(y)$ and $r'(x) \ge r(x)$. Thus

$$\begin{aligned}\delta &= r'(y) + r'(x) - r(y) - r(x) \\ &\le r'(x) - r(x) \\ &\le 3(r'(x) - r(x)).\end{aligned}$$

■

Theorem 3.9: *Let T be a splay tree with root t, and let Δ be the total variation of $r(T)$ caused by splaying a node x at depth d. We have*

$$\Delta \leq 3(r(t) - r(x)) - d + 2.$$

Proof: Splaying node x consists of $p = \lceil d/2 \rceil$ splaying substeps, each of which is a zig-zig or a zig-zag, except possibly the last one, which is a zig if d is odd. Let $r_0(x) = r(x)$ be the initial rank of x, and for $i = 1, \ldots, p$, let $r_i(x)$ be the rank of x after the ith substep and δ_i be the variation of $r(T)$ caused by the ith substep. By Lemma 3.8, the total variation Δ of $r(T)$ caused by splaying node x is given by

$$\begin{aligned} \Delta &= \sum_{i=1}^{p} \delta_i \\ &\leq \sum_{i=1}^{p} (3(r_i(x) - r_{i-1}(x)) - 2) + 2 \\ &= 3(r_p(x) - r_0(x)) - 2p + 2 \\ &\leq 3(r(t) - r(x)) - d + 2. \end{aligned}$$

■

By Theorem 3.9, if we make a payment of $3(r(t) - r(x)) + 2$ cyber-dollars towards the splaying of node x, we have enough cyber-dollars to maintain the invariant, keeping $r(v)$ cyber-dollars at each node v in T, and pay for the entire splaying work, which costs d dollars. Since the size of the root t is $2n + 1$, its rank $r(t) = \log(2n + 1)$. In addition, we have $r(x) < r(t)$. Thus, the payment to be made for splaying is $O(\log n)$ cyber-dollars. To complete our analysis, we have to compute the cost for maintaining the invariant when a node is inserted or deleted.

When inserting a new node v into a splay tree with n keys, the ranks of all the ancestors of v are increased. Namely, let $v_0, v_i, \ldots, v_d$ be the ancestors of v, where $v_0 = v$, v_i is the parent of v_{i-1}, and v_d is the root. For $i = 1, \ldots, d$, let $n'(v_i)$ and $n(v_i)$ be the size of v_i before and after the insertion, respectively, and let $r'(v_i)$ and $r(v_i)$ be the rank of v_i before and after the insertion, respectively. We have

$$n'(v_i) = n(v_i) + 1.$$

Also, since $n(v_i) + 1 \leq n(v_{i+1})$, for $i = 0, 1, \ldots, d-1$, we have the following for each i in this range:

$$r'(v_i) = \log(n'(v_i)) = \log(n(v_i) + 1) \leq \log(n(v_{i+1})) = r(v_{i+1}).$$

Thus, the total variation of $r(T)$ caused by the insertion is

$$\begin{aligned} \sum_{i=1}^{d} (r'(v_i) - r(v_i)) &\leq r'(v_d) + \sum_{i=1}^{d-1} (r(v_{i+1}) - r(v_i)) \\ &= r'(v_d) - r(v_0) \\ &\leq \log(2n + 1). \end{aligned}$$

Thus, a payment of $O(\log n)$ cyber-dollars is sufficient to maintain the invariant when a new node is inserted.

When deleting a node v from a splay tree with n keys, the ranks of all the ancestors of v are decreased. Thus, the total variation of $r(T)$ caused by the deletion is negative, and we do not need to make any payment to maintain the invariant. Therefore, we may summarize our amortized analysis in the following theorem.

Theorem 3.10: *Consider a sequence of m operations on a splay tree, each a search, insertion, or deletion, starting from an empty splay tree with zero keys. Also, let n_i be the number of keys in the tree after operation i, and n be the total number of insertions. The total running time for performing the sequence of operations is*

$$O\left(m + \sum_{i=1}^{m} \log n_i\right),$$

which is $O(m \log n)$.

In other words, the amortized running time of performing a search, insertion, or deletion in a splay tree is $O(\log n)$, where n is the size of the splay tree at the time. Thus, a splay tree can achieve logarithmic time amortized performance for implementing an ordered dictionary ADT. This amortized performance matches the worst-case performance of AVL trees, $(2,4)$ trees, and red-black trees, but it does so using a simple binary tree that does not need any extra balance information stored at each of its nodes. In addition, splay trees have a number of other interesting properties that are not shared by these other balanced search trees. We explore one such additional property in the following theorem (which is sometimes called the "Static Optimality" theorem for splay trees).

Theorem 3.11: *Consider a sequence of m operations on a splay tree, each a search, insertion, or deletion, starting from a tree T with no keys. Also, let $f(i)$ denote the number of times the item i is accessed in the splay tree, that is, its* **frequency**, *and let n be total number of items. Assuming that each item is accessed at least once, then the total running time for performing the sequence of operations is*

$$O\left(m + \sum_{i=1}^{n} f(i) \log(m/f(i))\right).$$

We leave the proof of this theorem as an exercise. The remarkable thing about this theorem is that it states that the amortized running time of accessing an item i is $O(\log(m/f(i)))$. For example, if a sequence of operations accesses some item i as many as $m/4$ times, then the amortized running time of each of these accesses is $O(1)$ when the dictionary is implemented with a splay tree. Contrast this to the $\Omega(\log n)$ time needed to access this item if the dictionary is implemented with an AVL tree, $(2,4)$ tree, or red-black tree. Thus, an additional nice property of splay trees is that they can "adapt" to the ways in which items are being accessed in a dictionary, so as to achieve faster running times for the frequently accessed items.

3.5 Skip Lists

An interesting data structure for efficiently realizing the ordered dictionary ADT is the ***skip list***. This data structure makes random choices in arranging the items in such a way that search and update times are logarithmic ***on average***.

Randomizing Data Structures and Algorithms

Interestingly, the notion of average time complexity used here does not depend on the probability distribution of the keys in the input. Instead, it depends on the use of a random-number generator in the implementation of the insertions to help decide where to place the new item. That is, the structure of the data structure and some algorithms that operate on it depend on the outcomes of random events. In this context, running time is averaged over all possible outcomes of the random numbers used when inserting items.

Because they are used extensively in computer games, cryptography, and computer simulations, methods that generate numbers that can be viewed as random numbers are built into most modern computers. Some methods, called ***pseudo-random number generators***, generate random-like numbers deterministically, starting with an initial number called a ***seed***. Other methods use hardware devices to extract "true" random numbers from nature. In any case, we will assume that our computer has access to numbers that are sufficiently random for our analysis.

The main advantage of using ***randomization*** in data structure and algorithm design is that the structures and methods that result are usually simple and efficient. We can devise a simple randomized data structure, called the skip list, that has a logarithmic time bound for searching, similar to what is achieved by the binary searching algorithm. Nevertheless, the logarithmic bound is ***expected*** for the skip list, while it is ***worst-case*** for binary searching in a lookup table. On the other hand, skip lists are much faster than lookup tables for dictionary updates.

Skip List Definition

A ***skip list*** S for dictionary D consists of a series of lists $\{S_0, S_1, \ldots, S_h\}$. Each list S_i stores a subset of the items of D sorted by a nondecreasing key plus items with two special keys, denoted $-\infty$ and $+\infty$, where $-\infty$ is smaller than every possible key that can be inserted in D and $+\infty$ is larger than every possible key that can be inserted in D. In addition, the lists in S satisfy the following:

- List S_0 contains every item of dictionary D (plus the special items with keys $-\infty$ and $+\infty$).
- For $i = 1, \ldots, h-1$, list S_i contains (in addition to $-\infty$ and $+\infty$) a randomly generated subset of the items in list S_{i-1}.
- List S_h contains only $-\infty$ and $+\infty$.

An example of a skip list is shown in Figure 3.46. It is customary to visualize a skip list S with list S_0 at the bottom and lists $S_1, \ldots, S_h$ above it. Also, we refer to h as the ***height*** of skip list S.

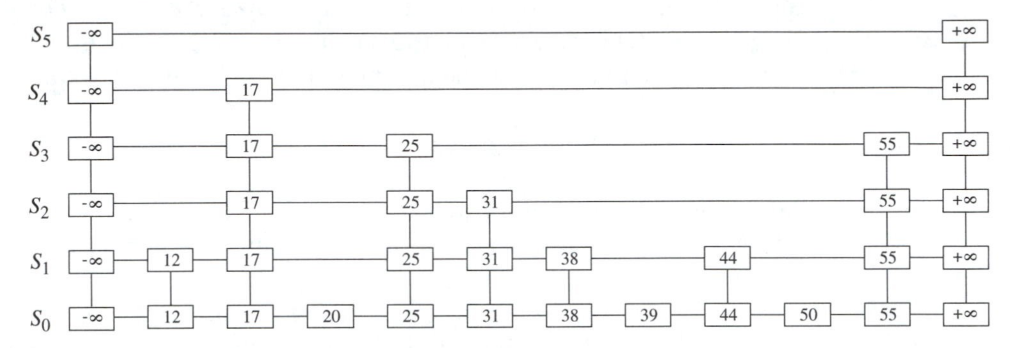

Figure 3.46: Example of a skip list.

Intuitively, the lists are set up so that S_{i+1} contains more or less every other item in S_i. As we shall see in the details of the insertion method, the items in S_{i+1} are chosen at random from the items in S_i by picking each item from S_i to also be in S_{i+1} with probability $1/2$. That is, in essence, we "flip a coin" for each item in S_i and place that item in S_{i+1} if the coin comes up "heads." Thus, we expect S_1 to have about $n/2$ items, S_2 to have about $n/4$ items, and, in general, S_i to have about $n/2^i$ items. In other words, we expect the height h of S to be about $\log n$. The halving of the number of items from one list to the next is not enforced as an explicit property of skip lists, however. Instead, randomization is used.

Using the position abstraction used for lists and trees, we view a skip list as a two-dimensional collection of positions arranged horizontally into ***levels*** and vertically into ***towers***. Each level is a list S_i and each tower contains positions storing the same item across consecutive lists. The positions in a skip list can be traversed using the following operations:

after(p): Return the position following p on the same level.

before(p): Return the position preceding p on the same level.

below(p): Return the position below p in the same tower.

above(p): Return the position above p in the same tower.

We conventionally assume that the above operations return a **null** position if the position requested does not exist. Without going into the details, we note that we can easily implement a skip list by means of a linked structure such that the above traversal methods each take $O(1)$ time, given a skip-list position p. Such a linked structure is essentially a collection of h doubly linked lists aligned at towers, which are also doubly linked lists.

3.5.1 Searching

Skip lists allow for simple dictionary search algorithms. In fact, all of the skip-list search methods are based on an elegant SkipSearch procedure, shown in Algorithm 3.47, that takes a key k and finds the item in a skip list S with the largest key (which is possibly $-\infty$) that is less than or equal to k.

Algorithm SkipSearch(k):
  Input: A search key k
  Output: Position in S whose item has the largest key less than or equal to k

  Let p be the top-most, left position of S (which should have at least 2 levels).
  while below(p) $\neq$ **null do**
    $p \leftarrow$ below(p)   {drop down}
    while key(after(p)) $\leq k$ **do**
      Let $p \leftarrow$ after(p)   {scan forward}
  return p.

Algorithm 3.47: Algorithm for searching in a skip list S.

Let us examine this algorithm more closely. We begin the SkipSearch method by setting a position variable p to the top-most, left position in the skip list S. That is, p is set to the position of the special item with key $-\infty$ in S_h. We then perform the following steps (see Figure 3.48):

1. If S.below(p) is null, then the search terminates—we are ***at the bottom*** and have located the largest item in S with key less than or equal to the search key k. Otherwise, we ***drop down*** to the next lower level in the present tower by setting $p \leftarrow S$.below(p).
2. Starting at position p, we move p forward until it is at the right-most position on the present level such that key(p) $\leq k$. We call this the ***scan forward*** step. Note that such a position always exists, since each level contains the special keys $+\infty$ and $-\infty$. In fact, after we perform the scan forward for this level, p may remain where it started. In any case, we then repeat the previous step.

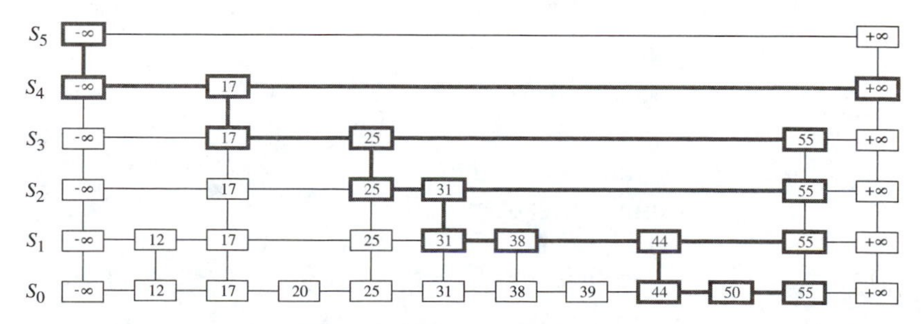

Figure 3.48: Example of a search in a skip list. The positions visited and the links traversed when searching (unsuccessfully) for key 52 are drawn with thick lines.

3.5.2 Update Operations

Given the SkipSearch method, it is easy to implement findElement(k)—we simply perform $p \leftarrow$ SkipSearch(k) and test whether or not key$(p) = k$. As it turns out, the expected running time of the SkipSearch algorithm is $O(\log n)$. We postpone this analysis, however, until after we discuss the update methods for skip lists.

Insertion

The insertion algorithm for skip lists uses randomization to decide how many references to the new item (k,e) should be added to the skip list. We begin the insertion of a new item (k,e) into a skip list by performing a SkipSearch(k) operation. This gives us the position p of the bottom-level item with the largest key less than or equal to k (note that p may be the position of the special item with key $-\infty$). We then insert (k,e) in this bottom-level list immediately after position p. After inserting the new item at this level, we "flip" a coin. That is, we call a method random() that returns a number between 0 and 1, and if that number is less than $1/2$, then we consider the flip to have come up "heads"; otherwise, we consider the flip to have come up "tails." If the flip comes up tails, then we stop here. If the flip comes up heads, on the other hand, then we backtrack to the previous (next higher) level and insert (k,e) in this level at the appropriate position. We again flip a coin; if it comes up heads, we go to the next higher level and repeat. Thus, we continue to insert the new item (k,e) in lists until we finally get a flip that comes up tails. We link together all the references to the new item (k,e) created in this process to create the ***tower*** for (k,e). We give the pseudo-code for this insertion algorithm for a skip list S in Algorithm 3.49 and we illustrate this algorithm in Figure 3.50. Our insertion algorithm uses an operation insertAfterAbove$(p,q,(k,e))$ that inserts a position storing the item (k,e) after position p (on the same level as p) and above position q, returning the position r of the new item (and setting internal references so that after, before, above, and below methods will work correctly for p, q, and r).

Algorithm SkipInsert(k,e):
  Input: Item (k,e)
  Output: None

```
p ← SkipSearch(k)
q ← insertAfterAbove(p, null, (k,e))        {we are at the bottom level}
while random() < 1/2 do
    while above(p) = null do
        p ← before(p)        {scan backward}
    p ← above(p)        {jump up to higher level}
    q ← insertAfterAbove(p, q, (k,e))        {insert new item}
```

Algorithm 3.49: Insertion in a skip list, assuming random() returns a random number between 0 and 1, and we never insert past the top level.

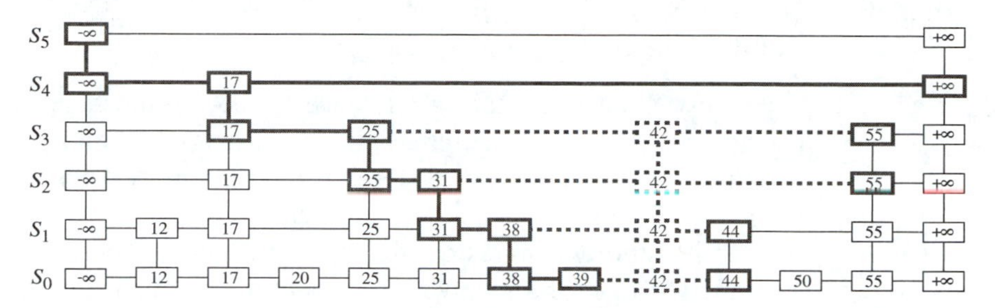

Figure 3.50: Insertion of an element with key 42 into the skip list of Figure 3.46. The positions visited and the links traversed are drawn with thick lines. The positions inserted to hold the new item are drawn with dashed lines.

Removal

Like the search and insertion algorithms, the removal algorithm for a skip list S is quite simple. In fact, it is even easier than the insertion algorithm. Namely, to perform a removeElement(k) operation, we begin by performing a search for the given key k. If a position p with key k is not found, then we return the NO_SUCH_KEY element. Otherwise, if a position p with key k is found (on the bottom level), then we remove all the positions above p, which are easily accessed by using above operations to climb up the tower of this item in S starting at position p. The removal algorithm is illustrated in Figure 3.51 and a detailed description of it is left as an exercise (R-3.19). As we show in the next subsection, the running time for removal in a skip list is expected to be $O(\log n)$.

Before we give this analysis, however, there are some minor improvements to the skip list data structure we would like to discuss. First, we don't need to store references to items at the levels above 0, because all that is needed at these levels are references to keys. Second, we don't actually need the above method. In fact, we don't need the before method either. We can perform item insertion and removal in strictly a top-down, scan-forward fashion, thus saving space for "up" and "prev" references. We explore the details of this optimization in an exercise (C-3.26).

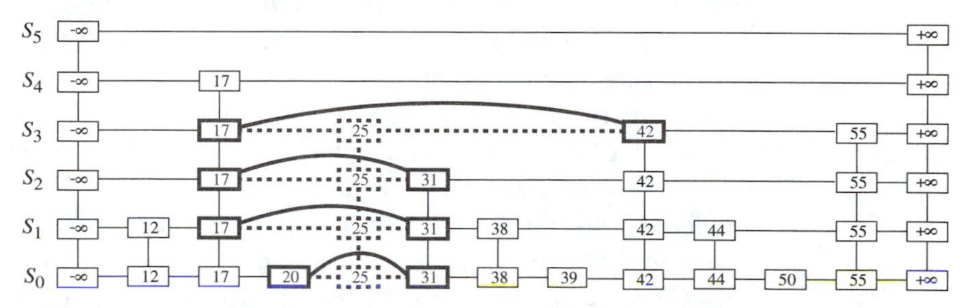

Figure 3.51: Removal of the item with key 25 from the skip list of Figure 3.50. The positions visited and the links traversed after the initial search are drawn with thick lines. The positions removed are drawn with dashed lines.

Maintaining the Top-most Level

A skip list S must maintain a reference to the top-most, left position in S as an instance variable, and must have a policy for any insertion that wishes to continue inserting a new item past the top level of S. There are two possible courses of action we can take, both of which have their merits.

One possibility is to restrict the top level, h, to be kept at some fixed value that is a function of n, the number of elements currently in the dictionary (from the analysis we will see that $h = \max\{10, 2\lceil \log n \rceil\}$ is a reasonable choice, and picking $h = 3\lceil \log n \rceil$ is even safer). Implementing this choice means that we must modify the insertion algorithm to stop inserting a new item once we reach the top-most level (unless $\lceil \log n \rceil < \lceil \log(n+1) \rceil$, in which case we can now go at least one more level, since the bound on the height is increasing).

The other possibility is to let an insertion continue inserting a new element as long it keeps returning heads from the random number generator. As we show in the analysis of skip lists, the probability that an insertion will go to a level that is more than $O(\log n)$ is very low, so this design choice should also work.

However, either choice will still result in our being able to perform element search, insertion, and removal in expected $O(\log n)$ time, which we will show in the next section.

3.5.3 A Probabilistic Analysis of Skip Lists

As we have shown above, skip lists provide a simple implementation of an ordered dictionary. In terms of worst-case performance, however, skip lists are not a superior data structure. In fact, if we don't officially prevent an insertion from continuing significantly past the current highest level, then the insertion algorithm can go into what is almost an infinite loop (it is not actually an infinite loop, however, since the probability of having a fair coin repeatedly come up heads forever is 0). Moreover, we cannot infinitely add elements to a list without eventually running out of memory. In any case, if we terminate item insertion at the highest level h, then the ***worst-case*** running time for performing the findElement, insertItem, and removeElement operations in a skip list S with n items and height h is $O(n+h)$. This worst-case performance occurs when the tower of every item reaches level $h-1$, where h is the height of S. However, this event has very low probability. Judging from this worst case, we might conclude that the skip list structure is strictly inferior to the other dictionary implementations discussed earlier in this chapter. But this would not be a fair analysis, for this worst-case behavior is a gross overestimate.

Because the insertion step involves randomization, a more honest analysis of skip lists involves a bit of probability. At first, this might seem like a major undertaking, for a complete and thorough probabilistic analysis could require deep mathematics. Fortunately, such an analysis is not necessary to understand the expected asymptotic behavior of skip lists. The informal and intuitive probabilistic analysis we give below uses only basic concepts of probability theory.

Bounding Height in a Skip List

Let us begin by determining the expected value of the height h of S (assuming that we do not terminate insertions early). The probability that a given item is stored in a position at level i is equal to the probability of getting i consecutive heads when flipping a coin, that is, this probability is $1/2^i$. Hence, the probability P_i that level i has at least one item is at most

$$P_i \leq \frac{n}{2^i},$$

for the probability that any one of n different events occurs is, at most, the sum of the probabilities that each occurs.

The probability that the height h of S is larger than i is equal to the probability that level i has at least one item, that is, it is no more than P_i. This means that h is larger than, say, $3\log n$ with probability at most

$$P_{3\log n} \leq \frac{n}{2^{3\log n}} = \frac{n}{n^3} = \frac{1}{n^2}.$$

More generally, given a constant $c > 1$, h is larger than $c\log n$ with probability at most $1/n^{c-1}$. That is, the probability that h is smaller than or equal to $c\log n$ is at least $1 - 1/n^{c-1}$. Thus, with high probability, the height h of S is $O(\log n)$.

Analyzing Search Time in a Skip List

Consider the running time of a search in skip list S, and recall that such a search involves two nested **while** loops. The inner loop performs a scan forward on a level of S as long as the next key is no greater than the search key k, and the outer loop drops down to the next level and repeats the scan forward iteration. Since the height h of S is $O(\log n)$ with high probability, the number of drop-down steps is $O(\log n)$ with high probability.

So we have yet to bound the number of scan forward steps we make. Let n_i be the number of keys examined while scanning forward at level i. Observe that, after the key at the starting position, each additional key examined in a scan-forward at level i cannot also belong to level $i+1$. If any of these items were on the previous level, we would have encountered them in the previous scan-forward step. Thus, the probability that any key is counted in n_i is $1/2$. Therefore, the expected value of n_i is exactly equal to the expected number of times we must flip a fair coin before it comes up heads. Let us denote this quantity with e. We have

$$e = \frac{1}{2} \cdot 1 + \frac{1}{2} \cdot (1 + e)$$

Thus, $e = 2$ and the expected amount of time spent scanning forward at any level i is $O(1)$. Since S has $O(\log n)$ levels with high probability, a search in S takes expected time $O(\log n)$. By a similar analysis, we can show that the expected running time of an insertion or a removal is $O(\log n)$.

Space Usage in a Skip List

Finally, let us turn to the space requirement of a skip list S. As we observed above, the expected number of items at level i is $n/2^i$, which means that the expected total number of items in S is

$$\sum_{i=0}^{h} \frac{n}{2^i} = n \sum_{i=0}^{h} \frac{1}{2^i} < 2n.$$

Hence, the expected space requirement of S is $O(n)$.

Table 3.52 summarizes the performance of a dictionary realized by a skip list.

Operation	Time
keys, elements	$O(n)$
findElement, insertItem, removeElement	$O(\log n)$ (expected)
findAllElements, removeAllElements	$O(\log n + s)$ (expected)

Table 3.52: Performance of a dictionary implemented with a skip list. We denote the number of items in the dictionary at the time the operation is performed with n, and the size of the iterator returned by operations findAllElements and removeAllElements with s. The expected space requirement is $O(n)$.

3.6 Java Example: AVL and Red-Black Trees

In this section, we describe a general binary search tree class, BinarySearchTree, and how it can be extended to produce either an AVL tree implementation or a red-black tree implementation. The BinarySearchTree class stores key-element pairs of class Item as the elements stored at the positions (nodes) of its underlying binary tree. The code for BinarySearchTree is shown in Code Fragments 3.54 through 3.56. Note that the underlying binary tree T is used only through the BinaryTree interface, where we assume that BinaryTree includes also methods expandExternal and removeAboveExternal (see Section 2.3.4). Thus, class BinarySearchTree takes advantage of code reuse.

The auxiliary method findPosition, based on the TreeSearch algorithm, is invoked by the findElement, insertItem, and removeElement methods. The instance variable actionPos stores the position where the most recent search, insertion, or removal ended. This instance variable is not necessary to the implementation of a binary search tree, but is useful to classes that will extend BinarySearchTree (see Code Fragments 3.58–3.59 and 3.62–3.63) to identify the position where the previous search, insertion, or removal has taken place. Position actionPos has the intended meaning provided it is used right after executing methods findElement, insertItem, and removeElement.

```
public class Item {
  private Object key, elem;
  protected Item (Object k, Object e) {
    key = k;
    elem = e;
  }
  public Object key() { return key; }
  public Object element() { return elem; }
  public void setKey(Object k) { key = k; }
  public void setElement(Object e) { elem = e; }
}
```

Code Fragment 3.53: Class for the key-element pairs stored in a dictionary.

```
/** Realization of a dictionary by means of a binary search tree */
public class BinarySearchTree implements Dictionary {
  Comparator C; // comparator
  BinaryTree T; // binary tree
  protected Position actionPos; // insertion position or parent of removed position

  public BinarySearchTree(Comparator c) {
    C = c;
    T = (BinaryTree) new NodeBinaryTree();
  }

  // auxiliary methods:
  /** Extract the key of the item at a given node of the tree. */
  protected Object key(Position position) {
    return ((Item) position.element()).key();
  }
  /** Extract the element of the item at a given node of the tree. */
  protected Object element(Position position) {
    return ((Item) position.element()).element();
  }
  /** Check whether a given key is valid. */
  protected void checkKey(Object key) throws InvalidKeyException {
    if(!C.isComparable(key))
      throw new InvalidKeyException("Key "+key+" is not comparable");
  }
```

Code Fragment 3.54: Class BinarySearchTree. (Continued in Code Fragment 3.55.)

```
/** Auxiliary method used by removeElement. */
protected void swap(Position swapPos, Position remPos){
  T.replaceElement(swapPos, remPos.element());
}
/** Auxiliary method used by findElement, insertItem, and removeElement. */
protected Position findPosition(Object key, Position pos) {
  if (T.isExternal(pos))
    return pos; // key not found and external node reached returned
  else {
    Object curKey = key(pos);
    if(C.isLessThan(key, curKey))
      return findPosition(key, T.leftChild(pos));
    else if(C.isGreaterThan(key, curKey)) // search in left subtree
      return findPosition(key, T.rightChild(pos)); // search in right subtree
    else
      return pos; // return internal node where key is found
  }
}

// methods of the dictionary ADT
public int size()  {
  return (T.size() - 1) / 2;
}

public boolean isEmpty() {
  return T.size() == 1;
}

public Object findElement(Object key) throws InvalidKeyException {
  checkKey(key); // may throw an InvalidKeyException
  Position curPos = findPosition(key, T.root());
  actionPos = curPos; // node where the search ended
  if (T.isInternal(curPos))
    return element(curPos);
  else
    return NO_SUCH_KEY;
}
```

Code Fragment 3.55: Class BinarySearchTree, continued from Code Fragment 3.54. (Continues in Code Fragment 3.56.)

```
public void insertItem(Object key, Object element)
  throws InvalidKeyException {
  checkKey(key); // may throw an InvalidKeyException
  Position insPos = T.root();
  do {
    insPos = findPosition(key, insPos);
    if (T.isExternal(insPos))
      break;
    else // the key already exists
      insPos = T.rightChild(insPos);
  } while (true);
  T.expandExternal(insPos);
  Item newItem = new Item(key, element);
  T.replaceElement(insPos, newItem);
  actionPos = insPos; // node where the new item was inserted
}

public Object removeElement(Object key) throws InvalidKeyException {
  Object toReturn;
  checkKey(key); // may throw an InvalidKeyException
  Position remPos = findPosition(key, T.root());
  if(T.isExternal(remPos)) {
    actionPos = remPos; // node where the search ended unsuccessfully
    return NO_SUCH_KEY;
  }
  else{
    toReturn = element(remPos); // element to be returned
    if (T.isExternal(T.leftChild(remPos)))
      remPos = T.leftChild(remPos);
    else if (T.isExternal(T.rightChild(remPos)))
      remPos = T.rightChild(remPos);
    else { // key is at a node with internal children
      Position swapPos = remPos; // find node for swapping items
      remPos = T.rightChild(swapPos);
      do
        remPos = T.leftChild(remPos);
      while (T.isInternal(remPos));
      swap(swapPos, T.parent(remPos));
    }
    actionPos = T.sibling(remPos); // sibling of the leaf to be removed
    T.removeAboveExternal(remPos);
    return toReturn;
  }
}
}
```

Code Fragment 3.56: Class BinarySearchTree. (Continued from Code Fragment 3.55.)

3.6.1 Java Implementation of AVL Trees

Let us now turn to the implementation details and analysis of using an AVL tree T with n internal nodes to implement an ordered dictionary of n items. The insertion and removal algorithms for T require that we are able to perform trinode restructurings and determine the difference between the heights of two sibling nodes. Regarding restructurings, we should extend the collection of operations of the binary tree ADT by adding the method restructure. It is easy to see that a restructure operation can be performed in $O(1)$ time if T is implemented with a linked structure (Section 2.3.4), which would not be the case with a vector (Section 2.3.4). Thus, we prefer a linked structure for representing an AVL tree.

Regarding height information, we can explicitly store the height of each internal node, v, in the node itself. Alternatively, we can store the ***balance factor*** of v at v, which is defined as the height of the left child of v minus the height of the right child of v. Thus, the balance factor of v is always equal to -1, 0, or 1, except during an insertion or removal, when it may become ***temporarily*** equal to -2 or $+2$. During the execution of an insertion or removal, the heights and balance factors of $O(\log n)$ nodes are affected and can be maintained in $O(\log n)$ time.

In Code Fragments 3.57–3.59, we show a Java implementation of a dictionary realized with an AVL tree. Class AVLItem, shown in Algorithm 3.57, extends the Item class used to represent a key-element item of a binary search tree. It defines an additional instance variable height, representing the height of the node. Class AVLTree, shown in full in Code Fragments 3.58 and 3.59, extends BinarySearchTree (Code Fragments 3.54–3.56). The constructor of AVLTree executes the superclass's constructor first, and then assigns a RestructurableNodeBinaryTree to T, which is a class that implements the binary tree ADT, and in addition supports method restructure for performing trinode restructurings. Class AVLTree inherits methods size, isEmpty, findElement, findAllElements, and removeAllElements from its superclass BinarySearchTree, but overrides methods insertItem and removeElement.

Method insertItem (Code Fragment 3.59) begins by calling the superclass's insertItem method, which inserts the new item and assigns the insertion position (node storing key 54 in Figure 3.12) to instance variable actionPos. The auxiliary method rebalance is then used to traverse the path from the insertion position to the root. This traversal updates the heights of all the nodes visited, and performs a trinode restructuring if necessary. Similarly, method removeElement (Code Fragment 3.59) begins by calling the superclass's removeElement method, which performs the removal of the item and assigns the position replacing the deleted one to instance variable actionPos. The auxiliary method rebalance is then used to traverse the path from the removed position to the root.

```
public class AVLItem extends Item {
  int height;
  AVLItem(Object k, Object e, int h) {
    super(k, e);
    height = h;
  }
  public int height() { return height; }
  public int setHeight(int h) {
    int oldHeight = height;
    height = h;
    return oldHeight;
  }
}
```

Code Fragment 3.57: Class implementing a node of an AVL tree. The height of the node in the tree is stored as an instance variable.

```
/** Realization of a dictionary by means of an AVL tree. */
public class AVLTree extends BinarySearchTree implements Dictionary {
  public AVLTree(Comparator c) {
    super(c);
    T = new RestructurableNodeBinaryTree();
  }
  private int height(Position p) {
    if(T.isExternal(p))
      return 0;
    else
      return ((AVLItem) p.element()).height();
  }
  private void setHeight(Position p) { // called only if p is internal
    ((AVLItem) p.element()).setHeight(1+Math.max(height(T.leftChild(p)),
                                                  height(T.rightChild(p))));
  }
  private boolean isBalanced(Position p) {
    // test whether node p has balance factor between -1 and 1
    int bf = height(T.leftChild(p)) - height(T.rightChild(p));
    return ((-1 <= bf) && (bf <= 1));
  }
  private Position tallerChild(Position p) {
    // return a child of p with height no smaller than that of the other child
    if(height(T.leftChild(p)) >= height(T.rightChild(p)))
      return T.leftChild(p);
    else
      return T.rightChild(p);
  }
```

Code Fragment 3.58: Constructor and auxiliary methods of class AVLTree.

```
/**
 * Auxiliary method called by insertItem and removeElement.
 * Traverses the path of T from the given node to the root. For
 * each node zPos encountered, recomputes the height of zPos and
 * performs a trinode restructuring if zPos is unbalanced.
 */
private void rebalance(Position zPos) {
  while (!T.isRoot(zPos)) {
    zPos = T.parent(zPos);
    setHeight(zPos);
    if (!isBalanced(zPos)) {
      // perform a trinode restructuring
      Position xPos = tallerChild(tallerChild(zPos));
      zPos = ((RestructurableNodeBinaryTree) T).restructure(xPos);
      setHeight(T.leftChild(zPos));
      setHeight(T.rightChild(zPos));
      setHeight(zPos);
    }
  }
}

// methods of the dictionary ADT

/** Overrides the corresponding method of the parent class. */
public void insertItem(Object key, Object element)
    throws InvalidKeyException {
  super.insertItem(key, element); // may throw an InvalidKeyException
  Position zPos = actionPos; // start at the insertion position
  T.replaceElement(zPos, new AVLItem(key, element, 1));
  rebalance(zPos);
}

/** Overrides the corresponding method of the parent class. */
public Object removeElement(Object key)
    throws InvalidKeyException {
  Object toReturn = super.removeElement(key);
                          // may throw an InvalidKeyException
  if(toReturn != NO_SUCH_KEY) {
    Position zPos = actionPos; // start at the removal position
    rebalance(zPos);
  }
  return toReturn;
}
```

Code Fragment 3.59: Auxiliary method rebalance and methods insertItem and removeElement of class AVLTree.

3.6.2 Java Implementation of Red-Black Trees

In Code Fragments 3.60–3.63, we show portions of a Java implementation of a dictionary realized by means of a red-black tree. Class RBTItem, shown in Code Fragment 3.60, extends the Item class used to represent a key-element item of a binary search tree. It defines an additional instance variable isRed, representing the color of the node, and methods to set and return it.

```
public class RBTItem extends Item {
  private boolean isRed;
  public RBTItem(Object k, Object elem, boolean color) {
    super(k, elem);
    isRed = color;
  }
  public boolean isRed() {return isRed;}
  public void makeRed() {isRed = true;}
  public void makeBlack() {isRed = false;}
  public void setColor(boolean color) {isRed = color;}
}
```

Code Fragment 3.60: Class implementing a node of a red-black tree.

```
/** Realization of a dictionary by means of a red-black tree. */
public class RBTree extends BinarySearchTree implements Dictionary {
  static boolean Red = true;
  static boolean Black = false;

  public RBTree(Comparator C) {
    super(C);
    T = new RestructurableNodeBinaryTree();
  }
```

Code Fragment 3.61: Instance variables and constructor of class RBTree.

Class RBTree, partially shown in Code Fragments 3.61–3.63, extends BinarySearchTree (Code Fragments 3.54–3.56). As in class AVLTree, the constructor of RBTree executes first the superclass's constructor, and then assigns to T a RestructurableNodeBinaryTree, which is a class that implements the binary tree ADT, and, in addition, supports the method restructure for performing trinode restructurings (rotations). Class RBTree inherits methods size, isEmpty, findElement, findAllElements, and removeAllElements from BinarySearchTree but overrides methods insertItem and removeElement. Several auxiliary methods of class RBTree are not shown.

Methods insertItem (Code Fragment 3.62) and removeElement (Code Fragment 3.63) call the corresponding methods of the superclass first and then rebalance the tree by calling auxiliary methods to perform rotations along the path from the update position (given by the instance variable actionPos inherited from the superclass) to the root.

```
public void insertItem(Object key, Object element)
    throws InvalidKeyException {
  super.insertItem(key, element); // may throw an InvalidKeyException
  Position posZ = actionPos; // start at the insertion position
  T.replaceElement(posZ, new RBTItem(key, element, Red));
  if (T.isRoot(posZ))
    setBlack(posZ);
  else
    remedyDoubleRed(posZ);
}

protected void remedyDoubleRed(Position posZ) {
  Position posV = T.parent(posZ);
  if (T.isRoot(posV))
    return;
  if (!isPosRed(posV))
    return;
  // we have a double red: posZ and posV
  if (!isPosRed(T.sibling(posV))) { // Case 1: trinode restructuring
    posV = ((RestructurableNodeBinaryTree) T).restructure(posZ);
    setBlack(posV);
    setRed(T.leftChild(posV));
    setRed(T.rightChild(posV));
  }
  else { // Case 2: recoloring
    setBlack(posV);
    setBlack(T.sibling(posV));
    Position posU = T.parent(posV);
    if (T.isRoot(posU))
      return;
    setRed(posU);
    remedyDoubleRed(posU);
  }
}
```

Code Fragment 3.62: Dictionary method insertItem and auxiliary method remedyDoubleRed of class RBTree.

```
public Object removeElement(Object key) throws InvalidKeyException {
  Object toReturn = super.removeElement(key);
  Position posR = actionPos;
  if (toReturn != NO_SUCH_KEY) {
    if (wasParentRed(posR) || T.isRoot(posR) || isPosRed(posR))
      setBlack(posR);
    else
      remedyDoubleBlack(posR);
  }
  return toReturn;
}
protected void remedyDoubleBlack(Position posR) {
  Position posX, posY, posZ;
  boolean oldColor;
  posX = T.parent(posR);
  posY = T.sibling(posR);
  if (!isPosRed(posY)) {
    posZ = redChild(posY);
    if (hasRedChild(posY)) { // Case 1: trinode restructuring
      oldColor = isPosRed(posX);
      posZ = ((RestructurableNodeBinaryTree) T).restructure(posZ);
      setColor(posZ, oldColor);
      setBlack(posR);
      setBlack(T.leftChild(posZ));
      setBlack(T.rightChild(posZ));
      return;
    }
    setBlack(posR);
    setRed(posY);
    if (!isPosRed(posX)) { // Case 2: recoloring
      if (!T.isRoot(posX))
        remedyDoubleBlack(posX);
      return;
    }
    setBlack(posX);
    return;
  } // Case 3: adjustment
  if (posY == T.rightChild(posX))
    posZ = T.rightChild(posY);
  else
    posZ = T.leftChild(posY);
  ((RestructurableNodeBinaryTree)T).restructure(posZ);
  setBlack(posY);
  setRed(posX);
  remedyDoubleBlack(posR);
}
```

Code Fragment 3.63: Method removeElement and its auxiliary method.

3.7 Exercises

Reinforcement

R-3.1 Insert items with the following keys (in the given order) into an initially empty binary search tree: 30, 40, 24, 58, 48, 26, 11, 13. Draw the tree after each insertion.

R-3.2 A certain Professor Amongus claims that the order in which a fixed set of elements is inserted into a binary search tree does not matter—the same tree results every time. Give a small example that proves Professor Amongus wrong.

R-3.3 Professor Amongus claims he has a "patch" to his claim from the previous exercise, namely, that the order in which a fixed set of elements is inserted into an AVL tree does not matter—the same AVL tree results every time. Give a small example that proves that Professor Amongus is still wrong.

R-3.4 Is the rotation done in Figure 3.12 a single or a double rotation? What about the rotation in Figure 3.15?

R-3.5 Draw the AVL tree resulting from the insertion of an item with key 52 into the AVL tree of Figure 3.15b.

R-3.6 Draw the AVL tree resulting from the removal of the item with key 62 from the AVL tree of Figure 3.15b.

R-3.7 Explain why performing a rotation in an n-node binary tree represented using a sequence takes $\Omega(n)$ time.

R-3.8 Is the multi-way search tree of Figure 3.17a a $(2,4)$ tree? Justify your answer.

R-3.9 An alternative way of performing a split at a node v in a $(2,4)$ tree is to partition v into v' and v'', with v' being a 2-node and v'' being a 3-node. Which of the keys k_1, k_2, k_3, or k_4 do we store at v's parent in this case? Why?

R-3.10 Professor Amongus claims that a $(2,4)$ tree storing a set of items will always have the same structure, regardless of the order in which the items are inserted. Show that Professor Amongus is wrong.

R-3.11 Consider the following sequence of keys:

$$(5,16,22,45,2,10,18,30,50,12,1).$$

Consider the insertion of items with this set of keys, in the order given, into:

a. An initially empty $(2,4)$ tree T'.
b. An initially empty red-black tree T''.

Draw T' and T'' after each insertion.

R-3.12 Draw four different red-black trees that correspond to the same $(2,4)$ tree using the correspondence rules described in the chapter.

R-3.13 Draw an example red-black tree that is not an AVL tree. Your tree should have at least 6 nodes, but no more than 16.

R-3.14 For each of the following statements about red-black trees, determine whether it is true or false. If you think it is true, provide a justification. If you think it is false, give a counterexample.

a. A subtree of a red-black tree is itself a red-black tree.
b. The sibling of an external node is either external or it is red.
c. Given a red-black tree T, there is an unique $(2,4)$ tree T' associated with T.
d. Given a $(2,4)$ tree T, there is a unique red-black tree T' associated with T.

R-3.15 Perform the following sequence of operations in an initially empty splay tree and draw the tree after each operation.

a. Insert keys 0, 2, 4, 6, 8, 10, 12, 14, 16, 18, in this order.
b. Search for keys 1, 3, 5, 7, 9, 11, 13, 15, 17, 19, in this order.
c. Delete keys 0, 2, 4, 6, 8, 10, 12, 14, 16, 18, in this order.

R-3.16 What does a splay tree look like if its items are accessed in increasing order by their keys?

R-3.17 How many trinode restructuring operations are needed to perform the zig-zig, zig-zag, and zig updates in splay trees? Use figures to explain your counting.

R-3.18 Draw an example skip list resulting from performing the following sequence of operations on the skip list in Figure 3.51: removeElement(38), insertItem(48,x), insertItem(24,y), removeElement(55). Assume the coin flips for the first insertion yield two heads followed by tails, and those for the second insertion yield three heads followed by tails.

R-3.19 Give a pseudo-code description of the removeElement dictionary operation, assuming the dictionary is implemented by a skip-list structure.

Creativity

C-3.1 Suppose we are given two ordered dictionaries S and T, each with n items, and that S and T are implemented by means of array-based ordered sequences. Describe an $O(\log n)$-time algorithm for finding the kth smallest key in the union of the keys from S and T (assuming no duplicates).

C-3.2 Design an algorithm for performing findAllElements(k) in an ordered dictionary implemented with an ordered array, and show that it runs in time $O(\log n + s)$, where n is the number of elements in the dictionary and s is the number of items returned.

C-3.3 Design an algorithm for performing the operation findAllElements(k) in an ordered dictionary implemented with a binary search tree T, and show that it runs in time $O(h+s)$, where h is the height of T and s is the number of items returned.

C-3.4 Describe how to perform the operation removeAllElements(k) in an ordered dictionary implemented with a binary search tree T, and show that this method runs in time $O(h+s)$, where h is the height of T and s is the size of the iterator returned.

C-3.5 Draw an example of an AVL tree such that a single removeElement operation could require $\Theta(\log n)$ trinode restructurings (or rotations) from a leaf to the root in order to restore the height-balance property. (Use triangles to represent subtrees that are not affected by this operation.)

C-3.6 Show how to perform operation removeAllElements(k) in a dictionary implemented with an AVL tree in time $O(s \log n)$, where n is the number of elements in the dictionary at the time the operation is performed and s is the size of the iterator returned by the operation.

C-3.7 If we maintain a reference to the position of the left-most internal node of an AVL tree, then operation first can be performed in $O(1)$ time. Describe how the implementation of the other dictionary methods needs to be modified to maintain a reference to the left-most position.

C-3.8 Show that any n-node binary tree can be converted to any other n-node binary tree using $O(n)$ rotations.

Hint: Show that $O(n)$ rotations suffice to convert any binary tree into a ***left chain***, where each internal node has an external right child.

C-3.9 Show that the nodes that become unbalanced in an AVL tree after operation expandExternal is performed, within the execution of an insertItem operation, may be nonconsecutive on the path from the newly inserted node to the root.

C-3.10 Let D be an ordered dictionary with n items implemented by means of an AVL tree. Show how to implement the following operation on D in time $O(\log n + s)$, where s is the size of the iterator returned:

findAllInRange(k_1, k_2): Return an iterator of all the elements in D with key k such that $k_1 \leq k \leq k_2$.

C-3.11 Let D be an ordered dictionary with n items implemented with an AVL tree. Show how to implement the following method for D in time $O(\log n)$:

countAllInRange(k_1, k_2): Compute and return the number of items in D with key k such that $k_1 \leq k \leq k_2$.

Note that this method returns a single integer.

Hint: You will need to extend the AVL tree data structure, adding a new field to each internal node and ways of maintaining this field during updates.

C-3.12 Show that at most one node in an AVL tree becomes unbalanced after operation removeAboveExternal is performed within the execution of a removeElement dictionary operation.

C-3.13 Show that at most one trinode restructure operation (which corresponds to one single or double rotation) is needed to restore balance after any insertion in an AVL tree.

C-3.14 Let T and U be $(2,4)$ trees storing n and m items, respectively, such that all the items in T have keys less than the keys of all the items in U. Describe an $O(\log n + \log m)$ time method for ***joining*** T and U into a single tree that stores all the items in T and U (destroying the old versions of T and U).

C-3.15 Repeat the previous problem for red-black trees T and U.

C-3.16 Justify Theorem 3.3.

C-3.17 The Boolean used to mark nodes in a red-black tree as being "red" or "black" is not strictly needed. Describe a scheme for implementing a red-black tree without adding any extra space to the binary search tree nodes. How does your scheme affect the running times for searching and updating a red-black tree?

C-3.18 Let T be a red-black tree storing n items, and let k be the key of an item in T. Show how to construct from T, in $O(\log n)$ time, two red-black trees T' and T'', such that T' contains all the keys of T less than k, and T'' contains all the keys of T greater than k. This operation destroys T.

C-3.19 A ***mergeable heap*** supports the operations insert(k,x), remove(k), unionWith(h), and minElement(), where the unionWith(h) operation performs a union of the mergeable heap h with the present one, destroying the old versions of both. Describe a concrete implementation of the mergeable heap ADT that achieves $O(\log n)$ performance for all its operations. For simplicity, you may assume that all keys in existing mergeable heaps are distinct, although this is not strictly necessary.

C-3.20 Consider a variation of splay trees, called ***half-splay trees***, where splaying a node at depth d stops as soon as the node reaches depth $\lfloor d/2 \rfloor$. Perform an amortized analysis of half-splay trees.

C-3.21 The standard splaying step requires two passes, one downward pass to find the node x to splay, followed by an upward pass to splay the node x. Describe a method for splaying and searching for x in one downward pass. Each substep now requires that you consider the next two nodes in the path down to x, with a possible zig substep performed at the end. Describe the details for performing each of the zig-zig, zig-zag, and zig substeps.

C-3.22 Describe a sequence of accesses to an n-node splay tree T, where n is odd, that results in T consisting of a single chain of internal nodes with external node children, such that the internal-node path down T alternates between left children and right children.

C-3.23 Justify Theorem 3.11. A way to establish this justification is to note that we can redefine the "size" of a node as the sum of the access frequencies of its children and show that the entire justification of Theorem 3.9 still goes through.

C-3.24 Suppose we are given a sorted sequence S of items $(x_0, x_1, \ldots, x_{n-1})$ such that each item x_i in S is given a positive integer weight a_i. Let A denote the total weight of all elements in S. Construct an $O(n \log n)$-time algorithm that builds a search tree T for S such that the depth of each item a_i is $O(\log A/a_i)$.

Hint: Find the item x_j with smallest j such that $\sum_{i=1}^{j} a_i < A/2$. Consider putting this item at the root and recursing on the two subsequences that this induces.

C-3.25 Design a linear-time algorithm for the previous problem.

C-3.26 Show that the methods above(p) and before(p) are not actually needed to efficiently implement a dictionary using a skip list. That is, we can implement item insertion and removal in a skip list using a strictly top-down, scan-forward approach, without ever using the above or before methods.

C-3.27 Describe how to implement the locator-based method before(ℓ) as well as the locator-based method closestBefore(k) in a dictionary realized using an ordered sequence. Do the same using an unordered sequence implementation. What are the running times of these methods?

C-3.28 Repeat the previous exercise using a skip list. What are the expected running times of the two locator-based methods in your implementation?

C-3.29 Suppose that each row of an $n \times n$ array A consists of 1's and 0's such that, in any row of A, all the 1's come before any 0's in that row. Assuming A is already in memory, describe a method running in $O(n \log n)$ time (not $O(n^2)$ time!) for counting the number of 1's in A.

C-3.30 Describe an efficient ordered dictionary structure for storing n elements that have an associated set of $k < n$ keys that come from a total order. That is, the set of keys is smaller than the number of elements. Your structure should perform all the ordered dictionary operations in $O(\log k + s)$ expected time, where s is the number of elements returned.

Projects

P-3.1 Implement the methods of the ordered dictionary ADT using an AVL tree, skip list, or red-black tree.

P-3.2 Providing a graphical animation of the skip-list operations. Visualize how items move up the skip list during insertions and are linked out of the skip list during removals.

Chapter Notes

Some of the data structures discussed above are extensively covered by Knuth in [119], and by Mehlhorn in [148]. AVL trees are due to Adel'son-Vel'skii and Landis [2]. Average-height analyses for binary search trees can be found in the books by Aho, Hopcroft, and Ullman [8] and Cormen, Leiserson, and Rivest [55]. The handbook by Gonnet and Baeza-Yates [81] contains a number of theoretical and experimental comparisons among dictionary implementations. Aho, Hopcroft, and Ullman [7] discuss $(2,3)$ trees, which are similar to $(2,4)$ trees. Red-black trees were defined by Bayer [23], and are discussed further by Guibas and Sedgewick [91]. Splay trees were invented by Sleator and Tarjan [189] (see also [200]). Additional reading can be found in the books by Mehlhorn [148] and Tarjan [200], and the chapter by Mehlhorn and Tsakalidis [152]. Knuth [119] is excellent additional reading that includes early approaches to balancing trees. Exercise C-3.25 is inspired by a paper by Mehlhorn [147]. Skip lists were introduced by Pugh [170]. Our analysis of skip lists is a simplification of a presentation given in the book by Motwani and Raghavan [157]. The reader interested in other probabilistic constructions for supporting the dictionary ADT is referred to the text by Motwani and Raghavan [157]. For a more in-depth analysis of skip lists, the reader is referred to papers on skip lists that have appeared [115, 163, 167].

Chapter

4 Sorting, Sets, and Selection

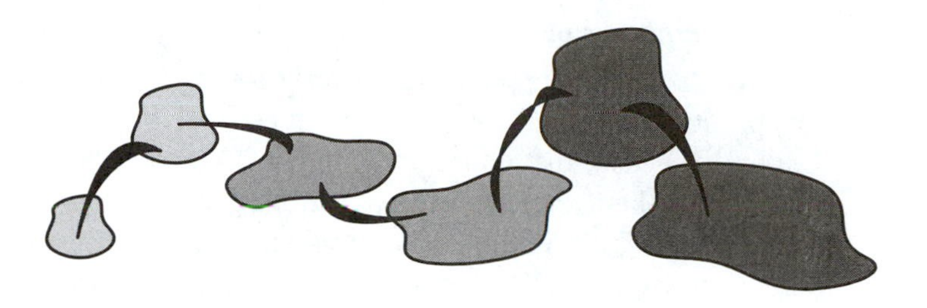

Contents

4.1 Merge-Sort 219

4.1.1 Divide-and-Conquer 219

4.1.2 Merge-Sort and Recurrence Equations 224

4.2 The Set Abstract Data Type 225

4.2.1 A Simple Set Implementation 226

4.2.2 Partitions with Union-Find Operations 227

4.2.3 A Tree-Based Partition Implementation 229

4.3 Quick-Sort 235

4.3.1 Randomized Quick-Sort 237

4.4 A Lower Bound on Comparison-Based Sorting 239

4.5 Bucket-Sort and Radix-Sort 241

4.5.1 Bucket-Sort 241

4.5.2 Radix-Sort 242

4.6 Comparison of Sorting Algorithms 244

4.7 Selection 245

4.7.1 Prune-and-Search 245

4.7.2 Randomized Quick-Select 245

4.7.3 Analyzing Randomized Quick-Select 246

4.8 Java Example: In-Place Quick-Sort 248

4.9 Exercises 251

The Second Law of Thermodynamics suggests that Nature tends toward disorder. Humans, on the other hand, prefer order. Indeed, there are several advantages to keeping data in order. For example, the binary search algorithm works correctly only for an ordered array or vector. Since computers are intended to be tools for humans, we devote this chapter to the study of sorting algorithms and their applications. We recall that the sorting problem is defined as follows. Let S be a sequence of n elements that can be compared to each other according to a total order relation, that is, it is always possible to compare two elements of S to see which is larger or smaller, or if the two of them are equal. We want to rearrange S in such a way that the elements appear in increasing order (or in nondecreasing order if there are equal elements in S).

We have already presented several sorting algorithms in the previous chapters. In particular, in Section 2.4.2, we presented a simple sorting scheme, which is called PQ-Sort, that consists of inserting elements into a priority queue and then extracting them in nondecreasing order, by means of a series of removeMin operations. If the priority queue is implemented by means of a sequence, then this algorithm runs in $O(n^2)$ time and corresponds to either insertion-sort or selection-sort, depending on whether the sequence is kept ordered or not. If the priority queue is implemented by means of a heap (Section 2.4.3) instead, then this algorithm runs in $O(n \log n)$ time and corresponds to the sorting method known as heap-sort.

In this chapter, we present several other sorting algorithms, together with the algorithmic design patterns they are based on. Two such algorithms, known as ***merge-sort*** and ***quick-sort***, are based on the divide-and-conquer pattern, which is widely applicable to other problems as well. Two other algorithms, ***bucket-sort*** and ***radix-sort***, are based instead on the bucket array approach utilized in hashing. We also introduce the ***set*** abstract data type and show how the merge technique used in the merge-sort algorithm can be used in the implementation of its methods. The set abstract data type has an important subtype known as the ***partition***, which supports the primary methods union and find and has a surprisingly fast implementation. Indeed, we show that a sequence of n union and find operations can be implemented in $O(n \log^* n)$ time, where $\log^* n$ is the number of times the logarithm function can be applied, starting at n, before reaching 1. This analysis provides a nontrivial example of amortized analysis.

In this chapter, we also discuss a lower bound proof for the sorting problem, showing that any comparison-based approach must perform at least $\Omega(n \log n)$ operations to sort n numbers. In some cases, however, we are not interested in sorting an entire set, but would just like to select the kth smallest element in the set instead. We show that this ***selection*** problem can, in fact, be solved much faster than the sorting problem. A Java implementation example concluding the chapter is for in-place quick-sort.

Throughout this chapter, we assume that a total order relation is defined over the elements to be sorted. If this relation is induced by a comparator (Section 2.4.1), we assume that a comparison test takes $O(1)$ time.

4.1 Merge-Sort

In this section, we present a sorting technique, called ***merge-sort***, which can be described in a simple and compact way using recursion.

4.1.1 Divide-and-Conquer

Merge-sort is based on an algorithmic design pattern called ***divide-and-conquer***. The divide-and-conquer paradigm can be described in general terms as consisting of the following three steps:

1. ***Divide:*** If the input size is smaller than a certain threshold (say, one or two elements), solve the problem directly using a straightforward method and return the solution so obtained. Otherwise, divide the input data into two or more disjoint subsets.
2. ***Recur:*** Recursively solve the subproblems associated with the subsets.
3. ***Conquer:*** Take the solutions to the subproblems and "merge" them into a solution to the original problem.

Merge-sort applies the divide-and-conquer technique to the sorting problem.

Using Divide-and-Conquer for Sorting

Recall that in the sorting problem we are given a collection of n objects, typically stored in a list, vector, array, or sequence, together with some comparator defining a total order on these objects, and we are asked to produce an ordered representation of these objects. For the sake of generality, we focus on the version of the sorting problem that takes a sequence S of objects as input, and returns S in sorted order. Specializations to other linear structures, such as lists, vectors, or arrays, are straightforward and left as exercises (R-4.3 and R-4.13). For the problem of sorting a sequence S with n elements, the three divide-and-conquer steps are as follows:

1. ***Divide:*** If S has zero or one element, return S immediately; it is already sorted. Otherwise (S has at least two elements), remove all the elements from S and put them into two sequences, S_1 and S_2, each containing about half of the elements of S; that is, S_1 contains the first $\lceil n/2 \rceil$ elements of S, and S_2 contains the remaining $\lfloor n/2 \rfloor$ elements.
2. ***Recur:*** Recursively sort sequences S_1 and S_2.
3. ***Conquer:*** Put the elements back into S by merging the sorted sequences S_1 and S_2 into a sorted sequence.

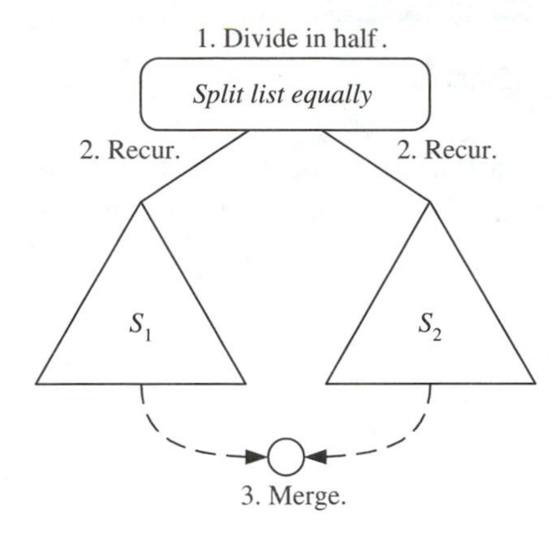

Figure 4.1: A visual schematic of the merge-sort algorithm.

We show a schematic for the merge-sort algorithm in Figure 4.1. We can also visualize an execution of the merge-sort algorithm by means of a binary tree T, called the ***merge-sort tree***. (See Figure 4.2.) Each node of T represents a recursive invocation (or call) of the merge-sort algorithm. We associate with each node v of T the sequence S that is processed by the invocation associated with v. The children of node v are associated with the recursive calls that process the subsequences S_1 and S_2 of S. The external nodes of T are associated with individual elements of S, corresponding to instances of the algorithm that make no recursive calls.

Figure 4.2 summarizes an execution of the merge-sort algorithm by showing the input and output sequences processed at each node of the merge-sort tree. This algorithm visualization in terms of the merge-sort tree helps us analyze the running time of the merge-sort algorithm. In particular, since the size of the input sequence roughly halves at each recursive call of merge-sort, the height of the merge-sort tree is about $\log n$ (recall that the base of log is 2 if omitted).

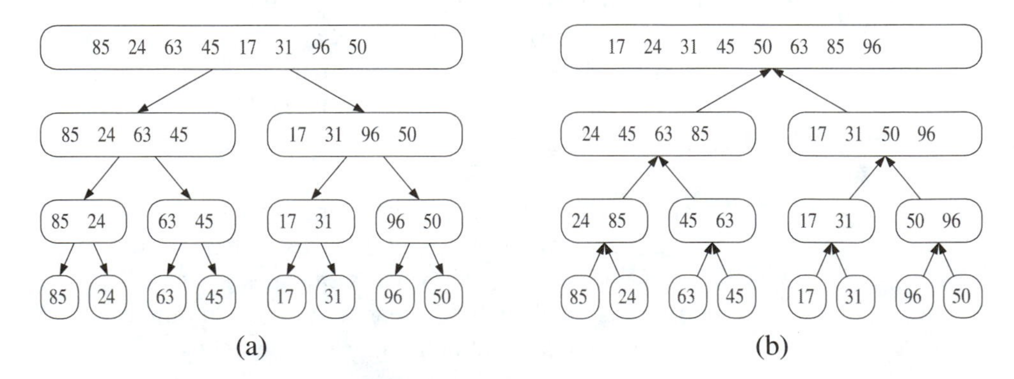

Figure 4.2: Merge-sort tree T for an execution of the merge-sort algorithm on a sequence with eight elements: (a) input sequences processed at each node of T; (b) output sequences generated at each node of T.

In reference to the divide step, we recall that the notation $\lceil x \rceil$ indicates the ***ceiling*** of x, that is, the smallest integer m, such that $x \leq m$. Similarly, the notation $\lfloor x \rfloor$ indicates the ***floor*** of x, that is, the largest integer k, such that $k \leq x$. Thus, the divide step divides the list S as equally as possible, which gives us the following.

Theorem 4.1: *The merge-sort tree associated with an execution of merge-sort on a sequence of size n has height* $\lceil \log n \rceil$.

We leave the justification of Theorem 4.1 as a simple exercise (R-4.1).

Having given an overview of merge-sort and an illustration of how it works, let us consider each of the steps of this divide-and-conquer algorithm in more detail. The divide and recur steps of the merge-sort algorithm are simple; dividing a sequence of size n involves separating it at the element with rank $\lceil n/2 \rceil$, and the recursive calls simply involve passing these smaller sequences as parameters. The difficult step is the conquer step, which merges two sorted sequences into a single sorted sequence.

Merging Two Sorted Sequences

Algorithm merge, in Algorithm 4.3, merges two sorted sequences, S_1 and S_2, by iteratively removing a smallest element from one of these two and adding it to the end of the output sequence, S, until one of these two sequences is empty, at which point we copy the remainder of the other sequence to the output sequence.

```
Algorithm merge(S1,S2,S):
  Input: Sequences S1 and S2 sorted in nondecreasing order, and an empty se-
    quence S
  Output: Sequence S containing the elements from S1 and S2 sorted in nonde-
    creasing order, with sequences S1 and S2 becoming empty
   while (not (S1.isEmpty() or S2.isEmpty()) do
     if S1.first().element() ≤ S2.first().element() then
       { move the first element of S1 at the end of S }
       S.insertLast(S1.remove(S1.first()))
     else
       { move the first element of S2 at the end of S }
       S.insertLast(S2.remove(S2.first()))
   { move the remaining elements of S1 to S }
   while (not S1.isEmpty()) do
     S.insertLast(S1.remove(S1.first()))
   { move the remaining elements of S2 to S }
   while (not S2.isEmpty()) do
     S.insertLast(S2.remove(S2.first()))
```

Algorithm 4.3: Algorithm merge for merging two sorted sequences.

We analyze the running time of the merge algorithm by making some simple observations. Let n_1 and n_2 be the number of elements of S_1 and S_2, respectively. Also, let us assume that the sequences S_1, S_2, and S are implemented so that access to, insertion into, and deletion from their first and last positions each take $O(1)$ time. This is the case for implementations based on circular arrays or doubly linked lists (Section 2.2.3). Algorithm merge has three **while** loops. Because of our assumptions, the operations performed inside each loop take $O(1)$ time each. The key observation is that during each iteration of one of the loops, one element is removed from either S_1 or S_2. Since no insertions are performed into S_1 or S_2, this observation implies that the overall number of iterations of the three loops is $n_1 + n_2$. Thus, the running time of algorithm merge is $O(n_1 + n_2)$, as we summarize:

Theorem 4.2: *Merging two sorted sequences S_1 and S_2 takes $O(n_1 + n_2)$ time, where n_1 is the size of S_1 and n_2 is the size of S_2.*

We show an example execution of algorithm merge in Figure 4.4.

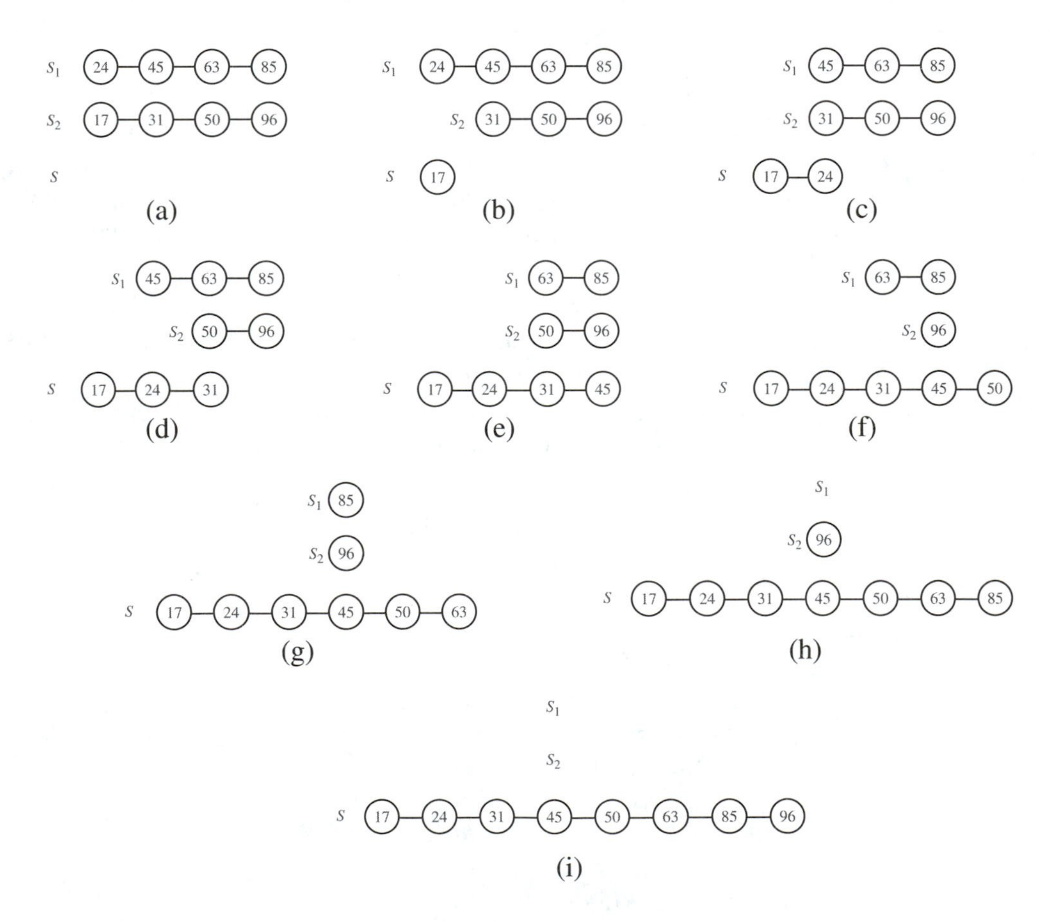

Figure 4.4: Example of execution of algorithm merge shown in Algorithm 4.3.

The Running Time of Merge-Sort

Having given the details of the merge-sort algorithm, let us analyze the running time of the entire merge-sort algorithm, assuming it is given an input sequence of n elements. For simplicity, let us also assume n is a power of 2. We leave it to an exercise (R-4.4) to show that the result of our analysis also holds when n is not a power of 2.

We analyze the merge-sort algorithm by referring to the merge-sort tree T. We call the ***time spent at a node*** v of T the running time of the recursive call associated with v, excluding the time taken waiting for the recursive calls associated with the children of v to terminate. In other words, the time spent at node v includes the running times of the divide and conquer steps, but excludes the running time of the recur step. We have already observed that the details of the divide step are straightforward; this step runs in time proportional to the size of the sequence for v. Also, as shown in Theorem 4.2, the conquer step, which consists of merging two sorted subsequences, also takes linear time. That is, letting i denote the depth of node v, the time spent at node v is $O(n/2^i)$, since the size of the sequence handled by the recursive call associated with v is equal to $n/2^i$.

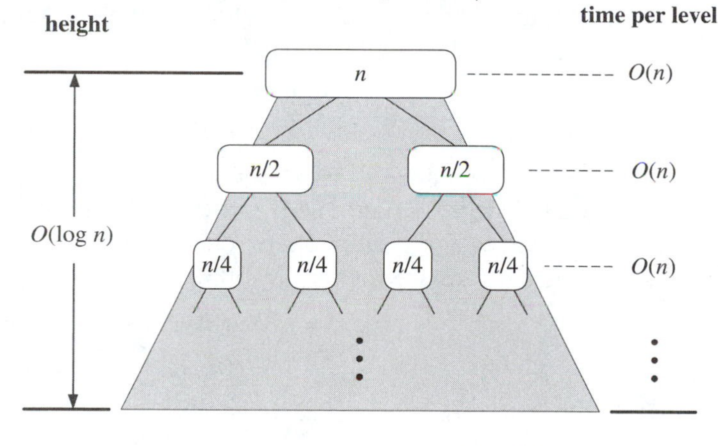

Figure 4.5: A visual analysis of the running time of merge-sort. Each node of the merge-sort tree is labeled with the size of its subproblem.

Looking at the tree T more globally, as shown in Figure 4.5, we see that, given our definition of "time spent at a node," the running time of merge-sort is equal to the sum of the times spent at the nodes of T. Observe that T has exactly 2^i nodes at depth i. This simple observation has an important consequence, for it implies that the overall time spent at all the nodes of T at depth i is $O(2^i \cdot n/2^i)$, which is $O(n)$. By Theorem 4.1, the height of T is $\log n$. Thus, since the time spent at each of the $\log n + 1$ levels of T is $O(n)$, we have the following result:

Theorem 4.3: *Merge-sort runs in $O(n \log n)$ time in the worst case.*

4.1.2 Merge-Sort and Recurrence Equations

There is another way to justify that the running time of the merge-sort algorithm is $O(n \log n)$. Let the function $t(n)$ denote the worst-case running time of merge-sort on an input sequence of size n. Since merge-sort is recursive, we can characterize function $t(n)$ by means of the following equalities, where function $t(n)$ is recursively expressed in terms of itself, as follows:

$$t(n) = \begin{cases} b & \text{if } n = 1 \\ t(\lceil n/2 \rceil) + t(\lfloor n/2 \rfloor) + cn & \text{otherwise} \end{cases}$$

where $b > 0$ and $c > 0$ are constants. A characterization of a function such as the one above is called a ***recurrence equation*** (Sections 1.1.4 and 5.2.1), since the function appears on both the left- and right-hand sides of the equal sign. Although such a characterization is correct and accurate, what we really desire is a big-Oh type of characterization of $t(n)$ that does not involve the function $t(n)$ itself (that is, we want a ***closed-form*** characterization of $t(n)$).

In order to provide a closed-form characterization of $t(n)$, let us restrict our attention to the case when n is a power of 2 We leave the problem of showing that our asymptotic characterization still holds in the general case as an exercise (R-4.4). In this case, we can simplify the definition of $t(n)$ to

$$t(n) = \begin{cases} b & \text{if } n = 1 \\ 2t(n/2) + cn & \text{otherwise.} \end{cases}$$

But, even so, we must still try to characterize this recurrence equation in a closed-form way. One way to do this is to iteratively apply this equation, assuming n is relatively large. For example, after one more application of this equation we can write a new recurrence for $t(n)$ as follows:

$$\begin{aligned} t(n) &= 2(2t(n/2^2) + (cn/2)) + cn \\ &= 2^2 t(n/2^2) + 2cn. \end{aligned}$$

If we apply the equation again, we get

$$t(n) = 2^3 t(n/2^3) + 3cn.$$

After applying this equation i times we get

$$t(n) = 2^i t(n/2^i) + icn.$$

The issue that remains, then, is to determine when to stop this process. To see when to stop, recall that we switch to the closed form $t(n) = b$ when $n = 1$, which occurs when $2^i = n$. In other words, this will occur when $i = \log n$. Making this substitution yields

$$\begin{aligned} t(n) &= 2^{\log n} t(n/2^{\log n}) + (\log n)cn \\ &= nt(1) + cn \log n \\ &= nb + cn \log n. \end{aligned}$$

That is, we get an alternative justification of the fact that $t(n)$ is $O(n \log n)$.

4.2 The Set Abstract Data Type

In this section, we introduce the ***set*** ADT. A ***set*** is a container of distinct objects. That is, there are no duplicate elements in a set, and there is no explicit notion of keys or even an order. Even so, we include our discussion of sets here in a chapter on sorting, because sorting can play an important role in efficient implementations of the operations of the set ADT.

Sets and Some of Their Uses

First, we recall the mathematical definitions of the ***union***, ***intersection***, and ***subtraction*** of two sets A and B:

$$\begin{aligned} A \cup B &= \{x : x \in A \text{ or } x \in B\}, \\ A \cap B &= \{x : x \in A \text{ and } x \in B\}, \\ A - B &= \{x : x \in A \text{ and } x \notin B\}. \end{aligned}$$

Example 4.4: *Most Internet search engines store, for each word x in their dictionary database, a set, $W(x)$, of Web pages that contain x, where each Web page is identified by a unique Internet address. When presented with a query for a word x, such a search engine need only return the Web pages in the set $W(x)$, sorted according to some proprietary priority ranking of page "importance." But when presented with a two-word query for words x and y, such a search engine must first compute the intersection $W(x) \cap W(y)$, and then return the Web pages in the resulting set sorted by priority. Several search engines use the set intersection algorithm described in this section for this computation.*

Fundamental Methods of the Set ADT

The fundamental methods of the set ADT, acting on a set A, are as follows:

union(B): Replace A with the union of A and B, that is, execute $A \leftarrow A \cup B$.

intersect(B): Replace A with the intersection of A and B, that is, execute $A \leftarrow A \cap B$.

subtract(B): Replace A with the difference of A and B, that is, execute $A \leftarrow A - B$.

We have defined the operations union, intersect, and subtract above so that they modify the contents of the set A involved. Alternatively, we could have defined these methods so that they do not modify A but instead return a new set.

4.2.1 A Simple Set Implementation

One of the simplest ways of implementing a set is to store its elements in an ordered sequence. This implementation is included in several software libraries for generic data structures, for example. Therefore, let us consider implementing the set ADT with an ordered sequence (we consider other implementations in several exercises). Any consistent total order relation among the elements of the set can be used, provided the same order is used for all the sets.

We implement each of the three fundamental set operations using a generic version of the merge algorithm that takes, as input, two sorted sequences representing the input sets, and constructs a sequence representing the output set, be it the union, intersection, or subtraction of the input sets.

The generic merge algorithm iteratively examines and compares the current elements a and b of the input sequences A and B, respectively, and finds out whether $a < b$, $a = b$, or $a > b$. Then, based on the outcome of this comparison, it determines whether it should copy one of the elements a and b to the end of the output sequence C. This determination is made based on the particular operation we are performing, be it a union, intersection, or subtraction. The next element of one or both sequences is then considered. For example, in a union operation, we proceed as follows:

- if $a < b$, we copy a to the output sequence and advance to the next element of A;
- if $a = b$, we copy a to the output sequence and advance to the next elements of A and B;
- if $a > b$, we copy b to the output sequence and advance to the next element of B.

Performance of Generic Merging

Let us analyze the running time of the generic merge algorithm. At each iteration, we compare two elements of the input sequences A and B, possibly copy one element to the output sequence, and advance the current element of A, B, or both. Assuming that comparing and copying elements takes $O(1)$ time, the total running time is $O(n_A + n_B)$, where n_A is the size of A and n_B is the size of B; that is, generic merging takes time proportional to the number of elements involved. Thus, we have the following:

Theorem 4.5: *The set ADT can be implemented with an ordered sequence and a generic merge scheme that supports operations* union, intersect, *and* subtract *in $O(n)$ time, where n denotes the sum of sizes of the sets involved.*

There is also a special and important version of the Set ADT that only applies when dealing with collections of disjoint sets.

4.2.2 Partitions with Union-Find Operations

A ***partition*** is a collection of disjoint sets. We define the methods of the partition ADT using locators (Section 2.4.4) to access the elements stored in a set. Each locator in this case is like a pointer, it provides immediate access to the position (node) where an element is stored in our partition.

makeSet(e): Create a singleton set containing the element e and return a locator ℓ for e.

union(A,B): Compute and return set $A \leftarrow A \cup B$.

find(ℓ): Return the set containing the element with locator ℓ.

Sequence Implementation

A simple implementation of a partition with a total of n elements is with a collection of sequences, one for each set, where the sequence for a set A stores locator nodes as its elements. Each locator node has a reference to its element e, which allows the execution of method element() of the locator ADT in $O(1)$ time, and a reference to the sequence storing e. (See Figure 4.6.) Thus, we can perform operation find(ℓ) in $O(1)$ time. Likewise, makeSet also takes $O(1)$ time. Operation union(A,B) requires that we join the two sequences into one and update the sequence references in the locators of one of the two. We choose to implement this operation by removing all the locators from the sequence with smaller size, and inserting them in the sequence with larger size. Hence, the operation union(A,B) takes time $O(\min(|A|,|B|))$, which is $O(n)$ because, in the worst case, $|A| = |B| = n/2$. Nevertheless, as shown below, an amortized analysis shows this implementation to be much better than appears from this worst-case analysis.

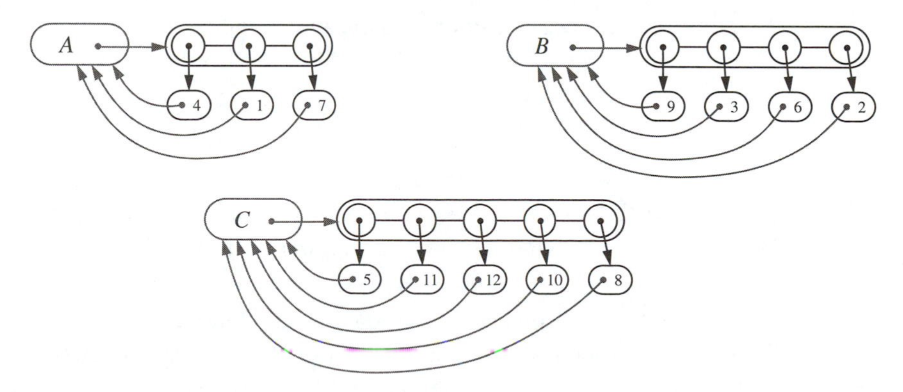

Figure 4.6: Sequence-based implementation of a partition consisting of three sets: $A = \{1,4,7\}$, $B = \{2,3,6,9\}$, and $C = \{5,8,10,11,12\}$.

Performance of the Sequence Implementation

The above sequence implementation is simple, but it is also efficient, as the following theorem shows.

Theorem 4.6: *Performing a series of n* makeSet, union, *and* find *operations, using the above sequence-based implementation, starting from an initially empty partition takes $O(n \log n)$ time.*

Proof: We use the accounting method and assume that one cyber-dollar can pay for the time to perform a find operation, a makeSet operation, or the movement of a locator node from one sequence to another in a union operation. In the case of a find or makeSet operation, we charge the operation itself 1 cyber-dollar. In the case of a union operation, however, we charge 1 cyber-dollar to each locator node that we move from one set to another. Note that we charge nothing to the union operations themselves. Clearly, the total charges to find and makeSet operations sum to be $O(n)$.

Consider, then, the number of charges made to locators on behalf of union operations. The important observation is that each time we move a locator from one set to another, the size of the new set at least doubles. Thus, each locator is moved from one set to another at most $\log n$ times; hence, each locator can be charged at most $O(\log n)$ times. Since we assume that the partition is initially empty, there are $O(n)$ different elements referenced in the given series of operations, which implies that the total time for all the union operations is $O(n \log n)$. ■

The amortized running time of an operation in a series of makeSet, union, and find operations, is the total time taken for the series divided by the number of operations. We conclude from the above theorem that, for a partition implemented using sequences, the amortized running time of each operation is $O(\log n)$. Thus, we can summarize the performance of our simple sequence-based partition implementation as follows.

Theorem 4.7: *Using a sequence-based implementation of a partition, in a series of n* makeSet, union, *and* find *operations starting from an initially empty partition, the amortized running time of each operation is $O(\log n)$.*

Note that in this sequence-based implementation of a partition, each find operation in fact takes worst-case $O(1)$ time. It is the running time of the union operations that is the computational bottleneck.

In the next section, we describe a tree-based implementation of a partition that does not guarantee constant-time find operations, but has amortized time much better than $O(\log n)$ per union operation.

4.2.3 A Tree-Based Partition Implementation

An alternative data structure for a partition with n elements uses a collection of trees to store the elements in sets, where each tree is associated with a different set. (See Figure 4.7.) In particular, we implement a tree T with a linked data structure, where each node u of T stores an element of the set associated with T, and a parent reference pointing to the parent node of u. If u is the root, then its parent reference points to itself. The nodes of the tree serve as the locators for the elements in the partition. Also, we identify each set with the root of its associated tree.

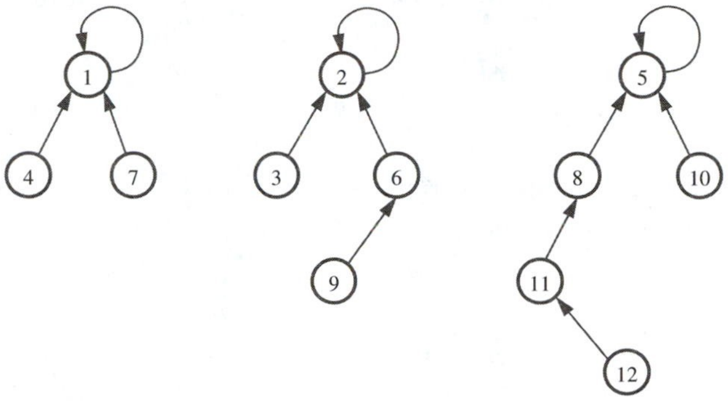

Figure 4.7: Tree-based implementation of a partition consisting of three disjoint sets: $A = \{1,4,7\}$, $B = \{2,3,6,9\}$, and $C = \{5,8,10,11,12\}$.

With this partition data structure, operation union is performed by making one of the two trees a subtree of the other (Figure 4.8b), which can be done in $O(1)$ time by setting the parent reference of the root of one tree to point to the root of the other tree. Operation find for a locator node ℓ is performed by walking up to the root of the tree containing the locator ℓ (Figure 4.8a), which takes $O(n)$ time in the worst case.

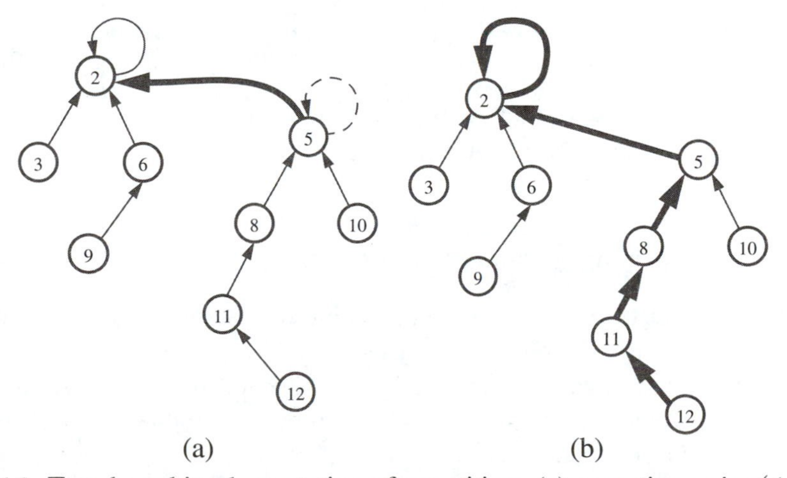

Figure 4.8: Tree-based implementation of a partition: (a) operation union(A,B); (b) operation find(ℓ), where ℓ denotes the locator for element 12.

Note that this representation of a tree is a specialized data structure used to implement a partition, and is not meant to be a realization of the tree abstract data type (Section 2.3). Indeed, the representation has only "upward" links, and does not provide a way to access the children of a given node. At first, this implementation may seem to be no better than the sequence-based data structure, but we add the following simple heuristics to make it run faster:

Union-by-Size: Store with each node v the size of the subtree rooted at v, denoted by $n(v)$. In a union operation, make the tree of the smaller set a subtree of the other tree, and update the size field of the root of the resulting tree.

Path Compression: In a find operation, for each node v that the find visits, reset the parent pointer from v to point to the root. (See Figure 4.9.)

These heuristics increase the running time of an operation by a constant factor, but as we show below, they significantly improve the amortized running time.

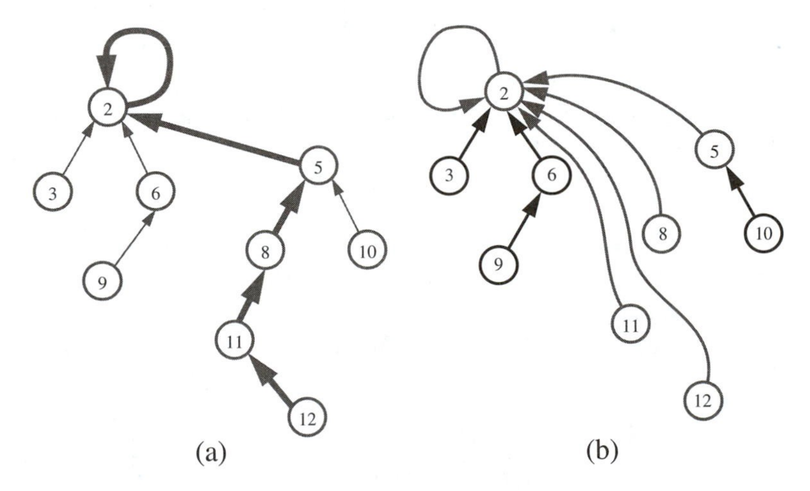

Figure 4.9: Path-compression heuristic: (a) path traversed by operation find on element 12; (b) restructured tree.

Defining a Rank Function

Let us analyze the running time of a series of n union and find operations on a partition that initially consists of n single-element sets.

For each node v that is a root, we recall that we have defined $n(v)$ to be the size of the subtree rooted at v (including v), and that we identified a set with the root of its associated tree.

We update the size field of v each time a set is unioned into v. Thus, if v is not a root, then $n(v)$ is the largest the subtree rooted at v can be, which occurs just before we union v into some other node whose size is at least as large as v's. For any node v, then, define the ***rank*** of v, which we denote as $r(v)$, as

$$r(v) = \lfloor \log n(v) \rfloor.$$

Thus, we immediately get that $n(v) \geq 2^{r(v)}$. Also, since there are at most n nodes in the tree of v, $r(v) \leq \lfloor \log n \rfloor$, for each node v.

Theorem 4.8: *If node w is the parent of node v, then*

$$r(v) < r(w).$$

Proof: We make v point to w only if the size of w before the union is at least as large as the size of v. Let $n(w)$ denote the size of w before the union and let $n'(w)$ denote the size of w after the union. Thus, after the union we get

$$\begin{aligned} r(v) &= \lfloor \log n(v) \rfloor \\ &< \lfloor \log n(v) + 1 \rfloor \\ &= \lfloor \log 2n(v) \rfloor \\ &\leq \lfloor \log(n(v) + n(w)) \rfloor \\ &= \lfloor \log n'(w) \rfloor \\ &\leq r(w). \end{aligned}$$

■

Put another way, this theorem states that ranks are ***monotonically*** increasing as we follow parent pointers up a tree. It also implies the following:

Theorem 4.9: *There are at most $n/2^s$ nodes of rank s, for $0 \leq s \leq \lfloor \log n \rfloor$.*

Proof: By the previous theorem, $r(v) < r(w)$, for any node v with parent w, and ranks are monotonically increasing as we follow parent pointers up any tree. Thus, if $r(v) = r(w)$ for two nodes v and w, then the nodes counted in $n(v)$ must be separate and distinct from the nodes counted in $n(w)$. By the definition of rank, if a node v is of rank s, then $n(v) \geq 2^s$. Therefore, since there are at most n nodes total, there can be at most $n/2^s$ that are of rank s. ■

Amortized Analysis

A surprising property of the tree-based partition data structure, when implemented using the union-by-size and path-compression heuristics, is that performing a series of n union and find operations takes $O(n \log^* n)$ time, where $\log^* n$ is the "iterated logarithm" function, which is the inverse of the ***tower-of-twos*** function $t(i)$:

$$t(i) = \begin{cases} 1 & \text{if } i = 0 \\ 2^{t(i-1)} & \text{if } i \geq 1. \end{cases}$$

That is,

$$\log^* n = \min\{i\colon\, t(i) \geq n\}.$$

Intuitively, $\log^* n$ is the number of times that one can iteratively take the logarithm (base 2) of a number before getting a number smaller than 2. Table 4.10 shows a few sample values of this function.

minimum n	$\log^* n$
1	0
2	1
$2^2 = 4$	2
$2^{2^2} = 16$	3
$2^{2^{2^2}} = 65,536$	4
$2^{2^{2^{2^2}}} = 2^{65,536}$	5

Table 4.10: Some sample values of $\log^* n$ and the minimum value of n needed to obtain this value.

As is demonstrated in Table 4.10, for all practical purposes, $\log^* n \leq 5$. It is an amazingly slow-growing function (but one that is growing nonetheless).

In order to justify our surprising claim that the time needed to perform n union and find operations is $O(n \log^* n)$, we divide the nodes into ***rank groups***. Nodes v and u are in the same rank group g if

$$g = \log^*(r(v)) = \log^*(r(u)).$$

Since the largest rank is $\lfloor \log n \rfloor$, the largest rank group is

$$\log^*(\log n) = \log^* n - 1.$$

We use rank groups to derive rules for an amortized analysis via the accounting method. We have already observed that performing a union takes $O(1)$ time. We charge each union operation 1 cyber-dollar to pay for this. Thus, we can concentrate on the find operations to justify our claim that performing all n operations takes $O(n \log^* n)$ time.

The main computational task in performing a find operation is following parent pointers up from a node u to the root of the tree containing u. We can account for all of this work by paying one cyber-dollar for each parent reference we traverse. Let v be some node along this path, and let w be v's parent. We use two rules for charging the traversal of this parent reference:

- If w is the root or if w is in a different rank group than v, then charge the find operation one cyber-dollar.
- Otherwise (w is not a root and v and w are in the same rank group), charge the node v one cyber-dollar.

Since there are most $\log^* n - 1$ rank groups, this rule guarantees that any find operation is charged at most $\log^* n$ cyber-dollars. Thus, this scheme accounts for the find operation, but we must still account for all the cyber-dollars we charged to nodes.

Observe that after we charge a node v then v will get a new parent, which is a node higher up in v's tree. Moreover, since ranks are monotonically increasing up a tree, the rank of v's new parent will be greater than the rank of v's old parent w. Thus, any node v can be charged at most the number of different ranks that are in v's rank group. Also, since any node in rank group 0 has a parent in a higher rank group, we can restrict our attention to nodes in rank groups higher than 0 (for we will always charge the find operation for examining a node in rank group 0). If v is in rank group $g > 0$, then v can be charged at most $t(g) - t(g-1)$ times before v has a parent in a higher rank group (and from that point on, v will never be charged again). In other words, the total number, C, of cyber-dollars that can ever be charged to nodes can be bound as

$$C \le \sum_{g=1}^{\log^* n - 1} n(g) \cdot (t(g) - t(g-1)),$$

where $n(g)$ denotes the number of nodes in rank group g.

Therefore, if we can derive an upper bound for $n(g)$, we can then plug that into the above equation to derive an upper bound for C. To derive a bound on $n(g)$, the number of nodes in rank group g, recall that the total number of nodes of any given rank s is at most $n/2^s$ (by Theorem 4.9). Thus, for $g > 0$,

$$\begin{aligned}
n(g) &\le \sum_{s=t(g-1)+1}^{t(g)} \frac{n}{2^s} \\
&= \frac{n}{2^{t(g-1)+1}} \sum_{s=0}^{t(g)-t(g-1)-1} \frac{1}{2^s} \\
&< \frac{n}{2^{t(g-1)+1}} \cdot 2 \\
&= \frac{n}{2^{t(g-1)}} \\
&= \frac{n}{t(g)}.
\end{aligned}$$

Plugging this bound into the bound given above for the total number of node charges C, we get

$$\begin{aligned}
C &< \sum_{g=1}^{\log^* n - 1} \frac{n}{t(g)} \cdot (t(g) - t(g-1)) \\
&\le \sum_{g=1}^{\log^* n - 1} \frac{n}{t(g)} \cdot t(g) \\
&= \sum_{g=1}^{\log^* n - 1} n \\
&\le n \log^* n.
\end{aligned}$$

Therefore, we have shown that the total cyber-dollars charged to nodes is at most $n \log^* n$. This implies the following:

Theorem 4.10: *Let P be a partition with n elements implemented by means of a collection of trees, as described above, using the union-by-size and path-compression heuristics. In a series of* union *and* find *operations performed on P, starting with a collection of single-element sets, the amortized running time of each operation is $O(\log^* n)$.*

The Ackermann Function

We can actually prove that the amortized running time of an operation in a series of n partition operations implemented as above is $O(\alpha(n))$, where $\alpha(n)$ is a function, called the inverse of the ***Ackermann function***, $\mathcal{A}$, that asymptotically grows even slower than $\log^* n$, but proving this is beyond the scope of this book.

Still, we define the Ackermann function here, so as to appreciate just how quickly it grows; hence, how slowly its inverse grows. We first define an indexed Ackermann function, $\mathcal{A}_i$, as follows:

$$\begin{aligned} \mathcal{A}_0(n) &= 2n && \text{for } n \geq 0 \\ \mathcal{A}_i(1) &= \mathcal{A}_{i-1}(2) && \text{for } i \geq 1 \\ \mathcal{A}_i(n) &= \mathcal{A}_{i-1}(\mathcal{A}_i(n-1)) && \text{for } i \geq 1 \text{ and } n \geq 2. \end{aligned}$$

In other words, the indexed Ackermann functions define a progression of functions, with each function growing much faster than the previous one:

- $\mathcal{A}_0(n) = 2n$ is the multiply-by-two function
- $\mathcal{A}_1(n) = 2^n$ is the power-of-two function
- $\mathcal{A}_2(n) = 2^{2^{\cdot^{\cdot^{\cdot^2}}}}$ (with n 2's) is the tower-of-twos function
- $\mathcal{A}_3(n)$ is the tower-of-tower-of-twos function
- and so on.

We then define the Ackermann function as $\mathcal{A}(n) = \mathcal{A}_n(n)$, which is an incredibly fast growing function. Likewise, its inverse, $\alpha(n) = \min\{m\colon \mathcal{A}(m) \geq n\}$, is an incredibly slow growing function.

We next return to sorting problem, discussing ***quick-sort***. Like merge-sort, this algorithm is also based on the ***divide-and-conquer*** paradigm, but it uses this technique in a somewhat opposite manner, as all the hard work is done ***before*** the recursive calls.

4.3 Quick-Sort

The quick-sort algorithm sorts a sequence S using a simple divide-and-conquer approach, whereby we divide S into subsequences, recur to sort each subsequence, and then combine the sorted subsequences by a simple concatenation. In particular, the quick-sort algorithm consists of the following three steps (see Figure 4.11):

1. ***Divide:*** If S has at least two elements (nothing needs to be done if S has zero or one element), select a specific element x from S, which is called the ***pivot***. As is common practice, choose the pivot x to be the last element in S. Remove all the elements from S and put them into three sequences:
   - L, storing the elements in S less than x
   - E, storing the elements in S equal to x
   - G, storing the elements in S greater than x.

   (If the elements of S are all distinct, E holds just one element—the pivot.)
2. ***Recur:*** Recursively sort sequences L and G.
3. ***Conquer:*** Put the elements back into S in order by first inserting the elements of L, then those of E, and finally those of G.

Like merge-sort, we can visualize quick-sort using a binary recursion tree, called the ***quick-sort tree***. Figure 4.12 visualizes the quick-sort algorithm, showing example input and output sequences for each node of the quick-sort tree.

Unlike merge-sort, however, the height of the quick-sort tree associated with an execution of quick-sort is linear in the worst case. This happens, for example, if the sequence consists of n distinct elements and is already sorted. Indeed, in this case, the standard choice of the pivot as the largest element yields a subsequence L of size $n-1$, while subsequence E has size 1 and subsequence G has size 0. Hence, the height of the quick-sort tree is $n-1$ in the worst case.

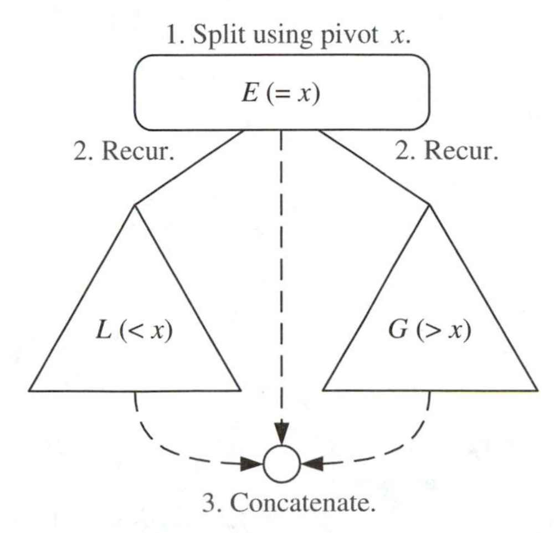

Figure 4.11: A visual schematic of the quick-sort algorithm.

Running Time of Quick-Sort

We can analyze the running time of quick-sort with the same technique used for merge-sort in Section 4.1.1. Namely, we identify the time spent at each node of the quick-sort tree T (Figure 4.12) and we sum up the running times for all the nodes. The divide step and the conquer step of quick-sort are easy to implement in linear time. Thus, the time spent at a node v of T is proportional to the ***input size*** $s(v)$ of v, defined as the size of the sequence handled by the invocation of quick-sort associated with node v. Since subsequence E has at least one element (the pivot), the sum of the input sizes of the children of v is at most $s(v) - 1$.

Given a quick-sort tree T, let s_i denote the sum of the input sizes of the nodes at depth i in T. Clearly, $s_0 = n$, since the root r of T is associated with the entire sequence. Also, $s_1 \leq n - 1$, since the pivot is not propagated to the children of r. Consider next s_2. If both children of r have nonzero input size, then $s_2 = n - 3$. Otherwise (one child of the root has zero size, the other has size $n - 1$), $s_2 = n - 2$. Thus, $s_2 \leq n - 2$. Continuing this line of reasoning, we obtain that $s_i \leq n - i$.

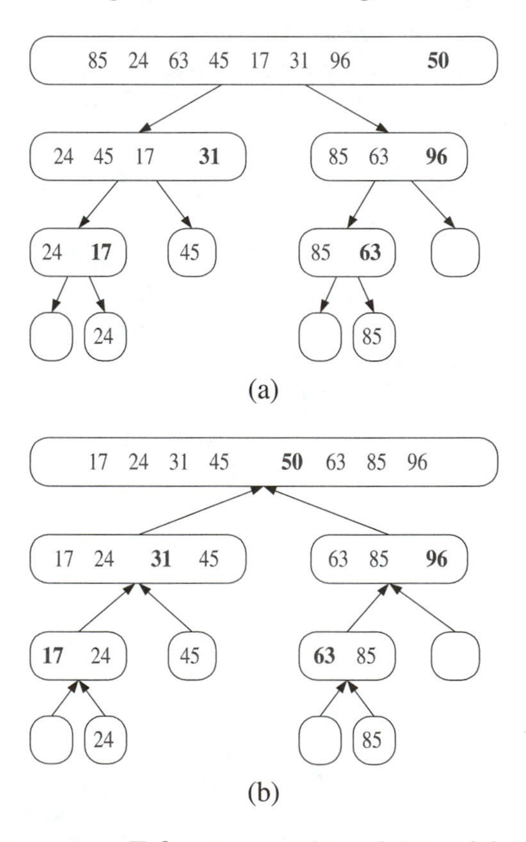

Figure 4.12: Quick-sort tree T for an execution of the quick-sort algorithm on a sequence with eight elements: (a) input sequences processed at each node of T; (b) output sequences generated at each node of T. The pivot used at each level of the recursion is shown in bold.

As observed in Section 4.3, the height of T is $n-1$ in the worst case. Thus, the worst-case running time of quick-sort is

$$O\left(\sum_{i=0}^{n-1} s_i\right), \text{ which is } O\left(\sum_{l=0}^{n-1} (n-i)\right) \text{ that is, } O\left(\sum_{i=1}^{n} i\right).$$

By Theorem 1.13, $\sum_{i=1}^{n} i$ is $O(n^2)$. Thus, quick-sort runs in $O(n^2)$ worst-case time.

Given its name, we would expect quick-sort to run quickly. However, the above quadratic bound indicates that quick-sort is slow in the worst case. Paradoxically, this worst-case behavior occurs for problem instances when sorting should be easy—if the sequence is already sorted. Still, note that the best case for quick-sort on a sequence of distinct elements occurs when subsequences L and G happen to have roughly the same size. Indeed, in this case we save one pivot at each internal node and make two equal-sized calls for its children. Thus, we save 1 pivot at the root, 2 at level 1, 2^2 at level 2, and so on. That is, in the best case, we have

$$\begin{aligned}
s_0 &= n \\
s_1 &= n-1 \\
s_2 &= n-(1+2) = n-3 \\
&\vdots \\
s_i &= n-(1+2+2^2+\cdots+2^{i-1}) = n-(2^i-1),
\end{aligned}$$

and so on. Thus, in the best case, T has height $O(\log n)$ and quick-sort runs in $O(n \log n)$ time. We leave the justification of this fact as an exercise (R-4.11).

The informal intuition behind the expected behavior of quick-sort is that at each invocation the pivot will probably divide the input sequence about equally. Thus, we expect the average running time quick-sort to be similar to the best-case running time, that is, $O(n \log n)$. We will see in the next section that introducing randomization makes quick-sort behave exactly as described above.

4.3.1 Randomized Quick-Sort

One common method for analyzing quick-sort is to assume that the pivot will always divide the sequence almost equally. We feel such an assumption would presuppose knowledge about the input distribution that is typically not available, however. For example, we would have to assume that we will rarely be given "almost" sorted sequences to sort, which are actually common in many applications. Fortunately, this assumption is not needed in order for us to match our intuition to quick-sort's behavior.

Since the goal of the partition step of the quick-sort method is to divide the sequence S almost equally, let us use a new rule to pick the pivot—choose a ***random element*** of the input sequence. As we show next, the resulting algorithm, called ***randomized quick-sort***, has an expected running time of $O(n \log n)$ given a sequence with n elements.

Theorem 4.11: *The expected running time of randomized quick-sort on a sequence of size n is $O(n \log n)$.*

Proof: We make use of a simple fact from probability theory:

> *The expected number of times that a fair coin must be flipped until it shows "heads" k times is $2k$.*

Consider now a particular recursive invocation of randomized quick-sort, and let m denote the size of the input sequence for this invocation. Say that this invocation is "good" if the pivot chosen creates subsequences L and G that have size at least $m/4$ and at most $3m/4$ each. Since the pivot is chosen uniformly at random and there are $m/2$ pivots for which this invocation is good, the probability that an invocation is good is $1/2$ (the same as the probability a coin comes up heads).

If a node v of the quick-sort tree T, as shown in Figure 4.13, is associated with a "good" recursive call, then the input sizes of the children of v are each at most $3s(v)/4$ (which is the same as $(s(v)/(4/3))$. If we take any path in T from the root to an external node, then the length of this path is at most the number of invocations that have to be made (at each node on this path) until achieving $\log_{4/3} n$ good invocations. Applying the probabilistic fact reviewed above, the expected number of invocations we must make until this occurs is $2\log_{4/3} n$ (if a path terminates before this level, that is all the better). Thus, the expected length of any path from the root to an external node in T is $O(\log n)$. Recalling that the time spent at each level of T is $O(n)$, the expected running time of randomized quick-sort is $O(n \log n)$. ■

We note that the expectation in the running time is taken over all the possible choices the algorithm makes, and is independent of any assumptions about the distribution of input sequences the algorithm is likely to encounter. Actually, by using powerful facts from probability, we can show that the running time of randomized quick-sort is $O(n \log n)$ with high probability. (See Exercise C-4.8.)

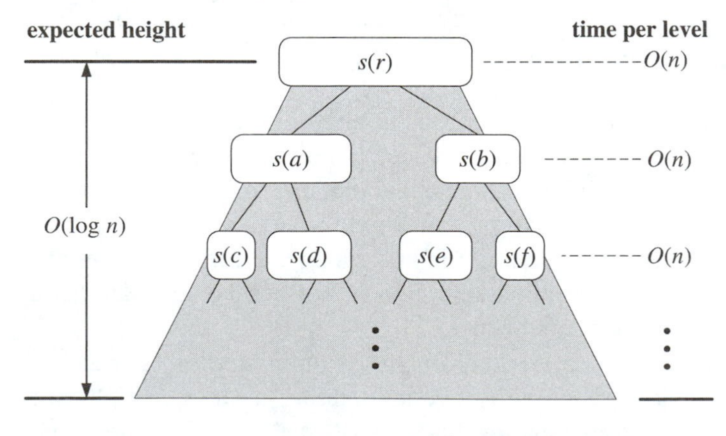

Figure 4.13: A visual time analysis of the quick-sort tree T.

4.4 A Lower Bound on Comparison-Based Sorting

Recapping our discussions on sorting to this point, we have described several methods with either a worst-case or expected running time of $O(n\log n)$ on an input sequence of size n. These methods include merge-sort and quick-sort, described in this chapter, as well as heap-sort, described in Section 2.4.4. A natural question to ask, then, is whether it is possible to sort any faster than in $O(n\log n)$ time.

In this section, we show that if the computational primitive used by a sorting algorithm is the comparison of two elements, then this is the best we can do—comparison-based sorting has an $\Omega(n\log n)$ worst-case lower bound on its running time. (Recall the notation $\Omega(\cdot)$ from Section 1.2.2.) To focus on the main cost of comparison-based sorting, let us only count the comparisons that a sorting algorithm performs. Since we want to derive a lower bound, this will be sufficient.

Suppose we are given a sequence $S = (x_0, x_1, \ldots, x_{n-1})$ that we wish to sort, and let us assume that all the elements of S are distinct (this is not a restriction since we are deriving a lower bound). Each time a sorting algorithm compares two elements x_i and x_j (that is, it asks, "is $x_i < x_j$?"), there are two outcomes: "yes" or "no." Based on the result of this comparison, the sorting algorithm may perform some internal calculations (which we are not counting here) and will eventually perform another comparison between two other elements of S, which again will have two outcomes. Therefore, we can represent a comparison-based sorting algorithm with a decision tree T. That is, each internal node v in T corresponds to a comparison and the edges from node v' to its children correspond to the computations resulting from either a "yes" or "no" answer (see Figure 4.14).

It is important to note that the hypothetical sorting algorithm in question probably has no explicit knowledge of the tree T. We simply use T to represent all the possible sequences of comparisons that a sorting algorithm might make, starting from the first comparison (associated with the root) and ending with the last comparison (associated with the parent of an external node) just before the algorithm terminates its execution.

Each possible initial ordering, or ***permutation***, of the elements in S will cause our hypothetical sorting algorithm to execute a series of comparisons, traversing a path in T from the root to some external node. Let us associate with each external node v in T, then, the set of permutations of S that cause our sorting algorithm to end up in v. The most important observation in our lower-bound argument is that each external node v in T can represent the sequence of comparisons for at most one permutation of S. The justification for this claim is simple: if two different permutations P_1 and P_2 of S are associated with the same external node, then there are at least two objects x_i and x_j, such that x_i is before x_j in P_1 but x_i is after x_j in P_2. At the same time, the output associated with v must be a specific reordering of S, with either x_i or x_j appearing before the other. But if P_1 and P_2 both cause the sorting algorithm to output the elements of S in this order, then that implies there is a way to trick the algorithm into outputting x_i and x_j in the wrong order. Since this cannot be allowed by a correct sorting algorithm, each external node of T must be associated with exactly one permutation of S. We use this property of the decision tree associated with a sorting algorithm to prove the following result:

Theorem 4.12: *The running time of any comparison-based algorithm for sorting an n-element sequence is $\Omega(n \log n)$ in the worst case.*

Proof: The running time of a comparison-based sorting algorithm must be greater than or equal to the height of the decision tree T associated with this algorithm, as described above. (See Figure 4.14.) By the above argument, each external node in T must be associated with one permutation of S. Moreover, each permutation of S must result in a different external node of T. The number of permutations of n objects is

$$n! = n(n-1)(n-2)\cdots 2\cdot 1.$$

Thus, T must have at least $n!$ external nodes. By Theorem 2.8, the height of T is at least $\log(n!)$. This immediately justifies the theorem, because there are at least $n/2$ terms that are greater than or equal to $n/2$ in the product $n!$; hence

$$\log(n!) \geq \log\left(\frac{n}{2}\right)^{\frac{n}{2}} = \frac{n}{2}\log\frac{n}{2},$$

which is $\Omega(n \log n)$. ■

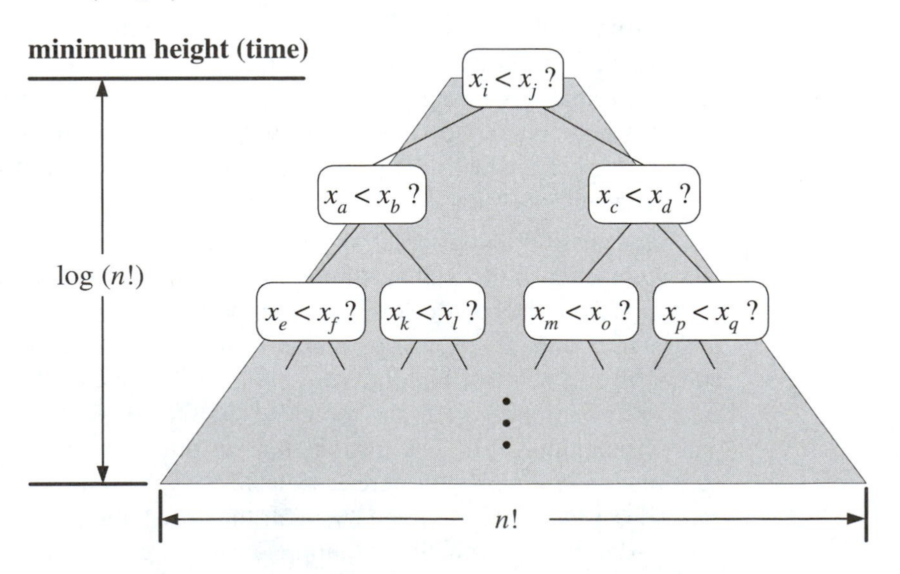

Figure 4.14: Visualizing the lower bound for comparison-based sorting.

4.5 Bucket-Sort and Radix-Sort

In the previous section, we showed that $\Omega(n \log n)$ time is necessary, in the worst case, to sort an n-element sequence with a comparison-based sorting algorithm. A natural question to ask, then, is whether there are other kinds of sorting algorithms that can be designed to run asymptotically faster than $O(n \log n)$ time. Interestingly, such algorithms exist, but they require special assumptions about the input sequence to be sorted. Even so, such scenarios often arise in practice, so discussing them is worthwhile. In this section, we consider the problem of sorting a sequence of items, each a key-element pair.

4.5.1 Bucket-Sort

Consider a sequence S of n items whose keys are integers in the range $[0, N-1]$, for some integer $N \geq 2$, and suppose that S should be sorted according to the keys of the items. In this case, it is possible to sort S in $O(n+N)$ time. It might seem surprising, but this implies, for example, that if N is $O(n)$, then we can sort S in $O(n)$ time. Of course, the crucial point is that, because of the restrictive assumption about the format of the elements, we can avoid using comparisons.

The main idea is to use an algorithm called ***bucket-sort***, which is not based on comparisons, but on using keys as indices into a bucket array B that has entries from 0 to $N-1$. An item with key k is placed in the "bucket" $B[k]$, which itself is a sequence (of items with key k). After inserting each item of the input sequence S into its bucket, we can put the items back into S in sorted order by enumerating the contents of the buckets $B[0], B[1], \ldots, B[N-1]$ in order. We give a pseudo-code description of bucket-sort in Algorithm 4.15.

Algorithm bucketSort(S):
    Input: Sequence S of items with integer keys in the range $[0, N-1]$
    Output: Sequence S sorted in nondecreasing order of the keys

```
let B be an array of N sequences, each of which is initially empty
for each item x in S do
   let k be the key of x
   remove x from S and insert it at the end of bucket (sequence) B[k]
for i ← 0 to N − 1 do
   for each item x in sequence B[i] do
      remove x from B[i] and insert it at the end of S
```

Algorithm 4.15: Bucket-sort.

It is easy to see that bucket-sort runs in $O(n+N)$ time and uses $O(n+N)$ space, just by examining the two **for** loops.

Thus, bucket-sort is efficient when the range N of values for the keys is small compared to the sequence size n, say $N = O(n)$ or $N = O(n \log n)$. Still, its performance deteriorates as N grows compared to n.

In addition, an important property of the bucket-sort algorithm is that it works correctly even if there are many different elements with the same key. Indeed, we described it in a way that anticipates such occurrences.

Stable Sorting

When sorting key-element items, an important issue is how equal keys are handled. Let $S = ((k_0, e_0), \ldots, (k_{n-1}, e_{n-1}))$ be a sequence of items. We say that a sorting algorithm is ***stable*** if, for any two items (k_i, e_i) and (k_j, e_j) of S, such that $k_i = k_j$ and (k_i, e_i) precedes (k_j, e_j) in S before sorting (that is, $i < j$), item (k_i, e_i) also precedes item (k_j, e_j) after sorting. Stability is important for a sorting algorithm because applications may want to preserve the initial ordering of elements with the same key.

Our informal description of bucket-sort in Algorithm 4.15 does not guarantee stability. This is not inherent in the bucket-sort method itself, however, for we can easily modify our description to make bucket-sort stable, while still preserving its $O(n + N)$ running time. Indeed, we can obtain a stable bucket-sort algorithm by always removing the ***first*** element from sequence S and from the sequences $B[i]$ during the execution of the algorithm.

4.5.2 Radix-Sort

One of the reasons that stable sorting is so important is that it allows the bucket-sort approach to be applied to more general contexts than to sort integers. Suppose, for example, that we want to sort items with keys that are pairs (k, l), where k and l are integers in the range $[0, N-1]$, for some integer $N \geq 2$. In a context such as this, it is natural to define an ordering on these items using the ***lexicographical*** (dictionary) convention, where $(k_1, l_1) < (k_2, l_2)$ if

- $k_1 < k_2$ or
- $k_1 = k_2$ and $l_1 < l_2$.

This is a pair-wise version of the lexicographic comparison function, usually applied to equal-length character strings (and it easily generalizes to tuples of d numbers for $d > 2$).

The ***radix-sort*** algorithm sorts a sequence of pairs such as S, by applying a stable bucket-sort on the sequence twice; first using one component of the pair as the ordering key and then using the second component. But which order is correct? Should we first sort on the k's (the first component) and then on the l's (the second component), or should it be the other way around?

Before we answer this question, we consider the following example.

Example 4.13: *Consider the following sequence S:*

$$S = ((3,3),(1,5),(2,5),(1,2),(2,3),(1,7),(3,2),(2,2)).$$

If we stably sort S on the first component, then we get the sequence

$$S_1 = ((1,5),(1,2),(1,7),(2,5),(2,3),(2,2),(3,3),(3,2)).$$

If we then stably sort this sequence S_1 using the second component, then we get the sequence

$$S_{1,2} = ((1,2),(2,2),(3,2),(2,3),(3,3),(1,5),(2,5),(1,7)),$$

which is not exactly a sorted sequence. On the other hand, if we first stably sort S using the second component, then we get the sequence

$$S_2 = ((1,2),(3,2),(2,2),(3,3),(2,3),(1,5),(2,5),(1,7)).$$

If we then stably sort sequence S_2 using the first component, then we get the sequence

$$S_{2,1} = ((1,2),(1,5),(1,7),(2,2),(2,3),(2,5),(3,2),(3,3)),$$

which is indeed sequence S lexicographically ordered.

So, from this example, we are led to believe that we should first sort using the second component and then again using the first component. This intuition is exactly right. By first stably sorting by the second component and then again by the first component, we guarantee that if two elements are equal in the second sort (by the first component), then their relative order in the starting sequence (which is sorted by the second component) is preserved. Thus, the resulting sequence is guaranteed to be sorted lexicographically every time. We leave the determination of how this approach can be extended to triples and other d-tuples of numbers to a simple exercise (R-4.15). We can summarize this section as follows:

Theorem 4.14: *Let S be a sequence of n key-element items, each of which has a key $(k_1, k_2, \ldots, k_d)$, where k_i is an integer in the range $[0, N-1]$ for some integer $N \geq 2$. We can sort S lexicographically in time $O(d(n+N))$ using radix-sort.*

As important as it is, sorting is not the only interesting problem dealing with a total order relation on a set of elements. There are some applications, for example, that do not require an ordered listing of an entire set, but nevertheless call for some amount of ordering information about the set. Before we study such a problem (called "selection"), let us step back and briefly compare all of the sorting algorithms we have studied so far.

4.6 Comparison of Sorting Algorithms

At this point, it might be useful for us to take a breath and consider all the algorithms we have studied in this book to sort an n-element sequence. As with many things in life, there is no clear "best" sorting algorithm, but we can offer some guidance and observations, based on the known properties of "good" algorithms.

If implemented well, ***insertion-sort*** runs in $O(n+k)$ time, where k is the number of inversions (that is, the number of pairs of elements out of order). Thus, insertion-sort is an excellent algorithm for sorting small sequences (say, less than 50 elements). Also, insertion-sort is quite effective for sorting sequences that are already "almost" sorted. By "almost," we mean that the number of inversions is small. But the $O(n^2)$-time performance of insertion-sort makes it a poor choice outside of these special contexts.

Merge-sort, on the other hand, runs in $O(n \log n)$ time in the worst case, which is optimal for comparison-based sorting methods. Still, experimental studies have shown that, since it is difficult to make merge-sort run in-place, the overheads needed to implement merge-sort make it less attractive than the in-place implementations of heap-sort and quick-sort for sequences that can fit entirely in a computer's main memory area. Even so, merge-sort is an excellent algorithm for situations where the input cannot all fit into main memory, but must be stored in blocks on an external memory device, such as a disk. In these contexts, the way that merge-sort processes runs of data in long merge streams makes the best use of all the data brought into main memory in a block from disk. (See Section 14.1.3.)

Experimental studies have shown that if an input sequence can fit entirely in main memory, then the in-place versions of quick-sort and heap-sort run faster than merge-sort. In fact, quick-sort tends, on average, to beat heap-sort in these tests. So, ***quick-sort*** is an excellent choice as a general-purpose, in-memory sorting algorithm. Indeed, it is included in the qsort sorting utility provided in C language libraries. Still, its $O(n^2)$ time worst-case performance makes quick-sort a poor choice in real-time applications where we must make guarantees on the time needed to complete a sorting operation.

In real-time scenarios where we have a fixed amount of time to perform a sorting operation and the input data can fit into main memory, the ***heap-sort*** algorithm is probably the best choice. It runs in $O(n \log n)$ worst-case time and can easily be made to execute in-place.

Finally, if our application involves sorting by integer keys or d-tuples of integer keys, then ***bucket-sort*** or ***radix-sort*** is an excellent choice, for it runs in $O(d(n+N))$ time, where $[0, N-1]$ is the range of integer keys (and $d = 1$ for bucket sort). Thus, if $d(n+N)$ is "below" $n \log n$ (formally, $d(n+N)$ is $o(n \log n)$), then this sorting method should run faster than even quick-sort or heap-sort.

Thus, our study of all these different sorting algorithms provides us with a versatile collection of sorting methods in our algorithm design "toolbox."

4.7 Selection

There are a number of applications in which we are interested in identifying a single element in terms of its rank relative to an ordering of the entire set. Examples include identifying the minimum and maximum elements, but we may also be interested in, say, identifying the ***median*** element, that is, the element such that half of the other elements are smaller and the remaining half are larger. In general, queries that ask for an element with a given rank are called ***order statistics***.

In this section, we discuss the general order-statistic problem of selecting the kth smallest element from an unsorted collection of n comparable elements. This is known as the ***selection*** problem. Of course, we can solve this problem by sorting the collection and then indexing into the sorted sequence at rank index $k-1$. Using the best comparison-based sorting algorithms, this approach would take $O(n \log n)$ time. Thus, a natural question to ask is whether we can achieve an $O(n)$ running time for all values of k, including the interesting case of finding the median, where $k = \lceil n/2 \rceil$.

4.7.1 Prune-and-Search

This may come as a small surprise, but we can indeed solve the selection problem in $O(n)$ time for any value of k. Moreover, the technique we use to achieve this result involves an interesting algorithmic design pattern. This design pattern is known as ***prune-and-search*** or ***decrease-and-conquer***. In applying this design pattern, we solve a given problem that is defined on a collection of n objects by pruning away a fraction of the n objects and recursively solving the smaller problem. When we have finally reduced the problem to one defined on a constant-sized collection of objects, then we solve the problem using some brute-force method. Returning back from all the recursive calls completes the construction. In some cases, we can avoid using recursion, in which case we simply iterate the prune-and-search reduction step until we can apply a brute-force method and stop.

4.7.2 Randomized Quick-Select

In applying the prune-and-search pattern to the selection problem, we can design a simple and practical method, called ***randomized quick-select***, for finding the kth smallest element in an unordered sequence of n elements on which a total order relation is defined. Randomized quick-select runs in $O(n)$ ***expected*** time, taken over all possible random choices made by the algorithm, and this expectation does not depend whatsoever on any randomness assumptions about the input distribution. We note though that randomized quick-select runs in $O(n^2)$ time in the ***worst-case*** time, the justification of which is left as an exercise (R-4.18). We also provide an exercise (C-4.24) on modifying randomized quick-select to get a ***deterministic*** selection algorithm that runs in $O(n)$ ***worst-case*** time. The existence of this deterministic algorithm is mostly of theoretical interest, however, since the constant factor hidden by the big-Oh notation is relatively large in this case.

Suppose we are given an unsorted sequence S of n comparable elements together with an integer $k \in [1,n]$. At a high level, the quick-select algorithm for finding the kth smallest element in S is similar in structure to the randomized quick-sort algorithm described in Section 4.3.1. We pick an element x from S at random and use this as a "pivot" to subdivide S into three subsequences L, E, and G, storing the elements of S less than x, equal to x, and greater than x, respectively. This is the prune step. Then, based on the value of k, we determine on which of these sets to recur. Randomized quick-select is described in Algorithm 4.16.

Algorithm quickSelect(S,k):
  Input: Sequence S of n comparable elements, and an integer $k \in [1,n]$
  Output: The kth smallest element of S

  if $n = 1$ **then**
    return the (first) element of S
  pick a random element x of S
  remove all the elements from S and put them into three sequences:

- L, storing the elements in S less than x
- E, storing the elements in S equal to x
- G, storing the elements in S greater than x.

  if $k \leq |L|$ **then**
    quickSelect(L,k)
  else if $k \leq |L| + |E|$ **then**
    return x {each element in E is equal to x}
  else
    quickSelect$(G, k - |L| - |E|)$ {note the new selection parameter}

Algorithm 4.16: Randomized quick-select algorithm.

4.7.3 Analyzing Randomized Quick-Select

We mentioned above that the randomized quick-select algorithm runs in expected $O(n)$ time. Fortunately, justifying this claim requires only the simplest of probabilistic arguments. The main probabilistic fact that we use is the ***linearity of expectation***. Recall that this fact states that if X and Y are random variables and c is a number, then $E(X+Y) = E(X) + E(Y)$ and $E(cX) = cE(X)$, where we use $E(\mathcal{Z})$ to denote the expected value of the expression $\mathcal{Z}$.

Let $t(n)$ denote the running time of randomized quick-select on a sequence of size n. Since the randomized quick-select algorithm depends on the outcome of random events, its running time, $t(n)$, is a random variable. We are interested in bounding $E(t(n))$, the expected value of $t(n)$. Say that a recursive invocation of randomized quick-select is "good" if it partitions S, so that the size of L and G is at most $3n/4$. Clearly, a recursive call is good with probability $1/2$. Let $g(n)$ denote the number of consecutive recursive invocations (including the present one) before getting a good invocation. Then

$$t(n) \leq bn \cdot g(n) + t(3n/4),$$

where $b > 0$ is a constant (to account for the overhead of each call). We are, of course, focusing on the case where n is larger than 1, for we can easily characterize in a closed form that $t(1) = b$. Applying the linearity of expectation property to the general case, then, we get

$$E\left(t(n)\right) \leq E\left(bn \cdot g(n) + t(3n/4)\right) = bn \cdot E\left(g(n)\right) + E\left(t(3n/4)\right).$$

Since a recursive call is good with probability $1/2$, and whether a recursive call is good or not is independent of its parent call being good, the expected value of $g(n)$ is the same as the expected number of times we must flip a fair coin before it comes up "heads." This implies that $E(g(n)) = 2$. Thus, if we let $T(n)$ be a shorthand notation for $E(t(n))$ (the expected running time of the randomized quick-select algorithm), then we can write the case for $n > 1$ as

$$T(n) \leq T(3n/4) + 2bn.$$

As with the merge-sort recurrence equation, we would like to convert this equation into a closed form. To do this, let us again iteratively apply this equation assuming n is large. So, for example, after two iterative applications, we get

$$T(n) \leq T((3/4)^2 n) + 2b(3/4)n + 2bn.$$

At this point, we see that the general case is

$$T(n) \leq 2bn \cdot \sum_{i=0}^{\lceil \log_{4/3} n \rceil} (3/4)^i.$$

In other words, the expected running time of randomized quick-select is $2bn$ times the sum of a geometric progression whose base is a positive number less than 1. Thus, by Theorem 1.12 on geometric summations, we obtain the result that $T(n)$ is $O(n)$. To summarize, we have:

Theorem 4.15: *The expected running time of randomized quick-select on a sequence of size n is $O(n)$.*

As we mentioned earlier, there is a variation of quick-select that does not use randomization and runs in $O(n)$ worst-case time. Exercise C-4.24 walks the interested reader through the design and analysis of this algorithm.

4.8 Java Example: In-Place Quick-Sort

Recall from Section 2.4.4 that a sorting algorithm is ***in-place*** if it uses only a constant amount of memory in addition to that needed for the objects being sorted themselves. The merge-sort algorithm, as we have described it above, is not in-place, and making it be in-place requires a more complicated merging method than the one we discuss in Section 4.1.1. In-place sorting is not inherently difficult, however. For, as with heap-sort, quick-sort can be adapted to be in-place.

Performing the quick-sort algorithm in-place requires a bit of ingenuity, however, for we must use the input sequence itself to store the subsequences for all the recursive calls. We show algorithm inPlaceQuickSort, which performs in-place quick-sort, in Algorithm 4.17. Algorithm inPlaceQuickSort assumes that the input sequence, S, has distinct elements. The reason for this restriction is explored in Exercise R-4.12. The extension to the general case is discussed in Exercise C-4.18. The algorithm accesses the elements of the input sequence, S, with rank-based methods. Hence, it runs efficiently provided S is implemented with an array.

Algorithm inPlaceQuickSort(S, a, b):
  Input: Sequence S of distinct elements; integers a and b
  Output: Sequence S with elements originally from ranks from a to b, inclusive, sorted in nondecreasing order from ranks a to b

  if $a \geq b$ **then return** {empty subrange}
  $p \leftarrow S$.elemAtRank(b) {pivot}
  $l \leftarrow a$ {will scan rightward}
  $r \leftarrow b - 1$ {will scan leftward}
  while $l \leq r$ **do**
    {find an element larger than the pivot}
    while $l \leq r$ **and** S.elemAtRank$(l) \leq p$ **do**
      $l \leftarrow l + 1$
    {find an element smaller than the pivot}
    while $r \geq l$ **and** S.elemAtRank$(r) \geq p$ **do**
      $r \leftarrow r - 1$
    if $l < r$ **then**
      S.swapElements$(S$.atRank$(l), S$.atRank$(r))$
  {put the pivot into its final place}
  S.swapElements$(S$.atRank$(l), S$.atRank$(b))$
  {recursive calls}
  inPlaceQuickSort$(S, a, l - 1)$
  inPlaceQuickSort$(S, l + 1, b)$

Algorithm 4.17: In-place quick-sort for a sequence implemented with an array.

In-place quick-sort modifies the input sequence using swapElements operations and does not explicitly create subsequences. Indeed, a subsequence of the input sequence is implicitly represented by a range of positions specified by a left-most rank l and a right-most rank r. The divide step is performed by scanning the sequence simultaneously from l forward and from r backward, swapping pairs of elements that are in reverse order, as shown in Figure 4.18. When these two indices "meet," subsequences L and G are on opposite sides of the meeting point. The algorithm completes by recursing on these two subsequences.

In-place quick-sort reduces the running time, caused by the creation of new sequences and the movement of elements between them, by a constant factor. We show a Java version of in-place quick-sort in Code Fragment 4.20.

Unfortunately, our implementation of quick-sort is, technically speaking, not quite in-place, as it still requires more than a constant amount of additional space. Of course, we are using no additional space for the subsequences, and we are using only a constant amount of additional space for local variables (such as l and r). So, where does this additional space come from? It comes from the recursion, for, recalling Section 2.1.1, we note that we need space for a stack proportional to the depth of the recursion tree for quick-sort, which is at least $\log n$ and at most $n-1$. In order to make quick-sort truly in-place, we must implement it nonrecursively (and not use a stack). The key detail for such an implementation is that we need an in-place way of determining the bounds for the left and right boundaries of the "current" subsequence. Such a scheme is not too difficult, however, and we leave the details of this implementation to an exercise (C-4.17).

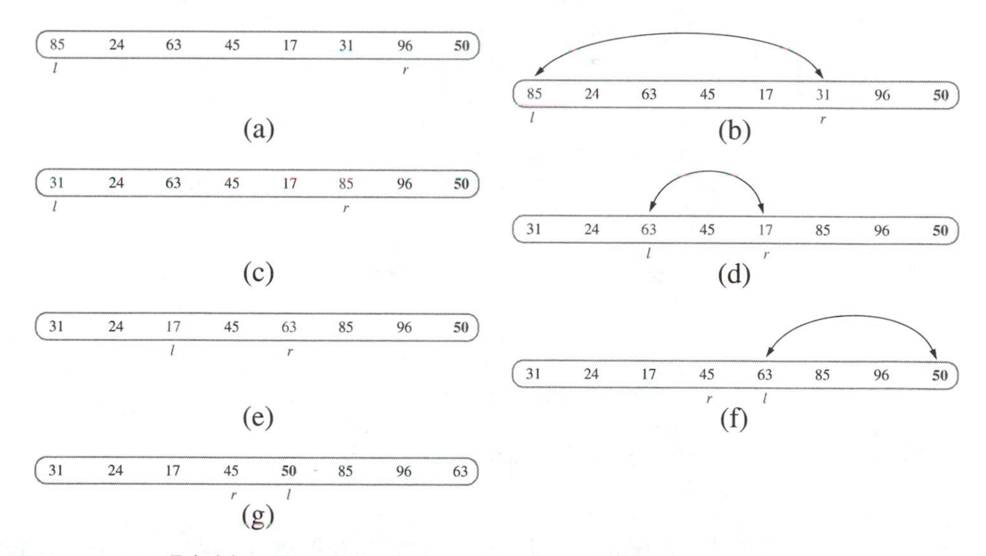

Figure 4.18: Divide step of in-place quick-sort. Index l scans the sequence from left to right, and index r scans the sequence from right to left. A swap is performed when l is at an element larger than the pivot and r is at an element smaller than the pivot. A final swap with the pivot completes the divide step.

```
/**
 * Sort the elements of sequence S in nondecreasing order according
 * to comparator c, using the quick-sort algorithm. Most of the work
 * is done by the auxiliary recursive method quickSortStep.
 **/
public static void quickSort (Sequence S, Comparator c) {
  if (S.size() < 2)
    return; // a sequence with 0 or 1 element is already sorted
  quickSortStep(S, c, 0, S.size()-1); // recursive sort method
}
/**
 * Sort in nondecreasing order the elements of sequence S between
 * ranks leftBound and rightBound, using a recursive, in-place,
 * implementation of the quick-sort algorithm.
 **/
private static void quickSortStep (Sequence S, Comparator c,
                                   int leftBound, int rightBound ) {
  if (leftBound >= rightBound)
    return;
  Object pivot = S.atRank(rightBound).element();
  int leftIndex = leftBound;      // will scan rightward
  int rightIndex = rightBound-1; // will scan leftward
  while (leftIndex <= rightIndex) {
    // scan rightward to find an element larger than the pivot
    while ( (leftIndex <= rightIndex) &&
          c.isLessThanOrEqualTo(S.atRank(leftIndex).element(), pivot) )
      leftIndex++;
    // scan leftward to find an element smaller than the pivot
    while ( (rightIndex >= leftIndex) &&
          c.isGreaterThanOrEqualTo(S.atRank(rightIndex).element(), pivot) )
      rightIndex--;
    if (leftIndex < rightIndex) // both elements were found
      S.swapElements(S.atRank(leftIndex), S.atRank(rightIndex));
  } // the loop continues until the indices cross
  // place the pivot by swapping it with the element at leftIndex
  S.swapElements(S.atRank(leftIndex), S.atRank(rightBound));
  // the pivot is now at leftIndex, so recur on both sides of it
  quickSortStep(S, c, leftBound, leftIndex-1);
  quickSortStep(S, c, leftIndex+1, rightBound);
}
```

Code Fragment 4.20: Java implementation of in-place quick-sort. It is assumed that the input sequence is implemented with an array and that it has distinct elements.

4.9 Exercises

Reinforcement

R-4.1 Give a complete justification of Theorem 4.1.

R-4.2 Give a pseudo-code description of the merge-sort algorithm. You can call the merge algorithm as a subroutine.

R-4.3 Give a pseudo-code description of a variation of the merge-sort algorithm that operates on an array instead of a general sequence.
Hint: Use an auxiliary array as a "buffer."

R-4.4 Show that the running time of the merge-sort algorithm on an n-element sequence is $O(n \log n)$, even when n is not a power of 2.

R-4.5 Suppose we are given two n-element sorted sequences A and B that should not be viewed as sets (that is, A and B may contain duplicate entries). Describe an $O(n)$-time method for computing a sequence representing the set $A \cup B$ (with no duplicates).

R-4.6 Show that $(X - A) \cup (X - B) = X - (A \cap B)$, for any three sets X, A, and B.

R-4.7 Suppose we implement the tree-based partition (union-find) data structure using only the union-by-size heuristic. What is the amortized running time of a sequence of n union and find operations in this case?

R-4.8 Provide pseudo-code descriptions for performing methods insert and remove on a set implemented with a sorted sequence.

R-4.9 Suppose we modify the deterministic version of the quick-sort algorithm so that, instead of selecting the last element in an n-element sequence as the pivot, we choose the element at rank (index) $\lfloor n/2 \rfloor$, that is, an element in the middle of the sequence. What is the running time of this version of quick-sort on a sequence that is already sorted?

R-4.10 Consider again the modification of the deterministic version of the quick-sort algorithm so that, instead of selecting the last element in an n-element sequence as the pivot, we choose the element at rank $\lfloor n/2 \rfloor$. Describe the kind of sequence that would cause this version of quick-sort to run in $\Theta(n^2)$ time.

R-4.11 Show that the best-case running time of quick-sort on a sequence of size n with distinct elements is $O(n \log n)$.

R-4.12 Suppose that algorithm inPlaceQuickSort (Algorithm 4.17) is executed on a sequence with duplicate elements. Show that, in this case, the algorithm correctly sorts the input sequence, but the result of the divide step may differ from the high-level description given in Section 4.3 and may result in inefficiencies. In particular, what happens in the partition step when there are elements equal to the pivot? Is the sequence E (storing the elements equal to the pivot) actually computed? Does the algorithm recur on the subsequences L and R, or on some other subsequences? What is the running time of the algorithm if all the elements of the input sequence are equal?

R-4.13 Give a pseudo-code description of the in-place version of quick-sort that is specialized to take an array as input, rather than a general sequence, and return that same array as output.

R-4.14 Which, if any, of the algorithms bubble-sort, heap-sort, merge-sort, and quick-sort are stable?

R-4.15 Describe a radix-sort method for lexicographically sorting a sequence S of triplets (k,l,m), where k, l, and m are integers in the range $[0,N-1]$, for some $N \geq 2$. How could this scheme be extended to sequences of d-tuples $(k_1,k_2,\ldots,k_d)$, where each k_i is an integer in the range $[0,N-1]$?

R-4.16 Is the bucket-sort algorithm in-place? Why or why not?

R-4.17 Give a pseudo-code description of an in-place quick-select algorithm.

R-4.18 Show that the worst-case running time of quick-select on an n-element sequence is $\Omega(n^2)$.

Creativity

C-4.1 Show how to implement method equals(B) on a set A, which tests whether $A = B$, in $O(|A|+|B|)$ time by means of a variation of the generic merge algorithm, assuming A and B are implemented with sorted sequences.

C-4.2 Give a variation of the generic merge algorithm for computing $A \oplus B$, which is the set of elements that are in A or B, but not in both.

C-4.3 Suppose that we implement the set ADT by representing each set using a balanced search tree. Describe and analyze algorithms for each of the methods in the set ADT.

C-4.4 Let A be a collection of objects. Describe an efficient method for converting A into a set. That is, remove all duplicates from A. What is the running time of this method?

C-4.5 Consider sets whose elements are (or can be mapped to) integers in the range $[0,N-1]$. A popular scheme for representing a set A of this type is by means of a Boolean vector, B, where we say that x is in A if and only if $B[x] =$ **true**. Since each cell of B can be represented with a single bit, B is sometimes referred to as a ***bit vector***. Describe efficient algorithms for performing the union, intersection, and subtraction methods of the set ADT assuming this representation. What are the running times of these methods?

C-4.6 Suppose we implement the tree-based partition (union-find) data structure using the union-by-size heuristic and a ***partial*** path-compression heuristic. The partial path compression in this case means that, after performing a sequence of pointer hops for a find operation, we update the parent pointer for each node u along this path to point to its grandparent. Show that the total running time of performing n union and find operations is still $O(n \log^* n)$.

C-4.7 Suppose we implement the tree-based partition (union-find) data structure using the union-by-size and path-compression heuristics. Show that the total running time of performing n union and find operations is $O(n)$ if all the unions come before all the finds.

C-4.8 Show that randomized quick-sort runs in $O(n \log n)$ time with probability $1 - 1/n^2$.

Hint: Use the ***Chernoff bound*** that states that if we flip a coin k times, then the probability that we get fewer than $k/16$ heads is less than $2^{-k/8}$.

C-4.9 Suppose we are given a sequence S of n elements, each of which is colored red or blue. Assuming S is represented as an array, give an in-place method for ordering S so that all the blue elements are listed before all the red elements. Can you extend your approach to three colors?

C-4.10 Suppose we are given an n-element sequence S such that each element in S represents a different vote in an election, where each vote is given as an integer representing the ID of the chosen candidate. Without making any assumptions about who is running or even how many candidates there are, design an $O(n \log n)$-time algorithm to see who wins the election S represents, assuming the candidate with the most votes wins.

C-4.11 Consider the voting problem from the previous exercise, but now suppose that we know the number $k < n$ of candidates running. Describe an $O(n \log k)$-time algorithm for determining who wins the election.

C-4.12 Show that any comparison-based sorting algorithm can be made to be stable, without affecting the asymptotic running time of this algorithm.

Hint: Change the way elements are compared with each other.

C-4.13 Suppose we are given two sequences A and B of n elements, possibly containing duplicates, on which a total order relation is defined. Describe an efficient algorithm for determining if A and B contain the same set of elements (possibly in different orders). What is the running time of this method?

C-4.14 Suppose we are given a sequence S of n elements, each of which is an integer in the range $[0, n^2 - 1]$. Describe a simple method for sorting S in $O(n)$ time.

Hint: Think of alternate ways of viewing the elements.

C-4.15 Let $S_1, S_2, \ldots, S_k$ be k different sequences whose elements have integer keys in the range $[0, N-1]$, for some parameter $N \geq 2$. Describe an algorithm running in $O(n+N)$ time for sorting all the sequences (not as a union), where n denotes the total size of all the sequences.

C-4.16 Suppose we are given a sequence S of n elements, on which a total order relation is defined. Describe an efficient method for determining whether there are two equal elements in S. What is the running time of your method?

C-4.17 Describe a nonrecursive, in-place version of the quick-sort algorithm. The algorithm should still be based on the same divide-and-conquer approach.

Hint: Think about how to "mark" the left and right boundaries of the current subsequence before making a recursive call from this one.

C-4.18 Modify Algorithm inPlaceQuickSort (Algorithm 4.17) to handle the general case efficiently when the input sequence, S, may have duplicate keys.

C-4.19 Let S be a sequence of n elements on which a total order relation is defined. An ***inversion*** in S is a pair of elements x and y such that x appears before y in S but $x > y$. Describe an algorithm running in $O(n \log n)$ time for determining the ***number*** of inversions in S.

Hint: Try to modify the merge-sort algorithm to solve this problem.

C-4.20 Let S be a sequence of n elements on which a total order relation is defined. Describe a comparison-based method for sorting S in $O(n+k)$ time, where k is the number of inversions in S (recall the definition of inversion from the previous problem).

Hint: Think of an in-place version of the insertion-sort algorithm that, after an linear-time preprocessing step, only swaps elements that are inverted.

C-4.21 Give a sequence of n integers with $\Omega(n^2)$ inversions. (Recall the definition of inversion from Exercise C-4.19.)

C-4.22 Let A and B be two sequences of n integers each. Given an integer x, describe an $O(n \log n)$-time algorithm for determining if there is an integer a in A and an integer b in B such that $x = a + b$.

C-4.23 Given an unordered sequence S of n comparable elements, describe an efficient method for finding the $\lceil \sqrt{n} \rceil$ items whose rank in an ordered version of S is closest to that of the median. What is the running time of your method?

C-4.24 This problem deals with the modification of the quick-select algorithm to make it deterministic, yet still run in $O(n)$ time on an n-element sequence. The idea is to modify the way we choose the pivot so that it is chosen deterministically, not randomly, as follows:

> Partition the set S into $\lceil n/5 \rceil$ groups of size 5 each (except possibly for one group). Sort each little set and identify the median element in this set. From this set of $\lceil n/5 \rceil$ "baby" medians, apply the selection algorithm recursively to find the median of the baby medians. Use this element as the pivot and proceed as in the quick-select algorithm.

Show that this deterministic method runs in $O(n)$ time by answering the following questions (please ignore floor and ceiling functions if that simplifies the mathematics, for the asymptotics are the same either way):

a. How many baby medians are less than or equal to the chosen pivot? How many are greater than or equal to the pivot?

b. For each baby median less than or equal to the pivot, how many other elements are less than or equal to the pivot? Is the same true for those greater than or equal to the pivot?

c. Argue why the method for finding the deterministic pivot and using it to partition S takes $O(n)$ time.

d. Based on these estimates, write a recurrence equation that bounds the worst-case running time $t(n)$ for this selection algorithm. (Note: In the worst case there are two recursive calls—one to find the median of the baby medians and one to then recur on the larger of L and G.)

e. Using this recurrence equation, show by induction that $t(n)$ is $O(n)$.

C-4.25 Bob has a set A of n nuts and a set B of n bolts, such that each nut in A has a unique matching bolt in B. Unfortunately, the nuts in A all look the same, and the bolts in B all look the same as well. The only kind of a comparison that Bob can make is to take a nut-bolt pair (a,b), such that $a \in A$ and $b \in B$, and test it to see if the threads of a are larger, smaller, or a perfect match with the threads of b. Describe an efficient algorithm for Bob to match up all of his nuts and bolts. What is the running time of this algorithm, in terms of nut-bolt tests that Bob must make?

C-4.26 Show how a deterministic $O(n)$-time selection algorithm can be used to design a quick-sort-like sorting algorithm that runs in $O(n \log n)$ ***worst-case*** time on an n-element sequence.

C-4.27 Given an unsorted sequence S of n comparable elements, and an integer k, give an $O(n \log k)$ expected-time algorithm for finding the $O(k)$ elements that have rank $\lceil n/k \rceil, 2\lceil n/k \rceil, 3\lceil n/k \rceil$, and so on.

Projects

P-4.1 Design and implement a stable version of the bucket-sort algorithm for sorting a sequence of n elements with integer keys taken from the range $[0, N-1]$, for $N \geq 2$. The algorithm should run in $O(n+N)$ time. Perform a series of benchmarking time trials to test whether this method does indeed run in this time, for various values of n and N, and write a short report describing the code and the results of these trials.

P-4.2 Implement merge-sort and deterministic quick-sort and perform a series of benchmarking tests to see which one is faster. Your tests should include sequences that are very "random" looking, as well as ones that are "almost sorted" or "almost reverse sorted." Write a short report describing the code and the results of these trials.

P-4.3 Implement deterministic and randomized versions of the quick-sort algorithm and perform a series of benchmarking tests to see which one is faster. Your tests should include sequences that are very "random" looking as well as ones that are "almost" sorted. Write a short report describing the code and the results of these trials.

P-4.4 Implement an in-place version of insertion-sort and an in-place version of quick-sort. Perform benchmarking tests to determine the range of values of n where quick-sort is, on average, faster than insertion-sort.

P-4.5 Design and implement an animation for one of the sorting algorithms described in this chapter. Your animation should illustrate the key properties of this algorithm in an intuitive manner, and should be annotated with text and/or sound so as to explain this algorithm to someone unfamiliar with it. Write a short report describing this animation.

P-4.6 Implement the partition (union-find) ADT using the tree-based approach with the union-by-size and path-compression heuristics.

Chapter Notes

Knuth's classic text on *Sorting and Searching* [119] contains an extensive history of the sorting problem and algorithms for solving it, starting with the census card sorting machines of the late 19th century. Huang and Langston [103] describe how to merge two sorted lists in-place in linear time. Our set ADT is derived from the set ADT of Aho, Hopcroft, and Ullman [8]. The standard quick-sort algorithm is due to Hoare [96]. A tighter analysis of randomized quick-sort can be found in the book by Motwani and Raghavan [157]. Gonnet and Baeza-Yates [81] provide experimental comparisons and theoretical analyses of a number of different sorting algorithms. The term "prune-and-search" originally comes from the computational geometry literature (such as in the work of Clarkson [47] and Megiddo [145, 146]). The term "decrease-and-conquer" is from Levitin [132].

The analysis we give for the partition data structure comes from Hopcroft and Ullman [99] (see also [7]). Tarjan [199] shows that a sequence of n union and find operations, implemented as described in this chapter, can be performed in $O(n\alpha(n))$ time, where $\alpha(n)$ is the very slow growing inverse of the Ackermann function, and this bound is tight in the worst case (see also [200]). Gabow and Tarjan [73] show that one can, in some cases, achieve a running time of $O(n)$, however.

Chapter

5 Fundamental Techniques

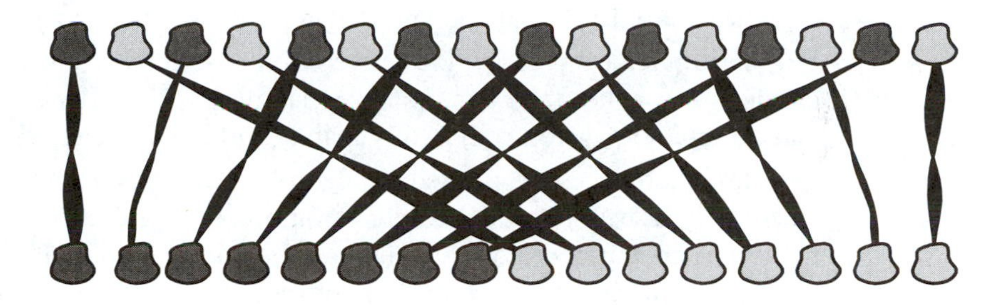

Contents

5.1 The Greedy Method 259

5.1.1 The Fractional Knapsack Problem 259

5.1.2 Task Scheduling 261

5.2 Divide-and-Conquer 263

5.2.1 Divide-and-Conquer Recurrence Equations 263

5.2.2 Integer Multiplication 270

5.2.3 Matrix Multiplication 272

5.3 Dynamic Programming 274

5.3.1 Matrix Chain-Product 274

5.3.2 The General Technique 278

5.3.3 The 0-1 Knapsack Problem 278

5.4 Exercises 282

A popular television network broadcasts two different shows about carpentry. In one show, the host builds furniture using specialized power tools, and in the other the host builds furniture using general-purpose hand tools. The specialized tools, used in the first show, are good at the jobs they are intended for, but none of them is very versatile. The tools in the second show are fundamental, however, because they can be used effectively for a wide variety of different tasks.

These two television shows provide an interesting metaphor for data structure and algorithm design. There are some algorithmic tools that are quite specialized. They are good for the problems they are intended to solve, but they are not very versatile. There are other algorithmic tools, however, that are ***fundamental*** in that they can be applied to a wide variety of different data structure and algorithm design problems. Learning to use these fundamental techniques is a craft, and this chapter is dedicated to developing the knowledge for using these techniques effectively.

The fundamental techniques covered in this chapter are the greedy method, divide-and-conquer, and dynamic programming. These techniques are versatile, and examples are given both in this chapter and in other chapters of this book.

The greedy method is used in algorithms for weighted graphs discussed in Chapter 7, as well as a data compression problem presented in Section 9.3. The main idea of this technique, as the name implies, is to make a series of greedy choices in order to construct an optimal solution (or close to optimal solution) for a given problem. In this chapter, we give the general structure for the greedy method and show how it can be applied to knapsack and scheduling problems.

Divide-and-conquer is used in the merge-sort and quick-sort algorithms of Chapter 4. The general idea behind this technique is to solve a given problem by dividing it into a small number of similar subproblems, recursively solve each of the subproblems until they are small enough to solve by brute force, and, after the recursive calls return, merge all the subproblems together to derive a solution to the original problem. In this chapter, we show how to design and analyze general divide-and-conquer algorithms and we give additional applications of this technique to the problems of multiplying big integers and large matrices. We also give a number of techniques for solving divide-and-conquer recurrence equations, including a general master theorem that can be applied to a variety of equations.

The dynamic programming technique might at first seem a bit mysterious, but it is quite powerful. The main idea is to solve a given problem by characterizing its subproblems using a small set of integer indices. The goal of this characterization is to allow an optimal solution to a subproblem to be defined by the combination of (possibly overlapping) solutions to even smaller subproblems. If we can construct such a characterization, which is the hardest step in using the dynamic programming technique, then we can build a rather straightforward algorithm that builds up larger subproblem solutions from smaller ones. This technique underlies the Floyd-Warshall transitive closure algorithm of Chapter 6. In this chapter, we describe the general framework of dynamic programming and give several applications, including to the 0-1 knapsack problem.

5.1 The Greedy Method

The first algorithmic technique we consider in this chapter is the ***greedy method***. We characterize this greedy method design pattern in terms of a general ***greedy-choice*** property, and we give two applications of its use.

The greedy method is applied to optimization problems, that is, problems that involve searching through a set of ***configurations*** to find one that minimizes or maximizes an ***objective function*** defined on these configurations. The general formula of the greedy method could not be simpler. In order to solve a given optimization problem, we proceed by a sequence of choices. The sequence starts from some well-understood starting configuration, and then iteratively makes the decision that seems best from all of those that are currently possible.

This greedy approach does not always lead to an optimal solution. But there are several problems that it does work optimally for, and such problems are said to possess the ***greedy-choice*** property. This is the property that a global optimal configuration can be reached by a series of locally optimal choices (that is, choices that are the best from among the possibilities available at the time), starting from a well-defined configuration.

5.1.1 The Fractional Knapsack Problem

Consider the ***fractional knapsack*** problem, where we are given a set S of n items, such that each item i has a positive benefit b_i and a positive weight w_i, and we wish to find the maximum-benefit subset that does not exceed a given weight W. If we are restricted to entirely accepting or rejecting each item, then we would have the 0-1 version of this problem (for which we give a dynamic programming solution in Section 5.3.3). Let us now allow ourselves to take arbitrary fractions of some elements, however. The motivation for this fractional knapsack problem is that we are going on a trip and we have a single knapsack that can carry items that together have weight at most W. In addition, we are allowed to break items into fractions arbitrarily. That is, we can take an amount x_i of each item i such that

$$0 \le x_i \le w_i \text{ for each } i \in S \quad \text{and} \quad \sum_{i \in S} x_i \le W.$$

The total benefit of the items taken is determined by the objective function

$$\sum_{i \in S} b_i (x_i / w_i).$$

Consider, for example, a student who is going to an outdoor sporting event and must fill a knapsack full of foodstuffs to take along. Each candidate foodstuff is something that can be easily divided into fractions, such as soda pop, potato chips, popcorn, and pizza.

Algorithm FractionalKnapsack(S, W):
Input: Set S of items, such that each item $i \in S$ has a positive benefit b_i and a positive weight w_i; positive maximum total weight W
Output: Amount x_i of each item $i \in S$ that maximizes the total benefit while not exceeding the maximum total weight W

```
for each item i ∈ S do
    x_i ← 0
    v_i ← b_i/w_i          {value index of item i}
w ← 0          {total weight}
while w < W do
    remove from S an item i with highest value index          {greedy choice}
    a ← min{w_i, W − w}          {more than W − w causes a weight overflow}
    x_i ← a
    w ← w + a
```

Algorithm 5.1: A greedy algorithm for the fractional knapsack problem.

This is one place where greed is good, for we can solve the fractional knapsack problem using the greedy approach shown in Algorithm 5.1.

The FractionalKnapsack algorithm can be implemented in $O(n \log n)$ time, where n is the number of items in S. Specifically, we use a heap-based priority queue (Section 2.4.3) to store the items of S, where the key of each item is its value index. With this data structure, each greedy choice, which removes the item with greatest value index, takes $O(\log n)$ time.

To see that the fractional knapsack problem satisfies the greedy-choice property, suppose that there are two items i and j such that

$$x_i < w_i, \quad x_j > 0, \quad \text{and} \quad v_i < v_j.$$

Let

$$y = \min\{w_i - x_i, x_j\}.$$

We could then replace an amount y of item j with an equal amount of item i, thus increasing the total benefit without changing the total weight. Therefore, we can correctly compute optimal amounts for the items by greedily choosing items with the largest value index. This leads to the following theorem.

Theorem 5.1: *Given a collection S of n items, such that each item i has a benefit b_i and weight w_i, we can construct a maximum-benefit subset of S, allowing for fractional amounts, that has a total weight W in $O(n \log n)$ time.*

This theorem shows how efficiently we can solve the fractional version of the knapsack problem. The all-or-nothing, or "0-1" version of the knapsack problem does not satisfy the greedy choice property, however, and solving this version of the problem is much harder, as we explore in Sections 5.3.3 and 13.3.4.

5.1.2 Task Scheduling

Let us consider another optimization problem. Suppose we are given a set T of n ***tasks***, such that each task i has a ***start time***, s_i, and a finish time, f_i (where $s_i < f_i$). Task i must start at time s_i and it is guaranteed to be finished by time f_i. Each task has to be performed on a ***machine*** and each machine can execute only one task at a time. Two tasks i and j are ***nonconflicting*** if $f_i \leq s_j$ or $f_j \leq s_i$. Two tasks can be scheduled to be executed on the same machine only if they are nonconflicting.

The ***task scheduling*** problem we consider here is to schedule all the tasks in T on the fewest machines possible in a nonconflicting way. Alternatively, we can think of the tasks as meetings that we must schedule in as few conference rooms as possible. (See Figure 5.2.)

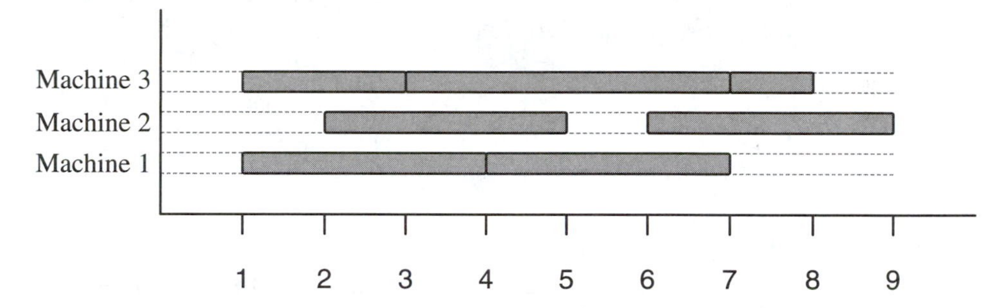

Figure 5.2: An illustration of a solution to the task scheduling problem, for tasks whose collection of pairs of start times and finish times is $\{(1,3), (1,4), (2,5), (3,7), (4,7), (6,9), (7,8)\}$.

In Algorithm 5.3, we describe a simple greedy algorithm for this problem.

Algorithm TaskSchedule(T):
  Input: A set T of tasks, such that each task has a start time s_i and a finish time f_i
  Output: A nonconflicting schedule of the tasks in T using a minimum number of machines

```
m ← 0            {optimal number of machines}
while T ≠ ∅ do
   remove from T the task i with smallest start time s_i
   if there is a machine j with no task conflicting with task i then
      schedule task i on machine j
   else
      m ← m+1            {add a new machine}
      schedule task i on machine m
```

Algorithm 5.3: A greedy algorithm for the task scheduling problem.

Correctness of Greedy Task Scheduling

In the algorithm TaskSchedule, we begin with no machines and we consider the tasks in a greedy fashion, ordered by their start times. For each task i, if we have a machine that can handle task i, then we schedule i on that machine. Otherwise, we allocate a new machine, schedule i on it, and repeat this greedy selection process until we have considered all the tasks in T.

The fact that the above TaskSchedule algorithm works correctly is established by the following theorem.

Theorem 5.2: *Given a set of n tasks specified by their start and finish times, Algorithm* TaskSchedule *produces a schedule of the tasks with the minimum number of machines in $O(n \log n)$ time.*

Proof: We can show that the above simple greedy algorithm, TaskSchedule, finds an optimal schedule on the minimum number of machines by a simple contradiction argument.

So, suppose the algorithm does not work. That is, suppose the algorithm finds a nonconflicting schedule using k machines but there is a nonconflicting schedule that uses only $k-1$ machines. Let k be the last machine allocated by our algorithm, and let i be the first task scheduled on k. By the structure of the algorithm, when we scheduled i, each of the machines 1 through $k-1$ contained tasks that conflict with i. Since they conflict with i and because we consider tasks ordered by their start times, all the tasks currently conflicting with task i must have start times less than or equal to s_i, the start time of i, and have finish times after s_i. In other words, these tasks not only conflict with task i, they all conflict with each other. But this means we have k tasks in our set T that conflict with each other, which implies it is impossible for us to schedule all the tasks in T using only $k-1$ machines. Therefore, k is the minimum number of machines needed to schedule all the tasks in T.

We leave as a simple exercise (R-5.2) the job of showing how to implement the Algorithm TaskSchedule in $O(n \log n)$ time. ■

We consider several other applications of the greedy method in this book, including two problems in string compression (Section 9.3), where the greedy approach gives rise to a construction known as Huffman coding, and graph algorithms (Section 7.3), where the greedy approach is used to solve shortest path and minimum spanning tree problems.

The next technique we discuss is the divide-and-conquer technique, which is a general methodology for using recursion to design efficient algorithms.

5.2 Divide-and-Conquer

The ***divide-and-conquer*** technique involves solving a particular computational problem by dividing it into one or more subproblems of smaller size, recursively solving each subproblem, and then "merging" or "marrying" the solutions to the subproblem(s) to produce a solution to the original problem.

We can model the divide-and-conquer approach by using a parameter n to denote the size of the original problem, and let $S(n)$ denote this problem. We solve the problem $S(n)$ by solving a collection of k subproblems $S(n_1)$, $S(n_2)$, ..., $S(n_k)$, where $n_i < n$ for $i = 1, \ldots, k$, and then merging the solutions to these subproblems.

For example, in the classic merge-sort algorithm (Section 4.1), $S(n)$ denotes the problem of sorting a sequence of n numbers. Merge-sort solves problem $S(n)$ by dividing it into two subproblems $S(\lfloor n/2 \rfloor)$ and $S(\lceil n/2 \rceil)$, recursively solving these two subproblems, and then merging the resulting sorted sequences into a single sorted sequence that yields a solution to $S(n)$. The merging step takes $O(n)$ time. This, the total running time of the merge-sort algorithm is $O(n \log n)$.

As with the merge-sort algorithm, the general divide-and-conquer technique can be used to build algorithms that have fast running times.

5.2.1 Divide-and-Conquer Recurrence Equations

To analyze the running time of a divide-and-conquer algorithm we utilize a ***recurrence equation*** (Section 1.1.4). That is, we let a function $T(n)$ denote the running time of the algorithm on an input of size n, and characterize $T(n)$ using an equation that relates $T(n)$ to values of the function T for problem sizes smaller than n. In the case of the merge-sort algorithm, we get the recurrence equation

$$T(n) = \begin{cases} b & \text{if } n < 2 \\ 2T(n/2) + bn & \text{if } n \geq 2, \end{cases}$$

for some constant $b > 0$, taking the simplifying assumption that n is a power of 2. In fact, throughout this section, we take the simplifying assumption that n is an appropriate power, so that we can avoid using floor and ceiling functions. Every asymptotic statement we make about recurrence equations will still be true, even if we relax this assumption, but justifying this fact formally involves long and boring proofs. As we observed above, we can show that $T(n)$ is $O(n \log n)$ in this case. In general, however, we will possibly get a recurrence equation that is more challenging to solve than this one. Thus, it is useful to develop some general ways of solving the kinds of recurrence equations that arise in the analysis of divide-and-conquer algorithms.

The Iterative Substitution Method

One way to solve a divide-and-conquer recurrence equation is to use the ***iterative substitution*** method, which is more colloquially known as the "plug-and-chug" method. In using this method, we assume that the problem size n is fairly large and we then substitute the general form of the recurrence for each occurrence of the function T on the right-hand side. For example, performing such a substitution with the merge-sort recurrence equation yields the equation

$$\begin{aligned} T(n) &= 2(2T(n/2^2) + b(n/2)) + bn \\ &= 2^2T(n/2^2) + 2bn. \end{aligned}$$

Plugging the general equation for T in again yields the equation

$$\begin{aligned} T(n) &= 2^2(2T(n/2^3) + b(n/2^2)) + 2bn \\ &= 2^3T(n/2^3) + 3bn. \end{aligned}$$

The hope in applying the iterative substitution method is that, at some point, we will see a pattern that can be converted into a general closed-form equation (with T only appearing on the left-hand side). In the case of the merge-sort recurrence equation, the general form is

$$T(n) = 2^iT(n/2^i) + ibn.$$

Note that the general form of this equation shifts to the base case, $T(n) = b$, when $n = 2^i$, that is, when $i = \log n$, which implies

$$T(n) = bn + bn\log n.$$

In other words, $T(n)$ is $O(n\log n)$. In a general application of the iterative substitution technique, we hope that we can determine a general pattern for $T(n)$ and that we can also figure out when the general form of $T(n)$ shifts to the base case.

From a mathematical point of view, there is one point in the use of the iterative substitution technique that involves a bit of a logical "jump." This jump occurs at the point where we try to characterize the general pattern emerging from a sequence of substitutions. Often, as was the case with the merge-sort recurrence equation, this jump is quite reasonable. Other times, however, it may not be so obvious what a general form for the equation should look like. In these cases, the jump may be more dangerous. To be completely safe in making such a jump, we must fully justify the general form of the equation, possibly using induction. Combined with such a justification, the iterative substitution method is completely correct and an often useful way of characterizing recurrence equations. By the way, the colloquialism "plug-and-chug," used to describe the iterative substitution method, comes from the way this method involves "plugging" in the recursive part of an equation for $T(n)$ and then often "chugging" through a considerable amount of algebra in order to get this equation into a form where we can infer a general pattern.

The Recursion Tree

Another way of characterizing recurrence equations is to use the ***recursion tree*** method. Like the iterative substitution method, this technique uses repeated substitution to solve a recurrence equation, but it differs from the iterative substitution method in that, rather than being an algebraic approach, it is a visual approach. In using the recursion tree method, we draw a tree R where each node represents a different substitution of the recurrence equation. Thus, each node in R has a value of the argument n of the function $T(n)$ associated with it. In addition, we associate an ***overhead*** with each node v in R, defined as the value of the nonrecursive part of the recurrence equation for v. For divide-and-conquer recurrences, the overhead corresponds to the running time needed to merge the subproblem solutions coming from the children of v. The recurrence equation is then solved by summing the overheads associated with all the nodes of R. This is commonly done by first summing values across the levels of R and then summing up these partial sums for all the levels of R.

Example 5.3: *Consider the following recurrence equation:*

$$T(n) = \begin{cases} b & \text{if } n < 3 \\ 3T(n/3) + bn & \text{if } n \geq 3. \end{cases}$$

This is the recurrence equation that we get, for example, by modifying the merge-sort algorithm so that we divide an unsorted sequence into three equal-sized sequences, recursively sort each one, and then do a three-way merge of three sorted sequences to produce a sorted version of the original sequence. In the recursion tree R for this recurrence, each internal node v has three children and has a size and an overhead associated with it, which corresponds to the time needed to merge the subproblem solutions produced by v's children. We illustrate the tree R in Figure 5.4. Note that the overheads of the nodes of each level sum to bn. Thus, observing that the depth of R is $\log_3 n$, we have that $T(n)$ is $O(n \log n)$.

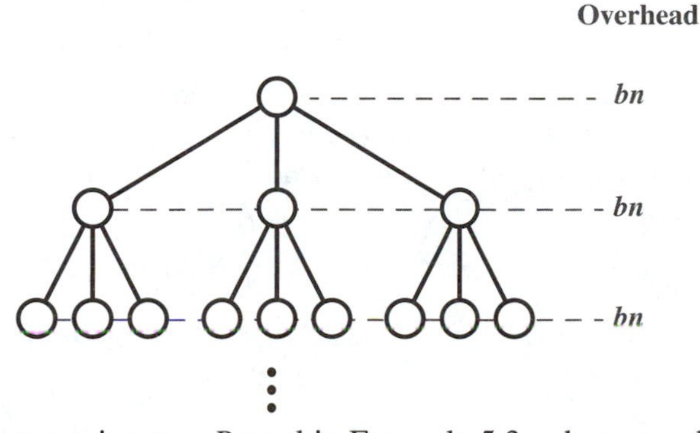

Figure 5.4: The recursion tree R used in Example 5.3, where we show the cumulative overhead of each level.

The Guess-and-Test Method

Another method for solving recurrence equations is the ***guess-and-test*** technique. This technique involves first making an educated guess as to what a closed-form solution of the recurrence equation might look like and then justifying that guess, usually by induction. For example, we can use the guess-and-test method as a kind of "binary search" for finding good upper bounds on a given recurrence equation. If the justification of our current guess fails, then it is possible that we need to use a faster-growing function, and if our current guess is justified "too easily," then it is possible that we need to use a slower-growing function. However, using this technique requires our being careful, in each mathematical step we take, in trying to justify that a certain hypothesis holds with respect to our current "guess." We explore an application of the guess-and-test method in the examples that follow.

Example 5.4: *Consider the following recurrence equation (assuming the base case $T(n) = b$ for $n < 2$):*

$$T(n) = 2T(n/2) + bn\log n.$$

This looks very similar to the recurrence equation for the merge-sort routine, so we might make the following as our first guess:

$$\textit{First guess: } T(n) \le cn\log n,$$

for some constant $c > 0$. We can certainly choose c large enough to make this true for the base case, so consider the case when $n \ge 2$. If we assume our first guess is an inductive hypothesis that is true for input sizes smaller than n, then we have

$$\begin{aligned} T(n) &= 2T(n/2) + bn\log n \\ &\le 2(c(n/2)\log(n/2)) + bn\log n \\ &= cn(\log n - \log 2) + bn\log n \\ &= cn\log n - cn + bn\log n. \end{aligned}$$

But there is no way that we can make this last line less than or equal to $cn\log n$ for $n \ge 2$. Thus, this first guess was not sufficient. Let us therefore try

$$\textit{Better guess: } T(n) \le cn\log^2 n,$$

for some constant $c > 0$. We can again choose c large enough to make this true for the base case, so consider the case when $n \ge 2$. If we assume this guess as an inductive hypothesis that is true for input sizes smaller then n, then we have

$$\begin{aligned} T(n) &= 2T(n/2) + bn\log n \\ &\le 2(c(n/2)\log^2(n/2)) + bn\log n \\ &= cn(\log^2 n - 2\log n + 1) + bn\log n \\ &= cn\log^2 n - 2cn\log n + cn + bn\log n \\ &\le cn\log^2 n, \end{aligned}$$

provided $c \ge b$. Thus, we have shown that $T(n)$ is indeed $O(n\log^2 n)$ in this case.

We must take care in using this method. Just because one inductive hypothesis for $T(n)$ does not work, that does not necessarily imply that another one proportional to this one will not work.

Example 5.5: *Consider the following recurrence equation (assuming the base case $T(n) = b$ for $n < 2$):*

$$T(n) = 2T(n/2) + \log n.$$

This recurrence is the running time for the bottom-up heap construction discussed in Section 2.4.4, which we have shown is $O(n)$. Nevertheless, if we try to prove this fact with the most straightforward inductive hypothesis, we will run into some difficulties. In particular, consider the following:

$$\text{First guess: } T(n) \leq cn,$$

for some constant $c > 0$. We can choose c large enough to make this true for the base case, certainly, so consider the case when $n \geq 2$. If we assume this guess as an inductive hypothesis that is true for input sizes smaller than n, then we have

$$\begin{aligned} T(n) &= 2T(n/2) + \log n \\ &\leq 2(c(n/2)) + \log n \\ &= cn + \log n. \end{aligned}$$

But there is no way that we can make this last line less than or equal to cn for $n \geq 2$. Thus, this first guess was not sufficient, even though $T(n)$ is indeed $O(n)$. Still, we can show this fact is true by using

$$\text{Better guess: } T(n) \leq c(n - \log n),$$

for some constant $c > 0$. We can again choose c large enough to make this true for the base case; in fact, we can show that it is true any time $n < 8$. So consider the case when $n \geq 8$. If we assume this guess as an inductive hypothesis that is true for input sizes smaller than n, then we have

$$\begin{aligned} T(n) &= 2T(n/2) + \log n \\ &\leq 2c((n/2) - \log(n/2)) + \log n \\ &= cn - 2c\log n + 2c + \log n \\ &= c(n - \log n) - c\log n + 2c + \log n \\ &\leq c(n - \log n), \end{aligned}$$

provided $c \geq 3$ and $n \geq 8$. Thus, we have shown that $T(n)$ is indeed $O(n)$ in this case.

The guess-and-test method can be used to establish either an upper or lower bound for the asymptotic complexity of a recurrence equation. Even so, as the above example demonstrates, it requires that we have developed some skill with mathematical induction.

The Master Method

Each of the methods described above for solving recurrence equations is ad hoc and requires mathematical sophistication in order to be used effectively. There is, nevertheless, one method for solving divide-and-conquer recurrence equations that is quite general and does not require explicit use of induction to apply correctly. It is the ***master method***. The master method is a "cook-book" method for determining the asymptotic characterization of a wide variety of recurrence equations. Namely, it is used for recurrence equations of the form

$$T(n) = \begin{cases} c & \text{if } n < d \\ aT(n/b) + f(n) & \text{if } n \geq d, \end{cases}$$

where $d \geq 1$ is an integer constant, $a > 0$, $c > 0$, and $b > 1$ are real constants, and $f(n)$ is a function that is positive for $n \geq d$. Such a recurrence equation would arise in the analysis of a divide-and-conquer algorithm that divides a given problem into a subproblems of size at most n/b each, solves each subproblem recursively, and then "merges" the subproblem solutions into a solution to the entire problem. The function $f(n)$, in this equation, denotes the total additional time needed to divide the problem into subproblems and merge the subproblem solutions into a solution to the entire problem. Each of the recurrence equations given above uses this form, as do each of the recurrence equations used to analyze divide-and-conquer algorithms given earlier in this book. Thus, it is indeed a general form for divide-and-conquer recurrence equations.

The master method for solving such recurrence equations involves simply writing down the answer based on whether one of the three cases applies. Each case is distinguished by comparing $f(n)$ to the special function $n^{\log_b a}$ (we will show later why this special function is so important).

Theorem 5.6 [The Master Theorem]: *Let $f(n)$ and $T(n)$ be defined as above.*

1. *If there is a small constant $\varepsilon > 0$, such that $f(n)$ is $O(n^{\log_b a - \varepsilon})$, then $T(n)$ is $\Theta(n^{\log_b a})$.*
2. *If there is a constant $k \geq 0$, such that $f(n)$ is $\Theta(n^{\log_b a} \log^k n)$, then $T(n)$ is $\Theta(n^{\log_b a} \log^{k+1} n)$.*
3. *If there are small constants $\varepsilon > 0$ and $\delta < 1$, such that $f(n)$ is $\Omega(n^{\log_b a + \varepsilon})$ and $af(n/b) \leq \delta f(n)$, for $n \geq d$, then $T(n)$ is $\Theta(f(n))$.*

Case 1 characterizes the situation where $f(n)$ is polynomially smaller than the special function, $n^{\log_b a}$. Case 2 characterizes the situation when $f(n)$ is asymptotically close to the special function, and Case 3 characterizes the situation when $f(n)$ is polynomially larger than the special function.

We illustrate the usage of the master method with a few examples (with each taking the assumption that $T(n) = c$ for $n < d$, for constants $c \geq 1$ and $d \geq 1$).

Example 5.7: *Consider the recurrence*

$$T(n) = 4T(n/2) + n.$$

In this case, $n^{\log_b a} = n^{\log_2 4} = n^2$. *Thus, we are in Case 1, for* $f(n)$ *is* $O(n^{2-\varepsilon})$ *for* $\varepsilon = 1$. *This means that* $T(n)$ *is* $\Theta(n^2)$ *by the master method.*

Example 5.8: *Consider the recurrence*

$$T(n) = 2T(n/2) + n\log n,$$

which is one of the recurrences given above. In this case, $n^{\log_b a} = n^{\log_2 2} = n$. *Thus, we are in Case 2, with* $k = 1$, *for* $f(n)$ *is* $\Theta(n\log n)$. *This means that* $T(n)$ *is* $\Theta(n\log^2 n)$ *by the master method.*

Example 5.9: *Consider the recurrence*

$$T(n) = T(n/3) + n,$$

which is the recurrence for a geometrically decreasing summation that starts with n. *In this case,* $n^{\log_b a} = n^{\log_3 1} = n^0 = 1$. *Thus, we are in Case 3, for* $f(n)$ *is* $\Omega(n^{0+\varepsilon})$, *for* $\varepsilon = 1$, *and* $af(n/b) = n/3 = (1/3)f(n)$. *This means that* $T(n)$ *is* $\Theta(n)$ *by the master method.*

Example 5.10: *Consider the recurrence*

$$T(n) = 9T(n/3) + n^{2.5}.$$

In this case, $n^{\log_b a} = n^{\log_3 9} = n^2$. *Thus, we are in Case 3, since* $f(n)$ *is* $\Omega(n^{2+\varepsilon})$ *(for* $\varepsilon = 1/2$*) and* $af(n/b) = 9(n/3)^{2.5} = (1/3)^{1/2}f(n)$. *This means that* $T(n)$ *is* $\Theta(n^{2.5})$ *by the master method.*

Example 5.11: *Finally, consider the recurrence*

$$T(n) = 2T(n^{1/2}) + \log n.$$

Unfortunately, this equation is not in a form that allows us to use the master method. We can put it into such a form, however, by introducing the variable $k = \log n$, *which lets us write*

$$T(n) = T(2^k) = 2T(2^{k/2}) + k.$$

Substituting into this the equation $S(k) = T(2^k)$, *we get that*

$$S(k) = 2S(k/2) + k.$$

Now, this recurrence equation allows us to use master method, which specifies that $S(k)$ *is* $O(k\log k)$. *Substituting back for* $T(n)$ *implies* $T(n)$ *is* $O(\log n \log\log n)$.

Rather than rigorously prove Theorem 5.6, we instead discuss the justification behind the master method at a high level.

If we apply the iterative substitution method to the general divide-and-conquer recurrence equation, we get

$$\begin{aligned} T(n) &= aT(n/b) + f(n) \\ &= a(aT(n/b^2) + f(n/b)) + f(n) = a^2T(n/b^2) + af(n/b) + f(n) \\ &= a^3T(n/b^3) + a^2f(n/b^2) + af(n/b) + f(n) \\ &\vdots \\ &= a^{\log_b n}T(1) + \sum_{i=0}^{\log_b n - 1} a^i f(n/b^i) \\ &= n^{\log_b a}T(1) + \sum_{i=0}^{\log_b n - 1} a^i f(n/b^i), \end{aligned}$$

where the last substitution is based on the identity $a^{\log_b n} = n^{\log_b a}$. Indeed, this equation is where the special function comes from. Given this closed-form characterization of $T(n)$, we can intuitively see how each of the three cases is derived. Case 1 comes from the situation when $f(n)$ is small and the first term above dominates. Case 2 denotes the situation when each of the terms in the above summation is proportional to the others, so the characterization of $T(n)$ is $f(n)$ times a logarithmic factor. Finally, Case 3 denotes the situation when the first term is smaller than the second and the summation above is a sum of geometrically decreasing terms that start with $f(n)$; hence, $T(n)$ is itself proportional to $f(n)$.

The proof of Theorem 5.6 formalizes this intuition, but instead of giving the details of this proof, we present two applications of the master method below.

5.2.2 Integer Multiplication

We consider, in this subsection, the problem of multiplying ***big integers***, that is, integers represented by a large number of bits that cannot be handled directly by the arithmetic unit of a single processor. Multiplying big integers has applications to data security, where big integers are used in encryption schemes.

Given two big integers I and J represented with n bits each, we can easily compute $I+J$ and $I-J$ in $O(n)$ time. Efficiently computing the product $I \cdot J$ using the common grade-school algorithm requires, however, $O(n^2)$ time. In the rest of this section, we show that by using the divide-and-conquer technique, we can design a subquadratic-time algorithm for multiplying two n-bit integers.

Let us assume that n is a power of two (if this is not the case, we can pad I and J with 0's). We can therefore divide the bit representations of I and J in half, with one half representing the ***higher-order*** bits and the other representing the ***lower-order*** bits. In particular, if we split I into I_h and I_l and J into J_h and J_l, then

$$\begin{aligned} I &= I_h 2^{n/2} + I_l, \\ J &= J_h 2^{n/2} + J_l. \end{aligned}$$

Also, observe that multiplying a binary number I by a power of two, 2^k, is trivial—it simply involves shifting left (that is, in the higher-order direction) the number I by k bit positions. Thus, provided a left-shift operation takes constant time, multiplying an integer by 2^k takes $O(k)$ time.

Let us focus on the problem of computing the product $I \cdot J$. Given the expansion of I and J above, we can rewrite $I \cdot J$ as

$$I \cdot J = (I_h 2^{n/2} + I_l) \cdot (J_h 2^{n/2} + J_l) = I_h J_h 2^n + I_l J_h 2^{n/2} + I_h J_l 2^{n/2} + I_l J_l.$$

Thus, we can compute $I \cdot J$ by applying a divide-and-conquer algorithm that divides the bit representations of I and J in half, recursively computes the product four products of $n/2$ bits each (as described above), and then merges the solutions to these subproducts in $O(n)$ time using addition and multiplication by powers of two. We can terminate the recursion when we get down to the multiplication of two 1-bit numbers, which is trivial. This divide-and-conquer algorithm has a running time that can be characterized by the following recurrence (for $n \geq 2$):

$$T(n) = 4T(n/2) + cn,$$

for some constant $c > 0$. We can then apply the master theorem to note that the special function $n^{\log_b a} = n^{\log_2 4} = n^2$ in this case; hence, we are in Case 1 and $T(n)$ is $\Theta(n^2)$. Unfortunately, this is no better than the grade-school algorithm.

The master method gives us some insight into how we might improve this algorithm. If we can reduce the number of recursive calls, then we will reduce the complexity of the special function used in the master theorem, which is currently the dominating factor in our running time. Fortunately, if we are a little more clever in how we define subproblems to solve recursively, we can in fact reduce the number of recursive calls by one. In particular, consider the product

$$(I_h - I_l) \cdot (J_l - J_h) = I_h J_l - I_l J_l - I_h J_h + I_l J_h.$$

This is admittedly a strange product to consider, but it has an interesting property. When expanded out, it contains two of the products we want to compute (namely, $I_h J_l$ and $I_l J_h$) and two products that can be computed recursively (namely, $I_h J_h$ and $I_l J_l$). Thus, we can compute $I \cdot J$ as follows:

$$I \cdot J = I_h J_h 2^n + [(I_h - I_l) \cdot (J_l - J_h) + I_h J_h + I_l J_l] 2^{n/2} + I_l J_l.$$

This computation requires the recursive computation of three products of $n/2$ bits each, plus $O(n)$ additional work. Thus, it results in a divide-and-conquer algorithm with a running time characterized by the following recurrence equation (for $n \geq 2$):

$$T(n) = 3T(n/2) + cn,$$

for some constant $c > 0$.

Theorem 5.12: *We can multiply two n-bit integers in $O(n^{1.585})$ time.*

Proof: We apply the master theorem with the special function $n^{\log_b a} = n^{\log_2 3}$; hence, we are in Case 1 and $T(n)$ is $\Theta(n^{\log_2 3})$, which is itself $O(n^{1.585})$. ■

Using divide-and-conquer, we have designed an algorithm for integer multiplication that is asymptotically faster than the straightforward quadratic-time method. We can actually do even better than this, achieving a running time that is "almost" $O(n \log n)$, by using a more complex divide-and-conquer algorithm called the ***fast Fourier transform***, which we discuss in Section 10.4.

5.2.3 Matrix Multiplication

Suppose we are given two $n \times n$ matrices X and Y, and we wish to compute their product $Z = XY$, which is defined so that

$$Z[i,j] = \sum_{k=0}^{e-1} X[i,k] \cdot Y[k,j],$$

which is an equation that immediately gives rise to a simple $O(n^3)$ time algorithm.

Another way of viewing this product is in terms of submatrices. That is, let us assume that n is a power of two and let us partition X, Y, and Z each into four $(n/2) \times (n/2)$ matrices, so that we can rewrite $Z = XY$ as

$$\begin{pmatrix} I & J \\ K & L \end{pmatrix} = \begin{pmatrix} A & B \\ C & D \end{pmatrix} \begin{pmatrix} E & F \\ G & H \end{pmatrix}.$$

Thus,

$$\begin{aligned} I &= AE + BG \\ J &= AF + BH \\ K &= CE + DG \\ L &= CF + DH. \end{aligned}$$

We can use this set of equations in a divide-and-conquer algorithm that computes $Z = XY$ by computing I, J, K, and L from the subarrays A through G. By the above equations, we can compute I, J, K, and L from the eight recursively computed matrix products on $(n/2) \times (n/2)$ subarrays, plus four additions that can be done in $O(n^2)$ time. Thus, the above set of equations give rise to a divide-and-conquer algorithm whose running time $T(n)$ is characterized by the recurrence

$$T(n) = 8T(n/2) + bn^2,$$

for some constant $b > 0$. Unfortunately, this equation implies that $T(n)$ is $O(n^3)$ by the master theorem; hence, it is no better than the straightforward matrix multiplication algorithm.

Interestingly, there is an algorithm known as ***Strassen's Algorithm***, that organizes arithmetic involving the subarrays A through G so that we can compute I, J, K, and L using just seven recursive matrix multiplications. It is somewhat mysterious how Strassen discovered these equations, but we can easily verify that they work correctly.

We begin Strassen's Algorithm by defining seven submatrix products:

$$\begin{aligned}
S_1 &= A(F-H)\\
S_2 &= (A+B)H\\
S_3 &= (C+D)E\\
S_4 &= D(G-E)\\
S_5 &= (A+D)(E+H)\\
S_6 &= (B-D)(G+H)\\
S_7 &= (A-C)(E+F).
\end{aligned}$$

Given these seven submatrix products, we can compute I as

$$\begin{aligned}
I &= S_5+S_6+S_4-S_2\\
&= (A+D)(E+H)+(B-D)(G+H)+D(G-E)-(A+B)H\\
&= AE+DE+AH+DH+BG-DG+BH-DH+DG-DE-AH-BH\\
&= AE+BG.
\end{aligned}$$

We can compute J as

$$\begin{aligned}
J &= S_1+S_2\\
&= A(F-H)+(A+B)H\\
&= AF-AH+AH+BH\\
&= AF+BH.
\end{aligned}$$

We can compute K as

$$\begin{aligned}
K &= S_3+S_4\\
&= (C+D)E+D(G-E)\\
&= CE+DE+DG-DE\\
&= CE+DG.
\end{aligned}$$

Finally, we can compute L as

$$\begin{aligned}
L &= S_1-S_7-S_3+S_5\\
&= A(F-H)-(A-C)(E+F)-(C+D)E+(A+D)(E+H)\\
&= AF-AH-AE+CE-AF+CF-CE-DE+AE+DE+AH+DH\\
&= CF+DH.
\end{aligned}$$

Thus, we can compute $Z=XY$ using seven recursive multiplications of matrices of size $(n/2)\times(n/2)$. Thus, we can characterize the running time $T(n)$ as

$$T(n)=7T(n/2)+bn^2,$$

for some constant $b>0$. Thus, by the master theorem, we have the following:

Theorem 5.13: *We can multiply two $n\times n$ matrices in $O(n^{\log 7})$ time.*

Thus, with a fair bit of additional complication, we can perform the multiplication for $n\times n$ matrices in time $O(n^{2.808})$, which is $o(n^3)$ time. As admittedly complicated as Strassen's matrix multiplication is, there are actually much more complicated matrix multiplication algorithms, with running times as low as $O(n^{2.376})$.

5.3 Dynamic Programming

In this section, we discuss the ***dynamic programming*** algorithm-design technique. This technique is similar to the divide-and-conquer technique, in that it can be applied to a wide variety of different problems. Conceptually, the dynamic programming technique is different from divide-and-conquer, however, because the divide-and-conquer technique can be easily explained in a sentence or two, and can be well illustrated with a single example. Dynamic programming takes a bit more explaining and multiple examples before it can be fully appreciated.

The extra effort needed to fully appreciate dynamic programming is well worth it, though. There are few algorithmic techniques that can take problems that seem to require exponential time and produce polynomial-time algorithms to solve them. Dynamic programming is one such technique. In addition, the algorithms that result from applications of the dynamic programming technique are usually quite simple—often needing little more than a few lines of code to describe some nested loops for filling in a table.

5.3.1 Matrix Chain-Product

Rather than starting out with an explanation of the general components of the dynamic programming technique, we start out instead by giving a classic, concrete example. Suppose we are given a collection of n two-dimensional matrices for which we wish to compute the product

$$A = A_0 \cdot A_1 \cdot A_2 \cdots A_{n-1},$$

where A_i is a $d_i \times d_{i+1}$ matrix, for $i = 0, 1, 2, \ldots, n-1$. In the standard matrix multiplication algorithm (which is the one we will use), to multiply a $d \times e$-matrix B times an $e \times f$-matrix C, we compute the (i, j)th entry of the product as

$$\sum_{k=0}^{e-1} B[i,k] \cdot C[k,j].$$

This definition implies that matrix multiplication is associative, that is, it implies that $B \cdot (C \cdot D) = (B \cdot C) \cdot D$. Thus, we can parenthesize the expression for A any way we wish and we will end up with the same answer. We will not necessarily perform the same number of primitive (that is, scalar) multiplications in each parenthesization, however, as is illustrated in the following example.

Example 5.14: *Let B be a 2×10-matrix, let C be a 10×50-matrix, and let D be a 50×20-matrix. Computing $B \cdot (C \cdot D)$ requires $2 \cdot 10 \cdot 20 + 10 \cdot 50 \cdot 20 = 10400$ multiplications, whereas computing $(B \cdot C) \cdot D$ requires $2 \cdot 10 \cdot 50 + 2 \cdot 50 \cdot 20 = 3000$ multiplications.*

The ***matrix chain-product*** problem is to determine the parenthesization of the expression defining the product A that minimizes the total number of scalar multiplications performed. Of course, one way to solve this problem is to simply enumerate all the possible ways of parenthesizing the expression for A and determine the number of multiplications performed by each one. Unfortunately, the set of all different parenthesizations of the expression for A is equal in number to the set of all different binary trees that have n external nodes. This number is exponential in n. Thus, this straightforward ("brute force") algorithm runs in exponential time, for there are an exponential number of ways to parenthesize an associative arithmetic expression (the number is equal to the nth ***Catalan number***, which is $\Omega(4^n/n^{3/2})$).

Defining Subproblems

We can improve the performance achieved by the brute force algorithm significantly, however, by making a few observations about the nature of the matrix chain-product problem. The first observation is that the problem can be split into ***subproblems***. In this case, we can define a number of different subproblems, each of which is to compute the best parenthesization for some subexpression $A_i \cdot A_{i+1} \cdots A_j$. As a concise notation, we use $N_{i,j}$ to denote the minimum number of multiplications needed to compute this subexpression. Thus, the original matrix chain-product problem can be characterized as that of computing the value of $N_{0,n-1}$. This observation is important, but we need one more in order to apply the dynamic programming technique.

Characterizing Optimal Solutions

The other important observation we can make about the matrix chain-product problem is that it is possible to characterize an optimal solution to a particular subproblem in terms of optimal solutions to its subproblems. We call this property the ***subproblem optimality*** condition.

In the case of the matrix chain-product problem, we observe that, no matter how we parenthesize a subexpression, there has to be some final matrix multiplication that we perform. That is, a full parenthesization of a subexpression $A_i \cdot A_{i+1} \cdots A_j$ has to be of the form $(A_i \cdots A_k) \cdot (A_{k+1} \cdots A_j)$, for some $k \in \{i, i+1, \ldots, j-1\}$. Moreover, for whichever k is the right one, the products $(A_i \cdots A_k)$ and $(A_{k+1} \cdots A_j)$ must also be solved optimally. If this were not so, then there would be a global optimal that had one of these subproblems solved suboptimally. But this is impossible, since we could then reduce the total number of multiplications by replacing the current subproblem solution by an optimal solution for the subproblem. This observation implies a way of explicitly defining the optimization problem for $N_{i,j}$ in terms of other optimal subproblem solutions. Namely, we can compute $N_{i,j}$ by considering each place k where we could put the final multiplication and taking the minimum over all such choices.

Designing a Dynamic Programming Algorithm

The above discussion implies that we can characterize the optimal subproblem solution $N_{i,j}$ as

$$N_{i,j} = \min_{i \leq k < j} \{N_{i,k} + N_{k+1,j} + d_i d_{k+1} d_{j+1}\},$$

where we note that

$$N_{i,i} = 0,$$

since no work is needed for a subexpression comprising a single matrix. That is, $N_{i,j}$ is the minimum, taken over all possible places to perform the final multiplication, of the number of multiplications needed to compute each subexpression plus the number of multiplications needed to perform the final matrix multiplication.

The equation for $N_{i,j}$ looks similar to the recurrence equations we derive for divide-and-conquer algorithms, but this is only a superficial resemblance, for there is an aspect of the equation $N_{i,j}$ that makes it difficult to use divide-and-conquer to compute $N_{i,j}$. In particular, there is a ***sharing of subproblems*** going on that prevents us from dividing the problem into completely independent subproblems (as we would need to do to apply the divide-and-conquer technique). We can, nevertheless, use the equation for $N_{i,j}$ to derive an efficient algorithm by computing $N_{i,j}$ values in a bottom-up fashion, and storing intermediate solutions in a table of $N_{i,j}$ values. We can begin simply enough by assigning $N_{i,i} = 0$ for $i = 0, 1, \ldots, n-1$. We can then apply the general equation for $N_{i,j}$ to compute $N_{i,i+1}$ values, since they depend only on $N_{i,i}$ and $N_{i+1,i+1}$ values, which are available. Given the $N_{i,i+1}$ values, we can then compute the $N_{i,i+2}$ values, and so on. Therefore, we can build $N_{i,j}$ values up from previously computed values until we can finally compute the value of $N_{0,n-1}$, which is the number that we are searching for. The details of this ***dynamic programming*** solution are given in Algorithm 5.5.

Algorithm MatrixChain($d_0, \ldots, d_n$):
  Input: Sequence $d_0, \ldots, d_n$ of integers
  Output: For $i, j = 0, \ldots, n-1$, the minimum number of multiplications $N_{i,j}$ needed to compute the product $A_i \cdot A_{i+1} \cdots A_j$, where A_k is a $d_k \times d_{k+1}$ matrix

```
for i ← 0 to n − 1 do
  N[i,i] ← 0
for b ← 1 to n − 1 do
  for i ← 0 to n − b − 1 do
    j ← i + b
    N[i,j] ← +∞
    for k ← i to j − 1 do
      N[i,j] ← min{N[i,j], N[i,k] + N[k+1,j] + d[i]d[k+1]d[j+1]}.
```

Algorithm 5.5: Dynamic programming algorithm for the matrix chain-product problem.

Analyzing the Matrix Chain-Product Algorithm

Thus, we can compute $N_{0,n-1}$ with an algorithm that consists primarily of three nested for-loops. The outside loop is executed n times. The loop inside is executed at most n times. And the inner-most loop is also executed at most n times. Therefore, the total running time of this algorithm is $O(n^3)$.

Theorem 5.15: *Given a chain-product of n two-dimensional matrices, we can compute a parenthesization of this chain that achieves the minimum number of scalar multiplications in $O(n^3)$ time.*

Proof: We have shown above how we can compute the optimal ***number*** of scalar multiplications. But how do we recover the actual parenthesization?

The method for computing the parenthesization itself is is actually quite straightforward. We modify the algorithm for computing $N_{i,j}$ values so that any time we find a new minimum value for $N_{i,j}$, we store, with $N_{i,j}$, the index k that allowed us to achieve this minimum. ■

In Figure 5.6, we illustrate the way the dynamic programming solution to the matrix chain-product problem fills in the array N.

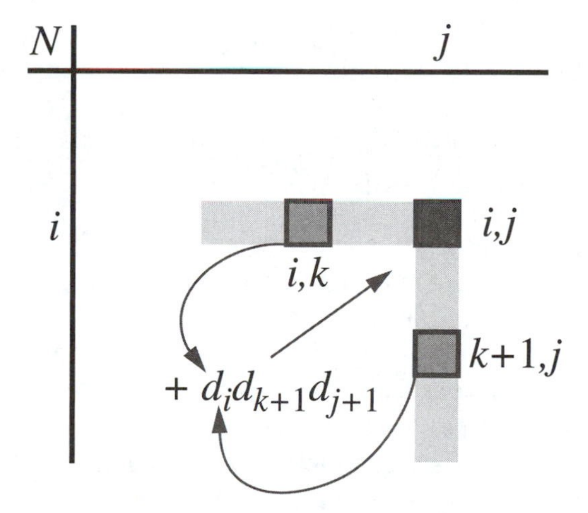

Figure 5.6: Illustration of the way the matrix chain-product dynamic-programming algorithm fills in the array N.

Now that we have worked through a complete example of the use of the dynamic programming method, let us discuss the general aspects of the dynamic programming technique as it can be applied to other problems.

5.3.2 The General Technique

The dynamic programming technique is used primarily for ***optimization*** problems, where we wish to find the "best" way of doing something. Often the number of different ways of doing that "something" is exponential, so a brute-force search for the best is computationally infeasible for all but the smallest problem sizes. We can apply the dynamic programming technique in such situations, however, if the problem has a certain amount of structure that we can exploit. This structure involves the following three components:

Simple Subproblems: There has to be some way of breaking the global optimization problem into subproblems, each having a similar structure to the original problem. Moreover, there should be a simple way of defining subproblems with just a few indices, like i, j, k, and so on.

Subproblem Optimality: An optimal solution to the global problem must be a composition of optimal subproblem solutions, using a relatively simple combining operation. We should not be able to find a globally optimal solution that contains suboptimal subproblems.

Subproblem Overlap: Optimal solutions to unrelated subproblems can contain subproblems in common. Indeed, such overlap improves the efficiency of a dynamic programming algorithm that stores solutions to subproblems.

Now that we have given the general components of a dynamic programming algorithm, we next give another example of its use.

5.3.3 The 0-1 Knapsack Problem

Suppose a hiker is about to go on a trek through a rain forest carrying a single knapsack. Suppose further that she knows the maximum total weight W that she can carry, and she has a set S of n different useful items that she can potentially take with her, such as a folding chair, a tent, and a copy of this book. Let us assume that each item i has an integer weight w_i and a benefit value b_i, which is the utility value that our hiker assigns to item i. Her problem, of course, is to optimize the total value of the set T of items that she takes with her, without going over the weight limit W. That is, she has the following objective:

$$\text{maximize} \sum_{i \in T} b_i \quad \text{subject to} \quad \sum_{i \in T} w_i \leq W.$$

Her problem is an instance of the ***0-1 knapsack problem***. This problem is called a "0-1" problem, because each item must be entirely accepted or rejected. We consider the fractional version of this problem in Section 5.1.1, and we study how knapsack problems arise in the context of Internet auctions in Exercise R-5.12.

A First Attempt at Characterizing Subproblems

We can easily solve the 0-1 knapsack problem in $\Theta(2^n)$ time, of course, by enumerating all subsets of S and selecting the one that has highest total benefit from among all those with total weight not exceeding W. This would be an inefficient algorithm, however. Fortunately, we can derive a dynamic programming algorithm for the 0-1 knapsack problem that runs much faster than this in most cases.

As with many dynamic programming problems, one of the hardest parts of designing such an algorithm for the 0-1 knapsack problem is to find a nice characterization for subproblems (so that we satisfy the three properties of a dynamic programming algorithm). To simplify the discussion, number the items in S as $1,2,\ldots,n$ and define, for each $k \in \{1,2,\ldots,n\}$, the subset

$$S_k = \{\text{items in } S \text{ labeled } 1,2,\ldots,k\}.$$

One possibility is for us to define subproblems by using a parameter k so that subproblem k is the best way to fill the knapsack using only items from the set S_k. This is a valid subproblem definition, but it is not at all clear how to define an optimal solution for index k in terms of optimal subproblem solutions. Our hope would be that we would be able to derive an equation that takes the best solution using items from S_{k-1} and considers how to add the item k to that. Unfortunately, if we stick with this definition for subproblems, then this approach is fatally flawed. For, as we show in Figure 5.7, if we use this characterization for subproblems, then an optimal solution to the global problem may actually contain a suboptimal subproblem.

(a)

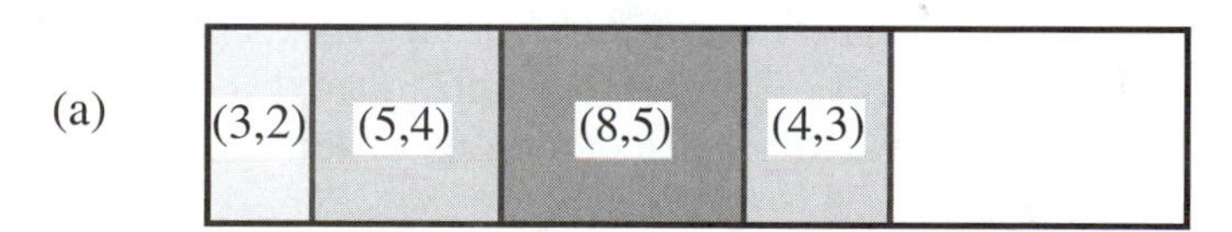

(b)

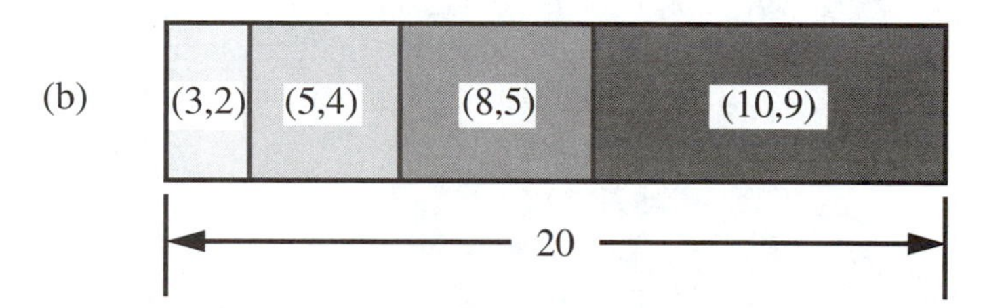

Figure 5.7: An example showing that our first approach to defining a knapsack subproblem does not work. The set S consists of five items denoted by the the (***weight***, ***benefit***) pairs $(3,2)$, $(5,4)$, $(8,5)$, $(4,3)$, and $(10,9)$. The maximum total weight is $W = 20$: (a) best solution with the first four items; (b) best solution with the first five items. We shade each item in proportion to its benefit.

A Better Subproblem Characterization

One of the reasons that defining subproblems only in terms of an index k is fatally flawed is that there is not enough information represented in a subproblem to provide much help for solving the global optimization problem. We can correct this difficulty, however, by adding a second parameter w. Let us therefore formulate each subproblem as that of computing $B[k,w]$, which is defined as the maximum total value of a subset of S_k from among all those subsets having total weight ***exactly*** w. We have $B[0,w] = 0$ for each $w \leq W$, and we derive the following relationship for the general case

$$B[k,w] = \begin{cases} B[k-1,w] & \text{if } w_k > w \\ \max\{B[k-1,w], B[k-1,w-w_k]+b_k\} & \text{else.} \end{cases}$$

That is, the best subset of S_k that has total weight w is either the best subset of S_{k-1} that has total weight w or the best subset of S_{k-1} that has total weight $w-w_k$ plus the item k. Since the best subset of S_k that has total weight w must either contain item k or not, one of these two choices must be the right choice. Thus, we have a subproblem definition that is simple (it involves just two parameters, k and w) and satisfies the subproblem optimization condition. Moreover, it has subproblem overlap, for the optimal way of summing exactly w to weight may be used by many future subproblems.

In deriving an algorithm from this definition, we can make one additional observation, namely, that the definition of $B[k,w]$ is built from $B[k-1,w]$ and possibly $B[k-1,w-w_k]$. Thus, we can implement this algorithm using only a single array B, which we update in each of a series of iterations indexed by a parameter k so that at the end of each iteration $B[w] = B[k,w]$. This gives us Algorithm 5.8 (01Knapsack).

Algorithm 01Knapsack(S,W):
  Input: Set S of n items, such that item i has positive benefit b_i and positive integer weight w_i; positive integer maximum total weight W
  Output: For $w = 0,\ldots,W$, maximum benefit $B[w]$ of a subset of S with total weight w

```
for w ← 0 to W do
  B[w] ← 0
for k ← 1 to n do
  for w ← W downto w_k do
    if B[w − w_k] + b_k > B[w] then
      B[w] ← B[w − w_k] + b_k
```

Algorithm 5.8: Dynamic programming algorithm for solving the 0-1 knapsack problem.

Analyzing the 0-1 Knapsack Dynamic Programming Algorithm

The running time of the 01Knapsack algorithm is dominated by the two nested for-loops, where the outer one iterates n times and the inner one iterates at most W times. After it completes we can find the optimal value by locating the value $B[w]$ that is greatest among all $w \leq W$. Thus, we have the following:

Theorem 5.16: *Given an integer W and a set S of n items, each of which has a positive benefit and a positive integer weight, we can find the highest benefit subset of S with total weight at most W in $O(nW)$ time.*

Proof: We have given Algorithm 5.8 (01Knapsack) for constructing the ***value*** of the maximum-benefit subset of S that has total weight at most W using an array B of benefit values. We can easily convert our algorithm into one that outputs the items in a best subset, however. We leave the details of this conversion as an exercise. ■

Pseudo-Polynomial-Time Algorithms

In addition to being another useful application of the dynamic programming technique, Theorem 5.16 states something very interesting. Namely, it states that the running time of our algorithm depends on a parameter W that, strictly speaking, is not proportional to the size of the input (the n items, together with their weights and benefits, plus the ***number*** W). Assuming that W is encoded in some standard way (such as a binary number), then it takes only $O(\log W)$ bits to encode W. Moreover, if W is very large (say $W = 2^n$), then this dynamic programming algorithm would actually be asymptotically slower than the brute force method. Thus, technically speaking, this algorithm is not a polynomial-time algorithm, for its running time is not actually a function of the ***size*** of the input.

It is common to refer to an algorithm such as our knapsack dynamic programming algorithm as being a ***pseudo-polynomial time*** algorithm, for its running time depends on the magnitude of a number given in the input, not its encoding size. In practice, such algorithms should run much faster than any brute-force algorithm, but it is not correct to say they are true polynomial-time algorithms. In fact, there is a theory known as ***NP-completeness***, which is discussed in Chapter 13, that states that it is very unlikely that anyone will ever find a true polynomial-time algorithm for the 0-1 knapsack problem.

Elsewhere in this book, we give additional applications of the dynamic programming technique for computing reachability in a directed graph (Section 6.4.2) and for testing the similarity of two strings (Section 9.4).

5.4 Exercises

Reinforcement

R-5.1 Let $S = \{a,b,c,d,e,f,g\}$ be a collection of objects with benefit-weight values as follows: a: $(12,4)$, b: $(10,6)$, c: $(8,5)$, d: $(11,7)$, e: $(14,3)$, f: $(7,1)$, g: $(9,6)$. What is an optimal solution to the fractional knapsack problem for S assuming we have a sack that can hold objects with total weight 18? Show your work.

R-5.2 Describe how to implement the TaskSchedule method to run in $O(n \log n)$ time.

R-5.3 Suppose we are given a set of tasks specified by pairs of the start times and finish times as $T = \{(1,2),(1,3),(1,4),(2,5),(3,7),(4,9),(5,6),(6,8),(7,9)\}$. Solve the task scheduling problem for this set of tasks.

R-5.4 Characterize each of the following recurrence equations using the master method (assuming that $T(n) = c$ for $n < d$, for constants $c > 0$ and $d \geq 1$).

a. $T(n) = 2T(n/2) + \log n$
b. $T(n) = 8T(n/2) + n^2$
c. $T(n) = 16T(n/2) + (n \log n)^4$
d. $T(n) = 7T(n/3) + n$
e. $T(n) = 9T(n/3) + n^3 \log n$

R-5.5 Use the divide-and-conquer algorithm, from Section 5.2.2, to compute $10110011 \cdot 10111010$ in binary. Show your work.

R-5.6 Use Strassen's matrix multiplication algorithm to multiply the matrices

$$X = \begin{pmatrix} 3 & 2 \\ 4 & 8 \end{pmatrix} \quad \text{and} \quad Y = \begin{pmatrix} 1 & 5 \\ 9 & 6 \end{pmatrix}.$$

R-5.7 A complex number $a + b\mathbf{i}$, where $\mathbf{i} = \sqrt{-1}$, can be represented by the pair (a,b). Describe a method performing only three real-number multiplications to compute the pair (e,f) representing the product of $a + b\mathbf{i}$ and $c + d\mathbf{i}$.

R-5.8 Boolean matrices are matrices such that each entry is 0 or 1, and matrix multiplication is performed by using AND for $\cdot$ and OR for $+$. Suppose we are given two $n \times n$ random Boolean matrices A and B, so that the probability that any entry in either is 1, is $1/k$. Show that if k is a constant, then there is an algorithm for multiplying A and B whose expected running time is $O(n^2)$. What if k is n?

R-5.9 What is the best way to multiply a chain of matrices with dimensions that are 10×5, 5×2, 2×20, 20×12, 12×4, and 4×60? Show your work.

R-5.10 Design an efficient algorithm for the matrix chain multiplication problem that outputs a fully parenthesized expression for how to multiply the matrices in the chain using the minimum number of operations.

R-5.11 Solve Exercise R-5.1 for the 0-1 knapsack problem.

R-5.12 Sally is hosting an Internet auction to sell n widgets. She receives m bids, each of the form "I want k_i widgets for d_i dollars," for $i = 1,2,\ldots,m$. Characterize her optimization problem as a knapsack problem. Under what conditions is this a 0-1 versus fractional problem?

Creativity

C-5.1 A native Australian named Anatjari wishes to cross a desert carrying only a single water bottle. He has a map that marks all the watering holes along the way. Assuming he can walk k miles on one bottle of water, design an efficient algorithm for determining where Anatjari should refill his bottle in order to make as few stops as possible. Argue why your algorithm is correct.

C-5.2 Consider the single ***machine scheduling*** problem where we are given a set T of tasks specified by their start times and finish times, as in the task scheduling problem, except now we have only one machine and we wish to maximize the number of tasks that this single machine performs. Design a greedy algorithm for this single machine scheduling problem and show that it is correct. What is the running time of this algorithm?

C-5.3 Describe an efficient greedy algorithm for making change for a specified value using a minimum number of coins, assuming there are four denominations of coins (called quarters, dimes, nickels, and pennies), with values 25, 10, 5, and 1, respectively. Argue why your algorithm is correct.

C-5.4 Give an example set of denominations of coins so that a greedy change making algorithm will not use the minimum number of coins.

C-5.5 In the ***art gallery guarding*** problem we are given a line L that represents a long hallway in an art gallery. We are also given a set $X = \{x_0, x_1, \ldots, x_{n-1}\}$ of real numbers that specify the positions of paintings in this hallway. Suppose that a single guard can protect all the paintings within distance at most 1 of his or her position (on both sides). Design an algorithm for finding a placement of guards that uses the minimum number of guards to guard all the paintings with positions in X.

C-5.6 Design a divide-and-conquer algorithm for finding the minimum and the maximum element of n numbers using no more than $3n/2$ comparisons.

C-5.7 Given a set P of n teams in some sport, a ***round-robin tournament*** is a collection of games in which each team plays each other team exactly once. Design an efficient algorithm for constructing a round-robin tournament assuming n is a power of 2.

C-5.8 Let a set of intervals $S = \{[a_0, b_0], [a_1, b_1], \ldots, [a_{n-1}, b_{n-1}]\}$ of the interval $[0, 1]$ be given, with $0 \le a_i < b_i \le 1$, for $i = 0, 1, \ldots, n-1$. Suppose further that we assign a height h_i to each interval $[a_i, b_i]$ in S. The ***upper envelope*** of S is defined to be a list of pairs $[(x_0, c_0), (x_1, c_1), (x_2, c_2), \ldots, (x_m, c_m), (x_{m+1}, 0)]$, with $x_0 = 0$ and $x_{m+1} = 1$, and ordered by x_i values, such that, for each subinterval $s = [x_i, x_{i+1}]$ the height of the highest interval in S containing s is c_i, for $i = 0, 1, \ldots, m$. Design an $O(n \log n)$-time algorithm for computing the upper envelope of S.

C-5.9 How can we modify the dynamic programming algorithm from simply computing the best benefit value for the 0-1 knapsack problem to computing the assignment that gives this benefit?

C-5.10 Suppose we are given a collection $A = \{a_1, a_2, \ldots, a_n\}$ of n positive integers that add up to N. Design an $O(nN)$-time algorithm for determining whether there is a subset $B \subset A$, such that $\sum_{a_i \in B} a_i = \sum_{a_i \in A-B} a_i$.

C-5.11 Let P be a convex polygon (Section 12.5.1). A ***triangulation*** of P is an addition of diagonals connecting the vertices of P so that each interior face is a triangle. The ***weight*** of a triangulation is the sum of the lengths of the diagonals. Assuming that we can compute lengths and add and compare them in constant time, give an efficient algorithm for computing a minimum-weight triangulation of P.

C-5.12 A ***grammar*** G is a way of generating strings of "terminal" characters from a nonterminal symbol S, by applying simple substitution rules, called ***productions***. If $B \rightarrow \beta$ is a production, then we can convert a string of the form $\alpha B \gamma$ into the string $\alpha\beta\gamma$. A grammar is in ***Chomsky normal form*** if every production is of the form "$A \rightarrow BC$" or "$A \rightarrow a$," where A, B, and C are nonterminal characters and a is a terminal character. Design an $O(n^3)$-time dynamic programming algorithm for determining if string $x = x_0x_1 \cdots x_{n-1}$ can be generated from start symbol S.

C-5.13 Suppose we are given an n-node rooted tree T, such that each node v in T is given a weight $w(v)$. An ***independent set*** of T is a subset S of the nodes of T such that no node in S is a child or parent of any other node in S. Design an efficient dynamic programming algorithm to find the maximum-weight independent set of the nodes in T, where the weight of a set of nodes is simply the sum of the weights of the nodes in that set. What is the running time of your algorithm?

Projects

P-5.1 Design and implement a big integer package supporting the four basic arithmetic operations.

P-5.2 Implement a system for efficiently solving knapsack problems. Your system should work for either fractional or 0-1 knapsack problems. Perform an experimental analysis to test the efficiency of your system.

Chapter Notes

The term "greedy algorithm" was coined by Edmonds [64] in 1971, although the concept existed before then. For more information about the greedy method and the theory that supports it, which is known as matroid theory, please see the book by Papadimitriou and Steiglitz [164].

The divide-and-conquer technique is a part of the folklore of data structure and algorithm design. The master method for solving divide-and-conquer recurrences traces its origins to a paper by Bentley, Haken, and Saxe [30]. The divide-and-conquer algorithm for multiplying two large integers in $O(n^{1.585})$ time is generally attributed to the Russians Karatsuba and Ofman [111]. The asymptotically fastest known algorithm for multiplying two n-digit numbers is an FFT-based algorithm by Schönhage and Strassen [181] that runs in $O(n \log n \log\log n)$ time.

Dynamic programming was developed in the operations research community and formalized by Bellman [26]. The matrix chain-product solution we described is due to Godbole [78]. The asymptotically fastest method is due to Hu and Shing [101, 102]. The dynamic programming algorithm for the knapsack problem is found in the book by Hu [100]. Hirchsberg [95] shows how to solve the longest common substring problem in the same time given above, but with linear space (see also [56]).

Part

II Graph Algorithms

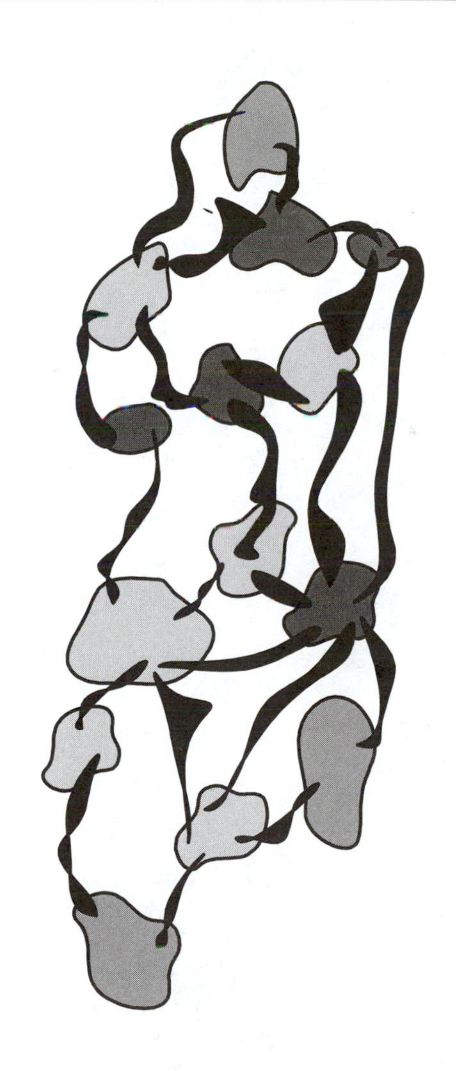

Chapter

6 Graphs

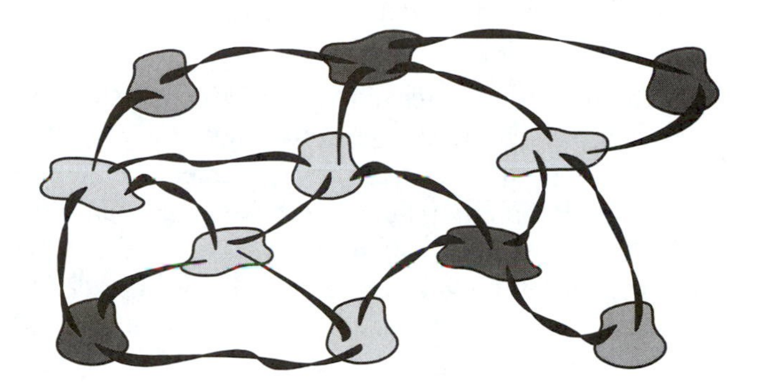

Contents

6.1 The Graph Abstract Data Type 289

6.1.1 Graph Methods 293

6.2 Data Structures for Graphs 296

6.2.1 The Edge List Structure 296

6.2.2 The Adjacency List Structure 299

6.2.3 The Adjacency Matrix Structure 301

6.3 Graph Traversal 303

6.3.1 Depth-First Search 303

6.3.2 Biconnected Components 307

6.3.3 Breadth-First Search 313

6.4 Directed Graphs 316

6.4.1 Traversing a Digraph 318

6.4.2 Transitive Closure 320

6.4.3 DFS and Garbage Collection 323

6.4.4 Directed Acyclic Graphs 325

6.5 Java Example: Depth-First Search 329

6.5.1 The Decorator Pattern 329

6.5.2 A DFS Engine 330

6.5.3 The Template Method Design Pattern 331

6.6 Exercises 335

Greek mythology tells of an elaborate labyrinth that was built to house the monstrous part bull, part man Minotaur. This labyrinth was so complex that neither beast nor human could escape it. No human, that is, until the Greek hero, Theseus, with the help of the king's daughter, Ariadne, decided to implement one of the algorithms discussed in this chapter. Theseus fastened a ball of thread to the door of the labyrinth and unwound it as he traversed the twisting passages in search of the monster. Theseus obviously knew about good algorithm design, for, after finding and defeating the beast, Theseus easily followed the string back out of the labyrinth to the loving arms of Ariadne.

Being able to determine which objects, such as labyrinth passages, are connected to which other objects may not always be as vitally important as it was in this story, but it is nevertheless fundamental. Connectivity information is present, for example, in city maps, where the objects are roads, and also in the routing tables for the Internet, where the objects are computers. Connectivity information is also present in the parent-child relationships defined by a binary tree, where the objects are tree nodes. Indeed, connectivity information can be defined by all kinds of relationships that exist between pairs of objects. The topic we study in this chapter—***graphs***—is therefore focused on representations and algorithms for dealing efficiently with such relationships. That is, a graph is a set of objects, called vertices, together with a collection of pairwise connections between them. By the way, this notion of a "graph" should not be confused with bar charts and function plots, as these kinds of "graphs" are unrelated to the topic of this chapter.

Graphs have applications in a host of different domains, including mapping (in geographic information systems), transportation (in road and flight networks), electrical engineering (in circuits), and computer networking (in the connections of the Internet). Because applications for graphs are so widespread and diverse, people have developed a great deal of terminology to describe different components and properties of graphs. Fortunately, since most graph applications are relatively recent developments, this terminology is fairly intuitive.

We therefore begin this chapter by reviewing much of this terminology and presenting the graph ADT, including some elementary properties of graphs. Having given the graph ADT, we then present, in Section 6.2, three main data structures for representing graphs. As with trees, traversals are important computations for graphs, and we discuss such computations in Section 6.3. We discuss directed graphs in Section 6.4, where relationships have a given direction, and connectivity problems become much more interesting. Finally, in Section 6.5, we give a case study of depth-first search in Java. This case study involves the use of two software engineering design patterns—the decorator pattern and the template method pattern—as well as a discussion of how depth-first search can be used for garbage collection.

6.1 The Graph Abstract Data Type

Viewed abstractly, a ***graph*** G is simply a set V of ***vertices*** and a collection E of pairs of vertices from V, called ***edges***. Thus, a graph is a way of representing connections or relationships between pairs of objects from some set V. Incidentally, some books use different terminology for graphs and refer to what we call vertices as ***nodes*** and what we call edges as ***arcs***. We use the terms "vertices" and "edges."

Edges in a graph are either ***directed*** or ***undirected***. An edge (u,v) is said to be ***directed*** from u to v if the pair (u,v) is ordered, with u preceding v. An edge (u,v) is said to be ***undirected*** if the pair (u,v) is not ordered. Undirected edges are sometimes denoted with set notation, as $\{u,v\}$, but for simplicity we use the pair notation (u,v), noting that in the undirected case (u,v) is the same as (v,u). Graphs are typically visualized by drawing the vertices as ovals or rectangles and the edges as segments or curves connecting pairs of ovals and rectangles.

Example 6.1: *We can visualize collaborations among the researchers of a certain discipline by constructing a graph whose vertices are associated with the researchers themselves, and whose edges connect pairs of vertices associated with researchers who have coauthored a paper or book. (See Figure 6.1.) Such edges are undirected because coauthorship is a* **symmetric relation***; that is, if A has coauthored something with B, then B necessarily has coauthored something with A.*

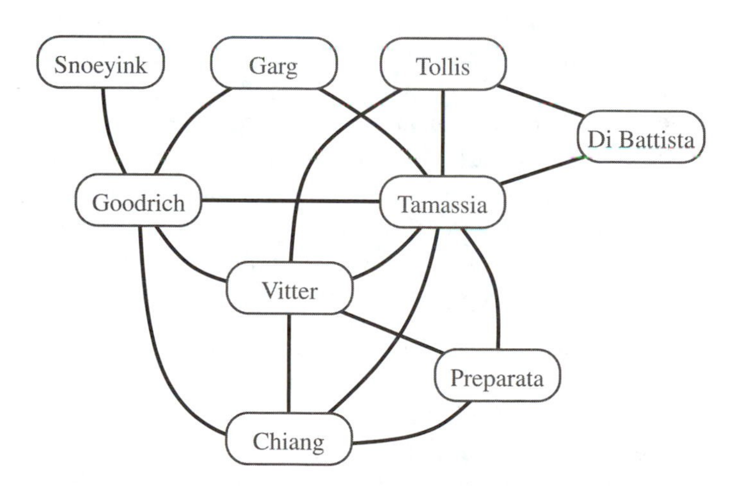

Figure 6.1: Graph of coauthorships among some authors.

Example 6.2: *We can associate with an object-oriented program a graph whose vertices represent the classes defined in the program, and whose edges indicate inheritance between classes. There is an edge from a vertex v to a vertex u if the class for v extends the class for u. Such edges are directed because the inheritance relation only goes in one direction (that is, it is* **asymmetric***).*

If all the edges in a graph are undirected, then we say the graph is an ***undirected graph***. Likewise, a ***directed graph***, also called a ***digraph***, is a graph whose edges are all directed. A graph that has both directed and undirected edges is often called a ***mixed graph***. Note that an undirected or mixed graph can be converted into a directed graph by replacing every undirected edge (u,v) by the pair of directed edges (u,v) and (v,u). It is often useful, however, to keep undirected and mixed graphs represented as they are, for such graphs have several applications.

Example 6.3: *A city map can be modeled by a graph whose vertices are intersections or dead ends, and whose edges are stretches of streets without intersections. This graph has both undirected edges, which correspond to stretches of two-way streets, and directed edges, which correspond to stretches of one-way streets. Thus, a graph modeling a city map is a mixed graph.*

Example 6.4: *Physical examples of graphs are present in the electrical wiring and plumbing networks of a building. Such networks can be modeled as graphs, where each connector, fixture, or outlet is viewed as a vertex, and each uninterrupted stretch of wire or pipe is viewed as an edge. Such graphs are actually components of much larger graphs, namely the local power and water distribution networks. Depending on the specific aspects of these graphs that we are interested in, we may consider their edges as undirected or directed, for, in principle, water can flow in a pipe and current can flow in a wire in either direction.*

The two vertices joined by an edge are called the ***end vertices*** of the edge. The end vertices of an edge are also known as the ***endpoints*** of that edge. If an edge is directed, its first endpoint is its ***origin*** and the other is the ***destination*** of the edge.

Two vertices are said to be ***adjacent*** if they are endpoints of the same edge. An edge is said to be ***incident*** on a vertex if the vertex is one of the edge's endpoints. The ***outgoing edges*** of a vertex are the directed edges whose origin is that vertex. The ***incoming edges*** of a vertex are the directed edges whose destination is that vertex. The ***degree*** of a vertex v, denoted $\deg(v)$, is the number of incident edges of v. The ***in-degree*** and ***out-degree*** of a vertex v are the number of the incoming and outgoing edges of v, and are denoted $\text{indeg}(v)$ and $\text{outdeg}(v)$, respectively.

Example 6.5: *We can study air transportation by constructing a graph G, called a* **flight network**, *whose vertices are associated with airports, and whose edges are associated with flights. (See Figure 6.2.) In graph G, the edges are directed because a given flight has a specific travel direction (from the origin airport to the destination airport). The endpoints of an edge e in G correspond respectively to the origin and destination for the flight corresponding to e. Two airports are adjacent in G if there is a flight that flies between them, and an edge e is incident upon a vertex v in G if the flight for e flies to or from the airport for v. The outgoing edges of a vertex v correspond to the out-bound flights from v's airport, and the incoming edges correspond to the in-bound flights to v's airport. Finally, the in-degree of a vertex v of G corresponds to the number of in-bound flights to v's airport, and the out-degree of a vertex v in G corresponds to the number of out-bound flights.*

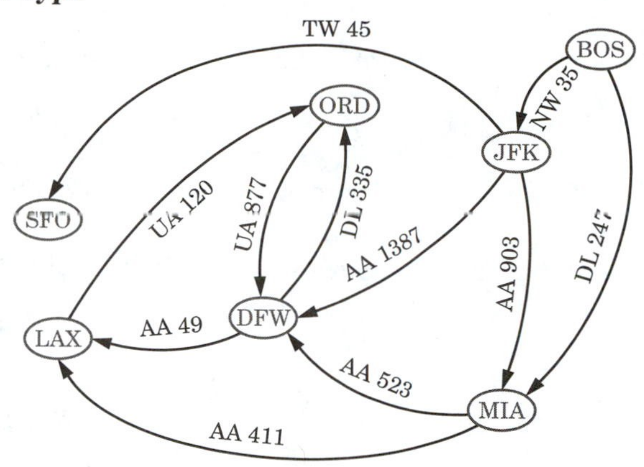

Figure 6.2: Example of a directed graph representing a flight network. The endpoints of edge UA 120 are LAX and ORD; hence, LAX and ORD are adjacent. The in-degree of DFW is 3, and the out-degree of DFW is 2.

The definition of a graph groups edges in a ***collection***, not a ***set***, thus allowing for two undirected edges to have the same end vertices, and for two directed edges to have the same origin and destination. Such edges are called ***parallel edges*** or ***multiple edges***. Parallel edges may exist in a flight network (Example 6.5), in which case multiple edges between the same pair of vertices could indicate different flights operating on the same route at different times of the day. Another special type of edge is one that connects a vertex to itself. In this case, we say that an edge (undirected or directed) is a ***self-loop*** if its two endpoints coincide. A self-loop may occur in a graph associated with a city map (Example 6.3), where it would correspond to a "circle" (a curving street that returns to its starting point).

With few exceptions, like those mentioned above, graphs do not have parallel edges or self-loops. Such graphs are said to be ***simple***. Thus, we can usually say that the edges of a simple graph are a ***set*** of vertex pairs (and not just a collection). Throughout this chapter, we shall assume that a graph is simple unless otherwise specified. This assumption simplifies the presentation of data structures and algorithms for graphs. Extending the results of this chapter to general graphs, with self-loops and/or parallel edges, is straightforward but tedious.

In the theorems that follow, we explore a few important properties of degrees and the number of edges in a graph. These properties relate the number of vertices and edges to each other and to the degrees of the vertices in a graph.

Theorem 6.6: *If G is a graph with m edges, then*

$$\sum_{v \in G} deg(v) = 2m.$$

Proof: An edge (u,v) is counted twice in the above summation; once by its endpoint u and once by its endpoint v. Thus, the total contribution of the edges to the degrees of the vertices is twice the number of edges. ■

Theorem 6.7: *If G is a directed graph with m edges, then*

$$\sum_{v \in G} indeg(v) = \sum_{v \in G} outdeg(v) = m.$$

Proof: In a directed graph, an edge (u,v) contributes one unit to the out-degree of its origin u and one unit to the in-degree of its destination v. Thus, the total contribution of the edges to the out-degrees of the vertices is equal to the number of edges, and similarly for the in-degrees. ■

Theorem 6.8: *Let G be a simple graph with n vertices and m edges. If G is undirected, then $m \leq n(n-1)/2$, and if G is directed, then $m \leq n(n-1)$.*

Proof: Suppose that G is undirected. Since no two edges can have the same endpoints and there are no self-loops, the maximum degree of a vertex in G is $n-1$ in this case. Thus, by Theorem 6.6, $2m \leq n(n-1)$. Now suppose that G is directed. Since no two edges can have the same origin and destination, and there are no self-loops, the maximum in-degree of a vertex in G is $n-1$ in this case. Thus, by Theorem 6.7, $m \leq n(n-1)$. ■

Put another way, Theorem 6.8 states that a simple graph with n vertices has $O(n^2)$ edges.

A ***path*** in a graph is a sequence of alternating vertices and edges that starts at a vertex and ends at a vertex, such that each edge is incident to its predecessor and successor vertex. A ***cycle*** is a path with the same start and end vertices. We say that a path is ***simple*** if each vertex in the path is distinct, and we say that a cycle is ***simple*** if each vertex in the cycle is distinct, except for the first and last one. A ***directed path*** is a path such that all the edges are directed and are traversed along their direction. A ***directed cycle*** is defined similarly.

Example 6.9: *Given a graph G representing a city map (see Example 6.3), we can model a couple driving from their home to dinner at a recommended restaurant as traversing a path though G. If they know the way, and don't accidentally go through the same intersection twice, then they traverse a simple path in G. Likewise, we can model the entire trip the couple takes, from their home to the restaurant and back, as a cycle. If they go home from the restaurant in a completely different way than how they went, not even going through the same intersection twice, then their entire round trip is a simple cycle. Finally, if they travel along one-way streets for their entire trip, then we can model their night out as a directed cycle.*

A ***subgraph*** of a graph G is a graph H whose vertices and edges are subsets of the vertices and edges of G, respectively. A ***spanning subgraph*** of G is a subgraph of G that contains all the vertices of the graph G. A graph is ***connected*** if, for any two vertices, there is a path between them. If a graph G is not connected, its maximal connected subgraphs are called the ***connected components*** of G. A ***forest*** is a graph without cycles. A ***tree*** is a connected forest, that is, a connected graph without cycles.

Note that this definition of a tree is somewhat different from the one given in Section 2.3. Namely, in the context of graphs, a tree has no root. Whenever there is ambiguity, the trees of Section 2.3 should be called ***rooted trees***, while the trees of this chapter should be called ***free trees***. The connected components of a forest are (free) trees. A ***spanning tree*** of a graph is a spanning subgraph that is a (free) tree.

Example 6.10: *Perhaps the most talked about graph today is the Internet, which can be viewed as a graph whose vertices are computers and whose (undirected) edges are communication connections between pairs of computers on the Internet. The computers and the connections between them in a single domain, like* wiley.com, *form a subgraph of the Internet. If this subgraph is connected, then two users on computers in this domain can send e-mail to one another without having their information packets ever leave their domain. Suppose the edges of this subgraph form a spanning tree. This implies that, even if a single connection goes down (for example, because someone pulls a communication cable out of the back of a computer in this domain), then this subgraph will no longer be connected.*

There are a number of simple properties of trees, forests, and connected graphs.

Theorem 6.11: *Let G be an undirected graph with n vertices and m edges. Then we have the following:*

- *If G is connected, then $m \geq n-1$.*
- *If G is a tree, then $m = n-1$.*
- *If G is a forest, then $m \leq n-1$.*

We leave the justification of this theorem as an exercise (C-6.1).

6.1.1 Graph Methods

As an abstract data type, a graph is a positional container of elements that are stored at the graph's vertices and edges. Namely, the ***positions*** in a graph are its vertices and edges. Hence, we can store elements in a graph at either its edges or its vertices (or both). In terms of an object-oriented implementation, this choice implies that we can define vertex and edge ADTs that extend the position ADT. Recall from Section 2.2.2 that a position has an element() method, which returns the element that is stored at this position. We can also use specialized iterators for vertices and edges, which allow us to iteratively enumerate a collection of vertices or edges, respectively. Since a graph is a positional container, the graph abstract data type supports the methods size(), isEmpty(), elements(), positions(), replaceElement(p,o), and swapElements(p,q), where p and q denote positions, and o denotes an object (that is, an element).

Graphs are a much richer abstract data type than those we have discussed in previous chapters. Their richness derives mostly from the two kinds of positions that help define a graph: vertices and edges. So as to present the methods for the graph ADT in as organized a way as possible, we divide the graph methods into three main categories: general methods, methods dealing with directed edges, and methods for updating and modifying graphs. In addition, in order to simplify the presentation, we denote a vertex position with v, an edge position with e, and an object (element) stored at a vertex or edge with o. Also, we do not discuss error conditions that may occur.

General Methods

We begin by describing the fundamental methods for a graph, which ignore the direction of the edges. Each of the following methods returns global information about a graph G:

numVertices(): Return the number of vertices in G.

numEdges(): Return the number of edges in G.

vertices(): Return an iterator of the vertices of G.

edges(): Return an iterator of the edges of G.

Unlike a tree (which has a root), a graph has no special vertex. Hence, we have a method that returns an arbitrary vertex of the graph:

aVertex(): Return a vertex of G.

The following accessor methods take vertex and edge positions as arguments:

degree(v): Return the degree of v.

adjacentVertices(v): Return an iterator of the vertices adjacent to v.

incidentEdges(v): Return an iterator of the edges incident upon v.

endVertices(e): Return an array of size 2 storing the end vertices of e.

opposite(v, e): Return the endpoint of edge e distinct from v.

areAdjacent(v, w): Return whether vertices v and w are adjacent.

Methods Dealing with Directed Edges

When we allow for some or all the edges in a graph to be directed, then there are several additional methods we should include in the graph ADT. We begin with some methods for dealing specifically with directed edges.

directedEdges(): Return an iterator of all directed edges.

undirectedEdges(): Return an iterator of all undirected edges.

destination(e): Return the destination of the directed edge e.

origin(e): Return the origin of the directed edge e.

isDirected(e): Return true if and only if the edge e is directed.

In addition, the existence of directed edges require that we have ways of relating vertices and edges in terms of directions:

inDegree(v): Return the in-degree of v.

outDegree(v): Return the out-degree of v.

inIncidentEdges(v): Return an iterator of all the incoming edges to v.

outIncidentEdges(v): Return an iterator of all the outgoing edges from v.

inAdjacentVertices(v): Return an iterator of all the vertices adjacent to v along incoming edges to v.

outAdjacentVertices(v): Return an iterator of all the vertices adjacent to v along outgoing edges from v.

Methods for Updating Graphs

We can also allow for update methods that add or delete edges and vertices:

insertEdge(v, w, o): Insert and return an undirected edge between vertices v and w, storing the object o at this position.

insertDirectedEdge(v, w, o): Insert and return a directed edge from vertex v to vertex w, storing the object o at this position.

insertVertex(o): Insert and return a new (isolated) vertex storing the object o at this position.

removeVertex(v): Remove vertex v and all its incident edges.

removeEdge(e): Remove edge e.

makeUndirected(e): Make edge e undirected.

reverseDirection(e): Reverse the direction of directed edge e.

setDirectionFrom(e, v): Make edge e directed away from vertex v.

setDirectionTo(e, v): Make edge e directed into vertex v.

There are admittedly a lot of methods in the graph ADT. The number of methods is to a certain extent unavoidable, however, since graphs are such rich structures. Graphs support two kinds of positions—vertices and edges—and even then allow for edges to be either directed or undirected. We need to have different methods for accessing and updating all these different positions, as well as dealing with the relationships that can exist between these different positions.

6.2 Data Structures for Graphs

There are several ways to realize the graph ADT with a concrete data structure. In this section, we discuss three popular approaches, usually referred to as the ***edge list*** structure, the ***adjacency list*** structure, and the ***adjacency matrix***. In all the three representations, we use a container (a list or vector, for example) to store the vertices of the graph. Regarding the edges, there is a fundamental difference between the first two structures and the latter. The edge list structure and the adjacency list structure only store the edges actually present in the graph, while the adjacency matrix stores a placeholder for every pair of vertices (whether there is an edge between them or not). As we will explain in this section, this difference implies that, for a graph G with n vertices and m edges, an edge list or adjacency list representation uses $O(n+m)$ space, whereas an adjacency matrix representation uses $O(n^2)$ space.

6.2.1 The Edge List Structure

The ***edge list*** structure is possibly the simplest, though not the most efficient, representation of a graph G. In this representation, a vertex v of G storing an element o is explicitly represented by a vertex object. All such vertex objects are stored in a container V, which would typically be a list, vector, or dictionary. If we represent V as a vector, for example, then we would naturally think of the vertices as being numbered. If we represent V as a dictionary, on the other hand, then we would naturally think of each vertex as being identified by a key that we associate with it. Note that the elements of container V are the vertex positions of graph G.

Vertex Objects

The vertex object for a vertex v storing element o has instance variables for

- A reference to o
- Counters for the number of incident undirected edges, incoming directed edges, and outgoing directed edges
- A reference to the position (or locator) of the vertex-object in container V.

The distinguishing feature of the edge list structure is not how it represents vertices, however, but the way in which it represents edges. In this structure, an edge e of G storing an element o is explicitly represented by an edge object. The edge objects are stored in a container E, which would typically be a list, vector, or dictionary (possibly supporting the locator pattern).

Edge Objects

The edge object for an edge e storing element o has instance variables for

- A reference to o
- A Boolean indicator of whether e is directed or undirected
- References to the vertex objects in V associated with the endpoint vertices of e (if the edge e is undirected) or to the origin and destination vertices of e (if the edge e is directed)
- A reference to the position (or locator) of the edge-object in container E.

We illustrate the edge list structure for a directed graph G in Figure 6.3.

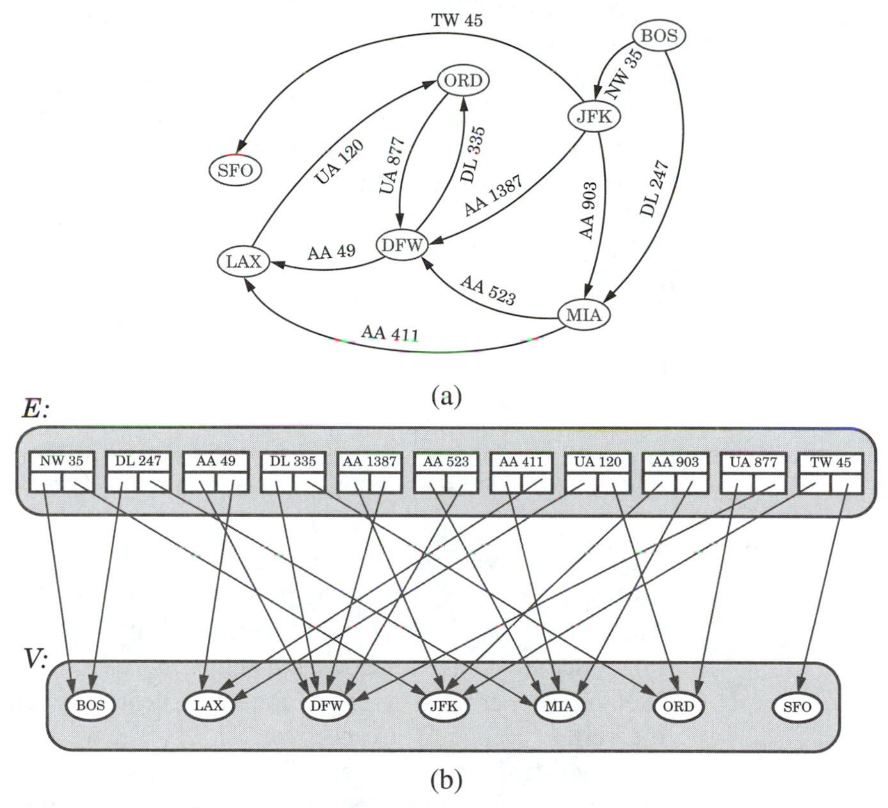

Figure 6.3: (a) A directed graph G; (b) schematic representation of the edge list structure for G. To avoid clutter, we do not show the following fields of the vertex objects: the three counters for the incident edges and the reference to the position (or locator) of the vertex-object in container V. Also, we do not show the following fields of the edge objects: the Boolean direction indicator and the reference to the position (or locator) of the edge-object in container E. Finally, we visualize the elements stored in the vertex and edge objects with the element names, instead of with actual references to the element objects.

The Edge List

The reason this structure is called the ***edge list*** structure is that the simplest and most common implementation of the container E is with a list. Even so, in order to be able to conveniently search for specific objects associated with edges, we may wish to implement E with a dictionary, in spite of our calling this the "edge list." We may also wish to implement the container V as a dictionary for the same reason. Still, in keeping with tradition, we call this structure the edge list structure.

The main feature of the edge list structure is that it provides direct access from edges to the vertices they are incident upon. This allows us to define simple algorithms for implementing the different edge-based methods of the graph ADT (for example, methods endVertices, origin, and destination). We can simply access the appropriate components of the given edge object to implement each such method.

Nevertheless, the "inverse" operation—that of accessing the edges that are incident upon a vertex—requires an exhaustive inspection of all the edges in E. Thus, incidentEdges(v) runs in time proportional to the number of edges in the graph, not in time proportional to the degree of vertex v, as we would like. In fact, even to check if two vertices v and w are adjacent, by the areAdjacent(v,w) method, requires that we search the entire edge list looking for the edge (v,w) or (w,v). Moreover, since removing a vertex involves removing all of its incident edges, the method removeVertex also requires a complete search of the edge list, E.

Performance

Important performance characteristics of the edge list structure, assuming that V and E are realized with doubly linked lists, include the following:

- Methods numVertices(), numEdges(), and size() are implemented in $O(1)$ time by accessing size fields associated with the lists V and/or E.
- The counters stored with each vertex object allow us to perform, in constant time, methods degree, inDegree, and outDegree.
- Methods vertices() and edges() are implemented by returning an iterator of the vertex or edge list, respectively. Likewise, we can implement iterators directedEdges() and undirectedEdges() extending an iterator for the list E to returning only those edges that are of the correct type.
- Since the containers V and E are lists implemented with a doubly linked list, we can insert vertices, and insert and remove edges, in $O(1)$ time.
- Methods incidentEdges, inIncidentEdges, outIncidentEdges, adjacentVertices, inAdjacentVertices, outAdjacentVertices, and areAdjacent all take $O(m)$ time, for to determine which edges are incident upon a vertex v we must inspect all edges.
- The update method removeVertex(v) takes $O(m)$ time, since it requires that we inspect all the edges to find and remove those incident upon v.

6.2.2 The Adjacency List Structure

The edge list representation is simple but has its limitations, for many methods that should be fast for individual vertices must instead examine the entire edge list to perform correctly. The ***adjacency list*** structure for a graph G extends the edge list structure, adding extra information that supports direct access to the incident edges (and thus to the adjacent vertices) of each vertex. While the edge list structure views the edge-vertex incidence relation only from the point of view of the edges, the adjacency list structure considers it from both viewpoints. This symmetric approach allows us to use the adjacency list structure to implement a number of vertex methods of the graph ADT much faster than is possible with the edge list structure, even though these two representations both use an amount of space proportional to the number of vertices and edges in the graph. The adjacency list structure includes all the structural components of the edge list structure plus the following:

- The vertex object v holds a reference to a container $I(v)$, called the ***incidence container***, that stores references to the edges incident on v. If directed edges are allowed, then we partition $I(v)$ into $I_{in}(v)$, $I_{out}(v)$, and $I_{un}(v)$, which store the in-coming, out-going, and undirected edges incident to v, respectively.
- The edge object for an edge (u,v) holds references to the positions (or locators) of the edge in the incidence containers $I(u)$ and $I(v)$.

The Adjacency List

Traditionally, the incidence container $I(v)$ for a vertex v is realized by means of a list, which is why we call this way of representing a graph the ***adjacency list*** structure. Still, there may be some contexts where we wish to represent an incidence container $I(v)$ as, say, a dictionary or a priority queue, so let us stick with thinking of $I(v)$ as a generic container of edge objects. If we want to support a graph representation that can represent a graph G potentially containing both directed and undirected edges, then we have, for each vertex, three incidence containers, $I_{in}(v)$, $I_{out}(v)$, and $I_{un}(v)$, that store references to the edge objects associated with the directed incoming, directed outgoing, and undirected edges incident on v, respectively.

The adjacency list structure provides direct access from both the edges to the vertices and from the vertices to their incident edges. Being able to provide access between vertices and edges in both directions allows us to speed up the performance of a number of the graph methods by using an adjacency list structure instead of an edge list structure. We illustrate the adjacency list structure of a directed graph in Figure 6.4. For a vertex v, the space used by the incidence container of v is proportional to the degree of v, that is, it is $O(\deg(v))$. Thus, by Theorem 6.6, the space requirement of the adjacency list structure is $O(n+m)$.

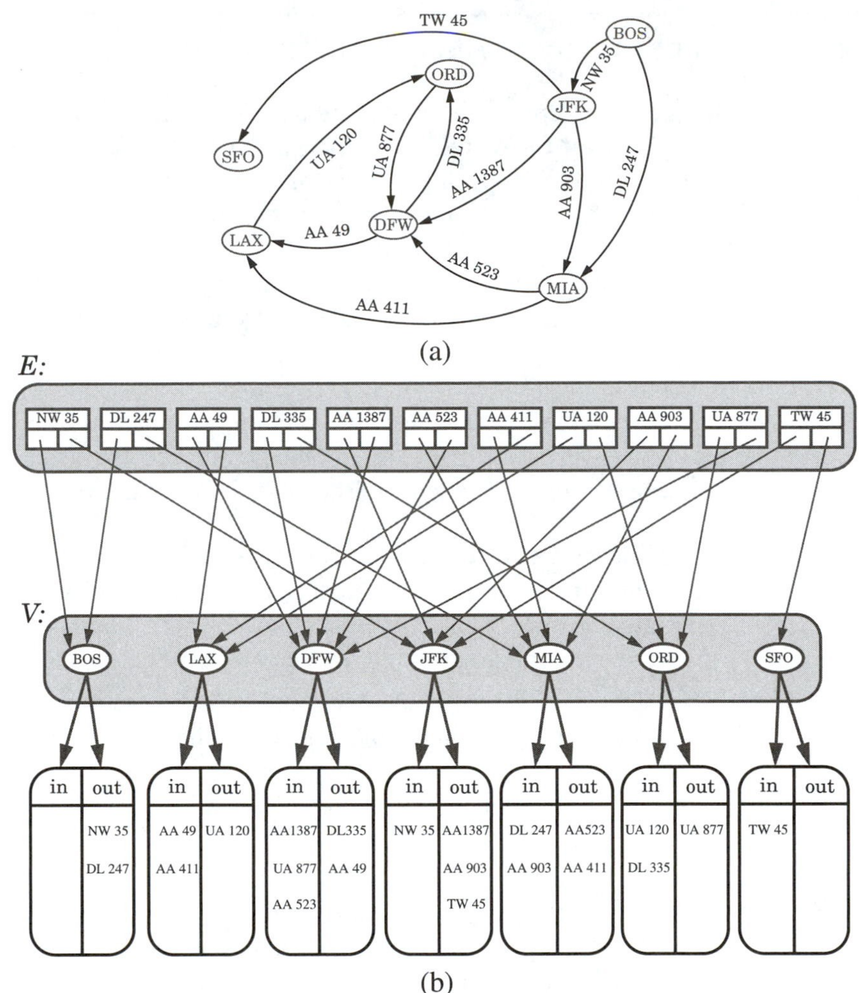

Figure 6.4: (a) A directed graph G; (b) schematic representation of the adjacency list structure of G. As in Figure 6.3, we visualize the elements of containers with names. Also, we only show the incidence containers for directed edges, since there are no undirected edges in this graph.

The adjacency list structure matches the performance of the edge list but also provides improved running time for the following methods:

- Methods returning iterators of incident edges or adjacent vertices for a vertex v can run in time proportional to their output size, that is, in $O(\deg(v))$ time.
- Method areAdjacent(u, v) can be performed by inspecting either the incidence container of u or that of v. By choosing the smaller of the two, we get $O(\min\{\deg(u), \deg(v)\})$ running time.
- Method removeVertex(v) requires calling incidentEdges(v) to identify the edges to be removed as a consequence of the operation. The subsequent $\deg(v)$ edge removals each take $O(1)$ time.

6.2.3 The Adjacency Matrix Structure

Like the adjacency list structure, the ***adjacency matrix*** representation of a graph also extends the edge-structure with an additional component. In this case, we augment the edge list with a matrix (a two-dimensional array) A that allows us to determine adjacencies between pairs of vertices in constant time. As we shall see, achieving this speedup comes at a price in the space usage of the data structure.

In the adjacency matrix representation, we number the vertices $0, 1, \ldots, n-1$, and we view the edges as being pairs of such integers. We represent the graph G with an $n \times n$ array, A, such that $A[i, j]$ stores a reference to the edge (i, j), if such an edge exists. If there is no edge (i, j), then $A[i, j]$ is null.

Specifically, the adjacency matrix extends the edge list structure as follows:

- A vertex object v also stores a distinct integer key in the range $0, 1, \ldots, n-1$, called the ***index*** of v. To simplify the discussion, we may refer to the vertex with index i simply as "vertex i."
- We keep a two-dimensional $n \times n$ array A, such that the cell $A[i, j]$ holds a reference to the edge e incident on vertices i and j, if such an edge exists. If the edge e, connecting vertices i and j, is undirected, then we store references to e in both $A[i, j]$ and $A[j, i]$. If there is no edge from vertex i to vertex j, then $A[i, j]$ references the null object (or some other indicator that this cell is associated with no edge).

Using an adjacency matrix A, we can perform method areAdjacent(v, w) in $O(1)$ time. We achieve this performance by accessing the vertices v and w to determine their respective indices i and j, and then testing whether the cell $A[i, j]$ is null or not. This performance achievement is traded off by an increase in the space usage, however, which is now $O(n^2)$, and in the running time of other methods. For example, methods such as incidentEdges and adjacentVerticesnow require that we examine an entire row or column of array A, which takes $O(n)$ time. The adjacency list structure is superior to the adjacency matrix in space, and is superior in time for all methods except for the areAdjacent method.

Historically, the adjacency matrix was the first representation used for graphs, with the adjacency matrix being defined strictly as a Boolean matrix, as follows:

$$A[i, j] = \begin{cases} 1 & \text{if } (i, j) \text{ is an edge} \\ 0 & \text{otherwise} \end{cases}$$

Thus, the adjacency matrix has a natural appeal as a mathematical structure (for example, an undirected graph has a symmetric adjacency matrix). Our adjacency matrix definition updates this historical perspective to an object-oriented framework. Most of the graph algorithms we examine will run most efficiently when acting upon a graph stored using the adjacency list representation. In some cases, however, a trade-off occurs, depending on how many edges are in the graph.

We illustrate an example adjacency matrix in Figure 6.5.

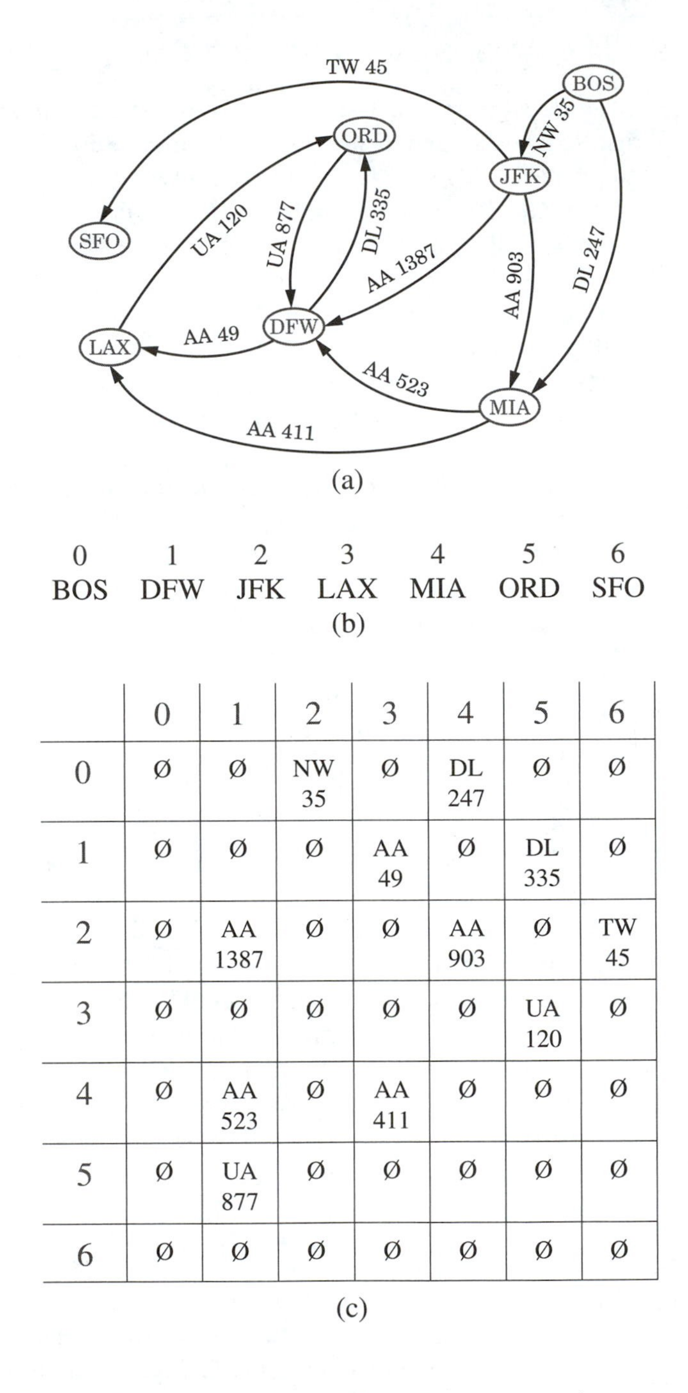

0	1	2	3	4	5	6
BOS	DFW	JFK	LAX	MIA	ORD	SFO

(b)

	0	1	2	3	4	5	6
0	∅	∅	NW 35	∅	DL 247	∅	∅
1	∅	∅	∅	AA 49	∅	DL 335	∅
2	∅	AA 1387	∅	∅	AA 903	∅	TW 45
3	∅	∅	∅	∅	∅	UA 120	∅
4	∅	AA 523	∅	AA 411	∅	∅	∅
5	∅	UA 877	∅	∅	∅	∅	∅
6	∅	∅	∅	∅	∅	∅	∅

(c)

Figure 6.5: Schematic representation of the adjacency matrix structure: (a) a directed graph G; (b) a numbering of its vertices; (c) the adjacency matrix A for G.

6.3 Graph Traversal

A ***traversal*** is a systematic procedure for exploring a graph by examining all of its vertices and edges. For example, a Web ***spider***, or ***crawler***, which is the data collecting part of a search engine, must explore a graph of hypertext documents by examining its vertices, which are the documents, and its edges, which are the hyperlinks between documents. A traversal is efficient if it visits all the vertices and edges in time proportional to their number, that is, in linear time.

6.3.1 Depth-First Search

The first traversal algorithm we consider is ***depth-first search*** (DFS) in an undirected graph. Depth-first search is useful for performing a number of computations on graphs, including finding a path from one vertex to another, determining whether or not a graph is connected, and computing a spanning tree of a connected graph.

Traversing a Graph via the Backtracking Technique

Depth-first search in an undirected graph G applies the ***backtracking*** technique and is analogous to wandering in a labyrinth with a string and a can of paint without getting lost. We begin at a specific starting vertex s in G, which we initialize by fixing one end of our string to s and painting s as "visited." The vertex s is now our "current" vertex—call our current vertex u. We then traverse G by considering an (arbitrary) edge (u,v) incident to the current vertex u. If the edge (u,v) leads us to an already visited (that is, painted) vertex v, then we immediately backtrack to vertex u. If, on the other hand, (u,v) leads to an unvisited vertex v, then we unroll our string, and go to v. We then paint v as "visited," and make it the current vertex, repeating the above computation. Eventually, we will get to a "dead end," that is, a current vertex u, such that all the edges incident on u lead to vertices already visited. Thus, taking any edge incident on u will cause us to return to u. To get out of this impasse, we roll our string back up, backtracking along the edge that brought us to u, going back to a previously visited vertex v. We then make v our current vertex and repeat the above computation for any edges incident upon v that we have not looked at before. If all of v's incident edges lead to visited vertices, then we again roll up our string and backtrack to the vertex we came from to get to v, and repeat the procedure at that vertex. Thus, we continue to backtrack along the path that we have traced so far until we find a vertex that has yet unexplored edges, at which point we take one such edge and continue the traversal. The process terminates when our backtracking leads us back to the start vertex s, and there are no more unexplored edges incident on s. This simple process traverses the edges of G in an elegant, systematic way. (See Figure 6.6.)

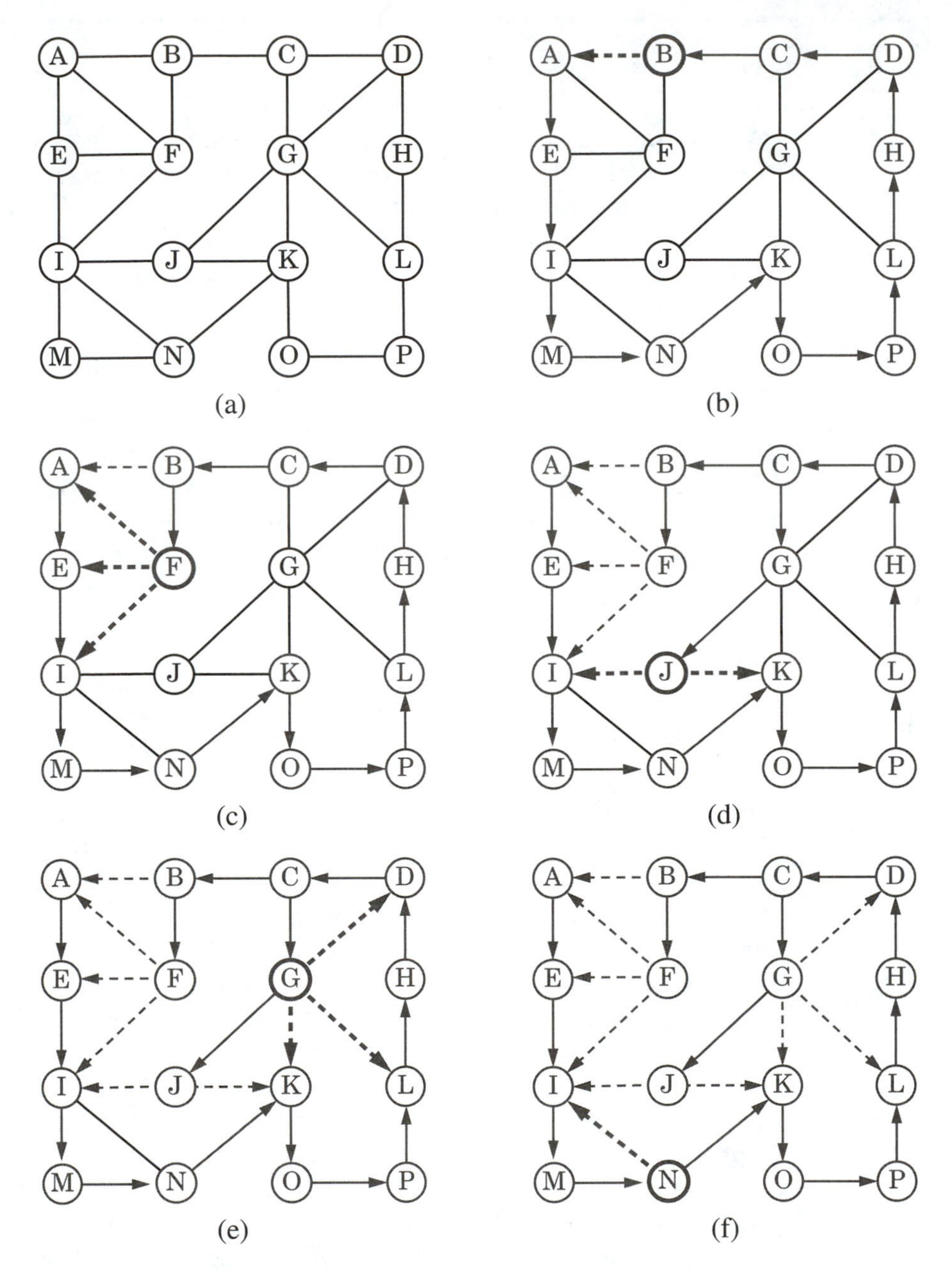

Figure 6.6: Example of depth-first search traversal on a graph starting at vertex A. Discovery edges are drawn with solid lines and back edges are drawn with dashed lines. The current vertex is drawn with a thick line: (a) input graph; (b) path of discovery edges traced from A until back edge (B,A) is hit; (c) reaching F, which is a dead end; (d) after backtracking to C, resuming with edge (C,G), and hitting another dead end, J; (e) after backtracking to G; (f) after backtracking to N.

Visualizing Depth-First Search

We can visualize a DFS traversal by orienting the edges along the direction in which they are explored during the traversal, distinguishing the edges used to discover new vertices, called ***discovery edges***, or ***tree edges***, from those that lead to already visited vertices, called ***back edges***. (See Figure 6.6f.) In the analogy above, discovery edges are the edges where we unroll our string when we traverse them, and back edges are the edges where we immediately return without unrolling any string. The discovery edges form a spanning tree of the connected component of the starting vertex s, called ***DFS tree***. We call the edges not in the DFS tree "back edges" because, assuming that the DFS tree is rooted at the start vertex, each such edge leads back from a vertex in this tree to one of its ancestors in the tree.

Recursive Depth-First Search

The pseudo-code for a DFS traversal starting at a vertex v follows our analogy with string and paint based on the backtracking technique. We use recursion to implement this approach. We assume that we have a mechanism (similar to the painting analogy) to determine if a vertex or edge has been explored or not, and to label the edges as discovery edges or back edges. A pseudo-code description of recursive DFS is given in Algorithm 6.7.

There are a number of observations that we can make about the depth-first search algorithm, many of which derive from the way the DFS algorithm partitions the edges of the undirected graph G into two groups, the discovery edges and the back edges. For example, since back edges always connect a vertex v to a previously visited vertex u, each back edge implies a cycle in G, consisting of the discovery edges from u to v plus the back edge (u,v).

Theorem 6.12, which follows, identifies some other important properties of the depth-first search traversal method.

Algorithm DFS(G,v):
  Input: A graph G and a vertex v of G
  Output: A labeling of the edges in the connected component of v as discovery edges and back edges

```
for all edges e in G.incidentEdges(v) do
  if edge e is unexplored then
    w ← G.opposite(v, e)
    if vertex w is unexplored then
      label e as a discovery edge
      recursively call DFS(G, w)
    else
      label e as a back edge
```

Algorithm 6.7: A Recursive description of the DFS algorithm.

Theorem 6.12: *Let G be an undirected graph on which a DFS traversal starting at a vertex s has been performed. Then the traversal visits all the vertices in the connected component of s, and the discovery edges form a spanning tree of the connected component of s.*

Proof: Suppose, for the sake of a contradiction, there is at least one vertex v in s's connected component not visited. Let w be the first unvisited vertex on some path from s to v (we may have $v = w$). Since w is the first unvisited vertex on this path, it has a neighbor u that was visited. But when we visited u, we must have considered the edge (u,w); hence, it cannot be correct that w is unvisited. Therefore, there are no unvisited vertices in s's connected component. Since we only mark edges when we go to unvisited vertices, we will never form a cycle with discovery edges, that is, the discovery edges form a tree. Moreover, this is a spanning tree because the depth-first search visits each vertex in the connected component of s. ■

Note that DFS is called exactly once on each vertex, and that every edge is examined exactly twice, once from each of its end vertices. Let m_s denote the number of edges in the connected component of vertex s. A DFS starting at s runs in $O(m_s)$ time provided the following conditions are satisfied:

- The graph is represented by a data structure with the following performance:
  - method incidentEdges(v) takes $O(\text{degree}(v))$ time
  - methods hasNext() and nextEdge() of the EdgeIterator returned by incidentEdges(v) each take $O(1)$ time
  - method opposite(v,e) takes $O(1)$ time.

  The adjacency list structure satisfies these properties; the adjacency matrix structure does not.
- We have a way to "mark" a vertex or edge as explored, and to test if a vertex or edge has been explored in $O(1)$ time. One way to do such marking is to extend the functionality of the node positions implementing vertices or edges to contain a visited flag. Another way is to use the decorator design pattern, which is discussed in Section 6.5.

Theorem 6.13: *Let G be a graph with n vertices and m edges represented with the adjacency list structure. A DFS traversal of G can be performed in $O(n+m)$ time. Also, there exist $O(n+m)$-time algorithms based on DFS for the following problems:*

- *Testing whether G is connected*
- *Computing a spanning forest of G*
- *Computing the connected components of G*
- *Computing a path between two vertices of G, or reporting that no such path exists*
- *Computing a cycle in G, or reporting that G has no cycles.*

We explore the details of the proof of this theorem in several exercises.

6.3.2 Biconnected Components

Let G be a connected graph. A ***separation edge*** of G is an edge whose removal disconnects G. A ***separation vertex*** is a vertex whose removal disconnects G. Separation edges and vertices correspond to single points of failure in a network; hence, we often wish to identify them. A connected graph G is ***biconnected*** if, for any two vertices u and v of G, there are two disjoint paths between u and v, that is, two paths sharing no common edges or vertices, except u and v. A ***biconnected component*** of G is a subgraph satisfying one of the following (see Figure 6.8):

- A subgraph of G that is biconnected and for which adding any additional vertices or edges of G would force it to stop being biconnected
- A single edge of G consisting of a separation edge and its endpoints.

If G is biconnected, it has one biconnected component: G itself. If G has no cycles, on the other hand, then each edge of G is a biconnected component. Biconnected components are important in computer networks, where vertices represent routers and edges represent connections, for even if a router in a biconnected component fails, messages can still be routed in that component using the remaining routers.

As stated in the following lemma, whose proof is left as an exercise (C-6.5), biconnectivity is equivalent to the absence of separation vertices and edges.

Lemma 6.14: *Let G be a connected graph. The following are equivalent:*

1. *G is biconnected.*
2. *For any two vertices of G, there is a simple cycle containing them.*
3. *G does not have separation vertices or separation edges.*

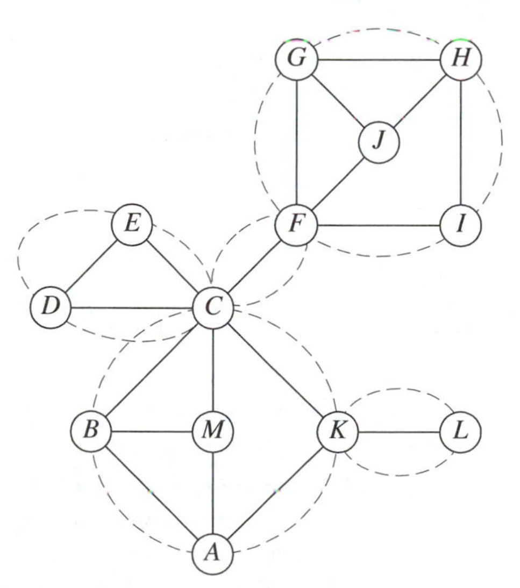

Figure 6.8: Biconnected components, shown circled with dashed lines. C, F, and K are separation vertices; (C,F) and (K,L) are separation edges.

Equivalence Classes and the Linked Relation

Any time we have a collection C of objects, we can define a Boolean relation, $R(x,y)$, for each pair x and y in C. That is, $R(x,y)$ is defined for each x and y in C as being either true or false. The relation R is an ***equivalence relation*** if it has the following properties:

- ***reflexive property***: $R(x,x)$ is true for each x in C.
- ***symmetric property***: $R(x,y) = R(y,x)$, for each pair x and y in C.
- ***transitive property***: If $R(x,y)$ is true and $R(y,z)$ is true, then $R(x,z)$ is true, for every x, y, and z in C.

For example, the usual "equals" operator (=) is an equivalence relation for any set of numbers. The ***equivalence class*** for any object x in C is the set of all objects y, such that $R(x,y)$ is true. Note that any equivalence relation R for a set C partitions the set C into disjoint subsets that consist of the equivalence classes of the objects in C.

We can define an interesting ***link relation*** on the edges of a graph G. We say two edges e and f of G are ***linked*** if $e = f$ or G has a simple cycle containing both e and f. The following lemma gives fundamental properties of the link relation.

Lemma 6.15: *Let G be a connected graph. Then,*

1. *The link relation forms an equivalence relation on the edges of G.*
2. *A biconnected component of G is the subgraph induced by an equivalence class of linked edges.*
3. *An edge e of G is a separation edge if and only if e forms a single-element equivalence class of linked edges.*
4. *A vertex v of G is a separation vertex if and only if v has incident edges in at least two distinct equivalence classes of linked edges.*

Proof: It is readily seen that the link relation is reflexive and symmetric. To show that it is transitive, suppose that edges f and g are linked, and edges g and h are linked. If $f = g$ or $g = h$, then $f = h$ or there is a simple cycle containing f and h; hence, f and h are linked. Suppose, then, that f, g, and h are distinct. That is, there is a simple cycle C_{fg} through f and g, and there is a simple cycle C_{gh} through g and h. Consider the graph obtained by the union of cycles C_{fg} and C_{gh}. While this graph may not be a simple cycle itself (although we could have $C_{fg} = C_{gh}$), it contains a simple cycle C_{fh} through f and h. Thus, f and h are linked. Therefore, the link relation is an equivalence relation.

The correspondence between equivalence classes of the link relation and biconnected components of G is a consequence of Lemma 6.14. ■

A Linked Approach to Computing Biconnected Components via DFS

Since the equivalence classes of the link relation on the edges of G are the same as the biconnected components, by Lemma 6.15, to construct the biconnected components of G we need only compute the equivalence classes of the link relation among G's edges. To perform this computation, let us begin with a DFS traversal of G, and construct an ***auxiliary graph*** B as follows (see Figure 6.9):

- The vertices of B are the edges of G.
- For every back edge e of G, let $f_1, \ldots, f_k$ be the discovery edges of G that form a cycle with e. Graph B contains the edges $(e, f_1), \ldots, (e, f_k)$.

Since there are $m - n + 1$ back edges and each cycle induced by a back edge has at most $O(n)$ edges, the graph B has at most $O(nm)$ edges.

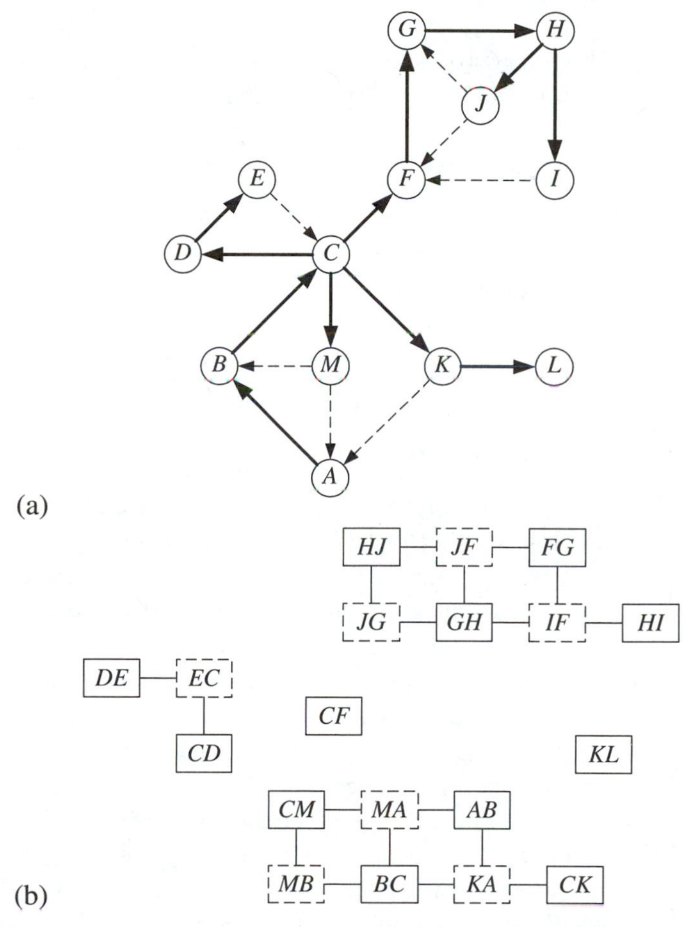

Figure 6.9: Auxiliary graph used to compute link components: (a) graph G on which a DFS traversal has been performed (the back edges are drawn with dashed lines); (b) auxiliary graph associated with G and its DFS traversal.

An $O(nm)$-Time Algorithm

From Figure 6.9, it appears that each connected component in B corresponds to an equivalence class in the link relation for the graph G. After all, we included an edge (e,f) in B for each back edge e found on the cycle containing f that was induced by e and the DFS spanning tree.

The following lemma, whose proof is left as an exercise (C-6.7), establishes a strong relationship between the graph B and the equivalence classes in the link relation on G's components of G, where, for brevity, we call the equivalence classes in the link relation the ***link components*** of G.

Lemma 6.16: *The connected components of the auxiliary graph B correspond to the link components of the graph G that induced B.*

Lemma 6.16 yields the following $O(nm)$-time algorithm for computing all the link components of a graph G with n vertices and m edges:

1. Perform a DFS traversal T on G.
2. Compute the auxiliary graph B by identifying the cycles of G induced by each back edge with respect to T.
3. Compute the connected components of B, for example, by performing a DFS traversal of the auxiliary graph B.
4. For each connected component of B, output the vertices of B (which are edges of G) as a link component of G.

From the identification of the link components in G, we can then determine the biconnected components, separation vertices, and separation edges of the graph G in linear time. Namely, after the edges of G have been partitioned into equivalence classes with respect to the link relation, the biconnected components, separation vertices, and separation edges of G can be identified in $O(n+m)$ time, using the simple rules listed in Lemma 6.15. Unfortunately, constructing the auxiliary graph B can take as much as $O(nm)$ time; hence, the bottleneck computation in this algorithm is the construction of B.

But note that we don't actually need all of the auxiliary graph B in order to find the biconnected components of G. We only need to identify the connected components in B. Thus, it would actually be sufficient if we were to simply compute a spanning tree for each connected component in B, that is, a spanning forest for B. Since the connected components in a spanning forest for B are the same as in the graph B itself, we don't actually need all the edges of B—just enough of them to construct a spanning forest of B.

Therefore, let us concentrate on how we can apply this more efficient spanning-forest approach to compute the equivalence classes of the edges of G with respect to the link relation.

A Linear-Time Algorithm

As outlined above, we can reduce the time required to compute the link components of G to $O(m)$ time by using an auxiliary graph of smaller size, which is a spanning forest of B. The algorithm is described in Algorithm 6.10.

Algorithm LinkComponents(G):
  Input: A connected graph G
  Output: The link components of G

```
Let F be an initially empty auxiliary graph.
Perform a DFS traversal of G starting at an arbitrary vertex s.
Add each DFS discovery edge f as a vertex in F and mark f "unlinked."
For each vertex v of G, let p(v) be the parent of v in the DFS spanning tree.
for each vertex v, in increasing rank order as visited in the DFS traversal do
  for each back edge e = (u,v) with destination v do
    Add e as a vertex of the graph F.
    {March up from u to s adding edges to F only as necessary.}
    while u ≠ s do
      Let f be the vertex in F corresponding to the discovery edge (u, p(u)).
      Add the edge (e, f) to F.
      if f is marked "unlinked" then
        Mark f as "linked."
        u ← p(u)
      else
        u ← s          {shortcut to the end of the while loop}
Compute the connected components of the graph F.
```

Algorithm 6.10: A linear-time algorithm for computing the link components. Note that a connected component in F consisting of an individual "unlinked" vertex corresponds to a separation edge (related only to itself in the link relation).

Let us analyze the running time of LinkComponents, from Algorithm 6.10. The initial DFS traversal of G takes $O(m)$ time. The main computation, however, is the construction of the auxiliary graph F, which takes time proportional to the number of vertices and edges of F. Note that at some point in the execution of the algorithm, each edge of G is added as a vertex of F. We use an accounting charge method to account for the edges of F. Namely, each time we add to F an edge (e,f), from a newly encountered back edge e to a discover edge f, let us charge this operation to f if f is marked "unlinked" and to e otherwise. From the construction of the inner while-loop, we see that we charge each vertex of F at most once during the algorithm using this scheme. We conclude that the construction of F takes $O(m)$ time. Finally, the computation of the connected components of F, which correspond to the link components of G, takes $O(m)$ time.

The correctness of the above algorithm follows from the fact that the graph F in LinkComponents is a spanning forest of the graph B mentioned in Lemma 6.16. For details, see Exercise C-6.8. Therefore we summarize with the following theorem, and give an example of LinkComponents in Figure 6.11.

Theorem 6.17: *Given a connected graph G with m edges, we can compute G's biconnected components, separation vertices, and separation edges in $O(m)$ time.*

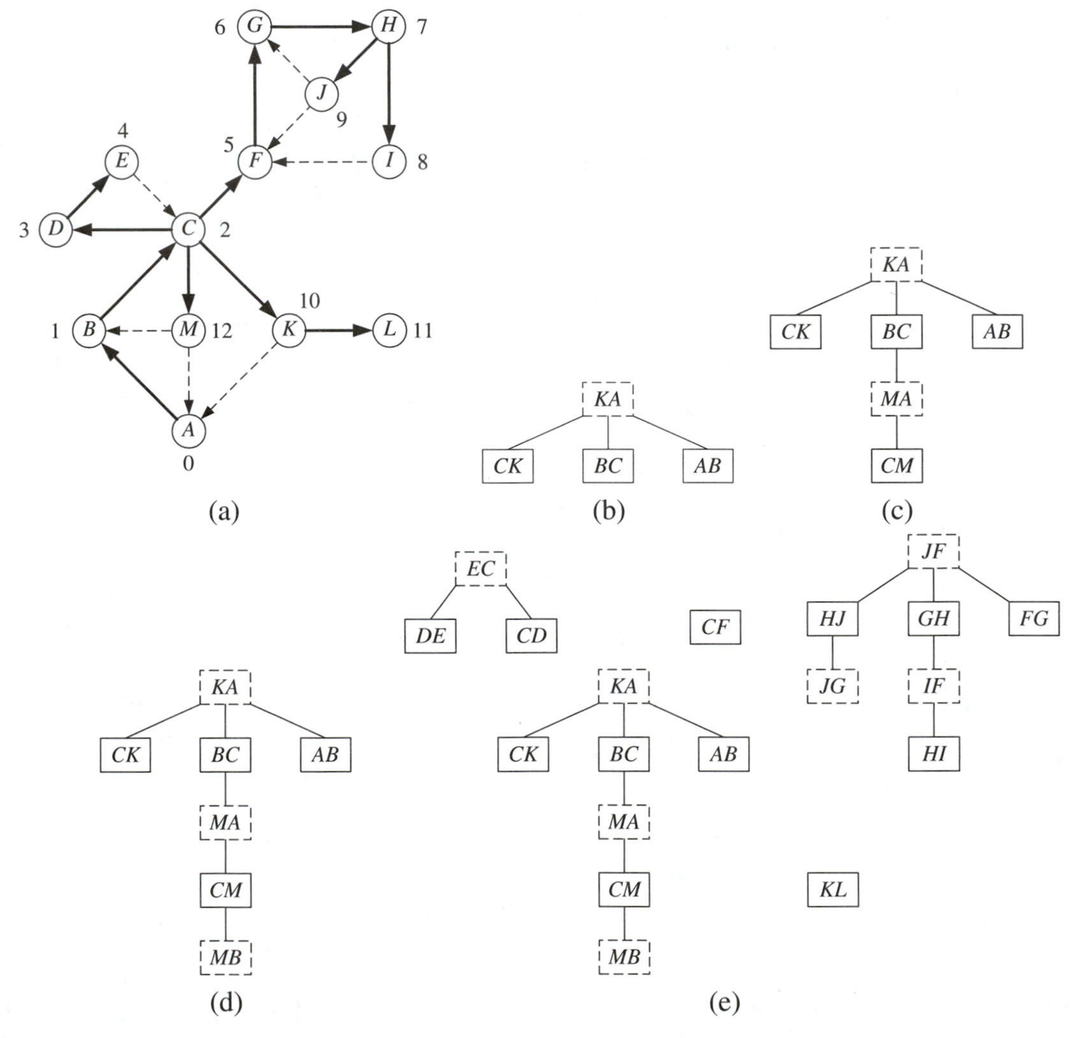

Figure 6.11: Sample execution of algorithm LinkComponents (Algorithm 6.10): (a) input graph G after a DFS traversal (the vertices are labeled by their rank in the visit order, and the back edges are drawn with dashed lines); auxiliary graph F after processing (b) back edge (K,A), (c) back edge (M,A), and (d) back edge $(M.B)$; (e) graph F at the end of the algorithm.

6.3.3 Breadth-First Search

In this section, we consider the ***breadth-first search*** (BFS) traversal algorithm. Like DFS, BFS traverses a connected component of a graph, and in so doing, defines a useful spanning tree. BFS is less "adventurous" than DFS, however. Instead of wandering the graph, BFS proceeds in rounds and subdivides the vertices into ***levels***. BFS can also be thought of as a traversal using a string and paint, with BFS unrolling the string in a more "conservative" manner.

BFS starts at a given vertex s, which is at level 0 and defines the "anchor" for our string. In the first round, we let out the string the length of one edge and we visit all the vertices we can reach without unrolling the string any farther. In this case, we visit, and paint as "visited," the vertices adjacent to the start vertex s—these vertices are placed into level 1. In the second round, we unroll the string the length of two edges and we visit all the new vertices we can reach without unrolling our string any farther. These new vertices, which are adjacent to level 1 vertices and not previously assigned to a level, are placed into level 2, and so on. The BFS traversal terminates when every vertex has been visited.

Pseudo-code for a BFS traversal starting at a vertex s is shown in Algorithm 6.12. We use auxiliary space to label edges, mark visited vertices, and store containers associated with levels. That is, the containers L_0, L_1, L_2, and so on, store the nodes that are in level 0, level 1, level 2, and so on. These containers could, for example, be implemented as queues. They also allow BFS to be nonrecursive.

Algorithm BFS(G,s):
 Input: A graph G and a vertex s of G
 Output: A labeling of the edges in the connected component of s as discovery edges and cross edges

```
create an empty container L_0
insert s into L_0
i ← 0
while L_i is not empty do
  create an empty container L_{i+1}
  for each vertex v in L_i do
    for all edges e in G.incidentEdges(v) do
      if edge e is unexplored then
        let w be the other endpoint of e
        if vertex w is unexplored then
          label e as a discovery edge
          insert w into L_{i+1}
        else
          label e as a cross edge
  i ← i+1
```

Algorithm 6.12: BFS traversal of a graph.

We illustrate a BFS traversal in Figure 6.13.

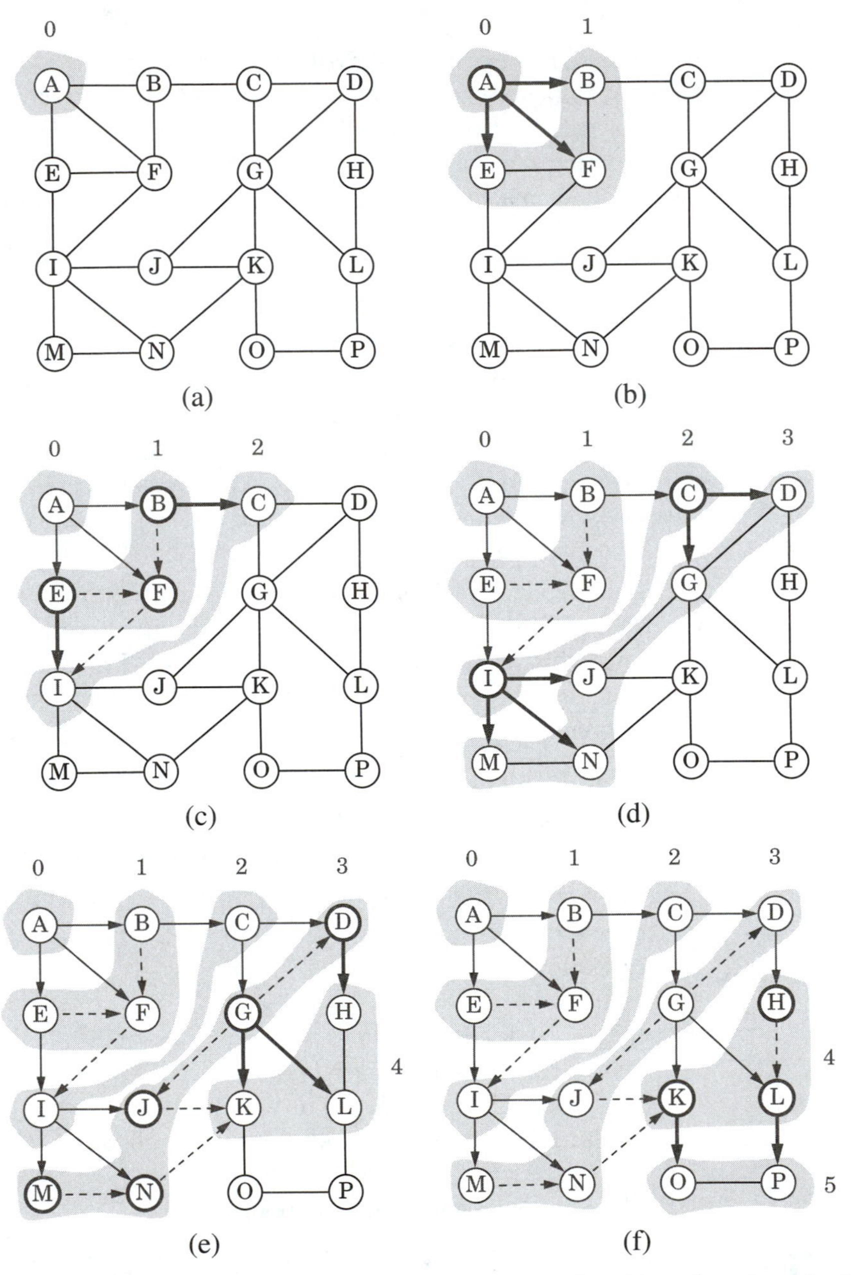

Figure 6.13: Example of breadth-first search traversal, where the edges incident on a vertex are explored by the alphabetical order of the adjacent vertices. The discovery edges are shown with solid lines and the cross edges are shown with dashed lines: (a) graph before the traversal; (b) discovery of level 1; (c) discovery of level 2; (d) discovery of level 3; (e) discovery of level 4; (f) discovery of level 5.

One of the nice properties of the BFS approach is that, in performing the BFS traversal, we can label each vertex by the length of a shortest path (in terms of the number of edges) from the start vertex s. In particular, if vertex v is placed into level i by a BFS starting at vertex s, then the length of a shortest path from s to v is i.

As with DFS, we can visualize the BFS traversal by orienting the edges along the direction in which they are explored during the traversal, and by distinguishing the edges used to discover new vertices, called ***discovery edges***, from those that lead to already visited vertices, called ***cross edges***. (See Figure 6.13f.) As with the DFS, the discovery edges form a spanning tree, which in this case we call the ***BFS tree***. We do not call the nontree edges "back edges" in this case, however, for none of them connects a vertex to one of its ancestors. Every nontree edge connects a vertex v to another vertex that is neither v's ancestor nor its descendent.

The BFS traversal algorithm has a number of interesting properties, some of which we state in the theorem that follows.

Theorem 6.18: *Let G be an undirected graph on which a BFS traversal starting at vertex s has been performed. Then:*

- *The traversal visits all the vertices in the connected component of s.*
- *The discovery edges form a spanning tree T of the connected component of s.*
- *For each vertex v at level i, the path of tree T between s and v has i edges, and any other path of G between s and v has at least i edges.*
- *If (u,v) is a cross edge, then the level numbers of u and v differ by at most 1.*

We leave the justification of this theorem as an exercise (C-6.20). The analysis of the running time of BFS is similar to the one of DFS.

Theorem 6.19: *Let G be a graph with n vertices and m edges represented with the adjacency list structure. A BFS traversal of G takes $O(n+m)$ time. Also, there exist $O(n+m)$-time algorithms based on BFS for the following problems:*

- *Testing whether G is connected*
- *Computing a spanning forest of G*
- *Computing the connected components of G*
- *Given a start vertex s of G, computing, for every vertex v of G, a path with the minimum number of edges between s and v, or reporting that no such path exists.*
- *Computing a cycle in G, or reporting that G has no cycles.*

Comparing BFS and DFS

By Theorem 6.19, the BFS traversal can do everything we claimed for the DFS traversal. There are a number of interesting differences between these two methods, however, and there are, in fact, a number of tasks that each can do better than the other. The BFS traversal is better at finding shortest paths in a graph (where distance is measured by the number of edges). Also, it produces a spanning tree such that all the nontree edges are cross edges. The DFS traversal is better for answering complex connectivity questions, such as determining if every pair of vertices in a graph can be connected by two disjoint paths. Also, it produces a spanning tree such that all the nontree edges are back edges. These properties only hold for undirected graphs, however. Nevertheless, as we explore in the next section, there are a number of interesting properties for the directed analogues of DFS and BFS.

6.4 Directed Graphs

In this section, we consider issues that are specific to directed graphs. Recall that a directed graph, which is also known as a ***digraph***, is a graph whose edges are all directed.

Reachability

A fundamental issue with directed graphs is the notion of ***reachability***, which deals with determining where we can get to in a directed graph. For example, in a computer network with unidirectional connections, such as those involving satellite connections, it is important to know whether we can reach every other node from any given node in the network. A traversal in a directed graph always goes along directed paths, that is, paths where all the edges are traversed according to their respective directions. Given vertices u and v of a digraph $\vec{G}$, we say that u ***reaches*** v (and v is ***reachable*** from u) if $\vec{G}$ has a directed path from u to v. We also say that a vertex v reaches an edge (w,z) if v reaches the origin vertex w of the edge.

A digraph $\vec{G}$ is ***strongly connected*** if, for any two vertices u and v of $\vec{G}$, u reaches v and v reaches u. A ***directed cycle*** of $\vec{G}$ is a cycle where all the edges are traversed according to their respective directions. (Note that $\vec{G}$ may have a cycle consisting of two edges with opposite direction between the same pair of vertices.) A digraph $\vec{G}$ is ***acyclic*** if it has no directed cycles. (See Figure 6.14 for some examples.)

The ***transitive closure*** of a digraph $\vec{G}$ is the digraph $\vec{G}^*$ such that the vertices of $\vec{G}^*$ are the same as the vertices of $\vec{G}$, and $\vec{G}^*$ has an edge (u,v), whenever $\vec{G}$ has a directed path from u to v. That is, we define $\vec{G}^*$ by starting with the digraph $\vec{G}$ and adding in an extra edge (u,v) for each u and v, such that v is reachable from u (and there isn't already an edge (u,v) in $\vec{G}$).

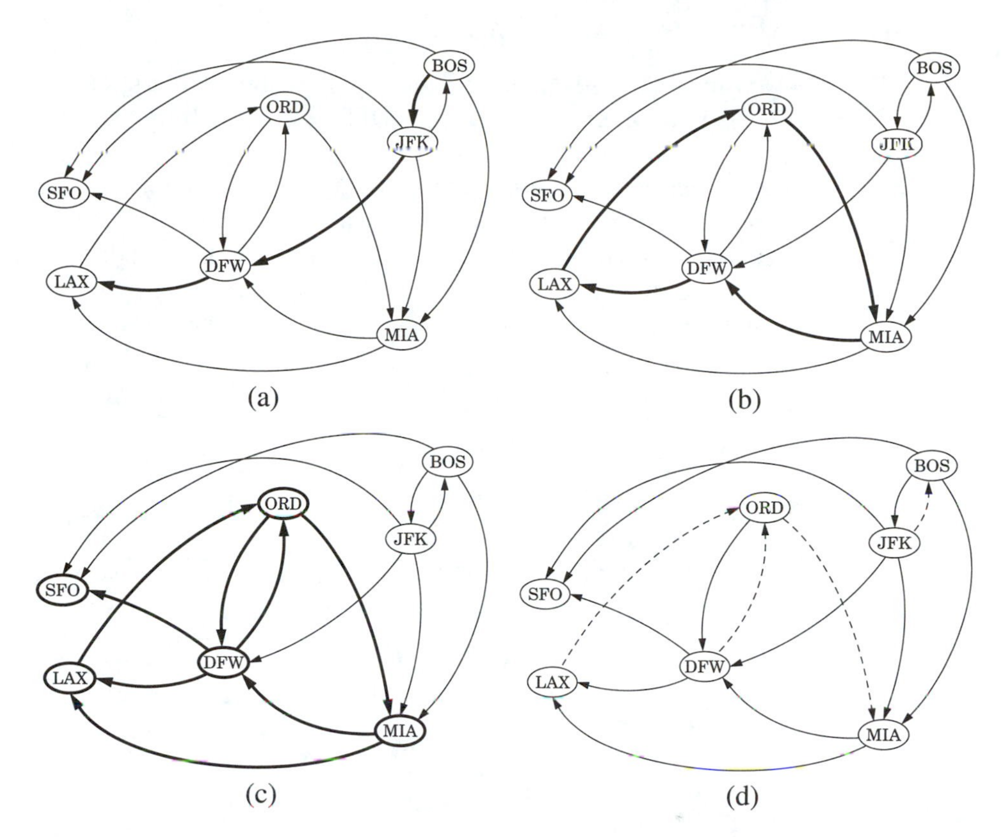

Figure 6.14: Examples of reachability in a digraph: (a) a directed path from BOS to LAX is drawn with thick lines; (b) a directed cycle (ORD, MIA, DFW, LAX, ORD) is drawn with thick lines; its vertices induce a strongly connected subgraph; (c) the subgraph of the vertices and edges reachable from ORD is shown with thick lines; (d) removing the dashed edges gives an acyclic digraph.

Interesting problems that deal with reachability in a digraph $\vec{G}$ include the following:

- Given vertices u and v, determine whether u reaches v.
- Find all the vertices of $\vec{G}$ that are reachable from a given vertex s.
- Determine whether $\vec{G}$ is strongly connected.
- Determine whether $\vec{G}$ is acyclic.
- Compute the transitive closure $\vec{G}^*$ of $\vec{G}$.

In the remainder of this section, we explore some efficient algorithms for solving these problems.

6.4.1 Traversing a Digraph

As with undirected graphs, we can explore a digraph in a systematic way with methods akin to the depth-first search (DFS) and breadth-first search (BFS) algorithms defined previously for undirected graphs (Sections 6.3.1 and 6.3.3). Such explorations can be used, for example, to answer reachability questions. The directed depth-first search and breadth-first search methods we develop in this section for performing such explorations are very similar to their undirected counterparts. In fact, the only real difference is that the directed depth-first search and breadth-first search methods only traverse edges according to their respective directions.

The directed version of DFS starting at a vertex v is illustrated in Figure 6.15.

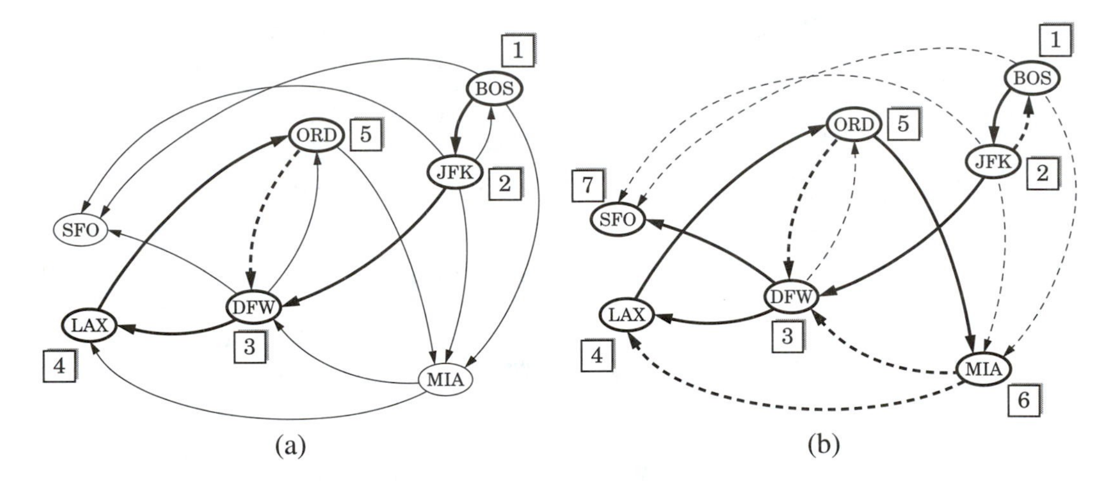

Figure 6.15: An example of a DFS in a digraph: (a) intermediate step, where, for the first time, an already visited vertex (DFW) is reached; (b) the completed DFS. The discovery edges are shown with thick solid lines, the back edges are shown with thick dashed lines, and the forward and cross edges are shown with dashed thin lines. The order in which the vertices are visited is indicated by a label next to each vertex. The edge (ORD,DFW) is a back edge, but (DFW,ORD) is a forward edge. Edge (BOS,SFO) is a forward edge, and (SFO,LAX) is a cross edge.

A directed DFS on a digraph $\vec{G}$ partitions the edges of $\vec{G}$ reachable from the starting vertex into ***discovery edges*** or ***tree edges***, which lead us to discover a new vertex, and ***nontree edges***, which take us to a previously visited vertex. The discovery edges form a tree rooted at the starting vertex, called the ***directed DFS tree***. Also, we can distinguish three kinds of nontree edges (see Figure 6.15b):

- ***back edges***, which connect a vertex to an ancestor in the DFS tree
- ***forward edges***, which connect a vertex to a descendent in the DFS tree
- ***cross edges***, which connect a vertex to a vertex that is neither its ancestor nor its descendent.

Theorem 6.20: *Let $\vec{G}$ be a digraph. Depth-first search on $\vec{G}$ starting at a vertex s visits all the vertices of $\vec{G}$ that are reachable from s. Also, the DFS tree contains directed paths from s to every vertex reachable from s.*

Proof: Let V_s be the subset of vertices of $\vec{G}$ visited by DFS starting at vertex s. We want to show that V_s contains s and every vertex reachable from s belongs to V_s. Suppose, for the sake of a contradiction, that there is a vertex w reachable from s that is not in V_s. Consider a directed path from s to w, and let (u,v) be the first edge on such a path taking us out of V_s, that is, u is in V_s but v is not in V_s. When DFS reaches u, it explores all the outgoing edges of u, and thus must also reach vertex v via edge (u,v). Hence, v should be in V_s, and we have obtained a contradiction. Therefore, V_s must contain every vertex reachable from s. ■

Analyzing the running time of the directed DFS method is analogous to that for its undirected counterpart. A recursive call is made for each vertex exactly once, and each edge is traversed exactly once (along its direction). Hence, if the subgraph reachable from a vertex s has m_s edges, a directed DFS starting at s runs in $O(n_s + m_s)$ time, provided the digraph is represented with an adjacency list.

By Theorem 6.20, we can use DFS to find all the vertices reachable from a given vertex, and hence to find the transitive closure of $\vec{G}$. That is, we can perform a DFS, starting from each vertex v of $\vec{G}$, to see which vertices w are reachable from v, adding an edge (v,w) to the transitive closure for each such w. Likewise, by repeatedly traversing digraph $\vec{G}$ with a DFS, starting in turn at each vertex, we can easily test whether $\vec{G}$ is strongly connected. Therefore, $\vec{G}$ is strongly connected if each DFS visits all the vertices of $\vec{G}$.

Theorem 6.21: *Let $\vec{G}$ be a digraph with n vertices and m edges. The following problems can be solved by an algorithm that runs in $O(n(n+m))$ time:*

- *Computing, for each vertex v of $\vec{G}$, the subgraph reachable from v*
- *Testing whether $\vec{G}$ is strongly connected*
- *Computing the transitive closure $\vec{G}^*$ of $\vec{G}$.*

Testing for Strong Connectivity

Actually, we can determine if a directed graph $\vec{G}$ is strongly connected much faster than $O(n(n+m))$ time, just using two depth-first searches.

We begin by performing a DFS of our directed graph $\vec{G}$ starting at an arbitrary vertex s. If there is any vertex of $\vec{G}$ that is not visited by this DFS, and is not reachable from s, then the graph is not strongly connected. So, if this first DFS visits each vertex of $\vec{G}$, then we reverse all the edges of $\vec{G}$ (using the reverseDirection method) and perform another DFS starting at s in this "reverse" graph. If every vertex of $\vec{G}$ is visited by this second DFS, then the graph is strongly connected, for each of the vertices visited in this DFS can reach s. Since this algorithm makes just two DFS traversals of $\vec{G}$, it runs in $O(n+m)$ time.

Directed Breadth-First Search

As with DFS, we can extend breadth-first search (BFS) to work for directed graphs. The algorithm still visits vertices level by level and partitions the set of edges into ***tree edges*** (or ***discovery edges***), which together form a directed ***breadth-first search*** tree rooted at the start vertex, and ***nontree edges***. Unlike the directed DFS method, however, the directed BFS method only leaves two kinds of nontree edges:

- ***back edges***, which connect a vertex to one of its ancestors, and
- ***cross edges***, which connect a vertex to another vertex that is neither its ancestor nor its descendent.

There are no forward edges, which is a fact we explore in an exercise (C-6.14).

6.4.2 Transitive Closure

In this section, we explore an alternative technique for computing the transitive closure of a digraph. That is, we describe a direct method for determining all pairs of vertices (v,w) in a directed graph such that w is reachable from v. Such information is useful, for example, in computer networks, for it allows us to immediately know if we can route a message from a node v to a node w, or whether it is appropriate to say "you can't get there from here" with respect to this message.

Let $\vec{G}$ be a digraph with n vertices and m edges. We compute the transitive closure of $\vec{G}$ in a series of rounds. We initialize $\vec{G}_0 = \vec{G}$. We also arbitrarily number the vertices of $\vec{G}$ as

$$v_1, v_2, \ldots, v_n.$$

We then begin the computation of the rounds, beginning with round 1. In a generic round k, we construct digraph $\vec{G}_k$ starting with $\vec{G}_k = \vec{G}_{k-1}$ and adding to $\vec{G}_k$ the directed edge (v_i, v_j) if digraph $\vec{G}_{k-1}$ contains both the edges (v_i, v_k) and (v_k, v_j). In this way, we will enforce a simple rule embodied in the lemma that follows.

Lemma 6.22: *For $i = 1, \ldots, n$, digraph $\vec{G}_k$ has an edge (v_i, v_j) if and only if digraph $\vec{G}$ has a directed path from v_i to v_j, whose intermediate vertices (if any) are in the set $\{v_1, \ldots, v_k\}$. In particular, $\vec{G}_n$ is equal to $\vec{G}^*$, the transitive closure of $\vec{G}$.*

This lemma suggests a simple ***dynamic programming*** algorithm (Section 5.3) for computing the transitive closure of $\vec{G}$, which is known as the ***Floyd-Warshall algorithm***. Pseudo-code for this method is given in Algorithm 6.16.

The running time of the Floyd-Warshall algorithm is easy to analyze. The main loop is executed n times and the inner loop considers each of $O(n^2)$ pairs of vertices, performing a constant-time computation for each pair. If we use a data structure, such as the adjacency matrix structure, that supports methods areAdjacent and insertDirectedEdge in $O(1)$ time, we have that the total running time is $O(n^3)$.

```
Algorithm FloydWarshall(G⃗):
    Input: A digraph G⃗ with n vertices
    Output: The transitive closure G⃗* of G⃗

    let v_1, v_2, ..., v_n be an arbitrary numbering of the vertices of G⃗
    G⃗_0 ← G⃗
    for k ← 1 to n do
        G⃗_k ← G⃗_{k-1}
        for i ← 1 to n, i ≠ k do
            for j ← 1 to n, j ≠ i,k do
                if both edges (v_i, v_k) and (v_k, v_j) are in G⃗_{k-1} then
                    if G⃗_k does not contain directed edge (v_i, v_j) then
                        add directed edge (v_i, v_j) to G⃗_k
    return G⃗_n
```

Algorithm 6.16: The Floyd-Warshall algorithm. This dynamic programming algorithm computes the transitive closure $\vec{G}^*$ of G by incrementally computing a series of digraphs $\vec{G}_0, \vec{G}_1, \ldots, \vec{G}_n$, for $k = 1, \ldots, n$.

The above description and analysis imply the following theorem.

Theorem 6.23: *Let $\vec{G}$ be a digraph with n vertices represented by the adjacency matrix structure. The Floyd-Warshall algorithm computes the transitive closure $\vec{G}^*$ of $\vec{G}$ in $O(n^3)$ time.*

Performance of the Floyd-Warshall Algorithm

We compare now the running time of the Floyd-Warshall algorithm with that of the more complicated algorithm of Theorem 6.21, which repeatedly performs a DFS n times, starting at each vertex.

If the digraph is represented by an adjacency matrix structure, then a DFS traversal takes $O(n^2)$ time (we explore the reason for this in an exercise). Thus, running DFS n times takes $O(n^3)$ time, which is no better than a single execution of the Floyd-Warshall algorithm

If the digraph is represented by an adjacency list structure, then running the DFS algorithm n times would take $O(n(n+m))$ time. Even so, if the graph is ***dense***, that is, if it has $\Theta(n^2)$ edges, then this approach still runs in $O(n^3)$ time.

Thus, the only case where the algorithm of Theorem 6.21 is better than the Floyd-Warshall algorithm is when the graph is not dense and is represented using an adjacency list structure.

We illustrate an example run of the Floyd-Warshall algorithm in Figure 6.17.

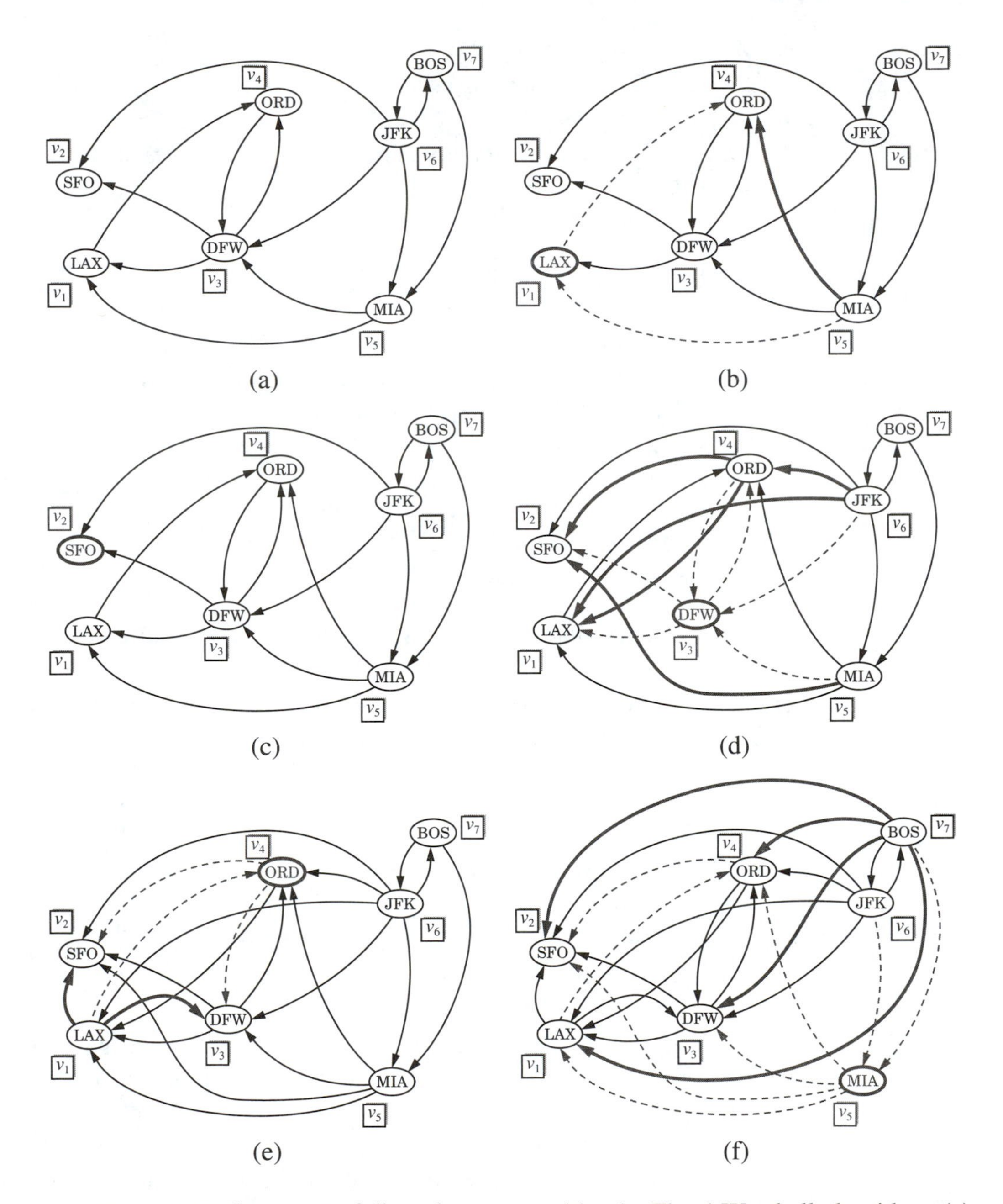

Figure 6.17: Sequence of digraphs computed by the Floyd-Warshall algorithm: (a) initial digraph $\vec{G} = \vec{G}_0$ and numbering of the vertices; (b) digraph $\vec{G}_1$; (c) $\vec{G}_2$; (d) $\vec{G}_3$; (e) $\vec{G}_4$; (f) $\vec{G}_5$. Note that $\vec{G}_5 = \vec{G}_6 = \vec{G}_7$. If digraph $\vec{G}_{k-1}$ has the edges (v_i, v_k) and (v_k, v_j), but not the edge (v_i, v_j), in the drawing of digraph $\vec{G}_k$, we show edges (v_i, v_k) and (v_k, v_j) with dashed thin lines, and edge (v_i, v_j) with a solid thick line.

6.4.3 DFS and Garbage Collection

In some languages, like C and C++, the memory space for objects must be explicitly allocated and deallocated by the programmer. This memory-allocation duty is often overlooked by beginning programmers, and, when done incorrectly, it can even be the source of frustrating programming errors for experienced programmers. Thus, the designers of other languages, like Java, place the burden of memory management on the run-time environment. A Java programmer does not have to explicitly deallocate the memory for some object when its life is over. Instead, the ***garbage collector*** mechanism deallocates the memory for such objects.

In Java, memory for most objects is allocated from a pool of memory called the "memory heap" (not to be confused with the heap data structure). In addition, the running threads (Section 2.1.2) store the space for their instance variables in their respective method stacks (Section 2.1.1). Since instance variables in the method stacks can refer to objects in the memory heap, all the variables and objects in the method stacks of running threads are called ***root objects***. All those objects that can be reached by following object references that start from a root object are called ***live objects***. The live objects are the active objects currently being used by the running program; these objects should ***not*** be deallocated. For example, a running Java program may store, in a variable, a reference to a sequence S that is implemented using a doubly linked list. The reference variable to S is a root object, while the object for S is a live object, as are all the node objects that are referenced from this object and all the elements that are referenced from these node objects.

From time to time, the Java virtual machine (JVM) may notice that available space in the memory heap is becoming scarce. At such times, the JVM can elect to reclaim the space that is being used for objects that are no longer live. This reclamation process is known as ***garbage collection***. There are several different algorithms for garbage collection, but one of the most used is the ***mark-sweep algorithm***.

The Mark-Sweep Algorithm

In the mark-sweep garbage collection algorithm, we associate a "mark" bit with each object that identifies if that object is live or not. When we determine at some point that garbage collection is needed, we suspend all other running threads and clear all of the mark bits of objects currently allocated in the memory heap. We then trace through the Java stacks of the currently running threads and we mark all of the (root) objects in these stacks as "live." We must then determine all of the other live objects—the ones that are reachable from the root objects. To do this efficiently, we should use the directed-graph version of the depth-first search traversal. In this case, each object in the memory heap is viewed as a vertex in a directed graph, and the reference from one object to another is viewed as an edge. By performing a directed DFS from each root object, we can correctly identify and mark each live object. This process is known as the "mark" phase. Once this process has completed, we then scan through the memory heap and reclaim any space that is being used for an object that has not been marked. This scanning process is known as the "sweep" phase, and when it completes, we resume running the suspended threads. Thus, the mark-sweep garbage collection algorithm will reclaim unused space in time proportional to the number of live objects and their references plus the size of the memory heap.

Performing DFS In-place

The mark-sweep algorithm correctly reclaims unused space in the memory heap, but there is an important issue we must face during the mark phase. Since we are reclaiming memory space at a time when available memory is scarce, we must take care not to use extra space during the garbage collection itself. The trouble is that the DFS algorithm, in the recursive way we have described it, can use space proportional to the number of vertices in the graph. In the case of garbage collection, the vertices in our graph are the objects in the memory heap; hence, we don't have this much memory to use. So our only alternative is to find a way to perform DFS in-place rather than recursively, that is, we must perform DFS using only a constant amount of additional storage.

The main idea for performing DFS in-place is to simulate the recursion stack using the edges of the graph (which in the case of garbage collection correspond to object references). Whenever we traverse an edge from a visited vertex v to a new vertex w, we change the edge (v,w) stored in v's adjacency list to point back to v's parent in the DFS tree. When we return back to v (simulating the return from the "recursive" call at w), we can now switch the edge we modified to point back to w. Of course, we need to have some way of identifying which edge we need to change back. One possibility is to number the references going out of v as 1, 2, and so on, and store, in addition to the mark bit (which we are using for the "visited" tag in our DFS), a count identifier that tells us which edges we have modified.

Using a count identifier of course requires an extra word of storage per object. This extra word can be avoided in some implementations, however. For example, many implementations of the Java virtual machine represent an object as a composition of a reference with a type identifier (which indicates if this object is an Integer or some other type) and as a reference to the other objects or data fields for this object. Since the type reference is always supposed to be the first element of the composition in such implementations, we can use this reference to "mark" the edge we changed when leaving an object v and going to some object w. We simply swap the reference at v that refers to the type of v with the reference at v that refers to w. When we return to v, we can quickly identify the edge (v,w) we changed, because it will be the first reference in the composition for v, and the position of the reference to v's type will tell us the place where this edge belongs in v's adjacency list. Thus, whether we use this edge-swapping trick or a count identifier, we can implement DFS in-place without affecting its asymptotic running time.

6.4.4 Directed Acyclic Graphs

Directed graphs without directed cycles are encountered in many applications. Such a digraph is often referred to as a ***directed acyclic graph***, or ***dag***, for short. Applications of such graphs include the following:

- Inheritance between C++ classes or Java interfaces
- Prerequisites between courses of a degree program
- Scheduling constraints between the tasks of a project.

Example 6.24: *In order to manage a large project, it is convenient to break it up into a collection of smaller tasks. The tasks, however, are rarely independent, because scheduling constraints exist between them. (For example, in a house building project, the task of ordering nails obviously precedes the task of nailing shingles to the roof deck.) Clearly, scheduling constraints cannot have circularities, because a circularity would make the project impossible. (For example, in order to get a job you need to have work experience, but in order to get work experience you need to have a job.) The scheduling constraints impose restrictions on the order in which the tasks can be executed. Namely, if a constraint says that task a must be completed before task b is started, then a must precede b in the order of execution of the tasks. Thus, if we model a feasible set of tasks as vertices of a directed graph, and we place a directed edge from v to w whenever the task for v must be executed before the task for w, then we define a directed acyclic graph.*

The above example motivates the following definition. Let $\vec{G}$ be a digraph with n vertices. A ***topological ordering*** of $\vec{G}$ is an ordering $(v_1, v_2, \ldots, v_n)$ of the vertices of $\vec{G}$ such that for every edge (v_i, v_j) of $\vec{G}$, $i < j$. That is, a topological ordering is an ordering such that any directed path in $\vec{G}$ traverses vertices in increasing order. (See Figure 6.18.) Note that a digraph may have more than one topological ordering.

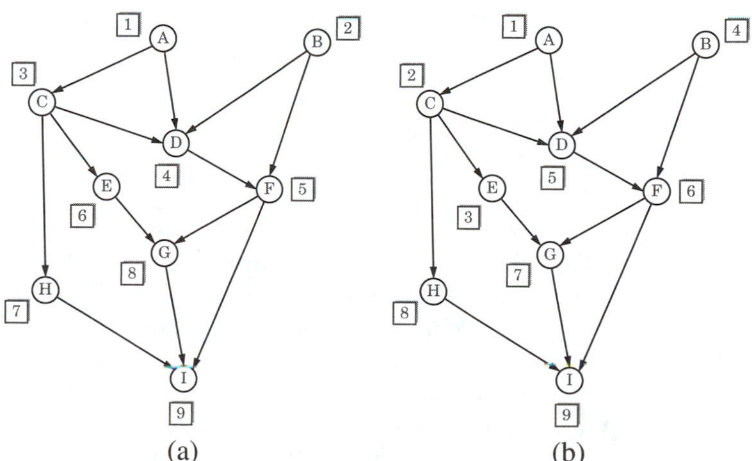

Figure 6.18: Two topological orderings of the same acyclic digraph.

Theorem 6.25: *A digraph has a topological ordering if and only if it is acyclic.*

Proof: The necessity (the "only if" part of the statement) is easy to demonstrate. Suppose $\vec{G}$ is topologically ordered. Assume, for the sake of a contradiction, that $\vec{G}$ has a cycle consisting of edges $(v_{i_0}, v_{i_1}), (v_{i_1}, v_{i_2}), \ldots, (v_{i_{k-1}}, v_{i_0})$. Because of the topological ordering, we must have $i_0 < i_1 < \cdots < i_{k-1} < i_0$, which is clearly impossible. Thus, $\vec{G}$ must be acyclic.

We now argue sufficiency (the "if" part). Suppose $\vec{G}$ is acyclic. We describe an algorithm to build a topological ordering for $\vec{G}$. Since $\vec{G}$ is acyclic, $\vec{G}$ must have a vertex with no incoming edges (that is, with in-degree 0). Let v_1 be such a vertex. Indeed, if v_1 did not exist, then in tracing a directed path from an arbitrary start vertex we would eventually encounter a previously visited vertex, thus contradicting the acyclicity of $\vec{G}$. If we remove v_1 from $\vec{G}$, together with its outgoing edges, the resulting digraph is still acyclic. Hence, the resulting digraph also has a vertex with no incoming edges, and we let v_2 be such a vertex. By repeating this process until $\vec{G}$ becomes empty, we obtain an ordering $v_1, \ldots, v_n$ of the vertices of $\vec{G}$. Because of the above construction, if (v_i, v_j) is an edge of $\vec{G}$, then v_i must be deleted before v_j can be deleted, and thus $i < j$. Thus, $v_1, \ldots, v_n$ is a topological ordering. ■

The above proof suggests Algorithm 6.19, called ***topological sorting***.

```
Algorithm TopologicalSort(G⃗):
  Input: A digraph G⃗ with n vertices.
  Output: A topological ordering v1,...,vn of G⃗ or an indication that G⃗ has a
     directed cycle.

  let S be an initially empty stack
  for each vertex u of G⃗ do
     incounter(u) ← indeg(u)
     if incounter(u) = 0 then
        S.push(u)
  i ← 1
  while S is not empty do
     u ← S.pop()
     number u as the i-th vertex vi
     i ← i + 1
     for each edge e ∈ G⃗.outIncidentEdges(u) do
        w ← G.opposite(u, e)
        incounter(w) ← incounter(w) − 1
        if incounter(w) = 0 then
           S.push(w)
  if S is empty then
     return "digraph G⃗ has a directed cycle"
```

Algorithm 6.19: Topological sorting algorithm.

Theorem 6.26: *Let $\vec{G}$ be a digraph with n vertices and m edges. The topological sorting algorithm runs in $O(n+m)$ time using $O(n)$ auxiliary space, and either computes a topological ordering of $\vec{G}$ or fails to number some vertices, which indicates that $\vec{G}$ has a directed cycle.*

Proof: The initial computation of in-degrees and setup of the incounter variables can be done with a simple traversal of the graph, which takes $O(n+m)$ time. We use an extra field in graph nodes or we use the decorator pattern, described in the next section, to associate counter attributes with the vertices. Say that a vertex u is ***visited*** by the topological sorting algorithm when u is removed from the stack S. A vertex u can be visited only when $\text{incounter}(u) = 0$, which implies that all its predecessors (vertices with outgoing edges into u) were previously visited. As a consequence, any vertex that is on a directed cycle will never be visited, and any other vertex will be visited exactly once. The algorithm traverses all the outgoing edges of each visited vertex once, so its running time is proportional to the number of outgoing edges of the visited vertices. Therefore, the algorithm runs in $O(n+m)$ time. Regarding the space usage, observe that the stack S and the incounter variables attached to the vertices use $O(n)$ space.

As a side effect, the algorithm also tests whether the input digraph $\vec{G}$ is acyclic. Indeed, if the algorithm terminates without ordering all the vertices, then the subgraph of the vertices that have not been ordered must contain a directed cycle. (See Figure 6.20.) ■

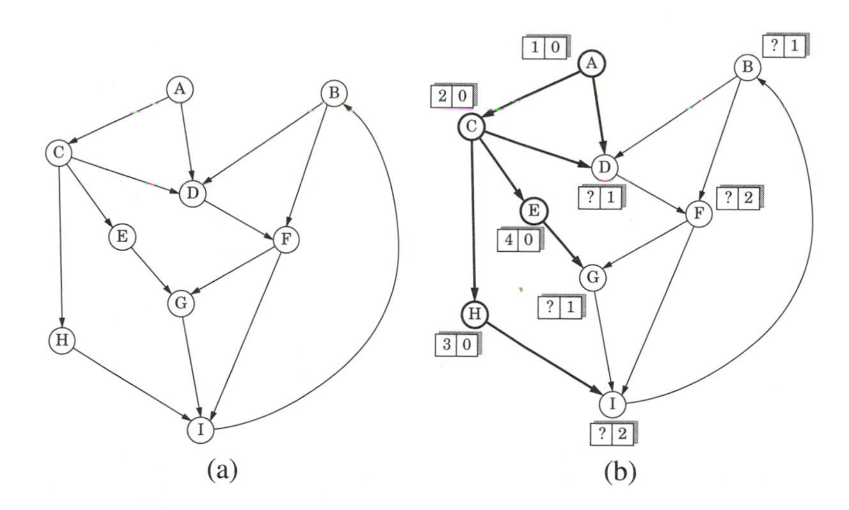

Figure 6.20: Detecting a directed cycle: (a) input digraph; (b) after algorithm TopologicalSort (Algorithm 6.19) terminates, the subgraph of the vertices with undefined number contains a directed cycle.

We visualize the topological sorting algorithm in Figure 6.21.

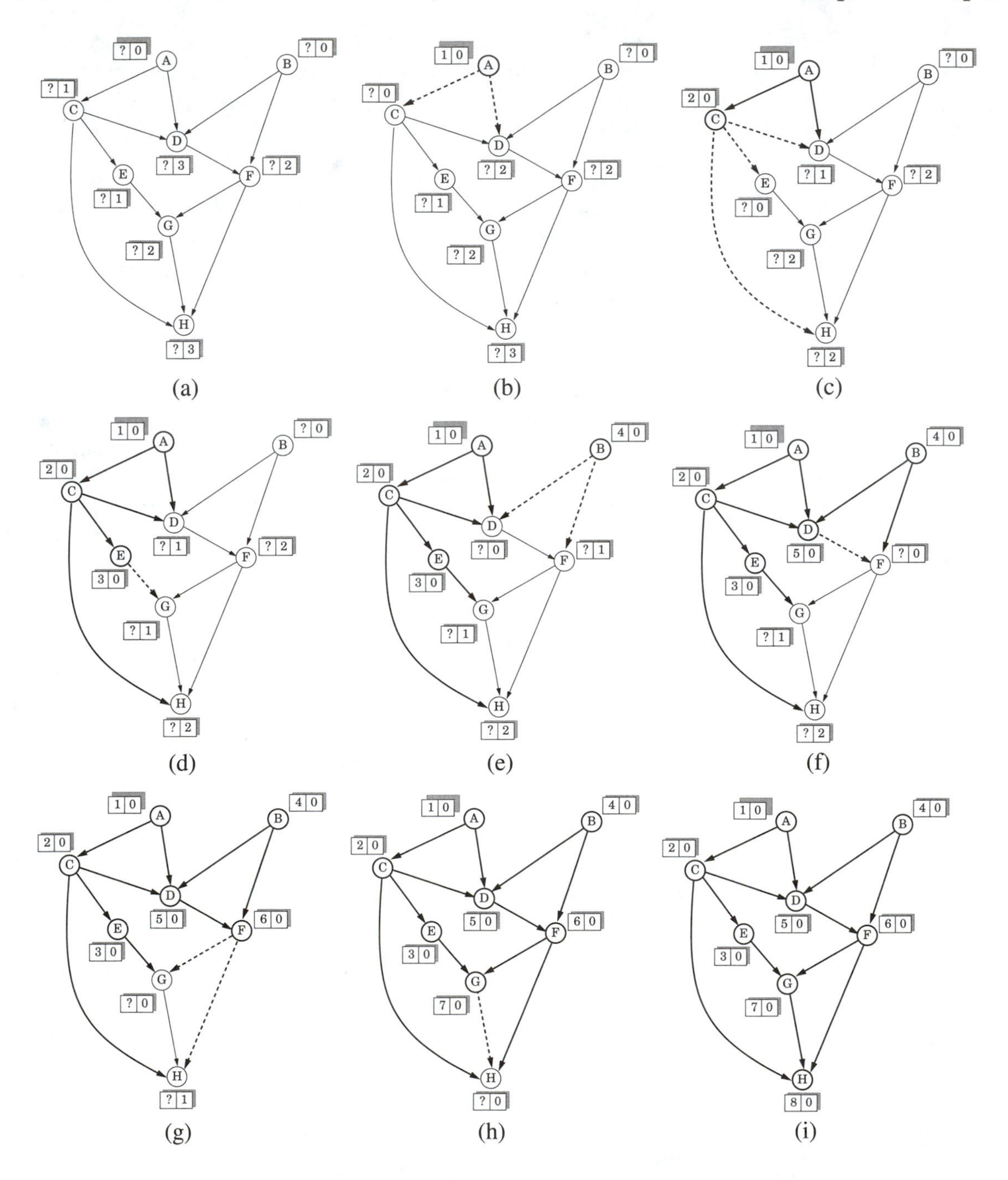

Figure 6.21: Example of a run of algorithm TopologicalSort (Algorithm 6.19): (a) initial configuration; (b–i) after each while-loop iteration. The vertex labels give the vertex number and the current incounter value. The edges traversed in previous iterations are drawn with thick solid lines. The edges traversed in the current iteration are drawn with thick dashed lines.

6.5 Java Example: Depth-First Search

In this section, we describe a case study implementation of the depth-first search algorithm in Java. This implementation is not simply an instantiation of the pseudo-code in Java, however, as it employs two interesting software engineering design patterns—the decorator pattern and the template method pattern.

6.5.1 The Decorator Pattern

Marking the explored vertices in a DFS traversal is an example of the ***decorator*** software engineering design pattern. The decorator pattern is used to add attributes or "decorations" to existing objects. Each attribute is identified by a specific decoration object, a, which acts as a kind of key identifying this attribute. Intuitively, the attribute a is the "name" of the decoration, and we then allow this attribute to take on different values for the different objects that are decorated with a attributes. The use of decorations is motivated by the need of some algorithms and data structures to add extra variables, or temporary scratch data, to objects that do not normally have such variables. Hence, a decoration is an (attribute, value) pair that can be dynamically attached to an object. For example, nodes in an AVL tree or red-black tree could be decorated with height or color attributes. In our DFS example, we would like to have "decorable" vertices and edges with an ***explored*** attribute and a Boolean value.

We can realize the decorator pattern for all positional containers by adding the following methods to the position ADT:

has(a): Tests whether the position has attribute a.

get(a): Returns the value of attribute a.

set(a, x): Sets to x the value of attribute a.

destroy(a): Removes attribute a and its associated value.

Implementing the Decorator Pattern

The above methods can be implemented by storing at each position a dictionary of the attributes and their values for that position, for example, in a small hash table. That is, the attributes, which can either be specific attribute objects or even string defining "names" for attributes, define the keys used in the hash table. Likewise, the values are simple base types or objects that assign a specific piece of data to given attributes. Such a hash table implementation provides a fast and efficient way to implement the methods of the decorator pattern. Indeed, although it is not shown, we use a small hash table in our DFS application to implement the decorator pattern.

6.5.2 A DFS Engine

In Code Fragment 6.22, we show the main Java "engine" for a recursive depth-first search traversal embodied in a class named "DFS."

```
/** Generic depth first search traversal of a graph using the template
  * method pattern. A subclass should override various methods to add
  * functionality to this traversal.    */
public abstract class DFS {
  /** The graph being traversed. */
  protected InspectableGraph G;
  /** The result of the traversal. */
  protected Object visitResult;
  /** Perform a depth first search traversal.
    * @param g Input graph.
    * @param start Start vertex of the traversal.
    * @param info Auxiliary information (to be used by subclasses).
    */
  public Object execute(InspectableGraph g, Vertex start, Object info) {
    G = g;
    for (PositionIterator pos = G.positions(); pos.hasNext(); )
      unVisit(pos.nextPosition());
    return null;
  }
  /**
    * Recursive template method for a generic DFS traversal.
    * @param v Start vertex of the traversal.
    */
  protected Object dfsTraversal(Vertex v) {
    initResult();
    startVisit(v);
    visit(v);
    for (EdgeIterator inEdges = G.incidentEdges(v); inEdges.hasNext(); ) {
      Edge nextEdge = inEdges.nextEdge();
      if (!isVisited(nextEdge)) { // found an unexplored edge, explore it
        visit(nextEdge);
        Vertex w = G.opposite(v, nextEdge);
        if (!isVisited(w)) { // w is unexplored, this is a discovery edge
          traverseDiscovery(nextEdge, v);
          if (!isDone())
            visitResult = dfsTraversal(w);
        }
        else // w is explored, this is a back edge
          traverseBack(nextEdge, v);
      }
    }
    finishVisit(v);
    return result();
  }
```

Code Fragment 6.22: Main variables and engine (dfsTraversal) for the DFS class.

6.5.3 The Template Method Design Pattern

The DFS class is defined so that its behavior can be specialized for any particular application. In Code Fragments 6.23 and 6.24, we show the methods that perform the specialization and decoration actions in the DFS class. The specialization is done by redefining the method execute, which activates the computation, and the following methods, which are called at various times by the recursive template method dfsTraversal.

- initResult(): called at the beginning of the execution of dfsTraversal.
- startVisit(Vertex v): also called at the beginning of dfsTraversal.
- traverseDiscovery(Edge e, Vertex v): called when traversing a discovery edge e out of v.
- traverseBack(Edge e, Vertex v): called when traversing a back edge e out of v.
- isDone(): called to determine whether to end the traversal early.
- finishVisit(Vertex v): called when we are done traversing all the incident edges of v.
- result(): called to return the output of dfsTraversal.

```
/** Auxiliary methods for specializing a generic DFS */
protected void initResult() {} // Initializes result (called first)
protected void startVisit(Vertex v) {} // Called when we first visit v
protected void finishVisit(Vertex v) {} // Called when we finish with v
protected void traverseDiscovery(Edge e, Vertex from) {} // Discovery edge
protected void traverseBack(Edge e, Vertex from) {} // Back edge
protected boolean isDone() { return false; } // Is DFS done early?
protected Object result() { return new Object(); } // The result of the DFS
```

Code Fragment 6.23: Auxiliary methods for specializing the template method dfsTraversal of class DFS (Code Fragment 6.22).

```
/** Attribute and its two values for the visit status of positions. */
protected static Object STATUS = new Object(); // The status attribute
protected static Object VISITED = new Object(); // Visited value
protected static Object UNVISITED = new Object(); // Unvisited value
/** Mark a position as visited.       */
protected void visit(Position p) { p.set(STATUS, VISITED); }
/** Mark a position as unvisited.     */
protected void unVisit(Position p) { p.set(STATUS, UNVISITED); }
/** Test if a position has been visited. */
protected boolean isVisited(Position p) { return (p.get(STATUS) == VISITED); }
```

Code Fragment 6.24: Methods visit, unVisit, and isVisited of class DFS (Code Fragment 6.22) implemented using decorable positions.

Definition of the Template Method Pattern

Our generic depth-first search traversal is based on the template method pattern, which describes a generic computation mechanism that can be specialized by redefining certain steps. That is, we define a generic class, Algorithm, that performs some useful and possibly complicated function while also calling a collection of named procedures at certain points. Initially, the procedures do nothing, but by extending the Algorithm class and redefining these methods to do interesting things, then we can construct a nontrivial computation. The Applet class in Java is an example use of this design pattern. In the case of our DFS application, we use the template method pattern for depth-first search assuming that the underlying graph is undirected, but it can easily be modified to work for directed graphs.

The way we identify the vertices and edges that have been already visited (explored) during the traversal is encapsulated in the calls to methods isVisited, visit, and unVisit. Our implementation (see Code Fragment 6.24) assumes that the vertex and edge positions support the decorator pattern, which we discuss next. (Alternatively, we can set up a dictionary of positions and store the visited vertices and edges in it.)

Using the DFS Template

For us to do anything interesting with the dfsTraversal, we must extend the DFS class and redefine some of the auxiliary methods of Code Fragment 6.23 to do something nontrivial. This approach conforms to the template method pattern, for these methods specialize the behavior of the template method dfsTraversal.

Class ConnectivityTesterDFS, given in Code Fragment 6.25, for instance, extends the DFS to create a program that tests whether the graph is connected. It counts the vertices reachable by a DFS traversal starting at a vertex and compares this number with the total number of vertices of the graph.

```
/** This class specializes DFS to determine whether the graph is connected. */
public class ConnectivityTesterDFS extends DFS {
  protected int reached;
  public Object execute(InspectableGraph g, Vertex start, Object info) {
    super.execute(g, start, info);
    reached = 0;
    if (!G.isEmpty()) {
      Vertex v = G.aVertex();
      dfsTraversal(v);
    }
    return (new Boolean(reached == G.numVertices()));
  }
  public void startVisit(Vertex v) { reached++; }
}
```

Code Fragment 6.25: Specialization of class DFS to test if the graph is connected.

Extending DFS for Path Finding

We can perform even more interesting algorithms by extending the DFS in more clever ways.

For example, Class FindPathDFS, given in Code Fragment 6.26, finds a path between a pair of given start and target vertices. It performs a depth-first search traversal beginning at the start vertex. We maintain the path of discovery edges from the start vertex to the current vertex. When we encounter an unexplored vertex, we add it to the end of the path, and when we finish processing a vertex, we remove it from the path. The traversal is terminated when the target vertex is encountered, and the path is returned as an iterator of vertices. Note that the path found by this class consists of discovery edges.

```
/** This class specializes DFS to find a path between the start vertex
  * and a given target vertex. */
public class FindPathDFS extends DFS {
  protected Sequence path;
  protected boolean done;
  protected Vertex target;
  /** @param info target vertex of the path
    * @return Iterator of the vertices in a path from the start vertex
    * to the target vertex, or an empty iterator if no such path
    * exists in the graph */
  public Object execute(InspectableGraph g, Vertex start, Object info) {
    super.execute(g, start, info);
    path = new NodeSequence();
    done = false;
    target = (Vertex) info; // target vertex is stored in info parameter
    dfsTraversal(start);
    return new VertexIteratorAdapter(path.elements());
  }
  protected void startVisit(Vertex v) {
    path.insertLast(v);
    if (v == target)
      done = true;
  }
  protected void finishVisit(Vertex v) {
    if (!done)
      path.remove(path.last());
  }
  protected boolean isDone() {
    return done;
  }
}
```

Code Fragment 6.26: Specialization of class DFS to find a path between the start vertex and a target vertex. The auxiliary class VertexIteratorAdapter provides an adapter from a sequence to a vertex iterator.

Extending DFS for Cycle Finding

We can also extend the DFS, as in Class FindCycleDFS, which is given in Code Fragment 6.27, to find a cycle in the connected component of a given vertex v. The algorithm performs a depth-first search traversal from v that terminates when a back edge is found. The method returns a (possibly empty) iterator of the cycle formed by the found back edge.

```
/** Specialize DFS to find a cycle in connected component of start vertex. */
public class FindCycleDFS extends DFS {
  protected Sequence cycle; // sequence of edges of the cycle
  protected boolean done;
  protected Vertex cycleStart, target;
  /** @return Iterator of edges of a cycle in the component of start vertex */
  public Object execute(InspectableGraph g, Vertex start, Object info) {
    super.execute(g, start, info);
    cycle = new NodeSequence();
    done = false;
    dfsTraversal(start);
    if (!cycle.isEmpty() && start != cycleStart) {
      PositionIterator pos = cycle.positions();
      while (pos.hasNext()) { // remove the edges from start to cycleStart
        Position p = pos.nextPosition();
        Edge e = (Edge) p.element();
        cycle.remove(p);
        if (g.areIncident(cycleStart, e)) break;
      }
    }
    return new EdgeIteratorAdapter(cycle.elements());
  }
  protected void finishVisit(Vertex v) {
    if ((!cycle.isEmpty()) && (!done)) cycle.remove(cycle.last());
  }
  protected void traverseDiscovery(Edge e, Vertex from) {
    if (!done) cycle.insertLast(e);
  }
  protected void traverseBack(Edge e, Vertex from) {
    if (!done) {
      cycle.insertLast(e); // back edge e creates a cycle
      cycleStart = G.opposite(from, e);
      done = true;
    }
  }
  protected boolean isDone() { return done; }
}
```

Code Fragment 6.27: Specialization of class DFS to find a cycle in the connected component of the start vertex. The auxiliary class EdgeIteratorAdapter provides an adapter from a sequence to an edge iterator.

6.6 Exercises

Reinforcement

R-6.1 Draw a simple undirected graph G that has 12 vertices, 18 edges, and 3 connected components. Why would it be impossible to draw G with 3 connected components if G had 66 edges?

R-6.2 Let G be a simple connected graph with n vertices and m edges. Explain why $O(\log m)$ is $O(\log n)$.

R-6.3 Draw a simple connected directed graph with 8 vertices and 16 edges such that the in-degree and out-degree of each vertex is 2. Show that there is a single (nonsimple) cycle that includes all the edges of your graph, that is, you can trace all the edges in their respective directions without ever lifting your pencil. (Such a cycle is called an ***Euler tour***.)

R-6.4 Bob loves foreign languages and wants to plan his course schedule to take the following nine language courses: LA15, LA16, LA22, LA31, LA32, LA126, LA127, LA141, and LA169. The course prerequisites are:

- LA15: (none)
- LA16: LA15
- LA22: (none)
- LA31: LA15
- LA32: LA16, LA31
- LA126: LA22, LA32
- LA127: LA16
- LA141: LA22, LA16
- LA169: LA32.

Find a sequence of courses that allows Bob to satisfy all the prerequisites.

R-6.5 Suppose we represent a graph G having n vertices and m edges with the edge list structure. Why, in this case, does the insertVertex method run in $O(1)$ time while the removeVertex method runs in $O(m)$ time?

R-6.6 Let G be a graph whose vertices are the integers 1 through 8, and let the adjacent vertices of each vertex be given by the table below:

vertex	adjacent vertices
1	(2, 3, 4)
2	(1, 3, 4)
3	(1, 2, 4)
4	(1, 2, 3, 6)
5	(6, 7, 8)
6	(4, 5, 7)
7	(5, 6, 8)
8	(5, 7)

Assume that, in a traversal of G, the adjacent vertices of a given vertex are returned in the same order as they are listed in the above table.

a. Draw G.
b. Order the vertices as they are visited in a DFS traversal starting at vertex 1.
c. Order the vertices as they are visited in a BFS traversal starting at vertex 1.

R-6.7 Would you use the adjacency list structure or the adjacency matrix structure in each of the following cases? Justify your choice.

a. The graph has 10,000 vertices and 20,000 edges, and it is important to use as little space as possible.
b. The graph has 10,000 vertices and 20,000,000 edges, and it is important to use as little space as possible.
c. You need to answer the query areAdjacent as fast as possible, no matter how much space you use.

R-6.8 Explain why the DFS traversal runs in $\Theta(n^2)$ time on an n-vertex simple graph that is represented with the adjacency matrix structure.

R-6.9 Draw the transitive closure of the directed graph shown in Figure 6.2.

R-6.10 Compute a topological ordering for the directed graph drawn with solid edges in Figure 6.14d.

R-6.11 Can we use a queue instead of a stack as an auxiliary data structure in the topological sorting algorithm shown in Algorithm 6.19?

R-6.12 Give the order in which the edges are labeled by the DFS traversal shown in Figure 6.6.

R-6.13 Repeat Exercise R-6.12 for Figure 6.13 illustrating a BFS traversal.

R-6.14 Repeat Exercise R-6.12 for Figure 6.15 illustrating a directed DFS traversal.

Creativity

C-6.1 Justify Theorem 6.11.

C-6.2 Describe the details of an $O(n+m)$-time algorithm for computing ***all*** the connected components of an undirected graph G with n vertices and m edges.

C-6.3 Let T be the spanning tree rooted at the start vertex produced by the depth-first search of a connected, undirected graph G. Argue why every edge of G, not in T, goes from a vertex in T to one of its ancestors, that is, it is a ***back edge***.

Hint: Suppose that such a nontree edge is a cross edge, and argue based upon the order the DFS visits the end vertices of this edge.

C-6.4 Suppose we wish to represent an n-vertex graph G using the edge list structure, assuming that we identify the vertices with the integers in the set $\{0,1,\ldots,n-1\}$. Describe how to implement the container E to support $O(\log n)$-time performance for the areAdjacent method. How are you implementing the method in this case?

C-6.5 Give a proof of Lemma 6.14

C-6.6 Show that if a graph G has at least three vertices, then it has a separation edge only if it has a separation vertex.

C-6.7 Give a proof of Lemma 6.16

C-6.8 Supply the details of the proof of correctness of algorithm LinkComponents (Algorithm 6.10).

C-6.9 Tamarindo University and many other schools worldwide are doing a joint project on multimedia. A computer network is built to connect these schools using communication links that form a free tree. The schools decide to install a file server at one of the schools to share data among all the schools. Since the transmission time on a link is dominated by the link setup and synchronization, the cost of a data transfer is proportional to the number of links used. Hence, it is desirable to choose a "central" location for the file server. Given a free tree T and a node v of T, the *eccentricity* of v is the length of a longest path from v to any other node of T. A node of T with minimum eccentricity is called a *center* of T.

a. Design an efficient algorithm that, given an n-node free tree T, computes a center of T.
b. Is the center unique? If not, how many distinct centers can a free tree have?

C-6.10 Show how to perform a BFS traversal using, as an auxiliary data structure a single queue instead of the level containers $L_0, L_1, \ldots$.

C-6.11 Show that, if T is a BFS tree produced for a connected graph G, then, for each vertex v at level i, the path of T between s and v has i edges, and any other path of G between s and v has at least i edges.

C-6.12 The time delay of a long-distance call can be determined by multiplying a small fixed constant by the number of communication links on the telephone network between the caller and callee. Suppose the telephone network of a company named RT&T is a free tree. The engineers of RT&T want to compute the maximum possible time delay that may be experienced in a long-distance call. Given a free tree T, the *diameter* of T is the length of a longest path between two nodes of T. Give an efficient algorithm for computing the diameter of T.

C-6.13 A company named RT&T has a network of n switching stations connected by m high-speed communication links. Each customer's phone is directly connected to one station in his or her area. The engineers of RT&T have developed a prototype video-phone system that allows two customers to see each other during a phone call. In order to have acceptable image quality, however, the number of links used to transmit video signals between the two parties cannot exceed 4. Suppose that RT&T's network is represented by a graph. Design an efficient algorithm that computes, for each station, the set of stations it can reach using no more than 4 links.

C-6.14 Explain why there are no forward nontree edges with respect to a BFS tree constructed for a directed graph.

C-6.15 Give a detailed pseudo-code description of the directed DFS traversal algorithm. How do we determine whether a nontree edge is a back edge, forward edge, or cross edge?

C-6.16 Explain why the strong connectivity testing algorithm given in Section 6.4.1 is correct.

C-6.17 Let G be an undirected graph G with n vertices and m edges. Describe an algorithm running in $O(n+m)$ time that traverses each edge of G exactly once in each direction.

C-6.18 An independent set of an undirected graph $G = (V,E)$ is a subset I of V, such that no two vertices in I are adjacent. That is, if $u, v \in I$, then $(u,v) \notin E$. A ***maximal independent set*** M is an independent set such that, if we were to add any additional vertex to M, then it would not be independent any longer. Every graph has a maximal independent set. (Can you see this? This question is not part of the exercise, but it is worth thinking about.) Give an efficient algorithm that computes a maximal independent set for a graph G. What is this method's running time?

C-6.19 An ***Euler tour*** of a directed graph $\vec{G}$ with n vertices and m edges is a cycle that traverses each edge of $\vec{G}$ exactly once according to its direction. Such a tour always exists if $\vec{G}$ is connected and the in-degree equals the out-degree of each vertex in $\vec{G}$. Describe an $O(n+m)$-time algorithm for finding an Euler tour of such a digraph $\vec{G}$.

C-6.20 Justify Theorem 6.18.

Projects

P-6.1 Implement a simplified graph ADT that has only methods relevant to undirected graphs and does not include update methods, using the adjacency matrix structure.

P-6.2 Implement the simplified graph ADT described in Project P-6.1, using the adjacency list structure.

P-6.3 Implement a generic BFS traversal using the template method pattern.

P-6.4 Implement the topological sorting algorithm.

P-6.5 Implement the Floyd-Warshall transitive closure algorithm.

Chapter Notes

The depth-first search method is a part of the "folklore" of computer science, but Hopcroft and Tarjan [98, 198] are the ones who showed how useful this algorithm is for solving several different graph problems. Knuth [118] discusses the topological sorting problem. The simple linear-time algorithm that we describe in Section 6.4.1 for determining if a directed graph is strongly connected is due to Kosaraju. The Floyd-Warshall algorithm appears in a paper by Floyd [69] and is based upon a theorem of Warshall [209]. The mark-sweep garbage collection method we describe is one of many different algorithms for performing garbage collection. We encourage the reader interested in further study of garbage collection to examine the book by Jones [110]. To learn about different algorithms for drawing graphs, please see the book chapter by Tamassia [194], the annotated bibliography of Di Battista *et al.* [58], or the book by Di Battista *et al.* [59].

The reader interested in further study of graph algorithms is referred to the books by Ahuja, Magnanti, and Orlin [9], Cormen, Leiserson, and Rivest [55], Even [68], Gibbons [77], Mehlhorn [149], and Tarjan [200], and the book chapter by van Leeuwen [205].

Chapter

7 Weighted Graphs

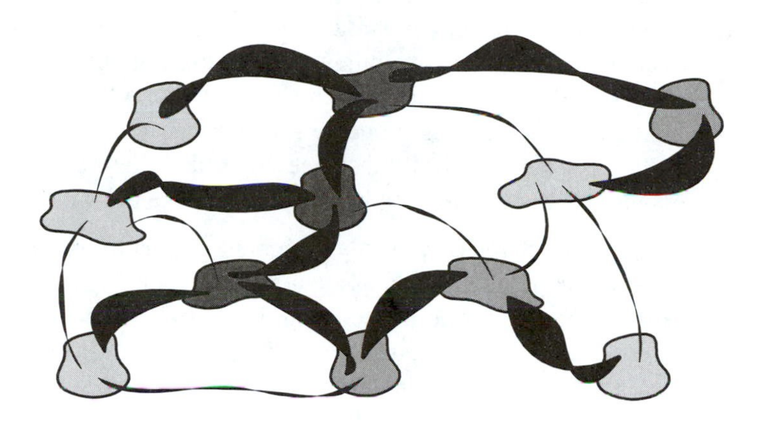

Contents

7.1 Single-Source Shortest Paths 341

7.1.1 Dijkstra's Algorithm 342

7.1.2 The Bellman-Ford Shortest Paths Algorithm 349

7.1.3 Shortest Paths in Directed Acyclic Graphs 352

7.2 All-Pairs Shortest Paths 354

7.2.1 A Dynamic Programming Shortest Path Algorithm . 354

7.2.2 Computing Shortest Paths via Matrix Multiplication . 355

7.3 Minimum Spanning Trees 360

7.3.1 Kruskal's Algorithm 362

7.3.2 The Prim-Jarník Algorithm 366

7.3.3 Barůvka's Algorithm 369

7.3.4 A Comparison of MST Algorithms 372

7.4 Java Example: Dijkstra's Algorithm 373

7.5 Exercises 376

As we saw in the previous chapter, the breadth-first search strategy can be used to find a shortest path from some starting vertex to every other vertex in a connected graph. This approach makes sense in cases where each edge is as good as any other, but there are many situations where this approach is not appropriate.

For example, we might be using a graph to represent a computer network (such as the Internet), and we might be interested in finding the fastest way to route a data packet between two computers. In this case, it is probably not appropriate for all the edges to be equal to each other, for some connections in a computer network are typically much faster than others (for example, some edges might represent slow phone-line connections while others might represent high-speed, fiber-optic connections). Likewise, we might want to use a graph to represent the roads between cities, and we might be interested in finding the fastest way to travel cross-country. In this case, it is again probably not appropriate for all the edges to be equal to each other, for some intercity distances will likely be much larger than others. Thus, it is natural to consider graphs whose edges are not weighted equally.

In this chapter, we study weighted graphs. A ***weighted graph*** is a graph that has a numeric label $w(e)$ associated with each edge e, called the ***weight*** of edge e. Edge weights can be integers, rational numbers, or real numbers, which represent a concept such as distance, connection costs, or affinity. We show an example of a weighted graph in Figure 7.1.

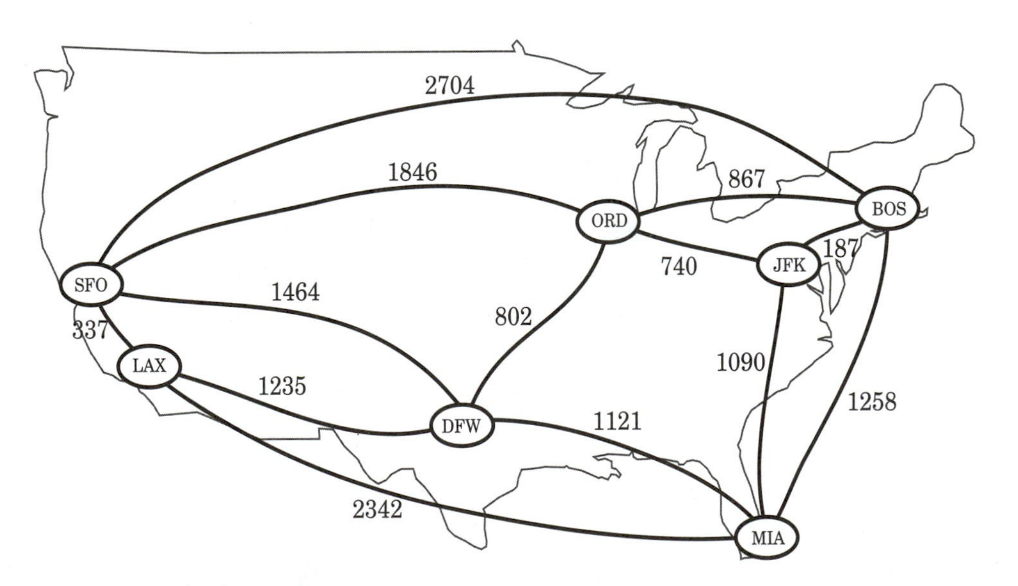

Figure 7.1: A weighted graph whose vertices represent major U.S. airports and whose edge weights represent distances in miles. This graph has a path from JFK to LAX of total weight 2,777 (going through ORD and DFW). This is the minimum weight path in the graph from JFK to LAX.

7.1 Single-Source Shortest Paths

Let G be a weighted graph. The ***length*** (or ***weight***) of a path P is the sum of the weights of the edges of P. That is, if P consists of edges $e_0, e_1, \ldots, e_{k-1}$ then the length of P, denoted $w(P)$, is defined as

$$w(P) = \sum_{i=0}^{k-1} w(e_i).$$

The ***distance*** from a vertex v to a vertex u in G, denoted $d(v,u)$, is the length of a minimum length path (also called ***shortest path***) from v to u, if such a path exists.

People often use the convention that $d(v,u) = +\infty$ if there is no path at all from v to u in G. Even if there is a path from v to u in G, the distance from v to u may not be defined, however, if there is a cycle in G whose total weight is negative. For example, suppose vertices in G represent cities, and the weights of edges in G represent how much money it costs to go from one city to another. If someone were willing to actually pay us to go from say JFK to ORD, then the "cost" of the edge (JFK,ORD) would be negative. If someone else were willing to pay us to go from ORD to JFK, then there would be a negative-weight cycle in G and distances would no longer be defined. That is, anyone can now build a path (with cycles) in G from any city A to another city B that first goes to JFK and then cycles as many times as he or she likes from JFK to ORD and back, before going on to B. The existence of such paths allows us to build arbitrarily low negative-cost paths (and in this case make a fortune in the process). But distances cannot be arbitrarily low negative numbers. Thus, any time we use edge weights to represent distances, we must be careful not to introduce any negative-weight cycles.

Suppose we are given a weighted graph G, and we are asked to find a shortest path from some vertex v to each other vertex in G, viewing the weights on the edges as distances. In this section, we explore efficient ways of finding all such ***single-source shortest paths***, if they exist.

The first algorithm we discuss is for the simple, yet common, case when all the edge weights in G are nonnegative (that is, $w(e) \geq 0$ for each edge e of G); hence, we know in advance that there are no negative-weight cycles in G. Recall that the special case of computing a shortest path when all weights are 1 was solved with the BFS traversal algorithm presented in Section 6.3.3.

There is an interesting approach for solving this ***single-source*** problem based on the ***greedy method*** design pattern (Section 5.1). Recall that in this pattern we solve the problem at hand by repeatedly selecting the best choice from among those available in each iteration. This paradigm can often be used in situations where we are trying to optimize some cost function over a collection of objects. We can add objects to our collection, one at a time, always picking the next one that optimizes the function from among those yet to be chosen.

7.1.1 Dijkstra's Algorithm

The main idea in applying the greedy method pattern to the single-source shortest-path problem is to perform a "weighted" breadth-first search starting at v. In particular, we can use the greedy method to develop an algorithm that iteratively grows a "cloud" of vertices out of v, with the vertices entering the cloud in order of their distances from v. Thus, in each iteration, the next vertex chosen is the vertex outside the cloud that is closest to v. The algorithm terminates when no more vertices are outside the cloud, at which point we have a shortest path from v to every other vertex of G. This approach is a simple, but nevertheless powerful, example of the greedy method design pattern.

A Greedy Method for Finding Shortest Paths

Applying the greedy method to the single-source, shortest-path problem, results in an algorithm known as ***Dijkstra's algorithm***. When applied to other graph problems, however, the greedy method may not necessarily find the best solution (such as in the so-called ***traveling salesman problem***, in which we wish to find the shortest path that visits all the vertices in a graph exactly once). Nevertheless, there are a number of situations in which the greedy method allows us to compute the best solution. In this chapter, we discuss two such situations: computing shortest paths and constructing minimum spanning trees.

In order to simplify the description of Dijkstra's algorithm, we assume, in the following, that the input graph G is undirected (that is, all its edges are undirected) and simple (that is, it has no self-loops and no parallel edges). Hence, we denote the edges of G as unordered vertex pairs (u,z). We leave the description of Dijkstra's algorithm so that it works for a weighted directed graph as an exercise (R-7.2).

In Dijkstra's algorithm, the cost function we are trying to optimize in our application of the greedy method is also the function that we are trying to compute—the shortest path distance. This may at first seem like circular reasoning until we realize that we can actually implement this approach by using a "bootstrapping" trick, consisting of using an approximation to the distance function we are trying to compute, which in the end will be equal to the true distance.

Edge Relaxation

Let us define a label $D[u]$ for each vertex u of G, which we use to approximate the distance in G from v to u. The meaning of these labels is that $D[u]$ will always store the length of the best path we have found ***so far*** from v to u. Initially, $D[v] = 0$ and $D[u] = +\infty$ for each $u \neq v$, and we define the set C, which is our "***cloud***" of vertices, to initially be the empty set $\emptyset$. At each iteration of the algorithm, we select a vertex u not in C with smallest $D[u]$ label, and we pull u into C. In the very first iteration we will, of course, pull v into C. Once a new vertex u is pulled into C, we then update the label $D[z]$ of each vertex z that is adjacent to u and is outside of

C, to reflect the fact that there may be a new and better way to get to z via u. This update operation is known as a ***relaxation*** procedure, for it takes an old estimate and checks if it can be improved to get closer to its true value. (A metaphor for why we call this a relaxation comes from a spring that is stretched out and then "relaxed" back to its true resting shape.) In the case of Dijkstra's algorithm, the relaxation is performed for an edge (u,z), such that we have computed a new value of $D[u]$ and wish to see if there is a better value for $D[z]$ using the edge (u,z). The specific edge relaxation operation is as follows:

Edge Relaxation:

if $D[u] + w((u,z)) < D[z]$ **then**
$D[z] \leftarrow D[u] + w((u,z))$.

Note that if the newly discovered path to z is no better than the old way, then we do not change $D[z]$.

The Details of Dijkstra's Algorithm

We give the pseudo-code for Dijkstra's algorithm in Algorithm 7.2. Note that we use a priority queue Q to store the vertices outside of the cloud C.

```
Algorithm DijkstraShortestPaths(G, v):
   Input: A simple undirected weighted graph G with nonnegative edge weights,
      and a distinguished vertex v of G
   Output: A label D[u], for each vertex u of G, such that D[u] is the distance from
      v to u in G
   D[v] ← 0
   for each vertex u ≠ v of G⃗ do
      D[u] ← +∞
   Let a priority queue Q contain all the vertices of G using the D labels as keys.
   while Q is not empty do
      {pull a new vertex u into the cloud}
      u ← Q.removeMin()
      for each vertex z adjacent to u such that z is in Q do
         {perform the relaxation procedure on edge (u,z)}
         if D[u] + w((u,z)) < D[z] then
            D[z] ← D[u] + w((u,z))
            Change to D[z] the key of vertex z in Q.
   return the label D[u] of each vertex u
```

Algorithm 7.2: Dijkstra's algorithm for the single-source shortest path problem for a graph G, starting from a vertex v.

We illustrate several iterations of Dijkstra's algorithm in Figures 7.3 and 7.4.

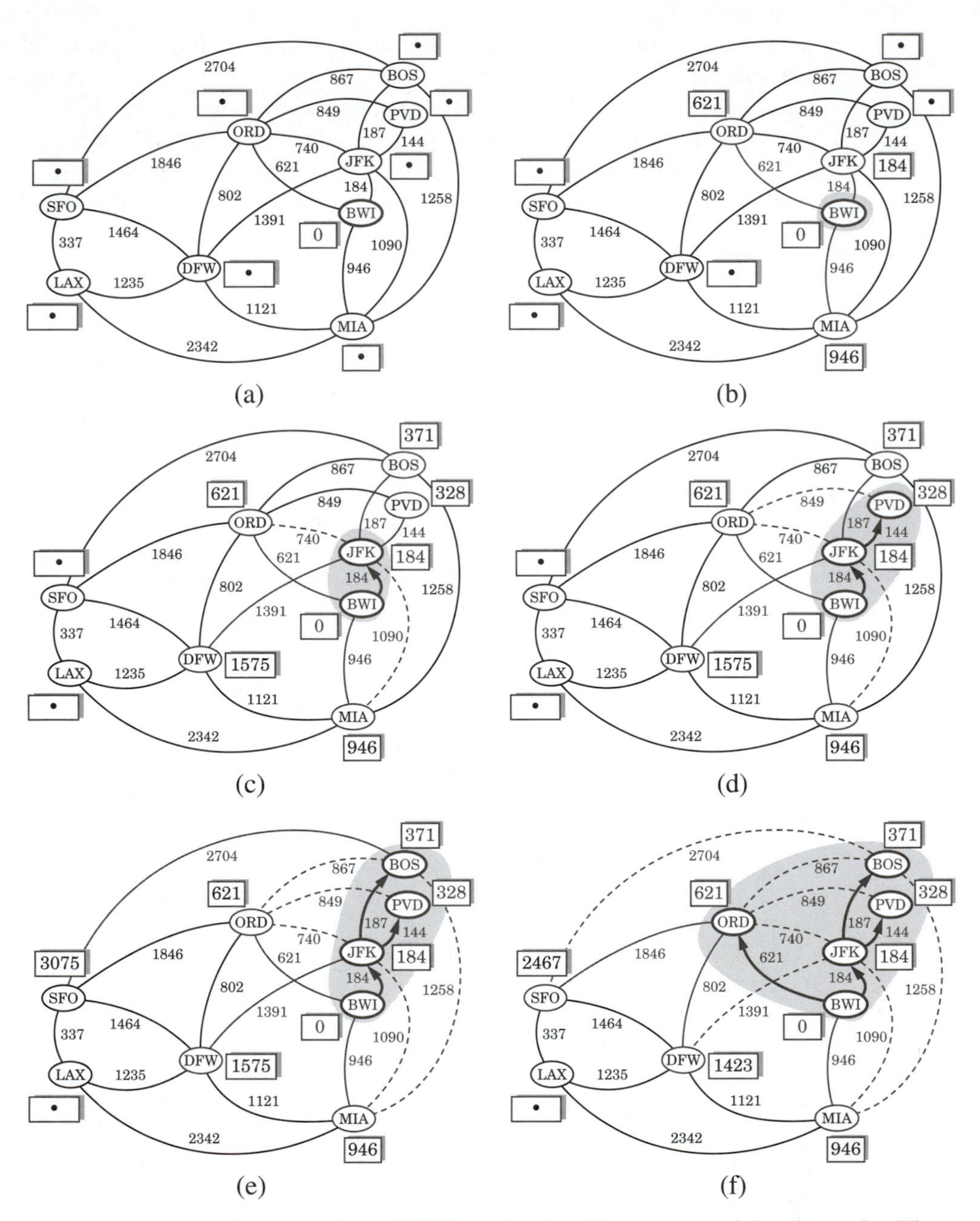

Figure 7.3: An execution of Dijkstra's algorithm on a weighted graph. The start vertex is BWI. A box next to each vertex u stores the label $D[u]$. The symbol • is used instead of $+\infty$. The edges of the shortest-path tree are drawn as thick arrows, and for each vertex u outside the "cloud" we show the current best edge for pulling in u with a solid line. (Continued in Figure 7.4.)

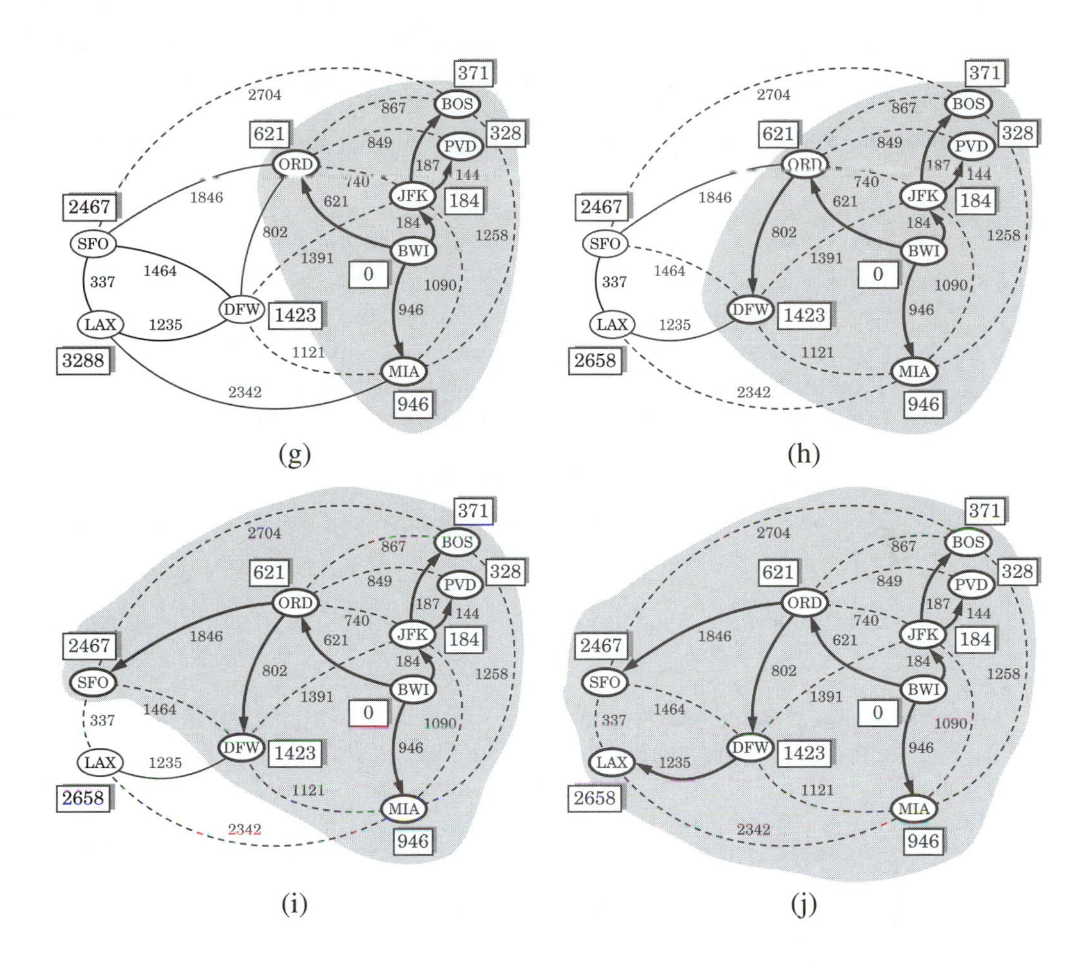

Figure 7.4: Visualization of Dijkstra's algorithm. (Continued from Figure 7.3.)

Why It Works

The interesting, and possibly even a little surprising, aspect of the Dijkstra algorithm is that, at the moment a vertex u is pulled into C, its label $D[u]$ stores the correct length of a shortest path from v to u. Thus, when the algorithm terminates, it will have computed the shortest-path distance from v to every vertex of G. That is, it will have solved the single-source shortest path problem.

It is probably not immediately clear why Dijkstra's algorithm correctly finds the shortest path from the start vertex v to each other vertex u in the graph. Why is it that the distance from v to u is equal to the value of the label $D[u]$ at the time vertex u is pulled into the cloud C (which is also the time u is removed from the priority queue Q)? The answer to this question depends on there being no negative-weight edges in the graph, for it allows the greedy method to work correctly, as we show in the lemma that follows.

Lemma 7.1: *In Dijkstra's algorithm, whenever a vertex u is pulled into the cloud, the label $D[u]$ is equal to $d(v,u)$, the length of a shortest path from v to u.*

Proof: Suppose that $D[t] > d(v,t)$ for some vertex t in V, and let u be the ***first*** vertex the algorithm pulled into the cloud C (that is, removed from Q), such that $D[u] > d(v,u)$. There is a shortest path P from v to u (for otherwise $d(v,u) = +\infty = D[u]$). Therefore, let us consider the moment when u is pulled into C, and let z be the first vertex of P (when going from v to u) that is not in C at this moment. Let y be the predecessor of z in path P (note that we could have $y = v$). (See Figure 7.5.) We know, by our choice of z, that y is already in C at this point. Moreover, $D[y] = d(v,y)$, since u is the ***first*** incorrect vertex. When y was pulled into C, we tested (and possibly updated) $D[z]$ so that we had at that point

$$D[z] \leq D[y] + w((y,z)) = d(v,y) + w((y,z)).$$

But since z is the next vertex on the shortest path from v to u, this implies that

$$D[z] = d(v,z).$$

But we are now at the moment when we are picking u, not z, to join C; hence,

$$D[u] \leq D[z].$$

It should be clear that a subpath of a shortest path is itself a shortest path. Hence, since z is on the shortest path from v to u,

$$d(v,z) + d(z,u) = d(v,u).$$

Moreover, $d(z,u) \geq 0$ because there are no negative-weight edges. Therefore,

$$D[u] \leq D[z] = d(v,z) \leq d(v,z) + d(z,u) = d(v,u).$$

But this contradicts the definition of u; hence, there can be no such vertex u. ■

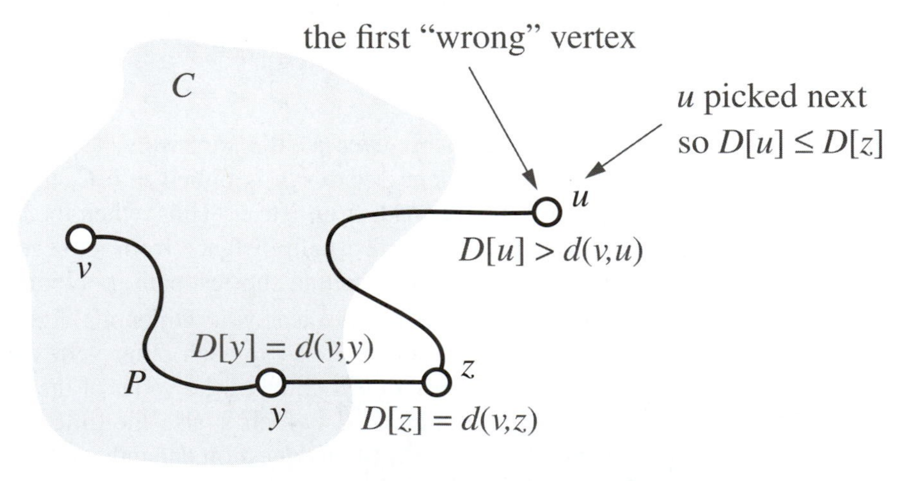

Figure 7.5: A schematic illustration for the justification of Theorem 7.1.

The Running Time of Dijkstra's Algorithm

In this section, we analyze the time complexity of Dijkstra's algorithm. We denote with n and m, the number of vertices and edges of the input graph G, respectively. We assume that the edge weights can be added and compared in constant time. Because of the high level of the description we gave for Dijkstra's algorithm in Algorithm 7.2, analyzing its running time requires that we give more details on its implementation. Specifically, we should indicate the data structures used and how they are implemented.

Let us first assume that we are representing the graph G using an adjacency list structure. This data structure allows us to step through the vertices adjacent to u during the relaxation step in time proportional to their number. It still does not settle all the details for the algorithm, however, for we must say more about how to implement the other main data structure in the algorithm—the priority queue Q.

An efficient implementation of the priority queue Q uses a heap (see Section 2.4.3). This allows us to extract the vertex u with smallest D label, by calling the removeMin method, in $O(\log n)$ time. As noted in the pseudo-code, each time we update a $D[z]$ label we need to update the key of z in the priority queue. If Q is implemented as a heap, then this key update can, for example, be done by first removing and then inserting z with its new key. If our priority queue Q supports the locator pattern (see Section 2.4.4), then we can easily implement such key updates in $O(\log n)$ time, since a locator for vertex z would allow Q to have immediate access to the item storing z in the heap (see Section 2.4.4). Assuming this implementation of Q, Dijkstra's algorithm runs in $O((n+m)\log n)$ time.

Referring back to Algorithm 7.2, the details of the running-time analysis are as follows:

- Inserting all the vertices in Q with their initial key value can be done in $O(n\log n)$ time by repeated insertions, or in $O(n)$ time using bottom-up heap construction (see Section 2.4.4).
- At each iteration of the **while** loop, we spend $O(\log n)$ time to remove vertex u from Q, and $O(\deg(v)\log n)$ time to perform the relaxation procedure on the edges incident on u.
- The overall running time of the **while** loop is
$$\sum_{v\in G}(1+\deg(v))\log n,$$
which is $O((n+m)\log n)$ by Theorem 6.6.

Thus, we have the following.

Theorem 7.2: *Given a weighted n-vertex graph G with m edges, each with a non-negative weight, Dijkstra's algorithm can be implemented to find all shortest paths from a vertex v in G in $O(m\log n)$ time.*

Note that if we wish to express the above running time as a function of n only, then it is $O(n^2\log n)$ in the worst case, since we have assumed that G is simple.

An Alternative Implementation for Dijkstra's Algorithm

Let us now consider an alternative implementation for the priority queue Q using an unsorted sequence. This, of course, requires that we spend $\Omega(n)$ time to extract the minimum element, but it allows for very fast key updates, provided Q supports the locator pattern (Section 2.4.4). Specifically, we can implement each key update done in a relaxation step in $O(1)$ time—we simply change the key value once we locate the item in Q to update. Hence, this implementation results in a running time that is $O(n^2+m)$, which can be simplified to $O(n^2)$ since G is simple.

Comparing the Two Implementations

We have two choices for implementing the priority queue in Dijkstra's algorithm: a locator-based heap implementation, which yields $O(m\log n)$ running time, and a locator-based unsorted sequence implementation, which yields an $O(n^2)$-time algorithm. Since both implementations would be fairly simple to code up, they are about equal in terms of the programming sophistication needed. These two implementations are also about equal in terms of the constant factors in their worst-case running times. Looking only at these worst-case times, we prefer the heap implementation when the number of edges in the graph is small (that is, when $m < n^2/\log n$), and we prefer the sequence implementation when the number of edges is large (that is, when $m > n^2/\log n$).

Theorem 7.3: *Given a simple weighted graph G with n vertices and m edges, such that the weight of each edge is nonnegative, and a vertex v of G, Dijkstra's algorithm computes the distance from v to all other vertices of G in $O(m\log n)$ time, or, alternatively, in $O(n^2)$ time.*

In Exercise R-7.3, we explore how to modify Dijkstra's algorithm to output a tree T rooted at v, such that the path in T from v to a vertex u is a shortest path in G from v to u. In addition, extending Dijkstra's algorithm for directed graphs is fairly straightforward. We cannot extend Dijkstra's algorithm to work on graphs with negative-weight edges, however, as Figure 7.6 illustrates.

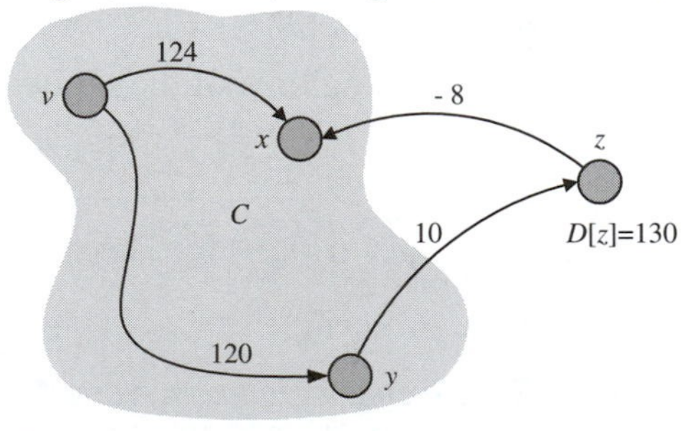

Figure 7.6: An illustration of why Dijkstra's algorithm fails for graphs with negative-weight edges. Bringing z into C and performing edge relaxations will invalidate the previously computed shortest path distance (124) to x.

7.1.2 The Bellman-Ford Shortest Paths Algorithm

There is another algorithm, which is due to Bellman and Ford, that can find shortest paths in graphs that have negative-weight edges. We must, in this case, insist that the graph be directed, for otherwise any negative-weight undirected edge would immediately imply a negative-weight cycle, where we traverse this edge back and forth in each direction. We cannot allow such edges, since a negative cycle invalidates the notion of distance based on edge weights.

Let $\vec{G}$ be a weighted directed graph, possibly with some negative-weight edges. The Bellman-Ford algorithm for computing the shortest-path distance from some vertex v in $\vec{G}$ to every other vertex in $\vec{G}$ is very simple. It shares the notion of edge relaxation from Dijkstra's algorithm, but does not use it in conjunction with the greedy method (which would not work in this context; see Exercise C-7.2). That is, as in Dijkstra's algorithm, the Bellman-Ford algorithm uses a label $D[u]$ that is always an upper bound on the distance $d(v,u)$ from v to u, and which is iteratively "relaxed" until it exactly equals this distance.

The Details of the Bellman-Ford Algorithm

The Bellman-Ford method is shown in Algorithm 7.7. It performs $n-1$ times a relaxation of every edge in the digraph. We illustrate an execution of the Bellman-Ford algorithm in Figure 7.8.

Algorithm BellmanFordShortestPaths($\vec{G}, v$):
  Input: A weighted directed graph $\vec{G}$ with n vertices, and a vertex v of $\vec{G}$
  Output: A label $D[u]$, for each vertex u of $\vec{G}$, such that $D[u]$ is the distance from v to u in $\vec{G}$, or an indication that $\vec{G}$ has a negative-weight cycle

  $D[v] \leftarrow 0$
  for each vertex $u \neq v$ of $\vec{G}$ **do**
    $D[u] \leftarrow +\infty$
  for $i \leftarrow 1$ to $n-1$ **do**
    for each (directed) edge (u,z) outgoing from u **do**
      {Perform the ***relaxation*** operation on (u,z)}
      if $D[u] + w((u,z)) < D[z]$ **then**
        $D[z] \leftarrow D[u] + w((u,z))$
  if there are no edges left with potential relaxation operations **then**
    return the label $D[u]$ of each vertex u
  else
    return "$\vec{G}$ contains a negative-weight cycle"

Algorithm 7.7: The Bellman-Ford single-source shortest-path algorithm, which allows for negative-weight edges.

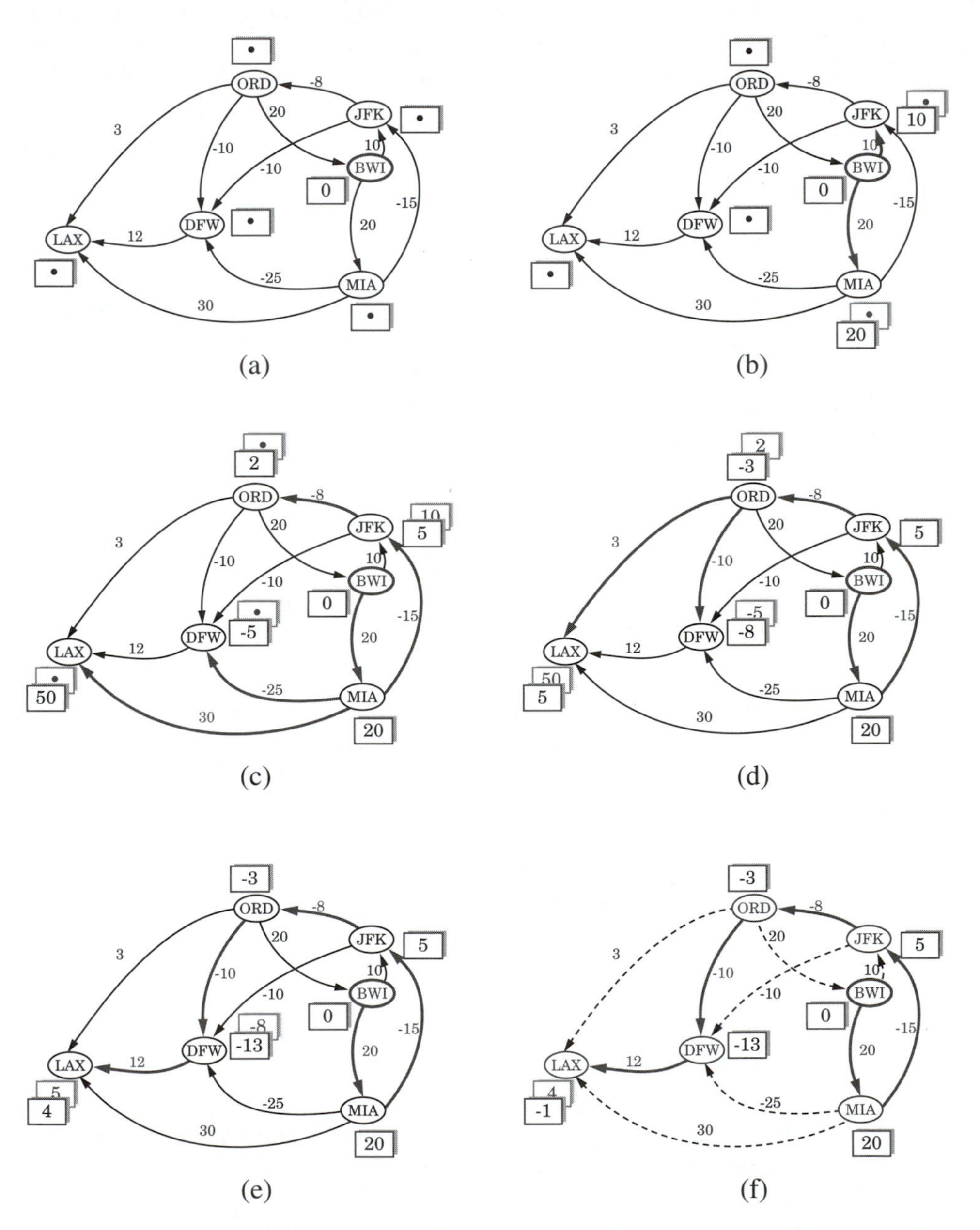

Figure 7.8: An illustration of an application of the Bellman-Ford algorithm. The start vertex is BWI. A box next to each vertex u stores the label $D[u]$, with "shadows" showing values revised during relaxations; the thick edges are causing such relaxations.

Lemma 7.4: *If at the end of the execution of Algorithm 7.7 there is an edge (u,z) that can be relaxed (that is, $D[u]+w((u,z)) < D[z]$), then the input digraph $\vec{G}$ contains a negative-weight cycle. Otherwise, $D[u] = d(v,u)$ for each vertex u in $\vec{G}$.*

Proof: For the sake of this proof, let us introduce a new notion of distance in a digraph. Specifically, let $d_i(v,u)$ denote the length of a path from v to u that is shortest among all paths from v to u that contain at most i edges. We call $d_i(v,u)$ the ***i*-edge distance** from v to u. We claim that after iteration i of the main for-loop in the Bellman-Ford algorithm $D[u] = d_i(v,u)$ for each vertex in $\vec{G}$. This is certainly true before we even begin the first iteration, for $D[v] = 0 = d_0(v,v)$ and, for $u \neq v$, $D[u] = +\infty = d_0(v,u)$. Suppose this claim is true before iteration i (we will now show that if this is the case, then this claim will be true after iteration i as well). In iteration i, we perform a relaxation step for every edge in the digraph. The i-edge distance $d_i(v,u)$, from v to a vertex u, is determined in one of two ways. Either $d_i(v,u) = d_{i-1}(v,u)$ or $d_i(v,u) = d_{i-1}(v,z)+w((z,u))$ for some vertex z in $\vec{G}$. Because we do a relaxation for ***every*** edge of $\vec{G}$ in iteration i, if it is the former case, then after iteration i we have $D[u] = d_{i-1}(v,u) = d_i(v,u)$, and if it is the latter case, then after iteration i we have $D[u] = D[z]+w((z,u)) = d_{i-1}(v,z)+w((z,u)) = d_i(v,u)$. Thus, if $D[u] = d_{i-1}(v,u)$ for each vertex u before iteration i, then $D[u] = d_i(v,u)$ for each vertex u after iteration i.

Therefore, after $n-1$ iterations, $D[u] = d_{n-1}(v,u)$ for each vertex u in $\vec{G}$. Now observe that if there is still an edge in $\vec{G}$ that can be relaxed, then there is some vertex u in $\vec{G}$, such that the n-edge distance from v to u is less than the $(n-1)$-edge distance from v to u, that is, $d_n(v,u) < d_{n-1}(v,u)$. But there are only n vertices in $\vec{G}$; hence, if there is a shortest n-edge path from v to u, it must repeat some vertex z in $\vec{G}$ twice. That is, it must contain a cycle. Moreover, since the distance from a vertex to itself using zero edges is 0 (that is, $d_0(z,z) = 0$), this cycle must be a negative-weight cycle. Thus, if there is an edge in $\vec{G}$ that can still be relaxed after running the Bellman-Ford algorithm, then $\vec{G}$ contains a negative-weight cycle. If, on the other hand, there is no edge in $\vec{G}$ that can still be relaxed after running the Bellman-Ford algorithm, then $\vec{G}$ does not contain a negative-weight cycle. Moreover, in this case, every shortest path between two vertices will have at most $n-1$ edges; hence, for each vertex u in $\vec{G}$, $D[u] = d_{n-1}(v,u) = d(v,u)$. ■

Thus, the Bellman-Ford algorithm is correct and even gives us a way of telling when a digraph contains a negative-weight cycle. The running time of the Bellman-Ford algorithm is easy to analyze. We perform the main for-loop $n-1$ times, and each such loop involves spending $O(1)$ time for each edge in $\vec{G}$. Therefore, the running time for this algorithm is $O(nm)$. We summarize as follows:

Theorem 7.5: *Given a weighted directed graph $\vec{G}$ with n vertices and m edges, and a vertex v of $\vec{G}$, the Bellman-Ford algorithm computes the distance from v to all other vertices of G or determines that $\vec{G}$ contains a negative-weight cycle in $O(nm)$ time.*

7.1.3 Shortest Paths in Directed Acyclic Graphs

As mentioned above, both Dijkstra's algorithm and the Bellman-Ford algorithm work for directed graphs. We can solve the single-source shortest paths problem faster than these algorithms can, however, if the digraph has no directed cycles, that is, it is a weighted directed acyclic graph (DAG).

Recall from Section 6.4.4 that a topological ordering of a DAG $\vec{G}$ is a listing of its vertices $(v_1, v_2, \ldots, v_n)$, such that if (v_i, v_j) is an edge in $\vec{G}$, then $i < j$. Also, recall that we can use the depth-first search algorithm to compute a topological ordering of the n vertices in an m-edge DAG $\vec{G}$ in $O(n+m)$ time. Interestingly, given a topological ordering of such a weighted DAG $\vec{G}$, we can compute all shortest paths from a given vertex v in $O(n+m)$ time.

The Details for Computing Shortest Paths in a DAG

The method, which is given in Algorithm 7.9, involves visiting the vertices of $\vec{G}$ according to the topological ordering, relaxing the outgoing edges with each visit.

Algorithm DAGShortestPaths($\vec{G}, s$):
  Input: A weighted directed acyclic graph (DAG) $\vec{G}$ with n vertices and m edges, and a distinguished vertex s in $\vec{G}$
  Output: A label $D[u]$, for each vertex u of $\vec{G}$, such that $D[u]$ is the distance from v to u in $\vec{G}$

  Compute a topological ordering $(v_1, v_2, \ldots, v_n)$ for $\vec{G}$
  $D[s] \leftarrow 0$
  for each vertex $u \neq s$ of $\vec{G}$ **do**
    $D[u] \leftarrow +\infty$
  for $i \leftarrow 1$ to $n-1$ **do**
    {Relax each outgoing edge from v_i}
    for each edge (v_i, u) outgoing from v_i **do**
      if $D[v_i] + w((v_i, u)) < D[u]$ **then**
        $D[u] \leftarrow D[v_i] + w((v_i, u))$
  Output the distance labels D as the distances from s.

Algorithm 7.9: Shortest path algorithm for a directed acyclic graph.

The running time of the shortest path algorithm for a DAG is easy to analyze. Assuming the digraph is represented using an adjacency list, we can process each vertex in constant time plus an additional time proportional to the number of its outgoing edges. In addition, we have already observed that computing the topological ordering of the vertices in $\vec{G}$ can be done in $O(n+m)$ time. Thus, the entire algorithm runs in $O(n+m)$ time. We illustrate this algorithm in Figure 7.10.

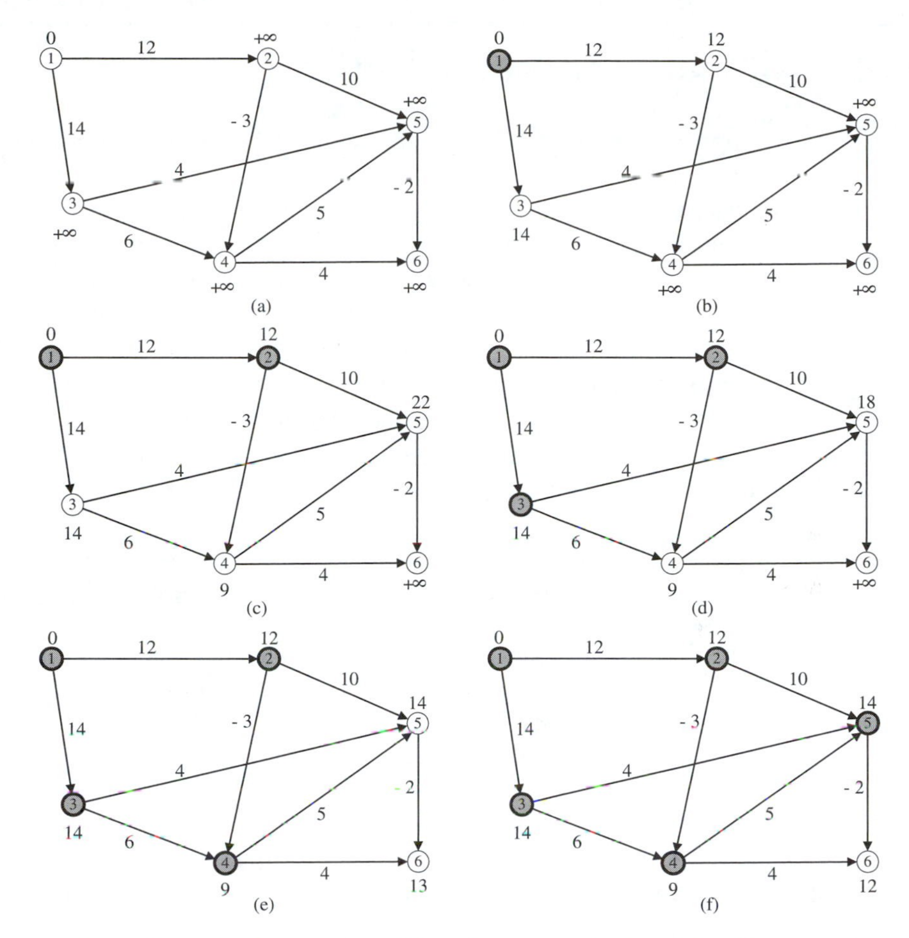

Figure 7.10: An illustration of the shortest-path algorithm for a DAG.

Theorem 7.6: DAGShortestPaths *computes the distance from a start vertex s to each other vertex in a directed n-vertex graph $\vec{G}$ with m edges in $O(n+m)$ time.*

Proof: Suppose, for the sake of a contradiction, that v_i is the first vertex in the topological ordering such that $D[v_i]$ is not the distance from s to v_i. First, note that $D[v_i] < +\infty$, for the initial D value for each vertex other than s is $+\infty$ and the value of a D label is only ever lowered if a path from s is discovered. Thus, if $D[v_j] = +\infty$, then v_j is unreachable from s. Therefore, v_i is reachable from s, so there is a shortest path from s to v_i. Let v_k be the penultimate vertex on a shortest path from s to v_i. Since the vertices are numbered according to a topological ordering, we have that $k < i$. Thus, $D[v_k]$ is correct (we may possibly have $v_k = s$). But when v_k is processed, we relax each outgoing edge from v_k, including the edge on the shortest path from v_k to v_i. Thus, $D[v_i]$ is assigned the distance from s to v_i. But this contradicts the definition of v_i; hence, no such vertex v_i can exist. ■

7.2 All-Pairs Shortest Paths

Suppose we wish to compute the shortest path distance between every pair of vertices in a directed graph $\vec{G}$ with n vertices and m edges. Of course, if $\vec{G}$ has no negative-weight edges, then we could run Dijkstra's algorithm from each vertex in $\vec{G}$ in turn. This approach would take $O(n(n+m)\log n)$ time, assuming $\vec{G}$ is represented using an adjacency list structure. In the worst case, this bound could be as large as $O(n^3 \log n)$. Likewise, if $\vec{G}$ contains no negative-weight cycles, then we could run the Bellman-Ford algorithm starting from each vertex in $\vec{G}$ in turn. This approach would run in $O(n^2 m)$ time, which, in the worst case, could be as large as $O(n^4)$. In this section, we consider algorithms for solving the all-pairs shortest path problem in $O(n^3)$ time, even if the digraph contains negative-weight edges (but not negative-weight cycles).

7.2.1 A Dynamic Programming Shortest Path Algorithm

The first all-pairs shortest path algorithm we discuss is a variation on an algorithm we have given earlier in this book, namely, the Floyd-Warshall algorithm for computing the transitive closure of a directed graph (Algorithm 6.16).

Let $\vec{G}$ be a given weighted directed graph. We number the vertices of $\vec{G}$ arbitrarily as $(v_1, v_2, \ldots, v_n)$. As in any dynamic programming algorithm (Section 5.3), the key construct in the algorithm is to define a parameterized cost function that is easy to compute and also allows us to ultimately compute a final solution. In this case, we use the cost function, $D^k_{i,j}$, which is defined as the distance from v_i to v_j using only intermediate vertices in the set $\{v_1, v_2, \ldots, v_k\}$. Initially,

$$D^0_{i,j} = \begin{cases} 0 & \text{if } i = j \\ w((v_i, v_j)) & \text{if } (v_i, v_j) \text{ is an edge in } \vec{G} \\ +\infty & \text{otherwise.} \end{cases}$$

Given this parameterized cost function $D^k_{i,j}$, and its initial value $D^0_{i,j}$, we can then easily define the value for an arbitrary $k > 0$ as

$$D^k_{i,j} = \min\{D^{k-1}_{i,j}, D^{k-1}_{i,k} + D^{k-1}_{k,j}\}.$$

In other words, the cost for going from v_i to v_j using vertices numbered 1 through k is equal to the shorter of two possible paths. The first path is simply the shortest path from v_i to v_j using vertices numbered 1 through $k-1$. The second path is the sum of the costs of the shortest path from v_i to v_k using vertices numbered 1 through $k-1$ and the shortest path from v_k to v_j using vertices numbered 1 through $k-1$. Moreover, there is no other shorter path from v_i to v_j using vertices of $\{v_1, v_2, \ldots, v_k\}$ than these two. If there was such a shorter path and it excluded v_k, then it would violate the definition of $D^{k-1}_{i,j}$, and if there was such a shorter path and it included v_k, then it would violate the definition of $D^{k-1}_{i,k}$ or $D^{k-1}_{k,j}$. In fact, note

Algorithm AllPairsShortestPaths($\vec{G}$):
  Input: A simple weighted directed graph $\vec{G}$ without negative-weight cycles
  Output: A numbering $v_1, v_2, \ldots, v_n$ of the vertices of $\vec{G}$ and a matrix D, such that $D[i,j]$ is the distance from v_i to v_j in $\vec{G}$

  let $v_1, v_2, \ldots, v_n$ be an arbitrary numbering of the vertices of $\vec{G}$
  for $i \leftarrow 1$ **to** n **do**
    for $j \leftarrow 1$ **to** n **do**
      if $i = j$ **then**
        $D^0[i,i] \leftarrow 0$
      if (v_i, v_j) is an edge in $\vec{G}$ **then**
        $D^0[i,j] \leftarrow w((v_i, v_j))$
      else
        $D^0[i,j] \leftarrow +\infty$
  for $k \leftarrow 1$ to n **do**
    for $i \leftarrow 1$ to n **do**
      for $j \leftarrow 1$ to n **do**
        $D^k[i,j] \leftarrow \min\{D^{k-1}[i,j], D^{k-1}[i,k] + D^{k-1}[k,j]\}$
  return matrix D^n

Algorithm 7.11: A dynamic programming algorithm to compute all-pairs shortest path distances in a digraph without negative cycles.

that this argument still holds even if there are negative cost edges in $\vec{G}$, just so long as there are no negative cost cycles. In Algorithm 7.11, we show how this cost-function definition allows us to build an efficient solution to the all-pairs shortest path problem.

The running time for this dynamic programming algorithm is clearly $O(n^3)$. Thus, we have the following theorem

Theorem 7.7: *Given a simple weighted directed graph $\vec{G}$ with n vertices and no negative-weight cycles, Algorithm 7.11 (*AllPairsShortestPaths*) computes the shortest-path distances between each pair of vertices of $\vec{G}$ in $O(n^3)$ time.*

7.2.2 Computing Shortest Paths via Matrix Multiplication

We can view the problem of computing the shortest-path distances for all pairs of vertices in a directed graph $\vec{G}$ as a matrix problem. In this subsection, we describe how to solve the all-pairs shortest-path problem in $O(n^3)$ time using this approach. We first describe how to use this approach to solve the all-pairs problem in $O(n^4)$ time, and then we show how this can be improved to $O(n^3)$ time by studying the problem in more depth. This matrix-multiplication approach to shortest paths is especially useful in contexts where we represent graphs using the adjacency matrix data structure.

The Weighted Adjacency Matrix Representation

Let us number the vertices of $\vec{G}$ as $(v_0, v_1, \ldots, v_{n-1})$, returning to the convention of numbering the vertices starting at index 0. Given this numbering of the vertices of $\vec{G}$, there is a natural weighted view of the adjacency matrix representation for a graph, where we define $A[i,j]$ as follows:

$$A[i,j] = \begin{cases} 0 & \text{if } i = j \\ w((v_i, v_j)) & \text{if } (v_i, v_j) \text{ is an edge in } \vec{G} \\ +\infty & \text{otherwise.} \end{cases}$$

(Note that this is the same definition used for the cost function $D^0_{i,j}$ from the previous subsection.)

Shortest Paths and Matrix Multiplication

In other words, $A[i,j]$ stores the shortest path distance from v_i to v_j using one or fewer edges in the path. Let us therefore use the matrix A to define another matrix A^2, such that $A^2[i,j]$ stores the shortest path distance from v_i to v_j using at most two edges. A path with at most two edges is either empty (a zero-edge path) or it adds an extra edge to a zero-edge or one-edge path. Therefore, we can define $A^2[i,j]$ as

$$A^2[i,j] = \min_{l=0,1,\ldots,n-1} \{A[i,l] + A[l,j]\}.$$

Thus, given A, we can compute the matrix A^2 in $O(n^3)$ time, by using an algorithm very similar to the standard matrix multiplication algorithm.

In fact, we can view this computation as a matrix multiplication in which we have simply redefined what the operators "plus" and "times" mean in the matrix multiplication algorithm (the programming language C++ specifically allows for such operator overloading). If we let "plus" be redefined to mean "min" and we let "times" be redefined to mean "+," then we can write $A^2[i,j]$ as a true matrix multiplication:

$$A^2[i,j] = \sum_{l=0,1,\ldots,n-1} A[i,l] \cdot A[l,j].$$

Indeed, this matrix-multiplication viewpoint is the reason why we have written this matrix as "A^2," for it is the square of the matrix A.

Let us continue this approach to define a matrix A^k, so that $A^k[i,j]$ is the shortest-path distance from v_i to v_j using at most k edges. Since a path with at most k edges is equivalent to a path with at most $k-1$ edges plus possibly one additional edge, we can define A^k so that

$$A^k[i,j] = \sum_{l=0,1,\ldots,n-1} A^{k-1}[i,l] \cdot A[l,j],$$

continuing the operator redefining so that "+" stands for "min" and "·" stands for "+."

The crucial observation is that if $\vec{G}$ contains no negative-weight cycles, then A^{n-1} stores the shortest-path distance between each pair of vertices in $\vec{G}$. This observation follows from the fact that any well-defined shortest path contains at most $n-1$ edges. If a path has more than $n-1$ edges, it must repeat some vertex; hence, it must contain a cycle. But a shortest path will never contain a cycle (unless there is a negative-weight cycle in $\vec{G}$). Thus, to solve the all-pairs shortest path problem, all we need to do is to multiply A times itself $n-1$ times. Since each such multiplication can be done in $O(n^3)$ time, this approach immediately gives us the following.

Theorem 7.8: *Given a weighted directed n-vertex graph $\vec{G}$ containing no negative-weight cycles, and the weighted adjacency matrix A for $\vec{G}$, the all-pairs shortest path problem for $\vec{G}$ can be solved by computing A^{n-1}, which can be performed in $O(n^4)$ time.*

In Section 10.1.4, we discuss an exponentiation algorithm for numbers, which can be applied in the present context of matrix multiplication to compute A^{n-1} in $O(n^3 \log n)$ time. We can actually compute A^{n-1} in $O(n^3)$ time, however, by taking advantage of additional structure present in the all-pairs shortest-path problem.

Matrix Closure

As observed above, if $\vec{G}$ contains no negative-weight cycles, then A^{n-1} encodes all the shortest-path distances between pairs of vertices in $\vec{G}$. A well-defined shortest path can contain no cycles; hence, a shortest path restricted to contain at most $n-1$ edges must be a true shortest path. Likewise, a shortest path containing at most n edges is a true shortest path, as is a shortest path containing at most $n+1$ edges, $n+2$ edges, and so on. Therefore, if $\vec{G}$ contains no negative-weight cycles, then

$$A^{n-1} = A^n = A^{n+1} = A^{n+2} = \cdots.$$

The ***closure*** of a matrix A is defined as

$$A^* = \sum_{l=0}^{\infty} A^l,$$

if such a matrix exists. If A is a weighted adjacency matrix, then $A^*[i, j]$ is the sum of all possible paths from v_i to v_j. In our case, A is the weighted adjacency matrix for a directed graph $\vec{G}$ and we have redefined "+" as "min." Thus, we can write

$$A^* = \min_{i=0,\ldots,\infty} \{A^i\}.$$

Moreover, since we are computing shortest path distances, the entries in A^{i+1} are never larger than the entries in A^i. Therefore, for the weighted adjacency matrix of an n-vertex digraph $\vec{G}$ with no negative-weight cycles,

$$A^* = A^{n-1} = A^n = A^{n+1} = A^{n+2} = \cdots.$$

That is, $A^*[i, j]$ stores the length of the shortest path from v_i to v_j.

Computing the Closure of a Weighted Adjacency Matrix

We can compute the closure A^* by divide-and-conquer in $O(n^3)$ time. Without loss of generality, we may assume that n is a power of two (if not, then pad the digraph $\vec{G}$ with extra vertices that have no in-going or out-going edges). Let us divide the set V of vertices in $\vec{G}$ into two equal-sized sets $V_1 = \{v_0, \ldots, v_{n/2-1}\}$ and $V_2 = \{v_{n/2}, \ldots, v_{n-1}\}$. Given this division, we can likewise divide the adjacency matrix A into four blocks, B, C, D, and E, each with $n/2$ rows and columns, defined as follows:

- B: weights of edges from V_1 to V_1
- C: weights of edges from V_1 to V_2
- D: weights of edges from V_2 to V_1
- E: weights of edges from V_2 to V_2.

That is,

$$A = \begin{pmatrix} B & C \\ D & E \end{pmatrix}.$$

We illustrate these four sets of edges in Figure 7.12.

Likewise, we can partition A^* into four blocks W, X, Y, and Z, as well, which are similarly defined.

- W: weights of shortest paths from V_1 to V_1
- X: weights of shortest paths from V_1 to V_2
- Y: weights of shortest paths from V_2 to V_1
- Z: weights of shortest paths from V_2 to V_2,

That is,

$$A^* = \begin{pmatrix} W & X \\ Y & Z \end{pmatrix}.$$

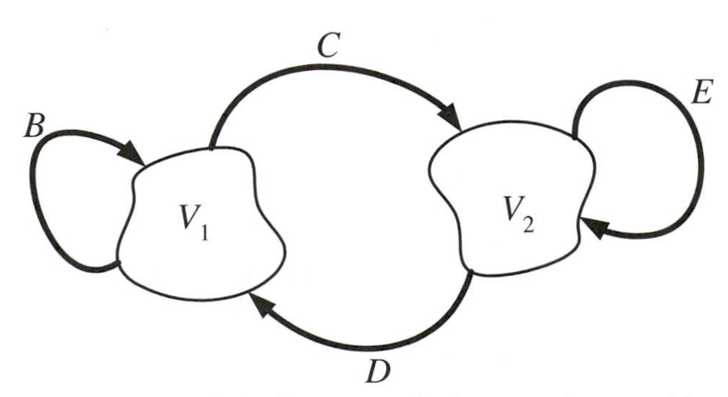

Figure 7.12: An illustration of the four sets of edges used to partition the adjacency matrix A in the divide-and-conquer algorithm for computing A^*.

Submatrix Equations

By these definitions and those above, we can derive simple equations to define W, X, Y, and Z directly from the submatrices B, C, D, and E.

- $W = (B + C \cdot E^* \cdot D)^*$, for paths in W consist of the closure of subpaths that either stay in V_1 or jump to V_2, travel in V_2 for a while, and then jump back to V_1.
- $X = W \cdot C \cdot E^*$, for paths in X consist of the closure of subpaths that start and end in V_1 (with possible jumps to V_2 and back), followed by a jump to V_2 and the closure of subpaths that stay in V_2.
- $Y = E^* \cdot D \cdot W$, for paths in Y consist of the closure of subpaths that stay in V_2, followed by a jump to V_1 and the closure of subpaths that start and end in V_1 (with possible jumps to V_2 and back).
- $Z = E^* + E^* \cdot D \cdot W \cdot C \cdot E^*$, for paths in Z consist of paths that stay in V_2 or paths that travel in V_2, jump to V_1, travel in V_1 for a while (with possible jumps to V_2 and back), jump back to V_2, and then stay in V_2.

Given these equations it is a simple matter to then construct a recursive algorithm to compute A^*. In this algorithm, we divide A into the blocks B, C, D, and E, as described above. We then recursively compute the closure E^*. Given E^*, we can then recursively compute the closure $(B + C \cdot E^* \cdot D)^*$, which is W.

Note that no other recursive closure computations are then needed to compute X, Y, and Z. Thus, after a constant number of matrix additions and multiplications, we can compute all the blocks in A^*. This gives us the following theorem.

Theorem 7.9: *Given a weighted directed n-vertex graph $\vec{G}$ containing no negative-weight cycles, and the weighted adjacency matrix A for $\vec{G}$, the all-pairs shortest path problem for $\vec{G}$ can be solved by computing A^*, which can be performed in $O(n^3)$ time.*

Proof: We have already argued why the computation of A^* solves the all-pairs shortest-path problem. Consider, then, the running time of the divide-and-conquer algorithm for computing A^*, the closure of the $n \times n$ adjacency matrix A. This algorithm consists of two recursive calls to compute the closure of $(n/2) \times (n/2)$ submatrices, plus a constant number of matrix additions and multiplications (using "min" for "+" and "+" for "·"). Thus, assuming we use the straightforward $O(n^3)$-time matrix multiplication algorithm, we can characterize the running time, $T(n)$, for computing A^* as

$$T(n) = \begin{cases} b & \text{if } n = 1 \\ 2T(n/2) + cn^3 & \text{if } n > 1, \end{cases}$$

where $b > 0$ and $c > 0$ are constants. Therefore, by the Master Theorem (5.6), we can compute A^* in $O(n^3)$ time. ■

7.3 Minimum Spanning Trees

Suppose we wish to connect all the computers in a new office building using the least amount of cable. Likewise, suppose we have an undirected computer network in which each connection between two routers has a cost for usage; we want to connect all our routers at the minimum cost possible. We can model these problems using a weighted graph G whose vertices represent the computers or routers, and whose edges represent all the possible pairs (u,v) of computers, where the weight $w((v,u))$ of edge (v,u) is equal to the amount of cable or network cost needed to connect computer v to computer u. Rather than computing a shortest path tree from some particular vertex v, we are interested instead in finding a (free) tree T that contains all the vertices of G and has the minimum total weight over all such trees. Methods for finding such trees are the focus of this section.

Problem Definition

Given a weighted undirected graph G, we are interested in finding a tree T that contains all the vertices in G and minimizes the sum of the weights of the edges of T, that is,

$$w(T) = \sum_{e \in T} w(e).$$

We recall from Section 6.1 that a tree such as this, which contains every vertex of a connected graph G, is said to be a ***spanning tree***. Computing a spanning tree T with smallest total weight is the problem of constructing a ***minimum spanning tree*** (or ***MST***).

The development of efficient algorithms for the minimum-spanning-tree problem predates the modern notion of computer science itself. In this section, we discuss two algorithms for solving the MST problem. These algorithms are all classic applications of the ***greedy method***. As was discussed in Section 5.1, we apply the greedy method by iteratively choosing objects to join a growing collection, by incrementally picking an object that minimizes some cost function.

The first MST algorithm we discuss is Kruskal's algorithm, which "grows" the MST in clusters by considering edges in order of their weights. The second algorithm we discuss is the Prim-Jarník algorithm, which grows the MST from a single root vertex, much in the same way as Dijkstra's shortest-path algorithm. We conclude this section by discussing a third algorithm, due to Barůvka, which applies the greedy approach in a parallel way.

As in Section 7.1.1, in order to simplify the description the algorithms, we assume, in the following, that the input graph G is undirected (that is, all its edges are undirected) and simple (that is, it has no self-loops and no parallel edges). Hence, we denote the edges of G as unordered vertex pairs (u,z).

A Crucial Fact about Minimum Spanning Trees

Before we discuss the details of these algorithms, however, let us give a crucial fact about minimum spanning trees that forms the basis of the algorithms. In particular, all the MST algorithms we discuss are based on the greedy method, which in this case depends crucially on the following fact. (See Figure 7.13.)

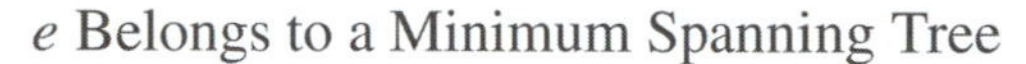

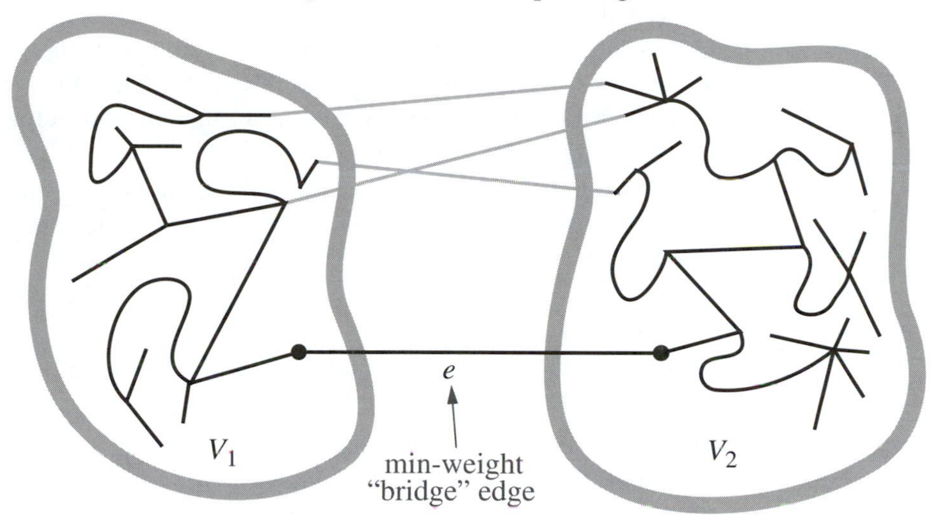

Figure 7.13: An illustration of the crucial fact about minimum spanning trees.

Theorem 7.10: *Let G be a weighted connected graph, and let V_1 and V_2 be a partition of the vertices of G into two disjoint nonempty sets. Furthermore, let e be an edge in G with minimum weight from among those with one endpoint in V_1 and the other in V_2. There is a minimum spanning tree T that has e as one of its edges.*

Proof: Let T be a minimum spanning tree of G. If T does not contain edge e, the addition of e to T must create a cycle. Therefore, there is some edge f of this cycle that has one endpoint in V_1 and the other in V_2. Moreover, by the choice of e, $w(e) \leq w(f)$. If we remove f from $T \cup \{e\}$, we obtain a spanning tree whose total weight is no more than before. Since T was a minimum spanning tree, this new tree must also be a minimum spanning tree. ■

In fact, if the weights in G are distinct, then the minimum spanning tree is unique; we leave the justification of this less crucial fact as an exercise (C-7.5).

In addition, note that Theorem 7.10 remains valid even if the graph G contains negative-weight edges or negative-weight cycles, unlike the algorithms we presented for shortest paths.

7.3.1 Kruskal's Algorithm

The reason Theorem 7.10 is so important is that it can be used as the basis for building a minimum spanning tree. In Kruskal's algorithm, it is used to build the minimum spanning tree in clusters. Initially, each vertex is in its own cluster all by itself. The algorithm then considers each edge in turn, ordered by increasing weight. If an edge e connects two different clusters, then e is added to the set of edges of the minimum spanning tree, and the two clusters connected by e are merged into a single cluster. If, on the other hand, e connects two vertices that are already in the same cluster, then e is discarded. Once the algorithm has added enough edges to form a spanning tree, it terminates and outputs this tree as the minimum spanning tree.

We give pseudo-code for Kruskal's method for solving the MST problem in Algorithm 7.14, and we show the working of this algorithm in Figures 7.15, 7.16, and 7.17.

Algorithm KruskalMST(G):
  Input: A simple connected weighted graph G with n vertices and m edges
  Output: A minimum spanning tree T for G

  for each vertex v in G **do**
    Define an elementary cluster $C(v) \leftarrow \{v\}$.
  Initialize a priority queue Q to contain all edges in G, using the weights as keys.
  $T \leftarrow \emptyset$ {T will ultimately contain the edges of the MST}
  while T has fewer than $n-1$ edges **do**
    $(u,v) \leftarrow Q$.removeMin()
    Let $C(v)$ be the cluster containing v, and let $C(u)$ be the cluster containing u.
    if $C(v) \neq C(u)$ **then**
      Add edge (v,u) to T.
      Merge $C(v)$ and $C(u)$ into one cluster, that is, union $C(v)$ and $C(u)$.
  return tree T

Algorithm 7.14: Kruskal's algorithm for the MST problem.

As mentioned before, the correctness of Kruskal's algorithm follows from the crucial fact about minimum spanning trees, Theorem 7.10. Each time Kruskal's algorithm adds an edge (v,u) to the minimum spanning tree T, we can define a partitioning of the set of vertices V (as in the theorem) by letting V_1 be the cluster containing v and letting V_2 contain the rest of the vertices in V. This clearly defines a disjoint partitioning of the vertices of V and, more importantly, since we are extracting edges from Q in order by their weights, e must be a minimum-weight edge with one vertex in V_1 and the other in V_2. Thus, Kruskal's algorithm always adds a valid minimum-spanning-tree edge.

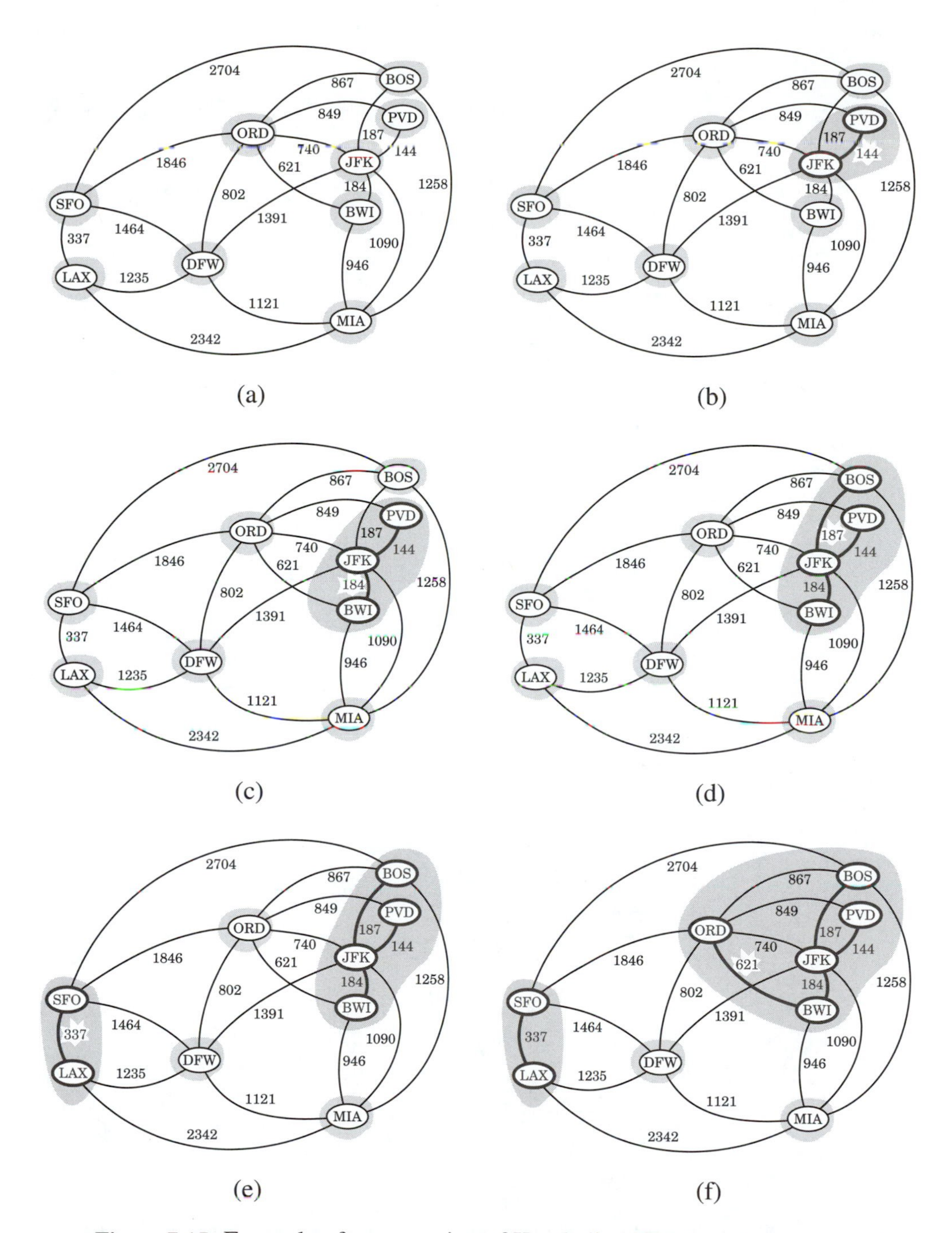

Figure 7.15: Example of an execution of Kruskal's MST algorithm on a graph with integer weights. We show the clusters as shaded regions and we highlight the edge being considered in each iteration (continued in Figure 7.16).

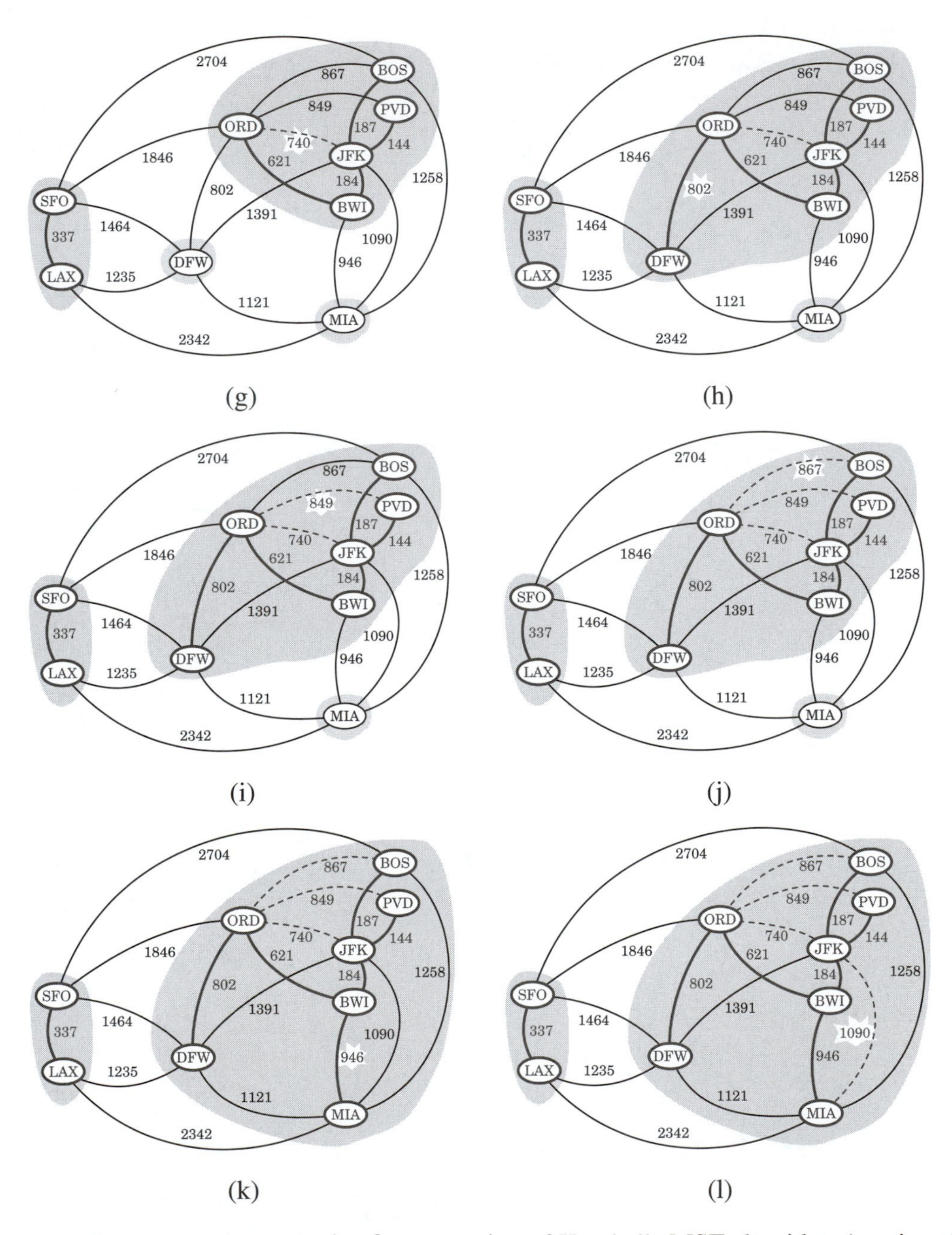

Figure 7.16: An example of an execution of Kruskal's MST algorithm (continued). Rejected edges are shown dashed. (continued in Figure 7.17).

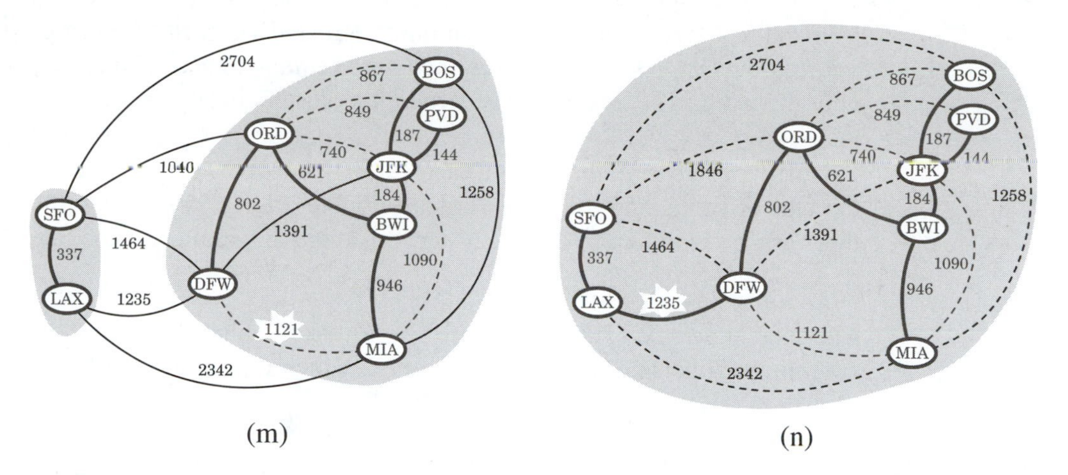

Figure 7.17: Example of an execution of Kruskal's MST algorithm (continued from Figures 7.15 and 7.16). The edge considered in (n) merges the last two clusters, which concludes this execution of Kruskal's algorithm.

Implementing Kruskal's Algorithm

We denote the number of vertices and edges of the input graph G with n and m, respectively. We assume that the edge weights can be compared in constant time. Because of the high level of the description we gave for Kruskal's algorithm in Algorithm 7.14, analyzing its running time requires that we give more details on its implementation. Specifically, we should indicate the data structures used and how they are implemented.

We implement the priority queue Q using a heap. Thus, we can initialize Q in $O(m \log m)$ time by repeated insertions, or in $O(m)$ time using bottom-up heap construction (see Section 2.4.4). In addition, at each iteration of the **while** loop, we can remove a minimum-weight edge in $O(\log m)$ time, which actually is $O(\log n)$, since G is simple.

A Simple Cluster Merging Strategy

We use a list-based implementation of a partition (Section 4.2.2) for the clusters. Namely, we represent each cluster C with an unordered linked list of vertices, storing, with each vertex v, a reference to its cluster $C(v)$. With this representation, testing whether $C(u) \neq C(v)$ takes $O(1)$ time. When we need to merge two clusters, $C(u)$ and $C(v)$, we move the elements of the ***smaller*** cluster into the larger one and update the cluster references of the vertices in the smaller cluster. Since we can simply add the elements of the smaller cluster at the end of the list for the larger cluster, merging two clusters takes time proportional to the size of the smaller cluster. That is, merging clusters $C(u)$ and $C(v)$ takes $O(\min\{|C(u)|, |C(v)|\})$ time. There are other, more efficient, methods for merging clusters (see Section 4.2.2), but this simple approach will be sufficient.

Lemma 7.11: *Consider an execution of Kruskal's algorithm on a graph with n vertices, where clusters are represented with sequences and with cluster references at each vertex. The total time spent merging clusters is $O(n \log n)$.*

Proof: We observe that each time a vertex is moved to a new cluster, the size of the cluster containing the vertex at least doubles. Let $t(v)$ be the number of times that vertex v is moved to a new cluster. Since the maximum cluster size is n,

$$t(v) \leq \log n.$$

The total time spent merging clusters in Kruskal's algorithm can be obtained by summing up the work done on each vertex, which is proportional to

$$\sum_{v \in G} t(v) \leq n \log n.$$

■

Using Lemma 7.11 and arguments similar to those used in the analysis of Dijkstra's algorithm, we conclude that the total running time of Kruskal's algorithm is $O((n+m)\log n)$, which can be simplified as $O(m \log n)$ since G is simple and connected.

Theorem 7.12: *Given a simple connected weighted graph G with n vertices and m edges, Kruskal's algorithm constructs a minimum spanning tree for G in time $O(m \log n)$.*

7.3.2 The Prim-Jarník Algorithm

In the Prim-Jarník algorithm, we grow a minimum spanning tree from a single cluster starting from some "root" vertex v. The main idea is similar to that of Dijkstra's algorithm. We begin with some vertex v, defining the initial "cloud" of vertices C. Then, in each iteration, we choose a minimum-weight edge $e = (v, u)$, connecting a vertex v in the cloud C to a vertex u outside of C. The vertex u is then brought into the cloud C and the process is repeated until a spanning tree is formed. Again, the crucial fact about minimum spanning trees comes to play, for by always choosing the smallest-weight edge joining a vertex inside C to one outside C, we are assured of always adding a valid edge to the MST.

Growing a Single MST

To efficiently implement this approach, we can take another cue from Dijkstra's algorithm. We maintain a label $D[u]$ for each vertex u outside the cloud C, so that $D[u]$ stores the weight of the best current edge for joining u to the cloud C. These labels allow us to reduce the number of edges that we must consider in deciding which vertex is next to join the cloud. We give the pseudo-code in Algorithm 7.18.

```
Algorithm PrimJarníkMST(G):
  Input: A weighted connected graph G with n vertices and m edges
  Output: A minimum spanning tree T for G

  Pick any vertex v of G
  D[v] ← 0
  for each vertex u ≠ v do
    D[u] ← +∞
  Initialize T ← ∅.
  Initialize a priority queue Q with an item ((u, null), D[u]) for each vertex u,
  where (u, null) is the element and D[u] is the key.
  while Q is not empty do
    (u, e) ← Q.removeMin()
    Add vertex u and edge e to T.
    for each vertex z adjacent to u such that z is in Q do
      {perform the relaxation procedure on edge (u, z)}
      if w((u, z)) < D[z] then
        D[z] ← w((u, z))
        Change to (z, (u, z)) the element of vertex z in Q.
        Change to D[z] the key of vertex z in Q.
  return the tree T
```

Algorithm 7.18: The Prim-Jarník algorithm for the MST problem.

Analyzing the Prim-Jarník Algorithm

Let n and m denote the number of vertices and edges of the input graph G, respectively. The implementation issues for the Prim-Jarník algorithm are similar to those for Dijkstra's algorithm. If we implement the priority queue Q as a heap that supports the locator-based priority queue methods (see Section 2.4.4), we can extract the vertex u in each iteration in $O(\log n)$ time.

In addition, we can update each $D[z]$ value in $O(\log n)$ time, as well, which is a computation considered at most once for each edge (u,z). The other steps in each iteration can be implemented in constant time. Thus, the total running time is $O((n+m)\log n)$, which is $O(m\log n)$. Hence, we can summarize as follows:

Theorem 7.13: *Given a simple connected weighted graph G with n vertices and m edges, the Prim-Jarník algorithm constructs a minimum spanning tree for G in $O(m\log n)$ time.*

We illustrate the Prim-Jarník algorithm in Figures 7.19 and 7.20.

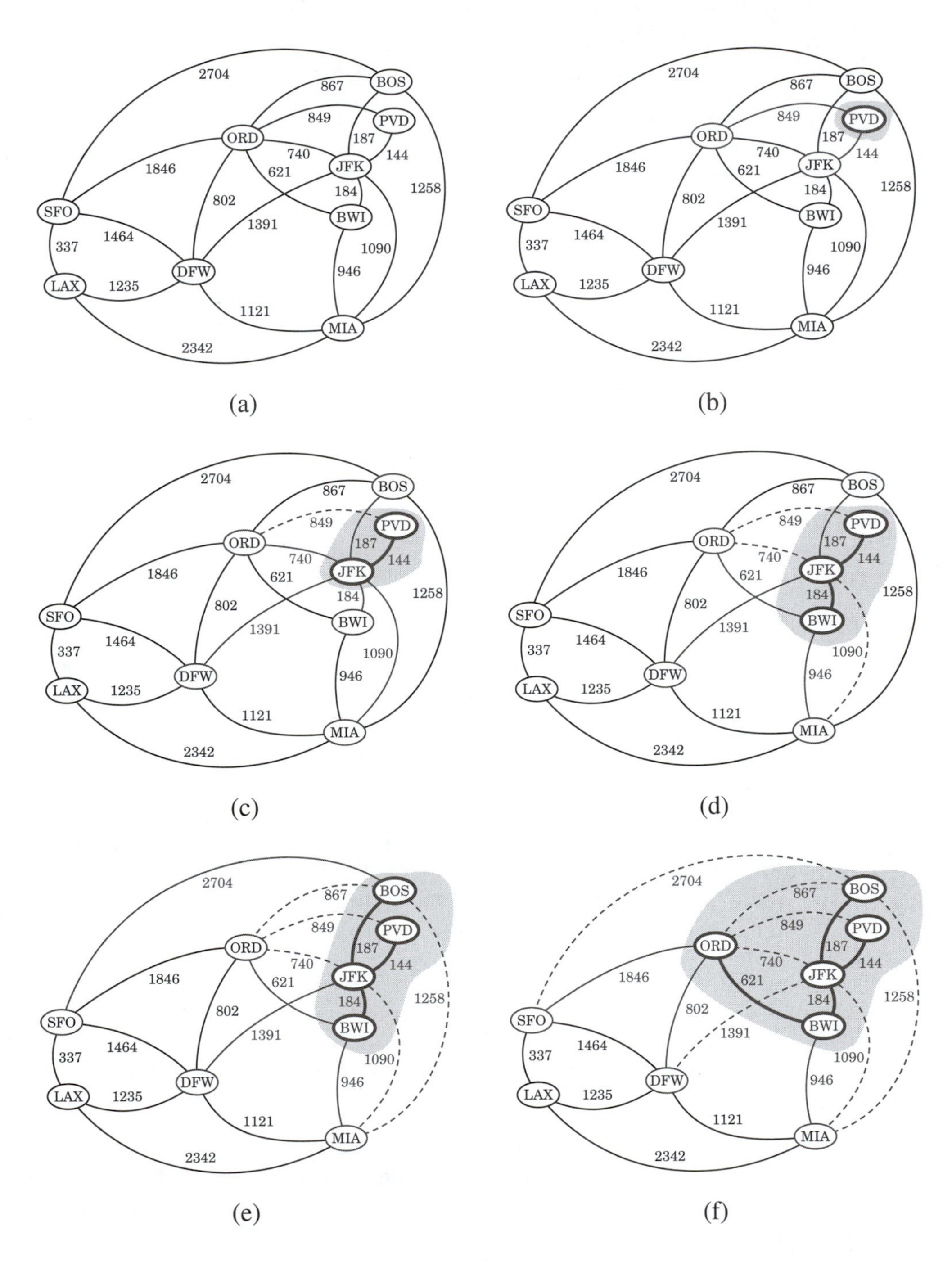

Figure 7.19: Visualizing the Prim-Jarník algorithm (continued in Figure 7.20).

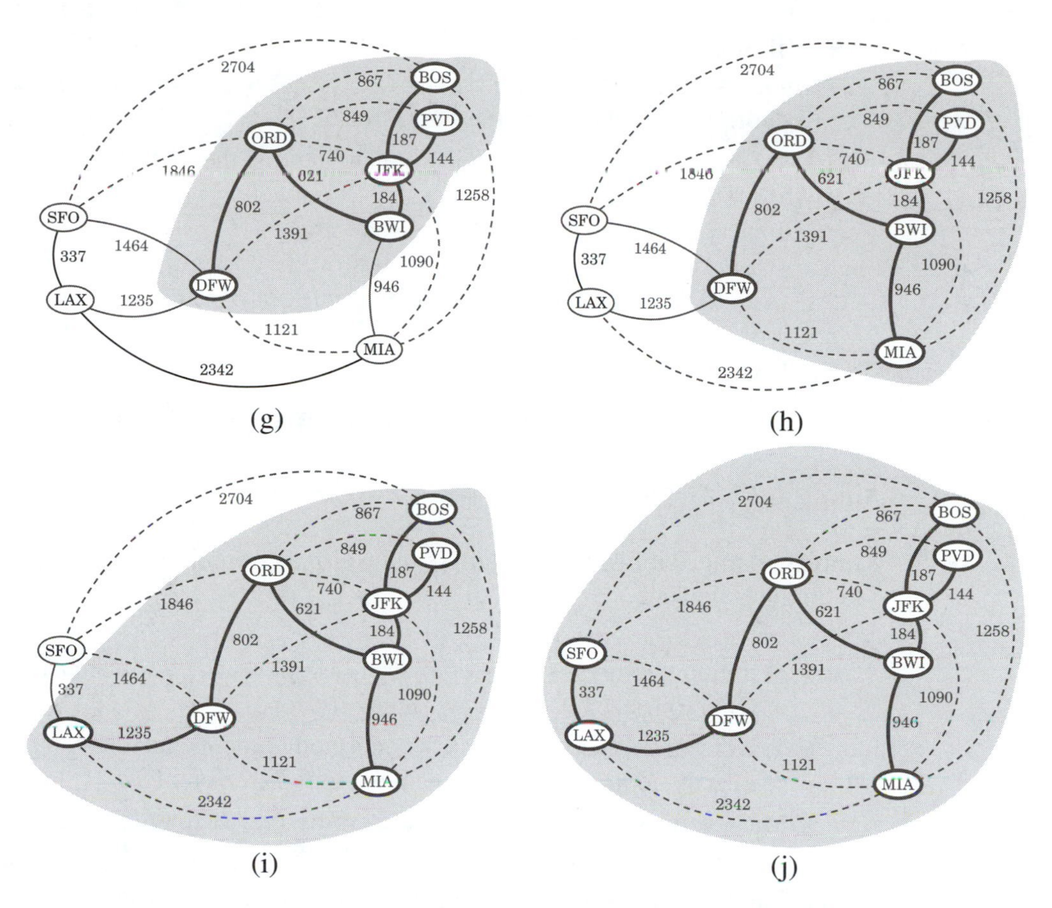

Figure 7.20: Visualizing the Prim-Jarník algorithm (continued from Figure 7.19).

7.3.3 Barůvka's Algorithm

Each of the two minimum-spanning-tree algorithms we have described previously has achieved its efficient running time by utilizing a priority queue Q, which could be implemented using a heap (or even a more sophisticated data structure). This usage should seem natural, for minimum-spanning-tree algorithms involve applications of the greedy method—and, in this case, the greedy method must explicitly be optimizing certain priorities among the vertices of the graph in question. It may be a bit surprising, but as we show in this section, we can actually design an efficient minimum-spanning-tree algorithm without using a priority queue. Moreover, what may be even more surprising is that the insight behind this simplification comes from the oldest known minimum-spanning-tree algorithm—the algorithm of Barůvka.

We present a pseudo-code description of Barůvka's minimum-spanning-tree algorithm in Algorithm 7.21, and we illustrate an execution of this algorithm in Figure 7.22.

Algorithm BarůvkaMST(G):
  Input: A weighted connected graph $G = (V, E)$ with n vertices and m edges
  Output: A minimum spanning tree T for G.

  Let T be a subgraph of G initially containing just the vertices in V.
  while T has fewer than $n-1$ edges $\{T$ is not yet an MST$\}$ **do**
    for each connected component C_i of T **do**
      $\{$Perform the MST edge addition procedure for cluster $C_i\}$
      Find the smallest-weight edge $e = (v, u)$, in E with $v \in C_i$ and $u \notin C_i$.
      Add e to T (unless e is already in T).
  return T

Algorithm 7.21: Pseudo-code for Barůvka's algorithm.

Implementing Barůvka's Algorithm

Implementing Barůvka's algorithm is quite simple, requiring only that we be able to do the following:

- Maintain the forest T subject to edge insertion, which we can easily support in $O(1)$ time each using an adjacency list for T
- Traverse the forest T to identify connected components (clusters), which we can easily do in $O(n)$ time using a depth-first search of T
- Mark vertices with the name of the cluster they belong to, which we can do with an extra instance variable for each vertex
- Identify a smallest-weight edge in E incident upon a cluster C_i, which we can do by scanning the adjacency lists in G for the vertices in C_i.

Like Kruskal's algorithm, Barůvka's algorithm builds the minimum spanning tree by growing a number of clusters of vertices in a series of rounds, not just one cluster, as was done by the Prim-Jarník algorithm. But in Barůvka's algorithm, the clusters are grown by applying the crucial fact about minimum spanning trees to each cluster simultaneously. This approach allows many more edges to be added in each round.

Why Is This Algorithm Correct?

In each iteration of Barůvka's algorithm, we choose the smallest-weight edge coming out of each connected component C_i of the current set T of minimum-spanning-tree edges. In each case, this edge is a valid choice, for if we consider a partitioning of V into the vertices in C_i and those outside of C_i, then the chosen edge e for C_i satisfies the condition of the crucial fact about minimum spanning trees (Theorem 7.10) for guaranteeing that e belongs to a minimum spanning tree.

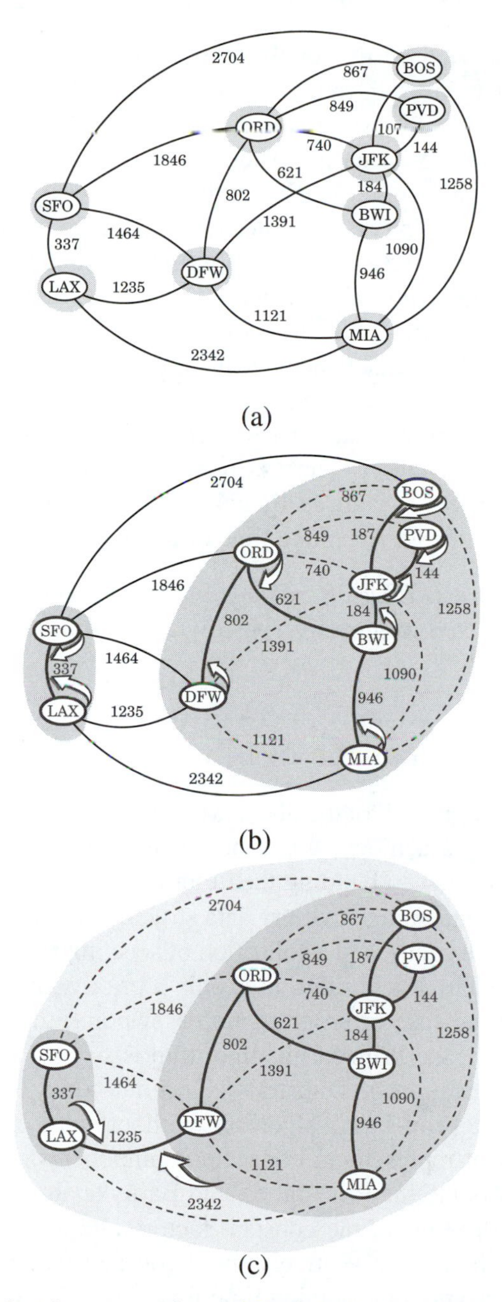

Figure 7.22: Example of an execution of Barůvka's algorithm. We show clusters as shaded regions. We highlight the edge chosen by each cluster with an arrow and we draw each such MST edge as a thick line. Edges determined not to be in the MST are shown dashed.

Analyzing Barůvka's Algorithm

Let us analyze the running time of Barůvka's algorithm (Algorithm 7.21). We can implement each round performing the searches to find the minimum-weight edge going out of each cluster by an exhaustive search through the adjacency lists of each vertex in each cluster. Thus, the total running time spent in searching for minimum-weight edges can be made to be $O(m)$, for it involves examining each edge (v,u) in G twice: once for v and once for u (since vertices are labeled with the number of the cluster they are in). The remaining computations in the main while-loop involve relabeling all the vertices, which takes $O(n)$ time, and traversing all the edges in T, which takes $O(n)$ time. Thus, each round in Barůvka's algorithm takes $O(m)$ time (since $n \le m$). In each round of the algorithm, we choose one edge coming out of each cluster, and we then merge each new connected component of T into a new cluster. Thus, each old cluster of T must merge with at least one other old cluster of T. That is, in each round of Barůvka's algorithm, the total number of clusters is reduced by half. Therefore, the total number of rounds is $O(\log n)$; hence, the total running time of Barůvka's algorithm is $O(m \log n)$. We summarize:

Theorem 7.14: *Barůvka's algorithm computes a minimum spanning tree for a connected weighted graph G with n vertices and m edges in $O(m \log n)$ time.*

7.3.4 A Comparison of MST Algorithms

Although each of the above MST algorithms has the same worst-case running time, each one achieves this running time using different data structures and different approaches to building the minimum spanning tree.

Concerning auxiliary data structures, Kruskal's algorithm uses a priority queue, to store edges, and a collection of sets, implemented with lists, to store clusters. The Prim-Jarník algorithm uses only a priority queue, to store vertex-edge pairs. Thus, from an ease of programming viewpoint, the Prim-Jarník algorithm is preferable. Indeed, the Prim-Jarník algorithm is so similar to Dijkstra's algorithm that an implementation of Dijkstra's algorithm could be converted into an implementation for the Prim-Jarník algorithm without much effort. Barůvka's algorithm requires a way of representing connected components. Thus, from an ease of programming viewpoint, the Prim-Jarník and Barůvka algorithms seem to be the best.

In terms of the constant factors, the three algorithms are fairly similar in that they both have relatively small constant factors in their asymptotic running times. The asymptotic running time for Kruskal's algorithm can be improved if the edges are given in sorted order by their weights (using the partition data structure of Section 4.2.2). Also, the running time of Barůvka's algorithm can be changed to be $O(n^2)$ in the worst case with a slight modification to the algorithm (which we explore in Exercise C-7.12). Thus, there is no clear winner among these three algorithms, although Barůvka's algorithm is the easiest of the three to implement.

7.4 Java Example: Dijkstra's Algorithm

In this section, we present Java code for performing Dijkstra's algorithm (Algorithm 7.2), assuming we are given an undirected graph with positive integer weights.

We express our implementation of Dijkstra's algorithm by means of an abstract class Dijkstra (Code Fragments 7.23–7.25), which declares the abstract method weight(e) to extract the weight of edge e. Class Dijkstra is meant to be extended by subclasses that implement method weight(e). See, for example, class MyDijkstra shown in Code Fragment 7.26.

```
/** Dijkstra's algorithm for the single-source shortest path problem
  * in an undirected graph whose edges have integer weights. Classes
  * extending ths abstract class must define the weight(e) method,
  * which extracts the weight of an edge. */
public abstract class Dijkstra {
  /** Execute Dijkstra's algorithm. */
  public void execute(InspectableGraph g, Vertex source) {
    graph = g;
    dijkstraVisit(source);
  }
  /** Attribute for vertex distances. */
  protected Object DIST = new Object();
  /** Set the distance of a vertex. */
  protected void setDist(Vertex v, int d) {
    v.set(DIST, new Integer(d));
  }
  /** Get the distance of a vertex from the source vertex. This method
    * returns the length of a shortest path from the source to u after
    * method execute has been called. */
  public int getDist(Vertex u) {
    return ((Integer) u.get(DIST)).intValue();
  }
  /** This abstract method must be defined by subclasses.
    * @return weight of edge e. */
  protected abstract int weight(Edge e);
  /** Infinity value. */
  public static final int INFINITE = Integer.MAX_VALUE;
  /** Input graph. */
  protected InspectableGraph graph;
  /** Auxiliary priority queue. */
  protected PriorityQueue Q;
```

Code Fragment 7.23: Class Dijkstra implementing Dijkstra's algorithm (continued in Code Fragments 7.24 and 7.25).

The algorithm is executed by method dijkstraVisit. A priority queue Q supporting locator-based methods (Section 2.4.4) is used. We insert a vertex u into Q with method insert, which returns the locator of u in Q. Following the decorator pattern, we "attach" to u its locator by means of method setLoc, and we retrieve the locator of u with method getLoc. Changing the label of a vertex z to d in the relaxation procedure is done with method replaceKey(ℓ, d), where ℓ is the locator of z.

```
/** The actual execution of Dijkstra's algorithm.
  * @param v source vertex. */
protected void dijkstraVisit (Vertex v) {
  // initialize the priority queue Q and store all the vertices in it
  Q = new ArrayHeap(new IntegerComparator());
  for (VertexIterator vertices = graph.vertices(); vertices.hasNext();) {
    Vertex u = vertices.nextVertex();
    int u_dist;
    if (u==v)
      u_dist = 0;
    else
      u_dist = INFINITE;
    // setDist(u, u_dist);
    Locator u_loc = Q.insert(new Integer(u_dist), u);
    setLoc(u, u_loc);
  }
  // grow the cloud, one vertex at a time
  while (!Q.isEmpty()) {
    // remove from Q and insert into cloud a vertex with minimum distance
    Locator u_loc = Q.min();
    Vertex u = getVertex(u_loc);
    int u_dist = getDist(u_loc);
    Q.remove(u_loc); // remove u from the priority queue
    setDist(u, u_dist); // the distance of u is final
    destroyLoc(u); // remove the locator associated with u
    if (u_dist == INFINITE)
      continue; // unreachable vertices are not processed
    // examine all the neighbors of u and update their distances
    for (EdgeIterator edges = graph.incidentEdges(u); edges.hasNext();) {
      Edge e = edges.nextEdge();
      Vertex z = graph.opposite(u,e);
      if (hasLoc(z)) { // check that z is in Q, i.e., it is not in the cloud
        int e_weight = weight(e);
        Locator z_loc = getLoc(z);
        int z_dist = getDist(z_loc);
        if ( u_dist + e_weight < z_dist ) // relaxation of edge e = (u,z)
          Q.replaceKey(z_loc, new Integer(u_dist + e_weight));
      }
    }
  }
}
```

Code Fragment 7.24: Method dijkstraVisit of class Dijkstra.

```
/** Attribute for vertex locators in the priority queue Q. */
protected Object LOC = new Object();
/** Check if there is a locator associated with a vertex. */
protected boolean hasLoc(Vertex v) {
  return v.has(LOC);
}
/** Get the locator in Q of a vertex. */
protected Locator getLoc(Vertex v) {
  return (Locator) v.get(LOC);
}
/** Associate with a vertex its locator in Q. */
protected void setLoc(Vertex v, Locator l) {
  v.set(LOC, l);
}
/** Remove the locator associated with a vertex. */
protected void destroyLoc(Vertex v) {
  v.destroy(LOC);
}
/** Get the vertex associated with a locator. */
protected Vertex getVertex(Locator l) {
  return (Vertex) l.element();
}
/** Get the distance of a vertex given its locator in Q. */
protected int getDist(Locator l) {
  return ((Integer) l.key()).intValue();
}
```

Code Fragment 7.25: Auxiliary methods of class Dijkstra. They assume that the vertices of the graph are decorable (continued from Algorithms 7.23 and 7.24).

```
/** A specialization of class Dijkstra that extracts edge weights from
  * decorations. */
public class MyDijkstra extends Dijkstra {
  /** Attribute for edge weights. */
  protected Object WEIGHT;
  /** Constructor that sets the weight attribute. */
  public MyDijkstra(Object weight_attribute) {
    WEIGHT = weight_attribute;
  }
  /** The edge weight is stored in attribute WEIGHT of the edge. */
  public int weight(Edge e) {
    return ((Integer) e.get(WEIGHT)).intValue();
  }
}
```

Code Fragment 7.26: Class MyDijkstra that extends Dijkstra and provides a concrete implementation of method weight(e).

7.5 Exercises

Reinforcement

R-7.1 Draw a simple, connected, weighted graph with 8 vertices and 16 edges, each with unique edge weights. Identify one vertex as a "start" vertex and illustrate a running of Dijkstra's algorithm on this graph.

R-7.2 Show how to modify Dijkstra's algorithm for the case when the graph is directed and we want to compute shortest ***directed paths*** from the source vertex to all the other vertices.

R-7.3 Show how to modify Dijkstra's algorithm to not only output the distance from v to each vertex in G, but also to output a tree T rooted at v, such that the path in T from v to a vertex u is actually a shortest path in G from v to u.

R-7.4 Draw a (simple) directed weighted graph G with 10 vertices and 18 edges, such that G contains a minimum-weight cycle with at least 4 edges. Show that the Bellman-Ford algorithm will find this cycle.

R-7.5 The dynamic programming algorithm of Algorithm 7.11 uses $O(n^3)$ space. Describe a version of this algorithm that uses $O(n^2)$ space.

R-7.6 The dynamic programming algorithm of Algorithm 7.11 computes only shortest-path distances, not actual paths. Describe a version of this algorithm that outputs the set of all shortest paths between each pair of vertices in a directed graph. Your algorithm should still run in $O(n^3)$ time.

R-7.7 Draw a simple, connected, undirected, weighted graph with 8 vertices and 16 edges, each with unique edge weights. Illustrate the execution of Kruskal's algorithm on this graph. (Note that there is only one minimum spanning tree for this graph.)

R-7.8 Repeat the previous problem for the Prim-Jarník algorithm.

R-7.9 Repeat the previous problem for Barůvka's algorithm.

R-7.10 Consider the unsorted sequence implementation of the priority queue Q used in Dijkstra's algorithm. In this case, what is the best-case running time of Dijkstra's algorithm $\Omega(n^2)$ on an n-vertex graph?

Hint: Consider the size of Q each time the minimum element is extracted.

R-7.11 Describe the meaning of the graphical conventions used in Figures 7.3 and 7.4 illustrating Dijkstra's algorithm. What do the arrows signify? How about thick lines and dashed lines?

R-7.12 Repeat Exercise R-7.11 for Figures 7.15 and 7.17 illustrating Kruskal's algorithm.

R-7.13 Repeat Exercise R-7.11 for Figures 7.19 and 7.20 illustrating the Prim-Jarník algorithm.

R-7.14 Repeat Exercise R-7.11 for Figure 7.22 illustrating Barůvka's algorithm.

Creativity

C-7.1 Give an example of an n-vertex simple graph G that causes Dijkstra's algorithm to run in $\Omega(n^2 \log n)$ time when its implemented with a heap for the priority queue.

C-7.2 Give an example of a weighted directed graph $\vec{G}$ with negative-weight edges, but no negative-weight cycle, such that Dijkstra's algorithm incorrectly computes the shortest-path distances from some start vertex v.

C-7.3 Consider the following greedy strategy for finding a shortest path from vertex *start* to vertex *goal* in a given connected graph.

1: Initialize *path* to *start*.
2: Initialize *VisitedVertices* to $\{start\}$.
3: If *start*=*goal*, return *path* and exit. Otherwise, continue.
4: Find the edge (*start*,v) of minimum weight such that v is adjacent to *start* and v is not in *VisitedVertices*.
5: Add v to *path*.
6: Add v to *VisitedVertices*.
7: Set *start* equal to v and go to step 3.

Does this greedy strategy always find a shortest path from *start* to *goal*? Either explain intuitively why it works, or give a counter example.

C-7.4★ Suppose we are given a weighted graph G with n vertices and m edges, such that the weight on each edge is an integer between 0 and n. Show that we can find a minimum spanning tree for G in $O(n \log^* n)$ time.

C-7.5 Show that if all the weights in a connected weighted graph G are distinct, then there is exactly one minimum spanning tree for G.

C-7.6 Design an efficient algorithm for finding a ***longest*** directed path from a vertex s to a vertex t of an acyclic weighted digraph $\vec{G}$. Specify the graph representation used and any auxiliary data structures used. Also, analyze the time complexity of your algorithm.

C-7.7 Suppose you are given a diagram of a telephone network, which is a graph G whose vertices represent switching centers, and whose edges represent communication lines between two centers. The edges are marked by their bandwidth. The bandwidth of a path is the bandwidth of its lowest bandwidth edge. Give an algorithm that, given a diagram and two switching centers a and b, will output the maximum bandwidth of a path between a and b.

C-7.8 NASA wants to link n stations spread over the country using communication channels. Each pair of stations has a different bandwidth available, which is known a priori. NASA wants to select $n-1$ channels (the minimum possible) in such a way that all the stations are linked by the channels and the total bandwidth (defined as the sum of the individual bandwidths of the channels) is maximum. Give an efficient algorithm for this problem and determine its worst-case time complexity. Consider the weighted graph $G = (V, E)$, where V is the set of stations and E is the set of channels between the stations. Define the weight $w(e)$ of an edge $e \in E$ as the bandwidth of the corresponding channel.

C-7.9 Suppose you are given a *timetable*, which consists of:

- A set $\mathcal{A}$ of n airports, and for each airport $a \in \mathcal{A}$, a minimum connecting time $c(a)$
- A set $\mathcal{F}$ of m flights, and the following, for each flight $f \in \mathcal{A}$:
  - Origin airport $a_1(f) \in \mathcal{A}$
  - Destination airport $a_2(f) \in \mathcal{A}$
  - Departure time $t_1(f)$
  - Arrival time $t_2(f)$.

Describe an efficient algorithm for the flight scheduling problem. In this problem, we are given airports a and b, and a time t, and we wish to compute a sequence of flights that allows one to arrive at the earliest possible time in b when departing from a at or after time t. Minimum connecting times at intermediate airports should be observed. What is the running time of your algorithm as a function of n and m?

C-7.10 As your reward for saving the Kingdom of Bigfunnia from the evil monster, "Exponential Asymptotic," the king has given you the opportunity to earn a big reward. Behind the castle there is a maze, and along each corridor of the maze there is a bag of gold coins. The amount of gold in each bag varies. You will be given the opportunity to walk through the maze, picking up bags of gold. You may enter only through the door marked "ENTER" and exit through the door marked "EXIT." (These are distinct doors.) While in the maze you may not retrace your steps. Each corridor of the maze has an arrow painted on the wall. You may only go down the corridor in the direction of the arrow. There is no way to traverse a "loop" in the maze. You will receive a map of the maze, including the amount of gold in and the direction of each corridor. Describe an algorithm to help you pick up the most gold.

C-7.11 Suppose we are given a directed graph $\vec{G}$ with n vertices, and let M be the $n \times n$ adjacency matrix corresponding to $\vec{G}$.

a. Let the product of M with itself (M^2) be defined, for $1 \leq i, j \leq n$, as follows:

$$M^2(i,j) = M(i,1) \odot M(1,j) \oplus \cdots \oplus M(i,n) \odot M(n,j),$$

where "$\oplus$" is the Boolean **or** operator and "$\odot$" is Boolean **and**. Given this definition, what does $M^2(i,j) = 1$ imply about the vertices i and j? What if $M^2(i,j) = 0$?

b. Suppose M^4 is the product of M^2 with itself. What do the entries of M^4 signify? How about the entries of $M^5 = (M^4)(M)$? In general, what information is contained in the matrix M^p?

c. Now suppose that $\vec{G}$ is weighted and assume the following:
   1: for $1 \leq i \leq n$, $M(i,i) = 0$.
   2: for $1 \leq i, j \leq n$, $M(i,j) = weight(i,j)$ if $(i,j) \in E$.
   3: for $1 \leq i, j \leq n$, $M(i,j) = \infty$ if $(i,j) \notin E$.

   Also, let M^2 be defined, for $1 \leq i, j \leq n$, as follows:

$$M^2(i,j) = \min\{M(i,1) + M(1,j), \ldots, M(i,n) + M(n,j)\}.$$

If $M^2(i,j) = k$, what may we conclude about the relationship between vertices i and j?

C-7.12 Show how to modify Barůvka's algorithm so that it runs in worst-case $O(n^2)$ time.

Projects

P-7.1 Implement Kruskal's algorithm assuming that the edge weights are integers.

P-7.2 Implement the Prim-Jarník algorithm assuming that the edge weights are integers.

P-7.3 Implement the Barůvka's algorithm assuming that the edge weights are integers.

P-7.4 Perform an experimental comparison of two of the minimum-spanning-tree algorithms discussed in this chapter (that is, two of Kruskal, Prim-Jarník, or Barůvka). Develop an extensive set of experiments to test the running times of these algorithms using randomly generated graphs.

Chapter Notes

The first known minimum-spanning-tree algorithm is due to Barůvka [22], and was published in 1926. The Prim-Jarník algorithm was first published in Czech by Jarník [108] in 1930 and in English in 1957 by Prim [169]. Kruskal published his minimum-spanning-tree algorithm in 1956 [127]. The reader interested in further study of the history of the minimum spanning tree problem is referred to the paper by Graham and Hell [89]. The current asymptotically fastest minimum-spanning-tree algorithm is a randomized method of Karger, Klein, and Tarjan [112] that runs in $O(m)$ expected time.

Dijkstra [60] published his single-source, shortest path algorithm in 1959. The Bellman-Ford algorithm is derived from separate publications of Bellman [25] and Ford [71].

The reader interested in further study of graph algorithms is referred to the books by Ahuja, Magnanti, and Orlin [9], Cormen, Leiserson, and Rivest [55], Even [68], Gibbons [77], Mehlhorn [149], and Tarjan [200], and the book chapter by van Leeuwen [205].

Incidentally, the running time for the Prim-Jarník algorithm, and also that of Dijkstra's algorithm, can actually be improved to be $O(n \log n + m)$ by implementing the queue Q with either of two more sophisticated data structures, the "Fibonacci Heap" [72] or the "Relaxed Heap" [61]. The reader interested in these implementations is referred to the papers that describe the implementation of these structures, and how they can be applied to the shortest-path and minimum-spanning-tree problems.

Chapter

8 Network Flow and Matching

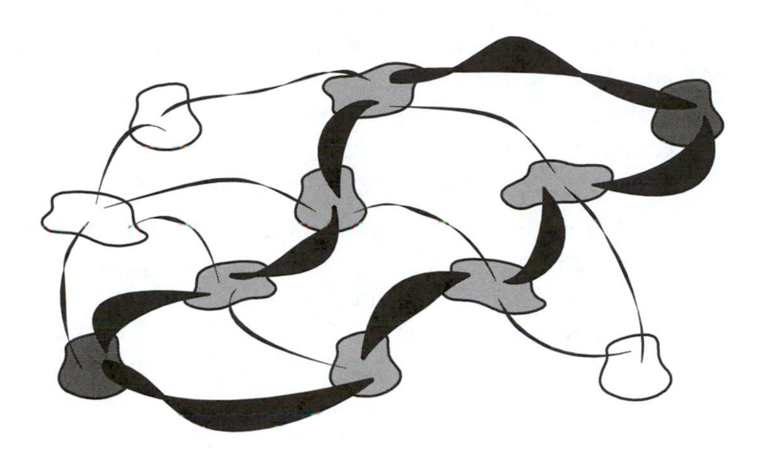

Contents

8.1 Flows and Cuts 383

8.1.1 Flow Networks 383

8.1.2 Cuts 385

8.2 Maximum Flow 387

8.2.1 Residual Capacity and Augmenting Paths 387

8.2.2 The Ford-Fulkerson Algorithm 390

8.2.3 Analyzing the Ford-Fulkerson Algorithm 392

8.2.4 The Edmonds-Karp Algorithm 393

8.3 Maximum Bipartite Matching 396

8.3.1 A Reduction to the Maximum Flow Problem 396

8.4 Minimum-Cost Flow 398

8.4.1 Augmenting Cycles 398

8.4.2 Successive Shortest Paths 400

8.4.3 Modified Weights 402

8.5 Java Example: Minimum-Cost Flow 405

8.6 Exercises 412

An important problem involving weighted graphs is the ***maximum flow*** problem. In this problem, we are given a weighted directed graph G, with each edge representing a "pipe" that can transport some commodity, with the weight of that edge representing the maximum amount it can transport. The maximum-flow problem is to find a way of transporting the maximum amount of the given commodity from some vertex s, called the ***source***, to some vertex t, called the ***sink***.

Example 8.1: *Consider a portion of the Internet modeled by a directed graph G in which each vertex represents a computer, each edge (u,v) represents a one-way communication channel from computer u to computer v, and the weight of each edge (u,v) represents the the bandwidth of the channel, that is, the maximum number of bytes that can be sent from u to v in one second. If we want to send a high-bandwidth streaming media connection from some computer s in G to some computer t in G, the fastest way to send this connection is to divide it into packets, and route these packets through G according to a maximum flow. (See Figure 8.1.)*

The maximum flow problem is closely related to the problem of finding the maximum way of matching vertices of one type in a graph with vertices of another type. We therefore also study the maximum matching problem, showing how the maximum flow problem can be used to solve it efficiently.

Sometimes we have many different maximum flows. Although all are maximum in terms of how much flow they produce, these flows may in fact be different in how much they cost. Thus, in this chapter we also study methods for computing maximum flows that are of minimum cost, when there are many different maximum flows and we have some way of measuring their relative costs. We conclude this chapter with a Java implementation of a minimum-cost flow algorithm.

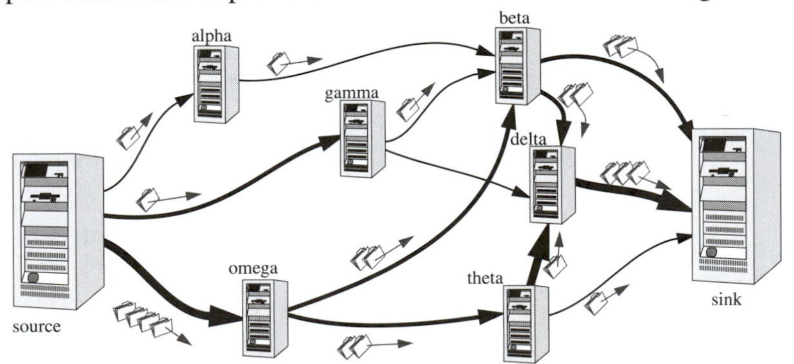

Figure 8.1: An example flow in a graph representing a computer network, with the bandwidth of thick edges being 4 MB/s, the bandwidth of medium edges being 2 MB/s., and the bandwidth of thin edges being 1 MB/s. We indicate the amount of data sent through an edge with folder icons, where each folder corresponds to one MB/s going through the channel. Note that the total amount of flow sent from the source to the sink (6 MB/s) is not maximum. Indeed, one additional MB/s can be pushed from the source to gamma, from gamma to delta, and from delta to the sink. After this extra flow is added, the total flow will be maximum.

8.1 Flows and Cuts

The above example illustrates the rules that a legal flow must obey. In order to precisely say what these rules are, let us carefully define what we mean by a flow.

8.1.1 Flow Networks

A ***flow network*** N consists of the following:

- A connected directed graph G with nonnegative integer weights on the edges, where the weight of an edge e is called the ***capacity*** $c(e)$ of e
- Two distinguished vertices, s and t, of G, called the ***source*** and ***sink***, respectively, such that s has no incoming edges and t has no outgoing edges.

Given such a labeled graph, the challenge is to determine the maximum amount of some commodity that can be pushed from s to t under the constraint that the capacity of an edge determines the maximum flow that can go along that edge. (See Figure 8.2.)

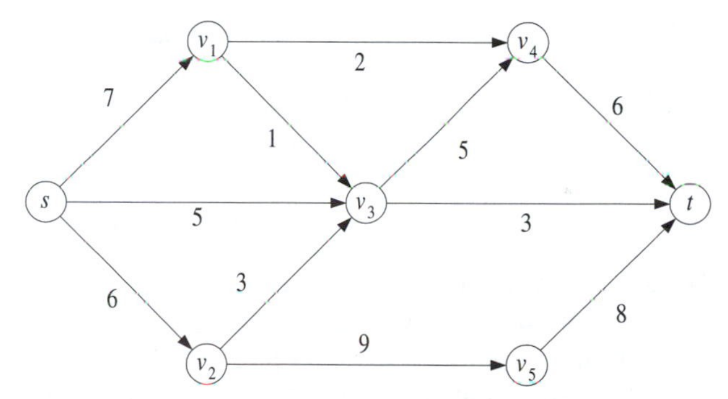

Figure 8.2: A flow network N. Each edge e of N is labeled with its capacity $c(e)$.

Of course, if we wish some commodity to flow from s to t, we need to be more precise about what we mean by a "flow." A ***flow*** for network N is an assignment of an integer value $f(e)$ to each edge e of G that satisfies the following properties:

- For each edge e of G,
$$0 \le f(e) \le c(e) \quad \textbf{(\textit{capacity rule})}.$$
- For each vertex v of G distinct from the source s and the sink t
$$\sum_{e \in E^-(v)} f(e) = \sum_{e \in E^+(v)} f(e) \quad \textbf{(\textit{conservation rule})},$$
where $E^-(v)$ and $E^+(v)$ denote the the sets of incoming and outgoing edges of v, respectively.

In other words, a flow must satisfy the edge capacity constraints and must, for every vertex v other than s and t, have the total amount of flow going out of v equal to the total amount of flow coming into v. Each of the above rules is satisfied, for example, by the flow illustrated in Figure 8.3.

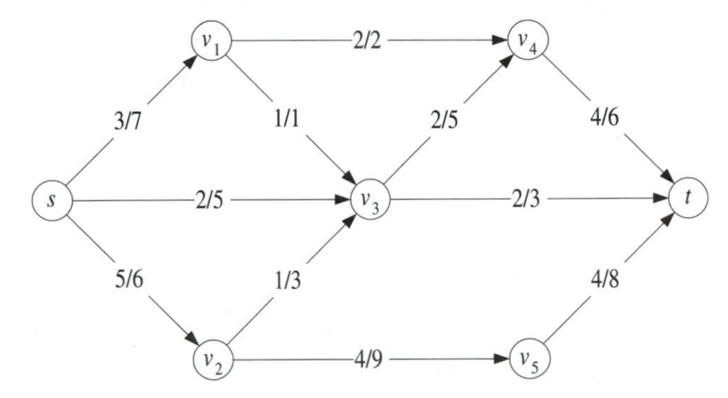

Figure 8.3: A flow f (of value $|f| = 10$) for the flow network N of Figure 8.2.

The quantity $f(e)$ is called the ***flow*** of edge e. The ***value*** of a flow f, which we denote by $|f|$, is equal to the total amount of flow coming out from the source s:

$$|f| = \sum_{e \in E^+(s)} f(e).$$

It is easy to show that the flow value is also equal to the total amount of flow going into the sink t (see Exercise R-8.1):

$$|f| = \sum_{e \in E^-(t)} f(e).$$

That is, a flow specifies how some commodity is pushed out from s, through the network N, and finally into the sink t. A ***maximum flow*** for flow network N is a flow with maximum value over all flows for N (see Figure 8.4). Since a maximum flow is using a flow network most efficiently, we are most interested in methods for computing maximum flows.

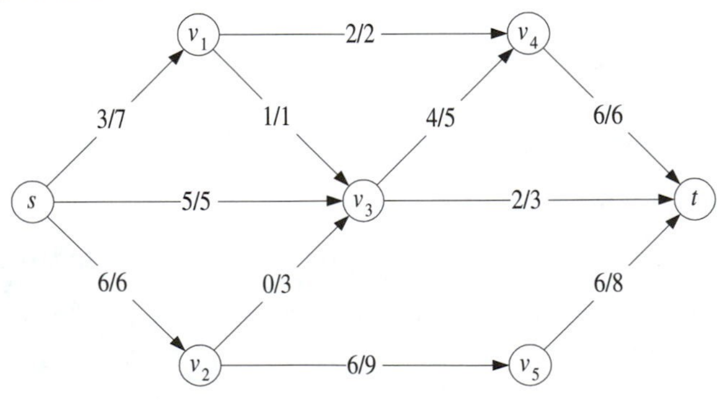

Figure 8.4: A maximum flow f^* (of value $|f^*| = 14$) for the flow network N of Figure 8.2.

8.1.2 Cuts

It turns out that flows are closely related to another concept, known as cuts. Intuitively, a cut is a division of the vertices of a flow network N into two sets, with s on one side and t on the other. Formally, a ***cut*** of N is a partition $\chi = (V_s, V_t)$ of the vertices of N such that $s \in V_s$ and $t \in V_t$. An edge e of N with origin $u \in V_s$ and destination $v \in V_t$ is said to be a ***forward edge*** of cut χ. An edge with origin in V_t and destination in V_s is said to be a ***backward edge***. We envision a cut as a separation of s and t in N done by cutting across edges of N, with forward edges going from s's side to t's side and backward edges going in the opposite direction. (See Figure 8.5.)

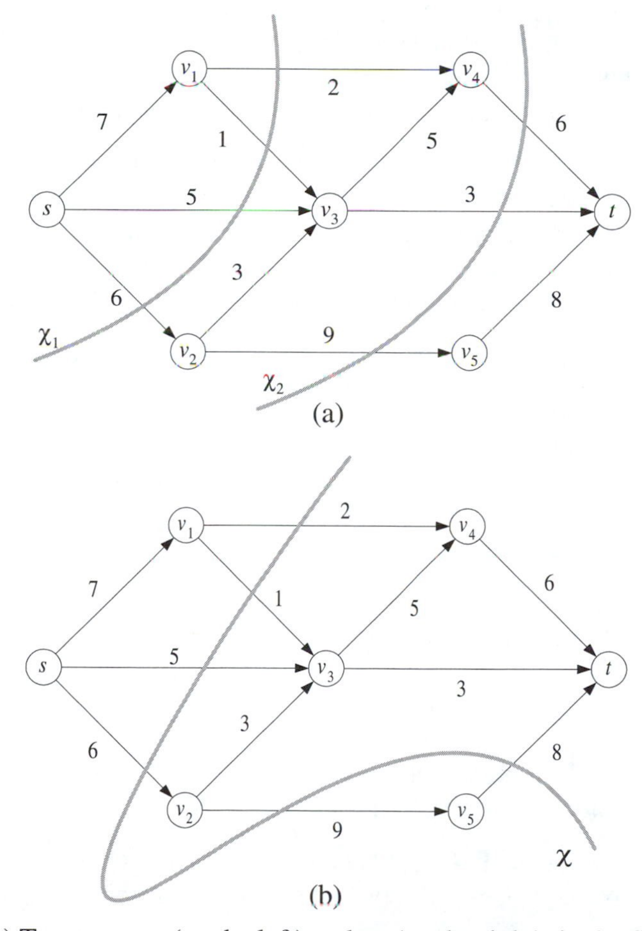

Figure 8.5: (a) Two cuts, χ_1 (on the left) and χ_2 (on the right), in the flow network N of Figure 8.2. These cuts have only forward edges and their capacities are $c(\chi_1) = 14$ and $c(\chi_2) = 18$. Cut χ_1 is a minimum cut for N. (b) A cut χ in N with both forward and backward edges. Its capacity is $c(\chi) = 22$.

Given a flow f for N, the ***flow across cut*** χ, denoted $f(\chi)$, is equal to the sum of the flows in the forward edges of χ minus the sum of the flows in the backward edges of χ. That is, $f(\chi)$ is the net amount of commodity that flows from s's side of χ to t's side of χ. The following lemma shows an interesting property of $f(\chi)$.

Lemma 8.2: *Let N be a flow network, and let f be a flow for N. For any cut χ of N, the value of f is equal to the flow across cut χ, that is, $|f| = f(\chi)$.*

Proof: Consider the sum

$$F = \sum_{v \in V_s} \left(\sum_{e \in E^+(v)} f(e) - \sum_{e \in E^-(v)} f(e) \right).$$

By the conservation rule, for each vertex v of V_s distinct from s, we have that $\sum_{e \in E^+(v)} f(e) - \sum_{e \in E^-(v)} f(e) = 0$. Thus, $F = |f|$.

On the other hand, for each edge e that is not a forward or a backward edge of cut χ, the sum F contains both the term $f(e)$ and the term $-f(e)$, which cancel each other, or neither the term $f(e)$ nor the term $-f(e)$. Thus, $F = f(\chi)$. ■

The above theorem shows that no matter where we cut a flow network to separate s and t, the flow across that cut is equal to the flow for the entire network. The ***capacity*** of cut χ, denoted $c(\chi)$, is the sum of the capacities of the forward edges of χ (note that we do not include the backward edges). The next lemma shows that a cut capacity $c(\chi)$ is an upper bound on any flow across χ.

Lemma 8.3: *Let N be a flow network, and let χ be a cut of N. Given any flow f for N, the flow across cut χ does not exceed the capacity of χ, that is, $f(\chi) \le c(\chi)$.*

Proof: Denote with $E^+(\chi)$ the forward edges of χ, and with $E^-(\chi)$ the backward edges of χ. By the definition of $f(\chi)$, we have

$$f(\chi) = \sum_{e \in E^+(\chi)} f(e) - \sum_{e \in E^-(\chi)} f(e).$$

Dropping nonpositive terms from the above sum, we obtain $f(\chi) \le \sum_{e \in E^+(\chi)} f(e)$. By the capacity rule, for each edge e, $f(e) \le c(e)$. Thus, we have

$$f(\chi) \le \sum_{e \in E^+(\chi)} c(e) = c(\chi).$$

■

By combining Lemmas 8.2 and 8.3, we obtain the following important result relating flows and cuts.

Theorem 8.4: *Let N be a flow network. Given any flow f for N and any cut χ of N, the value of f does not exceed the capacity of χ, that is, $|f| \le c(\chi)$.*

In other words, given any cut χ for a flow network N, the capacity of χ is an upper bound on any flow for N. This upper bound holds even for a ***minimum cut*** of N, which is a cut with minimum capacity, taken over all cuts of N. In the example of Figure 8.5, χ_1 is a minimum cut.

8.2 Maximum Flow

Theorem 8.4 implies that the value of a maximum flow is no more than the capacity of a minimum cut. We will show in this section that these two quantities are actually equal. In the process, we will outline an approach for constructing a maximum flow.

8.2.1 Residual Capacity and Augmenting Paths

In order to prove that a certain flow f is maximum, we need some way of showing that there is absolutely no more flow that can possibly be "squeezed" into f. Using the related concepts of residual capacity and augmenting paths, discussed next, we can provide just such a proof for when a flow f is maximum.

Residual Capacity

Let N be a flow network, which is specified by a graph G, capacity function c, source s, and sink t. Furthermore, let f be a flow for N. Given an edge e of G directed from vertex u to vertex v, the ***residual capacity*** from u to v with respect to the flow f, denoted $\Delta_f(u,v)$, is defined as

$$\Delta_f(u,v) = c(e) - f(e),$$

and the residual capacity from v to u is defined as

$$\Delta_f(v,u) = f(e).$$

Intuitively, the residual capacity defined by a flow f is any additional capacity that f has not fully taken advantage of in "pushing" its flow from s to t.

Let π be a path from s to t that is allowed to traverse edges in either the forward or backward direction, that is, we can traverse the edge $e = (u,v)$ from its origin u to its destination v or from its destination v to its origin u. Formally, a ***forward edge*** of π is an edge e of π such that, in going from s to t along path π, the origin of e is encountered before the destination of e. An edge of π that is not forward is said to be a ***backward edge***. Let us extend our definition of ***residual capacity*** to an edge e in π traversed from u to v, so that $\Delta_f(e) = \Delta_f(u,v)$. In other words,

$$\Delta_f(e) = \begin{cases} c(e) - f(e) & \text{if } e \text{ is a forward edge} \\ f(e) & \text{if } e \text{ is a backward edge.} \end{cases}$$

That is, the residual capacity of an edge e going in the forward direction is the additional capacity of e that f has yet to consume, but the residual capacity in the opposite direction is the flow that f has consumed (and could potentially "give back" if that allows for another flow of higher value).

Augmenting Paths

The residual capacity $\Delta_f(\pi)$ of a path π is the minimum residual capacity of its edges. That is,

$$\Delta_f(\pi) = \min_{e \in \pi} \Delta_f(e).$$

This value is the maximum amount of additional flow that we can possibly "push" down the path π without violating a capacity constraint. An ***augmenting path*** for flow f is a path π from the source s to the sink t with nonzero residual capacity, that is, for each edge e of π,

- $f(e) < c(e)$ if e is a forward edge
- $f(e) > 0$ if e is a backward edge.

We show in Figure 8.6 an example of an augmenting path.

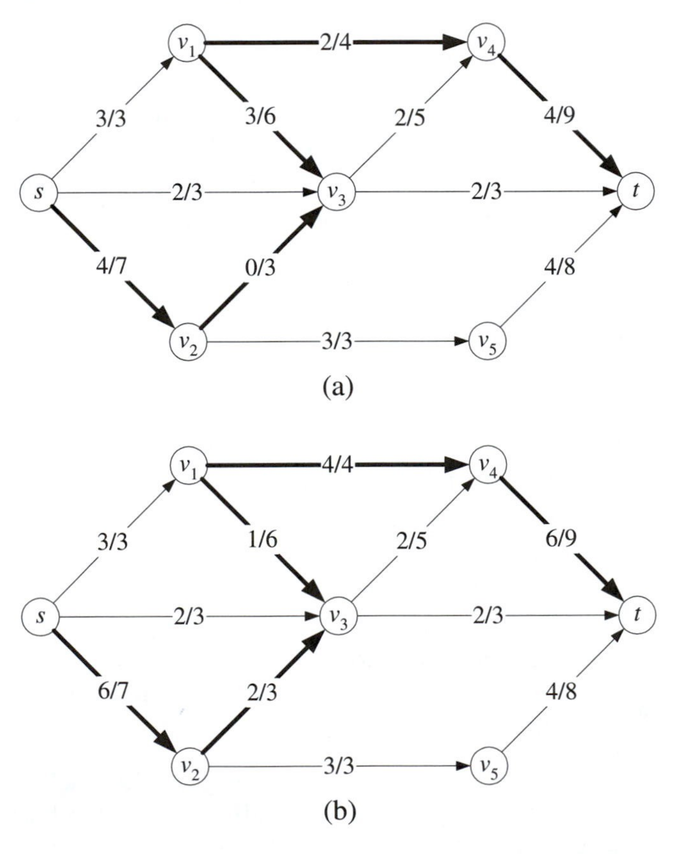

Figure 8.6: Example of an augmenting path: (a) network N, flow f, and an augmenting path π drawn with thick edges ((v_1, v_3) is a backward edge); (b) flow f' obtained from f by pushing $\Delta_f(\pi) = 2$ units of flow from s to t along path π.

As shown by the following lemma, we can always add the residual capacity of an augmenting path to an existing flow and get another valid flow.

Lemma 8.5: *Let π be an augmenting path for flow f in network N. There exists a flow f' for N of value $|f'| = |f| + \Delta_f(\pi)$.*

Proof: We compute the flow f' by modifying the flow of the edges of π:

$$f'(e) = \begin{cases} f(e) + \Delta_f(\pi) & \text{if } e \text{ is a forward edge} \\ f(e) - \Delta_f(\pi) & \text{if } e \text{ is a backward edge.} \end{cases}$$

Note that we subtract $\Delta_f(\pi)$ if e is a backward edge, for we are subtracting flow on e already taken by f in this case. In any case, because $\Delta_f(\pi) \geq 0$ is the minimum residual capacity of any edge in π, we will violate no capacity constraint on a forward edge by adding $\Delta_f(\pi)$ nor will we go below zero flow on any backward edge by subtracting $\Delta_f(\pi)$. Thus, f' is a valid flow for N, and the value of f' is $|f| + \Delta_f(\pi)$. ■

By Lemma 8.5, the existence of an augmenting path π for a flow f implies that f is not maximum. Also, given an augmenting path π, we can modify f to increase its value by pushing $\Delta_f(\pi)$ units of flow from s to t along path π, as shown in the proof of Lemma 8.5.

What if there is no augmenting path for a flow f in network N? In this case, we have that f is a maximum flow, as stated by the following lemma.

Lemma 8.6: *If a network N does not have an augmenting path with respect to a flow f, then f is a maximum flow. Also, there is a cut χ of N such that $|f| = c(\chi)$.*

Proof: Let f be a flow for N, and suppose there is no augmenting path in N with respect to f. We construct from f a cut $\chi = (V_s, V_t)$ by placing in set V_s all the vertices v, such that there is a path from the source s to vertex v consisting of edges of nonzero residual capacity. Such a path is called an augmenting path from s to v. Set V_t contains the remaining vertices of N. Since there is no augmenting path for flow f, the sink t of N is in V_t. Thus, $\chi = (V_s, V_t)$ satisfies the definition of a cut.

By the definition of χ, each forward edge and backward edge of cut χ has zero residual capacity, that is,

$$f(e) = \begin{cases} c(e) & \text{if } e \text{ is a forward edge of } \chi \\ 0 & \text{if } e \text{ is a backward edge of } \chi. \end{cases}$$

Thus, the capacity of χ is equal to the value of f. That is,

$$|f| = c(\chi).$$

By Theorem 8.4, we have that f is a maximum flow. ■

As a consequence of Theorem 8.4 and Lemma 8.6, we have the following fundamental result relating maximum flows and minimum cuts.

Theorem 8.7 (The Max-Flow, Min-Cut Theorem): *The value of a maximum flow is equal to the capacity of a minimum cut.*

8.2.2 The Ford-Fulkerson Algorithm

A classic algorithm, due to Ford and Fulkerson, computes a maximum flow in a network by applying the greedy method to the augmenting-path approach used to prove the Max-Flow, Min-Cut Theorem (Theorem 8.7).

The main idea of this ***Ford-Fulkerson algorithm*** is to incrementally increase the value of a flow in stages, where at each stage some amount of flow is pushed along an augmenting path from the source to the sink. Initially, the flow of each edge is equal to 0. At each stage, an augmenting path π is computed and an amount of flow equal to the residual capacity of π is pushed along π, as in the proof of Lemma 8.5. The algorithm terminates when the current flow f does not admit an augmenting path. Lemma 8.6 guarantees that f is a maximum flow in this case.

We provide a pseudo-code description of the Ford-Fulkerson solution to the problem of finding a maximum flow in Algorithm 8.7.

```
Algorithm MaxFlowFordFulkerson(N):
   Input: Flow network N = (G,c,s,t)
   Output: A maximum flow f for N
  for each edge e ∈ N do
    f(e) ← 0
  stop ← false
  repeat
    traverse G starting at s to find an augmenting path for f
    if an augmenting path π exists then
      { Compute the residual capacity Δ_f(π) of π }
      Δ ← +∞
      for each edge e ∈ π do
        if Δ_f(e) < Δ then
          Δ ← Δ_f(e)
      { Push Δ = Δ_f(π) units of flow along path π }
      for each edge e ∈ π do
        if e is a forward edge then
          f(e) ← f(e) + Δ
        else
          f(e) ← f(e) − Δ          {e is a backward edge}
    else
      stop ← true          {f is a maximum flow}
  until stop
```

Algorithm 8.7: The Ford-Fulkerson algorithm for computing a maximum flow in a network.

We visualize the Ford-Fulkerson algorithm in Figure 8.8.

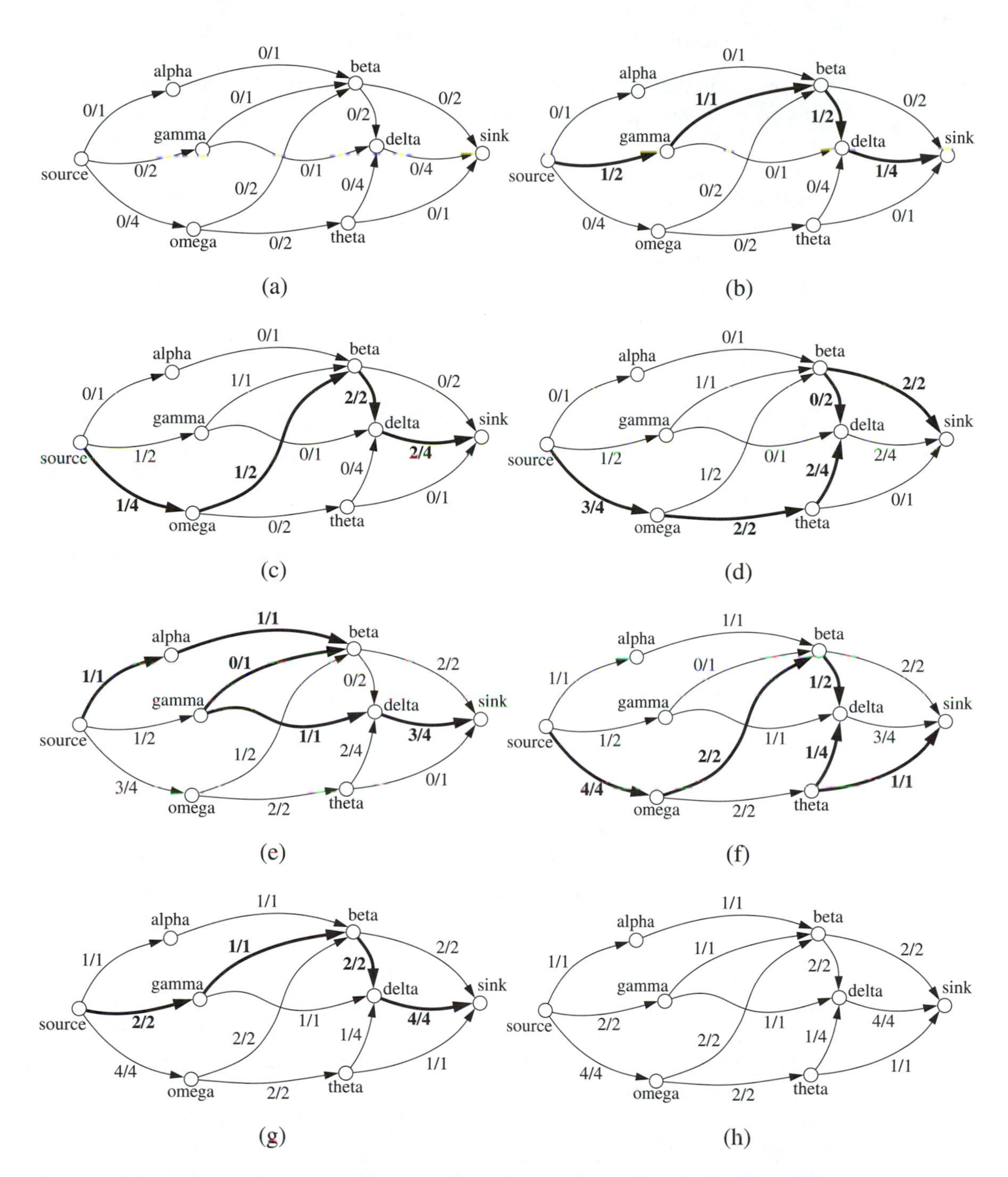

Figure 8.8: Example execution of the Ford-Fulkerson algorithm on the flow network of Figure 8.1. Augmenting paths are drawn with with thick lines.

Implementation Details

There are important implementation details for the Ford-Fulkerson algorithm that impact how we represent a flow and how we compute augmenting paths. Representing a flow is actually quite easy. We can label each edge of the network with an attribute representing the flow along that edge (Section 6.5). To compute an augmenting path, we use a specialized traversal of the graph G underlying the flow network. Such a traversal is a simple modification of either a DFS traversal (Section 6.3.1) or a BFS traversal (Section 6.3.3), where instead of considering all the edges incident on the current vertex v, we consider only the following edges:

- Outgoing edges of v with flow less than the capacity
- Incoming edges of v with nonzero flow.

Alternatively, the computation of an augmenting path with respect to the current flow f can be reduced to a simple path finding problem in a new directed graph R_f derived from G. The vertices of R_f are the same as the vertices of G. For each ordered pair of adjacent vertices u and v of G, we add a directed edge from u to v if $\Delta_f(u, v) > 0$. Graph R_f is called the ***residual graph*** with respect to flow f. An augmenting path with respect to flow f corresponds to a directed path from s to t in the residual graph R_f. This path can be computed by a DFS traversal of R_f starting at the source s. (See Sections 6.3 and 6.5.)

8.2.3 Analyzing the Ford-Fulkerson Algorithm

The analysis of the running time of the Ford-Fulkerson algorithm is a little tricky. This is because the algorithm does not specify the exact way to find augmenting paths and, as we shall see, the choice of augmenting path has a major impact on the algorithm's running time.

Let n and m be the number of vertices and edges of the flow network, respectively, and let f^* be a maximum flow. Since the graph underlying the network is connected, we have that $n \leq m+1$. Note that each time we find an augmenting path we increase the value of the flow by at least 1, since edge capacities and flows are integers. Thus, $|f^*|$, the value of a maximum flow, is an upper bound on the number of times the algorithm searches for an augmenting path. Also note that we can find an augmenting path by a simple graph traversal, such as a DFS or BFS traversal, which takes $O(m)$ time (see Theorems 6.13 and 6.19 and recall that $n \leq m+1$). Thus, we can bound the running time of the Ford-Fulkerson algorithm as being at most $O(|f^*|m)$. As illustrated in Figure 8.9, this bound can actually be attained for some choices of augmenting paths. We conclude that the Ford-Fulkerson algorithm is a pseudo-polynomial-time algorithm (Section 5.3.3), since its running time depends on both the size of the input and also the value of a numeric parameter. Thus, the time bound of the Ford-Fulkerson algorithm can be quite slow if $|f^*|$ is large and augmenting paths are chosen poorly.

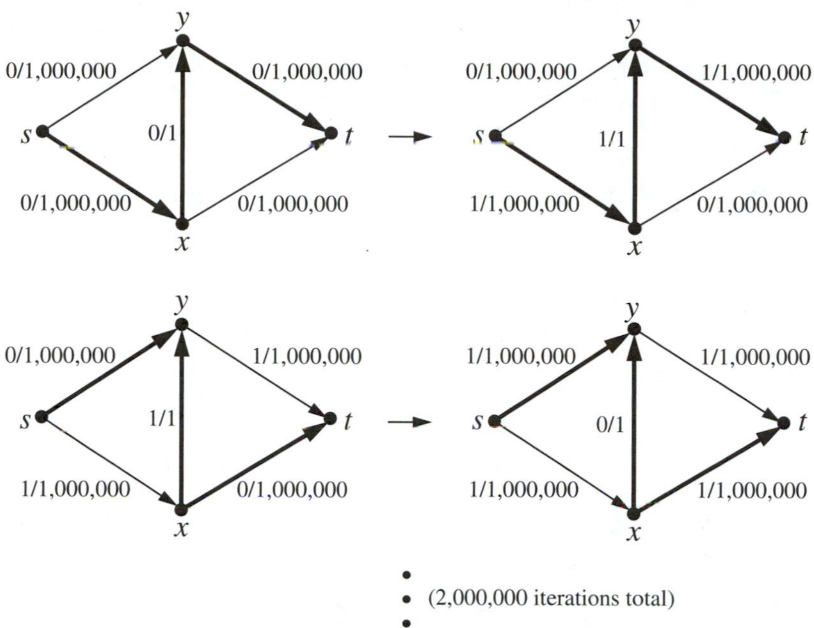

Figure 8.9: An example of a network for which the standard Ford-Fulkerson algorithm runs slowly. If the augmenting paths chosen by the algorithm alternate between (s,x,y,t) and (s,y,x,t), then the algorithm will make a total of $2,000,000$ iterations, even though two iterations would have sufficed.

8.2.4 The Edmonds-Karp Algorithm

The ***Edmonds-Karp algorithm*** is a variation of the Ford-Fulkerson algorithm. It uses a simple technique for finding good augmenting paths that results in faster running time. This technique is based on the notion of being "more greedy" in our application of the greedy method to the maximum-flow problem. Namely, at each iteration, we choose an augmenting path with the smallest number of edges, which can be easily done in $O(m)$ time by a modified BFS traversal. We will show that with these ***Edmonds-Karp augmentations***, the number of iterations is no more than nm, which implies an $O(nm^2)$ running time for the Edmonds-Karp algorithm.

We begin by introducing some notation. We call the ***length*** of a path π the number of edges in π. Let f be a flow for network N. Given a vertex v, we denote with $d_f(v)$ the minimum length of an augmenting path with respect to f from the source s to vertex v, and call this quantity the ***residual distance*** of v with respect to flow f.

The following discussion shows how residual distance of each vertex impacts the running time of the Edmonds-Karp algorithm.

Performance of the Edmonds-Karp Algorithm

We begin our analysis by noting that residual distance is nondecreasing over a sequence of Edmonds-Karp augmentations.

Lemma 8.8: *Let g be the flow obtained from flow f with an augmentation along a path π of minimum length. Then, for each vertex v,*

$$d_f(v) \leq d_g(v).$$

Proof: Suppose there is a vertex violating the above inequality. Let v be such a vertex with smallest residual distance with respect to g. That is,

$$d_f(v) > d_g(v) \tag{8.1}$$

and

$$d_g(v) \leq d_g(u), \text{ for each } u \text{ such that } d_f(u) > d_g(u). \tag{8.2}$$

Consider an augmenting path γ of minimum length from s to v with respect to flow g. Let u be the vertex immediately preceding v on γ, and let e be the edge of γ with endpoints u and v (see Figure 8.10). By the above definition, we have

$$\Delta_g(u,v) > 0. \tag{8.3}$$

Also, since u immediately precedes v in shortest path γ, we have

$$d_g(v) = d_g(u) + 1. \tag{8.4}$$

Finally, by (8.2) and (8.4), we have

$$d_f(u) \leq d_g(u). \tag{8.5}$$

We now show that $\Delta_f(u,v) = 0$. Indeed, if we had $\Delta_f(u,v) > 0$, we could go from u to v along an augmenting path with respect to flow f. This would imply

$$\begin{aligned} d_f(v) &\leq d_f(u) + 1 \\ &\leq d_g(u) + 1 \quad \text{by (8.5)} \\ &= d_g(v) \quad \text{by (8.4)}, \end{aligned}$$

thus contradicting (8.1).

Since $\Delta_f(u,v) = 0$ and, by (8.3), $\Delta_g(u,v) > 0$, the augmenting path π, which produces g from f, must traverse the edge e from v to u (see Figure 8.10). Hence,

$$\begin{aligned} d_f(v) &= d_f(u) - 1 \quad \text{because } \pi \text{ is a shortest path} \\ &\leq d_g(u) - 1 \quad \text{by (8.5)} \\ &\leq d_g(v) - 2 \quad \text{by (8.4)} \\ &< d_g(v). \end{aligned}$$

Thus, we have obtained a contradiction with (8.1), which completes the proof. ■

Intuitively, Lemma 8.8 implies that each time we do an Edmonds-Karp augmentation, the residual distance from s to any vertex v can only increase or stay the same. This fact gives us the following.

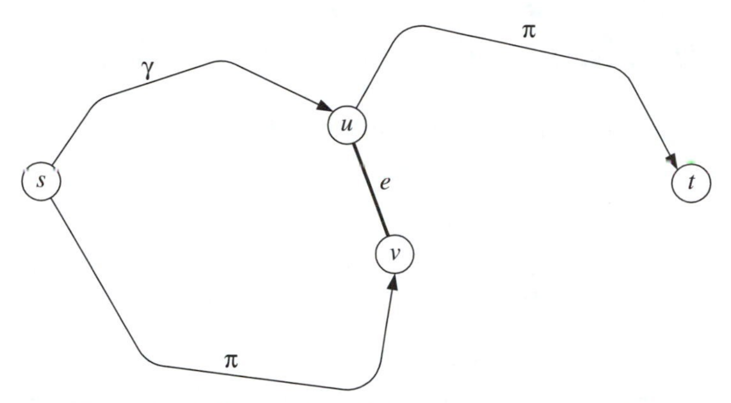

Figure 8.10: Illustration of the proof of Lemma 8.8.

Lemma 8.9: *When executing the Edmonds-Karp algorithm on a network with n vertices and m edges, the number of flow augmentations is no more than nm.*

Proof: Let f_i be the flow in the network before the i-th augmentation, and let π_i be the path used in such augmentation. We say that an edge e of π_i is a ***bottleneck*** for π_i if the residual capacity of e is equal to the residual capacity of π_i. Clearly, every augmenting path used by the Edmonds-Karp algorithm has at least one bottleneck.

Consider a pair of vertices u and v joined by an edge e, and suppose that edge e is a bottleneck for two augmenting paths π_i and π_k, with $i < k$, that traverse e from u to v. The above assumptions imply each of the following:

- $\Delta_{f_i}(u,v) > 0$
- $\Delta_{f_{i+1}}(u,v) = 0$
- $\Delta_{f_k}(u,v) > 0$.

Thus, there must be an intermediate j-th augmentation, with $i < j < k$ whose augmenting path π_j traverses edge e from v to u. We therefore obtain

$$\begin{aligned} d_{f_j}(u) &= d_{f_j}(v)+1 && \text{(because } \pi_j \text{ is a shortest path)} \\ &\geq d_{f_i}(v)+1 && \text{(by Lemma 8.8)} \\ &\geq d_{f_i}(u)+2 && \text{(because } \pi_i \text{ is a shortest path).} \end{aligned}$$

Since the residual distance of a vertex is always less than the number of vertices n, each edge can be a bottleneck at most n times during the execution of the Edmonds-Karp algorithm ($n/2$ times for each of the two directions in which it can be traversed by an augmenting path). Hence, the overall number of augmentations is no more than nm. ■

Since a single flow augmentation can be done in $O(m)$ time using a modified BFS strategy, we can summarize the above discussion as follows.

Theorem 8.10: *Given a flow network with n vertices and m edges, the Edmonds-Karp algorithm computes a maximum flow in $O(nm^2)$ time.*

8.3 Maximum Bipartite Matching

A problem that arises in a number of important applications is the ***maximum bipartite matching*** problem. In this problem, we are given a connected undirected graph with the following properties:

- The vertices of G are partitioned into two sets, X and Y.
- Every edge of G has one endpoint in X and the other endpoint in Y.

Such a graph is called a ***bipartite graph***. A ***matching*** in G is a set of edges that have no endpoints in common—such a set "pairs" up vertices in X with vertices in Y so that each vertex has at most one "partner" in the other set. The maximum bipartite matching problem is to find a matching with the greatest number of edges (over all matchings).

Example 8.11: *Let G be a bipartite graph where the set X represents a group of young men and the set Y represents a group of young women, who are all together at a community dance. Let there be an edge joining x in X and y in Y if x and y are willing to dance with one another. A maximum matching in G corresponds to a largest set of compatible pairs of men and women who can all be happily dancing at the same time.*

Example 8.12: *Let G be a bipartite graph where the set X represents a group of college courses and the set Y represents a group of classrooms. Let there be an edge joining x in X and y in Y if, based on its enrollment and audio-visual needs, the course x can be taught in classroom y. A maximum matching in G corresponds to a largest set of college courses that can be taught simultaneously without conflicting.*

These two examples provide a small sample of the kinds of applications that the maximum bipartite matching problem can be used to solve. Fortunately, there is a simple way of solving the maximum bipartite matching problem.

8.3.1 A Reduction to the Maximum Flow Problem

Let G be a bipartite graph whose vertices are partitioned into sets X and Y. We create a flow network H such that a maximum flow in H can be immediately converted into a maximum matching in G:

- We begin by including all the vertices of G in H, plus a new source vertex s and a new sink vertex t.
- Next, we add every edge of G to H, but direct each such edge so that it is oriented from the endpoint in X to the endpoint in Y. In addition, we insert a directed edge from s to each vertex in X, and a directed edge from each vertex in Y to t. Finally, we assign to each edge of H a capacity of 1.

Given a flow f for H, we use f to define a set M of edges of G using the rule that an edge e is in M whenever $f(e) = 1$. (See Figure 8.11.) We now show that the set M is a matching. Since the capacities in H are all 1, the flow through each edge of H is either 0 or 1. Moreover, since each vertex x in X has exactly one incoming edge, the conservation rule implies that at most one outgoing edge of x has nonzero flow. Similarly, since each vertex y in Y has exactly one outgoing edge, at most one incoming edge of y has nonzero flow. Thus, each vertex in X will be paired by M with at most one vertex in Y, that is, set M is a matching. Also, we can easily see that the size of M is equal to $|f|$, the value of flow f.

A reverse transformation can also be defined. Namely, given a matching M in graph G, we can use M to define a flow f for H using the following rules:

- For each edge e of H that is also in G, $f(e) = 1$ if $e \in M$ and $f(e) = 0$ otherwise.
- For each edge e of H incident to s or t, $f(e) = 1$ if v is an endpoint of some edge of M and $f(e) = 0$ otherwise, where v denotes the other endpoint of e.

It is easy to verify that f is a flow for H and the value of f is equal to the size of M.

Therefore, any maximum flow algorithm can be used to solve the maximum bipartite matching problem on a graph G with n vertices and m edges. Namely:

1. We construct network H from the bipartite graph G. This step takes $O(n+m)$ time. Network H has $n+2$ vertices and $n+m$ edges.
2. We compute a maximum for H using the standard Ford-Fulkerson algorithm. Since the value of the maximum flow is equal to $|M|$, the size of the maximum matching, and $|M| \leq n/2$, this step takes $O(n(n+m))$ time, which is $O(nm)$ because G is connected.

Therefore, we have the following.

Theorem 8.13: *Let G be a bipartite graph with n vertices and m edges. A maximum matching in G can be computed in $O(nm)$ time.*

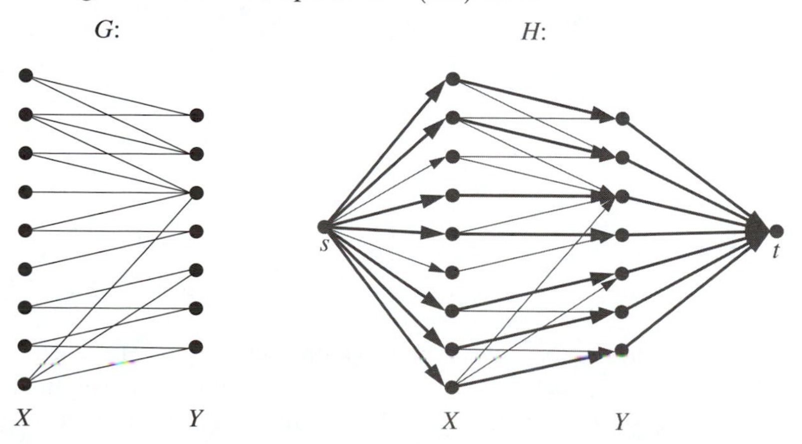

Figure 8.11: (a) A bipartite graph G. (b) Flow network H derived from G and a maximum flow in H; thick edges have unit flow and other edges have zero flow.

8.4 Minimum-Cost Flow

There is another variant of the maximum flow problem that applies in situations where there is a cost associated with sending a unit of flow through an edge. In this section, we extend the definition of a network by specifying a second nonnegative integer weight $w(e)$ for each edge e, representing the ***cost*** of edge e.

Given a flow f, we define the cost of f as

$$w(f) = \sum_{e \in E} w(e) f(e),$$

where E denotes the set of edges in the network. Flow f is said to be a ***minimum-cost flow*** if f has minimum cost among all flows of value $|f|$. The ***minimum-cost flow problem*** consists of finding a maximum flow that has the lowest cost over all maximum flows. A variation of the minimum-cost flow problem asks to find a minimum-cost flow with a given flow value. Given an augmenting path π with respect to a flow f, we define the cost of π, denoted $w(\pi)$, as the sum of the costs of the forward edges of π minus the sum of the costs of the backward edges of π.

8.4.1 Augmenting Cycles

An ***augmenting cycle*** with respect to flow f is an augmenting path whose first and last vertices are the same. In more mathematical terms, it is a directed cycle γ with vertices $v_0, v_1, \ldots, v_(k-1), v_k = v_0$, such that $\Delta_f(v_i, v_{i+1}) > 0$ for $i = 0, \ldots, k-1$ (see Figure 8.12). The definitions of residual capacity (given in Section 8.2.1) and cost (given above) also apply to an augmenting cycle. In addition, note that, since it is a cycle, we can add the flow of an augmenting cycle to an existing flow without changing its flow value.

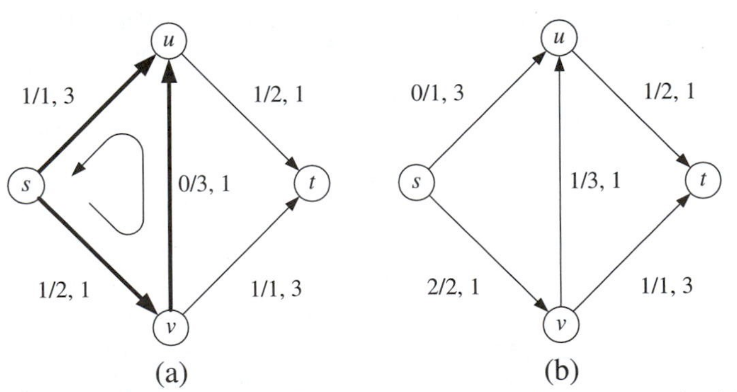

Figure 8.12: (a) Network with flow f, where each edge e is labeled with $f(e)/c(e), w(e)$. We have $|f| = 2$ and $w(f) = 8$. Augmenting cycle $\gamma = (s, v, u, s)$, drawn with thick edges. The residual capacity of γ is $\Delta_f(\gamma) = 1$. The cost of γ is $w(\gamma) = -1$. (b) Flow f' obtained from f by pushing one unit of flow along cycle γ. We have $|f'| = |f|$ and $w(f') = w(f) + w(\gamma)\Delta_f(\gamma) = 8 + (-1) \cdot 1 = 7$.

Adding the Flow from an Augmenting Cycle

The following lemma is analogous to Lemma 8.5, as it shows that a maximum flow can be changed into another maximum flow using an augmenting cycle.

Lemma 8.14: *Let γ be an augmenting cycle for flow f in network N. There exists a flow f' for N of value $|f'| = |f|$ and cost*

$$w(f') = w(f) + w(\gamma)\Delta_f(\gamma).$$

We leave the proof of Lemma 8.14 as an exercise (R-8.13).

A Condition for Minimum-Cost Flows

Note that Lemma 8.14 implies that if a flow f has an augmenting cycle of negative cost, then f does not have minimum cost. The following theorem shows that the converse is also true, giving us a condition for testing when a flow is in fact a minimum-cost flow.

Theorem 8.15: *A flow f has minimum cost among all flows of value $|f|$ if and only if there is no augmenting cycle of negative cost with respect to f.*

Proof: The "only-if" part follows immediately from Lemma 8.14. To prove the "if" part, suppose that flow f does not have minimum cost, and let g be a flow of value f with minimum cost. Flow g can be obtained from f by a series of augmentations along augmenting cycles. Since the cost of g is less than the cost of f, at least one of these cycles must have negative cost. ■

An Algorithmic Approach for Finding Minimum-Cost Flows

Theorem 8.15 suggests an algorithm for the minimum-cost flow problem based on repeatedly augmenting flow along negative-cost cycles. We first find a maximum flow f^* using the Ford-Fulkerson algorithm or the Edmonds-Karp algorithm. Next, we determine whether flow f^* admits a negative-cost augmenting cycle. The Bellman-Ford algorithm (Section 7.1.2) can be used to find a negative cycle in time $O(nm)$. Let w^* denote the total cost of the initial maximum flow f^*. After each execution of the Bellman-Ford algorithm, the cost of the flow decreases by at least one unit. Hence, starting from maximum flow f^*, we can compute a maximum flow of minimum cost in time $O(w^*nm)$. Therefore, we have the following:

Theorem 8.16: *Given an n-vertex flow network N with costs associated with its m edges, together with a maximum flow f^*, we can compute a maximum flow of minimum cost in $O(w^*nm)$ time, where w^* is the total cost of f^*.*

We can do much better than this, however, by being more careful in how we compute augmenting cycles, as we show in the remainder of this section.

8.4.2 Successive Shortest Paths

In this section, we present an alternative method for computing a minimum-cost flow. The idea is to start from an empty flow and build up to a maximum flow by a series of augmentations along minimum-cost paths. The following theorem provides the foundation of this approach.

Theorem 8.17: *Let f be a minimum-cost flow, and let f' be a the flow obtained by augmenting f along an augmenting path π of minimum cost. Flow f' is a minimum-cost flow.*

Proof: The proof is illustrated in Figure 8.13.

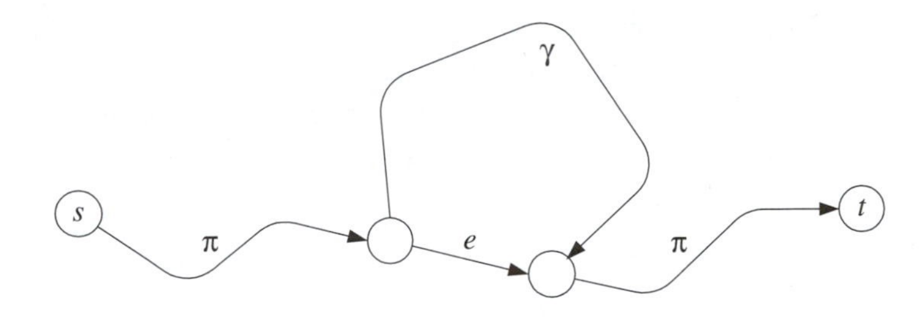

Figure 8.13: Illustration of the proof of Theorem 8.17.

Suppose, for the sake of a contradiction, that f' does not have minimum cost. By Theorem 8.15, f' has an augmenting cycle γ of negative cost. Cycle γ must have at least one edge e in common with path π and traverse e in the direction opposite to that of π, since otherwise γ would be an augmenting cycle of negative cost with respect to flow f, which is impossible, since f has minimum cost. Consider the path $\hat{\pi}$ obtained from π by replacing edge e with $\gamma - e$. The path $\hat{\pi}$ is an augmenting path with respect to flow f. Also path $\hat{\pi}$ has cost

$$w(\hat{\pi}) = w(\pi) + w(\gamma) < w(\pi).$$

This contradicts the assumption that π is an augmenting path of minimum cost with respect to flow f. ■

Starting from an initial null flow, we can compute a maximum flow of minimum cost by a repeated application of Theorem 8.17 (see Figure 8.14). Given the current flow f, we assign a weight to the edges of the residual graph R_f as follows (recall the definition of residual graph from Section 8.2.2). For each edge e, directed from u to v, of the original network, the edge of R_f from u to v, denoted (u, v), has weight $w(u, v) = w(e)$, while the edge (v, u) from v to u has weight $w(v, u) = -w(e)$. The computation of a shortest path in R_f can be done by using the Bellman-Ford algorithm (see Section 7.1.2) since, by Theorem 8.15, R_f does not have negative-cost cycles. Thus, we obtain a pseudo-polynomial-time algorithm (Section 5.3.3) that computes a maximum flow of minimum cost f^* in time $O(|f^*|nm)$.

An example execution of the above algorithm is shown in Figure 8.14.

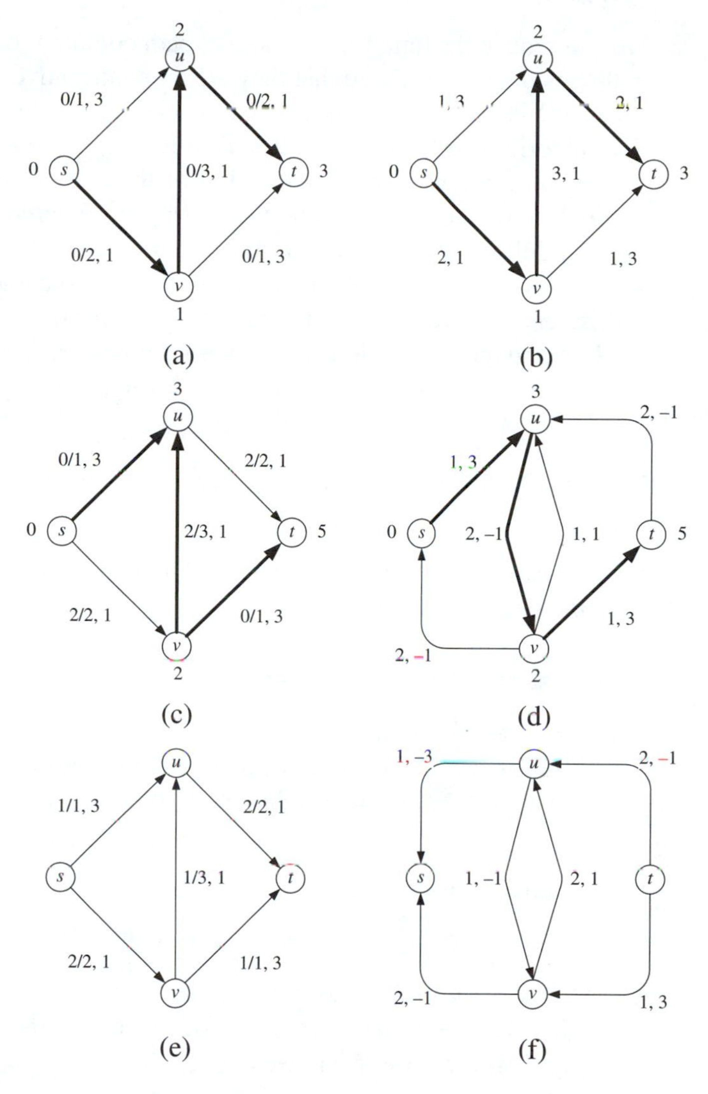

Figure 8.14: Example of computation of a minimum-cost flow by successive shortest path augmentations. At each step, we show the network on the left and the residual network on the right. Vertices are labeled with their distance from the source. In the network, each edge e is labeled with $f(e)/c(e), w(e)$. In the residual network, each edge is labeled with its residual capacity and cost (edges with zero residual capacity are omitted). Augmenting paths are drawn with thick lines. A minimum-cost flow is computed with two augmentations. In the first augmentation, two units of flow are pushed along path (s, v, u, t). In the second augmentation, one unit of flow is pushed along path (s, u, v, t).

8.4.3 Modified Weights

We can reduce the time for the shortest path computations by changing the weights in the residual graph R_f so that they are all nonnegative. After the modification, we can use Dijkstra's algorithm, which runs in $O(m \log n)$ time, instead of the Bellman-Ford algorithm, which runs in $O(nm)$ time.

We describe now the modification of the edge weights. Let f be the current minimum-cost flow. We denote with $d_f(v)$ the ***distance*** of vertex v from the source s in R_f, defined as the minimum weight of a path from s to v in R_f (the cost of an augmenting path from the source s to vertex v). Note that this definition of distance is different from the one used in Section 8.2.4 for the Edmonds-Karp algorithm.

Let g be the flow obtained from v by augmenting f along a minimum-cost path. We define a new set of edge weights w' for R_g, as follows (see Figure 8.15):

$$w'(u,v) = w(u,v) + d_f(u) - d_f(v).$$

Lemma 8.18: *For each edge (u,v) of residual network R_g, we have*

$$w'(u,v) \geq 0.$$

Also, a shortest path in R_g with the modified edge weights w' is also a shortest path with the original edge weights w.

Proof: We distinguish two cases.

Case 1: edge (u,v) exists in R_f.
In this case, the distance $d_f(v)$ of v from s, is no more than the distance $d_f(u)$ of u from s plus the weight $w(u,v)$ of edge (u,v), that is,

$$d_f(v) \leq d_f(u) + w(u,v).$$

Thus, we have

$$w'(u,v) \geq 0.$$

Case 2: edge (u,v) does not exist in R_f.
In this case, (v,u) must be an edge of the augmenting path used to obtained flow g from flow f and we have

$$d_f(u) = d_f(v) + w(v,u).$$

Since $w(v,u) = -w(u,v)$, we have

$$w'(u,v) = 0.$$

Given a path π of R_g from s to t, the cost $w'(\pi)$ of π with respect to the modified edge weights differs from the cost $c(\pi)$ of π by a constant:

$$w'(\pi) = w(\pi) + d_f(s) - d_f(t) = w(\pi) - d_f(t).$$

Thus, a shortest path in R_g with respect to the original weights is also a shortest path with respect to the modified weights. ■

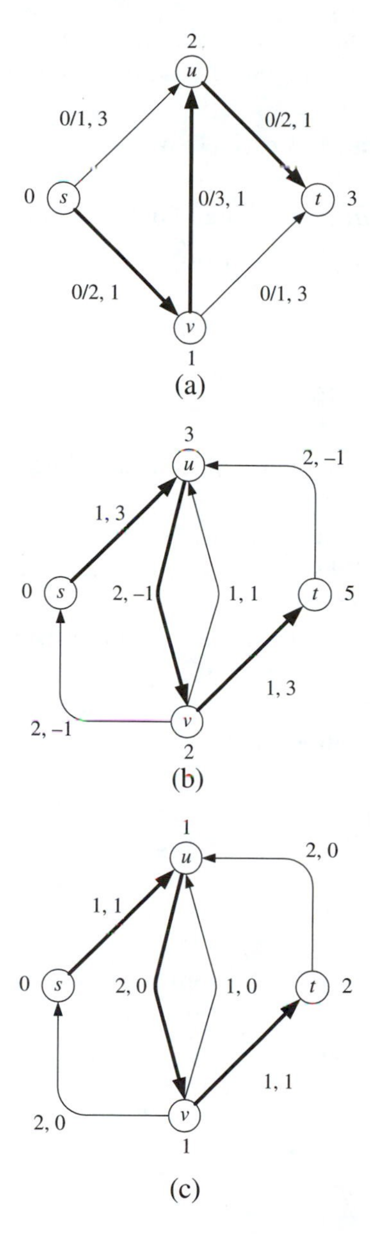

Figure 8.15: Modification of the edge costs in the computation of a minimum-cost flow by successive shortest path augmentations. (a) Flow network N_f with initial null flow f and shortest augmenting path $\pi_1 = (s, v, u, t)$ with cost $w_1 = w(\pi_1) = 3$. Each vertex is labeled with its distance d_f from the source. (Same as Figure 8.14.b.) (b) Residual network R_g after augmenting flow f by two units along path π and shortest path $\pi_2 = (s, u, v, t)$ with cost $w(\pi_2) = 5$. (Same as Figure 8.14.d.) (c) Residual network R_g with modified edge weights. Path π_2 is still a shortest path. However, its cost is decreased by w_1.

The complete algorithm for computing a minimum-cost flow using the successive shortest path method is given in Algorithm 8.16 (MinCostFlow).

```
Algorithm MinCostFlow(N):
   Input: Weighted flow network N = (G, c, w, s, t)
   Output: A maximum flow with minimum cost f for N
 for each edge e ∈ N do
   f(e) ← 0
 for each vertex v ∈ N do
   d(v) ← 0
 stop ← false
 repeat
   compute the weighted residual network R_f
   for each edge (u, v) ∈ R_f do
     w'(u, v) ← w(u, v) + d(u) − d(v)
   run Dijkstra's algorithm on R_f using the weights w'
   for each vertex v ∈ N do
     d(v) ← distance of v from s in R_f
   if d(t) < +∞ then
     {π is an augmenting path with respect to f}
     {Compute the residual capacity Δ_f(π) of π }
     Δ ← +∞
     for each edge e ∈ π do
       if Δ_f(e) < Δ then
         Δ ← Δ_f(e)
     { Push Δ = Δ_f(π) units of flow along path π }
     for each edge e ∈ π do
       if e is a forward edge then
         f(e) ← f(e) + Δ
       else
         f(e) ← f(e) − Δ          {e is a backward edge}
   else
     stop ← true          {f is a maximum flow of minimum cost}
 until stop
```

Algorithm 8.16: Successive shortest path algorithm for computing a minimum-cost flow.

We summarize this section in the following theorem:

Theorem 8.19: *A minimum-cost maximum flow f for a network with n vertices and m edges can be computed in $O(|f| m \log n)$ time.*

8.5 Java Example: Minimum-Cost Flow

In this section, we present portions of a Java implementation of Algorithm 8.16 (MinCostFlow), which computes a minimum-cost flow using successive augmentations along minimum-cost paths. The abstract class MinCostFlowTemplate, based on the template method pattern, implements the the core functionality of the algorithm. Any concrete class implementing the abstract class MinCostFlowTemplate should override the cost(e) and capacity(e) methods to return cost and capacity values for edge e specific to the application. The instance variables and the abstract methods, cost(e) and capacity(e), of class MinCostFlowTemplate are shown in Code Fragment 8.18. The core computation of a shortest augmenting path with method doOneIteration() is shown in Code Fragment 8.19.

The algorithm can be run either step-by-step, or at once. The two execute methods shown in Code Fragment 8.20 run the algorithm on the given flow network. The algorithm will run until either a given target value for the flow has been reached, or there are no more augmenting paths from the source (instance variable source_) to the sink (instance variable dest_). Optionally, the algorithm can be executed one augmenting path at a time, by first initializing the algorithm through method init(G,s,t) (Code Fragment 8.21), and then repeatedly calling doOneIteration(). Helper methods are shown in Code Fragment 8.22. To remove all auxiliary objects used by the algorithm, method cleanup() (not shown) can be called.

Code Fragment 8.23 contains methods for working with the residual graph. Method distance(v) returns the distance of a vertex v from the source of the residual graph. Method residualWeight(e) returns the modified weight of an edge e. Method isAtCapacity(v,e) is used to determine whether edge e has null residual capacity when traversed from endpoint vertex v. Additionally, calling method doOneIteration() returns an iterator over the edges in the current augmenting path. The results are reported by methods flow(e), and maximumFlow() (not shown).

Class MinCostFlowTemplate uses an auxiliary class MinCostFlowDijkstra (not shown) to compute shortest paths with Dijkstra's algorithm. Class MinCostFlowDijkstra is a specialization of the generic Dijkstra's shortest path algorithm provided by the JDSL library [195] (similar to the class given in Code Fragments 7.23–7.25). The main methods of MinCostFlowDijkstra are as follows. Method weight(e) returns the modified weight of edge e, as computed by method residualWeight(e) of class MinCostFlowTemplate. Method incidentEdges(v) is also overridden to consider only those incident edges of vertex v with nonzero residual capacity (this method, in effect, "removes" saturated edges from the residual graph). Additionally, through the use of decorations, MinCostFlowDijkstra keeps track of the flow bottlenecks on the current shortest paths through each node. Thus, at the end of each execution of MinCostFlowDijkstra, we know the minimum cost path from the source to the sink, as well as the maximum amount of flow that can be pushed along that path.

```
/**
 * Implementation of the minimum-cost flow algorithm based on
 * successive augmentations along minimum-cost paths. The algorithm
 * assumes that the graph has no negative-weight edges. The
 * implemetation uses the template-method pattern.
 */
public abstract class MinCostFlowTemplate {

  // instance variables
  protected MinCostFlowDijkstra dijkstra_;
  protected InspectableGraph graph_;
  protected Vertex source_;
  protected Vertex dest_;
  protected boolean finished_;
  protected int maximumFlow_;
  protected int targetFlow_;

  // various constants
  public final int ZERO = 0;
  public final int INFINITY = Integer.MAX_VALUE;

  // node decorations
  private final Object FLOW        = new Object();
  private final Object DISTANCE    = new Object();

  /**
   * Returns the cost for a specified edge. Should be overridden for
   * each specific implementation.
   * @param e Edge whose cost we want
   * @return int cost for edge e (non-negative) */
  protected abstract int cost(Edge e);

  /**
   * Returns the capacity for the specified edge. Should be
   * overridden for each specific implementation.
   * @param e Edge whose capacity we want
   * @return int capacity for edge e (non-negative) */
  protected abstract int capacity(Edge e);
```

Code Fragment 8.18: Instance variables and abstract methods of class MinCostFlowTemplate.

```
/**
 * Performs one iteration of the algorithm. The EdgeIterator it
 * returns contains the edges that were part of the associated path
 * from the source to the dest.
 *
 * @return EdgeIterator over the edges considered in the augmenting path */
public final EdgeIterator doOneIteration()
  throws jdsl.graph.api.InvalidEdgeException {
  EdgeIterator returnVal;
  runDijkstraOnResidualNetwork();
  updateDistances();
  // check to see if an augmenting path exists
  if (distance(dest_) < INFINITY) {
    EdgeIterator pathIter = dijkstra_.reportPath();
    int maxFlow = dijkstra_.reportPathFlow(dest_);
    maximumFlow_ += maxFlow;
    // push maxFlow along path now
    while (pathIter.hasNext()) {
      // check if it is a forward edge
      Edge e = pathIter.nextEdge();

      if (isForwardEdge(e)) {
        setFlow(e, flow(e) + maxFlow);
      } else {
        setFlow(e, flow(e) - maxFlow);
      }
    }
    pathIter.reset();
    returnVal = pathIter;
  } else {
    finished();
    returnVal = new EdgeIteratorAdapter(new ArrayObjectIterator(new Object[0]));
  }
  return returnVal;
}
```

Code Fragment 8.19: Method for computing a minimum-cost augmenting path in class MinCostFlowTemplate.

```
/**
 * Helper method to continually execute iterations of the algorithm
 * until it is finished.    */
protected final void runUntil() {
  while (shouldContinue()) {
    doOneIteration();
  }
}
/**
 * Execute the algorithm, which will compute the maximum flow
 * between source and dest in the Graph g.
 *
 * @param g a Graph
 * @param source of the flow
 * @param dest for the flow */
public final void execute(InspectableGraph g, Vertex source, Vertex dest)
  throws InvalidVertexException {
  init(g, source, dest);
  runUntil();
}
/**
 * Execute the algorithm, which will execute until the target flow
 * is reached, or no more flow is possible.
 *
 * @param g a Graph
 * @param source of the flow
 * @param dest for the flow */
public final void execute(InspectableGraph g, Vertex source, Vertex dest,
                          int target)
  throws InvalidVertexException {
  targetFlow_ = target;
  execute(g, source, dest);
}
```

Code Fragment 8.20: Methods for controlling the execution of the minimum-cost flow algorithm in class MinCostFlowTemplate.

```
/**
 * Initializes the algorithm.  Set up all local instance variables
 * and initialize all of the default values for the decorations.
 * Dijkstra's is also initialized.
 *
 * @param g a Graph
 * @param source of the flow
 * @param dest for the flow */
public void init(InspectableGraph g, Vertex source, Vertex dest)
  throws InvalidVertexException {
  if( !g.contains( source ) )
    throw new InvalidVertexException( source + " not contained in " + g );
  if( !g.contains( dest ) )
    throw new InvalidVertexException( dest + " not contained in " + g );
  graph_ = g;
  source_ = source;
  dest_ = dest;
  finished_ = false;
  maximumFlow_ = ZERO;
  targetFlow_ = INFINITY;
  // init dijkstra's
  dijkstra_ = new MinCostFlowDijkstra();
  dijkstra_.init(g, source);
  // initialize all the default values
  VertexIterator vertexIter = vertices();
  while (vertexIter.hasNext()) {
    Vertex u = vertexIter.nextVertex();
    setDistance(u, ZERO);
  }
  EdgeIterator edgeIter = edges();
  while (edgeIter.hasNext()) {
    Edge e = edgeIter.nextEdge();
    setFlow(e, ZERO);
  }
}
```

Code Fragment 8.21: Initialization method of class MinCostFlowTemplate.

```
/**
 * Helper method to copy all of the vertex distances from an
 * execution of Dijkstra's algorithm into local decorations so they
 * can be used in computing the residual network for the next
 * execution of Dijkstra's. */
protected void updateDistances() {
  // copy distances from residual network to our network
  VertexIterator vertexIter = vertices();
  while (vertexIter.hasNext()) {
    Vertex v = vertexIter.nextVertex();
    try {
      setDistance(v, dijkstra_.distance(v));
    } catch (InvalidQueryException iqe) {
      // vertex is unreachable; set distance to INFINITY
      setDistance(v, INFINITY);
    }
  }
}

/**
 * Helper method to execute Dijkstra's on the residual network. We
 * are sure to cleanup all past executions by first calling the
 * cleanup() method. */
protected void runDijkstraOnResidualNetwork() {
  dijkstra_.cleanup();
  dijkstra_.execute(graph_, source_, dest_);
}

/**
 * Helper method that is called exactly once when the algorithm is
 * finished executing. */
protected void finished() {
  finished_ = true;
}
```

Code Fragment 8.22: Helper methods of class MinCostFlowTemplate.

```
/**
 * Returns the distance of a vertex from the source.
 * @param v a vertex
 * @return the distance of v from the source
 * @throws InvalidQueryException if v has not been reached yet */
public final int distance(Vertex v) throws InvalidQueryException {
  try {
    return ((Integer)v.get(DISTANCE)).intValue();
  }
  catch (InvalidAttributeException iae) {
    throw new InvalidQueryException(v+" has not been reached yet");
  }
}
/**
 * Returns the modified weight of edge e in the current residual
 * graph. It can be calculated on the fly because distance
 * information is only updated after every iteration of the
 * algorithm.
 * @param e Edge to find residual weight for
 * @return int residual weight of e */
public final int residualWeight(Edge e) {
  // use the absolute value because if we traverse
  // the edge backwards, then w(v,u) = -w(u,v)
  return Math.abs( cost(e) +
                   distance(graph_.origin(e)) -
                   distance(graph_.destination(e)) );
}
/**
 * Determines whether edge e has null residual capacity when
 * traversed starting at endpoint v.
 * @param v Vertex from which edge is being considered
 * @param e Edge to check
 * @return boolean true if the edge is at capacity, false if not */
public final boolean isAtCapacity(Vertex v, Edge e) {
  // forward edges are full when capacity == flow
  if( v == graph_.origin( e ) )
    return (capacity(e) == flow(e));
  // back edges are full when flow == 0
  else
    return (flow(e) == 0);
}
```

Code Fragment 8.23: Methods distance residualWeight, and isAtCapacity of class MinCostFlowTemplate.

8.6 Exercises

Reinforcement

R-8.1 Show that for a flow f, the total flow out of the source is equal to the total flow into the sink, that is,

$$\sum_{e \in E^+(s)} f(e) = \sum_{e \in E^-(t)} f(e).$$

R-8.2 Answer the following questions on the flow network N and flow f shown in Figure 8.6a:

- What are the forward edges of augmenting path π? What are the backward edges?
- How many augmenting paths are there with respect to flow f? For each such path, list the sequence of vertices of the path and the residual capacity of the path.
- What is the value of a maximum flow in N?

R-8.3 Construct a minimum cut for the network shown in Figure 8.4 using the method in the proof of Lemma 8.6.

R-8.4 Illustrate the execution of the Ford-Fulkerson algorithm in the flow network of Figure 8.2.

R-8.5 Draw a flow network with 9 vertices and 12 edges. Illustrate an execution of the Ford-Fulkerson algorithm on it.

R-8.6 Find a minimum cut in the flow network of Figure 8.8a.

R-8.7 Show that, given a maximum flow in a network with m edges, a minimum cut of N can be computed in $O(m)$ time.

R-8.8 Find two maximum matchings for the bipartite graph of Figure 8.11a that are different from the maximum matching of Figure 8.11b.

R-8.9 Let G be a complete bipartite graph such that $|X| = |Y| = n$ and for each pair of vertices $x \in X$ and $y \in Y$, there is an edge joining x and y. Show that G has $n!$ distinct maximum matchings.

R-8.10 Illustrate the execution of the Ford-Fulkerson algorithm in the flow network of Figure 8.11b.

R-8.11 Illustrate the execution of the Edmonds-Karp algorithm in the flow network of Figure 8.8a.

R-8.12 Illustrate the execution of the Edmonds-Karp algorithm in the flow network of Figure 8.2.

R-8.13 Give a proof of Lemma 8.14.

R-8.14 Illustrate the execution minimum-cost flow algorithm based on successive augmentations along negative-cost cycles for the flow network of Figure 8.14a.

R-8.15 Illustrate the execution minimum-cost flow algorithm based on successive augmentations along minimum-cost paths for the flow network of Figure 8.2, where the cost of an edge (u,v) is given by $|\deg(u) - \deg(v)|$.

R-8.16 Is Algorithm 8.16 (MinCostFlow) a pseudo-polynomial-time algorithm?

Creativity

C-8.1 What is the worst-case running time of the Ford-Fulkerson algorithm if all edge capacities are bounded by a constant?

C-8.2 Improve the bound of Lemma 8.9 by showing that there are at most $nm/4$ augmentations in the Edmonds-Karp algorithm.

Hint: Use $d_f(u,t)$ in addition to $d_f(s,v)$.

C-8.3 Let N be a flow network with n vertices and m edges. Show how to compute an augmenting path with the largest residual capacity in $O((n+m)\log n)$ time.

C-8.4 Show that the Ford-Fulkerson algorithm runs in time $O(m^2 \log n \log |f^*|)$ when, at each iteration, the augmenting path with the largest residual capacity is chosen.

C-8.5 You want to increase the maximum flow of a network as much as possible, but you are only allowed to increase the capacity of one edge.

a. How do you find such an edge? (Give pseudo-code.) You may assume the existence of algorithms to compute max flow and min cut. What's the running time of your algorithm?
b. Is it always possible to find such an edge? Justify your answer.

C-8.6 Given a flow network N and a maximum flow f for N, suppose that the capacity of an edge e of N is decreased by one, and let N' be the resulting network. Give an algorithm for computing a maximum flow in network N' by modifying f.

C-8.7 Give an algorithm that determines, in $O(n+m)$ time, whether a graph with n vertices and m edges is bipartite.

C-8.8 Give an algorithm that determines what is the maximum number of edge-disjoint paths between two given vertices s and t of an undirected graph.

C-8.9 A taxi company receives pickup requests from n locations. There are m taxis available, where $m \geq n$, and the distance of taxi i to location j is d_{ij}. Give an algorithm for computing a dispatchment of n taxis to the n pickup locations that minimizes the total distance.

C-8.10 Give an algorithm for computing a flow of maximum value subject to the following two additional constraints:

a. Each edge e has a lower bound $\ell(e)$ on the flow through it.
b. There are multiple sources and sinks, and the value of the flow is computed as the total flow out of all the sources (equal to the total flow into all the sinks).

C-8.11 Show that, in a flow network with noninteger capacities, the Ford-Fulkerson algorithm may not terminate.

Projects

P-8.1 Design and implement an applet that animates the Ford-Fulkerson flow algorithm. Try to be creative about how you illustrate flow augmentation, residual capacity, and the actual flow itself.

P-8.2 Implement the Ford-Fulkerson flow algorithm using three different methods for finding augmenting paths. Perform a careful experimental comparison of these methods.

P-8.3 Implement the algorithm for computing a maximum bipartite matching. Show how to reuse an algorithm for computing a maximum flow.

P-8.4 Implement the Edmonds-Karp algorithm.

P-8.5 Implement the minimum-cost flow algorithm based on successive augmentations along negative-cost cycles.

P-8.6 Implement the minimum-cost flow algorithm based on successive augmentations along minimum-cost paths. Implement the variation that uses the Bellman-Ford algorithm and the variation that modifies the costs and uses Dijkstra's algorithm.

Chapter Notes

Ford and Fulkerson's network flow algorithm (8.2.2) is described in their book [71]. Edmonds and Karp [65] describe two methods for computing augmenting paths that cause the Ford-Fulkerson algorithm to run faster: shortest augmenting path (Section 8.2.4) and augmenting paths with maximum residual capacity (Exercise C-8.4). The minimum-cost flow algorithm based on successive augmentations along minimum-cost paths (Section 8.4.2) is also due to Edmonds and Karp [65].

The reader interested in further study of graph algorithms and flow networks is referred to the books by Ahuja, Magnanti, and Orlin [9], Cormen, Leiserson, and Rivest [55], Even [68], Gibbons [77], Mehlhorn [149], and Tarjan [200], and the book chapter by van Leeuwen [205].

Dan Polivy devloped the implementation of the minimum-cost flow algorithm given in Section 8.5.

Part

III Internet Algorithmics

Chapter 9 Text Processing

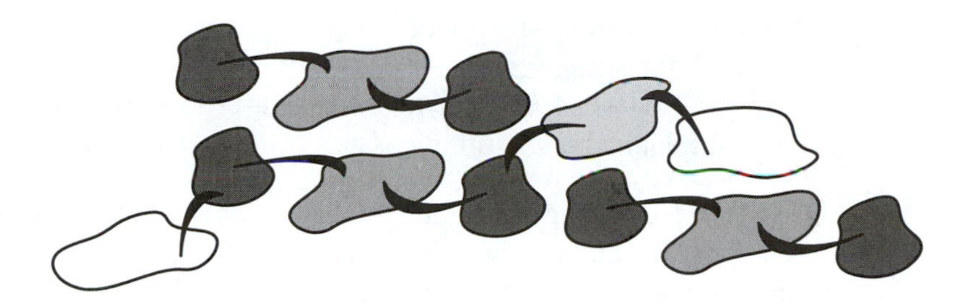

Contents

9.1 Strings and Pattern Matching Algorithms 419

9.1.1 String Operations 419

9.1.2 Brute Force Pattern Matching 420

9.1.3 The Boyer-Moore Algorithm 422

9.1.4 The Knuth-Morris-Pratt Algorithm 425

9.2 Tries 429

9.2.1 Standard Tries 429

9.2.2 Compressed Tries 433

9.2.3 Suffix Tries 435

9.2.4 Search Engines 439

9.3 Text Compression 440

9.3.1 The Huffman Coding Algorithm 441

9.3.2 The Greedy Method Revisited 442

9.4 Text Similarity Testing 443

9.4.1 The Longest Common Subsequence Problem 443

9.4.2 Applying Dynamic Programming to the LCS Problem 444

9.5 Exercises 447

Document processing is rapidly becoming one of the dominant functions of computers. Computers are used to edit documents, to search documents, to transport documents over the Internet, and to display documents on printers and computer screens. Web "surfing" and Web searching are becoming significant and important computer applications, and many of the key computations in all of this document processing involve character strings and string pattern matching. For example, the Internet document formats HTML and XML are primarily text formats, with added links to multimedia content. Making sense of the many terabytes of information on the Internet requires a considerable amount of text processing.

In this chapter, we study several fundamental text processing algorithms for quickly performing important string operations. We pay particular attention to algorithms for string searching and pattern matching, since these can often be computational bottlenecks in many document-processing applications. We also study some fundamental algorithmic issues involved in text processing, as well.

Text processing algorithms operate primarily on character strings. The terminology and notation for strings, as used in this chapter, is fairly intuitive, and it turns out that representing a string as an array of characters is quite simple and efficient. So we don't spend a lot of attention on string representations. Nevertheless, string processing often involves an interesting method for string pattern matching, and we study pattern matching algorithms in Section 9.1.

In Section 9.2, we study the trie data structure, which is a tree-based structure that allows for fast searching in a collection of strings.

We study an important text processing problem in Section 9.3, namely, the problem of compressing a document of text so that it fits more efficiently in storage or can be transmitted more efficiently over a network.

The final text processing problem we study, in Section 9.4, deals with how we can measure the similarity between two documents. All of these problems are topics that arise often in Internet computations, such as Web crawlers, search engines, document distribution, and information retrieval.

In addition to having interesting applications, the topics of this chapter also highlight some important algorithmic design patterns (see Chapter 5). In particular, in the section on pattern matching, we discuss the ***brute-force method***, which is often inefficient but has wide applicability. For text compression we study an application of the ***greedy method*** (Section 5.1), which often allows us to approximate solutions to hard problems, and for some problems such as our text compression application actually gives rise to optimal algorithms. Finally, in discussing text similarity, we give another application of ***dynamic programming*** (Section 5.3), which can be applied, in some special instances, to solve a problem in polynomial time that appears at first to require exponential time.

9.1 Strings and Pattern Matching Algorithms

Text documents are ubiquitous in modern computing, as they are used to communicate and publish information. From the perspective of algorithm design, such documents can be viewed as simple character strings. That is, they can be abstracted as a sequence of the characters that make up their content. Performing interesting searching and processing operations on such data, therefore, requires that we have efficient methods for dealing with character strings.

9.1.1 String Operations

At the heart of algorithms for processing text are methods for dealing with character strings. Character strings can come from a wide variety of sources, including scientific, linguistic, and Internet applications. Indeed, the following are examples of such strings:

P = `"CGTAAACTGCTTTAATCAAACGC"`
R = `"U.S. Men Win Soccer World Cup!"`
S = `"http://www.wiley.com/college/goodrich/"`.

The first string, P, comes from DNA applications, the last string, S, is the Internet address (URL) for the Web site that accompanies this book, and the middle string, R, is a fictional news headline. In this section, we present some of the useful operations that are supported by the string ADT for processing strings such as these.

Several of the typical string processing operations involve breaking large strings into smaller strings. In order to be able to speak about the pieces that result from such operations, we use the term ***substring*** of an m-character string P to refer to a string of the form $P[i]P[i+1]P[i+2]\cdots P[j]$, for some $0 \le i \le j \le m-1$, that is, the string formed by the characters in P from index i to index j, inclusive. Technically, this means that a string is actually a substring of itself (taking $i=0$ and $j=m-1$), so if we want to rule this out as a possibility, we must restrict the definition to ***proper*** substrings, which require that either $i>0$ or $j<m-1$. To simplify the notation for referring to substrings, let us use $P[i..j]$ to denote the substring of P from index i to index j, inclusive. That is,

$$P[i..j] = P[i]P[i+1]\cdots P[j].$$

We use the convention that if $i>j$, then $P[i..j]$ is equal to the ***null string***, which has length 0. In addition, in order to distinguish some special kinds of substrings, let us refer to any substring of the form $P[0..i]$, for $0 \le i \le m-1$, as a ***prefix*** of P, and any substring of the form $P[i..m-1]$, for $0 \le i \le m-1$, as a ***suffix*** of P. For example, if we again take P to be the string of DNA given above, then `"CGTAA"` is a prefix of P, `"CGC"` is a suffix of P, and `"TTAATC"` is a (proper) substring of P. Note that the null string is a prefix and a suffix of any other string.

The Pattern Matching Problem

In the classic ***pattern matching*** problem on strings, we are given a ***text*** string T of length n and a ***pattern*** string P of length m, and want to find whether P is a substring of T. The notion of a "match" is that there is a substring of T starting at some index i that matches P, character by character, so that

$$T[i] = P[0],\ T[i+1] = P[1],\ \ldots,\ T[i+m-1] = P[m-1].$$

That is,

$$P = T[i..i+m-1].$$

Thus, the output from a pattern matching algorithm is either an indication that the pattern P does not exist in T or the starting index in T of a substring matching P.

To allow for fairly general notions of a character string, we typically do not restrict the characters in T and P to come explicitly from a well-known character set, like the ASCII or Unicode character sets. Instead, we typically use the general symbol Σ to denote the character set, or ***alphabet***, from which the characters of T and P can come. This alphabet Σ can, of course, be a subset of the ASCII or Unicode character sets, but it could also be more general and is even allowed to be infinite. Nevertheless, since most document processing algorithms are used in applications where the underlying character set is finite, we usually assume that the size of the alphabet Σ, denoted with $|\Sigma|$, is a fixed constant.

Example 9.1: *Suppose we are given the text string*

$T =$ `"abacaabaccabacabaabb"`

and the pattern string

$P =$ `"abacab"`.

Then P is a substring of T. Namely, $P = T[10..15]$.

In this section, we present three different pattern matching algorithms.

9.1.2 Brute Force Pattern Matching

The ***brute force*** algorithmic design pattern is a powerful technique for algorithm design when we have something we wish to search for or when we wish to optimize some function. In applying this technique in a general situation, we typically enumerate all possible configurations of the inputs involved and pick the best of all these enumerated configurations.

Brute-Force Pattern Matching

In applying this technique to design the ***brute-force pattern matching*** algorithm, we derive what is probably the first algorithm that we might think of for solving the pattern matching problem—we simply test all the possible placements of P relative to T. This approach, shown in Algorithm 9.1, is quite simple.

Algorithm BruteForceMatch(T,P):
  Input: Strings T (text) with n characters and P (pattern) with m characters
  Output: Starting index of the first substring of T matching P, or an indication that P is not a substring of T

```
for i ← 0 to n − m {for each candidate index in T} do
   j ← 0
   while (j < m and T[i + j] = P[j]) do
      j ← j + 1
   if j = m then
      return i
return "There is no substring of T matching P."
```

Algorithm 9.1: Brute-force pattern matching.

The brute-force pattern matching algorithm could not be simpler. It consists of two nested loops, with the outer loop indexing through all possible starting indices of the pattern in the text, and the inner loop indexing through each character of the pattern, comparing it to its potentially corresponding character in the text. Thus, the correctness of the brute-force pattern matching algorithm follows immediately.

The running time of brute-force pattern matching in the worst case is not good, however, because, for each candidate index in T, we can perform up to m character comparisons to discover that P does not match T at the current index. Referring to Algorithm 9.1, we see that the outer for-loop is executed at most $n-m+1$ times, and the inner loop is executed at most m times. Thus, the running time of the brute-force method is $O((n-m+1)m)$, which is $O(nm)$. Thus, in the worst case, when n and m are roughly equal, this algorithm has a quadratic running time.

In Figure 9.2 we illustrate the execution of the brute-force pattern matching algorithm on the strings T and P from Example 9.1.

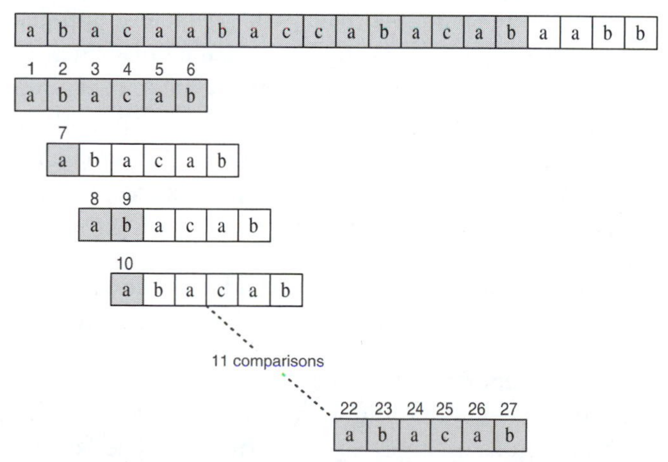

Figure 9.2: Example run of the brute-force pattern matching algorithm. The algorithm performs 27 character comparisons, indicated above with numerical labels.

9.1.3 The Boyer-Moore Algorithm

At first, we might feel that it is always necessary to examine every character in T in order to locate a pattern P as a substring. But this is not always the case, for the ***Boyer-Moore*** (***BM***) pattern matching algorithm, which we study in this section, can sometimes avoid comparisons between P and a sizable fraction of the characters in T. The only caveat is that, whereas the brute-force algorithm can work even with a potentially unbounded alphabet, the BM algorithm assumes the alphabet is of fixed, finite size. It works the fastest when the alphabet is moderately sized and the pattern is relatively long.

In this section, we describe a simplified version of the original BM algorithm. The main idea is to improve the running time of the brute-force algorithm by adding two potentially time-saving heuristics:

Looking-Glass Heuristic: When testing a possible placement of P against T, begin the comparisons from the end of P and move backward to the front of P.

Character-Jump Heuristic: During the testing of a possible placement of P against T, a mismatch of text character $T[i] = c$ with the corresponding pattern character $P[j]$ is handled as follows. If c is not contained anywhere in P, then shift P completely past $T[i]$ (for it cannot match any character in P). Otherwise, shift P until an occurrence of character c in P gets aligned with $T[i]$.

We will formalize these heuristics shortly, but at an intuitive level, they work as an integrated team. The looking-glass heuristic sets up the other heuristic to allow us to avoid comparisons between P and whole groups of characters in T. In this case at least, we can get to the destination faster by going backwards, for if we encounter a mismatch during the consideration of P at a certain location in T, then we are likely to avoid lots of needless comparisons by significantly shifting P relative to T using the character-jump heuristic. The character-jump heuristic pays off big if it can be applied early in the testing of a potential placement of P against T.

Therefore, let us define how the character-jump heuristics can be integrated into a string pattern matching algorithm. To implement this heuristic, we define a function $\mathsf{last}(c)$ that takes a character c from the alphabet and specifies how far we may shift the pattern P if a character equal to c is found in the text that does not match the pattern. In particular, we define $\mathsf{last}(c)$ as follows:

- If c is in P, $\mathsf{last}(c)$ is the index of the last (right-most) occurrence of c in P. Otherwise, we conventionally define $\mathsf{last}(c) = -1$.

If characters can be used as indices in arrays, then the last function can be easily implemented as a lookup table. We leave the method for computing this table efficiently as a simple exercise (R-9.6). The last function will give us all the information we need to perform the character-jump heuristic. In Algorithm 9.3, we show the BM pattern matching method. The jump step is illustrated in Figure 9.4.

Algorithm BMMatch(T,P):
  Input: Strings T (text) with n characters and P (pattern) with m characters
  Output: Starting index of the first substring of T matching P, or an indication that P is not a substring of T

```
compute function last
i ← m − 1
j ← m − 1
repeat
  if P[j] = T[i] then
    if j = 0 then
      return i            {a match!}
    else
      i ← i − 1
      j ← j − 1
  else
    i ← i + m − min(j, 1 + last(T[i]))          { jump step }
    j ← m − 1
until i > n − 1
return "There is no substring of T matching P."
```

Algorithm 9.3: The Boyer-Moore pattern matching algorithm.

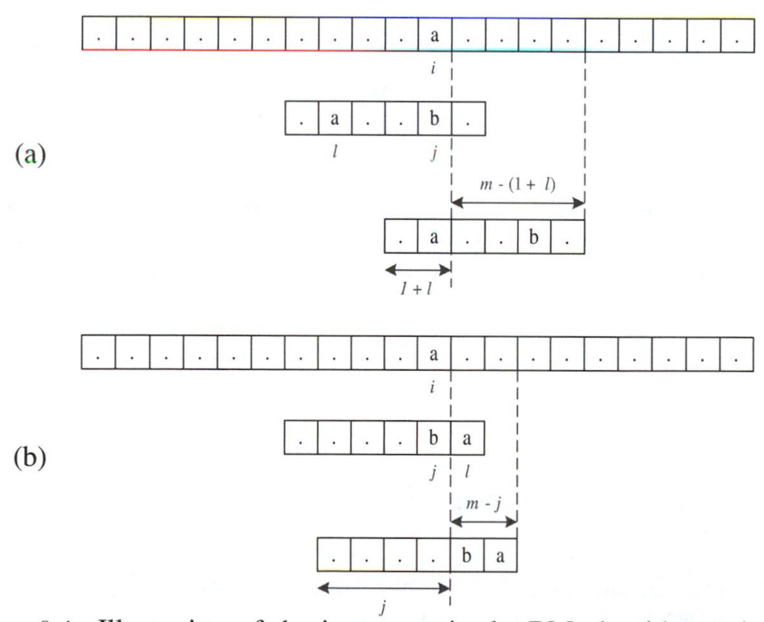

Figure 9.4: Illustration of the jump step in the BM algorithm, where l denotes last$(T[i])$. We distinguish two cases: (a) $1+l \leq j$, where we shift the pattern by $j-l$ units; (b) $j < 1+l$, where we shift the pattern by one unit.

In Figure 9.5, we illustrate the execution of the Boyer-Moore pattern matching algorithm on a similar input string as in Example 9.1.

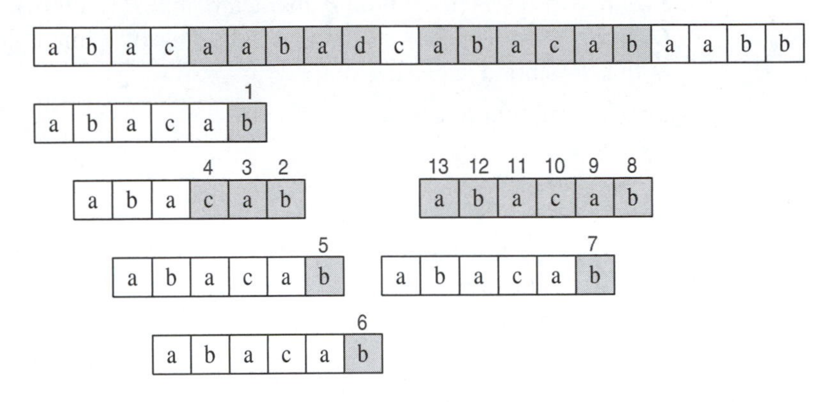

The $\mathsf{last}(c)$ function:

c	a	b	c	d
$\mathsf{last}(c)$	4	5	3	-1

Figure 9.5: An illustration of the BM pattern matching algorithm. The algorithm performs 13 character comparisons, which are indicated with numerical labels.

The correctness of the BM pattern matching algorithm follows from the fact that each time the method makes a shift, it is guaranteed not to "skip" over any possible matches. For $\mathsf{last}(c)$ is the location of the ***last*** occurrence of c in P.

The worst-case running time of the BM algorithm is $O(nm+|\Sigma|)$. Namely, the computation of the last function takes time $O(m+|\Sigma|)$ and the actual search for the pattern takes $O(nm)$ time in the worst case, the same as the brute-force algorithm. An example of a text-pattern pair that achieves the worst case is

$$T = \overbrace{aaaaaa\cdots a}^{n}$$
$$P = b\overbrace{aa\cdots a}^{m-1}.$$

The worst-case performance, however, is unlikely to be achieved for English text.

Indeed, the BM algorithm is often able to skip over large portions of the text. (See Figure 9.6.) There is experimental evidence that on English text, the average number of comparisons done per text character is approximately 0.24 for a five-character pattern string. The payoff is not as great for binary strings or for very short patterns, however, in which case the KMP algorithm, discussed in Section 9.1.4, or, for very short patterns, the brute-force algorithm, may be better.

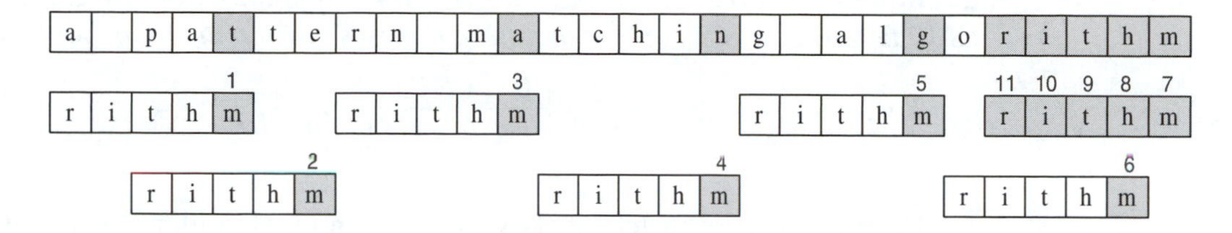

Figure 9.6: Execution of the Boyer-Moore algorithm on an English text and pattern, where a significant speedup is achieved. Note that not all text characters are examined.

We have actually presented a simplified version of the Boyer-Moore (BM) algorithm. The original BM algorithm achieves running time $O(n+m+|\Sigma|)$ by using an alternative shift heuristic to the partially matched text string, whenever it shifts the pattern more than the character-jump heuristic. This alternative shift heuristic is based on applying the main idea from the Knuth-Morris-Pratt pattern matching algorithm, which we discuss next.

9.1.4 The Knuth-Morris-Pratt Algorithm

In studying the worst-case performance of the brute-force and BM pattern matching algorithms on specific instances of the problem, such as that given in Example 9.1, we should notice a major inefficiency. Specifically, we may perform many comparisons while testing a potential placement of the pattern against the text, yet if we discover a pattern character that does not match in the text, then we throw away all the information gained by these comparisons and start over again from scratch with the next incremental placement of the pattern. The Knuth-Morris-Pratt (or "KMP") algorithm, discussed in this section, avoids this waste of information and, in so doing, it achieves a running time of $O(n+m)$, which is optimal in the worst case. That is, in the worst case any pattern matching algorithm will have to examine all the characters of the text and all the characters of the pattern at least once.

The Failure Function

The main idea of the KMP algorithm is to preprocess the pattern string P so as to compute a ***failure function*** f that indicates the proper shift of P so that, to the largest extent possible, we can reuse previously performed comparisons. Specifically, the failure function $f(j)$ is defined as the length of the longest prefix of P that is a suffix of $P[1..j]$ (note that we did ***not*** put $P[0..j]$ here). We also use the convention that $f(0)=0$. Later, we will discuss how to compute the failure function efficiently. The importance of this failure function is that it "encodes" repeated substrings inside the pattern itself.

Example 9.2: *Consider the pattern string $P =$ "abacab" from Example 9.1. The KMP failure function $f(j)$ for the string P is as shown in the following table:*

j	0	1	2	3	4	5
$P[j]$	a	b	a	c	a	b
$f(j)$	0	0	1	0	1	2

The KMP pattern matching algorithm, shown in Algorithm 9.7, incrementally processes the text string T comparing it to the pattern string P. Each time there is a match, we increment the current indices. On the other hand, if there is a mismatch and we have previously made progress in P, then we consult the failure function to determine the new index in P where we need to continue checking P against T. Otherwise (there was a mismatch and we are at the beginning of P), we simply increment the index for T (and keep the index variable for P at its beginning). We repeat this process until we find a match of P in T or the index for T reaches n, the length of T (indicating that we did not find the pattern P in T).

The main part of the KMP algorithm is the while-loop, which performs a comparison between a character in T and a character in P each iteration. Depending upon the outcome of this comparison, the algorithm either moves on to the next characters in T and P, consults the failure function for a new candidate character in P, or starts over with the next index in T. The correctness of this algorithm follows from the definition of the failure function. The skipped comparisons are actually unnecessary, for the failure function guarantees that all the ignored comparisons are redundant—they would involve comparing characters we already know match.

Algorithm KMPMatch(T,P):
  Input: Strings T (text) with n characters and P (pattern) with m characters
  Output: Starting index of the first substring of T matching P, or an indication that P is not a substring of T

```
f ← KMPFailureFunction(P)        {construct the failure function f for P}
i ← 0
j ← 0
while i < n do
  if P[j] = T[i] then
    if j = m − 1 then
      return i − m + 1        {a match!}
    i ← i + 1
    j ← j + 1
  else if j > 0 {no match, but we have advanced in P} then
    j ← f(j − 1)        {j indexes just after prefix of P that must match}
  else
    i ← i + 1
return "There is no substring of T matching P."
```

Algorithm 9.7: The KMP pattern matching algorithm.

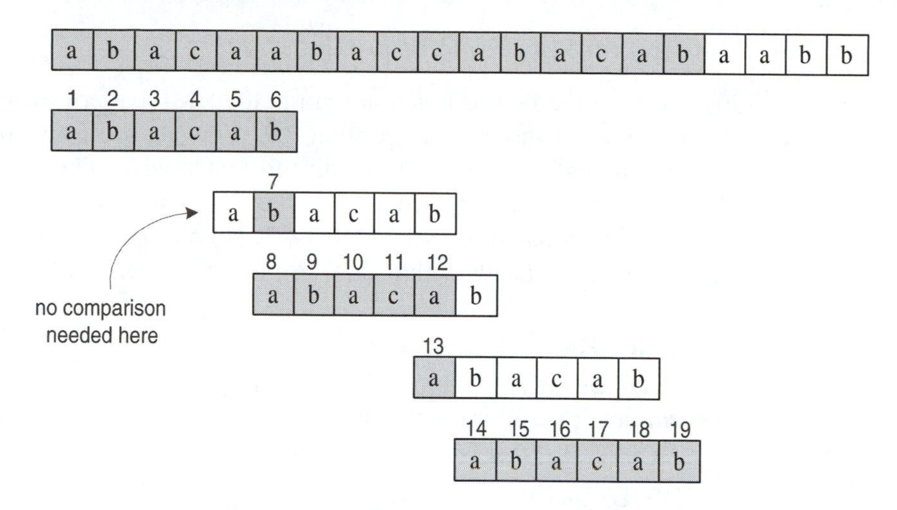

Figure 9.8: An illustration of the KMP pattern matching algorithm. The failure function f for this pattern is given in Example 9.2. The algorithm performs 19 character comparisons, which are indicated with numerical labels.

In Figure 9.8, we illustrate the execution of the KMP pattern matching algorithm on the same input strings as in Example 9.1. Note the use of the failure function to avoid redoing one of the comparisons between a character of the pattern and a character of the text. Also note that the algorithm performs fewer overall comparisons than the brute-force algorithm run on the same strings (Figure 9.2).

Performance

Excluding the computation of the failure function, the running time of the KMP algorithm is clearly proportional to the number of iterations of the while-loop. For the sake of the analysis, let us define $k = i - j$. Intuitively, k is the total amount by which the pattern P has been shifted with respect to the text T. Note that throughout the execution of the algorithm, we have $k \leq n$. One of the following three cases occurs at each iteration of the loop.

- If $T[i] = P[j]$, then i increases by 1, and k does not change, since j also increases by 1.
- If $T[i] \neq P[j]$ and $j > 0$, then i does not change and k increases by at least 1, since in this case k changes from $i - j$ to $i - f(j-1)$, which is an addition of $j - f(j-1)$, which is positive because $f(j-1) < j$.
- If $T[i] \neq P[j]$ and $j = 0$, then i increases by 1 and k increases by 1, since j does not change.

Thus, at each iteration of the loop, either i or k increases by at least 1 (possibly both); hence, the total number of iterations of the while-loop in the KMP pattern matching algorithm is at most $2n$. Of course, achieving this bound assumes that we have already computed the failure function for P.

Constructing the KMP Failure Function

To construct the failure function used in the KMP pattern matching algorithm, we use the method shown in Algorithm 9.9. This algorithm is another example of a "bootstrapping" process quite similar to that used in the KMPMatch algorithm. We compare the pattern to itself as in the KMP algorithm. Each time we have two characters that match, we set $f(i) = j+1$. Note that since we have $i > j$ throughout the execution of the algorithm, $f(j-1)$ is always defined when we need to use it.

Algorithm KMPFailureFunction(P):
  Input: String P (pattern) with m characters
  Output: The failure function f for P, which maps j to the length of the longest prefix of P that is a suffix of $P[1..j]$

```
i ← 1
j ← 0
f(0) ← 0
while i < m do
  if P[j] = P[i] then
    {we have matched j+1 characters}
    f(i) ← j+1
    i ← i+1
    j ← j+1
  else if j > 0 then
    {j indexes just after a prefix of P that must match}
    j ← f(j−1)
  else
    {we have no match here}
    f(i) ← 0
    i ← i+1
```

Algorithm 9.9: Computation of the failure function used in the KMP pattern matching algorithm. Note how the algorithm uses the previous values of the failure function to efficiently compute new values.

Algorithm KMPFailureFunction runs in $O(m)$ time. Its analysis is analogous to that of algorithm KMPMatch. Thus, we have:

Theorem 9.3: *The Knuth-Morris-Pratt algorithm performs pattern matching on a text string of length n and a pattern string of length m in $O(n+m)$ time.*

The running time analysis of the KMP algorithm may seem a little surprising at first, for it states that, in time proportional to that needed just to read the strings T and P separately, we can find the first occurrence of P in T. Also, it should be noted that the running time of the KMP algorithm does not depend on the size of the alphabet.

9.2 Tries

The pattern matching algorithms presented in the previous section speed up the search in a text by preprocessing the pattern (to compute the failure function in the KMP algorithm or the last function in the BM algorithm). In this section, we take a complementary approach, namely, we present string searching algorithms that preprocess the text. This approach is suitable for applications where a series of queries is performed on a fixed text, so that the initial cost of preprocessing the text is compensated by a speedup in each subsequent query (for example, a Web site that offers pattern matching in Shakespeare's *Hamlet* or a search engine that offers Web pages on the *Hamlet* topic).

A ***trie*** (pronounced "try") is a tree-based data structure for storing strings in order to support fast pattern matching. The main application for tries is in information retrieval. Indeed, the name "trie" comes from the word "re*trie*val." In an information retrieval application, such as a search for a certain DNA sequence in a genomic database, we are given a collection S of strings, all defined using the same alphabet.

The primary query operations that tries support are pattern matching and ***prefix matching***. The latter operation involves being given a string X, and looking for all the strings in S that contain X as a prefix.

9.2.1 Standard Tries

Let S be a set of s strings from alphabet Σ, such that no string in S is a prefix of another string. A ***standard trie*** for S is an ordered tree T with the following properties (see Figure 9.10):

- Each node of T, except the root, is labeled with a character of Σ.
- The ordering of the children of an internal node of T is determined by a canonical ordering of the alphabet Σ.
- T has s external nodes, each associated with a string of S, such that the concatenation of the labels of the nodes on the path from the root to an external node v of T yields the string of S associated with v.

Thus, a trie T represents the strings of S with paths from the root to the external nodes of T. Note the importance of assuming that no string in S is a prefix of another string. This ensures that each string of S is uniquely associated with an external node of T. We can always satisfy this assumption by adding a special character that is not in the original alphabet Σ at the end of each string.

An internal node in a standard trie T can have anywhere between 1 and d children, where d is the size of the alphabet. There is an edge going from the root r to one of its children for each character that is first in some string in the collection S.

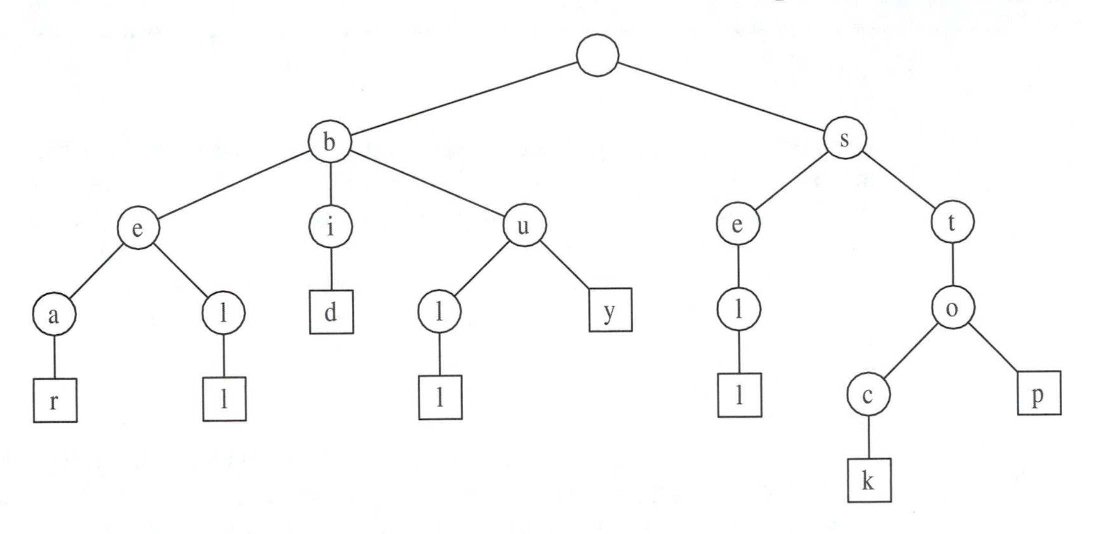

Figure 9.10: Standard trie for the strings {bear, bell, bid, bull, buy, sell, stock, stop}.

In addition, a path from the root of T to an internal node v at depth i corresponds to an i-character prefix $X[0..i-1]$ of a string X of S. In fact, for each character c that can follow the prefix $X[0..i-1]$ in a string of the set S, there is a child of v labeled with character c. In this way, a trie concisely stores the common prefixes that exist among a set of strings.

If there are only two characters in the alphabet, then the trie is essentially a binary tree, although some internal nodes may have only one child (that is, it may be an improper binary tree). In general, if there are d characters in the alphabet, then the trie will be a multi-way tree where each internal node has between 1 and d children. In addition, there are likely to be several internal nodes in a standard trie that have fewer than d children. For example, the trie shown in Figure 9.10 has several internal nodes with only one child. We can implement a trie with a tree storing characters at its nodes.

The following theorem provides some important structural properties of a standard trie:

Theorem 9.4: *A standard trie storing a collection S of s strings of total length n from an alphabet of size d has the following properties:*

- *Every internal node of T has at most d children*
- *T has s external nodes*
- *The height of T is equal to the length of the longest string in S*
- *The number of nodes of T is $O(n)$.*

Performance

The worst case for the number of nodes of a trie occurs when no two strings share a common nonempty prefix; that is, except for the root, all internal nodes have one child.

A trie T for a set S of strings can be used to implement a dictionary whose keys are the strings of S. Namely, we perform a search in T for a string X by tracing down from the root the path indicated by the characters in X. If this path can be traced and terminates at an external node, then we know X is in the dictionary. For example, in the trie in Figure 9.10, tracing the path for "bull" ends up at an external node. If the path cannot be traced or the path can be traced but terminates at an internal node, then X is not in the dictionary. In the example in Figure 9.10, the path for "bet" cannot be traced and the path for "be" ends at an internal node. Neither such word is in the dictionary. Note that in this implementation of a dictionary, single characters are compared instead of the entire string (key).

It is easy to see that the running time of the search for a string of size m is $O(dm)$, where d is the size of the alphabet. Indeed, we visit at most $m+1$ nodes of T and we spend $O(d)$ time at each node. For some alphabets, we may be able to improve the time spent at a node to be $O(1)$ or $O(\log d)$ by using a dictionary of characters implemented in a hash table or lookup table. However, since d is a constant in most applications, we can stick with the simple approach that takes $O(d)$ time per node visited.

From the above discussion, it follows that we can use a trie to perform a special type of pattern matching, called ***word matching***, where we want to determine whether a given pattern matches one of the words of the text exactly. (See Figure 9.11.) Word matching differs from standard pattern matching since the pattern cannot match an arbitrary substring of the text, but only one of its words. Using a trie, word matching for a pattern of length m takes $O(dm)$ time, where d is the size of the alphabet, independent of the size of the text. If the alphabet has constant size (as is the case for text in natural languages and DNA strings), a query takes $O(m)$ time, proportional to the size of the pattern. A simple extension of this scheme supports prefix matching queries. However, arbitrary occurrences of the pattern in the text (for example, the pattern is a proper suffix of a word or spans two words) cannot be efficiently performed.

To construct a standard trie for a set S of strings, we can use an incremental algorithm that inserts the strings one at a time. Recall the assumption that no string of S is a prefix of another string. To insert a string X into the current trie T, we first try to trace the path associated with X in T. Since X is not already in T and no string in S is a prefix of another string, we will stop tracing the path at an ***internal*** node v of T before reaching the end of X. We then create a new chain of node descendents of v to store the remaining characters of X. The time to insert X is $O(dm)$, where m is the length of X and d is the size of the alphabet. Thus, constructing the entire trie for set S takes $O(dn)$ time, where n is the total length of the strings of S.

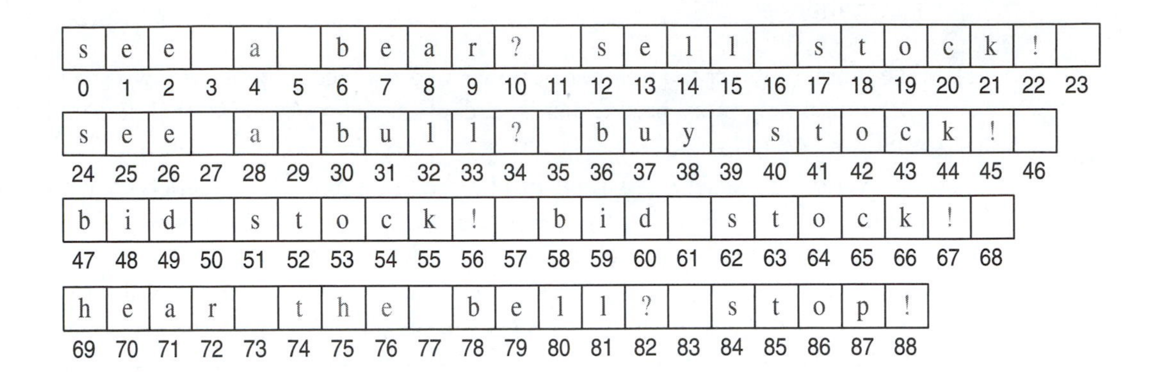

(a)

(b)

Figure 9.11: Word matching and prefix matching with a standard trie: (a) an example text that is to be searched; (b) a standard trie for the words in the text (with articles and prepositions, which are also known as ***stop words***, excluded). We show external nodes augmented with indications of the corresponding word positions.

There is a potential space inefficiency in the standard trie that has prompted the development of the ***compressed trie***, which is also known (for historical reasons) as the ***Patricia trie***. Namely, there are potentially a lot of nodes in the standard trie that have only one child, and the existence of such nodes is a waste, for it implies that the total number of nodes in the tree could be more than the number of words in the corresponding text.

We discuss the compressed trie data structure in the next subsection.

9.2.2 Compressed Tries

A ***compressed trie*** is similar to a standard trie but it ensures that each internal node in the trie has at least two children. It enforces this rule by compressing chains of single-child nodes into individual edges. (See Figure 9.12.) Let T be a standard trie. We say that an internal node v of T is ***redundant*** if v has one child and is not the root. For example, the trie of Figure 9.10 has eight redundant nodes. Let us also say that a chain of $k \geq 2$ edges,

$$(v_0, v_1)(v_1, v_2) \cdots (v_{k-1}, v_k),$$

is ***redundant*** if

- v_i is redundant for $i = 1, \ldots, k-1$
- v_0 and v_k are not redundant.

We can transform T into a compressed trie by replacing each redundant chain $(v_0, v_1) \cdots (v_{k-1}, v_k)$ of $k \geq 2$ edges into a single edge (v_0, v_k), relabeling v_k with the concatenation of the labels of nodes $v_1, \ldots, v_k$.

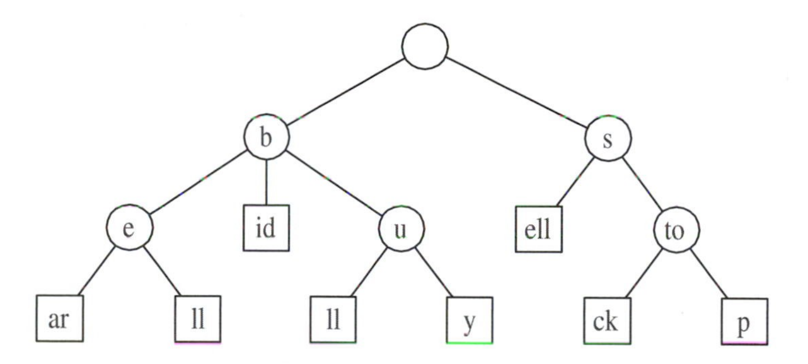

Figure 9.12: Compressed trie for the strings {bear, bell, bid, bull, buy, sell, stock, stop}. Compare this with the standard trie shown in Figure 9.10.

Thus, nodes in a compressed trie are labeled with strings, which are substrings of strings in the collection, rather than with individual characters. The advantage of a compressed trie over a standard trie is that the number of nodes of the compressed trie is proportional to the number of strings and not to their total length, as shown in the following theorem (compare with Theorem 9.4).

Theorem 9.5: *A compressed trie storing a collection S of s strings from an alphabet of size d has the following properties:*

- *Every internal node of T has at least two children and at most d children*
- *T has s external nodes*
- *The number of nodes of T is $O(s)$.*

The attentive reader may wonder whether the compression of paths provides any significant advantage, since it is offset by a corresponding expansion of the node labels. Indeed, a compressed trie is truly advantageous only when it is used as an ***auxiliary*** index structure over a collection of strings already stored in a primary structure, and is not required to actually store all the characters of the strings in the collection. Given this auxiliary structure, however, the compressed trie is indeed quite efficient.

Suppose, for example, that the collection S of strings is an array of strings $S[0]$, $S[1]$, ..., $S[s-1]$. Instead of storing the label X of a node explicitly, we represent it implicitly by a triplet of integers (i, j, k), such that $X = S[i][j..k]$; that is, X is the substring of $S[i]$ consisting of the characters from the jth to the kth included. (See the example in Figure 9.13. Also compare with the standard trie of Figure 9.11.)

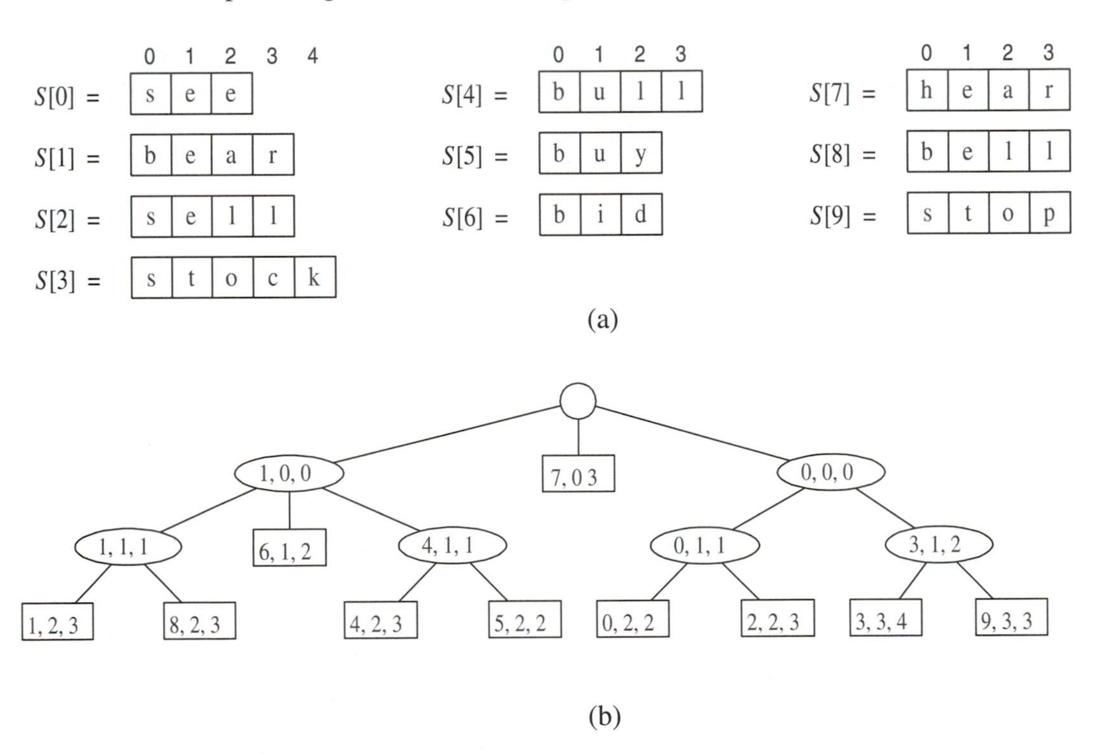

Figure 9.13: (a) Collection S of strings stored in an array. (b) Compact representation of the compressed trie for S.

This additional compression scheme allows us to reduce the total space for the trie itself from $O(n)$ for the standard trie to $O(s)$ for the compressed trie, where n is the total length of the strings in S and s is the number of strings in S. We must still store the different strings in S, of course, but we nevertheless reduce the space for the trie. In the next section, we present an application where the collection of strings can also be stored compactly.

9.2.3 Suffix Tries

One of the primary applications for tries is for the case when the strings in the collection S are all the suffixes of a string X. Such a trie is called the ***suffix trie*** (also known as a ***suffix tree*** or ***position tree***) of string X. For example, Figure 9.14a shows the suffix trie for the eight suffixes of string "`minimize`".

For a suffix trie, the compact representation presented in the previous section can be further simplified. Namely, we can construct the trie so that the label of each vertex is a pair (i, j) indicating the string $X[i..j]$. (See Figure 9.14b.) To satisfy the rule that no suffix of X is a prefix of another suffix, we can add a special character, denoted with \$, that is not in the original alphabet Σ at the end of X (and thus to every suffix). That is, if string X has length n, we build a trie for the set of n strings $X[i..n-1]\$$, for $i = 0, \ldots, n-1$.

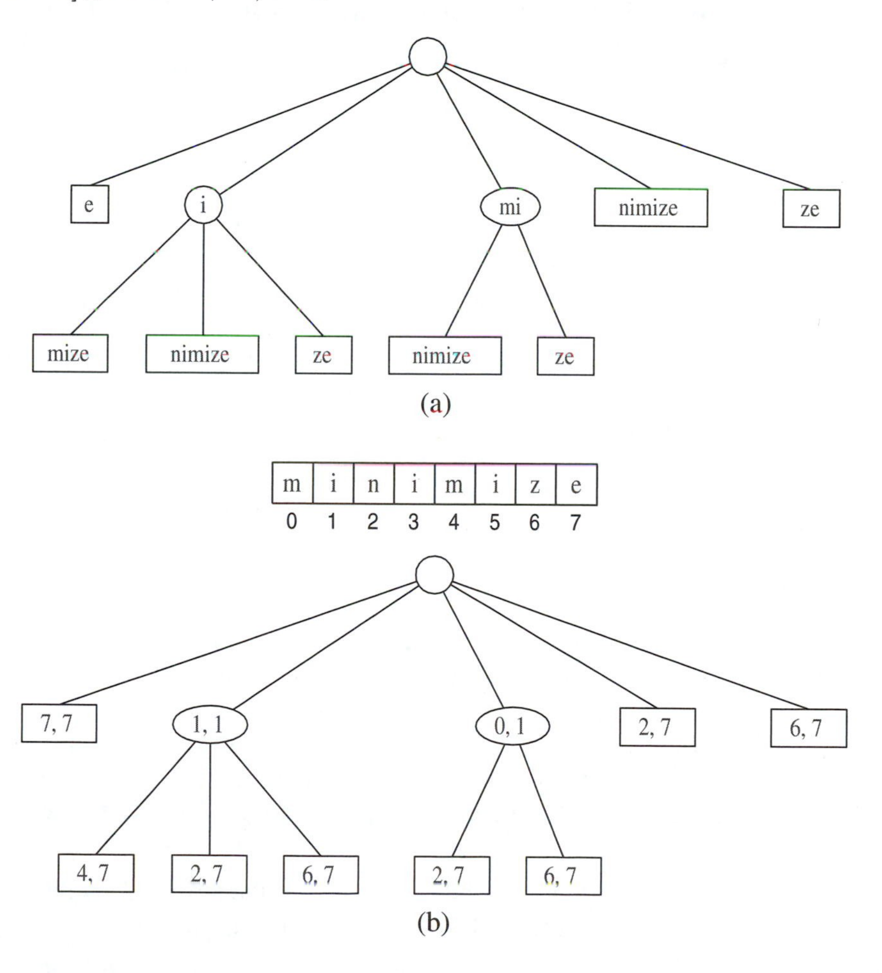

Figure 9.14: (a) Suffix trie T for the string $X =$ "`minimize`", (b) Compact representation of T, where pair (i, j) denotes $X[i..j]$.

Saving Space

Using a suffix trie allows us to save space over a standard trie by using several space compression techniques, including those used for the compressed trie. The advantage of the compact representation of tries now becomes apparent for suffix tries. Since the total length of the suffixes of a string X of length n is

$$1+2+\cdots+n=\frac{n(n+1)}{2},$$

storing all the suffixes of X explicitly would take $O(n^2)$ space. Even so, the suffix trie represents these strings implicitly in $O(n)$ space, as formally stated in the following theorem.

Theorem 9.6: *The compact representation of a suffix trie T for a string X of length n uses $O(n)$ space.*

Construction

We can construct the suffix trie for a string of length n with an incremental algorithm like the one given in Section 9.2.1. This construction takes $O(dn^2)$ time because the total length of the suffixes is quadratic in n. However, the (compact) suffix trie for a string of length n can be constructed in $O(n)$ time with a specialized algorithm, different from the one for general tries. This linear-time construction algorithm is fairly complex, however, and is not reported here. Still, we can take advantage of the existence of this fast construction algorithm when we want to use a suffix trie to solve other problems.

Using a Suffix Trie

The suffix trie T for a string X can be used to efficiently perform pattern matching queries on text X. Namely, we can determine whether a pattern P is a substring of X by trying to trace a path associated with P in T. P is a substring of X if and only if such a path can be traced. The details of the pattern matching algorithm are given in Algorithm 9.15, which assumes the following additional property on the labels of the nodes in the compact representation of the suffix trie:

> If node v has label (i,j) and Y is the string of length y associated with the path from the root to v (included), then $X[j-y+1..j]=Y$.

This property ensures that we can easily compute the start index of the pattern in the text when a match occurs.

```
Algorithm suffixTrieMatch(T, P):
    Input: Compact suffix trie T for a text X and pattern P
    Output: Starting index of a substring of X matching P or an indication that P
        is not a substring of X
    p ← P.length() { length of suffix of the pattern to be matched }
    j ← 0 { start of suffix of the pattern to be matched }
    v ← T.root()
    repeat
      f ← true { flag indicating that no child was successfully processed }
      for each child w of v do
        i ← start(v)
        if P[j] = T[i] then
          { process child w }
          x ← end(w) − i + 1
          if p ≤ x then
            { suffix is shorter than or of the same length of the node label }
            if P[j..j + p − 1] = X[i..i + p − 1] then
              return i − j { match }
            else
              return "P is not a substring of X"
          else
            { suffix is longer than the node label }
            if P[j..j + x − 1] = X[i..i + x − 1] then
              p ← p − x { update suffix length }
              j ← j + x { update suffix start index }
              v ← w
              f ← false
              break out of the for loop
    until f or T.isExternal(v)
    return "P is not a substring of X"
```

Algorithm 9.15: Pattern matching with a suffix trie. We denote the label of a node v with $(\mathsf{start}(v), \mathsf{end}(v))$, that is, the pair of indices specifying the substring of the text associated with v.

Suffix Trie Properties

The correctness of algorithm suffixTrieMatch follows from the fact that we search down the trie T, matching characters of the pattern P one at a time until one of the following events occurs:

- We completely match the pattern P
- We get a mismatch (caught by the termination of the for-loop without a break-out)
- We are left with characters of P still to be matched after processing an external node.

Let m be the size of pattern P and d be the size of the alphabet. In order to determine the running time of algorithm suffixTrieMatch, we make the following observations:

- We process at most $m+1$ nodes of the trie
- Each node processed has at most d children
- At each node v processed, we perform at most one character comparison for each child w of v to determine which child of v needs to be processed next (which may possibly be improved by using a fast dictionary to index the children of v)
- We perform at most m character comparisons overall in the processed nodes
- We spend $O(1)$ time for each character comparison.

Performance

We conclude that algorithm suffixTrieMatch performs pattern matching queries in $O(dm)$ time (and would possibly run even faster if we used a dictionary to index children of nodes in the suffix trie). Note that the running time does not depend on the size of the text X. Also, the running time is linear in the size of the pattern, that is, it is $O(m)$, for a constant-size alphabet. Hence, suffix tries are suited for repetitive pattern matching applications, where a series of pattern matching queries is performed on a fixed text.

We summarize the results of this section in the following theorem.

Theorem 9.7: *Let X be a text string with n characters from an alphabet of size d. We can perform pattern matching queries on X in $O(dm)$ time, where m is the length of the pattern, with the suffix trie of X, which uses $O(n)$ space and can be constructed in $O(dn)$ time.*

We explore another application of tries in the next subsection.

9.2.4 Search Engines

The World Wide Web contains a huge collection of text documents (Web pages). Information about these pages is gathered by a program called a ***Web crawler***, which then stores this information in a special dictionary database. A Web ***search engine*** allows users to retrieve relevant information from this database, thereby identifying relevant pages on the Web containing given keywords. In this section, we present a simplified model of a search engine.

Inverted Files

The core information stored by a search engine is a dictionary, called an ***inverted index*** or ***inverted file***, storing key-value pairs (w, L), where w is a word and L is a collection of references to pages containing word w. The keys (words) in this dictionary are called ***index terms*** and should be a set of vocabulary entries and proper nouns as large as possible. The elements in this dictionary are called ***occurrence lists*** and should cover as many Web pages as possible.

We can efficiently implement an inverted index with a data structure consisting of the following:

- An array storing the occurrence lists of the terms (in no particular order)
- A compressed trie for the set of index terms, where each external node stores the index of the occurrence list of the associated term.

The reason for storing the occurrence lists outside the trie is to keep the size of the trie data structure sufficiently small to fit in internal memory. Instead, because of their large total size, the occurrence lists have to be stored on disk.

With our data structure, a query for a single keyword is similar to a word matching query (see Section 9.2.1). Namely, we find the keyword in the trie and we return the associated occurrence list.

When multiple keywords are given and the desired output is the pages containing ***all*** the given keywords, we retrieve the occurrence list of each keyword using the trie and return their intersection. To facilitate the intersection computation, each occurrence list should be implemented with a sequence sorted by address or with a dictionary (see, for example, the generic merge computation discussed in Section 4.2).

In addition to the basic task of returning a list of pages containing given keywords, search engines provide an important additional service by ***ranking*** the pages returned by relevance. Devising fast and accurate ranking algorithms for search engines is a major challenge for computer researchers and electronic commerce companies.

9.3 Text Compression

In this section, we consider another text processing application, ***text compression***. In this problem, we are given a string X defined over some alphabet, such as the ASCII or Unicode character sets, and we want to efficiently encode X into a small binary string Y (using only the characters 0 and 1). Text compression is useful in any situation where we are communicating over a low-bandwidth channel, such as a slow modem line or wireless connection, and we wish to minimize the time needed to transmit our text. Likewise, text compression is also useful for storing collections of large documents more efficiently, so as to allow for a fixed-capacity storage device to contain as many documents as possible.

The method for text compression explored in this section is the ***Huffman code***. Standard encoding schemes, such as the ASCII and Unicode systems, use fixed-length binary strings to encode characters (with 7 bits in the ASCII system and 16 in the Unicode system). A Huffman code, on the other hand, uses a variable-length encoding optimized for the string X. The optimization is based on the use of character ***frequencies***, where we have, for each character c, a count $f(c)$ of the number of times c appears in the string X. The Huffman code saves space over a fixed-length encoding by using short code-word strings to encode high-frequency characters and long code-word strings to encode low-frequency characters.

To encode the string X, we convert each character in X from its fixed-length code word to its variable-length code word, and we concatenate all these code words in order to produce the encoding Y for X. In order to avoid ambiguities, we insist that no code word in our encoding is a prefix of another code word in our encoding. Such a code is called a ***prefix code***, and it simplifies the decoding of Y in order to get back X. (See Figure 9.16.) Even with this restriction, the savings produced by a variable-length prefix code can be significant, particularly if there is a wide variance in character frequencies (as is the case for natural language text in almost every spoken language).

Huffman's algorithm for producing an optimal variable-length prefix code for X is based on the construction of a binary tree T that represents the code. Each node in T, except the root, represents a bit in a code word, with each left child representing a "0" and each right child representing a "1." Each external node v is associated with a specific character, and the code word for that character is defined by the sequence of bits associated with the nodes in the path from the root of T to v. (See Figure 9.16.) Each external node v has a ***frequency*** $f(v)$, which is simply the frequency in X of the character associated with v. In addition, we give each internal node v in T a frequency, $f(v)$, that is the sum of the frequencies of all the external nodes in the subtree rooted at v.

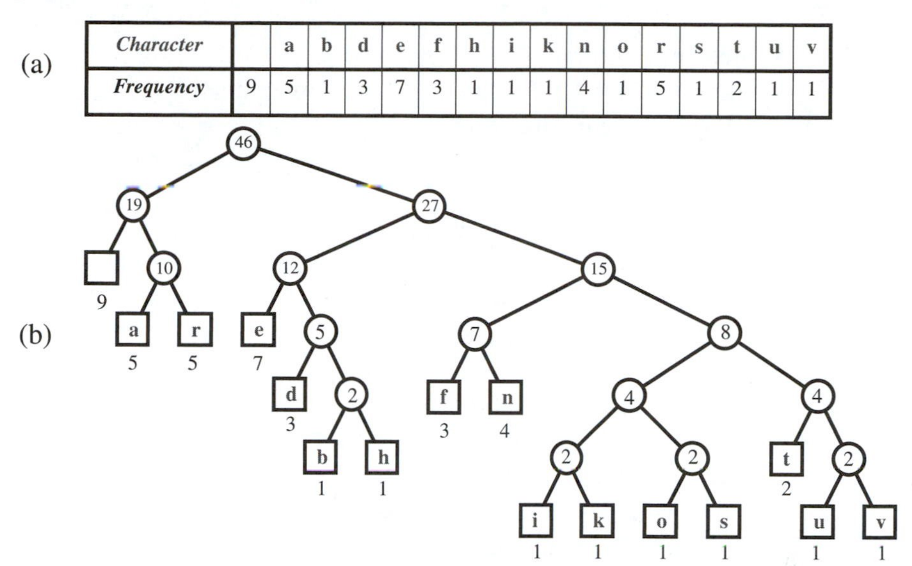

(a)

Character		a	b	d	e	f	h	i	k	n	o	r	s	t	u	v
Frequency	9	5	1	3	7	3	1	1	1	4	1	5	1	2	1	1

Figure 9.16: An illustration of an example Huffman code for the input string $X =$ `"a fast runner need never be afraid of the dark"`: (a) frequency of each character of X; (b) Huffman tree T for string X. The code for a character c is obtained by tracing the path from the root of T to the external node where c is stored, and associating a left child with 0 and a right child with 1. For example, the code for "a" is 010, and the code for "f" is 1100.

9.3.1 The Huffman Coding Algorithm

The Huffman coding algorithm begins with each of the d distinct characters of the string X to encode being the root node of a single-node binary tree. The algorithm proceeds in a series of rounds. In each round, the algorithm takes the two binary trees with the smallest frequencies and merges them into a single binary tree. It repeats this process until only one tree is left. (See Algorithm 9.17.)

Each iteration of the while-loop in Huffman's algorithm can be implemented in $O(\log d)$ time using a priority queue represented with a heap. In addition, each iteration takes two nodes out of Q and adds one in, a process that will be repeated $d-1$ times before exactly one node is left in Q. Thus, this algorithm runs in $O(n + d\log d)$ time. Although a full justification of this algorithm's correctness is beyond our scope here, we note that its intuition comes from a simple idea—any optimal code can be converted into an optimal code in which the code words for the two lowest-frequency characters, a and b, differ only in their last bit. Repeating the argument for a string with a and b replaced by a character c, gives the following:

Theorem 9.8: *Huffman's algorithm constructs an optimal prefix code for a string of length n with d distinct characters in $O(n + d\log d)$ time.*

```
Algorithm Huffman(X):
   Input: String X of length n with d distinct characters
   Output: Coding tree for X

   Compute the frequency f(c) of each character c of X.
   Initialize a priority queue Q.
   for each character c in X do
      Create a single-node binary tree T storing c.
      Insert T into Q with key f(c).
   while Q.size() > 1 do
      f1 ← Q.minKey()
      T1 ← Q.removeMin()
      f2 ← Q.minKey()
      T2 ← Q.removeMin()
      Create a new binary tree T with left subtree T1 and right subtree T2.
      Insert T into Q with key f1 + f2.
   return tree Q.removeMin()
```

Algorithm 9.17: Huffman coding algorithm.

9.3.2 The Greedy Method Revisited

Huffman's algorithm for building an optimal encoding is an example application of an algorithmic design pattern called the ***greedy method***. We recall from Section 5.1 that this design pattern is applied to optimization problems, where we are trying to construct some structure while minimizing or maximizing some property of that structure.

Indeed, the Huffman coding algorithm closely follows the general formula for the greedy method pattern. Namely, in order to solve the given optimization code problem using the greedy method, we proceed by a sequence of choices. The sequence starts from a well-understood starting condition, and computes the cost for that initial condition. Finally, we iteratively make additional choices by identifying the decision that achieves the best cost improvement from all of the choices that are currently possible. This approach does not always lead to an optimal solution, but it does indeed find the optimal prefix code when used according to the approach of Huffman's algorithm.

This global optimality for the Huffman coding algorithm is due to the fact that the optimal prefix coding problem possesses the ***greedy-choice*** property. This is the property that a global optimal condition can be reached by a series of locally optimal choices (that is, choices that are each the current best from among the possibilities available at the time), starting from a well-defined starting condition. In fact, the problem of computing an optimal variable-length prefix code is just one example of a problem that possesses the greedy-choice property.

9.4 Text Similarity Testing

A common text processing problem, which arises in genetics and software engineering, is to test the similarity between two text strings. In a genetics application, the two strings could correspond to two strands of DNA, which could, for example, come from two individuals, who we will consider genetically related if they have a long subsequence common to their respective DNA sequences. Likewise, in a software engineering application, the two strings could come from two versions of source code for the same program, and we may wish to determine which changes were made from one version to the next. In addition, the data gathering systems of search engines, which are called Web ***spiders*** or ***crawlers***, must be able to distinguish between similar Web pages to avoid needless Web page requests. Indeed, determining the similarity between two strings is considered such a common operation that the Unix/Linux operating systems come with a program, called `diff`, for comparing text files.

9.4.1 The Longest Common Subsequence Problem

There are several different ways we can define the similarity between two strings. Even so, we can abstract a simple, yet common, version of this problem using character strings and their subsequences. Given a string X of size n, a ***subsequence*** of X is any string that is of the form

$$X[i_1]X[i_2]\cdots X[i_k], \quad i_j < i_{j+1} \text{ for } j = 1,\ldots,k;$$

that is, it is a sequence of characters that are not necessarily contiguous but are nevertheless taken in order from X. For example, the string $AAAG$ is a subsequence of the string $CGATAATTGAGA$. Note that the concept of ***subsequence*** of a string is different from the one of ***substring*** of a string, defined in Section 9.1.1.

Problem Definition

The specific text similarity problem we address here is the ***longest common subsequence*** (LCS) problem. In this problem, we are given two character strings, X of size n and Y of size m, over some alphabet and are asked to find a longest string S that is a subsequence of both X and Y.

One way to solve the longest common subsequence problem is to enumerate all subsequences of X and take the largest one that is also a subsequence of Y. Since each character of X is either in or not in a subsequence, there are potentially 2^n different subsequences of X, each of which requires $O(m)$ time to determine whether it is a subsequence of Y. Thus, the brute-force approach yields an exponential algorithm that runs in $O(2^n m)$ time, which is very inefficient. In this section, we discuss how to use ***dynamic programming*** (Section 5.3) to solve the longest common subsequence problem much faster than this.

9.4.2 Applying Dynamic Programming to the LCS Problem

We can solve the LCS problem much faster than exponential time using dynamic programming. As mentioned in Section 5.3, one of the key components of the dynamic programming technique is the definition of simple subproblems that satisfy the subproblem optimization and subproblem overlap properties.

Recall that in the LCS problem, we are given two character strings, X and Y, of length n and m, respectively, and are asked to find a longest string S that is a subsequence of both X and Y. Since X and Y are character strings, we have a natural set of indices with which to define subproblems—indices into the strings X and Y. Let us define a subproblem, therefore, as that of computing the length of the longest common subsequence of $X[0..i]$ and $Y[0..j]$, denoted $L[i,j]$.

This definition allows us to rewrite $L[i,j]$ in terms of optimal subproblem solutions. We consider the following two cases. (See Figure 9.18.)

Case 1: $X[i] = Y[j]$

Let $c = X[i] = Y[j]$. We claim that a longest common subsequence of $X[0..i]$ and $Y[0..j]$ ends with c. To prove this claim, let us suppose it is not true. There has to be some longest common subsequence $X[i_1]X[i_2]\ldots X[i_k] = Y[j_1]Y[j_2]\ldots Y[j_k]$. If $X[i_k] = c$ or $Y[j_k] = c$, then we get the same sequence by setting $i_k = i$ and $j_k = j$. Alternately, if $X[j_k] \neq c$, then we can get an even longer common subsequence by adding c to the end. Thus, a longest common subsequence of $X[0..i]$ and $Y[0..j]$ ends with $c = X[i] = Y[j]$. Therefore, we set

$$L[i,j] = L[i-1,j-1]+1 \quad \text{if } X[i] = Y[j]. \tag{9.1}$$

Case 2: $X[i] \neq Y[j]$

In this case, we cannot have a common subsequence that includes both $X[i]$ and $Y[j]$. That is, a common subsequence can end with $X[i]$, $Y[j]$, or neither, but not both. Therefore, we set

$$L[i,j] = \max\{L[i-1,j], L[i,j-1]\} \quad \text{if } X[i] \neq Y[j]. \tag{9.2}$$

In order to make Equations 9.1 and 9.2 make sense in the boundary cases when $i=0$ or $j=0$, we define $L[i,-1]=0$ for $i=-1,0,1,\ldots,n-1$ and $L[-1,j]=0$ for $j=-1,0,1,\ldots,m-1$.

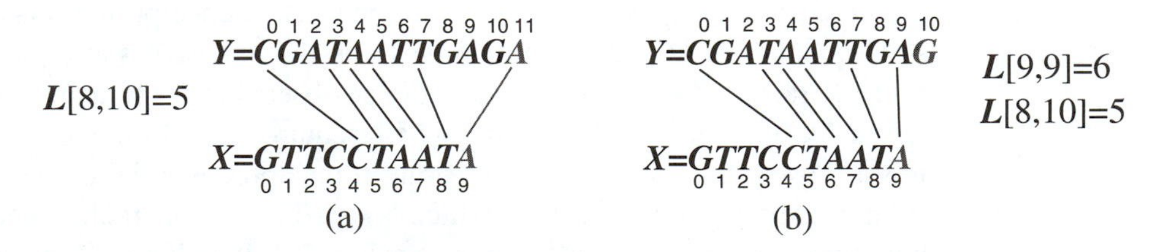

Figure 9.18: The two cases in the definition of $L[i,j]$: (a) $X[i]=Y[j]$; (b) $X[i] \neq Y[j]$.

The LCS Algorithm

The above definition of $L[i,j]$ satisfies subproblem optimization, for we cannot have a longest common subsequence without also having longest common subsequences for the subproblems. Also, it uses subproblem overlap, because a subproblem solution $L[i,j]$ can be used in several other problems (namely, the problems $L[i+1,j]$, $L[i,j+1]$, and $L[i+1,j+1]$).

Turning this definition of $L[i,j]$ into an algorithm is actually quite straightforward. We initialize an $(n+1)\times(m+1)$ array, L, for the boundary cases when $i=0$ or $j=0$. Namely, we initialize $L[i,-1]=0$ for $i=-1,0,1,\ldots,n-1$ and $L[-1,j]=0$ for $j=-1,0,1,\ldots,m-1$. (This is a slight abuse of notation, since in reality, we would have to index the rows and columns of L starting with 0.) Then, we iteratively build up values in L until we have $L[n-1,m-1]$, the length of a longest common subsequence of X and Y. We give a pseudo-code description of how this approach results in a dynamic programming solution to the longest common subsequence (LCS) problem in Algorithm 9.19. Note that the algorithm stores only the $L[i,j]$ values, not the matches.

Algorithm LCS(X,Y):
  Input: Strings X and Y with n and m elements, respectively
  Output: For $i=0,\ldots,n-1$, $j=0,\ldots,m-1$, the length $L[i,j]$ of a longest common subsequence of $X[0..i]$ and $Y[0..j]$

```
for i ← −1 to n − 1 do
  L[i, −1] ← 0
for j ← 0 to m − 1 do
  L[−1, j] ← 0
for i ← 0 to n − 1 do
  for j ← 0 to m − 1 do
    if X[i] = Y[j] then
      L[i, j] ← L[i − 1, j − 1] + 1
    else
      L[i, j] ← max{L[i − 1, j], L[i, j − 1]}
return array L
```

Algorithm 9.19: Dynamic programming algorithm for the LCS problem.

Performance

The running time of Algorithm 9.19 is easy to analyze, for it is dominated by two nested for-loops, with the outer one iterating n times and the inner one iterating m times. Since the if-statement and assignment inside the loop each requires $O(1)$ primitive operations, this algorithm runs in $O(nm)$ time. Thus, the dynamic programming technique can be applied to the longest common subsequence problem to improve significantly over the exponential-time brute-force solution to the LCS problem.

Algorithm LCS (9.19) computes the length of the longest common subsequence (stored in $L[n-1,m-1]$), but not the subsequence itself. As shown in the following theorem, a simple postprocessing step can extract the longest common subsequence from the array L returned by the algorithm.

Theorem 9.9: *Given a string X of n characters and a string Y of m characters, we can find the longest common subsequence of X and Y in $O(nm)$ time.*

Proof: We have already observed that Algorithm LCS computes the ***length*** of a longest common subsequence of the input strings X and Y in $O(nm)$ time. Given the table of $L[i,j]$ values, constructing a longest common subsequence is straightforward. One method is to start from $L[n-1,m-1]$ and work back through the table, reconstructing a longest common subsequence from back to front. At any position $L[i,j]$, we determine whether $X[i]=Y[j]$. If this is true, then we take $X[i]$ as the next character of the subsequence (noting that $X[i]$ is ***before*** the previous character we found, if any), moving next to $L[i-1,j-1]$. If $X[i]\neq Y[j]$, then we move to the larger of $L[i,j-1]$ and $L[i-1,j]$. (See Figure 9.20.) We stop when we reach a boundary entry (with $i=-1$ or $j=-1$). This method constructs a longest common subsequence in $O(n+m)$ additional time. ■

L	-1	0	1	2	3	4	5	6	7	8	9	10	11
-1	0	0	0	0	0	0	0	0	0	0	0	0	0
0	0	0	1	1	1	1	1	1	1	1	1	1	1
1	0	0	1	1	2	2	2	2	2	2	2	2	2
2	0	0	1	1	2	2	2	3	3	3	3	3	3
3	0	1	1	1	2	2	2	3	3	3	3	3	3
4	0	**1**	1	1	2	2	2	3	3	3	3	3	3
5	0	1	1	1	**2**	2	2	3	4	4	4	4	4
6	0	1	1	2	2	**3**	3	3	4	4	5	5	5
7	0	1	1	2	2	3	**4**	4	4	4	5	5	6
8	0	1	1	2	3	3	4	5	**5**	5	5	5	6
9	0	1	1	2	3	4	4	5	5	5	6	6	**6**

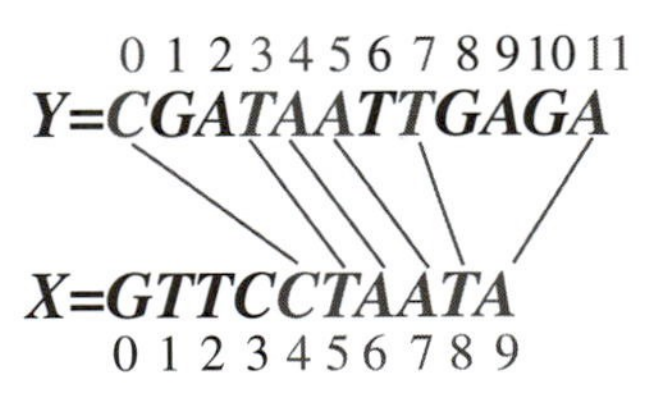

Figure 9.20: Illustration of the algorithm for constructing a longest common subsequence from the array L.

9.5 Exercises

Reinforcement

R-9.1 How many nonempty prefixes of the string $P =$ `"aaabbaaa"` are also suffixes of P?

R-9.2 Draw a figure illustrating the comparisons done by the brute-force pattern matching algorithm for the case when the text is `"aaabaadaabaaa"` and the pattern is `"aabaaa"`.

R-9.3 Repeat the previous problem for the BM pattern matching algorithm, not counting the comparisons made to compute the last function.

R-9.4 Repeat the previous problem for the KMP pattern matching algorithm, not counting the comparisons made to compute the failure function.

R-9.5 Compute a table representing the last function used in the BM pattern matching algorithm for the pattern string

`"the quick brown fox jumped over a lazy cat"`

assuming the following alphabet (which starts with the space character):

$$\Sigma = \{\ ,a,b,c,d,e,f,g,h,i,j,k,l,m,n,o,p,q,r,s,t,u,v,w,x,y,z\}.$$

R-9.6 Assuming that the characters in alphabet Σ can be enumerated and can index arrays, give an $O(m+|\Sigma|)$ time method for constructing the last function from an m-length pattern string P.

R-9.7 Compute a table representing the KMP failure function for the pattern string `"cgtacgttcgtac"`.

R-9.8 Draw a standard trie for the following set of strings:

{`abab`, `baba`, `ccccc`, `bbaaaa`, `caa`, `bbaacc`, `cbcc`, `cbca`}.

R-9.9 Draw a compressed trie for the set of strings given in Exercise R-9.8.

R-9.10 Draw the compact representation of the suffix trie for the string

`"minimize minime"`.

R-9.11 What is the longest prefix of the string `"cgtacgttcgtacg"` that is also a suffix of this string?

R-9.12 Draw the frequency table and Huffman tree for the following string:

`"dogs do not spot hot pots or cats"`.

R-9.13 Show how to use dynamic programming to compute the longest common subsequence between the two strings `"babbabab"` and `"bbabbaaab"`.

R-9.14 Show the longest common subsequence table L for the two strings

$$X = \texttt{"skullandbones"}$$
$$Y = \texttt{"lullabybabies"}.$$

What is a longest common subsequence between these strings?

Creativity

C-9.1 Give an example of a text T of length n and a pattern P of length m that force the brute-force pattern matching algorithm to have a running time that is $\Omega(nm)$.

C-9.2 Give a justification of why the KMPFailureFunction method (Algorithm 9.9) runs in $O(m)$ time on a pattern of length m.

C-9.3 Show how to modify the KMP string pattern matching algorithm so as to find ***every*** occurrence of a pattern string P that appears as a substring in T, while still running in $O(n+m)$ time. (Be sure to catch even those matches that overlap.)

C-9.4 Let T be a text of length n, and let P be a pattern of length m. Describe an $O(n+m)$-time method for finding the longest prefix of P that is a substring of T.

C-9.5 Say that a pattern P of length m is a ***circular substring*** of a text T of length n if there is an index $0 \leq i < m$, such that $P = T[n-m+i..n-1] + T[0..i-1]$, that is, if P is a substring of T or P is equal to the concatenation of a suffix of T and a prefix of T. Give an $O(n+m)$-time algorithm for determining whether P is a circular substring of T.

C-9.6 The KMP pattern matching algorithm can be modified to run faster on binary strings by redefining the failure function as

$$f(j) = \text{the largest } k < j \text{ such that } P[0..k-2]\overline{P[k-1]} \text{ is a suffix of } P[1..j],$$

where $overlineP[k]$ denotes the complement of the kth bit of P. Describe how to modify the KMP algorithm to be able to take advantage of this new failure function and also give a method for computing this failure function. Show that this method makes at most n comparisons between the text and the pattern (as opposed to the $2n$ comparisons needed by the standard KMP algorithm given in Section 9.1.4).

C-9.7 Modify the simplified BM algorithm presented in this chapter using ideas from the KMP algorithm so that it runs in $O(n+m)$ time.

C-9.8 Show how to perform prefix matching queries using a suffix trie.

C-9.9 Give an efficient algorithm for deleting a string from a standard trie and analyze its running time.

C-9.10 Give an efficient algorithm for deleting a string from a compressed trie and analyze its running time.

C-9.11 Describe an algorithm for constructing the compact representation of a suffix trie and analyze its running time.

C-9.12 Let T be a text string of length n. Describe an $O(n)$-time method for finding the longest prefix of T that is a substring of the reversal of T.

C-9.13 Describe an efficient algorithm to find the longest palindrome that is a suffix of a string T of length n. Recall that a ***palindrome*** is a string that is equal to its reversal. What is the running time of your method?

C-9.14 Given a sequence $S = (x_0, x_1, x_2, \ldots, x_{n-1})$ of numbers, describe an $O(n^2)$-time algorithm for finding a longest subsequence $T = (x_{i_0}, x_{i_1}, x_{i_2}, \ldots, x_{i_{k-1}})$ of numbers, such that $i_j < i_{j+1}$ and $x_{i_j} > x_{i_{j+1}}$. That is, T is a longest decreasing subsequence of S.

C-9.15 Describe an $O(n \log n)$-time algorithm for the previous problem.

C-9.16 Show that a sequence of n distinct numbers contains a decreasing or increasing subsequence of size at least $\lfloor \sqrt{n} \rfloor$.

C-9.17 Define the ***edit distance*** between two strings X and Y of length n and m, respectively, to be the number of edits that it takes to change X into Y. An edit consists of a character insertion, a character deletion, or a character replacement. For example, the strings `"algorithm"` and `"rhythm"` have edit distance 6. Design an $O(nm)$-time algorithm for computing the edit distance between X and Y.

C-9.18 Let A, B, and C be three length-n character strings taken over the same constant-sized alphabet Σ. Design an $O(n^3)$-time algorithm for finding a longest substring that is common to all three of A, B, and C.

C-9.19 Consider the pattern matching algorithm that always returns "no" when asked to determine whether a pattern P of length m is contained in a text T of length n, with both taken over the same alphabet of size d for some constant $d > 1$. Give a big-Oh characterization of the probability that this simple algorithm incorrectly determines whether or not P is a substring in T, assuming that all possible pattern strings of length m are equally likely? Your bound must be $o(1)$.

Hint: This is a remarkably accurate algorithm when m is large.

C-9.20 Suppose A, B, and C are three integer arrays representing the ASCII or Unicode values of three character strings, each of size n. Given an arbitrary integer x, design an $O(n^2 \log n)$-time algorithm to determine if there exist numbers $a \in A$, $b \in B$, and $c \in C$, such that $x = a + b + c$.

C-9.21 Give an $O(n^2)$-time algorithm for the previous problem.

C-9.22 Suppose each character c in a constant-sized alphabet Σ has an integer worth, $w(c)$. Two players are going to play a game, given a string P of length $2n$ taken over Σ. In each turn, a player must select and remove either the first or last character in P, reducing its length by one. The goal of each player is to maximize the total worth of all his or her selected characters. Give an $O(n^2)$-time algorithm for computing the optimal strategy for the first player.

Hint: Use dynamic programming.

C-9.23 Design an $O(n)$-time non-losing strategy for the first player in the game of the previous exercise. Your strategy does not have to be optimal, but it should be guaranteed to end in a tie or better for the first player.

Projects

P-9.1 Perform an experimental analysis, using documents found on the Internet, of the efficiency (number of character comparisons performed) of at least two different pattern matching algorithms for varying-length patterns.

P-9.2 Implement a compression and decompression scheme that is based on Huffman coding.

P-9.3 Create classes that implement a standard and compressed trie for a set of ASCII strings. Each class should have a constructor that takes a list of strings as an argument, and the class should have a method that tests whether a given string is stored in the trie.

P-9.4 Implement the simplified search engine described in Section 9.2.4 for the pages of a small Web site. Use all the words in the pages of the site as index terms, excluding stop words such as articles, prepositions, and pronouns.

P-9.5 Implement a search engine for the pages of a small Web site by adding a page-ranking feature to the simplified search engine described in Section 9.2.4. Your page-ranking feature should return the most relevant pages first. Use all the words in the pages of the site as index terms, excluding stop words, such as articles, prepositions, and pronouns.

P-9.6 Design and implement dynamic programming and greedy methods for solving the longest common subsequence (LCS) problem. Run experiments comparing the running times of these two methods to the quality of the solutions they produce.

P-9.7 Implement an algorithm that can take any string of text and produce a Huffman code for it.

Chapter Notes

The KMP algorithm is described by Knuth, Morris, and Pratt in their journal article [122]. Boyer and Moore published their algorithm in the same year [36]. In their article, Knuth *et al.* [122] also prove that the BM algorithm runs in linear time. More recently, Cole [49] shows that the BM algorithm makes at most $3n$ character comparisons in the worst case, and this bound is tight. All of the algorithms presented in this chapter are also discussed in the book chapter by Aho [6], albeit in a more theoretical framework. The reader interested in further study of string pattern matching algorithms is referred to the book by Stephen [193] and the book chapters by Aho [6] and Crochemore and Lecroq [56].

The trie was invented by Morrison [156] and is discussed extensively in the classic *Sorting and Searching* book by Knuth [119]. The name "Patricia" is short for "Practical Algorithm to Retrieve Information Coded in Alphanumeric" [156]. McCreight [139] shows how to construct suffix tries in linear time. An introduction to the field of information retrieval, which includes a discussion of search engines for the Web, is provided in the book by Baeza-Yates and Ribeiro-Neto [21]. The application of the greedy method we gave to the coding problem comes from Huffman [104].

Chapter

10 Number Theory and Cryptography

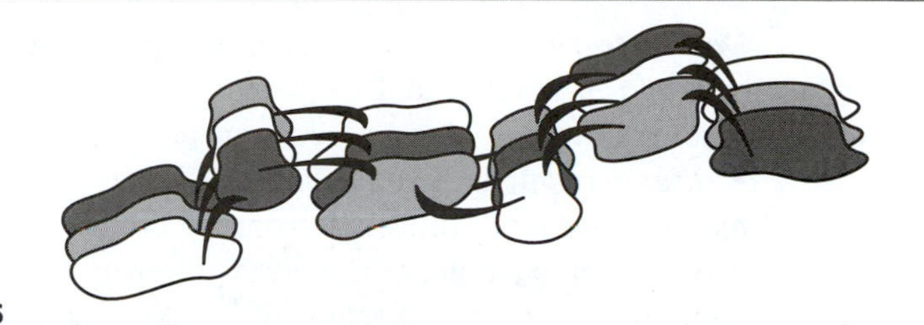

Contents

10.1 Fundamental Algorithms Involving Numbers 453

10.1.1 Some Facts from Elementary Number Theory 453

10.1.2 Euclid's GCD Algorithm 455

10.1.3 Modular Arithmetic 458

10.1.4 Modular Exponentiation 462

10.1.5 Modular Multiplicative Inverses 464

10.1.6 Primality Testing 466

10.2 Cryptographic Computations 471

10.2.1 Symmetric Encryption Schemes 473

10.2.2 Public-Key Cryptosystems 475

10.2.3 The RSA Cryptosystem 476

10.2.4 The El Gamal Cryptosystem 479

10.3 Information Security Algorithms and Protocols 481

10.3.1 One-way Hash Functions 481

10.3.2 Timestamping and Authenticated Dictionaries 482

10.3.3 Coin Flipping and Bit Commitment 483

10.3.4 The Secure Electronic Transaction (SET) Protocol . 484

10.3.5 Key Distribution and Exchange 486

10.4 The Fast Fourier Transform 488

10.4.1 Primitive Roots of Unity 489

10.4.2 The Discrete Fourier Transform 491

10.4.3 The Fast Fourier Transform Algorithm 495

10.4.4 Multiplying Big Integers 497

10.5 Java Example: FFT 500

10.6 Exercises 508

Computers today are used for a multitude of sensitive applications. Customers utilize electronic commerce to make purchases and pay their bills. Businesses use the Internet to share sensitive company documents and interact with business partners. And universities use networks of computers to store personal information about students and their grades. Such sensitive information can be potentially damaging if it is altered, destroyed, or falls into the wrong hands. In this chapter, we discuss several powerful algorithmic techniques for protecting sensitive information, so as to achieve the following goals:

- ***Data integrity***: Information should not be altered without detection. For example, it is important to prevent the modification of purchase orders or other contractually binding documents transmitted electronically.
- ***Authentication***: Individuals and organizations that are accessing or communicating sensitive information must be correctly identified, that is, authenticated. For example, corporations offering telecommuting arrangements to their employees should set up an authentication procedure for accessing corporate databases through the Internet.
- ***Authorization***: Agents that are performing computations involving sensitive information must be authorized to perform those computations.
- ***Nonrepudiation***: In transactions that imply a contract, the parties that have agreed to that contract must not have the ability of backing out of their obligations without being detected.
- ***Confidentiality***: Sensitive information should be kept secret from individuals who are not authorized to see that information. That is, we must ensure that data is viewed by the sender and by the receiver, but not by unauthorized parties who can eavesdrop on the communication. For example, many email messages are meant to be confidential.

Many of the techniques we discuss in this chapter for achieving the above goals utilize number theory. Thus, we begin this chapter by discussing a number of important number theory concepts and algorithms. We describe the ancient, yet surprisingly efficient, Euclid's algorithm for computing greatest common divisors, as well as algorithms for computing modular exponents and inverses. In addition, because prime numbers play such a crucial role in cryptographic computations, we discuss efficient methods for testing if numbers are prime. We show how many of these number theory algorithms can be used in cryptographic algorithms that implement computer security services. We focus on encryption and digital signatures, including the popular RSA scheme. We also discuss, in this chapter, several protocols that can be built from these algorithms.

We conclude by discussing the fast Fourier transform (FFT), a general divide-and-conquer technique that can solve many problems with multiplication-like properties. We show how it use FFT to efficiently multiply polynomial and big integers. We also give a Java implementation of the FFT algorithm for multiplying big integers, and we empirically compare the performance of this algorithm to a standard multiplication method for big integers.

10.1 Fundamental Algorithms Involving Numbers

In this section we discuss several fundamental algorithms for performing important computations involving numbers. We describe efficient methods for computing exponents modulo n, for computing multiplicative inverses modulo n, and for testing if an integer n is prime. All of these computations have several important applications, including forming the critical algorithms in well-known cryptographic computations. But before we can present these algorithms, we must first present some basic facts from number theory. Throughout this discussion, we assume that all variables are integers. Also, proofs of some mathematical facts are left as exercises.

10.1.1 Some Facts from Elementary Number Theory

To get us started, we need some facts from elementary number theory, including some notation and definitions. Given positive integers a and b, we use the notation

$$a|b$$

to indicate that a ***divides*** b, that is, b is a multiple of a. If $a|b$, then we know that there is some integer k, such that $b = ak$. The following properties of divisibility follow immediately from this definition.

Theorem 10.1: *Let a, b, and c be arbitrary integers. Then*

- *If $a|b$ and $b|c$, then $a|c$.*
- *If $a|b$ and $a|c$, then $a|(ib + jc)$, for all integers i and j.*
- *If $a|b$ and $b|a$, then $a = b$ or $a = -b$.*

Proof: See Exercise R-10.1. ■

An integer p is said to be a ***prime*** if $p \geq 2$ and its only divisors are the trivial divisors 1 and p. Thus, in the case that p is prime, $d|p$ implies $d = 1$ or $d = p$. An integer greater than 2 that is not prime is said to be ***composite***. So, for example, 5, 11, 101, and 98 711 are prime, whereas 25 and 10 403 ($= 101 \cdot 103$) are composite. We also have the following:

Theorem 10.2 (Fundamental Theorem of Arithmetic): *Let $n > 1$ be an integer. Then there is a unique set of prime numbers $\{p_1, \ldots, p_k\}$ and positive integer exponents $\{e_1, \ldots, e_k\}$, such that*

$$n = p_1^{e_1} \cdots p_k^{e_k}.$$

The product $p_1^{e_1} \cdots p_k^{e_k}$ is known as the ***prime decomposition*** of n in this case. Theorem 10.2 and the notion of unique prime decomposition is the basis of several cryptographic schemes.

The Greatest Common Divisor (GCD)

The ***greatest common divisor*** of positive integers a and b, denoted $\gcd(a,b)$, is the largest integer that divides both a and b. Alternatively, we could say that $\gcd(a,b)$ is the number c, such that if $d|a$ and $d|b$, then $d|c$. If $\gcd(a,b) = 1$, we say that a and b are ***relatively prime***. We extend the notion of greatest common divisor to a pair of arbitrary integers by the following two rules:

- $\gcd(a,0) = \gcd(0,a) = a$.
- $\gcd(a,b) = \gcd(|a|,|b|)$, which takes care of negative values.

Thus, $\gcd(12,0) = 12$, $\gcd(10403,303) = 101$, and $\gcd(-12,78) = 6$.

The Modulo Operator

A few words about the ***modulo operator*** (mod) are in order. Recall that $a \bmod n$ is the remainder of a when divided by n. That is,

$$r = a \bmod n$$

means that

$$r = a - \lfloor a/n \rfloor n.$$

In other words, there is some integer q, such that

$$a = qn + r.$$

Note, in addition, that $a \bmod n$ is always an integer in the set $\{0,1,2,\ldots,n-1\}$, even when a is negative.

It is sometimes convenient to talk about ***congruence*** modulo n. If

$$a \bmod n = b \bmod n,$$

we say that a is ***congruent*** to b modulo n, which we call the ***modulus***, and we write

$$a \equiv b \pmod{n}.$$

Therefore, if $a \equiv b \bmod n$, then $a - b = kn$ for some integer k.

Relating the Modulo Operator and the GCD

The following theorem gives an alternative characterization of the greatest common divisor. Its proof makes use of the modulo operator.

Theorem 10.3: *For any positive integers a and b, $\gcd(a,b)$ is the smallest positive integer d such that $d = ia + jb$ for some integers i and j. In other words, if d is the smallest positive integer linear combination of a and b, then $d = \gcd(a,b)$.*

Proof: Suppose d is the smallest integer such that $d = ia + jb$ for integers i and j. Note that, immediately from the definition of d, any common divisor of both a and b is also a divisor of d. Thus, $d \geq \gcd(a,b)$. To complete the proof, we need to show that $d \leq \gcd(a,b)$.

Let $h = \lfloor a/d \rfloor$. That is, h is the integer such that $a \bmod d = a - hd$. Then

$$\begin{aligned} a \bmod d &= a - hd \\ &= a - h(ia + jb) \\ &= (1 - hi)a + (-hj)b. \end{aligned}$$

In other words, $a \bmod d$ is also an integer linear combination of a and b. Moreover, by the definition of the modulo operator, $a \bmod d < d$. But d is the smallest positive integer linear combination of a and b. Thus, we must conclude that $a \bmod d = 0$, which implies that $d|a$. In addition, by a similar argument, we get that $d|b$. Thus, d is a divisor of both a and b, which implies $d \leq \gcd(a,b)$. ■

As we will show in Section 10.1.3, this theorem shows that the gcd function is useful for computing multiplicative modular inverses. In the next subsection, we show how to quickly compute the gcd function.

10.1.2 Euclid's GCD Algorithm

To compute the greatest common divisor of two numbers, we can use one of the oldest algorithms known, Euclid's algorithm. This algorithm is based on the following property of $\gcd(a,b)$:

Lemma 10.4: *Let a and b be two positive integers. For any integer r, we have*

$$\gcd(a,b) = \gcd(b, a - rb).$$

Proof: Let $d = \gcd(a,b)$ and $c = \gcd(b, a - rb)$. That is, d is the largest integer such that $d|a$ and $d|b$, and c is the largest integer such that $c|b$ and $c|(a - rb)$. We want to prove that $d = c$. By the definition of d, the number

$$(a - rb)/d = a/d - r(b/d)$$

is an integer. Thus, d divides both a and $a - rb$; hence, $d \leq c$.

By the definition of c, $k = b/c$ must be an integer, since $c|b$. Moreover, the number

$$(a - rb)/c = a/c - rk$$

must also be an integer, since $c|(a - rb)$. Thus, a/c must also be an integer, that is, $c|a$. Therefore, c divides both a and b; hence, $c \leq d$. We conclude then that $d = c$. ■

Lemma 10.4 leads us easily to an ancient algorithm, known as Euclid's algorithm, for computing the greatest common divisor (GCD) of two numbers, shown next in Algorithm 10.1.

```
Algorithm EuclidGCD(a,b):
   Input: Nonnegative integers a and b
   Output: gcd(a,b)
  if b = 0 then
     return a
  return EuclidGCD(b, a mod b)
```

Algorithm 10.1: Euclid's GCD algorithm.

An example of the execution of Euclid's algorithm is shown in Table 10.2.

	1	2	3	4	5	6	7
a	412	260	152	108	44	20	4
b	260	152	108	44	20	4	0

Table 10.2: Example of an execution of Euclid's algorithm to compute $\gcd(412,260) = 4$. The arguments a and b of each recursive invocation of method EuclidGCD(412,260) are shown left-to-right, with the column headings showing the level of recursion in the EuclidGCD method.

Analyzing Euclid's Algorithm

The number of arithmetic operations performed by method EuclidGCD(a,b) is proportional to the number of recursive calls. So to bound the number of arithmetic operations performed by Euclid's algorithm we need only bound the number of recursive calls. First, we observe that after the first call, the first argument is always larger than the second one. For $i > 0$, let a_i be the first argument of the ith recursive call of method EuclidGCD. Clearly, the second argument of a recursive call is equal to a_{i+1}, the first argument of the next call. Also, we have

$$a_{i+2} = a_i \bmod a_{i+1},$$

which implies that the sequence of the a_i's is strictly decreasing. We will now show that the sequence decreases quickly. Specifically, we claim that

$$a_{i+2} < \frac{1}{2}a_i.$$

To prove the claim, we distinguish two cases:

Case 1: $a_{i+1} \leq \frac{1}{2}a_i$. Since the sequence of the a_i's is strictly decreasing, we have

$$a_{i+2} < a_{i+1} \leq \frac{1}{2}a_i.$$

Case 2: $a_{i+1} > \frac{1}{2}a_i$. In this case, since $a_{i+2} = a_i \bmod a_{i+1}$, we have

$$a_{i+2} = a_i \bmod a_{i+1} = a_i - a_{i+1} < \frac{1}{2}a_i.$$

Thus, the size of the first argument to the EuclidGCD method decreases by half with every other recursive call. We may therefore summarize the above analysis as follows.

Theorem 10.5: *Let a and b be two positive integers. Euclid's algorithm computes* $\gcd(a,b)$ *by executing* $O(\log \max(a,b))$ *arithmetic operations.*

We note that the complexity bound here is based on counting arithmetic operations. We can in fact improve the constant factor in the above bound by taking advantage of the fact that in modern times Euclid's algorithm should be implemented on a digital computer.

Binary Euclid's Algorithm

A variation of Euclid's algorithm, called the ***Binary Euclid's Algorithm***, takes into account the fact that integer division by 2 in a computer is faster than division by a general integer, since it can be accomplished by the ***right-shift*** native processor instruction. The binary Euclid's algorithm is shown in Algorithm 10.3. Like the original Euclid's algorithm, it computes the greatest common divisor of two integers, a and b, in $O(\log \max(a,b))$ arithmetic operations, though with a smaller constant factor. The justification of its correctness and the asymptotic analysis of its running time are explored in Exercise C-10.1.

Algorithm EuclidBinaryGCD(a,b):
    Input: Nonnegative integers a and b
    Output: $\gcd(a,b)$

  if $a = 0$ **then**
      return b
  else if $b = 0$ **then**
      return a
  else if a is even and b is even **then**
      return $2 \cdot$ EuclidBinaryGCD$(a/2, b/2)$
  else if a is even and b is odd **then**
      return EuclidBinaryGCD$(a/2, b)$
  else if a is odd and b is even **then**
      return EuclidBinaryGCD$(a, b/2)$
  else
      $\{a$ is odd and b is odd$\}$
      return EuclidBinaryGCD$(|a-b|/2, b)$

Algorithm 10.3: The Binary Euclid's Algorithm for computing the greatest common divisor of two nonnegative integers.

10.1.3 Modular Arithmetic

Let Z_n denote the set of nonnegative integers less than n:

$$Z_n = \{0, 1, \cdots, (n-1)\}.$$

The set Z_n is also called the set of ***residues*** modulo n, because if $b = a \bmod n$, b is sometimes called the ***residue*** of a modulo n. Modular arithmetic in Z_n, where operations on the elements of Z_n are performed $\bmod n$, exhibits properties similar to those of traditional arithmetic, such as the associativity, commutativity, distributivity of addition and multiplication, and the existence of identity elements 0 and 1 for addition and multiplication, respectively. Moreover, in any arithmetic expression, reducing each of its subexpressions modulo n produces the same result as computing the entire expression and then reducing that value modulo n. Also, every element x in Z_n has an ***additive inverse***, that is, for each $x \in Z_n$, there is a $y \in Z_n$ such that $x + y \bmod n = 0$. For example, the additive inverse of 5 modulo 11 is 6.

When it comes to multiplicative inverses, however, an important difference arises. Let x be an element of Z_n. A ***multiplicative inverse*** of x is an element $z^{-1} \in Z_n$ such that $xx^{-1} \equiv 1 \bmod n$. For example, the multiplicative inverse of 5 modulo 9 is 2, that is, $5^{-1} = 2$ in Z_9. As in standard arithmetic, 0 does not have a multiplicative inverse in Z_n. Interestingly, some nonzero elements also may not have a multiplicative inverse in Z_n. For example, 3 does not have a multiplicative inverse in Z_9. However, if n is prime, then every element $x \neq 0$ of Z_n has a multiplicative inverse in Z_n (1 is its own multiplicative inverse).

Theorem 10.6: *An element $x > 0$ of Z_n has a multiplicative inverse in Z_n if and only if $\gcd(x, n) = 1$ (that is, either $x = 1$ or x does not divide n).*

Proof: Suppose that $\gcd(x, n) = 1$. By Theorem 10.3, there are integers i and j such that $ix + jn = 1$. This implies $ix \bmod n = 1$, that is, $i \bmod n$ is the multiplicative inverse of x in Z_n, which proves the "if" part of the theorem.

To prove the "only if" part, suppose, for a contradiction, that $x > 1$ divides n, and there is an element y such that $xy \equiv 1 \bmod n$. We have $xy = kn + 1$, for some integer k. Thus, we have found integers $i = y$ and $j = -k$ such that $ix + jn = 1$. By Theorem 10.3, this implies that $\gcd(x, n) = 1$, a contradiction. ■

If $\gcd(x, n) = 1$, we say x and n are ***relatively prime*** (1 is relatively prime to all other numbers). Thus, Theorem 10.6 implies that x has a multiplicative inverse in Z_n if and only if x is relatively prime to n. In addition, Theorem 10.6 implies that the sequence $0, x, 2x, 3x, \ldots, (n-1)x$ is simply a reordering of the elements of Z_n, that is, it is a permutation of the elements Z_n, as shown in the following.

Corollary 10.7: *Let $x > 0$ be an element of Z_n such that $\gcd(x, n) = 1$. Then*

$$Z_n = \{ix : i = 0, 1, \ldots, n-1\}.$$

Proof: See Exercise R-10.7. ■

In Table 10.4, we show the multiplicative inverses of the elements of Z_{11} as an example. When the multiplicative inverse x^{-1} of x exists in Z_n, the notation y/x in an expression taken modulo n means "$yx^{-1} \bmod n$."

x	0	1	2	3	4	5	6	7	8	9	10
$x^{-1} \bmod 11$		1	6	4	3	9	2	8	7	5	10

Table 10.4: Multiplicative inverses of the elements of Z_{11}.

Fermat's Little Theorem

We now have enough machinery for our first major theorem, which is known as ***Fermat's Little Theorem***.

Theorem 10.8 (Fermat's Little Theorem): *Let p be a prime, and let x be an integer such that $x \bmod p \neq 0$. Then*

$$x^{p-1} \equiv 1 \pmod{p}.$$

Proof: It is sufficient to prove the result for $0 < x < p$, because

$$x^{p-1} \bmod p = (x \bmod p)^{p-1} \bmod p,$$

since we can reduce each subexpression "x" in "x^{p-1}" modulo p.

By Corollary 10.7, we know that for $0 < x < p$, the set $\{1, 2, \ldots, p-1\}$ and the set $\{x \cdot 1, x \cdot 2, \ldots, x \cdot (p-1)\}$ contain exactly the same elements. So when we multiply the elements of the sets together, we get the same value, namely, we get

$$1 \cdot 2 \cdots (p-1) = (p-1)!.$$

In other words,

$$(x \cdot 1) \cdot (x \cdot 2) \cdots (x \cdot (p-1)) \equiv (p-1)! \pmod{p}.$$

If we factor out the x terms, we get

$$x^{p-1}(p-1)! \equiv (p-1)! \pmod{p}.$$

Since p is prime, every nonnull element in Z_p has a multiplicative inverse. Thus, we can cancel the term $(p-1)!$ from both sides, yielding $x^{p-1} \equiv 1 \bmod p$, the desired result. ■

In Table 10.5, we show the powers of the nonnull elements of Z_{11}. We observe the following interesting patterns:

- The last column of the table, with the values $x^{10} \bmod 11$ for $x = 1, \cdots, 10$, contains all ones, as given by Fermat's Little Theorem.
- In row 1, a subsequence of one element (1), is repeated ten times.
- In row 10, a subsequence of two elements, ending with 1, is repeated five times, since $10^2 \bmod 11 = 1$.
- In rows 3, 4, 5, and 9, a subsequence of five elements, ending with 1, is repeated twice.
- In each of the rows 2, 6, 7, and 8, the ten elements are all distinct.
- The lengths of the subsequences forming the rows of the table, and their number of repetitions, are the divisors of 10, that is, 1, 2, 5, and 10.

x	x^2	x^3	x^4	x^5	x^6	x^7	x^8	x^9	x^{10}
1	1	1	1	1	1	1	1	1	1
2	4	8	5	10	9	7	3	6	1
3	9	5	4	1	3	9	5	4	1
4	5	9	3	1	4	5	9	3	1
5	3	4	9	1	5	3	4	9	1
6	3	7	9	10	5	8	4	2	1
7	5	2	3	10	4	6	9	8	1
8	9	6	4	10	3	2	5	7	1
9	4	3	5	1	9	4	3	5	1
10	1	10	1	10	1	10	1	10	1

Table 10.5: Successive powers of the elements of Z_{11} modulo 11.

Euler's Theorem

Euler's ***totient function*** of a positive integer n, denoted $\phi(n)$, is defined as the number of positive integers less than or equal to n that are relatively prime to n. That is, $\phi(n)$ is equal to the number of elements in Z_n that have multiplicative inverses in Z_n. If p is a prime, then $\phi(p) = p - 1$. Indeed, since p is prime, each of the numbers $1, 2, \ldots, p-1$ are relatively prime to it, and $\phi(p) = p - 1$.

What if n isn't a prime number? Suppose $n = pq$, where p and q are primes. How many numbers are relatively prime to n? Well, initially, we observe that there are pq positive integers between 1 and n. However, q of them (including n) are multiples of p, and so they have a gcd of p with n. Similarly, there are p multiples of q (again, including n). Those multiples can't be counted in $\phi(n)$. Thus, we see that

$$\phi(n) = pq - q - (p - 1) = (p - 1)(q - 1).$$

Euler's totient function is closely related to an important subset of Z_n known as the ***multiplicative group*** for Z_n, which is denoted as Z_n^*. The set Z_n^* is defined to be the set of integers between 1 and n that are relatively prime to n. If n is prime, then Z_n^* consists of the $n-1$ nonzero elements in Z_n, that is, $Z_n^* = \{1,2,\ldots,n-1\}$ if n is prime. In general, Z_n^* contains $\phi(n)$ elements.

The set Z_n^* possesses several interesting properties, with one of the most important being that this set is closed under multiplication modulo n. That is, for any pair of elements a and b of Z_n^*, we have that $c = ab \bmod n$ is also in Z_n^*. Indeed, by Theorem 10.6, a and b have multiplicative inverses in Z_n. To see that Z_n^* has this closure property, let $d = a^{-1}b^{-1} \bmod n$. Clearly, $cd \bmod n = 1$, which implies that d is the multiplicative inverse of c in Z_n. Thus, again applying Theorem 10.6, we have that c is relatively prime to n, that is, $c \in Z_n^*$. In algebraic terminology, we say that Z_n^* is a ***group***, which is a shorthand way of saying that each element in Z_n^* has a multiplicative inverse and multiplication in Z_n^* is associative, has an identity, and is closed in Z_n^*.

The fact that Z_n^* has $\phi(n)$ elements and is a multiplicative group naturally leads to an extension of Fermat's Little Theorem. Recall that, in Fermat's Little Theorem, the exponent is $p-1 = \phi(p)$, since p is prime. As it turns out, a generalized form of Fermat's Little Theorem is true, too. This generalized form is presented in the following, which is known as ***Euler's Theorem***.

Theorem 10.9 (Euler's Theorem): *Let n be a positive integer, and let x be an integer such that $\gcd(x,n) = 1$. Then*

$$x^{\phi(n)} \equiv 1 \pmod{n}.$$

Proof: The proof technique is similar to that of Fermat's Little Theorem. Denote the elements of set Z_n^*, the multiplicative group for Z_n, as $u_1, u_2, \ldots, u_{\phi(n)}$. By the closure property of Z_n^* and Corollary 10.7,

$$Z_n^* = \{xu_i : i = 1, \cdots, \phi(n)\},$$

that is, multiplying elements in Z_n^* by x modulo n merely permutes the sequence $u_1, u_2, \ldots, u_{\phi(n)}$. Thus, multiplying together the elements of Z_n^*, we obtain

$$(xu_1) \cdot (xu_2) \cdots (xu_{\phi(n)}) \equiv u_1\, u_2 \cdots u_{\phi(n)} \pmod{n}.$$

Again, we collect a term $x^{\phi(n)}$ on one side, giving us the congruence

$$x(u_1\, u_2 \cdots u_{\phi(n)}) \equiv u_1\, u_2 \cdots u_{\phi(n)} \pmod{n}.$$

Dividing by the product of the u_i's, gives us $x^{\phi(n)} \equiv 1 \bmod n$. ■

Theorem 10.9 gives a closed-form expression for the multiplicative inverses. Namely, if x and n are relatively prime, we can write

$$x^{-1} \equiv x^{\phi(n)-1} \pmod{n}.$$

Generators

Given a prime p and an integer a between 1 and $p-1$, the ***order*** of a is the smallest exponent $e > 1$ such that

$$a^e \equiv 1 \bmod q.$$

A ***generator*** (also called ***primitive root***) of Z_p is an element g of Z_p with order $p-1$. We use the term "generator" for such an element a, because the repeated exponentiation of a can generate all of Z_p^*. For example, as shown in Table 10.5, the generators of Z_{11} are 2, 6, 7, and 8. Generators play an important role in many computations, including the Fast Fourier Transform algorithm discussed in Section 10.4. The existence of generators is established by the following theorem, stated without proof.

Theorem 10.10: *If p is a prime, then set Z_p has $\phi(p-1)$ generators.*

10.1.4 Modular Exponentiation

We address first exponentiation. The main issue in this case is to find a method other than the obvious brute-force. Before we describe an efficient algorithm, however, let us review the naive algorithm, for it already contains an important technique.

Brute-Force Exponentiation

One of the most important considerations in any exponentiation algorithms is to keep any intermediate results from getting too large. Suppose we want to compute, say $30\,192^{43\,791} \bmod 65\,301$. Multiplying 30 192 by itself 43 791 times and ***then*** taking the result modulo 65 301 will yield unpredictable results in most programming languages due to arithmetic overflows. Thus, we should take the modulo at each iteration, as shown in Algorithm 10.6.

Algorithm NaiveExponentiation(a,p,n):
  Input: Integers a, p, and n
  Output: $r = a^p \bmod n$

  $r \leftarrow 1$
  for $i \leftarrow 1$ **to** p **do**
    $r \leftarrow (r \cdot a) \bmod n$
  return r

Algorithm 10.6: A brute-force method for modular exponentiation.

This "naive" exponentiation algorithm is correct, but it is not very efficient, for it takes $\Theta(p)$ iterations to compute the modular exponentiation of a number to the power p. With large exponents, this running time is quite slow. Fortunately, there is a better method.

The Repeated Squaring Algorithm

A simple but important observation for an improved exponentiation algorithm is that squaring a number a^p is equivalent to multiplying its exponent p by two. In addition, multiplying two numbers a^p and a^q is equivalent to computing $a^{(p+q)}$. Let us therefore write an exponent p as a binary number $p_{b-1} \ldots p_0$, that is,

$$p = p_{b-1}2^{b-1} + \cdots + p_0 2^0.$$

Of course, each of the p_i's is either 1 or 0. Using the above observation, we can compute $a^p \bmod n$ by a variation of Horner's rule to evaluate polynomials, where the polynomial in question is the above binary expansion of the exponent p. Specifically, define q_i as the number whose binary representation is given by the leftmost i bits of p, that is, q_i is written in binary as $p_{b-1} \ldots p_{b-i}$. Clearly, we have $p = q_b$. Note that $q_1 = p_{b-1}$ and we can define q_i recursively as

$$q_i = 2q^{i-1} + p_{b-i} \quad \text{for} \quad 1 < i \le b.$$

Thus, we can evaluate $a^p \bmod n$ with the recursive computation, called the ***repeated squaring*** method, given in Algorithm 10.7.

The main idea of this algorithm is to consider each bit of the exponent p in turn by dividing p by two until p goes to zero, squaring the current product Q_i for each such bit. In addition, if the current bit is a one (that is, p is odd), then we multiply in the base, a, as well. To see why this algorithm works, define, for $i = 1, \ldots, b$,

$$Q_i = a^{q_i} \bmod n.$$

From the recursive definition of q_i, we derive the following definition of Q_i:

$$\begin{aligned} Q_i &= (Q_{i-1}^2 \bmod n)a^{p_{b-i}} \bmod n \quad \text{for} \quad 1 < i \le b \\ Q_1 &= a^{p_{b-1}} \bmod n. \end{aligned} \tag{10.1}$$

It is easy to verify that $Q_b = a^p \bmod n$.

Algorithm FastExponentiation(a, p, n):
  Input: Integers a, p, and n
  Output: $r = a^p \bmod n$

```
if p = 0 then
   return 1
if p is even then
   t ← FastExponentiation(a, p/2, n)  { p is even, so t = a^(p/2) mod n }
   return t^2 mod n
t ← FastExponentiation(a, (p − 1)/2, n)  { p is odd, so t = a^((p−1)/2) mod n }
return a(t^2 mod n) mod n
```

Algorithm 10.7: Algorithm FastExponentiation for modular exponentiation using the repeated squaring method. Note that, since the modulo operator is applied after each arithmetic operation in method FastExponentiation, the size of the operands of each multiplication and modulo operation is never more than $2\lceil \log_2 n \rceil$ bits.

p	12	6	3	1	0
r	1	12	8	2	1

Table 10.8: Example of an execution of the repeated squaring algorithm for modular exponentiation. For each recursive invocation of FastExponentiation$(2,12,13)$, we show the second argument, p, and the output value $r = 2^p \bmod 13$.

We show a sample execution of the repeated squaring algorithm for modular exponentiation in Table 10.8.

The running time of the repeated squaring algorithm is easy to analyze. Referring to Algorithm 10.7, a constant number of arithmetic operations are performed, excluding those in the recursive call. Also, in each each recursive call, the exponent p gets halved. Thus, the number of recursive calls and arithmetic operations is $O(\log p)$. We may therefore summarize as follows.

Theorem 10.11: *Let a p, and n be positive integers, with $a < n$. The repeated squaring algorithm computes $a^p \bmod n$ using $O(\log p)$ arithmetic operations.*

10.1.5 Modular Multiplicative Inverses

We turn now to the problem of computing multiplicative inverses in Z_n. First, we recall Theorem 10.6, which states that a nonnegative element x of Z_n admits an inverse if and only if $\gcd(x,n) = 1$. The proof of Theorem 10.6 actually suggests a way to compute $x^{-1} \bmod n$. Namely, we should find the integers i and j referred to by Theorem 10.3, such that

$$ix + jn = \gcd(x,n) = 1.$$

If we can find such integers i and j, we immediately obtain

$$i \equiv x^{-1} \bmod n.$$

The computation of the integers i and j referred to by Theorem 10.3 can be done with a variation of Euclid's algorithm, called ***Extended Euclid's Algorithm***.

Extended Euclid's Algorithm

Let a and b be positive integers, and denote with d their greatest common divisor,

$$d = \gcd(a,b).$$

Let $q = a \bmod b$ and r be the integer such that $a = rb + q$, that is,

$$q = a - rb.$$

Euclid's algorithm is based on the repeated application of the formula

$$d = \gcd(a,b) = \gcd(b,q),$$

which immediately follows from Lemma 10.4.

Suppose that the recursive call of the algorithm, with arguments b and q, also returns integers k and l, such that

$$d = kb + lq.$$

Recalling the definition of r, we have

$$d = kb + lq = kb + l(a - rb) = la + (k - lr)b.$$

Thus, we have

$$d = ia + jb, \qquad \text{for } i = l \text{ and } j = k - lr.$$

This last equation suggests a method to compute the integers i and j. This method, known as the extended Euclid's algorithm, is shown in Algorithm 10.9. We present, in Table 10.10, a sample execution of this algorithm. Its analysis is analogous to that of Euclid's algorithm.

Theorem 10.12: *Let a and b be two positive integers. The extended Euclid's algorithm for computing a triplet of integers (d,i,j) such that*

$$d = \gcd(a,b) = ia + jb,$$

executes $O(\log \max(a,b))$ arithmetic operations.

Corollary 10.13: *Let x be an element of Z_n such that $\gcd(x,n) = 1$. The multiplicative inverse of x in Z_n can be computed with $O(\log n)$ arithmetic operations.*

Algorithm ExtendedEuclidGCD(a,b):
  Input: Nonnegative integers a and b
  Output: Triplet of integers (d,i,j) such that $d = \gcd(a,b) = ia + jb$
 if $b = 0$ **then**
  return $(a,1,0)$
 $q \leftarrow a \bmod b$
 Let r be the integer such that $a = rb + q$
 $(d,k,l) \leftarrow$ ExtendedEuclidGCD(b,q)
 return $(d,l,k - lr)$

Algorithm 10.9: Extended Euclid's algorithm.

a	412	260	152	108	44	20	4
b	260	152	108	44	20	4	0
r	1	1	1	2	2	5	
i	12	-7	5	-2	1	0	1
j	-19	12	-7	5	-2	1	0

Table 10.10: Execution of ExtendedEuclidGCD(a,b), for $a = 412$ and $b = 260$, to compute (d,i,j) such that $d = \gcd(a,b) = ia + jb$. For each recursive invocation, we show the arguments a and b, variable r, and output values i and j. The output value d is always $\gcd(412,260) = 4$.

10.1.6 Primality Testing

Prime numbers play an important role in computations involving numbers, including cryptographic computations. But how do we test whether a number n is prime, particularly if it is large?

Testing all possible divisors of n is computationally infeasible for large n. Alternatively, Fermat's Little Theorem (Theorem 10.8) seems to suggest an efficient solution. Perhaps we can somehow use the equation

$$a^{p-1} \equiv 1 \bmod p$$

to form a test for p. That is, let us pick a number a, and raise it to the power $p-1$. If the result is ***not*** 1, then the number p is definitely not prime. Otherwise, there's a chance it is. Would repeating this test for various values of a prove that p is prime? Unfortunately, the answer is "no." There is a class of numbers, called ***Carmichael numbers***, that have the property that $a^{n-1} \equiv 1 \bmod n$ for all $1 \le a \le n-1$, but n is composite. The existence of these numbers ruins such a simple test as that proposed above. Example Carmichael numbers are 561 and 1105.

A Template for Primality Testing

While the above "probabilistic" test won't work, there are several related tests that will, by making more sophisticated use of Fermat's Little Theorem. These probabilistic tests of primality are based on the following general approach. Let n be an odd integer that we want to test for primality, and let $\mathsf{witness}(x,n)$ be a Boolean function of a random variable x and n with the following properties:

1. If n is prime, then $\mathsf{witness}(x,n)$ is always false. So if $\mathsf{witness}(x,n)$ is true, then n is definitely composite.
2. If n is composite, then $\mathsf{witness}(x,n)$ is false with probability $q < 1$.

The function witness is said to be a ***compositeness witness function*** with error probability q, for q bounds the probability that witness will incorrectly identify a composite number as possibly prime. By repeatedly computing $\mathsf{witness}(x,n)$ for independent random values of the parameter x, we can determine whether n is prime with an arbitrarily small error probability. The probability that $\mathsf{witness}(x,n)$ would incorrectly return "false" for k independent random x's, when n is a composite number, is q^k. A generic probabilistic primality testing algorithm based on this observation is shown in Algorithm 10.11. This algorithm, which is described using a design technique known as the template method pattern, assumes that we have a compositeness witness function, witness, that satisfies the two conditions above. In order to turn this template into a full-blown algorithm, we need only specify the details of how to pick random numbers x and compute $\mathsf{witness}(x,n)$, the composite witness function.

```
Algorithm RandomizedPrimalityTesting(n, k):
  Input: Odd integer n ≥ 2 and confidence parameter k
  Output: An indication of whether n is composite (which is always correct) or
    prime (which is incorrect with error probability 2^{-k})
  {This method assumes we have a compositeness witness function witness(x, n)
  with error probability q < 1.}
  t ← ⌈k/log_2(1/q)⌉
  for i ← 1 to t do
    x ← random()
    if witness(x, n) then
      return "composite"
  return "prime"
```

Algorithm 10.11: A template for a probabilistic primality testing algorithm based on a compositeness witness function witness(x,n). We assume that the auxiliary method random() picks a value at random from the domain of the random variable x.

If the method RandomizedPrimalityTesting$(n,k,$witness$)$ returns "composite," we know with certainty that n is composite. However, if the method returns "prime," the probability that n is actually composite is no more than 2^{-k}. Indeed, suppose that n is composite but the method returns "prime." We have that the witness function witness(x,n) has evaluated to true for t random values of x. The probability of this event is q^t. From the relation between the confidence parameter k, the number of iterations t, and the error probability q of the witness function established by the first statement of the method, we have that $q^t \leq 2^{-k}$. The second argument, k, of the template method RandomizedPrimalityTesting is a ***confidence parameter***.

The Solovay-Strassen Primality Testing Algorithm

The ***Solovay-Strassen algorithm*** for primality testing is a specialization of the template method RandomizedPrimalityTesting. The compositeness witness function used by this algorithm is based on some number-theoretic facts, which we review below.

Let p be an odd prime. An element $a > 0$ of Z_p is said to be a ***quadratic residue*** if it is the square of some element x of Z_p, that is,

$$a \equiv x^2 \pmod{p}$$

For $a \geq 0$, the ***Legendre symbol*** $\left(\frac{a}{p}\right)$ is defined by:

$$\left(\frac{a}{b}\right) = \begin{cases} 1 & \text{if } a \bmod p \text{ is a quadratic residue} \\ 0 & \text{if } a \bmod p = 0 \\ -1 & \text{otherwise.} \end{cases}$$

The notation for the Legendre symbol should not be confused with the division operation. It can be shown (see Exercise C-10.2) that

$$\left(\frac{a}{p}\right) \equiv a^{\frac{p-1}{2}} \pmod{p}.$$

We generalize the Legendre symbol by removing the restriction that p be a prime. Let n be a positive odd integer with prime decomposition

$$n = p_1^{e_1} \cdots p_k^{e_k}.$$

For $a \geq 0$, the ***Jacobi symbol***,

$$\left(\frac{a}{n}\right),$$

is defined by the following equation:

$$\left(\frac{a}{n}\right) = \prod_{i=1}^{k} \left(\frac{a}{p_i}\right)^{e_i} = \left(\frac{a}{p_1}\right)^{e_1} \cdot \left(\frac{a}{p_1}\right)^{e_1} \cdots \left(\frac{a}{p_k}\right)^{e_k}.$$

Like the Legendre symbol, the Jacobi symbol is equal to either 0, 1, or -1. We show in Algorithm 10.12 a recursive method for computing the Jacobi symbol. The justification of its correctness is omitted (see Exercise C-10.5).

Algorithm Jacobi(a, b):
Input: Integers a and b
Output: The value of the Jacobi symbol $\left(\frac{a}{b}\right)$

```
if a = 0 then
  return 0
else if a = 1 then
  return 1
else if a mod 2 = 0 then
  if (b^2 − 1)/8 mod 2 = 0 then
    return Jacobi(a/2, b)
  else
    return −Jacobi(a/2, b)
else if (a − 1)(b − 1)/4 mod 2 = 0 then
  return Jacobi(b mod a, a)
else
  return −Jacobi(b mod a, a)
```

Algorithm 10.12: Recursive computation of the Jacobi symbol.

If n is prime, then the Jacobi symbol $\left(\frac{a}{n}\right)$ is the same as the Legendre symbol. Thus, for any element a of Z_n, we have

$$\left(\frac{a}{n}\right) \equiv a^{\frac{n-1}{2}} \pmod{n}, \tag{10.2}$$

when n is prime. If n is composite, there may be values of a such that Equation 10.2 is still satisfied. So, if Equation 10.2 is satisfied, then we say that n is an ***Euler pseudo-prime*** with base a. The following lemma, given without proof, gives a property of Euler pseudo-primes that yields a compositeness witness function.

Lemma 10.14: *Let n be a composite number. There are at most $(n-1)/2$ positive values of a in Z_n such that n is an Euler pseudo-prime with base a.*

The Solovay-Strassen primality testing algorithm uses the following compositeness witness function:

$$\mathsf{witness}(x,n) = \begin{cases} \mathit{false} & \text{if } n \text{ is an Euler pseudo-prime with base } x \\ \mathit{true} & \text{otherwise,} \end{cases}$$

where x is a random integer with $1 < x \leq n-1$. By Lemma 10.14, this function has error probability $q \leq 1/2$. The Solovay-Strassen primality testing algorithm can be expressed as a specialization of the template method RandomizedPrimalityTesting (Algorithm 10.11) that redefines the auxiliary methods witness(x,n) and random$()$, as shown in Algorithm 10.13.

Algorithm witness(x,n):
  return (Jacobi(x,n) mod n) $\neq$ FastExponentiation $\left(x, \frac{n-1}{2}, n\right)$

Algorithm random$()$:
  return a random integer between 1 and $n-1$

Algorithm 10.13: Solovay-Strassen algorithm obtained by specializing the auxiliary methods of algorithm RandomizedPrimalityTesting (Algorithm 10.11).

The analysis of the running time of the Solovay-Strassen algorithm is simple. Since the error probability of the compositeness witness function is no more than $1/2$, we can set $q = 2$, which implies that the number of iterations equal to the confidence parameter k. At each iteration, the computation of witness(x,n) takes $O(\log n)$ arithmetic operations (see Theorem 10.11 and Exercise C-10.5). We conclude as follows.

Theorem 10.15: *Given an odd positive integer n and a confidence parameter $k > 0$, the Solovay-Strassen algorithm determines whether n is prime with error probability 2^{-k} by performing $O(k \log n)$ arithmetic operations.*

The Rabin-Miller Primality Testing Algorithm

We now describe the ***Rabin-Miller algorithm*** for primality testing. It is based on Fermat's Little Theorem (Theorem 10.8) and on the following lemma.

Lemma 10.16: *Let $p > 2$ be a prime. If x is an element of Z_p such that*

$$x^2 \equiv 1 \pmod{p},$$

then either

$$x \equiv 1 \pmod{p}$$

or

$$x \equiv -1 \pmod{p}.$$

A ***nontrivial square root of the unity*** in Z_n is defined as an integer $1 < x < n-1$ such that

$$x^2 \equiv 1 \pmod{n}.$$

Lemma 10.16 states that if n is prime, there are no nontrivial square roots of the unity in Z_n.

For an odd integer n, let the binary representation of $n-1$ be

$$r_{b-1}r_{b-2}\cdots r_1 r_0.$$

Define s_i as the number whose binary representation is given by the leftmost i bits of $n-1$, that is, s_i is written in binary as

$$r_{b-1}\cdots r_{b-i}.$$

Given an integer x, define the element X_i of Z_n as

$$X_i = x^{s_i} \bmod n.$$

The Rabin-Miller algorithm defines its compositeness witness function (that is, $\mathsf{witness}(x,n)$) so that it is true if and only if $x^{n-1} \bmod n \neq 1$. X_i is a nontrivial square root of the unity for some $1 < i < b-1$. The computation of this function is easier than it may seem. Indeed, if we compute $x^{n-1} \bmod n$ using the repeated squaring algorithm (Algorithm 10.7), the integers X_i are just a byproduct of the computation (see Exercise C-10.6). The error probability is provided by the following lemma, stated without proof.

Lemma 10.17: *Let n be a composite number. There are at most $(n-1)/4$ positive values of x in Z_n such that the Rabin-Miller compositeness witness function $\mathsf{witness}(x,n)$ returns true.*

We conclude as follows.

Theorem 10.18: *Given an odd positive integer n and a confidence parameter $k > 0$, the Rabin-Miller algorithm determines whether n is prime, with error probability 2^{-k}, by performing $O(k \log n)$ arithmetic operations.*

The Rabin-Miller algorithm is widely used in practice for primality testing.

Finding Prime Numbers

A primality testing algorithm can be used to select a random prime in a given range, or with a prespecified number of bits. We exploit the following result from number theory, stated without proof.

Theorem 10.19: *The number, $\pi(n)$, of primes that are less than or equal to n is $\Theta(n/\ln n)$. In fact, if $n \geq 17$, then $n/\ln n < \pi(n) < 1.26n/\ln n$.*

In the above theorem, $\ln n$ is the natural logarithm of n, that is, the logarithm of n in base e, where e is Euler's number, a transcendental number whose first few digits are $2.71828182845904523536\ldots$.

A consequence of Theorem 10.19 is that a random integer n is prime with probability $1/\ln n$. Thus, to find a prime with a given number b of bits, we generate random b-bit odd numbers and test them for primality until we find a prime number.

Theorem 10.20: *Given an integer b and a confidence parameter k, a random prime with b bits can be selected with error probability 2^{-k} by performing $O(kb)$ arithmetic operations.*

10.2 Cryptographic Computations

The Internet is enabling a growing number of activities, such as correspondence (email), shopping (Web stores), and financial transactions (online banking), to be performed electronically. However, the Internet itself is an insecure transmission network: data transmitted over the Internet travels through several intermediate specialized computers, called ***routers***, which can observe the data and potentially modify it.

A variety of cryptographic techniques have been developed to support secure communication over an insecure network such as the Internet. In particular, cryptography research has developed the following useful cryptographic computations:

- ***Encryption/decryption***: A message M to be transmitted, called the ***plaintext***, is transformed into an unrecognizable string of characters C, called the ***ciphertext***, before being sent over the network. This transformation is known as ***encryption***. After the ciphertext C is received, it is converted back to the plaintext M using an inverse transformation (that depends on additional secret information). This reverse transformation is called ***decryption***. An essential ingredient in encryption is that it should be computationally infeasible for an outsider to transform C back to M (without knowing the secret information possessed by the receiver).
- ***Digital signatures***: The author of a message M computes a message S that is derived from M and secret information known by the author. The message S is a ***digital signature*** if another party can easily verify that only the author of M could have computed S in a reasonable amount of time.

Using Cryptographic Computations for Information Security Services

The computations of encryption and digital signatures are sometimes combined with other cryptographic computations, some of which we discuss later in this chapter. Still, the two techniques above are already sufficient to support the information security services discussed in the introduction:

- ***Data integrity***: Computing a digital signature S of a message M not only helps us determine the author of M, it also verifies the integrity of M, for a modification to M would produce a different signature. So, to perform a data integrity check we can perform a verification test that S is, in fact, a digital signature for the message M.
- ***Authentication***: The above cryptographic tools can be used for authentication in two possible ways. In ***password*** authentication schemes, a user will type a user-id and password in a client application, with this combination being immediately encrypted and sent to an authenticator. If the encrypted user-id and password combination matches that in a user database, then the individual is authenticated (and the database never stores passwords in plaintext). Alternatively, an authenticator can issue a challenge to a user in the form of a random message M that the user must immediately digitally sign for authentication.
- ***Authorization***: Given a scheme for authentication, we can issue authorizations by keeping lists, called ***access control lists***, that are associated with sensitive data or computations that should be accessed only by authorized individuals. Alternatively, the holder of a right to sensitive data or computations can digitally sign a message C that authorizes a user to perform certain tasks. For example, the message could be of the form, "I U.S. Corporation vice president give person x permission to access our fourth quarter earnings data."
- ***Confidentiality***: Sensitive information can be kept secret from nonauthorized agents by encrypting it.
- ***Nonrepudiation***: If we make the parties negotiating a contract, M, digitally sign that message, then we can have a way of proving that they have seen and agreed to the content of the message M.

This section gives an introduction to cryptographic computations. Conventional names of personae, such as Alice, Bob, and Eve, are used to denote the parties involved in a cryptographic protocol. We focus primarily on ***public-key cryptography***, which is based on the number-theoretic properties and algorithms discussed in the previous section. Still, before we introduce the concepts of public-key cryptography, we briefly discuss an alternate approach to encryption.

10.2.1 Symmetric Encryption Schemes

As mentioned above, a fundamental problem in cryptography is confidentiality, that is, sending a message from Alice to Bob so that a third party, Eve, cannot gain any information from an intercepted copy of the message. Moreover, we have observed that confidentiality can be achieved by ***encryption schemes***, or ***ciphers***, where the message M to be transmitted, called the ***plaintext***, is ***encrypted*** into an unrecognizable string of characters C, called the ***ciphertext***, before being sent over the network. After the ciphertext C is received, it is decrypted back to the plaintext M using an inverse transformation called ***decryption***.

Secret Keys

In describing the details of an encryption scheme, we must explain all the steps needed in order to encrypt a plaintext M into a ciphertext C, and how to then decrypt that ciphertext back to M. Moreover, in order for Eve to be unable to extract M from C, there must be some secret information that is kept private from her.

In traditional cryptography, a common ***secret key*** k is shared by Alice and Bob, and is used to both encrypt and decrypt the message. Such schemes are also called ***symmetric encryption*** schemes, since k is used for both encryption and decryption and the same secret is shared by both Alice and Bob.

Substitution Ciphers

A classic example of a symmetric cipher is a ***substitution cipher***, where the secret key is a permutation π of the characters of the alphabet. Encrypting plaintext M into ciphertext C consists of replacing each character x of M with character $y = \pi(x)$. Decryption can be easily performed by knowing the permutation function π. Indeed, M is derived from C by replacing each character y of C with character $x = \pi^{-1}(y)$. The ***Caesar cipher*** is an early example of a substitution cipher, where each character x is replaced by character

$$y = x + k \bmod n,$$

where n is the size of the alphabet and $1 < k < n$ is the secret key. This substitution scheme is known as the "Caesar cipher," for Julius Caesar is known to have used it with $k = 3$.

Substitution ciphers are quite easy to use, but they are not secure. Indeed, the secret key can be quickly inferred using ***frequency analysis***, based on the knowledge of the frequency of the various letters, or groups of consecutive letters in the text language.

The One-Time Pad

Secure symmetric ciphers exist. Indeed, the most secure cipher known is a symmetric cipher. It is the ***one-time pad***. In this cryptosystem, Alice and Bob each share a random bit string K as large as any message they might wish to communicate. The string K is the symmetric key, for to compute a ciphertext C from a message M, Alice computes

$$C = M \oplus K,$$

where "$\oplus$" denotes the bitwise exclusive-or operator. She can send C to Bob using any reliable communication channel, even one on which Eve is eavesdropping, because the ciphertext C is computationally indistinguishable from a random string. Nevertheless, Bob can easily decrypt the ciphertext message C by computing $C \oplus K$, since

$$\begin{aligned} C \oplus K &= (M \oplus K) \oplus K \\ &= M \oplus (K \oplus K) \\ &= M \oplus \mathbf{0} \\ &= M, \end{aligned}$$

where $\mathbf{0}$ denotes the bit string of all 0's the same length as M. This scheme is clearly a symmetric cipher system, since the key K is used for encryption and decryption.

The one-time pad is computationally efficient, for bitwise exclusive-or is one of the fastest operators that computers can perform. Also, as already mentioned, the one-time pad is incredibly secure. Nevertheless, the one-time pad cryptosystem is not widely used. The main trouble with this system is that Alice and Bob must share a very large secret key. Moreover, the security of the one-time pad depends crucially on the fact that the secret key K is used only once. If K is reused, there are several simple cryptoanalyses that can break this system. For practical cryptosystems, we prefer secret keys that can be reused and are smaller than the messages they encrypt and decrypt.

Other Symmetric Ciphers

Secure and efficient symmetric ciphers do exist. They are referred to by their acronyms or colorful names, such as "3DES," "IDEA," "Blowfish," and "Rijndael" (pronounce "Rhine-doll"). They perform a sequence of complex substitution and permutation transformations on the bits of the plaintext. While these systems are important in many applications, they are only mildly interesting from an algorithmic viewpoint; hence, they are out of the scope of this book. They run in time proportional to the length of the message being encrypted or decrypted. Thus, we mention that these algorithms exist and are fast, but in this book we do not discuss any of these efficient symmetric ciphers in any detail.

10.2.2 Public-Key Cryptosystems

A major problem with symmetric ciphers is ***key transfer***, or how to distribute the secret key for encryption and decryption. In 1976, Diffie and Hellman described an abstract system that would avoid these problems, the ***public-key cryptosystem***. While they didn't actually publish a particular public-key system, they discussed the features of such a system. Specifically, given a message M, encryption function E, and decryption function D, the following four properties must hold:

1. $D(E(M)) = M$.
2. Both E and D are easy to compute.
3. It is computationally infeasible[1] to derive D from E.
4. $E(D(M)) = M$.

In retrospect, these properties seem fairly common sense. The first property merely states that, once a message has been encrypted, applying the decryption procedure will restore it. Property two is perhaps more obvious. In order for a cryptosystem to be practical, encryption and decryption must be computationally fast.

The third property is the start of the innovation. It means that E only goes one way; it is computationally infeasible to invert E, unless you already know D. Thus, the encryption procedure E can be made public. Any party can send a message, while only one knows how to decrypt it.

If the fourth property holds, then the mapping is one-to-one. Thus, the cryptosystem is a solution to the ***digital signature*** problem. Given an electronic message from Bob to Alice, how can we prove that Bob actually sent it? Bob can apply his decryption procedure to some signature message M. Any other party can then verify that Bob actually sent the message by applying the public encryption procedure E. Since only Bob knows the decryption function, only Bob can generate a signature message which can be correctly decoded by the function E.

Public-key cryptography is the basis of modern cryptography. Its economic importance is fast growing, since it provides the security infrastructure of all electronic transactions over the Internet.

The design of public-key cryptosystems can be described in general terms. The idea is to find a very tough problem in computer science, and then somehow tie the cryptosystem to it. Ideally, one arrives at an actual proof that breaking the cryptosystem is computationally equivalent to solving the difficult problem. There's a large class of problems, called ***NP-complete***, which do not have known polynomial time algorithms for their solution. (See Chapter 13.) In fact, it is widely believed that there are none. Then, to generate the particular encryption and decryption keys, we create a particular set of parameters for this problem. Encrypting then means turning the message into an instance of the problem. The recipient can use secret information (the decryption key) to solve the puzzle effortlessly.

[1] The concept of computational difficulty is formalized in Chapter 13.

10.2.3 The RSA Cryptosystem

Some care must be taken in how a computationally difficult problem is tied to a cryptosystem. One of the earlier public-key cryptosystems, the Merkle-Hellman system, linked encryption to something called the knapsack problem, which is ***NP***-complete. Unfortunately, the problems the system generates turn out to be a special subclass of the knapsack problem that can be easily solved. So designing public-key cryptosystems has its share of subtleties.

Probably the most well-known public-key cryptosystem is also one of the oldest, and is tied to the difficulty of factoring large numbers. It is named ***RSA*** after its inventors, Rivest, Shamir, and Adleman.

In this cryptosystem, we begin by selecting two large primes, p and q. Let $n = pq$ be their product and recall that $\phi(n) = (p-1)(q-1)$. Encryption and decryption keys e and d are selected so that

- e and $\phi(n)$ are relatively prime
- $ed \equiv 1 \pmod{\phi(n)}$.

The second condition means that d is the multiplicative inverse of $e \bmod \phi(n)$. The pair of values n and e form the public key, while d is the private key. In practice, e is chosen either randomly or as one of the following numbers: 3, 17, or 65 537.

The rules for encrypting and decrypting with RSA are simple. Let us assume, for simplicity, that the plaintext is an integer M, with $0 < M < n$. If M is a string, we can view it as an integer by concatenating the bits of its characters. The plaintext M is encrypted into ciphertext C with one modular exponentiation using the encryption key e as the exponent:

$$\boxed{C \leftarrow M^e \bmod n \quad \text{(RSA encryption).}}$$

The decryption of ciphertext C is also performed with an exponentiation, using now the decryption key d as the exponent:

$$\boxed{M \leftarrow C^d \bmod n \quad \text{(RSA decryption).}}$$

The correctness of the above encryption and decryption rules is justified by the following theorem.

Theorem 10.21: *Let p and q be two odd primes, and define $n = pq$. Let e be relatively prime with $\phi(n)$ and let d be the multiplicative inverse of e modulo $\phi(n)$. For each integer x such that $0 < x < n$,*

$$x^{ed} \equiv x \pmod{n}.$$

Proof: Let $y = x^{ed} \bmod n$. We want to prove that $y = x$. Because of the way we have selected e and d, we can write $ed = k\phi(n) + 1$, for some integer k. Thus, we have

$$y = x^{k\phi(n)+1} \bmod n.$$

We distinguish two cases.

Case 1: x does not divide n. We rewrite y as follows:

$$\begin{aligned} y &= x^{k\phi(n)+1} \bmod n \\ &= x x^{k\phi(n)} \bmod n \\ &= x(x^{\phi(n)} \bmod n)^k \bmod n. \end{aligned}$$

By Theorem 10.9 (Euler's theorem), we have $x^{\phi(n)} \bmod n = 1$, which implies $y = x \cdot 1^k \bmod n = x$.

Case 2: x divides n. Since $n = pq$, with p and q primes, x is a multiple of either p or q. Suppose x is a multiple of p, that is, $x = hp$ for some positive integer h. Clearly, x cannot be a multiple of q as well, since otherwise x would be greater than $n = pq$, a contradiction. Thus, $\gcd(x,q) = 1$ and by Theorem 10.9 (Euler's theorem), we have

$$x^{\phi(q)} \equiv 1 \pmod{q}.$$

Since $\phi(n) = \phi(p)\phi(q)$, raising both sides of the above congruence to the power of $k\phi(q)$, we obtain

$$x^{k\phi(n)} \equiv 1 \pmod{q},$$

which we rewrite as

$$x^{k\phi(n)} = 1 + iq,$$

for some integer i. Multiplying both sides of the above equality by x, and recalling that $x = hp$ and $n = pq$, we obtain:

$$\begin{aligned} x^{k\phi(n)+1} &= x + xiq \\ &= x + hpiq \\ &= x + (hi)n. \end{aligned}$$

Thus, we have

$$y = x^{k\phi(n)+1} \bmod n = x.$$

In either case, we have shown that $y = x$, which concludes the proof of the theorem. ■

Using RSA for Digital Signatures

The symmetry of the encryption and decryption functions implies that the RSA cryptosystem directly supports digital signatures. Indeed, a digital signature S for message M is obtained by applying the decryption function to M, that is,

$$\boxed{S \leftarrow M^d \bmod n \quad \text{(RSA signature).}}$$

The verification of the digital signature S is now performed with the encryption function, that is, by checking that

$$\boxed{M \equiv S^e \pmod{n} \quad \text{(RSA verification).}}$$

The Difficulty of Breaking RSA

Note that, even if we know the value e, we cannot figure out d unless we know $\phi(n)$. Most cryptography researchers generally believe that breaking RSA requires that we compute $\phi(n)$ and that this requires factoring n. While there is no ***proof*** that factorization is computationally difficult, a whole series of famous mathematicians have worked on the problem over the past few hundred years. Especially if n is large ($\approx$ 200 digits), it will take a very long time to factor it. To give you an idea of the state of the art, mathematicians were quite excited when a nationwide network of computers was able to factor the ninth Fermat number, $2^{512}-1$. This number has "only" 155 decimal digits. Barring a major breakthrough, the RSA system will remain secure. For if technology somehow advances to a point where it is feasible to factor 200 digit numbers, we need only choose an n with three or four hundred digits.

Analysis and Setup for RSA Encryption

The running time of RSA encryption, decryption, signature, and verification is simple to analyze. Indeed, each such operation requires a constant number of modular exponentiations, which can be performed with method FastExponentiation (Algorithm 10.7).

Theorem 10.22: *Let n be the modulus used in the RSA cryptosystem. RSA encryption, decryption, signature, and verification each take $O(\log n)$ arithmetic operations.*

To set up the RSA cryptosystem, we need to generate the public and private key pair. Namely, we need to compute the private key (d,p,q) and the public key (e,n) that goes with it. This involves the following computations:

- Selection of two random primes p and q with a given number of bits. This can be accomplished by testing random integers for primality, as discussed at the end of Section 10.1.6.
- Selection of an integer e relatively prime to $\phi(n)$. This can be done by picking random primes less than $\phi(n)$ until we find one that does not divide $\phi(n)$. In practice, it is sufficient to check small primes from a list of known primes (often $e=3$ or $e=17$ will work).
- Computing the multiplicative inverse d of e in $Z_{\phi(n)}$. This can be done using the extended Euclid's algorithm (Corollary 10.13).

We have previously explained algorithms for each of these number theory problems in this chapter.

10.2.4 The El Gamal Cryptosystem

We have seen that the security of the RSA cryptosystem is related to the difficulty of factoring large numbers. It is possible to construct cryptosystems based on other difficult number-theoretic problems. We now consider the El Gamal cryptosystem, named after its inventor, Taher El Gamal, which is based on the difficulty of a problem called the "discrete logarithm."

The Discrete Logarithm

When we're working with the real numbers, $\log_b y$ is the value x, such that $b^x = y$. We can define an analogous discrete logarithm. Given integers b and n, with $b < n$, the ***discrete logarithm*** of an integer y to the base b is an integer x, such that

$$b^x \equiv y \bmod n.$$

The discrete logarithm is also called ***index***, and we write

$$x = \mathrm{ind}_{b,n} y.$$

While it is quite efficient to raise numbers to large powers modulo p (recall the repeated squaring algorithm, Algorithm 10.7), the inverse computation of the discrete logarithm is much harder. The El Gamal system relies on the difficulty of this computation.

El Gamal Encryption

Let p be a prime, and g be a generator of Z_p. The private key x is an integer between 1 and $p-2$. Let $y = g^x \bmod p$. The public key for El Gamal encryption is the triplet (p, g, y). If taking discrete logarithms is as difficult as it is widely believed, releasing $y = g^x \bmod p$ does not reveal x.

To encrypt a plaintext M, a random integer k relatively prime to $p-1$ is selected, and the following pair of values is computed:

$$\begin{aligned} a &\leftarrow g^k \bmod p \\ b &\leftarrow My^k \bmod p \end{aligned} \quad \text{(El Gamal encryption).}$$

The ciphertext C consists of the pair (a, b) computed above.

El Gamal Decryption

The decryption of the ciphertext $C = (a, b)$ in the El Gamal scheme, to retrieve the plaintext M, is simple:

$$M \leftarrow b/a^x \bmod p \quad \text{(El Gamal decryption).}$$

In the above expression, the "division" by a^x should be interpreted in the context of modular arithmetic, that is, M is multiplied by the inverse of a^x in Z_p. The correctness of the El Gamal encryption scheme is easy to verify. Indeed, we have

$$\begin{aligned} b/a^x \bmod p &= My^k(a^x)^{-1} \bmod p \\ &= Mg^{xk}(g^{kx})^{-1} \bmod p \\ &= M. \end{aligned}$$

Using El Gamal for Digital Signatures

A variation of the above scheme provides a digital signature. Namely, a signature for message M is a pair $S = (a,b)$ obtained by selecting a random integer k relatively prime to $p-1$ (which, of course, equals $\phi(p)$) and computing

$$\begin{aligned} a &\leftarrow g^k \bmod p \\ b &\leftarrow k^{-1}(M - xa) \bmod (p-1) \end{aligned} \quad \text{(El Gamal signature).}$$

To verify a digital signature $S = (a,b)$, we check that

$$y^a a^b \equiv g^M \pmod{p} \quad \text{(El Gamal verification).}$$

The correctness of the El Gamal digital signature scheme can be seen as follows:

$$\begin{aligned} y^a a^b \bmod p &= ((g^x \bmod p)^a \bmod p)((g^k \bmod p)^{k^{-1}(M-xa) \bmod (p-1)} \bmod p) \\ &= g^{xa} g^{kk^{-1}(M-xa) \bmod (p-1)} \bmod p \\ &= g^{xa+M-xa} \bmod p \\ &= g^M \bmod p. \end{aligned}$$

Analysis of El Gamal Encryption

The analysis of the performance of the El Gamal cryptosystem is similar to that of RSA. Namely, we have the following.

Theorem 10.23: *Let n be the modulus used in the El Gamal cryptosystem. El Gamal encryption, decryption, signature, and verification each take $O(\log n)$ arithmetic operations.*

10.3 Information Security Algorithms and Protocols

Once we have some tools, like the fundamental algorithms involving numbers and the public-key encryption methods, we can start to compose them with other algorithms to provide needed information security services. We discuss several such protocols in this section, many of which use, in addition to the algorithms discussed above, the topic we discuss next.

10.3.1 One-way Hash Functions

Public-key cryptosystems are often used in conjunction with a ***one-way hash function***, also called a ***message digest*** or ***fingerprint***. We provide an informal description of such a function next. A formal discussion is beyond the scope of this book.

A ***one-way hash function*** H maps a string (message) M of arbitrary length to an integer $d = H(M)$ with a fixed number of bits, called the ***digest*** of M, that satisfies the following properties:

1. Given a string M, the digest of M can be computed quickly.
2. Given the digest d of M, but not M, it is computationally infeasible to find M.

A one-way hash function is said to be ***collision-resistant*** if, given a string M, it is computationally infeasible to find another string M' with the same digest, and is said to be ***strongly collision-resistant*** if it is computationally infeasible to find two strings M_1 and M_2 with the same digest.

Several functions believed to be strongly collision-resistant, one-way hash functions have been devised. The ones used most in practice are MD5, which produces a 128-bit digest, and SHA-1, which produces a 160-bit digest. We examine now some applications of one-way hashing.

A first application of one-way hash functions is to speed up the construction of digital signatures. If we have a collision-resistant, one-way hash function, we can sign the digest of a message instead of the message itself, that is, the signature S is given by:

$$S = D(H(M)).$$

Except for small messages, hashing the message and signing the digest is faster, in practice, than signing the message directly. Also, this procedure overcomes a significant restriction of the RSA and El Gamal signature schemes, namely that the message M must be less than the modulus n. For example, when using MD5, we can sign messages of arbitrary length using a fixed modulus n that is only required to be greater than 2^{128}.

10.3.2 Timestamping and Authenticated Dictionaries

The next application is ***timestamping***. Alice has a document M and wants to obtain a certification that the document M exists at the present time t.

In one method for timestamping, Alice uses the services of a trusted third party, Trevor, to provide timestamping. Alice can send M to Trevor and have him sign a new document M' consisting of the concatenation of M and t. While this approach works, it has the drawback that Trevor can see M. A collision-resistant, one-way hash function H can eliminate the problem. Alice computes the digest d of M using H, and asks Trevor to sign a new message M'' consisting of the concatenation of d and t.

Authenticated Dictionaries

In fact, we can define another method for timestamping that does not require that we fully trust Trevor. This alternative method is based on the concept of an ***authenticated dictionary***.

In an authenticated dictionary, the third party, Trevor, collects a dictionary database of items. In the timestamping application, the items are the digests of documents that need to be timestamped as existing on a certain date. In this case, however, we do not trust Trevor's signed statement that a digest d of Alice's document M exists on a certain date t. Instead, Trevor computes a digest D of the entire dictionary and he publishes D in a location where timestamping cannot be questioned (such as the classified section of a well-known newspaper). In addition, Trevor responds to Alice with partial digest D' that summarizes all the items in the dictionary except for Alice's document digest d.

For this scheme to work effectively, there should be a function f such that $D = f(D', d)$, with f being easy to compute (for Alice). But this function should be one-way in the sense that, given an arbitrary y, it should be computationally difficult (for Trevor) to compute an x such that $D = f(x, y)$. Given such a function, we can rely on Trevor to compute the digest of all the documents he receives and publish that digest to the public location. For it is computationally infeasible for Trevor to fabricate a response that would indicate that a value d was in the dictionary when in fact it was not. Thus, the key component of this protocol is the existence of the one-way function f. In the remainder of this subsection we explore a possible method for constructing a function f suitable for an authenticated dictionary.

Hash Trees

An interesting data structure approach, known as the ***hash tree*** scheme, can be used to implement an authenticated dictionary. This structure supports the initial construction of the dictionary database followed by query operations or membership responses for each item.

A hash tree T for a set S stores the elements of S at the external nodes of a complete binary tree T and a hash value $h(v)$ at each node v, which combines the hash of its children using a well-known, one-way hash function. In the timestamping application the items stored at the external nodes of T are themselves digests of documents to be timestamped as existing on a particular day. The authenticated dictionary for S consists of the hash tree T plus the publication of the value $h(r)$ stored in the root r of T. An element x is proven to belong to S by reporting the values stored at the nodes on the path in T from the node storing x to the root, together with the values of all nodes that have siblings on this path.

Given such a path p, Alice can recompute the hash value $h(r)$ of the root. Moreover, since T is a complete binary tree, she need only perform $O(\log n)$ calls to the hash function h to compute this value, where n is the number of elements in S.

10.3.3 Coin Flipping and Bit Commitment

We now present a protocol that allows Alice and Bob to ***flip a random coin*** by exchanging email messages or otherwise communicating over a network. Let H be a strongly collision-resistant, one-way hash function. The interaction between Alice and Bob consists of the following steps:

1. Alice picks a number x and computes the digest $d = H(x)$, sending d to Bob.
2. After receiving d, Bob sends Alice his guess of whether x is odd or even.
3. Alice announces the result of the coin flip: if Bob has guessed correctly, the result is heads; if not, it is tails. She also sends to Bob x as proof of the result.
4. Bob verifies that Alice has not cheated, that is, that $d = H(x)$.

The strong collision-resistance requirement is essential, since otherwise Alice could come up with two numbers, one odd and one even, with the same digest d, and would be able to control the outcome of the coin flip.

Related to coin flipping is ***bit commitment***. In this case, Alice wants to commit to a value n (which could be a single bit or an arbitrary string) without revealing it to Bob. Once Alice reveals n, Bob wants to verify that she has not cheated. For example, Alice may want to prove to Bob that she can predict whether a certain stock will be up ($n = 1$), down ($n = -1$), or unchanged ($n = 0$) tomorrow. Using a strongly collision-resistant, one-way hash function H, the protocol goes as follows:

1. She sends Bob x plus the digest of the concatenation of x, y, and n. In keeping with tradition in cryptographic literature, we denote the concatenation of strings a and b with "$a||b$" in this chapter. Thus, using this notation, Alice sends Bob $d = H(x||y||n)$. Note that Bob is unable to figure out n from x and d.
2. At the close of trading the next day, when n becomes publicly known, Alice sends y to Bob for verification.
3. Bob verifies that Alice has not cheated, that is, $d = H(x||y||n)$.

10.3.4 The Secure Electronic Transaction (SET) Protocol

Our final application is significantly more complex and involves the combined use of encryption, digital signatures, and one-way hashing. It is actually a simplified version of the ***SET*** (secure electronic transaction) protocol for secure credit card payment over the Internet.

Alice wants to purchase a book from Barney (an Internet bookstore) using a credit card issued by Lisa (a bank). Alice is concerned about privacy: on one hand, she does not want Barney to see her credit card number; on the other hand, she does not want Lisa to know which book she purchased from Barney. However, she wants Barney to send her the book, and Lisa to send the payment to Barney. Finally, Alice also wants to ensure that the communication between Barney, Lisa, and herself is kept confidential even if someone is eavesdropping over the Internet. Using a strongly collision-resistant, one-way hash function H, the protocol is described in Algorithm 10.14.

Properties of the SET Protocol

The following observations show that the confidentiality, integrity, nonrepudiation, and authentication requirements of the protocol are satisfied.

- Barney cannot see Alice's credit card number, which is stored in the payment slip P. Barney has the digest p of P. However, he cannot compute P from p since H is one-way. Barney also has the ciphertext C_L of a message that contains P. However, he cannot decrypt C_L since he does not have Lisa's private key.
- Lisa cannot see the book ordered by Alice, which is stored in the purchase order O. Lisa has the digest o of O. However, she cannot compute O from o since H is one-way.
- The digital signature S provided by Alice serves a dual purpose. It allows Barney to verify the authenticity of Alice's purchase order O, and Alice to verify the authenticity of Alice's payment slip P.
- Alice cannot deny that she ordered the specific book indicated in O and to have charged her credit card for the given amount indicated in P. Indeed, since H is collision-resistant, she cannot forge a different purchase order and/or payment slip that hash to the same digests o and p.
- All communication between the parties uses public-key encryption and ensures confidentiality, even in the presence of eavesdroppers.

Thus, although it is somewhat intricate, the SET protocol illustrates how cryptographic computations can be composed to perform a nontrivial electronic commerce operation.

1. Alice prepares two documents, a purchase order O stating that she intends to order the book from Barney, and a payment slip P, providing Lisa the card number to be used in the transaction, and the amount to be charged. Alice computes digests
$$o = H(O)$$
$$p = H(P),$$
and produces a digital signature S for the digest of the concatenation of o and p, that is,
$$S = D_A(H(o||p)) = D(H(H(O)||H(P))),$$
where D_A is the function used by Alice to sign, based on her private key. Alice encrypts the concatenation of o, P, and S with Lisa's public key, which yields ciphertext
$$C_L = E_L(o||P||S).$$
She also encrypts with Barney's public key the concatenation of O, p, and S, yielding ciphertext
$$C_B = E_B(O||p||S).$$
She sends to Barney C_L and C_B.
2. Barney retrieves O, p, and S by decrypting C_B with his private key. He verifies the authenticity of the purchase order O with Alice's public key by checking that
$$E_A(S) = H(H(O)||p),$$
and forwards C_L to Lisa.
3. Lisa retrieves o, P, and S by decrypting C_L with her private key. She verifies the authenticity of the payment slip P with Alice's public key by checking that
$$E_A(S) = H(o||H(P)),$$
and verifies that P indicates a payment to Barney. She then creates an authorization message M that consists of a transaction number, Alice's name, and the amount she agreed to pay. Lisa computes the signature T of M, and sends the pair (M,T) encrypted with Barney's public key to Barney, that is, $C_M = E_B(M||T)$.
4. Barney retrieves M and T by decrypting C_M and verifies the authenticity of the authorization message M with Lisa's public key, by checking that $E_L(T) = M$. He verifies that the name in M is Alice's, and that the amount is the correct price of the book. He fulfills the order by sending the book to Alice and requests the payment from Lisa by sending her the transaction number encrypted with Lisa's public key.
5. Lisa pays Barney and charges Alice's credit card account.

Algorithm 10.14: Simplified version of the SET protocol.

10.3.5 Key Distribution and Exchange

A public-key cryptosystem assumes that public keys are known to all the parties. For example, if Alice wants to send a confidential message to Bob, she needs to know Bob's public key. Similarly, if Alice wants to verify Bob's digital signature, she needs Bob's public key as well. How does Alice get Bob's public key? Bob can just send it to Alice, but if Eve can intercept the communication between Bob and Alice, she could replace Bob's public key with her key, and thus trick Alice into revealing her message meant for Bob, or believing that a message was signed by Bob, while it was signed instead by Eve.

Digital Certificates

A solution to the problem requires the introduction of a third party, Charlie, who is trusted by all the participants in a protocol. It is further assumed that each participant has Charlie's public key. Charlie issues each participant a ***certificate***, which is a statement digitally signed by Charlie that contains the name of the participant and its public key. Bob now sends Alice the certificate issued to him by Charlie. Alice extracts Bob's public key from the certificate and verifies its authenticity by using Charlie's public key (recall the assumption that each participant has Charlie's public key). Certificates are widely used in practical public-key applications. Their format is described in the ***X.509*** ITU (International Telecommunication Union) standard. In addition to the subject of the certificate and its public key, a certificate also contains a unique serial number and an expiration date. An issuer of certificates is called a ***certificate authority*** (CA).

In a realistic setting, the protocols described in the previous section should be modified by introducing certificates to distribute public keys. Also, the certificates should be validated using the CA's public key.

Certificate Revocation

Private keys are sometimes lost, stolen, or otherwise compromised. When this happens, the CA should revoke the certificate for that key. For example, Bob may have kept his private key in a file on his laptop computer. If the laptop is stolen, Bob should request the CA to immediately revoke his certificate, since otherwise the thief could impersonate Bob. The CA periodically publishes a ***certificate revocation list*** (CRL), which consists of the signed list of the serial numbers of all the unexpired certificates that have been revoked together with a timestamp.

When validating a certificate, a participant should also get the latest CRL from the CA, and verify that that the certificate has not been revoked. The age of the CRL (difference between the current time and the timestamp) provides a measure of risk for the participant examining a certificate. Alternately, there are several online schemes for checking the validity of a given digital certificate using a networked server that stores revocation information.

Using Public Keys for Symmetric Key Exchange

Public key cryptography overcomes the critical bottleneck of symmetric key cryptosystems, since, in a public key cryptosystem, there is no need to distribute secret keys before engaging in a secure communication. Unfortunately, this advantage comes at a cost, as the existing public-key cryptosystems take much longer to encrypt and decrypt than existing symmetric cryptosystems. Thus, in practice, public-key cryptosystems are often used in conjunction with symmetric cryptosystems, to overcome the challenge of exchanging secret keys in order to set up a symmetric cryptographic communication channel.

For example, if Alice wants to set up a secure communication channel with Bob, she and Bob can perform the following set of steps.

1. Alice computes a random number x, computes her digital signature S of x, and encrypts the pair (x,S) using Bob's public key, sending the resulting ciphertext C to Bob.
2. Bob decrypts C using his private key, and verifies that Alice sent it to him by checking the signature S.
3. Bob can then show Alice that he has indeed received x, by encrypting x with Alice's public key, and sending it back to her.

From this point on, they can use the number x as the secret key in a symmetric cryptosystem.

Diffie-Hellman Secret Key Exchange

If Alice and Bob are communicating using a medium that is reliable but perhaps not private, there is another scheme they can use to compute a secret key that they can then share for future symmetric encryption communications. This scheme is called ***Diffie-Hellman key exchange***, and consists of the following steps:

1. Alice and Bob agree (publicly) on a large prime n and a generator g in Z_n.
2. Alice chooses a random number x and sends Bob $B = g^x \bmod n$.
3. Bob chooses a random number y and sends Alice $A = g^y \bmod n$.
4. Alice computes $K = A^x \bmod n$.
5. Bob computes $K' = B^y \bmod n$.

Clearly, $K = K'$, so Alice and Bob can now use K (respectively, K') to communicate using a symmetric cryptosystem.

10.4 The Fast Fourier Transform

A common bottleneck computation in many cryptographic systems is the multiplication of large integers and polynomials. The fast Fourier transform is a surprising and efficient algorithm for multiplying such objects. We describe this algorithm first for multiplying polynomials and we then show how this approach can be extended to large integers.

A polynomial represented in ***coefficient form*** is described by a coefficient vector $\mathbf{a} = [a_0, a_1, \ldots, a_{n-1}]$ as follows:

$$p(x) = \sum_{i=0}^{n-1} a_i x^i.$$

The ***degree*** of such a polynomial is the largest index of a nonzero coefficient a_i. A coefficient vector of length n can represent polynomials of degree at most $n-1$.

The coefficient representation is natural, in that it is simple and allows for several polynomial operations to be performed quickly. For example, given a second polynomial described using a coefficient vector $\mathbf{b} = [b_0, b_1, \ldots, b_{n-1}]$ as

$$q(x) = \sum_{i=0}^{n-1} b_i x^i,$$

we can easily add $p(x)$ and $q(x)$ component-wise to produce their sum,

$$p(x) + q(x) = \sum_{i=0}^{n-1} (a_i + b_i) x^i.$$

Likewise, the coefficient form for $p(x)$ allows us to evaluate $p(x)$ efficiently, by ***Horner's rule*** (Exercise C-1.16), as

$$p(x) = a_0 + x(a_1 + x(a_2 + \cdots + x(a_{n-2} + x a_{n-1}) \cdots)).$$

Thus, with the coefficient representation, we can add and evaluate degree-$(n-1)$ polynomials in $O(n)$ time.

Multiplying two polynomials $p(x)$ and $q(x)$, as defined above in coefficient form, is not straightforward, however. To see the difficulty, consider $p(x)q(x)$:

$$p(x)q(x) = a_0 b_0 + (a_0 b_1 + a_1 b_0)x + (a_0 b_2 + a_1 b_1 + a_2 b_0)x^2 + \cdots + a_{n-1} b_{n-1} x^{2n-2}.$$

That is,

$$p(x)q(x) = \sum_{i=0}^{2n-2} c_i x^i, \quad \text{where} \quad c_i = \sum_{j=0}^{i} a_j b_{i-j}, \quad \text{for } i = 0, 1, \ldots, 2n-2.$$

This equation defines a vector $\mathbf{c} = [c_0, c_1, \ldots, c_{2n-1}]$, which we call the ***convolution*** of the vectors $\mathbf{a}$ and $\mathbf{b}$. For symmetry reasons, we view the convolution as a vector of size $2n$, defining $c_{2n-1} = 0$. We denote the convolution of $\mathbf{a}$ and $\mathbf{b}$ as $\mathbf{a} * \mathbf{b}$. If we apply the definition of the convolution directly, then it will take us $\Theta(n^2)$ time to multiply the two polynomials p and q.

The ***fast Fourier transform*** (***FFT***) algorithm allows us to perform this multiplication in $O(n \log n)$ time. The improvement of the FFT is based on an interesting observation. Namely, that another way of representing a degree-$(n-1)$ polynomial is by its value on n distinct inputs. Such a representation is unique because of the following theorem.

Theorem 10.24 [The Interpolation Theorem for Polynomials]: *Given a set of n points in the plane, $S = \{(x_0, y_0), (x_1, y_1), (x_2, y_2), \ldots, (x_{n-1}, y_{n-1})\}$, such that the x_i's are all distinct, there is a unique degree-$(n-1)$ polynomial $p(x)$ with $p(x_i) = y_i$, for $i = 0, 1, \ldots, n-1$.*

Suppose, then, that we can represent a polynomial not by its coefficients, but instead by its value on a collection of different inputs. This theorem suggests an alternative method for multiplying two polynomials p and q. In particular, evaluate p and q for $2n$ different inputs $x_0, x_1, \ldots, x_{2n-1}$ and compute the representation of the product of p and q as the set

$$\{(x_0, p(x_0)q(x_0)), (x_1, p(x_1)q(x_1)), \ldots, (x_{2n-1}, p(x_{2n-1})q(x_{2n-1}))\}.$$

Such a computation would clearly take just $O(n)$ time given the $2n$ input-output pairs for each of p and q.

The challenge, then, to effectively using this approach to multiply p and q is to come up quickly with $2n$ input-output pairs for p and q. Applying Horner's rule to $2n$ different inputs would take us $\Theta(n^2)$ time, which is not asymptotically any faster than using the convolution directly. So Horner's rule is of no help here. Of course, we have full freedom in how we choose the set of $2n$ inputs for our polynomials. That is, we have full discretion to choose inputs that are easy to evaluate. For example, $p(0) = a_0$ is a simple case. But we have to choose a set of $2n$ easy inputs to evaluate p on, not just one. Fortunately, the mathematical concept we discuss next provides a convenient set of inputs that are collectively easier to use to evaluate a polynomial than applying Horner's rule $2n$ times.

10.4.1 Primitive Roots of Unity

A number ω is a ***primitive nth root of unity***, for $n \geq 2$, if it satisfies the following properties:

1. $\omega^n = 1$, that is, ω is an nth root of 1.
2. The numbers $1, \omega, \omega^2, \ldots, \omega^{n-1}$ are distinct.

Note that this definition implies that a primitive nth root of unity has a multiplicative inverse, $\omega^{-1} = \omega^{n-1}$, for

$$\omega^{-1}\omega = \omega^{n-1}\omega = \omega^n = 1.$$

Thus, we can speak in a well-defined fashion of negative exponents of ω, as well as positive ones.

The notion of a primitive nth root of unity may, at first, seem like a strange definition with few examples. But it actually has several important instances. One important one is the complex number

$$e^{2\pi i/n} = \cos(2\pi/n) + \mathbf{i}\sin(2\pi/n),$$

which is a primitive nth root of unity, when we take our arithmetic over the complex numbers, where $\mathbf{i} = \sqrt{-1}$.

Primitive nth roots of unity have a number of important properties, including the following three ones.

Lemma 10.25 (Cancellation Property): *If ω is an nth root of unity, then, for any integer $k \neq 0$, with $-n < k < n$,*

$$\sum_{j=0}^{n-1} \omega^{kj} = 0.$$

Proof: Since $\omega^k \neq 1$,

$$\sum_{j=0}^{n-1} \omega^{kj} = \frac{(\omega^k)^n - 1}{\omega^k - 1} = \frac{(\omega^n)^k - 1}{\omega^k - 1} = \frac{1^k - 1}{\omega^k - 1} = \frac{1 - 1}{\omega^k - 1} = 0$$

■

Lemma 10.26 (Reduction Property): *If ω is a primitive $(2n)$th root of unity, then ω^2 is a primitive nth root of unity.*

Proof: If $1, \omega, \omega^2, \ldots, \omega^{2n-1}$ are distinct, then $1, \omega^2, (\omega^2)^2, \ldots, (\omega^2)^{n-1}$ are also distinct. ■

Lemma 10.27 (Reflective Property): *If ω is a primitive nth root of unity and n is even, then*

$$\omega^{n/2} = -1.$$

Proof: By the cancellation property, for $k = n/2$,

$$\begin{aligned}
0 &= \sum_{j=0}^{n-1} \omega^{(n/2)j} \\
&= \omega^0 + \omega^{n/2} + \omega^n + \omega^{3n/2} + \cdots + \omega^{(n/2)(n-2)} + \omega^{(n/2)(n-1)} \\
&= \omega^0 + \omega^{n/2} + \omega^0 + \omega^{n/2} + \cdots + \omega^0 + \omega^{n/2} \\
&= (n/2)(1 + \omega^{n/2}).
\end{aligned}$$

Thus, $0 = 1 + \omega^{n/2}$. ■

An interesting corollary to the reflective property, which motivates its name, is the fact that if ω is a primitive nth root of unity and $n \geq 2$ is even, then

$$\omega^{k+n/2} = -\omega^k.$$

10.4.2 The Discrete Fourier Transform

Let us now return to the problem of evaluating a polynomial defined by a coefficient vector $\mathbf{a}$ as

$$p(x) = \sum_{i=0}^{n-1} a_i x^i,$$

for a carefully chosen set of input values. The technique we discuss in this section, called the ***Discrete Fourier Transform*** (DFT), is to evaluate $p(x)$ at the nth roots of unity, $\omega^0, \omega^1, \omega^2, \ldots, \omega^{n-1}$. Admittedly, this gives us just n input-output pairs, but we can "pad" our coefficient representation for p with 0's by setting $a_i = 0$, for $n \le i \le 2n-1$. This padding would let us view p as a degree-$(2n-1)$ polynomial, which would in turn let us use the primitive $(2n)$th roots of unity as inputs for a DFT for p. Thus, if we need more input-output values for p, let us assume that the coefficient vector for p has already been padded with as many 0's as necessary.

Formally, the Discrete Fourier Transform for the polynomial p represented by the coefficient vector $\mathbf{a}$ is defined as the vector $\mathbf{y}$ of values

$$y_j = p(\omega^j),$$

where ω is a primitive nth root of unity. That is,

$$y_j = \sum_{i=0}^{n-1} a_i \omega^{ij}.$$

In the language of matrices, we can alternatively think of the vector $\mathbf{y}$ of y_j values and the vector $\mathbf{a}$ as column vectors, and say that

$$\mathbf{y} = F\mathbf{a},$$

where F is an $n \times n$ matrix such that $F[i,j] = \omega^{ij}$.

The Inverse Discrete Fourier Transform

Interestingly, the matrix F has an inverse, F^{-1}, so that $F^{-1}(F(\mathbf{a})) = \mathbf{a}$ for all $\mathbf{a}$. The matrix F^{-1} allows us to define an ***inverse Discrete Fourier Transform***. If we are given a vector $\mathbf{y}$ of the values of a degree-$(n-1)$ polynomial p at the nth roots of unity, $\omega^0, \omega^1, \ldots, \omega^{n-1}$, then we can recover a coefficient vector for p by computing

$$\mathbf{a} = F^{-1}\mathbf{y}.$$

Moreover, the matrix F^{-1} has a simple form, in that $F^{-1}[i,j] = \omega^{-ij}/n$. Thus, we can recover the coefficient a_i as

$$a_i = \sum_{j=0}^{n-1} y_j \omega^{-ij}/n.$$

The following lemma justifies this claim, and is the basis of why we refer to F and F^{-1} as "transforms."

Lemma 10.28: *For any vector* $\mathbf{a}$, $F^{-1} \cdot F\mathbf{a} = \mathbf{a}$.

Proof: Let $A = F^{-1} \cdot F$. It is enough to show that $A[i,j] = 1$ if $i = j$, and $A[i,j] = 0$ if $i \neq j$. That is, $A = I$, where I is the ***identity matrix***. By the definitions of F^{-1}, F, and matrix multiplication,

$$A[i,j] = \frac{1}{n} \sum_{k=0}^{n-1} \omega^{-ik} \omega^{kj}.$$

If $i = j$, then this equation reduces to

$$A[i,i] = \frac{1}{n} \sum_{k=0}^{n-1} \omega^{0} = \frac{1}{n} \cdot n = 1.$$

So, consider the case when $i \neq j$, and let $m = j - i$. Then the ijth entry of A can be written as

$$A[i,j] = \frac{1}{n} \sum_{k=0}^{n-1} \omega^{mk},$$

where $-n < m < n$ and $m \neq 0$. By the cancellation property for a primitive nth root of unity, the right-hand side of the above equation reduces to 0; hence,

$$A[i,j] = 0,$$

for $i \neq j$. ■

Given the DFT and the inverse DFT, we can now define our approach to multiplying two polynomials p and q.

The Convolution Theorem

To use the discrete Fourier transform and its inverse to compute the convolution of two coefficient vectors, $\mathbf{a}$ and $\mathbf{b}$, we apply the following steps, which we illustrate in a schematic diagram, as shown in Figure 10.15.

1. Pad $\mathbf{a}$ and $\mathbf{b}$ each with n 0's and view them as column vectors to define
$$\mathbf{a}' = [a_0, a_1, \ldots, a_{n-1}, 0, 0, \ldots, 0]^T$$
$$\mathbf{b}' = [b_0, b_1, \ldots, b_{n-1}, 0, 0, \ldots, 0]^T.$$
2. Compute the Discrete Fourier Transforms $\mathbf{y} = F\mathbf{a}'$ and $\mathbf{z} = F\mathbf{b}'$.
3. Multiply the vectors $\mathbf{y}$ and $\mathbf{z}$ component-wise, defining the simple product $\mathbf{y} \cdot \mathbf{z} = F\mathbf{a}' \cdot F\mathbf{b}'$, where
$$(\mathbf{y} \cdot \mathbf{z})[i] = (F\mathbf{a}' \cdot F\mathbf{b}')[i] = F\mathbf{a}'[i] \cdot F\mathbf{b}'[i] = y_i \cdot z_i,$$
for $i = 1, 2, \ldots, 2n-1$.
4. Compute the inverse Discrete Fourier Transform of this simple product. That is, compute $\mathbf{c} = F^{-1}(F\mathbf{a}' \cdot F\mathbf{b}')$.

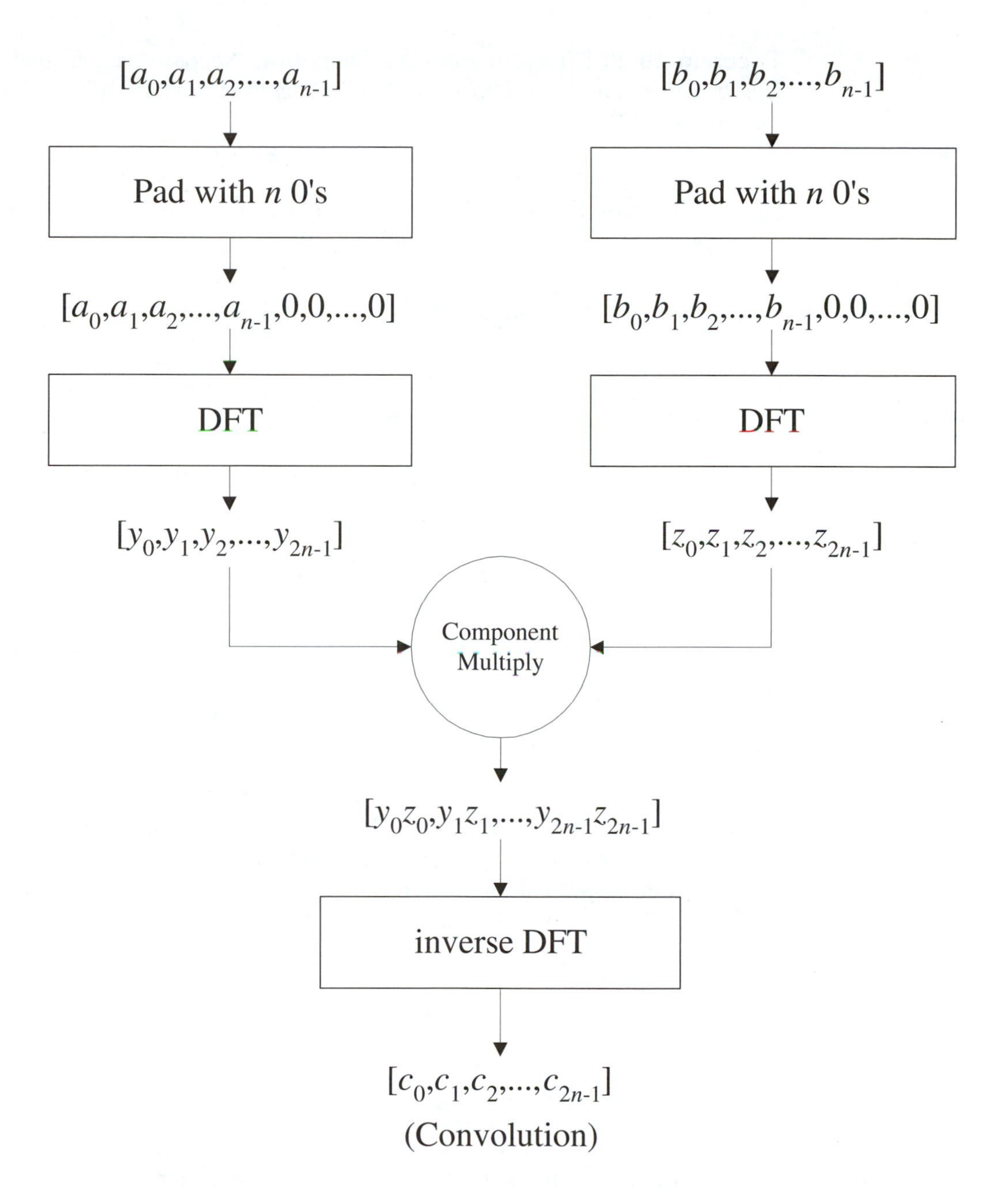

Figure 10.15: An illustration of the Convolution Theorem, to compute $\mathbf{c} = \mathbf{a} * \mathbf{b}$.

The reason the above approach works is because of the following.

Theorem 10.29 [The Convolution Theorem]: *Suppose we are given two n-length vectors $\mathbf{a}$ and $\mathbf{b}$ padded with 0's to $2n$-length vectors $\mathbf{a}'$ and $\mathbf{b}'$, respectively. Then $\mathbf{a} * \mathbf{b} = F^{-1}(F\mathbf{a}' \cdot F\mathbf{b}')$.*

Proof: We will show that $F(\mathbf{a} * \mathbf{b}) = F\mathbf{a}' \cdot F\mathbf{b}'$. So, consider $A = F\mathbf{a}' \cdot F\mathbf{b}'$. Since the second halves of $\mathbf{a}'$ and $\mathbf{b}'$ are padded with 0's,

$$\begin{aligned} A[i] &= \left(\sum_{j=0}^{n-1} a_j \omega^{ij}\right) \cdot \left(\sum_{k=0}^{n-1} b_k \omega^{ik}\right) \\ &= \sum_{j=0}^{n-1} \sum_{k=0}^{n-1} a_j b_k \omega^{i(j+k)}, \end{aligned}$$

for $i = 0, 1, \ldots, 2n-1$. Consider, next, $B = F(\mathbf{a} * \mathbf{b})$. By the definition of convolution and the DFT,

$$B[i] = \sum_{l=0}^{2n-1} \sum_{j=0}^{2n-1} a_j b_{l-j} \omega^{il}.$$

Substituting k for $l - j$, and changing the order of the summations, we get

$$B[i] = \sum_{j=0}^{2n-1} \sum_{k=-j}^{2n-1-j} a_j b_k \omega^{i(j+k)}.$$

Since b_k is undefined for $k < 0$, we can start the second summation above at $k = 0$. In addition, since $a_j = 0$ for $j > n-1$, we can lower the upper limit in the first summation above to $n-1$. But once we have made this substitution, note that the upper limit on the second summation above is always at least n. Thus, since $b_k = 0$ for $k > n-1$, we may lower the upper limit on the second summation to $n-1$. Therefore,

$$B[i] = \sum_{j=0}^{n-1} \sum_{k=0}^{n-1} a_j b_k \omega^{i(j+k)},$$

which proves the theorem. ■

We now have a method for computing the multiplication of two polynomials that involves computing two DFTs, doing a simple linear-time component-wise multiplication, and computing an inverse DFT. Thus, if we can find a fast algorithm for computing the DFT and its inverse, then we will have a fast algorithm for multiplying two polynomials. We describe such a fast algorithm, which is known as the "fast Fourier transform," next.

10.4.3 The Fast Fourier Transform Algorithm

The ***Fast Fourier Transform*** (FFT) Algorithm computes a Discrete Fourier Transform (DFT) of an n-length vector in $O(n \log n)$ time. In the FFT algorithm, we apply the divide-and-conquer approach to polynomial evaluation by observing that if n is even, we can divide a degree-$(n-1)$ polynomial

$$p(x) = a_0 + a_1 x + a_2 x^2 + \cdots + a_{n-1} x^{n-1}$$

into two degree-$(n/2-1)$ polynomials

$$\begin{aligned} p^{\text{even}}(x) &= a_0 + a_2 x + a_4 x^2 + \cdots + a_{n-2} x^{n/2-1} \\ p^{\text{odd}}(x) &= a_1 + a_3 x + a_5 x^2 + \cdots + a_{n-1} x^{n/2-1} \end{aligned}$$

and noting that we can combine these two polynomials into p using the equation

$$p(x) = p^{\text{even}}(x^2) + x p^{\text{odd}}(x^2).$$

The DFT evaluates $p(x)$ at each of the nth roots of unity, $\omega^0, \omega^1, \omega^2, \ldots, \omega^{n-1}$. Note that, by the reduction property, the values $(\omega^2)^0, \omega^2, (\omega^2)^2, (\omega^2)^3, \ldots, (\omega^2)^{n-1}$ are $(n/2)$th roots of unity. Thus, we can evaluate each of $p^{\text{even}}(x)$ and $p^{\text{odd}}(x)$ at these values, and we can reuse those same computations in evaluating $p(x)$. This observation is used in Algorithm 10.16 (FFT) to define the, which takes as input an n-length coefficient vector $\mathbf{a}$ and a primitive nth root of unity ω. For the sake of simplicity, we assume that n is a power of two.

Algorithm $\mathsf{FFT}(\mathbf{a}, \omega)$:

Input: An n-length coefficient vector $\mathbf{a} = [a_0, a_1, \ldots, a_{n-1}]$ and a primitive nth root of unity ω, where n is a power of 2

Output: A vector $\mathbf{y}$ of values of the polynomial for $\mathbf{a}$ at the nth roots of unity

```
if n = 1 then
   return y = a.
x ← ω^0          {x will store powers of ω, so initially x = 1.}
{Divide Step, which separates even and odd indices}
a^even ← [a_0, a_2, a_4, ..., a_{n-2}]
a^odd ← [a_1, a_3, a_5, ..., a_{n-1}]
{Recursive Calls, with ω^2 as (n/2)th root of unity, by the reduction property}
y^even ← FFT(a^even, ω^2)
y^odd ← FFT(a^odd, ω^2)
{Combine Step, using x = ω^i}
for i ← 0 to n/2 − 1 do
   y_i ← y_i^even + x · y_i^odd
   y_{i+n/2} ← y_i^even − x · y_i^odd          {Uses reflective property}
   x ← x · ω
return y
```

Algorithm 10.16: Recursive FFT algorithm.

The Correctness of the FFT Algorithm

The pseudo-code description in Algorithm 10.16 for the FFT algorithm is deceptively simple, so let us say a few words about why it works correctly. First, note that the base case of the recursion, when $n = 1$, correctly returns a vector $\mathbf{y}$ with the one entry, $y_0 = a_0$, which is the leading and only term in the polynomial $p(x)$ in this case.

In the general case, when $n \geq 2$, we separate $\mathbf{a}$ into its even and odd instances, $\mathbf{a}^{\text{even}}$ and $\mathbf{a}^{\text{odd}}$, and recursively call the FFT using ω^2 as the $(n/2)$th root of unity. As we have already mentioned, the reduction property of a primitive nth root of unity, allows us to use ω^2 in this way. Thus, we may inductively assume that

$$\begin{aligned} y_i^{\text{even}} &= p^{\text{even}}(\omega^{2i}) \\ y_i^{\text{odd}} &= p^{\text{odd}}(\omega^{2i}). \end{aligned}$$

Let us therefore consider the for-loop that combines the values from the recursive calls. Note that in the i iteration of the loop, $x = \omega^i$. Thus, when we perform the assignment statement

$$y_i \leftarrow y_i^{\text{even}} + x y_i^{\text{odd}},$$

we have just set

$$\begin{aligned} y_i &= p^{\text{even}}((\omega^2)^i) + \omega^i \cdot p^{\text{odd}}((\omega^2)^i) \\ &= p^{\text{even}}((\omega^i)^2) + \omega^i \cdot p^{\text{odd}}((\omega^i)^2) \\ &= p(\omega^i), \end{aligned}$$

and we do this for each index $i = 0, 1, \ldots, n/2 - 1$. Similarly, when we perform the assignment statement

$$y_{i+n/2} \leftarrow y_i^{\text{even}} - x y_i^{\text{odd}},$$

we have just set

$$y_{i+n/2} = p^{\text{even}}((\omega^2)^i) - \omega^i \cdot p^{\text{odd}}((\omega^2)^i).$$

Since ω^2 is a primitive $(n/2)$th root of unity, $(\omega^2)^{n/2} = 1$. Moreover, since ω is itself a primitive nth root of unity,

$$\omega^{i+n/2} = -\omega^i,$$

by the reflection property. Thus, we can rewrite the above identity for $y_{i+n/2}$ as

$$\begin{aligned} y_{i+n/2} &= p^{\text{even}}((\omega^2)^{i+(n/2)}) - \omega^i \cdot p^{\text{odd}}((\omega^2)^{i+(n/2)}) \\ &= p^{\text{even}}((\omega^{i+(n/2)})^2) + \omega^{i+n/2} \cdot p^{\text{odd}}((\omega^{i+(n/2)})^2) \\ &= p(\omega^{i+n/2}), \end{aligned}$$

and this will hold for each $i = 0, 1, \ldots, n/2 - 1$. Thus, the vector $\mathbf{y}$ returned by the FFT algorithm will store the values of $p(x)$ at each of the nth roots of unity.

Analyzing the FFT Algorithm

The FFT algorithm follows the divide-and-conquer paradigm, dividing the original problem of size n into two subproblems of size $n/2$, which are solved recursively. We assume that each arithmetic operation performed by by algorithms takes $O(1)$ time. The divide step as well as the combine step for merging the recursive solutions, each take $O(n)$ time. Thus, we can characterize the running time $T(n)$ of the FFT algorithm using the recurrence equation

$$T(n) = 2T(n/2) + bn,$$

for some constant $b > 0$. By the Master Theorem (5.6), $T(n)$ is $O(n \log n)$. Therefore, we can summarize our discussion as follows.

Theorem 10.30: *Given an n-length coefficient vector* **a** *defining a polynomial $p(x)$, and a primitive nth root of unity, ω, the* FFT *algorithm evaluates $p(x)$ at each of the nth roots of unity, ω^i, for $i = 0, 1, \ldots, n-1$, in $O(n \log n)$ time.*

There is also an inverse FFT algorithm, which computes the inverse DFT in $O(n \log n)$ time. The details of this algorithm are similar to those for the FFT algorithm and are left as an exercise (R-10.14). Combining these two algorithms in our approach to multiplying two polynomials $p(x)$ and $q(x)$, given their n-length coefficient vectors, we have an algorithm for computing this product in $O(n \log n)$ time.

By the way, this approach for using the FFT algorithm and its inverse to compute the product of two polynomials can be extended to the problem of computing the product of two large integers. We discuss this method next.

10.4.4 Multiplying Big Integers

Let us revisit the problem studied in Section 5.2.2. Namely, suppose we are given two big integers I and J that use at most N bits each, and we are interested in computing $I \cdot J$. The main idea of the method we describe in this section is to use the FFT algorithm to compute this product. Of course, a major challenge in utilizing the FFT algorithmic design pattern in this way is to define integer arithmetic so that it gives rise to primitive roots of unity (see, for example, Exercise C-10.8).

The algorithm we describe here assumes that we can break I and J up into words of $O(\log N)$ bits each, such that arithmetic on each word can be done using built-in operations in our computer model in constant time. This is a reasonable assumption, since it takes $\lceil \log N \rceil$ bits just to represent the number N itself. The number system we use for the FFT in this case is to perform all arithmetic modulo p, for a suitably chosen prime number p, which itself can be represented in a single word of at most $O(\log N)$ bits. The specific prime modulus p we choose is to find small integers $c \geq 1$ and $n \geq 1$, such that $p = cn + 1$ is prime and $N / \lfloor \log p \rfloor \leq n/2$. For the sake of the simplicity of our description, let us additionally assume that n is a power of two.

In general, we would expect c in the above definition of p to be $O(\log n)$, since a fundamental theorem from number theory states that a random odd number in the range $[1,n]$ is prime with probability $\Omega(1/\log n)$. That is, we expect p to be represented with $O(\log N)$ bits. Given this prime number p, our intent is to perform all arithmetic in the FFT modulo p. Since we are performing this arithmetic on the words of a large vector of integers, we also want the size of each word to be less than half of that used to represent p, so we can represent the product of any two words without having the modulo-p arithmetic "wipe out" any pairwise products of words. For example, the following values of p work well for modern computers:

- If $n \leq 2^{10} = 1024$, then we choose $p = 25 \cdot 2^{10} + 1 = 25601$ as our prime modulus, which can be represented using a 15-bit word. Moreover, since $p > 2^{14}$ in this case, such a choice allows us to multiply numbers whose representations are as large as 2^{10} words of 7 bits each.
- If $n \leq 2^{27} = 134217728$, then we choose $p = 15 \cdot 2^{27} + 1 = 2013265921$ as our prime modulus, which uses a 31-bit word. Moreover, since $p > 2^{30}$ in this case, we can multiply numbers whose representations are as large as 2^{27} words of 15 bits each, or 240MB.

Given a prime $p = cn + 1$, for reasonably small $c \geq 1$, and n defined so that $N/\lfloor \log p \rfloor$ is $O(n)$, we define $m = \lfloor (\log p)/2 \rfloor$. We view I and J respectively as being vectors $\mathbf{a}$ and $\mathbf{b}$ of words that use m bits each, extended with as many 0's as needed to make $\mathbf{a}$ and $\mathbf{b}$ both have length n, with at least the last half of their higher-order terms being 0. We can write I and J as

$$
\begin{aligned}
I &= \sum_{i=0}^{n-1} a_i 2^{mi} \\
J &= \sum_{i=0}^{n-1} b_i 2^{mi}.
\end{aligned}
$$

Moreover, we choose n so that the first $n/2$ of the a_i's and b_i's are nonzero at most. Thus, we can represent the product $K = I \cdot J$, as

$$
K = \sum_{i=0}^{n-1} c_i 2^{mi}.
$$

Once we have a prime number $p = cn + 1$, for a reasonably small integer $c \geq 1$, we find an integer x that is a generator of the group Z_p^* (see Section 10.1). That is, we find x such that $x^i \bmod p$ is different for $i = 0, 1, \ldots, p-1$. Given such a generator, x, then we can use $\omega = x^c \bmod p$ as a primitive nth root of unity (assuming all multiplication and addition is done modulo p). That is, each of $(x^c)^i \bmod p$ are distinct for $i = 0, 1, 2, \ldots, n-1$, but, by Fermat's Little Theorem (Theorem 10.8),

$$
\begin{aligned}
(x^c)^n \bmod p &= x^{cn} \bmod p \\
&= x^{p-1} \bmod p \\
&= 1.
\end{aligned}
$$

In order to compute the product of the big N-bit integers I and J, recall that view I and J, respectively, as extended n-length vectors $\mathbf{a}$ and $\mathbf{b}$ of words having m bits each (with at least the $n/2$ higher-order words being all 0's). Note that, since $m = \lfloor \log p/2 \rfloor$, we have that $2^m < p$. Thus, each of the terms in $\mathbf{a}$ and $\mathbf{b}$ is already reduced modulo p without us having to do any additional work, and any product of two of these terms is also reduced modulo p.

To compute $K = I \cdot J$, we then apply the Convolution Theorem, using the FFT and inverse FFT algorithms, to compute the convolution $\mathbf{c}$ of $\mathbf{a}$ and $\mathbf{b}$. In this computation we use ω, as defined above, as the primitive nth root of unity, and we perform all the internal arithmetic (including the component-wise products of the transformed versions of $\mathbf{a}$ and $\mathbf{b}$) modulo p.

The terms in the convolution $\mathbf{c}$ are all less than p, but in order to build a representative of $K = I \cdot J$, we actually need each term to be represented using exactly m bits. Thus, after we have the convolution $\mathbf{c}$, we must compute the product K as

$$K = \sum_{i=0}^{n-1} c_i 2^{mi}.$$

This final computation is not as difficult as it looks, however, since multiplying by a power of two in binary is just a shifting operation. Moreover, p is $O(2^{m+1})$, so the above summation just involves propagating some groups of carry bits from one term to the next. Thus, this final construction of a binary representation of K as a vector of words of m bits each can be done in $O(n)$ time. Since applying the Convolution Theorem as described above takes $O(n \log n)$ time, this gives us the following.

Theorem 10.31: *Given two N-bit integers I and J, we can compute the product $K = I \cdot J$ in $O(N)$ time, assuming that arithmetic involving words of size $O(\log N)$ can be done in constant time.*

Proof: The number n is chosen so that it is $O(N/\log N)$. Thus a running time of $O(n \log n)$ is $O(N)$, assuming that arithmetic operations involving words of size $O(\log N)$ can be done in constant time. ■

In some cases, we cannot assume that arithmetic involving $O(\log n)$-size words can be done in constant time, but instead, we must pay constant time for every bit operation. In this model it is still possible to use the FFT to multiply two N-bit integers, but the details are somewhat more complicated and the running time increases to $O(N \log N \log \log N)$.

In Section 10.5, we study some important implementation issues related to the FFT algorithm, including an experimental analysis of how well it performs in practice.

10.5 Java Example: FFT

There are a number of interesting implementation issues related to the FFT algorithm, which we discuss in this section. We begin with the description of a big integer class that performs multiplication using the recursive version of the FFT, as described above in pseudo-code in Algorithm 10.16. We show the declaration of this class and its important instance variables and constants in Code Fragment 10.17. A significant detail in these declarations includes our defining the primitive nth root of unity, OMEGA. Our choice of 31^{15} derives from the fact that 31 is a generator for Z_p^* for the prime number $15 \cdot 2^{27} + 1$. We know 31 is a generator for this Z_p^*, because of a theorem from number theory. This theorem states that an integer x is a generator of Z_p^* if and only if $x^{\phi(p)/q} \bmod p$ is not equal to 1 for any prime divisor q of $\phi(p)$, where $\phi(p)$ is the Euler totient function defined in Section 10.1. For our particular p, $\phi(p) = 15 \cdot 2^{27}$; hence, the only prime divisors q we need to consider are 2, 3, and 5.

```
import java.lang.*;
import java.math.*;
import java.util.*;

public class BigInt {
  protected int signum=0;                    // neg = -1, 0 = 0, pos = 1
  protected int[] mag;                       // magnitude in little-endian format
  public final static int MAXN=134217728;   // Maximum value for n
  public final static int ENTRYSIZE=15;      // Bits per entry in mag
  protected final static long P=2013265921; // The prime 15*2^{27}+1
  protected final static int OMEGA=440564289; // Root of unity 31^{15} mod P
  protected final static int TWOINV=1006632961; // 2^{-1} mod P
```

Code Fragment 10.17: Declarations and instance variables for a big integer class that supports multiplication using the FFT algorithm.

A Recursive FFT Implementation

We show the multiplication method of our big integer class, BigInt, in Code Fragment 10.18, and, in Code Fragment 10.19, we show our implementation of the recursive FFT algorithm. Note that we use a variable, prod, to store the product that is used in the subsequent two expressions. By factoring out this common subexpression we can avoid performing this repeated computation twice. In addition, note that all modular arithmetic is performed as **long** operations. This requirement is due to the fact that P uses 31 bits, so that we may need to perform additions and subtractions that would overflow a standard-size integer. Instead, we perform all arithmetic as **long** operations and then store the result back to an **int**.

```
public BigInt multiply(BigInt val) {
  int n = makePowerOfTwo(Math.max(mag.length,val.mag.length))*2;
  int signResult = signum * val.signum;
  int[] A = padWithZeros(mag,n);  // copies mag into A padded w/ 0's
  int[] B = padWithZeros(val.mag,n); // copies val.mag into B padded w/ 0's
  int[] root = rootsOfUnity(n);       // creates all n roots of unity
  int[] C = new int[n];               // result array for A*B
  int[] AF = new int[n];              // result array for FFT of A
  int[] BF = new int[n];              // result array for FFT of B
  FFT(A,root,n,0,AF);
  FFT(B,root,n,0,BF);
  for (int i=0; i<n; i++)
    AF[i] = (int)(((long)AF[i]*(long)BF[i]) % P);  // Component multiply
  reverseRoots(root);                 // Reverse roots to create inverse roots
  inverseFFT(AF,root,n,0,C);          // Leaves inverse FFT result in C
  propagateCarries(C);                // Convert C to right no. bits per entry
  return new BigInt(signResult,C);
  }
```

Code Fragment 10.18: The multiplication method for a big integer class that supports multiplication using a recursive FFT algorithm.

```
public static void FFT(int[] A, int[] root, int n, int base, int[] Y) {
  int prod;
  if (n==1) {
    Y[base] = A[base];
    return;
    }
  inverseShuffle(A,n,base);     // inverse shuffle to separate evens and odds
  FFT(A,root,n/2,base,Y);      // results in Y[base] to Y[base+n/2-1]
  FFT(A,root,n/2,base+n/2,Y); // results in Y[base+n/2] to Y[base+n-1]
  int j = A.length/n;
  for (int i=0; i<n/2; i++) {
    prod = (int)(((long)root[i*j]*Y[base+n/2+i]) % P);
    Y[base+n/2+i] = (int)(((long)Y[base+i] + P - prod) % P);
    Y[base+i] = (int)(((long)Y[base+i] + prod) % P);
    }
}
public static void inverseFFT(int[] A, int[] root, int n, int base, int[] Y) {
  int inverseN = modInverse(n);      // n^{-1}
  FFT(A,root,n,base,Y);
  for (int i=0; i<n; i++)
    Y[i] = (int)(((long)Y[i]*inverseN) % P);
}
```

Code Fragment 10.19: A recursive implementation of the FFT algorithm.

Avoiding Repeated Array Allocation

The pseudo-code for the recursive FFT algorithm calls for the allocation of several new arrays, including $\mathbf{a}^{\text{even}}$, $\mathbf{a}^{\text{odd}}$, $\mathbf{y}^{\text{even}}$, $\mathbf{y}^{\text{odd}}$, and $\mathbf{y}$. Allocating all of these arrays with each recursive call could prove to be a costly amount of extra work. If it can be avoided, saving this additional allocation of arrays could significantly improve the constant factors in the $O(n \log n)$ time (or $O(N)$ time) performance of the FFT algorithm.

Fortunately, the structure of FFT allows us to avoid this repeated array allocation. Instead of allocating many arrays, we can use a single array, A, for the input coefficients and use a single array, Y, for the answers. The main idea that allows for this usage is that we can think of the arrays A and Y as partitioned into subarrays, each one associated with a different recursive call. We can identify these subarrays using just two variables, base, which identifies the base address of the subarray, and n, which identifies the size of the subarray. Thus, we can avoid the overhead associated with allocating lots of small arrays with each recursive call.

The Inverse Shuffle

Having decided that we will not allocate new arrays during the FFT recursive calls, we must deal with the fact that the FFT algorithm involves performing separate computations on even and odd indices of the input array. In the pseudo-code of Algorithm 10.16, we use new arrays $\mathbf{a}^{\text{even}}$ and $\mathbf{a}^{\text{odd}}$, but now we must use subarrays in A for these vectors. Our solution for this memory management problem is to take the current n-cell subarray in A, and divide it into two subarrays of size $n/2$. One of the subarrays will have the same base as A, while the other has base $\text{base} + n/2$. We move the elements at even indices in A to the lower half and we move elements at odd indices in A to the upper half. In doing so, we define an interesting permutation known as the ***inverse shuffle***. This permutation gets its name from its resemblance to the inverse of the permutation we would get by cutting the array A in half and shuffling it perfectly as if it were a deck of cards. (See Figure 10.20.)

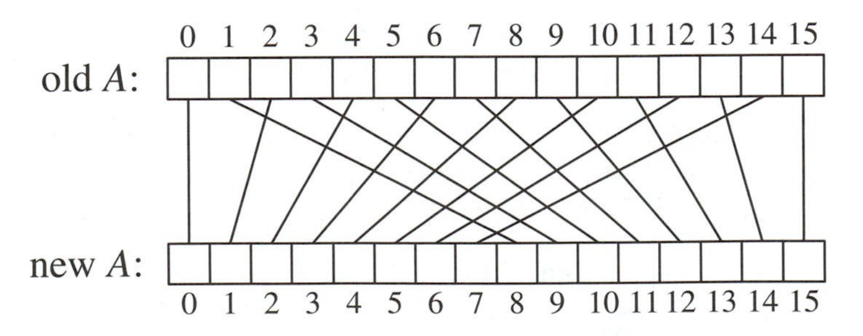

Figure 10.20: An illustration of the inverse shuffle permutation.

Precomputing Roots of Unity and Other Optimizations

There are a number of additional optimizations that we utilized in our FFT implementation. In Code Fragment 10.21, we show some of the important support methods for our implementation, including the computation of the inverse n^{-1}, the inverse shuffle permutation, the precomputation of all the nth roots of unity, propagation of the carries after the convolution has been computed modulo p.

```
protected static int modInverse(int n) { // assumes n is power of two
  int result = 1;
  for (long twoPower = 1; twoPower < n; twoPower *= 2)
    result = (int)(((long)result*TWOINV) % P);
  return result;
}
protected static void inverseShuffle(int[] A, int n, int base) {
  int shift;
  int[] sp = new int[n];
  for (int i=0; i<n/2; i++) { // Unshuffle A into the scratch space
    shift = base + 2*i;
    sp[i] = A[shift];          // an even index
    sp[i+n/2] = A[shift+1];    // an odd index
    }
  for (int i=0; i<n; i++)
    A[base+i] = sp[i];         // copy back to A
}
protected static int[] rootsOfUnity(int n) { //assumes n is power of 2
  int t = MAXN;
  int nthroot = OMEGA;
  for (int t = MAXN; t>n; t /= 2)  // Find prim. nth root of unity
    nthroot = (int)(((long)nthroot*nthroot) % P);
  int[] roots = new int[n];
  int r = 1;              // r will run through all nth roots of unity
  for (int i=0; i<n; i++) {
    roots[i] = r;
    r = (int)(((long)r*nthroot) % P);
    }
  return roots;
}
protected static void propagateCarries(int[] A) {
  int i, carry;
  carry = 0;
  for (i=0; i<A.length; i++) {
    A[i] = A[i] + carry;
    carry = A[i] >>> ENTRYSIZE;
    A[i] = A[i] - (carry << ENTRYSIZE);
    }
  }
```

Code Fragment 10.21: Support methods for a recursive FFT.

An Iterative FFT Implementation

There are additional time improvements that can be made in the FFT algorithm, which involve replacing the recursive version of the algorithm with an iterative version. Our iterative FFT is a part of an alternate big integer class, called FastInt. The multiplication method for this class is shown in Code Fragment 10.22.

```
public FastInt multiply(FastInt val) {
  int n = makePowerOfTwo(Math.max(mag.length,val.mag.length))*2;
  logN = logBaseTwo(n);                  // Log of n base 2
  reverse = reverseArray(n,logN);        // initialize reversal lookup table
  int signResult = signum * val.signum;
  int[] A = padWithZeros(mag,n);  // copies mag into A padded w/ 0's
  int[] B = padWithZeros(val.mag,n); // copies val.mag into B padded w/ 0's
  int[] root = rootsOfUnity(n);          // creates all n roots of unity
  FFT(A,root,n);                         // Leaves FFT result in A
  FFT(B,root,n);                         // Leaves FFT result in B
  for (int i=0; i<n; i++)
    A[i] = (int) (((long)A[i]*B[i]) % P);     // Component-wise multiply
  reverseRoots(root);                    // Reverse roots to create inverse roots
  inverseFFT(A,root,n);                  // Leaves inverse FFT result in A
  propagateCarries(A);                   // Convert A to right no. of bits/entry
  return new FastInt(signResult,A);
}
```

Code Fragment 10.22: The multiplication method for an iterative FFT.

Computing the FFT in Place

From Code Fragment 10.22, we already can see a difference between this and the multiply method for the recursive version of the FFT. Namely, we are now performing the FFT in-place. That is, the array A is being used for both the input and output values. This saves us the extra work of copying between output and input arrays. In addition, we compute the logarithm of n, base two, and store this in a static variable, as this logarithm is used repeatedly in calls to the iterative FFT algorithm.

Avoiding Recursion

The main challenge in avoiding recursion in an in-place version of the FFT algorithm is that we have to figure out a way of performing all the inverse shuffles in the input array A. Rather than performing each inverse shuffle with each iteration, we instead perform all the inverse shuffles in advance, assuming that n, the size of the input array, is a power of two.

In order to figure out the net effect of the permutation we would get by repeated and recursive inverse shuffle operations, let us consider how the inverse shuffles move data around with each recursive call. In the first recursive call, of course, we perform an inverse shuffle on the entire array A. Note how this permutation operates at the bit level of the indices in A. It brings all elements at addresses that have a 0 as their least significant bit to the bottom half of A. Likewise, it brings all elements at addresses that have a 1 as their least significant bit to the top half of A. That is, if an element starts out at an address with b as its least significant bit, then it ends up at an address with b as its most significant bit. The least significant bit in an address is the determiner of which half of A an element winds up in. In the next level of recursion, we repeat the inverse shuffle on each half of A. Viewed again at the bit level, for $b = 0,1$, these recursive inverse shuffles take elements originally at addresses with b as their second least significant bit, and move them to addresses that have b as their second most significant bit. Likewise, for $b = 0,1$, the ith levels of recursion move elements originally at address with b as their ith least significant bit, to addresses with b as their ith most significant bit. Thus, if an element starts out at an address with binary representation $[b_{l-1}\dots b_2b_1b_0]$, then it ends up at an address with binary representation $[b_0b_1b_2\dots b_{l-1}]$, where $l = \log_2 n$. That is, we can perform all the inverse shuffles in advance just by moving elements in A to the address that is the bit reversal of their starting address in A. To perform this permutation, we build a permutation array, reverse, in the multiply method, and then use this in the bitReversal method called inside the FFT method to permute the elements in the input array A according to this permutation. The resulting iterative version of the FFT algorithm is shown in Code Fragment 10.23.

```
public static void FFT(int[] A, int[] root, int n) {
  int prod,term,index;        // Values for common subexpressions
  int subSize = 1;            // Subproblem size
  bitReverse(A,logN);         // Permute A by bit reversal table
  for (int lev=1; lev<=logN; lev++) {
    subSize *= 2;             // Double the subproblem size.
    for (int base=0; base<n-1; base += subSize) { // Iterate subproblems
      int j = subSize/2;
      int rootIndex = A.length/subSize;
      for (int i=0; i<j; i++) {
        index = base + i;
        prod = (int) (((long)root[i*rootIndex]*A[index+j]) % P);
        term = A[index];
        A[index+j] = (int) (((long)term + P - prod) % P);
        A[index] = (int) (((long)term + prod) % P);
      }
    }
  }
}
public static void inverseFFT(int[] A, int[] root, int n) {
  int inverseN = modInverse(n);     // n^{-1}
  FFT(A,root,n);
  for (int i=0; i<n; i++)
    A[i] = (int) (((long)A[i]*inverseN) % P);
}
```

Code Fragment 10.23: An iterative implementation of the FFT algorithm.

```
protected static void bitReverse(int[] A, int logN) {
  int[] temp = new int[A.length];
  for (int i=0; i<A.length; i++)
    temp[reverse[i]] = A[i];
  for (int i=0; i<A.length; i++)
    A[i] = temp[i];
}
protected static int[] reverseArray(int n, int logN) {
  int[] result = new int[n];
  for (int i=0; i<n; i++)
    result[i] = reverse(i,logN);
  return result;
}
protected static int reverse(int N, int logN) {
  int bit=0;
  int result=0;
  for (int i=0; i<logN; i++) {
    bit = N & 1;
    result = (result << 1) + bit;
    N = N >>> 1;
    }
  return result;
  }
```

Code Fragment 10.24: Support methods for an iterative implementation of the FFT algorithm. Other support methods are like those in the recursive implementation.

We show the additional support methods used by the iterative FFT algorithm in Code Fragment 10.24. All of these support methods deal with the operation of computing the reverse permutation table and then using it to perform the bit-reversal permutation on A.

Experimental Results

Of course, the goal of using the FFT algorithm for big integer multiplication is to perform this operation in $O(n\log n)$ time, on integers represented as n-word vectors, as opposed to the standard $O(n^2)$ multiplication algorithm taught in grade schools. In addition, we designed an iterative version of the FFT algorithm with the goal of improving the constant factors in the running time of this multiplication method. To test these goals in practice, we designed a simple experiment.

In this experiment, we randomly generated ten big integers that consisted of 2^s words of 15 bits each, for $s = 7, 8, \ldots, 16$, and we multiplied them in consecutive pairs, producing nine products for each value of s. We timed the execution time for performing these products, and compared these times to those for multiplying integers represented with the same number of bits in a standard implementation of the Java BigInteger class. The results of this experiment are shown in Figure 10.25. The running times are shown in milliseconds. The experiment was performed in the Sun Java virtual machine for JDK 1.2 on a Sun Ultra5 with a 360MHz processor and 128MB of memory.

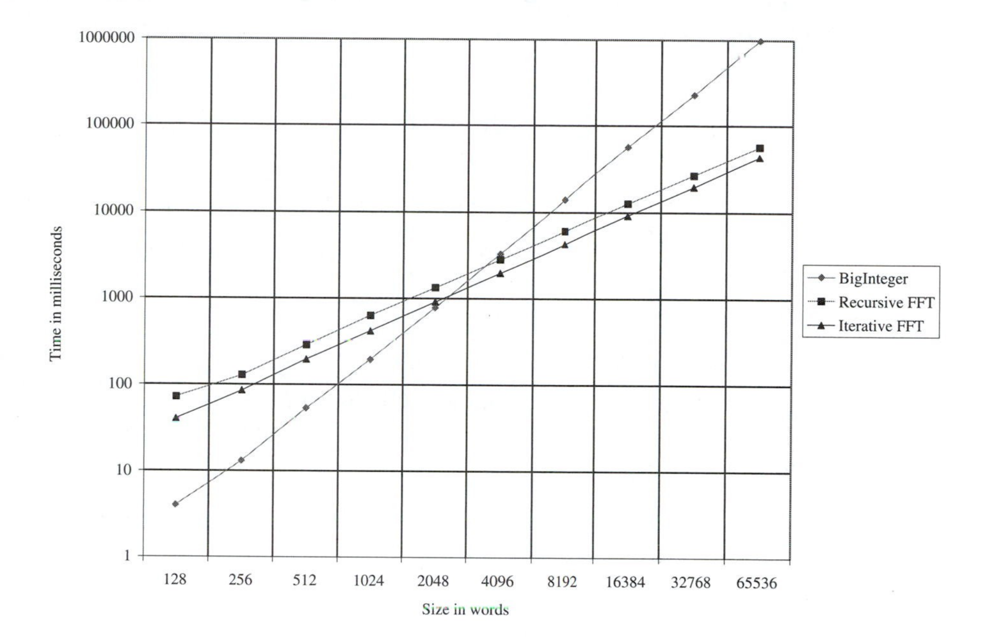

Figure 10.25: Running times for integer multiplication. The chart shows running times for multiplying integers made up of various numbers of words of 15 bits each (for the FFT), or the equivalent size for a standard BigInteger implementation. Note that the scales are logarithmic for both the x- and y-axes.

Note that we display the results of the experiment on a log-log scale. This choice corresponds to the power test (Section 1.6.2) and allows us to see the relative costs of the different implementations much clearer than we would see on a standard linear scale. Since $\log n^c = c \log n$, the slope of a line on a log-log scale correlates exactly with the exponent of a polynomial in a standard linear scale. Likewise the height of a line on a log-log scale corresponds to a constant of proportionality. The chart in Figure 10.25 displays time using base-ten on the y-axis and base-two on the x-axis. Using the fact that $\log_2 10$ is approximately 3.322, we indeed see that the running time of the standard multiplication algorithm is $\Theta(n^2)$, whereas the running time of the FFT algorithms is close to linear. Likewise, we note that the constant factor in the iterative FFT algorithm implementation is about 70% of the constant for the recursive FFT algorithm implementation. Also note the significant trade-off that exists between the FFT-based methods and the standard multiplication algorithm. At the small end of the scale, the FFT-based methods are ten times slower than the standard algorithm, but at the high end of the scale they are more than ten times faster!

10.6 Exercises

Reinforcement

R-10.1 Prove Theorem 10.1.

R-10.2 Show the execution of method EuclidGCD(14300, 5915) by constructing a table similar to Table 10.2.

R-10.3 Write a nonrecursive version of Algorithm EuclidGCD.

R-10.4 Show the execution of method EuclidBinaryGCD(14300, 5915) by constructing a table similar to Table 10.2.

R-10.5 Show the existence of additive inverses in Z_p, that is, prove that for each $x \in Z_p$, there is a $y \in Z_p$, such that $x + y \bmod p = 0$.

R-10.6 Construct the multiplication table of the elements of Z_{11}, where the element in row i and column j $(0 \le i, j \le 10)$ is given by $i \cdot j \bmod 11$.

R-10.7 Prove Corollary 10.7.

R-10.8 Give an alternative proof of Theorem 10.6 and Corollary 10.7 that does not use Theorem 10.3.

R-10.9 Show the execution of method FastExponentiation(5, 12, 13) by constructing a table similar to Table 10.8.

R-10.10 Write a nonrecursive version of Algorithm ExtendedEuclidGCD.

R-10.11 Extend Table 10.10 with two rows giving the values of ia and jb at each step of the algorithm and verify that $ia + jb = 1$.

R-10.12 Show the execution of method ExtendedEuclidGCD(412, 113) by constructing a table similar to Table 10.10.

R-10.13 Compute the multiplicative inverses of the numbers 113, 114, and 127 in Z_{299}.

R-10.14 Describe the inverse FFT algorithm, which computes the inverse DFT in $O(n \log n)$ time. That is, show how to reverse the roles of $\mathbf{a}$ and $\mathbf{y}$ and change the assignments so that, for each output index, we have

$$a_i = \frac{1}{n} \sum_{j=1}^{n-1} y_j \omega^{-ij}.$$

R-10.15 Prove a more general form of the reduction property of primitive roots of unity. Namely, show that, for any integer $c > 0$, if ω is a primitive (cn)th root of unity, then ω^c is a primitive nth root of unity.

R-10.16 Write in the form $a + b\mathbf{i}$ the complex nth roots of unity for $n = 4$ and $n = 8$.

R-10.17 What is the bit-reversal permutation, reverse, for $n = 16$?

R-10.18 Use the FFT and inverse FFT to compute the convolution of $\mathbf{a} = [1, 2, 3, 4]$ and $\mathbf{b} = [4, 3, 2, 1]$. Show the output of each component as in Figure 10.15.

R-10.19 Use the convolution theorem to compute the product of the polynomials $p(x) = 3x^2 + 4x + 2$ and $q(x) = 2x^3 + 3x^2 + 5x + 3$.

R-10.20 Compute the discrete Fourier transform of the vector $[5,4,3,2]$ using arithmetic modulo $17 = 2^4 + 1$. Use the fact that 5 is a generator of Z_{17}^*.

R-10.21 Construct a table showing an example of the RSA cryptosystem with parameters $p = 17$, $q = 19$, and $e = 5$. The table should have two rows, one for the plaintext M and the other for the ciphertext C. The columns should correspond to integer values in the range $[10,20]$ for M.

Creativity

C-10.1 Justify the correctness of the binary Euclid's algorithm (Algorithm 10.3) and analyze its running time.

C-10.2 Let p be an odd prime.

a. Show that Z_p has exactly $(p-1)/2$ quadratic residues.
b. Show that
$$\left(\frac{a}{b}\right) \equiv a^{\frac{p-1}{2}} \pmod{p}.$$
c. Give a randomized algorithm for finding a quadratic residue of Z_p in expected $O(1)$ time.
d. Discuss the relationship between quadratic residues and the quadratic probing technique for collision resolution in hash tables (see Section 2.5.5 and Exercise C-2.35).

C-10.3 Let p be a prime. Give an efficient alternative algorithm for computing the multiplicative inverse of an element of Z_p that is not based on the extended Euclid's algorithm. What is the running time of your algorithm?

C-10.4 Show how to modify Algorithm ExtendedEuclidGCD to compute the multiplicative inverse of an element in Z_n using arithmetic operations on operands with at most $2\lceil \log_2 n \rceil$ bits.

C-10.5 Prove the correctness of method Jacobi(a,b) (Algorithm 10.12) for computing the Jacobi symbol. Also, show that this method executes $O(\log \max(a,b)$ arithmetic operations.

C-10.6 Give a pseudo-code description of the compositeness witness function of the Rabin-Miller algorithm.

C-10.7 Describe a divide-and-conquer algorithm, not based on the FFT, for multiplying two degree-n polynomials with integer coefficients in $O(n^{\log_2 3})$ time, assuming that elementary arithmetic operations on any two integers run in constant time.

C-10.8 Prove that $\omega = 2^{4b/m}$ is a primitive mth root of unity when multiplication is taken modulo $(2^{2b} + 1)$, for any integer $b > 0$.

C-10.9 Given degree-n polynomials $p(x)$ and $q(x)$, describe an $O(n \log n)$-time method for multiplying the derivative of $p(x)$ by the derivative of $q(x)$.

C-10.10 Describe a version of the FFT that works when n is a power of 3 by dividing the input vector into three subvectors, recursing on each one, and then merging the subproblem solutions. Derive a recurrence equation for the running time of this algorithm and solve this recurrence using the Master Theorem.

C-10.11 Suppose you are given a set of real numbers $X = \{x_0, x_1, \ldots, x_{n-1}\}$. Note that, by the Interpolation Theorem for Polynomials, there is a unique degree-$(n-1)$ polynomial $p(x)$, such that $p(x_i) = 0$ for $i = 0, 1, \ldots, n-1$. Design a divide-and-conquer algorithm that can construct a coefficient representation of this $p(x)$ in $O(n \log^2 n)$ time.

Projects

P-10.1 Write a class that contains methods for modular exponentiation and computing modular inverses.

P-10.2 Implement the randomized primality testing algorithms by Rabin-Miller and by Solovay-Strassen. Test the results of these algorithms on randomly generated 32-bit integers using the confidence parameters 7, 10, and 20, respectively.

P-10.3 Implement a simplified RSA cryptosystem for integer messages with a Java class that provides methods for encrypting, decrypting, signing, and verifying a signature.

P-10.4 Implement a simplified El Gamal cryptosystem for integer messages with a Java class that provides methods for encrypting, decrypting, signing, and verifying a signature.

Chapter Notes

An introduction to number theory is provided in books by Koblitz [123] and Kranakis [125]. The classic textbook on numerical algorithms is the second volume of Knuth's series on ***The Art of Computer Programming*** [121]. Algorithms for number theoretic problems are also presented in the books by Bressoud and Wagon [40] and by Bach and Shallit [20]. The Solovay-Strassen randomized primality testing algorithm appears in [190, 191]. The Rabin-Miller algorithm is presented in [171].

The book by Schneier [180] describes cryptographic protocols and algorithms in detail. Applications of cryptography to network security are covered in the book by Stallings [192]. The RSA cryptosystem is named after the initials of its inventors, Rivest, Shamir, and Adleman [173]. The El Gamal cryptosystem is named after its inventor [75]. The hash tree structure was introduced by Merkle [153, 154]. The one-way ***accumulator*** function is introduced in [27, 179].

The Fast Fourier Transform (FFT) appears in a paper by Cooley and Tukey [54]. It is also discussed in books by Aho, Hopcroft, and Ullman [7], Baase [19], Cormen, Leiserson, and Rivest [55], Sedgewick [182, 183], and Yap [213], all of which were influential in the discussion given above. In particular, the fast integer multiplication algorithm implementation given above is fashioned after the QuickMul algorithm of Yap and Li. For information on additional applications of the FFT, the interested reader is referred to books by Brigham [41] and Elliott and Rao [66], and the chapter by Emiris and Pan [67]. Sections 10.1 and 10.2 are based in part on a section of an unpublished manuscript of Achter and Tamassia [1].

Chapter

11 Network Algorithms

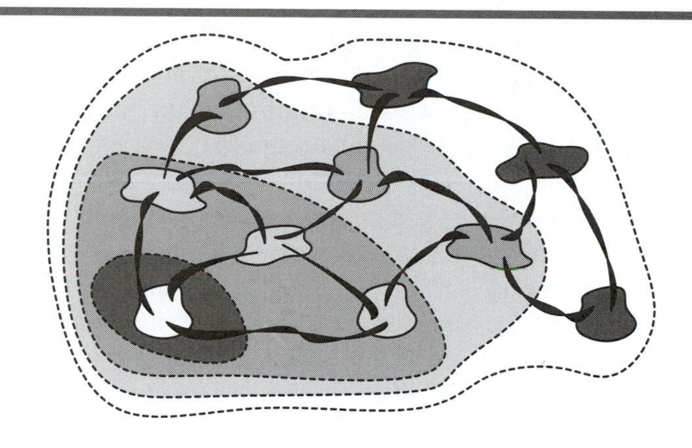

Contents

11.1 Complexity Measures and Models 513

11.1.1 The Networking Protocol Stack 513

11.1.2 The Message-Passing Model 514

11.1.3 Complexity Measures for Network Algorithms 516

11.2 Fundamental Distributed Algorithms 517

11.2.1 Leader Election in a Ring 517

11.2.2 Leader Election in a Tree 521

11.2.3 Breadth-First Search 523

11.2.4 Minimum Spanning Trees 528

11.3 Broadcast and Unicast Routing 530

11.3.1 The Flooding Algorithm for Broadcast Routing . . . 530

11.3.2 The Distance Vector Algorithm for Unicast Routing . 532

11.3.3 The Link-State Algorithm for Unicast Routing 534

11.4 Multicast Routing 535

11.4.1 Reverse Path Forwarding 535

11.4.2 Center-Based Trees 537

11.4.3 Steiner Trees 538

11.5 Exercises 541

Network algorithms are written to execute on a computer network, and these algorithms include those that specify how specialized computers, called ***routers***, send data packets through the network. The computer network is modeled as a graph, with the vertices representing processors, or routers, and the edges representing communications channels. (See Figure 11.1.) Algorithms that run on such networks are unconventional, because the inputs to such algorithms are typically spread throughout the network and the execution of such algorithms is distributed across the processors in the network.

We begin our study of network algorithms, then, by considering several fundamental distributed algorithms. These algorithms address some basic issues that are encountered in network algorithms, including leader election and building spanning trees. We examine each algorithm in both a synchronous setting, where processors can operate in "lock step" in a series of "rounds," and an asynchronous setting, where processors can run at relatively different speeds. In some cases, dealing with asynchrony introduces new complications, but in diverse networks, such as the Internet, asynchrony is a reality that must be dealt with effectively.

A major class of network algorithms are ***routing*** algorithms, which specify how to move information packets between various computers in a network. Good routing algorithms should route packets so as to arrive at their destinations quickly and reliably, while also being "fair" to other packets in the network. One challenge to designing good routing algorithms is that these goals are somewhat contradictory, since fairness sometimes conflicts with speedy packet delivery. Another challenge is that the processing needed to implement a routing scheme should also be fast and efficient. We therefore focus the second part of this chapter on routing algorithms, including methods for the following communication patterns:

- ***Broadcast routing***, which sends a packet to every computer
- ***Unicast routing***, which sends a packet to a specific computer
- ***Multicast routing***, which sends a packet to a group of computers.

We will study these routing algorithms by analyzing the costs involved in setting up the algorithm and also in routing messages using that algorithm. Before we discuss how these and other network algorithms work, however, we should explain a bit more about the computational model in which they are designed to operate.

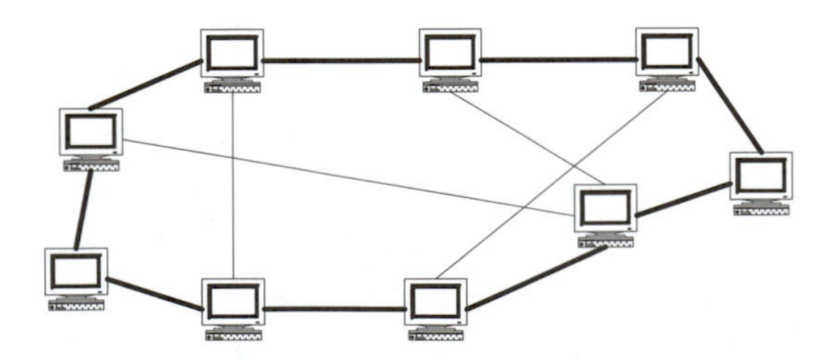

Figure 11.1: A computational network, whose vertices are processors and edges are communication links. Bold edges define a simple cycle known as a ***ring*** network.

11.1 Complexity Measures and Models

Before we can fully study network algorithms, we need to better understand how networks, such as the Internet, work. Specifically, we need to explore how interprocessor communication is performed, modeled, and analyzed.

11.1.1 The Networking Protocol Stack

One way to get a handle on the way a network, such as the Internet, functions is in terms of a layered networking model, having the following conceptual layers:

- ***Physical layer:*** This is the layer where raw bits are transmitted across some medium, such as electrical wires or fiber-optic cables. The design decisions for this layer have mostly to do with engineering techniques for representing 1's and 0's, maximizing transmission bandwidth, and minimizing transmission noise.
- ***Data-link layer:*** This is the layer that handles the methods for breaking data into subunits called ***frames*** and transmitting data from one computer, through the physical layer, to another. A typical example includes the point-to-point protocol, which describes how to send data between two physically connected computers.
- ***Network layer:*** This layer is concerned with methods for breaking data into ***packets*** (different than frames) and routing those packets from computer to computer through the entire network. Algorithmic issues concerned with this layer deal with methods for routing packets through the network and for breaking and reassembling packets. The primary Internet protocol used in this layer is the ***Internet Protocol***, or ***IP***. This protocol uses a "best effort" approach, which means that no performance guarantees are made and some packets may even be lost.
- ***Transport layer:*** This layer accepts data from various applications, splits it up into smaller units if need be, and passes these to the network layer in a fashion that fulfills specific guarantees on reliability and congestion control. The two primary Internet protocols that exist in this layer are the ***Transmission Control Protocol (TCP)***, which provides error-free, end-to-end, connection-oriented transmission between two machines on the Internet, and the ***User Datagram Protocol (UDP)***, which is a connectionless, best-effort protocol.
- ***Application layer:*** This is the layer at which applications operate, using the lower-level protocols. Examples of Internet applications include electronic mail (SMTP), file transfer (FTP and SCP), virtual terminals (TELNET and SSH), the World Wide Web (HTTP), and the Domain Name Service (DNS), which maps host names (such as www.cs.brown.edu) to IP addresses (such as 128.148.32.110).

11.1.2 The Message-Passing Model

We say very little about the details of the networking protocol stack in this chapter. Instead, the network algorithms we discuss operate in a computational model that abstracts the functionality provided by the various layers in the above ***network protocol stack***. Still, understanding the different layers of the network protocol stack allows us to tie concepts in our distributed computational model to specific functions and protocols in a real network, such as the Internet.

There are several possible ways of abstracting the functionality of a network in a way that would allow us to describe network algorithms. In this chapter, we will use a ***message-passing model*** that is commonly used to describe such ***distributed algorithms***, where loosely coupled processors communicate in order to solve computational problems. The alternative model of ***parallel algorithms*** is introduced in Section 14.2. In a parallel algorithm, tightly coupled multiple processors cooperate and coordinate, often through a shared memory space.

In the distributed message passing model, which will be our exclusive focus in this chapter, the network is modeled as a graph, where the vertices correspond to processors and the edges correspond to fixed connections between processors that do not change throughout the computation. Each edge e supports message passing between the two processors associated with the endpoints of e. Messages can be sent only in one direction if e is directed, and in both directions if e is undirected. For example, at the network layer of the Internet, vertices correspond to specialized computers called ***IP routers***, each identified by a unique numeric code called ***IP address***, and the messages exchanged by them are basic data transmission units called ***IP packets***. Alternatively, vertices could correspond to server computers on the Internet and edges could correspond to permanent TCP/IP connections that are maintained between various pairs of servers.

As the name implies, in the message passing model, information is communicated in the network by exchanging messages. Each processor in the network is assigned a unique numeric ***identifier*** (for example, it could be the IP address of a router or host on the Internet). Moreover, we assume that each processor knows its neighbors in the network, and that it communicates directly only with its neighbors. In some cases, we may even allow each processor to know the total number of processors in the network, but in many instances this global knowledge is unavailable or unnecessary.

Another important consideration in network algorithms is whether or not algorithms have to cope with potential changes to the network while they are running. During the execution of an algorithm, processors may fail (or "crash"), network connections may go down, and we could have some processors remain active but perform faulty or even malicious computations. Ideally, we would like distributed algorithms to be dynamic, that is, be able to respond to changes in the network, and be fault-tolerant, that is, be able to recover correctly and gracefully from failures. Nevertheless, the techniques for making distributed algorithms fully robust are fairly intricate; hence, they are beyond the scope of this book. Therefore, in this chapter, we assume that the topology of the network does not change and that processors remain active and nonfaulty while the network is executing a distributed algorithm. That is, we assume the network remains ***static*** during algorithm execution.

One of the most important considerations in the message-passing model for distributed computing is the assumption we make about the synchronization of processors in the network. There are several possible choices we can make regarding synchronization, but the following are the two most utilized models in distributed algorithm design:

- ***Synchronous model***: In this model, each processor has an internal clock that times program execution and the clocks of all the processors are synchronized. Also, we assume that the execution speeds of the processors are uniform and each processor takes the same amount of time to perform the same operation (such as an addition or comparison). Finally, we assume that it takes the same amount of time to send a message through any connection in the network.
- ***Asynchronous model***: In this model, we make no assumptions about any internal clocks that the processors might have. Moreover, we do not assume that the speeds of the processors are necessarily similar. Thus, the steps in an asynchronous algorithm are determined by conditions or ***events***, not by clock "ticks." Still, there are some reasonable timing assumptions that we make to allow algorithms to perform their tasks effectively. First, we assume that each communication channel, represented by an edge, is a first-in, first-out (FIFO) queue that can buffer an arbitrary number of messages. That is, the messages that are sent on an edge are stored in a buffer for that edge so that the messages arrive in the same order they are sent. Second, we assume that while processor speeds can vary, they are not arbitrarily different from one another. That is, there is a basic ***fairness*** assumption that guarantees that if a processor p has an event enabling p to perform a task, then p will eventually perform that task.

In addition to these two extreme versions of the distributed computing model, we can also consider intermediate versions, where processors have clocks, but these clocks are not perfectly synchronized. Thus, in such an intermediate model we cannot assume that processors compute in "lock step," but we can nevertheless make choices based on "time out" events where processors do not respond after a lengthy period of time. Although such intermediate models more closely match the actual timing properties of real networks, such as the Internet, we nevertheless find it useful to restrict our attention to the synchronous and asynchronous models described above. Algorithms designed for the synchronous model are usually quite simple and can often be translated into algorithms that work in the asynchronous model. In addition, algorithms designed for the asynchronous model will certainly still function correctly in an intermediate model that has limited synchronization.

11.1.3 Complexity Measures for Network Algorithms

In traditional algorithm design, as studied in other chapters of this book, the primary complexity measures used to determine the efficiency of an algorithm are running time and memory space used. These complexity measures do not immediately translate into the domain of network algorithms, however, since they implicitly assume that a computation is performed on a single computer, not a network of computers. In network algorithms, inputs are spread across the computers of the network and computations must be carried out across many computers on the network. Thus, we must take some care to characterize the performance parameters of network algorithms.

The complexity measures for comparing traditional algorithms have natural counterparts in distributed algorithms, but there are also complexity measures unique in the network setting. In this chapter, we focus on the following complexity measures:

- ***Computational rounds***: Several network algorithms proceed through a series of global rounds so as to eventually converge on a solution. The number of rounds needed for convergence can therefore be used as a crude approximation of time. In synchronous algorithms, these rounds are determined by clock ticks, whereas in asynchronous algorithms these rounds are often determined by propagating "waves" of events across the network.
- ***Space:*** The amount of space needed by a computation can be used even for network algorithms, but it must be qualified as to whether it is a ***global*** bound on the total space used by all computers in the algorithm or a ***local*** bound on how much space is needed per computer involved.
- ***Local running time:*** While it is difficult to analyze the global running time needed for a computation, particularly for asynchronous algorithms, we can nevertheless analyze the amount of local computing time needed for a particular computer to participate in a network algorithm. If all computers in an algorithm are essentially performing the same type of function, then a single local running time bound can suffice for all. But if there are several different classes of computers participating in an algorithm, we should characterize the local running time needed for each class of computer.
- ***Message complexity***: This parameter measures the total number of messages (of size at most logarithmic in the number of processors) that are sent between all pairs of computers during the computation. For example, if a message M is routed through p edges to get from one computer to another, we would say that the message complexity of this communication is $p|M|$, where $|M|$ denotes the length of M (in words).

Finally, if there is some other obvious complexity measure that we are trying to optimize in a network algorithm (such as profit in an online auction protocol or retrieval cost in an online caching scheme), then we should include bounds on these complexities as well.

11.2 Fundamental Distributed Algorithms

Complexity measures for network algorithms are often best thought of as being functions of some intuitive notions of the "size" of the problem we are trying to solve. For example, the size of a problem could be expressed in terms of the following parameters:

- The number of words used to express the input;
- The number of processor deployed; and
- The number of communication connections between processors.

Thus, to properly analyze the complexity measures for a network algorithm we must formalize what we mean by the size of the problem for that algorithm.

To make these notions more concrete, we study several fundamental distributed algorithms in this section, analyzing their performance using some of the above complexity measures. The specific problems we study are chosen both to illustrate fundamental distributed algorithm techniques as well as methods for analyzing network algorithms.

11.2.1 Leader Election in a Ring

The first problem we address is ***leader election*** in a ring network. In this problem, we are given a network of n processors that are connected in a ring, that is, the graph of the network is a simple cycle of n vertices. The goal is to identify one of the n processors as the "leader," and have all the other processors agree on this selection. We describe an algorithm for the case where the ring is a directed cycle. Exercise C-11.1 considers the case of an undirected ring.

We begin by describing a synchronous solution. The main idea of the synchronous solution is to select the leader as the processor with the smallest identifier. The challenge is that in a ring there is no obvious place to start. So we start the computation everywhere. At the beginning of the algorithm each processor sends its identifier to the next processor in the ring. In the subsequent rounds, each processor performs the following computations:

1. It receives an identifier i from its predecessor in the ring
2. It compares i to its own identifier
3. It sends the minimum of these two values to its successor in the ring.

If a processor ever receives its own identifier from its predecessor, then this processor knows that it must have the smallest identifier and hence, it is the leader. This processor can then send a message around the ring informing all the other processors that it is the leader.

We give a description of the above method in Algorithm 11.2. A sample execution of the algorithm is illustrated in Figure 11.3.

```
Algorithm RingLeader(id):
  Input: The unique identifier, id, for the processor running this algorithm
  Output: The smallest identifier of a processor in the ring

  M ← [Candidate is id]
  Send message M to the successor processor in the ring.
  done ← false
  repeat
    Get message M from the predecessor processor in the ring.
    if M = [Candidate is i] then
      if i = id then
        M ← [Leader is id]
        done ← true
      else
        m ← min{i, id}
        M ← [Candidate is m]
    else
      {M is a "Leader is" message}
      done ← true
    Send message M to the next processor in the ring.
  until done
  return M          {M is a "Leader is" message}
```

Algorithm 11.2: A synchronous algorithm run by each processor in a directed ring to determine a "leader" for that ring of processors.

Before we analyze algorithm RingLeader, let us first convince ourselves that it works correctly. Let n be the number of processors. Each processor begins by sending its identifier in the first round. Then, in the next $n-1$ rounds, each processor accepts a "candidate is" message, computes the minimum m of the identifier i in the message and its own identifier *id*, and transmits identifier m to the next processor with a "candidate is" message. Let ℓ be the smallest identifier of a processor in the ring. The first message sent by processor ℓ will traverse the entire ring and will come back unchanged to processor ℓ. At that point, processor ℓ will realize that it is the leader and will inform all the other processors with a "leader is" message that will traverse the entire ring over the next n rounds . It should be noted that the number n of processors used in the above analysis does not have to be known by the processors. Also, observe that there are no deadlocks in the algorithm, that is, no two processors are both waiting on messages that need to come from the other.

Let us now analyze the performance of algorithm RingLeader. First, in terms of the number of rounds, the first "candidate is" message from the leader takes n rounds to traverse the ring. Also, the "leader is" message initiated by the leader takes n more rounds to reach all the other processors. Thus, there are $2n$ rounds.

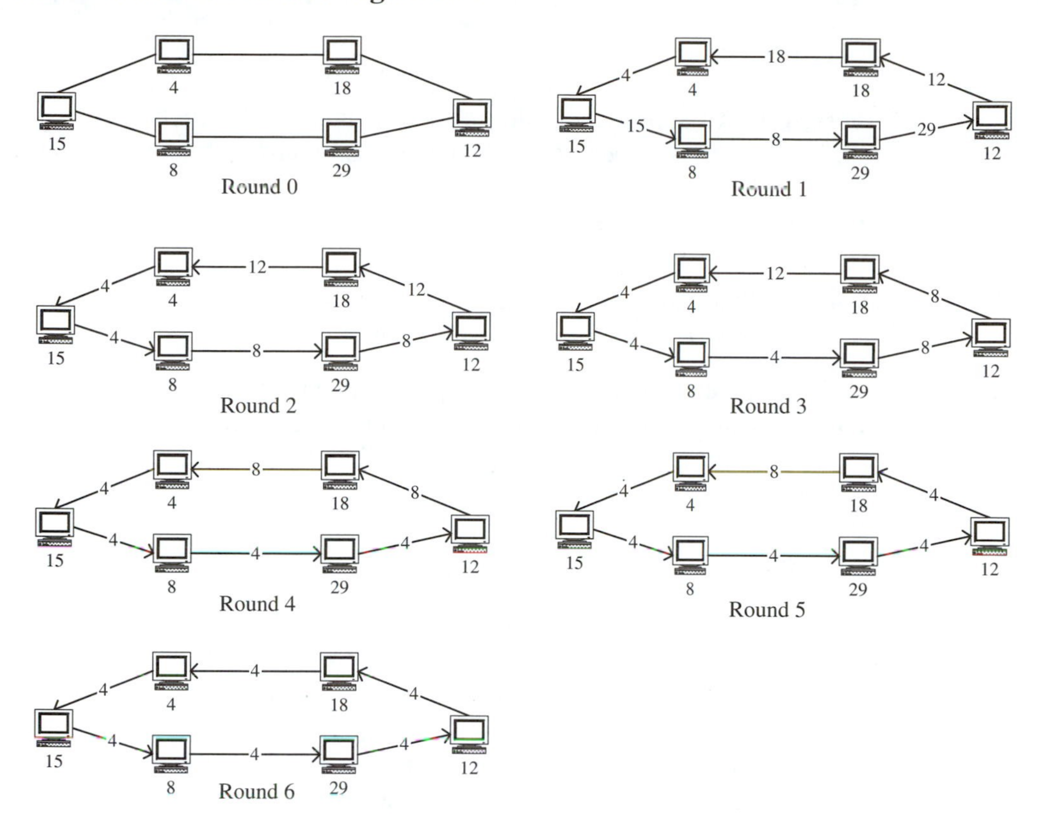

Figure 11.3: An illustration of the algorithm for synchronous leader election in a ring. The initial configuration is labeled as "Round 0." For each successive round, we label each edge with the "candidate is" message sent along the edge. We do not show the final rounds where processor 4 informs the other processors that it is the leader with a "leader is" message.

We analyze now the message complexity of the algorithm. We distinguish two phases in the algorithm.

1. The first phase consists of the first n rounds where the processors are sending "candidate is" messages and are propagating them on. In this phase, each processor sends and receives one message in each round. Thus, $O(n^2)$ messages are sent in the first phase.
2. The second phase consists of the next n rounds where the "leader is" message makes its way around the ring. In this phase, a processor continues sending "candidate is" messages until the "leader is" message reaches it. At this point, it forwards the "leader is" message and stops. Thus, in this phase, the leader will send one message, the successor of the leader will send two messages, its successor will send three messages, and so on. Thus, the total number of messages sent in the second phase is $\sum_{i=1}^{n} i$, which is $O(n^2)$.

We conclude as follows.

Theorem 11.1: *Suppose we are given an n-node distributed directed ring network, N, with distinct node identifiers but no distinguished leader. The* RingLeader *algorithm finds a leader in N using a total of $O(n^2)$ messages. Moreover, the total message complexity of the algorithm is $O(n^2)$.*

Proof: We have already seen that $O(n^2)$ messages are sent. Since each message uses $O(1)$ words, the total message complexity is $O(n^2)$. ■

It is possible to improve the message complexity for leader election in a ring by modifying algorithm RingLeader so that it requires fewer messages. We explore two possible modifications in Exercises C-11.2 and C-11.3.

Asynchronous Leader Election

Algorithm 11.2 (RingLeader) was described and analyzed under the synchronous model. Moreover, we structured each round so that it would consist of a a message receiving step, a processing step, and a message sending step. Indeed, this is the typical structure of synchronous distributed algorithms.

In an asynchronous algorithm, we cannot assume that the processors move in "lock step" any longer. Instead, processing is determined by events, not clock ticks. Still, the above algorithm for leader election in a ring also works in the asynchronous model. The correctness of the algorithm did not actually depend on the processors acting synchronously. It only depended on each processor receiving messages from its predecessor in the same sequence as they were sent. This condition still holds in the asynchronous model.

We summarize our study of leader election in a ring in the following theorem.

Theorem 11.2: *Given a directed ring with n processors, algorithm* RingLeader *performs leader election with $O(n^2)$ message complexity. For each processor, the local computing time is $O(n)$ and the local space used is $O(1)$. Algorithm* RingLeader *works under both the synchronous and asynchronous models. In the synchronous model, its overall running time is $O(n)$.*

Leader election might seem like a contrived problem at first, but it actually has many applications. Any time we need to compute a global function of a subset of nodes in a network, we essentially have to perform a leader election. For example, computing the sum of the values stored at computers connected in a ring, or the minimum or maximum of such values, can be solved by an algorithm similar to the leader-election algorithm given above.

Of course, processors are not always connected in a ring. So, in the next section, we explore the scenario when processors are connected in a (free) tree.

11.2.2 Leader Election in a Tree

If the network is a (free) tree, electing a leader is much simpler than in a ring, since a tree has a natural starting place for the computation: the external nodes.

Asynchronous Leader Election in a Tree

An asynchronous leader election algorithm for a tree is shown in Algorithm 11.5. Again, we choose the processor with the smallest identifier as the leader. The algorithm assumes that a processor can perform a constant-time ***message check*** on an incident edge to see if a message has arrived from that edge.

The main idea of Algorithm TreeLeader is to use two phases. In the ***accumulation phase***, identifiers flow in from the external nodes of the tree. Each node keeps track of the minimum identifier ℓ received from its neighbors, and after it receives identifiers from all but one neighbor, it sends identifier ℓ to that neighbor. At some point, a node receives identifiers from all its neighbors. This node, called ***accumulation node***, determines the leader. We illustrate this accumulation phase in Figure 11.4. Once we have the leader identified at one node, we start the ***broadcast phase***. In the broadcast phase, the accumulation node broadcasts the identifier of the leader toward the external nodes. Note that a tie condition may occur where two adjacent nodes become accumulation nodes. In this case, they broadcast to their respective "halves" of the tree. Any node in the tree, even an external node, can be an accumulation node, depending on the relative speed of the processors.

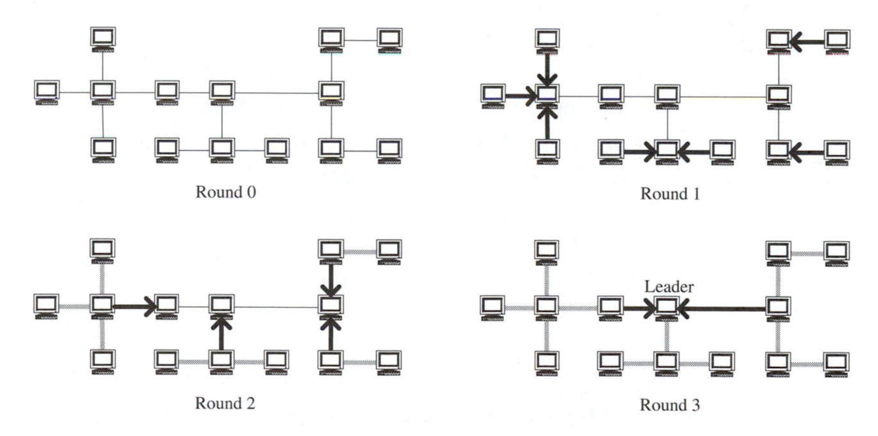

Figure 11.4: An illustration of the algorithm for finding a leader in a tree. We only show the accumulation phase. Edges that have carried no message yet are shown with thin lines. Edges with messages flowing in that round are drawn as thick arrows. Grey lines denote edges that have transported a message in a previous round.

```
Algorithm TreeLeader(id):
  Input: The unique identifier, id, for the processor running this algorithm
  Output: The smallest identifier of a processor in the tree
   {Accumulation Phase}
   let d be the number of neighbors of processor id          {d ≥ 1}
   m ← 0          {counter for messages received}
   ℓ ← id         {tentative leader}
   repeat
     {begin a new round}
     for each neighbor j do
       check if a message from processor j has arrived
       if a message M = [Candidate is i] from j has arrived then
         ℓ ← min{i, ℓ}
         m ← m + 1
   until m ≥ d − 1
   if m = d then
     M ← [Leader is ℓ]
     for each neighbor j ≠ k do
       send message M to processor j
     return M          {M is a " leader is" message}
   else
     M ← [Candidate is ℓ]
     send M to the neighbor k that has not sent a message yet
   {Broadcast Phase}
   repeat
     {begin a new round}
     check if a message from processor k has arrived
     if a message M from k has arrived then
       m ← m + 1
       if M = [Candidate is i] then
         ℓ ← min{i, ℓ}
         M ← [Leader is ℓ]
         for each neighbor j do
           send message M to processor j
       else
         {M is a " leader is" message}
         for each neighbor j ≠ k do
           send message M to processor j
   until m = d
   return M          {M is a " leader is" message}
```

Algorithm 11.5: An algorithm for computing a leader in a tree of processors. In the synchronous version of the algorithm, all the processors begin a round at the same time until they stop.

Synchronous Leader Election in a Tree

In the synchronous version of the algorithm, all the processors begin a round at the same time. Thus, the messages in the accumulation phase flow into the accumulation node like the reverse of ripples in a pond after a stone is dropped in. Likewise, in the broadcast phase, the messages propagate out from the accumulation node like ripples in a pond in the forward direction. That is, in the accumulation phase messages march into the "center" of the tree, and in the broadcast phase messages march out.

The ***diameter*** of a graph is the length of a longest path between any two nodes in the graph. For a tree, the diameter is achieved by a path between two external nodes. Interestingly, note that the number of rounds in the synchronous version of the algorithm is exactly equal to the diameter of the tree.

Performance of Tree Leader Election Algorithms

Analyzing the message complexity of the asynchronous tree leader election algorithm is fairly straightforward. During the accumulation phase, each processor sends one "candidate is" message. During the broadcast phase, each processor sends at most one "leader is" message. Each message has $O(1)$ size. Thus, the message complexity is $O(n)$.

We now study the local running time of the synchronous algorithm under the assumption that we ignore the time spent waiting to begin a round. The algorithm for processor i takes time $O(d_i D)$, where d_i is the number of neighbors of processor i, and D is the diameter of the tree. Also, processor i uses space d_i to keep track of the neighbors that have sent messages.

We summarize our study of leader election in a tree in the following theorem.

Theorem 11.3: *Given a (free) tree with n nodes and with diameter D, algorithm* TreeLeader *performs leader election with $O(n)$ message complexity. Algorithm* TreeLeader *works under both the synchronous and asynchronous models. In the synchronous model, for each processor i, the local computing time is $O(d_i D)$ and the local space used is $O(d_i)$, where d_i is the number of neighbors of processor i.*

11.2.3 Breadth-First Search

Suppose we have a general connected network of processors and we have identified a specific vertex s in this network as a source node. In Section 6.3.3, we discuss a centralized algorithm for constructing a breadth-first search for a graph G starting at a source node s. In this section, we describe distributed algorithms for solving this problem.

Synchronous BFS

We first describe a simple synchronous breadth-first search (BFS) algorithm. The main idea of this algorithm is to proceed in "waves" that propagate outward from the source vertex s to construct a BFS tree layer-by-layer from the top down. The synchronization of the processors will benefit us greatly, in this case, to make the propagation process completely coordinated.

We begin the algorithm by identifying s as an "external node" in the current BFS tree, which is just s at this point. Then, in each round, each external node v sends a message to all of its neighbors that have not contacted v earlier, informing them that v would like to make them its children in the BFS tree. These nodes respond by picking v as their parent, if they have not already chosen some other node as their parent.

We illustrate this algorithm in Figure 11.6 and we give the pseudo-code for it in Algorithm 11.7.

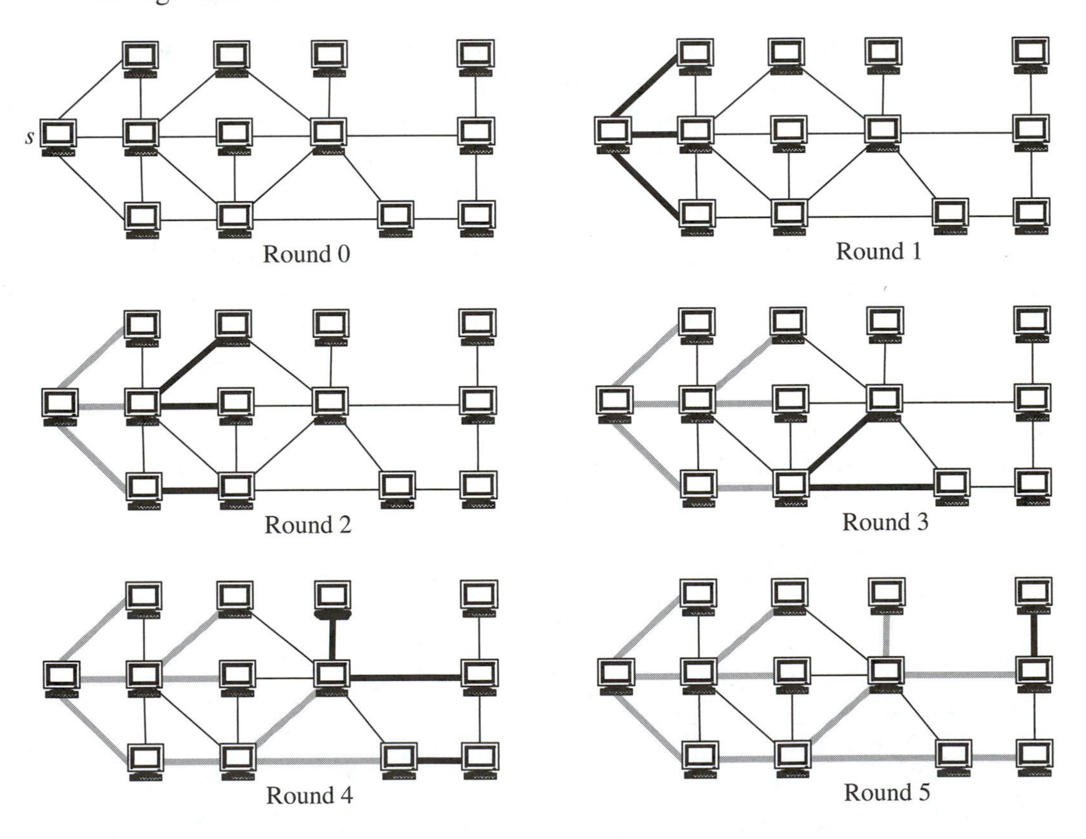

Figure 11.6: An illustration of the synchronized BFS algorithm. The thick edges are those of the BFS tree, with the black thick edges being the ones chosen in the current round.

Algorithm SynchronousBFS(v, s):
Input: The identifier v of the node (processor) executing this algorithm and the identifier s of the start node of the BFS traversal
Output: For each node v, its parent in a BFS tree rooted at s

repeat
  {begin a new round}
  if $v = s$ **or** v has received a message from one of its neighbors **then**
    set parent(v) to be a node requesting v to become its child (or **null**, if $v = s$)
    for each node w adjacent to v that has not contacted v yet **do**
      send a message to w asking w to become a child of v
until $v = s$ or v has received a message

Algorithm 11.7: A synchronous algorithm for computing a breadth-first search tree in a connected network of processors.

Analyzing algorithm SynchronousBFS is simple. In each round, we propagate out another level of the BFS tree. Thus, the running time of this algorithm is proportional to the depth of the BFS tree. In addition, we send at most one message on each edge in each direction over the entire computation. Thus, the number of messages sent in a network of n nodes and m edges is $O(n+m)$. Thus, this algorithm is quite efficient. But it admittedly makes considerable use of the synchronization of processors.

Asynchronous BFS

We can make the above BFS algorithm asynchronous at the expense of additional messages to keep things coordinated. Also, we require each processor to know the total number of processors in the network.

Rather than relying on synchronized clocks to determine each round in the computation, we will now have the source node s send out a "pulse" message that triggers the other processors to perform the next round in the computation. By using this pulse technique, we can still have the computation propagate out level by level. The pulsing process itself is like breathing—there is a ***pulse-down phase***, where a signal is passed down the BFS tree from the root s, and a ***pulse-up phase*** where a signal is combined from the external nodes back up the tree to the root s.

The processors at the external nodes can only go from one round to the next if they have received a new pulse-down signal from their respective parents. Likewise, the root s will not issue a new pulse-down signal until it has received all the pulse-up signals from its children. In this way, we can be sure that the processors are operating in rough synchronization (at the granularity of the rounds). We describe the asynchronous BFS algorithm in detail in Algorithm 11.8.

```
Algorithm AsynchronousBFS(v, s, n):
  Input: The identifier v of the processor running this algorithm, the identifier
    s of the start node of the BFS traversal, and the number n of nodes in the
    network
  Output: For each node v, its parent in the BFS tree rooted at s

  C ← ∅            {verified BFS children for v}
  set A to be the set of neighbors of v          {candidate BFS children for v}
  repeat
    {begin a new round}
    if parent(v) is defined or v = s then
      if parent(v) is defined then
        wait for a pulse-down message from parent(v)
      if C is not empty then
        {v is an internal node in the BFS tree}
        send a pulse-down message to all nodes in C
        wait for a pulse-up message from all nodes in C
      else
        {v is an external node in the BFS tree}
        for each node u in A do
          send a make-child message to u
        for each node u in A do
          get a message M from u and remove u from A
          if M is an accept-child message then
            add u to C
      send a pulse-up message to parent(v)
    else
      {v ≠ s has no parent yet.}
      for each node w in A do
        if w has sent v a make-child message then
          remove w from A          {w is no longer a candidate child for v}
          if parent(v) is undefined then
            parent(v) ← w
            send an accept-child message to w
          else
            send a reject-child message to w
  until (v has received message done) or (v = s and has pulsed-down n − 1 times)
  send a done message to all the nodes in C
```

Algorithm 11.8: An asynchronous algorithm for computing a breadth-first search tree in a connected network of processors. This algorithm is to be run simultaneously by each node v in the network. The possible messages are pulse-down, pulse-up, make-child, accept-child, reject-child, and done.

Performance

This asynchronous BFS algorithm is admittedly more complicated than its synchronous counterpart. The computation still operates in a series of rounds, however. In each round, the root node s sends "pulse-down" messages down the partially constructed BFS tree. When these messages reach the external level of the tree, the current external nodes attempt to extend the BFS tree one more level, by issuing "make-child" messages to candidate children. When these candidates respond, either by accepting the invitation to become a child or rejecting it, the processors send a "pulse-up" message that propagates back up to s. The root s then starts the whole process all over again.

Since the BFS tree can have height at most $n-1$ nodes, node s repeats the pulsing action for $n-1$ times, just to make sure that each node in the network has been included in the BFS tree. Thus, the synchronization from round to round is done completely via message passing. A current external node will not operate until it gets a "pulse-down" message, and it will not issue a "pulse-up" message until it has heard back from all of its candidate children (who either accept or reject an invitation to become children). The BFS tree grows level-by-level just as in the synchronous algorithm.

The number of messages needed to perform all of this coordination is more than that needed in the synchronous algorithm, however. Each edge in the network still has at most one "make-child" message and a response in each direction. Thus, the total message complexity for accepting and rejecting make-child requests is $O(m)$, where m is the number of edges in the network. But with each round of the algorithm we need to propagate all the "pulse-down" and "pulse-up" messages. Since they only travel along edges of the BFS tree, there are at most $O(n)$ pulse-up and pulse-down messages sent each round. Given that the source operates for $n-1$ rounds, there are at most $O(n^2)$ messages that are issued for the pulse coordinate. Therefore, the total message complexity of the algorithm is $O(n^2+m)$, where m is the number of edges in the network. This bound can be further simplified to just $O(n^2)$, since m is $O(n^2)$.

Thus, we summarize the above discussion with the following theorem.

Theorem 11.4: *Given a network G with n vertices and m edges, we can compute a breadth-first spanning tree in G in the asynchronous model using only $O(n^2)$ messages.*

In Exercise C-11.4, we explore how to improve the running time of the asynchronous breadth-first search algorithm to be $O(nh+m)$, where h is the height of the BFS tree.

11.2.4 Minimum Spanning Trees

We recall that a ***minimum spanning tree*** (MST) of a weighted graph is a spanning subgraph that is a tree and that has minimum weight (Section 7.3). In this section, we describe an efficient distributed algorithm for this problem. Before we provide the details, we first review an efficient sequential algorithm for finding an MST due to Barůvka (Section 7.3.3). The algorithm starts with each node of G in its own connected component of (zero) tree edges. It then proceeds, in a series of rounds, to add tree edges to join connected components and thereby build up an MST. As with all MST algorithms, it is based on the fact that, for any partition $\{V_1, V_2\}$ of the vertices into two nonempty subsets, if e is a minimum-weight edge joining V_1 and V_2, then e belongs to a minimum spanning tree. (See Theorem 7.10.)

For the sake of simplicity, let us assume that all the edge weights are unique. Recall that, initially, each node of the graph is in its own (trivial) connected component and the initial set, T, of tree edges is empty. At a high level, Barůvka's algorithm then performs the following computations:

while there is more than one connected component defined by T **do**
  for each connected component C in parallel **do**
    choose the smallest edge e joining c to another component
    add e to the set T of tree edges

Barůvka's algorithm performs the above computations for each connected component in parallel, and therefore finds tree edges quickly. Note, in fact, that in each round, we are guaranteed to join each connected component with at least one other. Thus, the number of connected components decreases by a factor of 2 with each round (defined by an iteration of the while loop), which implies that the total number of rounds is logarithmic in the number of vertices.

Barůvka's Algorithm in a Distributed Setting

Let us implement a distributed Barůvka's algorithm for the synchronous model (the asynchronous version of this algorithm is left as Exercise C-11.7). There are two critical computations that need to be performed in each round—we have to determine all the connected components and we need to determine the minimum outgoing edge from each one (recall that we are assuming that edge weights are unique, so the minimum outgoing edge from a component will also be unique). (See Figure 11.9.)

We assume that, for each node v, v stores a list of the edges of T that are incident on v. Thus, each node v belongs to a tree, but v only stores information about its neighbors in T. In each round, the leader election algorithm in a tree from Section 11.2.2 is used twice as an auxiliary method:

1. To identify each connected component
2. To find, for each connected component, the minimum-weight edge joining a component to another component.

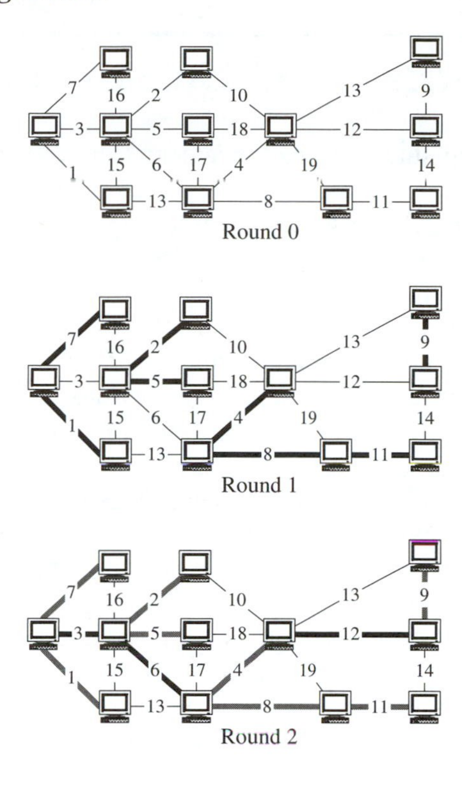

Figure 11.9: An illustration of a synchronous distributed version of Barůvka's algorithm. The thick edges identify MST edges, with the black thick edges being the ones chosen in the given round.

A round operates as follows. To identify the connected components, the leader-election computation is performed using the identifier of each node. Thus, each component gets identified by the smallest identifier of its nodes. Next, each node v computes the minimum-weight edge e incident on v, such that the endpoints of e are in different connected components. If there is no such edge, we use a fictitious edge with infinite weight. Leader election is then performed again using the edges associated with each vertex and their weights, which yields, for each connected component C, the minimum-weight edge connecting C to another component. Note that we can detect the end of the algorithm as the round in which we compute the weight of the minimum-weight edge to be infinity.

Let n and m denote the number of nodes and edges, respectively. To analyze the message complexity of the distributed version of Barůvka's algorithm, note that $O(m)$ constant-size messages are sent at each round. Thus, since there are $O(\log n)$ rounds, the overall message complexity is $O(m \log n)$. In Exercise C-11.6, we examine a way to improve the message complexity for synchronous MST to $O(m + n \log n)$, and in Exercise C-11.7, we challenge the reader to find an asynchronous MST algorithm that still has message complexity $O(m \log n)$.

11.3 Broadcast and Unicast Routing

Having studied some fundamental distributed algorithms, let us now turn to two problems common in communication networks—***broadcast routing*** and ***unicast routing***. Broadcast routing is a message that is sent from one processor to all other processors in a network. This form of communication is used when information on a single processor must be shared with all other processors in the network. Unicast routing, on the other hand, involves setting up data structures in a network so as to support point-to-point communication, where a single processor has a message that it wishes to have relayed to another processor.

When discussing routing algorithms in the remaining subsections, we refer to a processor as a ***router***. We recall our assumption that the network is fixed and does not change over time. Thus, we restrict ourselves to the study of static routing algorithms. We also make the assumption that the messages exchanged by the routers have constant size, which implies that the message complexity is proportional to the total number of messages exchanged. Throughout the section, we denote with n and m the number of nodes and edges of the network, respectively.

We begin our discussion with broadcast routing and then cover unicast routing and multicast routing. The algorithms presented in this section are simplified versions of those used for packet routing in the Internet.

11.3.1 The Flooding Algorithm for Broadcast Routing

The ***flooding*** algorithm for broadcast routing is quite simple and requires virtually no setup. However, its routing cost is high.

A router s wishing to send a message M to all other routers in the network begins by simply sending M to its neighbors. When a router $v \neq s$ receives a flooding message M from an adjacent router u, v simply rebroadcasts M to all its neighbors, except for u itself. Of course, left unmodified, this algorithm will cause an "infinite loop" of messages on any network that contains a cycle; a network without cycles has a simple routing algorithm, however, as we explore in an exercise (C-11.5).

Flooding with a Hop Counter

To avoid the infinite loop problem, we must associate some memory, or ***state***, with the main actors in the flooding algorithm. One possibility is that we add a ***hop counter*** to each message M and decrement the hop counter for M each time a router processes M. If a hop counter ever reaches 0, we then discard the message it belongs to. If we initialize the hop counter for a message M to the diameter of the network, then we can reach all the routers while avoiding the creation of an infinite number of messages.

Flooding with Sequence Numbers

Another possibility is to store a hash table (or another efficient dictionary data structure) at each router that keeps track of which messages the router has already processed. When a router x originates a broadcast message, it assigns a unique ***sequence number*** k to it. Thus, a flooding message is tagged by the pair (x,k). When a router receives a message with tag (x,k), it checks whether (x,k) is in its table. If so, it simply discards the message. Otherwise, it adds (x,k) to the table and rebroadcasts the message to its neighbors.

This approach will certainly eliminate the infinite loop problem, but it is not space efficient. So a common heuristic to use is to have each router keep only the latest sequence number for each other router in the network, with the assumption being that if a router receives a message originated by x with sequence number k, it has probably already processed all the messages sent by x with sequence numbers less than k.

Analysis of Flooding Algorithms

To analyze flooding algorithms, we begin by noting that there is no setup cost other than having each router know the number n of routers in the network, and possibly the diameter D of the network. If we use the hop-counter heuristic, then there is no additional space needed at the routers. If we use the sequence-number heuristic, on the other hand, then the space needed by each router is $O(n)$ in the worst case. In both cases, the expected time required by a router to process a message is proportional to the number of neighbors of the router, since search and insertion in a hash table have $O(1)$ expected running time (see Section 2.5.3).

We now analyze the message complexity of flooding algorithms. When using the hop-counter heuristic, the message complexity is $O((d_{\max}-1)^D)$ in the worst case, where $d_{\max}$ is the maximum degree of the routers in our network. When using the sequence-number heuristic, the message complexity is $O(m)$, since we end up sending a message along every edge in the network. Since m is usually much smaller than $(d_{\max}-1)^D$, sequence numbers are generally preferable to hop counters. In either case, however, the flooding algorithm is only efficient for messages we are willing to ***broadcast*** to all other routers in our network.

Still, the flooding algorithm is guaranteed to send a message M from its source to each destination in the fewest number of hops in the synchronized network model. That is, it always finds a shortest routing path. Given the overheads involved in the flooding algorithm, however, it would be nice to have an algorithm that can route messages along shortest paths more efficiently. The algorithm we discuss next does just this by performing some setup computations for determining good routes in a network.

11.3.2 The Distance Vector Algorithm for Unicast Routing

The first unicast routing algorithm we discuss is a distributed version of a classic algorithm for finding shortest paths in a graph attributed to Bellman and Ford (Section 7.1.2). We assume that we have a positive weight $w(e)$ assigned to each edge e of the network, which represents the cost of sending a message through e. For example, the weight could represent the average "latency" of the communication link.

The unicast routing problem is to set up data structures at the nodes of the network that support the efficient routing of a message from an origin node to a destination node.

The ***distance vector*** algorithm always routes along shortest paths. The main idea of this algorithm is for each router x to store a bucket array called the ***distance vector*** of router x, which stores the length of the best known path from x to every other router y in the network, denoted $D_x[y]$, and the first edge (connection) of such a path, denoted $C_x[y]$. Initially, for each edge (x,y), we assign

$$D_x[y] = D_y[x] = w(x,y)$$

and

$$C_x[y] = C_y[x] = (x,y).$$

All other D_x entries are set equal to $+\infty$. We then perform a series of rounds that iteratively refine each distance vector to find possibly better paths until every distance vector stores the actual distance to all other routers.

Distributed Relaxation

The setup of the distance vector algorithm consists of a series of rounds. In turn, each round consists of a collection of ***relaxation*** steps. At the beginning of a round, each router sends its distance vector to all of its immediate neighbors in the network. After a router x has received the current distance vectors from each of its neighbors, it performs the following local computation for $n-1$ rounds:

for each router w connected to x **do**
  for each router y in the network **do**
    { ***relaxation*** }
    if $D_w[y] + w(x,w) < D_x[y]$ **then**
      {a better route from x to y through w has been found}
      $D_x[y] \leftarrow D_w[y] + w(x,w)$.
      $C_x[y] \leftarrow (x,w)$.

Performance

Since each vertex x sends a vector of size n to each of its neighbors in each round, the time and message complexity for x to complete a round is $O(d_x n)$, where d_x is the degree of x and n is the number of routers in the network. Recall that we iterate this algorithm for $n-1$ rounds. In fact, we can improve this to D rounds, where D is the diameter of the network, as the distance vectors will not change after that many rounds.

After the setup, the distance vector of a router x stores the actual distances of x to the other routers in the network and the first edge of such paths. Therefore, once we have performed this setup, the routing algorithm is quite simple: if a router x receives a message intended for router y, x sends y along the edge $C_x[y]$.

Correctness of the Distance Vector Algorithm

The correctness of the distance vector algorithm follows by a simple inductive argument:

Lemma 11.5: *At the end of round i, each distance vector stores the shortest path to every other router restricted to visit at most i other routers along the way.*

This fact is true at the beginning of the algorithm, and the relaxations done in each round ensure that it will be true after each round as well.

Analysis of the Distance Vector Algorithm

Let us analyze the complexity of the distance vector algorithm. Unlike the flooding algorithm, discussed in Section 11.3.1, the distance vector algorithm has a significant setup cost. The total number of messages passed in each round is proportional to n times the sum of all the degrees in the network. This is because the number of messages sent and received at a router x is $O(d_x n)$, where d_x denotes the degree of x. Thus, there are $O(nm)$ messages per round. Hence, the total message complexity for the setup of the distance vector algorithm is $O(Dnm)$, which is $O(n^2 m)$ in the worst case.

After the setup is completed, each router stores a bucket array with $n-1$ elements, which takes $O(n)$ space, and processes a message in $O(1)$ expected time. Note that the local space requirement matches that of the flooding algorithm under the sequence-number heuristic. Since the distance vector algorithm finds shortest paths, like the flooding algorithm, but does so during the setup computation, it can be viewed as trading off setup costs for subsequent efficient message delivery.

11.3.3 The Link-State Algorithm for Unicast Routing

The last static routing algorithm we discuss is a distributed version of a classic shortest path algorithm due to Dijkstra. As in the distance vector algorithm description, we assume that the edges have positive weights. Whereas the distance vector algorithm performed its setup in a series of rounds that each required only local communication between adjacent routers, the link-state algorithm computes a single communication round that requires lots of global communication throughout the entire network.

The ***link-state algorithm*** proceeds as follows. The setup begins with each router x broadcasting the weights of its incident edges (that is, the "status" of x) to all other routers in the network, using a flooding routing algorithm with sequence numbers (which requires no prior setup, see Section 11.3.1). After this broadcast phase, each router knows the entire network and can run Dijkstra's shortest path algorithm on it to determine the shortest path from it to every other router y and the first edge $C_x[y]$ of such a path. This internal computation takes $O(m \log n)$ time using standard implementations of Dijkstra's algorithm, or $O(n \log n + m)$ using more sophisticated data structures (recall Section 7.1.1).

As in the distance-vector algorithm, the data structure constructed by the setup at each router has $O(n)$ space and supports the processing of a message in $O(1)$ expected time.

Let us now analyze the total message complexity of the setup in the link-state algorithm. A total of m constant-size messages are broadcast, each of which causes m messages to be sent by the flooding algorithm in turn. Thus, the overall message complexity of the setup is $O(m^2)$.

Comparison of Broadcast and Unicast Routing Algorithms

We compare the performance of the three static routing algorithms discussed in this section in Table 11.10. Note that we are not including the internal computation time that is required of a router that is participating in a preprocessing setup computation in this table.

Algorithm	messages	local space	local time	routing time
Flooding w/ hop count	$O(1)$	$O(1)$	$O(d)$	$O((d-1)^D)$
Flooding w/ seq. no.	$O(1)$	$O(n)$	$O(d)$	$O(m)$
Distance vector	$O(Dnm)$	$O(n)$	$O(1)$	$O(p)$
Link state	$O(m^2)$	$O(n)$	$O(1)$	$O(p)$

Table 11.10: Asymptotic performance bounds for static routing algorithms. We use the following notation for the network and routing parameters: n, number of nodes; m, number of edges; d, maximum node degree; D, diameter; and p, number of edges in a shortest routing path. Note that p, d, and D are all less than n.

11.4 Multicast Routing

So far, we have studied routing algorithms for two types of communication—broadcast and unicast routing—which can be viewed as being at the two extremes of a spectrum. Somewhere in the middle of this spectrum is ***multicast routing***, which involves communication with a subset of hosts on a network, called a ***multicast group***.

11.4.1 Reverse Path Forwarding

The reverse path forwarding (RPF) algorithm adapts the flooding algorithms for broadcast routing to multicast routing. It is designed to work in conjunction with the existing shortest-path routing tables available at every router, in order to broadcast a multicast message along the shortest path tree from a source.

The method begins with a host that wishes to send a message to a group g. The host sends that message to its local router s in order for s to then send the message to all of its neighboring routers. When a router x receives, from one if its neighbors y, a multicast message that originated at the router s, x checks its local routing table to see if y is on x's shortest path to s. If y is not on x's shortest path to s, then (assuming all the routing tables are correct and consistent) the link from y to x is not in the shortest path tree from s. Thus, in this case, x simply discards the packet sent from y and sends back to y a special ***prune*** message, which includes the name of the source s and the group g. This prune message tells y to stop sending multicast messages from s intended for group g (and, if possible, not to send any multicast messages from s along this link no matter what the group is). If, on the other hand, y is on x's shortest path to s, then x replicates the message and sends it out to all of its neighboring routers, except for y itself. For, in this case, the link from y to x is on the shortest path tree from s (again, assuming that all the routing tables are correct and consistent).

This mode of broadcast communication extends outward from s along the shortest path tree T from s until it floods the entire network. The fact that the algorithm broadcasts a multicast message to every router in the network is wasteful if only a small fraction of the routers on the network have clients wishing to receive multicast messages that are sent to the group g.

To deal with this waste, the RPF algorithm provides an additional type of message pruning. In particular, if a router x, at an external node of T, determines that it has no clients on its local network that are interested in receiving messages for the group g, then x issues a prune message to its parent y in T telling y to stop sending it messages from s to the group g. This message in effect tells y to remove the external node x from the tree T.

Pruning

These prune messages can, of course, be issued by many external nodes of T in parallel; hence, we can have many external nodes of T removed at the same time. Moreover, the removal of some external nodes of T may create new external nodes. So, the RPF algorithm has each router x continually test if it has become an external node in T and, if x has, then it should test if it has any client hosts on its local network that are interested in receiving multicast messages for the group g. Again, if there are no such clients, then x sends its parent in T a prune message for multicast messages from s to the group g. This external-node pruning continues until all remaining external nodes in T have clients wishing to receive multicast messages to the group g. At this point the RPF algorithm has reached a steady state.

This steady state cannot be locked in forever, however, for we may have some client hosts in our network that wish to start receiving messages for the group g. That is, we may have at least one client h wishing to ***join*** the group g. Since the RPF provides no explicit way for clients to join a group, the only way h can start to receive multicasts to group g is if h's router x is receiving those packets. But if x has been pruned from T, then this will not happen. Thus, one additional component of the RPF algorithm is that the prunes that are stored at a node in the Internet are timed out after a certain amount of time.

When such a time-out occurs, say for a prune coming from a router z to the router x holding z's previous prune message, then x resumes sending multicast packets for the group g to z. Therefore, if a router really intends not to receive or process certain types of multicast messages, then it must continually inform its upstream neighbors of this desire by using prune messages. For this reason, the RPF algorithm is not an efficient method for performing multicast routing.

Performance

In terms of message efficiency, the RPF initially sends out $O(m)$ messages, where m is the number of connections (edges) in the network. After the first wave of prunes propagate through the network, however, the complexity of multicasting reduces to $O(n)$ messages per multicast message, where n is the number of routers. And this is further reduced as additional prune messages are processed. In terms of additional storage at the routers, the RPF algorithm is not too efficient, for it requires that each router store every prune message it receives until that prune message times out. In the worst case, then, a router x may have to store as many as $O(|\mathcal{S}| \cdot |\mathcal{G}|d_x)$ prune messages, where $\mathcal{S}$ is the set of sources, $\mathcal{G}$ is the set of groups, and d_x is the degree of x in the network. Thus, as we have already observed, the RPF algorithm is not efficient.

11.4.2 Center-Based Trees

A multicast algorithm with message efficiency better than that of the reverse path forwarding algorithm is the ***center-based trees*** method. In this algorithm, we choose, for each group g, a single router z on the network that will act as the "center" or "rendezvous" node for the group g. The router z forms the root node of the multicast tree T for g, which is used for sending messages to routers that are a part of this group. Any source wishing to send a multicast message to the group g first sends that message toward the center z. In the simplest form of the center-based trees algorithm, this message proceeds all the way to z, and once it is received by z, then z broadcasts this message to all the nodes in T. Thus, each router x that is represented by a node in T knows that if x receives a multicast message for g from its parent in T, then x replicates this message and sends it to all of its neighbors that correspond to its children in T. Likewise, in the simplest form of the center-based trees method, if x receives a multicast message from any other neighbor different than its parent in T, then it sends this message up the tree to z. Such a message is coming from some source and should be sent up to z before being multicast to T.

As mentioned above, we must explicitly maintain the multicast tree T for each group g. Thus, we must provide a way for routers to ***join*** the group g. A join operation for a router x begins by having x send a join message toward the center node z. Any other router y receiving a join message from a neighbor t looks up to see which of y's neighbors u is on the shortest path to z, and then y creates and stores an internal record indicating that y now has a child t and a parent u in the tree T. If y was already in the tree T (that is, there was already a record saying that u was y's parent in T), then this completes the join operation—the router x is now a connected external node in the tree T. If y was not already in the tree T, however, then y propagates the join message up to its (new) parent u in T. (See Figure 11.11.)

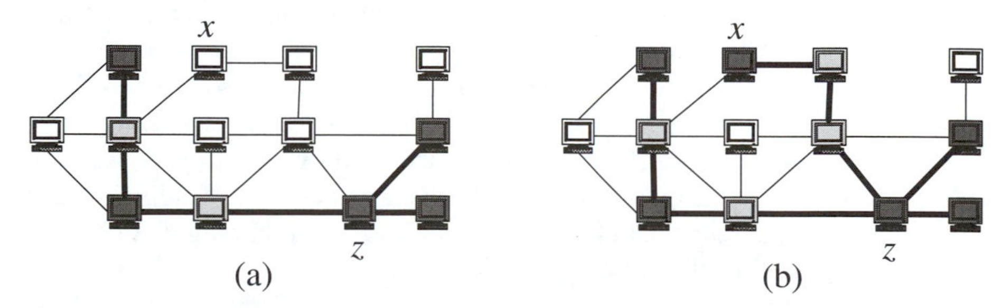

Figure 11.11: An illustration of the center-based trees protocol. (a) A multicast tree centered at z, with thick edges being tree edges, dark gray nodes being group members, and light gray nodes being routers that simply propagate messages; (b) the multicast tree after x joins. Notice that x could have joined using just one edge and no additional intermediate nodes, but the route to z would not be a shortest path.

Performance

For routers wishing to leave group g, either through explicit ***leave*** messages or because a join record times out, we essentially reverse the action we performed for a join. In terms of efficiency, the center-based trees method only sends messages along T, the multicast tree for group g, so its message complexity is $O(|T|)$ for each multicast. In addition, since each router only stores the local structure of T, the maximum number of records that need to be stored at any router x is $O(|\mathcal{G}|d_x)$, where $\mathcal{G}$ is the set of groups and d_x is the degree of x in the network. Therefore, the center-based tree algorithm has the benefit of efficiency that comes from always sending multicast messages for a group g along a single tree T. This tree may not be the most efficient tree for sending such a message, however.

11.4.3 Steiner Trees

The main goal of the Steiner tree algorithm is to optimize the total cost of all the edges we are using to build the multicast tree for a group g. Formally, we let $G = (V, E)$ denote our network, with V being the set of routers, and we define a cost metric, $c(e)$, for the edges of G. Additionally, we assume we are given a subset S of V that indicates the routers in our network that belong to the group g. The ***Steiner tree*** T for S is the tree of minimum total cost that connects all the nodes in S. Note that if $|S| = 1$, then T is a single node, that if $|S| = 2$, then T is the shortest path between the two nodes in S, and if $|S| = |V|$, then T is the minimum spanning tree for T. Thus, for these special cases, we can easily construct the optimal tree, T, joining the nodes of S and we can use this tree for all multicasts to the group g, as in the center-based trees algorithm. Unfortunately, solving the general case of the Steiner tree problem is ***NP***-hard (Section 13.2.1); hence, we should try to employ some heuristic algorithm that can approximate the Steiner tree.

The Steiner tree approximation algorithm we describe is based on the minimum spanning tree algorithm described above (in Section 11.2.4). It uses information already available at each router in the network and is known as the ***distance network*** algorithm, for it operates on a graph G', derived from G, known as the distance network for S. The graph G' is formed by taking the vertices of S as its nodes, and connecting each pair of such nodes with an edge. The cost $c'(e)$ of an edge $e = (v, w)$ in G' is exactly the distance between v and w in G, that is, the length of the shortest path from v to w in G (we are assuming that G is undirected here). The specific algorithm is as follows:

1. Construct a representation of the distance network, G' for S.
2. Find a minimum spanning tree (MST) T_M in G'.
3. Translate T_M into a tree T_A in G by taking the shortest path from v to w for each edge (v, w) in T_M.
4. Find the MST T_D in the subgraph of G induced by the nodes of T_A.
5. Remove from T_D any paths leading to external nodes not in S.

The last two steps provide some additional improvement to the tree T_A, which is already a good approximation to the Steiner tree, T_S.

Lemma 11.6: $|T_A| \le |T_S|(2-2/k)$, *where* $k = |S|$.

Proof: Consider the Steiner tree, T_S, which connects the nodes of S optimally in G. Consider further the walk, W, formed by taking a continuous (depth-first) traversal around the boundary of T_S. That is, imagine that T_S is the map of some set of roads that we then walk along always staying on the right side of the road. Thus, $|W| = 2|T_S|$. Subdivide W into the set of k paths connecting pairs of nodes of S that are visited consecutively in the walk W, subdividing W only at the first visit we make to each node. (See Figure 11.12a.) Let P denote the set of $k-1$ paths that remain after removing the path of highest cost from this set. Thus, $|P| \le (2-2/k)|T_S|$. Let P' denote the set of paths formed by replacing each path p in P, which goes from a node v to a node w in S, with the shortest path from v to w. Thus, $|P'| \le |P|$. Finally, let T' denote the set of edges in the distance network formed by replacing each path in P' with its corresponding edge in the distance network for S. (See Figure 11.12b.) Observe that T' is a spanning tree in the distance network for S; hence, $|T_A| \le |T'|$. Therefore, $|T_A| \le (2-2/k)|T_S|$. ■

Since T_D is no worse than T_A, the above lemma implies $|T_D| \le (2-2/k)|T_S|$.

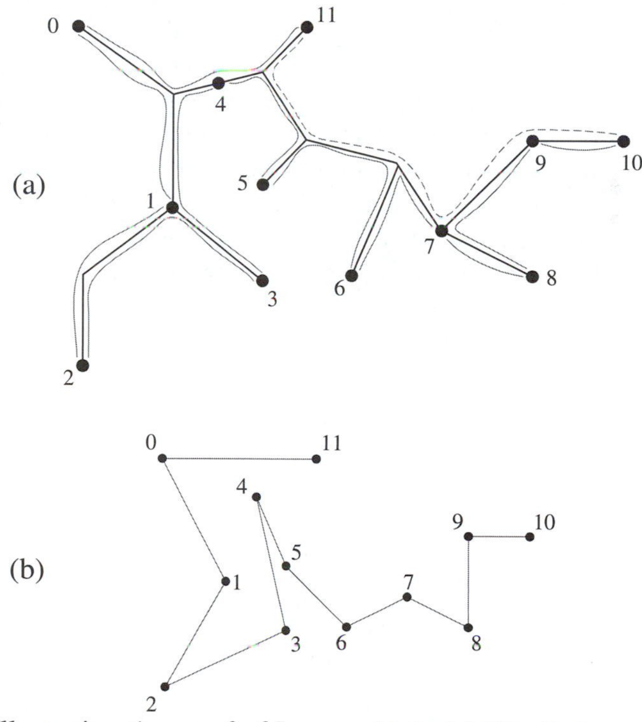

Figure 11.12: Illustrating the proof of Lemma 11.6: (a) The Steiner tree, T_S, with the vertices in S highlighted and the walk W partitioned into $k = 12$ paths. The highest-cost path is shown dashed. (b) The tree T' in the distance network.

Analysis

In addition to producing a good approximation to the Steiner tree the distance network algorithm also is easy to implement in a network setting. The distance network itself is implicitly represented by the distance vectors that could be stored at each router in the network (after either the link-state or distance-vector algorithm). Thus, if each router knows which routers belong to the group g, then there is no additional computation needed to form the distance network G'. Finding a minimum spanning tree in G', then, can be done using the distributed minimum spanning tree algorithm described above in Section 11.2.4, where rather than having nodes examine just their adjacent connections in a single round, we have each node in S consider all possible shortest paths to other nodes in S. But if each node stores a distance vector to all other nodes in the network, we do not need to query other nodes to determine the distance to those other nodes. We only need to determine, in each round for each node x in S, the shortest path to another node in S that is not in the same connected component as x. We can do this by having x send messages in G to the other nodes in S, ordered by their distance, asking that other node if it is in the same connected component as x. That is, each step of the distributed algorithm can be performed by routing messages in G. Since each such message will require at most D hops, where D is the diameter of G, this implies that we can find T_A using at most $O(k^2D)$ messages. If we wish to additionally compute the tree T_D, then we must perform an additional MST algorithm in G itself, which can be done using $O(n\log n + m)$ messages. Thus, this approximation algorithm to the Steiner tree problem has an efficient message complexity.

Still, this algorithm is only suited for groups that are fairly stable over time, since any modification to a group requires that we build a new multicast tree for that tree from scratch. Note, therefore, that each of the multicast algorithms we discuss has some drawbacks. Indeed, there is still considerable algorithmic work that can be done to come up with new more-efficient multicast routing algorithms.

11.5 Exercises

Reinforcement

R-11.1 Draw a picture that illustrates the messages sent in each round of the synchronous algorithm for electing a leader in a 10-node ring.

R-11.2 Draw a picture that illustrates the messages sent in each round of the synchronous algorithm for electing a leader in a 10-node tree. Design the processing so that two nodes "tie" for leader.

R-11.3 Draw a figure that illustrates how the synchronous BFS algorithm works. Your figure should result in a BFS tree with at least five levels.

R-11.4 Draw a figure that illustrates how the asynchronous BFS algorithm works. Your figure should result in a BFS tree with at least three levels and should show both the pulse-down and pulse-up actions.

R-11.5 Draw a computer network that causes the synchronous distributed minimum spanning tree derived from Barůvka's algorithm to run for four rounds. Show the edge choices made in each round.

R-11.6 Give a pseudo-code description of the algorithm that a computer performs to route a flooding message that uses a hop counter.

R-11.7 Give a pseudo-code description of the algorithm that a computer performs to route a flooding message that uses a sequence number.

R-11.8 Give a pseudo-code description of the algorithm that a computer performs to route a unicast message after it has already performed the setup for the link state or distance vector algorithm.

R-11.9 Draw a figure that illustrates how the distance vector works in a network of at least 10 nodes. Your illustration should show a computation that takes at least three rounds to stabilize.

R-11.10 Exactly how many messages are sent to perform the link state setup algorithm in a network of 10 nodes and 20 edges, assuming each node already knows the state of its incident edges?

R-11.11 Draw a figure that illustrates three prune operations in the reverse-path forwarding multicasting algorithm.

R-11.12 Draw a figure that shows that the center-based trees approach to multicast routing can use twice as many edges as the Steiner tree approach.

R-11.13 Draw a figure that shows that the reverse-path forwarding approach to multicast routing can use more than the Steiner tree approach.

Creativity

C-11.1 Extend the leader election algorithm to the case where the network is an undirected cycle and messages can be passed in either direction.

Hint: View an undirected cycle as the union of two directed cycles.

C-11.2 Consider the problem of electing a leader processor in a ring of $n \geq 4$ processors, each of which has a unique id. Assuming that all the processors know the value of n, design a synchronous randomized algorithm whose expected running time is $O(n)$ and whose expected message complexity is also $O(n)$.

Hint: Use the fact that that if each of $n \geq 4$ processors independently decides to send a message with probability $4/n$, then the expected number of processors that send messages is 4 and the probability that no processor sends a message is less than $1/2$.

C-11.3 Consider the problem of electing a leader processor in a ring of n processors, each of which has a unique id. Design a synchronous deterministic algorithm whose running time and message complexity is $O(n \log n)$.

Hint: Consider an algorithm with $\log n$ phases, where you have each processor who, in phase i, thinks it might be the leader, send out a "probe" message in each direction that goes 2^i hops and comes back if it finds no processor with lower id value.

C-11.4 Design an asynchronous breadth-first search (BFS) algorithm for a network of n vertices and m edges that has a total message complexity that is $O(nh+m)$, where h is the height of the BFS tree.

Hint: Extend the "pulse-down" and "pulse-up" messages so that the root s can know the exact round in which the BFS tree is completely constructed.

C-11.5 Suppose a connected network G contains no cycles; that is, G is a (free) tree. Describe a way to number the nodes in G so that any node x stores only $O(1)$ information, but we can route a message from a computer y to a computer z in G without any detours.

C-11.6 Describe a synchronous distributed algorithm for finding a minimum spanning tree in a weighted network of n vertices and m edges having a message complexity that is $O(m+n\log n)$.

Hint: Consider that advantage that comes from first sorting the edges incident on each vertex.

C-11.7 Describe an asynchronous distributed algorithm for finding a minimum spanning tree in a weighted network of n vertices and m edges having a message complexity that is $O(m \log n)$.

Hint: Consider using a "pulsing" strategy that counts the rounds the algorithm is performing.

C-11.8 Describe a modification to the distributed minimum spanning tree algorithm described in class so that we do not need to assume that the weights of the edges are unique.

Hint: Describe a local tie-breaking rule so that under this rule the minimum spanning tree is unique.

C-11.9 Consider a passive dynamic version of the flooding algorithm using sequence numbers that is resilient against network partitions occurring while the algorithm is running. The main idea of this approach is to have each router that initiates a flooding broadcast to store old messages for a sufficient amount of time longer than any anticipated network failure. Each router still stores the latest sequence number for a flooding message coming from each other router. But now if a router x receives a flooding message y with a sequence number i more than 1 greater than x's previously recorded sequence number j from y, then x initiates a reply flooding message that requests that y resend its messages $j+1$ through $i-1$. Show how accommodating for this "fix" could result in infinitely looping flooding messages.

C-11.10 Consider a version of the flooding algorithm using sequence numbers or hop counters, where each time a router x is unable to forward a message M onto an adjacent router y (for example, because the connection (x,y) is down), then x buffers the message in a queue. Your algorithm should work in a ***dynamic*** setting, where communication links can fail and be restored. Design your protocol so that when a link (x,y) is restored, x sends to y all the messages that had previously been queued up on this connection. Show how this allows for flooding messages to be sent robustly even in the presence of temporary network partitions. How much additional space is needed to implement this solution? How should this algorithm be modified to allow for computers that are permanently disconnected from the network?

C-11.11 Let G be a network represented as a graph, whose n nodes represent routers and whose m edges represent connections. Suppose further that G is static (that is, it doesn't change) and that there is a spanning tree T defined on the nodes of G. T need not be a minimum spanning tree, but it includes all the nodes of G and, for each node v of G, v stores its neighbors in G and it also knows which of these are also neighbors in T. Describe how to utilize the tree T to improve the message complexity for performing the link-state shortest path setup algorithm (which builds the routing tables for shortest-path routing). What is the message complexity of this revised algorithm?

C-11.12 Suppose that a routing algorithm, such as link state or distance vector, has completed its setup phase on a stable network (with no link changes). That is, each router i stores a vector D, such that $D[j]$ stores the distance from router i to router j, together with the name of the next hop on the path to j. Design an efficient algorithm that allows all the routers to verify that all their routing tables are correct. What is the message complexity of this algorithm?

C-11.13 Suppose that we are implementing multicasting using the center-based tree approach, so each member of the multicast group dynamically enters the group by sending a join message toward the root of the tree, and the path this message traverses forms a new path in the center-based tree (joining up at some previous node of the center-based tree). Members leave the tree in a similar, but reversed, manner. Describe how to modify the join algorithm, so that each time some router x wants to join the group it is automatically connected to the node in the center-based tree that is closest to x (note that this node might not actually be a member of the group).

C-11.14 Show how to extend your solution to the previous problem so that rather than finding the closest tree node to a new router x it instead finds the closest group member to x. This node is an ideal candidate for an ***anycast*** request, which requests that any member of a certain group respond to a certain query.

C-11.15 Suppose we use digital signatures in the standard flooding algorithm (using sequence numbers), so that each router wanting to send a flooding message must sign that message. During transmission, if any router receives a packet that was not correctly signed by its source router, then this packet is discarded. Still, this algorithm allows a source x to sign two different flooding messages with the same sequence number and send those out to different neighbors at the same time. Describe an algorithm for detecting if such a problem occurs, assuming that the network is biconnected and x is the only "bad" router. What is the message complexity of your algorithm?

Projects

P-11.1 Use a network access protocol, like "ping " or "HTTP" to collect the following statistics on four hosts on the Internet that are physically on four different continents on the earth (that is, four of the following: North America, South America, Europe, Asia, Africa, Australia, Antarctica):

- The minimum, average, standard deviation, and maximum round-trip time taken over 50 consecutive packet requests (all within a few seconds of each other). Plot your data as a scatter plot, with x-axis representing each round-trip and the y-axis representing round-trip time.
- The average round-trip time, taken over 10 consecutive packet requests (all within a few seconds of each other), but repeated at least every 4 hours over at least 2 days. Ideally, you should repeat your experiment of 10 pings every hour for 5 days (using a background process). Plot your data with time-of-day as the x-axis, and round-trip time as the y-axis, and overlay the statistics from all four hosts as line plots on the same graph.

P-11.2 Do an experimental comparison of the approximation algorithm for the Steiner tree multicasting approach with the center-based trees approach. Is the edge usage significantly better for one of these approaches? If so, under what assumptions about the distribution of join requests?

Chapter Notes

The reader interested in further study in distributed algorithms is referred to the excellent books by Lynch [137], Peleg [166], and Tel [202]. The reader interested in further reading on computer networks and protocols is referred to the books by Comer [52], Huitema [105], and indTanenbaum [196]. The distributed implementation of Barůvka's algorithm is due to Galleger *et al.* [74]. A simple way to implement it in an asynchronous network is due to Awerbuch [18].

Part

IV Additional Topics

Chapter

12 Computational Geometry

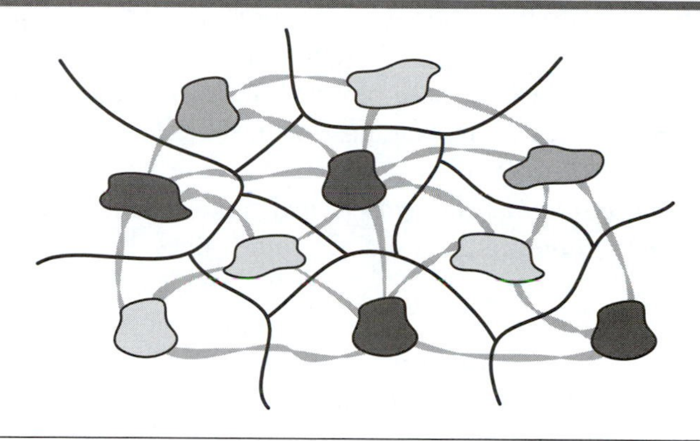

Contents

12.1 Range Trees 549

12.1.1 One-Dimensional Range Searching 550

12.1.2 Two-Dimensional Range Searching 553

12.2 Priority Search Trees 556

12.2.1 Constructing a Priority Search Tree 557

12.2.2 Searching in a Priority Search Tree 558

12.2.3 Priority Range Trees 560

12.3 Quadtrees and k-D Trees 561

12.3.1 Quadtrees 561

12.3.2 k-D Trees 563

12.4 The Plane Sweep Technique 565

12.4.1 Orthogonal Segment Intersection 565

12.4.2 Finding a Closest Pair of Points 568

12.5 Convex Hulls 572

12.5.1 Representations of Geometric Objects 572

12.5.2 Point Orientation Testing 574

12.5.3 Basic Properties of Convex Hulls 576

12.5.4 The Gift Wrapping Algorithm 578

12.5.5 The Graham Scan Algorithm 580

12.6 Java Example: Convex Hull 583

12.7 Exercises 587

We live in a multi-dimensional geometric world. Physical space itself is three-dimensional, for we can use three coordinates, x, y, and z, to describe points in space. Completely describing the orientation of the tip of a robot arm actually requires six dimensions, for we use three dimensions to describe the position of the tip in space, plus three more dimensions to describe the angles the tip is in (which are typically called pitch, roll, and yaw). Describing the state of an airplane in flight takes at least nine dimensions, for we need six to describe its orientation in the same manner as for the tip of a robot arm, and we need three more to describe the plane's velocity. In fact, these physical representations are considered "low-dimensional," particularly in applications in machine learning or computational biology, where 100- and 1000-dimensional spaces are not unusual. This chapter is directed at ***computational geometry***, which studies data structures and algorithms for dealing with geometric data, such as points, lines, and polygons.

There are actually a great number of different data structures and algorithms for processing multi-dimensional geometric data, and it is beyond the scope of this chapter to discuss all of them. Instead, we provide an introduction to some of the more interesting ones in this chapter. We begin with a discussion of ***range trees***, which can store multi-dimensional points so as to support a special kind of search operation, called a ***range-searching query***, and we also include an interesting variant of the range tree called the ***priority search tree***. Finally, we discuss a class of data structures, called ***partition trees***, which partition space into cells, and focus on variants known as ***quadtrees*** and ***k-d trees***.

We follow this discussion by introducing a general-purpose algorithmic design pattern, called the ***plane-sweep*** technique, which is particularly useful for solving two-dimensional geometric problems. We illustrate the applicability of this technique by showing how it can be used to solve two-dimensional computational geometry problems, by reducing them to a series of one-dimensional problems. Specifically, we apply the plane-sweep technique to the computation of the intersections of a set of orthogonal line segments and to the identification of a pair of points with minimum distance from a set of points. The plane-sweep technique can be used for many additional problems, some of which we explore in exercises at the end of this chapter.

We conclude this chapter by studying a problem that has applications in computer graphics, statistics, geographic information systems, robotics, and computer vision. In this problem, known as the ***convex hull*** problem, we are interested in finding the smallest convex set that contains a given set of points. Constructing such a set allows us to define the "boundary" of a set of points; hence, this problem also raises some interesting issues about how to represent geometric objects and perform geometric tests.

12.1 Range Trees

Multi-dimensional data arise in a variety of applications, including statistics and robotics. The simplest type of multi-dimensional data are d-dimensional points, which can be represented by a sequence $(x_0, x_1, \ldots, x_{d-1})$ of numeric ***coordinates***. In business applications, a d-dimensional point may represent the various attributes of a product or an employee in a database. For example, televisions in an electronics catalog would probably have different attribute values for price, screen size, weight, height, width, and depth. Multi-dimensional data can also come from scientific applications, where each point represents attributes of individual experiments or observations. For example, heavenly objects in an astronomy sky survey would probably have different attribute values for brightness (or apparent magnitude), diameter, distance, and position in the sky (which is itself two-dimensional).

A natural query operation to perform on a set of multi-dimensional points is a ***range-search query***, which is a request to retrieve all points in a multi-dimensional collection whose coordinates fall within given ranges. For example, a consumer wishing to buy a new television may request, from an electronic store's catalog, all units that have a screensize between 24 and 27 inches, and have a price between \$200 and \$400. Alternately, an astronomer interested in studying asteroids may request all heavenly objects that are at a distance between 1.5 and 10 astronomical units, have an apparent magnitude between $+1$ and $+15$, and have a diameter between 0.5 and $1,000$ kilometers. The range tree data structure, which we discuss in this section, can be used to answer such queries.

Two-Dimensional Range-Search Queries

To keep the discussion simple, let us focus on two-dimensional range-searching queries. Exercise C-12.6 addresses how the corresponding two-dimensional range tree data structure can be extended to higher dimensions. A ***two-dimensional dictionary*** is an ADT for storing key-element items such that the key is a pair (x,y) of numbers, called the ***coordinates*** of the element. A two-dimensional dictionary D supports the following fundamental query operation:

findAllInRange(x_1, x_2, y_1, y_2): Return all the elements of D with coordinates (x,y) such that $x_1 \leq x \leq x_2$ and $y_1 \leq y \leq y_2$.

Operation findAllInRange is the ***reporting*** version of the range-searching query, because it asks for all the items satisfying the range constraints. There is also a ***counting*** version of the range query, in which we are simply interested in the number of items in that range. We present data structures for realizing a two-dimensional dictionary in the remainder of this section.

12.1.1 One-Dimensional Range Searching

Before we proceed to two-dimensional searching, we make a slight digression to study ***one-dimensional range searching***, where, given an ordered dictionary D, we want to perform the following query operation:

findAllInRange(k_1, k_2): Return all the elements in dictionary D with key k such that $k_1 \leq k \leq k_2$.

Let us discuss how we can use a binary search tree T representing dictionary D (see Chapter 3) to perform query findAllInRange(k_1, k_2). We use a recursive method 1DTreeRangeSearch that takes as arguments the range parameters k_1 and k_2 and a node v in T. If node v is external, we are done. If node v is internal, we have three cases, depending on the value of key(v), the key of the item stored at node v:

- key$(v) < k_1$: We recurse on the right child of v.
- $k_1 \leq$ key$(v) \leq k_2$: We report element(v) and recurse on both children of v.
- key$(v) > k_2$: We recurse on the left child of v.

We describe this search procedure in Algorithm 12.1 (1DTreeRangeSearch) and illustrate it in Figure 12.2. We perform operation findAllInRange(k_1, k_2) by calling 1DTreeRangeSearch$(k_1, k_2, T.$root$())$. Intuitively, method 1DTreeRangeSearch is a modification of the standard binary-tree search method (Algorithm 3.5), allowing search for "both" keys k_1 and k_2.

Algorithm 1DTreeRangeSearch(k_1, k_2, v):
 Input: Search keys k_1 and k_2, and a node v of a binary search tree T
 Output: The elements stored in the subtree of T rooted at v, whose keys are greater than or equal to k_1 and less than or equal to k_2

```
if T.isExternal(v) then
   return ∅
if k1 ≤ key(v) ≤ k2 then
   L ← 1DTreeRangeSearch(k1, k2, T.leftChild(v))
   R ← 1DTreeRangeSearch(k1, k2, T.rightChild(v))
   return L ∪ {element(v)} ∪ R
else if key(v) < k1 then
   return 1DTreeRangeSearch(k1, k2, T.rightChild(v))
else if k2 < key(v) then
   return 1DTreeRangeSearch(k1, k2, T.leftChild(v))
```

Algorithm 12.1: Recursive method for one-dimensional range search in a binary search tree.

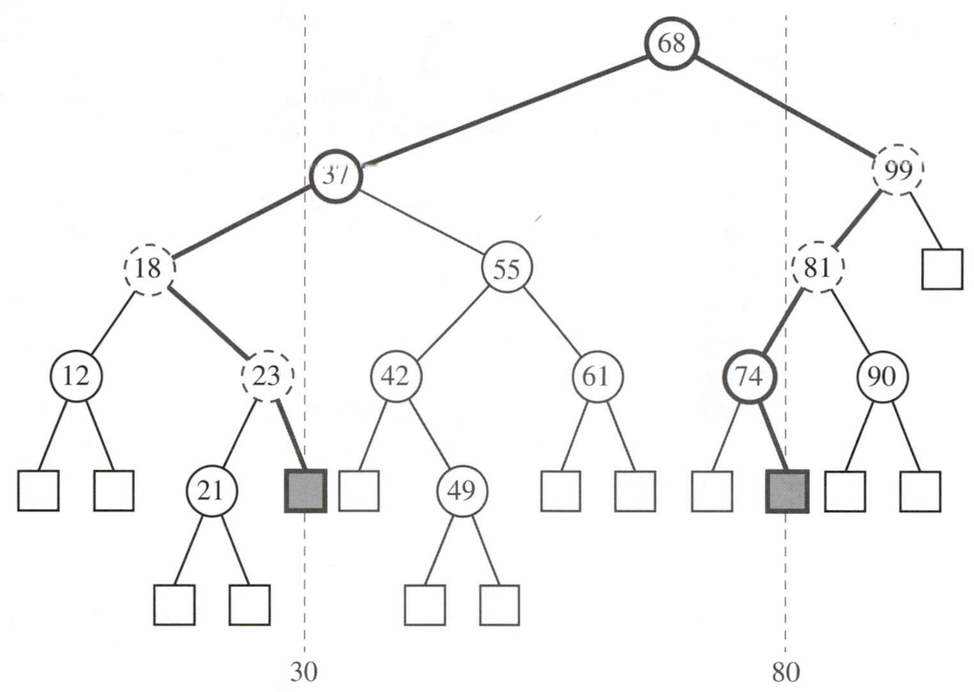

Figure 12.2: One-dimensional range search using a binary search tree for $k_1 = 30$ and $k_2 = 80$. Paths P_1 and P_2 of boundary nodes are drawn with thick lines. The boundary nodes storing items with key outside the interval $[k_1, k_2]$ are drawn with dashed lines. There are ten inside nodes.

Performance

We now analyze the running time of algorithm 1DTreeRangeSearch. In our analysis, we assume, for simplicity, that T does not contain items with key k_1 or k_2. The extension of the analysis to the general case is left as an exercise.

Let P_1 the search path traversed when performing a search in tree T for key k_1. Path P_1 starts at the root of T and ends at an external node of T. Define a path P_2 similarly with respect to k_2. We identify each node v of T as belonging to one of following three groups (see Figure 12.2):

- Node v is a ***boundary node*** if v belongs to P_1 or P_2; a boundary node stores an item whose key may be inside or outside the interval $[k_1, k_2]$.
- Node v is an ***inside node*** if v is not a boundary node and v belongs to a subtree rooted at a right child of a node of P_1 or at a left child of a node of P_2; an internal inside node stores an item whose key is inside the interval $[k_1, k_2]$.
- Node v is an ***outside node*** if v is not a boundary node and v belongs to a subtree rooted at a left child of a node of P_1 or at a right child of a node of P_2; an internal outside node stores an item whose key is outside the interval $[k_1, k_2]$.

Consider the execution of algorithm 1DTreeRangeSearch(k_1, k_2, r), where r is the root of T. We traverse a path of boundary nodes, calling the algorithm recursively either on the left or on the right child, until we reach either an external node or an internal node w (which may be the root) with key in the range $[k_1, k_2]$. In the first case (we reach an external node), the algorithm terminates returning the empty set. In the second case, the execution continues by calling the algorithm recursively at both of w's children. We know that node w is the bottommost node common to paths P_1 and P_2. For each boundary node v visited from this point on, we either make a single call at a child of v, which is also a boundary node, or we make a call at one child of v that is a boundary node and the other child that is an inside node. Once we visit an inside node, we will visit all of its (inside node) descendents.

Since we spend a constant amount of work per node visited by the algorithm, the running time of the algorithm is proportional to the number of nodes visited. We count the nodes visited as follows:

- We visit no outside nodes.
- We visit at most $2h+1$ boundary nodes, where h is the height of T, since boundary nodes are on the search paths P_1 and P_2 and they share at least one node (the root of T).
- Each time we visit an inside node v, we also visit the entire subtree T_v of T rooted at v and we add all the elements stored at internal nodes of T_v to the reported set. If T_v holds s_v items, then it has $2s_v + 1$ nodes. The inside nodes can be partitioned into j disjoint subtrees $T_1, \ldots, T_j$ rooted at children of boundary nodes, where $j \leq 2h$. Denoting with s_i the number of items stored in tree T_i, we have that the total number of inside nodes visited is

$$\sum_{i=1}^{j}(2s_i + 1) = 2s + j \leq 2s + 2h.$$

Therefore, at most $2s+4h+1$ nodes of T are visited and operation findAllInRange runs in $O(h+s)$ time. If we wish to minimize h in the worst case, we should choose T to be a balanced binary search tree, such as an AVL tree (Section 3.2) or a red-black tree (Section 3.3.3), so that h is $O(\log n)$. Moreover, by using a balanced binary search tree, we can additionally perform operations insertItem and removeElement in $O(\log n)$ time each. We summarize:

Theorem 12.1: *A balanced binary search tree supports one-dimensional range searching in an ordered dictionary with n items:*

- *The space used is $O(n)$.*
- *Operation* findAllInRange *takes $O(\log n + s)$ time, where s is the number of elements reported.*
- *Operations* insertItem *and* removeElement *each take $O(\log n)$ time.*

12.1.2 Two-Dimensional Range Searching

The two-dimensional range tree (Figure 12.3) is a data structure realizing the two-dimensional dictionary ADT. It consists of a ***primary*** structure, which is a balanced binary search tree T, together with a number of ***auxiliary*** structures. Specifically, as we describe below, each internal node in the primary structure T stores a reference to a related auxiliary structure. The function of the primary structure, T, is to support searching based on x-coordinates. To also support searching in terms of the y-coordinates, we use a collection of auxiliary data structures, each of which is a one-dimensional range tree that uses y-coordinates as its keys. The primary structure of T is a balanced binary search tree built using the x-coordinates of the items as the keys. An internal node v of T stores the following data:

- An item, whose coordinates are denoted by $x(v)$ and $y(v)$, and whose element is denoted by element(v).
- A one-dimensional range tree $T(v)$ that stores the same set of items as the subtree rooted at v in T (including v), but using the y-coordinates as keys.

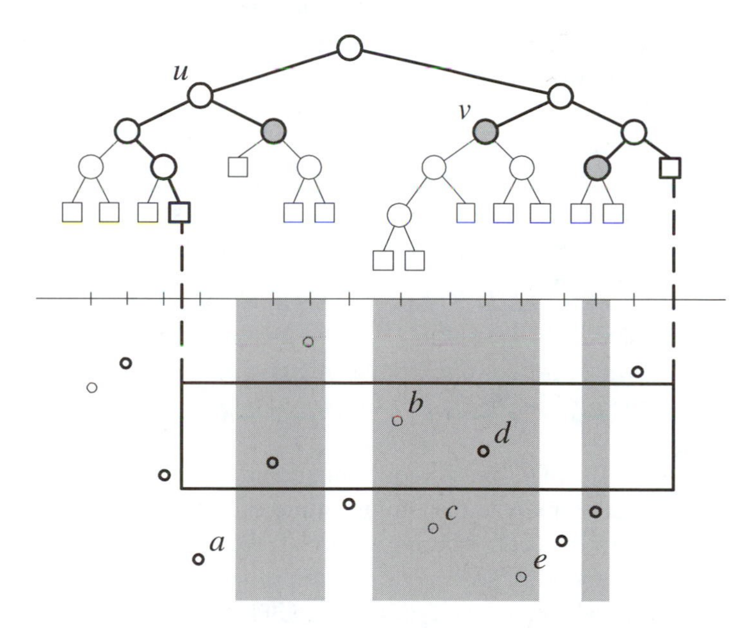

Figure 12.3: A set of items with two-dimensional keys represented by a two-dimensional range tree, and a range search on it. The primary structure T is shown. The nodes of T visited by the search algorithm are drawn with thick lines. The boundary nodes are white-filled, and the allocation nodes are grey-filled. Point a, stored at boundary node u, is outside the search range. The grey vertical strips cover the points stored at the auxiliary structures of the allocation nodes. For example, the auxiliary structure of node v stores points b, c, d, and e.

Lemma 12.2: *A two-dimensional range tree storing n items uses $O(n \log n)$ space and can be constructed in $O(n \log n)$ time.*

Proof: The primary structure uses $O(n)$ space. There are n secondary structures. The size of an auxiliary structure is proportional to the number of items stored in it. An item stored at node v of the primary structure T is also stored at each auxiliary structure $T(u)$ such that u is an ancestor of v. Since tree T is balanced, node v has $O(\log n)$ ancestors. Hence, there are $O(\log n)$ copies of the item in the auxiliary structures. Thus, the total space used is $O(n \log n)$. The construction algorithm is left as an exercise (C-12.2). ■

The algorithm for operation findAllInRange(x_1, x_2, y_1, y_2) begins by performing what is essentially a one-dimensional range search on the primary structure T for the range $[x_1, x_2]$. Namely, we traverse down tree T in search of inside nodes. We make one important modification, however: when we reach an inside node v, instead of recursively visiting the subtree rooted at v, we perform a one-dimensional range search for the interval $[y_1, y_2]$ in the auxiliary structure of v.

We call ***allocation nodes*** the inside nodes of T that are children of boundary nodes. The algorithm visits the boundary nodes and the allocation nodes of T, but not the other inside nodes. Each boundary node v is classified by the algorithm as a ***left node***, ***middle node***, or ***right node***. A middle node is in the intersection of the search paths P_1 for x_1 and P_2 for x_2. A left node is in P_1 but not in P_2. A right node is in P_2 but not in P_1. At each allocation node v, the algorithm executes a one-dimensional range search on the auxiliary structure $T(v)$ for the y-range $[y_1, y_2]$.

We give the details of this method in Algorithm 12.4 (see also Figure 12.3).

Theorem 12.3: *A two-dimensional range tree T for a set of n items with two-dimensional keys uses $O(n \log n)$ space and can be constructed in $O(n \log n)$ time. Using T, a two-dimensional range-search query takes time $O(\log^2 n + s)$, where s is the number of elements reported.*

Proof: The space requirement and construction time follow from Lemma 12.2. We now analyze the running time of a range-search query performed with Algorithm 12.4 (2DTreeRangeSearch). We account for the time spent at each boundary node and allocation node of the primary structure T. The algorithm spends a constant amount of time at each boundary node. Since there are $O(\log n)$ boundary nodes, the overall time spent at the boundary nodes is $O(\log n)$. For each allocation node v, the algorithm spends $O(\log n_v + s_v)$ time doing a one-dimensional range search in auxiliary structure $T(v)$, where n_v is the number of items stored in $T(v)$ and s_v is the number of elements returned by the range search in $T(v)$. Denoting with A the set of allocation nodes, we have that the total time spent at the allocation nodes is proportional to $\sum_{v \in A}(\log n_v + s_v)$. Since $|A|$ is $O(\log n)$, $n_v \leq n$ and $\sum_{v \in A} \leq s$, we have that the overall time spent at the allocation nodes is $O(\log^2 n + s)$. We conclude that a two-dimensional range search takes $O(\log^2 n + s)$ time. ■

```
Algorithm 2DTreeRangeSearch(x1,x2,y1,y2,v,t):
  Input: Search keys x1, x2, y1, and y2; node v in the primary structure T of a
    two-dimensional range tree; type t of node v
  Output: The items in the subtree rooted at v whose coordinates are in the x-
    range [x1,x2] and in the y-range [y1,y2]
  if T.isExternal(v) then
    return ∅
  if x1 ≤ x(v) ≤ x2 then
    if y1 ≤ y(v) ≤ y2 then
      M ← {element(v)}
    else
      M ← ∅
    if t = "left" then
      L ← 2DTreeRangeSearch(x1,x2,y1,y2,T.leftChild(v),"left")
      R ← 1DTreeRangeSearch(y1,y2,T.rightChild(v))
    else if t = "right" then
      L ← 1DTreeRangeSearch(y1,y2,T.leftChild(v))
      R ← 2DTreeRangeSearch(x1,x2,y1,y2,T.rightChild(v),"right")
    else
      { t = "middle }
      L ← 2DTreeRangeSearch(x1,x2,y1,y2,T.leftChild(v),"left")
      R ← 2DTreeRangeSearch(x1,x2,y1,y2,T.rightChild(v),"right")
  else
    M ← ∅
    if x(v) < x1 then
      L ← ∅
      R ← 2DTreeRangeSearch(x1,x2,y1,y2,T.rightChild(v),t)
    else
      { x(v) > x2 }
      L ← 2DTreeRangeSearch(x1,x2,y1,y2,T.leftChild(v),t)
      R ← ∅
    return L ∪ M ∪ R
```

Algorithm 12.4: Recursive method for two-dimensional range search in a two-dimensional range tree. The initial method call is 2DTreeRangeSearch$(x_1,x_2,y_1,y_2,T.\text{root}(),$"middle"$)$. The algorithm is called recursively on all the boundary nodes with respect to the x-range $[x_1,x_2]$. Parameter t indicates whether v is a left, middle, or right boundary node.

12.2 Priority Search Trees

In this section, we present the ***priority search tree*** structure, which can answer ***three-sided*** range queries on a set S of items with two-dimensional keys:

findAllInRange(x_1,x_2,y_1): Return all the items of S with coordinates (x,y) such that $x_1 \leq x \leq x_2$ and $y_1 \leq y$.

Geometrically, this query asks us to return all points between two vertical lines ($x = x_1$ and $x = x_2$) and above a horizontal line ($y = y_1$).

A ***priority search tree*** for set S is a binary tree storing the items of S that behaves like a binary search tree with respect to the x-coordinates, and like a heap with respect to the y-coordinates. For simplicity, let us assume that all the items of S have distinct x and y-coordinates. If set S is empty, T consists of a single external node. Otherwise, let $\bar{p}$ be the topmost item of of S, that is, the item with with maximum y-coordinate. We denote with $\hat{x}$ the median x-coordinate of the items in $S - \{\bar{p}\}$, and with S_L and S_R the subsets of $S - \{\bar{p}\}$ with items having x-coordinate less than or equal to $\hat{x}$ and greater than $\hat{x}$, respectively. We recursively define the priority search tree T for S as follows:

- The root T stores item $\bar{p}$ and the median x-coordinate $\hat{x}$.
- The left subtree of T is a priority search tree for S_L.
- The right subtree of T is a priority search tree for S_R.

For each internal node v of T, we denote with $\bar{p}(v)$, $\bar{x}(v)$, and $\bar{y}(v)$ the topmost item stored at v and its coordinates. Also, we denote with $\hat{x}(v)$ the median x-coordinate stored at v. An example of a priority search tree is shown in Figure 12.5.

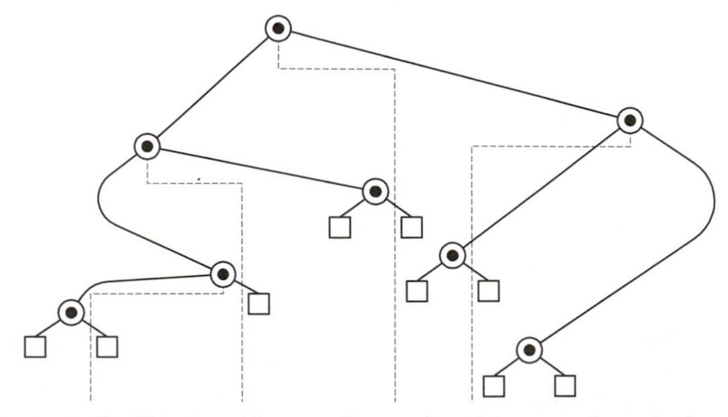

Figure 12.5: A set S of items with two-dimensional keys and a priority search tree T for S. Each internal node v of T is drawn as a circle around point $\bar{p}(v)$. The median x-coordinate $\hat{x}(v)$ is represented by a dashed line below node v that separates the items stored in the left subtree of v from those stored in the right subtree.

12.2.1 Constructing a Priority Search Tree

The y-coordinates of the items stored at the nodes of a priority search tree T satisfy the heap-order property (Section 2.4.3). That is, if u is the parent of v, then $\bar{y}(u) > \bar{y}(v)$. Also, the median x-coordinates stored at the nodes of T define a binary search tree (Section 3.1.2). These two facts motivate the term "priority search tree." Let us therefore explain how to construct a priority search tree from a set S of n two-dimensional items. We begin by sorting S by increasing x-coordinate, and then call the recursive method buildPST(S) shown in Algorithm 12.6.

Algorithm buildPST(S):
  Input: A sequence S of n two-dimensional items, sorted by x-coordinate
  Output: A priority search tree T for S

  Create an elementary binary tree T consisting of single external node v
  if !S.isEmpty() **then**
    Traverse sequence S to find the item $\bar{p}$ of S with highest y-coordinate
    Remove $\bar{p}$ from S
    $\bar{p}(v) \leftarrow \bar{p}$
    $\hat{p} \leftarrow S$.elemAtRank($\lceil S$.size()$/2\rceil$)
    $\hat{x}(v) \leftarrow x(\hat{p})$
    Split S into two subsequences, S_L and S_R, where S_L contains the items up to $\hat{p}$ (included), and S_R contains the remaining items
    $T_L \leftarrow$ buildPST(S_L)
    $T_R \leftarrow$ buildPST(S_R)
    T.expandExternal(v)
    Replace the left child of v with T_L
    Replace the right child of v with T_R
  return T

Algorithm 12.6: Recursive construction of a priority search tree.

Lemma 12.4: *Given a set S of n two-dimensional items, a priority search tree for S uses $O(n)$ space, has height $O(\log n)$, and can be built in $O(n \log n)$ time.*

Proof: The $O(n)$ space requirement follows from the fact that every internal node of the priority search tree T stores a distinct item of S. The height of T follows from the halving of the number of nodes at each level. The preliminary sorting of the items of S by x-coordinate can be done in $O(n \log n)$ time using an asymptotically optimal sorting algorithm, such as heap sort or merge sort. The running time $T(n)$ of method buildPST (Algorithm 12.6) is characterized by the recurrence, $T(n) = 2T(n/2) + bn$, for some constant $b > 0$. Therefore, by the Master Theorem (5.6), $T(n)$ is $O(n \log n)$. ■

12.2.2 Searching in a Priority Search Tree

We now show how to perform a three-sided range query findAllInRange(x_1,x_2,y_1) on a priority search tree T. We traverse down T in a fashion similar to that of a one-dimensional range-search for the range $[x_1,x_2]$. One important difference, however, is that we only continue searching in the subtree of a node v if $y(v) \geq y_1$. We give the details of the algorithm for three-sided range searching in Algorithm 12.7 (PSTSearch) and we illustrate the execution of the algorithm in Figure 12.8.

Algorithm PSTSearch(x_1,x_2,y_1,v):
Input: Three-sided range, defined by x_1, x_2, and y_1, and a node v of a priority search tree T
Output: The items stored in the subtree rooted at v with coordinates (x,y), such that $x_1 \leq x \leq x_2$ and $y_1 \leq y$

```
if ȳ(v) < y1 then
    return ∅
if x1 ≤ x̄(v) ≤ x2 then
    M ← {p̄(v)}           {we should output p̄(v)}
else
    M ← ∅
if x1 ≤ x̂(v) then
    L ← PSTSearch(x1,x2,y1,T.leftChild(v))
else
    L ← ∅
if x̂(v) ≤ x2 then
    R ← PSTSearch(x1,x2,y1,T.rightChild(v))
else
    R ← ∅
return L ∪ M ∪ R
```

Algorithm 12.7: Three-sided range searching in a priority search tree T. The algorithm is initially called with PSTSearch$(x_1,x_2,y_1,T.\text{root}())$.

Note that we have defined three-sided ranges to have a left, right, and bottom side, and to be unbounded at the top. This restriction was made without loss of generality, however, for we could have defined our three-sided range queries using any three sides of a rectangle. The priority search tree from such an alternate definition is similar to the one defined above, but "turned on its side."

Let us analyze the running time of method PSTSearch for answering a three-sided range-search query on a priority search tree T storing a set of n items with two-dimensional keys. We denote with s the number of items reported. Since we spend $O(1)$ time for each node we visit, the running time of method PSTSearch is proportional to the number of visited nodes.

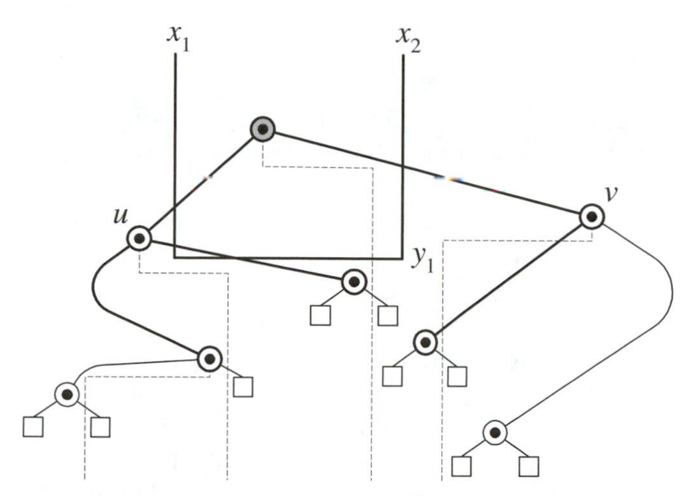

Figure 12.8: Three-sided range-searching in a priority search tree. The nodes visited are drawn with thick lines. The nodes storing reported items are grey-filled.

Each node v visited by method PSTSearch is classified as follows:

- Node v is a ***boundary node*** if it is on the search path for x_1 or x_2 when viewing T as a binary search tree on the median x-coordinate stored at its nodes. The item stored at an internal boundary node may be inside or outside the three-sided range. By Lemma 12.4, the height of T is $O(\log n)$. Thus, there are $O(\log n)$ boundary nodes.
- Node v is an ***inside node*** if it is internal, it is not a boundary node, and $\bar{y}(v) \geq y_1$. The item stored at an internal node is inside the three-sided range. The number of inside nodes is no more than the number s of items reported.
- Node v is a ***terminal node*** if it is not a boundary node and, if internal, $\bar{y}(v) < y_1$. The item stored at an internal terminal node is outside the three-sided range. Each terminal node is the child of a boundary node or of an inside node. Thus, the number of terminal nodes is at most twice the number of boundary nodes plus inside nodes. Hence, there are $O(\log n + s)$ terminal nodes.

We conclude that PSTSearch visits $O(\log n + s)$ nodes, giving us the following.

Theorem 12.5: *A priority search tree T storing n items with two-dimensional keys uses $O(n)$ space and can be constructed in $O(n \log n)$ time. Using T, a three-sided range queries takes $O(\log n + s)$ time, where s is the number of items reported.*

Of course, three-sided range queries are not as general as regular (four-sided) range queries, which can be answered in $O(\log^2 n + k)$ time using the range tree data structure discussed in the previous section. Still, priority search trees can be used to speed up the running time of answering standard four-sided, two-dimensional range queries. The resulting data structure, which is known as the ***priority range tree***, uses priority search trees as auxiliary structures in a way that achieves the same space bound as traditional range trees. We discuss this data structure next.

12.2.3 Priority Range Trees

Let T be a balanced binary search tree storing n items with two-dimensional keys, ordered according to their x-coordinates. We show how to augment T with priority search trees as auxiliary structures to answer (four-sided) range queries. The resulting data structure is called a ***priority range tree***.

To convert T into a priority range tree, we visit each internal node v of T other than the root and construct, as an auxiliary structure, a priority search tree $T(v)$ for the items stored in the subtree of T rooted at v. If v is a left child, $T(v)$ answers range queries for three-side ranges unbounded on the right. If v is a right child, $T(v)$ answers range queries for three-side ranges unbounded on the left. By Lemmas 12.2 and 12.4, a priority range tree uses $O(n \log n)$ space and can be constructed in $O(n \log n)$ time. The method for performing a two dimensional range query in a priority range tree is given in Algorithm 12.9 (PSTRangeSearch).

Algorithm PSTRangeSearch(x_1, x_2, y_1, y_2, v):
 Input: Search keys x_1, x_2, y_1, and y_2; node v in the primary structure T of a priority range tree
 Output: The items in the subtree rooted at v whose coordinates are in the x-range $[x_1, x_2]$ and in the y-range $[y_1, y_2]$

```
if T.isExternal(v) then
   return ∅
if x1 ≤ x(v) ≤ x2 then
   if y1 ≤ y(v) ≤ y2 then
      M ← {element(v)}
   else
      M ← ∅
   L ← PSTSearch(x1, y1, y2, T(leftChild(v)).root())
   R ← PSTSearch(x2, y1, y2, T(rightChild(v)).root())
   return L ∪ M ∪ R
else if x(v) < x1 then
   return PSTRangeSearch(x1, x2, y1, y2, T.rightChild(v))
else
   { x2 < x(v) }
   return PSTRangeSearch(x1, x2, y1, y2, T.leftChild(v))
```

Algorithm 12.9: Range searching in a priority range tree T. The algorithm is initially called with PSTRangeSearch$(x_1, x_2, y_1, y_2, T.\text{root}())$.

Theorem 12.6: *A priority range tree T for a set of n items with two-dimensional keys uses $O(n \log n)$ space and can be constructed in $O(n \log n)$ time. Using T, a two-dimensional range-search query takes time $O(\log n + s)$, where s is the number of elements reported.*

12.3 Quadtrees and k-D Trees

Multi-dimensional data sets often come from large applications; hence, we often desire linear-space structures for storing them. A general framework for designing such linear-space structures for d-dimensional data, where the dimensionality d is assumed to be a fixed constant, is based on an approach called the partition tree.

A ***partition tree*** is a rooted tree T that has at most n external nodes, where n is the number of d-dimensional points in our given set S. Each external node of a partition tree T stores a different small subset from S. Each internal node v in a partition tree T corresponds to a region of d-dimensional space, which is then divided into some number c of different cells or regions associated with v's children. For each region R associated with a child u of v, we require that all the points in u's subtree fall inside the region R. Ideally, the c different cells for v's children should easily be distinguished using a constant number of comparisons and arithmetic calculations.

12.3.1 Quadtrees

The first partition tree data structure we discuss is the ***quadtree***. The main application for quadtrees is for sets of points that come from images, where x- and y-coordinates are integers, because the data points come from image pixels. In addition, they exhibit their best properties if the distributions of points is fairly nonuniform, with some areas being mostly empty and others being dense.

Suppose we are given a set S of n points in the plane. In addition, let R denote a square region that contains all the points of S (for example, R could be a bounding box of a 2048×2048 image that produced the set S). The quadtree data structure is a partition tree T such that the root r of T is associated with the region R. To get to the next level in T, we subdivide R into four equal-sized squares R_1, R_2, R_3, and R_4, and we associate each square R_i with a potential child of the root r. Specifically, we create a child v_i of r, if the square R_i contains a point in S. If a square R_i contains no points of S, then we create no child of r for it. This process of refining R into the squares R_1, R_2, R_3, and R_4 is called a ***split***.

The ***quadtree*** T is defined by recursively performing a split at each child v of r if necessary. That is, each child v of r has a square region R_i associated with it, and if the region R_i for v contains more than one point of S, then we perform a split at v, subdividing R_i into four equal-sized squares and repeating the above subdivision process at v. We continue in this manner, splitting squares that contain more than one point into four subsquares, and recursing on the nonempty subsquares, until we have separated all the points of S into individual squares. We then store each point p in S at the external node of T that corresponds to the smallest square in the subdivision process that contains p. We store at each internal node v a concise representation of the split that we performed for v.

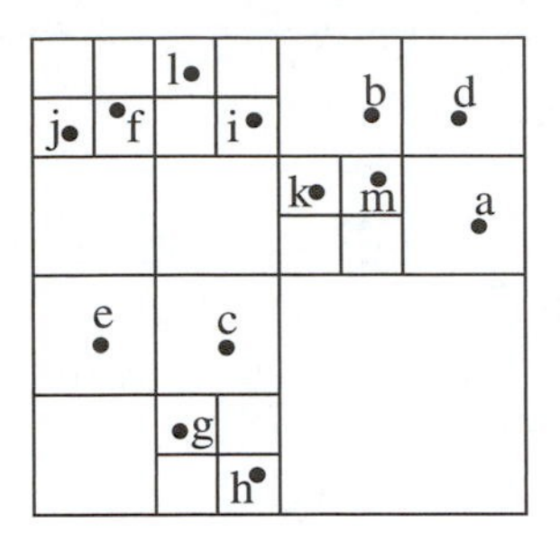

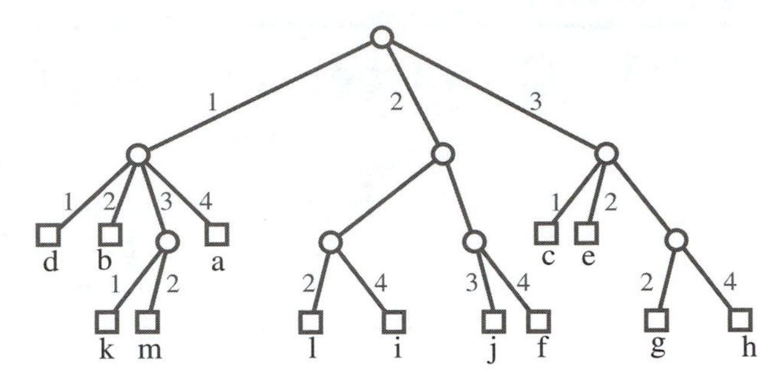

Figure 12.10: A quadtree. We illustrate an example point set and its corresponding quadtree data structure.

We illustrate an example point set and an associated quadtree in Figure 12.10. Note, however, that, contrary to the illustration, there is potentially no upper bound on the depth of a quadtree, as we have previously defined. For example, our point set S could contain two points that are very close to one another, and it may take a long sequence of splits before we separate these two points. Thus, it is customary for quadtree designers to specify some upper bound D on the depth of T. Given a set S of n points in the plane, we can construct a quadtree T for S so as to spend $O(n)$ time building each level of T. Thus, in the worst case, constructing such a depth-bounded quadtree takes $O(Dn)$ time.

Answering Range Queries with a Quadtree

One of the queries that quadtrees are often used to answer is range searching. Suppose that we are given a rectangle A aligned with the coordinate axes, and are asked to use a quadtree T to return all the points in S that are contained in A. The method for answering this query is quite simple. We start with the root r of T, and we compare the region R for r to A. If A and R do not intersect at all, then we are done—there are no points in the subtree rooted at r that fall inside A. Alternatively, if A completely contains R, then we simply enumerate all the external node descendents of r. These are two simple cases. If instead R and A intersect, but A does not completely contain R, then we recursively perform this search on each child v of r.

Performance

In performing such a range-searching query, we can traverse the entire tree T and not produce any output in the worst case. Thus, the worst-case running time for performing a range query in a depth D quadtree, with n external nodes is $O(Dn)$. From a worst-case point of view, answering a range-searching query with a quadtree is actually worse than a brute-force search through the set S, which would take $O(n)$ time to answer a two-dimensional range query. In practice, however, the quadtree typically allows for range-searching queries to be processed faster than this.

12.3.2 k-D Trees

There is a drawback to quadtrees, which is that they do not generalize well to higher dimensions. In particular, each node in a four-dimensional analogue of a quadtree can have as many as 16 children. Each internal node in a d-dimensional quadtree can have has many as 2^d children. To overcome the out-degree drawback for storing data from dimensions higher than three, data structure designers often consider alternative partition tree structures that are binary.

Another kind of partition data structure is the k-d tree, which is similar to quadtree structure, but is binary. The k-d tree data structure is actually a family of partition tree data structures, all of which are binary partition trees for storing multi-dimensional data. Like the quadtree data structure, each node v in a k-d tree is associated with a rectangular region R, although in the case of k-d trees this region is not necessarily square. The difference is that, when it comes time to perform a split operation for a node v in a k-d tree, it is done with a single line that is perpendicular to one of the coordinate axes. For three- or higher-dimensional data sets, this "line" is an axis-aligned hyperplane. Thus, no matter the dimensionality, a k-d tree is a binary tree, for we resolve a split by associating the part of v's region R to the "left" of the splitting line with v's left child, and associating the part of v's region R to the "right" of the splitting line with v's right child. As with the quadtree structure, we stop performing splits if the number of points in a region falls below some fixed constant threshold. (See Figure 12.11.)

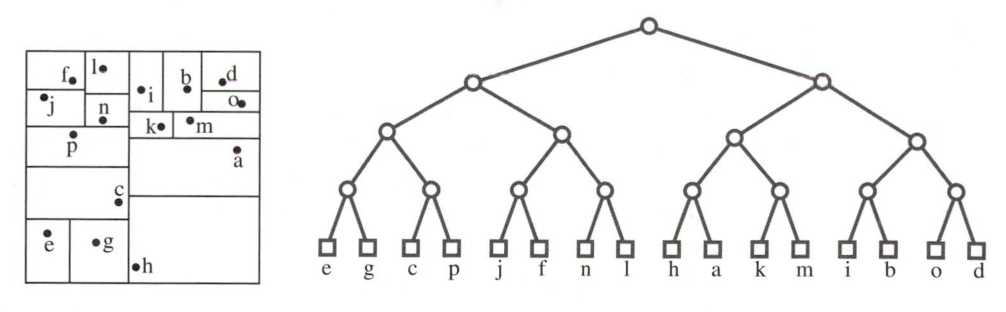

Figure 12.11: An example k-d tree.

There are fundamentally two different kinds of k-d trees, ***region-based*** k-d trees and ***point-based*** k-d trees. Region-based k-d trees are essentially binary versions of quadtrees. Each time a rectangular region R needs to be split in a region-based k-d tree, the region R is divided exactly in half by a line perpendicular to the longest side of R. If there is more than one longest side of R, then they are split in a "round robin" fashion. On the other hand, point-based k-d trees, perform splits based on the distribution of points inside a rectangular region. The k-d tree of Figure 12.11 is point-based.

The method for splitting a rectangle R containing a subset $S' \subseteq S$ in a point-based k-d tree involves two steps. In the first step, we determine the dimension i that has the largest variation in dimension i from among those points in S'. This can be done, for example, by finding, for each dimension j, the points in S' with minimum and maximum dimension j values, and taking i to be the dimension with the largest gap between these two values. In the second step, we determine the median dimension i value from among all those points in S', and we split R with a line going through this median perpendicular to the dimension i axis. Thus, the split for R divides the set of points in S' in half, but may not divide the region R itself very evenly. Using a linear-time median-finding method (Section 4.7), this splitting step can be performed in $O(k|S'|)$ time. Therefore, the running time for building a k-d tree for a set of n points can be characterized by the following recurrence equation: $T(n) = 2T(n/2) + kn$, which is $O(kn \log n)$. Moreover, since we divide the size of the set of points associated with a node in two with each split, the height of T is $\lceil \log n \rceil$. Figure 12.11 illustrates a point-based k-d tree built using this algorithm.

The advantage of point-based k-d trees is that they are guaranteed to have nice depth and construction times. The drawback of point-based schemes is that they may give rise to "long-and-skinny" rectangular regions, which are usually considered bad for most k-d tree query methods. In practice, however, such long-and-skinny regions are rare, and most of the rectangular regions associated with the nodes of a k-d tree are "boxy."

Using k-d Trees for Nearest Neighbor Searching

Let us discuss how k-d trees can be used to answer queries. In particular, let us focus on nearest-neighbor searching, where we are given a query point p and asked to find the point in S that is closest to p. A good way to use a k-d tree T to answer such a query is as follows. We first search down the tree T to locate the external node v with smallest rectangular region R that contains p. Any points of S that fall in R or in the region associated with v's sibling are then compared to find a current closest neighbor, q. We can then define a sphere centered at p and containing q as a current nearest-neighbor sphere, s. Given this sphere, we then perform a traversal of T (with a bottom-up traversal being preferred) to find any regions associated with external nodes of T that intersect s. If, during this traversal, we find a point closer than q, then we update the reference q to refer to this new point and we update the sphere s to contain this new point. We do not visit any nodes that have regions not intersecting s. When we have exhausted all possible alternatives, we output the current point q as the nearest neighbor of p. In the worst case, this method may take $O(n)$ time, but there are many different analytic and experimental analyses that suggest that the average running time is more like $O(\log n)$, using some reasonable assumptions about the distribution of points in S. In addition, there are a number of useful heuristics for speeding up this search in practice, with one of the best being the ***priority*** searching strategy, which says that we should explore subtrees of T in order of the distance of their associated regions to p.

12.4 The Plane Sweep Technique

In this section, we study a technique that can be applied to many different geometric problems. The main idea is to turn a static two-dimensional problem into a dynamic one-dimensional problem, which we solve using a sequence of insertion, removal, and query operations. Rather than present this technique in an abstract setting, however, we illustrate its use on a number of concrete examples.

12.4.1 Orthogonal Segment Intersection

The first problem we solve using the plane-sweep technique is that of finding all the intersecting pairs among a set of n line segments. Of course, we could apply a brute-force algorithm to check every pair of segments to see whether they intersect. Since the number of pairs is $n(n-1)/2$, this algorithm takes $O(n^2)$ time, since we can test any pair for intersection in constant time. If all the pairs intersect, this algorithm is optimal. Still, we would like to have a faster method for the case where the number of intersecting pairs is small or there are no intersections at all. Specifically, if s is the number of intersecting pairs, we would like to have an output sensitive algorithm whose running time depends on both n and s. We shall present an algorithm that uses the plane-sweep technique and runs in $O(n\log n + s)$ time for the case when the input set of segments consists of n ***orthogonal segments***, meaning that each segment in the set is either horizontal or vertical.

One-Dimensional Range Searching Revisited

Before we proceed with our algorithm, we make a slight digression to review a problem discussed previously in this chapter.

This problem is the one-dimensional range-searching problem, in which we wish to dynamically maintain a dictionary of numbers (that is, points on a number line), subject to insertions and deletions and queries of the following form:

findAllInRange(k_1, k_2): Return an enumeration of all the elements in D with key k, such that $k_1 \leq k \leq k_2$.

We show in Section 12.1.1 how we can use any balanced binary search tree, such as an AVL tree or a red-black tree, to maintain such a dictionary in order to achieve $O(\log n)$ time for point insertion and removal, and $O(\log n + s)$ time for answering findAllInRange queries, where n is the number of points in the dictionary at the time and s is the number of returned points in the range. We will not make use of the details of this algorithm, only its existence, so a reader who skipped Section 12.1.1 can safely take this result on faith and not have to worry about how it is achieved.

A Collection of Range-Searching Problems

Let us return to the problem at hand, which is to compute all intersecting pairs of segments from a collection of n horizontal and vertical segments. The main idea of the algorithm for solving this problem is to reduce this two-dimensional problem to a collection of one-dimensional range-searching problems. Namely, for each vertical segment v, we consider the vertical line $l(v)$ through v, and plunge into the "one-dimensional world" of line $l(v)$. (See Figure 12.13a and b.) Only the vertical segment v and the intersections of horizontal segments with $l(v)$ exist in this world. In particular, segment v corresponds to an interval of $l(v)$, a horizontal segment h intersecting $l(v)$ corresponds to a point on $l(v)$, and the horizontal segments crossing v correspond to the points on $l(v)$ contained in the interval.

Thus, if we are given the set $S(v)$ of horizontal segments intersecting line $l(v)$, then determining those that intersect segment v is equivalent to performing a range search in $S(v)$ using the y coordinates of the segments as keys and the interval given by the y-coordinates of the endpoints of segment v as the selection range.

The Plane-Sweep Segment Intersection Algorithm

Suppose we are given a set of n horizontal and vertical segments in the plane. We will determine all pairs of intersecting segments in this set by using the ***plane sweep*** technique and the collective approach suggested by the above idea. This algorithm involves simulating the sweeping of a vertical line l, over the segments, moving from left to right, starting at a location to the left of all the input segments. During the sweep, the set of horizontal segments currently intersected by the sweep line is maintained by means of insertions into and removals from a dictionary ordered by y-coordinate. When the sweep encounters a vertical segment v, a range query on the dictionary is performed to find the horizontal segments intersecting v.

Specifically, during the sweep, we maintain an ordered dictionary S storing horizontal segments with their keys given by their y-coordinates. The sweep pauses at certain ***events*** that trigger the ***actions*** shown in Table 12.12 and illustrated in Figure 12.13.

Event	Action
left endpoint of a horizontal segment h	insert h into dictionary S
right endpoint of a horizontal segment h	remove h from dictionary S
vertical segment v	perform a range search on S with selection range given by the y-coordinates of the endpoints of v

Table 12.12: Events triggering actions in the plane-sweep algorithm for orthogonal segment intersection.

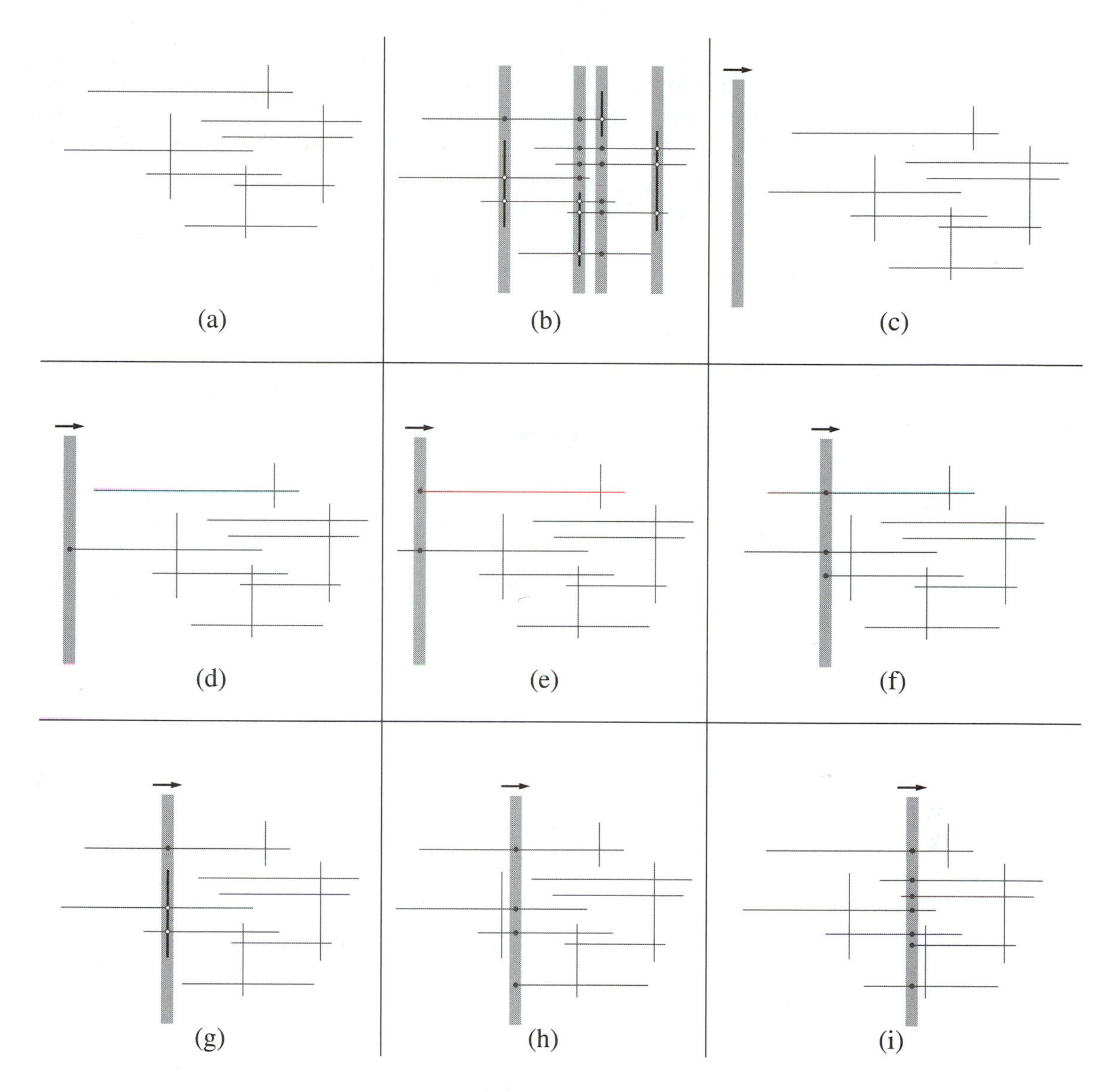

Figure 12.13: Plane sweep for orthogonal segment intersection: (a) a set of horizontal and vertical segments; (b) the collection of one-dimensional range-search problems; (c) beginning of the plane sweep (the ordered dictionary S of horizontal segments is empty); (d) the first (left-endpoint) event, causing an insertion into S; (e) the second (left-endpoint) event, causing another insertion into S; (f) the third (left-endpoint) event, causing yet another insertion into S; (g) the first vertical-segment event, causing a range search in S (two intersections reported); (h) the next (left-endpoint) event, causing an insertion into S; (i) a left-endpoint event three events later, causing an insertion into S.

Performance

To analyze the running time of this plane-sweep algorithm, first note that we must identify all the events and sort them by x-coordinate. An event is either an endpoint of a horizontal segment or a vertical segment. Hence, the number of events is at most $2n$. When sorting the events, we compare them by x-coordinate, which takes $O(1)$ time. Using one of the asymptotically optimal sorting algorithms, such as heap-sort (Section 2.4.4) or merge-sort (Section 4.1), we can order the events in $O(n \log n)$ time. The operations performed on the dictionary S are insertions, removals, and range searches. Each time an operation is executed, the size of S is at most $2n$. We implement S as an AVL tree (Section 3.2), or as a red-black tree (Section 3.3.3), so that insertions and deletions each take $O(\log n)$ time. As we have reviewed above (and seen in Section 12.1.1), range searching in an n-element ordered dictionary can be performed in $O(\log n + s)$ time, using $O(n)$ space, where s is the number of items reported. Let us characterize, then, the running time of a range search triggered by a vertical segment v as $O(\log n + s(v))$, where $s(v)$ is the number of horizontal segments currently in the dictionary S that intersect v. Thus, indicating the set of vertical segments with V, the running time of the sweep is

$$O\left(2n\log n + \sum_{v \in V}(\log n + s(v))\right).$$

Since the sweep goes through all the segments, the sum of $s(v)$ over all the vertical segments encountered is equal to the total number s of intersecting pairs of segments. Hence, we conclude that the sweep takes time $O(n \log n + s)$.

In summary, the complete segment intersection algorithm, outlined above, consists of the event sorting step followed by the sweep step. Sorting the events takes $O(n \log n)$ time, while sweeping takes $O(n \log n + s)$ time. Thus, the running time of the algorithm is $O(n \log n + s)$.

12.4.2 Finding a Closest Pair of Points

Another geometric problem that can be solved using the plane sweep technique involves the concept of ***proximity***, which is the relationship of ***distance*** that exists between geometric objects. Specifically, we focus on the ***closest pair*** problem, which consists of finding a pair of points p and q that are at a minimum distance from each other in a set of n points. This pair is said to be a closest pair. We will use the Euclidean definition of the distance between two points a and b:

$$\mathsf{dist}(a,b) = \sqrt{(x(a) - x(b))^2 + (y(a) - y(b))^2},$$

where $x(p)$ and $y(p)$ respectively denote the x- and y-coordinates of the point p. Applications of the closest pair problem include the verification of mechanical parts and integrated circuits, where it is important that certain separation rules between components be respected.

A Plane-Sweep Algorithm

A straightforward "brute-force" algorithm for solving the closest pair problem is to compute the distance between every pair of points and select a pair with minimum distance. Since the number of pairs is $n(n-1)/2$, this algorithm takes $O(n^2)$ time. We can apply a more clever strategy, however, which avoids checking all the pairs of points.

It turns out that we can effectively apply the plane-sweep technique to the closest pair problem. We solve the closest pair problem, in this case, by imagining that we sweep the plane by a vertical line from left to right, starting at a position to the left of all n of the input points. As we sweep the line across the plane, we keep track of the closest pair seen so far, and of all those points that are "near" the sweep line. We also keep track of the distance, d, between the closest pair seen so far. In particular, as we illustrate in Figure 12.14, while sweeping through the points from left to right, we maintain the following data:

- A closest pair (a,b) among the points encountered, and the distance $d = \mathsf{dist}(a,b)$
- An ordered dictionary S that stores the points lying in a strip of width d to the left of the sweep line and uses the y-coordinates of points as keys.

Each input point p corresponds to an event in this plane sweep. When the sweep line encounters a point p, we perform the following actions:

1. We update dictionary S by removing the points at horizontal distance greater than d from p, that is, each point r such that $x(p) - x(r) > d$.
2. We find the closest point q to the left of p by searching in dictionary S (we will say in a moment how this is done). If $\mathsf{dist}(p,q) < d$, then we update the current closest pair and distance by setting $a \leftarrow p$, $b \leftarrow q$, and $d \leftarrow \mathsf{dist}(p,q)$.
3. We insert p into S.

Clearly, we can restrict our search of the closest point q to the left of p to the points in dictionary S, since all other points will have distance greater than d. What we want are those points in S that lie within the half-circle $C(p,d)$ of radius d centered at and to the left of point p. (See Figure 12.15.) As a first approximation, we can get the points in the enclosing $d \times 2d$ rectangular box $B(p,d)$ of $C(p,d)$ (Figure 12.15) by performing a range search (Section 12.1.1) on S for the points in S with y-coordinates in the interval of keys $[y(p) - d, y(p) + d]$. We examine such points, one by one, and find the closest to p, denoted q. Since the operations performed on dictionary S are range searches, insertions, and removals of points, we implement S by means of an AVL tree or red-black tree.

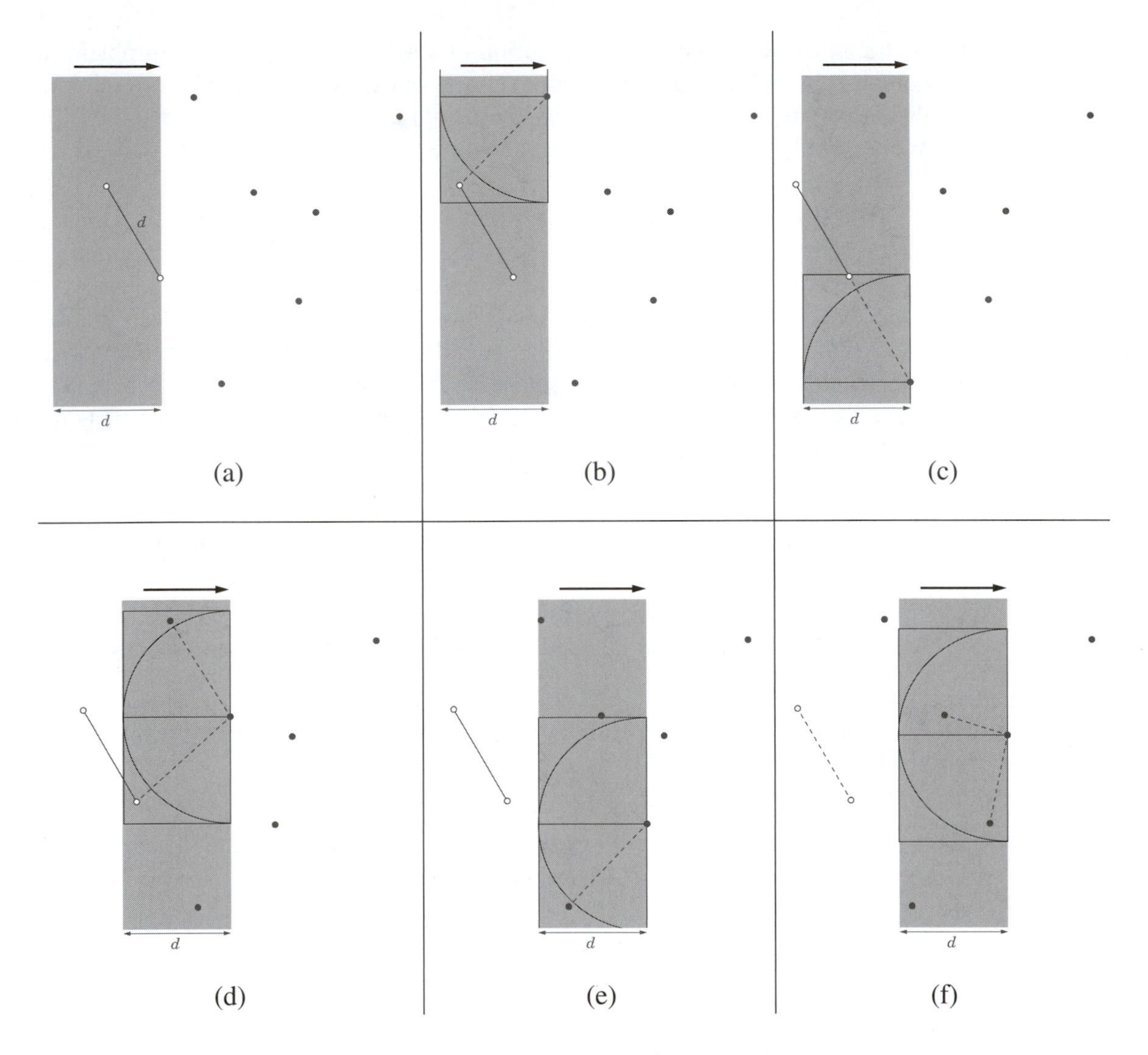

Figure 12.14: Plane sweep for the closest pair problem: (a) the first minimum distance d and closest pair (highlighted); (b) the next event (box $B(p,d)$ contains a point, but the half-circle $C(p,d)$ is empty); (c) next event ($C(p,d)$ again is empty, but a point is removed from S); (d) next event (with $C(p,d)$ again empty). The dictionary S contains the points in the grey strip of width d; (e) a point p is encountered (and a point removed from S), with $B(p,d)$ containing 1 point, but $C(p,d)$ containing none; thus, the minimum distance d and closest pair (a,b) stay the same; (f) a point p encountered with $C(p,d)$ containing 2 points (and a point is removed from S).

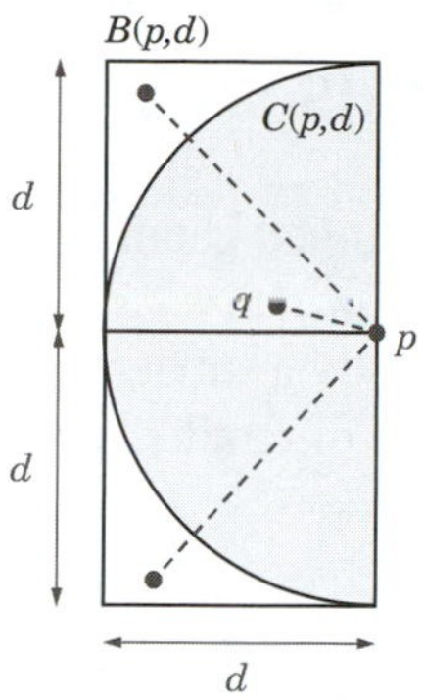

Figure 12.15: Box $B(p,d)$ and half-circle $C(p,d)$.

The following intuitive property, whose proof is left as an exercise (R-12.3), is crucial to the analysis of the running time of the algorithm.

Theorem 12.7: *A rectangle of width d and height $2d$ can contain at most six points such that any two points are at distance at least d.*

Thus, there are at most six points of S that lie in the box $B(p,d)$. So the range-search operation on S, to find the points in $B(p,d)$, takes time $O(\log n + 6)$, which is $O(\log n)$. Also, we can find the point in $B(p,d)$ closest to p in $O(1)$ time.

Before we begin the sweep, we sort the points by x-coordinate, and store them in an ordered list X. The list X is used for two purposes:

- To get the next point to be processed
- To identify the points to be removed from dictionary S.

We keep references to two positions in the list X, which we denote as firstInStrip and lastInStrip. Position lastInStrip keeps track of the new point to be inserted into S, while position firstInStrip keeps track of the left-most point in S. By advancing lastInStrip one step at a time, we find the new point to be processed. By using firstInStrip, we identify the points to be removed from S. Namely, while we have

$$x(\text{point}(\text{firstInStrip})) < x(\text{point}(\text{lastInStrip}) - d,$$

we perform operation removeElement(y(point(firstInStrip))) on dictionary S and advance firstInStrip.

Let n be the number of input points. Our analysis of the plane-sweep algorithm for the closest pair problem is based on the following observations:

- The preliminary sorting by x-coordinate takes time $O(n\log n)$.
- Each point is inserted once and removed once from dictionary S, which has size at most n; hence, the total time for inserting and removing elements in S is $O(n\log n)$.
- By Theorem 12.7, each range query in S takes $O(\log n)$ time. We execute such a range query each time we process a new point. Thus, the total time spent for performing range queries is $O(n\log n)$.

We conclude that we can compute a closest pair in a set of n points in time $O(n\log n)$.

12.5 Convex Hulls

One of the most studied geometric problems is that of computing the convex hull of a set of points. Informally speaking, the ***convex hull*** of a set of points in the plane is the shape taken by a rubber band that is placed "around the points" and allowed to shrink to a state of equilibrium. (See Figure 12.16.)

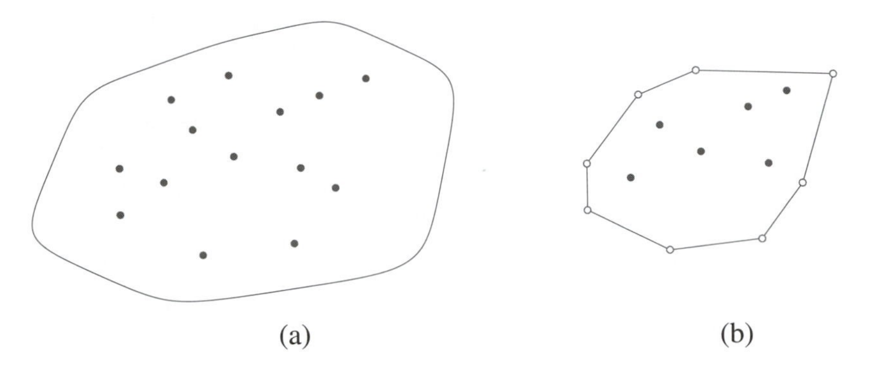

Figure 12.16: The convex hull of a set of points in the plane: (a) an example "rubber band" placed around the points; (b) the convex hull of the points.

The convex hull corresponds to the intuitive notion of a "boundary" of a set of points and can be used to approximate the shape of a complex object. Indeed, computing the convex hull of a set of points is a fundamental operation in computational geometry. Before we describe the convex hull and algorithms to compute it in detail, we need to first discuss some representational issues for geometric data objects.

12.5.1 Representations of Geometric Objects

Geometric algorithms take geometric objects of various types as their inputs. The basic geometric objects in the plane are points, lines, segments, and polygons.

There are many ways of representing planar geometric objects. Rather than give separate ADT's for points, lines, segments, and polygons, which would be appropriate for a book on geometric algorithms, we instead assume we have intuitive representations for these objects. Even so, we briefly mention some of the choices that we can make regarding geometric representations.

We can represent a point in the plane by a pair (x,y) that stores the x and y Cartesian coordinates for that point. While this representation is quite versatile, it is not the only one. There may be some applications where a different representation may be better (such as representing a point as the intersection between two nonparallel lines).

Lines, Segments, and Polygons

We can represent a line l as a triple (a,b,c), such that these values are the coefficients a, b, and c of the linear equation

$$ax+by+c=0$$

associated with l. Alternatively, we may specify instead two different points, q_1 and q_2, and associate them with the line that goes through both. Given the Cartesian coordinates (x_1,y_1) of q_1 and (x_2,y_2) of q_2, the equation of the line l through q_1 and q_2 is given by

$$\frac{x-x_1}{x_2-x_1}=\frac{y-y_1}{y_2-y_1},$$

from which we derive

$$a=(y_2-y_1);\;\; b=-(x_2-x_1);\;\; c=y_1(x_2-x_1)-x_1(y_2-y_1).$$

A line segment s is typically represented by the pair (p,q) of points in the plane that form s's endpoints. We may also represent s by giving the line through it, together with a range of x- and y-coordinates, that restrict this line to the segment s. (Why is it insufficient to include just a range of x- or y-coordinates?)

We can represent a polygon P by a circular sequence of points, called the ***vertices*** of P. (See Figure 12.17.) The segments between consecutive vertices of P are called the ***edges*** of P. Polygon P is said to be ***nonintersecting***, or ***simple***, if intersections between pairs of edges of P happen only at a common endpoint vertex. A polygon is ***convex*** if it is simple and all its internal angles are less than π.

Our discussion of different ways of representing points, lines, segments, and polygons is not meant to be exhaustive. It is meant simply to indicate the different ways we can implement these geometric objects.

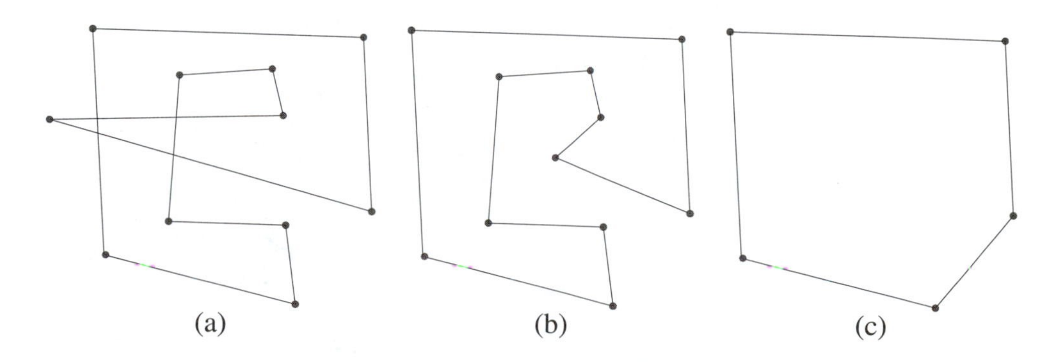

Figure 12.17: Examples of polygons: (a) intersecting, (b) simple, (c) convex.

12.5.2 Point Orientation Testing

An important geometric relationship, which arises in many geometric algorithms, and particularly for convex hull construction, is ***orientation***. Given an ordered triplet (p,q,r) of points, we say that (p,q,r) makes a ***left turn*** and is oriented ***counterclockwise*** if the angle that stays on the left-hand side when going from p to q and then to r is less than π. If the angle on the right-hand side is less than π instead, then we say that (p,q,r) makes a ***right turn*** and is oriented ***clockwise***. (See Figure 12.18.) It is possible that the angles of the left- and right-hand sides are both equal to π, in which case the three points actually do not make a turn, and we say that their orientation is ***collinear***.

Given a triplet (p_1,p_2,p_3) of three points $p_1=(x_1,y_1)$, $p_2=(x_2,y_2)$, and $p_3=(x_3,y_3)$, in the plane, let $\Delta(p_1,p_2,p_3)$ be the determinant defined by

$$\Delta(p_1,p_2,p_3)=\begin{vmatrix} x_1 & y_1 & 1 \\ x_2 & y_2 & 1 \\ x_3 & y_3 & 1 \end{vmatrix}=x_1y_2-x_2y_1+x_3y_1-x_1y_3+x_2y_3-x_3y_2. \quad (12.1)$$

The function $\Delta(p_1,p_2,p_3)$ is often called the "signed area" function, because its absolute value is twice the area of the (possibly degenerate) triangle formed by the points p_1, p_2, and p_3. In addition, we have the following important fact relating this function to orientation testing.

Theorem 12.8: *The orientation of a triplet (p_1,p_2,p_3) of points in the plane is counterclockwise, clockwise, or collinear, depending on whether $\Delta(p_1,p_2,p_3)$ is positive, negative, or zero, respectively.*

We sketch the proof of Theorem 12.8; we leave the details as an exercise (R-12.4). In Figure 12.18, we show a triplet (p_1,p_2,p_3) of points such that $x_1<x_2<x_3$. Clearly, this triplet makes a left turn if the slope of segment p_2p_3 is greater than the slope of segment p_1p_2. This is expressed by the following question:

$$\text{Is } \frac{y_3-y_2}{x_3-x_2}>\frac{y_2-y_1}{x_2-x_1}\ ? \quad (12.2)$$

By the expansion of $\Delta(p_1,p_2,p_3)$ shown in 12.1, we can verify that inequality 12.2 is equivalent to $\Delta(p_1,p_2,p_3)>0$.

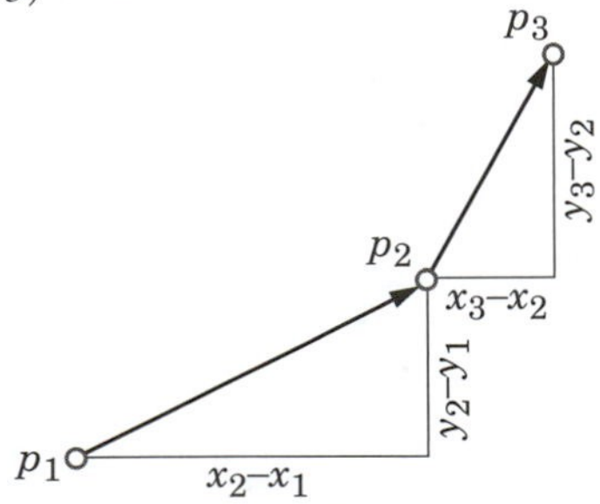

Figure 12.18: An example of a left turn. The differences between the coordinates between p_1 and p_2 and the coordinates of p_2 and p_3 are also illustrated.

Example 12.9: *Using the notion of orientation, let us consider the problem of testing whether two line segments s_1 and s_2 intersect. Specifically, Let $s_1 = \overline{p_1q_1}$ and $s_2 = \overline{p_2q_2}$ be two segments in the plane. s_1 and s_2 intersect if and only if* ***one of*** *the following two conditions is verified:*

1. (a) (p_1,q_1,p_2) and (p_1,q_1,q_2) *have different orientations,* **and**
   (b) (p_2,q_2,p_1) and (p_2,q_2,q_1) *have different orientations.*
2. (a) (p_1,q_1,p_2), (p_1,q_1,q_2), (p_2,q_2,p_1) and (p_2,q_2,q_1) *are all collinear,* **and**
   (b) *the x-projections of s_1 and s_2 intersect,* **and**
   (c) *the y-projections of s_1 and s_2 intersect.*

Condition 1 is illustrated in Figure 12.19. We also show, in Table 12.20, the respective orientation of the triplets (p_1,q_1,p_2), (p_1,q_1,q_2), (p_2,q_2,p_1), and (p_2,q_2,q_1) in each of the four cases for Condition 1. A complete proof is left as an exercise (R-12.5). Note that the conditions also hold if s_1 and/or s_2 is a degenerate segment with coincident endpoints.

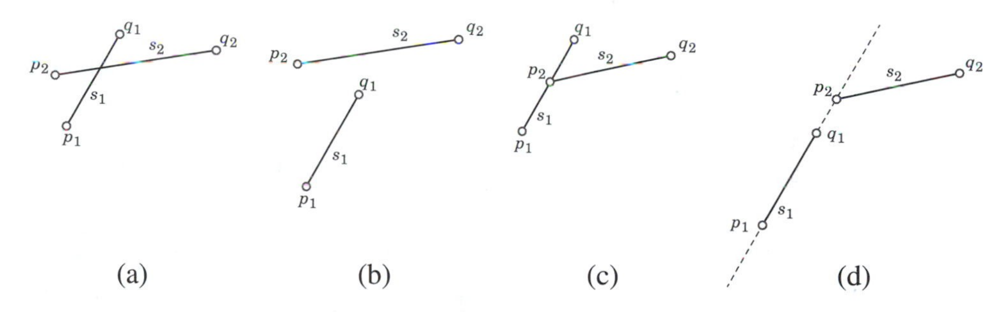

Figure 12.19: Examples illustrating four cases of Condition 1 of Example 12.9.

case	(p_1,q_1,p_2)	(p_1,q_1,q_2)	(p_2,q_2,p_1)	(p_2,q_2,q_1)	intersection?
(a)	CCW	CW	CW	CCW	yes
(b)	CCW	CW	CW	CW	no
(c)	COLL	CW	CW	CCW	yes
(d)	COLL	CW	CW	CW	no

Table 12.20: The four cases shown in Figure 12.19 for the orientations specified by Condition 1 of Example 12.9, where CCW stands for counterclockwise, CW stands for clockwise, and COLL stands for collinear.

12.5.3 Basic Properties of Convex Hulls

We say that a region R is ***convex*** if any time two points p and q are in R, the entire line segment $\overline{pq}$ is also in R. The ***convex hull*** of a set of points S is the boundary of the smallest convex region that contains all the points of S inside it or on its boundary. The notion of "smallest" refers to either the perimeter or area of the region, both definitions being equivalent. The convex hull of a set of points S in the plane defines a convex polygon, and the points of S on the boundary of the convex hull define the vertices of this polygon. The following example describes an application of the convex hull problem in a robot motion planning problem.

Example 12.10: *A common problem in robotics is to identify a trajectory from a start point s to a target point t that avoids a certain obstacle. Among the many possible trajectories, we would like to find one that is as short as possible. Let us assume that the obstacle is a polygon P. We can compute a shortest trajectory from s to t that avoids P with the following strategy (see Figure 12.21):*

- *We determine if the line segment $\ell = \overline{st}$ intersects P. If it does not intersect, then ℓ is the shortest trajectory avoiding P.*
- *Otherwise, if $\overline{st}$ intersects P, then we compute the convex hull H of the vertices of polygon P plus points s and t. Note that s and t subdivide the convex hull H into two polygonal chains, one going clockwise from s to t and one going counterclockwise from s to t.*
- *We select and return the shortest of the two polygonal chains with endpoints s and t on H.*

This shortest chain is the shortest path in the plane that avoids the obstacle P.

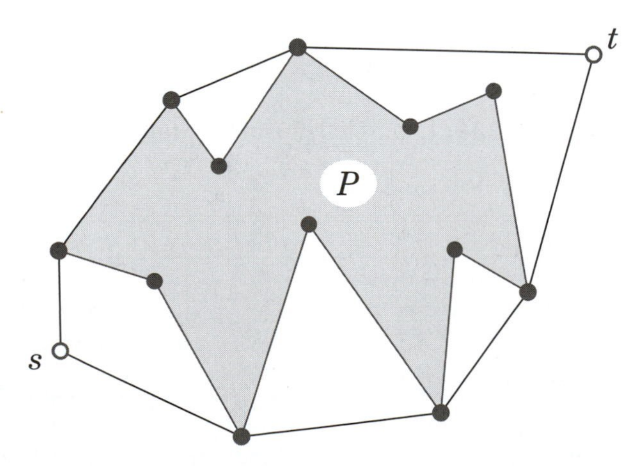

Figure 12.21: An example shortest trajectory from a point s to a point t that avoids a polygonal obstacle P; the trajectory is a clockwise chain from s to t.

There are a number of applications of the convex hull problem, including partitioning problems, shape testing problems, and separation problems. For example, if we wish to determine whether there is a half-plane (that is, a region of the plane on one side of a line) that completely contains a set of points A but completely avoids a set of points B, it is enough to compute the convex hulls of A and B and determine whether they intersect each other.

There are many interesting geometric properties associated with convex hulls. The following theorem provides an alternate characterization of the points that are on the convex hull and of those that are not.

Theorem 12.11: *Let S be a set of planar points with convex hull H. Then*

- *A pair of points a and b of S form an edge of H if and only if all the other points of S are contained on one side of the line through a and b.*
- *A point p of S is a vertex of H if and only if there exists a line l through p, such that all the other points of S are contained in the same half-plane delimited by l (that is, they are all on the same side of l).*
- *A point p of S is not a vertex of H if and only if p is contained in the interior of a triangle formed by three other points of S or in the interior of a segment formed by two other points of S.*

The properties expressed by Theorem 12.11 are illustrated in Figure 12.22. A complete proof of them is left as an exercise (R-12.6). As a consequence of Theorem 12.11, we can immediately verify that, in any set S of points in the plane, the following ***critical*** points are always on the boundary of the convex hull of S:

- A point with minimum x-coordinate
- A point with maximum x-coordinate
- A point with minimum y-coordinate
- A point with maximum y-coordinate.

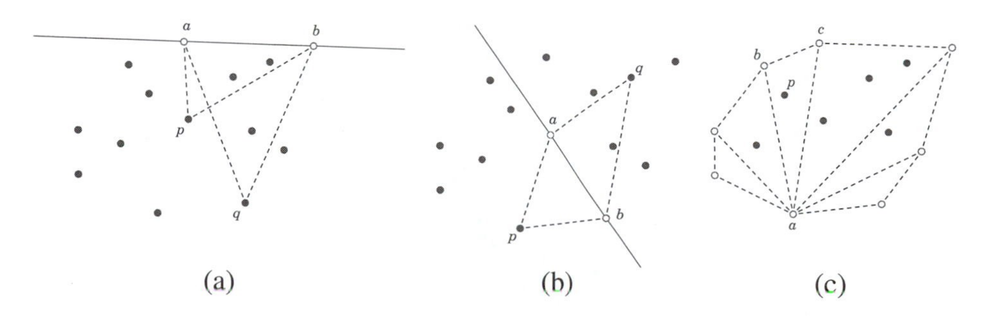

Figure 12.22: Illustration of the properties of the convex hull given in Theorem 12.11: (a) points a and b form an edge of the convex hull; (b) points a and b do not form an edge of the convex hull; (c) point p is not on the convex hull.

12.5.4 The Gift Wrapping Algorithm

Theorem 12.11 basically states that we can identify a particular point, say one with minimum y-coordinate, that provides an initial starting configuration for an algorithm that computes the convex hull. The ***gift wrapping*** algorithm for computing the convex hull of a set of points in the plane is based on just such a starting point, and can be intuitively described as follows (see Figure 12.23):

1. View the points as pegs implanted in a level field, and imagine that we tie a rope to the peg corresponding to the point a with minimum y-coordinate (and minimum x-coordinate if there are ties). Call a the ***anchor point***, and note that a is a vertex of the convex hull.
2. Pull the rope to the right of the anchor point and rotate it counterclockwise until it touches another peg, which corresponds to the next vertex of the convex hull.
3. Continue rotating the rope counterclockwise, identifying a new vertex of the convex hull at each step, until the rope gets back to the anchor point.

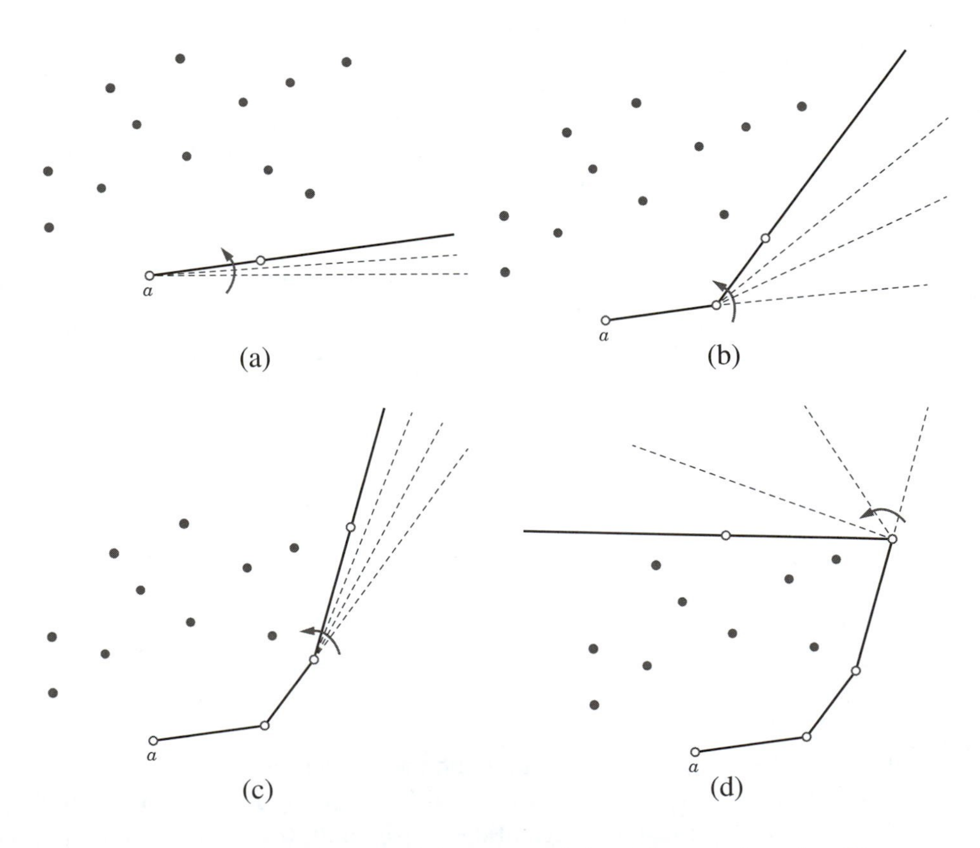

Figure 12.23: Initial four wrapping steps of the gift wrapping algorithm.

Each time we rotate our "rope" around the current peg until it hits another point, we perform an operation called a ***wrapping*** step. Geometrically, a wrapping step involves starting from a given line L known to be tangent to the convex hull at the current anchor point a, and determining the line through a and another point in the set making the smallest angle with L. Implementing this wrapping step does not require trigonometric functions and angle calculations, however. Instead, we can perform a wrapping step by means of the following theorem, which follows from Theorem 12.11.

Theorem 12.12: *Let S be a set of points in the plane, and let a be a point of S that is a vertex of the convex hull H of S. The next vertex of H, going counterclockwise from a, is the point p, such that triplet (a,p,q) makes a left turn with every other point q of S.*

Recalling the discussion from Section 2.4.1, let us define a comparator $C(a)$ that uses the orientation of (a,p,q) to compare two points p and q of S. That is, $C(a)$.isLess(p,q) returns true if triplet (a,p,q) makes a left turn. We call the comparator $C(a)$ the ***radial*** comparator, as it compares points in terms of their radial relationships around the anchor point a. By Theorem 12.12, the vertex following a counterclockwise on the hull is simply the minimum point with respect to the radial comparator $C(a)$.

Performance

We can now analyze the running time of the gift wrapping algorithm. Let n be the number of points of S, and let $h \leq n$ be the number of vertices of the convex hull H of S. Let $p_0, \ldots, p_{h-1}$ be the vertices of H. Finding the anchor point $a = p_0$ takes $O(n)$ time. Since with each wrapping step of the algorithm we discover a new vertex of the convex hull, the number of wrapping steps is equal to h. Step i is a minimum-finding computation based on radial comparator $C(p_{i-1})$, which runs in $O(n)$ time, since determining the orientation of a triplet takes $O(1)$ time and we must examine all the points of S to find the smallest with respect to $C(p_{i-1})$. We conclude that the gift wrapping algorithm runs in time $O(hn)$, which is $O(n^2)$ in the worst case. Indeed, the worst case for the gift wrapping algorithm occurs when $h = n$, that is, when all the points are on the convex hull.

The worst-case running time of the gift wrapping algorithm in terms of n is therefore not very efficient. This algorithm is nevertheless reasonably efficient in practice, however, for it can take advantage of the (common) situation when h, the number of hull points, is small relative to the number of input points, n. That is, this algorithm is an ***output sensitive*** algorithm—an algorithm whose running time depends on the size of the output. Gift wrapping has a running time that varies between linear and quadratic, and is efficient if the convex hull has few vertices. In the next section, we will see an algorithm that is efficient for all hull sizes, although it is slightly more complicated.

12.5.5 The Graham Scan Algorithm

A convex hull algorithm that has an efficient running time no matter how many points are on the boundary of the convex is the ***Graham scan*** algorithm. The Graham scan algorithm for computing the convex hull H of a set P of n points in the plane consists of the following three phases:

1. We find a point a of P that is a vertex of H and call it the ***anchor point***. We can, for example, pick as our anchor point a the point in P with minimum y-coordinate (and minimum x-coordinate if there are ties).
2. We sort the remaining points of P (that is, $P - \{a\}$) using the radial comparator $C(a)$, and let S be the resulting sorted list of points. (See Figure 12.24.) In the list S, the points of P appear sorted counterclockwise "by angle" with respect to the anchor point a, although no explicit computation of angles is performed by the comparator.

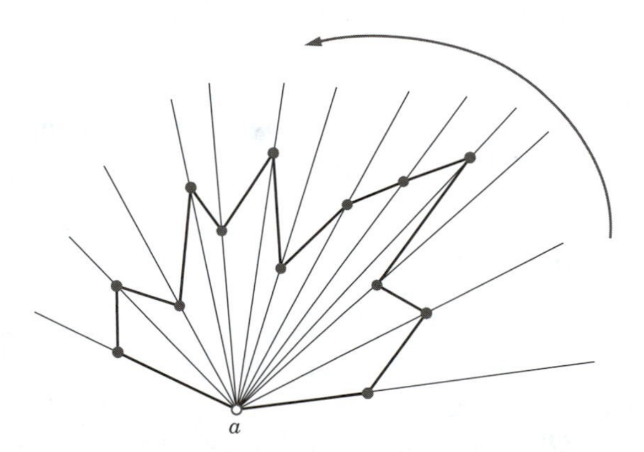

Figure 12.24: Sorting around the anchor point in the Graham scan algorithm.

3. After adding the anchor point a at the first and last position of S, we ***scan*** through the points in S in (radial) order, maintaining at each step a list H storing a convex chain "surrounding" the points scanned so far. Each time we consider new point p, we perform the following test:

   (a) If p forms a left turn with the last two points in H, or if H contains fewer than two points, then add p to the end of H.
   (b) Otherwise, remove the last point in H and repeat the test for p.

   We stop when we return to the anchor point a, at which point H stores the vertices of the convex hull of P in counterclockwise order.

The details of the scan phase (Phase 3) are spelled out in Algorithm Scan, described in Algorithm 12.25. (See Figure 12.26.)

```
Algorithm Scan(S,a):
  Input: A list S of points in the plane beginning with point a, such that a is on the
    convex hull of S and the remaining points of S are sorted counterclockwise
    around a
  Output: List S with only convex hull vertices remaining
  S.insertLast(a)          {add a copy of a at the end of S}
  prev ← S.first()          {so that prev = a initially}
  curr ← S.after(prev)          {the next point is on the current convex chain}
  repeat
    next ← S.after(curr)          {advance}
    if points (point(prev), point(curr), point(next)) make a left turn then
      prev ← curr
    else
      S.remove(curr)          { point curr is not in the convex hull}
      prev ← S.before(prev)
    curr ← S.after(prev)
  until curr = S.last()
  S.remove(S.last())          {remove the copy of a}
```

Algorithm 12.25: The scan phase of the Graham scan convex hull algorithm. (See Figure 12.26.) Variables *prev*, *curr*, and *next* are positions (Section 2.2.2) of the list S. We assume that an accessor method point(*pos*) is defined that returns the point stored at position *pos*. We give a simplified description of the algorithm that works only if S has at least three points, and no three points of S are collinear.

Performance

Let us now analyze the running time of the Graham scan algorithm. We denote the number of points in P (and S) with n. The first phase (finding the anchor point) clearly takes $O(n)$ time. The second phase (sorting the points around the anchor point) takes $O(n \log n)$ time provided we use one of the asymptotically optimal sorting algorithms, such as heap-sort (Section 2.4.4) or merge-sort (Section 4.1). The analysis of the scan (third) phase is more subtle.

To analyze the scan phase of the Graham scan algorithm, let us look more closely at the **repeat** loop of Algorithm 12.25. At each iteration of the loop, either variable *next* advances forward by one position in the list S (successful **if** test), or variable *next* stays at the same position but a point is removed from S (unsuccessful **if** test). Hence, the number of iterations of the **repeat** loop is at most $2n$. Therefore, each statement of algorithm Scan is executed at most $2n$ times. Since each statement requires the execution of $O(1)$ elementary operations in turn, algorithm Scan takes $O(n)$ time. In conclusion, the running time of the Graham scan algorithm is dominated by the second phase, where sorting is performed. Thus, the Graham scan algorithm runs in $O(n \log n)$ time.

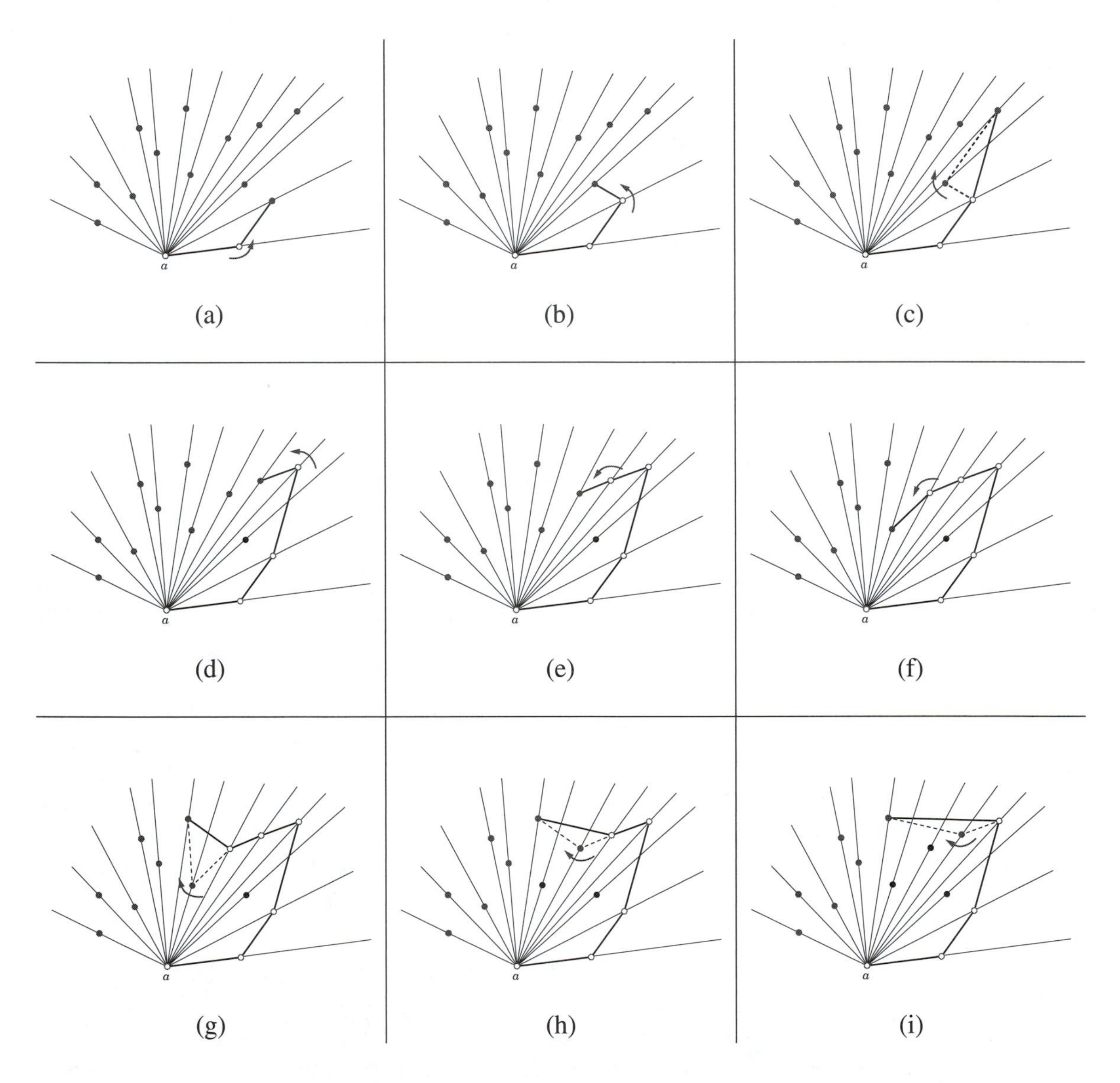

Figure 12.26: Third phase of the Graham scan algorithm (see Algorithm 12.25).

12.6 Java Example: Convex Hull

We described the Graham scan algorithm (Algorithm 12.25) assuming it avoided any ***degeneracies***, that is, input configurations that involve annoying special cases (such as coincident or collinear points). When implementing the Graham scan algorithm, however, it is important to handle all possible input configurations. For example, two or more of the points may be coincident, and some triplets of points may be collinear.

In Code Fragments 12.27–12.29, we show a Java implementation of the Graham scan algorithm. The main method is grahamScan (Code Fragment 12.27), which uses several auxiliary methods. Because of the degenerate point configurations that may occur, several special situations are handled by method grahamScan.

- The input list is first copied into sequence hull, which will be returned at the end of the execution (method copyInputPoints of Code Fragment 12.28).
- If the input has zero or one point (the output is the same as the input) return.
- If there are two input points, then if the two points are coincident, remove one of them and return.
- The anchor point is computed and removed, together with all the points coincident with it (method anchorPointSearchAndRemove of Code Fragment 12.28). If zero or one point is left, reinsert the anchor point and return.
- If none of the above special cases arises, that is, at least two points are left, sort the points counterclockwise around the anchor point with method sortPoints (Code Fragment 12.28), which passes a ConvexHullComparator (a comparator that allows for a generic sorting algorithm sorting algorithm to sort points counterclockwise radially around a point, as needed in Algorithm 12.25).
- In preparation for the Graham scan, we remove any initial collinear points in the sorted list, except the farthest one from the anchor point (method removeInitialIntermediatePoints of Code Fragment 12.29).
- The scan phase of the algorithm is performed calling method scan of Code Fragment 12.29.

In general, when we implement computational geometry algorithms we must take special care to handle all possible "degenerate" cases.

```
public class ConvexHull {
  private static Sequence hull;
  private static Point2D anchorPoint;
  private static GeomTester2D geomTester = new GeomTester2DImpl();
  // public class method
  public static Sequence grahamScan (Sequence points) {
    Point2D p1, p2;
    copyInputPoints(points); // copy into hull the sequence of input points
    switch (hull.size()) {
    case 0: case 1:
      return hull;
    case 2:
      p1 = (Point2D)hull.first().element();
      p2 = (Point2D)hull.last().element();
      if (geomTester.areEqual(p1,p2))
        hull.remove(hull.last());
      return hull;
    default:   // at least 3 input points
      // compute anchor point and remove it together with coincident points
      anchorPointSearchAndRemove();
      switch (hull.size()) {
      case 0: case 1:
        hull.insertFirst(anchorPoint);
        return hull;
      default:   // at least 2 input points left besides the anchor point
        sortPoints();// sort the points in hull around the anchor point
        // remove the (possible) initial collinear points in hull except the
        // farthest one from the anchor point
        removeInitialIntermediatePoints();
        if (hull.size() == 1)
          hull.insertFirst(anchorPoint);
        else { // insert the anchor point as first and last element in hull
          hull.insertFirst(anchorPoint);
          hull.insertLast(anchorPoint);
          scan(); // Graham's scan
          // remove one of the two copies of the anchor point from hull
          hull.remove(hull.last());
        }
        return hull;
      }
    }
  }
```

Code Fragment 12.27: Method grahamScan in the Java implementation of the Graham scan algorithm.

```
private static void copyInputPoints (Sequence points) {
  // copy into hull the sequence of input points
  hull = new NodeSequence();
  Enumeration pe = points.elements();
  while (pe.hasMoreElements()) {
    Point2D p = (Point2D)pe.nextElement();
    hull.insertLast(p);
  }
}
private static void anchorPointSearchAndRemove () {
  // compute the anchor point and remove it from hull together with
  // all the coincident points
  Enumeration pe = hull.positions();
  Position anchor = (Position)pe.nextElement();
  anchorPoint = (Point2D)anchor.element();
  // hull contains at least three elements
  while (pe.hasMoreElements()) {
    Position pos = (Position)pe.nextElement();
    Point2D p = (Point2D)pos.element();
    int aboveBelow = geomTester.aboveBelow(anchorPoint,p);
    int leftRight = geomTester.leftRight(anchorPoint,p);
    if (aboveBelow == GeomTester2D.BELOW ||
        aboveBelow == GeomTester2D.ON &&
        leftRight == GeomTester2D.LEFT) {
      anchor = pos;
      anchorPoint = p;
    }
    else
      if (aboveBelow == GeomTester2D.ON &&
          leftRight == GeomTester2D.ON)
        hull.remove(pos);
  }
  hull.remove(anchor);
}
private static void sortPoints() {
  // sort the points in hull around the anchor point
  SortObject sorter = new ListMergeSort();
  ConvexHullComparator comp = new ConvexHullComparator(anchorPoint,
                                                      geomTester);
  sorter.sort(hull,comp);
}
```

Code Fragment 12.28: Auxiliary methods copyInputPoints, anchorPointSearchAndRemove, and sortPoints called by method grahamScan of Code Fragment 12.27.

```
private static void removeInitialIntermediatePoints() {
  // remove the (possible) initial collinear points in hull except the
  // farthest one from the anchor point
  boolean collinear = true;
  while (hull.size() > 1 && collinear) {
    Position pos1 = hull.first();
    Position pos2 = hull.after(pos1);
    Point2D p1 = (Point2D)pos1.element();
    Point2D p2 = (Point2D)pos2.element();
    if (geomTester.leftRightTurn(anchorPoint,p1,p2) ==
        GeomTester2D.COLLINEAR)
      if (geomTester.closest(anchorPoint,p1,p2) == p1)
        hull.remove(pos1);
      else
        hull.remove(pos2);
    else
      collinear = false;
  }
}
private static void scan() {
  // Graham's scan
  Position first = hull.first();
  Position last = hull.last();
  Position prev = hull.first();
  Position curr = hull.after(prev);
  do {
    Position next = hull.after(curr);
    Point2D prevPoint = (Point2D)prev.element();
    Point2D currPoint = (Point2D)curr.element();
    Point2D nextPoint = (Point2D)next.element();
    if (geomTester.leftRightTurn(prevPoint,currPoint,nextPoint) ==
        GeomTester2D.LEFT_TURN)
      prev = curr;
    else {
      hull.remove(curr);
      prev = hull.before(prev);
    }
    curr = hull.after(prev);
  }
  while (curr != last);
}
}
```

Code Fragment 12.29: Auxiliary methods removeInitialIntermediatePoints and scan called by method grahamScan of Code Fragment 12.27.

12.7 Exercises

Reinforcement

R-12.1 Extend the analysis of the running time of Algorithm 12.1 1DTreeRangeSearch to the case where the binary search tree T contains k_1 and/or k_2.

R-12.2 Verify that the absolute value of the function $\Delta(p_1, p_2, p_3)$ is twice the area of the triangle formed by the points p_1, p_2, and p_3 in the plane.

R-12.3 Provide a complete proof of Theorem 12.7.

R-12.4 Provide a complete proof of Theorem 12.8.

R-12.5 Provide a complete proof of Example 12.9.

R-12.6 Provide a complete proof of Theorem 12.11.

R-12.7 Provide a complete proof of Theorem 12.12.

R-12.8 What would be the worst-case space usage of a range tree, if the primary structure were not required to have $O(\log n)$ height?

R-12.9 Given a binary search tree T built on the x-coordinates of a set of n objects, describe an $O(n)$ time method for computing $\min_x(v)$ and $\max_x(v)$ for each node v in T.

R-12.10 Show that the high_y values in a priority search tree satisfy the heap-order property.

R-12.11 Argue that the algorithm for answering three-sided range-searching queries with a priority search tree is correct.

R-12.12 What is the worst-case depth of a k-d tree defined on n points in the plane? What about in higher dimensions?

R-12.13 Suppose a set S contains n two-dimensional points whose coordinates are all integers in the range $[0,N]$. What is the worst-case depth of a quadtree defined on S?

R-12.14 Draw a quadtree for the following set of points, assuming a 16×16 bounding box:

$$\{(1,2),(4,10),(14,3),(6,6),(3,15),(2,2),(3,12),(9,4),(12,14)\}.$$

R-12.15 Construct a k-d tree for the point set of Exercise R-12.14.

R-12.16 Construct a priority search tree for the point set of Exercise R-12.14.

Creativity

C-12.1 The $\min_x(v)$ and $\max_x(v)$ labels used in the two-dimensional range tree are not strictly needed. Describe an algorithm for performing a two-dimensional range-searching query in a two-dimensional range tree, where each internal node of the primary structure only stores a key(v) label (which is the x-coordinate of its element). What is the running time of your method?

C-12.2 Give a pseudo-code description of an algorithm for constructing a range tree from a set of n points in the plane in $O(n \log n)$ time.

C-12.3 Describe an efficient data structure for storing a set S of n items with ordered keys, so as to support a rankRange(a,b) method, which enumerates all the items with keys whose ***rank*** in S is in the range $[a,b]$, where a and b are integers in the interval $[0,n-1]$. Describe methods for object insertions and deletion, and characterize the running times for these and the rankRange method.

C-12.4 Design a static data structure (which does not support insertions and deletions) that stores a two-dimensional set S of n points and can answer queries of the form countAllIn Range(a,b,c,d), in $O(\log^2 n)$ time, which return the number of points in S with x-coordinates in the range $[a,b]$ and y-coordinates in the range $[c,d]$. What is the space used by this structure?

C-12.5 Design a data structure for answering countAllInRange queries (as defined in the previous exercise) in $O(\log n)$ time.

Hint: Think of storing auxiliary structures at each node that are "linked" to the structures at neighboring nodes.

C-12.6 Show how to extend the two-dimensional range tree so as to answer d-dimensional range-searching queries in $O(\log^d n)$ time for a set of d-dimensional points, where $d \geq 2$ is a constant.

Hint: Design a recursive data structure that builds a d-dimensional structure using $(d-1)$-dimensional structures.

C-12.7 Suppose we are given a range-searching data structure D that can answer range-searching queries for a set of n points in d-dimensional space for any fixed dimension d (like 8, 10, or 20) in time that is $O(\log^d n + k)$, where k is the number of answers. Show how to use D to answer the following queries for a set S of n rectangles in the plane:

- findAllContaining(x,y): Return an enumeration of all rectangles in S that contain the point (x,y).
- findAllIntersecting(a,b,c,d): Return an enumeration of all rectangles that intersect the rectangle with x-range $[a,b]$ and y-range $[c,d]$.

What is the running time needed to answer each of these queries?

C-12.8 Let S be a set of n intervals of the form $[a,b]$, where $a < b$. Design an efficient data structure that can answer, in $O(\log n + k)$ time, queries of the form contains(x), which asks for an enumeration of all intervals in S that contain x, where k is the number of such intervals. What is the space usage of your data structure?

C-12.9 Describe an efficient method for inserting an object into a (balanced) priority search tree. What is the running time of this method?

C-12.10 Suppose we are given an array-based sequence S of n nonintersecting segments $s_0, \ldots, s_{n-1}$ with endpoints on the lines $y = 0$ and $y = 1$, and ordered from left to right. Given a point q with $0 < y(q) < 1$, design an algorithm that in $O(\log n)$ time computes the segment s_i of S immediately to right of q, or reports that q is to the right of all the segments.

C-12.11 Give an $O(n)$-time algorithm for testing whether a point q is inside, outside, or on the boundary of a nonintersecting polygon P with n vertices. Your algorithm should also work correctly for the case when the y-coordinate of q is equal to the y-coordinate of one or more vertices of P.

C-12.12 Design an $O(n)$-time algorithm to test whether a given n-vertex polygon is convex. You should not assume that P is nonintersecting.

C-12.13 Let S be a collection of segments. Give an algorithm for determining whether the segments of S form a polygon. Allow the polygon to be intersecting, but do not allow two vertices of the polygon to be coincident.

C-12.14 Let S be a collection of n line segments in the plane. Give an algorithm to enumerate all k pairs of intersecting segments in S in $O((n+k)\log n)$.

Hint: Use the plane-sweep technique, including segments intersections as events. Note that you cannot know these events in advance, but it is always possible to know the next event to process as you are sweeping.

C-12.15 Design a data structure for convex polygons that uses linear space and supports the point inclusion test in logarithmic time.

C-12.16 Given a set P of n points, design an efficient algorithm for constructing a nonintersecting polygon whose vertices are the points of P.

C-12.17 Design an $O(n^2)$-time algorithm for testing whether a polygon with n vertices is nonintersecting. Assume that the polygon is given by the list of its vertices.

C-12.18 Give examples of configurations of input points for which the simplified Graham scan algorithm, given in Algorithm 12.25, does not work correctly.

C-12.19 Let P be a set of n points in the plane. Modify the Graham scan algorithm to compute, for every point p of P that is not a vertex of the convex hull, either a triangle with vertices in P, or a segment with endpoints in P that contains p in its interior.

C-12.20 Given a set S of points in the plane, define the ***Voronoi diagram*** of S to be the set of regions $V(p)$, called ***Voronoi cells***, defined, for each point p in S, as the set of all points q in the plane such that p is a closest neighbor of q in S.

a. Show that each cell in a Voronoi diagram is convex.
b. Show that if p and q are a closest pair of points in the set S, then the Voronoi cells $V(p)$ and $V(q)$ touch.
c. Show that a point p is on the boundary of the convex hull of the set S if and only if the Voronoi cell $V(p)$ for p is unbounded.

C-12.21 Given a set S of points in the plane, define the ***Delaunay triangulation*** of S to be the set of all triangles (p,q,r) such that p, q, and r are in S and the circle defined to have these points on its boundary is empty—it contains no points of S in its interior.

a. Show that if p and q are a closest pair of points in the set S, then p and q are joined by an edge in the Delaunay triangulation.
b. Show that the Voronoi cells $V(p)$ and $V(q)$ share an edge in the Voronoi diagram of a point set S if and only if p and q are joined by an edge in the Delaunay triangulation of S.

Projects

P-12.1 Produce an animation of the gift wrapping and Graham scan algorithms for computing the convex hull of a set of points.

P-12.2 Implement a class supporting range-searching queries with a range tree or priority range tree data structure.

P-12.3 Implement the quadtree and k-d tree data structures and perform an experimental study comparing their performance on range-searching queries.

Chapter Notes

The convex hull algorithm we present in this chapter is a variant of an algorithm given by Graham [88]. The plane sweep algorithm we present for intersecting orthogonal line segments is due to Bentley and Ottmann [31]. The closest point algorithm we present combines ideas of Bentley [28] and Hinrichs *et al.* [94].

There are several excellent books for computational geometry, including books by Edelsbrunner [63], Mehlhorn [150], O'Rourke [160], Preparata and Shamos [168], and handbooks edited by Goodman and O'Rourke [83], and Pach [162]. Other sources for further reading include survey papers by Aurenhammer [17], Lee and Preparata [129], and book chapters by Goodrich [84], Lee [128], and Yao [212]. Also, the books by Sedgewick [182, 183] contain several chapters on computational geometry, which have some very nice figures. Indeed, the figures in Sedgewick's books have inspired many of the figures we present in this book.

Multi-dimensional search trees are discussed in books by Mehlhorn [150], Samet [175, 176], and Wood [211]. Please see these books for an extensive discussion of the history of multi-dimensional search trees, including various data structures for solving range queries. Priority search trees are due to McCreight [140], although Vuillemin [208] introduced this structure earlier under the name "Cartesian trees." They are also known as "treaps," as described by McCreight [140] and Aragon and Seidel [12]. Edelsbrunner [62] shows how priority search trees can be used to answer two-dimensional range queries. Arya and Mount [14] present the balanced box decomposition tree, and they show how it can be used to solve approximate range searching [15]. The reader interested in recent developments for range-searching data structures is referred to the book chapters by Agarwal [3, 4] or the survey paper by Matoušek [138]. Luca Vismara developed the implementation of the convex hull algorithm given in Section 12.6.

Chapter

13 NP-Completeness

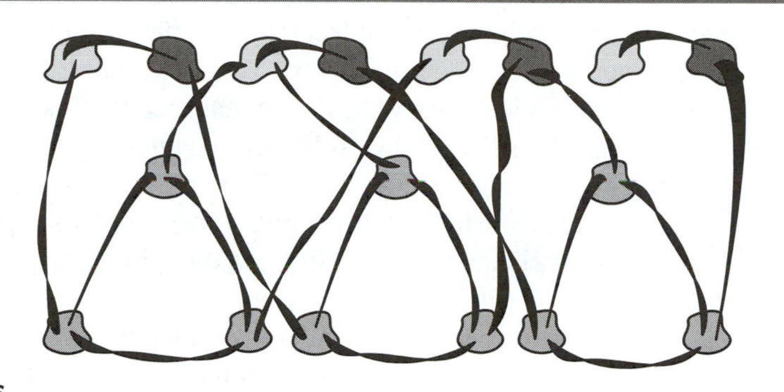

Contents

13.1 P and NP **593**
13.1.1 Defining the Complexity Classes **P** and **NP** 594
13.1.2 Some Interesting Problems in **NP** 597
13.2 NP-Completeness **599**
13.2.1 Polynomial-Time Reducibility and **NP**-Hardness . . . 600
13.2.2 The Cook-Levin Theorem 600
13.3 Important NP-Complete Problems **603**
13.3.1 CNF-SAT and 3SAT 605
13.3.2 VERTEX-COVER 608
13.3.3 CLIQUE and SET-COVER 610
13.3.4 SUBSET-SUM and KNAPSACK 612
13.3.5 HAMILTONIAN-CYCLE and TSP 615
13.4 Approximation Algorithms **618**
13.4.1 Polynomial-Time Approximation Schemes 619
13.4.2 A 2-Approximation for VERTEX-COVER 622
13.4.3 A 2-Approximation for a Special Case of TSP 623
13.4.4 A Logarithmic Approximation for SET-COVER . . . 625
13.5 Backtracking and Branch-and-Bound **627**
13.5.1 Backtracking 627
13.5.2 Branch-and-Bound 632
13.6 Exercises **638**

Some computational problems are hard. We rack our brains to find efficient algorithms for solving them, but time and time again we fail. It would be nice if we could prove that finding an efficient algorithm is impossible in such cases. Such a proof would be a great relief when an efficient algorithm evades us, for then we could take comfort from the fact that no efficient algorithm exists for this problem. Unfortunately, such proofs are typically even harder to come by than efficient algorithms.

Still, all is not frustration, for the topics we discuss in this chapter let us show that certain problems are indeed computationally hard. The proofs involve a concept known as ***NP-completeness***. This concept allows us to rigorously show that finding an efficient algorithm for a certain problem is at least as hard as finding efficient algorithms for ***all*** the problems in a large class of problems called "***NP***." The formal notion of "efficient" we use here is that a problem has an algorithm running in time proportional to a polynomial function of its input size, n. (Recall that this notion of efficiency was already mentioned in Section 1.2.2.) That is, we consider an algorithm "efficient" if it runs in time $O(n^k)$ on any input of size n, for some constant $k > 0$. Even so, the class ***NP*** contains some extremely difficult problems, for which polynomial-time solutions have eluded researchers for decades. Therefore, while showing that a problem is ***NP***-complete is admittedly not the same as proving that an efficient algorithm for the problem is impossible, it is nevertheless a powerful statement. Basically, showing that a problem L is ***NP***-complete says that, although we have been unable to find an efficient algorithm for L, neither has any computer scientist who has ever lived! Indeed, most computer scientists strongly believe it is impossible to solve any ***NP***-complete problem in polynomial time.

In this chapter, we formally define the class ***NP*** and its related class ***P***, and we show how to prove that some problems are ***NP***-complete. We also discuss some of the best known of the ***NP***-complete problems, showing that each one is at least as hard as every other problem in ***NP***. These problems include satisfiability, vertex cover, knapsack, and traveling salesperson problems.

We do not stop there, however, for many of these problems are quite important, in that they are related to optimization problems whose solution in the real world can oftentimes save money, time, or other resources. Thus, we also discuss some ways of dealing with ***NP***-completeness in this chapter. One of the most effective methods is to construct polynomial-time approximation algorithms for ***NP***-complete problems. Although such algorithms do not usually produce optimal solutions, they oftentimes come close to being optimal. In fact, in some cases we can provide a guarantee of how close an approximation algorithm will come to an optimal solution. We explore several such situations in this chapter.

We conclude this chapter by covering techniques that often work well for dealing with ***NP***-complete problems in practice. We present, in particular, ***backtracking*** and ***branch-and-bound***, which construct algorithms that run in exponential time in the worst case, but nevertheless take advantage of situations where faster time is possible. We give Java examples of both techniques.

13.1 P and NP

In order to study ***NP***-completeness, we need to be more precise about running time. Namely, instead of the informal notion of input size as the number of "items" that form the input (see Chapter 1), we define the ***input size***, n, of a problem to be the number of bits used to encode an input instance. We also assume that characters and numbers in the input are encoded using a reasonable binary encoding scheme, so that each character uses a constant number of bits and each integer $M > 0$ is represented with at most $c \log M$ bits, for some constant $c > 0$. In particular, we disallow ***unary encoding***, where an integer M is represented with M 1's.

Recall that we have, for the rest of this book, defined the input size n to be the number of "items" in an input. Let us for the moment, however, refer to the number of items in an input as N and the number of bits to encode an input as n. Thus, if M is the largest integer in an input, then $N + \log M \leq n \leq cN \log M$, for some constant $c > 0$. Formally, we define the worst-case ***running time*** of an algorithm A to be the worst-case time taken by A as a function of n, taken over all possible inputs having an encoding with n bits. Fortunately, as we show in the following lemma, most algorithms running in polynomial time in terms of N still result in polynomial-time algorithms in terms of n. We define an algorithm to be ***c-incremental*** if any primitive operation involving one or two objects represented with b bits results in an object represented with at most $b + c$ bits, for $c \geq 0$. For example, an algorithm using multiplication as a primitive operation may not be c-incremental for any constant c. Of course, we can include a routine in a c-incremental algorithm to perform multiplication, but we should not count this routine as a primitive operation here.

Lemma 13.1: *If a c-incremental algorithm A has a worst-case running time $t(N)$ in the RAM model, as a function of the number of input items, N, for some constant $c > 0$, then A has running time $O(n^2 t(n))$, in terms of the number, n, of bits in a standard nonunary encoding of the input.*

Proof: Note that $N \leq n$. Thus, $t(N) \leq t(n)$. Likewise, each primitive operation in the algorithm A, involving one or two objects represented with $b \geq 1$ bits, can be performed using at most db^2 bitwise operations, for some constant $d \geq 1$, since c is a constant. Such primitive operations include all comparison, control flow, and basic non-multiplicative arithmetic operations. Moreover, in N steps of a c-incremental algorithm, the largest any object's representation can become is $cN + b$, where b is the maximum size of any input object. But, $cN + b \leq (c+1)n$. Thus, every step in A will take at most $O(n^2)$ bit steps to complete. ■

Therefore, any "reasonable" algorithm that runs in polynomial time in terms of the number of input items will also run in polynomial time in terms of the number of input bits. Thus, for the remainder of this chapter, we may revert to using n as input size and number of "items" with the understanding that any "polynomial-time" algorithm must run in polynomial time in terms of the number of input bits.

13.1.1 Defining the Complexity Classes P and NP

By Lemma 13.1, we know that, for the problems discussed in this book, such as graph problems, text processing, or sorting, our previous polynomial-time algorithms translate into polynomial-time algorithms in the bit model. Even the repeated squaring algorithm (Section 10.1.4) for computing powers of an integer x runs in a polynomial number of bit operations if we apply it to raise x to a number that is represented using $O(\log n)$ bits. Thus, the notion of polynomial time is quite useful as a measure for tractability.

Moreover, the class of polynomials is closed under addition, multiplication, and composition. That is, if $p(n)$ and $q(n)$ are polynomials, then so are $p(n) + q(n)$, $p(n) \cdot q(n)$, and $p(q(n))$. Thus, we can combine or compose polynomial-time algorithms to construct new polynomial-time algorithms.

Decision Problems

To simplify our discussion, let us restrict our attention for the time being to ***decision problems***, that is, to computational problems for which the intended output is either "yes" or "no." In other words, a decision problem's output is a single bit, which is either 0 or 1. For example, each of the following are decision problems:

- Given a string T and a string P, does P appear as a substring of T?
- Given two sets S and T, do S and T contain the same set of elements?
- Given a graph G with integer weights on its edges, and an integer k, does G have a minimum spanning tree of weight at most k?

In fact, the last problem illustrates how we can often turn an ***optimization problem***, where we are trying to minimize or maximize some value, into a decision problem. Namely, we can introduce a parameter k and ask if the optimal value for the optimization problem is at most or at least k. Note that if we can show that a decision problem is hard, then its related optimization version must also be hard.

Problems and Languages

We say that an algorithm A ***accepts*** an input string x if A outputs "yes" on input x. Thus, we can view a ***decision problem*** as actually being just a set L of strings—the strings that should be accepted by an algorithm that correctly solves the problem. Indeed, we used the letter "L" to denote a decision problem, because a set of strings is often referred to as a ***language***. We can extend this language-based viewpoint further to say that an algorithm A ***accepts*** a language L if A outputs "yes" for each x in L and outputs "no" otherwise. Throughout this chapter, we assume that if x is in an improper syntax, then an algorithm given x will output "no." (Note: Some texts also allow for the possibility of A going into an infinite loop and never outputting anything on some inputs, but we are restricting our attention in this book to algorithms, that is, computations that terminate after a finite number of steps.)

The Complexity Class **P**

The ***complexity class P*** is the set of all decision problems (or languages) L that can be accepted in worst-case polynomial time. That is, there is an algorithm A that, if $x \in L$, then on input x, A outputs "yes" in $p(n)$ time, where n is the size of x and $p(n)$ is a polynomial. Note that the definition of ***P*** doesn't say anything about the running time for rejecting an input—when an algorithm A outputs "no." Such cases refer to the ***complement*** of a language L, which consists of all binary strings that are not in L. Still, given an algorithm A that accepts a language L in polynomial time, $p(n)$, we can easily construct a polynomial-time algorithm that accepts the complement of L. In particular, given an input x, we can construct a complement algorithm B that simply runs A for $p(n)$ steps, where n is the size of x, terminating A if it attempts to run more than $p(n)$ steps. If A outputs "yes," then B outputs "no." Likewise, if A outputs "no" or if A runs for at least $p(n)$ steps without outputting anything, then B outputs "yes." In either case, the complement algorithm B runs in polynomial time. Therefore, if a language L, representing some decision problem, is in ***P***, then the complement of L is also in ***P***.

The Complexity Class **NP**

The ***complexity class NP*** is defined to include the complexity class ***P*** but allow for the inclusion of languages that may not be in ***P***. Specifically, with ***NP*** problems, we allow algorithms to perform an additional operation:

- choose(b): this operation chooses in a nondeterministic way a bit (that is, a value that is either 0 or 1) and assigns it to b.

When an algorithm A uses the choose primitive operation, then we say A is ***non-deterministic***. We state that an algorithm A ***nondeterministically accepts*** a string x if there exists a set of outcomes to the choose calls that A could make on input x such that A would ultimately output "yes." In other words, it is as if we consider all possible outcomes to choose calls and only select those that lead to acceptance if there is such a set of outcomes. Note this is not the same as random choices.

The complexity class ***NP*** is the set of decision problems (or languages) L that can be nondeterministically accepted in polynomial time. That is, there is a non-deterministic algorithm A that, if $x \in L$, then, on input x, there is a set of outcomes to the choose calls in A so that it outputs "yes" in $p(n)$ time, where n is the size of x and $p(n)$ is a polynomial. Note that the definition of ***NP*** does not address the running time for a rejection. Indeed, we allow for an algorithm A accepting a language L in polynomial time $p(n)$ to take much more than $p(n)$ steps when A outputs "no." Moreover, because nondeterministic acceptance could involve a polynomial number of calls to the choose method, if a language L is in ***NP***, the complement of L is not necessarily also in ***NP***. Indeed, there is a complexity class, called **co-*NP***, that consists of all languages whose complement is in ***NP***, and many researchers believe **co-*NP*** $\neq$ ***NP***.

An Alternate Definition of NP

There is actually another way to define the complexity class ***NP***, which might be more intuitive for some readers. This alternate definition of ***NP*** is based on deterministic verification, instead of nondeterministic acceptance. We say that a language L can be ***verified*** by an algorithm A if, given any string x in L as input, there is another string y such that A outputs "yes" on input $z = x + y$, where we use the symbol "+" to denote concatenation. The string y is called a ***certificate*** for membership in L, for it helps us certify that x is indeed in L. Note that we make no claims about verifying when a string is not in L.

This notion of verification allows us to give an alternate definition of the complexity class ***NP***. Namely, we can define ***NP*** to be the set of all languages L, defining decision problems, such that L can be verified in polynomial time. That is, there is a (deterministic) algorithm A that, for any x in L, verifies using some certificate y that x is indeed in L in polynomial time, $p(n)$, including the time A takes to read its input $z = x + y$, where n is the size of x. Note that this definition implies that the size of y is less than $p(n)$. As the following theorem shows, this verification-based definition of ***NP*** is equivalent to the nondeterminism-based definition given above.

Theorem 13.2: *A language L can be (deterministically) verified in polynomial time if and only if L can be nondeterministically accepted in polynomial time.*

Proof: Let us consider each possibility. Suppose first that L can be verified in polynomial time. That is, there is a deterministic algorithm A (making no use of choose calls) that can verify in polynomial time $p(n)$ that a string x is in L when given a polynomial-length certificate y. Therefore, we can construct a nondeterministic algorithm B that takes the string x as input and calls the choose method to assign the value of each bit in y. After B has constructed a string $z = x + y$, it then calls A to verify that $x \in L$ given the certificate y. If there exists a certificate y such that A accepts z, then there is clearly a set of nondeterministic choices for B that result in B outputting "yes" itself. In addition, B will run in $O(p(n))$ steps.

Next, suppose that L can be nondeterministically accepted in polynomial time. That is, there is a nondeterministic algorithm A that, given a string x in L, performs $p(n)$ steps, which may include choose steps, such that, for some sequence of outcomes to these choose steps, A will output "yes." There is a deterministic verification algorithm B that, given x in L, uses as its certificate y the ordered concatenation of all the outcomes to choose calls that A makes on input x in order to ultimately output "yes." Since A runs in $p(n)$ steps, where n is the size of x, the algorithm B will also run in $O(p(n))$ steps given input $z = x + y$. ■

The practical implication of this theorem is that, since both definitions of ***NP*** are equivalent, we can use either one for showing that a problem is in ***NP***.

The $\mathbf{P} = \mathbf{NP}$ Question

Computer scientists do not know for certain whether $P = NP$ or not. Indeed, researchers don't even know for sure whether or not $P = NP \cap$ co-NP. Still, the vast majority of researchers believe that P is different than both NP and co NP, as well as their intersection. In fact, the problems we discuss next are examples of problems in NP that many believe are not in P.

13.1.2 Some Interesting Problems in NP

Another way of interpreting Theorem 13.2 is that it implies we can always structure a nondeterministic algorithm so that all of its choose steps are performed first and the rest of the algorithm is just a verification. We illustrate with several examples in this subsection this approach of showing interesting decision problems to be in NP. Our first example is for a graph problem.

HAMILTONIAN-CYCLE is the problem that takes a graph G as input and asks whether there is a simple cycle in G that visits each vertex of G exactly once and then returns to its starting vertex. Such a cycle is called an Hamiltonian cycle of G.

Lemma 13.3: HAMILTONIAN-CYCLE *is in NP*.

Proof: Let us define a nondeterministic algorithm A that takes, as input, a graph G encoded as an adjacency list in binary notation, with the vertices numbered 1 to N. We define A to first iteratively call the choose method to determine a sequence S of $N+1$ numbers from 1 to N. Then, we have A check that each number from 1 to N appears exactly once in S (for example, by sorting S), except for the first and last numbers in S, which should be the same. Then, we verify that the sequence S defines a cycle of vertices and edges in G. A binary encoding of the sequence S is clearly of size at most n, where n is the size of the input. Moreover, both of the checks made on the sequence S can be done in polynomial time in n.

Observe that if there is a cycle in G that visits each vertex of G exactly once, returning to its starting vertex, then there is a sequence S for which A will output "yes." Likewise, if A outputs "yes," then it has found a cycle in G that visits each vertex of G exactly once, returning to its starting point. That is, A nondeterministically accepts the language HAMILTONIAN-CYCLE. In other words, HAMILTONIAN-CYCLE is in NP. ■

Our next example is a problem related to circuit design testing. A ***Boolean circuit*** is a directed graph where each node, called a ***logic gate***, corresponds to a simple Boolean function, AND, OR, or NOT. The incoming edges for a logic gate correspond to inputs for its Boolean function and the outgoing edges correspond to outputs, which will all be the same value, of course, for that gate. (See Figure 13.1.) Vertices with no incoming edges are ***input*** nodes and a vertex with no outgoing edges is an ***output*** node.

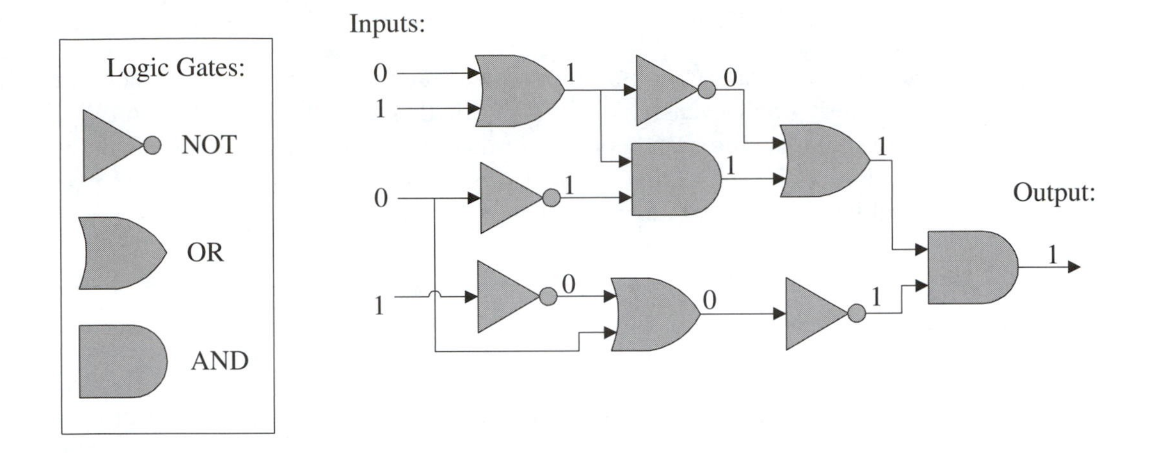

Figure 13.1: An example Boolean circuit.

CIRCUIT-SAT is the problem that takes as input a Boolean circuit with a single output node, and asks whether there is an assignment of values to the circuit's inputs so that its output value is "1." Such an assignment of values is called a ***satisfying assignment***.

Lemma 13.4: CIRCUIT-SAT *is in **NP**.*

Proof: We construct a nondeterministic algorithm for accepting CIRCUIT-SAT in polynomial time. We first use the choose method to "guess" the values of the input nodes as well as the output value of each logic gate. Then, we simply visit each logic gate g in C, that is, each vertex with at least one incoming edge. We then check that the "guessed" value for the output of g is in fact the correct value for g's Boolean function, be it an AND, OR, or NOT, based on the given values for the inputs for g. This evaluation process can easily be performed in polynomial time. If any check for a gate fails, or if the "guessed" value for the output is 0, then we output "no." If, on the other hand, the check for every gate succeeds and the output is "1," the algorithm outputs "yes." Thus, if there is indeed a satisfying assignment of input values for C, then there is a possible collection of outcomes to the choose statements so that the algorithm will output "yes" in polynomial time. Likewise, if there is a collection of outcomes to the choose statements so that the algorithm outputs "yes" in polynomial time algorithm, there must be a satisfying assignment of input values for C. Therefore, CIRCUIT-SAT is in ***NP***. ■

The next example illustrates how a decision version of an optimization problem can be shown to be in ***NP***. Given a graph G, a ***vertex cover*** for G is a subset C of vertices such that, for every edge (v,w) of G, $v \in C$ or $w \in C$ (possibly both). The optimization goal is to find as small a vertex cover for G as possible.

VERTEX-COVER is the decision problem that takes a graph G and an integer k as input, and asks whether there is a vertex cover for G containing at most k vertices.

Lemma 13.5: *VERTEX-COVER is in **NP***

Proof: Suppose we are given an integer k and a graph G, with the vertices of G numbered from 1 to N. We can use repeated calls to the choose method to construct a collection C of k numbers that range from 1 to N. As a verification, we insert all the numbers of C into a dictionary and then we examine each of the edges in G to make sure that, for each edge (v,w) in G, v is in C or w is in C. If we ever find an edge with neither of its end-vertices in G, then we output "no." If we run through all the edges of G so that each has an end-vertex in C, then we output "yes." Such a computation clearly runs in polynomial time.

Note that if G has a vertex cover of size at most k, then there is an assignment of numbers to define the collection C so that each edge of G passes our test and our algorithm outputs "yes." Likewise, if our algorithm outputs "yes," then there must be a subset C of the vertices of size at most k, such that C is a vertex cover. Thus, VERTEX-COVER is in ***NP***. ■

Having given some interesting examples of problems in ***NP***, let us now turn to the definition of the concept of ***NP***-completeness.

13.2 NP-Completeness

The notion of nondeterministic acceptance of a decision problem (or language) is admittedly strange. There is, after all, no conventional computer that can efficiently perform a nondeterministic algorithm with many calls to the choose method. Indeed, to date no one has shown how even an unconventional computer, such as a quantum computer or DNA computer, can efficiently simulate any nondeterministic polynomial-time algorithm using a polynomial amount of resources. Certainly, we can deterministically simulate a nondeterministic algorithm by trying out, one by one, all possible outcomes to the choose statements that the algorithm makes. But this simulation would become an exponential-time computation for any nondeterministic algorithm that makes at least n^{ε} calls to the choose method, for any fixed constant $\varepsilon > 0$. Indeed, there are hundreds of problems in the complexity class ***NP*** for which most computer scientists strongly believe there is no conventional deterministic method for solving them in polynomial time.

The usefulness of the complexity class ***NP***, therefore, is that it formally captures a host of problems that many believe to be computationally difficult. In fact, there are some problems that are provably at least as hard as every other problem in ***NP***, as far as polynomial-time solutions are concerned. This notion of hardness is based on the concept of polynomial-time reducibility, which we now discuss.

13.2.1 Polynomial-Time Reducibility and **NP**-Hardness

We say that a language L, defining some decision problem, is ***polynomial-time reducible*** to a language M, if there is a function f computable in polynomial time, that takes an input x to L, and transforms it to an input $f(x)$ of M, such that $x \in L$ if and only if $f(x) \in M$. In addition, we use a shorthand notation, saying $L \xrightarrow{\text{poly}} M$ to signify that language L is polynomial-time reducible to language M.

We say that a language M, defining some decision problem, is ***NP-hard*** if every other language L in ***NP*** is polynomial-time reducible to M. In more mathematical notation, M is ***NP***-hard, if, for every $L \in \boldsymbol{NP}$, $L \xrightarrow{\text{poly}} M$. If a language M is ***NP***-hard and it is also in the class ***NP*** itself, then M is ***NP-complete***. Thus, an ***NP***-complete problem is, in a very formal sense, one of the hardest problems in ***NP***, as far as polynomial-time computability is concerned. For, if anyone ever shows that an ***NP***-complete problem L is solvable in polynomial time, then that immediately implies that every other problem in the entire class ***NP*** is solvable in polynomial time. For, in this case, we could accept any other ***NP*** language M by reducing it to L and then running the algorithm for L. In other words, if anyone finds a deterministic polynomial-time algorithm for even one ***NP***-complete problem, then $\boldsymbol{P} = \boldsymbol{NP}$.

13.2.2 The Cook-Levin Theorem

At first, it might appear that the definition of ***NP***-completeness is too strong. Still, as the following theorem shows, there is at least one ***NP***-complete problem.

Theorem 13.6 (The Cook-Levin Theorem): CIRCUIT-SAT *is **NP**-complete.*

Proof: Lemma 13.4 shows that CIRCUIT-SAT is in ***NP***. Thus, we have yet to show this problem is ***NP***-hard. That is, we need to show that every problem in ***NP*** is polynomial-time reducible to CIRCUIT-SAT. So, consider a language L, representing some decision problem that is in ***NP***. Since L is in ***NP***, there is a deterministic algorithm D that accepts any x in L in polynomial-time $p(n)$, given a polynomial-sized certificate y, where n is the size of x. The main idea of the proof is to build a large, but polynomial-sized, circuit C that simulates the algorithm D on an input x in such a way that C is satisfiable if and only if there is a certificate y such that D outputs "yes" on input $z = x + y$.

Recall (from Section 1.1.2) that any deterministic algorithm, such as D, can be implemented on a simple computational model (called the Random Access Machine, or RAM) that consists of a CPU and a bank M of addressable memory cells. In our case, the memory M contains the input, x, the certificate, y, the working storage, W, that D needs to perform its computations, and the code for the algorithm D itself. The working storage W for D includes all the registers used for temporary calculations and the stack frames for the procedures that D calls during its execution. The topmost such stack frame in W contains the program counter

(PC) that identifies where D currently is in its program execution. Thus, there are no memory cells in the CPU itself. In performing each step of D, the CPU reads the next instruction i, which is pointed to by the PC, and performs the calculation indicated by i, be it a comparison, arithmetic operation, a conditional jump, a step in procedure call, etc., and then updates the PC to point to the next instruction to be performed. Thus, the current state of D is completely characterized by the contents of its memory cells. Moreover, since D accepts an x in L in a polynomial $p(n)$ number of steps, where n is the size of x, then the entire effective collection of its memory cells can be assumed to consist of just $p(n)$ bits. For in $p(n)$ steps, D can access at most $p(n)$ memory cells. Note also that the size of D's code is constant with respect to the sizes of x, y, and even W. We refer to the $p(n)$-sized collection M of memory cells for an execution of D as the ***configuration*** of the algorithm D.

The heart of the reduction of L to CIRCUIT-SAT depends on our constructing a Boolean circuit that simulates the workings of the CPU in our computational model. The details of such a construction are beyond the scope of this book, but it is well known that a CPU can be designed as a Boolean circuit consisting of AND, OR, and NOT gates. Moreover, let us further take for granted that this circuit, including its address unit for connecting to a memory of $p(n)$ bits, can be designed so as to take a configuration of D as input and provide as output the configuration resulting from processing the next computational step. In addition, this simulation circuit, which we will call S, can be constructed so as to consist of at most $cp(n)^2$ AND, OR, and NOT gates, for some constant $c > 0$.

To then simulate the entire $p(n)$ steps of D, we make $p(n)$ copies of S, with the output from one copy serving as the input for the next. (See Figure 13.2.) Part of the input for the first copy of S consists of "hard wired" values for the program for D, the value of x, the initial stack frame (complete with PC pointing to the first instruction of D), and the remaining working storage (initialized to all 0's). The only unspecified true inputs to the first copy of S are the cells of D's configuration for the certificate y. These are the true inputs to our circuit. Likewise, we ignore all the outputs from the final copy of S, except the single output that indicates the answer from D, with "1" for "yes" and "0" for "no." The total size of the circuit C is $O(p(n)^3)$, which of course is still polynomial in the size of x.

Consider an input x that D accepts for some certificate y after $p(n)$ steps. Then there is an assignment of values to the input to C corresponding to y, such that, by having C simulate D on this input and the hard-wired values for x, we will ultimately have C output a "1." Thus, C is satisfiable in this case. Conversely, consider a case when C is satisfiable. Then there is a set of inputs, which correspond to the certificate y, such that C outputs a "1." But, since C exactly simulates the algorithm D, this implies that there is an assignment of values to the certificate y, such that D outputs "yes." Thus, D will verify x in this case. Therefore, D accepts x with certificate y if and only if C is satisfiable. ■

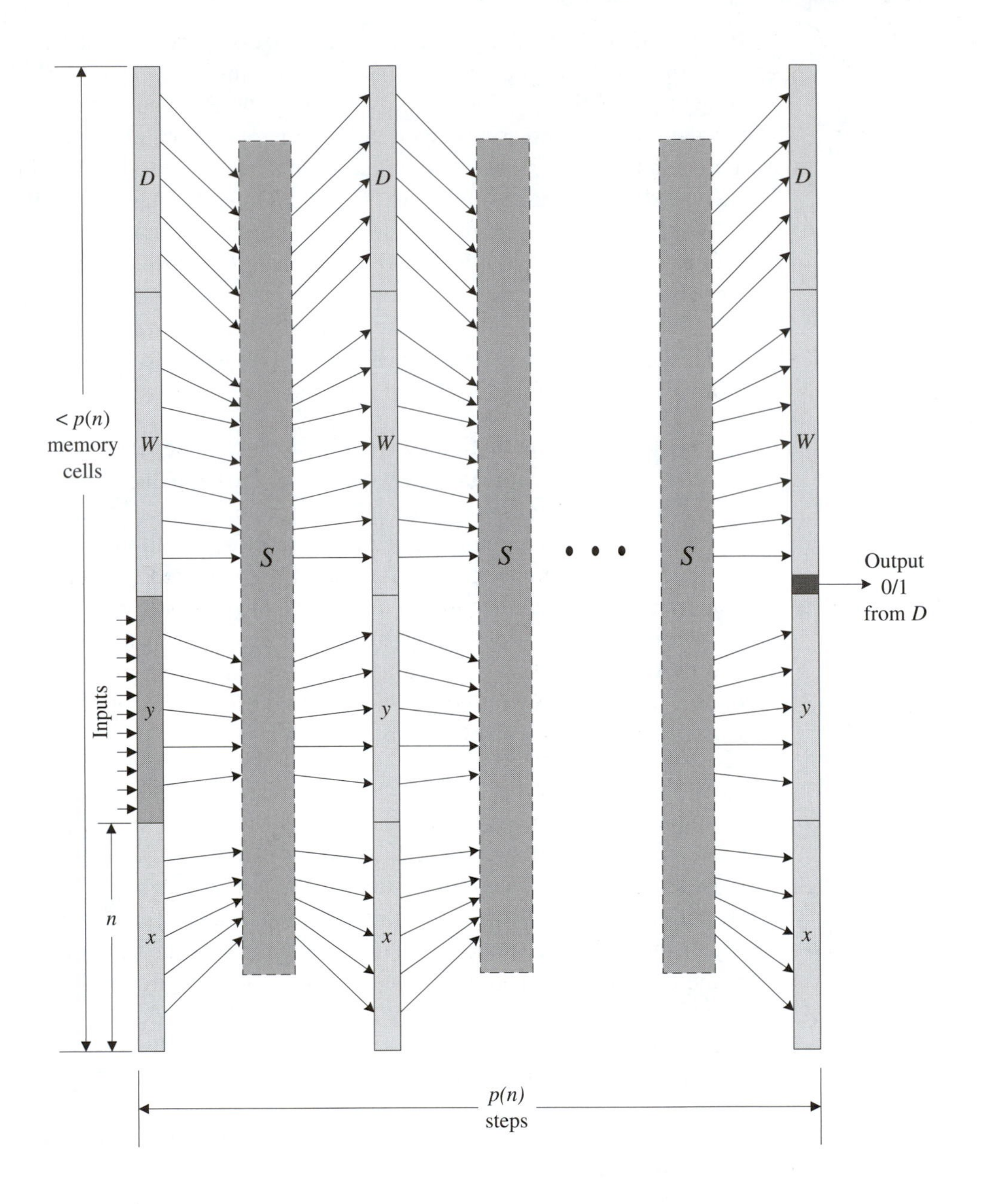

Figure 13.2: An illustration of the circuit used to prove that CIRCUIT-SAT is ***NP***-hard. The only true inputs correspond to the certificate, y. The problem instance, x, the working storage, W, and the program code, D, are initially "hard wired" values. The only output is the bit that determines if the algorithm accepts x or not.

13.3 Important NP-Complete Problems

So there is indeed an ***NP***-complete problem. But proving this fact was admittedly a tiring exercise, even taking into account the major shortcut we took in assuming the existence of the simulation circuit S. Fortunately, now that we are armed with one problem that is proven to be ***NP***-complete "from scratch," we can prove other problems are ***NP***-complete using simple polynomial-time reductions. We explore a number of such reductions in this section.

Given just a single ***NP***-complete problem, we can now use polynomial-time reducibility to show other problems to be ***NP***-complete. In addition, we will make repeated use of the following important lemma about polynomial-time reducibility.

Lemma 13.7: *If* $L_1 \xrightarrow{\text{poly}} L_2$ *and* $L_2 \xrightarrow{\text{poly}} L_3$*, then* $L_1 \xrightarrow{\text{poly}} L_3$*.*

Proof: Since $L_1 \xrightarrow{\text{poly}} L_2$, any instance x for L_1 can be converted in polynomial-time $p(n)$ into an instance $f(x)$ for L_2, such that $x \in L_1$ if and only if $f(x) \in L_2$, where n is the size of x. Likewise, since $L_2 \xrightarrow{\text{poly}} L_3$, any instance y for L_2 can be converted in polynomial-time $q(m)$ into an instance $g(y)$ for L_3, such that $y \in L_2$ if and only if $g(y) \in L_3$, where m is the size of y. Combining these two constructions, any instance x for L_1 can be converted in time $q(k)$ into an instance $g(f(x))$ for L_3, such that $x \in L_1$ if and only if $g(f(x)) \in L_3$, where k is the size of $f(x)$. But, $k \le p(n)$, since $f(x)$ is constructed in $p(n)$ steps. Thus, $q(k) \le q(p(n))$. Since the composition of two polynomials always results in another polynomial, this inequality implies that $L_1 \xrightarrow{\text{poly}} L_3$. ■

In this section we establish several important problems to be ***NP***-complete, using this lemma. All of the proofs have the same general structure. Given a new problem L, we first prove that L is in ***NP***. Then, we reduce a known ***NP***-complete problem to L in polynomial time, showing L to be ***NP***-hard. Thus, we show L to be in ***NP*** and also ***NP***-hard; hence, L has been shown to be ***NP***-complete. (Why not do the reduction in the other direction?) These reductions generally take one of three forms:

- ***Restriction***: This form shows a problem L is ***NP***-hard by noting that a known ***NP***-complete problem M is actually just a special case of L.
- ***Local replacement***: This forms reduces a known ***NP***-complete problem M to L by dividing instances of M and L into "basic units," and then showing how each basic unit of M can be locally converted into a basic unit of L.
- ***Component design***: This form reduces a known ***NP***-complete problem M to L by building components for an instance of L that will enforce important structural functions for instances of M. For example, some components might enforce a "choice" while others enforce an "evaluation" function.

The latter of the three above forms tends to be the most difficult to construct; it is the form used, for example, by the proof of the Cook-Levin Theorem (13.6).

In Figure 13.3, we illustrate the problems we prove are ***NP***-complete, together with the problems they are reduced from and the technique used in each polynomial-time reduction.

In the remainder of this section we study some important ***NP***-complete problems. We treat most of them in pairs, with each pair addressing an important class of problems, including problems involving Boolean formulas, graphs, sets, and numbers. We begin with two problems involving Boolean formulas.

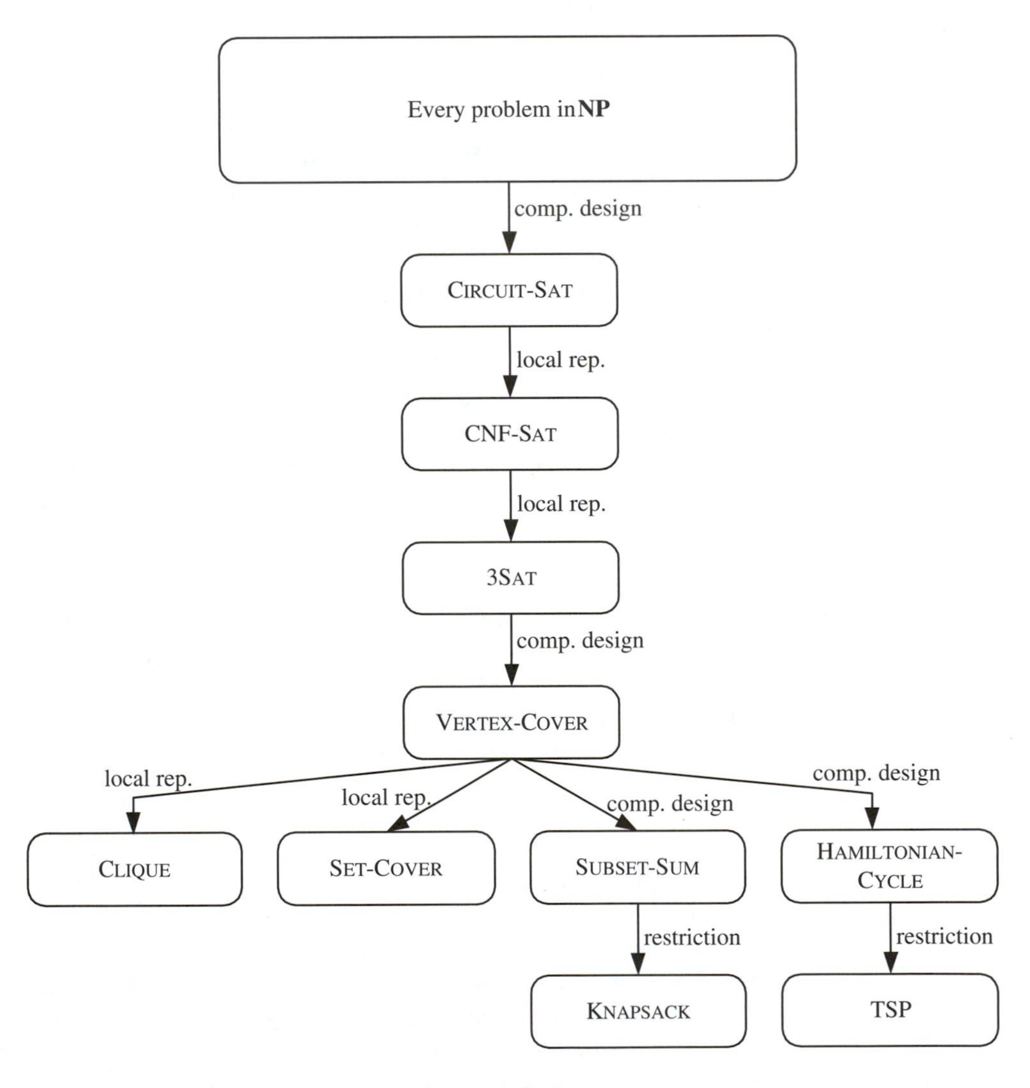

Figure 13.3: Illustration of the reductions used in some fundamental ***NP***-completeness proofs. Each directed edge denotes a polynomial-time reduction, with the label on the edge indicating the primary form of that reduction. The topmost reduction is the Cook-Levin Theorem.

13.3.1 CNF-SAT and 3SAT

The first reductions we present are for problems involving Boolean formulas. A Boolean formula is a parenthesized expression that is formed from Boolean variables using Boolean operations, such as OR (+), AND (·), NOT (drawn as a bar over the negated subexpression), IMPLIES (→), and IF-AND-ONLY-IF (↔). A Boolean formula is in ***conjunctive normal form*** (CNF) if it is formed as a collection of subexpressions, called ***clauses***, that are combined using AND, with each clause formed as the OR of Boolean variables or their negation, called ***literals***. For example, the following Boolean formula is in CNF:

$$(\overline{x_1}+x_2+x_4+\overline{x_7})(x_3+\overline{x_5})(\overline{x_2}+x_4+\overline{x_6}+x_8)(x_1+x_3+x_5+\overline{x_8}).$$

This formula evaluates to 1 if x_2, x_3, and x_4 are 1, where we use 0 for **false** and 1 for **true**. CNF is called a "normal" form, because any Boolean formula can be converted into this form.

CNF-SAT

Problem CNF-SAT takes a Boolean formula in CNF form as input and asks if there is an assignment of Boolean values to its variables so that the formula evaluates to 1.

It is easy to show that CNF-SAT is in ***NP***, for, given a Boolean formula S, we can construct a simple nondeterministic algorithm that first "guesses" an assignment of Boolean values for the variables in S and then evaluates each clause of S in turn. If all the clauses of S evaluate to 1, then S is satisfied; otherwise, it is not.

To show that CNF-SAT is ***NP***-hard, we will reduce the CIRCUIT-SAT problem to it in polynomial time. So, suppose we are given a Boolean circuit, C. Without loss of generality, we assume that each AND and OR gate has two inputs and each NOT gate has one input. To begin the construction of a formula S equivalent to C, we create a variable x_i for each input for the entire circuit C. One might be tempted to limit the set of variables to just these x_i's and immediately start constructing a formula for C by combining subexpressions for inputs, but in general this approach will not run in polynomial time. (See Exercise C-13.3.) Instead, we create a variable y_i for each output of a gate in C. Then, we create a short formula B_g that corresponds to each gate g in C as follows:

- If g is an AND gate with inputs a and b (which could be either x_i's or y_i's) and output c, then $B_g = (c \leftrightarrow (a \cdot b))$.
- If g is an OR gate with inputs a and b and output c, then $B_g = (c \leftrightarrow (a+b))$.
- If g is a NOT gate with input a and output b, then $B_g = (b \leftrightarrow \overline{a})$.

We wish to create our formula S by taking the AND of all of these B_g's, but such a formula would not be in CNF. So our method is to first convert each B_g to be in CNF, and then combine all of these transformed B_g's by AND operations to define the CNF formula S.

a	b	c	$B = (c \leftrightarrow (a \cdot b))$
1	1	1	1
1	1	0	0
1	0	1	0
1	0	0	1
0	1	1	0
0	1	1	1
0	0	1	0
0	0	0	1

DNF formula for $\overline{B} = a \cdot b \cdot \overline{c} + a \cdot \overline{b} \cdot c + \overline{a} \cdot b \cdot c + \overline{a} \cdot \overline{b} \cdot c$

CNF formula for $B = (\overline{a} + \overline{b} + c) \cdot (\overline{a} + b + \overline{c}) \cdot (a + \overline{b} + \overline{c}) \cdot (a + b + \overline{c})$.

Figure 13.4: A truth table for a Boolean formula B over variables a, b, and c. The equivalent formula for $\overline{B}$ in DNF, and equivalent formula for B in CNF.

To convert a Boolean formula B into CNF, we construct a truth table for B, as shown in Figure 13.4. We then construct a short formula D_i for each table row that evaluates to 0. Each D_i consists of the AND of the variables for the table, with the variable negated if and only if its value in that row is 0. We create a formula D by taking the OR of all the D_i's. Such a formula, which is the OR of formulas that are the AND of variables or their negation, is said to be in ***disjunctive normal form***, or ***DNF***. In this case, we have a DNF formula D that is equivalent to $\overline{B}$, since it evaluates to 1 if and only if B evaluates to 0. To convert D into a CNF formula for B, we apply, to each D_i, De Morgan's Laws, which establish that

$$\overline{(a+b)} = \overline{a} \cdot \overline{b} \quad \text{and} \quad \overline{(a \cdot b)} = \overline{a} + \overline{b}.$$

From Figure 13.4, we can replace each B_g that is of the form $(c \leftrightarrow (a \cdot b))$, by

$$(\overline{a} + \overline{b} + c)(\overline{a} + b + \overline{c})(a + \overline{b} + \overline{c})(a + b + \overline{c}),$$

which is in CNF. Likewise, for each B_g that is of the form $(b \leftrightarrow \overline{a})$, we can replace B_g by the equivalent CNF formula

$$(\overline{a} + \overline{b})(a + b).$$

We leave the CNF substitution for a B_g of the form $(c \leftrightarrow (a+b))$ as an exercise (R-13.2). Substituting each B_g in this way results in a CNF formula S' that corresponds exactly to each input and logic gate of the circuit, C. To construct the final Boolean formula S, then, we define $S = S' \cdot y$, where y is the variable that is associated with the output of the gate that defines the value of C itself. Thus, C is satisfiable if and only if S is satisfiable. Moreover, the construction from C to S builds a constant-sized subexpression for each input and gate of C; hence, this construction runs in polynomial time. Therefore, this local-replacement reduction gives us the following.

Theorem 13.8: CNF-SAT *is* ***NP****-complete.*

3SAT

Consider the 3SAT problem, which takes a Boolean formula S that is in conjunctive normal form (CNF) with each clause in S having exactly three literals, and asks if S is satisfiable. Recall that a Boolean formula is in CNF if it is formed by the AND of a collection of clauses, each of which is the OR of a set of literals. For example, the following formula could be an instance of 3SAT:

$$(\overline{x_1}+x_2+\overline{x_7})(x_3+\overline{x_5}+x_6)(\overline{x_2}+x_4+\overline{x_6})(x_1+x_5+\overline{x_8}).$$

Thus, the 3SAT problem is a restricted version of the CNF-SAT problem. (Note that we cannot use the restriction form of ***NP***-hardness proof, however, for this proof form only works for reducing a restricted version to its more general form.) In this subsection, we show that 3SAT is ***NP***-complete, using the local replacement form of proof. Interestingly, the 2SAT problem, where every clause has exactly two literals, can be solved in polynomial time. (See Exercises C-13.4 and C-13.5.)

Note that 3SAT is in ***NP***, for we can construct a nondeterministic polynomial-time algorithm that takes a CNF formula S with 3-literals per clause, guesses an assignment of Boolean values for S, and then evaluates S to see if it is equal to 1.

To prove that 3SAT is ***NP***-hard, we reduce the CNF-SAT problem to it in polynomial time. Let C be a given Boolean formula in CNF. We perform the following local replacement for each clause C_i in C:

- If $C_i = (a)$, that is, it has one term, which may be a negated variable, then we replace C_i with $S_i = (a+b+c)\cdot(a+\overline{b}+c)\cdot(a+b+\overline{c})\cdot(a+\overline{b}+\overline{c})$, where b and c are new variables not used anywhere else.
- If $C_i = (a+b)$, that is, it has two terms, then we replace C_i with the subformula $S_i = (a+b+c)\cdot(a+b+\overline{c})$, where c is a new variable not used anywhere else.
- If $C_i = (a+b+c)$, that is, it has three terms, then we set $S_i = C_i$.
- If $C_i = (a_1+a_2+a_3+\cdots+a_k)$, that is, it has $k > 3$ terms, then we replace C_i with $S_i = (a_1+a_2+b_1)\cdot(\overline{b_1}+a_3+b_2)\cdot(\overline{b_2}+a_4+b_3)\cdots(\overline{b_{k-3}}+a_{k-1}+a_k)$, where $b_1,b_2,\ldots,b_{k-1}$ are new variables not used anywhere else.

Notice that the value assigned to the newly introduced variables is completely irrelevant. No matter what we assign them, the clause C_i is 1 if and only if the small formula S_i is also 1. Thus, the original clause C is 1 if and only if S is 1. Moreover, note that each clause increases in size by at most a constant factor and that the computations involved are simple substitutions. Therefore, we have shown how to reduce an instance of the CNF-SAT problem to an equivalent instance of the 3SAT problem in polynomial time. This, together with the earlier observation about 3SAT belonging to ***NP***, gives us the following theorem.

Theorem 13.9: *3SAT is **NP**-complete.*

13.3.2 VERTEX-COVER

Recall from Lemma 13.5 that VERTEX-COVER takes a graph G and an integer k and asks if there is a vertex cover for G containing at most k vertices. Formally, VERTEX-COVER asks if there is a subset C of vertices of size at most k, such that for each edge (v,w), we have $v \in C$ or $w \in C$. We showed, in Lemma 13.5, that VERTEX-COVER is in ***NP***. The following example motivates this problem.

Example 13.10: *Suppose we are given a graph G representing a computer network where vertices represent routers and edges represent physical connections. Suppose further that we wish to upgrade some of the routers in our network with special new, but expensive, routers that can perform sophisticated monitoring operations for incident connections. If we would like to determine if k new routers are sufficient to monitor every connection in our network, then we have an instance of* VERTEX-COVER *on our hands.*

Let us now show that VERTEX-COVER is ***NP***-hard, by reducing the 3SAT problem to it in polynomial time. This reduction is interesting in two respects. First, it shows an example of reducing a logic problem to a graph problem. Second, it illustrates an application of the component design proof technique.

Let S be a given instance of the 3SAT problem, that is, a CNF formula such that each clause has exactly three literals. We construct a graph G and an integer k such that G has a vertex cover of size at most k if and only if S is satisfiable. We begin our construction by adding the following:

- For each variable x_i used in the formula S, we add two vertices in G, one that we label with x_i and the other we label with $\overline{x_i}$. We also add the edge $(x_i, \overline{x_i})$ to G. (Note: These labels are for our own benefit; after we construct the graph G we can always relabel vertices with integers if that is what an instance of the VERTEX-COVER problem should look like.)

Each edge $(x_i, \overline{x_i})$ is a "truth-setting" component, for, with this edge in G, a vertex cover must include at least one of x_i or $\overline{x_i}$. In addition, we add the following:

- For each clause $C_i = (a+b+c)$ in S, we form a triangle consisting of three vertices, $i1$, $i2$, and $i3$, and three edges, $(i1,i2)$, $(i2,i3)$, and $(i3,i1)$.

Note that any vertex cover will have to include at least two of the vertices in $\{i1,i2,i3\}$ for each such triangle. Each such triangle is a "satisfaction-enforcing" component. We then connect these two types of components, by adding, for each clause $C_i = (a+b+c)$, the edges $(i1,a)$, $(i2,b)$, and $(i3,c)$. (See Figure 13.5.) Finally, we set the integer parameter $k = n+2m$, where n is the number of variables in S and m is the number of clauses. Thus, if there is a vertex cover of size at most k, it must have size exactly k. This completes the construction of an instance of the VERTEX-COVER problem.

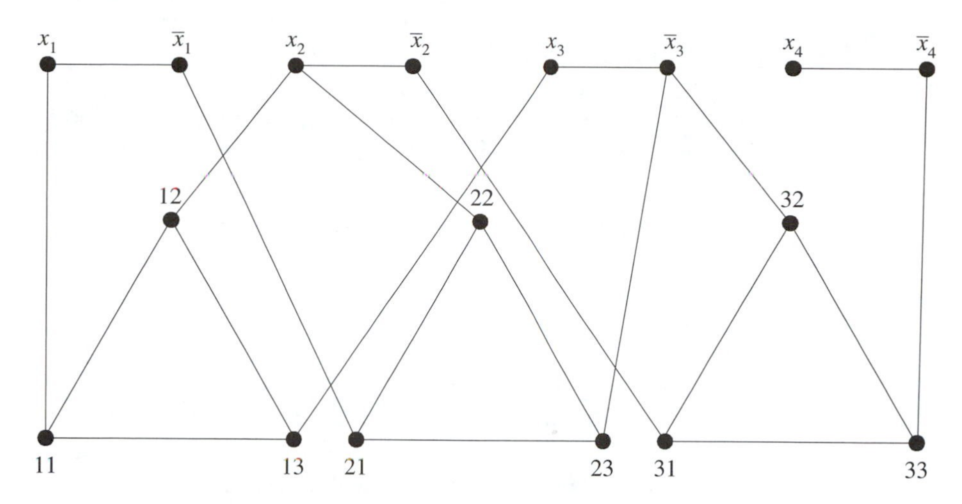

Figure 13.5: Example graph G as an instance of the VERTEX-COVER problem constructed from the formula $S = (x_1 + x_2 + x_3) \cdot (\overline{x_1} + x_2 + \overline{x_3}) \cdot (\overline{x_2} + \overline{x_3} + \overline{x_4})$.

This construction clearly runs in polynomial time, so let us consider its correctness. Suppose there is an assignment of Boolean values to variables in S so that S is satisfied. From the graph G constructed from S, we can build a subset of vertices C that contains each literal a (in a truth-setting component) that is assigned 1 by the satisfying assignment. Likewise, for each clause $C_i = (a+b+c)$, the satisfying assignment sets at least one of a, b, or c to 1. Whichever one of a, b, or c is 1 (picking arbitrarily if there are ties), we include the other two in our subset C. This C is of size $n+2m$. Moreover, notice that each edge in a truth-setting component and clause-satisfying component is covered, and two of every three edges incident on a clause-satisfying component are also covered. In addition, notice that an edge incident to a component associated clause C_i that is not covered by a vertex in the component must be covered by the node in C labeled with a literal, for the corresponding literal in C_i is 1.

Suppose then the converse, namely that there is a vertex cover C of size at most $n+2m$. By construction, this set must have size exactly $n+2m$, for it must contain one vertex from each truth-setting component and two vertices from each clause-satisfying component. This leaves one edge incident to a clause-satisfying component that is not covered by a vertex in the clause-satisfying component; hence, this edge must be covered by the other endpoint, which is labeled with a literal. Thus, we can assign the literal in S associated with this node 1 and each clause in S is satisfied; hence, all of S is satisfied. Therefore, S is satisfiable if and only if G has a vertex cover of size at most k. This gives us the following.

Theorem 13.11: VERTEX-COVER *is* ***NP****-complete.*

As mentioned before, the above reduction illustrates the component design technique. We constructed truth-setting and clause-satisfying components in our graph G to enforce important properties in the clause S.

13.3.3 CLIQUE and SET-COVER

As with the VERTEX-COVER problem, there are several problems that involve selecting a subset of objects from a larger set so as to optimize the size the subset can have while still satisfying an important property. In this subsection, we study two more such problems, CLIQUE and SET-COVER.

CLIQUE

A ***clique*** in a graph G is a subset C of vertices such that, for each v and w in C, with $v \neq w$, (v,w) is an edge. That is, there is an edge between every pair of distinct vertices in C. Problem CLIQUE takes a graph G and an integer k as input and asks whether there is a clique in G of size at least k.

We leave as a simple exercise (R-13.7) to show that CLIQUE is in ***NP***. To show CLIQUE is ***NP***-hard, we reduce the VERTEX-COVER problem to it. Therefore, let (G,k) be an instance of the VERTEX-COVER problem. For the CLIQUE problem, we construct the complement graph G^c, which has the same vertex set as G, but has the edge (v,w), with $v \neq w$, if and only if (v,w) is not in G. We define the integer parameter for CLIQUE as $n-k$, where k is the integer parameter for VERTEX-COVER. This construction runs in polynomial time and serves as a reduction, for G^c has a clique of size at least $n-k$ if and only if G has a vertex cover of size at most k. (See Figure 13.6.)

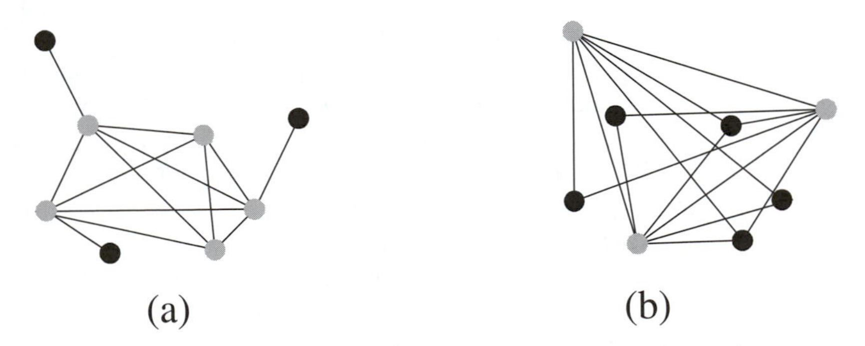

Figure 13.6: A graph G illustrating the proof that CLIQUE is ***NP***-hard. (a) Shows the graph G with the nodes of a clique of size 5 shaded in grey. (b) Shows the graph G^c with the nodes of a vertex cover of size 3 shaded in grey.

Therefore, we have the following.

Theorem 13.12: CLIQUE *is* ***NP****-complete.*

Note how simple the above proof by local replacement is. Interestingly, the next reduction, which is also based on the local replacement technique, is even simpler.

SET-COVER

Problem SET-COVER takes a collection of m sets S_1, S_2, ..., S_m and an integer parameter k as input, and asks whether there is a subcollection of k sets S_{i_1}, S_{i_2}, ..., S_{i_k}, such that

$$\bigcup_{i=1}^{m} S_i = \bigcup_{j=1}^{k} S_{i_j}.$$

That is, the union of the subcollection of k sets includes every element in the union of the original m sets.

We leave it to an exercise (R-13.14) to show SET-COVER is in ***NP***. As to the reduction, we note that we can define an instance of SET-COVER from an instance G and k of VERTEX-COVER. Namely, for each each vertex v of G, there is set S_v, which contains the edges of G incident on v. Clearly, there is a set cover among these sets S_v's of size k if and only if there is a vertex cover of size k in G. (See Figure 13.7.)

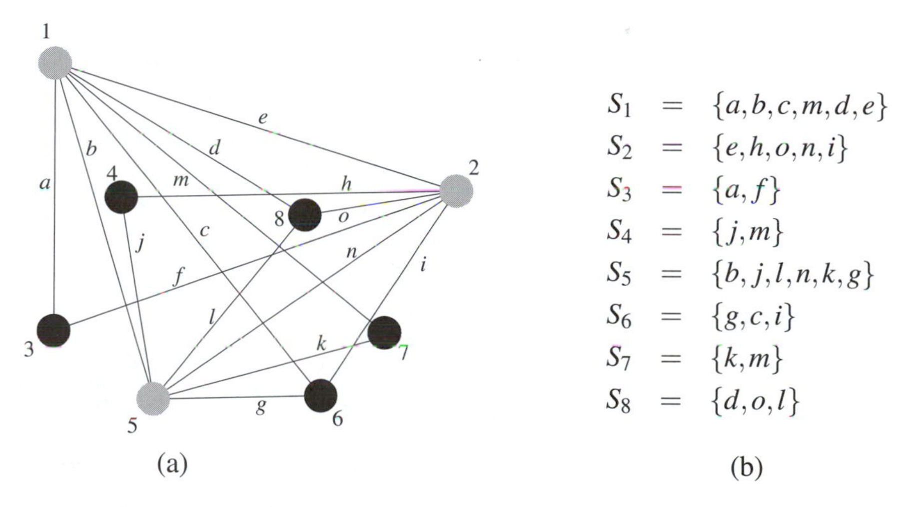

Figure 13.7: A graph G illustrating the proof that SET-COVER is ***NP***-hard. The vertices are numbered 1 through 8 and the edges are given letter labels a through o. (a) Shows the graph G with the nodes of a vertex cover of size 3 shaded in grey. (b) Shows the sets associated with each vertex in G, with the subscript of each set identifying the associated vertex. Note that $S_1 \cup S_2 \cup S_5$ contains all the edges of G.

Thus, we have the following.

Theorem 13.13: *SET-COVER is **NP**-complete.*

This reduction illustrates how easily we can covert a graph problem into a set problem. In the next subsection we show how we can actually reduce graph problems to number problems.

13.3.4 SUBSET-SUM and KNAPSACK

Some hard problems involve only numbers. In such cases, we must take extra care to use the size of the input in bits, for some numbers can be very large. To clarify the role that the size of numbers can make, researchers say that a problem L is ***strongly NP-hard*** if L remains ***NP***-hard even when we restrict the value of each number in the input to be bounded by a polynomial in the size (in bits) of the input. An input x of size n would satisfy this condition, for example, if each number i in x was represented using $O(\log n)$ bits. Interestingly, the number problems we study in this section are not strongly ***NP***-hard. (See Exercises C-13.12 and C-13.13.)

SUBSET-SUM

In the SUBSET-SUM problem, we are given a set S of n integers and an integer k, and we are asked if there is a subset of integers in S that sum to k. This problem could arise, for example, as in the following.

Example 13.14: *Suppose we have an Internet web server, and we are presented with a collection of download requests. For each each download request we can easily determine the size of the requested file. Thus, we can abstract each web request simply as an integer—the size of the requested file. Given this set of integers, we might be interested in determining a subset of them that exactly sums to the bandwidth our server can accommodate in one minute. Unfortunately, this problem is an instance of* SUBSET-SUM. *Moreover, because it is* ***NP****-complete, this problem will actually become harder to solve as our web server's bandwidth and request-handling ability improves.*

SUBSET-SUM might at first seem easy, and indeed showing it belongs to ***NP*** is straightforward. (See Exercise R-13.15.) Unfortunately, it is ***NP***-complete, as we now show. Let G and k be given as an instance of the VERTEX-COVER problem. Number the vertices of G from 1 to n and the edges G from 1 to m, and construct the ***incidence matrix*** H for G, defined so that $H[i,j]=1$ if and only if the edge numbered j is incident on the vertex numbered i; otherwise, $H[i,j]=0$. (See Figure 13.8.)

We use H to define some admittedly large (but still polynomial-sized) numbers to use as inputs to the SUBSET-SUM problem. Namely, for each row i of H, which encodes all the edges incident on vertex i, we construct the number

$$a_i = 4^{m+1} + \sum_{j=1}^{m} H[i,j]4^j.$$

Note that this number adds in a different power of 4 for each 1-entry in the ith row of $H[i,j]$, plus a larger power of 4 for good measure. The collection of a_i's defines an "incidence component" to our reduction, for each power of 4 in an a_i, except for the largest, corresponds to a possible incidence between vertex i and some edge.

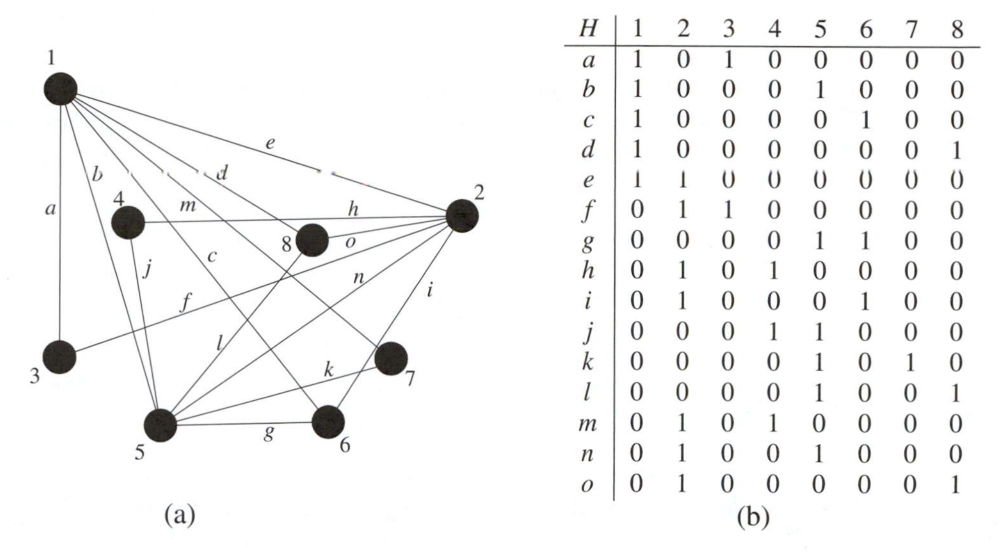

H	1	2	3	4	5	6	7	8
a	1	0	1	0	0	0	0	0
b	1	0	0	0	1	0	0	0
c	1	0	0	0	0	1	0	0
d	1	0	0	0	0	0	0	1
e	1	1	0	0	0	0	0	0
f	0	1	1	0	0	0	0	0
g	0	0	0	0	1	1	0	0
h	0	1	0	1	0	0	0	0
i	0	1	0	0	0	1	0	0
j	0	0	0	1	1	0	0	0
k	0	0	0	0	1	0	1	0
l	0	0	0	0	1	0	0	1
m	0	1	0	1	0	0	0	0
n	0	1	0	0	1	0	0	0
o	0	1	0	0	0	0	0	1

Figure 13.8: A graph G illustrating the proof that SUBSET-SUM is ***NP***-hard. The vertices are numbered 1 through 8 and the edges are given letter labels a through o. (a) Shows the graph G; (b) shows the incidence matrix H for G. Note that there is a 1 for each edge in one or more of the columns for vertices 1, 2, and 5.

In addition to the above incidence component, we also define an "edge-covering component," where, for each edge j, we define a number

$$b_j = 4^j.$$

We then set the sum we wish to attain with a subset of these numbers as

$$k' = k4^{m+1} + \sum_{j=1}^{m} 2 \cdot 4^j,$$

where k is the integer parameter for the VERTEX-COVER instance.

Let us consider, then, how this reduction, which clearly runs in polynomial time, actually works. Suppose graph G has a vertex cover $C = \{i_1, i_2, \ldots, i_k\}$, of size k. Then we can construct a set of values adding to k' by taking every a_i with an index in C, that is, each a_{i_r} for $r = 1, 2, \ldots, k$. In addition, for each edge numbered j in G, if only one of j's endpoints is included in C, then we also include b_j in our subset. This set of numbers sums to k', for it includes k values of 4^{m+1} plus 2 values of each 4^j (either from two a_{i_r}'s such that this edge has both endpoints in C or from one a_{i_r} and one b_j if C contains just one endpoint of edge j).

Suppose there is a subset of numbers that sums to k'. Since k' contains k values of 4^{m+1}, it must include exactly k a_i's. Let us include vertex i in our cover for each such a_i. Such a set is a cover, for each edge j, which corresponds to a power 4^j, must contribute two values to this sum. Since only one value can come from a b_j, one must have come from at least one of the chosen a_i's. Thus, we have:

Theorem 13.15: SUBSET-SUM *is* ***NP***-*complete.*

KNAPSACK

In the KNAPSACK problem, illustrated in Figure 13.9, we are given a set S of items, numbered 1 to n. Each item i has an integer size, s_i, and worth, w_i. We are also given two integer parameters, s, and w, and are asked if there is a subset, T, of S such that

$$\sum_{i \in T} s_i \leq s, \quad \text{and} \quad \sum_{i \in T} w_i \geq w.$$

Problem KNAPSACK defined above is the decision version of the optimization problem "0-1 knapsack" discussed in Section 5.3.3.

We can motivate the KNAPSACK problem with the following Internet application.

Example 13.16: *Suppose we have s widgets that we are interested in selling at an Internet auction web site. A prospective buyer i can bid on multiple lots by saying that he or she is interested in buying s_i widgets at a total price of w_i dollars. If multiple-lot requests, such as this, cannot be broken up (that is, buyer i wants exactly s_i widgets), then determining if we can earn w dollars from this auction gives rise to the* KNAPSACK *problem. (If lots can be broken up, then our auction optimization problem gives rise to the fractional knapsack problem, which can be solved efficiently using the greedy method of Section 5.1.1.)*

The KNAPSACK problem is in ***NP***, for we can construct a nondeterministic polynomial-time algorithm that guesses the items to place in our subset T and then verifies that they do not violate the s and w constraints, respectively.

KNAPSACK is also ***NP***-hard, as it actually contains the SUBSET-SUM problem as a special case. In particular, any instance of numbers given for the SUBSET-SUM problem can correspond to the items for an instance of KNAPSACK with each $w_i = s_i$ set to a value in the SUBSET-SUM instance and the targets for the size s and worth w both equal to k, where k is the integer we wish to sum to for the SUBSET-SUM problem. Thus, by the restriction proof technique, we have the following.

Theorem 13.17: KNAPSACK *is **NP**-complete.*

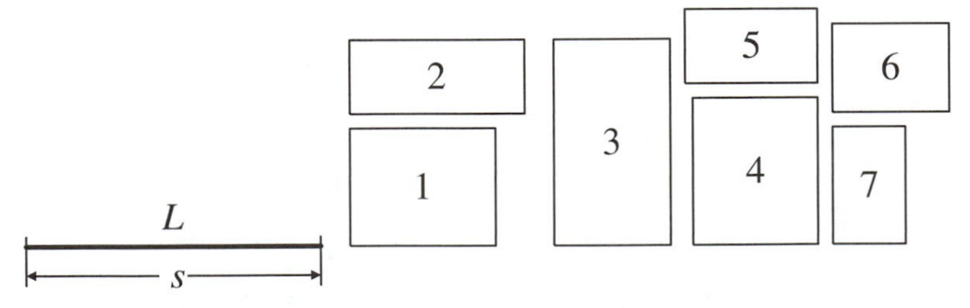

Figure 13.9: A geometric view of the KNAPSACK problem. Given a line L of length s, and a collection of n rectangles, can we translate a subset of the rectangles to have their bottom edge on L so that the total area of the rectangles touching L is at least w? Thus, the width of rectangle i is s_i and its area is w_i.

13.3.5 HAMILTONIAN-CYCLE and TSP

The last two ***NP***-complete problems we consider involve the search for certain kinds of cycles in a graph. Such problems are useful for optimizing the travel of robots and printer-plotters, for example.

HAMILTONIAN-CYCLE

Recall, from Lemma 13.3, that HAMILTONIAN-CYCLE is the problem that takes a graph G and asks if there is a cycle in G that visits each vertex in G exactly once, returning to its starting vertex. (See Figure 13.10a.) Also recall, from Lemma 13.3, that HAMILTONIAN-CYCLE is in ***NP***. To show that this problem is ***NP***-complete, we will reduce VERTEX-COVER to it, using a component design type of reduction.

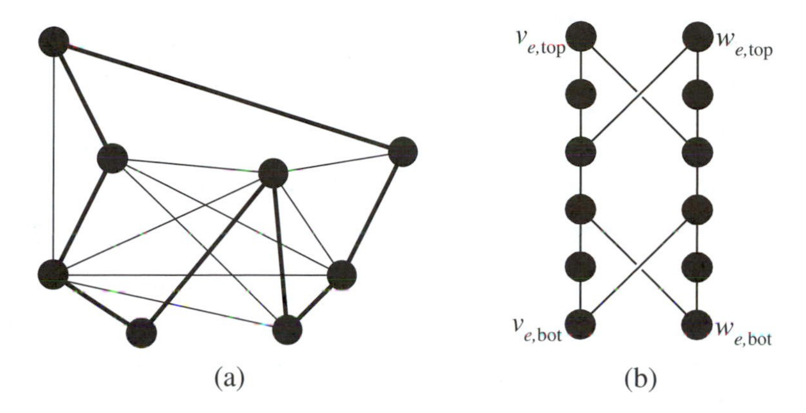

Figure 13.10: Illustrating the HAMILTONIAN-CYCLE problem and its ***NP***-completeness proof. (a) Shows an example graph with a Hamiltonian cycle shown in bold. (b) Illustrates a cover-enforcer subgraph H_e used to show that HAMILTONIAN-CYCLE is ***NP***-hard.

Let G and k be a given instance of the VERTEX-COVER problem. We will construct a graph H that has a Hamiltonian cycle if and only if G has a vertex cover of size k. We begin by including a set of k initially disconnected vertices $X = \{x_1, x_2, \ldots, x_k\}$ to H. This set of vertices will serve as a "cover-choosing" component, for they will serve to identify which nodes of G should be included in a vertex cover. In addition, for each edge $e = (v, w)$ in G we create a "cover-enforcer" subgraph H_e in H. This subgraph H_e has 12 vertices and 14 edges as shown in Figure 13.10b.

Six of the vertices in the cover-enforcer H_e for $e = (v, w)$ correspond to v and the other six correspond to w. Moreover, we label two vertices in cover-enforcer H_e corresponding to v as $v_{e,\text{top}}$ and $v_{e,\text{bot}}$, and we label two vertices in H_e corresponding to w as $w_{e,\text{top}}$ and $w_{e,\text{bot}}$. These are the only vertices in H_e that will be connected to any other vertices in H outside of H_e.

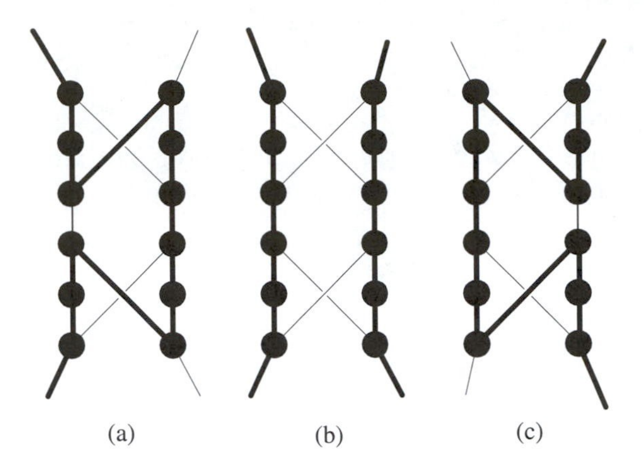

Figure 13.11: The three possible ways that a Hamiltonian cycle can visit the edges in a cover-enforcer H_e.

Thus, a Hamiltonian cycle can visit the nodes of H_e in only one of three possible ways, as shown in Figure 13.11.

We join the important vertices in each cover-enforcer H_e to other vertices in H in two ways, one that corresponds to the cover-choosing component and one that corresponds to the cover-enforcing component. For the cover-choosing component, we add an edge from each vertex in X to every vertex $v_{e,\text{top}}$ and every vertex $v_{e,\text{bot}}$. That is, we add $2kn$ edges to H, where n is the number of vertices in G.

For the cover-enforcing component, we consider each vertex v in G in turn. For each such v, let $\{e_1, e_2, \ldots, e_{d(v)}\}$ be a listing of the edges of G that are incident upon v. We use this listing to create edges in H by joining $v_{e_i,\text{bot}}$ in H_{e_i} to $v_{e_{i+1},\text{top}}$ in $H_{e_{i+1}}$, for $i = 1, 2, \ldots, d-1$. (See Figure 13.12.) We refer to the H_{e_i} components joined in this way as belonging to the ***covering thread*** for v. This completes the construction of the graph H. Note that this computation runs in polynomial time in the size of G.

We claim that G has a vertex cover of size k if and only if H has a Hamiltonian cycle. Suppose, first, that G has a vertex cover of size k. Let $C = \{v_{i_1}, v_{i_2}, \ldots, v_{i_k}\}$ be such a cover. We construct a Hamiltonian cycle in H, by connecting a series of paths P_j, where each P_j starts at x_j and ends at x_{j+1}, for $j = 1, 2, \ldots, k-1$, except for the last path P_k, which starts at x_k and ends at x_1. We form such a path P_j as follows. Start with x_j, and then visit the entire covering thread for v_{i_j} in H, returning to x_{j+1} (or x_1 if $j = k$). For each cover-enforcer subgraph H_e in the covering thread for v_{i_j}, which is visited in this P_j, we write, without loss of generality, e as (v_{i_j}, w). If w is not also in C, then we visit this H_e as in Figure 13.11a or Figure 13.11c (with respect to v_{i_j}). Instead, if w is also in C, then we visit this H_e as in Figure 13.11b. In this way we will visit each vertex in H exactly once, since C is a vertex cover for G. Thus, this cycle we construct is in fact a Hamiltonian cycle.

Suppose, conversely, that H has a Hamiltonian cycle. Since this cycle must visit all the vertices in X, we break this cycle up into k paths, P_1, P_2, ..., P_k, each

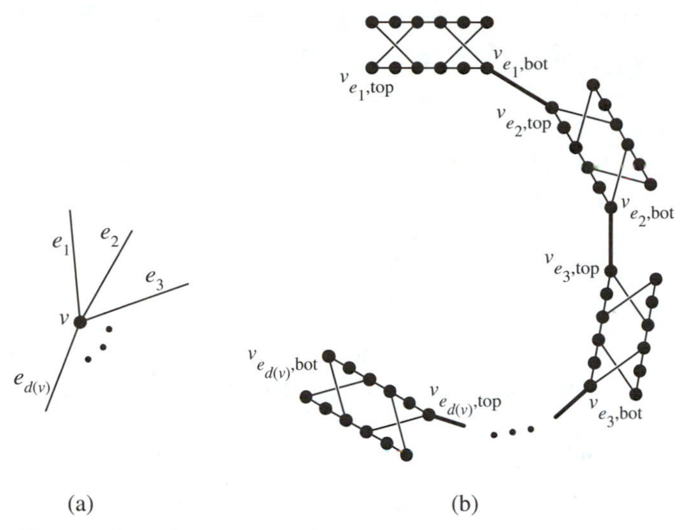

Figure 13.12: Connecting the cover-enforcers. (a) A vertex v in G and its set of incident edges $\{e_1, e_2, \ldots, e_{d(v)}\}$. (b) The connections made between the H_{e_i}'s in H for the edges incident upon v.

of which starts and ends at a vertex in X. Moreover, by the structure of the cover-enforcer subgraphs H_e and the way that we connected them, each P_j must traverse a portion (possibly all) of a covering thread for a vertex v in G. Let C be the set of all such vertices in G. Since the Hamiltonian cycle must include the vertices from every cover-enforcer H_e and every such subgraph must be traversed in a way that corresponds to one (or both) of e's endpoints, C must be a vertex cover in G.

Therefore, G has a vertex cover of size k if and only if H has a Hamiltonian cycle. This gives us the following.

Theorem 13.18: HAMILTONIAN-CYCLE *is* ***NP****-complete.*

TSP

In the ***traveling salesperson problem***, or language TSP, we are given an integer parameter k and a graph G, such that each edge e in G is assigned an integer cost $c(e)$, and we are asked if there is a cycle in G that visits all the vertices in G (possibly more than once) and has total cost at most k. Showing that TSP is in ***NP*** is as easy as guessing a sequence of vertices and then verifying that it forms a cycle of cost at most k in G. Showing that TSP is ***NP***-complete is also easy, as it contains the HAMILTONIAN-CYCLE problem as a special case. Namely, given an instance G of the HAMILTONIAN-CYCLE problem, we can create an instance of TSP by assigning each edge in G the cost $c(e) = 1$ and setting the integer parameter $k = n$, where n is the number of vertices in G. Therefore, using the restriction form of reduction, we get the following.

Theorem 13.19: TSP *is* ***NP****-complete.*

13.4 Approximation Algorithms

One way of dealing with *NP*-completeness for optimization problems is to use an ***approximation algorithm***. Such an algorithm typically runs much faster than an algorithm that strives for an exact solution, but it is not guaranteed to find the best solution. In this section, we study methods for constructing and analyzing approximation algorithms for hard optimization problems.

The general situation is that we have some problem instance x, which could be an encoding of a set of numbers, a graph, etc., as discussed above. In addition, for the problem we are interested in solving for x, there will often be a large number of ***feasible*** solutions for x, which define a set $\mathcal{F}$ of such feasible solutions.

We also have a cost function, c, that determines a numeric cost $c(S)$ for any solution $S \in \mathcal{F}$. In the general optimization problem, we are interested in finding a solution S in $\mathcal{F}$, such that

$$c(S) = OPT = \min\{c(T) : T \in \mathcal{F}\}.$$

That is, we want a solution with minimum cost. We could also formulate a maximization version of the optimization problem, as well, which would simply involve replacing the above "min" with "max." To keep the discussion in this section simple, however, we will typically take the view that, unless otherwise stated, our optimization goal is a minimization.

The goal of an approximation algorithm is to come as close to the optimum value as possible in a reasonable amount of time. As we have been doing for this entire chapter, we take the view in this section that a reasonable amount of time is at most polynomial time.

Ideally, we would like to provide a guarantee of how close an approximation algorithm comes to the optimal value, OPT. We say that a ***δ-approximation*** algorithm for a particular optimization problem is an algorithm that returns a feasible solution S (that is, $S \in \mathcal{F}$), such that

$$c(S) \le \delta OPT,$$

for a minimization problem. For a maximization problem, a δ-approximation algorithm would guarantee $OPT \le \delta c(S)$. Or, in general, we have

$$\delta \le \max\{c(S)/OPT, OPT/c(S)\}.$$

In the remainder of this section, we study problems for which we can construct δ-approximation algorithms for various values of δ. We begin with the ideal situation as far as approximation factors are concerned.

13.4.1 Polynomial-Time Approximation Schemes

There are some problems for which we can construct δ-approximation algorithms that run in polynomial-time with $\delta = 1 + \varepsilon$, for any fixed value $\varepsilon > 0$. The running time of such a collection of algorithms depends both on n, the size of the input, and also on the fixed value ε. We refer to such a collection of algorithms as a ***polynomial-time approximation scheme***, or ***PTAS***. When we have a polynomial-time approximation scheme for a given optimization problem, we can tune our performance guarantee based on how much time we can afford to spend. Ideally, the running time is polynomial in both n and $1/\varepsilon$, in which case we have a ***fully polynomial-time approximation scheme***.

Polynomial-time approximation schemes take advantage of a property that some hard problems possess, namely, that they are rescalable. A problem is said to be ***rescalable*** if an instance x of the problem can be transformed into an equivalent instance x' (that is, one with the same optimal solution) by scaling the cost function, c. For example, TSP is rescalable. Given an instance G of TSP, we can construct an equivalent instance G' by multiplying the distance between every pair of vertices by a scaling factor s. The traveling salesperson tour in G' will be the same as in G, although its cost will now be multiplied by s.

A Fully Polynomial-Time Approximation Scheme for KNAPSACK

To be more concrete, let us give a fully polynomial approximation scheme for the optimization version of a well-known problem, KNAPSACK (Sections 5.1.1 and 13.3.4). In the optimization version of this problem, we are given a set S of items, numbered 1 to n, together with a size constraint, s. Each item i in S is given an integer size, s_i, and worth, w_i, and we are asked to find a subset, T, of S, such that T maximizes the worth

$$w = \sum_{i \in T} w_i \quad \text{while satisfying} \quad \sum_{i \in T} s_i \leq s.$$

We desire a PTAS that produces a $(1+\varepsilon)$-approximation, for any given fixed constant ε. That is, such an algorithm should find a subset T' satisfying the size constraint such that if we define $w' = \sum_{i \in T'} w_i$, then

$$OPT \leq (1+\varepsilon)w',$$

where OPT is the optimal worth summation, taken over all possible subsets satisfying the total size constraint. To prove that this inequality holds, we will actually prove that

$$w' \geq (1 - \varepsilon/2)OPT,$$

for $0 < \varepsilon < 1$. This will be sufficient, however, since, for any fixed $0 < \varepsilon < 1$,

$$\frac{1}{1 - \varepsilon/2} < 1 + \varepsilon.$$

To derive a PTAS for KNAPSACK, we take advantage of the fact that this problem is rescalable. Suppose we are given a value of ε with $0 < \varepsilon < 1$. Let $w_{\max}$ denote the maximum worth of any item in S. Without loss of generality, we assume that the size of each item is at most s (for an item larger than this could not fit in the knapsack). Thus, the item with worth $w_{\max}$ defines a lower bound for the optimal value. That is, $w_{\max} \le OPT$. Likewise, we can define an upper bound on the optimal solution by noting that the knapsack can at most contain all n items in S, each of which has worth at most $w_{\max}$. Thus, $OPT \le n w_{\max}$. To take advantage of the rescalability of KNAPSACK, we round each worth value w_i to $w_i{}'$, the nearest smaller multiple of $M = \varepsilon w_{\max}/2n$. Let us denote the rounded version of S as S', and let us also use OPT' to denote the solution for this rounded version S'. Note that, by simple substitution, $OPT \le 2n^2M/\varepsilon$. Moreover, $OPT' \le OPT$, since we rounded every worth value in S down to form S'. Thus, $OPT' \le 2n^2M/\varepsilon$.

Therefore, let us turn to our solution for the rounded version S' of the KNAPSACK problem for S. Since every worth value in S' is a multiple of M, any achievable worth of a collection of items taken from S' is also a multiple of M. Moreover, there are just $N = \lceil 2n^2/\varepsilon \rceil$ such multiples that need to be considered, because of the upper bound on OPT'. We can use dynamic programming (Section 5.3) to construct an efficient algorithm for finding the optimal worth for S'. In particular, let us define the parameter,

$$s[i, j] = \text{the size of the smallest set of items in } \{1,2,\ldots,j\} \text{ with worth } iM.$$

The key insight to the design of a dynamic programming algorithm for solving the rounded KNAPSACK problem is the observation that we can write

$$s[i, j] = \min\{s[i, j-1],\ s_j + s[i-(w_j{}'/M), j-1]\},$$

for $i = 1,2,\ldots,N$, and $j = 1,2,\ldots,n$. (See Figure 13.13.)

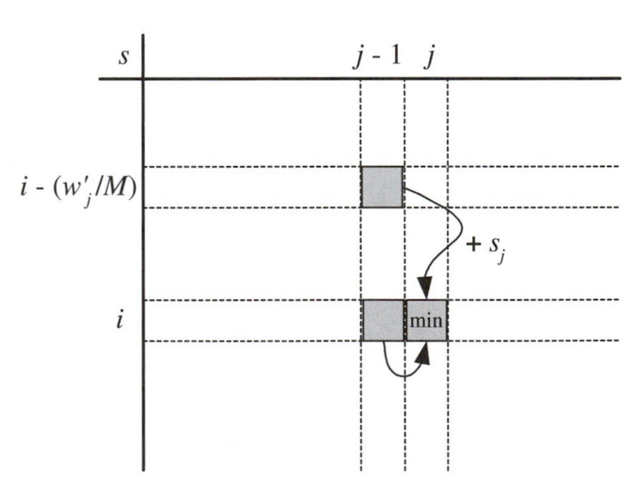

Figure 13.13: Illustration of the equation for $s[i, j]$ used in the dynamic program for the scaled version of KNAPSACK.

The above equation for $s[i,j]$ follows from the fact that item j will either contribute or not contribute to the smallest way of achieving worth iM from the items in $\{1,2,\ldots,j\}$. In addition, note that for the base case, $j=0$, when no items at all are included in the knapsack, then

$$s[i,0] = +\infty,$$

for $i = 1,2,\ldots,N$. That is, such a size is undefined. In addition,

$$s[0,j] = 0,$$

for $j = 1,2,\ldots,n$, since we can always achieve worth 0 by including no items in the knapsack. The optimal value is defined by

$$OPT' = \max\{iM\colon s[i,n] \leq s\}.$$

This is the value that is output by our PTAS algorithm.

Analysis of the PTAS for Knapsack

We can easily convert the above description into a dynamic programming algorithm that computes OPT' in $O(n^3/\varepsilon)$ time. Such an algorithm gives us the value of an optimal solution, but we can easily translate the dynamic programming algorithm for computing the size into one for the actual set of items.

Let us consider, then, how good an approximation OPT' is for OPT. Recall that we reduced the worth w_i of each item i by at most $M = \varepsilon w_{\max}/2n$. Thus,

$$OPT' \geq OPT - \varepsilon w_{\max}/2,$$

since the optimal solution can contain at most n items. Since $OPT \geq w_{\max}$, this in turn implies that

$$OPT' \geq OPT - \varepsilon OPT/2 = (1-\varepsilon/2)OPT.$$

Thus, $OPT \leq (1+\varepsilon)OPT'$, which was what we wished to prove. The running time of our approximation algorithm is $O(n^3/\varepsilon)$. Our scheme of designing an efficient algorithm for any given $\varepsilon > 0$ gives rise to a fully polynomial approximation scheme, since the running time is polynomial in both n and $1/\varepsilon$. This fact gives us the following.

Theorem 13.20: *The* Knapsack *optimization problem has a fully polynomial approximation scheme that achieves a $(1+\varepsilon)$-approximation factor in $O(n^3/\varepsilon)$ time, where n is the number of items in the* Knapsack *instance and $0 < \varepsilon < 1$ is a given fixed constant.*

13.4.2 A 2-Approximation for VERTEX-COVER

It is not always possible to design a polynomial-time approximation scheme for a hard problem, let alone a fully polynomial-time approximation scheme. In such cases, we would still like good approximations, of course, but we will have to settle for an approximation factor that is not arbitrarily close to 1, as we had in the previous subsection. In this subsection, we describe how we can achieve a 2-approximation algorithm for a well-known ***NP***-complete problem, the VERTEX-COVER problem (Section 13.3.2). In the optimization version of this problem, we are given a graph G and we are asked to produce the smallest set C that is a vertex cover for G, that is, such that every edge in G is incident on some vertex in C.

Our approximation algorithm is based on the greedy method, and is rather simple. It involves picking an edge in the graph, adding both its endpoints to the cover, and then deleting this edge and its incident edges from the graph. The algorithm repeats this process until no edges are left. We give the details for this approach in Algorithm 13.14.

Algorithm VertexCoverApprox(G):
  Input: A graph G
  Output: A small vertex cover C for G

```
C ← ∅
while G still has edges do
  select an edge e = (v,w) of G
  add vertices v and w to C
  for each edge f incident to v or w do
    remove f from G
return C
```

Algorithm 13.14: A 2-approximation algorithm for VERTEX-COVER.

We leave the details of how to implement this algorithm in $O(n+m)$ time as a simple exercise (R-13.18). Let us consider, then, why this algorithm is a 2-approximation. First, observe that each edge $e=(v,w)$ selected by the algorithm, and used to add v and w to C, must be covered in any vertex cover. That is, any vertex cover for G must contain v or w (possibly both). The approximation algorithm adds both v and w to C in such a case. When the approximation algorithm completes, there are no uncovered edges left in G, for we remove all the edges covered by the vertices v and w when we add them to C. Thus, C forms a vertex cover of G. Moreover, the size of C is at most twice that of an optimal vertex cover for G, since, for every two vertices we add to C, one of these vertices must belong to the optimal cover. Therefore, we have the following.

Theorem 13.21: *Given a graph with n vertices and m edges, the optimization version of* VERTEX-COVER *has a 2-approximation algorithm taking $O(n+m)$ time.*

13.4.3 A 2-Approximation for a Special Case of TSP

In the optimization version of the traveling salesperson problem, or TSP, we are given a weighted graph G, such that each edge e in G has an integer weight $c(e)$, and we are asked to find a minimum-weight cycle in G that visits all vertices in G. In this section we describe a simple 2-approximation algorithm for a special case of the TSP optimization problem.

The Triangle Inequality

Consider an instance of TSP such that the edge weights satisfy the ***triangle inequality***. That is, for any three edges (u,v), (v,w), and (u,w) in G, we have

$$c((u,v)) + c((v,w)) \geq c((u,w)),$$

Also, suppose that every pair of vertices in G is connected by an edge, that is, G is a complete graph. These properties, which hold for any distance metric, imply that the optimal tour of G will visit each vertex exactly once; hence, let us consider only Hamiltonian cycles as possible solutions of TSP.

The Approximation Algorithm

Our approximation algorithm takes advantage of the above properties of G to design a very simple TSP approximation algorithm, which has just three steps. In the first step we construct a minimum-spanning tree, M, of G (Section 7.3). In the second step we construct an Euler-tour traversal, E, of M, that is, a traversal of M that starts and ends at the same vertex and traverses each edge of M exactly once in each direction (Section 2.3.3). In the third step we construct a tour T from E by marching through the edges of E, but each time we have two edges (u,v) and (v,w) in E, such that v has already been visited, we replace these two edges by the edge (u,w) and continue. In essence, we are constructing T as a a preorder traversal of M. This three-step algorithm clearly runs in polynomial-time. (See Figure 13.15.)

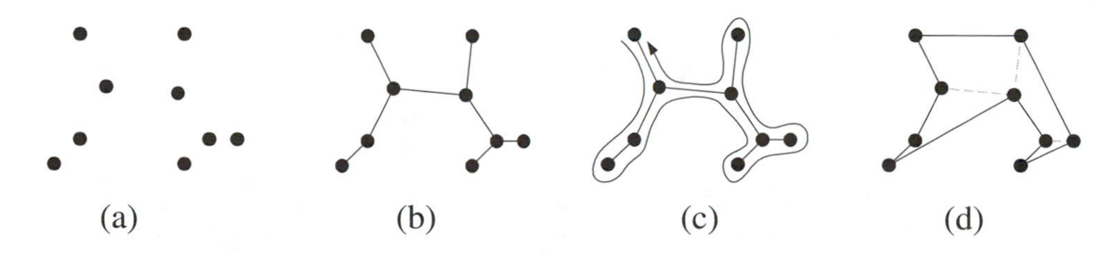

Figure 13.15: Example run of the approximation algorithm for TSP for a graph satisfying the triangle inequality: (a) a set S of points in the plane, with Euclidean distance defining the costs of the edges (not shown); (b) the minimum-spanning tree, M, for S, (c) an Euler tour, E, of M; (d) the approximate TSP tour, T.

Analysis of the TSP Approximation Algorithm

The analysis of why this algorithm achieves an approximation factor of 2 is also simple. Let us extend our notation so that $c(H)$ denotes the total weight of the edges in a subgraph H of G. Let T' be the optimal tour for the graph G. If we delete any edge from T' we get a path, which is, of course, also a spanning tree. Thus,

$$c(M) \leq c(T').$$

We can also easily relate the cost of E to that of M, as

$$c(E) = 2c(M),$$

since the Euler tour E visits each edge of M exactly once in each direction. Finally, note that, by the triangle inequality, when we construct our tour T, each time we replace two edges (u, v) and (v, w) with the edge (u, w), we do not increase the cost of the tour. That is,

$$c(T) \leq c(E).$$

Therefore, we have

$$c(T) \leq 2c(T').$$

(See Figure 13.16.)

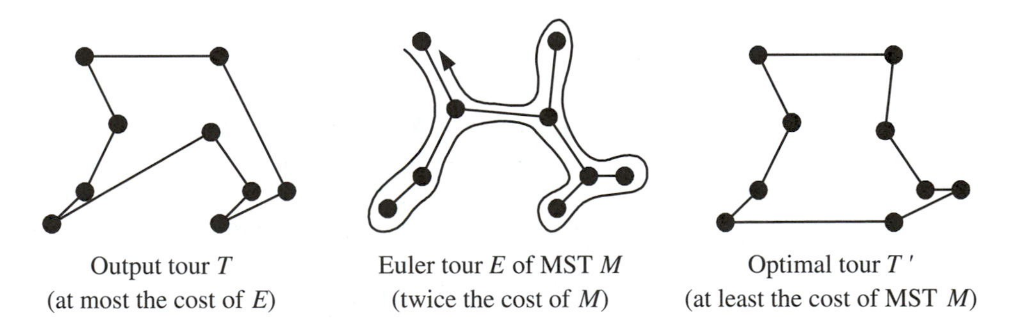

Figure 13.16: Illustrating the proof that MST-based algorithm is a 2-approximation for the TSP optimization problem.

We may summarize this discussion as follows.

Theorem 13.22: *If a weighted graph G is complete and has edge weights satisfying the triangle inequality, then there is a 2-approximation algorithm for the* TSP *optimization problem for G that runs in polynomial time.*

This theorem depends heavily on the fact that the cost function on the graph G satisfies the triangle inequality. In fact, without this assumption, no constant-factor approximation algorithm for the optimization version of TSP exists that runs in polynomial time, unless $\boldsymbol{P} = \boldsymbol{NP}$. (See Exercise C-13.14.)

13.4.4 A Logarithmic Approximation for SET-COVER

There are some cases when achieving even a constant-factor approximation in polynomial time is difficult. In this section, we study one of the best known of such problems, the SET-COVER problem (Section 13.3.3). In the optimization version of this problem, we are given a collection of sets $S_1, S_2, \ldots, S_m$, whose union is a universe U of size n, and we are asked to find the smallest integer k, such that there is a subcollection of k sets $S_{i_1}, S_{i_2}, \ldots, S_{i_k}$ with

$$U = \bigcup_{i=1}^{m} S_i = \bigcup_{j=1}^{k} S_{i_j}.$$

Although it is difficult to find a constant-factor approximation algorithm that runs in polynomial time for this problem, we can design an efficient algorithm that has an approximation factor of $O(\log n)$. As with several other approximation algorithms for hard problems, this algorithm is based on the greedy method (Section 5.1).

A Greedy Approach

Our algorithm selects sets S_{i_j} one at a time, each time selecting the set that has the most uncovered elements. When every element in U is covered, we are done. We give a simple pseudo-code description in Algorithm 13.17.

Algorithm SetCoverApprox(S):
  Input: A collection S of sets $S_1, S_2, \ldots, S_m$ whose union is U
  Output: A small set cover C for S

```
C ← ∅            {The set cover we are building}
E ← ∅            {The set of covered elements from U}
while E ≠ U do
   select a set S_i that has the maximum number of uncovered elements
   add S_i to C
   E ← E ∪ S_i
Return C.
```

Algorithm 13.17: An approximation algorithm for SET-COVER.

This algorithm runs in polynomial time. (See Exercise R-13.19.)

Analyzing the Greedy SET-COVER Algorithm

To analyze the approximation factor of the above greedy SET-COVER algorithm, we will use an amortization argument based on a charging scheme (Section 1.5). Namely, each time our approximation algorithm selects a set S_j we will charge the elements of S_j for its selection.

Specifically, consider the moment in our algorithm when a set S_j is added to C, and let k be the number of previously uncovered elements in S_j. We must pay a total charge of 1 to add this set to C, so we charge each previously uncovered element i of S_j a charge of

$$c(i) = 1/k.$$

Thus, the total size of our cover is equal to the total charges made by our algorithm. That is,

$$|C| = \sum_{i \in U} c(i).$$

To prove an approximation bound, we will consider the charges made to the elements in each subset S_j that belongs to an optimal cover, C'. So, suppose that S_j belongs to C'. Let us write $S_j = \{x_1, x_2, \ldots, x_{n_j}\}$ so that S_j's elements are listed in the order in which they are covered by our algorithm (we break ties arbitrarily). Now, consider the iteration in which x_1 is first covered. At that moment, S_j has not yet been selected; hence, whichever set is selected must have at least n_j uncovered elements. Thus, x_1 is charged at most $1/n_j$. So let us consider, then, the moment our algorithm charges an element x_l of S_j. In the worst case, we will have not yet chosen S_j (indeed, our algorithm may never choose this S_j). Whichever set is chosen in this iteration has, in the worst case, at least $n_j - l + 1$ uncovered elements; hence, x_l is charged at most $1/(n_j - l + 1)$. Therefore, the total amount charged to all the elements of S_j is at most

$$\sum_{l=1}^{n_j} \frac{1}{n_l - l + 1} = \sum_{l=1}^{n_j} \frac{1}{l},$$

which is the familiar Harmonic number, H_{n_j}. It is well known (for example, see the Appendix) that H_{n_j} is $O(\log n_j)$. Let $c(S_j)$ denote the total charges given to all the elements of a set S_j that belongs to the optimal cover C'. Our charging scheme implies that $c(S_j)$ is $O(\log n_j)$. Thus, summing over the sets of C', we obtain

$$\begin{aligned} \sum_{S_j \in C'} c(S_j) &\leq \sum_{S_j \in C'} b \log n_j \\ &\leq b|C'| \log n, \end{aligned}$$

for some constant $b \geq 1$. But, since C' is a set cover,

$$\sum_{i \in U} c(i) \leq \sum_{S_j \in C'} c(S_j)$$

Therefore,

$$|C| \leq b|C'| \log n.$$

This fact gives us the following result.

Theorem 13.23: *The optimization version of the* SET-COVER *problem has an $O(\log n)$-approximation polynomial-time algorithm for finding a cover of a collection of sets whose union is a universe of size n.*

13.5 Backtracking and Branch-and-Bound

In the above sections, we showed many problems to be ***NP***-complete. Thus, unless $P = NP$, which the vast majority of computer scientists believes is not true, it is impossible to solve any of these problems in polynomial time. Nevertheless, many of these problems arise in real-life applications where solutions to them need to be found, even if finding these solutions may take a long time. Thus, in this section, we address techniques for dealing with ***NP***-completeness that have shown much promise in practice. These techniques allow us to design algorithms that can find solutions to hard problems, often in a reasonable amount of time. In this section, we study the methods of ***backtracking*** and ***branch-and-bound***.

13.5.1 Backtracking

The backtracking design pattern is a way to build an algorithm for some hard problem L. Such an algorithm searches through a large, possibly even exponential-size, set of possibilities in a systematic way. The search strategy is typically optimized to avoid symmetries in problem instances for L and to traverse the search space so as to find an "easy" solution for L if such a solution exists.

The ***backtracking*** technique takes advantage of the inherent structure that many ***NP***-complete problems possess. Recall that acceptance for an instance x in a problem in ***NP*** can be verified in polynomial time given a polynomial-sized certificate. Oftentimes, this certificate consists of a set of "choices," such as the values assigned to a collection of Boolean variables, a subset of vertices in a graph to include in a special set, or a set of objects to include in a knapsack. Likewise, the verification for a certificate often involves a simple test of whether or not the certificate demonstrates a successful configuration for x, such as satisfying a formula, covering all the edges in a graph, or conforming to certain performance criteria. In such cases, we can use the ***backtracking*** algorithm, given in Algorithm 13.18, to systematically search for a solution to our problem, if such a problem exists.

The backtracking algorithm traverses through possible "search paths" to locate solutions or "dead ends." The configuration at the end of such a path consists of a pair (x,y), where x is the remaining subproblem to be solved and y is the set of choices that have been made to get to this subproblem from the original problem instance. Initially, we give the backtracking algorithm the pair $(x,\emptyset)$, where x is our original problem instance. Anytime the backtracking algorithm discovers that a configuration (x,y) cannot lead to a valid solution no matter how additional choices are made, then it cuts off all future searches from this configuration and "backtracks" to another configuration. In fact, this approach gives the backtracking algorithm its name.

Algorithm Backtrack(x):
  Input: A problem instance x for a hard problem
  Output: A solution for x or "no solution" if none exists
  $F \leftarrow \{(x, \emptyset)\}$. {$F$ is the "frontier" set of subproblem configurations}
  while $F \neq \emptyset$ **do**
    select from F the most "promising" configuration (x, y)
    expand (x, y) by making a small set of additional choices
    let (x_1, y_1), (x_2, y_2), ..., (x_k, y_k) be the set of new configurations.
    for each new configuration (x_i, y_i) **do**
      perform a simple consistency check on (x_i, y_i)
      if the check returns "solution found" **then**
        return the solution derived from (x_i, y_i)
      if the check returns "dead end" **then**
        discard the configuration (x_i, y_i) {Backtrack}
      else
        $F \leftarrow F \cup \{(x_i, y_i)\}$ {(x_i, y_i) starts a promising search path}
  return "no solution"

Algorithm 13.18: The template for a backtracking algorithm.

Filling in the Details

In order to turn the backtracking strategy into an actual algorithm, we need only fill in the following details:

1. Define a way of selecting the most "promising" candidate configuration from the frontier set F.
2. Specify the way of expanding a configuration (x, y) into subproblem configurations. This expansion process should, in principle, be able to generate all feasible configurations, starting from the initial configuration, $(x, \emptyset)$.
3. Describe how to perform a simple consistency check for a configuration (x, y) that returns "solution found," "dead end," or "continue."

If F is a stack, then we get a depth-first search of the configuration space. In fact, in this case we could even use recursion to implement F automatically as a stack. Alternatively, if F is a queue, then we get a breadth-first search of the configuration space. We can also imagine other data structures to implement F, but as long as we have an intuitive notion of how to select the most "promising" configuration from F with each iteration, then we have a backtracking algorithm.

So as to make this approach more concrete, let us work through an application of the backtracking technique to the CNF-SAT problem.

A Backtracking Algorithm for CNF-SAT

Recall that in the CNF-SAT problem we are given a Boolean formula S in conjunctive normal form (CNF) and are asked if S is satisfiable. To design a backtracking algorithm for CNF-SAT, we will systematically make tentative assignments to the variables in S and see if such assignments make S evaluate immediately to 1 or 0, or yield a new formula S' for which we could continue making tentative value assignments. Thus, a configuration in our algorithm will consist of a pair (S', y), where S' is a Boolean formula in CNF, and y is an assignment of values to Boolean variables not in S' such that making these assignments in S results in the formula S'.

To formulate our backtracking algorithm, then, we need to give the details of each of the three components to the backtracking algorithm. Given a frontier F of configurations, we make our most "promising" choice, which is the subformula S' with the smallest clause. Such a formula is the most constrained of all the formulas in F; hence, we would expect it to hit a dead end most quickly if that is indeed its destiny.

Let us consider, then, how to generate subproblems from a subformula S'. We do this by locating a smallest clause C in S', and picking a variable x_i that appears in C. We then create two new subproblems that are associated with our assigning $x_i = 1$ and $x_i = 0$ respectively.

Finally, we must say how to process S' to perform a consistency check for an assignment of a variable x_i in S'. We begin this processing by reducing any clauses containing x_i based on the assigned 0 or 1 value of x_i (depending on the choice we made). If this reduction results in a new clause with a single literal, x_j or $\overline{x_j}$, we also perform the appropriate value assignment to x_j to make this single-literal clause satisfied. We then process the resulting formula to propagate the assigned value of x_j. If this new assignment in turn results in a new single-literal clause, we repeat this process until we have no more single-literal clauses. If at any point we discover a contradiction (that is, clauses x_i and $\overline{x_i}$, or an empty clause), then we return "dead end." If we reduce the subformula S' all the way to the constant 1, then we return "solution found," along with all the variable assignments we made to reach this point. Otherwise, we derive a new subformula, S'', such that each clause has at least two literals, along with the value assignments that lead from the original formula S to S''. We call this operation the ***reduce*** operation for propagating an assignment of value to x_i in S'.

Fitting all of these pieces into the template for the backtracking algorithm results in an algorithm that solves the CNF-SAT problem in about as fast a time as we can expect. In general, the worst-case running time for this algorithm is still exponential, but the backtracking can often speed things up. Indeed, if every clause in the given formula has at most two literals, then this algorithm runs in polynomial time. (See Exercise C-13.4.)

Java Example: A Backtracking Solution for SUBSET-SUM

To be even more concrete, let us consider a Java backtracking solution for the ***NP***-hard SUBSET-SUM problem. Recall from Section 13.3.4 that in the SUBSET-SUM problem we are given a set S of n integers and an integer k, and we are asked if there is a subset of integers in S that sum to k.

To make the decision easier for determining whether a configuration is a dead end or not, let us assume that the integers in S are given in nondecreasing order as $S = \{a_0, a_1, \ldots, a_{n-1}\}$. Given this choice, we then define the three main components of our backtracking algorithm as follows:

1. For our way of selecting the most "promising" candidate configuration, we make a choice common in many backtracking algorithms. Namely, we will use recursion to perform a depth-first search of the configuration space. Thus, our method stack will automatically keep track of unexplored configurations for us.
2. For our procedure for specifying the way of expanding a configuration (x, y) into subproblem configurations, let us simply "march" down the sequence of integers in S in order. Thus, having a configuration that has already considered the subset $S_i = \{a_0, \ldots, a_i\}$, we simply need to generate the two possible configurations determined by whether we use a_{i+1} or not.
3. The final major component of our backtracking algorithm is a way to perform a consistency check that returns "solution found," "dead end," or "continue." To aid in this test, we will again use the fact that the integers in S are sorted. Suppose we have already considered integers in the subset $S_i = \{a_0, \ldots, a_i\}$ and are now considering a_{i+1}. There is a simple two-fold consistency test we can perform at this point. Let k_i denote the sum of the elements in S_i that we have tentatively chosen to belong to our selection, and let the sum of the remaining integers be
$$r_{i+1} = \sum_{j=i+1}^{n-1} a_j.$$
The first part of our test is to confirm that
$$k \geq k_i + a_{i+1}.$$
If this condition fails, then we are "overshooting" k. Moreover, since S is sorted, any a_j with $j > i+1$ will also overshoot k; hence, we are at a dead end in this case. For the second part of our test, we confirm that
$$k \leq k_i + r_{i+1}.$$
If this condition fails, then we are "undershooting" k, and there is no hope for us to reach k with the remaining set of integers in S; hence, we are also at a dead end in this case. If both tests succeed, then we consider a_{i+1} and proceed.

We give the Java code for this method in Code Fragment 13.19.

```
/**
 * Method to find a subset of an array of integers summing to k, assuming:
 * - the array a is sorted in nondecreasing order,
 * - we have already considered the elements up to index i,
 * - the ones we have chosen add up to sum,
 * - the set that are left sum to reamin.
 * The function returns "true" and prints the subset if it is found.
 * Should be first called as findSubset(a,k,-1,0,t), where t is total.
 */
public static boolean findSubset(int[] a, int k, int i, int sum, int remain) {
  /* Test conditions for expanding this configuration */
  if (i+1 >= a.length) return false; // safety check that integers remain
  if (sum + remain < k) return false; // we're undershooting k
  int next = a[i+1];                  // the next candidate integer
  if (sum + next > k) return false; // we're overshooting k
  if (sum + next == k) {            // we've found a solution!
    System.out.print(k + "=" + next); // begin printing solution
    return true;
    }
  if (findSubset(a, k, i+1, sum+next, remain−next)) {
    System.out.print("+" + next);     // solution includes a[i+1]
    return true;
    }
  else    // backtracking - solution doesn't include a[i+1]
    return findSubset(a, k, i+1, sum, remain);
}
```

Code Fragment 13.19: A Java implementation of a backtracking algorithm for the SUBSET-SUM problem.

Note that we have defined the searching method, findSubset, recursively, and we use that recursion both for the backtracking and also for printing a solution when it is found. Also note that each recursive call takes $O(1)$ time, since an array is passed as a reference to the base address. Thus, the worst-case running time of this method is $O(2^n)$, where n is the number of integers we are considering. We hope, of course, that for typical problem instances the backtracking will avoid this worst case, either by quickly finding a solution or by using the conditions for dead ends to prune away many useless configurations.

There is a minor improvement we can make to the findSubset method if we can faithfully trust that it is always called correctly. Namely, we can drop the safety test for integers that are left to be considered. For, if there are no more integers to consider, then remain $= 0$. Thus, sum + remain $<$ k, since we would have terminated this path of searching for a solution earlier had we overshot k or hit k exactly. Still, although we could, in theory, drop this test for remaining integers, we keep this test in our code for safety reasons, just in case someone calls our method incorrectly.

13.5.2 Branch-and-Bound

The backtracking algorithm is effective for decision problems, but it is not designed for optimization problems, where, in addition to having some feasibility condition be satisfied for a certificate y associated with an instance x, we also have a cost function $f(x)$ that we wish to minimize or maximize (without loss of generality, let us assume the cost function should be minimized). Nevertheless, we can extend the backtracking algorithm to work for such optimization problems, and in so doing derive the algorithmic design pattern known as ***branch-and-bound***.

The branch-and-bound design pattern, given in Algorithm 13.20, has all the elements of backtracking, except that rather than simply stopping the entire search process any time a solution is found, we continue processing until the best solution is found. In addition, the algorithm has a scoring mechanism to always choose the most promising configuration to explore in each iteration. Because of this approach, branch-and-bound is sometimes called a ***best-first search*** strategy.

Algorithm Branch-and-Bound(x):
    Input: A problem instance x for a hard optimization (minimization) problem
    Output: An optimal solution for x or "no solution" if none exists

    $F \leftarrow \{(x, \emptyset)\}$ {Frontier set of subproblem configurations}
    $b \leftarrow (+\infty, \emptyset)$ {Cost and configuration of current best solution}
    while $F \neq \emptyset$ **do**
        select from F the most "promising" configuration (x, y)
        expand (x, y), yielding new configurations $(x_1, y_1), \ldots, (x_k, y_k)$
        for each new configuration (x_i, y_i) **do**
            perform a simple consistency check on (x_i, y_i)
            if the check returns "solution found" **then**
                if the cost c of the solution for (x_i, y_i) beats b **then**
                    $b \leftarrow (c, (x_i, y_i))$
                else
                    discard the configuration (x_i, y_i)
            if the check returns "dead end" **then**
                discard the configuration (x_i, y_i) {Backtrack}
            else
                if $lb(x_i, y_i)$ is less than the cost of b **then**
                    $F \leftarrow F \cup \{(x_i, y_i)\}$ {(x_i, y_i) starts a promising search path}
                else
                    discard the configuration (x_i, y_i) {A "bound" prune}
    return b

Algorithm 13.20: The template for a branch-and-bound algorithm. This algorithm assumes the existence of a function, $lb(x_i, y_i)$, that returns a lower bound on the cost of any solution derived from the configuration (x_i, y_i).

To provide for the optimization criterion of always selecting the "most promising" configuration, we extend the three assumptions for a backtracking algorithm to add one more condition:

- For any configuration (x,y), we assume we have a function, $lb(x,y)$, that returns a lower bound on the cost of any solution that is derived from this configuration.

The only strict requirement for $lb(x,y)$, then, is that it must be less than or equal to the cost of any derived solution. But, as should be clear from the branch-and-bound description, if this lower bound is more accurate, the algorithm's efficiency improves.

A Branch-and-Bound Algorithm for TSP

To make the branch-and-bound approach more concrete, let us consider how it can be applied to solve the optimization version of the traveling salesperson (TSP) problem. In the optimization version of this problem, we are given a graph G with a cost function $c(e)$ defined for each edge e in G, and we wish to find the smallest total-cost tour that visits every vertex in G, returning back to its starting vertex.

We can design an algorithm for TSP by computing for each edge $e = (v,w)$, the minimum-cost path that begins at v and ends at w while visiting all other vertices in G along the way. To find such a path, we apply the branch-and-bound technique. We generate the path from v to w in $G - \{e\}$ by augmenting a current path by one vertex in each loop of the branch-and-bound algorithm.

- After we have built a partial path P, starting, say, at v, we only consider augmenting P with vertices in not in P.
- We can classify a partial path P as a "dead end" if the vertices not in P are disconnected in $G - \{e\}$.
- To define the lower bound function, lb, we can use the total cost of the edges in P plus $c(e)$. This will certainly be a lower bound for any tour that will be built from e and P.

In addition, after we have run the algorithm to completion for one edge e in G, we can use the best path found so far over all tested edges, rather than restarting the current best solution b at $+\infty$. The running time of the resulting algorithm will still be exponential in the worst-case, but it will avoid a considerable amount of unnecessary computation in practice. The TSP problem is of considerable interest, as it has many applications, so such a solution could be of use in practice if the number of vertices in the input graph is not too high. In addition, there are a number of other heuristics that can be added to the search for an optimal TSP tour, but these are beyond the scope of this book.

Java Example: A Branch-and-Bound Solution for KNAPSACK

To be even more concrete, let us describe a Java implementation of a branch-and-bound solution to the KNAPSACK problem. In the optimization version of this problem, we are given a set S of items, numbered 0 to $n-1$. Each item i is given an integer size, s_i, and worth, w_i. We are also given an integer parameter, *size*, and asked for a subset, T, of S such that $\sum_{i \in T} s_i \leq size$ and the total worth of items in T, $worth = \sum_{i \in T} w_i$, is maximized.

Let us begin by borrowing some ideas from the greedy algorithm for solving the fractional KNAPSACK problem (Section 5.1.1). Namely, let us assume that the items in S are sorted in nonincreasing order by w_i/s_i values. We will process them in this order, so that we are considering items by decreasing gain, starting with the element with maximum gain, that is, the item with maximum worth for its size. Our configuration, then, will be defined by a subset S_i of the first i items in S based on this order. So the indices of the items in S_i are in the range 0 to $i-1$ (and let us define S_0 to be the empty configuration having index -1).

We begin by placing the configuration for S_0 into a priority queue, P. Then, in each iteration of the branch-and-bound algorithm, we select the most promising configuration c in P. If i is the index of the last item considered for c, then we expand c into two new configurations, one that includes item $i+1$ and one that excludes it. Note that every configuration that satisfies the size constraint is a valid solution to the KNAPSACK problem. Thus, if either of the two new configurations is valid and better than the best solution found so far, we update our current best to be the better of the two, and continue the loop.

In order to select configurations that are most promising, of course, we need a way of scoring configurations by their potential value. Since in the KNAPSACK problem we are interested in maximizing a worth, rather than minimizing a cost, we score configurations by computing an upper bound on their potential worth. Specifically, given a configuration c, which has considered items with indices 0 to i, we compute an upper bound for c by starting with the total worth w_c for c and see how much more worth we can add to c if we were to augment c with a solution to a fractional KNAPSACK problem taken from the remaining items in S. Recalling that the items in S are sorted by nonincreasing w_i/s_i values, let k be the largest index such that $\sum_{j=i+1}^{k} s_j \leq size - s_c$, where s_c is the size of all the items already in configuration c. The items indexed $i+1$ to k are the best remaining items that completely fit in the knapsack. To compute our upper bound for c, then, we consider adding all these elements to c plus as much of item $k+1$ (if it exists) as will fit. Namely, our upper bound for c is defined as follows:

$$\text{upper}(c) = w_c + \sum_{j=i+1}^{k} w_j + \left(size - s_c - \sum_{j=i+1}^{k} s_j \right) \frac{w_{k+1}}{s_{k+1}}.$$

If $k = n-1$, then assume that $w_{k+1}/s_{k+1} = 0$.

We give code fragments from the Java branch-and-bound solution based on this approach in Code Fragments 13.21, 13.22, and 13.23.

```
/**
 * Method to find an optimal solution to KNAPSACK problem, given:
 * - s, indexed array of the sizes
 * - w, index array of element worth (profit)
 * - indexes of s and w are sorted by w[i]/s[i] values
 * - size, the total size constraint
 * It returns an external-node Configuration object for optimal solution.
 */
public static Configuration solve(int[] s, int[] w, long size) {
  /* Create priority queue for selecting current best configurations */
  PriorityQueue p = DoublePriorityQueue();
  /* Create root configuration */
  Configuration root = new Configuration(s,w,size);
  double upper = root.getUpperBound(); // upper bound for root
  Configuration curBest = root; // the current best solution
  p.insertItem(new Double(-upper), root); // add root configuration to p
  /* generate new configurations until all viable solutions are found */
  while (!p.isEmpty()) {
    double curBound = -((Double)p.minKey()).doubleValue(); // we want max
    Configuration curConfig = (Configuration) p.removeMin();
    if (curConfig.getIndex() >= s.length-1) continue; // nothing to expand
    /* Expand this configuration to include the next item */
    Configuration child = curConfig.expandWithNext();
    /* Test if new child has best valid worth seen so far */
    if ((child.getWorth() > curBest.getWorth()) && (child.getSize() <= size))
      curBest = child;
    /* Test if new child is worth expanding further */
    double newBound = child.getUpperBound();
    if (newBound > curBest.getWorth())
      p.insertItem( new Double(-newBound), child);
    /* Expand the current configuration to exclude the next item */
    child = curConfig.expandWithoutNext();
    /* Test if new child is worth expanding further */
    newBound = child.getUpperBound();
    if (newBound > curBest.getWorth())
      p.insertItem( new Double(-newBound), child);
  }
  return curBest;
}
```

Code Fragment 13.21: The engine method for the branch-and-bound solution to the KNAPSACK problem. The class DoublePriorityQueue, which is not shown, is a priority queue specialized to hold objects with Double keys. Note that the key values used in the priority queue are made negative, since we are interested in maximizing worth, not minimizing cost. Also note that when we expand a configuration without adding the next element, we don't check if this is a better solution, since its worth is the same as its parent.

```
class Configuration {
  protected int index; // index of the last element considered
  protected boolean in; // true iff the last element is in the tentative sol'n
  protected long worth; // total worth of all elements in this solution
  protected long size; // total size of all elements in this solution
  protected Configuration parent; // configuration deriving this one
  protected static int[] s;
  protected static int[] w;
  protected static long bagSize;
  /** The initial configuration - is only called for the root config. */
  Configuration(int[] sizes, int[] worths, long sizeConstraint) {
    /* Set static references to the constraints for all configurations */
    s = sizes;
    w = worths;
    bagSize = sizeConstraint;
    /* Set root configuration values */
    index = −1;
    in = false;
    worth = 0L;
    size = 0L;
    parent = null;
  }
  /** Default constructor */
  Configuration() { /* Assume default initial values */ }
  /** Expand this configuration to one that includes next item */
  public Configuration expandWithNext() {
    Configuration c = new Configuration();
    c.index = index + 1;
    c.in = true;
    c.worth = worth + w[c.index];
    c.size = size + s[c.index];
    c.parent = this;
    return c;
  }
  /** Expand this configuration to one that doesn't include next item */
  public Configuration expandWithoutNext() {
    Configuration c = new Configuration();
    c.index = index + 1;
    c.in = false;
    c.worth = worth;
    c.size = size;
    c.parent = this;
    return c;
  }
```

Code Fragment 13.22: The Configuration class and its methods for constructing and expanding configurations. These are used in the branch-and-bound solution to the KNAPSACK problem. This class is continued in Code Fragment 13.23.

```
/** Get this configuration's index */
public long getIndex() {
  return index;
}
/** Get this configuration's size */
public long getSize() {
  return size;
}
/** Get this configuration's worth */
public long getWorth() {
  return worth;
}
/** Get this configuration's upper bound on future potential worth */
public double getUpperBound() {
  int g;  // index for greedy solution
  double bound = worth; // start from current worth
  long curSize=0L;
  long sizeConstraint = bagSize - size;
  /* Greedily add items until remaining size is overflowed */
  for (g=index+1; (curSize <= sizeConstraint) && (g < s.length); g++) {
    curSize += s[g];
    bound += (double) w[g];
    }
  if (g < s.length) {
    bound -= w[g]; // roll back to worth that fit
    /* Add fractional component of the extra greedy item */
    bound += (double) (bagSize - size)*w[g]/s[g];
  }
  return bound;
}
/** Print a solution from this configuration */
public void printSolution() {
  Configuration c = this; // start with external-node Configuration
  System.out.println("(Size,Worth) = " + c.size + "," + c.worth);
  System.out.print("index-size-worth list = [");
  for (; c.parent != null; c = c.parent)  // march up to root
    if (c.in) { // print index, size, and worth of next included item
      System.out.print("(" + c.index);
      System.out.print("," + s[c.index]);
      System.out.print("," + w[c.index] + ")");
    }
  System.out.println("]");
}
```

Code Fragment 13.23: The support methods for the Configuration class, of Code Fragment 13.22, used in the branch-and-bound solution to the KNAPSACK problem. The method for computing upper bounds is particularly important.

13.6 Exercises

Reinforcement

R-13.1 Professor Amongus has shown that a decision problem L is polynomial-time reducible to an $\boldsymbol{NP}$-complete problem M. Moreover, after 80 pages of dense mathematics, he has also just proven that L can be solved in polynomial time. Has he just proven that $\boldsymbol{P} = \boldsymbol{NP}$? Why or why not?

R-13.2 Use a truth table to convert the Boolean formula $B = (a \leftrightarrow (b + c))$ into an equivalent formula in CNF. Show the truth table and the intermediate DNF formula for $\overline{B}$.

R-13.3 Show that the problem SAT, which takes an arbitrary Boolean formula S as input and asks if S is satisfiable, is $\boldsymbol{NP}$-complete.

R-13.4 Consider the problem DNF-SAT, which takes a Boolean formula S in disjunctive normal form (DNF) as input and asks if S is satisfiable. Describe a deterministic polynomial-time algorithm for DNF-SAT.

R-13.5 Consider the problem DNF-DISSAT, which takes a Boolean formula S in disjunctive normal form (DNF) as input and asks if S is dissatisfiable, that is, there is an assignment of Boolean values to the variables of S so that it evaluates to 0. Show that DNF-DISSAT is $\boldsymbol{NP}$-complete.

R-13.6 Convert the Boolean formula $B = (x_1 \leftrightarrow x_2) \cdot (\overline{x_3} + x_4 x_5) \cdot (\overline{x_1 x_2} + x_3 \overline{x_4})$ into CNF.

R-13.7 Show that the CLIQUE problem is in $\boldsymbol{NP}$.

R-13.8 Given the CNF formula $B = (x_1) \cdot (\overline{x_2} + x_3 + x_5 + \overline{x_6}) \cdot (x_1 + x_4) \cdot (x_3 + \overline{x_5})$, show the reduction of B into an equivalent input for the 3SAT problem.

R-13.9 Given $B = (x_1 + \overline{x_2} + x_3) \cdot (x_4 + x_5 + \overline{x_6}) \cdot (x_1 + \overline{x_4} + \overline{x_5}) \cdot (x_3 + x_4 + x_6)$, draw the instance of VERTEX-COVER that is constructed by the reduction from 3SAT of the Boolean formula B.

R-13.10 Draw an example of a graph with 10 vertices and 15 edges that has a vertex cover of size 2.

R-13.11 Draw an example of a graph with 10 vertices and 15 edges that has a clique of size 6.

R-13.12 Professor Amongus has just designed an algorithm that can take any graph G with n vertices and determine in $O(n^k)$ time whether or not G contains a clique of size k. Does Professor Amongus deserve the Turing Award for having just shown that $\boldsymbol{P} = \boldsymbol{NP}$? Why or why not?

R-13.13 Is there a subset of the numbers in $\{23, 59, 17, 47, 14, 40, 22, 8\}$ that sums to 100? What about 130? Show your work.

R-13.14 Show that the SET-COVER problem is in $\boldsymbol{NP}$.

R-13.15 Show that the SUBSET-SUM problem is in $\boldsymbol{NP}$.

R-13.16 Draw an example of a graph with 10 vertices and 20 edges that has a Hamiltonian cycle. Also, draw an example of a graph with 10 vertices and 20 edges that does not have a Hamiltonian cycle.

R-13.17 The ***Manhattan distance*** between two points (a,b) and (c,d) in the plane is $|a-c|+|b-d|$. Using Manhattan distance to define the cost between every pair of points, find an optimal traveling salesperson tour of the following set of points: $\{(1,1),(2,8),(1,5),(3,-4),(5,6),(-2,-6)\}$.

R-13.18 Describe in detail how to implement Algorithm 13.14 in $O(n+m)$ time on an n-vertex graph with m edges. You may use the traditional operation-count measure of running time in this case.

R-13.19 Describe the details of an efficient implementation of Algorithm 13.17 and analyze its running time.

R-13.20 Give an example of a graph G with at least 10 vertices such that the greedy 2-approximation algorithm for VERTEX-COVER given above is guaranteed to produce a suboptimal vertex cover.

R-13.21 Give a complete, weighted graph G, such that its edge weights satisfy the triangle inequality but the MST-based approximation algorithm for TSP does not find an optimal solution.

R-13.22 Give a pseudo-code description of the backtracking algorithm for CNF-SAT.

R-13.23 Give a recursive pseudo-code description of the backtracking algorithm, assuming the search strategy should visit configurations in a depth-first fashion.

R-13.24 Give a pseudo-code description of the branch-and-bound algorithm for TSP.

R-13.25 The branch-and-bound program in Section 13.5.2, for solving the KNAPSACK problem, uses a Boolean flag to determine when an item is included in a solution or not. Show that this flag is redundant. That is, even if we remove this field, there is a way (using no additional fields) to tell if an item is included in a solution or not.

Creativity

C-13.1 Show that we can deterministically simulate in polynomial time any nondeterministic algorithm A that runs in polynomial time and makes at most $O(\log n)$ calls to the choose method, where n is the size of the input to A.

C-13.2 Show that every language L in $\boldsymbol{P}$ is polynomial-time reducible to the language $M=\{5\}$, that is, the language that simply asks if the binary encoding of the input is equal to 5.

C-13.3 Show how to construct a Boolean circuit C such that, if we create variables only for the inputs of C and then try to build a Boolean formula that is equivalent to C, then we will create a formula exponentially larger than an encoding of C.

Hint: Use recursion to repeat subexpressions in a way that doubles their size each time they are used.

C-13.4 Show that the backtracking algorithm given in Section 13.5.1 for the CNF-SAT problem runs in polynomial time if every clause in the given Boolean formula has at most two literals. That is, it solves 2SAT in polynomial time.

C-13.5 Consider the 2SAT version of the CNF-SAT problem, in which every clause in the given formula S has exactly two literals. Note that any clause of the form $(a+b)$ can be thought of as two implications, $(\overline{a} \rightarrow b)$ and $(\overline{b} \rightarrow a)$. Consider a graph G from S, such that each vertex in G is associated with a variable, x, in S, or its negation, $\overline{x}$. Let there be a directed edge in G from $\overline{a}$ to b for each clause equivalent to $(\overline{a} \rightarrow b)$. Show that S is not satisfiable if and only if there is a variable x such that there is a path in G from x to $\overline{x}$ and a path from $\overline{x}$ to x. Derive from this rule a polynomial time algorithm for solving this special case of the CNF-SAT problem. What is the running time of your algorithm?

C-13.6 Suppose an oracle has given you a magic computer, C, that when given any Boolean formula B in CNF will tell you in one step if B is satisfiable or not. Show how to use C to construct an actual assignment of satisfying Boolean values to the variables in any satisfiable formula B. How many calls do you need to make to C in the worst case in order to do this?

C-13.7 Define SUBGRAPH-ISOMORPHISM as the problem that takes a graph G and another graph H and determines if H is a subgraph of G. That is, there is a mapping from each vertex v in H to a vertex $f(v)$ in G such that, if (v,w) is an edge in H, then $(f(v), f(w))$ is an edge in G. Show that SUBGRAPH-ISOMORPHISM is ***NP***-complete.

C-13.8 Define INDEPENDENT-SET as the problem that takes a graph G and an integer k and asks if G contains an independent set of vertices of size k. That is, G contains a set I of vertices of size k such that, for any v and w in I, there is no edge (v,w) in G. Show that INDEPENDENT-SET is ***NP***-complete.

C-13.9 Define HYPER-COMMUNITY to be the problem that takes a collection of n web pages and an integer k, and determines if there are k web pages that all contain hyperlinks to each other. Show that HYPER-COMMUNITY is ***NP***-complete.

C-13.10 Define PARTITION as the problem that takes a set $S = \{s_1, s_2, \ldots, s_n\}$ of numbers and asks if there is a subset T of S such that

$$\sum_{s_i \in T} s_i = \sum_{s_i \in S-T} s_i.$$

That is, it asks if there is a partition of the numbers into two groups that sum to the same value. Show that PARTITION is ***NP***-complete.

C-13.11 Show that the HAMILTONIAN-CYCLE problem on directed graphs is ***NP***-complete.

C-13.12 Show that the SUBSET-SUM problem is solvable in polynomial time if the input is given in a unary encoding. That is, show that SUBSET-SUM is not strongly ***NP***-hard. What is the running time of your algorithm?

C-13.13 Show that the KNAPSACK problem is solvable in polynomial time if the input is given in a unary encoding. That is, show that KNAPSACK is not strongly ***NP***-hard. What is the running time of your algorithm?

C-13.14 Consider the general optimization version of the TSP problem, where the underlying graph need not satisfy the triangle inequality. Show that, for any fixed value $\delta \geq 1$, there is no polynomial-time δ-approximation algorithm for the general TSP problem unless $P = NP$.

Hint: Reduce HAMILTONIAN-CYCLE to this problem by defining a cost function for a complete graph H for the n-vertex input graph G so that edges of H also in G have cost 1 but edges of H not in G have cost δn more than 1.

C-13.15 Consider the special case of TSP where the vertices correspond to points in the plane, with the cost defined on an edge for every pair (p,q) being the usual Euclidean distance between p and q. Show that an optimal tour will not have any pair of crossing edges.

C-13.16 Derive an efficient backtracking algorithm for the HAMILTONIAN-CYCLE problem.

C-13.17 Derive an efficient backtracking algorithm for the KNAPSACK decision problem.

C-13.18 Derive an efficient branch-and-bound algorithm for the KNAPSACK optimization problem.

C-13.19 Derive a new lower bound function, *lb*, for a branch-and-bound algorithm for solving the TSP optimization problem. Your function should always be greater than or equal to the *lb* function used in Section 13.5.2, but still be a valid lower bound function. Describe an example where your *lb* is strictly greater than the *lb* function used in Section 13.5.2.

Projects

P-13.1 Design and implement a backtracking algorithm for the CNF-SAT problem. Compare the running time of your algorithm on a rich set of instances of 2SAT and 3SAT.

P-13.2 Design and implement a branch-and-bound algorithm for the TSP problem. Use at least two different definitions for the lower bound function, *lb*, and test the effectiveness of each.

P-13.3 Possibly working in a group, design and implement a branch-and-bound algorithm for the TSP problem as well as a polynomial-time approximation algorithm for TSP. Test the efficiency and effectiveness of these two implementations for finding traveling salesperson tours for sets of points in the plane with Euclidean distance defining the costs between pairs.

P-13.4 Implement a backtracking algorithm for HAMILTONIAN-CYCLE. For various values of n, test its effectiveness for finding Hamiltonian cycles when the number of edges is $2n$, $\lceil n \log n \rceil$, and $10n$, and $20\lceil n^{1.5} \rceil$.

P-13.5 Do an empirical comparison of using dynamic programming and backtracking for the SUBSET-SUM problem.

P-13.6 Do an empirical comparison of using dynamic programming and branch-and-bound for the KNAPSACK problem.

Chapter Notes

Computing models are discussed in the textbooks by Lewis and Papadimitriou [133], Savage [177] and Sipser [187].

The proof sketch of the Cook-Levin Theorem (13.6) given in this chapter is an adaptation of a proof sketch of Cormen, Leiserson, and Rivest [55]. Cook's original theorem [53] showed that CNF-SAT was ***NP***-complete, and Levin's original theorem [131] was for a tiling problem. We refer to Theorem 13.6 as the "Cook-Levin" theorem in honor of these two seminal papers, for their proofs were along the same lines as the proof sketch given for Theorem 13.6. Karp [113] demonstrated several more problems to be ***NP***-complete, and subsequently hundreds of other problems have been shown to be ***NP***-complete. Garey and Johnson [76] give a very nice discussion of ***NP***-completeness as well as a catalog of many important ***NP***-complete and ***NP***-hard problems.

The reductions given in this chapter that use local replacement and restriction are well-known in the computer science literature; for example, see Garey and Johnson [76] or Aho, Hopcroft, and Ullman [7]. The component design proof that VERTEX-COVER is ***NP***-complete is an adaptation of a proof of Garey and Johnson [76], as is the component design proof that HAMILTONIAN-CYCLE is ***NP***-complete, which itself is a combination of two reductions by Karp [113]. The component design proof that SUBSET-SUM is ***NP***-complete is an adaptation of a proof of Cormen, Leiserson, and Rivest [55].

The discussion of backtracking and branch-and-bound is modeled after discussions by Lewis and Papadimitriou [133] and Brassard and Bratley [38], where backtracking is intended for decision problems and branch-and-bound is for optimization problems. Nevertheless, our discussion is also influenced by Neapolitan and Naimipour [159], who alternatively view backtracking as a heuristic search that uses a depth-first search of a configuration space and branch-and-bound as a heuristic search that uses breadth-first or best-first search with a lower bound function to perform pruning. The technique of backtracking itself dates to early work of Golomb and Baumert [80].

General discussions of approximation algorithms can be found in several other books, including those by Hochbaum [97] and Papadimitriou and Steiglitz [165], as well as the chapter by Klein and Young [116]. The PTAS for KNAPSACK is modeled after a result of Ibarra and Kim [106], as presented by Klein and Young [116]. Papadimitriou and Steiglitz attribute the 2-approximation for VERTEX-COVER to Gavril and Yannakakis. The 2-approximation algorithm for the special case of TSP is due to Rosenkrantz, Stearns, and Lewis [174]. The $O(\log n)$-approximation for SET-COVER, and its proof, follow from work of Chvátal [46], Johnson [109], and Lovász [136].

Chapter

14 Algorithmic Frameworks

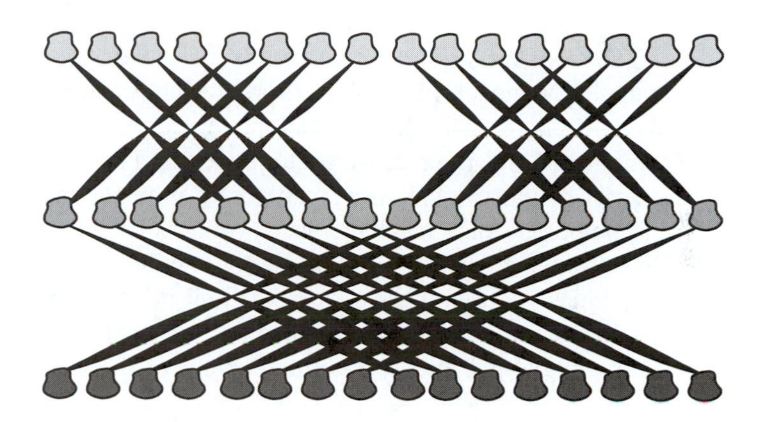

Contents

14.1 External-Memory Algorithms 645

14.1.1 Hierarchical Memory Management 646

14.1.2 (a,b) Trees and B-Trees 649

14.1.3 External-Memory Sorting 654

14.2 Parallel Algorithms 657

14.2.1 Parallel Models of Computation 657

14.2.2 Simple Parallel Divide-and-Conquer 659

14.2.3 Sequential Subsets and Brent's Theorem 659

14.2.4 Recursive Doubling 661

14.2.5 Parallel Merging and Sorting 664

14.2.6 Finding the Diameter of a Convex Polygon 665

14.3 Online Algorithms 667

14.3.1 Caching Algorithms 668

14.3.2 Auction Strategies 674

14.3.3 Competitive Search Trees 676

14.4 Exercises 680

For the most part, we have stuck with one computational framework in this book. This framework, which is formally known as the random-access machine (or RAM), consists of a single processor connected to a single, potentially unbounded, memory. Moreover, we have focused primarily on the study of algorithms that accept a single input and then process that input to produce an output. This framework has served us well, and it models the majority of computations that algorithm designers encounter. But it nevertheless has its limitations, as there are several natural and well-motivated computational contexts where this framework does not apply. We study three such frameworks in this chapter.

The first framework we address is for an extension of the memory component of the RAM model. In this framework, which is called the ***external memory*** model, we try to more realistically model the memory hierarchy that is present in modern computers. In particular, we try to model the fact that memory is divided into fast internal memory, which has small access time but small capacity, and slow external memory, which has large access time but large capacity. Designing efficient algorithms with this memory hierarchy in mind requires some modifications to the techniques we used when we assumed all memory had the same access times. In this chapter, we examine some specific changes that should be made for searching and sorting to make these algorithms efficient for external memory.

Another important variation on the traditional RAM framework that we consider is for parallel algorithms. That is, we consider algorithms that can utilize multiple processors working in concert to solve a problem. In parallel algorithm design, we desire solutions that improve upon known sequential algorithms by as close to a linear factor in the number of processors as is possible. We study several important parallel algorithms, including algorithms for parallel arithmetic, searching, and sorting, looking at ways we can exploit a parallel extension of the RAM model that allows for multiple processors.

The final framework we examine in this chapter challenges the viewpoint that an algorithm is just a function that maps an input to an output. In the framework of online algorithms we consider an algorithm to be a server that must process a sequence of client requests that are processed over time. The response from one request must be fully processed before we can examine and process the next. This model is motivated by the way computers are often used on the Internet to process computational requests from remote users. The challenge in designing algorithms for this model is that a choice we make on one request might make the time needed for processing a future request much longer. To analyze the effectiveness of an online algorithm's choices, then, we often compare its behavior to that of an offline algorithm that knows the sequence of client requests in advance. Such an analysis is known as a competitive analysis, and it forms a natural analogue to the worst-case time complexity we have been using throughout this book for algorithms that map inputs to outputs.

14.1 External-Memory Algorithms

There are several computer applications that must deal with a large amount of data. Examples include the analysis of scientific data sets, the processing of financial transactions, and the organization and maintenance of databases (such as telephone directories). In fact, the amount of data that must be dealt with is often too large to fit entirely in the internal memory of a computer.

The Memory Hierarchy

In order to accommodate large data sets, computers have a ***hierarchy*** of different kinds of memories, which vary in terms of their size and distance from the CPU. Closest to the CPU are the internal registers that the CPU itself uses. Access to such locations is very fast, but there are relatively few such locations. At the second level in the hierarchy is the ***cache*** memory. This memory is considerably larger than the register set of a CPU, but accessing it takes longer (and there may even be multiple caches with progressively slower access times). At the third level in the hierarchy is the ***internal memory***, which is also known as ***main memory***, ***core memory***, or random-access memory (RAM). The internal memory is considerably larger than the cache memory, but also requires more time to access. Finally, at the highest level in the hierarchy is the ***external memory***, which usually consists of disks, CDs, or tapes. This memory is very large, but it is also very slow. Thus, the memory hierarchy for computers can be viewed as consisting of four levels, each of which is larger and slower than the previous level. (See Figure 14.1.)

In most applications, however, only two levels really matter—the one that can hold all the data items in our problem and the level just below that one. Bringing data items in and out of the higher memory that can hold all items will typically be the computational bottleneck in this case.

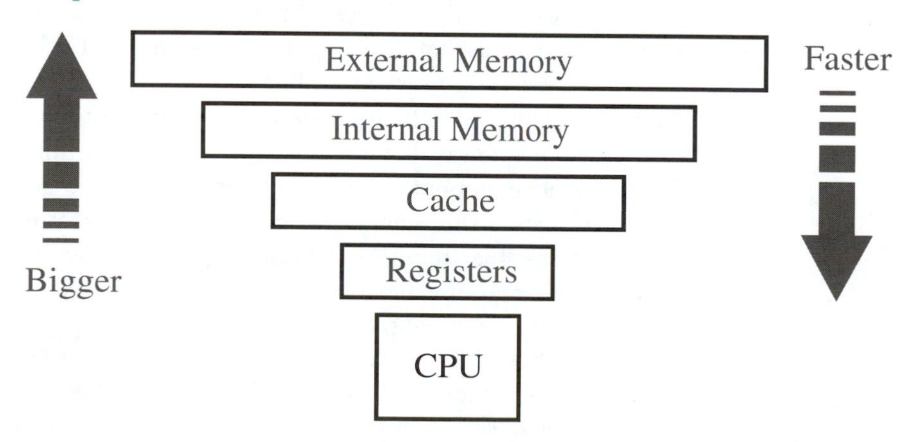

Figure 14.1: The memory hierarchy.

Caches and Disks

The specific two levels that matter most depend on the size of the problem we are trying to solve. For a problem that can fit entirely in main memory, the important two levels are the cache memory and the internal memory. Access times for internal memory can be as much as 10 to 100 times longer than those for cache memory. It is desirable, therefore, to be able to perform most memory accesses in cache memory. For a problem that does not fit entirely in main memory, on the other hand, the important two levels are the internal memory and the external memory. Here the differences are even more dramatic, for access times for disks, the usual general-purpose external-memory device, are typically as much as 100000 to 1000000 times longer than those for internal memory.

To put this latter figure into perspective, imagine there is a student in Baltimore who wants to send a request-for-money message to his parents in Chicago. If the student sends his parents an e-mail message, it can arrive at their home computer in about five seconds. Think of this mode of communication as corresponding to an internal-memory access by a CPU. A mode of communication, corresponding to an external-memory access that is 500000 times slower, would be for the student to walk to Chicago and deliver his message in person, which would take about a month if he can average 20 miles per day. Thus, we should make as few accesses to external memory as possible.

In this section, we discuss general strategies for hierarchical memory management and present methods for external-memory searching and sorting.

14.1.1 Hierarchical Memory Management

Most algorithms are not designed with the memory hierarchy in mind, in spite of the great variance between access times for the different levels. Indeed, all of the algorithm analyses described in this book so far have assumed that all memory accesses are equal. This assumption might seem, at first, to be a great oversight—and one we are only addressing now in the final chapter—but there are two fundamental justifications for why it is actually a reasonable assumption to make.

The first justification is that it is often necessary to assume that all memory accesses take the same amount of time, since specific device-dependent information about memory sizes is often hard to come by. In fact, information about memory size may be impossible to get. For example, a Java program that is designed to run on many different computer platforms cannot be defined in terms of a specific computer architecture configuration. We can certainly use architecture-specific information, if we have it (and we will show how to exploit such information later in this chapter). But once we have optimized our software for a certain architecture configuration, our software will no longer be device-independent. Fortunately, such optimizations are not always necessary, primarily because of the second justification for the equal-time, memory-access assumption.

The second justification for the memory-access equality assumption is that operating system designers have developed general mechanisms that allow for most memory accesses to be fast. These mechanisms are based on two important ***locality-of-reference*** properties that most software possesses:

- **Temporal locality**: If a program accesses a certain memory location, then it is likely to access this location again in the near future. For example, it is quite common to use the value of a counter variable in several different expressions, including one to increment the counter's value. In fact, a common adage among computer architects is that "a program spends ninety percent of its time in ten percent of its code."
- **Spatial locality**: If a program accesses a certain memory location, then it is likely to access other locations that are near this one. For example, a program using an array is likely to access the locations of this array in a sequential or near-sequential manner.

Computer scientists and engineers have performed extensive software profiling experiments to justify the claim that most software possesses both of these kinds of locality-of-reference. For example, a for-loop used to scan through an array will exhibit both kinds of locality.

Caching and Blocking

Temporal and spatial localities have, in turn, given rise to two fundamental design choices for two-level computer memory systems (which are present in the interface between cache memory and internal memory, and also in the interface between internal memory and external memory).

The first design choice is called ***virtual memory***. This concept consists of providing an address space as large as the capacity of the secondary-level memory, and of transferring into the primary-level memory, data located in the secondary level, when they are addressed. Virtual memory does not limit the programmer to the constraint of the internal memory size. The concept of bringing data into primary memory is called ***caching***, and it is motivated by temporal locality. For, by bringing data into primary memory, we are hoping that it will be accessed again soon, and we will be able to quickly respond to all the requests for this data that come in the near future.

The second design choice is motivated by spatial locality. Specifically, if data stored at a secondary-level memory location l is accessed, then we bring into primary-level memory a large block of contiguous locations that include the location l. (See Figure 14.2.) This concept is known as ***blocking***, and it is motivated by the expectation that other secondary-level memory locations close to l will soon be accessed. In the interface between cache memory and internal memory, such blocks are often called ***cache lines***, and in the interface between internal memory and external memory, such blocks are often called ***pages***.

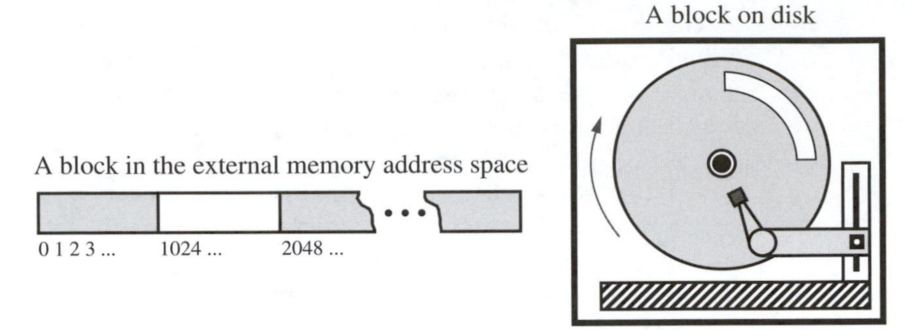

Figure 14.2: Blocks in external memory.

Incidentally, blocking for disk and CD-ROM drives is also motivated by the properties of these hardware technologies. For a reading arm on a disk or CD-ROM takes a relatively long time to position itself for reading a certain location, but, once the arm is positioned, it can quickly read many contiguous locations, because the medium it is reading is spinning very fast. (See Figure 14.2.) Even without this motivation, however, blocking is fully justified by the spatial locality property that most programs have.

Thus, when implemented with caching and blocking, virtual memory often allows us to perceive secondary-level memory as being faster than it really is. There is still a problem, however. Primary-level memory is much smaller than secondary-level memory. Moreover, because memory systems use blocking, any program of substance will likely reach a point where it requests data from secondary-level memory, but the primary memory is already full of blocks. In order to fulfill the request and maintain our use of caching and blocking, we must remove some block from primary memory to make room for a new block from secondary memory in this case. Deciding how to do this eviction brings up a number of interesting data structure and algorithm design issues that we discuss in the remainder of this section.

A Model for External Searching

The first problem we address is that of implementing a dictionary for a large collection of items that do not fit in primary memory. Recall that a dictionary stores key-element pairs (items) subject to insertions, removals, and key-based searches. Since one of the main applications of large dictionaries is in database systems, we refer to the secondary-memory blocks as ***disk blocks***. Likewise, we refer to the transfer of a block between secondary memory and primary memory as a ***disk transfer***. Even though we use this terminology, the search techniques we discuss in this section apply also when the primary memory is the CPU cache and the secondary memory is the main (internal) memory. We use the disk-based viewpoint because it is concrete and also because it is more prevalent.

14.1.2 (a,b) Trees and B-Trees

Recalling the great time difference that exists between main memory accesses and disk accesses, the main goal of maintaining a dictionary in external memory is to minimize the number of disk transfers needed to perform a query or update. In fact, the difference in speed between disk and internal memory is so great that we should be willing to perform a considerable number of internal-memory accesses if they allow us to avoid a few disk transfers. Let us, therefore, analyze the performance of dictionary implementations by counting the number of disk transfers each would require to perform the standard dictionary search and update operations.

Let us first consider some external-memory inefficient dictionary implementations based on sequences. If the sequence representing a dictionary is implemented as an unsorted, doubly linked list, then insert and remove can be performed with $O(1)$ transfers each, assuming we know which block holds an item to be removed. But, in this case, searching requires $\Theta(n)$ transfers in the worst case, since each link hop we perform could access a different block. This search time can be improved to $O(n/B)$ transfers (see Exercise C-14.1), where B denotes the number of nodes of the list that can fit into a block, but this is still poor performance. We could alternately implement the sequence using a sorted array. In this case, a search performs $O(\log_2 n)$ transfers, via binary search, which is a nice improvement. But this solution requires $\Theta(n/B)$ transfers to implement an insert or remove operation in the worst case, for we may have to access all blocks to move elements up or down. Thus, sequence dictionary implementations are not external-memory efficient.

If sequence implementations are inefficient, then perhaps we should consider the logarithmic-time, internal-memory strategies that use balanced binary trees (for example, AVL trees or red-black trees) or other search structures with logarithmic average-case query and update times (for example, skip lists or splay trees). These methods store the dictionary items at the nodes of a binary tree or of a graph. In the worst case, each node accessed for a query or update in one of these structures will be in a different block. Thus, these methods all require $O(\log_2 n)$ transfers in the worst case to perform a query or update operation. This is good, but we can do better. In particular, we can perform dictionary queries and updates using only $O(\log_B n) = O(\log n/\log B)$ transfers.

A Better Approach

The main idea for improving the external-memory performance of the dictionary implementations discussed above is that we should be willing to perform up to $O(B)$ internal-memory accesses to avoid a single disk transfer, where B denotes the size of a block. The hardware and software that drives the disk performs this many internal-memory accesses just to bring a block into internal memory, and this is only a small part of the cost of a disk transfer. Thus, $O(B)$ high-speed, internal-memory accesses are a small price to pay to avoid a time-consuming disk transfer.

(a,b) Trees

To reduce the importance of the performance difference between internal-memory accesses and external-memory accesses for searching, we can represent our dictionary using a multi-way search tree (Chapter 3). This approach gives rise to a generalization of the $(2,4)$ tree data structure to a structure known as the (a,b) tree.

Formally, an (a,b) tree is a multi-way search tree such that each node has between a and b children and stores between $a-1$ and $b-1$ items. The algorithms for searching, inserting, and removing elements in an (a,b) tree are straightforward generalizations of the corresponding ones for $(2,4)$ trees. The advantage of generalizing $(2,4)$ trees to (a,b) trees is that a generalized class of trees provides a flexible search structure, where the size of the nodes and the running time of the various dictionary operations depends on the parameters a and b. By setting the parameters a and b appropriately with respect to the size of disk blocks, we can derive a data structure that achieves good external-memory performance.

An (a,b) ***tree***, where a and b are integers, such that $2 \le a \le (b+1)/2$, is a multi-way search tree T with the following additional restrictions:

Size Property: Each internal node has at least a children, unless it is the root, and has at most b children.

Depth Property: All the external nodes have the same depth.

Theorem 14.1: *The height of an (a,b) tree storing n items is $\Omega(\log n/\log b)$ and $O(\log n/\log a)$.*

Proof: Let T be an (a,b) tree storing n elements, and let h be the height of T. We justify the theorem by establishing the following bounds on h:

$$\frac{1}{\log b}\log(n+1) \le h \le \frac{1}{\log a}\log\frac{n+1}{2}+1.$$

By the size and depth properties, the number n'' of external nodes of T is at least $2a^{h-1}$ and at most b^h. By Theorem 3.3, $n'' = n+1$. Thus

$$2a^{h-1} \le n+1 \le b^h.$$

Taking the logarithm in base 2 of each term, we get

$$(h-1)\log a + 1 \le \log(n+1) \le h\log b.$$

■

We recall that in a multi-way search tree T, each node v of T holds a secondary structure $D(v)$, which is itself a dictionary (Section 3.3.1). If T is an (a,b) tree, then $D(v)$ stores at most b items. Let $f(b)$ denote the time for performing a search in a $D(v)$ dictionary. The search algorithm in an (a,b) tree is exactly like the one for multi-way search trees given in Section 3.3.1. Hence, searching in an (a,b) tree

T with n items takes $O(\frac{f(b)}{\log a}\log n)$. Note that if b is a constant (and thus a is also), then the search time is $O(\log n)$, independent of the specific implementation of the secondary structures.

The main application of (a,b) trees is for dictionaries stored in external memory (for example, on a disk or CD-ROM). Namely, to minimize disk accesses, we select the parameters a and b so that each tree node occupies a single disk block (so that $f(b) = 1$ if we wish to simply count block transfers). Providing the right a and b values in this context gives rise to a data structure known as the B-tree, which we will describe shortly. Before we describe this structure, however, let us discuss how insertions and removals are handled in (a,b) trees.

Insertion and Removal in an (a,b) Tree

The insertion algorithm for an (a,b) tree is similar to that for a $(2,4)$ tree. An overflow occurs when an item is inserted into a b-node v, which becomes an illegal $(b+1)$-node. (Recall that a node in a multi-way tree is a ***d*-node** if it has d children.) To remedy an overflow, we split node v by moving the median item of v into the parent of v and replacing v with a $\lceil (b+1)/2 \rceil$-node v' and a $\lfloor (b+1)/2 \rfloor$-node v''. We can now see the reason for requiring $a \leq (b+1)/2$ in the definition of an (a,b) tree. Note that as a consequence of the split, we need to build the secondary structures $D(v')$ and $D(v'')$.

Removing an element from an (a,b) tree is also similar to what was done for $(2,4)$ trees. An underflow occurs when a key is removed from an a-node v, distinct from the root, which causes v to become an illegal $(a-1)$-node. To remedy an underflow, we either perform a transfer with a sibling of v that is not an a-node or we perform a fusion of v with a sibling that is an a-node. The new node w resulting from the fusion is a $(2a-1)$-node. Here, we see another reason for requiring $a \leq (b+1)/2$. Note that as a consequence of the fusion, we need to build the secondary structure $D(w)$.

Table 14.3 shows the running time of the main operations of a dictionary realized by means of an (a,b) tree T.

Method	Time
findElement	$O\left(\frac{f(b)}{\log a}\log n\right)$
insertItem	$O\left(\frac{g(b)}{\log a}\log n\right)$
removeElement	$O\left(\frac{g(b)}{\log a}\log n\right)$

Table 14.3: Time complexity of the main methods of a dictionary realized by an (a,b) tree. We let $f(b)$ denote the time to search a b-node and $g(b)$ the time to split or fuse a b-node. We also denote the number of elements in the dictionary with n. The space complexity is $O(n)$.

The bounds in Table 14.3 are based on the following assumptions and facts:

- The (a,b) tree T is represented using the data structure described in Section 3.3.1, and the secondary structure of the nodes of T support search in $f(b)$ time, and split and fusion operations in $g(b)$ time, for some functions $f(b)$ and $g(b)$, which can be made to be $O(1)$ in the context where we are only counting disk transfers.
- The height of an (a,b) tree storing n elements is at most $O((\log n)/(\log a))$ (Theorem 14.1).
- A search visits $O((\log n)/(\log a))$ nodes on a path between the root and an external node, and spends $f(b)$ time per node.
- A transfer operation takes $f(b)$ time.
- A split or fusion operation takes $g(b)$ time and builds a secondary structure of size $O(b)$ for the new node(s) created.
- An insertion or removal of an element visits $O((\log n)/(\log a))$ nodes on a path between the root and an external node, and spends $g(b)$ time per node.

Thus, we may summarize as follows.

Theorem 14.2: *An (a,b) tree implements an n-item dictionary to support performing insertions and removals in $O((g(b)/\log a)\log n)$ time, and performing find queries in $O((f(b)/\log a)\log n)$ time.*

B-Trees

A specialized version of the (a,b) tree data structure, which is an efficient method for maintaining a dictionary in external memory, is the data structure known as the "B-tree." (See Figure 14.4.) A ***B-tree of order*** d is simply an (a,b) tree with $a = \lceil d/2 \rceil$ and $b = d$. Since we discussed the standard dictionary query and update methods for (a,b) trees above, we restrict our discussion here to the analysis of the external-memory performance of B-trees.

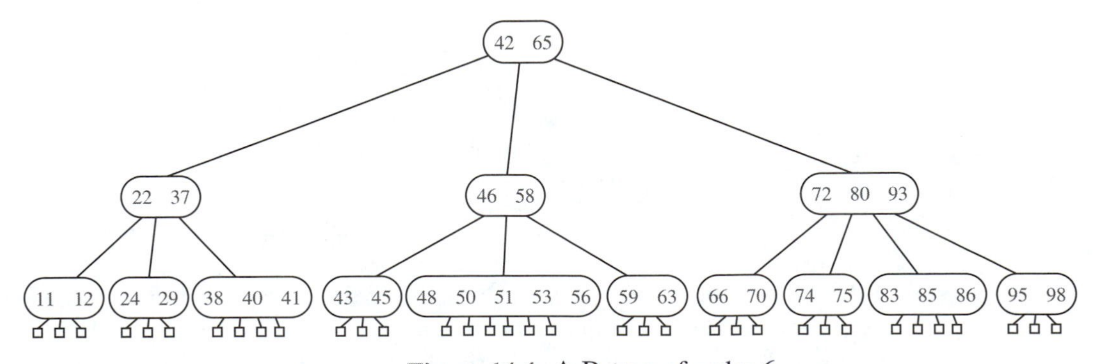

Figure 14.4: A B-tree of order 6.

Parameterizing B-trees for External Memory

The most important observation about B-trees is that we can choose d so that the d children references and the $d-1$ keys stored at a node can all fit into a single disk block. That is, we choose d so that

$$d \text{ is } \Theta(B).$$

This choice also implies that we may assume that a and b are $\Theta(B)$ in the analysis of the search and update operations on (a,b) trees. Also, recall that we are interested primarily in the number of disk transfers needed to perform various operations. Thus, the choice for d also implies that

$$f(b) = c,$$

and

$$g(b) = c,$$

for some constant $c \geq 1$, for each time we access a node to perform a search or an update operation, we need only perform a single disk transfer. That is, $f(b)$ and $g(b)$ are both $O(1)$. As we have already observed above, each search or update requires that we examine at most $O(1)$ nodes for each level of the tree. Therefore, any dictionary search or update operation on a B-tree requires only

$$\begin{aligned} O(\log_{\lceil d/2 \rceil} n) &= O(\log n / \log B) \\ &= O(\log_B n) \end{aligned}$$

disk transfers. For example, an insert operation proceeds down the B-tree to locate the node in which to insert the new item. If the node would ***overflow*** (to have $d+1$ children) because of this addition, then this node is ***split*** into two nodes that have $\lfloor (d+1)/2 \rfloor$ and $\lceil (d+1)/2 \rceil$ children, respectively. This process is then repeated at the next level up, and will continue for at most $O(\log_B n)$ levels. Likewise, in a remove operation, we remove an item from a node, and, if this results in a node ***underflow*** (to have $\lceil d/2 \rceil - 1$ children), then we either move references from a sibling node with at least $\lceil d/2 \rceil + 1$ children or we need to perform a ***fusion*** operation of this node with its sibling (and repeat this computation at the parent). As with the insert operation, this will continue up the B-tree for at most $O(\log_B n)$ levels. Thus, we have the following:

Theorem 14.3: *A B-tree with n items executes $O(\log_B n)$ disk transfers in a search or update operation, where B is the number of items that can fit in one block.*

The requirement that each internal node have at least $\lceil d/2 \rceil$ children implies that each disk block used to support a B-tree is at least half full. Analytical and experimental study of the average block usage in a B-tree is that it is closer to 67%, which is quite good.

14.1.3 External-Memory Sorting

In addition to data structures, such as dictionaries, that need to be implemented in external memory, there are many algorithms that must also operate on input sets that are too large to fit entirely into internal memory. In this case, the objective is to solve the algorithmic problem using as few block transfers as possible. The most classic domain for such external-memory algorithms is the sorting problem.

A Lower Bound for External-Memory Sorting

As we discussed above, there can be a big difference between an algorithm's performance in internal memory and its performance in external memory. For example, the performance of the radix-sorting algorithm is bad in external memory, yet good in internal memory. Other algorithms, such as the merge-sort algorithm, are reasonably good in both internal memory and external memory, however. The number of block transfers performed by the traditional merge-sorting algorithm is $O((n/B)\log_2 n)$, where B is the size of disk blocks. While this is much better than the $O(n)$ block transfers performed by an external version of radix sort, it is, nevertheless, not the best that is achievable for the sorting problem. In fact, we can show the following lower bound, whose proof is beyond the scope of this book.

Theorem 14.4: *Sorting n elements stored in external memory requires*

$$\Omega\left(\frac{n}{B}\cdot\frac{\log(n/B)}{\log(M/B)}\right)$$

block transfers, where M is the size of the internal memory.

The ratio M/B is the number of external memory blocks that can fit into internal memory. Thus, this theorem is saying that the best performance we can achieve for the sorting problem is equivalent to the work of scanning through the input set (which takes $\Theta(n/B)$ transfers) at least a logarithmic number of times, where the base of this logarithm is the number of blocks that fit into internal memory. We will not formally justify this theorem, but we will show how to design an external-memory sorting algorithm whose running time comes within a constant factor of this lower bound.

Multi-way Merge-Sort

An efficient way to sort a set S of n objects in external memory amounts to a simple external-memory variation on the familiar merge-sort algorithm. The main idea behind this variation is to merge many recursively sorted lists at a time, thereby reducing the number of levels of recursion. Specifically, a high-level description of this ***multi-way merge-sort*** method is to divide S into d subsets S_1, S_2, ..., S_d of roughly equal size, recursively sort each subset S_i, and then simultaneously merge all d sorted lists into a sorted representation of S. If we can perform the merge process using only $O(n/B)$ disk transfers, then, for large enough values of n, the total number of transfers performed by this algorithm satisfies the following recurrence:

$$t(n) = d \cdot t(n/d) + cn/B,$$

for some constant $c \geq 1$. We can stop the recursion when $n \leq B$, since we can perform a single block transfer at this point, getting all of the objects into internal memory, and then sort the set with an efficient internal-memory algorithm. Thus, the stopping criterion for $t(n)$ is

$$t(n) = 1 \quad \text{if } n/B \leq 1.$$

This implies a closed-form solution that $t(n)$ is $O((n/B)\log_d(n/B))$, which is

$$O((n/B)\log(n/B)/\log d).$$

Thus, if we can choose d to be $\Theta(M/B)$, then the worst-case number of block transfers performed by this multi-way merge-sort algorithm will be within a constant factor of the lower bound given in Theorem 14.4. We choose

$$d = (1/2)M/B.$$

The only aspect of this algorithm left to specify, then, is how to perform the d-way merge using only $O(n/B)$ block transfers.

We perform the d-way merge by running a "tournament." We let T be a complete binary tree with d external nodes, and we keep T entirely in internal memory. We associate each external node i of T with a different sorted list S_i. We initialize T by reading into each external node i, the first object in S_i. This has the effect of reading into internal memory the first block of each sorted list S_i. For each internal-node parent v of two external nodes, we then compare the objects stored at v's children and we associate the smaller of the two with v. We then repeat this comparison test at the next level up in T, and the next, and so on. When we reach the root r of T, we will associate the smallest object from among all the lists with r. This completes the initialization for the d-way merge. (See Figure 14.5.)

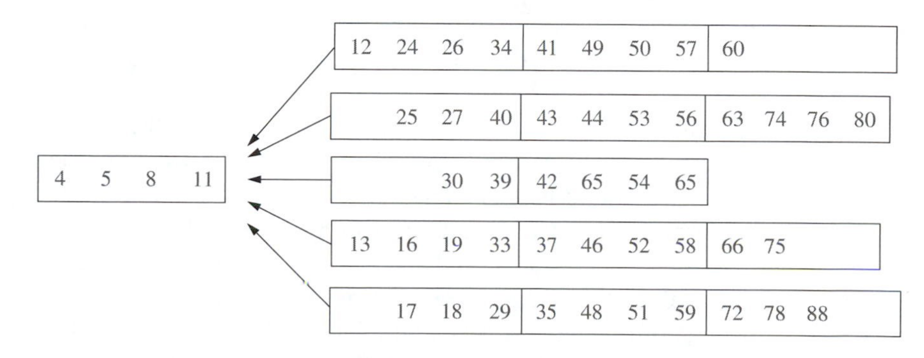

Figure 14.5: A d-way merge. We show a five-way merge with $B = 4$.

In a general step of the d-way merge, we move the object o associated with the root r of T into an array we are building for the merged list S'. We then trace down T, following the path to the external node i that o came from. We then read into i the next object in the list S_i. If o was not the last element in its block, then this next object is already in internal memory. Otherwise, we read in the next block of S_i to access this new object (if S_i is now empty, associate with the node i a pseudo-object with key $+\infty$). We then repeat the minimum computations for each of the internal nodes from i to the root of T. This again gives us the complete tree T. We then repeat this process of moving the object from the root of T to the merged list S', and rebuilding T until T is empty of objects. Each step in the merge takes $O(\log d)$ time; hence, the internal time for the d-way merge is $O(n \log d)$. The number of transfers performed in a merge is $O(n/B)$, since we scan each list S_i in order once and we write out the merged list S' once. Thus, we have:

Theorem 14.5: *Given an array-based sequence S of n elements stored in external memory, we can sort S using $O((n/B)\log(n/B)/\log(M/B))$ transfers and $O(n \log n)$ internal CPU time, where M is the size of the internal memory and B is the size of a block.*

Achieving "Near" Machine Independence

Using B-trees and external sorting algorithms can produce significant reductions in the number of block transfers. The most important piece of information that made such reductions possible was knowing the value of B, the size of a disk block (or cache line). This information is, of course, machine-dependent, but it is one of the few truly machine-dependent pieces of information that are needed, with one of the others being the ability to store keys continuously in arrays.

From our description of B-trees and external sorting, we might think that we also require low-level access to the external-memory device driver, but this is not strictly needed in order to achieve the claimed results to within a constant factor. In particular, in addition to knowing the block size, the only other thing we need to know is that large arrays of keys are partitioned into blocks of continuous cells. This allows us to implement the "blocks" in B-trees and our external-memory sorting algorithm as separate B-sized arrays, which we call ***pseudo-blocks***. If arrays are allocated to blocks in the natural way, any such pseudo-block will be allocated to at most two real blocks. Thus, even if we are relying on the operating system to perform block replacement (for example, using FIFO, LRU, or the Marker policy discussed later in Section 14.3), we can be sure that accessing any pseudo-block takes at most two, that is, $O(1)$, real block transfers. By using pseudo-blocks then, instead of real blocks, we can implement the dictionary ADT to achieve search and update operations that use only $O(\log_B n)$ block transfers. We can, therefore, design external-memory data structures and algorithms without taking complete control of the memory hierarchy from the operating system.

14.2 Parallel Algorithms

In this section we discuss parallel algorithms and some fundamental parallel algorithmic techniques, including simple parallel divide-and-conquer, sequential subsets, Brent's theorem, recursive doubling and parallel prefix, and parallel merging and sorting. All of these techniques have proven useful for designing a host of efficient parallel algorithms. We conclude the section by giving an application of some of these techniques to the problem of finding the diameter of a convex polygon.

14.2.1 Parallel Models of Computation

Extending the RAM model to allow for multiple processors gives rise to a parallel model known as the Parallel RAM, or ***PRAM***. This is the synchronous parallel model in which all processors share a common memory. Because of its conceptual simplicity, this model seems to be a model which almost all parallel computers emulate in one way or another. The PRAM model is also well suited for discovering the inherent parallelism that may be present in a problem. Finally, the PRAM model seems ideally suited for finding general paradigms which can be used to develop efficient parallel algorithms.

Parallel Efficiency

In the sequential setting, we say that an algorithm is "good" if it has a running time that is at most $O(n^k)$ for some constant k, that is, it runs in polynomial time. As addressed in Chapter 13, a problem is considered "tractable" if there is a polynomial-time algorithm that solves it. The corresponding notion in the parallel setting is to say that an algorithm is good if its running time is $O(\log^{k_1} n)$ using $O(n^{k_2})$ processors, where k_1 and k_2 are constants, that is, it runs in polylog time using a polynomial number of processors. Analogously, in the language of complexity theory, one says that a problem belongs to the class *NC* if there is an algorithm solving it which is good in this sense.

In the sequential setting, once it is known that a problem can be solved in polynomial time, the goal shifts to finding an algorithm that solves the problem as fast as possible. Likewise, in the parallel setting, once it is known that a problem is in *NC*, the goal shifts to finding an algorithm that solves the problem and minimizes the product $T(n) * P(n)$ (in the asymptotic sense), where $T(n)$ is the time complexity of the algorithm and $P(n)$ is the number of processors used by the algorithm. That is, if $Seq(n)$ denotes the sequential running time to solve a certain problem, then we want $T(n) * P(n)$ to be as close to $Seq(n)$, in the asymptotic sense, as possible. This goal is motivated from the fact that a single processor can simulate the computations of $P(n)$ processors by performing a step of each in a round-robin fashion. (See Section 2.1.2.)

We say that a parallel algorithm is ***optimal*** if its $T(n) * P(n)$ product matches the sequential lower bound for the problem it solves. Technically, this definition allows a sequential algorithm (with $P(n) = 1$) to also be an optimal parallel algorithm. So, given that $T(n) * P(n)$ is close to $Seq(n)$ for some problem, the secondary goal is to minimize $T(n)$, the running time. The motivation for these two goals is that any existing machine, with say k processors (a constant), can simulate an algorithm that is efficient in this sense to get the maximum amount of speedup. The k processors can simulate each time step of the $P(n)$ processors in $\lceil P(n)/k \rceil$ time, by having each of the k processors perform the work of $\lceil P(n)/k \rceil$ processors. This approach results in an algorithm that runs in $O(T(n)P(n)/k + T(n))$ time. In addition, any lower bound for the sequential running time necessary to solve a certain problem immediately becomes a lower bound for the product $T(n) * P(n)$ (because a sequential machine can simulate a PRAM algorithm with these bounds in $O(T(n) * P(n))$ time).

Versions of the PRAM Model

There are basically three different versions of the PRAM model, each differing from the other in how it resolves memory conflicts. (Recall that in all PRAM models the processors operate synchronously.) The most restrictive version is the Exclusive-Read, Exclusive-Write (or EREW) PRAM, in which no simultaneous reads or simultaneous writes are allowed. If we allow more than one processor to simultaneously read from the same memory cell, but still restrict concurrent writes, then we get the Concurrent-Read, Exclusive-Write (or CREW) PRAM. Finally, if we allow more than one processor to simultaneously write to the same memory cell, then we get the most powerful model, the Concurrent-Read, Concurrent-Write (or CRCW) PRAM. The method of resolving write conflicts varies, but the two most common methods are based on defining the model based on one of the following rules:

- Restrict all processors writing to the same location to be writing the same value.
- When $k > 1$ processors are writing simultaneously to the same location, allow exactly one of these processors to succeed (arbitrarily).

As an example of a CRCW PRAM algorithm, suppose we are given a Boolean array A and asked to compute the common OR of all the bits in A. We can initialize the output bit o to 0, and assign a processor to each bit in A. Then, we can have each processor assigned to a bit that is 1 to write the value 1 to o. This simple algorithm allows us to compute the OR of n bits in $O(1)$ time using n processors in the CRCW PRAM model (using either of the above rules to resolve write conflicts).

This simple example shows the power of the CRCW PRAM model, but this model is considered unrealistic by many researchers. Thus, all of the other algorithms described in this section will be for the CREW PRAM and EREW PRAM models.

14.2.2 Simple Parallel Divide-and-Conquer

The parallel divide-and-conquer technique is the exact analogue of the classic sequential divide-and-conquer technique. The approach is as follows. Given some problem, we divide the problem into a small number of subproblems, similar in structure to the original problem, but smaller in size, and then solve each subproblem recursively in parallel. In order to have an efficient algorithm, we must then be able to merge the subproblem solutions quickly in parallel, once the parallel recursive call returns.

As an easy example of using this technique, consider the problem of computing the sum of n integers (the same technique works for any associative operation). Let us assume that the input is an array containing the n integers, and is already resident in memory. For simplicity, let us also assume that n is a power of two. Divide the array into two subarrays comprising $n/2$ integers each, and find the sum of the integers in each subarray recursively in parallel. After the parallel recursive call returns, we can compute the sum of all n integers by adding the sums computed from each subarray. Since this can be done in $O(1)$ time, the time complexity $T(n)$ satisfies the recurrence equation $T(n) = T(n/2) + c$, which implies that $T(n) = O(\log n)$. The number of processors $P(n)$ needed for this computation can be expressed in the recurrence equation $P(n) = \max\{2P(n/2), 1\}$, which has solution $P(n) = O(n)$. Note that the $T(n) * P(n)$ product in this case is $O(n \log n)$, which is off by a factor of $\log n$ from optimal. In the next subsection we discuss two methods which can be used to reduce the number of processors so that the $T(n) * P(n)$ product is optimal, that is, $O(n)$.

14.2.3 Sequential Subsets and Brent's Theorem

The ***sequential subsets*** technique and ***Brent's theorem*** both involve constructing an efficient parallel algorithm from existing algorithms, which may not be very efficient themselves. We begin our discussion with the sequential subsets technique. The main idea behind this technique is to perform a limited amount of sequential preprocessing on small subsets of the problem to be solved, and then apply a parallel algorithm to finish solving the problem. In some instances, there may also be some sequential post-processing that needs to be done on each subset after the parallel algorithm completes. We illustrate how this technique could be applied to the n-integer summation problem. First, we could divide the array into $n/\log n$ subarrays of $\log n$ elements each, and, assigning one processor to each subarray, sum the elements of each sequentially. Then, we could apply the parallel divide-and-conquer procedure described in the previous subsection to sum the $n/\log n$ partial sums just computed. The preprocessing step would run in $O(\log n)$ time using $O(n/\log n)$ processors, as would the parallel divide-and-conquer step. Thus, this would result in an optimal $T(n) * P(n)$ product of $O(n)$ for computing the sum of n integers.

Brent's Theorem

Brent's theorem is also a technique for reducing the number of processors needed to solve a particular problem. If an algorithm is designed so that a large number of processors are idle during much of the computation, then Brent's theorem may be of use. This theorem is summarized as follows.

Theorem 14.6: *Any synchronous parallel algorithm that runs in T time steps and consists of a total of N operations can be simulated by P processors in time that is*

$$O(\lfloor N/P \rfloor + T).$$

Proof: (Sketch) Let N_i be the number of operations performed at step i in the parallel algorithm. The P processors can simulate step i of the algorithm in $O(\lceil N_i/P \rceil)$ time. Thus, the total running time is $O(\lfloor N/P \rfloor + T)$, since

$$\begin{aligned}\sum_{i=1}^{T} \lceil N_i/P \rceil &\le \sum_{i=1}^{T} (\lfloor N_i/P \rfloor + 1) \\ &\le \lfloor N/P \rfloor + T.\end{aligned}$$

■

There are two qualifications we must make to Brent's theorem before we can apply it in the PRAM model, however. First, we must be able to compute N_i at the beginning of step i in $O(\lceil N_i/P \rceil)$ time using P processors. That is, we must know how many operations are actually to be performed in step i. And, second, we must know exactly how to assign each processor to its job. That is, we must be able to direct each processor to the $O(\lceil N_i \rceil / P)$ operations it is to perform in simulating step i.

As an example of an application of Brent's theorem, consider the summation problem again. Recall the divide-and-conquer summation algorithm presented above. Although the algorithm ran in $O(\log n)$ time and used $O(n)$ processors, it only performed $O(n)$ total operations. Thus, by applying Brent's theorem we have an alternate method for solving this problem in $O(\log n)$ time using $O(n/\log n)$ processors. The qualifications to Brent's theorem are easily solved in this case, since the number of operations performed in step i is exactly half the number performed in step $i-1$. More specifically, we will take $\lceil \log n \rceil$ time simulating the first step (when all n processors are active), $\lceil \log n/2 \rceil$ time simulating the second step, $\lceil \log n/4 \rceil$ time for the third, and so on. This clearly sums to $O(\log n)$, giving us an alternative method for summing n integers in $O(\log n)$ time using $O(n/\log n)$ processors.

14.2.4 Recursive Doubling

Recursive doubling is a technique that can be thought of as being a complement of the divide-and-conquer paradigm—whereas divide-and-conquer is a top-down technique, recursive doubling is a bottom-up technique. The main idea is that we start with small subsets, and iteratively combine them in pairs until we have solved the whole problem. We describe the recursive doubling technique with an example: ***list ranking***. In the list ranking problem we are given a linked list represented as an array of pointers resident in memory, and are asked to compute the distance from the tail of each element in the list. We discuss here the classic parallel algorithm for this problem. The main idea is to assign a processor to each element in the list, and at each time step set each element's pointer to the pointer of its successor. With each iteration, the distance that each element has "looked ahead" is doubled, hence, in at most $O(\log n)$ iterations, each element will be pointing at the tail. More specifically, let $p(v)$ denote the pointer from v, and let *tail* denote the node which is the tail of the list. Also store a label $r(v)$ with each node v, which is initially 1 for all nodes except the tail (whose r label is 0). This label will eventually store the rank of v in the list. In each time step one performs the following operation for each node v in parallel (see Figure 14.6):

if $p(v) \neq tail$ **then**
  $r(v) := r(p(v)) + r(v);$ { the ranking step }
  $p(v) := p(p(v));$ { the "doubling" step }.

Thus, we have the following:

Theorem 14.7: *We can find, for each node v in an n-node list L, the distance from v to the tail in $O(\log n)$ time using $O(n)$ processors in the CREW PRAM model.*

Note that the above $T(n) * P(n)$ product is a $\log n$ factor from optimal.

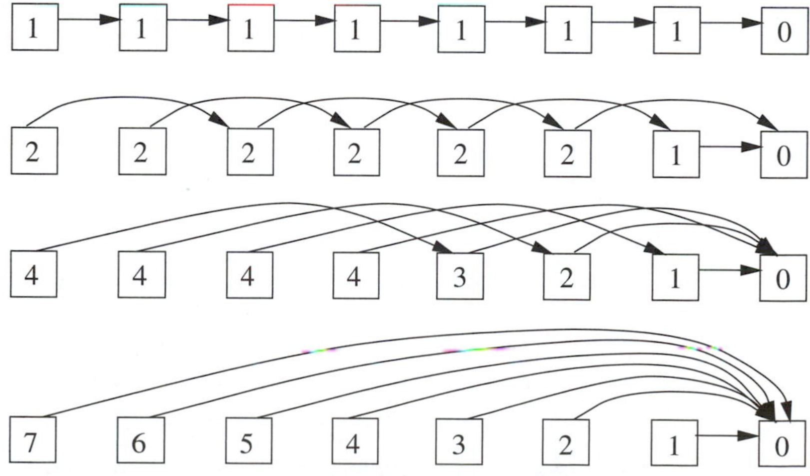

Figure 14.6: Recursive doubling applied to the list ranking problem.

Parallel Prefix

There is a related problem, the ***parallel prefix*** problem, which can also be solved by recursive doubling. We are given a list $A = (a_1, a_2, \ldots, a_n)$ of integers, and wish to compute all the prefix sums $s_k = \sum_{i=1}^{k} a_i$. Using the recursive doubling technique we can easily do this in $O(\log n)$ time using $O(n)$ processors (see Figure 14.7). The method is basically the same as that given above for list ranking.

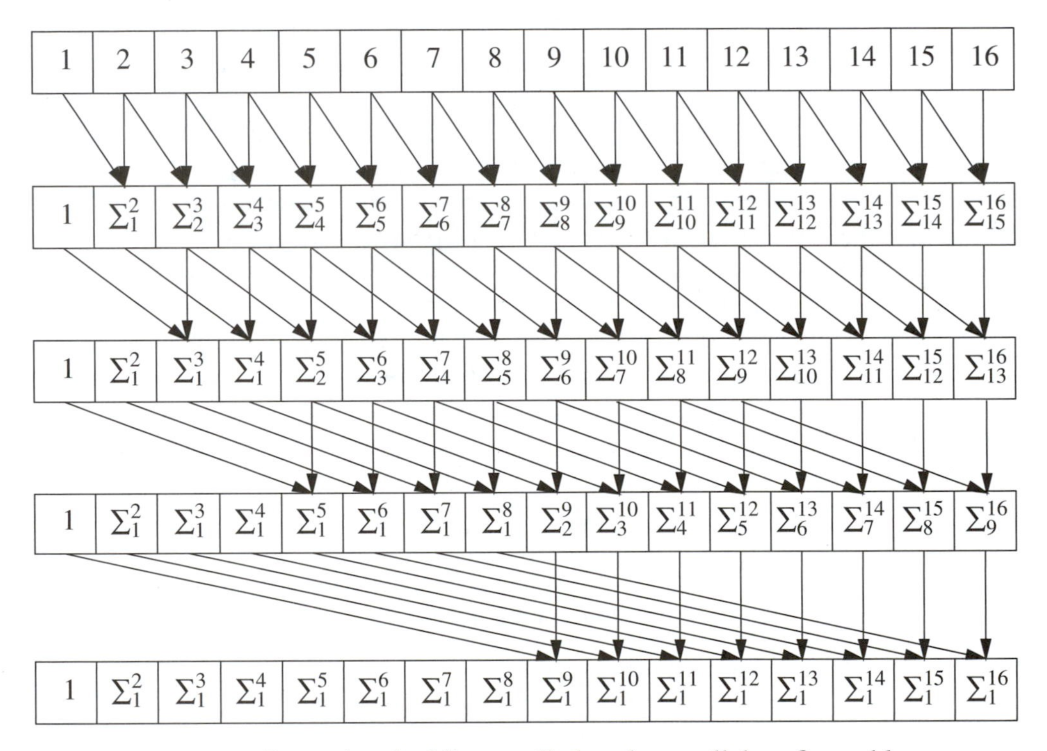

Figure 14.7: Recursive doubling applied to the parallel prefix problem.

Unlike the list ranking problem, we can easily make a fairly straightforward application of the sequential subsets technique to the parallel prefix problem. In this case, we can reduce the number of processors to $O(n/\log n)$ and still achieve an $O(\log n)$ running time, giving us an optimal $T(n) * P(n)$ product. The method for doing this is the following. Divide the array A into $n/\log n$ subarrays of size $\log n$ each and compute the sum of each subarray sequentially using a single processor. Then proceed with the prefix computation just as before, using these partial sums as the elements. After completing the prefix computation on these elements, we simply "backtrack" through each of the $n/\log n$ subarrays, one processor per subarray, to compute all the partial sums. (See Figure 14.8.)

The parallel prefix problem arises as a subproblem in a number of other list manipulation problems. We illustrate this with two examples.

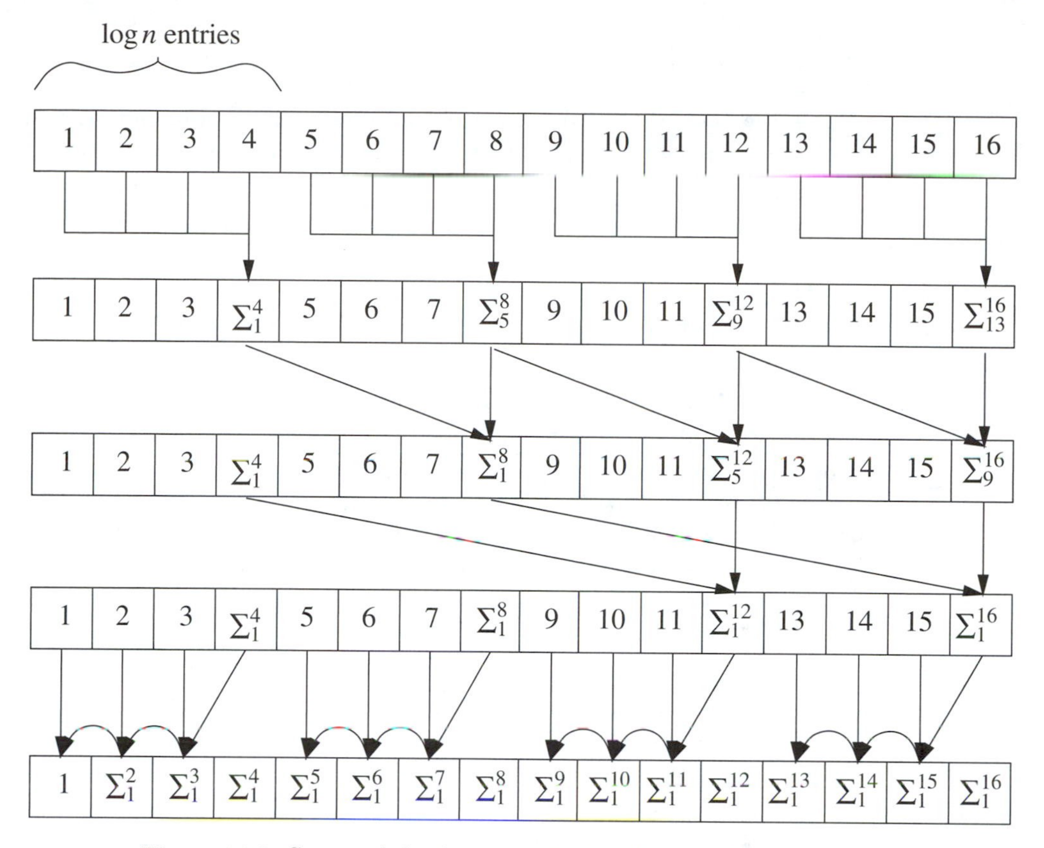

Figure 14.8: Sequential subsets applied to the parallel prefix problem.

First, consider the following array compression problem: given an n-element array A in which each element is flagged as being either "marked" or "unmarked," construct an array B listing the marked elements of A in order as they appear in A (that is, B is the marked subsequence of A). The method is to associate a value of 1 with each marked element and a value of 0 with each unmarked element. By performing a parallel prefix computation, we can determine the rank in the compressed list B for each marked element in A. It is then an easy operation to write each marked element in A to its appropriate position in B. This can clearly be done in $O(\log n)$ time using $O(n)$ processors.

Second, consider the ***array splitting*** problem: given an array A consisting of n integers, decompose A into subarrays A_1, A_2, ..., A_m, such that each A_i consists of repetitions of the same integer, which differs from the integer repeated in A_{i-1} and the one repeated in A_{i+1} (that is, $k \in A_i$ implies $k \notin A_{i-1}$ and $k \notin A_{i+1}$). This can be done by associating a value of 1 with each element in A and performing the combining step of the parallel prefix algorithm for each element as long as all the preceding elements are identical. This will give us the rank of each element a in its subarray. We could then perform another parallel prefix operation to determine which subarray, A_i, a belongs to (that is, determining the value of i).

14.2.5 Parallel Merging and Sorting

Merging two sorted lists or sorting n numbers are computations that are easy to perform efficiently in the sequential model but nontrivial to perform efficiently in parallel. There has been a considerable amount of work done on these two problems, with the most efficient merging algorithm being able to merge two sorted lists in $O(\log n)$ time using $n/\log n$ processors. The most efficient sorting algorithm can sort n numbers in $O(\log n)$ time using n processors. Moreover, some of these algorithms can even be made to run in the EREW PRAM model in these same asymptotic bounds.

Unfortunately, the most efficient parallel merging and sorting algorithms are too involved to describe in detail here. Let us instead describe a simple method for merging two sorted n-element lists A and B of distinct elements in $O(\log n)$ time using n processors in the CREW PRAM model. For any element x, define the ***rank*** of x in A or B as the number of elements in that list that are less than or equal to x. Our algorithm finds the rank in B of each item in A and the rank in A of each item in B. In particular, we assign a processor to each item in A and B, and perform a binary search to find where that item would go in the other list. This takes $O(\log n)$ time, since all the binary searches are performed in parallel. Once a processor, which is assigned to an item x in $A \cup B$, knows x's rank i in A and its rank j in B, then that processor can immediately write x to the location $i + j$ in the output merged array. Thus, we can merge A and B in $O(\log n)$ time using n processors.

Once we know how to quickly merge two sorted lists in parallel, we can use this as a subroutine in a parallel version of the merge sort algorithm. Specifically, to sort a set S, we divide S into two sets S_1 and S_2 of equal size and recursively sort each in parallel. Once we have S_1 and S_2 sorted, then we use the parallel merging algorithm to merge them into one sorted list. The total number of processors needed is n, since we assign to each subproblem a number of processors equal to its size. Likewise, the running time $T(n)$ of the algorithm is characterized by the recurrence equation, $T(n) = T(n/2) + b\log n$, for some constant b, which implies $T(n)$ is $O(\log^2 n)$. Thus, we have the following:

Theorem 14.8: *Given a set S of n items, we can sort S in $O(\log^2 n)$ time using n processors in the CREW PRAM model.*

Note that the above algorithm is an example of the simple parallel divide-and-conquer pattern. We explore in Exercise C-14.23 how to merge two sorted arrays in $O(\log n)$ time using $O(n/\log n)$ processors, which yields a work-optimal parallel sorting algorithm. As mentioned above, we can actually sort n items in $O(\log n)$ time using n processors in the EREW PRAM model by using a more sophisticated algorithm. Although we do not describe this algorithm here, we know this fact is useful for building other efficient parallel algorithms. We give an example of such an application in the next subsection, applying merging and sorting (and some of the other techniques presented above) to a geometric problem.

14.2.6 Finding the Diameter of a Convex Polygon

Consider the following problem: given a convex polygon P, find the farthest pair of points on P. This is the same as computing the ***diameter*** of P, that is, the distance between a farthest pair of points on P. It is easy to see that for any P there is a farthest pair of points which are both vertices of P. Thus, we can easily solve this problem in $O(\log n)$ time using $O(n^2)$ processors (using the simple divide-and-conquer technique to compute the maximum distance between all $O(n^2)$ pairs of vertices). We can do much better than this, however, by taking advantage of some of the geometric structure present in the problem and by using some of the techniques presented above. In this section, we present an algorithm DIAMETER to solve the diameter-finding problem in $O(\log n)$ time using $O(n/\log n)$ processors, which is optimal.

Note that any farthest pair of points p and q must be ***antipodal*** vertices of P. Points p and q are antipodal if there are two parallel lines L_1 and L_2 tangent to the polygon P such that L_1 contains p and L_2 contains q. This clearly restricts the number of pairs one must consider from $O(n^2)$ to $O(n)$, but there is still a problem with how we enumerate all the antipodal pairs of vertices efficiently in parallel. The cyclic ordering of the vertices around P determines a direction for each edge.

Treating each edge as a vector, translate this set of edge vectors to the origin. Any line through the origin of this vector diagram intersects two sectors which correspond to antipodal vertices. (See Figure 14.9.)

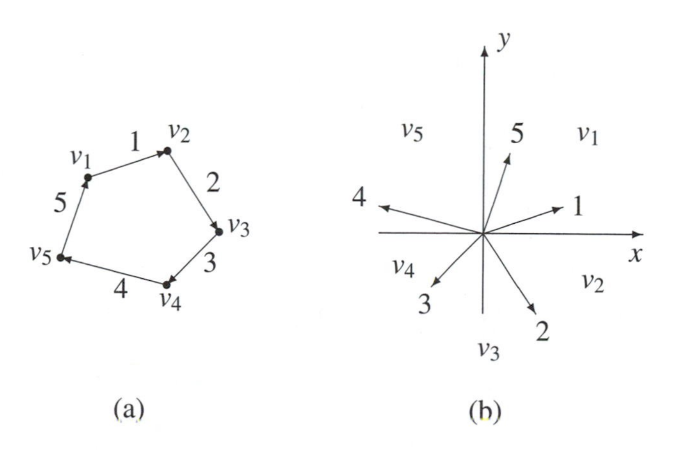

Figure 14.9: Treating edges as vectors, translate these edges to the origin. Note that vertices in the polygon (a) correspond to sectors in the vector diagram (b).

Since we wish to find all antipodal vertices in $O(\log n)$ time, we cannot use the method of rotating a line containing the origin through the set of vectors. Neither can we assign a processor to each region (corresponding to some vertex v) and then enumerate all other vertices which are antipodal to v by binary searches, for there can be $O(n)$ such vertices for any v, and, besides, we only have $O(n/\log n)$ processors at our disposal. Instead, we divide the set of vectors into two sets, divided by the x-axis, rotate all the vectors below the x-axis by 180°, and use a parallel merging procedure to enumerate all antipodal vertices. Then, by taking a maximum over the $O(n)$ pairs we find a farthest pair of vertices in P. (See Algorithm 14.10.)

Algorithm DIAMETER(P):
   Input: A convex polygon $P = (v_1, v_2, \ldots, v_n)$.
   Output: Two farthest points, p and q, in P.
1. Using the cyclic ordering of the vertices of P as determining a direction on each edge, and treating edges as vectors, translate the set of edge vectors to the origin.
2. Tag the vectors in the vector diagram that are above the x-axis "red" and the vectors below the x-axis "blue."
3. Rotate each blue vector by an angle of 180°.
   {The red vectors and blue vectors are now similarly ordered by angle.}
4. Use a fast parallel merging algorithm to merge these two sorted lists.
5. **for** each vector v **do**
      Use the sorted list to compute the two vectors of opposite color that precede v and succeed v in the merged list.
      Identify each such pair (a,b) as an antipodal pair.
6. Find the maximum of all the distances between antipodal vertices to find a farthest pair of vertices in P.

Algorithm 14.10: Algorithm for finding two farthest points in a convex polygon P.

Theorem 14.9: *Algorithm DIAMETER correctly finds a farthest pair of points in an n-vertex convex polygon P in $O(\log n)$ time using $O(n/\log n)$ processors in the CREW PRAM model.*

Proof: The correctness of the algorithm DIAMETER follows from the fact that in rotating the vectors below the x-axis by 180° all sectors which were opposite before (that is, both intersected by the same line through the origin) are now overlapping. We turn to the complexity bounds. Note that Steps 1, 2, 3, and 5 could be solved in $O(1)$ time if we were using $O(n)$ processors, since we are doing $O(1)$ work for each of $O(n)$ objects in each of these steps. Thus we can perform each of these steps in $O(\log n)$ time using $O(n/\log n)$ processors. We have already observed that Steps 4 and 6 can be done in $O(\log n)$ time using $O(n/\log n)$ processors (see Exercise C-14.23). ■

14.3 Online Algorithms

An ***online algorithm*** responds to a sequence of ***service requests***, each an associated ***cost***. For example, a web page replacement policy maintains pages in a cache, subject to a sequence of access requests, with the cost of a web page request being zero if the page is in the cache and one if the page is outside the cache. In an ***online*** setting, the algorithm must completely finish responding to a service request before it can receive the next request in the sequence. If an algorithm is given the entire sequence of service requests in advance, it is said to be an ***offline*** algorithm. To analyze an online algorithm we often employ a competitive analysis, where we compare a particular online algorithm A to an optimal offline algorithm, OPT. Given a particular sequence $P = (p_1, p_2, \ldots, p_n)$ of service requests, let $cost(A,P)$ denote the cost of A on P and let $cost(OPT,P)$ denote the cost of the optimal algorithm on P. The algorithm A is said to be ***c-competitive*** for P if

$$cost(A,P) \leq c \cdot cost(OPT,P) + b,$$

for some constant $b \geq 0$. If A is c-competitive for every sequence P, then we simply say that A is c-competitive, and we call c the ***competitive ratio*** of A. If $b = 0$, then we say that the algorithm A has a ***strict*** competitive ratio of c.

The Renter's Dilemma

A well-known online problem, best explained with a story, is the ***renter's dilemma***. Alice has decided to try out a music streaming service to listen to some songs by *The Streamin' Meemees*. Each time Alice streams a song, it costs her x dollars to "rent" the song, as her software does not allow for replays without paying again. Suppose it costs y dollars to buy all the songs on *The Streamin' Meemees* new album. Let us say, for the sake of the story, that y is 10 times larger than x, that is, $y = 10x$. The dilemma for Alice is to decide if and when she should buy the album instead of streaming songs one at a time. For example, if she buys before streaming any songs and then decides she doesn't like any, then she has spent 10 times more than she should. But if she streams many times and never buys the album, then she will spend potentially even more than 10 times more than she should. In fact, if she streams songs n times, then this strategy of always "renting" will cause her to spend $n/10$ times as many dollars as she should. That is, a strategy of buying the first time has a worst-case competitive ratio of 10 and the always-rent strategy has a worst-case competitive ratio of $n/10$. Neither of these choices is good.

Fortunately, Alice has a strategy with a competitive ratio of 2. Namely, she can rent for 10 times and then buy the album. The worst-case scenario is that she never listens to the album she just bought. So, she has spent $10x + y = 2y$ dollars, when she should have spent y; hence, this strategy has a competitive ratio of 2. In fact, no matter how much bigger y is than x, if Alice first rents for y/x times, and then buys, she will have a competitive ratio of 2.

14.3.1 Caching Algorithms

There are several web applications that must deal with revisiting information presented in web pages. These revisits have been shown to exhibit localities of reference, both in time and in space. To exploit these localities of reference, it is often advantageous to store copies of web pages in a ***cache*** memory, so these pages can be quickly retrieved when requested again. In particular, suppose we have a cache memory that has m "slots" that can contain web pages. We assume that a web page can be placed in any slot of the cache. This is known as a ***fully associative*** cache.

As a browser executes, it requests different web pages. Each time the browser requests such a web page l, the browser determines (using a quick test) if l is unchanged and currently contained in the cache. If l is contained in the cache, then the browser satisfies the request using the cached copy. If l is not in the cache, however, the page for l is requested over the Internet and transferred into the cache. If one of the m slots in the cache is available, then the browser assigns l to one of the empty slots. But if all the m cells of the cache are occupied, then the computer must determine which previously viewed web page to evict before bringing in l to take its place. There are, of course, many different policies that can be used to determine the page to evict. Some of the better-known page replacement policies include the following (see Figure 14.11):

- **First-in, First-out (FIFO)**: Evict the page that has been in the cache the longest, that is, the page that was transferred to the cache furthest in the past.
- **Least recently used (LRU)**: Evict the page whose last request occurred furthest in the past.

In addition, we can consider a simple and purely random strategy:

- **Random**: Choose a page at random to evict from the cache.

The Random strategy is one of the easiest policies to implement, for it only requires a random or pseudo-random number generator. The overhead involved in implementing this policy is an $O(1)$ additional amount of work per page replacement. Moreover, there is no additional overhead for each page request, other than to determine whether a page request is in the cache or not. Still, this policy makes no attempt to take advantage of any temporal or spatial localities that a user's browsing exhibits.

The FIFO strategy is quite simple to implement, as it only requires a queue Q to store references to the pages in the cache. Pages are enqueued in Q when they are referenced by a browser, and then are brought into the cache. When a page needs to be evicted, the computer simply performs a dequeue operation on Q to determine which page to evict. Thus, this policy also requires $O(1)$ additional work per page replacement. Also, the FIFO policy incurs no additional overhead for page requests. Moreover, it tries to take some advantage of temporal locality.

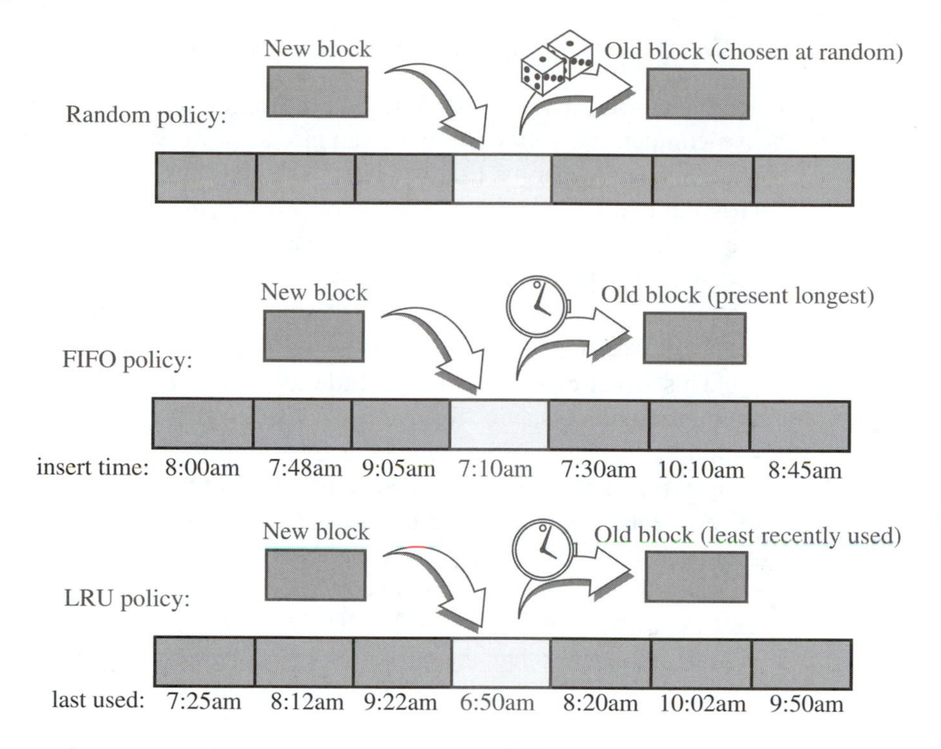

Figure 14.11: The Random, FIFO, and LRU page replacement policies.

The LRU strategy goes a step further than the FIFO strategy, which assumes that the page that has been in the cache the longest among all those present is the least likely to be requested in the near future. For the LRU strategy explicitly takes advantage of temporal locality as much as possible, by always evicting the page that was least-recently used. From a policy point of view, this is an excellent approach, but it is costly from an implementation point of view. That is, its way of optimizing temporal and spatial locality is fairly costly. Implementing the LRU strategy requires the use of a priority queue Q that supports searching for existing pages, for example, using special pointers or "locators." If Q is implemented with a sorted sequence based on a linked list, then the overhead for each page request and page replacement is $O(1)$. Whenever we insert a page in Q or update its key, the page is assigned the highest key in Q and is placed at the end of the list, which can also be done in $O(1)$ time. Even though the LRU strategy has constant-time overhead, using the above implementation, the constant factors involved, in terms of the additional time overhead and the extra space for the priority queue Q, make this policy less attractive from a practical point of view.

Since these different page replacement policies have different trade-offs between implementation difficulty and the degree to which they seem to take advantage of localities, it is natural for us to ask for some kind of comparative analysis of these methods to see which one, if any, is the best.

A Worst-Case Competitive Analysis of FIFO and LRU

From a worst-case point of view, the FIFO and LRU strategies have fairly unattractive competitive behavior. For example, suppose we have a cache containing m pages, and consider the FIFO and LRU methods performing page replacement for a program that has a loop that repeatedly requests $m+1$ pages in a cyclic order. Both the FIFO and LRU policies perform badly on such a sequence of page requests, because they perform a page replacement on every page request. Thus, from a worst-case point of view, these policies are almost the worst we can imagine—they require a page replacement on every page request.

This worst-case analysis is a little too pessimistic, however, for it focuses on each protocol's behavior for one bad sequence of page requests. An ideal analysis would be to compare these methods over all possible page-request sequences. Of course, this is impossible to do exhaustively, but there have been a great number of experimental simulations done on page-request sequences derived from real programs. The experiments have focused primarily on the Random, FIFO, and LRU policies. Based on these experimental comparisons, the ordering of policies, from best to worst, is as follows: (1) LRU, (2) FIFO, and (3) Random. In fact, LRU is significantly better than the others on typical request sequences, but it still has poor performance in the worst case, as the following theorem shows.

Theorem 14.10: *The FIFO and LRU page replacement policies for a cache with m pages have competitive ratio at least m.*

Proof: We observed above that there is a sequence $P = (p_1, p_2, \ldots, p_n)$ of web page requests causing FIFO and LRU to perform a page replacement with each request—the loop of $m+1$ requests. We compare this performance with that of the optimal offline algorithm, *OPT*, which, in the case of the page replacement problem, is to evict from the cache the page that is requested the furthest into the future. This strategy can only be implemented, of course, in the offline case, when we are given the entire sequence P in advance, unless the algorithm is "prophetic." When applied to the loop sequence, the *OPT* policy will perform a page replacement once every m requests (for it evicts the most recently referenced page each time, as this one is referenced furthest in the future). Thus, both FIFO and LRU are c-competitive on this sequence P, where

$$c = \frac{n}{n/m} = m.$$

Observe that if any portion $P' = (p_i, p_{i+1}, \ldots, p_j)$ of P makes requests to m different pages (with p_{i-1} and/or p_{j+1} not being one of them), then even the optimal algorithm must evict one page. In addition, the most number of pages the FIFO and LRU policies evict for such a portion P' is m, each time evicting a page that was referenced prior to p_i. Therefore, FIFO and LRU have a competitive ratio of m, and this is the best possible competitive ratio for these strategies in the worst case. ■

The Randomized Marker Algorithm

Even though the deterministic FIFO and LRU policies can have poor worst-case competitive ratios compared to the "prophetic" optimal algorithm, we can show that a randomized policy that attempts to simulate LRU has a good competitive ratio. Specifically, let us study the competitive ratio of a randomized strategy that tries to emulate the LRU policy. From a strategic viewpoint, this policy, which is known as the ***Marker strategy***, emulates the best aspects of the deterministic LRU policy, while using randomization to avoid the worst-case situations that are bad for the LRU strategy. The policy for Marker is as follows:

- **Marker**: Associate, with each page in the cache, a Boolean variable "marked," which is initially set to "false" for every page in the cache. If a browser requests a page that is already in the cache, that page's marked variable is set to "true." Otherwise, if a browser requests a page that is not in the cache, a random page whose marked variable is "false" is evicted and replaced with the new page, whose marked variable is immediately set to "true." If all the pages in the cache have marked variables set to "true," then all of them are reset to "false." (See Figure 14.12.)

Competitive Analysis for a Randomized Online Algorithm

Armed with the above policy definition, we would now like to perform a competitive analysis of the Marker strategy. Before we can do this analysis, however, we must first define what we mean by the competitive ratio of a randomized online algorithm. Since a randomized algorithm A, like the Marker policy, can have many different possible runs, depending upon the random choices it makes, we define such an algorithm to be ***c-competitive*** for a sequence of requests P if

$$E(cost(A,P)) \leq c \cdot cost(OPT,P) + b,$$

for some constant $b \geq 0$, where $E(cost(A,P))$ denotes the expected cost of algorithm A on the sequence P (with this expectation taken over all possible random choices for the algorithm A). If A is c-competitive for every sequence P, then we simply say that A is c-competitive, and we call c the ***competitive ratio*** for A.

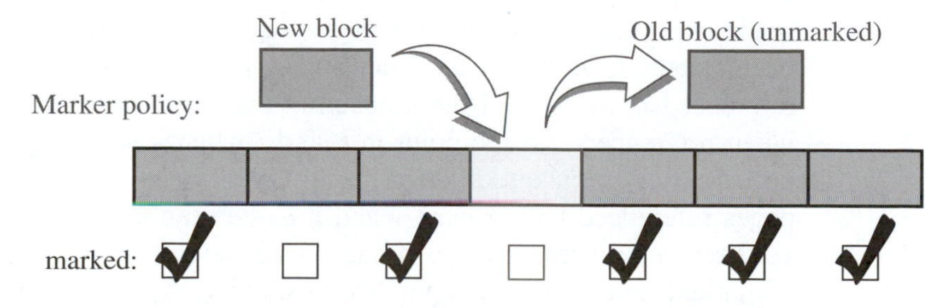

Figure 14.12: The Marker page replacement policy.

Theorem 14.11: *The Marker page policy for a cache with m pages has competitive ratio $2\log m$.*

Proof: Let $P = (p_1, p_2, \ldots, p_n)$ be a sufficiently long sequence of page requests. The Marker policy implicitly partitions the requests in P into ***rounds***. Each round begins with all the pages in the cache having "false" marked labels, and a round ends when all the pages in the cache have "true" marked labels (with the next request beginning the next round, since the policy then resets each such label to "false"). Consider the ith round in P, and call a page requested in round i ***fresh*** if it is not in the Marker policy's cache at the beginning of round i. Also, we refer to a page in the Marker's cache that has a false marked label ***stale***. Thus, at the beginning of a round i, all the pages in the Marker policy's cache are stale. Let m_i denote the number of fresh pages referenced in the ith round, and let b_i denote the number of pages that are in the cache for the OPT algorithm at the beginning of round i and are not in the cache for the Marker policy at this time. Since the Marker policy has to perform a page replacement for each of the m_i requests, algorithm OPT must perform at least $m_i - b_i$ page replacements in round i. (See Figure 14.13.) In addition, since each of the pages in the Marker policy's cache at the end of round i are requested in round i, algorithm OPT must perform at least b_{i+1} page replacements in round i. Thus, the algorithm OPT must perform at least

$$\max\{m_i - b_i, b_{i+1}\} \geq \frac{m_i - b_i + b_{i+1}}{2}$$

page replacements in round i. Summing over all k rounds in P then, we see that algorithm OPT must perform at least the following number of page replacements:

$$L = \sum_{i=1}^{k} \frac{m_i - b_i + b_{i+1}}{2} = (b_{k+1} - b_1)/2 + \frac{1}{2}\sum_{i=1}^{k} m_i.$$

Next, let us consider the expected number of page replacements performed by the Marker policy.

We have already observed that the Marker policy has to perform at least m_i page replacements in round i. It may actually perform more than this, however, if it evicts stale pages that are then requested later in the round. Thus, the expected number of page replacements performed by the Marker policy is $m_i + n_i$, where n_i is the expected number of stale pages that are referenced in round i after having been evicted from the cache. The value n_i is equal to the sum, over all stale pages referenced in round i, of the probability that these pages are outside of the cache when referenced. At the point in round i when a stale page v is referenced, the probability that v is out of the cache is at most f/g, where f is the number of fresh pages referenced before page v and g is the number of stale pages that have not yet been referenced. This is because each reference to a fresh page evicts some unmarked stale page at random. The cost to the Marker policy will be highest then, if all m_i requests to fresh pages are made before any requests to stale pages. So, assuming this worst-case viewpoint, the expected number of evicted stale pages

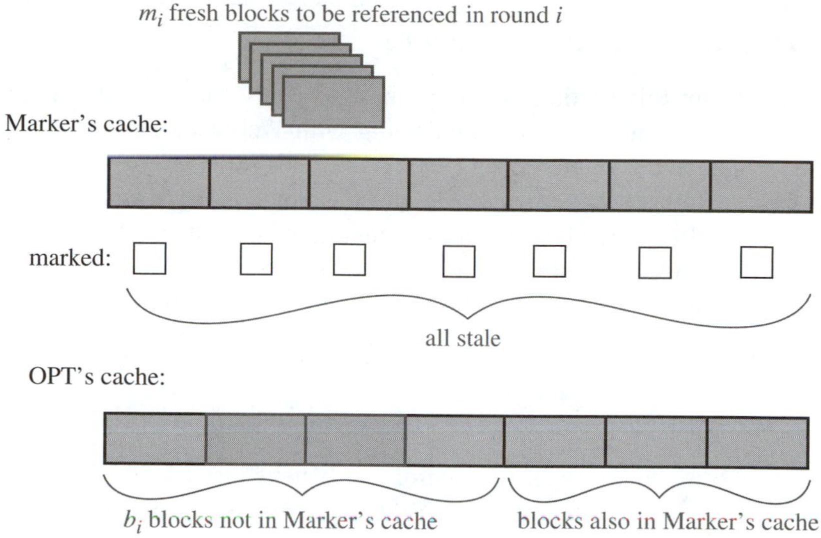

m_i fresh blocks to be referenced in round i

Marker's cache:

marked:

all stale

OPT's cache:

b_i blocks not in Marker's cache

blocks also in Marker's cache

Figure 14.13: The state of Marker's cache and OPT's cache at the beginning of round i.

referenced in round i can be bounded as follows:

$$\begin{aligned} n_i &\leq \frac{m_i}{m} + \frac{m_i}{m-1} + \frac{m_i}{m-2} + \cdots + \frac{m_i}{m_i+1} \\ &\leq m_i \sum_{j=1}^{m} \frac{1}{j}, \end{aligned}$$

since there are $m - m_i$ references to stale pages in round i. Noting that this summation is known as the mth harmonic number, which is denoted H_m, we have

$$n_i \leq m_i H_m.$$

Thus, the expected number of page replacements performed by the Marker policy is at most

$$U = \sum_{i=1}^{k} m_i(H_m + 1) = (H_m + 1) \sum_{i=1}^{k} m_i.$$

Therefore, the competitive ratio for the Marker policy is at most

$$\begin{aligned} \frac{U}{L} &= \frac{(H_m+1)\sum_{i=1}^{k} m_i}{(1/2)\sum_{i=1}^{k} m_i} \\ &= 2(H_m+1). \end{aligned}$$

Using an approximation for H_m, namely that $H_m \leq \log m$, the competitive ratio for the Marker policy is at most $2\log m$. ■

Thus, the competitive analysis shows that the Marker policy is fairly efficient.

14.3.2 Auction Strategies

In this section, we show how to apply the competitive analysis to some simple algorithmic problems dealing with Web auctions. The general setting is that we have a single object, like an antique, work of art, or piece of jewelry, that has an integer value between 1 and B dollars, that we wish to sell at a Web auction. At this particular auction, we must provide an algorithm A in advance that will accept bids one-at-a-time, in an online fashion, such that A will accept or reject the current bid before it is shown the next (if there is a next bid, of course). Our goal is to maximize the amount that A will accept for our precious object.

Competitive Analysis for a Maximization Problem

Since we wish to maximize a benefit instead of minimizing a cost in this problem, we need to slightly redefine what we mean by a c-competitive algorithm. In particular, we say that a maximization algorithm is c-competitive if

$$cost(A,P) \geq cost(OPT,P)/c + b,$$

for some constant $b \geq 0$. As with the minimization case, if $b = 0$, then we say the maximization algorithm is strictly c-competitive.

If we don't know how many bids to accept, however, then a deterministic algorithm hasn't much choice but to accept the first bid, since it might be the only one. But, for the sake of the competitive analysis, if we compare this strategy against an adversary that knows the bids to expect, then we must have a competitive ratio that is B. This poor competitive ratio is due to the fact that $P_1 = (1,B)$ and $P_2 = (1)$ are both valid bid sequences. Since we don't know whether to expect P_1 or P_2, we must take the 1 dollar bid as soon as we see it, whereas an adversary knowing the sequence is P_1 will wait for the bid of B dollars. If we know the number, n, of bids to expect, however, we can do better.

Theorem 14.12: *If the number of bids, n, is known, then there is a deterministic algorithm for the auctioning problem with a competitive ratio that is $O(\sqrt{B})$.*

Proof: The algorithm to achieve this competitive ratio is quite simple: accept the first bid over $\lfloor\sqrt{B}\rfloor$. If no such bid materializes, then accept the last bid. To analyze the competitive ratio, there are two cases.

1. Suppose no bid over $\lfloor\sqrt{B}\rfloor$ is given. Let m be the maximum bid given. Then, in the worst case we may accept a bid for 1 dollar while the offline algorithm accepts the bid for m. Thus, we achieve a competitive ratio of $m \leq \lfloor\sqrt{B}\rfloor$.
2. Suppose a bid over $\lfloor\sqrt{B}\rfloor$ is given. Let m be the maximum bid given. Then, in the worst case we may accept a bid for $\lfloor\sqrt{B}\rfloor + 1$ while the offline algorithm accepts the bid for m. Thus, we achieve a competitive ratio of $m/(\lfloor\sqrt{B}\rfloor + 1)$. This value is, of course, less than $\sqrt{B}$. ■

This competitive ratio is admittedly not very good, but it is, nevertheless, the best possible for a deterministic algorithm.

Theorem 14.13: *If the number of bids, n, is known, then no deterministic algorithm for the auctioning problem can have a competitive ratio better than $\Omega(\sqrt{B})$.*

Proof: Let A be a deterministic algorithm for the auctioning problem, and let $b = \lfloor \sqrt{B} \rfloor$. Consider the behavior of A on the sequence $P = (b, B)$, which is given online. There are two cases.

1. If A accepts b, then the adversary clearly can achieve the bid of B; hence, the competitive ratio is $\Omega(\sqrt{B})$ in this case.
2. Suppose A does not accept b in P. Since A is online, at the point it rejects the bid b it cannot distinguish if it is given the sequence P or the sequence $Q = (b, 1)$ instead. Thus, we can consider A's behavior on Q. Since A doesn't know the next bid it will receive at the point it must decide on b, then A will be forced to accept the bid 1 in this case. Thus, in this case, A's competitive ratio is b, which is $\Omega(\sqrt{B})$.

■

Thus, a deterministic algorithm cannot achieve a very good competitive ratio for the auctioning problem.

Randomized Thresholding

Let us consider using a randomized algorithm for the auctioning problem. In this case, we can achieve a much improved competitive ratio, even when the algorithm does not know the number of bids to expect in advance, by using a ***randomized thresholding*** technique. The idea is as follows.

The algorithm A picks an integer i at random from the set $\{0, 1, 2, \ldots, \log B\}$ and accepts the first bid it receives that is greater than or equal to 2^i. As the following theorem shows, this randomized thresholding algorithm achieves a competitive ratio of $O(\log B)$.

Theorem 14.14: *The randomized thresholding algorithm achieves a competitive ratio that is $O(\log B)$.*

Proof: Let P be a given sequence of bids and let m be the largest bid in P. Then the offline algorithm achieves a bid of m. Recall that the competitive ratio of a randomized algorithm is based on its expected cost, which, in the case of the auctioning problem, should be viewed as a "benefit" since we are trying to maximize the accepted bid. The expected value of the bid accepted by A is at least $m/(1 + \log B)$, since A will accept m with probability $1/(1 + \log B)$. Therefore, the competitive ratio for A is at most $1 + \log B$. ■

In the next subsection, we show how the competitive analysis can be applied to data structure design.

14.3.3 Competitive Search Trees

In this subsection, we present a simple adaptive tree-based dictionary structure that is balanced and competitive. Our approach is based on a ***potential energy*** parameter stored at each node in the tree. As updates and queries are performed, the potential energies of tree nodes are increased or decreased. Whenever the potential energy of a node reaches a ***threshold*** level, we rebuild the subtree rooted at that node. We show that, in spite of its simplicity, such a scheme is competitive.

Energy-Balanced Binary Search Trees

Recall that a ***dictionary*** holds pairs of ordered keys and elements, subject to update and query operations. A common way of implementing the dictionary ADT is to use a balanced binary search tree, which maintains balance by local rotation operations. Typically, such rotations are fast, but if the tree has auxiliary structures, rotations are often slow. We describe a simple tree structure that achieves balance without rotations, by using a potential energy parameter stored at each node and partial rebuilding. Our approach does not use any explicit balancing rules. Instead, it uses potential labels on the nodes, which allow it to be adaptive, competitive, and arguably simpler than previous approaches.

An ***energy-balanced tree*** is a binary search tree T in which each node v stores an element e such that all elements in v's left subtree are less than or equal to e and all elements in v's right subtree are greater than or equal to e. Each node v in T maintains a parameter n_v, which is the number of elements stored in the subtree rooted at v (including v). More importantly, each node v in T also maintains a potential energy parameter, p_v. Insertions and removals are handled as in standard (unbalanced) binary search trees, with one small modification. Every time we perform an update operation, which traverses a path from the root of T to some node w in T, we increment p_v by 1 for each node v in this path. If there is no node v in this path such that $p_v \geq n_v/2$, then we are done. Otherwise, let v be the highest node in T such that $p_v \geq n_v/2$. We rebuild the subtree rooted at v as a complete binary tree, and we zero out the potential fields of each node in this subtree (including v itself). This is the entire algorithm for performing updates.

This simple strategy immediately implies the following.

Theorem 14.15: *The worst-case height of the energy-balanced tree is $O(\log n)$, and the amortized time for performing updates in such a tree is $O(\log n)$.*

Proof: It is enough to show that $n_w < n_v/4$, for any node v with sibling w. So suppose not. Then, since the last rebalance at v and w's parent, z, (when the size of v and w's subtrees were equal) the number of removals in w's subtree plus the number of insertions in v's subtree must have been at least $3n_v/4$. That is, $p_z \geq 3n_v/4$. At this point in time, $n_z = n_w + n_v < 5n_v/4$. Hence, $p_z \geq 3n_v/4 > (3/5)n_z$. But this cannot occur, since we would have rebuilt the subtree at z as soon as $p_z > n_z/2$.

The above fact immediately implies that the height of the search tree T is $O(\log n)$; hence, the worst-case time for any search is $O(\log n)$. Moreover, each time a rebuilding computation is performed to rebuild the subtree rooted at a node v, $p_v \geq n_v/2$. That is, p_v is $O(n_v)$. Since it takes $O(n_v)$ time to rebuild the subtree rooted at v, this fact implies that we can charge the p_v previous operations that deposited "energy" at the node v for this rebuilding computation. Since the depth of the energy balanced tree is $O(\log n)$ and any update operation will deposit energy in a root-to-leaf path, this fact in turn implies that each update operation will be charged at most $O(\log n)$ times for rebuilding computations. Thus, the amortized time needed to perform update operations in an energy-balanced search tree is also $O(\log n)$. ■

Biased Energy-Balanced Search Trees

Our potential energy approach can be further extended to adapt a dictionary to biased distributions of accesses and updates. We augment the tree T in this case so that each node v stores an ***access count***, a_v, which counts the number of times that the element stored at v has been accessed. Each time a node is accessed in a search we increment its access count. We also now increment the potential energy parameter of each node on the path from v to the root. We keep the insertion algorithm the same, but now, whenever we remove a node v, we increment the potential energy of each node on the path from v to the root by a_v. Let A_v denote the cumulative access counts for all nodes in the subtree rooted at v in T. We do a rebuilding step any time the potential energy of a node rises to be more than a quarter of its access value, that is, when $p_v \geq A_v/4$. In this adapted binary search tree, we rebuild the subtree so that nodes are nearly balanced by their access counts, that is, we try to balance children by their A_v values. Specifically, there is a linear-time tree-building algorithm (see Exercise C-3.25) that can guarantee that for any node v with parent z, $A_z \geq 3A_v/2$. For any nonroot node v, we use $\hat{A}_v$ to denote the size of the subtree rooted at v plus the weight of the item stored at v's parent z (so $A_z = A_v + \hat{A}_w$, where w denotes v's sibling).

Lemma 14.16: *For any node v with sibling w, $\hat{A}_w \geq A_v/8$.*

Proof: Suppose, for the sake of proving a contradiction, that $\hat{A}_w < A_v/8$. Then, since the last rebalance at v and w's parent, z, (when $\hat{A}'_w \geq A'_v/2$, where $\hat{A}'_w$ and A'_v denote the old values of $\hat{A}_w$ and A_v respectively) the total weight of removals in w's subtree plus the number of insertions and accesses in v's subtree, plus accesses ending at v's parent, must have been at least $3A_v/8$. That is, $p_z \geq 3A_v/8$. At this point in time, $A_z = \hat{A}_w + A_v < 9A_v/8$. Hence, $p_z \geq 3A_v/8 > A_z/3$. But this cannot occur, since we would have rebuilt the subtree at z as soon as $p_z > A_z/4$. ■

The implication of the above fact is that an element having current access frequency a is stored at a node at depth $O(\log A/a)$ in the search tree, where A is the current total access frequency of all nodes in the tree, as the following theorem shows. This lemma immediately implies the following.

Theorem 14.17: *An element having current access frequency a is stored at depth $O(\log A/a)$, where A is the current total access frequency of all nodes.*

Proof: By the previous lemma, the total access count for the subtree root at a node v is at least a constant factor larger than the total access counts for v's children. Thus, the depth of any node v in the tree is at most $O(\log A/a_v)$. ■

Before we analyze our biased energy-balanced tree, we first establish the following technical lemma. This lemma is used to analyze the time needed to process the operations in a subsequence S_v, of the entire operation sequence S, formed by all operations that access or update the element at a given node v.

Lemma 14.18: *Let A_i denote the total access counts of all nodes present in the dynamic biased energy-balanced tree (for S) after we perform the ith operation in S_v. Then*

$$\sum_{i=1}^{m} \log A_i/i$$

is

$$O(m \log \hat{A}/m),$$

where $m = |S_v|$ and $\hat{A}$ is the total access counts for all elements referenced in S.

Proof: Let us assume for the sake of analysis that m is a power of 2, that is, that $m = 2^k$, for some k. Note that

$$\begin{aligned} \sum_{i=1}^{m} \log \frac{A_i}{i} &\le \sum_{i=1}^{m} \log \frac{\hat{A}}{i} = \sum_{i=1}^{m} \log \left(\frac{\hat{A}}{m}\right)\left(\frac{m}{i}\right) \\ &= \sum_{i=1}^{m} \log \frac{\hat{A}}{m} + \sum_{i=1}^{m} \log \frac{m}{i} = m \log \frac{\hat{A}}{m} + \sum_{i=1}^{m} \log \frac{m}{i}. \end{aligned}$$

Thus, to establish the lemma we need only bound the the last term above (the summation term). Note that

$$\begin{aligned} \sum_{i=1}^{m} \log \frac{m}{i} &= \sum_{i=1}^{2^k} \log \frac{2^k}{i} \le \sum_{i=1}^{2^k} \log \frac{2^k}{2^{\lfloor \log i \rfloor}} = \sum_{i=1}^{2^k} k - \lfloor \log i \rfloor \\ &\le \sum_{j=1}^{k} j 2^{k-j} = 2^k \sum_{j=1}^{k} \frac{j}{2^j} \le 2 \cdot 2^k = 2m. \end{aligned}$$

■

The above lemma is needed to relate the access counts seen so far in a sequence of updates and accesses to the access counts for the entire sequence. An oracle, which we call the ***biased-tree oracle***, knowing the sequence in advance could construct a static tree based on known access counts, so that the running time for each access or update at a node v is $O(\log \hat{A}/\hat{a}_v)$, where $\hat{a}_v$ denotes the total access count for the element at node v.

Theorem 14.19: *The energy-balanced search tree achieves amortized performance for update operations at each node v that is $O(\log \hat{A}/\hat{a}_v)$, which is within a constant factor of the performance achievable by the biased-tree oracle.*

Proof: Let S be a sequence of n dictionary operations and let T be the static tree built by the biased-tree oracle. Consider a subsequence S_v of S formed by all operations that access or update the element at a given node v. Let A_i denote the total access counts of all nodes present in the dynamic adaptable energy-balanced tree (for S) after we perform the ith operation in S_v. Note that the amortized running time for performing the ith operation in S_v using the energy-balanced tree is proportional to the future depth of v in the energy-balanced tree, which will be at most $O(\log A_i/i)$. Thus, the amortized time required for our performing all operations in S_v is proportional to at most

$$\sum_{i=1}^{m} \log A_i/i,$$

whereas the total time required of the implementation of the biased-tree oracle is proportional to

$$m \log \hat{A}/\hat{a}_v = m \log \hat{A}/m,$$

where $m = |S_v|$. However, by Lemma 14.18

$$\sum_{i=1}^{m} \log A_i/i$$

is

$$O(m \log \hat{A}/m),$$

which implies that the time performance of the energy-balanced approach on S_v is at most a constant factor more than the time performance achievable by the biased-tree oracle. Therefore, a similar claim holds for the processing of all of S. ■

Thus, in spite of their simplicity, biased energy-balanced search trees are efficient and competitive.

14.4 Exercises

Reinforcement

R-14.1 Describe, in detail, the insertion and removal algorithms for an (a,b) tree.

R-14.2 Suppose T is a multi-way tree in which each internal node has at least five and at most eight children. For what values of a and b is T a valid (a,b) tree?

R-14.3 For what values of d is the tree T of the previous exercise an order-d B-tree?

R-14.4 Draw the order-7 B-tree resulting from inserting the following keys (in this order) into an initially empty tree T:

$$(4,40,23,50,11,34,62,78,66,22,90,59,25,72,64,77,39,12).$$

R-14.5 Show each level of recursion in performing a four-way, external-memory merge-sort of the sequence given in the previous exercise.

R-14.6 Consider the generalization of the renter's dilemma where Alice can buy or rent her skis separate from her boots. Say that renting skis costs a dollars, whereas buying skis costs b dollars. Likewise, say that renting boots costs c dollars, whereas buying boots costs b dollars. Describe a 2-competitive online algorithm for Alice to try to minimize the costs for going skiing subject to the uncertainty of her not knowing how many times she will continue to go skiing in the future.

R-14.7 Consider an initially empty memory cache consisting of four pages. How many page misses does the LRU algorithm incur on the following page request sequence: $(2,3,4,1,2,5,1,3,5,4,1,2,3)$?

R-14.8 Consider an initially empty memory cache consisting of four pages. How many page misses does the FIFO algorithm incur on the following page request sequence: $(2,3,4,1,2,5,1,3,5,4,1,2,3)$?

R-14.9 Consider an initially empty memory cache consisting of four pages. How many page misses does the marker algorithm incur on the following page request sequence: $(2,3,4,1,2,5,1,3,5,4,1,2,3)$? Show the random choices your algorithm made.

R-14.10 Consider an initially empty memory cache consisting of four pages. Construct a sequence of memory requests that would cause the marker algorithm to go through four rounds.

R-14.11 Show how a recursive-doubling parallel algorithm would compute the parallel prefixes of the sequence $(1,4,20,12,7,15,32,10,9,18,11,45,22,50,5,16)$.

Creativity

C-14.1 Show how to implement a dictionary in external memory, using an unordered sequence so that updates require only $O(1)$ transfers and updates require $O(n/B)$ transfers in the worst case, where n is the number of elements and B is the number of list nodes that can fit into a disk block.

C-14.2 Change the rules that define red-black trees so that each red-black tree T has a corresponding $(4,8)$ tree, and vice versa.

C-14.3 Describe a modified version of the B-tree insertion algorithm so that each time we create an overflow because of a split of a node v, we redistribute keys among all of v's siblings such that each sibling holds roughly the same number of keys (possibly cascading the split up to the parent of v). What is the minimum fraction of each block that will always be filled using this scheme?

C-14.4 Another possible external-memory dictionary implementation is to use a skip list, but to collect consecutive groups of $O(B)$ nodes, in individual blocks, on any level in the skip list. In particular, we define an ***order-d B-skip list*** to be such a representation of a skip-list structure, where each block contains at least $\lceil d/2 \rceil$ list nodes and at most d list nodes. Let us also choose d in this case to be the maximum number of list nodes from a level of a skip list that can fit into one block. Describe how we should modify the skip-list insertion and removal algorithms for a B-skip list so that the expected height of the structure is $O(\log n / \log B)$.

C-14.5 Suppose that instead of having the node-search function $f(d) = 1$ in an order-d B-tree T, we instead have $f(d) = \log d$. What does the asymptotic running time of performing a search in T now become?

C-14.6 Describe how to use a B-tree to implement the queue ADT so that the total number of disk transfers needed to process a sequence of n enqueue and dequeue operations is $O(n/B)$.

C-14.7 Describe how to use a B-tree to implement the partition (union-find) ADT (from Section 4.2.2) so that the union and find operations each use at most $O(\log n / \log B)$ disk transfers.

C-14.8 Suppose we are given a sequence S of n elements with integer keys such that some elements in S are colored "blue" and some elements in S are colored "red." In addition, say that a red element e ***pairs*** with a blue element f if they have the same key value. Describe an efficient external-memory algorithm for finding all the red-blue pairs in S. How many disk transfers does your algorithm perform?

C-14.9 Consider the page caching problem where the memory cache can hold m pages, and we are given a sequence P of n requests taken from a pool of $m+1$ possible pages. Describe the optimal strategy for the offline algorithm and show that it causes at most $m + n/m$ page misses in total, starting from an empty cache.

C-14.10 Consider the page caching strategy based on the ***least frequently used*** (LFU) rule, where the page in the cache that has been accessed the least often is the one that is evicted when a new page is requested. If there are ties, LFU evicts the least frequently used page that has been in the cache the longest. Show that there is a sequence P of n requests that causes LFU to miss $\Omega(n)$ times for a cache of m pages, whereas the optimal algorithm will miss only m times.

C-14.11 Show that LRU is m-competitive for any sequence of n page requests, where m is the size of the memory cache.

C-14.12 Show that FIFO is m-competitive for any sequence of n page requests, where m is the size of the memory cache.

C-14.13 What is the expected number of block replacements performed by the Random policy on a cache of size m, for an access sequence of length n, that iteratively accesses $m+1$ blocks in a cyclic fashion (assuming n is much larger than m)?

C-14.14 Show that the Marker algorithm is H_m-competitive when the size of the cache is m and there are $m+1$ possible pages that can be accessed, where m denotes the mth Harmonic number.

C-14.15 Show how to merge two sorted n-element arrays A and B of distinct elements in $O(\log n)$ time using $O(n/\log n)$ processors in the CREW PRAM model.

C-14.16 Show how an EREW PRAM E with p processors can simulate any CREW PRAM C with p processors so that each parallel step on C can be simulated in $O(\log p)$ time on E.

C-14.17 Describe a parallel algorithm for multiplying two $n \times n$ matrices in $O(\log^2 n)$ time using n^3 processors.

C-14.18 Describe a parallel algorithm for the CRCW PRAM model that computes the AND of n bits in $O(1)$ time using n processors.

C-14.19 Describe a parallel algorithm for the CRCW PRAM model that computes the maximum of n numbers in $O(1)$ time using $O(n^2)$ processors.

C-14.20★ Describe a parallel algorithm for the CRCW PRAM model that computes the maximum of n numbers in $O(\log\log n)$ time using $O(n)$ processors.

Hint: Apply parallel divide-and-conquer where you first divide the set of numbers into $\sqrt{n}$ groups of size $\sqrt{n}$ each.

C-14.21 Describe a parallel algorithm for the CREW PRAM that can sort a sequence S of n integers in the range $[1,c]$, for some constant $c > 1$, in $O(\log n)$ time using $O(n/\log n)$ processors.

C-14.22 Describe a parallel algorithm for the CREW PRAM that computes in $O(\log n)$ time with n processors the convex hull of a set of n points in the plane (see Chapter 12) that are stored in an array in sorted order by their x-coordinates (you may assume points have distinct x-coordinates).

C-14.23 Let A and B be two sorted arrays of n integers each. Describe a method for merging A and B into a single sorted array C in $O(\log n)$ time using $O(n/\log n)$ processors in the CREW PRAM.

Hint: Start out by assigning a processor to every $\lceil \log n \rceil$-th cell in A (respectively, B) and performing a binary search for this item in the other array.

Projects

P-14.1 Write a class that implements all the methods of a dictionary given in Section 2.5 by means of an (a,b) tree, where a and b are integer constants.

P-14.2 Implement the B-tree data structure, assuming that the block size is 1,000 and that keys are integers. Test the number of "disk transfers" needed to process a sequence of dictionary operations.

Chapter Notes

Knuth [119] has very nice discussions about external-memory sorting and searching, and Ullman [203] discusses external memory structures for database systems. The reader interested in the study of the architecture of hierarchical memory systems is referred to the book chapter by Burger *et al.* [43] or the book by Hennessy and Patterson [93]. The handbook by Gonnet and Baeza-Yates [81] compares the performance of a number of different sorting algorithms, many of which are external-memory algorithms. B-trees were invented by Bayer and McCreight [24] and Comer [51] provides a very nice overview of this data structure. The books by Mehlhorn [148] and Samet [176] also have nice discussions about B-trees and their variants. Aggarwal and Vitter [5] study the I/O complexity of sorting and related problems, establishing upper and lower bounds, including the lower bound for sorting given in this chapter. Goodrich *et al.* [87] study the I/O complexity of several computational geometry problems. The reader interested in further study of I/O-efficient algorithms is encouraged to examine the survey paper of Vitter [206].

For a good general introduction to parallel algorithm design, please see the books by JáJá [107], Reif [172], Leighton [130], and Akl and Lyons [11]. For discussions of more recent developments in parallel algorithm design, please see the chapters by Atallah and Chen [16] and Goodrich [84]. Brent [39] presented the design pattern for what we call "Brent's Theorem" in 1976. Kruskal *et al.* [126] study the parallel prefix problem and its applications, and Cole and Vishkin [50] study this and the list ranking problem in detail. In [186] Shiloach and Vishkin give an algorithm for merging two sorted lists which runs in $O(\log n)$ time using $O(n/\log n)$ processors in the CREW PRAM model, which is clearly optimal. In [204] Valiant shows that $O(\log\log n)$ time is possible when using $O(n)$ processors, when only comparisons are counted. In [34] Borodin and Hopcroft show that Valiant's algorithm can in fact be implemented in the CREW PRAM model, still running in $O(\log\log n)$ time and using $O(n)$ processors. In [10] Ajtai, Komlós, and Szemerédi show that one can sort n numbers in optimal $O(\log n)$ time using $O(n)$ processors in the EREW PRAM model. Unfortunately, their result is largely of theoretic interest, because the constant involved in the time complexity is very large. Cole [48] has given an elegant $O(\log n)$ time sorting algorithm for the EREW PRAM model using $O(n)$ processors in which the constants involved are reasonable, however. The parallel algorithm for finding the diameter of a convex polygon is a parallel adaptation of an algorithm of Shamos [185].

The reader interested in further study of the competitive analysis of other online algorithms is referred to the book by Borodin and El-Yaniv [33] or the paper by Koutsoupias and Papadimitriou [124]. The marker caching algorithm and the online auctioning algorithms are discussed in the book by Borodin and El-Yaniv; the discussion of the marker algorithm given above is modeled after a similar discussion in the book by Motwani and Raghavan [157]. The discussion of competitive search trees is based on a paper by Goodrich [85]. Overmars [161] introduces the concept of partial rebuilding for keeping data structures balanced. Exercises C-14.11 and C-14.12 come from Sleator and Tarjan [188].

Appendix

Useful Mathematical Facts

In this appendix, we give several useful mathematical facts. We begin with some combinatorial definitions and facts.

Logarithms and Exponents

The logarithm function is defined as

$$\log_b a = c \qquad \text{if} \qquad a = b^c.$$

The following identities hold for logarithms and exponents:

1. $\log_b ac = \log_b a + \log_b c$
2. $\log_b a/c = \log_b a - \log_b c$
3. $\log_b a^c = c \log_b a$
4. $\log_b a = (\log_c a)/\log_c b$
5. $b^{\log_c a} = a^{\log_c b}$
6. $(b^a)^c = b^{ac}$
7. $b^a b^c = b^{a+c}$
8. $b^a/b^c = b^{a-c}$.

In addition, we have the following:

Theorem A.1: *If $a > 0$, $b > 0$, and $c > a + b$, then*

$$\log a + \log b \leq 2\log c - 2.$$

The ***natural logarithm*** function $\ln x = \log_e x$, where $e = 2.71828\ldots$, is the value of the following progression:

$$e = 1 + \frac{1}{1!} + \frac{1}{2!} + \frac{1}{3!} + \cdots.$$

In addition,

$$e^x = 1 + \frac{x}{1!} + \frac{x^2}{2!} + \frac{x^3}{3!} + \cdots$$

$$\ln(1+x) = x - \frac{x^2}{2!} + \frac{x^3}{3!} - \frac{x^4}{4!} + \cdots.$$

There are a number of useful inequalities relating to these functions (which derive from these definitions).

Theorem A.2: *If $x > -1$,*

$$\frac{x}{1+x} \leq \ln(1+x) \leq x.$$

Theorem A.3: *For $0 \leq x < 1$,*

$$1+x \leq e^x \leq \frac{1}{1-x}.$$

Theorem A.4: *For any two positive real numbers x and n,*

$$\left(1+\frac{x}{n}\right)^n \leq e^x \leq \left(1+\frac{x}{n}\right)^{n+x/2}.$$

Integer Functions and Relations

The "floor" and "ceiling" functions are defined respectively as follows:

1. $\lfloor x \rfloor =$ the largest integer less than or equal to x.
2. $\lceil x \rceil =$ the smallest integer greater than or equal to x.

The ***modulo*** operator is defined for integers $a \geq 0$ and $b > 0$ as

$$a \bmod b = a - \left\lfloor \frac{a}{b} \right\rfloor b.$$

The ***factorial*** function is defined as

$$n! = 1 \cdot 2 \cdot 3 \cdot \cdots \cdot (n-1)n.$$

The binomial coefficient is

$$\binom{n}{k} = \frac{n!}{k!(n-k)!},$$

which is equal to the number of different ***combinations*** we can define by choosing k different items from a collection of n items (where the order does not matter). The name "binomial coefficient" derives from the ***binomial expansion***:

$$(a+b)^n = \sum_{k=0}^{n} \binom{n}{k} a^k b^{n-k}.$$

We also have the following relationships.

Theorem A.5: *If $0 \leq k \leq n$, then*

$$\left(\frac{n}{k}\right)^k \leq \binom{n}{k} \leq \frac{n^k}{k!}.$$

Theorem A.6 (Stirling's Approximation):

$$n! = \sqrt{2\pi n}\left(\frac{n}{e}\right)^n \left(1 + \frac{1}{12n} + \varepsilon(n)\right),$$

where $\varepsilon(n)$ is $O(1/n^2)$.

The ***Fibonacci progression*** is a numeric progression such that $F_0 = 0$, $F_1 = 1$, and $F_n = F_{n-1} + F_{n-2}$ for $n \geq 2$.

Theorem A.7: *If F_n is defined by the Fibonacci progression, then F_n is $\Theta(g^n)$, where $g = (1+\sqrt{5})/2$ is the so-called* **golden ratio**.

Summations

There are a number of useful facts about summations.

Theorem A.8: *Factoring summations:*

$$\sum_{i=1}^{n} af(i) = a\sum_{i=1}^{n} f(i),$$

provided a does not depend upon i.

Theorem A.9: *Reversing the order:*

$$\sum_{i=1}^{n}\sum_{j=1}^{m} f(i,j) = \sum_{j=1}^{m}\sum_{i=1}^{n} f(i,j).$$

One special form of summation is a ***telescoping sum***:

$$\sum_{i=1}^{n}(f(i) - f(i-1)) = f(n) - f(0),$$

which often arises in the amortized analysis of a data structure or algorithm.

The following are some other facts about summations that often arise in the analysis of data structures and algorithms.

Theorem A.10:

$$\sum_{i=1}^{n} i = \frac{n(n+1)}{2}.$$

Theorem A.11:

$$\sum_{i=1}^{n} i^2 = \frac{n(n+1)(2n+1)}{6}.$$

Theorem A.12: *If $k \geq 1$ is an integer constant, then*

$$\sum_{i=1}^{n} i^k \text{ is } \Theta(n^{k+1}).$$

Another common summation is the ***geometric sum***

$$\sum_{i=0}^{n} a^i,$$

for any fixed real number $0 < a \neq 1$.

Theorem A.13:

$$\sum_{i=0}^{n} a^i = \frac{1-a^{n+1}}{1-a}$$

for any real number $0 < a \neq 1$.

Theorem A.14:

$$\sum_{i=0}^{\infty} a^i = \frac{1}{1-a}$$

for any real number $0 < a < 1$.

There is also a combination of the two common forms, called the ***linear exponential*** summation, which has the following expansion:

Theorem A.15: *For* $0 < a \neq 1$, *and* $n \geq 2$,

$$\sum_{i=1}^{n} ia^i = \frac{a-(n+1)a^{(n+1)}+na^{(n+2)}}{(1-a)^2}.$$

The nth ***harmonic number*** H_n is defined as

$$H_n = \sum_{i=1}^{n} \frac{1}{i}.$$

Theorem A.16: *If* H_n *is the nth harmonic number, then* H_n *is* $\ln n + \Theta(1)$.

Useful Mathematical Techniques

To determine whether a function is little-oh or little-omega of another, it is sometimes helpful to apply the following rule.

Theorem A.17 (L'Hôpital's Rule): *If we have* $\lim_{n\to\infty} f(n) = +\infty$ *and we have* $\lim_{n\to\infty} g(n) = +\infty$, *then* $\lim_{n\to\infty} f(n)/g(n) = \lim_{n\to\infty} f'(n)/g'(n)$, *where* $f'(n)$ *and* $g'(n)$ *denote the derivatives of* $f(n)$ *and* $g(n)$ *respectively.*

In deriving an upper or lower bound for a summation, it is often useful to ***split a summation*** as follows:

$$\sum_{i=1}^{n} f(i) = \sum_{i=1}^{j} f(i) + \sum_{i=j+1}^{n} f(i).$$

Another useful technique is to ***bound a sum by an integral***. If f is a nondecreasing function, then, assuming the following terms are defined,

$$\int_{a-1}^{b} f(x)\,dx \leq \sum_{i=a}^{b} f(i) \leq \int_{a}^{b+1} f(x)\,dx.$$

Bibliography

[1] J. D. Achter and R. Tamassia, "Selected topics in algorithms." Manuscript, 1993.

[2] G. M. Adel'son-Vel'skii and Y. M. Landis, "An algorithm for the organization of information," *Doklady Akademii Nauk SSSR*, vol. 146, pp. 263–266, 1962. English translation in *Soviet Math. Dokl.*, **3**, 1259–1262.

[3] P. K. Agarwal, "Geometric partitioning and its applications," in *Computational Geometry: Papers from the DIMACS Special Year* (J. E. Goodman, R. Pollack, and W. Steiger, eds.), American Mathematical Society, 1991.

[4] P. K. Agarwal, "Range searching," in *Handbook of Discrete and Computational Geometry* (J. E. Goodman and J. O'Rourke, eds.), ch. 31, pp. 575–598, Boca Raton, FL: CRC Press LLC, 1997.

[5] A. Aggarwal and J. S. Vitter, "The input/output complexity of sorting and related problems," *Commun. ACM*, vol. 31, pp. 1116–1127, 1988.

[6] A. V. Aho, "Algorithms for finding patterns in strings," in *Handbook of Theoretical Computer Science* (J. van Leeuwen, ed.), vol. A. Algorithms and Complexity, pp. 255–300, Amsterdam: Elsevier, 1990.

[7] A. V. Aho, J. E. Hopcroft, and J. D. Ullman, *The Design and Analysis of Computer Algorithms*. Reading, MA: Addison-Wesley, 1974.

[8] A. V. Aho, J. E. Hopcroft, and J. D. Ullman, *Data Structures and Algorithms*. Reading, MA: Addison-Wesley, 1983.

[9] R. K. Ahuja, T. L. Magnanti, and J. B. Orlin, *Network Flows: Theory, Algorithms, and Applications*. Englewood Cliffs, NJ: Prentice Hall, 1993.

[10] M. Ajtai, J. Komlós, and E. Szemerédi, "Sorting in $c \log n$ parallel steps," *Combinatorica*, vol. 3, pp. 1–19, 1983.

[11] S. G. Akl and K. A. Lyons, *Parallel Computational Geometry*. Prentice Hall, 1993.

[12] C. Aragon and R. Seidel, "Randomized search trees," in *Proc. 30th Annu. IEEE Sympos. Found. Comput. Sci.*, pp. 540–545, 1989.

[13] K. Arnold and J. Gosling, *The Java Programming Language*. The Java Series, Reading, Mass.: Addison-Wesley, 1996.

[14] S. Arya and D. M. Mount, "Approximate nearest neighbor queries in fixed dimensions," in *Proc. 4th ACM-SIAM Sympos. Discrete Algorithms*, pp. 271–280, 1993.

[15] S. Arya and D. M. Mount, "Approximate range searching," in *Proc. 11th Annu. ACM Sympos. Comput. Geom.*, pp. 172–181, 1995.

[16] M. J. Atallah and D. Z. Chen, "Deterministic parallel computational geometry," in *Handbook of Computational Geometry* (J.-R. Sack and J. Urrutia, eds.), pp. 155–200, Amsterdam: Elsevier Science Publishers B.V. North-Holland, 2000.

[17] F. Aurenhammer, "Voronoi diagrams: A survey of a fundamental geometric data structure," *ACM Comput. Surv.*, vol. 23, pp. 345–405, Sept. 1991.

[18] B. Awerbuch, "Optimal distributed algorithms for minimum weight spanning tree, counting, leader election and related problems," in *19th ACM Symp. on Theory of Computing*, pp. 230–240, 1987.

[19] S. Baase, *Computer Algorithms: Introduction to Design and Analysis*. Reading, Mass.: Addison-Wesley, 2nd ed., 1988.

[20] E. Bach and J. Shallit, *Algorithmic Number Theory, Volume I: Efficient Algorithms*. MIT Press, 1996.

[21] R. Baeza-Yates and B. Ribeiro-Neto, *Modern Information Retrieval*. Reading, Mass.: Addison-Wesley, 1999.

[22] O. Baruvka, "O jistem problemu minimalnim," *Praca Moravske Prirodovedecke Spolecnosti*, vol. 3, pp. 37–58, 1926. (in Czech).

[23] R. Bayer, "Symmetric binary B-trees: Data structure and maintenance," *Acta Informatica*, vol. 1, no. 4, pp. 290–306, 1972.

[24] R. Bayer and McCreight, "Organization of large ordered indexes," *Acta Inform.*, vol. 1, pp. 173–189, 1972.

[25] R. Bellman, "On a routing problem," *Quarterly of Applied Mathematics*, vol. 16, no. 1, pp. 87–90, 1958.

[26] R. E. Bellman, *Dynamic Programming*. Princeton, NJ: Princeton University Press, 1957.

[27] J. Benaloh and M. de Mare, "One-way accumulators: A decentralized alternative to digital signatures," in *Advances in Cryptology—EUROCRYPT 93*, vol. 765 of *Lecture Notes in Computer Science*, pp. 274–285, 1993.

[28] J. L. Bentley, "Multidimensional divide-and-conquer," *Commun. ACM*, vol. 23, no. 4, pp. 214–229, 1980.

[29] J. L. Bentley, "Programming pearls: Thanks, heaps," *Communications of the ACM*, vol. 28, pp. 245–250, 1985.

[30] J. L. Bentley, D. Haken, and J. B. Saxe, "A general method for solving divide-and-conquer recurrences," *SIGACT News*, vol. 12, no. 3, pp. 36–44, 1980.

[31] J. L. Bentley and T. A. Ottmann, "Algorithms for reporting and counting geometric intersections," *IEEE Trans. Comput.*, vol. C-28, pp. 643–647, Sept. 1979.

[32] G. Booch, *Object-Oriented Analysis and Design with Applications*. Redwood City, CA: Benjamin/Cummings, 1994.

[33] A. Borodin and R. El-Yaniv, *Online Computation and Competitive Analysis*. New York: Cambridge University Press, 1998.

[34] A. Borodin and J. E. Hopcroft, "Routing, merging, and sorting on parallel models of computation," *J. Comput. Syst. Sci.*, vol. 30, no. 1, pp. 130–145, 1985.

[35] C. B. Boyer and U. C. Merzbach, *A History of Mathematics*. New York: John Wiley & Sons, Inc., 2nd ed., 1991.

[36] R. S. Boyer and J. S. Moore, "A fast string searching algorithm," *Communications of the ACM*, vol. 20, no. 10, pp. 762–772, 1977.

[37] G. Brassard, "Crusade for a better notation," *SIGACT News*, vol. 17, no. 1, pp. 60–64, 1985.

[38] G. Brassard and P. Bratley, *Fundamentals of Algorithmics*. Enlewood Cliffs, NJ: Prentice Hall, 1996.

[39] R. P. Brent, "Fast multiple-precision evaluation of elementary functions," *J. ACM*, vol. 23, pp. 242–251, 1976.

[40] D. Bressoud and S. Wagon, *A Course in Computational Number Theory*. Key College Publishing, 2000.

[41] E. O. Brigham, *The Fast Fourier Transform*. Englewood Cliffs, NJ: Prentice-Hall, 1974.

[42] T. Budd, *An Introduction to Object-Oriented Programming*. Reading, Mass.: Addison-Wesley, 1991.

[43] D. Burger, J. R. Goodman, and G. S. Sohi, "Memory systems," in *The Computer Science and Engineering Handbook* (A. B. Tucker, Jr., ed.), ch. 18, pp. 447–461, CRC Press, 1997.

[44] L. Cardelli and P. Wegner, "On understanding types, data abstraction and polymorphism," *ACM Computing Surveys*, vol. 17, no. 4, pp. 471–522, 1985.

[45] S. Carlsson, "Average case results on heapsort," *BIT*, vol. 27, pp. 2–17, 1987.

[46] V. Chvátal, "A greedy heuristic for the set-covering problem," *Math. Oper. Res.*, vol. 4, pp. 233–235, 1979.

[47] K. L. Clarkson, "Linear programming in $O(n3^{d^2})$ time," *Inform. Process. Lett.*, vol. 22, pp. 21–24, 1986.

[48] R. Cole, "Parallel merge sort," *SIAM J. Comput.*, vol. 17, no. 4, pp. 770–785, 1988.

[49] R. Cole, "Tight bounds on the complexity of the Boyer-Moore pattern matching algorithm," *SIAM Journal on Computing*, vol. 23, no. 5, pp. 1075–1091, 1994.

[50] R. Cole and U. Vishkin, "Faster optimal parallel prefix sums and list ranking," *Inform. Comput.*, vol. 81, pp. 334–352, June 1989.

[51] D. Comer, "The ubiquitous B-tree," *ACM Comput. Surv.*, vol. 11, pp. 121–137, 1979.

[52] D. Comer, *Computer Networks and Internets*. Englewood Cliffs, NJ: Prentice Hall, 1997.

[53] S. Cook, "The complexity of theorem proving procedures," in *30th ACM Symp. on Theory of Computing*, pp. 151–158, 1971.

[54] J. W. Cooley and J. W. Tukey, "An algorithm for the machine calculation of complex Fourier series," *Mathematics of Computation*, vol. 19, no. 90, pp. 297–301, 1965.

[55] T. H. Cormen, C. E. Leiserson, and R. L. Rivest, *Introduction to Algorithms*. Cambridge, MA: MIT Press, 1990.

[56] M. Crochemore and T. Lecroq, "Pattern matching and text compression algorithms," in *The Computer Science and Engineering Handbook* (A. B. Tucker, Jr., ed.), ch. 8, pp. 162–202, CRC Press, 1997.

[57] S. A. Demurjian, Sr., "Software design," in *The Computer Science and Engineering Handbook* (A. B. Tucker, Jr., ed.), ch. 108, pp. 2323–2351, CRC Press, 1997.

[58] G. Di Battista, P. Eades, R. Tamassia, and I. G. Tollis, "Algorithms for drawing graphs: an annotated bibliography," *Comput. Geom. Theory Appl.*, vol. 4, pp. 235–282, 1994.

[59] G. Di Battista, P. Eades, R. Tamassia, and I. G. Tollis, *Graph Drawing: Algorithms for Geometric Representations of Graphs*. Englewood Cliffs, NJ: Prentice Hall, 1998.

[60] E. W. Dijkstra, "A note on two problems in connexion with graphs," *Numerische Mathematik*, vol. 1, pp. 269–271, 1959.

[61] J. R. Driscoll, H. N. Gabow, R. Shrairaman, and R. E. Tarjan, "Relaxed heaps: An alternative to Fibonacci heaps with applications to parallel computation.," *Commun. ACM*, vol. 31, pp. 1343–1354, 1988.

[62] H. Edelsbrunner, "A note on dynamic range searching," *Bull. EATCS*, vol. 15, pp. 34–40, 1981.

[63] H. Edelsbrunner, *Algorithms in Combinatorial Geometry*, vol. 10 of *EATCS Monographs on Theoretical Computer Science*. Heidelberg, West Germany: Springer-Verlag, 1987.

[64] J. Edmonds, "Matroids and the greedy algorithm," *Mathematical Programming*, vol. 1, pp. 126–136, 1971.

[65] J. Edmonds and R. M. Karp, "Theoretical improvements in the algorithmic efficiency for network flow problems," *Journal of the ACM*, vol. 19, pp. 248–264, 1972.

[66] D. F. Elliott and K. R. Rao, *Fast Transform Algorithms, Analyses, and Applications*. New York: Academic Press, 1982.

[67] I. Z. Emiris and V. Y. Pan, "Applications of FFT," in *Algorithms and Theory of Computation Handbook* (M. J. Atallah, ed.), ch. 17, pp. 17–1–17–30, CRC Press, 1999.

[68] S. Even, *Graph Algorithms*. Potomac, Maryland: Computer Science Press, 1979.

[69] R. W. Floyd, "Algorithm 97: Shortest path," *Communications of the ACM*, vol. 5, no. 6, p. 345, 1962.

[70] R. W. Floyd, "Algorithm 245: Treesort 3," *Communications of the ACM*, vol. 7, no. 12, p. 701, 1964.

[71] L. R. Ford, Jr. and D. R. Fulkerson, *Flows in Networks*. Princeton, NJ: Princeton University Press, 1962.

[72] M. L. Fredman and R. E. Tarjan, "Fibonacci heaps and their uses in improved network optimization algorithms," *J. ACM*, vol. 34, pp. 596–615, 1987.

[73] H. N. Gabow and R. E. Tarjan, "A linear-time algorithm for a special case of disjoint set union," *SIAM Journal on Computing*, vol. 30, no. 2, pp. 209–221, 1985.

[74] R. G. Gallager, P. A. Humblet, and P. M. Spira, "A distributed algorithm for minimum-weight spanning trees," *ACM Transactions on Programming Languages and Systems*, vol. 5, no. 1, pp. 66–77, 1983.

[75] T. E. Gamal, "A public key cryptosystem and a signature scheme based on discrete logarithms," *IEEE Transactions on Information Theory*, vol. IT–31, no. 4, pp. 469–472, 1985.

[76] M. R. Garey and D. S. Johnson, *Computers and Intractability: A Guide to the Theory of NP-Completeness*. New York, NY: W. H. Freeman, 1979.

[77] A. M. Gibbons, *Algorithmic Graph Theory*. Cambridge, UK: Cambridge University Press, 1985.

[78] S. S. Godbole, "On efficient computation of matrix chain products," *IEEE Transactions on Computers*, vol. C-22, no. 9, pp. 864–866, 1973.

[79] A. Goldberg and D. Robson, *Smalltalk-80: The Language*. Reading, Mass.: Addison-Wesley, 1989.

[80] S. Golomb and L. Baumert, "Backtrack programming," *Journal of the ACM*, vol. 12, pp. 516–524, 1965.

[81] G. H. Gonnet and R. Baeza-Yates, *Handbook of Algorithms and Data Structures in Pascal and C*. Reading, Mass.: Addison-Wesley, 1991.

[82] G. H. Gonnet and J. I. Munro, "Heaps on heaps," *SIAM Journal on Computing*, vol. 15, no. 4, pp. 964–971, 1986.

[83] J. E. Goodman and J. O'Rourke, eds., *Handbook of Discrete and Computational Geometry*. CRC Press LLC, 1997.

[84] M. T. Goodrich, "Parallel algorithms in geometry," in *Handbook of Discrete and Computational Geometry* (J. E. Goodman and J. O'Rourke, eds.), ch. 36, pp. 669–682, Boca Raton, FL: CRC Press LLC, 1997.

[85] M. T. Goodrich, "Competitive tree-structured dictionaries," in *11th ACM-SIAM Symp. on Discrete Algorithms*, pp. 494–495, 2000.

[86] M. T. Goodrich, M. Handy, B. Hudson, and R. Tamassia, "Accessing the internal organization of data structures in the JDSL library," in *Proc. Workshop on Algorithm Engineering and Experimentation* (M. T. Goodrich and C. C. McGeoch, eds.), vol. 1619 of *Lecture Notes Comput. Sci.*, pp. 124–139, Springer-Verlag, 1999.

[87] M. T. Goodrich, J.-J. Tsay, D. E. Vengroff, and J. S. Vitter, "External-memory computational geometry," in *Proc. 34th Annu. IEEE Sympos. Found. Comput. Sci.*, pp. 714–723, 1993.

[88] R. L. Graham, "An efficient algorithm for determining the convex hull of a finite planar set," *Inform. Process. Lett.*, vol. 1, pp. 132–133, 1972.

[89] R. L. Graham and P. Hell, "On the history of the minimum spanning tree problem," *Annals of the History of Computing*, vol. 7, no. 1, pp. 43–57, 1985.

[90] R. L. Graham, D. E. Knuth, and O. Patashnik, *Concrete Mathematics*. Reading, Mass.: Addison-Wesley, 1989.

[91] L. J. Guibas and R. Sedgewick, "A dichromatic framework for balanced trees," in *Proc. 19th Annu. IEEE Sympos. Found. Comput. Sci.*, Lecture Notes Comput. Sci., pp. 8–21, Springer-Verlag, 1978.

[92] Y. Gurevich, "What does $O(n)$ mean?," *SIGACT News*, vol. 17, no. 4, pp. 61–63, 1986.

[93] J. Hennessy and D. Patterson, *Computer Architecture: A Quantitative Approach*. San Francisco: Morgan Kaufmann, 2nd ed., 1996.

[94] K. Hinrichs, J. Nievergelt, and P. Schorn, "Plane-sweep solves the closest pair problem elegantly," *Inform. Process. Lett.*, vol. 26, pp. 255–261, 1988.

[95] D. S. Hirchsberg, "A linear space algorithm for computing maximal common subsequences," *Communications of the ACM*, vol. 18, no. 6, pp. 341–343, 1975.

[96] C. A. R. Hoare, "Quicksort," *The Computer Journal*, vol. 5, pp. 10–15, 1962.

[97] D. Hochbaum (ed.), *Approximation Algorithms for NP-Hard Problems*. Boston, MA: PWS Publishers, 1996.

[98] J. E. Hopcroft and R. E. Tarjan, "Efficient algorithms for graph manipulation," *Communications of the ACM*, vol. 16, no. 6, pp. 372–378, 1973.

[99] J. E. Hopcroft and J. D. Ullman, "Set merging algorithms," *SIAM Journal on Computing*, vol. 2, no. 4, pp. 294–303, 1979.

[100] T. C. Hu, *Combinatorial Algorithms*. Reading, Mass.: Addison-Wesley, 1981.

[101] T. C. Hu and M. T. Shing, "Computations of matrix chain products, part i," *SIAM Journal on Computing*, vol. 11, no. 2, pp. 362–373, 1982.

[102] T. C. Hu and M. T. Shing, "Computations of matrix chain products, part ii," *SIAM Journal on Computing*, vol. 13, no. 2, pp. 228–251, 1984.

[103] B. Huang and M. Langston, "Practical in-place merging," *Communications of the ACM*, vol. 31, no. 3, pp. 348–352, 1988.

[104] D. A. Huffman, "A method for the construction of minimum-redundancy codes," *Proceedings of the IRE*, vol. 40, no. 9, pp. 1098–1101, 1952.

[105] C. Huitema, *Routing in the Internet*. Englewood Cliffs, NJ: Prentice Hall, 2nd ed., 2000.

[106] O. H. Ibarra and C. E. Kim, "Fast approximation algorithms for the knapsack and sum of subset problems," *Journal of the ACM*, vol. 9, pp. 463–468, 1975.

[107] J. JáJá, *An Introduction to Parallel Algorithms*. Reading, Mass.: Addison-Wesley, 1992.

[108] V. Jarnik, "O jistem problemu minimalnim," *Praca Moravske Prirodovedecke Spolecnosti*, vol. 6, pp. 57–63, 1930. (in Czech).

[109] D. S. Johnson, "Approximation algorithms for combinatorial problems," *J. Comput. Syst. Sci.*, vol. 9, pp. 256–278, 1974.

[110] R. E. Jones, *Garbage Collection: Algorithms for Automatic Dynamic Memory Management*. John Wiley and Sons, 1996.

[111] A. Karatsuba and Y. Ofman, "Multiplication of multidigit numbers on automata," *Doklady Akademii Nauk SSSR*, vol. 145, pp. 293–294, 1962. (In Russian).

[112] D. R. Karger, P. Klein, and R. E. Tarjan, "A randomized linear-time algorithm to find minimum spanning trees," *Journal of the ACM*, vol. 42, pp. 321–328, 1995.

[113] R. Karp, "Reducibility among combinatorical problems of computer computaions," in *Complexity of Computer Computations* (E. Miller and J. W. Thatcher, eds.), pp. 88–104, New York: Plenum Press, 1972.

[114] R. M. Karp and V. Ramachandran, "Parallel algorithms for shared memory machines," in *Handbook of Theoretical Computer Science* (J. van Leeuwen, ed.), pp. 869–941, Amsterdam: Elsevier/The MIT Press, 1990.

[115] P. Kirschenhofer and H. Prodinger, "The path length of random skip lists," *Acta Informatica*, vol. 31, pp. 775–792, 1994.

[116] P. N. Klein and N. E. Young, "Approximation algorithms," in *Algorithms and Theory of Computation Handbook* (M. J. Atallah, ed.), ch. 34, pp. 34–1–34–19, CRC Press, 1999.

[117] D. E. Knuth, *Fundamental Algorithms*, vol. 1 of *The Art of Computer Programming*. Reading, MA: Addison-Wesley, 1st ed., 1968.

[118] D. E. Knuth, *Fundamental Algorithms*, vol. 1 of *The Art of Computer Programming*. Reading, MA: Addison-Wesley, 2nd ed., 1973.

[119] D. E. Knuth, *Sorting and Searching*, vol. 3 of *The Art of Computer Programming*. Reading, MA: Addison-Wesley, 1973.

[120] D. E. Knuth, "Big omicron and big omega and big theta," in *SIGACT News*, vol. 8, pp. 18–24, 1976.

[121] D. E. Knuth, *Seminumerical Algorithms*, vol. 2 of *The Art of Computer Programming*. Reading, MA: Addison-Wesley, 3rd ed., 1998.

[122] D. E. Knuth, J. H. Morris, Jr., and V. R. Pratt, "Fast pattern matching in strings," *SIAM Journal on Computing*, vol. 6, no. 1, pp. 323–350, 1977.

[123] N. Koblitz, *A Course in Number Theory and Cryptography*. Springer-Verlag, 1987.

[124] E. Koutsoupias and C. H. Papadimitriou, "On the k-server conjecture," *Journal of the ACM*, vol. 42, no. 5, pp. 971–983, 1995.

[125] E. Kranakis, *Primality and Cryptography*. John Wiley and Sons, 1986.

[126] C. P. Kruskal, L. Rudolph, and M. Snir, "The power of parallel prefix," *IEEE Trans. Comput.*, vol. C-34, pp. 965–968, 1985.

[127] J. B. Kruskal, Jr., "On the shortest spanning subtree of a graph and the traveling salesman problem," *Proc. Amer. Math. Soc.*, vol. 7, pp. 48–50, 1956.

[128] D. T. Lee, "Computational geometry," in *The Computer Science and Engineering Handbook* (A. B. Tucker, Jr., ed.), ch. 6, pp. 111–140, CRC Press, 1997.

[129] D. T. Lee and F. P. Preparata, "Computational geometry: a survey," *IEEE Trans. Comput.*, vol. C-33, pp. 1072–1101, 1984.

[130] F. T. Leighton, *Introduction to Parallel Algorithms and Architectures: Arrays, Trees, Hypercubes*. San Mateo, CA: Morgan-Kaufmann, 1992.

[131] L. A. Levin, "Universal sorting problems," *Problemy Peredachi Informatsii*, vol. 9, no. 3, pp. 265–266, 1973. In Russian.

[132] A. Levitin, "Do we teach the right algorithm design techniques?," in *30th ACM SIGCSE Symp. on Computer Science Education*, pp. 179–183, 1999.

[133] H. R. Lewis and C. H. Papadimitriou, *Elements of the Theory of Computation*. Upper Saddle River, New Jersey: Prentice-Hall, 2nd ed., 1998.

[134] T. Lindholm and F. Yellin, *The Java Virtual Machine Specification*. Reading, Mass.: Addison-Wesley, 1997.

[135] B. Liskov and J. Guttag, *Abstraction and Specification in Program Development*. Cambridge, Mass./New York: The MIT Press/McGraw-Hill, 1986.

[136] L. Lovász, "On the ratio of optimal integral and fractional covers," *Discrete Math.*, vol. 13, pp. 383–390, 1975.

[137] N. A. Lynch, *Distributed Algorithms*. San Francisco: Morgan Kaufmann, 1996.

[138] J. Matoušek, "Geometric range searching," *ACM Comput. Surv.*, vol. 26, pp. 421–461, 1994.

[139] E. M. McCreight, "A space-economical suffix tree construction algorithm," *Journal of Algorithms*, vol. 23, no. 2, pp. 262–272, 1976.

[140] E. M. McCreight, "Priority search trees," *SIAM J. Comput.*, vol. 14, no. 2, pp. 257–276, 1985.

[141] C. J. H. McDiarmid and B. A. Reed, "Building heaps fast," *Journal of Algorithms*, vol. 10, no. 3, pp. 352–365, 1989.

[142] C. C. McGeoch, "Analyzing algorithms by simulation: Variance reduction techniques and simulation speedups," *ACM Computing Surveys*, vol. 24, no. 2, pp. 195–212, 1992.

[143] C. C. McGeoch, "Toward an experimental method for algorithm simulation," *INFORMS Journal on Computing*, vol. 8, no. 1, pp. 1–15, 1996.

[144] C. C. McGeoch, D. Precup, and P. R. Cohen, "How to find the Big-Oh of your data set (and how not to)," in *Advances in Intelligent Data Analysis*, vol. 1280 of *Lecture Notes in Computer Science*, pp. 41–52, Springer-Verlag, 1997.

[145] N. Megiddo, "Linear-time algorithms for linear programming in R^3 and related problems," *SIAM J. Comput.*, vol. 12, pp. 759–776, 1983.

[146] N. Megiddo, "Linear programming in linear time when the dimension is fixed," *J. ACM*, vol. 31, pp. 114–127, 1984.

[147] K. Mehlhorn, "A best possible bound for the weighted path length of binary search trees," *SIAM Journal on Computing*, vol. 6, no. 2, pp. 235–239, 1977.

[148] K. Mehlhorn, *Data Structures and Algorithms 1: Sorting and Searching*, vol. 1 of *EATCS Monographs on Theoretical Computer Science*. Heidelberg, Germany: Springer-Verlag, 1984.

[149] K. Mehlhorn, *Data Structures and Algorithms 2: Graph Algorithms and NP-Completeness*, vol. 2 of *EATCS Monographs on Theoretical Computer Science*. Heidelberg, Germany: Springer-Verlag, 1984.

[150] K. Mehlhorn, *Data Structures and Algorithms 3: Multi-dimensional Searching and Computational Geometry*, vol. 3 of *EATCS Monographs on Theoretical Computer Science*. Heidelberg, Germany: Springer-Verlag, 1984.

[151] K. Mehlhorn and S. Näher, *LEDA: a Platform for Combinatorial and Geometric Computing*. Cambridge, UK: Cambridge University Press, 1999.

[152] K. Mehlhorn and A. Tsakalidis, "Data structures," in *Handbook of Theoretical Computer Science* (J. van Leeuwen, ed.), vol. A. Algorithms and Complexity, pp. 301–341, Amsterdam: Elsevier, 1990.

[153] R. C. Merkle, "Protocols for public key cryptosystems," in *Proc. Symp. on Security and Privacy*, IEEE Computer Society Press, 1980.

[154] R. C. Merkle, "A certified digital signature," in *Advances in Cryptology—CRYPTO '89* (G. Brassard, ed.), vol. 435 of *Lecture Notes in Computer Science*, pp. 218–238, Springer-Verlag, 1990.

[155] M. H. Morgan, *Vitruvius: The Ten Books on Architecture*. New York: Dover Publications, Inc., 1960.

[156] D. R. Morrison, "PATRICIA—practical algorithm to retrieve information coded in alphanumeric," *Journal of the ACM*, vol. 15, no. 4, pp. 514–534, 1968.

[157] R. Motwani and P. Raghavan, *Randomized Algorithms*. New York, NY: Cambridge University Press, 1995.

[158] D. R. Musser and A. Saini, *STL Tutorial and Reference Guide: C++ Programming with the Standard Template Library*. Reading, Mass.: Addison-Wesley, 1996.

[159] R. Neapolitan and K. Naimipour, *Foundations of Algorithms Using C++ Pseudocode*. Boston: Jones and Bartlett Publishers, 1998.

[160] J. O'Rourke, *Computational Geometry in C*. Cambridge University Press, 1994.

[161] M. H. Overmars, *The Design of Dynamic Data Structures*, vol. 156 of *Lecture Notes Comput. Sci.* Heidelberg, West Germany: Springer-Verlag, 1983.

[162] J. Pach, ed., *New Trends in Discrete and Computational Geometry*, vol. 10 of *Algorithms and Combinatorics*. Springer-Verlag, 1993.

[163] T. Papadakis, J. I. Munro, and P. V. Poblete, "Average search and update costs in skip lists," *BIT*, vol. 32, pp. 316–332, 1992.

[164] C. H. Papadimitriou and K. Steiglitz, "Some complexity results for the traveling salesman problem," in *Proc. 8th Annu. ACM Sympos. Theory Comput.*, pp. 1–9, 1976.

[165] C. H. Papadimitriou and K. Steiglitz, *Combinatorial Optimization: Algorithms and Complexity*. Englewood Cliffs, NJ: Prentice Hall, 1982.

[166] D. Peleg, *Distributed Computing: A Locally-Sensitive Approach*. Philadelphia: SIAM, 2000.

[167] P. V. Poblete, J. I. Munro, and T. Papadakis, "The binomial transform and its application to the analysis of skip lists," in *Proceedings of the European Symposium on Algorithms (ESA)*, pp. 554–569, 1995.

[168] F. P. Preparata and M. I. Shamos, *Computational Geometry: An Introduction*. New York, NY: Springer-Verlag, 1985.

[169] R. C. Prim, "Shortest connection networks and some generalizations," *Bell Syst. Tech. J.*, vol. 36, pp. 1389–1401, 1957.

[170] W. Pugh, "Skip lists: a probabilistic alternative to balanced trees," *Commun. ACM*, vol. 33, no. 6, pp. 668–676, 1990.

[171] M. O. Rabin, "A probabilistic algorithm for testing primality," *Journal of Number Theory*, vol. 12, 1980.

[172] J. H. Reif, *Synthesis of Parallel Algorithms*. San Mateo, CA: Morgan Kaufmann Publishers, Inc., 1993.

[173] R. L. Rivest, A. Shamir, and L. Adleman, "A method for obtaining digital signatures and public-key cryptosystems," *Communications of the ACM*, vol. 21, no. 2, pp. 120–126, 1978.

[174] D. J. Rosenkrantz, R. E. Stearns, and P. M. Lewis, "An analysis of several heuristics for the traveling salesman problem," *SIAM J. on Computing*, vol. 6, pp. 563–581, 1977.

[175] H. Samet, *Applications of Spatial Data Structures: Computer Graphics, Image Processing, and GIS*. Reading, MA: Addison-Wesley, 1990.

[176] H. Samet, *The Design and Analysis of Spatial Data Structures*. Reading, MA: Addison-Wesley, 1990.

[177] J. E. Savage, *Models of Computation: Exploring the Power of Computing*. Addison-Wesley, 1998.

[178] R. Schaffer and R. Sedgewick, "The analysis of heapsort," *Journal of Algorithms*, vol. 15, no. 1, pp. 76–100, 1993.

[179] B. Schneier, *Applied cryptography: protocols, algorithms, and sourcecode in C*. New York: John Wiley and Sons, Inc., 1994.

[180] B. Schneier, *Applied Cryptography: Protocols, Algorithms, and Source Code in C*. New York, NY, USA: John Wiley and Sons, Inc., second ed., 1996.

[181] A. Schönhage and V. Strassen, "Schnelle multiplikation grosser zahlen," *Computing*, vol. 7, no. 1, pp. 37–44, 1971.

[182] R. Sedgewick, *Algorithms*. Reading, MA: Addison-Wesley, 1st ed., 1983.

[183] R. Sedgewick, *Algorithms in C++*. Reading, MA: Addison-Wesley, 1992.

[184] R. Sedgewick and P. Flajolet, *An Introduction to the Analysis of Algorithms*. Reading, Mass.: Addison-Wesley, 1996.

[185] M. I. Shamos, "Geometric complexity," in *Proc. 7th Annu. ACM Sympos. Theory Comput.*, pp. 224–233, 1975.

[186] Y. Shiloach and U. Vishkin, "Finding the maximum, merging and sorting in a parallel computation model," *J. Algorithms*, vol. 2, pp. 88–102, 1981.

[187] M. Sipser, *Introduction to the Theory of Computation*. PWS Publishing Co., 1997.

[188] D. D. Sleator and R. E. Tarjan, "Amortized efficiency of list update and paging rules," *Commun. ACM*, vol. 28, pp. 202–208, 1985.

[189] D. D. Sleator and R. E. Tarjan, "Self-adjusting binary search trees," *J. ACM*, vol. 32, no. 3, pp. 652–686, 1985.

[190] R. Solovay and V. Strassen, "A fast Monte-Carlo test for primality," *SIAM Journal on Computing*, vol. 6, no. 1, pp. 84–85, 1977.

[191] R. Solovay and V. Strassen, "Erratum: A fast Monte-Carlo test for primality," *SIAM Journal on Computing*, vol. 7, no. 1, 1978.

[192] W. Stallings, *Cryptography and network security: principles and practice*. Upper Saddle River, NJ 07458, USA: Prentice-Hall, Inc., second ed., 1999.

[193] G. A. Stephen, *String Searching Algorithms*. World Scientific Press, 1994.

[194] R. Tamassia, "Graph drawing," in *Handbook of Discrete and Computational Geometry* (J. E. Goodman and J. O'Rourke, eds.), ch. 44, pp. 815–832, Boca Raton, FL: CRC Press LLC, 1997.

[195] R. Tamassia, M. T. Goodrich, L. Vismara, M. Handy, G. Shubina, R. Cohen, B. Hudson, R. S. Baker, N. Gelfand, and U. Brandes, "JDSL: The data structures library in Java," *Dr. Dobb's Journal*, vol. 323, April 2001.

[196] A. S. Tanenbaum, *Computer Networks*. Englewood Cliffs, NJ: Prentice Hall, 1996.

[197] R. Tarjan and U. Vishkin, "An efficient parallel biconnectivity algorithm," *SIAM J. Comput.*, vol. 14, pp. 862–874, 1985.

[198] R. E. Tarjan, "Depth first search and linear graph algorithms," *SIAM Journal on Computing*, vol. 1, no. 2, pp. 146–160, 1972.

[199] R. E. Tarjan, "A class of algorithms which require nonlinear time to maintain disjoint sets," *J. Comput. System Sci.*, vol. 18, pp. 110–127, 1979.

[200] R. E. Tarjan, *Data Structures and Network Algorithms*, vol. 44 of *CBMS-NSF Regional Conference Series in Applied Mathematics*. Philadelphia, PA: Society for Industrial and Applied Mathematics, 1983.

[201] R. E. Tarjan, "Amortized computational complexity," *SIAM J. Algebraic Discrete Methods*, vol. 6, no. 2, pp. 306–318, 1985.

[202] G. Tel, *Introduction to Distributed Algorithms*. New York: Cambridge University Press, 1994.

[203] J. D. Ullman, *Principles of Database Systems*. Potomac, MD: Computer Science Press, 1983.

[204] L. Valiant, "Parallelism in comparison problems," *SIAM J. Comput.*, vol. 4, no. 3, pp. 348–355, 1975.

[205] J. van Leeuwen, "Graph algorithms," in *Handbook of Theoretical Computer Science* (J. van Leeuwen, ed.), vol. A. Algorithms and Complexity, pp. 525–632, Amsterdam: Elsevier, 1990.

[206] J. S. Vitter, "Efficient memory access in large-scale computation," in *Proc. 8th Sympos. Theoret. Aspects Comput. Sci.*, Lecture Notes Comput. Sci., Springer-Verlag, 1991.

[207] J. S. Vitter and P. Flajolet, "Average-case analysis of algorithms and data structures," in *Algorithms and Complexity* (J. van Leeuwen, ed.), vol. A of *Handbook of Theoretical Computer Science*, pp. 431–524, Amsterdam: Elsevier, 1990.

[208] J. Vuillemin, "A unifying look at data structures," *Commun. ACM*, vol. 23, pp. 229–239, 1980.

[209] S. Warshall, "A theorem on boolean matrices," *Journal of the ACM*, vol. 9, no. 1, pp. 11–12, 1962.

[210] J. W. J. Williams, "Algorithm 232: Heapsort," *Communications of the ACM*, vol. 7, no. 6, pp. 347–348, 1964.

[211] D. Wood, *Data Structures, Algorithms, and Performance*. Reading, Mass.: Addison-Wesley, 1993.

[212] F. F. Yao, "Computational geometry," in *Algorithms in Complexity* (R. A. Earnshaw and D. Wyvill, eds.), pp. 345–490, Amsterdam: Elsevier, 1990.

[213] C. K. Yap, *Fundamental Problems in Algorithmic Algebra*. Oxford University Press, 1999.

Index

δ-approximation, 618
c-incremental, 593
2SAT, 607, 640
3SAT, 607, 608

abstract data type
  dictionary, 114–115, 141
  graph, 289–295
  list, 69–70
  partition, 227–234
  priority queue, 94–95, 112–113
  queue, 61
  sequence, 73–74
  set, 225–234
  stack, 57
  string, 419–420
  tree, 77–78
  vector, 65
(a,b) tree, 650–652
  depth property, 650
  size property, 650
accepting a string, 594
access control lists, 472
accounting method, 36–37
Achter, 510
Ackermann function, 234, 256
acyclic, 316
additive inverse, 458
Adel'son-Vel'skii, 216
adjacency list, 296, 299
adjacency matrix, 296, 301
adjacent, 290
Adleman, 476
Agarwal, 590
Aggarwal, 683
Aho, 137, 216, 256, 450, 510, 642
Ahuja, 338, 379, 414
Ajtai, 683
Akl, 683
algorithm, 4
algorithm analysis, 8–33
  average case, 11
  worst case, 11
alphabet, 420
amortization, 34–41, 80, 133, 191–194, 215, 227–234, 427, 625–626, 676–679
  accounting method, 36–37
  potential function, 37–38
ancestor, 75, 315
anchor point, 578–581
antipodal, 665
antisymmetric property, 94
anycast, 544
approximation algorithm, 618
approximation algorithms, 618–626
Aragon, 590
arc, 289
Archimedes, 4, 54
Ariadne, 288
Arnold, 137
array splitting, 663
art gallery guarding, 283
Arya, 590
asymmetric relation, 289
asymptotic notation, 13–33
  big-Oh, 13–16
  big-Omega, 16
  big-Theta, 16
  little-oh, 18
  little-omega, 18
Atallah, 683
auction algorithm, 674–675
audit trail, 115
augmenting cycle, 398
augmenting path, 388
Aurenhammer, 590
authenticated dictionary, 482
AVL tree, 152–158, 206, 569
  balance factor, 206
  height-balance property, 152
Awerbuch, 544

Baase, 510
back edge, 305, 318, 320, 336
backtracking, 303, 627–631, 642
Baeza-Yates, 216, 256, 450, 683
balance factor, 206
balanced search tree, 162
Barůvka, 379
Barůvka's algorithm, 369–372, 528–529
Baumert, 642
Bayer, 216, 683
Bellman, 284, 379
Bellman-Ford algorithm, 349–351
Bentley, 137, 284, 590
Bertrand's Postulate, 126
best-first search, 632
BFS, *see* breadth-first search

BFS tree, 315
biconnected, 307
biconnected component, 307
big integers, 270
big-Oh notation, 13–16, 54
big Omega notation, 16
big-Theta notation, 16
Binary Euclid's Algorithm, 457
binary search, 142–145
binary search tree, 145–151
    insertion, 148
    removal, 149–150
    rotation, 155
    trinode restructure, 155
binary tree, 76, 84–92, 220
    complete, 99
    left child, 76
    level, 84
    linked structure, 92
    proper, 76
    right child, 76
    vector representation, 90–91
binomial expansion, 686
bipartite graph, 396
bit commitment, 483
bit vector, 252
blocking, 647
Booch, 137
Boolean circuit, 597
bootstrapping, 161
Borodin, 683
bottleneck, 395
boundary node, 551
Boyer, 54, 450
branch-and-bound, 632–634, 639, 641, 642
Brassard, 54, 642
Bratley, 642
breadth-first search, 313–316, 320, 523–527
Brent, 683
Brent's theorem, 659, 660
Brigham, 510
broadcast routing, 530–531
brute force, 420
brute-force pattern matching, 420
B-tree, 652–653
bubble-sort, 137
bucket array, 116
bucket-sort, 241–242
Budd, 137
Burger, 683

cache, 645
cache line, 647
caching algorithms, 668–673
call-by-value, 60
capacity rule, 383
Cardelli, 137
Carlsson, 137
Carmichael numbers, 466
Cartesian coordinates, 572
Cartesian tree, 590
Catalan number, 275
certificate, 486, 596
certificate authority, 486
certificate revocation list, 486
character-jump heuristic, 422
Chen, 683
Chernoff bound, 253
child, 75
children, 75
Chomsky normal form, 284
Chvátal, 642
CIRCUIT-SAT, 598, 600–602, 605
Clarkson, 256
clauses, 605
clearable table, 34
CLIQUE, 610, 638
clique, 610
clockwise, 574
closed form, 12
closest pairs, 568–571
closure, 357
CNF, ***see*** conjunctive normal form
CNF-SAT, 605–607, 628, 629, 640, 642
co-*NP*, 595, 597
coefficient form, 488
Cole, 450, 683
collinear, 574
collision resolution, 116, 120–127
collision-resistant, 481
Comer, 544, 683
comparator, 95, 218, 579, 583
    radial, 579, 580, 583
competitive search trees, 676–679
complement, 595
complete binary tree, 99
complexity class, 595
component design, 603
composite, 453
compositeness witness function, 466
compression map, 117, 119
computational geometry, 548–590
    closest pairs, 568–571
    convex hull, 572–583
    degeneracies, 575, 583
    orientation, 574–575
    plane sweep, 566–571

proximity, 568
representations, 572–573
segment intersection, 565–568
conditional probability, 29
confidentiality, 452
congruence, 454
congruent, 454
conjunctive normal form, 605, 607
connected components, 292, 306, 315
conservation rule, 383
container, 137
contradiction, 25
contrapositive, 25
convex hull, 572–583, 590
gift wrapping, 578–579
Graham scan algorithm, 580–583
convexity, 573, 576
convolution, 488
Convolution Theorem, 492
Cook, 642
Cook-Levin Theorem, 600
Cooley, 510
coordinates, 549
core memory, 645
Cormen, 216, 338, 379, 414, 510, 642
cost, 398
counterclockwise, 574
Crochemore, 450
cross edge, 315, 318, 320
cryptography, 471–480
El Gamal cryptosystem, 479–480
RSA cryptosystem, 476–478
cursor, 70
cut, 385
cyber-dollar, 36
cycle, 292
directed, 292
cyptograph
public-key, 475–480

DAG, ***see*** directed acyclic graph
data integrity, 452, 472
data structure, 4
secondary, 161
decision problem, 594
decision tree, 239
decorator pattern, 329–332
decrease-and-conquer, ***see*** prune-and-search
decryption, 471
degree, 290, 488
Delaunay triangulation, 590
DeMorgan's Law, 25
Demurjian, 137
depth, 79–80
depth-bounded tree, 159
depth-first search, 303–306
descendent, 75, 315
design patterns
amortization, 39–41
brute force, 420
comparator, 95
decorator, 329–332
divide-and-conquer, 219–221, 235, 263–273
dynamic programming, 274–281, 444–446
greedy method, 442
iterator, 74
locator, 112–113
position, 68
prune-and-search, 245–247
template method, 332
destination, 290
DFS, ***see*** depth-first search
DFS tree, 305
DFT, ***see*** Discrete Fourier Transform
Di Battista, 137, 338
diameter, 135, 523, 665
dictionary, 114–127, 141–216
(2,4) tree, 163–169
abstract data type, 114–115, 141
AVL tree, 152–158
binary search tree, 145–151
hash table, 116–127
log file, 115
lookup table, 142–145
ordered, 114, 141
red-black tree, 170–184
skip list, 195–202
unordered, 114, 115
update operations, 148, 149, 154, 157, 198, 199
Diffie-Hellman key exchange, 487
digital signature, 471
El Gamal, 480
RSA, 477
digraph, 316
Dijkstra, 379
Dijkstra's algorithm, 342–348, 373–376
directed acyclic graph, 325–327
directed cycle, 316
directed DFS tree, 318
discovery edge, 305, 315, 318, 320
Discrete Fourier Transform, 491–494
discrete logarithm, 479
disjunctive normal form, 606
distance, 341

distance vector, 532
distance vector algorithm, 532–533
distributed algorithms, 514–517
 message-passing model, 514–516
distributed computing
 asynchronous model, 515
 synchronous model, 515
divide-and-conquer, 219–221, 235, 263–273, 659
division method, 119
DNF, ***see*** disjunctive normal form
DNF-DISSAT, 638
DNF-SAT, 638
d-node, 159
double black, 177
double hashing, 124
double red, 172
down-heap bubbling, 104, 109
dynamic programming, 274–281, 320, 443–446

Edelsbrunner, 590
edge, 289, 573
 destination, 290
 end vertices, 290
 incident, 290
 multiple, 291
 origin, 290
 outgoing, 290
 parallel, 291
 self-loop, 291
edge capacity, 383
edge list, 296, 298
edit distance, 449
Edmonds, 284, 414
Edmonds-Karp algorithm, 393–395
Edmonds-Karp augmentations, 393
El-Yaniv, 683
Elliott, 510
El Gamal cryptosystem, 479–480
Emiris, 510
encryption schemes, 473
end vertices, 290
endpoints, 290
energy-balanced trees, 676–679
equivalence class, 308
equivalence relation, 308
Euclid's algorithm, 455–457
 binary, 457
 extended, 464–465
Euler pseudo-prime, 469
Euler tour, 335, 338
Euler tour traversal, 87, 137
Euler's Theorem, 461

Even, 338, 379, 414
event, 28
expected value, 29
exponent, 23
Extended Euclid's Algorithm, 464
external memory, 644–656, 683
external-memory algorithm, 645–656
external-memory sorting, 654–656

factorial, 686
failure function, 425
fairness, 515
Fast Fourier Transform, 488–507, 510
Fermat's Little Theorem, 459
FFT, ***see*** Fast Fourier Transform
Fibonacci progression, 687
FIFO, 61, 656
first-in first-out, 61
Flajolet, 54
flip a random coin, 483
flow, ***see*** network flow
flow network, 383
Floyd, 137
Floyd-Warshall algorithm, 320, 338
Ford, 379
Ford-Fulkerson algorithm, 387–395
forest, 292
forward edge, 318
frame, 59
Fulkerson, 414
fully polynomial-time approximation scheme, 619
Fundamental Theorem of Arithmetic, 453
fusion, 167, 651, 653

Gabow, 256
Galleger, 544
garbage collection, 323–324
 mark-sweep, 323
Garey, 642
Gauss, 22
Gavril, 642
GCD, ***see*** greatest common divisor
generator, 462
generic merge algorithm, 226
geometric sum, 687
Gibbons, 338, 379, 414
gift wrapping, 578–579
Godbole, 284
Golberg, 137
golden ratio, 687
Golomb, 642
Gonnet, 137, 216, 256, 683
Goodman, 590

Goodrich, 590, 683
googol, 17
Gosling, 137
Graham, 54, 379, 590
Graham scan algorithm, 580–583
grammar, 284
graph, 288–338, 340–379
  abstract data type, 289–295
  acyclic, 316
  bipartite, 396
  breadth-first search, 313–316, 318–320
  connected, 292, 315
  data structures, 296–301
    adjacency list, 299–301
    adjacency matrix, 301
    edge list, 296–298
  dense, 321
  depth-first search, 303–306, 318–320
  digraph, 316
  directed, 289, 290, 316–327
    acyclic, 325–327
    strongly connected, 316
  methods, 293–295
  mixed, 290
  reachability, 316–317, 320–321
  shortest paths, 320–321
  simple, 291
  traversal, 303–316
  undirected, 289, 290
  weighted, 340–379
greatest common divisor, 454–457
  Euclid's algorithm, 455–457
greedy method, 259–262, 341, 342, 442
greedy-choice, 259, 442
group, 461
guess-and-test, 266–267
Guibas, 216
Guttag, 137

Haken, 284
HAMILTONIAN-CYCLE, 597, 615, 617, 641, 642
Harmonic number, 626
harmonic number, 688
hash code, 117, 118
hash function, 117, 124–126
  2-universal, 125
  one-way, 481
hash table, 116–127
  bucket array, 116
  capacity, 116
  chaining, 121
  clustering, 124
  collision, 116
  collision resolution, 120–127
  double hashing, 124
  linear probing, 123
  open addressing, 124
  quadratic probing, 124
  secondary clustering, 124
  universal hashing, 125–127
hash value, 118
header, 70
heap, 99–111
  bottom-up construction, 109–111
heap-order property, 99
heap-sort, 107–111, 218
height, 79–80
height-balance property, 152, 154, 157
Hell, 379
Hennessy, 683
hierarchical, 56
Hinrichs, 590
Hirchsberg, 284
Hoare, 256
Hochbaum, 642
Hopcroft, 137, 216, 256, 338, 510, 642, 683
Horner's method, 52
Horner's rule, 488
Hu, 284
Huang, 256
Huffman, 450
Huffman coding, 440–441
Huitema, 544

Ibarra, 642
identity matrix, 492
in-degree, 290
in-place, 248, 324
incidence container, 299
incidence matrix, 612
incident, 290
incoming edges, 290
independent, 28, 30
independent set, 284
INDEPENDENT-SET, 640
index, ***see*** discrete logarithm
induction, 25–26
inorder traversal, 146, 150, 155
input size, 593
insertion-sort, 98, 218
inside node, 551
integer multiplication, 270–272
internal memory, 645
inverse shuffle, 502
inversion, 254
IP routers, 514
items, 114

iterative substitution, 264
iterator, 74

Jacobi symbol, 468
JáJá, 137, 683
Jarník, 379
Java Virtual Machine, 64, 137
JDSL, 137
Johnson, 642
Jones, 338
Josephus problem, 133

Karatsuba, 284
Karger, 379
Karp, 137, 414, 642
k-D tree, 563–564
key, 94, 114, 115, 159
key transfer, 475
Kim, 642
Klein, 379, 642
KNAPSACK, 614, 619–621, 634, 639–642
knapsack problem, 259–260, 278–281
Knuth, 54, 137, 216, 256, 338, 450, 683
Komlós, 683
Kosaraju, 338
Koutsoupias, 683
Kruskal, 379, 683
Kruskal's algorithm, 362–366

L'Hôpital's Rule, 688
Landis, 216
Langston, 256
language, 594
last node, 99
last-in first-out, 57
LCS, ***see*** longest common subsequence
leader election, 517–523
leaves, 75
Lecroq, 450
LEDA, 137
Lee, 590
left child, 76
left subtree, 76
left turn, 574
Legendre symbol, 467
Leighton, 683
Leiserson, 216, 338, 379, 414, 510, 642
level, 84, 313
level numbering, 90
level order traversal, 134
Levin, 642
Lewis, 642
lexicographical, 242
LIFO, 57
Lindholm, 137
line, 572
linear exponential, 688
linear probing, 123
linearity of expectation, 29, 246
link components, 310
link relation, 308
link-state algorithm, 534–535
linked list
    doubly linked, 70–73
linked structure, 92
Liskov, 137
list, 68–72, 115
    abstract data type, 69–72
list ranking, 661
literals, 605
little-oh notation, 18
little-omega notation, 18
live objects, 323
load factor, 122
local replacement, 603
locality-of-reference, 647
locator pattern, 112–113
log file, 115, 121
logarithm, 23, 685
    natural, 685
longest common subsequence, 443–446
looking-glass heuristic, 422
lookup table, 142–145
loop invariant, 27
Lovász, 642
LRU, 656
Lynch, 544
Lyons, 683

machine scheduling, 283
Magnanti, 338, 379, 414
main memory, 645
mark-sweep algorithm, 323
Marker strategy, 671
master method, 268–270
matching, 396
matrix chain-product, 274–277
matrix closure, 357–359
matroid theory, 284
Max-Flow, Min-Cut Theorem, 389
maximal independent set, 338
maximum bipartite matching, 396–397
maximum flow, ***see*** network flow
McCreight, 450, 590, 683
McDiarmid, 137
McGeoch, 54
median, 245
Megiddo, 256

Mehlhorn, 216, 338, 379, 414, 590, 683
memory hierarchy, 645
memory management, 323, 646–648, 668–673
merge-sort, 219–224
  multi-way, 654–656
  tree, 220
mergeable heap, 215
Merzbach, 54
message-passing model, 514–516
method stack, 59–60
minimum cut, 386
minimum spanning tree, 360–372, 528
  Barůvka's algorithm, 369–372, 528–529
  Kruskal's algorithm, 362–366, 372
  Prim-Jarnik algorithm, 366–367, 372
minimum-cost flow, 398–405
Minotaur, 288
modular arithmetic, 62, 126, 454, 458–462, 686
modular exponentiation, 462–464
modular multiplicative inverse, 464
modulus, 454
Moore, 450
Morris, 450
Morrison, 450
Motwani, 216, 256, 683
Mount, 590
MST, ***see*** minimum spanning tree
multi-way search tree, 159
multi-way tree, 159–162
multicast routing, 535–540
multiplicative group, 461
multiplicative inverse, 458, 464
multiprogramming, 63
Munro, 137
mutually independent, 28

Naimipour, 642
natural logarithm, 685
Neapolitan, 642
network flow, 382–414
  augmenting cycle, 398
  augmenting path, 388
  backward edge, 385
  bottleneck, 395
  capacity rule, 383
  conservation rule, 383
  cut, 385–386
  cut capacity, 386
  edge capacity, 383
  Edmonds-Karp algorithm, 393–395
  flow across a cut, 386
  flow network, 383–385
  flow value, 384
  Ford-Fulkerson algorithm, 387–395
  forward edge, 385
  Max-Flow, Min-Cut Theorem, 389
  maximum flow problem, 384, 387
  minimum cut, 386
  minimum-cost flow, 398–405
  residual capacity, 387
  residual distance, 393
  residual graph, 392
network protocol stack, 514
networking protocol stack, 513–514
  application layer, 513
  data-link layer, 513
  network layer, 513
  physical layer, 513
  transport layer, 513
node, 68, 75, 77, 289
  ancestor, 75
  balanced, 154
  boundary, 551
  child, 75
  descendent, 75
  external, 75
  inside, 551
  internal, 75
  outside, 551
  parent, 75
  redundant, 433
  root, 75
  sibling, 75
  size, 191
  unbalanced, 154
nontree edge, 318, 320
NP, 595, 596
NP-completeness, 592–642
NP-hard, 600
null string, 419
number theory, 453–471

O'Rourke, 590
object-oriented design, 137
objective function, 259
Ofman, 284
one-time pad, 474
one-way hash function, 481
online algorithm, 667–679
open addressing, 123, 124
optimization problem, 278, 594
order statistic, 245
orientation, 574, 575
origin, 290
Orlin, 338, 379, 414
orthogonal segments, 565
Ottmann, 590

out-degree, 290
outgoing edge, 290
output sensitive, 565, 579
outside node, 551
overflow, 164, 653
Overmars, 683

P, 595
Pach, 590
palindrome, 449
Pan, 510
Papadimitriou, 284, 642, 683
parallel algorithm, 657–666
parallel prefix, 662
parent, 75
PARTITION, 640
partition, 227–234
partition tree, 561
password, 472
Patashnik, 54
path, 292
    directed, 292
    length, 341
    simple, 292
    weight, 341
path compression, 230
path length, 134
pattern matching, 419–428
    Boyer-Moore algorithm, 422–425
    brute force, 420–422
    Knuth-Morris-Pratt algorithm, 425–428
Patterson, 683
Peleg, 544
plane sweep, 566–571, 590
point, 572
polygon, 572, 573, 576
    convex, 573
    edges, 573
    non-intersecting, 573
    simple, 573
    vertices, 573
polynomial, 52
polynomial-time approximation scheme, 619
polynomial-time reducible, 600
position, 68, 77, 196
potential function, 37–38
power test, 46
PRAM model, 657
    CRCW, 658
    CREW, 658
    EREW, 658
Pratt, 450
prefix, 419
prefix averages, 31
prefix code, 440
prefix sum, 33
Preparata, 590
Prim, 379
Prim-Jarnik algorithm, 366–367
primality testing, 466–471
    Rabin-Miller algorithm, 470
    Slovay-Strassen algorithm, 467–469
prime, 453
prime decomposition, 453
primitive operations, 9–12, 36
primitive root, 462
primitive root of unity, 489
priority queue, 94–113, 218
    heap implementation, 100–106
    sequence implementation, 96–98
priority range tree, 560–561
priority search tree, 556–559
probability, 28–30
probability space, 28
program counter, 60
proximity, 568
prune-and-search, 245–247
pseudo-blocks, 656
pseudo-code, 7–8
pseudo-polynomial time, 281
pseudo-random number generators, 195
PTAS, ***see*** polynomial-time approximation scheme
public-key cryptography, 472, 475–480
public-key cryptosystem, 475
Pugh, 216

quadratic probing, 124
quadratic residue, 467
quadtree, 561–562
queue, 61–64
    abstract data type, 61
    array implementation, 61–63
quick-sort, 234–238
    tree, 235

Rabin-Miller algorithm, 470
radix-sort, 242–243
Raghavan, 216, 256, 683
RAM, ***see*** random-access machine
Ramachandran, 137
random variable, 29
random-access machine, 9, 644
randomization, 195, 196
randomized quick-select, 245
randomized quick-sort, 237
randomized thresholding, 675
range searching
    one-dimensional, 550–552

three-sided, 556
range tree, 549–561
range-search query, 549
rank, 142, 231
rank groups, 232
Rao, 510
ratio test, 45
reachability, 316
recurrence equation, 12, 224, 263–270
recursion, 12, 60
recursion tree, 265
recursive doubling, 661
red-black tree, 170–184, 209, 569
depth property, 170
external property, 170
internal property, 170
recoloring, 174
root property, 170
Reed, 137
reflexive property, 94, 308
rehashing, 122
Reif, 683
relatively prime, 454, 458
relaxation, 343, 349
renter's dilemma, 667
repeated squaring, 463
rescalable, 619
residual capacity, 387
residual distance, 393
residual graph, 392
residue, 458
restriction, 603
restructure
trinode, 155
Ribeiro-Neto, 450
right child, 76
right subtree, 76
right turn, 574
Rivest, 216, 338, 379, 414, 476, 510, 642
Robson, 137
root, 75
root objects, 323
Rosenkrantz, 642
rotation, 155, 157
double, 155
single, 155
round-robin, 64
router, 530
routing
broadcast, 530–531
center-based trees, 537–538
distance vector algorithm, 532–533
link-state algorithm, 534–535
multicast, 535–540
reverse path forwarding, 535–536
unicast, 532–535
RPF, ***see*** reverse path forwarding
RSA, 476
RSA cryptosystem, 476–478
running time, 4–6, 10–12

Samet, 590, 683
sample space, 28
SAT, 638
satisfying assignment, 598
Saxe, 284
scan forward, 197
Schaffer, 137
Schönhage, 284
search engine, 225, 439
secondary clustering, 124
security algorithms, 481–487
Sedgewick, 54, 137, 216, 510, 590
seed, 195
segment, 572, 573
segment intersection, 565–568
Seidel, 590
selection, 245–247
selection-sort, 97, 218
self-loop, 291
sentinel, 70, 115
separate chaining, 121
separation edge, 307
separation vertex, 307
sequence, 73–74
abstract data type, 73–74
sequential subsets, 659
SET, 484
set, 225–234
SET-COVER, 610, 611, 625, 626, 638, 642
Shamir, 476
Shamos, 590, 683
Shiloach, 683
Shing, 284
shortest path, 341–359
Bellman-Ford algorithm, 349–351
Dijkstra's algorithm, 342–348, 373–376
matrix multiplication, 355–359
sibling, 75
sieve algorithm, 136
sink, 382, 383
skip list, 195–202
analysis, 200–202
insertion, 198–199
levels, 196
removal, 199–200
searching, 197–198

towers, 196
update operations, 198–200
Sleator, 216, 683
Solovay-Strassen algorithm, 467
sorting, 96, 218–224, 235–243
bucket-sort, 241–242
external-memory, 654–656
heap-sort, 107–111
in-place, 108, 248
insertion-sort, 98
lower bound, 239–240
merge-sort, 219–224
priority-queue, 96
quick-sort, 235–238
radix-sort, 242–243
selection-sort, 97
stable, 242
source, 382, 383
space usage, 4
spanning forest, 306, 315
spanning subgraph, 292
spanning tree, 293, 303, 305, 306, 313, 315, 316, 360
splay tree, 185–194
split, 164, 653
stable, 242
stack, 57–60
abstract data type, 57
array implementation, 57–58
start time, 261
Stearns, 642
Steiglitz, 284, 642
Steiner trees, 538–540
Stephen, 450
Stirling's Approximation, 686
STL, 137
stop words, 431, 450
Strassen, 284
Strassen's Algorithm, 272
string
abstract data type, 419–420
null, 419
pattern matching, ***see*** pattern matching
prefix, 419
suffix, 419
strongly collision-resistant, 481
strongly connected, 316
strongly ***NP***-hard, 612
subgraph, 292
SUBGRAPH-ISOMORPHISM, 640
subproblem optimality, 275, 278
subproblem overlap, 278
subsequence, 443
SUBSET-SUM, 612–614, 630, 638, 642
substring, 419
subtree, 75
suffix, 419
summation, 21, 687
geometric, 21
symmetric encryption, 473–474
symmetric property, 308
symmetric relation, 289
Szemerédi, 683

Tamassia, 137, 338, 510
Tarjan, 54, 137, 216, 256, 338, 379, 414, 683
task scheduling, 261
Tel, 544
telescoping sum, 35, 687
template method pattern, 332
text compression, 440–441
Theseus, 288
thread, 63–64
timestamping, 482
topological ordering, 325–327
total order, 94
totient function, 460
tower, 198
tower-of-twos, 231
trailer, 70
transfer, 167
transitive closure, 316, 319
transitive property, 94, 308
traveling salesman problem, 342
traveling salesperson problem, 617
treap, 590
tree, 75–137, 292
abstract data type, 77–78
binary, ***see*** binary tree
child node, 75
depth, 79–80
external node, 75
height, 79–80
internal node, 75
level, 84
linked structure, 93
multi-way, 159–162
multidimensional, 549–564
node, 75
ordered, 76
parent node, 75
root node, 75
tree edge, 318, 320
tree traversal, 81–83, 86–89
Euler tour, 88–89
generic, 88–89
inorder, 87

level order, 134
postorder, 82–83, 86
preorder, 81, 86
triangle inequality, 623
triangulation, 284
trie, 429–439
compressed, 433
standard, 429
trinode restructuring, 155, 173
Tsakalidis, 216
TSP, 617, 619, 623, 624, 633, 641, 642
Tukey, 510
two-dimensional dictionary, 549
(2,4) tree, 163–169
depth property, 163
size property, 163

Ullman, 137, 216, 256, 510, 642, 683
unary encoding, 593
underflow, 167, 653
unicast routing, 530, 532–535
union-by-size, 230
union-find, 227–234
universal hashing, 125–127
unordered dictionary, 114
up-heap bubbling, 102
upper envelope, 283

Valiant, 683
van Leeuwen, 338, 379, 414
vector, 65–67, 115, 142
abstract data type, 65
verification, 596
vertex, 289
degree, 290
in-degree, 290
out-degree, 290
vertex cover, 598
VERTEX-COVER, 599, 608–613, 615, 622, 642
virtual memory, 647
Vishkin, 137, 683
Vismara, 590
Vitter, 54, 683
Voronoi diagram, 589
Vuillemin, 590

Web crawler, 303, 443
Web spider, 303, 443
Wegner, 137
Williams, 137
Wood, 137, 590

X.509, 486

Yannakakis, 642
Yao, 590
Yap, 510
Yellin, 137
Young, 642

zig, 186, 192
zig-zag, 186, 192
zig-zig, 185, 192